HUMAN
DEVELOPMENT

SEVENTH EDITION

HUMAN DEVELOPMENT

Diane E. Papalia
Sally Wendkos Olds
Ruth Duskin Feldman

McGraw Hill

Boston, Massachusetts   Burr Ridge, Illinois   Dubuque, Iowa
Madison, Wisconsin   New York, New York   San Francisco, California   St. Louis, Missouri

McGraw-Hill

A Division of The McGraw·Hill Companies

HUMAN DEVELOPMENT

Acknowledgments begin on page 723 and on this page by
reference.

This book is printed on acid-free paper.

2 3 4 5 6 7 8 9 0   VNH   VNH   9 0 9 8

ISBN 0-07-048772-3

Library of Congress Catalogue Number: 97-073170

INTERNATIONAL EDITION

When ordering this title, use ISBN 0-07-115461-2.

This book was set in Palatino by York Graphic Services, Inc.
The editors were Leslye Jackson, Michelle E. Cox,
Jeannine Ciliotta, and David A. Damstra; the production
supervisors were Leroy Young and Kathryn Porzio.
The designer was Joan O'Connor.
The photo editor was Inge King.
Cover photo: Bob Daemmrich, Stock, Boston
Von Hoffmann was printer and binder.

Part-Opening Photo Credits

Part 1 J. M. Trois / Explorer / Photo Researchers / *Part 2*
David Young-Wolff / PhotoEdit / *Part 3* Lauren Lantos /
The Picture Cube / *Part 4* Bob Daemmrich / The Image
Works / *Part 5* L. Koolvoord / The Image Works / *Part 6*
John Eastcott & Yva Momatiuk / The Image Works / *Part
7* Wayne Hoy / The Picture Cube

Chapter-Opening Photo Credits

Chapter 1 Scott J. Witte / The Picture Cube / *Chapter 2*
P. Wysocki / Explorer / Photo Researchers / *Chapter 3*
Bob Daemmrich / The Image Works / *Chapter 4* Erika
Stone / *Chapter 5* Nancy Richmond / The Image Works /
Chapter 6 Ellen Senisi / The Image Works / *Chapter 7*
CLEO Photo / The Picture Cube / *Chapter 8* Bill
Bachmann / PhotoEdit / *Chapter 9* Richard Shock /
Gamma-Liaison / *Chapter 10* Will and Deni McIntyre /
Photo Researchers / *Chapter 11* Bob Daemmrich / Stock,
Boston / *Chapter 12* Bob Daemmrich / The Image Works
/ *Chapter 13* Spencer Grant / Stock, Boston / *Chapter 14*
USDA / Science Source / Photo Researchers / *Chapter 15*
Bachmann / Photo Researchers / *Chapter 16* Elaine
Rebman / Photo Researchers, Inc. / *Chapter 17* Bachmann
/ The Image Works / *Chapter 18* Dennis Stock / Magnum

Lifespan Photo Credits

Chapter 1 Peg Skorpinski / *Chapter 3* Neil Michel / Axiom
/ *Chapter 5* Courtesy of Mary Main / *Chapter 7* Julia
Miller / *Chapter 9* Courtesy of Victor Cicirelli / *Chapter 11*
Michael Marsland / Yale University, Office of Public
Affairs / *Chapter 12* Kay Hinton / Emory University
Photography / *Chapter 14* Courtesy of Matilda White
Riley / *Chapter 17* L. A. Cicero / Stanford University
News Service

ABOUT THE AUTHORS

 As a professor, **Diane E. Papalia** taught thousands of undergraduates at the University of Wisconsin-Madison. She received her bachelor's degree, majoring in psychology, from Vassar College, and both her master's degree in child development and family relations and her Ph.D. in life-span developmental psychology from West Virginia University. She has published numerous articles in such professional journals as *Human Development, International Journal of Aging and Human Development, Sex Roles, Journal of Experimental Child Psychology,* and *Journal of Gerontology.* Most of these papers have dealt with her major research focus, cognitive development from childhood through old age. She is especially interested in intelligence in old age and in factors that contribute to the maintenance of intellectual functioning in late adulthood. She is a Fellow in the Gerontological Society of America. She is the coauthor, with Sally Wendkos Olds, of *A Child's World,* now in its seventh edition, and of *Adult Development and Aging,* with Cameron J. Camp and Ruth Duskin Feldman.

 **Sally Wendkos Olds** is an award-winning professional writer who has written more than 200 articles in leading magazines and is the author or coauthor of six books addressed to general readers, in addition to the three textbooks she has coauthored with Dr. Papalia. Her book *The Complete Book of Breast-feeding,* a classic since its publication in 1972, has been issued in a completely updated and expanded edition, and is now in press for its third edition. She is also the author of *The Working Parents' Survival Guide* and *The Eternal Garden: Seasons of Our Sexuality,* and the coauthor of *Raising a Hyperactive Child* (winner of The Family Service Association of America National Media Award) and *Helping Your Child Find Values to Live By.* She received her bachelor's degree from The University of Pennsylvania, where she majored in English literature and minored in psychology. She was elected to Phi Beta Kappa and was graduated summa cum laude.

 **Ruth Duskin Feldman** is an award-winning writer. She is the author or coauthor of four books addressed to general readers, including *Whatever Happened to the Quiz Kids? Perils and Profits of Growing Up Gifted.* She was coauthor of the Fourth Edition of Diane E. Papalia and Sally Wendkos Olds's *Human Development* and is coauthor, with Dr. Papalia and Cameron J. Camp, of *Adult Development and Aging.* A former teacher, she has developed educational materials for all levels from elementary school through college. She has written for numerous newspapers and national magazines on education and other topics and has lectured extensively throughout the United States. She prepared the test banks to accompany the Fifth Edition of *Human Development* and the Sixth Edition of another Papalia/Olds text, *A Child's World,* as well as the *Study Guide with Readings* to accompany the Fifth, Sixth, and Seventh Editions of *A Child's World.* She received her bachelor's degree from Northwestern University, where she was graduated with highest distinction and was elected to Phi Beta Kappa.

To our husbands,
Jonathan L. Finlay,
David Mark Olds,
and Gilbert Feldman
—our loved and loving partners
in growth and development

CONTENTS IN BRIEF

CONTENTS

LIST OF BOXES

PREFACE

As we have emphasized in the previous six editions of *Human Development*, both change and continuity govern human development throughout life. This book, too, has changed and developed, along with its authors; yet it has maintained an underlying continuity of purpose, outlook, tone, and style.

Although this seventh edition retains the scope, emphasis, level, and much of the flavor of earlier editions, it also contains a number of significant changes. Some of these represent growth and development in our thinking as a result of our ongoing personal and professional experience. An important part of that experience has been our work on two other college textbooks, *A Child's World* (for courses in child development) and *Adult Development and Aging*, which has helped refine our thinking about life-span development.

One notable change in this edition is the expansion of the author team. Ruth Duskin Feldman, who drafted the fourth edition of this book and who, with Diane E. Papalia and Cameron J. Camp, coauthored the new textbook *Adult Development and Aging*, has been added as a coauthor of this edition, bringing a fresh perspective to the organization and writing of the text. (About the Authors on page v details the professional backgrounds of all three authors.)

Cameron J. Camp, a prominent psychologist specializing in applied research in gerontology, has had a major consulting role in this edition of *Human Development*, substantially enlarging and updating the research base of the chapters dealing with the adult portions of the life span. Formerly a research professor of psychology at the University of New Orleans, Dr. Camp is now research scientist at the Myers Research Institute of Menorah Park Center for the Aging in Cleveland, Ohio. He has served on the editorial boards of several professional journals, including *Adult Development*, *Contemporary Psychology*, *Cognitive Aging*, *Educational Gerontology*, and *Experimental Aging Research*, and is a leader in designing interventions for persons with dementia.

✔ OUR AIMS FOR THIS EDITION

The primary goals of this seventh edition are the same as those of the first six: to emphasize the continuity of development throughout the life span and the interrelationships among the physical, cognitive, and psychosocial realms of development. We are still asking the same basic questions: What are the many influences upon people that stem from their genes, their upbringing, and the society they live in? How do these influences interact to make people living at the turn of the twenty-first century the way they are? What factors are likely to affect us in the future? How do experiences at one time of life influence future development? How much control do people have over their lives? How are people like one another? How is each person unique? What is normal? What is cause for concern? In seeking to sharpen and refine our answers to these questions, we continue to synthesize theories and research findings and to help students think critically about controversial issues.

✔ THE SEVENTH EDITION: AN OVERVIEW

ORGANIZATION

There are two major approaches to the study of human development: the *chronological approach* (describing all aspects of development at each period of life) and the *topical approach* (focusing on one aspect of development at a time). We have chosen the *chronological* approach, which provides a sense of the multifaceted sweep of human development, as we get to know first the developing person-to-be in the womb, then the infant and toddler, then the young child, the schoolchild, the adolescent, the young adult, the adult at midlife, and the person in late adulthood.

In line with our chronological approach, we have divided this book into seven parts. After an introductory chapter about research methods and theoretical perspectives, Parts One through Seven discuss physical, cognitive, and psychosocial development during each of the periods of the life span mentioned above. We conclude with a chapter on the end of life.

CONTENT

This new edition continues to provide comprehensive coverage of physical, cognitive, and psychosocial development from conception to death and to integrate theoretical, research-related, and practical concerns. In this revision, we have made a special effort to draw on the most recent information available. We discuss much new research and several new theories, many published during the mid-1990s.

Because we believe that all parts of life are important, challenging, and full of opportunities for growth and change, we provide evenhanded treatment of all periods of the life span, taking care not to overemphasize some while slighting others. In this edition we have greatly strengthened our coverage of young, middle, and late adulthood.

This edition also continues to expand our cross-cultural coverage, reflecting the diversity of the population in the United States and in other countries around the world. Our photo illustrations show an ever greater commitment to depicting this diversity.

As in previous editions, we illustrate and enliven the text with real, personal examples, some of them from the authors' own lives. The chapters on childhood include many incidents in the life of Diane Papalia's daughter, Anna. Chapter 1 begins with the story of Anna's development of proficiency with language, which serves as a springboard for the discussion of several developmental issues.

As in previous editions, we have reorganized some material to make it more effective and have added completely new sections. We have also added tables and figures and updated statistics. Among the important topics given new or greatly revised coverage are the following:

■ *New sections:* Paul B. Baltes's life-span developmental approach, the ethological and contextual perspectives, reaction range and canalization, Esther Thelen's work challenging the traditional maturational explanation of infants' motor development, the origins of conscience, a neo-Piagetian view of self-concept development, self-esteem and helplessness in early childhood, Alice Miller's theory of "poisonous pedagogy," the effects of early childhood education in preventing juvenile delinquency, emotional intelligence, Daniel Levinson's research on women's life structures, models of career development, working at home, Lawrence Kohlberg's seventh stage of moral development, extending the life span, metamemory in late adulthood, the self-concept model of personality, Laura Carstensen's socioemotional selectivity theory, continuity theory, and productive aging.

■ *Important revisions and expansions:* Discussions of research methods, the prenatal environment, the human immunodeficiency virus (HIV) and acquired immune deficiency syndrome (AIDS), low birthweight, sudden infant death syndrome (SIDS), language and literacy, attachment, young children's theories of mind, early memory development, early emotional development, childhood health problems and issues, the effects of poverty, learning disabilities and attention deficit hyperactivity disorder (ADHD), drug use and abuse, sexual behavior and sexual risk taking, the origins of homosexuality and homosexual relationships throughout adulthood, diet and cholesterol, obesity, the effects of smoking, premenstrual syndrome, trait models of personality, cohabitation, domestic violence, dealing with infertility, stepparenthood, expertise and intelligence, practical problem solving, sensory changes of aging, women's health, stress and health, postformal thought, creativity, research on women's development, patterns of marital relationships and characteristics of long-term marriages, the revolving door syndrome, the sandwich generation, grandparenthood (including kinship care), memory systems, improving cognition and memory, theories of aging, Alzheimer's disease, depression, the "oldest old," education in late adulthood, activity theory, retirement options, preparing for retirement, abuse of the elderly, and cross-cultural customs regarding death and bereavement.

SPECIAL FEATURES IN THIS EDITION

New to this edition is a series called *Life-Span Issues,* one for each period of the life span. These extended essays, integrated at appropriate points in the text, explore a variety of topics: Do attachment patterns span generations? How does culture affect sibling relationships throughout life? How does faith change across the life span? Are age-based roles obsolete?

As in the past, this edition also includes three kinds of boxed material:

■ *Window on the World* boxes offer focused glimpses of human development in societies other than our own (in addition to the cross-cultural coverage in the main body of the text). These boxes highlight the fact that people grow up, live, and thrive in many different kinds of cultures, under many different influences. Among the new, significantly updated, or expanded topics: female genital mutilation; Daniel Offer's work on the "universal adolescent"; cross-cultural conceptions of love; cross-cultural perspectives on moral development; Japanese women's experience of menopause; aging in Asia; and work, retirement, and health care in China.

■ *Practically Speaking* boxes build bridges between academic study and everyday life by showing ways to apply research findings on various aspects of human development. Among the new, expanded, or substantially updated topics: progress in immunizing preschoolers, the reliability of young children's eyewitness testimony, "good-enough" parenting, dealing with underemployment, how dual-earner couples cope, the estrogen decision, preventing caregiver burnout, new environments for an aging population, and options for living arrangements for older adults.

■ *Food for Thought* boxes explore important, cutting-edge, or controversial research-related issues. Some of these include new or significantly expanded or updated discussions of the pros and cons of genetic testing; early signs of the development of conscience; intelligence tests as predictors of job performance; young, middle-aged, and older adults' ideas about personality change at midlife; the influence of personality on longevity; and near-death experiences.

LEARNING AIDS

New to this edition are *Questions for Thought and Discussion* at the end of each chapter, which challenge students to interpret, apply, or evaluate information presented in the text. We also continue to provide a number of other teaching and learning aids:

- *Part overviews:* At the beginning of each part, an overview introduces the period of life discussed in the chapters that follow. In this edition, the part overviews have been revised to stress the interaction of physical, cognitive, and psychosocial aspects of development.
- *Chapter-opening outlines:* At the beginning of each chapter, an outline clearly previews the major topics included in the chapter.
- *Chapter overviews:* At the beginning of each chapter, a one-paragraph overview introduces the material to be discussed.
- *"Ask Yourself" questions:* At the beginning of each chapter, a few key questions highlight important issues addressed in the chapter.
- *Chapter summaries:* At the end of every chapter, a series of brief statements, organized by the major topics in the chapter, clearly restate the most important points.
- *Key terms:* Whenever an important new term is introduced in the text, it is highlighted in **bold-face italic** and defined, both in the text and, sometimes more formally, in the end-of-book Glossary.
- *End-of-chapter lists of key terms:* At the end of every chapter, key terms are listed in the order in which they first appear and are cross-referenced to pages where they are defined.
- *Glossary:* The extensive Glossary at the back of the book gives definitions of key terms and indicates the pages on which they first appear.
- *Bibliography:* A complete listing of references enables students to evaluate the sources of major statements of fact or theory.
- *Indexes:* Separate indexes, by subject and by author, appear at the end of the book.
- *Illustrations:* Many points in the text are underscored visually through carefully selected drawings, graphs, and photographs. The illustration program includes new figures and many full-color photographs.
- The *Resource Guide* at the front of the book helps interested readers seek information and assistance with regard to practical concerns related to topics discussed in the book.

✔ SUPPLEMENTARY MATERIALS

Human Development, Seventh Edition, is accompanied by a complete learning and teaching package. Each component of this package has been thoroughly revised and expanded to include important new course material. The package consists of a *Student Study Guide with Readings* by Thomas Crandell and Corinne Crandell of Broome Community College, an *Instructor's Manual* by Marion Mason of Bloomsburg University, and a *Test Bank* by Thomas Moye of Coe College. Computerized versions of the Study Guide and Test Bank are available for IBM and Macintosh computers. The *Human Development* supplements package also includes a newly revised set of full-color overhead transparencies. Annotated lists of *Recommended Readings* for students who want to explore issues in greater depth, formerly included in the text, will now be found in the Study Guide.

In addition, the text will continue to be supplemented regularly by a newsletter for adopters. The *Human Development Update* newsletter highlights recent research and current issues related to the themes of the text.

The *Human Development Electronic Image Bank CD-ROM* contains more than 100 useful images and a computer projection system divided into two separate programs: The Interactive Slide Show and the Slide Show Editor. The Interactive Slide Show allows you to play a preset slide show containing selected images. The Slide Show Editor allows you to customize and create your own slide show. You can add slides anywhere you like in the presentation and incorporate any audio or visual files you'd like, as well as create title screens. You also may use the CD-ROM images with your own presentation software (PowerPoint, etc.).

The *McGraw-Hill Psychology Video Library* contains a wide selection of developmental videos. Contact your local McGraw-Hill sales representative for a complete listing of what is available.

The *AIDS Booklet,* Third Edition, by Frank D. Cox of Santa Barbara City College, is a brief but comprehensive introduction to the acquired immune deficiency syndrome, which is caused by HIV (human immunodeficiency virus) and related viruses.

The *Critical Thinker,* written by Richard Mayer and Fiona Goodchild of the University of California, Santa Barbara, uses excerpts from introductory psychology textbooks to show students how to think critically about psychology. Either this or the AIDS booklet is available at no charge to first-year adopters of our textbook or can be purchased separately.

Guide to Life-Span Development for Future Nurses and *Guide to Life-Span Development for Future Educators* are new course supplements that help students apply the concepts of human development to the education and nursing professions. Each supplement contains information, exercises, and sample tests designed to help students prepare for certification and understand human development from these professional perspectives.

The *Human Development Interactive Videodisc Set*, produced by Roger Ray of Rollins College, brings lifespan development to life with instant access to more than 30 brief video segments from the highly acclaimed *Seasons of Life* series.

Primis Custom Publishing allows you to create original works or tailor existing materials to suit your students' needs. All you need to do is organize chapters from your McGraw-Hill textbook to match your course syllabus. You control the number of chapters, pieces of art, and end-of-chapter materials appropriate for your course. You may also include your own materials in the book. In a few weeks after consulting with your McGraw-Hill sales representative, you can have a professionally printed and bound book delivered to your bookstore.

Annual Editions: Human Development, published by Dushkin/McGraw-Hill, is a collection of more than 40 articles on topics related to the latest research and thinking in human development. *Annual Editions* is updated on an annual basis, and there are a number of features designed to make it particularly useful, including a topic guide, an annotated table of contents, and unit overviews. Consult your sales representative for more details.

✔ ACKNOWLEDGMENTS

We would like to express our gratitude to the many friends and colleagues who, through their work and their interest, helped us clarify our thinking about human development. We are especially grateful for the valuable help given by those who reviewed the sixth edition of *Human Development* and the manuscript drafts of this seventh edition; their evaluations and suggestions helped greatly in the preparation of this new edition. These reviewers, who are affiliated with both two- and four-year institutions include:

Nancy R. Ahlander	Ricks College
Daniel R. Bellack	Trident Technical College
Shirley Cassara	Bunker Hill Community College
Sandra Ciccarelli	Gulf Coast Community College
Bill Dibiase	Delaware County Community College
Jean Edwards	Jones County Junior College
Joan T. Erber	Florida International University
Wade Gladin	Bob Jones University
Bert Hayslip, Jr.	University of North Texas
Karen S. Holbrook	Frostburg State University
Debra Lee Hollister	Valencia Community College
Dale A. Lund	University of Utah
Allyssa McCabe	University of Massachusetts, Lowell
Karla Miley	Black Hawk College
Robin K. Montvilo	Rhode Island College
Catherine S. Murray	St. Joseph's University
Eileen S. Nelson	James Madison University
Stuart I. Offenbach	Purdue University
Robert H. Poresky	Kansas State University
Karen Rook	University of California, Irvine
Bruce R. Stam	Chemeketa Community College
Tamina Toray	Western Oregon State College

We appreciate the strong support we have had from our publisher. We would like to express our special thanks to Jane Vaicunas, editorial director; Leslye Jackson, sponsoring editor of this book; Jeannine Ciliotta, our capable, clear-thinking development editor; David A. Damstra, our dedicated, expert production editor; Mary Farrell, copy editor; and Beth Kaufman and Amy Mack, who edited the supplements and helped in many other ways. Deborah M. Evans coordinated the preparation of the Bibliography and assisted with the Glossary; Linda Camp and Kim Gelé also provided valuable help with the Bibliography. Inge King, photo editor of all seven editions of *Human Development*, again used her sensitivity, her interest, and her good eye to find outstanding photographs. Joan O'Connor and the artists working with her produced a creative, unique cover and book design.

Diane E. Papalia
Sally Wendkos Olds
Ruth Duskin Feldman

TO THE STUDENT

When you look through your family photo album, do you wonder about the people whose images are frozen there at a succession of moments in time? When you see that snapshot of your mother on her first bicycle, do you suppose that she had trouble learning to ride? Did she take a lot of spills? And why is she smiling shyly in that photo of her taken on the first day of school? Was she nervous about meeting her teacher? There she is with your father on their wedding day. Did their lives turn out as they had hoped? There is your mother, holding you as a baby. How did that little girl on a bike turn into the woman with an infant in her arms? How did *you* become the person you are today? How will you become the person you will be tomorrow?

Snapshots tell us little about the processes of inward and outward change that make up a human life. Even a series of home movies or videotapes, which can follow people from moment to moment as they grow older, will not capture a progression of changes so subtle that we often cannot detect them until after they have occurred. The processes that produce those changes—the processes by which human beings develop across time—are the subject of this book.

HOW THIS BOOK APPROACHES HUMAN DEVELOPMENT

Each human being is like all other people in some ways but different in other ways. This book, too, is like other books about human development in some ways, but different in others. It shows its "personality" in the topics it discusses, the way it treats them, and how it illustrates and organizes them. Its uniqueness grows out of its authors' personalities, experiences, and outlooks, and the way they mesh in collaboration.

Before introducing the study of human development, we will introduce some of our own ideas on the subject—the assumptions and beliefs that underlie this book—so that you may keep them in mind as you read.

- *We respect all periods of the life span.* We believe that people have the potential to change as long as they live. The changes of early life are especially dramatic, as almost helpless newborns transform themselves into competent, exploring children. Change during adulthood can be striking, too. Even very old people can show growth, and the experience of dying can be a final attempt to come to terms with one's life—in short, to develop. This book is organized chronologically, each part dealing with a period of the life span. To capture the continuous character of development, many chapters contain special essays on life-span issues, such as (in Chapter 1) whether early personality traits predict midlife development.

- *We believe in human resilience.* We believe that people can often bounce back from difficult early circumstances or stressful experiences. A traumatic incident or a severely deprived childhood may well have grave emotional consequences, but the life histories of countless people show that a single experience—even one as painful as the death of a parent in childhood—is not likely to cause irreversible damage. A nurturing environment can help a child overcome the effects of early deprivation or trauma.

- *We believe that people help shape their own development.* They actively affect their own environment and then respond to the environmental forces they have helped bring about. When infants babble and coo, they encourage adults to talk to them, and this talk in turn stimulates the babies' language development. Teenagers' burgeoning sexuality may evoke their parents' fears of growing older and regrets for lost youth; the parents' reactions, in turn, may affect the teenagers' attitudes toward the changes they are undergoing. Older adults shape their own development by

deciding when to retire from paid work, by taking up new activities, and by forming new relationships.

- *We believe that all domains of development are interrelated.* Although we look separately at physical, cognitive, and psychosocial development, we recognize that each of these aspects of development is entwined with the others, and we point out many of these connections. For example, sleep habits and nutrition can affect memory, and researchers have found possible links between personality and disease.

- *We celebrate cultural diversity.* People are a part of a wide array of cultures that exhibit the richness and complexity of human aspirations and experience. Since what happens around and to people affects them in many ways, we look at development in the context in which it occurs. We examine cross-cultural differences at appropriate points throughout the text. In addition, every chapter has a "Window on the World" box that focuses on some aspect of a culture other than the dominant one in the United States.

- *We believe that knowledge is useful.* There are two kinds of research, and each complements the other. *Basic* research is conducted in the spirit of intellectual inquiry with no direct practical goal in mind; it often leads to *applied* research, which addresses immediate problems. In each chapter, "Practically Speaking" boxes present research-based information on specific problems, and "Food for Thought" boxes raise thought-provoking, controversial issues—many based on cutting-edge research.

STUDYING REAL PEOPLE IN THE REAL WORLD

Ultimately, it is *you* who must apply what you learn from this book. Real people are not abstractions. They are living, working, loving, laughing, weeping, question-asking, decision-making human beings. Observe the adults and children about you. Pay attention to them as they confront the challenges of everyday life. Think about your own experiences and how they relate to the concepts and issues discussed in this book. With the insights you gain as you proceed through your study of human development, you will be able to look at yourself and at every person you see with new eyes; and you may be able to help yourself and others live happier, more fulfilled lives.

RESOURCES

Throughout this book we discuss many medical and psychological issues and disorders. You may want more detailed information on specific conditions for academic or for personal reasons. To help you in your search, we provide the following listing, which includes organizations that offer information, counseling, or other help. Of course, it is not all-inclusive; there are many other organizations in addition to those listed here.

If a topic in which you are interested is not included, look in your local telephone directory under "Associations," "Social Service Organizations," or "Human Services Organizations" or in the *Encyclopedia of Associations* in your local library.

Telephone numbers and addresses listed here are subject to change without notice; the same is true of fax numbers and e-mail addresses and websites. For information about tollfree numbers, dial 1-800-555-1212.

✔ ADOPTIVE AND STEPFAMILIES

Adoptive Families of America
3333 Highway 100 North
Minneapolis MN 55422
tel. 612-535-4829; fax 612-535-7808;
tollfree 800-372-3300
Umbrella organization for adoptive parent support groups; offers information and support in adoption and adoptive family problems; 24-hour hotline.

National Adoptive Information Clearinghouse
5640 Nicholas Lane suite 300
Rockville MD 20852
tel 301-231-6512; fax 301-984-8527
Information on all aspects of adoption, including intercountry adoption, adoption of children with special needs, state and federal adoption laws.

Stepfamily Foundation
333 West End Avenue
New York NY 10023

tel 212-877-3244; fax 212-362-7030
e-mail: stepfamily@aol.com; internet: stepfamily.org
Counseling; information packets; seminars for social workers and medical personnel; cable show "Family Matters" in Manhattan.

✔ AGING

AARP (American Association of Retired Persons)
A Path for Caregivers Stock no. D12957
AARP Fulfillment EE0294
PO Box 22796
Long Beach CA 90801-5796
Publication that gives information on AARP programs and publications to support caregivers; free.

Alliance for Aging
2021 K Street NW, suite 305
Washington DC 20006-1003
tel 202-293-2856; fax 202-785-8574
Works to increase private and public research on aging; operates speakers' bureau; compiles statistics; publications.

Eldercare Locator
800-677-1116
Nationwide resource for older people and caregivers: puts callers in touch with help in their area for legal assistance, housing, adult day care, home health, or any other type of service available for older individuals.

Gray Panthers
PO Box 21477
Washington DC 20009-9477
tel 202-466-3132; fax 202-466-3133; tollfree 800-280-5362
Consciousness-raising group that organizes local groups; focus on 8 national issues, including health care and affordable housing.

Lifespan Resources
1212 Roosevelt
Ann Arbor MI 48104
tel 313-663-9891; fax 313-973-7645
Designs, implements, and develops innovations for programs involving youth and senior citizens, emphasizing mentoring.

Senior Masters
77 Leland Farm Road
Ashland MA 01721
tel 508-881-8052
Encourages seniors to remain active by volunteering or working in an area that interests them; provides information about activities, newsletter, guidebook.

Widowed Persons Service
c/o AARP
601 E Street NW
Washington DC 20049
tel 202-434-2260; fax 202-434-6474
e-mail astudner@AARP.org
Provides widowed "partners" for the newly widowed, all ages, to help in the adjustment period.

✔ ALCOHOL AND DRUG ABUSE

Al-Anon Family Group Headquarters
200 Park Avenue, room 814
New York, NY 10003
800-356-9996
Offers information and help to family and friends of people with drinking and drug problems.

Alcoholics Anonymous World Services
475 Riverside Drive
New York, NY 10115
212 870 3400
The largest and most successful organization in the world for recovery from alcoholism, through meetings and peer support. All services are free.

Center for Substance Abuse and Treatment
1-800-662-HELP
A 24-hour hotline sponsored by the federal government and affiliated with the National Institute of Drug Abuse.

✔ ALZHEIMER'S DISEASE

Alzheimer's Association
800-272-3900
Main national organization providing support and information for people with Alzheimer's disease and their families.

American Health Assistance Foundation
800-437-2423
Provides $500 grants to people with less than $10,000 in assets; publishes pamphlets on Alzheimer's disease and its effect on caregivers.

✔ BIRTH DEFECTS AND DISEASES

National Down Syndrome Congress
1605 Chantilly Drive, suite 250
Atlanta GA 30324
tel 404-633-1555; fax 404-633-2817; tollfree 800-232-NDSC
Clearinghouse for information on Down Syndrome.

National Muscular Dystrophy Association
3300 East Sunrise Drive
Tucson, AZ 85718
602-529-2000
Supplies general information about the disease and services offered.

Spina Bifida Information and Referral
4590 MacArthur Boulevard NW, suite 250
Washington, DC 20007
800-621-3141
Provides general information and referrals.

✔ CANCER

American Cancer Society
1599 Clifton Road NE
Atlanta, GA 30329
800-ACS-2345
For free information on almost any concern about cancer, this number will aid you in finding local resources.

Memorial Sloan-Kettering Cancer Center
1275 York Avenue
New York NY 10021
tel 212-639-3573; fax 212-639-3576
Internet http://www.mskcc.org
The Center offers a number of counseling services, including physician referral, clinical genetics service, prevention programs, a post-treatment resource program, and a cancer information service at 1-800-4CANCER.

✔ CHILD ABUSE AND ADVOCACY

American Coalition for Abuse Awareness
PO Box 27959
1858 Park Road NW, 2d floor
Washington DC 20038-7959
tel 202-462-4688; fax 202-462-4689
e-mail acaad@aol.com
Champions rights of victims and survivors of childhood sexual abuse; provides information on legal issues.

Childhelp USA
1345 N. El Centro Avenue, suite 630
Los Angeles CA 90028-8216
800-423-4453
website http://www.charities.org/chidhelp/index.html.
Dedicated to treatment and prevention of child abuse; operates residential centers, recovery programs, referral services; 24-hour hotline.

✔ DEATH AND DYING

Choice in Dying
200 Varick Street
New York, NY 10014
212-366-5540
A national nonprofit organization that advocates the rights of dying patients through professional and public education. Choice in Dying distributes, free of charge, state-specific forms for medical power of attorney or executing a living will.

The National Hospice Organization
1901 N. Moore Street, suite 901
Arlington VA 22209
tel 703-243-5900; fax 703-525-5762
Source of information on developments in hospice care and changing attitudes toward death and dying.

Well Spouse Foundation
PO Box 801
New York NY 10023
212-724-5209
Provides information and support for husbands and wives who are caring for a terminally ill spouse.

✔ DISABILITIES

Center on Human Policy
305 S. Crouse Avenue
Syracuse NY 13244-2280
tel 315-443-3851; fax 315-443-4338; tollfree 800-894-0826
e-mail thechp@sued.syr.edu
Disseminates information on laws, regulations and programs affecting those with disabilities, especially developmental disabilities.

Disability Resources
4 Glatter Lane
Centereach NY 11720-1032
516-585-0290
e-mail jklaubere@suffold.lib.ny.us
Provides information to help those with disabilities to live independently.

National Information Center for Children and Youth with Disabilities
PO Box 1492
Washington DC 20013
tel 202-884-8200; fax 202-884-8441; tollfree 800-695-0285

e-mail nichcy@aed.org
website http://aed.org/nichcy/index.html
Provides information to parents, educators, caregivers, and advocates to help children and youth with disabilities participate at home, in school, in the community.

Pilot Parents
3610 Dodge Street, suite 101
Omaha NE 68131
tel 401-346-5220; fax 402-346-5253
Support for new parents of children with special needs; parent matching program matches experienced parents with parents of newly diagnosed children to share expertise and experiences.

✔ DIVORCE/CUSTODY

Fathers Rights and Equality Exchange
701 Welch Road, suite 323
Palo Alto CA 94304
tel 415-853-6877; e-mail FREE@VIX.com
website http://www.vix.love/free
Offers educational programs, referrals, and support for noncustodial divorced fathers.

Joint Custody Association
10606 Wilkins Avenue
Los Angeles CA 90024
tel 310-475-5352; fax 310-474-4859
Disseminates information on joint custody for children of divorce; assists children, parents, attorneys, and jurists.

✔ EDUCATION AND CHILDCARE

ChildCare Action Campaign
330 Seventh Avenue, 17th floor
New York, NY 10001
212-239-0138
National coalition of leaders from various institutions and organizations serves as an advocacy group offering information on many aspects of child care through individual information sheets, a bimonthly newsletter, and audio training tapes for family day care providers.

National Association for the Education of Young Children
1509 16th Street NW
Washington, DC 20036-1426
800-424-2460
Professional association that accredits child-care centers and preschools around the country, holds regional and national meetings, and distributes publications for both professionals and parents.

✔ FAMILY SUPPORT

Alternative Family Project
PO Box 16631
San Francisco CA 94116
415-566-5683
Provides affordable therapy for nontraditional families.

Family Research Council
700 13th Street, suite 500
Washington DC 20005
tel 202-393-2100; fax 202-393-2134
Provides expertise and information on issues such as impact of parental absence, community support for single parents, adolescent pregnancy, teen suicide.

Mother's Network
70 West 36 Street, suite 900
New York NY 10018
tollfree 800-779-6667; fax 212-239-0535
Provides information on services and products for parents with
children under 5.

Parents Without Partners
401 North Michigan Avenue
Chicago IL 60611-4267
tel 312-644-6610; fax 312-321-6869; tollfree 800-637-7974
Provides information on problems of single parents.

✔ GRANDPARENTING

AARP Grandparenting Information Center
202-424-2296
Connects grandparents with local support groups and resources;
works with national and local agencies involved in child care, aging
issues, and legal and family services.

Foster Grandparents Program
1100 Vermont Avenue NW room 6100
Washington DC 50525
202-606-4849
Offers information and counseling for those who wish to participate
in foster grandparent programs.

Grandparents'-Children's Rights, Inc.
5728 Bayonne Avenue
Haslett MI 48840
517-339-8663
Information and counseling for grandparents whose relationship with
grandchildren is changed or broken by divorce: problems with custodial
grandparenting, visitation rights, stepgrandchildren, other issues.

Grandparents Raising Grandchildren
Barbara Kirkland
PO Box 104
Colleyville TX 76034
tel 817-577-0435
Information on issues; support for starting local self-help groups.

✔ INFANT MORTALITY

Compassionate Friends, Inc.
P.O. Box 3696
Oak Brook, IL 60522-3696
708-990-0010
Offers support to bereaved parents and siblings of infants and older
children through 660 chapters in the United States.

National Sudden Infant Death Syndrome Clearinghouse
8201 Greensboro Drive, Suite 600
McLean, VA 22102
703-821-8955
Provides resources and information.

✔ MENTAL HEALTH

National Institute of Mental Health
Public Inquiries Branch
5600 Fishers Lane, room 7C02
Rockville, MD 20857
310-443-4513
Federally sponsored agency that answers questions about depression
and other psychological disorders.

✔ MISSING AND RUNAWAY CHILDREN

Child Find
P.O. Box 277
New Paltz, NY 12561
800-I AM LOST
Hotline to report disappearances or sightings.

National Center for Missing and Exploited Children
2101 Wilson Boulevard, suite 550
Arlington, VA 22201
Hotline to report disappearances or sightings.

National Runaway Switchboard
3080 North Lincoln Avenue
Chicago, IL 60657
800-621-4000
Confidential crisis intervention and referral for runaway homeless
youth and their families, and youth in crisis throughout the country.

✔ PREGNANCY AND CHILDBIRTH

Center for the Study of Multiple Birth
333 East Superior Street, suite 464
Chicago IL 60611
312-266-9093
Disseminates information on the risks of multiple births; resource
center for media and the public.

International Childbirth Education Association
P.O. Box 20048
Minneapolis, MN 55420
800-624-4934
Offers a free catalog of materials on pregnancy, childbirth, and child
care.

Resolve
1310 Broadway
Somerville MA 02144-1731
617-623-0744
National, nonprofit organization that offers counseling services to
infertile couples.

✔ SEXUALLY TRANSMITTED DISEASES AND AIDS

American Foundation for the Prevention of Venereal Disease
799 Broadway, suite 638
New York, NY 10003
212-759-2069
Publishes a booklet and other educational materials on sexually
transmitted diseases.

AIDS Hotline
800-342-AIDS
Run by the Centers for Disease Control, this 24-hour hotline provides
basic information on AIDS, HIV testing, prevention, and referral to
treatment centers.

VD/STD National Hotline
800-227-8922
Provides basic information on sexually transmitted diseases, as well
as referrals to free or low-cost clinics in your area.

HUMAN DEVELOPMENT

CHAPTER ONE

ABOUT HUMAN DEVELOPMENT

There is nothing permanent except change.

Heraclitus, Fragment (sixth century B.C.)

ASK YOURSELF

✔ What can you gain from the study of human development?

✔ What are the major changes in the course of human life, and what common and individual influences affect people?

✔ How has the study of human development evolved, and what issues are involved in studying the life span?

✔ How do social scientists study people, and what are some advantages and pitfalls of the various methods?

✔ What major theoretical perspectives try to explain human development, and what are their strengths and weaknesses?

T he study of human development is endlessly fascinating because it is the study of real lives: yours, the reader's; ours, the authors'; and those of millions of people around the world. Human development and its study are also extremely complex, for development is subject to many influences. Understanding these influences and the ways they interact is not only of academic interest; such knowledge can have enormous practical usefulness—for example, when a child seems to have a problem in learning to talk.

To illustrate this point, we'd like to introduce Anna Victoria Finlay. When Anna—who was born in Chile—was 8 weeks old, Jonathan Finlay, her adoptive father, flew to Santiago and brought her home to her adoptive mother, Diane E. Papalia, one of the authors of this book. Anna was already cooing—making happy squeals, gurgles, and vowel sounds—and, in the manner of parents around the world, Diane and Jonathan began to coo back and talk to their baby. At about 6 months Anna added consonants to her "speech" and began to babble. At 11 months, she said her first word: "Hi." She added three more words to her vocabulary during the next month and a few more soon after her first birthday. Anna seemed to be right on schedule in becoming a talker.

Then Anna's progress slowed. By the time she was 2½, her parents began to worry. Anna seemed to understand what was said to her, but she spoke only a few words and was not putting them together in two-word sentences—though the average child does this considerably earlier, at about 18 months of age. Diane and Jonathan mentioned their anxieties to their pediatrician, who suggested language assessment at a speech clinic. There, the speech pathologist told them that although Anna's language comprehension was normal, at the age of 30 months she had the expressive language of a 15-month-old child.

"Was it something I did?" Diane asked, struck by the possible irony that she, a developmental psychologist, might have contributed to Anna's language delay. The speech pathologist reassured both parents. Speech, she told them, may be late in developing for a number of reasons unrelated to the child's intelligence or home environment. She recommended a two-pronged program of language therapy.

One aspect was language stimulation. A speech and language therapist played with Anna, using toys to teach such concepts as *up-down*, *soft-hard*, and *big-little*. The therapist helped Anna to say her words more clearly and communicate more effectively. The other part of Anna's language therapy rested with her parents. Since her infancy, Jonathan and Diane had generally spoken to their daughter in the simplified type of speech that most adults use almost automatically with babies. Now they were encouraged to simplify their speech even further. Instead of asking Anna, "Want to get up on Mommy's lap?" for example, they were to ask, "Want up?" Diane and Jonathan carried out this suggestion, gradually moving to more complex usage as Anna's speech improved. They also expanded on whatever Anna said and talked about whatever she showed interest in; and, when reading aloud to her, they used an effective new technique (described later in this chapter) to encourage active participation and provide feedback.

After 4 months of language therapy, Diane and Jonathan received good news: at 3 years, 4 months, Anna had the usual vocabulary for her age. By 3 years, 9 months of age, her vocabulary was at an *advanced* level—4 years, 4 months. In addition, she was speaking sentences that averaged 5 to 7 words each, including some of up to 10 words.

By age 4, Anna was chattering away constantly, making requests, asking questions, issuing comments. She would tell her mother, "Do your happy face, Mommy. Do your crying face." She could name her favorite books, sing "Eensy Weensy Spider," and use pronouns and past and future tenses correctly.

At this writing, Anna is a cheerful, lively 10-year-old. She loves to read and to be read to, and is also an imaginative storyteller. As a fifth-grade project, she wrote a research report on a dinosaur called the Iguanadon.

In many ways, language is a good illustration of the study of human development; it involves both the change and the consistency that are typical of development, and it lends itself to study by all the basic methods used by investigators in the field. Of course, language, like any other aspect of human development, cannot be studied in a vacuum. In order to determine how best to help Anna, it was first necessary to rule out any physical or mental impediment or emotional problem that might be interfering with normal language development. Then, too, language affects other aspects of development. Language is a tool for thought—for classifying objects, grasping inferences and analogies, and thinking about ideas. Thus it is essential to normal mental development. The ability to use language effectively can also have an enormous effect on a child's—or an adult's—self-esteem and social relationships. As we discuss other aspects of human development throughout this book, we will look for linkages among them.

■ In this chapter, we begin with concepts fundamental to the study of human development. We sketch the history of the field, describe methods used by its practitioners, point out ethical considerations in research, and present the theoretical perspectives of some of the field's most influential thinkers. ■

✔ HUMAN DEVELOPMENT: BASIC CONCEPTS

The field of *human development* focuses on the scientific study of ways in which people change, as well as ways in which they stay the same, from conception to death. Change is most obvious in childhood, but occurs throughout life. Indeed, the

Besides being an enjoyable shared activity, reading with a child—as Anna's father is doing with her—is an important way to help language skills develop. *(Erika Stone)*

changes in a human being over the course of a lifetime are too numerous, too diverse, and often too random to study usefully. Developmentalists—professionals who study human development—therefore focus on *developmental change*. Developmental change is *systematic* in that it is coherent and organized. It is *adaptive* in that it is aimed at dealing with the ever-changing internal and external conditions of existence. It may take more than one route and may or may not have a definite goal; but there is some connection between the often-imperceptible changes of which it is composed.

There are two kinds of developmental change: quantitative and qualitative. ***Quantitative change*** is a change in number or amount, such as an increase in height and weight or in Anna's vocabulary. ***Qualitative change*** is a change in kind, structure, or organization, such as Anna's development from a nonverbal infant to a child who understands and speaks a language. Qualitative change is marked by the appearance of new phenomena that could not have been predicted from earlier functioning. Speech is one such phenomenon.

Despite such changes, most people show an underlying continuity, or consistency of personality and behavior. For example, about 10 to 15 percent of children are consistently shy, another 10 to 15 percent are very sociable, and most children fall between these extremes. Although various influences can modify these traits somewhat, the psychologist Jerome Kagan (1989) found that they persist to a moderate degree through at least the first 7½ years, especially in children at one extreme or the other. Research on adults has shown that certain characteristics—extraversion (or outgoingness), neuroticism, conscientiousness, agreeableness, and openness to new experiences—seem to be set by the age of 30.

As the field of human development became a scientific discipline, its goals evolved to include *description*, *explanation*, *prediction*, and *modification* of behavior. By looking at language development, we can see how these four functions work together. For example, to *describe* the time when most normal children say their first word or the extent of their vocabulary at a certain age, developmentalists observe large groups of children and establish norms, or averages, for behavior at various ages. They then attempt to *explain* what causes or influences the observed behavior; for example, how children acquire and learn to use language, and why a child may not progress at the usual rate. This knowledge may make it possible to *predict* what language ability at a given age can tell about later behavior. (Might Anna's language delay at age 2½, if untreated, have predicted reading problems later on?) Finally, awareness of how language develops may be used to *modify* behavior by intervening to promote optimal development, as Anna's therapist did in designing her treatment program.

An understanding of adult development, too, can have practical implications. It can help people deal with life's transitions: a woman returning to work after maternity leave, a person making a career change or about to retire, a widow or widower dealing with loss, someone coping with a terminal illness.

Students of development are interested in factors that affect everyone, but they also want to know why one person turns out so different from another. Because human development is complex, scientists cannot always answer that question. However, developmentalists have learned much about what people need to develop normally, how they react to the many influences upon and within them, and how they can best fulfill their potential.

PERIODS OF THE LIFE SPAN

In this book we divide the human life span into eight periods: (1) prenatal, (2) infancy and toddlerhood, (3) early childhood, (4) middle childhood, (5) adolescence, (6) young adulthood, (7) middle adulthood, and (8) late adulthood. These age divisions are approximate and somewhat arbitrary. This is especially true of adulthood, when there are no clear-cut social or physical landmarks, such as starting school and entering puberty, to signal a shift from one period to another. Still, at least in most western societies today, each period has characteristic events and concerns (see Table 1-1).

ASPECTS OF DEVELOPMENT

One reason for the complexity of human development is that changes occur in many different aspects of the self. To simplify discussion, we talk separately about *physical development, cognitive development,* and *psychosocial development* at each period of life, but actually these aspects of development are intertwined. Each affects the others.

Changes in the body, the brain, sensory capacities, and motor skills are part of *physical development* and may influence other aspects of development. For example, a child who has a hearing loss may be at risk of delayed language development. During puberty, dramatic physiological and hormonal changes affect the developing sense of self. In some older adults, physical changes in the brain cause intellectual and personality deterioration. Although physical development is in part genetically programmed, research now suggests that people can control their own physical development to a greater extent than was once thought possible.

Changes in mental abilities, such as learning, memory, reasoning, thinking, and language, constitute *cognitive development.* The ability to speak depends on the development of physical structures in the mouth and brain. A baby's growing memory contributes to the emotional experience of *separation anxiety,* the fear that the mother will not return once she has gone away. If children could not remember the past and anticipate the future, they would not be as likely to worry about the mother's absence.

TABLE 1-1

Major Developments in Eight Periods of the Life Span

Age Period	Major Developments
Prenatal stage (conception) to birth)	Basic body structure and organs form. Physical growth is most rapid in life span. Vulnerability to environmental influences is great.
Infancy and toddlerhood (birth to age 3)	Newborn is dependent but competent. All senses operate at birth. Physical growth and development of motor skills are rapid. Ability to learn and remember is present, even in early weeks of life. Comprehension and speech develop rapidly. Self-awareness develops in second year. Attachments to parents and others form toward end of first year. Interest in other children increases.
Early childhood (3 to 6 years)	Fine and gross motor skills and strength improve. Behavior is largely egocentric, but understanding of other people's perspectives grows. Cognitive immaturity leads to some illogical ideas about the world. Play, creativity, and imagination become more elaborate. Independence, self-control, and self-care increase. Family is still focus of life, although other children become more important.
Middle childhood (6 to 12 years)	Physical growth slows. Strength and athletic skills improve. Egocentrism diminishes. Children begin to think logically, although largely concretely. Memory and language skills increase. Cognitive gains enable children to benefit from formal schooling. Self-concept develops, affecting self-esteem. Peers assume central importance.
Adolescence (12 to about 20 years)	Physical changes are rapid and profound. Reproductive maturity arrives. Ability to think abstractly and use scientific reasoning develops. Adolescent egocentrism persists in some behaviors. Search for identity becomes central. Peer groups help develop and test self-concept. Relationships with parents are generally good.
Young adulthood (20 to 40 years)	Physical health peaks, then declines slightly. Cognitive abilities assume more complexity. Decisions are made about intimate relationships. Most people marry, most become parents. Career choices are made.
Middle age (40 to 65 years)	Some deterioration of physical health, stamina, and prowess takes place. Women experience menopause. Wisdom and practical problem-solving skills are high; ability to solve novel problems declines. Sense of identity continues to develop. Double responsibilities of caring for children and elderly parents may cause stress. Launching of children typically leaves empty nest. For some, career success and earning powers peak; for others, burnout occurs.

(Continued)

TABLE 1-1 (Cont.)

Major Developments in Eight Periods of the Life Span

Age Period	Major Developments
	Search for meaning in life assumes central importance.
	For some, there may be a midlife crisis.
Late adulthood (65 years and over)	Most people are healthy and active, although health and physical abilities decline somewhat.
	Slowing of reaction time affects many aspects of functioning.
	Most people are mentally alert. Although intelligence and memory may deteriorate in some areas, most people find ways to compensate.
	Retirement from work force may create more leisure time but may reduce economic circumstances.
	People need to cope with losses in many areas (loss of one's own faculties, loss of loved ones) and their own impending death.

Personality is a person's unique and relatively consistent way of feeling, reacting, and behaving. *Social development* refers to changes in relationships with others. Taken together, they constitute *psychosocial development*. Changes in this realm can affect cognitive and physical functioning. For example, anxiety about taking a test can impair performance. Social support can help people cope with the potentially negative effects of stress on their physical and mental health. Conversely, physical and cognitive capacities can affect psychosocial development. They contribute greatly to self-esteem and can affect social acceptance and choice of occupation.

INDIVIDUAL DIFFERENCES

Throughout this book, we talk about average ages for the occurrence of certain phenomena: the first word, the first menstruation, the development of abstract thought. But these ages are *merely* averages. Although people typically proceed through the same general sequence of development, there is a wide range of individual differences. Only when deviation from a norm is extreme is there cause to consider a person's development exceptionally advanced or delayed.

Not only rates but also results of development vary. People differ in height, weight, and body build; in constitutional factors such as health and energy level; in comprehension of complex ideas; and in emotional reactions. Their lifestyles differ too: the work they do, how well they do it, and how much they like it; the homes and communities they live in and how they feel about them; the people they see and the relationships they have; and how they spend their leisure time.

Individual differences increase as people grow older. Children pass the same milestones in development at nearly the same ages. Many changes of childhood seem to be tied to *maturation* of the body and brain—the unfolding of a definite sequence of physical changes and behavior patterns, including readiness to master new abilities such as walking and talking. Later, differences in life experience play a greater role.

INFLUENCES ON DEVELOPMENT

Development is subject to many influences. Some originate with *heredity*, the inborn genetic endowment that human beings receive from their biological parents. Others come from the external *environment*, the world outside the self, beginning in the womb. But this distinction soon blurs: people change their world even as it changes them. A baby girl born with a cheerful disposition, for example, is likely to get positive reactions from adults, which strengthen her trust that her smiles will be rewarded and motivate her to smile more.

In discussing how people develop, we look at influences that affect many or most people and also at those which affect people differently, such as gender, race, ethnicity, culture, lifestyle, family constellation, and socioeconomic status (social class, education, occupation, and income). We also look at the presence or absence of physical or mental disabilities. Some experiences are purely individual; others are common to certain groups—to age groups, to generations, or to people who live in or were raised in particular societies and cultures at particular times.

Normative and Nonnormative Influences

Some researchers distinguish between normative and nonnormative influences on development (Baltes, Reese, & Lipsitt, 1980).

An event is *normative* when it occurs in a similar way for most people in a given group. *Normative age-graded influences* are highly similar for people in a particular age group. They include biological events (such as puberty and menopause) as well as cultural events (such as entry into formal education and retirement from paid employment).

Normative history-graded influences are common to a particular *cohort:* a group of people who share a similar experience, in this case, growing up at the same time in the same place. Some examples are the political turmoil in the United States during the 1960s and 1970s in reaction to the war in Vietnam, the massive famines in Africa during the 1980s and 1990s, and the violent conflicts in eastern Europe in the 1990s. Also in this category are such cultural developments as the changing roles of women, the use of anesthesia during childbirth, and the impact of television and computers.

Nonnormative life events are unusual events that have a major impact on individual lives. They are either typical events that happen to a person at an atypical time of life (such as the death of a parent when a child is young) or atypical events (such as being in an airplane crash or having a birth defect). They can also, of course, be happy events, like Anna's adoption. Whether such an event is positive or negative, it is likely to cause stress when a person does not expect it. People often help create their own nonnormative life events—by, say, applying for a new job or taking up a risky hobby such as skydiving—and thus participate actively in their own development.

Timing of Influences: Critical Periods

A *critical period* is a specific time during development when a given event has its greatest impact. For example, if a woman receives x-rays, takes certain drugs, or contracts certain diseases at specific times during pregnancy, the fetus may show specific ill effects. The amount and kind of damage to the fetus will vary, depending on the nature of the "shock" and on its timing.

The concept of critical periods has been applied to psychological development as well. Lenneberg (1969) proposed a critical period for language development, before puberty. But although evidence for critical periods of physical development, particularly fetal development, is undeniable, for other aspects of development the concept is very controversial. The human organism may be particularly *sensitive* to certain psychological experiences at certain times of life, but later events can often reverse the effects of early ones.

Normative history-graded influences, such as the impact of home computers, can affect an entire cohort. Children who learn to use computers at an early age are likely to grow up more comfortable with this technological tool than their parents—and may even think differently. *(Shackman/Monkmeyer)*

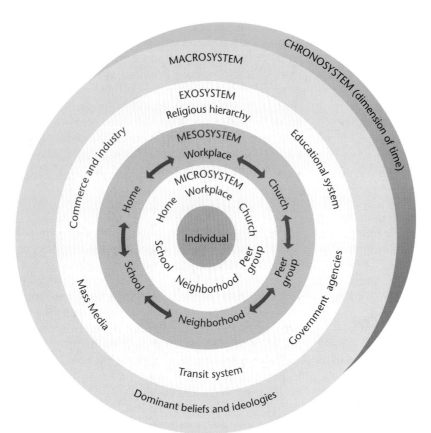

FIGURE 1-1
Ecological view of influences on development. Concentric circles indicate the most intimate environment (innermost area) to the broadest—all within the dimension of time. (*Source: Based on Cole & Cole, 1989.*)

Influences in Context: An Ecological Approach

An important way of classifying influences is by immediacy of impact. Urie Bronfenbrenner's (1979, 1986, 1994) *ecological approach* to development identifies five levels of environmental influence, from the most intimate to the broadest (see Figure 1-1). He describes them as "a set of nested structures, each inside the other like a set of Russian dolls" (1994, p. 1645). To understand individual development, we must study a person in the context of these multiple environments.

■ The *microsystem* is the everyday environment of home, school, work, or neighborhood. It includes face-to-face bidirectional relationships with parents, siblings, caregivers, classmates, and teachers. Influences flow back and forth: How, for example, does a new baby affect the parents' lives? How do their attitudes affect the baby?

■ The *mesosystem* is the interlocking of various microsystems that contain the developing person—in other words, a system of microsystems. These may include linkages between home and school, home and work, or the family and the peer group. When parents and teachers collab-

orate in educational planning, for example, children tend to do better in school.

■ The *exosystem* refers to linkages between two or more settings, at least one of which does not contain the developing person but affects him or her indirectly. Three that are especially likely to influence children's development are the parents' workplaces, parents' social networks, and links between family and community. For example, a mother who is frustrated at work may mistreat her children.

■ The *macrosystem* consists of overarching cultural patterns, such as dominant beliefs, ideologies, and economic and political systems. How is a person affected by living in a capitalist or socialist society?

■ The *chronosystem* adds the dimension of time: the influence of normative or nonnormative change or constancy in the person and the environment. This can include changes in family structure, place of residence, or employment, as well as larger cultural changes such as wars and economic cycles.

By looking at systems that affect individuals in and beyond the family, this ecological approach shows the variety of influences on human development. The relative importance of each system may vary from one society to another and from one cultural group to another within the same society. This is one reason for doing cross-cultural research.

THE ROLE OF CULTURE

When adults in the Kpelle tribe in central Liberia were asked to sort 20 objects, they consistently sorted on the basis of functional categories (that is, they matched a knife with an orange or a potato with a hoe). Western psychologists associate functional sorting with a low level of thought; but since the Kpelle kept saying that this was how a "wise man" would do it, the experimenter finally asked, "How would a fool do it?" He then received the "higher-order" categories he had originally expected—four neat piles with food in one, tools in another, and so on (Glick, 1975, p. 636).

Cross-cultural research can tell us which aspects of development are universal (and thus seem to be intrinsic to the human condition) and which are culturally determined. For example, no matter where children live, they learn to speak in the same sequence, advancing from cooing and babbling to single words and then to simple combinations of words. The sentences of toddlers around the world are structured similarly, though the words vary. Such findings suggest that the capacity for learning language is inborn. On the other hand, culture can exert a surprisingly large influence on early motor development. African babies, whose parents often prop them in a sitting position and bounce them on their feet, tend to sit and walk earlier than American babies (Rogoff & Morelli, 1989).

This book discusses several influential theories developed from research on western people that do not hold up when tested on people from other cultures—theories about gender roles, abstract thinking, moral reasoning, and a number of other topics. In each chapter, we look at people in cultures other than the dominant one in the United States to show how closely human development is tied to society and culture and to try to understand development in a variety of settings.

✔ HUMAN DEVELOPMENT: HOW THE STUDY HAS EVOLVED

Human development has, of course, been going on as long as human beings have existed; but formal scientific study of human development is rela-

Compulsory vaccination of children helped curb a smallpox epidemic in New Jersey during the 1880s, saving many lives. The discovery of germs and immunization paved the way for the study of child development by showing that adults can affect what happens to children. *(National Library of Medicine)*

tively new. There have been dramatic changes both in the way adults look at children and in the way psychologists view adult development.

STUDYING CHILDHOOD

According to the French historian Philippe Ariès (1962), not until the seventeenth century were children seen as qualitatively different from adults; before that, children were considered simply smaller, weaker, and less intelligent. Ariès based his opinion on historical sources. Old paintings showed children dressed like their elders. Documents described children working long hours, leaving their parents at early ages for apprenticeships, and suffering brutality at the hands of adults. Ariès's view has been widely accepted. However, the psychologist David Elkind (1986) found recognition of children's special nature in the Bible and in the works of the ancient Greeks and Romans. And after examining autobiographies, diaries, and literature going back to the sixteenth century, Linda A. Pollock (1983) makes a strong argument that children have historically been seen and treated differently from adults.

Although people throughout history have held various ideas about what children are like and how they should be raised, not until the nineteenth century did several important trends prepare the way for the scientific study of child development. By that time, scientists had unlocked the mystery of conception and were beginning to argue about the relative importance of heredity and environment. The discovery of germs and immunization allowed parents to protect their children from the plagues and fevers that had made survival so uncertain. Adults came to feel more responsible for the way children developed, instead of simply accepting misfortune or misbehavior as the workings of fate. Because of an abundance of cheap labor, children were less needed as workers, and new laws protecting them from long workdays let them spend more time in school. The new science of psychology taught that people could understand themselves by learning what had influenced them as children.

STUDYING ADOLESCENCE, ADULTHOOD, AND AGING

Adolescence was not considered a separate phase of development until the early twentieth century, when G. Stanley Hall, a pioneer in child study, published a book called *Adolescence* (1904/1916). This popular (if unscientific) work stimulated thought and discussion about what then came to be known as a separate period of life.

Hall was also one of the first psychologists to become interested in aging. In 1922, at age 78, he published *Senescence: The Last Half of Life.* Six years later, Stanford University opened the first major scientific research unit devoted to aging. But not until a generation later did this area of study blossom. By 1946, the National Institutes of Health (NIH) had set up a large-scale research unit, and specialized organizations and journals were reporting the latest findings.

Since the late 1930s, a number of long-term studies have focused on adults. The Grant Study of Adult Development followed Harvard University students through adulthood. In the mid-1950s Bernice Neugarten and her associates at the University of Chicago began studies of middle-aged people, and K. Warner Schaie launched the still-ongoing Seattle Longitudinal Study of adult intelligence. In the late 1950s, Paul Costa and Robert McCrae began a study of personality traits in thousands of adults of all ages in Boston and Baltimore.

These and other studies have added much to our understanding of human development. We still, however, know more about children and the elderly than we do about those in between. The growing number of studies on young and middle-aged adults should yield fruit in years to come.

STUDYING THE LIFE SPAN

Full life-span studies in the United States grew out of programs designed to follow children through adulthood. The Stanford Studies of Gifted Children (begun in 1921 under the direction of Lewis Terman) continue to trace the development of people (now in old age) who were identified as unusually intelligent in childhood. Other major studies that began around 1930—the Fels Research Institute Study, the Berkeley Growth and Guidance Studies, and the Oakland (Adolescent) Growth Study—have given us much information on long-term development.

Today most psychologists recognize that human development goes on throughout life. Each period of the life span is influenced by what occurred before and will affect what is to come. This concept of a lifelong process of development is known as *life-span development.* Scientific study of life-span development is the primary task of life-span developmental psychology. The idea that development goes on throughout life suggests that each part of the life span has its own unique characteristics and value; no part is more or less important than any other.

Paul B. Baltes (1987), a leader in shaping the concept and study of life-span development, has identified key features of a life-span developmental approach. Among them are:

■ *Multidirectionality:* According to Baltes, development throughout life involves a balance of growth and decline. As people gain in one area, they may lose in another, and at varying rates. Children grow mostly in one direction—up—both in size and in abilities. In adulthood the balance gradually shifts. Some capacities, such as vocabulary, continue to increase; others, such as the ability to solve unfamiliar problems, normally diminish; and some new attributes, such as wisdom, may emerge.
■ *Plasticity:* Many skills can be significantly modified with training and practice, even in late life, but the potential for change is not unbounded. Researchers now are testing the limits of improvement in memory training.
■ *History and context:* Each person develops within

a specific set of circumstances or conditions defined by time and place. During the course of development, human beings influence, and are influenced by, their historical and social context. They not only respond to their environment but interact with and change it.

■ *Multiple causation:* Because development has a variety of causes, to view behavior from the standpoint of psychology alone would be incomplete. The study of human development requires a partnership of scholars from many fields. How, for example, can we fully understand the psychological impact of menopause without knowing about the biological changes occurring in a woman's body or about the ways different cultures regard this transition?

In keeping with a life-span developmental approach, students of human development draw on many disciplines, including psychology, sociology, anthropology, biology, family studies, education, and medicine. This book includes findings from research in all these fields.

LIFE-SPAN ISSUE
CAN EARLY PERSONALITY TRAITS PREDICT MIDLIFE DEVELOPMENT?

John A. Clausen is professor of sociology emeritus and director of the Institute of Human Development at the University of California at Berkeley. When he arrived at Berkeley after directing research at the National Institute of Mental Health, the three life-span studies known collectively as the Berkeley Longitudinal Studies had been going on for three decades, and the participants were in their thirties. Clausen devoted the next three decades to carrying on this work. His book American Lives *(1993) draws on those 60 years of research to tease out connections between personality traits shown in childhood and at midlife.*
(Photo: Peg Skorpinski)

Stuart Campbell, orphaned at age 6 by his mother's death and his alcoholic father's abandonment, was raised in near poverty by his stern but loving grandmother. In 1932, at age 11, he became one of more than 500 children recruited for the Berkeley Longitudinal Studies. The study in which Stuart was enrolled was the Oakland (Adolescent) Growth Study, initially designed to assess social and emotional development through the senior high school years. Twenty years later, a full-scale

follow-up study began; ultimately, more than 300 of the participants in the three studies were followed into old age.

All participants had medical examinations, and their family histories and current family situations were recorded. They took periodic intelligence and psychological tests, including personality inventories (instruments that yield quantitative ratings of certain traits or groups of traits). The researchers developed detailed life histories of 60 participants, including Stuart Campbell, on the basis of recorded data and interviews.

Eventually the research began to focus on a theoretical construct (phenomenon) that the personality inventories called "planful competence," a combination of self-confidence, intellectual commitment, and dependable effectiveness. Of the 60 youngsters, Stuart Campbell had the highest score for planful competence.

At first, the investigators were most interested in how people develop planful competence. Parenting that combined high standards, loving support, and firm control emerged as a major influence. Later the central question became the extent to which planful competence persists and affects success in life.

Clausen (1993), analyzing the results of the study, concluded that planful competence helps people mobilize resources and cope with difficulties. Planful competence did not *guarantee* success, nor did its absence ensure failure. But it did turn out to be the most powerful influence on the course of a person's life. The personalities of people who as teenagers had shown planful competence changed less than those of less competent teenagers. Competent teenagers made good choices in adolescence and early adulthood, which often led to promising opportunities (scholarships, good jobs, and competent spouses); less competent teenagers made poorer early decisions and then tended to lead crisis-ridden lives.

Stuart Campbell, for example, in junior high school and high school was judged to be unusually mature, intelligent, and mentally healthy, with a good sense of humor. He knew by age 17 that he wanted to be a doctor. He became a pediatrician, married early, went through an amicable divorce, married again (this time happily), had five children, and established a home and a solid professional and civic reputation in an upper-middle-class community. He was a strong family man, a man who could be counted on. At age 61, he was self-confident, intellectually involved, and dependable, as well as outgoing, warm, agreeable, and modestly assertive—all qualities he had shown since early adolescence.

Although the report of these studies is entitled *American Lives,* it actually is a report of only some American lives. The participants were a cohort born in the 1920s in one part of the country (the San Francisco Bay area) and—like most of the people living there at the time—were almost entirely white, mostly native-born, Christian, and middle-class. Thus the findings might not apply to people of other races, religions, or ethnic or socioeconomic backgrounds. Also, of the approximately

200 participants who dropped out, a disproportionate number were from families with financial or interpersonal problems, making the study group even less representative of the total population. Still, the findings can be useful as an indication of the persistence of personality traits throughout adulthood and of human beings' ability to help shape their own lives.

✔ HUMAN DEVELOPMENT: RESEARCH METHODS

The purpose of research such as the life-span studies just described is to draw conclusions about the world and the human beings who inhabit it. Although researchers in various branches of the physical and social sciences use varying methods, the *scientific method* refers to principles and processes that characterize scientific inquiry in any field: identification of the problem to be studied; formulation of *hypotheses* (explanations or predictions that can be tested); collection of *data* (information obtained through research); statistical analysis to determine whether the data support the hypothesis; and public dissemination of findings so that other observers can check, learn from, analyze, repeat, and build on the work. Only by following these principles and processes can developmentalists produce sound conclusions that explain and predict human behavior.

Two key issues at the outset of any investigation are how the participants will be chosen—the sampling method—and how the data will be collected. These decisions often depend on what questions the research is intended to answer. All these issues play a part in a research design, or plan.

SAMPLING

How can we be sure that the results of research are true in general and not just for the participants? First of all, we need to control who gets into the study. Because studying an entire *population* (a group to which we want to apply the findings) is usually too costly and time-consuming, investigators select a *sample,* a smaller group within the population. But, as we saw with the Oakland (Adolescent) Growth Study, it is important to make sure that a sample does not leave out or greatly underrepresent major segments of the group under study. Otherwise the results cannot properly be *generalized*, or applied to the population as a whole.

One way to ensure representatives is by *random selection,* in which each person in a population has an equal and independent chance of being chosen. One way to select a random sample of the students in a human development class, for example, would be to put all their names into a hat, shake it, and then draw out a certain number of names. A random sample, especially a large one, is likely to represent the population well, that is, to show relevant characteristics and behavior in the same proportion in which they are found in the entire group.

FORMS OF DATA COLLECTION

Common ways of gathering data include self-reports (verbal reports of a person's own thoughts, feelings, or actions), tests and other behavioral measures, and observation (see Table 1-2). Researchers may use one or more of these data collection techniques in any research design.

Self-Reports: Diaries, Interviews, and Questionnaires

The simplest form of self-report is a *diary* or log. People may be asked, for example, to record the foods they eat each day, the times when they feel depressed, or the times when they forget something. Other types of self-reports are interviews and questionnaires.

In a face-to-face or telephone *interview,* researchers ask questions about attitudes, opinions, or behavior. For example, interviews with nearly a hundred 7- to 18-year-olds who attended a private girls' school in Ohio formed the basis of a study on how girls negotiate the transition to womanhood (Brown & Gilligan, 1992). To reach more people, researchers sometimes distribute a printed *questionnaire,* which participants fill out and return.

Interviews or questionnaires often cover such topics as parent-child relationships, sexual activities, and occupational goals. By questioning a large number of people, investigators get a broad picture—at least of what the respondents *say* they believe or do or did. But some people forget when and how events actually took place, and others consciously or unconsciously distort their replies to please the researchers. Also, how a question is asked, and by whom, can affect the answer. When researchers at the National Institute on Drug Abuse reworded a question about alcohol use to indicate that a "drink" meant "more than a few

vantage is flexibility: the researcher is free to explore avenues of inquiry that arise during the course of the study. But case studies have shortcomings. From studying Genie, for instance, we learn much about the development of a single child, but not how well the information applies to people in general. Furthermore, case studies cannot explain behavior with certainty, because there is no way to test their conclusions. Even though it seems reasonable that Genie's severely deprived environment caused her language deficiency, it is impossible to know whether she would have developed normally if she had had a normal upbringing.

Correlational Studies

A *correlational study* is an attempt to find a *correlation,* or statistical relationship, between *variables*—phenomena that change or vary among people or can be varied for purposes of research. Correlations are expressed in terms of direction (positive or negative) and magnitude (degree). Two variables that are related *positively* increase or decrease together. A positive, or direct, correlation between blood pressure and risk of heart attack would exist if we found that people with high blood pressure are more likely to have heart attacks than people with low blood pressure. Two variables have a *negative,* or inverse, correlation if, as one increases, the other decreases. Studies in Shanghai, China, and a number of other countries show a negative correlation between educational level and the risk of dementia due to Alzheimer's disease. In other words, less schooling is associated with more dementia (Katzman, 1993).

Correlations are reported as numbers ranging from −1.0 (a perfect negative relationship) to +1.0 (a perfect positive relationship). Perfect correlations are rare. The closer a correlation comes to +1.0 or −1.0, the stronger the relationship, either positive or negative. A correlation of zero means that the variables have no relationship (see Figure 1-2, page 17).

Correlations allow us to *predict* one variable on the basis of another. If, for example, we found a positive correlation between watching televised violence and fighting, we would predict that children who watch violent shows are more likely to get into fights. The greater the magnitude of the correlation between two variables, the greater the ability to predict one from the other.

Although correlations suggest *possible* causes for outcomes, they do *not* allow us to draw conclusions about cause and effect. We cannot conclude, for example, that high blood pressure *causes* heart attacks; we can conclude *only* that the two variables are related. It is possible that a third variable—perhaps an inborn predisposition or lifestyle factor—causes *both* high blood pressure and a heightened risk of heart attack. To be sure that one variable causes another, we would need to design a controlled experiment—something that, in studying human beings, is often not possible for practical or ethical reasons. (See Box 1-1 for a discussion of ethical issues in research.)

Playing with babies is work for the psychologist Tiffany Field, who studies children by laboratory observation. At a child development center affiliated with a university medical school and hospital, Field follows up high-risk infants to assess the effects of early social interactions. *(Roe DiBona)*

BOX 1-1   FOOD FOR THOUGHT

ETHICS OF RESEARCH

Should research that might harm its participants ever be undertaken? How can we balance the possible benefits to humanity against the risk of intellectual, emotional, or physical injury to individuals?

Since the 1970s, federally mandated committees have been set up at colleges, universities, and other institutions to review proposed research from an ethical standpoint. The American Psychological Association's guidelines cover such points as protection of research participants from harm and loss of dignity; guarantees of privacy and confidentiality, informed consent, avoidance of deception, and the right to decline or withdraw from an experiment at any time; and the responsibility of investigators to correct any undesirable effects. Still, researchers often face troubling ethical questions concerning participants' rights.

RIGHT TO INFORMED CONSENT

Informed consent exists when participants voluntarily agree to be in a study, are competent to give consent, are fully aware of the risks as well as the potential benefits, and are not being exploited. However, some potential research participants, such as very young children or demented persons, may not be capable of giving consent. When parents, school personnel, or caregivers consent to a child's or a demented person's participation in research, can we be sure that they are acting in that person's best interests?

The National Commission for the Protection of Human Subjects of Biomedical and Behavioral Research (1978) recommends that children age 7 or over should be asked to give their own consent to take part in research and that children's objections should be overruled only if the research promises direct benefit to the child, as in the use of an experimental drug to cure a debilitating disease. On the other hand, studies that seek the causes and treatments for Alzheimer's disease need participants whose mental status may preclude their being fully or even partially aware of what is involved. What if a person gives consent and later forgets having done so? Current practice, to be on the safe side, is to ask *both* participants and caregivers for consent.

Obviously, informed consent cannot exist when participants are deceived about the nature of a study. Suppose that children are told they are trying out a new game when they are actually being tested on their reactions to success or failure? Suppose that adults are told they are participating in a study on learning when they are really being tested on their willingness to inflict pain? Experiments like these, which cannot be carried out without deception, have been done, and they have added significantly to our knowledge, but at the cost of the participants' right to know what they were getting involved in.

RIGHT TO SELF-ESTEEM

Should people be subjected to research that may damage their self-esteem? Studies on limits of memory, for example, have a built-in "failure factor": the researcher keeps asking questions until the participant is unable to answer. Might this inevitable failure affect a participant's self-confidence? Similarly, when researchers publish findings that middle-class children are academically superior to poor children, unintentional harm may be done to the latter's self-esteem. Furthermore, such studies may affect teachers' expectations and students' performance.

RIGHT TO PRIVACY

Is it ethical to use one-way mirrors and hidden cameras to observe people without their knowledge? How can we protect the confidentiality of personal information that participants may reveal in interviews or questionnaires (for example, about income or family relationships or even about illegal activities, such as smoking marijuana or shoplifting)?

Despite the stringent rules and vastly improved ethical climate that prevail today, specific situations often call for hard judgments. Everyone who is in the field of human development has to accept the responsibility to try to do good and, at the very least, to do no harm.

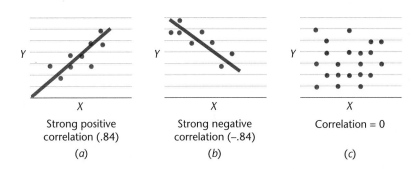

FIGURE 1-2
Correlational studies may find positive or negative correlations or no correlation. In a positive, or direct, correlation (a), data, plotted on a graph, cluster around a line showing that one variable (*X*) increases as the other variable (*Y*) increases. In a negative, or inverse, correlation (b), one variable (*X*) increases as the other variable (*Y*) decreases. No correlation, or a zero correlation, exists (c) when increases and decreases in two variables show no consistent relationship (that is, data plotted on a graph show no pattern).

Experiments

An *experiment* is a rigorously controlled procedure in which the investigator, called the *experimenter,* manipulates variables to learn how one affects another. Scientific experiments must be conducted and reported in such a way that another investigator can *replicate* them, that is, repeat them in exactly the same way with different participants to verify the results and conclusions. Figure 1-3 shows how an experiment might be designed.

Groups and Variables To conduct an experiment, the experimenter needs to divide the participants into two kinds of groups. An *experimental group* is composed of people who are to be exposed to the experimental manipulation, or *treatment*—the phenomenon the researcher wants to study. Afterward, the effect of the treatment will be measured one or more times. A *control group*

is composed of people who are similar to the experimental group but do not receive the treatment. An experiment must include one or more of each type of group. Ideally, as we've already discussed, to ensure that the results will be generalizable to people outside the study, the sample should be randomly selected.

To see how an experiment actually works, let's look at how one team of researchers (Whitehurst, Falco, et al., 1988) designed an experiment to find out what effect a certain method of reading aloud to children might have on their language and vocabulary skills. In this method, parents read picture books to the children, encourage the children's active participation, and give frequent, age-based feedback. In the read-aloud experiment, the researchers compared two groups of middle-class children ages 21 to 35 months. In the *experimental group*, the parents adopted the new reading method (the treatment); in the *control group*, the

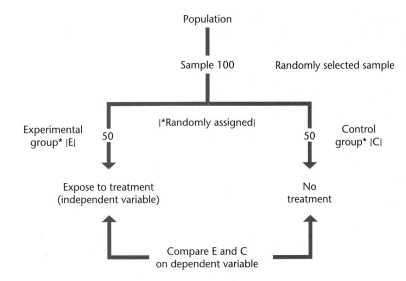

Conclusion: Any difference between the experimental group and the control group is due to treatment received by the experimental group.

FIGURE 1-3
Design for an experiment. This experiment takes a random sample from the larger population being studied, randomly assigns participants to either the experimental (E) or control (C) group, and exposes the experimental group to a treatment that is not given to the control group. By comparing the two groups after the experimental group has received the treatment, the researcher can conclude that any difference between them is due to the experimental treatment.

parents simply read aloud as they usually did. The parents of the children in the experimental group asked the children challenging open-ended questions rather than questions calling for simple yes-no answers. (Instead of asking, "Is the cat asleep?" they would ask, "What is the cat doing?") They expanded on the children's answers, corrected wrong answers, gave alternative possibilities, and bestowed praise. After 1 month of the program, the children in the experimental group were 8.5 months ahead of the control group in level of speech and 6 months ahead in vocabulary; 9 months later, the experimental group was still 6 months ahead of the controls. It is fair to conclude, then, that this reading method improved the children's language and vocabulary skills. (And that is why Diane and Jonathan adopted it in reading to Anna.)

In the experiment just described, the type of reading approach was the *independent variable,* and the children's language skills were the *dependent variable.* An **independent variable** is something over which the experimenter has direct control. A **dependent variable** is something that may or may not change as a result of changes in the independent variable; in other words, it *depends* on the independent variable. In an experiment, a researcher manipulates the independent variable to see how changes in it will affect the dependent variable.

Random Assignment If an experiment finds a significant difference in the performance of the experimental and control groups, how do we know

that the cause was the independent variable? For example, in the read-aloud experiment, how can we be sure that the reading method and not some other factor (such as intelligence) caused the difference in language development of the two groups? The answer lies in controlling who gets the treatment. This can be done by randomly assigning the participants to experimental and control groups so that each person has an equal chance of being assigned to either group. If assignment is random and the sample is large enough, differences in such factors as age, sex, race, IQ, and socioeconomic status will be evenly distributed so that the groups are as alike as possible in every respect except for the variable to be tested.

Laboratory, Field, and Natural Experiments Methods such as random assignment are most easily used in *laboratory experiments.* In a laboratory experiment the participants are brought to a special place where they experience conditions manipulated by the experimenter. The experimenter records the participants' reactions to these conditions, perhaps comparing them with their own or other participants' behavior under different conditions.

Not all experiments can be readily done in the laboratory. A *field experiment* is a controlled study conducted in a setting that is part of everyday life, such as a child's home or school. The experiment in which parents adopted a new way of reading aloud was a field experiment.

Laboratory and field experiments differ in two

Experiments use strictly controlled procedures that manipulate variables to determine how one affects another. To study emotional resiliency, this research project at the University of California at San Francisco monitors the heart rate and blood pressure of young children as they explain their feelings in response to a hand puppet's happy or angry face. *(James Wilson/Woodfin Camp & Assoc.)*

important respects. One is the *degree of control* exerted by the experimenter; the other is the degree to which findings can be *generalized* beyond the study situation. Laboratory experiments are more rigidly controlled and thus are easier to replicate. However, the results may be less generalizable to real life; because of the artificiality of the situation, participants may not act as they normally would.

When, for practical or ethical reasons, it is impossible to conduct a true experiment, a *natural experiment* may provide a way of studying certain events. A natural experiment compares people who have been accidentally "assigned" to separate groups by circumstances of life—members of one group who were exposed, say, to famine or a sexually transmitted disease or a birth defect or advanced education, and members of another group who were not. Natural experiments, because they do not try to manipulate behavior, are actually correlational studies.

Combining Experimentation with Other Designs There is no one "right" way to study human beings. Many questions can be approached from several angles, each yielding different kinds of information. Experiments have important advantages over other research designs: the ability to establish cause-and-effect relationships and to permit replication. However, experiments can be too artificial and too narrowly focused. Greater understanding of human development can result from designing experiments to pursue leads suggested by other kinds of studies. For example, the case study of Genie suggests that exposure to speech is related to language development. To examine this relationship further, we could design an experiment to see what kinds of verbal stimulation best promote language development. Similarly, observations of how parents talk to children can generate hypotheses and inspire experiments to test them.

STUDYING AGE EFFECTS:
QUASI-EXPERIMENTAL METHODS

If we want to study effects of age—or rather, of processes associated with age, such as hormonal changes, or changes in the brain—we are asking a question about a causal relationship. The appropriate research design would seem to be an experiment. But such an experiment can't be done, because age can't be controlled. Developmental processes vary among individuals, and investiga-

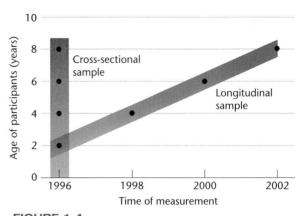

FIGURE 1-4
The two most common ways to obtain data about age-related development. In a *cross-sectional* study, people of different ages are measured at one time. Here, groups of 2-, 4-, 6-, and 8-year-olds were tested in 1996 to obtain data about age differences in performance. In a *longitudinal* study, the same people are measured more than once. Here, a sample of children were first measured in 1996, when they were 2 years old; follow-up testing will be done in 1998, 2000, and 2002, when the children are 4, 6, and 8, respectively. This technique shows age changes in performance.

tors can't randomly assign people to age groups to control for the variations. Therefore, most studies of age effects use a special type of correlational design called a *quasi-experiment*. A **quasi-experiment** looks something like an experiment; but, like a natural experiment, it lacks the critical feature that all true experiments must have: control based on random assignment.

The two most common quasi-experimental designs used to study human development are *longitudinal* and *cross-sectional* studies (see Figure 1-4). Because each of these designs has drawbacks, researchers have also devised *sequential* designs.

Longitudinal and Cross-sectional Studies

In a **longitudinal study,** such as the one Stuart Campbell participated in, researchers study the same people more than once, sometimes years apart, to measure changes that occur with age. They may measure a single characteristic, such as vocabulary size, IQ, height, or aggressiveness. Or they may look at several aspects of development, to find relationships among them.

In a **cross-sectional study,** people of different ages are assessed at one time. Cross-sectional studies provide information about *differences* in development among different age groups rather than about *changes* in the same person. In one cross-sectional study, people in six age groups from age 6 to late adulthood took a battery of cognitive tests. Middle-aged people scored highest, and young children and older adults scored lowest (Papalia, 1972). We could not necessarily conclude from these findings, however, that when the middle-aged participants became older, their performance would drop. The older participants may, as a cohort (generation), have had poorer education or other experiences that affected their performance, so that they may *never* have scored as high as the middle-aged participants. The only way to see whether change occurs in a particular person is to conduct a longitudinal study.

Each of these designs has strengths and weaknesses. Longitudinal studies are sensitive to individual patterns of change; by repeatedly studying the same people, researchers can track data about individuals. Also, *within* a study, they avoid the effects of cohort membership. However, a longitudinal study done on a particular cohort may not apply to a different cohort. (In other words, a study done with people born in 1930 may not apply to people born in 1990.) Furthermore, longitudinal studies are more time-consuming and expensive than cross-sectional studies; it is hard to follow a large group of participants over the years, to maintain records, and to keep the study going despite turnover in research personnel. Then there is the problem of attrition: participants may die or drop out. Another likely difficulty is bias in the sample: people who volunteer for such studies, and especially those who stay with them, tend to be above average in intelligence and socioeconomic status. Also, results can be affected by repeated testing: people may do better in later tests because they have become familiar with test materials and procedures.

Advantages of cross-sectional research include speed and economy; data can be gathered fairly quickly from large number of people. And, since participants are assessed only once, there is no problem of attrition. A drawback of cross-sectional studies is that they mask individual differences by looking only at group averages. Their major disadvantage, however, is the one we've already mentioned: they cannot eliminate cohort influences on people born at different times. Cross-sectional studies are sometimes interpreted as yielding information about developmental changes in groups or individuals, but such information is often misleading.

Sequential Studies

The *cross-sequential study* is one of several sequential strategies designed to overcome the drawbacks of longitudinal and cross-sectional studies. This method combines the other two: researchers assess a cross-sectional sample more than once to determine differences in each age cohort over a period of time. Most sequential research has focused on intelligence and seems to provide a more accurate assessment of intellectual functioning in adulthood than cross-sectional or longitudinal studies. For example, sequential studies have provided clear evidence of cohort effects on intellectual performance (Schaie, 1990). Their major drawbacks—and they can be daunting—involve time, effort, and complexity. Sequential designs require large numbers of participants and the collection and analysis of huge amounts of data over a period of years. Interpreting their findings and conclusions can demand a high degree of sophistication.

✔ HUMAN DEVELOPMENT: THEORETICAL PERSPECTIVES

Developmentalists have come up with many explanations, or theories, about why people behave as they do. A *theory* is a coherent set of related concepts that seeks to organize and explain data gathered through research. Theories are dynamic; they change to incorporate new findings, and they serve as a continuing source of hypotheses to be tested by research. Sometimes research supports a hypothesis and the theory on which it was based. At other times, scientists must modify their theories to account for unexpected data.

No one theory of human development is universally accepted, and no one theory explains all facets of development. Different investigators look from different perspectives at how human beings develop. Their perspectives influence the questions they ask, the research methods they use, and the ways they interpret data. Therefore, to evaluate and interpret research, it is important to know the researcher's theoretical perspective.

Some theories give more weight to innate factors (heredity), others to environment or experience—though most contemporary theories acknowledge the interaction of the two. Theories also differ as to whether they emphasize quantitative or qualitative development and as to whether they view development as continuous or discontinuous. Stage theorists see development as a series of separate steps rising from one level to the next, with rests on the "landings"; other theories see development as a gradual, continuous process, like walking up a ramp.

Let's look at key features of five perspectives (summarized in Table 1-4) that underlie influential theories and research on human development: (1) *psychoanalytic* (which focuses on emotions); (2) *learning* (which emphasizes observable behavior); (3) *cognitive* (which stresses thought processes); (4) *ethological* (which focuses on the evolutionary underpinnings of behavior); and (5) *contextual* (which emphasizes the impact of the social and cultural context). A sixth perspective, the *humanistic* perspective, is discussed in Chapter 13.

PSYCHOANALYTIC PERSPECTIVE

The ***psychoanalytic perspective*** is concerned with unconscious forces that motivate human behavior; it seeks to describe *qualitative* change. This view originated at the beginning of the twentieth century, when a Viennese physician named Sigmund Freud developed *psychoanalysis,* a therapeutic approach aimed at giving people insight into unconscious emotional conflicts. The psychoanalytic perspective has been expanded and modified by other theorists, including Erik H. Erikson and Jean Baker Miller.

Sigmund Freud: Psychosexual Theory

Sigmund Freud (1856–1939) wanted to devote himself to medical research, but limited funds and barriers to academic advancement for Jews in Austria forced him into the private practice of medicine. One of his main interests was neurology, the study of the brain and treatment of disorders of the nervous system, a branch of medicine then in its infancy. To relieve symptoms with no apparent physical cause, Freud asked questions designed to summon up long-buried memories. He concluded that the source of emotional disturbances lay in repressed traumatic experiences of early childhood.

Freud (1935/1953, 1933/1964a, 1940/1964b) believed that personality is formed in the first few years of life, as children deal with conflicts between their inborn biological, sexually related

The Viennese physician Sigmund Freud developed an original, influential, and controversial theory of psychosexual development in childhood, based on his adult patients' recollections. His daughter, Anna, shown here with her father, followed in his professional footsteps and constructed her own theories of personality development. *(Mary Evans/Sigmund Freud Copyrights)*

urges and the requirements of society. He proposed that these conflicts occur in an unvarying, maturation-based sequence of stages of ***psychosexual development,*** in which pleasure shifts from one body zone to another—from the mouth to the anus and then to the genitals. At each stage, the behavior that is the chief source of gratification changes—from feeding to elimination and eventually to sexual activity.

Of the five stages of personality development that Freud described (see Table 1-5), he considered the first three—those of the first few years of life—crucial. He suggested that if children receive too little or too much gratification in any of these stages, they are at risk of *fixation*—an arrest in development—and may need help to move beyond that stage. He believed that evidence of childhood fixation shows up in adult personality. For example, babies whose needs are not met during the *oral stage* of infancy, when feeding is the main source of sensual pleasure, may grow up to become nail-

TABLE 1-4

Five Perspectives on Human Development

Perspective	Important Theories	Basic Beliefs	Technique Used	Stage-Oriented	Causal Emphasis
Psychoanalytic	Freud's psychosexual theory	Behavior is controlled by powerful unconscious urges	Clinical observation	Yes	Innate factors modified by experience
	Erikson's psychosocial theory	Personality is influenced by society and develops through a series of crises.	Clinical observation	Yes	Interaction of innate and experiential factors
	Miller's relational theory	Personality develops in the context of emotional relationships.	Clinical observation	No	Interaction of innate and experiential factors
Learning	Behaviorism, or traditional learning theory (Pavlov, Skinner, Watson)	People are responders; the environment controls behavior.	Rigorous scientific (experimental) procedures	No	Experience
	Social-learning (social-cognitive) theory (Bandura)	Children learn in a social context, by observing and imitating models; person is an active contributor to learning.	Rigorous scientific (experimental) procedures	No	Experience modified by innate factors
Cognitive	Piaget's cognitive-stage theory	Qualitative changes in thought between infancy and adolescence. Person is active initiator of development.	Flexible interviews; meticulous observation	Yes	Interaction of innate and experiential factors
	Information-processing theory	Human beings are processors of symbols.	Laboratory research; technological monitoring of physiologic responses	No	Interaction of innate and experiential factors
Ethological	Bowlby's and Ainsworth's attachment theory	Human beings have the adaptive mechanisms to survive; critical or sensitive periods are stressed; biological and evolutionary basis for behavior and predisposition toward learning are important.	Naturalistic and laboratory observation	No	Interaction of innate and experiential factors
Contextual	Vygotsky's sociocultural theory	Child's sociocultural context has an important impact on development.	Cross-cultural research; observation of child interacting with more competent person	No	Experience

TABLE 1-5

Developmental Stages According to Various Theories

Psychosexual Stages (Freud)	Psychosocial Stages (Erikson)	Cognitive Stages (Piaget)
Oral (birth to 12–18 months). Baby's chief source of pleasure involves mouth-oriented activities (sucking and eating).	*Basic trust versus mistrust (birth to 12–18 months).* Baby develops sense of whether world is a good and safe place. Virtue: hope.	*Sensorimotor (birth to 2 years).* Infant gradually becomes able to organize activities in relation to the environment through sensory and motor activity.
Anal (12–18 months to 3 years). Child derives sensual gratification from withholding and expelling feces. Zone of gratification is anal region.	*Autonomy versus shame and doubt (12–18 months to 3 years).* Child develops a balance of independence over doubt and shame. Virtue: will.	*Preoperational (2 to 7 years).* Child develops a representational system and uses symbols such as words to represent people, places, and events.
Phallic (3 to 6 years). Child becomes attached to parent of the other sex and later identifies with same-sex parent. Zone of gratification shifts to genital region.	*Initiative versus guilt (3 to 6 years).* Child develops initiative when trying out new things and is not overwhelmed by failure. Virtue: purpose.	
Latency (6 years to puberty). Time of relative calm between more turbulent stages.	*Industry versus inferiority (6 years to puberty).* Child must learn skills of the culture or face feelings of incompetence. Virtue: skill.	*Concrete operations (7 to 12 years).* Child can solve problems logically if they are focused on the here and now.
Genital (puberty through adulthood). Time of mature adult sexuality.	*Identity versus identity confusion (puberty to young adulthood).* Adolescent must determine own sense of self or experience confusion about roles. Virtue: fidelity.	*Formal operations (12 years through adulthood).* Person can think abstractly, deal with hypothetical situations, and think about possibilities.
	Intimacy versus isolation (young adulthood). Person seeks to make commitments to others; if unsuccessful, may suffer from isolation and self-absorption. Virtue: love.	
	Generativity versus stagnation (middle adulthood). Mature adult is concerned with establishing and guiding the next generation or else feels personal impoverishment. Virtue: care.	
	Integrity versus despair (late adulthood). Elderly person achieves acceptance of own life, allowing acceptance of death, or else despairs over inability to relive life. Virtue: wisdom.	

Note: All ages are approximate.

The psychoanalyst Erik H. Erikson departed from Freudian theory in emphasizing societal, rather than chiefly biological, influences on personality. Erikson described development as proceeding through eight crises, or turning points, throughout the life span. *(UPI/Bettmann Newsphotos)*

biters or develop "bitingly" critical personalities. Babies who receive so *much* oral pleasure that they do not want to abandon this stage may become compulsive eaters or smokers. A person who, as a toddler, had too-strict toilet training may be fixated at the *anal stage,* when the chief source of pleasure was moving the bowels. Such a person may have a "constipated" personality: obsessively clean and neat or rigidly tied to schedules and routines. Or the person may be defiantly messy.

According to Freud, a key event in psychosexual development occurs during the *phallic stage* of early childhood, when the site of pleasure shifts to the genitals. Boys develop sexual attachment to their mothers and girls to their fathers, and they regard the same-sex parent as a rival. The boy learns that little girls do not have penises, assumes that they were cut off, and worries that his father will castrate him too. The girl experiences what Freud called *penis envy* and blames her mother for not having given her a penis. Children eventually resolve their anxiety by identifying with the same-sex parent and move into the relatively calm *latency stage* of middle childhood. They become socialized, develop skills, and learn about themselves and society. The *genital stage,* the final one, lasts throughout adulthood. The physical changes of puberty reawaken the *libido,* the energy that fuels the sex drive. The sexual urges of the phallic stage, repressed during latency, now resurface to flow in socially approved channels, which Freud defined as heterosexual relations with persons outside the family.

Freud proposed three hypothetical parts of the personality: the id, the ego, and the superego. Newborns are governed by the *id,* a source of motives and desires that is present at birth. The id seeks immediate satisfaction under the *pleasure principle.* When gratification is delayed (as when they have to wait for food), infants begin to see themselves as separate from the outside world. The *ego,* which represents reason or common sense, develops sometime during the first year of life and operates under the *reality principle.* The ego's aim is to find realistic ways to gratify the id. At about age 5 or 6, as the child identifies with the parent of the same sex, the *superego* develops. The **superego,** which includes the conscience, incorporates socially approved "shoulds" and "should nots" into the child's own value system. The early superego is rigid and rules by guilt; with maturity, the superego becomes more realistic and flexible under control of the ego.

Erik Erikson: Psychosocial Theory

Erik Erikson (1902–1994), a German-born psychoanalyst, was part of Freud's inner circle in Vienna until he fled from the threat of Nazism and came to the United States in 1933. His broad personal and professional experience led him to modify and extend Freudian theory by emphasizing the influence of society on the developing personality. Unlike Freud, who saw civilization as an impediment to biological drives, Erikson stressed how society can shape the development of the ego, or self. A girl growing up on a Sioux Indian reservation, where females are trained to serve their hunter husbands, will develop different personality patterns and different skills from a girl growing up in a wealthy family in turn-of-the-century Vienna, as most of Freud's patients did.

Whereas Freud maintained that early childhood experiences permanently shape personality, Erikson contended that ego development continues throughout life. Erikson's (1950, 1985; Erikson, Erikson, & Kivnick, 1986) theory of **psychosocial development** covers eight stages across the life span (listed in Table 1-5 and discussed in later chapters). Each stage involves a "crisis" in personality, a major issue that is particularly important at that time and will remain an issue to some degree throughout life. The crises emerge according to a maturational timetable and must be satisfactorily resolved for healthy ego development.

Successful resolution of each of the eight crises requires the balancing of a positive trait and a corresponding negative one. Although the positive quality should predominate, some degree of the negative is needed too. The crisis of infancy, for example, is *trust versus mistrust*. People need to trust the world and the people in it, but they also need to learn some mistrust to protect themselves from danger. The successful outcome of each crisis is the development of a particular "virtue" or strength—in this first crisis, the virtue of hope.

A major theme for Erikson, particularly in adolescence but also throughout adult life, was the quest for *identity*, which he defined as confidence in one's inner continuity amid change. He himself, growing up in Germany as the son of a Danish mother and a Jewish adoptive father, had felt confusion about his identity. He never knew his biological father; he floundered before settling on a vocation; and when he came to the United States, he needed to redefine his identity as an immigrant. All these issues found echoes in the "identity crises" he observed among disturbed adolescents, soldiers in combat, and members of minority groups (Erikson, 1968, 1973; R. I. Evans, 1967). Erikson believed that men must develop a sense of identity before they can engage in intimate relationships but that women first strive for intimacy and then define themselves through a mate.

Jean Baker Miller: Relational Theory

Jean Baker Miller (b. 1927), a psychiatrist who founded the Stone Center for Developmental Services and Studies at Wellesley College, originally criticized the classic psychoanalytic theories as male-oriented, and thus as failing to adequately explain women's development. She and her colleagues came to believe that such theories do not describe well what occurs in men, either.

According to Miller's (1991) **relational theory**, personality growth occurs within relationships. The concept of self begins in dynamic interaction with another. The infant identifies with the first caregiver, not because of who that person *is* but because of what the person *does*. The baby responds to other people's emotions, becomes comfortable when others are comfortable, and acts to build closer relationships. During toddlerhood and early childhood, rather than striving for au-

According to the psychiatrist Jean Baker Miller's relational theory, personality growth—beginning in infancy—occurs within emotional connections, not separate from them. *(C. Fatta Studio, Boston/Courtesy of Wellesley College)*

tonomy and individuation, both boys and girls continue to place the highest importance on intimate connections. However, a split between male and female development occurs during the school years, when girls' interest in relationships, family, and emotional issues is encouraged, while boys are steered toward competition and personal achievement. This dichotomy widens during adolescence and adulthood, to the detriment of both men and women. Women's growth within relationships is devalued, and men's deficiencies in participating in growth-fostering relationships are not addressed early enough.

Evaluation of Psychoanalytic Perspective

Freud's theory made historic contributions and has generated considerable debate. Freud made us aware of unconscious thoughts and emotions, the ambivalence of early parent-child relationships, and the presence from birth of sexual urges. His psychoanalytic method greatly influenced modern-day psychotherapy. However, Freud's theory grew out of his place in history and in society. Much of it seems to demean women, no doubt because of its roots in the male-dominated social system of a Victorian-era European culture. Also, Freud based his theories about normal development not on a population of average children but on a clientele of upper-middle-class adults in therapy. His narrow concentration on biological and maturational factors and on early experience does not take into account other, and later, influences on personality. His theories, like those of Erikson and other psychoanalytic theorists, are hard to test. Research has questioned or invalidated many of his concepts, for example, his idea that the superego and gender identity are outcomes of children's conflicts during the phallic stage (Emde, 1992).

Erikson's theory has held up better, especially in its emphasis on social and cultural influences and on development beyond adolescence. However, Erikson, too, has been criticized for taking the male as the norm for healthy development. Miller's theory, which highlights the importance of relationships and does not consider female development a deviation from the norm, is quite new and, like Freud's and Erikson's, is based largely on clinical observation.

A key issue among psychoanalytic theorists is whether healthy development rests more on individuation (development of the self) or on connectedness (relationships with other people). A newer model (Guisinger & Blatt, 1994) seeks to combine these concepts. According to this model, healthy development for both men and women depends on the lifelong interaction of a continually maturing individuality with a continually maturing sense of connectedness.

LEARNING PERSPECTIVE

The *learning perspective* is concerned, not with unconscious forces, but with behavior that can be observed and studied objectively and scientifically. Learning theorists maintain that development results from *learning*, a long-lasting change in behavior based on experience, or adaptation to the environment. Learning theorists see development as *continuous* (rather than occurring in stages) and emphasize *quantitative* development (changes in amount rather than kind). Two important learning theories are behaviorism and social-learning (or social-cognitive) theory.

Behaviorism

Behaviorism describes observed behavior as a predictable response to experience. Although biology sets limits on what people do, behaviorists view the environment as much more influential. They hold that human beings at all ages learn about the world the same way other animals do: by reacting to conditions, or aspects of their environment, that they find pleasing, painful, or threatening. Thus behaviorists look for events that determine whether or not a particular behavior will be repeated.

Behavioral research deals with two kinds of learning: classical conditioning and operant conditioning.

Classical Conditioning   Eager to capture Anna's memorable moments on film, Jonathan took pictures of her smiling, crawling, and showing off her other achievements. Whenever the flash went off, Anna blinked. One evening, when Anna was 11 months old, she saw Jonathan hold the camera up to his eye and she blinked *before* the flash. She had learned to associate the camera with the bright light, so that the sight of the camera activated her blinking reflex.

Anna's blinking is an example of *classical conditioning*, a kind of learning in which a person or animal learns a response to a stimulus that did not originally evoke it, after the stimulus is repeatedly associated with a stimulus that *does* elicit the response. Figure 1-5 shows the steps in classical conditioning:

1   *Before conditioning:* Anna blinks when the flash goes off. Blinking is an automatic, reflexive response to bright light. The light, therefore, is an unconditioned stimulus; it automatically brings an unlearned (unconditioned) response. The camera is a neutral stimulus; without the flash, it does not ordinarily cause blinking.
2   *During conditioning:* Since Jonathan often takes photos indoors, Anna repeatedly sees the camera with the light. When her father holds up the camera, the light flashes, and Anna blinks.
3   *After conditioning:* Anna blinks at the sight of the camera alone. She has learned to associate the camera with the light and to respond in the same way to both. The camera has become a conditioned stimulus; after repeatedly being linked with the light, it now produces blinking as a conditioned response.

The principles of classical conditioning were developed by the Russian physiologist Ivan Pavlov (1849–1936), who devised experiments in which dogs learned to salivate at the sound of a bell that rang at feeding time. The American behaviorist

Stage 1: Before conditioning

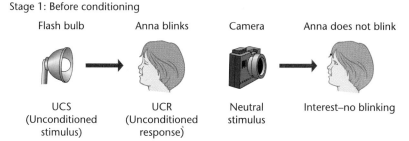

UCS automatically produces UCR. Neutral stimulus does not produce blinking.

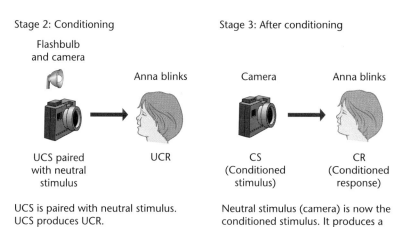

FIGURE 1-5

Classical conditioning occurs in three stages. The neutral stimulus eventually produces a conditioned response.

John B. Watson (1878–1958) applied stimulus-response theories of learning to children. Watson claimed that he could mold any infant in any way he chose. Using classical conditioning, he taught one baby, known as "Little Albert," to fear furry white objects (see Chapter 4).

Operant Conditioning Baby Terrell lies peacefully in his crib. When he happens to smile, his mother goes over to the crib, picks him up, and plays with him. Later his father does the same thing. As this sequence continues to occur, Terrell learns that something he does (smiling) can produce something he likes (loving attention from a parent), and so he keeps smiling to attract his parents' attention. An originally accidental response has become a deliberate, conditioned response.

This kind of learning is called **operant conditioning** because the individual learns from the consequences of "operating" on the environment. The American psychologist B. F. Skinner (1904–1990) formulated the principles of operant conditioning on the basis of work primarily with rats and pigeons. Skinner (1938) maintained that the same principles applied to human beings. He found that

an organism will tend to repeat a response that has been reinforced and will suppress a response that has been punished. **Reinforcement** is a consequence of behavior that increases the likelihood that the behavior will be repeated; in Terrell's case, his parents' attention reinforces his smiling (see Figure 1-6). **Punishment** is a consequence of behavior that *decreases* the likelihood of repetition. Whether a consequence is reinforcing or punishing depends on the person. What is reinforcing for one person may be punishing for another.

Reinforcement can be either positive or negative. *Positive reinforcement* consists of *giving* a reward, such as food, gold stars, money, or praise or the picking up of a baby. *Negative reinforcement* consists of *taking away* something the individual does not like (known as an *aversive* event), such as a loud noise. Negative reinforcement is sometimes confused with punishment. However, they are different. Punishment suppresses a behavior by *bringing on* an aversive event (such as spanking a child or giving an electric shock to an animal) or by *withdrawing* a positive event (such as watching television). Negative reinforcement encourages repetition of a behavior by *removing* an aversive event.

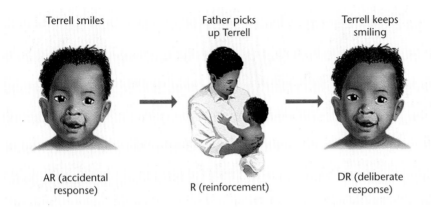

Terrell smiles

Father picks
up Terrell

Terrell keeps
smiling

AR (accidental
response)

R (reinforcement)

DR (deliberate
response)

FIGURE 1-6
Operant, or instrumental,
conditioning.

Reinforcement is most effective when it immediately follows a behavior. If a response is no longer reinforced, it will eventually return to its original (baseline) level. This is called **extinction.** If, after a while, no one picks up Terrell when he smiles, he may not stop smiling, but will smile less often than if his smiles still brought reinforcement.

Intermittent reinforcement—reinforcing a response at certain times and not at others—produces more durable behaviors than reinforcing it every time. That is because, when the reinforcement ends, it takes longer for a person to realize it. Thus parents who only occasionally give in to a child's temper tantrum encourage such behavior even more than if they gave in every time and then stopped. If they had been reinforcing every tantrum, the child would recognize almost at once when the tantrum was no longer producing the desired result.

Shaping is a technique used to bring about a new response by reinforcing responses that are more and more like the desired one. For example, in helping 5-year-old Joey learn to throw a ball more accurately, his mother first gave him lavish praise if his throw came within a few feet of its intended target. Gradually she bestowed praise only after the ball came closer and closer to the mark. Shaping is often part of *behavioral modification,* a form of operant conditioning used to eliminate undesirable behavior or to instill positive behavior, such as obeying classroom rules. Behavioral modification is particularly effective among children with special needs, such as mentally handicapped or emotionally disturbed youngsters.

Social-Learning (Social-Cognitive) Theory

Social-learning theory, an outgrowth of behaviorism, maintains that children, in particular, learn social behaviors by observing and imitating models

(usually their parents). Albert Bandura (b. 1925), a professor of psychology at Stanford University, developed many of the principles of modern social-learning theory, also known as social-cognitive theory, which today is more influential than behaviorism.

Social-learning theory differs from behaviorism in several ways (Bandura, 1977, 1989). First, it regards the learner as an active contributor to his or her learning. Whereas both behaviorists and social-learning theorists see the environment as molding the child, social-learning theorists believe that the child also acts upon the environment and, in fact, *creates* the environment to some extent. One child's hostile behavior creates a negative, rejecting environment; another child's cheerful, cooperative demeanor creates a positive, accepting environment.

Second, although social-learning theorists, like behaviorists, emphasize laboratory experimentation, they believe that theories based on animal research cannot explain human behavior. People learn in a social context, and human learning is more complex than simple conditioning.

Third, social-learning theory acknowledges the importance of cognition. It maintains that children's cognitive response to their perceptions, rather than a reflexive response to reinforcement or punishment, is central to development.

Of particular importance in social-learning theory is observation and imitation of models. Children acquire new abilities through *observational learning*—by watching others. They demonstrate their learning by imitating the model, sometimes when the model is no longer present. However, learning can occur even if the child does not imitate the observed behavior. According to social-learning theory, imitation of models is the most important element in the way children learn a language, deal with aggression, develop a moral sense, and learn gender-appropriate behaviors.

Children actively advance their own social learning by choosing the models they imitate. The choice is influenced by characteristics of the model, the child, and the environment. A child may choose one parent over the other. Or the child may choose another adult (say, a teacher, a television personality, a sports figure, or a drug dealer) in addition to, or instead of, either parent. Children tend to imitate people of high status and people whose personalities are similar to their own. A child with aggressive tendencies is more likely to imitate Rambo than Mr. Rogers.

The specific behavior children imitate depends on what they perceive as valued in their culture. If all the teachers in Carlos's school are women, he will not model their behavior, thinking that would not be "manly." However, if he meets a male teacher he likes, he may change his mind about the value of teachers as models.

Cognitive factors, such as the ability to pay attention and to mentally organize sensory information, affect the way people incorporate observed behavior into their own. Cognitive processes are at work as people observe models, learn "chunks" of behavior, and mentally put the chunks together into new, complex behavior patterns. A woman who tries to model her tennis serve on Steffi Graf's and her backhand on Monica Seles's will integrate both strokes into her own style of play.

Evaluation of Learning Perspective

Behaviorists and social-learning theorists have helped make the study of human development more scientific. Their terms are defined precisely, and their theories can be tested in the laboratory. By stressing environmental influences, learning theories help explain cultural differences in behavior (Horowitz, 1992). However, they underplay the importance of heredity and biology. And, since they apply the same principles to behavior from infancy through adulthood, they do not deal with age-related development.

Behaviorism has been useful in designing therapies to effect rapid changes in behavior (such as giving up smoking) or to teach new behaviors (such as using the toilet). However, because behaviorists are not interested in the causes of symptoms, they may eliminate one undesirable behavior (say, stealing) by punishing it, only to see the substitution of another negative behavior (say,

bed-wetting), leaving the basic problem unresolved.

By acknowledging cognitive influences on behavior and the active role people play in their own learning, social-learning theory serves as a bridge between behaviorism and the cognitive perspective.

COGNITIVE PERSPECTIVE

The *cognitive perspective* is concerned with *qualitative changes* in thought processes and the behavior that reflects these changes. It views people as active, growing beings with their own internal impulses and patterns of development. It sees every normal person, from infancy on, as a doer who actively constructs his or her world.

The Cognitive-Stage Theory of Jean Piaget

Much of what we know about how children think is due to the work of the Swiss theoretician Jean Piaget (1896–1980). As a young man studying in Paris, Piaget set out to standardize the tests Alfred Binet had developed to assess the intelligence of French schoolchildren. Piaget became intrigued by the children's wrong answers, finding in them clues to their thought processes. From his observations of his own and other children, Piaget created a comprehensive theory of how cognitive development results in a growing ability to acquire and use knowledge about the world.

Piaget's *clinical method* combined observation with flexible questioning. To find out how children think, Piaget followed up their answers with more questions. In this way, he discovered, for example, that a typical 4-year-old believed that pennies or flowers were more numerous when arranged in a line than when heaped or piled up.

Piaget believed that the core of intelligent behavior is an inborn ability to adapt to the environment. Building on their sensory, motor, and reflex capacities, young children learn about and act upon their surroundings. By feeling a pebble, or exploring the boundaries of a room, they develop a more accurate picture of their world.

Piaget described cognitive development as occurring in a series of stages (listed in Table 1-5 and discussed in later chapters). At each stage a child develops a new way of thinking about and responding to the environment. Thus, each stage constitutes a qualitative change from one type of thought and behavior to another. Each stage builds on the one before and lays the foundation for the

The Swiss psychologist Jean Piaget studied children's cognitive development by observing and talking with his own youngsters and others. *(Yves DeBraine/Black Star)*

next. Piaget believed that all people go through the same stages in the same order, though the timing varies.

According to Piaget, cognitive growth occurs through three interrelated principles: organization, adaptation, and equilibration. These principles operate at all stages of development and affect all interactions with the environment.

Cognitive *organization* is a tendency to create increasingly complex systems of knowledge. From infancy on, people organize what they know into mental representations of reality that help them make sense of their world. Within these representations lie cognitive structures called *schemes:* organized patterns of behavior that a person uses to think about and act in a situation. An infant has simple schemes for sucking, looking, and so forth. From the first days of life, infants begin to vary and combine schemes. Babies develop different schemes for sucking at the breast, a bottle, or a thumb. At first, schemes for looking and grasping operate independently. Later, infants integrate these separate schemes into a single scheme that allows them to look at an object while holding it. As children acquire more information, their schemes become more and more complex, progressing from ways to perform motor actions to concrete thinking about sensory perceptions, and eventually to abstract thought.

Adaptation is Piaget's term for the way a person deals with new information. Adaptation involves two steps: (1) *assimilation,* taking in information and incorporating it into existing cognitive structures, or ways of thinking, and (2) *accommodation,* changing one's ideas, or cognitive structures, to include the new knowledge. A breastfed baby who begins to suck on a rubber nipple is showing assimilation—using an old scheme to deal with a new object or situation. When the infant discovers that sucking on a bottle requires somewhat different tongue and mouth movements from those used to suck on a breast, she accommodates by modifying the old scheme. She has adapted her original sucking scheme to deal with a new experience: the bottle. Thus, assimilation and accommodation work together to produce cognitive growth.

Equilibration is a constant striving for equilibrium—a state of balance between a child and the outside world and among the child's own cognitive structures. The need for equilibrium leads a child to shift from assimilation to accommodation. When children cannot handle new experiences with their existing structures, they organize new mental patterns, restoring equilibrium.

Neo-Piagetians and the Information-Processing Approach

The newer *information-processing approach* analyzes the mental processes underlying intelligent behavior: perception, attention, memory, and problem solving. Scientists who pursue this approach study how people acquire, transform, and use sensory information through active manipulation of symbols, or mental images. Like Piaget, information-processing theorists see people as active thinkers about their world; but, unlike Piaget, they do not propose stages of development.

Neo-Piagetian developmental psychologists have extended and modified Piaget's theory by integrating it with the information-processing approach. Robbie Case (1985, 1992), a prominent neo-Piagetian, maintains that children develop cognitively by becoming more efficient at processing information (rather than through equilibration, as Piaget believed). One way to do this is through practice. According to Case, there is a limit to the number of schemes a child can keep in mind. A child who practices a skill, such as counting or reading, becomes able to do it faster, more proficiently, almost automatically, freeing some mental "space" for additional information and more complex problem solving. Maturation of the child's neurological processes also expands available memory capacity. Case has outlined a series of stages similar to Piaget's. His theory is being extended to such disparate domains as emotional development and learning disabilities.

Evaluation of Cognitive Perspective

Piaget was the forerunner of today's "cognitive revolution" with its emphasis on internal mental processes, as opposed to classical learning theory's concern with external influences and overt behaviors. Piaget, who wrote more than 40 books and more than 100 articles, has inspired more research on children's cognitive development than any other theorist. Among the important offshoots of his theory are Lawrence Kohlberg's cognitive-developmental theories of gender identity and moral reasoning (discussed in Chapters 7, 10, and 12).

Piaget's careful observations have yielded a wealth of information, including some surprising insights. Who, for example, would have thought that not until age 6 or 7 do even very bright children realize that a ball of clay that has been rolled into a "worm" before their eyes still contains the same amount of clay? Of that an infant might think that a person who has moved out of sight may no longer exist? Piaget has shown us that children's minds are not miniatures of adults' minds. Understanding how children think makes it easier for parents to teach them and helps teachers know how and when to introduce topics into the curriculum.

Yet Piaget spoke primarily of the "average" child and took little notice of individual differences or of ways in which culture, education, and motivation affect performance. He said little about emotional and personality development. Many of his ideas emerged not from rigorous research but from informal observation. More recent research suggests that he seriously underestimated the abilities of young children. Some contemporary psychologists question his clearly demarcated stages of cognitive growth, viewing cognitive development as more gradual and continuous (Flavell, 1992).

The information-processing approach provides a valuable way of assessing intelligence and gathering information about the development of memory and other cognitive processes. However, it pays little or no attention to such important aspects of cognitive development as creativity, motivation, and social interaction.

The neo-Piagetian approach, and Case's model in particular, is a promising attempt to explain the processes by which qualitative changes in cognition occur and the constraints on learning at any given stage. Because of its emphasis on efficiency of processing, it helps account for individual differences in cognitive ability. The theory is still being developed and is in need of more supporting research (P. H. Miller, 1993).

ETHOLOGICAL PERSPECTIVE

The *ethological perspective* focuses on biological and evolutionary bases of behavior. In the 1930s, two European zoologists, Konrad Lorenz and Niko Tinbergen, developed the scientific discipline of *ethology*, the study of the behavior of species of animals in their natural surroundings or in the laboratory. Ethologists rely mostly on naturalistic observation. They believe that, for each species, a variety of innate, species-specific behaviors have evolved to increase its odds of survival. In the 1950s, the British psychologist John Bowlby extended ethological principles to human development.

Imprinting and Attachment

In one well-known study, Lorenz (1957) waddled, honked, and flapped his arms, and got newborn ducklings to follow him as they would the mother duck. Lorenz showed that newly hatched ducklings will follow the first moving object they see, whether or not it is a member of their own species, and they become increasingly attached to it. Usually, this first attachment is to the mother; but if the natural course of events is disturbed, other attachments (like the one to Lorenz) can form. This phenomenon is called *imprinting,* and Lorenz believed that it is automatic and irreversible.

Imprinting, said Lorenz, is the result of a *predisposition toward learning:* the readiness of an organism's nervous system to acquire certain information during a brief critical (or sensitive) period in early life. If ducklings had no object to follow during the critical period after birth, imprinting would not occur. Similarly, among goats and cows, certain ritual behaviors occur right after birth. If these rituals are prevented or interrupted, mother and offspring will not recognize each other. The results for the young animal are devastating: physical withering and death or abnormal development.

Does something similar to imprinting happen between human newborns and their mothers? Bowlby (1951) was convinced of the importance of the mother-baby bond and warned against separating mother and baby without providing good substitute caregiving. His conviction arose partly from examining ethological studies of bonding in animals and partly from seeing disturbed children in a psychoanalytic clinic in London. Mary Ainsworth, originally a junior colleague of Bowlby, studied how African and American babies become attached to their mothers and devised the now-famous "Strange Situation," which we describe in Chapter 5, to measure attachment. Research on attachment is based on the belief that infant and parent are biologically predisposed to becoming attached to each other and that such attachment is important for the baby's survival.

Evaluation of Ethological Perspective

The ethological perspective challenges us to look beyond the immediate adaptive value of a behavior for an individual to its function in promoting the survival of the species. So far, this approach has been applied chiefly to a few specific developmental issues, such as attachment between infant and caregiver and interaction between peers, but has had little to say about other aspects of human development, such as language and abstract thought. Its methods may be more suited to studying animals than people. Ethological research does, however, point up the value of naturalistic observation, which can be fruitfully combined with other methods (P. H. Miller, 1993).

CONTEXTUAL PERSPECTIVE

According to the *contextual perspective,* human development can be understood only in its social context. The individual is not a separate entity interacting with the environment but an inseparable part of it. The developing person acts upon and changes the environment, as the constantly shifting environment acts upon and changes the person. This emphasis on the context of development, which finds echoes in Bronfenbrenner's ecological approach, contrasts with the picture of the solitary individual drawn by Piaget and information-processing theorists.

Contextualists emphasize individual differences. Individuals set goals within a particular context as they perceive it and then select new goals within the new context which they seek out or which then presents itself. Success depends on how appropriate behavior is to its context. For example, making fishing boats may be highly adaptive behavior on an island until the coming of a factory whose polluted discharge kills the fish.

Vygotsky's Sociocultural Theory

The noted Russian psychologist Lev Semenovich Vygotsky (1896–1934) earned a degree in law and maintained a special interest in language and literature. His interest in cognitive development arose from his efforts to help blind, deaf, and mentally retarded children fulfill their potential. During the social upheaval following the Russian revolution in 1919, radical new theories such as Vygotsky's received a warm reception; but he fell out of favor during the Stalinist period (1927–1953). With the translation of his work into English and the increasing recognition of sociocultural contexts of development and of the importance of cross-cultural research, his views have become more influential.

Vygotsky's (1978) *sociocultural theory* is concerned mainly with higher mental activities and has important implications for education and cognitive testing. Its focus is the active, goal-setting child in a social-historical-cultural context. Its emphasis is on how social interaction with adults can fulfill a child's potential for learning. According to Vygotsky, adults must direct and organize a child's learning before a child can master and internalize it.

Vygotsky's best-known concept is the *zone of proximal development (ZPD).* (*Proximal* means "near.") Children in the zone of proximal development for a particular task (such as multiplying fractions) can almost, but not quite, perform the task on their own. With the right kind of teaching, however, they can accomplish it successfully. A good teacher identifies a child's ZPD and helps the child stretch beyond it. Then the adult gradually withdraws support until the child can perform the task unaided. Researchers have applied the metaphor of scaffolds—the temporary platforms on which construction workers stand—to this way of teaching (Wood, 1980; Wood, Bruner, & Ross, 1976). *Scaffolding* is the temporary support that parents or teachers give a child to do a task.

Evaluation of Contextual Perspective

The contextual perspective, and Vygotsky's theory in particular, suggests that the development of children from one culture or one group within a culture (such as white, middle-class Americans) may not be an appropriate norm for children from other societies or cultural groups. Tests based on Vygotsky's theory, which focus on a child's potential, present a welcome change from standard intelligence tests that assess only what the child has already learned; and many children may benefit from the sort of guidance Vygotsky prescribes. However, the concept of the ZPD may not lend itself to precise measurement. It also leaves unan-

swered questions: for example, how influential are a child's motivation and learning ability? Furthermore, the theory pays little attention to developmental issues, such as the role of maturation (P. H. Miller, 1993).

Our final word in this introductory chapter is that this entire book is far from the final word. Although we have tried to incorporate the most important and the most up-to-date information about the ways in which people develop, developmentalists are constantly learning more. As you read the text, you are certain to come up with your own questions. By thinking about them, and perhaps eventually conducting research to find answers, it is possible that you yourself, now just embarking on the study of human development, will someday add to our knowledge about the interesting species to which we all belong.

✔ SUMMARY

HUMAN DEVELOPMENT: BASIC CONCEPTS

- Human development is the scientific study of the quantitative and qualitative ways people change and do not change over time. Qualitative change is marked by the appearance of new phenomena that cannot be predicted from earlier functioning. Developmental change is systematic and adaptive.
- The study of human development focuses on describing, explaining, predicting, and modifying development.
- The various aspects of development (physical, cognitive, and psychosocial development) do not occur in isolation. Each affects the others.
- Influences on development are both internal (hereditary) and external (environmental). Influences that affect large groups of people are called either *normative age-graded* or *normative history-graded*. *Nonnormative* life events are unusual in themselves or in their timing.
- According to Bronfenbrenner's ecological approach, environmental influences on development occur at five levels: microsystem, mesosystem, exosystem, macrosystem, and chronosystem.
- Cross-cultural research can indicate whether certain aspects of development are universal or culturally influenced.

HUMAN DEVELOPMENT: HOW THE STUDY HAS EVOLVED

- The scientific study of child development began in the nineteenth century. Adolescence was not considered a separate phase of development until the twentieth century work of G. Stanley Hall. Hall was also one of the first psychologists to study aging, which did not become a major area of study until the 1940s.
- As researchers became interested in following development into adulthood, life-span development expanded as a subject for study. Today most developmentalists recognize that development continues throughout life.
- Key features of Baltes's life-span developmental approach are multidirectionality, plasticity, the importance of history and context, and multiple causation.

HUMAN DEVELOPMENT: RESEARCH METHODS

- Research based on the scientific method is characterized by identification of a problem, formulation of hypotheses, collection of data, statistical analysis to determine whether the data support the hypothesis, and public dissemination of findings.

- Random selection of a research sample can ensure generalizability.
- Forms of data collection include self-reports (diaries, interviews, and questionnaires); tests and other behavioral measures; and naturalistic or laboratory observation.
- Three basic designs used in developmental research are case studies, correlational studies, and experiments. Case studies are studies of individuals. Correlational studies show the direction and magnitude of a relationship between variables. Only experiments can establish causal relationships, but case studies and correlational studies can provide hypotheses or predictions to be tested by experimental research.
- In an experiment, the experimenter manipulates the independent variable to see its effect on the dependent variable. Experiments must be rigorously controlled so as to be valid and replicable. Random assignment of participants to experimental or control groups can control for unforeseen factors.
- Laboratory experiments are easiest to control and replicate, but findings of field experiments may be more generalizable beyond the study situation.
- Natural experiments, which actually are correlational studies, may be useful in situations in which true experiments would be impractical or unethical.
- The two major methods of studying age effects are cross-sectional and longitudinal. Both of these are quasi-experimental because of the fact that age cannot be controlled. Cross-sectional studies describe age differences; longitudinal studies describe age changes. Sequential strategies seek to overcome the weaknesses of these two designs.
- Ethical issues in research on human development include informed consent, self-esteem, and privacy of participants. In a carefully designed study, researchers consider its effect on the participants, as well as its potential benefit to the field.

HUMAN DEVELOPMENT: THEORETICAL PERSPECTIVES

- A theory is a coherent set of related concepts, which seeks to organize and explain data, the information obtained from research. Theories attempt to explain, interpret, and predict behavior and to guide future research. Many influential theories of human development stem from one of five theoretical perspectives: psychoanalytic, learning, cognitive, ethological, and contextual.
- Psychoanalytic theories focus on the underlying forces that motivate behavior. Freud described a series of psychosexual stages, based on maturation, in which gratification shifts from one body zone to another. Erikson proposed eight stages of psychosocial development, each involving the resolution of a crisis. Jean Baker Miller's relational theory holds that personality growth occurs within emotional connections.
- The learning perspective views human development primarily as a response to external events. Its focus is on observable behaviors and quantitative change. Behaviorists, such as Watson and Skinner, have shown that behavior can be altered by classical or operant conditioning. Social-learning theory, proposed by Bandura, stresses observational learning and imitation of models.
- The cognitive perspective emphasizes qualitative change, seeing people as active contributors to their own development. Piaget's cognitive-stage theory describes four stages in cognitive development: sensorimotor, preoperational, concrete operations, and formal operations. The information-processing approach analyzes processes underlying intelligent behavior, focusing on perception, attention, memory, and problem solving.
- The ethological perspective of Lorenz, Bowlby, and Ainsworth focuses on the biological and evolutionary bases of behavior, particularly with regard to critical periods for development of attachment.
- The contextual perspective views the individual within a shifting social context. Vygotsky's sociocultural theory emphasizes how social interaction with adults can help children learn.

✔ KEY TERMS

human development (page 3)
quantitative change (3)
qualitative change (3)
personality (6)
maturation (6)
heredity (6)
environment (6)
cohort (7)
critical period (7)
ecological approach (8)
life-span development (10)
scientific method (12)
hypotheses (12)
data (12)
sample (12)
random selection (12)
naturalistic observation (13)
laboratory observation (13)
observer bias (14)
case study (14)
correlational study (15)
experiment (17)

experimental group (17)
control group (17)
independent variable (18)
dependent variable (18)
quasi-experiment (19)
longitudinal study (19)
cross-sectional study (19)
cross-sequential study (20)
theory (20)
psychoanalytic perspective (21)
psychosexual development (21)
id (24)
ego (24)
superego (24)
psychosocial development (24)
relational theory (25)
learning perspective (26)
learning (26)
behaviorism (26)
classical conditioning (26)
operant conditioning (27)
reinforcement (27)

punishment (27)
extinction (28)
shaping (28)
social-learning theory (28)
observational learning (28)
cognitive perspective (29)
organization (30)
schemes (30)
adaptation (30)
assimilation (30)
accommodation (30)
equilibration (30)
information-processing approach (30)
ethological perspective (31)
imprinting (31)
contextual perspective (32)
sociocultural theory (32)
zone of proximal development (ZPD) (32)
scaffolding (33)

✔ QUESTIONS FOR THOUGHT AND DISCUSSION

1 What reasons do you have for wanting to learn more about human development?
2 Can you think of ways in which some aspect of your development has affected one or more other aspects?
3 Can you describe some of the influences that helped make you the person you are today? How might you be different if you had grown up in a culture other than your own?
4 Because of ethical limitations on experimentation with humans, researchers often must rely on correlative studies to suggest links, for example, between smoking and lung cancer or between aggression and televised violence. How would you evaluate the usefulness of information gained from such studies?
5 Some people have raised ethical objections to behaviorists' goal of controlling or shaping behavior. If developmentalists could mold children to eliminate antisocial behavior, should they?
6 What contributions can animal research make to the study of human beings? What might be some limitations of such research?

Beginnings

From the moment of conception, human beings undergo complex processes of development. Changes that occur during the earliest periods of the life span are broader and faster-paced than any a person will ever experience again.

Because human beings are whole persons, all aspects of their development are intimately connected, even in the womb. Fetuses whose ears and brains have physically developed enough to hear sounds from the outside world seem to retain a memory of these sounds after birth. The physical growth of the brain before and after birth makes possible a great burst of cognitive and emotional development.

Learning is not just a matter of the mind; infants learn through their physical movements where their bodies end and everything else begins. As they drop toys, splash water, and hurl sand, they learn how their bodies can change their world. Physical gestures precede and often accompany early attempts to speak, which alter social relationships. Of course, without the motor coordination to form sounds, babies would not be able to speak at all.

Thus as we look at prenatal development in Chapter 2, at the physical development of infants and toddlers in Chapter 3, at their cognitive development in Chapter 4, and at their psychosocial development in Chapter 5, we see from the beginning how these various aspects of development affect one another.

CHAPTER TWO

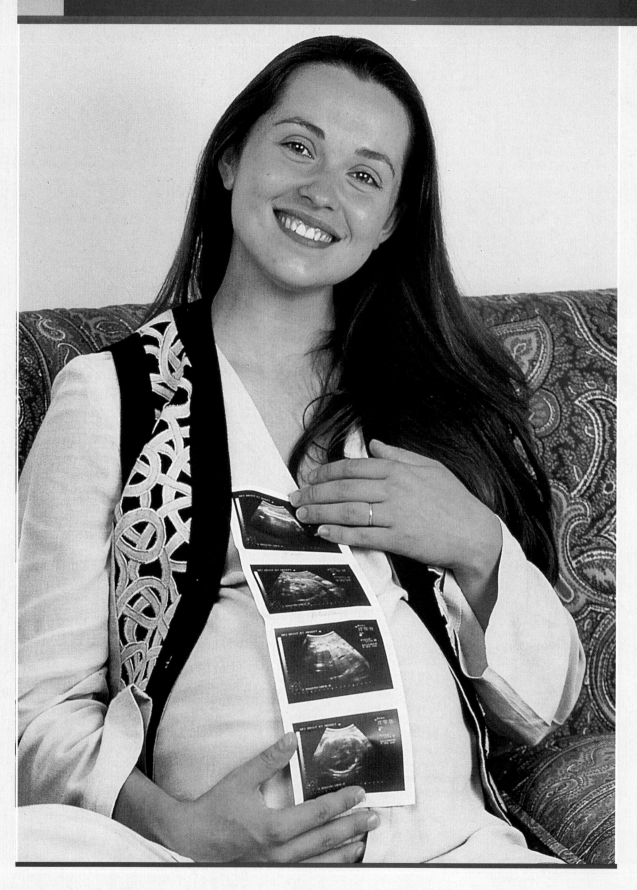

FORMING A NEW LIFE

If I could have watched you grow as a magical mother might, if I could have seen through my magical transparent belly, there would have been such ripening within. . . .

Anne Sexton, 1966

The beginning of human life has always inspired wonder and curiosity. The beginning for you, as for everyone, came long before you gave your first yell upon leaving the womb. Every human being's biological beginning is a split-second event when a single spermatozoon, one of millions of sperm cells from the father, joins an ovum (egg cell), one of the several hundred thousand ova produced and stored in the mother's body. Which sperm meets which ovum has tremendous implications for the new person.

The science of *genetics* is the study of heredity—the inborn factors, inherited from the biological parents, that affect a person's development. When ovum and sperm unite, they give the new life a unique genetic makeup, which influences a wide range of characteristics from color of eyes and hair to health, intellect, and personality. In hereditary endowment, the sperm and the ovum are partial microcosms of the two human beings, man and woman, who bring the new life into existence.

■ In this chapter we describe how this important union of ovum and sperm comes about and how the biological inheritance interacts with environmental influences within and outside the womb. We trace the course of prenatal development (development before birth), describe influences upon it, and report on techniques to monitor and even intervene in it. ■

✔ CONCEPTION

Fertilization, or conception, is the process by which sperm and ovum combine to create a single cell called a *zygote*. During *gestation,* the approximately 9-month or 266-day period of development between conception and birth, the zygote duplicates itself again and again by cell division.

It develops first into an embryo, then into a fetus, and finally emerges as a complex human being with billions of cells specializing in different functions.

HOW DOES FERTILIZATION TAKE PLACE?

A girl is born with all the ova she will ever have: about 400,000. At birth, these immature ova are in her two ovaries (see Figure 2-1), each ovum in its own small sac, or *follicle*. The ovum—only about one-fourth the size of the period that ends this sentence—is the largest cell in the human body. In a mature woman, *ovulation,* the rupture of a mature follicle in either ovary and expulsion of its ovum, occurs about once every 28 days until menopause. The ovum is swept along through the fallopian tube by tiny hair cells, called *cilia,* toward the uterus, or womb. Fertilization normally occurs during the brief time the ovum is passing through the fallopian tube.

The tadpolelike sperm—only $\frac{1}{600}$ inch from head to tail—is one of the smallest cells in the body. Sperm are much more active than ova, and there are many more of them. Sperm are produced in the testicles (testes), or reproductive glands, of a mature male (Figure 2-1) at the rate of several hundred million a day and are ejaculated in the semen at sexual climax. They enter the vagina and try to swim through the cervix (the opening of the uterus) and into the fallopian tubes, but only a tiny fraction make it that far. Since sperm cells have odor receptors, like those in the nose, they may locate a fertile ovum by its scent (Parmentier et al., 1992).

Fertilization is most likely if intercourse occurs on the day of ovulation or during the five days before (Wilcox, Weinberg, & Baird, 1995). Contrary to popular belief, the timing of intercourse does not affect the sex of the baby (Wilcox et al., 1995).

If fertilization does not occur, the ovum and any sperm cells in the woman's body die. The sperm are absorbed by the woman's white blood cells, and the ovum passes through the uterus and exits through the vagina.

WHAT CAUSES MULTIPLE BIRTHS?

Unlike most animals, the human baby usually comes into the world alone. Multiple births are thought to occur in two ways. If the mother's body releases two ova within a short time (or sometimes, perhaps, if a single ovum splits) and then both are fertilized, the resulting babies are *dizygotic twins,* usually called *fraternal twins.* This is the most common type of multiple birth. If a single *fertilized* ovum splits into two, the babies that result from this cell division are *monozygotic twins,* usually called *identical twins.* Triplets, quadruplets, and other multiple births can result from either of these processes or a combination of both.

Monozygotic twins have the same genetic endowment and are the same sex: dizygotic twins, who are created from different sperm cells and usually from different ova, are no more alike in hereditary makeup than any other siblings and may be the same sex or different sexes. However, in part because of differences in prenatal as-well as postnatal experience, monozygotic twins differ in some respects. They may not be identical in **temperament** (disposition, or style of approaching and reacting to situations). In some physical characteristics, such as hair whorls, dental patterns, and handedness, they may be mirror images of

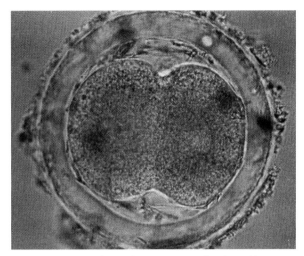

Fertilization takes place when a sperm cell unites with an ovum to form a single new cell. The fertilized ovum shown here has begun to grow by cell division. It will eventually differentiate into 800 billion or more cells with specialized functions. *(Petit Format/Science Source/Photo Researchers)*

each other; one may be left-handed and the other right-handed. One may have a cleft palate (incomplete fusion of the roof of the mouth), whereas the other does not. There have even been rare cases in which abnormal prenatal development resulted in monozygotic twins of opposite sex (L. Wright, 1995).

Monozygotic twins—about one-third of all twins—seem to be a result of an "accident" of prenatal development; their incidence is about the same in all ethnic groups. Dizygotic twins are most common among African Americans, white northern Europeans, and east Indians and are least com-

FIGURE 2-1
Human reproductive systems.

Female

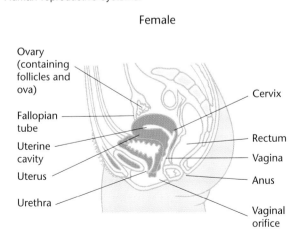

Male

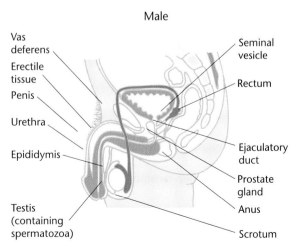

mon among other Asians (Behrman, 1992). These differences may be due to hormonal tendencies that may make women of some ethnic groups more likely to release more than one ovum at the same time. Dizygotic twins are more likely to be born in third or later pregnancies, to older women, and in families with a history of fraternal twins. In recent years, more dizygotic twins have been born because of increased use of fertility drugs, which spur ovulation. Multiple births rose from 19.3 per thousand in 1980 to 25.7 per thousand in 1994 (Guyer, Strobino, Ventura, MacDorman, & Martin, 1996).

✔ MECHANISMS OF HEREDITY

Heredity alone does not, of course, define a human being; environmental influences are important too. However, before we can weigh the roles of heredity and environment, we need to see how heredity works.

GENES AND CHROMOSOMES

The basic unit of heredity is the *gene.* Genes determine inherited characteristics; they contain all the hereditary material passed from biological parents to children. Each cell in the human body contains an estimated 100,000 genes, which are made of the chemical *deoxyribonucleic acid (DNA).* DNA carries the biochemical instructions that tell the cells how to make the proteins that enable them to carry out each specific body function. Each gene seems to be located by function in a definite position on a rod-shaped structure called a *chromosome.*

Normally every cell in the body except the sex cells, or *gametes* (sperm and ovum), has 23 pairs of chromosomes—46 in all. The sperm and the ovum have only 23 each; through a complex process of cell division called *meiosis,* the gametes receive only one chromosome from each pair. Thus, when sperm and ovum fuse at conception, they produce a zygote with 46 chromosomes, half from the father and half from the mother (see Figure 2-2). Meiotic division is random, producing, except for monozygotic twins, a different combination of genes for each child.

At conception, the single-celled zygote has all the biological information needed to guide its development into a human baby. This happens through *mitosis,* a process by which the cells divide in half over and over again. Each division creates

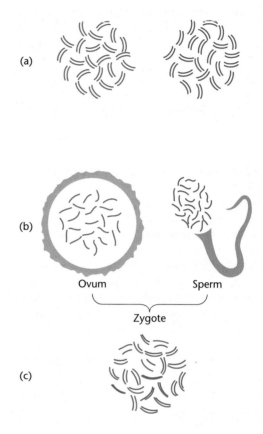

FIGURE 2-2
Hereditary composition of the zygote. (a) Body cells of women and men contain 23 pairs of chromosomes, which carry the genes, the basic units of inheritance. (b) Each gamete, or sex cell (ovum or sperm), has only 23 single chromosomes because of a special kind of cell division (meiosis) in which the total number of chromosomes is halved. (c) At fertilization, the 23 chromosomes from the sperm join the 23 from the ovum so that the zygote receives 46 chromosomes, arranged in 23 pairs.

a duplicate of the original cell, with the same hereditary information. When development is normal, each cell (except the gametes) continues to have 46 chromosomes identical to those in the original zygote.

WHAT DETERMINES SEX?

In many villages in Nepal, it is common for a man whose wife has borne no male babies to take a second wife. In some other societies, a woman's failure to produce sons is justification for divorce. The irony in these customs is that it is normally the father's sperm that determines a child's sex. Let's see how.

At the moment of conception, the 23 chromosomes from the sperm and the 23 from the mother's ovum form into 23 pairs. Twenty-two pairs are **autosomes,** chromosomes that are not related to sexual expression. The twenty-third pair are *sex chromosomes*—one from the father and one from the mother—which govern the baby's sex.

Sex chromosomes are either *X chromosomes* or *Y chromosomes*. The sex chromosome of every ovum is an X chromosome, but the sperm may contain either an X or a Y chromosome. The Y chromosome contains the gene for maleness, the *SRY gene*. When an ovum (X) is fertilized by an X-carrying sperm, the zygote formed is XX, a female. When an ovum (X) is fertilized by a Y-carrying sperm, the resulting zygote is XY, a male (see Figure 2-3).

Still, if nothing further happens prenatally, the embryo will develop female sexual characteristics. For the embryo to develop male characteristics, certain events must occur about 6 to 8 weeks after conception. At this time human male embryos normally start producing the male hormone testosterone. It is exposure to steady, high levels of testosterone that results in the development of a male body plan with male sexual organs. Even a child with the masculine genetic endowment (XY) will retain the female body plan unless exposed prenatally to ongoing high levels of self-produced male hormones.

Until recently, then, it was assumed that femaleness is a genetic "default setting," which will be operative unless a gene for maleness and a resulting exposure to male hormone overrides it. Now, however, researchers have found a gene on the X chromosome, the *DDS gene*, which—if a fetus has *two* copies of it instead of only one—seems able to disrupt male development by overriding the SRY gene on the Y chromosome (Bardoni et al., 1994). Thus the development of femaleness may be a more genetically active process than was previously thought.

PATTERNS OF GENETIC TRANSMISSION

During the 1860s, Gregor Mendel, an Austrian monk who experimented with plants, laid the foundation for our understanding of patterns of inheritance in all living things. He cross-bred pea plants that produced only yellow seeds with pea plants that produced only green seeds. The resulting hybrid plants produced yellow seeds, meaning, he said, that yellow was *dominant* over green. Yet when he bred the yellow-seeded hybrids

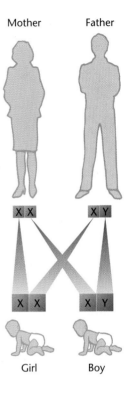

Father has an X chromosome and a Y chromosome. Mother has two X chromosomes. Male baby receives an X chromosome from the mother and a Y chromosome from the father. Female baby receives X chromosomes from both mother and father

FIGURE 2-3
Determination of sex. Females have two X chromosomes; males have an X chromosome and a Y chromosome. Since all babies receive an X chromosome from the mother, sex is determined by whether an X or a Y chromosome is received from the father.

with each other, only 75 percent of their offspring had yellow seeds, while the other 25 percent had green seeds. This proved, Mendel said, that a hereditary characteristic can be *recessive*, that is, carried by an organism that does not express, or show, it.

Mendel also tried breeding for two traits at once. Crossing pea plants that produced round yellow seeds with plants that produced wrinkled green seeds, he found that color and shape were independent of each other. Mendel thus showed that hereditary traits are transmitted separately.

Today we know that the genetic picture in humans is far more complex than Mendel imagined. It is hard to find a single normal trait that people inherit through simple dominant transmission other than the ability to curl the tongue lengthwise! Let's look at various ways in which people inherit characteristics.

These 2-year-old monozygotic twins look so much alike that at first glance they could be mistaken for one child sitting by a mirror. Monozygotic twins have exactly the same genetic heritage, but may differ in temperament and other respects because of differences in prenatal and postnatal experience. *(John Coletti/The Picture Cube)*

Dominant and Recessive Inheritance

If you are a "tongue curler," you inherited this ability through *dominant inheritance*. If you are a redhead but both your parents have dark hair, *recessive inheritance* operated. How do these two types of inheritance work?

Genes that can produce alternative expressions of a characteristic (such as ability or inability to curl the tongue) are called *alleles*. Every person receives a pair of alleles for a given characteristic, one from each biological parent. When both alleles are the same, the person is *homozygous* for the characteristic; when they are different, the person is *heterozygous*. In *dominant inheritance*, when a person is heterozygous for a particular trait, the dominant allele governs. In other words, when an offspring receives alleles for two contradictory traits, only one of them, the dominant one, will be expressed. *Recessive inheritance*, the expression of a recessive trait, occurs only when a person receives the recessive allele from both parents.

If you inherited one allele for tongue-curling ability from each parent, you are homozygous for tongue curling and you express the trait. If, say, your mother passed on an allele for the ability and your father passed on an allele lacking it, you are heterozygous. Since the ability is dominant and its lack is recessive, you can curl your tongue. But if you received the recessive allele from both parents, you would not be a tongue curler.

Many traits are transmitted by *polygenic inheritance,* the interaction of several genes. For example, skin color is the result of three or more sets of genes on three different chromosomes. These genes work together to produce different amounts of brown pigment, resulting in hundreds of shades of skin. Polygenic inheritance is one reason that simple dominance and recessiveness cannot explain the inheritance of such complex human traits as intelligence. The other main reason has to do with *multifactorial transmission,* the interaction of genetic and environmental factors.

Genotypes and Phenotypes: Multifactorial Transmission

If you can curl your tongue, that ability is part of your *phenotype*, the array of observable characteristics through which your *genotype*, or underlying genetic makeup, is expressed. Except for monozygotic twins, no two people have the same genotype.

As Figure 2-4 shows, the same phenotype may arise from different genotypes: either a homozygous combination of two dominant alleles or a heterozygous combination of one dominant allele and one recessive allele. If you are heterozygous for tongue curling and you have four children with someone who is also heterozygous for the trait, the statistical probability is that one child will be homozygous for the ability, one will be homozygous lacking it, and the other two will be heterozygous. Thus three of your children will have phenotypes for tongue curling (they will be able to curl their tongues), but this ability will arise from two different genotypes (homozygous and heterozygous).

Tongue curling has a strong genetic base; but for most traits, experience modifies the expression of the genotype. Let's say that Steven has inherited musical talent. If he takes music lessons and practices regularly, he may delight his family with his performances. If his family likes and encourages classical music, he may play Bach preludes; if the other children on his block influence him to prefer popular music, he may eventually form a rock group. However, if from early childhood he is not

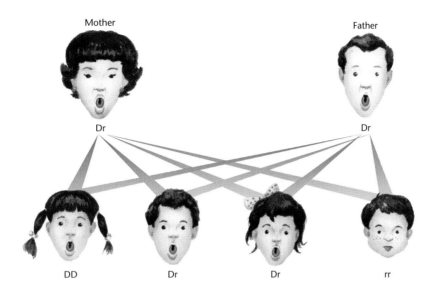

FIGURE 2-4

Phenotypes and genotypes. Because of dominant inheritance, the same observable phenotype (in this case, the ability to curl the tongue lengthwise) can result from two different genotypes (genetic patterns). This mother's and father's genotypes are heterozygous; each has one dominant gene (D) for the ability and one recessive gene (r) lacking the ability. Since the ability is dominant, both can curl their tongues. Each child receives one gene for this trait from each parent. Statistical averages predict that three out of four children in this family will express the trait in their phenotypes (that is, be able to curl their tongues). Two of these three children (*center*) will have heterozygous genotypes (Dr), like the parents; the third child (*left*) with the same phenotype will have a homozygous genotype (DD). The fourth child (*right*) will receive recessive genes from both parents and will be unable to curl the tongue. A phenotype expressing a recessive characteristic (such as inability to curl the tongue) must have a homozygous genotype (rr).

encouraged and not motivated, and if he has no access to a musical instrument or to music lessons, his genotype for musical ability may not be expressed in his phenotype.

Some physical characteristics (including height and weight) and most psychological characteristics (such as intelligence and personality traits, as well as musical ability) are the result of multifactorial transmission. Later in this chapter we discuss how environmental influences interact with the genetic endowment to influence many aspects of development.

GENETIC AND CHROMOSOMAL ABNORMALITIES

Each year about 6 percent of babies born in the United States (out of a total of 3.9 million born in 1995, according to preliminary estimates) are born with physical or mental disabilities. These babies account for about 22.4 percent of deaths in infancy. Most of the serious malformations involve the circulatory or central nervous systems (Guyer et al., 1996; Wegman, 1994; see Table 2-1).

It is in genetic defects and diseases that we see most clearly the operation of dominant and recessive transmission in humans, and also the operation of a variation, *sex-linked inheritance.* Some defects are due to abnormalities in genes or chromosomes. Some are due to mutations—minor alterations in genes or chromosomes that often produce harmful characteristics. Many disorders arise when an inherited predisposition interacts with an environmental factor, either before or after birth. Spina bifida (a defect in the closure of the vertebral canal) and cleft palate probably result from multifactorial transmission. Hyperactivity is one of a number of behavioral disorders thought to be transmitted multifactorially.

Not all genetic or chromosomal abnormalities show up at birth. Symptoms of Tay-Sachs disease (a degenerative disease of the central nervous system that occurs mainly among Jews of eastern European ancestry) and sickle-cell anemia (a blood disorder most common among African Americans) may not appear until at least 6 months of age; cystic fibrosis, not until age 4; and glaucoma and Huntington's disease (a progressive degener-

TABLE 2-1

Birth Defects

Problem	Characteristics of the Condition	Who Is at Risk	What Can Be Done
Alpha$_1$ antitrypsin deficiency	Enzyme deficiency that can lead to cirrhosis of the liver in early infancy and pulmonary emphysema and degenerative lung disease in middle age.	1 in 1,000 white births	No treatment.
Alpha thalassemia	Severe anemia that reduces ability of the blood to carry oxygen; nearly all affected infants are stillborn or die soon after birth.	Primarily families of Malaysian, African, and southeast Asian descent	Frequent blood transfusions.
Beta thalassemia (Cooley's anemia)	Severe anemia resulting in weakness, fatigue, and frequent illness; usually fatal in adolescence or young adulthood.	Primarily families of Mediterranean descent	Frequent blood transfusions.
Cystic fibrosis	Body makes too much mucus, which collects in the lungs and digestive tract; children do not grow normally and usually do not live beyond age 30, although some live longer; the most common inherited *lethal* defect among white people.	1 in 2,000 white births	Daily physical therapy to loosen mucus; antibiotics for lung infections; enzymes to improve digestion; gene therapy (in experimental stage); lung transplants (in experimental stage).
Down syndrome	Minor-to-severe mental retardation caused by an extra twenty-first chromosome; the most common chromosomal defect.	1 in 350 babies born to women over age 35; 1 in 800 born to all women	No treatment, although programs of intellectual stimulation are effective.
Duchenne's muscular dystrophy	Fatal disease found only in males, marked by muscle weakness; minor mental retardation is common; respiratory failure and death usually occur in young adulthood.	1 in 7,000 male births	No treatment.
Hemophilia	Excessive bleeding, usually affecting males rather than females; in its most severe form, can lead to crippling arthritis in adulthood.	1 in 10,000; families with a history of hemophilia	Frequent transfusions of blood with clotting factors.

TABLE 2-1 (*Cont.*)

Birth Defects

Problem	Characteristics of the Condition	Who Is at Risk	What Can Be Done
Neural-tube defects. Two types of neural-tube defects together constitute the most common serious type of birth defect in the United States:			
Anencephaly	Absence of brain tissue; infants are stillborn or die soon after birth.	1 in 1,000	No treatment.
Spina bifida	Incompletely closed spinal canal, resulting in muscle weakness or paralysis and loss of bladder and bowel control; often accompanied by hydrocephalus, an accumulation of spinal fluid in the brain, which can lead to mental retardation.	1 in 1,000	Surgery to close spinal canal prevents further injury; shunt placed in brain drains excess fluid and prevents mental retardation.
Phenylketonuria (PKU)	Metabolic disorder resulting in mental retardation.	1 in 14,000 births	Special diet begun in first few weeks of life can offset mental retardation.
Polycystic kidney disease	*Infantile form:* enlarged kidneys, leading to respiratory problems and congestive heart failure. *Adult form:* kidney pain, kidney stones, and hypertension resulting in chronic kidney failure; symptoms usually begin around age 30.	1 in 1,000	Kidney transplants.
Sickle-cell anemia	Deformed, fragile red blood cells that can clog the blood vessels, depriving the body of oxygen; symptoms include severe pain, stunted growth, frequent infections, leg ulcers, gallstones, susceptibility to pneumonia, and stroke.	1 in 500 African Americans	Painkillers, transfusions for anemia, antibiotics for infections.
Tay-Sachs disease	Degenerative disease of the brain and nerve cells, resulting in death before age 5.	1 in 3,000 eastern European Jews, rarer in other groups	No treatment.

SOURCE: Adapted from Tisdale, 1988, pp. 68–69.

ation of the nervous system) usually not until middle age.

Defects Transmitted by Dominant Inheritance

Most of the time, normal genes are dominant over those carrying abnormal traits, but sometimes an abnormal trait is carried by a dominant gene. When one parent has a dominant abnormal gene and one normal gene and the other parent has two normal genes, each of their children will have a 50-50 chance of inheriting the abnormal gene (see Figure 2-5). Because the abnormal gene is dominant, every child who receives it will have the defect. The defect cannot be of a kind that kills a person before the age of reproduction: if it did, the defect could not be passed to the next generation. Among the 1,800 disorders known to be transmitted by dominant inheritance are achondroplasia (a type of dwarfism) and Huntington's disease.

Through *genome imprinting,* some genes seem to be temporarily imprinted, or chemically altered, in either the mother or the father. These genes, when transmitted to offspring, have different effects than do comparable genes from the other parent. An imprinted gene will dominate one that has not

been imprinted. Genome imprinting may explain why, for example, children who inherit Huntington's disease from their fathers are far more likely to be affected at an early age than children who inherit the Huntington's gene from their mothers (Sapienza, 1990).

Defects Transmitted by Recessive Inheritance

Many defects transmitted by recessive genes are killers early in life. Some, such as Tay-Sachs disease and sickle-cell anemia, are more common among certain ethnic groups, which, through inbreeding (marriage within the group) have passed down recessive characteristics (see Table 2-2.)

Recessive defects are expressed only if a child receives the same recessive gene from each biological parent. Suppose that only one parent, say, the father, has a faulty recessive gene. If he is homozygous for the trait, that is, if he has two alleles for it, he has the disorder; if he is heterozygous, that is, if he has one normal and one defective allele, he is a *carrier* for the defect but does not suffer from it. In either case, none of his children will have it; but he can pass on the defective gene to them, and they have a 50-50 chance of being car-

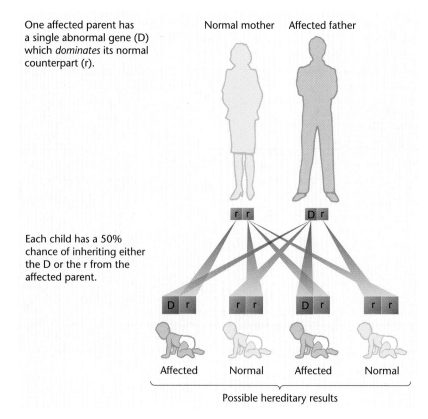

One affected parent has a single abnormal gene (D) which *dominates* its normal counterpart (r).

Normal mother   Affected father

Each child has a 50% chance of inheriting either the D or the r from the affected parent.

Affected   Normal   Affected   Normal

Possible hereditary results

FIGURE 2-5
Dominant inheritance of a birth defect.

TABLE 2-2

Chances of Genetic Disorders for Various Ethnic Groups

If You Are	The Chance Is About	That
African American	1 in 12 7 in 10	You are a carrier of sickle-cell anemia. You will have milk intolerance as an adult.
African American and male	1 in 10	You have a hereditary predisposition to develop hemolytic anemia after taking sulfa or other drugs.
African American and female	1 in 50	You have a hereditary predisposition to develop hemolytic anemia after taking sulfa or other drugs.
White	1 in 25 1 in 80	You are a carrier of cystic fibrosis. You are a carrier of phenylketonuria (PKU).
Jewish (Ashkenazic)	1 in 30 1 in 100	You are a carrier of Tay-Sachs disease. You are a carrier of familial dysautonomia.
Italian American or Greek American	1 in 10	You are a carrier of beta thalassemia.
Armenian or Jewish (Sephardic)	1 in 45	You are a carrier of familial Mediterranean fever.
Afrikaner (white South African)	1 in 330	You have porphyria.
Asian	almost 100%	You will have milk intolerance as an adult.

SOURCE: Adapted from Milunsky, 1992, p. 122.

riers and of passing it on to future generations. If *both* parents carry the abnormal recessive gene (see Figure 2-6), although *they* are unaffected, each child has 1 chance in 4 of inheriting the abnormal gene from both of them and suffering the disorder, as well as 1 chance in 2 of being a carrier.

Defects Transmitted by Sex-linked Inheritance

If you have trouble distinguishing red from green, you are probably male and you probably inherited your color blindness from your mother. In *sex-linked inheritance,* certain recessive traits linked to genes on the sex chromosomes are transmitted differently to male and female children. Red-green color blindness is one of these sex-linked conditions. Another is hemophilia, a disorder in which blood does not clot when it should.

Sex-linked recessive traits, which are carried on one of the X chromosomes of an unaffected mother, almost always show up only in male children, since there is no opposite dominant trait on the Y chromosome they received from the father. Females typically do not have such disorders because a normal gene on the X chromosome from the father overrides the defective gene on the X chro-

mosome from the mother. Each son of a normal man and a woman who is a carrier has a 50 percent chance of inheriting the mother's harmful gene—and the disorder—and a 50 percent chance of receiving the mother's normal X chromosome and being unaffected (see Figure 2-7). Daughters have a 50 percent chance of being carriers. An affected father can never pass on such a gene to his sons, since he contributes a Y chromosome to them; but he can pass on the gene to his daughters, who then become carriers.

In rare instances, a female does inherit a sex-linked condition. For example, if her father is a hemophiliac and her mother happens to be a carrier for the disorder, the daughter has a 50 percent chance of receiving the abnormal X chromosome from each parent and having the disease.

Chromosomal Abnormalities

About 1 in every 156 children born in western countries is estimated to have a chromosomal abnormality (Milunsky, 1992). Some of these abnormalities are inherited; others result from accidents during prenatal development and are not likely to recur in the same family.

Both parents, usually unaffected, carry a normal gene (D), which dominates its abnormal recessive counterpart (r).

The odds for each child are:
1. 25% risk of inheriting a "double dose" of r genes which may cause a serious birth defect
2. 25% chance of inheriting two D's, thus being unaffected
3. 50% chance of being a carrier as both parents are

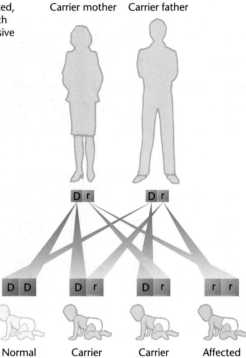

FIGURE 2-6
Recessive inheritance of a birth defect.

In the most common form, the female sex chromosome of an unaffected mother carries one abnormal gene and one normal one (X). The father has one normal male X and Y chromosome complement.

The odds for each *male* child are 50/50:
1. 50% risk of inheriting the abnormal X and the disorder
2. 50% chance of inheriting normal X and Y chromosomes
For each *female* child, the odds are:
1. 50% chance of inheriting one abnormal X, to be a carrier like mother
2. 50% chance of inheriting no abnormal genes

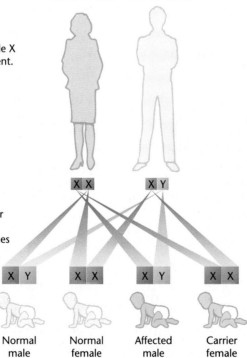

FIGURE 2-7
Sex-linked inheritance of a birth defect.

Some chromosomal disorders, such as Klinefelter syndrome, are caused by an extra sex chromosome (shown by the pattern XXY). Others, such as Turner syndrome, result from a missing sex chromsome (XO). Characteristics of the most common sex chromosome disorders are shown in Table 2-3.

Other chromosomal abnormalities occur in the autosomes. *Down syndrome,* the most common of these, is responsible for about one-third of all cases of moderate-to-severe mental retardation. The condition is also called *trisomy 21,* because it is usually caused by an extra twenty-first chromosome or the translocation of part of the twenty-first chromosome onto another chromosome. The most obvious physical characteristic associated with the disorder is a downward-sloping skinfold at the inner corners of the eyes. Other signs are a small head; a flat nose; a protruding tongue; motor retardation; and defective heart, gastrointestinal tract, eyes, and ears.

About 1 in every 700 babies born alive has Down syndrome (Hayes & Batshaw, 1993). The risk is greatest with older parents: the chances rise from 1 such birth in 2,000 among 25-year-old mothers to 1 in 40 for women over 45. The risk also rises with the father's age, especially among men over 50 (Abroms & Bennett, 1981). DNA analysis has

This kindergartner making Valentine cookies in school has Down syndrome. Although her cognitive potential is limited, loving care and patient teaching are likely to help her achieve much more than was once thought possible for such children. *(Bob Daemmrich/Stock, Boston)*

TABLE 2-3

Sex Chromosome Abnormalities

Pattern/Name	Characteristic*	Incidence	Treatment
XYY	Male; tall stature; tendency to low IQ, especially verbal.	1 in 1,000 male births	No special treatment
XXX (triple X)	Female, normal appearance, menstrual irregularities, learning disorders, mental retardation.	1 in 1,000 female births	Special education
XXY (Kleinfelter)	Male, sterility, underdeveloped secondary sex characteristics, small testes, learning disorders.	1 in 1,000 male births	Hormone therapy, special education
XO (Turner)	Female, short stature, webbed neck, impaired spatial abilities, no menstruation, sterility, underdeveloped sex organs, incomplete development of secondary sex characteristics.	1 in 3,500 female births	Hormone therapy, special education
Fragile X	Minor-to-severe mental retardation; symptoms, which are more severe in males, include delayed speech and motor development, speech impairments, and hyperactivity; the most common *inherited* form of mental retardation.	1 in 1,200 male births; 1 in 2,000 female births	Educational and behavioral therapies when needed

*Not every affected person has every characteristic.

shown that the extra chromosome seems to come from the mother's ovum in 95 percent of cases (Antonarakis & Down Syndrome Collaborative Group, 1991): the other 5 percent of cases seem to be related to the father.

The prognosis for children with Down syndrome is brighter than was once thought. Many live at home until adulthood and then enter small group homes. Many can support themselves; they tend to do well in structured job situations. More than 70 percent of people with Down syndrome live into their sixties, but they are at special risk of developing Alzheimer's disease (Hayes & Batshaw, 1993).

Genetic counseling can help prospective parents assess their risk of bearing children with genetic or chromosomal defects (see Box 2-1). Today, researchers are rapidly identifying genes that cause many serious diseases and disorders. Their work is likely to lead to widespread genetic testing, a prospect that involves dangers as well as benefits (see Box 2-2).

✔ NATURE AND NURTURE: INFLUENCES OF HEREDITY AND ENVIRONMENT

Which is more important—nature or nurture? The answer to this classic question differs for different traits. Some physical characteristics, such as eye color and blood type, are clearly inherited. As we

Monozygotic twins separated at birth are sought after by researchers who want to study the impact of genes on personality. These twins, adopted by different families and not reunited till age 31, both became firefighters. Was this a coincidence, or did it reflect the influence of heredity? *(Bob Sacha)*

have already mentioned, phenotypes for more complex traits having to do with health, intelligence, and personality are subject to both hereditary and environmental forces. And even if a trait is strongly influenced by heredity, the environment can often have a substantial impact, since genetic influences are rarely immutable.

STUDYING HEREDITY AND ENVIRONMENT

Researchers use a variety of methods to study the effects of heredity and environment. The best way to study genetic influences on animal behavior is to breed the animals for certain traits, such as aggressiveness. For ethical reasons, such studies cannot be done on human beings. Scientists therefore have relied on three types of correlational research: family, adoption, and twin studies (Plomin, 1990; Plomin, Owen, & McGuffin, 1994).

Heritability is a statistical estimate of how great a contribution heredity makes toward individual differences in a specific trait at a certain time within a given population. Researchers measure heritability by calculating the incidence of a given trait, or the degree of similarity for that trait, in members of the same family, in monozygotic twins as compared with dizygotic twins, and in adoptive children as compared with their adopted and biological parents. Such studies have found that the heritability of traits rarely exceeds 50 percent, leaving a great deal of room for environmental influence (Plomin, 1990; Plomin et al., 1994).

Family (Kinship) Studies

In family studies, researchers measure the degree to which biological relatives share certain traits and the extent to which the closeness of the genetic relationship is associated with the degree of similarity. If the correlation is strong, the researchers can infer a genetic influence. However, family studies cannot rule out environmental influences (Plomin, 1990). A family study alone cannot tell us whether obese children of obese parents inherited the tendency or whether they are fat because their diet is like that of their parents.

Adoption Studies

Adoption studies look at similarities between adopted children and their adoptive families and also between adopted children and their biological families. When adopted children are more like

BOX 2-1　　PRACTICALLY SPEAKING

GENETIC COUNSELING FOR PROSPECTIVE PARENTS

Genetic counseling helps people who believe that they may be at high risk of bearing a child with a birth defect to find out how great the risk is. People who have already had a child with a genetic defect, who have a family history of hereditary illness, who suffer from conditions known or suspected to be inherited, or who come from ethnic groups at higher-than-average risk of passing on genes for certain diseases can get information about their likelihood of producing affected children.

A genetic counselor may be a pediatrician, an obstetrician, a family doctor, or a genetic specialist. The counselor takes a thorough family history and gives the prospective parents and any existing children physical examinations. Laboratory investigations of blood, skin, urine, or fingerprints may be performed. Chromosomes from body tissues may be analyzed and photographed, and the photographs enlarged and arranged according to size and structure on a chart called a *karyotype.* This chart can show chromosomal abnormalities and can indicate whether a person who appears normal might transmit genetic defects to a child (see accompanying figure in this box).

On the basis of these tests, the counselor calculates the mathematical odds of having an afflicted child. Prospective parents who feel the risk is too high may choose to have one partner sterilized, may consider adoption or another type of conception (see Chapter 13), or may choose to terminate a pregnancy. A genetic counselor does not give advice. Rather, the coun-

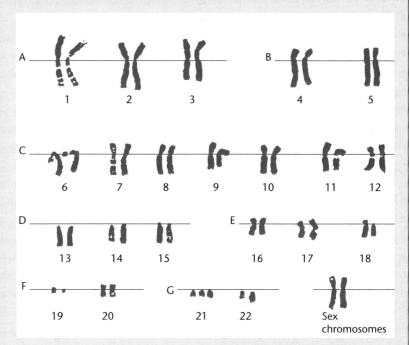

selor helps clients understand the mathematical risk of a particular condition, explains its implications, and presents information about alternative courses of action. A prediction that a child may be born with a hereditary disorder does not necessarily mean that nothing can be done about it. For example, children born with the enzyme disorder phenylketonuria (PKU) will be mentally retarded if untreated; but if put on a special diet within the first 3 to 6 weeks of life, they develop normally.

Geneticists have made a great contribution to avoidance of birth defects. For example, since so many Jewish couples have been tested for Tay-Sachs genes, far fewer Jewish babies have been born with the disease; in fact, it is

A karyotype is a photograph that shows the chromosomes when they are separated and aligned for cell division. We know that this is a karyotype of a person with Down syndrome, because there are three chromosomes instead of the usual two on chromosome 21. Since pair 23 consists of two X's, we know that this is the karyotype of a female. (*Source: Babu & Hirschhorn, 1992; March of Dimes, 1987.*)

now far more likely to affect non-Jewish babies (Kaback et al., 1993). A national registry could help identify people who may be at risk of specific birth defects, provide preventive services, and help agencies meet the needs of affected people and their families.

BOX 2-2　　FOOD FOR THOUGHT

GENETIC TESTING: BENEFITS AND RISKS

What is your risk of developing colon cancer or Alzheimer's disease? Genetic testing, formerly done mainly for reproductive counseling, is becoming more common as scientists find ways of identifying people genetically likely to develop a variety of diseases and disorders.

The Human Genome Project, a 15-year, $3 billion research effort under the joint leadership of the National Institutes of Health and the U.S. Department of Energy, is designed to map the chromosomal locations of all the estimated 100,000 human genes and identify those which cause particular disorders. The first phase of this mapping was completed in 1996.

The genetic information gained from such research could save many lives and improve the quality of many others by increasing our ability to predict, control, treat, and cure disease. A person who learns of a genetic predisposition to lung cancer might be motivated to stop smoking. A woman who has a genetic tendency for breast cancer might be advised to undergo earlier and more frequent breast examinations. A person with a tendency toward high cholesterol might be given a special diet or medication. *Gene therapy* (repairing or replacing abnormal genes) is now in the experimental stages and may become a therapeutic option within the next decade (Freeman, Whartenby, & Abraham, 1992). In the meantime, genetic information may help people make important decisions—not only whether to have children and with whom, but what type of occupation to pursue and what climate to live in. It will also allow more time to plan what to do in the event of illness or death (Post, 1994).

Still, the prospect of widespread genetic testing is controversial. One major concern is *genetic determinism:* the misconception that a person with a gene for a disease is bound to get the disease. Actually, most diseases involve a complex combination of genes or depend in part on lifestyle or other environmental factors. Furthermore, our genetic knowledge is far from infallible. For example, research that seemed to identify a specific gene for alcoholism has not been confirmed by other investigators (Holden, 1994).

If a gene that controls alcoholism were to be identified, and a test developed for it, there would be pressure to screen airline pilots and other workers whose health and sobriety might affect public safety or welfare. But is it fair to use a genetic profile to deny employment to a currently healthy person? Discrimination on the basis of genetic information has already occurred—even though tests may be imprecise and unreliable, people deemed at risk of a disease may never develop it, and testing is largely unregulated (Rennie, 1994; Voelker, 1993). One informal survey found 50 cases in which people had been

their biological parents and siblings in a particular trait (say, obesity), we see the influence of heredity. When they resemble their adoptive families more, we see the influence of environment. Some studies, such as the Colorado Adoption Project (DeFries, Plomin, & Fulker, 1994), compare the resemblance between adoptive siblings with the resemblance between genetically related siblings.

Studies of Twins

This method compares monozygotic twins, who came from the same egg and sperm and thus have the same genetic makeup, with same-gender dizygotic twins, who are no more similar genetically than other siblings. When monozygotic twins are more alike in a trait than dizygotic twins, we see the likely effects of heredity. Studies of monozygotic twins who were separated in infancy and reared apart have found strong resemblances between the twins. Such findings support a hereditary basis for many physical and psychological characteristics.

UNTANGLING HEREDITY AND ENVIRONMENT

The effects of heredity and environment are difficult to untangle. For one thing, human beings continue developing throughout life, and development generally reflects a combination of the two forces. Also, the mechanisms by which environment operates cannot be described as precisely as those of heredity. Nor can controlled comparisons

BOX 2-2 *(Cont.)*

GENETIC TESTING: BENEFITS AND RISKS

denied jobs, insurance claims, and other benefits because of their genes (Gruson, 1992).

A panel of experts has recommended that testing be voluntary, that employers be forbidden to collect genetic information unless it is clear that a worker's performance will be affected, and that insurers be prevented from considering genetic risk in issuing or pricing insurance policies (Institute of Medicine, IOM, 1993). A number of states have passed or are considering laws prohibiting job or insurance discrimination on the basis of genetic information; and the federal Equal Employment Opportunity Commission (EEOC) has ruled such job discrimination illegal under the Americans with Disabilities Act (ADA).

Psychologically, it might be extremely anxiety-producing for a person to learn that she or he has the gene for an incurable disease. What is the point of knowing you

have a potentially debilitating condition if you cannot do anything about it? For this reason, the Institute of Medicine (1993) panel recommended against genetic testing for diseases for which there is no known cure. On the other hand, some people who have family histories of a disease might be relieved once they know the worst that is likely to happen (Wiggins et al., 1992).

What about privacy? Although medical data are supposed to be confidential, it is almost impossible to keep such information private. A study at the University of Minnesota found that at least 50 people had access to each patient's medical charts (Gruson, 1992). Then, do parents, children, or siblings have a legitimate claim to information about a patient that may affect them? (Rennie, 1994)

Specific issues have to do with testing of children. Whose decision should it be to have a child

tested—the parent's or the child's? Should a child be tested to benefit a sibling or someone else? How will a child be affected by learning that he or she is likely to develop a disease twenty, thirty, or fifty years later? Will the child grow up thinking "There's something wrong with me"? Will parents who learn that a child has a gene for an incurable disease feel or act differently toward the child? Will they become overprotective? (Wertz, Fanos, & Reilly, 1994) Or will they be afraid of becoming too attached to a child who may die young? (E. Marshall, 1993) If routine testing of newborns showed that a presumed biological father was not really the father of the child, might that information lead him to reject the child? (Voelker, 1993)

Finally, genetic testing can be extremely costly. Given limited economic resources, the need for it must be weighed against other medical priorities (Post, 1994).

be made, since no two children—not even twins growing up in the same household—have exactly the same environment.

Today, most developmentalists see the relationship between genetic and environmental factors as fundamentally intertwined. Let's look at some ways in which heredity and environment work together.

Reaction Range and Canalization

Although some physical traits, such as eye color and blood type, are clearly inherited, many characteristics vary within genetic limits. Developmentalists explain this variance through the concepts of *reaction range* and *canalization*.

For many traits that are influenced by heredity, there is a **reaction range**—a range of potential ex-

pressions of the trait, depending on environmental conditions. Body size, for example, depends largely on biological processes, which are genetically regulated. Even so, a range of sizes is possible, depending upon environmental opportunities and constraints and a person's own behavior. In societies in which nutrition has drastically improved, an entire generation has grown up to tower over the generation before. The better-fed children share their parents' genes but have responded to a healthier world. Once a society's average diet becomes adequate for more than one generation, however, children tend to grow to heights similar to their parents'. Ultimately, height has genetic limits: we don't see people who are only a foot tall, or any who are 10 feet tall.

Heredity can influence whether a reaction range

is wide or narrow. For example, a child born with a defect producing mild retardation is more able to respond to a favorable environment than a child born with severe limitations.

The metaphor of *canalization* may help explain why heredity is more powerful for some traits than for others. After a heavy storm, the rainwater that has fallen on a pavement has to go somewhere. If the street has potholes, the water will fill them. However, if deep canals have been dug along the edges of the street, the water will flow into the canals rather than into the holes in the center. Some human characteristics, such as eye color, are so strongly programmed by the genes that they are said to be highly canalized: there is little opportunity for variance in their expression. Certain behaviors also develop along genetically "dug" channels; it takes an extreme change in environment to alter their course.

Behaviors that depend largely on *maturation* (see Chapter 1) seem to appear when a child is ready. Normal babies follow a typical sequence of motor development: crawling, walking, and running, in that order, at certain approximate ages. Still, this development is not completely canalized; experience can affect its pace and timing.

Cognition and personality are more subject to variations in experience: the kinds of families children grow up in, the schools they attend, and the people they encounter. Consider language. Before children can talk, they must reach a certain level of neurological and muscular maturation. No 6-month-old could speak this sentence, no matter how enriched the infant's home life might be. Yet environment does play a large part in language development. If parents encourage babies' first sounds by talking back to them, children are likely to start to speak earlier than if their early vocalizing is ignored. Heredity, then, lays the foundation for development, but environment affects the pace at which "construction" proceeds and the form of the structure.

What Makes Siblings Alike or Different?

Although two children in the same family may bear a striking physical resemblance to each other, in intellect and personality siblings tend to be more different than alike (Plomin, 1989). Indeed, their family environment seems to make them more different as experience compounds the effects of differences in heredity. From childhood on, people create their environments, both by the choices they make—what they do and with whom—and by the responses they evoke from others; and these choices and responses are influenced by their unique genetic makeup (Bouchard, 1994; Plomin, 1990, 1996; Plomin et al., 1994; Scarr, 1992).

For example, a child who has inherited artistic talent may spend a great deal of time creating "masterpieces" in solitude, while a sibling who is athletically inclined spends more time playing ball with others; and these differences are accentuated as children grow older and encounter more experiences outside the family. Furthermore, since each child is genetically different, the parents tend to react to them differently and treat them differently (Bouchard, 1994; Plomin, 1996; Scarr, 1992). Genes also influence how children respond to parental treatment and what the outcome of that treatment will be (Plomin et al., 1994). Certain events, such as illnesses and school experiences, may affect one child and not another. All these interwoven factors contribute to what have been called *nonshared environmental effects*—the unique environment in which each child in a family grows up. While heredity accounts for most of the similarity between siblings, the nonshared environment accounts for much of the difference (Plomin et al., 1994; Plomin, 1996).

SOME CHARACTERISTICS INFLUENCED BY HEREDITY AND ENVIRONMENT

Keeping in mind the difficulty of unraveling the influences of heredity and environment, let's look more closely at their roles in producing certain kinds of characteristics (see Table 2-4).

Physical and Physiological Traits

Not only do monozygotic twins generally look alike; they are also more *concordant* (alike) than dizygotic twins in their risk for such medical disorders as hypertension (high blood pressure), heart disease, rheumatoid arthritis, peptic ulcers, and epilepsy (Plomin et al., 1994). Obesity, too, is strongly influenced by heredity. It is twice as likely that both monozygotic twins will be overweight as that both dizygotic twins will be (Stunkard, Harris, Pedersen, & McClearn, 1990). However, the environment also affects weight gain. The kind and amount of food eaten in a particular home or in a particular social or ethnic group and the amount of exercise that is encouraged can affect whether or not someone becomes obese.

TABLE 2-4

Some Conditions and Characteristics Showing Genetic Influence

Condition/Characteristic	Genetic Influence*
Behavioral and personality dimensions:	
General intelligence	Substantial
Verbal reasoning	Substantial
Vocational interest	Substantial
Scholastic achievement	Substantial
Processing speed	Substantial
Spatial reasoning	Substantial
Memory	Substantial
Extraversion	Substantial
Neuroticism	Substantial
Openness	Substantial
Conscientiousness	Substantial
Agreeableness	Substantial
Behavioral and personality disorders:	
Reading disability	Substantial
Major affective disorder (depression)	Substantial
Autism	Substantial
Alzheimer's disease	Substantial
Schizophrenia	Substantial
Alcoholism	Modest
Specific language disorder	Some evidence
Panic disorder	Some evidence
Eating disorder	Some evidence
Antisocial personality disorder	Some evidence
Tourette syndrome	Some evidence

Note: Heritability rarely exceeds .50, or 50 percent.
SOURCE: Based on information in Plomin et al., 1994; Bouchard, 1994.

Our days on earth seem to be greatly affected by our genes. For example, male monozygotic twins are more concordant for incidence of strokes than male dizygotic twins—17.7 percent compared with 3.6 percent (Brass, Isaacsohn, Merikangas, & Robinette, 1992). In one study, adopted children whose biological parents had died before age 50 were twice as likely to have died young themselves as adopted children whose biological parents had lived past 49 (Sorenson, Nielsen, Andersen, & Teasdale, 1988). Still, sound health and fitness practices can increase longevity by tempering predispositions toward certain illnesses such as cancer and heart disease.

Intelligence

Heredity seems to exert a strong influence on general intelligence, as measured by intelligence (IQ) tests, and on specific abilities as well—more clearly so with age (Plomin et al., 1994). Apparently, many genes, each with its own small effect, combine to establish a range of possible reactions to a range of possible experiences (Weinberg, 1989).

Evidence for the role of heredity in intelligence has emerged from adoption and twin studies. Adopted children's IQs have been compared with IQs of their adoptive siblings and parents and with the IQs or educational levels of their biological mothers, from whom they had been separated since the first week of life. Concordances with the biological mothers have been consistently higher than they have been with the family members children have lived with (J. Horn, 1983; Scarr & Weinberg, 1983).

Heredity seems to play a more important role in cognitive ability as people grow older, reaching a heritability as high as 80 percent (Plomin et al., 1994). In adoption studies, young siblings score similarly, whether related by blood or adoption, but adolescents' scores have zero correlation with those of their adoptive siblings. Furthermore, the adolescents' IQs correlate more closely with their

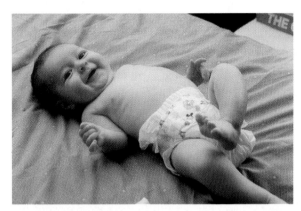

According to longitudinal research, the usually cheerful mood of a baby like 4-month-old Annie is largely the result of inborn temperament but may also be influenced by experience. *(Nancy Olds)*

biological mothers' levels of schooling than with their adoptive parents' IQs. Apparently family environment is more influential for younger children, but adolescents are more apt to find their own niche in life by actively selecting environments compatible with their hereditary abilities and interests (Scarr & Weinberg, 1983).

Longitudinal twin studies, too, have found that the genetic influence on intelligence increases with age. Monozygotic twins tend to grow more alike in IQ from infancy to adolescence, while dizygotic twins become less alike (Chipuer, Rovine, & Plomin, 1990). Still, genetics accounts only in part for variations in intelligence; an enriched or impoverished environment can substantially affect its development and expression (Neisser et al., 1995; see Chapter 8).

Personality

Personality encompasses a person's overall pattern of character, behavioral, temperamental, emotional, and mental traits. Something so complicated cannot be ascribed to any one major influence, either hereditary or environmental. Still, specific aspects of personality appear to be inherited, at least in part. Analyses of five groupings of traits—extraversion, neuroticism, conscientiousness, agreeableness, and openness to experience—suggest a heritability of about .40. Setting aside variances attributable to measurement error brings heritability closer to .66 (Bouchard, 1994).

In 1956, two psychiatrists and a pediatrician (A.

Thomas & Chess, 1984; A. Thomas, Chess, & Birch, 1968) launched the New York Longitudinal Study (NYLS), which followed 133 children from infancy into adulthood. These studies (more fully described in Chapter 5) found that temperament seems to be inborn. The researchers looked at how active children were; how regular they were in hunger, sleep, and bowel habits; how readily they accepted new people and situations; how they adapted to changes in routine; how sensitive they were to noise, bright lights, and other sensory stimuli; how intensely they responded; whether they tended to be cheerful or sad; and whether they persisted at tasks or were easily distracted. The children varied enormously in all these characteristics, almost from birth, and the variances tended to continue. However, the environment, too, was important; many children changed their behavioral style, apparently reacting to special experiences or parental handling.

Other studies suggest ethnic differences in inborn temperament. If a western newborn's nose is briefly pressed with a cloth, the baby will normally turn away or swipe at the cloth. Chinese babies are more likely to open their mouths immediately to restore breathing, without a fight (Freedman, 1979). Four-month-old American babies react more strongly than Irish babies to stimulating sights, loud sounds, and strong smells, by crying, fussing, kicking, arching their backs, and otherwise showing irritability; and Irish babies react more strongly than Chinese babies (Kagan et al., 1994). Furthermore, such temperamental differences in infants tend to predict how fearful or outgoing they will be as toddlers (Kagan & Snidman, 1991a, 1991b). Shyness and sociability, then, may vary genetically among cultures.

A major body of research strongly suggests that shyness and its opposite, boldness, are inborn characteristics that tend to stay with people throughout life (Plomin, 1989). Jerome Kagan, a professor of psychology at Harvard University, and his colleagues have studied about 400 children longitudinally, starting in infancy (DiLalla, Kagan, & Reznick, 1994; Garcia-Coll, Kagan, & Reznick, 1984; Kagan, 1989; Kagan, Reznick, Clarke, Snidman, & Garcia-Coll, 1984; Kagan, Reznick, & Gibbons, 1989; Reznick et al., 1986; Robinson, Kagan, Reznick, & Corley, 1992). Shyness, or what these researchers call "inhibition to the unfamiliar," was marked in about 15 percent of the children, first showing up in infancy and persisting in most cases until at least early adolescence. Boldness—comfort in strange situations—was especially strong in another 10 to 15 percent. Most of the children fell between the two extremes.

Both the genetic influence and the stability of the traits were strongest for the children at either extreme. Furthermore, these personality characteristics were associated with physiological signs, such as hormonal and brain activity, that may give clues to the heritability of the traits. The shyest children tended to have blue eyes and thin faces and to be subject to allergies, constipation, and unusual fears. When asked to solve problems or learn new information, they had higher and less variable heart rates than the other children, and the pupils of their eyes dilated more. The boldest children tended to be boys, to be energetic and spontaneous, and to have very low heart rates.

In another study, 2-year-olds who had been adopted soon after birth closely resembled their biological mothers in shyness. However, these babies also resembled their adoptive mothers, showing an environmental influence as well as a genetic one (Daniels & Plomin, 1985). The parents of shy babies tended to have less active social lives, exposing neither themselves nor their babies to new social situations. Thus, although a *tendency* toward shyness may be inherited, the environment can either accentuate or modify the tendency. Some shy children, especially those who are not extremely shy, may become more outgoing and spontaneous, apparently in response to parents' efforts to help them become more comfortable with new people and situations. Likewise, whether a bold child becomes a bully depends largely on upbringing. And what parents do tends to reflect what their society values.

Personality Disorders

Certain personality disorders illustrate the interrelationship of heredity and environment. There is evidence for a strong hereditary influence on schizophrenia, alcoholism, and depression. (The latter two are discussed later in this book.) They all tend to run in families and to show greater concordance between monozygotic twins than between dizygotic twins. However, heredity alone does not produce such disorders; an inherited tendency can be triggered by environmental factors.

For example, many studies suggest that schizophrenia, a disorder marked by loss of contact with reality and by such symptoms as hallucinations and delusions, has a strong genetic component (Gottesman, 1993; Plomin et al., 1994; Plomin & Rende, 1991). Still, since not all monozygotic twins are concordant for the illness, it cannot be purely genetic. But the contributing environmental causes are unknown ("Schizophrenia Update," 1995).

Infantile autism is a rare and severe developmental disorder marked by inability to communicate with or respond to other people. Infantile autism develops within the first 2½ years of life, often as early as the fourth month, and it continues to affect the child throughout life. Boys are 4 to 5 times more likely than girls to be afflicted (American Psychiatric Association, APA, 1994). An autistic baby fails to notice the emotional signals of others (Sigman, Kasari, Kwon, & Yirmiya, 1992); parents cannot get the infant to cuddle or make eye contact with them. About 3 out of 4 autistic children are mentally retarded (APA, 1994), but they often do well on tests of manipulative or visual-spatial skill and may perform unusual mental feats, such as memorizing entire train schedules. They may scream when their place at the table is changed, insist on always carrying a particular object (such as a rubber band), obsessively repeat a behavior (such as hand flapping), and engage in self-injurious behavior (such as head banging). Some autistic children never learn to speak but can sing a wide repertory of songs.

Although "cold and unresponsive" parents once were blamed for causing autism, it is now recognized as a biological disorder of the nervous system (Mauk, 1993). Interference with brain development seems to occur either during early prenatal life or during the first or second year after birth (Courchesne, Yeung-Courchesne, Press, Hesselink, & Jernigan, 1988). Autism is probably inherited; concordance between monozygotic twins is more than 4 times as high as between dizygotic twins— 96 percent versus 23 percent (Ritvo, Freeman, Mason-Brothers, Mo, & Ritvo, 1985).

✔ PRENATAL DEVELOPMENT

Of the many influences that affect a new life, some of the most far-reaching come during the nine months before birth. What turns a single fertilized ovum into a creature with a specific shape and pattern? Recent research has found that an identifiable group of genes is responsible for this transformation in vertebrates, presumably including human beings. These genes produce molecules called *morphogens,* which are switched on after fertilization and begin sculpting arms, hands, fingers, vertebrae, ribs, a brain, and other body parts (Riddle, Johnson, Laufer, & Tabin, 1993; Krauss, Concordet, & Ingham, 1993; Echeland et al., 1993).

Likewise, only recently have we become aware of some of the myriad environmental influences that can affect the developing fetus. The role of the father, for example, used to be almost ignored. Today we know that various environmental factors can affect a man's sperm and the children he conceives. The mother's role has been recognized far longer, but we are still discovering many factors that can affect her fetus.

In this section we describe the three stages of gestation, or prenatal development. Then we discuss environmental factors that can affect the developing person-to-be, assess techniques for determining whether development is proceeding normally, and explain the importance of prenatal care.

STAGES OF PRENATAL DEVELOPMENT

Prenatal development takes place in three stages: germinal, embryonic, and fetal. Table 2-5 gives a month-by-month description.

Germinal Stage (Fertilization to about 2 Weeks)

During the *germinal stage,* the organism divides, becomes more complex, and is implanted in the wall of the uterus (see Figure 2-8).

Within 36 hours after fertilization, the single-celled zygote enters a period of rapid cell division (mitosis). Seventy-two hours after fertilization, it has divided into 32 cells; a day later it has 64 cells. This division continues until the original single cell has developed into the 800 billion or more specialized cells that make up the human body.

While the fertilized ovum is dividing, it is also making its way down the fallopian tube to the uterus, a journey of 3 or 4 days. By the time it gets there, its form has changed into a fluid-filled sphere, a *blastocyst,* which then floats freely in the uterus for a day or two. Some cells around the edge of the blastocyst cluster on one side to form the *embryonic disk,* a thickened cell mass from which the baby will develop. This mass is already differentiating into two layers. The upper layer, the *ectoderm,* will become the outer layer of skin, the nails, hair, teeth, sensory organs, and the nervous system, including the brain and spinal cord. The lower layer, the *endoderm,* will become the digestive system, liver, pancreas, salivary glands, and respiratory system. Later a middle layer, the *mesoderm,* will develop and differentiate into the inner layer of skin, muscles, skeleton, and excretory and circulatory systems.

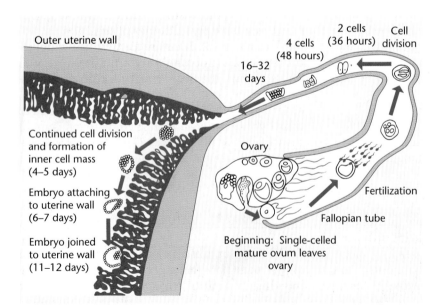

FIGURE 2-8

Early development of a human embryo. This simplified diagram shows the progress of the ovum as it leaves the ovary, as it is fertilized in the fallopian tube, and as it then divides while traveling to the lining of the uterus. It is implanted in the uterus, where it will grow larger and more complex until it is ready to be born.

TABLE 2-5

Development of Embryo and Fetus

Month	Description
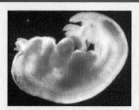 1 month	During the first month, growth is more rapid than at any other time during prenatal or postnatal life: the embryo reaches a size 10,000 times greater than the zygote. By the end of the first month, it measures about ½ inch in length. Blood flows through its veins and arteries, which are very small. It has a minuscule heart, beating 65 times a minute. It already has the beginnings of a brain, kidneys, liver, and digestive tract. The umbilical cord, its lifeline to the mother, is working. By looking very closely through a microscope, it is possible to see the swellings on the head that will eventually become eyes, ears, mouth, and nose. Its sex cannot yet be determined.
 7 weeks	By the end of the second month, the fetus is less than 1 inch long and weighs only ¹/₁₃ ounce. Its head is half its total body length. Facial parts are clearly developed, with tongue and teeth buds. The arms have hands, fingers, and thumbs, and the legs have knees, ankles, and toes. It has a thin covering of skin and can make handprints and footprints. Bone cells appear at about 8 weeks. Brain impulses coordinate the function of the organ system. Sex organs are developing; the heartbeat is steady. The stomach produces digestive juices; the liver, blood cells. The kidneys remove uric acid from the blood. The skin is now sensitive enough to react to tactile stimulation. If an aborted 8-week-old fetus is stroked, it reacts by flexing its trunk, extending its head, and moving back its arms.
  3 months	By the end of the third month, the fetus weighs about 1 ounce and measures about 3 inches in length. It has fingernails, toenails, eyelids (still closed), vocal cords, lips, and a prominent nose. Its head is still large—about one-third its total length—and its forehead is high. Sex can be easily determined. The organ systems are functioning, and so the fetus may now breathe, swallow amniotic fluid into the lungs and expel it, and occasionally urinate. Its ribs and vertebrae have turned into cartilage. The fetus can now make a variety of specialized responses: it can move its legs, feet, thumbs, and head; its mouth can open and close and swallow. If its eyelids are touched, it squints; if its palm is touched, it makes a partial fist; if its lip is touched, it will suck; and if the sole of the foot is stroked, the toes will fan out. These reflexes will be present at birth but will disappear during the first months of life.
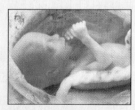 4 months	The body is catching up to the head, which is now only one-fourth the total body length, the same proportion it will be at birth. The fetus now measures 8 to 10 inches and weighs about 6 ounces. The umbilical cord is as long as the fetus and will continue to grow with it. The placenta is now fully developed. The mother may be able to feel the fetus kicking, a movement known as *quickening,* which some societies and religious groups consider the beginning of human life. The reflex activities that appeared in the third month are now brisker because of increased muscular development.
 5 months	The fetus, now weighing about 12 ounces to 1 pound and measuring about 1 foot, begins to show signs of an individual personality. It has definite sleep-wake patterns, has a favorite position in the uterus (called its *lie*), and becomes more active—kicking, stretching, squirming, and even hiccuping. By putting an ear to the mother's abdomen, it is possible to hear the fetal heartbeat. The sweat and sebaceous glands are functioning. The respiratory system is not yet adequate to sustain life outside the womb; a baby born at this time does not usually survive. Coarse hair has begun to grow for eyebrows and eyelashes, fine hair is on the head, and a woolly hair called *lanugo* covers the body.

TABLE 2-5 (*Cont.*)

Development of Embryo and Fetus

Month	Description
 6 months	The rate of fetal growth has slowed down a little—by the end of the sixth month, the fetus is about 14 inches long and weighs 1¼ pounds. It has fat pads under the skin; the eyes are complete, opening, closing, and looking in all directions. It can hear, it cries, and it can make a fist with a strong grip. A fetus born during the sixth month still has only a slight chance of survival, because the breathing apparatus has not matured. However, some fetuses of this age do survive outside the womb.
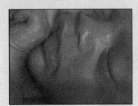 7 months	By the end of the seventh month, the fetus, 16 inches long and weighing 3 to 5 pounds, now has fully developed reflex patterns. It cries, breathes, swallows, and may suck its thumb. The lanugo may disappear at about this time, or it may remain until shortly after birth. Head hair may continue to grow. The chances that a fetus weighing at least 3½ pounds will survive are fairly good, provided it receives intensive medical attention. It will probably need to be kept in an isolette until a weight of 5 pounds is attained.
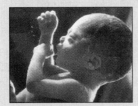 8 months	The 8-month-old fetus is 18 to 20 inches long and weighs between 5 and 7 pounds. Its living quarters are becoming cramped, and so its movements are curtailed. During this month and the next, a layer of fat is developing over the fetus's entire body, which will enable it to adjust to varying temperatures outside the womb.
 9 months–newborn	About a week before birth, the fetus stops growing, having reached an average weight of about 7½ pounds and a length of about 20 inches, with boys tending to be a little longer and heavier than girls. Fat pads continue to form, the organ systems are operating more efficiently, the heart rate increases, and more wastes are expelled through the umbilical cord. The reddish color of the skin is fading. At birth, the fetus will have been in the womb for about 266 days, although gestational age is usually estimated at 280 days, since most doctors date the pregnancy from the mother's last menstrual period.

Note: Even in these early stages, individuals differ. The figures and descriptions given here represent averages.

During the germinal stage, other parts of the blastocyst develop into organs that nurture and protect the unborn child: the placenta, the umbilical cord, and the amniotic sac. The *placenta,* which has several important functions, is connected to the embryo by the *umbilical cord.* Through this cord the placenta delivers oxygen and nourishment to the developing baby and removes its body wastes. The placenta also helps combat internal infection and gives the unborn child immunity to various diseases. It produces the hormones that support pregnancy, prepare the mother's breasts for lactation, and eventually stimulate the uterine contractions that will expel the baby from the mother's body. The *amniotic sac* is a fluid-filled membrane that encases the developing baby, protecting it and giving it room to move.

The *trophoblast*, the outer cell layer of the blastocyst, produces tiny threadlike structures that penetrate the lining of the uterine wall and enable the blastocyst to cling there until it is implanted (attached to the uterine lining). When it is fully implanted in the uterus, the blastocyst, which by that time has about 150 cells, is an embryo.

Embryonic Stage (2 to 8–12 Weeks)

During the **embryonic stage,** the second stage of gestation, the organs and major body systems—respiratory, digestive, and nervous—develop rapidly. This is a critical period, when the embryo is most vulnerable to influences of the prenatal environment (see Figure 2-9). An organ system or structure that is still developing at the time of exposure is most likely to be affected; a structure or organ that is already formed is in least danger. Almost all developmental birth defects (such as cleft palate, incomplete or missing limbs, blindness, and deafness) occur during the first *trimester* (3-month period) of pregnancy; defects that occur later in pregnancy are likely to be less serious than those occurring in the first 3 months.

The most severely defective embryos usually do not survive beyond the first trimester. A ***spontaneous abortion,*** commonly called a *miscarriage,* is the expulsion from the uterus of an embryo or fetus that is unable to survive outside the womb. Most miscarriages result from abnormal pregnancies; about 50 to 70 percent involve chromosomal abnormalities. About one-third (31 percent) of all conceptions end in miscarriage (Wilcox et al., 1988), and 3 out of 4 miscarriages occur within the first trimester (J. F. Miller et al., 1980). Women are at higher risk of miscarriage if they smoke, drink alcohol or coffee, have miscarried in the past, experience vaginal bleeding during pregnancy, are over 35, or have uterine abnormalities, endocrine problems, or certain infections (Apgar & Churgay, 1993; Mishell, 1993).

Males are more likely than females to be spontaneously aborted or stillborn (dead at birth). Thus, although about 120 to 170 males are conceived for every 100 females, only 106 boys are born for every 100 girls. Males' greater vulnerability continues after birth: more of them die early in life, and at every age they are more susceptible to many disorders, with the result that there are only 96 males for every 100 females in the United States (U.S. Department of Health and Human Services, USDHHS, 1982, 1996). Part of the explanation for male vulnerability may be that all zygotes start out with the female body plan. The fact that males undergo more alteration than females during early development may account at least in part for their poorer survival rates. Other possibilities are that the X chromosome may contain genes that protect females, that the Y chromosome may contain harmful genes, or that the sexes may have dif-

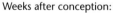

Weeks after conception:

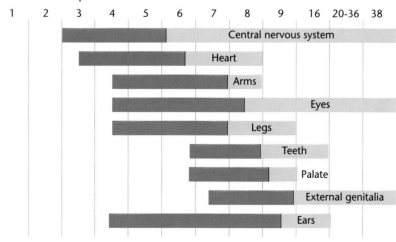

FIGURE 2-9
When birth defects occur. Body parts and systems are most vulnerable to damage when they are developing most rapidly (shaded periods) generally within the first trimester of pregnancy. *Note*: Intervals of time are not all equal. (*Source: J. E. Brody, 1995c; data from March of Dimes.*)

ferent mechanisms for providing immunity to infections and diseases.

Fetal Stage (8–12 Weeks to Birth)

With the appearance of the first bone cells at about 8 weeks, the embryo begins to become a fetus, and by 12 weeks the developing baby is fully in the *fetal stage,* the final stage of gestation. During this period, the fetus grows rapidly to about 20 times its previous length, and organs and body systems become more complex. Right up to birth, "finishing touches" such as fingernails, toenails, and eyelids develop.

Fetuses are not passive passengers in their mothers' wombs. They kick, turn, flex their bodies, do somersaults, squint, swallow, make fists, hiccup, and suck their thumbs. They respond to sound and vibrations, showing that they can hear and feel (Bernard & Sontag, 1947; Kisilevsky, Muir, & Low, 1992; Sontag & Richards, 1938; Sontag & Wallace, 1934, 1936). Their brains continue to develop, and they seem to be able to learn and remember (De-Casper & Spence, 1986). The activities of fetuses vary in amount and kind, and their heart rates vary in regularity and speed. Some of these patterns seem to persist into adulthood, supporting the idea that temperament is inborn.

Males develop more slowly than females from the early fetal period into adulthood. At 20 weeks after conception, males are, on average, 2 weeks behind females; at 40 weeks they are 4 weeks behind; and they continue to lag behind till maturity.

MATERNAL FACTORS IN PRENATAL DEVELOPMENT

Although a fetus can withstand many shocks and stresses, a healthy prenatal environment can give it the best start in life. Since the prenatal environment is the mother's body, she is greatly responsible for the earliest environmental influences on her child-to-be.

Much of what we know about prenatal hazards we have learned either from animal research or from reports by mothers, after childbirth, on what they ate while they were pregnant, what drugs they took, how much radiation they were exposed to, what illnesses they had, and so forth. Both methods have limitations: it is not always accurate to apply findings from animals to human beings, and women do not always remember what they did during pregnancy. Because of ethical considerations, it is impossible to set up controlled experiments that might provide more definitive answers. Nevertheless, we know a great deal about prenatal influences.

Particular factors in the prenatal environment affect different fetuses differently. Some environmental factors that are **teratogenic** (birth defect–producing) in some cases have little or no effect in other cases. The timing of an environmental event, its intensity, and its interaction with other factors may be relevant (refer back to Figure 2-9). Also, heredity may play a crucial role: vulnerability may depend on a gene either in the fetus or in the mother (Kolata, 1995). One study found that fetuses with a particular variant of a growth gene, called *transforming growth factor alpha,* have six times more risk than other fetuses of developing a cleft palate if the mother smokes while pregnant (Hwang et al., 1995). Other influences on prenatal development may turn out to be similarly multifactorial.

Nutrition

A woman's diet before she conceives can affect her child's future health. Her diet during pregnancy may be even more vital. Pregnant women who gain between 22 and 46 pounds are less likely to miscarry or to bear babies who are stillborn or whose weight at birth is dangerously low (Abrams & Parker, 1990). Gaining too little is riskier than gaining too much. Many women gain less than they should, in part because of societal pressures to look thin. Giving dietary supplements to malnourished pregnant women results in bigger, healthier, more active, and more visually alert infants (J. L. Brown, 1987; Vuori et al., 1979).

A well-balanced daily diet for pregnant women includes a variety of foods from each of the following categories: grains (bread, cereal, rice, and pasta); fruits and vegetables rich in vitamin C; dark-green vegetables; other fruits and vegetables (including yellow ones rich in vitamin A); protein (meat and meat alternatives); dairy products; and fats and oils. Women need to eat more than usual when pregnant: typically, 300 to 500 more calories a day, including extra protein (Winick, 1981). Teenagers, women who are ill or undernourished or under stress, and women who took birth control pills until shortly before pregnancy need extra nutrients (J. E. Brown, 1983).

Only recently have we learned of the critical importance of folic acid (a B vitamin) in a pregnant woman's diet. For some time, scientists have known that China has the highest incidence in the world of babies born with the neural-tube defects anencephaly and spina bifida, but it was not until the 1980s that researchers linked that fact with the timing of the babies' conception. Traditionally, Chinese couples marry in January or February and try to conceive as soon as possible. That means pregnancies often begin in the winter, when rural women have little access to fresh fruits and vegetables, important sources of folic acid. After medical detective work established the lack of folic acid as a cause of neural-tube defects, China embarked on a massive program to give folic acid supplements to prospective mothers (Tyler, 1994). In the United States, women of childbearing age are now urged to include this vitamin in their diets, even before becoming pregnant (American Academy of Pediatrics [AAP] Committee on Genetics, 1993).

Newer research points to a multifactorial effect. A randomized study in Dublin found that women who gave birth to babies with neural-tube defects were much more likely than women who gave birth to normal babies to have inherited a certain defective enzyme. This enzyme causes the fetus to be exposed to a toxic substance unless the mother gets large amounts of folic acid (Mills et al., 1995).

Physical Activity

Moderate exercise does not seem to endanger the fetuses of healthy women; an expectant mother can continue to jog, cycle, swim, play tennis, and so forth. Regular exercise prevents constipation and improves respiration, circulation, muscle tone, and skin elasticity, all of which contribute to a more comfortable pregnancy and an easier, safer delivery. A study of 45 women in midpregnancy who pedaled exercise bicycles found that only when the women were at the point of exhaustion did their fetuses show any decline in heart rate. Even then, the decline was short-lived; normal heart response returned within half an hour after the exercise stopped. And all the babies except two who had unrelated complications were healthy at birth (Carpenter et al., 1988).

Employment during pregnancy generally entails no special risk. However, a survey of 1,470 nurses found that strenuous working conditions, occupational fatigue, and long working hours may be associated with a greater risk of premature birth (Luke et al., 1995).

The American College of Obstetrics and Gynecology's (1994) guidelines encourage women in low-risk pregnancies to be guided by their own stamina and abilities. The safest course seems to be for pregnant women to exercise moderately, not pushing themselves and not raising their heart rate above 150, and to taper off at the end of each session rather than stop abruptly.

Drug Intake

Practically everything an expectant mother takes in makes its way to the uterus. Drugs may cross the placenta, just as oxygen, carbon dioxide, and water do. Vulnerability is greatest in the first few months of gestation, when development is most rapid. Some problems resulting from prenatal exposure to drugs can be treated if the presence of a drug in a baby's body can be detected early.

What are the effects on children of the mother's use of specific drugs during pregnancy? Let's look first at medical drugs; then at alcohol, nicotine, and caffeine; and finally at widely used, though illegal, drugs: marijuana, opiates, and cocaine.

Medical Drugs Medical drugs known to be harmful include the antibiotics streptomycin and tetracycline; the sulfanomides; excessive amounts of vitamins A, B_6, C, D, and K; certain barbiturates, opiates, and other central nervous system depressants; several hormones, including birth control pills, progestin, diethylstilbestrol (DES), androgen, and synthetic estrogen; Accutane, a drug often prescribed for severe acne; and even aspirin. The American Academy of Pediatrics (AAP) Committee on Drugs (1994) recommends that *no* medication be prescribed for a pregnant or breastfeeding woman unless it is essential for her health or her child's.

The effects of taking a drug during pregnancy do not always show up immediately. In the late 1940s and early 1950s, the synthetic hormone diethylstilbestrol (DES) was widely prescribed (ineffectually, as it turned out) to prevent miscarriage. Not until years later, when the daughters of

A mother who drinks during pregnancy risks having a child born with fetal alcohol syndrome, as this 4-year-old boy was. *(George Steinmetz)*

women who had taken DES during pregnancy reached puberty, did about 1 in 1,000 develop a rare form of vaginal or cervical cancer (Melnick, Cole, Anderson, & Herbst, 1987). "DES daughters" also have had more trouble bearing their own children than other women do, with higher risks of miscarriage or premature delivery (A. Barnes et al., 1980).

Alcohol Each year in the United States, more than 40,000 babies are born with alcohol-related birth defects. About 1 infant in 750 suffers from *fetal alcohol syndrome (FAS),* a combination of slowed prenatal and postnatal growth, facial and bodily malformations, and disorders of the central nervous system. Problems related to the central nervous system can include poor sucking response, brain-wave abnormalities, and sleep disturbances in infancy; and, throughout childhood, slow information processing, short attention span, restlessness, irritability, hyperactivity, learning disabilities, and motor impairments.

Some FAS problems recede after birth. Others, such as retardation, learning disabilities, and hyperactivity, tend to persist into adulthood. Unfortunately, enriching these children's education or general environment does not seem to enhance their cognitive development (Spohr, Willms, & Steinhausen, 1993; Streissguth et al., 1991).

The number of children known to have FAS has increased more than sixfold since 1979, to 6.7 per 10,000 births (Centers for Disease Control and Prevention, CDC, 1995d). However, it is not clear whether this represents a real increase in the number of infants with FAS or merely an increase in awareness and reporting of the problem. For every child with fetal alcohol syndrome, as many as 10 others may be born with *fetal alcohol effects,* a less severe condition that can include mental retardation, retardation of intrauterine growth, and minor congenital abnormalities.

Even moderate drinking may harm the fetus. A study of nearly 32,000 pregnancies found that having one or two drinks a day can raise the risk of growth retardation. The risk increased sharply with heavier alcohol intake (Mills, Graubard, Harley, Rhoads, & Berendes, 1984). In another study, infants whose mothers averaged one alcoholic drink a day while pregnant processed information more slowly; the more the mothers drank, the greater the effect (Jacobson, Jacobson, Sokol, Martier, & Ager, 1993). Still another study linked maternal alcohol consumption during pregnancy with infant leukemia (Shu et al., 1996).

The interrelationship among developmental realms, as well as the bidirectional influences in a child's life, are seen in the ways a mother's alcohol use affects her baby's physical, cognitive, and emotional development. A study of 44 white, middle-class mothers and babies found that the babies of mothers who had drunk even moderate amounts of alcohol while pregnant were more irritable at 1 year of age than babies whose mothers did not drink during pregnancy. The babies' crying, whining, and tantrums annoyed their mothers, interfering with the bonding between them, which may be important to a child's emotional development. These babies also tended to have low scores on tests of cognitive development (O'Connor, Sigman, & Kasari, 1993).

Since there is no safe level of drinking during pregnancy, it is best to avoid alcohol from the time a woman begins *thinking* about becoming pregnant until she stops breastfeeding (AAP Committee on Substance Abuse, 1993). About one-fifth of the women who know they are pregnant drink, according to the National Maternal and Infant Health Survey. Of 13,417 women who gave birth in 1988—the most recent year for which a population sample that large is available—nearly 21 percent reported that they had drunk alcohol after learning they were pregnant, and more than 45 percent had imbibed during the previous 3 months. Women who smoked heavily were more than twice as likely to drink as nonsmokers (CDC, 1995b). There still is a need, then, to educate women not to use alcohol if they are, or may be, pregnant.

Nicotine   How harmful is nicotine to an unborn baby? An estimate based on data from almost 100 studies is that cigarette smoking by pregnant women causes the deaths of about 5,600 babies every year in the United States, as well as 115,000 miscarriages (DiFranza & Lew, 1995). Of the deaths, 1,900 are cases of *sudden infant death syndrome (SIDS)*, in which an apparently healthy infant is unexpectedly found dead; the other 3,700 infants die by the age of 1 month, many of them because they are too small to survive. Smoking during pregnancy is estimated to contribute to the births of 53,000 low-birthweight babies (weighing less than 5½ pounds at birth) annually and 22,000 babies who need intensive care.

Although this is the first comprehensive attempt to measure the extent of the problem, previous research has established that pregnant smokers are at higher risk than nonsmokers of bearing low-birthweight babies and of complications ranging from bleeding during pregnancy to death of the fetus or newborn (Armstrong, McDonald, & Sloan, 1992; Chomitz, Cheung, & Lieberman, 1995; Landesman-Dwyer & Emanuel, 1979; McDonald, Armstrong, & Sloan, 1992; Sexton & Hebel, 1984). Women who cut down on smoking during pregnancy tend to have bigger babies than those who continue to smoke at the same rate (Li, Windsor, Perkins, Goldenberg, & Lowe, 1993).

Smoking during pregnancy seems to have some of the same effects on children when they reach school age as drinking during pregnancy: poor attention span, hyperactivity, learning problems, perceptual-motor and linguistic problems, social maladjustment, poor IQ scores, low grade placement, and minimal brain dysfunction (Landesman-Dwyer & Emanuel, 1979; Naeye & Peters, 1984; D. Olds, Henderson, & Tatelbaum, 1994a, 1994b; Streissguth et al., 1984; J. T. Wright et al., 1983). However, since women who smoke during pregnancy also tend to smoke after the birth, it is hard to separate the effects of prenatal and post-natal exposure. In one study of 2,256 children ages 4 to 11, those whose mothers smoked at least a pack a day after pregnancy were twice as likely to be anxious, disobedient, or hyperactive or to exhibit some other behavior problem than were children of nonsmokers. The effect was more pronounced in children whose mothers smoked more than a pack a day. And the risk was not lessened if the mother had stopped smoking during pregnancy but resumed afterward (Weitzman, Gortmaker, & Sobol, 1992). It is possible that smoking during pregnancy may alter the child's brain structure or function, with resulting long-term effects on behavior; that passive exposure to cigarette smoke after birth may affect a child's central nervous system; that smoking may alter the mother's behavior, thus affecting her child's; or that mothers who smoke may be less tolerant of their children's behavior.

Caffeine   Can the caffeine a pregnant woman swallows in coffee, tea, cola, or chocolate cause trouble for her fetus? One study suggests that the amount of caffeine in 1½ to 3 cups of coffee a day may nearly double the risk of miscarriage, and drinking more than 3 cups nearly triples the risk (Infante-Rivard, Fernández, Gauthier, David, & Rivard, 1993). These findings appear to conflict with those of another study, which suggested that drinking up to 3 cups of coffee a day during pregnancy does not increase the risk of miscarriage or affect fetal development (Mills et al., 1993). Because serious questions remain, the U.S. Food and Drug Administration recommends that pregnant women avoid or use sparingly any food, beverages, or drugs that contain caffeine.

Marijuana   Findings about marijuana use by pregnant women are mixed. Some evidence suggests that heavy use can lead to birth defects. A Canadian study found temporary neurological disturbances, such as tremors and startles, as well as higher rates of low birthweight in the infants of marijuana smokers (Fried, Watkinson, & Willan, 1984). And a study in the United States found that marijuana use just before and during pregnancy was linked with acute lymphoblastic leukemia, a childhood cancer, possibly because of pesticide contamination of the cannabis leaves (Robison et al., 1989).

In Jamaica (West Indies), where marijuana use is common, researchers who analyzed infants' cries concluded that a mother's heavy marijuana use affects her infant's nervous system (B. M. Lester

& Dreher, 1989). On the other hand, in another study, 3-day-old infants of mothers who had used marijuana prenatally showed no difference from a control group of nonexposed newborns; and at 1 month, the exposed babies were more alert and sociable and less irritable (Dreher, Nugent, & Hudgins, 1994). The authors of this study suggest that rural Jamaican women who use marijuana are likely to be better educated, to have higher income, and to have more adults living in the household and that these factors may combine to create a more favorable child-rearing environment. Thus scientists cannot look at a single factor, such as marijuana use, in isolation, but must explore the cultural context in which it occurs. Still, the safest course for women of childbearing age is *not* to use marijuana.

Opiates   Women addicted to morphine, heroin, and codeine are likely to bear premature, addicted babies who will be addicted to the same drugs and suffer the effects of addiction until at least age 6. Addicted newborns are restless and irritable and often suffer tremors, convulsions, fever, vomiting, and breathing difficulties. They are twice as likely to die soon after birth as nonaddicted babies (Cobrinick, Hood, & Chused, 1959; Henly & Fitch, 1966; Ostrea & Chavez, 1979). As older babies, they cry often and are less alert and less responsive (Strauss, Lessen-Firestone, Starr, & Ostrea, 1975). In early childhood they weigh less, are shorter, are less well adjusted, and score lower on tests of perceptual and learning abilities (G. Wilson, McCreary, Kean, & Baxter, 1979). Later, these children tend not to do well in school, to be unusually anxious in social situations, and to have trouble making friends (Householder, Hatcher, Burns, & Chasnoff, 1982).

Cocaine   Cocaine use seems to interfere with the flow of blood through the placenta, and it may act on fetal brain chemicals to cause behavioral change. A pregnant woman's use of cocaine is associated with a higher risk of spontaneous abortion, prematurity, low birthweight, small head circumference, and neurological problems. These babies are not as alert as other babies and not as responsive, either emotionally or cognitively (Alessandri, Sullivan, Imaizumi, & Lewis, 1993; Chasnoff et al., 1989; Chasnoff, Griffith, Freier, & Murray, 1992; Eisen et al., 1991; Hadeed & Siegel, 1989; Kliegman, Madura, Kiwi, Eisenberg, & Yamashita, 1994; Lester et al., 1991; Singer et al., 1994;

B. Zuckerman et al., 1989). Later, organizational and language skills and emotional attachment may suffer (Azuma & Chasnoff, 1993; Hawley & Disney, 1992).

The far-reaching impact of cocaine exemplifies both the interconnectedness of development and its bidirectional influences. The mother's psychological reasons for using cocaine—which then affects her physically, cognitively, and emotionally—produce effects on her baby in all three domains. A baby's initial reaction to the drug may be worsened by the early environment. Drug-abusing parents are impaired themselves and often depressed, and these conditions frequently lead to child abuse or neglect. Children of addicted mothers often face other environmental risks, such as poverty and unstable homes.

The children's own behavior affects their cognitive and emotional progress. For example, cocaine-exposed newborns do not show the kind of learning called *habituation* (see Chapter 4), in which a baby stops responding to a stimulus that is presented repeatedly. This may affect the ability to regulate attention (Mayes, Granger, Frank, Schottenfeld, & Bornstein, 1993); and a very short attention span interferes with learning. Also, the lethargic or irritable behavior of a cocaine-affected infant is not likely to inspire loving feelings. In early childhood, many of these children have trouble loving their parents, making friends, and playing normally (Lester et al., 1991). Still, some studies have shown resilience in cocaine-exposed infants. Often—especially if they had good prenatal care—they catch up in weight, length, and head circumference by 1 year of age (Racine, Joyce, & Anderson, 1993; Weathers, Crane, Sauvain, & Blackhurst, 1993).

Human Immunodeficiency Virus (HIV) Infection and AIDS

Acquired immune deficiency syndrome (AIDS) is a disease caused by the human immunodeficiency virus (HIV), which undermines effective functioning of the immune system. A fetus may become infected with HIV if the mother has AIDS or has the virus in her blood. The contents of the mother's blood are shared with the fetus through the placenta, and blood is a carrier of HIV. After birth, the virus can be transmitted through breast milk. Women most often contract HIV by intravenous drug use or by sexual intercourse with an infected person, usually a drug user. The chances that an infected woman will transmit the virus to her baby during pregnancy are about 1 in 4 (Connor, Sperling, Gelber, et al., 1994; Gabiano et al., 1992) but can be cut to about 1 in 12 by giving the drug zidovudine, commonly called AZT, to expectant mothers with HIV (Connor et al., 1994).

The prospects for children born with HIV infection have improved somewhat. Current research indicates that the progress of the disease, at least in some of these children, is not as fast as was previously thought, even without treatment. While some develop full-blown AIDS by their first or second birthday, others live for years without apparently being affected much, if at all (European Collaborative Study, 1994; Nozyce et al., 1994). In a recent study of 42 children and adolescents, ages 9 to 16, who had acquired HIV prenatally, 10 youngsters—nearly 1 out of 4—were living without symptoms and had relatively intact immune systems (Grubman et al., 1995). Most of the remaining youngsters, who had AIDS or chronic HIV-related symptoms that significantly affected their daily functioning, had not shown the signs until after 4 years of age. About three-fourths of the total group were attending regular schools, and the rest were enrolled in special education programs. This report, while giving some cause for hope, also carries a caution: often children with HIV who appear to be healthy may not be diagnosed in the early stages.

Advances in the prevention, detection, and treatment of HIV infection in infants include the successful use of AZT to curtail transmission, the recognition that women with HIV should not breastfeed, and the availability of new drugs to treat AIDS-related pneumonia. The American Academy of Pediatrics (AAP) now recommends that all pregnant women be given the opportunity for voluntary, confidential testing (AAP Provisional Committee on Pediatrics AIDS, 1995). Women who test HIV-positive can then receive information about how to protect their babies.

Other Maternal Illness

Some illnesses contracted during pregnancy can have serious effects on the developing fetus. Medical advances have lowered the risks of many serious illnesses. Some can be prevented by immunization. Also, tests can now determine whether pregnant women and their fetuses may have been infected by viruses or parasites, and if so, the woman can be treated.

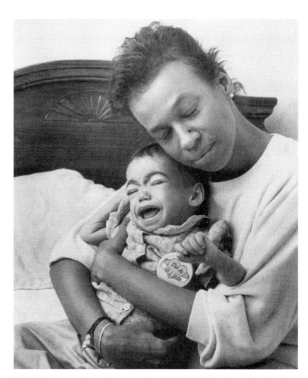

This 26-year-old mother contracted AIDS from her husband, who had gotten it from a former girlfriend, an intravenous drug user. The father died first of this modern plague, then the 21-month-old baby, and lastly the mother. *(Fred R. Conrad/The New York Times)*

Rubella (German measles), if contracted by a mother before the eleventh week of pregnancy, is almost certain to cause deafness and heart defects in the baby. However, between 13 and 16 weeks of pregnancy, the chances of such effects are only about 1 in 3, and after 16 weeks, they are almost nonexistent (E. Miller, Cradock-Watson, & Pollock, 1982). Such defects are rare these days, since most children are inoculated against rubella, making it unlikely that a pregnant woman will catch the disease. A woman who is not yet pregnant can find out through a blood test whether she is immune, and, if not, she can be immunized.

Diabetes, tuberculosis, and syphilis can cause problems in fetal development, and gonorrhea and genital herpes can have harmful effects on the baby at the time of delivery. The incidence of genital herpes simplex virus (HSV) has increased among newborns, who can acquire the disease from the mother or father either at or soon after birth (Sullivan-Bolyai, Hull, Wilson, & Corey, 1983). Newborns with HSV may suffer blindness, other abnormalities, or death.

A mild infection called *toxoplasmosis*, caused by a parasite harbored in the bodies of cattle, sheep, and pigs and in the intestinal tracts of cats, typically produces either no symptoms or symptoms like those of the common cold. In a pregnant woman, however, it can cause brain damage, blindness, or death of the baby. To avoid infection, expectant mothers should not eat raw or very rare meat, should not handle cats, and should not dig in a garden where cat feces are buried. Women who have a cat should have it checked for the disease, should not feed it raw meat, and should not empty the litter box.

Maternal Age

In recent years, as more women have delayed childbearing until the mid-thirties or even the forties, researchers have studied the risk of birth-related complications. Older pregnant women are more likely to suffer complications and possibly even death due to diabetes, high blood pressure, or severe bleeding. Also, there is greater likelihood of miscarriage, premature delivery, retarded fetal growth, stillbirth, and birth defects. However, due to widespread screening for fetal defects, deliveries of malformed fetuses after the age of viability have decreased (Cunningham & Leveno, 1995). A Canadian study found that, although the overall fetal death rate has declined since 1961 for women of all ages, the risk of stillbirth remains greater for women over 35. Still, in absolute numbers the risk of fetal death among older mothers is low—about 6 per 1,000, as compared with 3 per 1,000 when the mother is 35 or under (Fretts, Schmittdiel, McLean, Usher, & Goldman, 1995). For prospective older mothers who are basically healthy, these findings are encouraging.

Incompatibility of Blood Types

Heredity can interact with the prenatal environment to cause incompatibility of blood type between mother and baby, most commonly due to the *Rh factor,* a protein substance found in the blood of most people. When a fetus's blood contains this protein (is Rh-positive) but the mother's blood does not (is Rh-negative), antibodies in the mother's blood may attack the fetus. The result can be miscarriage or stillbirth, jaundice, anemia, heart defects, mental retardation, or death soon after birth. Usually the first Rh-positive baby of an Rh-negative mother is not affected, but with each pregnancy the risk becomes greater. A vaccine administered to an Rh-negative mother within 3 days after childbirth or abortion will prevent her body from making antibodies that will attack future Rh-positive fetuses. Babies already affected by Rh incompatibility can receive blood transfusions, sometimes even before birth.

Medical X-rays

We have known for more than 65 years that radiation can cause gene mutations (D. P. Murphy, 1929). Since the greatest damage seems to occur early in pregnancy, radiation exposure should be avoided, especially during the first 3 months (Kleinman, Cooke, Machlin, & Kessel, 1983). Today ultrasound, which we discuss later in this chapter, makes medical x-rays less necessary.

Environmental Hazards

Chemicals, radiation, extremes of heat and humidity, and other hazards of modern life can affect prenatal development. Infants exposed prenatally to high levels of lead score lower on tests of cognitive abilities than those exposed to low or moderate levels (Bellinger, Leviton, Watermaux, Needleman, & Rabinowitz, 1987; Needleman & Gatsonis, 1990). Children exposed prenatally to heavy metals have higher rates of childhood illness and lower levels of performance on a children's intelligence test (Lewis, Worobey, Ramsay, & McCormack, 1992). Women who work with chemicals used in manufacturing semiconductor chips have about twice the rate of miscarriage as other female workers (Markoff, 1992).

Nuclear radiation is especially dangerous. It affected Japanese infants after the atomic bomb explosions in Hiroshima and Nagasaki (Yamazaki & Schull, 1990) and German infants after the spill-out at the nuclear power plant at Chernobyl in the Soviet Union (West Berlin Human Genetics Institute, 1987). In utero exposure to radiation has been linked to greater risk of mental retardation, small head size, chromosomal malformations, Down syndrome, seizures, and poor performance on IQ tests and in school. The critical period seems to be 8 through 15 weeks after fertilization (Yamazaki & Schull, 1990).

PATERNAL FACTORS IN PRENATAL DEVELOPMENT

The father, too, can transmit environmentally caused defects. A man's exposure to lead, marijuana and tobacco smoke, large amounts of alcohol and radiation, DES, and certain pesticides may result in the production of abnormal sperm (R. Lester & Van Theil, 1977). Children of men who are electrical or electronic workers, auto mechanics, miners, printers, paper or pulp mill workers, and aircraft industry workers are more likely than other children to develop tumors in the nervous system (M. R. Spitz & Johnson, 1985). According to one study, fathers whose diet is low in vitamin C are more likely to have children with birth defects and certain types of cancer (Fraga et al., 1991).

One harmful environmental influence on both mother and baby is nicotine from a father's smoking. In one study, babies of fathers who smoked were lighter at birth by about 4 ounces per pack of cigarettes smoked per day by the father, or the cigar or pipe equivalent (D. H. Rubin, Krasilnikoff, Leventhal, Weile, & Berget, 1986). Another study found that children of men who smoked were twice as likely as other children to develop cancer in adulthood (Sandler, Everson, Wilcox, & Browder, 1985). In both studies, however, it was hard to distinguish between prebirth and childhood exposure to smoke.

A man's use of cocaine can cause birth defects in his children. The cocaine seems to attach itself to his sperm, and this cocaine-bearing sperm then enters the ovum at conception. Other toxins, such as lead and mercury, may "hitchhike" onto sperm in the same way (Yazigi, Odem, & Polakoski, 1991). One route for the transmission of cocaine from sperm to baby may lie with the mother. When a cocaine-using woman has sexual intercourse, the man's sperm in her reproductive tract may pick up the drug and carry it to the ovum.

A later paternal age (averaging in the late thirties) is associated with increases in several rare conditions, including Marfan syndrome (deformities of the head and limbs), dwarfism, and a bone malformation (G. Evans, 1976). Advanced age of the father may also be a factor in about 5 percent of cases of Down syndrome (Antonarakis & Down Syndrome Collaborative Group, 1991). More male than female cells undergo mutations, and mutations may increase with paternal age. Older fathers may therefore be a significant source of birth defects in their children (Crow, 1993, 1994).

PRENATAL ASSESSMENT

Not long ago, almost the only decision parents had to make about their babies before birth was the de-

cision to conceive; most of what happened in the intervening months was beyond their control. Now we have an array of tools to assess fetal development and well-being. Techniques for prenatal diagnosis of birth defects, coupled with the legal availability of abortion and the possibility of fetal therapy, have encouraged many couples who have troubling medical histories to go ahead and take a chance on conception.

Amniocentesis

In *amniocentesis,* a sample of the fluid in the amniotic sac, in which the fetus floats, is withdrawn and analyzed. This fluid contains fetal cells, and its analysis enables physicians to detect the presence of about 200 (out of 4,000) genetic defects, all recognizable chromosomal disorders, and other problems, including neural-tube defects (Milunsky, 1992). Amniocentesis can also reveal the sex of the fetus, which may help in diagnosing a sex-linked disorder such as hemophilia. In some cultures in which male births are prized, the procedure has been used for "sex screening" of fetuses (see Box 2-3).

Amniocentesis is recommended for pregnant women if they are at least 35 years old, if they and their partners are both known carriers of diseases such as Tay-Sachs or sickle-cell anemia, or if they or their partners have a family history of such conditions as Down syndrome, spina bifida, Rh disease, or muscular dystrophy. Although amniocentesis is generally considered safe, reliable and accurate, one large-scale study found a slightly higher risk of miscarriage in women who had the procedure (Tabor et al., 1986). Amniocentesis is usually done between the fifteenth and eighteenth weeks of pregnancy. Women who have the test done earlier may greatly increase their risk of miscarriage, which is more common during the first trimester.

One study found a 2.2 percent risk of miscarriage when amniocentesis is done between the eleventh and fourteenth weeks of gestation, as compared with 0.2 percent between the sixteenth and nineteenth weeks (Brumfield et al., 1996). In a Canadian study, tested babies were no more likely than those who were untested to have problems relating to intelligence, language, or behavior. They did seem to be at slightly greater risk, however, of ear infections and middle ear abnormalities, though their hearing was not affected (Finegan et al., 1990).

BOX 2-3 WINDOW ON THE WORLD

ANCIENT CULTURES AND NEW TECHNOLOGY

What happens when state-of-the-art technology is applied in the service of ancient cultural mores?

Both amniocentesis and ultrasound were developed to detect birth defects; coincidentally, they disclose the sex of the fetus. In the past twenty years, since these procedures became available in China and India, where male babies have traditionally been preferred over female babies and where efforts to fight poverty depend on holding down the birth rate, thousands of women have undergone amniocentesis or ultrasound solely to determine the sex of their unborn children. Many female fetuses have been aborted, with the result that in both populations males now predominate (Burns, 1994; Kristof, 1993).

Females fare poorly in many male-dominated Asian countries. Girls often receive less food, less schooling, and poorer medical care than boys. Sons are wanted because they carry on the family name and family traditions, perform religious rituals, and often support aging parents. Since daughters usually go to live with their in-laws after marriage, their economic value to parents is limited. Furthermore, their dowry can be costly; in India, although such payments are technically outlawed, in practice the expected sum can be more than 10 times a rural family's entire income for a year (J. F. Burns, 1994). One Indian woman pregnant with a fifth daughter burst into tears, crying that her husband would throw her out of the house if she did not produce a son (Weisman, 1988).

In recent years, as a result of the new medical technology, fewer girls have been born. In China, where the government has decreed that families have no more than one child, an estimated 12 percent of female fetuses were aborted in 1993. In one county alone, ultrasound was used in 2,316 cases, resulting in 1,006 abortions of female fetuses (Kristof, 1993). Laws to ban such testing except for medical reasons have been adopted, but their effectiveness is yet to be determined.

In India, ending a pregnancy just because the fetus is female has been against the law for several years, but the practice has continued; child welfare organizations estimate that tens of thousands of such abortions take place every year. As a result of protests by feminist groups and health officials, a new law was passed by the Indian Parliament in 1994 imposing fines and prison sentences on doctors or patients who give or take prenatal tests solely to determine the sex of the fetus. However, the penalties apply only to clinics, laboratories, and hospitals; thousands of mobile clinics equipped with compact ultrasound machines are beyond the reach of the law. Some women's advocates object to prosecuting women, whose husbands often are the ones who make the decision to abort (J. F. Burns, 1994).

In the face of the continuing pressure to bear sons, there is grave doubt about how effectively such a law can be enforced. Unless social attitudes or economic realities change, the net effect may be to drive families back to the ancient practice—outlawed under British colonial laws more than 100 years ago, but still common—of killing baby girls soon after birth or neglecting them so badly that they die of illness or starvation (J. F. Burns, 1994).

Chorionic Villus Sampling

In *chorionic villus sampling (CVS),* tissue from the ends of villi—hairlike projections of the membrane around the embryo, which are made up of fetal cells—are tested for the presence of birth defects and disorders. This procedure can be performed between 8 and 13 weeks of pregnancy (earlier than amniocentesis), and it yields results sooner (within about a week). However, one study found almost a 5 percent greater chance of miscarriage or neonatal death (death of a newborn) after CVS than after amniocentesis. Also, since CVS diagnoses can be ambiguous, women may need to undergo amniocentesis anyway (D'Alton & DeCherney, 1993).

Maternal Blood Tests

A blood sample taken from the mother between the sixteenth and eighteenth weeks of pregnancy can be tested for the amount of alpha fetoprotein (AFP) it contains. This *maternal blood test* is appropriate for women at risk of bearing children with defects in the formation of the brain or spinal cord, such as anencephaly or spina bifida, which may be detected by high AFP levels. To confirm or refute the presence of suspected conditions, ultrasound or amniocentesis, or both, may be performed.

Blood tests from samples taken between the fifteenth and twentieth weeks of gestation—for AFP and two hormones (unconjugated estriol and chorionic gonadotropin)—can predict about 60 percent of cases of Down syndrome. The diagnosis can then be confirmed by amniocentesis. This blood test is particularly important for women under 35, who bear 80 percent of all Down syndrome babies, because they are not usually targeted to receive amniocentesis (Haddow et al., 1992).

Blood tests can identify carriers of such diseases as sickle-cell anemia, Tay-Sachs disease, and thalassemia (a blood disorder that affects people of Mediterranean origin). And they can reveal the sex of a fetus, which can be of help in identifying sex-linked disorders (Lo et al., 1989). The recent discovery that fetal cells can be isolated from the mother's blood and then analyzed should make it possible to detect even more disorders (Simpson & Elias, 1993).

Ultrasound

Some parents see their baby for the first time in a *sonogram.* This picture of the uterus, fetus, and placenta is created by **ultrasound,** high-frequency sound waves directed into the mother's abdomen. Ultrasound provides the clearest images yet of a fetus in the womb, with little or no discomfort to the mother. Ultrasound is used to measure fetal growth, to judge gestational age, to detect multiple pregnancies, to evaluate uterine abnormalities, to detect major structural abnormalities in the fetus, to determine whether a fetus has died, and to guide other procedures such as amniocentesis. Results from ultrasound can suggest what other procedures may be needed (D'Alton & DeCherney, 1993).

Physicians use ultrasound to guide them in doing a fetal biopsy (a test on a sample of fetal skin) to diagnose certain disorders. But fetal biopsy is experimental, its safety and accuracy still in question (D'Alton & DeCherney, 1993). Moreover, a recent report indicates that ultrasound screening does not reduce fetal and neonatal death (Ewigman et al., 1993). So there seems to be no reason to use it in low-risk pregnancies, especially since some research suggests that frequently repeated ultrasound may affect fetal growth (Newnham, Evans, Michael, Stanley, & Landau, 1993).

Umbilical Cord Blood Sampling

By inserting a needle into tiny blood vessels of the umbilical cord under the guidance of ultrasound,

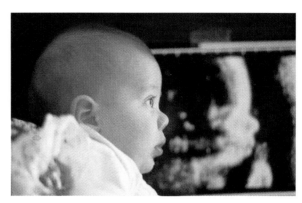

This 6-month-old baby is shown next to an ultrasound picture taken during his fourth month of gestation. Ultrasound is a popular diagnostic tool that presents an immediate image of the fetus in the womb. *(J. Pavlovsky/Sygma)*

doctors can take samples of a fetus's blood. They can then get a blood count, examine liver function, and assess various other body functions. This procedure, called *umbilical cord sampling,* can test for infection, anemia, certain metabolic disorders and immunodeficiencies, and heart failure, and it seems to offer promise for identifying still other conditions. But the technique is associated with miscarriage, bleeding from the umbilical cord, early labor, and infection (Chervenak, Isaacson, & Mahoney, 1986; Kolata, 1988). It should be used only when diagnostic information cannot be obtained by safer means (D'Alton & DeCherney, 1993).

Preimplantation Genetic Diagnosis

Preimplantation genetic diagnosis can identify genetic defects in embryos of four to eight cells, which were conceived by in vitro fertilization (fertilization outside the mother's body; see Chapter 13). In one study, researchers extracted and examined a single cell for cystic fibrosis (Handyside, Lesko, Tarin, Winston, & Hughes, 1992). Defective embryos were not implanted in the mother's body.

Embryoscopy

Embryoscopy, insertion of a tiny viewing scope into a pregnant woman's abdomen, can provide a clear look at embryos as young as 6 weeks. The procedure is promising for early diagnosis and treatment of embryonic and fetal abnormalities (Quintero, Abuhamad, Hobbins, & Mahoney, 1993).

Fetal Therapy

Sometimes conditions detected by the methods described above can be corrected in the womb. Fetuses can swallow and absorb medicines, nutrients, vitamins, and hormones that are injected into the amniotic fluid. Blood can be transfused through the umbilical cord as early as the eighteenth week of pregnancy, and drugs that might not pass through the placenta can be injected through the cord. Even surgery has been performed in the womb, though most current thinking favors waiting until after birth (Marwick, 1993).

PRENATAL CARE

Prenatal care has become widespread in the United States, but its form and quality vary greatly due to the absence of uniform national standards and guaranteed financial coverage. The percentage of pregnant women who start care during the first trimester of pregnancy has grown since 1970; still, in 1994 about 20 percent of expectant mothers did not get care until after the first trimester. And 4.4 percent received no care until the last trimester or no care at all (Guyer et al., 1996; USDHHS, 1996). Women most at risk of bearing low-birthweight babies—teenage, unmarried, and some minority women, and women with little education—get the least prenatal care (S. S. Brown, 1985; Ingram, Makuc, & Kleinman, 1986; National Center for Health Statistics, 1994a; J. D. Singh, Forrest, & Torres, 1989; USDHHS, 1996; see Figure 2-10).

By contrast, any pregnant woman in, for example, Belgium, Denmark, Germany, France, Ireland, Netherlands, Norway, Spain, Switzerland, Great Britain, or Israel can experience good maternity care. Every woman in these countries is entitled to health services and social support including free or very-low-cost prenatal and postnatal care and paid maternity leave from work. The women tend to seek early prenatal care, which enables them to begin receiving such benefits as transportation privileges and preferential hospital booking for delivery. Typically, a general practitioner coordinates care with a midwife and an obstetrician; the midwife provides most of the prenatal care and attends the birth unless the pregnancy is considered high-risk.

Early prenatal care is important because research demonstrates that it reduces maternal and infant death and other birth complications. It should include medical care and screening for treatable defects and diseases, plus educational, social, and nutritional services. First-time mothers particularly need information about pregnancy, childbirth, and infant care. Poor women who get prenatal care benefit by being put in touch with other needed social services, and they are more likely to get care for their infants after birth (Shiono & Behrman, 1995).

Early prenatal care has the potential for reducing the incidence of low birthweight (discussed

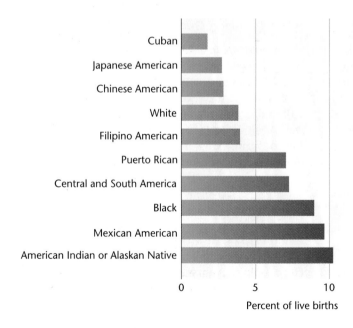

FIGURE 2-10
Proportion of American mothers with late or no prenatal care, according to race and ethnicity. Figures are for 1993. Late prenatal care begins in the last 3 months of pregnancy. (*Source: Data from USDHHS, 1996.*)

more fully in Chapter 3). Unfortunately, most prenatal care programs in the United States start too late to effectively address this problem, and they are not designed to attack its causes, such as maternal smoking. Instead, the main focus is on screening for major complications (Shiono & Behrman, 1995).

A national panel has recommended that prenatal care be restructured to provide more visits early in the pregnancy and fewer in the last trimester and that it be targeted to the specific needs of the woman and the fetus. In addition, care needs to be made more accessible to poor women and those from disadvantaged groups. In fact, care should begin before pregnancy. Prepregnancy counseling could make more women aware, for example, of the importance of getting enough folic acid in their diet and making sure that they are immune to rubella (Shiono & Behrman, 1995).

Good prenatal care can give every child the best possible chance for entering the world in good condition to meet the challenges of life outside the womb—challenges we will discuss in the next three chapters.

✔ SUMMARY

CONCEPTION

- Fertilization is the process by which sperm and ovum unite to form a one-celled zygote. During gestation, the zygote duplicates by cell division and becomes first an embryo and then a fetus.

- Although conception usually results in single births, multiple births can occur. Dizygotic (fraternal) twins have different genetic makeups and may be of different sexes; monozygotic (identical) twins have the same genetic makeup. Larger multiple births result from either one of these processes or a combination of the two.

MECHANISMS OF HEREDITY

- The basic unit of heredity is the gene, which is made up of DNA. Chromosomes carry the genes that determine inherited characteristics.

- At conception, each normal human being receives 23 chromosomes from the mother and 23 from the father. These align into 23 pairs of chromosomes—22 pairs of autosomes and 1 pair of sex chromosomes.

- A child who receives an X chromosome from each parent will be female. If a Y chromosome is contributed by the father, a male child will be conceived.

- Most normal human characteristics are transmitted by polygenic inheritance (the interaction of several genes) or multifactorially. Birth defects and disorders are more likely to result from simple dominant, recessive, or sex-linked transmission or from chromosomal abnormalities.

- Through genetic counseling, prospective parents can receive information about the mathematical odds of having children with certain birth defects. Genetic testing to identify people likely to develop certain diseases is likely to become more widespread as scientists complete the identification and location of all human genes.

NATURE AND NURTURE: INFLUENCES OF HEREDITY AND ENVIRONMENT

- Today, developmentalists look at the interaction of heredity and environment rather than attribute development exclusively to one factor or the other. Family studies, adoption studies, and studies of twins have found the heritability of most traits to be no more than 50 percent. Developmentalists use the concepts of reaction range and canalization to describe the interrelationship of heredity and environment.

- Heredity accounts for most of the similarity between siblings; the nonshared environment accounts for much of the difference.

- Obesity, longevity, intelligence, shyness, and temperament are examples of characteristics influenced by an interaction of heredity and environment. Schizophrenia, alcoholism, and depression are examples of emotional and behavioral disorders influenced by both factors.

PRENATAL DEVELOPMENT

■ Prenatal development occurs in three stages: the germinal stage, the embryonic stage, and the fetal stage.

■ Nearly all birth defects and three-quarters of all spontaneous abortions occur during the first 3 months of pregnancy.

■ The unborn baby is affected by the prenatal environment. Important factors affecting the mother include nutrition, physical activity, drug intake, illness, maternal age, incompatibility of blood type, medical x-rays, and external environmental hazards. Factors involving the father are also important. Environmental factors that can produce birth defects are called *teratogenic*.

■ Amniocentesis, chorionic villus sampling, maternal blood testing, ultrasound, umbilical cord sampling, preimplantation genetic diagnosis, and embryoscopy are techniques used to determine whether a fetus is developing normally.

■ Prenatal care, especially if begun early in a pregnancy, can reduce maternal and infant death and other birth complications.

✔ KEY TERMS

genetics (page 40)
fertilization (40)
zygote (40)
gestation (40)
ovulation (40)
dizygotic twins (41)
monozygotic twins (41)
temperament (41)
gene (42)
deoxyribonucleic acid (DNA) (42)
chromosome (42)
gametes (42)
autosomes (43)
sex chromosomes (43)
alleles (44)
homozygous (44)

heterozygous (44)
dominant inheritance (44)
recessive inheritance (44)
polygenic inheritance (44)
multifactorial transmission (44)
phenotype (44)
genotype (44)
sex-linked inheritance (49)
Down syndrome (51)
heritability (52)
genetic counseling (53)
karyotype (53)
reaction range (55)
canalization (56)
nonshared environmental effects (56)

concordant (56)
germinal stage (60)
embryonic stage (63)
spontaneous abortion (63)
fetal stage (64)
teratogenic (64)
fetal alcohol syndrome (FAS) (66)
amniocentesis (71)
chorionic villus sampling (CVS) (72)
maternal blood test (72)
ultrasound (73)
umbilical cord sampling (73)
preimplantation genetic diagnosis (73)
embryoscopy (73)

✔ QUESTIONS FOR THOUGHT AND DISCUSSION

1 To prevent the transmission of hereditary disorders, should genetic counseling be made compulsory for all people wanting to get married? Or just for people in certain categories? Give reasons.

2 Would you want to know that you had a gene predisposing you to lung cancer? To Alzheimer's disease? If you had a family history of either of these diseases, would you want your child to be tested for the genes?

3 In what ways are you more like your mother and in what ways like your father? How are you similar and dissimilar to your siblings? Which differences would you guess come chiefly from heredity and which from environment?

4 In American culture, many people consider shyness undesirable. How should a parent handle a shy child? Is it best to accept the child's temperament or try to change it?

5 Hundreds of adults now alive suffered gross abnormalities of development because their mothers took the tranquilizer thalidomide during pregnancy. As a result, the use of thalidomide was banned in the United States and certain other countries. Now thalidomide has been found to be effective in treating or controlling many illnesses from cancer to leprosy. Should its use for these purposes be permitted even though there is a risk that pregnant women might take it?

6 Does society's interest in protecting an unborn child justify coercive measures against pregnant

women who ingest alcohol or other drugs that could harm the fetus? If so, what form should such measures take?

7 In the United States, women who undergo ultrasound or amniocentesis are given the choice of whether or not they will be told their unborn babies' sex. Suppose it became known that substantial numbers of American women were aborting their fetuses for reasons of sex preference. In that case, would you favor a law forbidding use of a prenatal diagnostic procedure to reveal the sex of a fetus?

CHAPTER THREE

PHYSICAL DEVELOPMENT DURING THE FIRST THREE YEARS

The experiences of the first three years of life are almost entirely lost to us, and when we attempt to enter into a small child's world, we come as foreigners who have forgotten the landscape and no longer speak the native tongue.

Selma Fraiberg, The Magic Years, 1959

A newborn baby is, in an extreme sense, an immigrant. After struggling through a difficult passage, the newcomer is faced with much more than learning a language and customs. A baby must start to breathe, eat, adapt to the climate, and respond to confusing surroundings—a mighty challenge for someone who weighs but a few pounds and whose organ systems are not fully mature. As we'll see, infants normally arrive with body systems and senses ready to meet that challenge.

■ In this chapter we see how babies come into the world. We describe how newborn babies look, how their body systems work, and how their brains grow. We discuss ways to assess their health, and how birth trauma and low birthweight can affect development. We then describe how children develop physically during the first 3 years of life, with particular attention to sleep-and-wake cycles, the importance of nutrition, and early sensory and motor development. ■

✔ BIRTH

Birth is both a beginning and an end: the climax of all that has happened from the moment of fertilization. The uterine contractions that expel the fetus begin as mild tightenings of the uterus. A woman may have felt similar contractions at times during the final months of pregnancy, but she may recognize birth contractions as the "real thing" because of their greater regularity and intensity.

As in many animal species, maturation of the fetus determines when birth begins—typically, 266 days after conception. The process is controlled by the fetus's brain. When vital organs, such as the lungs, are ready for life outside the womb, en-

docrine changes in the fetus signal the mother's body to produce large quantities of estrogen, which stimulate the uterus to contract and the cervix to dilate, or widen (Nathanielsz, 1995). Thus, from the start, human beings act upon their environment to create the necessary conditions for development.

STAGES OF CHILDBIRTH

Childbirth, or labor, takes place in four overlapping stages (see Figure 3-1). The *first stage*, the longest, typically lasts 12 hours or more for a woman having her first child. There is a great deal of variability, however, and in later births the first stage tends to be shorter. During this stage, uterine contractions cause the cervix to dilate. At first, contractions occur about every 8 to 10 minutes and last about 30 seconds; toward the end of labor, they may come every 2 minutes and last 60 to 90 seconds.

Much of the discomfort of labor is caused by the stretching of the lower part of the uterus, especially the cervix. Before the cervix can dilate sufficiently to let the baby's head pass through, it needs to soften and thin out, through a process called *effacement*. Effacement and early dilation begin during the last weeks of pregnancy. If a woman's cervix dilates quickly during labor, she will feel little or no pain; but if her cervix is rigid and is forcibly dilated by the contractions of her uterus, the contractions will be painful.

The *second stage* typically lasts about 1½ hours or less. It begins when the baby's head begins to move through the cervix into the vaginal canal, and it ends when the baby emerges completely from the mother's body. It is also known as the "pushing" stage, since the mother feels the urge to push to help the baby in its efforts to leave her body by bearing down hard with her abdominal muscles at each contraction. If this stage lasts longer than 2 hours, signaling that the baby needs more help, a doctor may grasp the baby's head with forceps to pull it out of the mother's body. At the end of this stage, the baby is born; but it is still attached to the placenta in the mother's body by the umbilical cord, which must be cut and clamped.

During the *third stage,* which lasts about 5 to 30 minutes, the placenta and the remainder of the umbilical cord are expelled from the mother. The couple of hours after delivery constitute the *fourth stage,* when the mother rests in bed while her recovery is monitored.

METHODS OF DELIVERY

The primary concerns in choosing a method for delivering a baby are the comfort of the mother and, especially, the safety of both mother and baby. Recently, as safety has become more assured in most normal births in developed countries, health workers have focused on making the experience more pleasant and on meeting emotional needs by bringing the father and other family members into the process.

Medicated Delivery

Most societies have evolved techniques to hasten delivery, make labor easier, and lessen discomfort. General anesthesia, which renders the woman completely unconscious, is rarely used today. More common is regional (local) anesthesia, which blocks the nerve pathways that would carry the sensation of pain to the brain; or the mother can receive a relaxing analgesic. All these drugs pass through the placenta to enter the fetal blood supply and tissues.

A number of studies indicate that obstetric medication may pose dangers to the baby. Children appear to have shown immediate effects in poorer motor and physiological responses (A. D. Murray, Dolby, Nation, & Thomas, 1981) and, through the first year, in slower motor development (Brackbill & Broman, 1979). In one study (A. D. Murray et al., 1981), the babies born in medicated deliveries had caught up by 1 month of age, but their mothers felt differently about them. Why? An alert infant, who nurses eagerly, generates positive feelings in the mother. If the first encounters between mother and baby do not draw a strong reaction from the baby, the mother's early impressions of her baby may in-

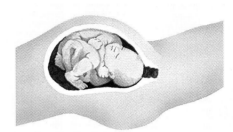

(a) First stage

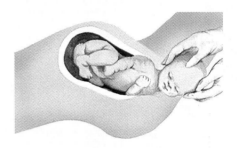

(b) Second stage

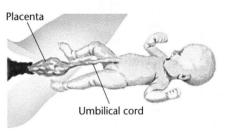

Placenta

Umbilical cord

(c) Third stage

FIGURE 3-1
The first three stages of childbirth. (a) During the first stage of labor, a series of stronger and stronger contractions dilates the cervix, the opening to the mother's womb. (b) During the second stage, the baby's head moves down the birth canal and emerges from the vagina. (c) During the brief third stage, the placenta and umbilical cord are expelled from the womb. Then the cord is cut. During the fourth stage, recovery from delivery (not shown), the mother's uterus contracts and she begins her recovery. *(Source: Adapted from Lagercrantz & Slotkin, 1986.)*

terfere with bonding between them. On the other hand, it is possible that mothers who choose unmedicated deliveries may have more positive feelings about becoming parents, and these feelings may affect how they act with their babies.

Some research suggests, however, that medicated delivery may *not* be harmful. When babies born to medicated and nonmedicated mothers were compared on strength, tactile sensitivity, activity, irritability, and sleep patterns, no evidence

In a Lamaze class, this expectant mother learns breathing and muscular exercises to make labor easier, and the prospective father learns how to assist her through labor and delivery. *(Lawrence Migdale/Photo Researchers)*

of any drug effect appeared (Kraemer, Korner, Anders, Jacklin, & Dimiceli, 1985). The authors of this study suggest that earlier research which was poorly designed and misleading may have kept appropriate drugs from some mothers, making them suffer unnecessary discomfort, and may have caused mothers who did receive drugs to feel guilty. Because the mother is the only person who can gauge her pain and because she is one of the two people most concerned about her child's well-being, she should be the one who decides about obstetric medication.

Natural and Prepared Childbirth

Two alternative methods of childbirth have been developed to minimize the use of drugs while maximizing the parents' active involvement. In 1914 a British physician, Dr. Grantly Dick-Read, claimed that pain in childbirth was not inevitable but was caused mostly by fear. To eliminate fear, he advocated *natural childbirth:* educating women about the physiology of reproduction and training them in physical fitness and in breathing and relaxation during delivery. By mid-century, Dr. Fernand Lamaze was using the *prepared childbirth* method of obstetrics. This technique substitutes controlled physical responses to the sensations of uterine contractions for the old responses of fear and pain.

The Lamaze method has become very popular in the United States. It entails learning about the anatomy and physiology involved in childbirth to reduce fear, training in such techniques as rapid breathing and panting "in sync" with the contractions to ease pain, and concentrating on sensations other than the contractions. The mother learns to relax her muscles as a conditioned response to the voice of her "coach" (usually the father or a friend). The coach attends classes with her, takes part in the delivery, and helps with the exercises. This support enhances her sense of self-worth and reassures her that she will not be alone at the time of birth (Wideman & Singer, 1984).

Cesarean Delivery

Cesarean delivery is a surgical procedure to remove the baby from the uterus by cutting through the abdomen. In 1995, according to preliminary data, 20.8 percent of babies born in the United States were delivered in this way, as compared with only 5.5 percent in 1970. However, the rate of cesarean births has been falling since 1989 (CDC, 1993; Guyer et al., 1996). The operation is commonly performed when labor does not progress as quickly as it should, when the fetus seems to be in trouble, or when the mother is bleeding vaginally. Often a cesarean is needed when the fetus is in the breech position (feet first) or in the transverse position (lying crosswise in the uterus), or when its head is too big to pass through the mother's pelvis. Surgical deliveries are more likely when the birth involves a first baby, a large baby, or an older mother. Thus the increase in cesarean rates since 1970 is in part a reflection of a proportional increase in first births, a rise in average birthweight, and a trend toward later childbirth. (Parrish, Holt, Easterling, Connell, & LeGerfo, 1994).

Cesarean deliveries have a superior safety record in delivering breech babies (Sachs et al., 1983), but there is little evidence that they improve the survival rates of very-low-birthweight infants—those weighing 3½ pounds or less (Malloy, Rhoads, Schramm, & Land, 1989). A comparison among 21 countries found no association between national cesarean rates and birth outcomes (Notzon, 1990).

Disadvantages of cesarean deliveries include a longer hospital stay and recovery, greater expense, and the physical and psychological impacts of surgery (Sachs et al., 1983). About 4 percent of cesareans result in serious complications, such as bleeding and infections (K. B. Nelson, Dambrosia, Ting, & Grether, 1996). In addition, there may be an important risk in bypassing the experience of labor, which may help the baby adjust to life outside the womb (Lagercrantz & Slotkin, 1986).

The struggle to be born apparently stimulates the infant's body to produce huge amounts of two stress hormones, adrenaline and noradrenaline. The surge of these hormones at birth clears the lungs of excess fluid to permit breathing, mobilizes stored fuel to nourish cells, and sends blood to the heart and brain. All this activity helps the baby survive such hardships as lack of food and low levels of oxygen in the first hours of life. Also, by making the baby more alert and ready to interact with another person, these hormones may promote the mother-infant bond. Babies born by emergency cesarean surgery, after the onset of labor, show levels of stress hormones almost as high as in vaginally born infants; but babies born through elective cesarean deliveries *before labor has begun* do not experience this surge of hormones, which seems to be triggered by contractions of the mother's uterus. Many of these babies have trouble breathing, possibly because smaller amounts of stress hormones are released during birth (Lagercrantz & Slotkin, 1986).

Critics of current childbirth practices claim that many cesareans are unnecessary, especially in the United States, where cesarean birth rates are among the highest in the world (Notzon, 1990). However, the increasingly common practice of vaginal delivery in subsequent births after an initial cesarean delivery may be ill-advised. A study of 6,138 women in Nova Scotia who gave birth after a previous cesarean section found twice the risk of major complications to the mother (such as rupture of the uterus) when vaginal delivery was attempted (McMahon, Luther, Bowes, & Olshan, 1996).

Medical Monitoring

Electronic fetal monitoring is the use of machinery to track the fetus's heartbeat during labor and delivery. This procedure is intended to detect a lack of oxygen, which may lead to brain damage; it can provide valuable information in high-risk deliveries, including those of low-birthweight babies and those in which the fetus seems to be in distress.

In 1992, electronic fetal monitoring was used in 77 percent of births in the United States (Wegman, 1994). Yet monitoring has drawbacks when used routinely in low-risk pregnancies. It is costly; it restricts the mother's movements during labor; and, most important, it has an extremely high "false positive" rate, suggesting that fetuses are in trouble when they are not. Such warnings may prompt doctors to deliver by the riskier cesarean method rather than vaginally (K. B. Nelson et al., 1996). Research has found that electronic fetal monitoring results in twice as many cesarean deliveries without corresponding improvements in outcome (Leveno et al., 1986; T. Lewin, 1988). Among babies that had shown abnormal heartbeats during monitoring, infants delivered by cesarean section were as likely to have cerebral palsy as those delivered vaginally (K. B. Nelson et al., 1996).

SETTINGS FOR CHILDBIRTH

In the Netherlands, pregnancy and labor are thought of as normal events that require medical intervention only when there is a specific reason. About 35 percent of Dutch babies are born at home, and about 43 percent of deliveries are attended by midwives (Treffers, Eskes, Kleiverda, & van Alten, 1990). Most of these births are to women deemed to be at low risk, and their outcomes compare very favorably with hospital births attended by obstetricians.

By contrast, 99 percent of American babies are born in hospitals, and most of these births are attended by physicians (Guyer, Strobino, Ventura, & Singh, 1995). Many hospitals are big and impersonal, with rules that sometimes seem designed more for the smooth functioning of the institution than for the benefit of the patient. Some women with good medical histories and normal pregnancies therefore opt for more intimate, less impersonal settings in their homes or in small, homelike birth centers that offer prenatal care; and some expectant mothers—5.5 percent in 1994—choose to be attended by midwives (Guyer et al., 1996). In recent years, many hospitals have established their own birth centers, where fathers or other birth coaches may remain with the mothers during labor and delivery. Many hospitals also have rooming-

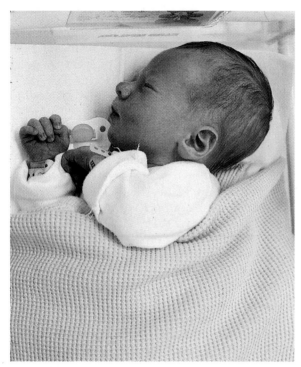

This 1-day-old boy's head is temporarily elongated from its passage through the birth canal. This "molding" of the head during birth occurs because the bones of the skull have not yet fused. *(Joseph Nettis/Stock, Boston)*

in policies, which allow babies to stay in their mothers' rooms for much or all of the day.

Freestanding maternity or birth centers are usually staffed principally by nurse-midwives, with one or more physicians and nurse-assistants. They are designed for low-risk, uncomplicated births with discharge the same day, and they appear to be a safe alternative to hospital delivery in such circumstances (Guyer et al., 1995).

Of course, low-risk pregnancies and uncomplicated births can proceed well under almost any arrangement. However, since there may be a sudden emergency during any birth, it is vital to have backup plans. A good freestanding birth center will have a contract with an ambulance service, an agreement with a local hospital, and on-premises equipment for resuscitation and administration of oxygen. Plans for a home birth should include arrangements for emergency transportation to a nearby hospital.

In many cultures, childbearing women are attended by a *doula,* an experienced mother who can furnish emotional support. In a study of 412 women having their first babies in an American hospital, 212 had a doula with them, and 200 did not (Kennell, Klaus, McGrath, Robertson, & Hinkley, 1991). The group attended by doulas had shorter labor, less anesthesia, and fewer forceps and cesarean deliveries. These findings argue for a female companion as part of the childbirth support team.

The new ways of giving birth have important implications. First, techniques that minimize drugs may give the baby a better start in life. Second, the active participation of both parents can reinforce family attachments. And third, women's assuming a major decision-making role in the birth of their children is representative of the growing tendency for people to take responsibility for their own health. The significant element is *choice.* Children born in a variety of ways and places can grow up physically and psychologically healthy.

✔ THE NEWBORN

The first 4 weeks of life are the ***neonatal period***—a time of transition from life in the uterus, when a fetus is supported entirely by its mother, to an independent existence. What are the physical characteristics of newborn babies? How are they equipped for this crucial transition? How can we assess their health and development?

SIZE AND APPEARANCE

An average ***neonate,*** or newborn, is about 20 inches long and weighs about 7½ pounds. At birth, 95 percent of full-term babies weigh between 5½ and 10 pounds and are between 18 and 22 inches long. Boys tend to be slightly longer and heavier than girls, and a firstborn child is likely to weigh less at birth than later-borns. Size at birth is related to race, sex, parents' size, and the mother's nutrition and health, and tends to predict relative size later in childhood (Behrman, 1992).

In their first few days, neonates lose as much as 10 percent of their body weight, primarily because of a loss of fluids. They begin to gain weight again at about the fifth day and are generally back to birthweight by the tenth to the fourteenth day. Light full-term infants lose less weight than heavy infants, and firstborns lose less than later-borns (Behrman, 1992).

New babies have distinctive features, including a large head (one-fourth the body length) and a receding chin (which makes it easier to nurse). At first, a neonate's head may be long and misshapen because of the "molding" that eased its passage through the mother's pelvis. This temporary molding was possible because an infant's skull bones are not yet fused; they will not be completely joined for 18 months. The places on the head where the bones have not yet grown together—the soft spots, or *fontanels*—are covered by a tough membrane; the fontanels will close within the first month of life. Since the cartilage in the baby's nose also is malleable, the trip through the birth canal may leave the nose looking squashed for a few days.

Many newborns have a pinkish cast because their skin is so thin that it barely covers the capillaries through which blood flows. During the first few days, some neonates are very hairy because some of the *lanugo,* a fuzzy prenatal hair, has not yet fallen off. All new babies are covered with *vernix caseosa* ("cheesy varnish"), an oily protection against infection that dries within the first few days.

BODY SYSTEMS

The newborn's need to survive puts a host of new demands on the body systems. Before birth, blood circulation, breathing, nourishment, elimination of waste, and temperature regulation were accomplished through the mother's body. After birth, babies must do all of this themselves (see Table 3-1). Most newborns do it so well that nobody even remarks on the feat.

Circulatory System

Before birth, the fetus and mother have separate circulatory systems and separate heartbeats; but the fetus's blood is cleansed through the umbilical cord, which carries "used" blood to the placenta and returns a fresh supply. After birth, the baby's circulatory system must operate on its own. A neonate's heartbeat is fast and irregular, and blood pressure does not stabilize until about the tenth day of life.

Respiratory System

The fetus gets oxygen through the umbilical cord, which also carries away carbon dioxide. A newborn needs much more oxygen than before and must now get the oxygen on its own. Most babies start to breathe as soon as they are exposed to air. If breathing does not begin within about 5 minutes, the baby may suffer permanent brain injury caused by *anoxia,* lack of oxygen. Because infants' lungs have only one-tenth as many air sacs as those of adults, infants (especially those born prematurely) are susceptible to respiratory problems.

Gastrointestinal System

In the uterus, the fetus relies on the umbilical cord to bring food from the mother and to carry fetal body wastes away. At birth, babies have a strong sucking reflex to help them take in milk, and their own gastrointestinal secretions to digest it. During the first few days infants secrete *meconium,* a stringy, greenish-black waste matter formed in the fetal intestinal tract. When their bowels and bladder are full, their sphincter muscles open automatically; a baby will not be able to control these muscles for many months.

TABLE 3-1

A Comparison of Prenatal and Postnatal Life

Characteristic	Prenatal Life	Postnatal Life
Environment	Amniotic fluid	Air
Temperature	Relatively constant	Fluctuates with atmosphere
Stimulation	Minimal	All senses stimulated by various stimuli
Nutrition	Dependent on mother's blood	Dependent on external food and functioning of digestive system
Oxygen supply	Passed from maternal bloodstream via placenta	Passed from neonate's lungs to pulmonary blood vessels
Metabolic elimination	Passed into maternal bloodstream via placenta	Discharged by skin, kidneys, lungs, and gastrointestinal tract

SOURCE: Timiras, 1972, p. 74.

Three or four days after birth, about half of all babies (and a larger proportion of babies born prematurely) develop *neonatal jaundice:* their skin and eyeballs look yellow. This kind of jaundice is caused by the immaturity of the liver; usually it is not serious and has no long-term effects. It is treated by putting the baby under fluorescent lights and by giving medicine. Medicinal treatment is especially important for babies in poor families and in countries where special lights are not available (Valaes, Petmezaki, Henschke, Drummon, & Kappas, 1994). Jaundice that is not monitored and treated promptly may result in brain damage. In the United States, this seems to be occurring more often because tightened medical insurance benefits have shortened hospital stays after birth.

Temperature Regulation

The layers of fat that develop during the last two months of fetal life enable healthy full-term infants to keep their body temperature constant after birth despite changes in air temperature. Newborn babies also maintain body temperature by increasing their activity when air temperature drops.

THE BRAIN AND REFLEX BEHAVIOR

What makes newborns respond to a nipple? What tells them to start the sucking movements that allow them to control their intake of milk? Such responses are functions of the *central nervous system*—the brain and *spinal cord* (a bundle of nerves running through the backbone)—and of a growing peripheral network of nerves, which eventually reaches every part of the body. Through this network, sensory messages travel to the brain and motor commands travel back. Neurological growth is what permits the rapid motor and cognitive development that takes place during infancy.

Development of the Central Nervous System

The brain's growth before and after birth (Behrman, 1992; Casaer, 1993; M. W. Cowan, 1979; Kolb, 1989) is fundamental to future development. In the uterus an estimated 250,000 brain cells form every minute through cell division (mitosis); by birth most of the 100 billion nerve cells in a mature brain are already formed but are not yet fully developed. The brain at birth is only 25 percent of its adult weight. It reaches about 70 percent of its

eventual weight during the first year and 80 percent by the end of the second year. It then continues to grow more slowly until, by age 12, it is almost adult size. Increases in brain weight and volume can be measured before birth by ultrasound and after birth by the circumference of the baby's head. These measurements provide a check on whether the brain is growing normally.

The number of cells in the central nervous system increases most rapidly between the twenty-fifth week of gestation and the first few months after birth. By the time of birth, the growth spurt of the *brain stem* (the part of the brain responsible for such basic bodily functions as breathing and heart rate), the spinal cord, and much of the *cerebrum,* the front and largest portion of the brain, has almost run its course (see Figure 3-2). However, the *cerebellum* (the part of the brain that maintains balance and motor coordination) grows fastest during the first year of life. When a particular part of the brain is growing most rapidly, it is most vulnerable to damage. Thus cerebral palsy is most likely to result from injuries occurring during the middle period of gestation—though a major trauma at any point, even after birth, can result in cerebral palsy or mental retardation, or both.

There are two main kinds of brain cells: neurons and glial cells. *Neurons,* or nerve cells, are the cells that send and receive information. *Glial cells* form the "glue" of the brain; they support and protect the neurons. Most of the neurons in the *cerebral cortex*—the outer part of the cerebrum, which is responsible for thinking and problem solving—germinate by 20 weeks of gestation.

Neurons do not spring up fully formed. At first they are simply cell bodies with a nucleus, or center, composed of deoxyribonucleic acid (DNA), which contains the cell's genetic programming. As the brain grows, these rudimentary cells migrate to various parts of it. As they differentiate to perform various functions, they sprout *axons* and *dendrites.* These narrow, branching extensions send signals to other neurons and receive incoming messages through connections called *synapses,* the nervous system's communication links. The full timetable for differentation is not known exactly. We do know that some changes in the primary visual cortex (the part of the cerebral cortex that controls vision) occur between 25 and 32 weeks of gestation, whereas in the cerebellum differentiation comes later and lasts until the end of the second year.

In a newborn infant, the subcortical structures

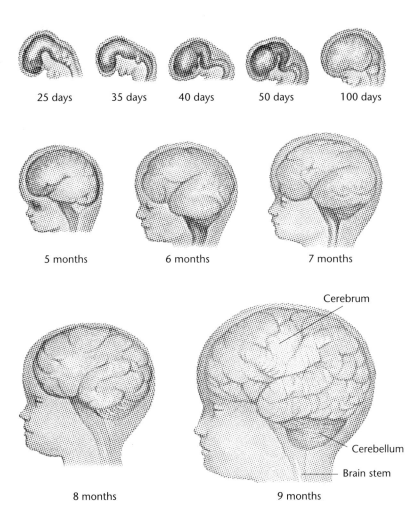

25 days   35 days   40 days   50 days   100 days

5 months   6 months   7 months

Cerebrum

8 months   9 months

Cerebellum

Brain stem

FIGURE 3-2
Fetal brain development from 25 days of gestation through birth. The brain stem, which controls basic biological functions such as breathing, develops first. As the brain grows, the front part expands greatly to form the cerebrum (the large, convoluted upper mass). Specific areas of the cerebral cortex (the gray outer covering of the brain) have specific functions, such as sensory and motor activity; but large areas are "uncommitted" and thus are free for higher cognitive activity, such as thinking, remembering, and problem solving. The subcortex (the brain stem and other structures below the cortical layer) handles reflex behavior and other lower-level functions. The cerebellum, which maintains balance and motor coordination, grows most rapidly during the first year of life. *(Source: Adapted from Restak, 1984.)*

(those below the cortex) are the most fully developed; cells in the cerebral cortex are not yet well connected. *Positron emission tomography* (PET), a tool for measuring brain activity, suggests that this is because there are too many connections, not too few. The prenatal brain produces more cells and synapses than it needs. Those which are not used or do not function well die out after birth. This pruning of excess cells and connections helps create an efficient nervous system. Connections among cortical cells continue to improve throughout childhood and into adult life, allowing more flexible and more advanced motor and cognitive functioning.

How the Environment Influences Brain Development

Until the middle of the twentieth century, scientists believed that the brain grew in an unchangeable, genetically determined pattern. We now know that the brain can be "molded" by experience, especially during early life, when it is growing most quickly and organizing itself.

Early experiences can have lasting effects on the capacity of the central nervous system to learn and store information (Greenough, Black, & Wallace, 1987; Wittrock, 1980). Chronic malnutrition of a fetus and fetal alcohol syndrome can result in brain damage; and undernourishment during the critical period just after birth can have a similar effect.

Animal experiments show that impoverished cognitive experience during early life can leave a permanent imprint on the brain. Kittens have been fitted with goggles that allowed them to see only vertical lines. In maturity, these cats were unable to see horizontal lines and bumped into horizontal boards in front of them. Other kittens, whose goggles allowed them to see only horizontal lines, grew up blind to vertical columns (H. V. Hirsch & Spinelli, 1970). This does not happen when the same procedure is carried out with adult cats. Apparently, early experience can modify the "wiring" of the visual cortex: during their formative period, neurons in that part of the brain become programmed to respond only to lines running in the direction the kittens are permitted to see. It appears that, if certain cortical connections are not made early in life, these circuits "shut down" forever.

By the same token, a stimulating environment can enhance brain growth and functioning. In a series of experiments (Rosenzweig, 1984; Rosenzweig & Bennett, 1976), rats and other animals were raised in cages with wheels to run on, rocks to climb on, levers to manipulate, or other animals to interact with. These animals were then compared with littermates raised in standard cages or in isolation. The "enriched" animals had heavier brains with thicker cortical layers, more cells in the visual cortex, more complex cells, and higher levels of neurochemical activity (making it easier to form connections between cells). Similar (though smaller) differences showed up when older animals were exposed to differing environments, suggesting that positive change is possible even in adult life.

The implications of these findings for human development—and for social policy—are profound. Children deprived of stimulation early in life may be left with permanently stunted brains. One report therefore calls for intensive educational programs to enrich the environments of underprivileged children from the first month of life (Carnegie Corporation, 1994). Data on brain development have already sparked successful efforts to stimulate the physical and mental development of children with Down syndrome, to keep aging people mentally alert, and to help victims of brain damage recover function.

A Newborn's Reflexes

When babies (or adults) blink at a bright light, they are acting involuntarily. Such automatic responses to external stimulation are called *reflex behaviors.*

Human beings have an array of reflexes, many of which are present by the time of birth or soon after (see Table 3-2). Some of these *primitive reflexes,* or newborn reflexes, such as rooting for food, are needed for early survival. Others may be part of humanity's evolutionary legacy. One example is the grasping reflex, by which infant monkeys hold on to the hair of their mothers' bodies.

Normally, the primitive reflexes disappear during the first year or so. For example, the Moro, or

"startle," reflex drops out at 2 to 3 months, and rooting for the nipple drops out at about 9 months. Other reflexes, which continue to serve protective functions—such as blinking, yawning, coughing, gagging, sneezing, shivering, and the pupillary reflex (dilation of the pupils in the dark)—remain.

Disappearance of the primitive reflexes on schedule is a sign that the cortex is maturing and developing normally, enabling a shift from reflex to voluntary behavior. Thus we can evaluate a baby's neurological development by seeing whether certain reflexes are present or absent. One of the first tests after birth is for normal reflexes.

What is normal, however, varies somewhat from culture to culture; some reflex behaviors do not seem to be universal (D. G. Freedman, 1979). For example, differences show up in the Moro reflex. To elicit this reflex, the baby's body is lifted, supporting the head. Then the head support is released, and the head is allowed to drop. White newborns reflexively extend both arms and legs, cry persistently, and move about agitatedly. Navajo babies, however, do not extend their limbs in the same way, rarely cry, and almost immediately stop any agitated motion. It seems unlikely that such reflexive differences displayed soon after birth have much, if anything, to do with the cultural environment. Instead, it would seem that such instinctive behaviors show genetic variability among ethnic groups.

MEDICAL AND BEHAVIORAL SCREENING

The first few weeks, days, and even minutes after birth are crucial for development. It is important, then, to know as soon as possible whether a baby has any problem that needs special care.

Immediate Medical Assessment: The Apgar Scale

One minute after delivery, and then again 5 minutes after birth, most babies are assessed using the *Apgar scale* (see Table 3-3). Its name, after its developer, Dr. Virginia Apgar (1953), helps us remember its five subtests: *a*ppearance (color), *p*ulse (heart rate), *g*rimace (reflex irritability), *a*ctivity (muscle tone), and *r*espiration (breathing). The newborn is rated 0, 1, or 2 on each measure, for a maximum score of 10. A 5-minute score of 7 to 10 is considered normal. A score below 7 means the baby needs help to establish breathing; a score below 4 means the baby needs immediate life-

or standard neurological testing (Behrman & Vaughan, 1983).

✔ SURVIVAL AND HEALTH DURING INFANCY

Although the great majority of births result in normal, healthy babies, some infants are born very small, remain in the womb too long, are born dead, or suffer other complications that put them at risk of dying or of physical, cognitive, or personality problems. What causes such complications? How many babies die during infancy, and why? What can be done to prevent debilitating childhood diseases (see Box 3-1)? How can we ensure that babies will live, grow, and develop as they should?

COMPLICATIONS OF CHILDBIRTH

For a small minority of babies, the passage through the birth canal is a particularly harrowing journey. About 2 newborns in 1,000 are injured in the process (Wegman, 1994). *Birth trauma* (injury sustained at the time of birth) may be caused by anoxia (oxygen deprivation), diseases or infections, or mechanical injury. Sometimes the trauma leaves permanent brain damage, causing mental retardation, behavior problems, or even death. Low birthweight and early or late birth, which are more common, also can impair a baby's chances of survival and well-being.

Low Birthweight

In 1993, 7.2 percent of babies born in the United States (up from 6.8 percent in 1970) had *low birthweight:* they weighed less than 2,500 grams (5½ pounds) at birth. Much of this increased prevalence of low birthweight is attributed to the rise in multiple births (see Chapter 2). Very-low-birthweight babies weigh 1,500 grams (3⅓ pounds) or less; in 1994 they accounted for 1.3 percent of births (Guyer et al., 1996).

Low-birthweight babies fall into two categories. Babies born before completing the thirty-seventh week of gestation are called *preterm (premature) infants;* they may or may not be the appropriate size for their gestational age. *Small-for-date infants,* who may or may not be preterm, weigh less than 90 percent of all babies of the same gestational age. Their delay in fetal growth is generally the result of inadequate prenatal nutrition. Preventing

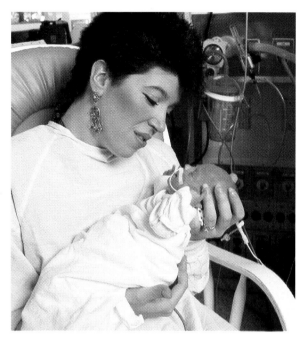

The tiniest babies thrive on human touch. This mother's holding and stroking of her low-birthweight baby girl will help establish a bond between mother and child, and will also help the baby grow and be more alert. *(Hank Morgan/Science Source/Photo Researchers)*

low birthweight and intervening when it occurs can increase the number of babies who survive the neonatal period and the first year of life.

Who Is Likely to Have a Low-Birthweight Baby? Factors increasing the likelihood of having an underweight baby (see Table 3-5) include: (1) *demographic factors,* such as race, age, education, and marital status; (2) *medical factors predating the pregnancy,* such as previous abortions, stillbirths, or medical conditions; (3) *medical factors associated with the current pregnancy,* such as vaginal bleeding, infections, or too little weight gain; and (4) *prenatal behavioral and environmental factors,* such as poor nutrition, inadequate prenatal care, smoking, use of alcohol and drugs, and exposure to stress or to toxic substances.

Many of these factors are interrelated, and socioeconomic status cuts across almost all of them. Teenagers' higher risk of having low-birthweight babies may stem more from malnutrition and inadequate prenatal care than from age, since teenagers who become pregnant are likely to be poor. At least one-fifth of all low birthweights are attributed to smoking; but when the mother is underweight and does not gain enough weight during pregnancy, smoking—in combination with

BOX 3-1 PRACTICALLY SPEAKING

IMMUNIZATION FOR BETTER HEALTH

By the middle of the twentieth century, immunization beginning in infancy seemed to have banished such widespread and often fatal childhood diseases as measles, rubella (German measles), mumps, pertussis (whopping cough), diphtheria, and poliomyelitis, at least in the United States. Then, between 1980 and 1985, the proportion of 1- to 4-year-olds who were immunized against the major childhood illnesses dropped; and between 1985 and 1990, mumps, measles, rubella, and pertussis cases rose (USDHHS, 1992). American preschoolers were less likely to be protected against childhood diseases than preschoolers in Denmark, France, West Germany, Netherlands, Norway, England, and Wales (B. C. Williams, 1990), where publicly subsidized health surveillance offers easy access at little or no cost. (In the United States, many children are not covered by health insurance, and those who are insured often have no preventive-care coverage.)

Since 1990, probably because of renewed attention to the need to vaccinate children, both rates and number of cases of mumps, measles, rubella, and pertussis in the United States have shown a generally downward trend, but there was an increase in measles and rubella in 1994 (USDHHS, 1996). According to an expert panel of the Institute of Medicine (1994), more than 90 percent of the nation's children begin their immunizations on schedule, and more than 90 percent are fully inoculated by age 5, when it is required for school attendance. However, there is often a lag in obtaining the recommended shots. One report found that fewer than half the 2-year-olds in major American cities had gotten all their required shots, and those who did get them all had not received them at recommended intervals (Zell, Dietz, Stevenson, Cochi, & Bruce, 1994; Table 3-4 shows current recommendations). However, by 1994, about 2 out of 3 of the nation's 2-year-olds were fully protected (Children's Defense Fund, 1996). Immunization rates are lower among minority groups and poor families (Institute of Medicine, 1994; USDHHS, 1996).

In 1994 Congress appropriated more than $800 million to improve community education, to make vaccines more available and less costly, and to provide free vaccine to the uninsured and those on Medicaid (Children's Defense Fund, 1995; Leary, 1994b). By 1995, the proportion of 19- to 35-month-old children who were fully vaccinated had reached about 75 percent; but 1 in 4 children still lacked at least one of the required shots (Children's Defense Fund, 1996).

New and improved vaccines are being devised. For example, in 1995, the federal government approved a vaccine for chicken pox. It is recommended for all children over 1 year old and for adolescents and adults who have not had the disease (CDC, 1996a).

Immunization is cost-effective. Every dollar spent to immunize against measles, mumps, and rubella saves $13.40 as compared with the cost of treating these illnesses, and every dollar spent on pertussis immunization saves $11.10 (Harvey, 1990).

---

these factors—accounts for nearly two-thirds of cases of retarded fetal growth. Even before pregnancy, women can cut down their chances of having a low-birthweight baby by eating well, not smoking or using drugs, drinking little or no alcohol, and getting good medical care (Chomitz et al., 1995; Shiono & Behrman, 1995).

Although the United States is more successful than any other country in the world in *saving* low-birthweight babies, the rate of such births to American women is higher than in 21 European, Asian, and Middle East nations (UNICEF, 1996). Worse still, the rates of low birthweight for African American babies are higher than the rates in 73 other countries, including a number of African, Asian, and South American nations (UNICEF, 1992). In the United States, African American babies are more than twice as likely as white babies to be born perilously small (see Table 3-6); and Puerto Rican babies are about one and a half times as likely as white babies to have low birthweight. Rates for other minorities are about the same as for white births (Chomitz et al., 1995; USDHHS, 1996).

The higher rates for African American women may in part reflect greater poverty, less education, less prenatal care, and a greater incidence of teenage and unwed pregnancy. However, such differences do not fully explain the disparities; Hispanic women, too, tend to have limited education and to lack early prenatal care. Also, even college-

TABLE 3-4

Recommended Childhood Immunization Schedule*

Vaccine	Birth	1 mo.	2 mo.	4 mo.	6 mo.	12 mo.	15 mo.	18 mo.	4–6 yr.	11–12 yr.	14–16 yr.
Hepatitis B	Hep B-1		Hep B-2		Hep B-3					Hep B	
Diphtheria, tetanus, pertussis			DTP	DTP	DTP		DTP		DTP	TD†	
H. influenzae, type b			Hib	Hib	Hib		Hib				
Polio			OPV	OPV	OPV				OPV		
Measles, mumps, rubella							MMR		MMR or MMR		
Varicella zoster virus vaccine							Var			Var	

*Vaccines are listed under the routinely recommended ages. Bars indicate range of acceptable ages for vaccination. Shaded bars (indicate *catch-up vaccination:* at 11–12 years of age, hepatitis B vaccine should be administered to children not previously vaccinated, and Varicella Zoster Virus vaccine should be administered to children not previously vaccinated who lack a reliable history of chickenpox. †Tetanus and diphtheria toxoids. SOURCE: Adapted from AAP Committee on Infectious Diseases, 1996.

TABLE 3-5

Principal Maternal Risk Factors for Delivering Underweight Infants

Category	Risks	Category	Risks
Demographic and socio-economic factors	Age (under 17 or over 40) Race (black) Poverty Unmarried Low level of education	Conditions of current pregnancy	Multiple pregnancy (twins or more) Poor weight gain (less than 14 pounds) Less than 6 months since previous pregnancy Low blood pressure Hypertension or toxemia Certain infections, such as rubella and urinary infections Vaginal bleeding in the first or second trimester Placental problems Anemia or abnormal blood count Fetal abnormalities Incompetent cervix Spontaneous premature rupture of membranes
Medical risks predating current pregnancy	No children or more than four Low weight for height or short stature Genital or urinary abnormalities or past surgery Diseases such as diabetes or chronic hypertension Lack of immunity to certain infections, such as rubella Poor obstetric history, including previous low-birthweight infant and multiple miscarriages Genetic factors in the mother (such as low weight at her own birth)	Lifestyle factors	Smoking Poor nutritional status Abuse of alcohol and other substances Exposure to DES and other toxins, including those in the workplace High altitude Stress
		Risks involving health care	Absent or inadequate prenatal care Premature delivery by cesarean section or induced labor

SOURCES: Adapted from S. S. Brown, 1985; additional data from Chomitz et al., 1995; Nathanielsz, 1995; Shiono & Behrman, 1995; Wegman, 1992.

TABLE 3-6

Comparison of Black and White Infants: Low Birthweight and Mortality*

	Low Birthweight (less than 5 pounds, or 2500 grams), % of births (1995[†])	Very Low Birthweight (less than 3.3 pounds, or 1500 grams), % of births (1994)	Infant Mortality Rate, per 1000 (1995[†])	Neonatal Mortality Rate per 1000 (1995[†])	Postneonatal Mortality Rate per 1000 (1995[†])	Decline in Infant Mortality Rate, 1970-1995[†]
Black infants	13.0	3.0	14.9	9.6	5.3	55.3%
White infants	6.2	1.0	6.3	4.0	2.2	64.2%

*Note: Black infants are more likely than white infants to die in the first year from sudden infant death syndrome, respiratory distress syndrome, infections, injuries, disorders related to short gestation and low birthweight, pneumonia and influenza, and as a result of maternal complications of pregnancy.
[†]Preliminary data.
SOURCES: Guyer et al., 1996; Rosenberg et al., 1996.

educated black women are more likely than white women to bear low-birthweight babies (S. S. Brown, 1985; Chomitz et al., 1995; Schoendorf, Hogue, Kleinman, & Rowley, 1992). This may be due to poorer general health, or it may stem from specific health problems that span generations. In any case, the high proportion of low-birthweight babies in the African American population is the major factor in the high mortality rates of black babies.

Consequences of Low Birthweight The most pressing fear for very small babies is that they will die in infancy. Because their immune systems are not fully developed, they are especially vulnerable to infection. Their reflexes may not be mature enough to perform functions basic to survival, such as sucking, and they may need to be fed intravenously (through the veins). Because they have insufficient fat to insulate them and to generate heat, it is hard for them to stay warm enough. Respiratory distress syndrome, also called *hyaline membrane disease,* is common. Many preterm babies with very low birthweight lack surfactant, an essential lung-coating substance that keeps air sacs from collapsing; they may breathe irregularly or stop breathing altogether and die.

Administering surfactant to high-risk preterm neonates has increased their survival rate (Corbet et al., 1995; Horbar et al., 1993), allowing some infants who weigh as little as 750 grams (1 pound 10 ounces) to survive. However, these rescue efforts are extremely costly—as much as $1 million or more for one baby!—and often leave the infant with long-term health or developmental problems (Shiono & Behrman, 1995). Health care, education,

and child care for the 3.5 to 4 million children up to 15 years old whose weight was low at birth costs nearly $6 billion more than if these children had been born with normal weight (Lewit, Baker, Corman, & Shiono, 1995).

Still, many low-birthweight babies who survive the dangerous early days do fairly well, owing in part to follow-up support. In an analysis of 80 studies published since 1979, only about a 6-point difference in average IQ showed up between children of low and normal birthweight, and both were in the normal range for intelligence—97.7 as compared with 103.78 (Aylward, Pfeiffer, Wright, & Verhulst, 1989). *Very*-low-birthweight babies have a less promising prognosis. In one study, about half of a sample of eighty-eight 7-year-olds who had weighed less than 3.3 pounds at birth needed special education, compared with 15 percent of a normal-weight, full-term control group (G. Ross, Lipper, & Auld, 1991). When low-birthweight children reach school age, those who weighed the least at birth have the most behavioral, social, attention, and language problems (Klebanov, Brooks-Gunn, & McCormick, 1994).

Male babies with very low birthweight are more likely than female babies to have long-range problems. In a nationwide study of more than 1,000 infants born before 32 weeks of gestation, about the same number of boy and girl babies died during the first month; but boys who survived to age 5 were three times as likely to have impairments that caused them to need special education, interfered with everyday activities, or imposed burdens on the child, caregivers, or society (Verloove-Vanhorick et al., 1994).

Treatment of Low-Birthweight Babies Much of the increase in neonatal survival is due to improved care of low-birthweight babies. Anemic babies are given iron supplements; babies with low blood sugar are fed glucose intravenously; and babies with jaundice are given medicine or are put under fluorescent lights. A low-birthweight baby is placed in an *isolette* (an antiseptic, temperature-controlled crib) and fed through tubes. To counteract the sensory impoverishment of life in an isolette, hospital workers and parents give these small babies special handling. Gentle massage seems to foster growth, behavioral organization, weight gain, motor activity, and alertness (T. M. Field, 1986; Schanberg & Field, 1987).

Some parents, anxious about the health of a low-birthweight baby and fearful that the infant may die, are afraid of becoming too attached; they may feel uncomfortable with the baby and refrain from touching the infant (Stern & Hildebrandt, 1986). Frequent visits can give parents a more realistic idea of how the baby is doing and help them become more relaxed. Regularly visited babies seem to recover faster and leave the hospital sooner (Levy-Shiff, Hoffman, Mogilner, Levinger, & Mogilner, 1990; Zeskind & Iacino, 1984).

A child's prospects for overcoming the early disadvantage of low birthweight depend on several interacting factors. One is the family's socioeconomic circumstances (Aylward et al., 1989; McGauhey, Starfield, Alexander, & Ensminget, 1991; G. Ross et al., 1991). Another is the amount of stimulation in the caregiving environment.

A large-scale study (Infant Health & Development Program, IHDP, 1990) followed 985 preterm, low-birthweight babies in eight parts of the United States—most of them from poor inner-city families—from birth to age 3. The parents of one-third of the babies received counseling and information about the children's health and development and learned games and activities to play with their children; at 1 year, these babies entered an educational day care program. At 30 months, children in this experimental group were more persistent, enthusiastic, and competent than a control group of low-birthweight children whose parents had not received counseling (Spiker, Ferguson, & Brooks-Gunn, 1993). At age 3, when the program stopped, the experimental group members were doing better on cognitive and social measures, were much less likely to show mental retardation, and had fewer behavioral problems than the control group (Brooks-Gunn, Klebanov, Liaw, & Spiker, 1993).

However, two years later, at age 5, the children in the experimental group who had had the lowest birthweights no longer held a cognitive edge over children in the control group. Furthermore, having been in the program made no difference in health or behavior, regardless of how low the birthweight had been. It seems, then, that for such an intervention to be effective, it needs to continue beyond age 3 (Brooks-Gunn et al., 1994).

Other studies of the full IHDP sample underline the importance of what goes on in the home. Children from nonstimulating homes, who got little parental attention and care, were more likely to be undersized and to do poorly on cognitive tests than children from more favorable home environments (Kelleher et al., 1993). Those whose cognitive performance stayed high had mothers who scored high themselves on cognitive tests and who were responsive and stimulating. Babies who had more than one risk factor (such as poor neonatal health combined with having a mother who did not receive counseling or was less well educated or less responsive) fared the worst (Liaw & Brooks-Gunn, 1993).

These studies make clear the need to look at human development in context. The studies show how biological and environmental influences interact, before and after birth; they show the complex consequences of such influences on all aspects of development; and they show that some resiliency is possible even among babies born with serious complications.

Postmaturity

As many as 7 percent of pregnant women have not gone into labor 2 weeks after the due date, or 42 weeks after the last menstrual period. At that point, a baby is considered *postmature.* Postmaturity can last as long as 5 weeks. Postmature babies tend to be long and thin, because they have kept growing in the womb but have had an insufficient blood supply toward the end of gestation. Possibly because the placenta has aged and become less efficient, it may provide less oxygen. The baby's greater size also complicates labor: the mother has to deliver a baby the size of a normal 1-month-old.

Since postmature fetuses are at higher risk of brain damage or even death, doctors sometimes induce labor with drugs or perform cesarean deliveries. However, if the due date has been miscalculated, a baby who is actually premature may be delivered. To help make the decision, doctors monitor the baby's status with ultrasound to see whether the heart rate speeds up when the fetus moves; if not, the baby may be short of oxygen. Another test involves examining the volume of amniotic fluid; a low level may mean the baby is not getting enough food.

LIFE-SPAN ISSUE
CAN A SUPPORTIVE ENVIRONMENT OVERCOME EFFECTS OF BIRTH COMPLICATIONS?

 Children's vulnerability and resiliency are major research interests of Emmy E. Werner, professor of human development at the University of California, Davis. Most studies of these topics have been short-term and have focused on middle childhood and adolescence. An important exception is the Kauai Longitudinal Study. For more than three decades, Werner and a research team of pediatricians, psychologists, public health workers, and social workers have followed 698 children born in 1955 on the Hawaiian island of Kauai, from the prenatal period through birth, and then into young adulthood.

Can a favorable environment overcome the effects of birth injuries, low birthweight, or other complications of birth? According to a 30-year longitudinal study of all babies born on Kauai, Hawaii, in 1955, the answer is yes (Werner, 1987, 1995).

Kauai was chosen as the site for the research for several reasons. First, its population is stable, so attrition would be—and was—low. Second, because the island is part of the United States, families had access to high-quality medical, educational, and social services. Third, the 40,000 multiethnic inhabitants had diverse socioeconomic and educational levels and lifestyles.

The researchers interviewed the mothers; recorded their personal, family, and reproductive histories; monitored the course of their pregnancies; and interviewed them again when the children were 1, 2, and 10 years old. They also observed the children interacting with their parents at home and gave them aptitude, achievement, and personality tests in elementary and high school. The children's teachers reported on their progress and their behavior. The young people themselves were interviewed at ages 18 and 30. The researchers also reviewed records of community agencies and police and court files.

Of the original 1,000 live births, 865 children survived to age 2 with no apparent physical, cognitive, or social abnormalities. Stress at birth took its biggest toll during the first two years of life: all of the deaths during the first month and three-fourths of the deaths before the second birthday were attributed to birth complications. As time went on, however, the role of the environment became more pronounced.

Among the children who had suffered problems at or before birth, physical and psychological development was seriously impaired *only* when they grew up in persistently poor environmental circumstances. From toddlerhood on, unless the early damage was so serious as to require institutionalization, those children who had a stable and enriching environment did well (Werner, 1985, 1987). In fact, they had fewer language, perceptual, emotional, and school problems than children who had *not* experienced unusual stress at birth but who had suffered "environmental trauma" by receiving little intellectual stimulation or emotional support at home (Werner, 1989; Werner et al., 1968). The children who showed the worst health problems and whose development was most retarded were those who had been exposed to *both* reproductive problems and stressful experiences (Werner, 1987). Given a supportive environment, then, children—even those who have suffered significant birth complications—can overcome a poor start in life.

Even more remarkable is the resilience of children who escape damage despite *multiple* sources of stress. Even when birth complications were combined with such environmental risks as chronic poverty, family discord, divorce, or parents who were mentally ill, a large minority of children came through relatively unscathed. Of the 276 children who at age 2 had been identified as having four or more risk factors, two-thirds developed serious learning or behavior problems by the age of 10 or, by age 18, had become pregnant, gotten in trouble with the law, or become emotionally troubled. Yet by age 30, one-third of these highly at-risk children had managed to become "competent, confident, and caring adults" (Werner, 1995, p. 82).

Protective factors fell into three categories: (1) individual attributes that may be largely genetic, such as energy, sociability, and intelligence, (2) affectionate ties with at least one supportive family member, and (3) rewards at school, work, or church that provide a sense of meaning and control over one's life (Werner, 1987). While the home environment seemed to have the most marked effect in childhood, the individuals' own qualities made more difference in their lives and in the environments they chose as adults (Werner, 1995).

DEATH DURING INFANCY

One of the most tragic losses is the death of an infant. Great strides have been made in protecting

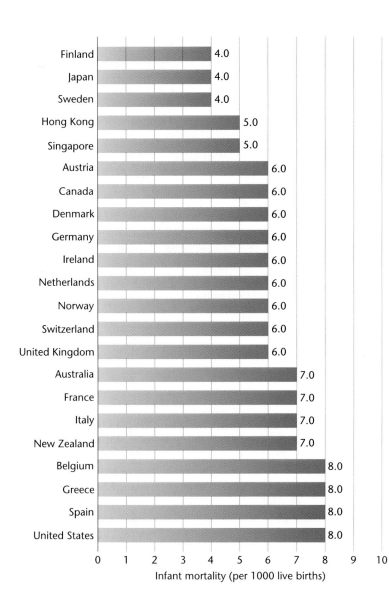

FIGURE 3-3
Infant mortality rates in industrialized countries, 1994. A nation's infant mortality rate is one indicator of its health status. The United States—along with Belgium, Greece, and Spain—has the highest infant mortality among 22 industrialized nations, largely because of its very high mortality rate for minority babies (see Table 3-6). Most nations, including the United States, have shown improvement in recent years. *(Source: Data from UNICEF, 1996. Note: Figures have been rounded.)*

the lives of new babies, but these improvements are not evenly distributed throughout the population. Too many babies still die, some of them without warning and for no apparent reason.

Trends in Infant Mortality

In the United States, the *infant mortality rate*— the proportion of babies who die within the first year of life—is now the lowest ever. In 1995, according to preliminary data, there were 7.5 deaths in the first year for every 1,000 live births, compared with 26 per 1,000 in 1960 (Guyer et al., 1995; Guyer et al., 1996; Rosenberg et al., 1996). Although more than two-thirds of these deaths take place during the first 4 weeks (USDHHS, 1996),

there has been a rapid drop in *neonatal mortality* (deaths during the first 4 weeks) since the 1960s, due mainly to medical advances in keeping very small babies alive and in treating sick newborns. *Postneonatal mortality* (after the first 4 weeks) has also declined, largely because of better nutrition and sanitation. However, because of the greater decline in neonatal mortality, an increased proportion of infant deaths occur after the first month, often in poor families with little or no access to medical care.

Death in infancy is still far too prevalent. American babies have a poorer chance of reaching their first birthday than babies in many other industrialized countries (Guyer et al., 1996; see Figure 3-3). The infant mortality rate in the United States in 1993 was higher than the mortality rate in any other age group below ages 55 to 64 (USDHHS, 1996).

Birth defects were the leading cause of infant mortality in 1995, according to preliminary data; second were disorders related to low birthweight; third was sudden infant death syndrome (SIDS), which is discussed in the next section; then came respiratory distress syndrome (Guyer et al., 1996).

Although infant mortality has declined for both black and white babies (refer back to Table 3-6), the rates for white babies have fallen more. Black babies are still dying at nearly two and a half times the rate of white babies—14.9 as compared with 6.3 per 1,000 live births, according to preliminary 1995 data (Guyer et al., 1996). Latino infants, as a group, die at only slightly higher rates than non-Hispanic white babies (Wegman, 1993, 1994). White newborns are more likely to die of birth defects than of other causes, whereas black neonates are most likely to die of disorders related to low birthweight.

These facts raise troubling questions. Why, in a wealthy country like the United States, is infant mortality not declining faster? Why does the large disparity between black and white babies continue? Although physicians have the knowledge and technology to diagnose and treat high-risk pregnancies and help vulnerable infants, this know-how has not equally benefited all babies.

Sudden Infant Death Syndrome

Sudden infant death syndrome (SIDS), sometimes called "crib death," is the sudden death of any infant under 1 year of age in which the cause of death remains unexplained after a thorough investigation that includes an autopsy. In 1995, according to preliminary data, about 3,300 babies were victims of SIDS (Guyer et al., 1996). SIDS occurs most often between 2 and 4 months of age (Willinger, 1995).

Babies who succumb to SIDS are likely to be black, male, and of low birthweight. Often their mothers are young, unmarried, and poor; have received little or no prenatal care; have been ill during pregnancy; smoke or abuse drugs, or both; and have had another baby less than a year before the one who died. The fathers, too, are likely to be young and to smoke (Babson & Clark, 1983; C. E. Hunt & Brouillette, 1987; Kleinberg, 1984; Klonoff-Cohen et al., 1995; E. A. Mitchell et al., 1993; D. C. Shannon & Kelly, 1982a, 1982b; USDHHS, 1990).

The risk of SIDS is worsened by low socioeconomic circumstances, but SIDS also strikes infants in advantaged families.

What causes SIDS? The condition is not contagious, nor is it caused by choking or vomiting. One theory suggests a neurological anomaly, perhaps an abnormality in brain chemistry. Studies point to difficulties in the regulation of respiratory control (C. E. Hunt & Brouillette, 1987), in making the transition from sleep to wakefulness (Schechtman, Harper, Wilson, & Southall, 1992), or in arousal and ability to turn the head to avoid suffocation (K. A. Waters, Gonzalez, Jean, Morielli, & Brouillette, 1996). It seems likely that SIDS results from a combination of factors. An underlying biological defect may make some infants vulnerable, during a critical period in their development, to certain contributing or triggering factors, such as exposure to smoke or sleeping on the stomach (Cutz, Perrin, Hackman, & Czegledy-Nagy, 1996). However, some SIDS-labeled deaths may actually be the result of accidents (Bass, Kravath, & Glass, 1986).

Strong support for the connection with parental smoking has come from several studies (Haglund, 1993; E. A. Mitchell et al., 1993; Schoendorf & Kiely, 1992). In one nationally representative sample, the mother's smoking during pregnancy was the *only* risk factor independently associated with SIDS; perhaps 30 percent of SIDS could be prevented if pregnant women did not smoke (J. A. Taylor & Sanderson, 1995). The mother's smoking during pregnancy appears to affect the lungs of babies with SIDS, and these changes in the lungs may be a contributing factor (Cutz et al., 1996). Passive exposure to smoke is also a risk factor after birth; the more smoking around the baby, the greater the risk. If a breastfeeding mother smokes, her baby is not protected against SIDS, as the infant would be if she did not smoke (Klonoff-Cohen et al., 1995). Exposure to smoke, both before and after birth, seems related to changes in brain development (Milerad & Sundell, 1993). The 1993 International State of the Art Conference on SIDS recommended that parents and other caregivers stop smoking completely; at the very least, they should smoke less, and not around the baby.

A clue to what happens in SIDS has emerged from the discovery of a cell defect in a chemical receptor in the brain stem. This defect may prevent SIDS babies from awakening when they are breathing too much stale air containing carbon dioxide trapped under their blankets (Kinney et al., 1995). This may be especially likely to happen when the baby is sleeping face down; and it may be why SIDS deaths are more common in winter, when babies tend to be more heavily covered or tightly wrapped. Since many infants sleep face down at least part of the time, and relatively few succumb to SIDS, SIDS babies may be deficient in a protective mechanism that allows an infant to become aroused enough to turn the head when breathing is restricted (K. A. Waters et al., 1996).

Data from the United States (J. A. Taylor et al., 1996), Tasmania (an Australian island), the Netherlands, New Zealand, the United Kingdom, and other countries support the relationship between SIDS and sleeping on the stomach. SIDS rates fell by as much as 50 to 70 percent following recommendations by the American Academy of Pediatrics and medical societies in other nations, as well as by the 1993 International State of the Art Conference on SIDS, that healthy babies be put to sleep on the back or side (Dwyer, Ponsonby, Blizzard, Newman, & Cochrane, 1995; Hunt, 1996; Willinger, Hoffman, & Hartford, 1994). The only babies who should still be put to bed stomach down are premature infants with respiratory distress and infants with swallowing or upper-airway difficulties or other special problems (AAP Task Force on Infant Positioning and SIDS, 1992; Dwyer, Ponsonby, Newman, & Gibbons, 1991). To keep a baby's temperature within a healthy range, caregivers should feel the baby's upper chest or nape of the neck, the face, and the forehead, and should remove outdoor clothing when taking the baby inside or into a car. A feverish infant may need less clothing and blankets (Köhler & Markestad, 1993).

✔ EARLY PHYSICAL DEVELOPMENT

Fortunately, most infants do survive, develop normally, and grow up healthy. What principles govern their development? How do infants, who seem to do almost nothing but sleep and eat, become busy, active 3-year-olds? What are their typical growth patterns, and what nourishment do they need? How do their sensory and motor abilities develop?

PRINCIPLES OF DEVELOPMENT

Both before and after birth, development proceeds according to two fundamental principles. Growth and motor development occur from top to bottom and from the center of the body outward.

The *cephalocaudal principle* (from Greek and Latin, meaning "head to tail") dictates that development proceeds from the head to the lower parts of the body. An embryo's head, brain, and eyes develop earliest and are disproportionately large until the other parts catch up. At 2 months of gestation, the embryo's head is half the length of the body. By the time of birth, the head is only one-fourth the length of the body but is still disproportionately large; it becomes less so as the child grows (see Figure 3-4). Although the brain of a 1-

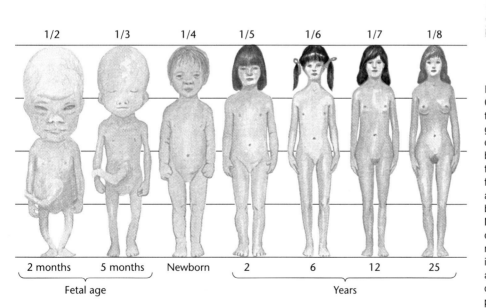

| 1/2 | 1/3 | 1/4 | 1/5 | 1/6 | 1/7 | 1/8 |

| 2 months | 5 months | Newborn | 2 | 6 | 12 | 25 |

Fetal age   Years

FIGURE 3-4
Changes in proportions of the human body during growth. The most striking change is that the head becomes smaller relative to the rest of the body. The fractions indicate head size as a proportion of total body length at several ages. More subtle is the stability of the trunk proportion (from neck to crotch). The increasing leg proportion is almost exactly the reverse of the decreasing head proportion.

TABLE 3-7

States of Arousal in Infancy

State	Eyes	Breathing	Movements	Responsiveness
Regular sleep	Closed; no eye movement	Regular and slow	None, except for sudden, generalized startles	Cannot be aroused by mild stimuli
Irregular sleep	Closed; occasional rapid eye movements	Irregular	Muscles twitch, but no major movements	Sounds or light bring smiles or grimaces in sleep
Drowsiness	Open or closed	Irregular	Somewhat active	May smile, startle, suck, or have erections in response to stimuli
Alert inactivity	Open	Even	Quiet; may move head, limbs, and trunk while looking around	An interesting environment (with people or things to watch) may initiate or maintain this state
Waking activity and crying	Open	Irregular	Much activity	External stimuli (such as hunger, cold, pain, being restrained, or being put down) bring about more activity, perhaps starting with soft whimpering and gentle movements and turning into a rhythmic crescendo of crying or kicking, or perhaps beginning and enduring as uncoordinated thrashing and spasmodic screeching

SOURCES: Adapted from information in Prechtl & Beintema, 1964; Wolff, 1966.

year-old is 70 percent of its adult weight, the rest of the body is only about 10 to 20 percent of adult weight. Infants also learn to use the upper parts of the body before the lower parts. Babies see objects before they can control their trunk, and they learn to do many things with their hands long before they can do much with their legs.

According to the *proximodistal principle* (from Latin, "near to far"), development proceeds from parts near the center of the body to outer ones. The embryo's head and trunk develop before the limbs, and the arms and legs before the fingers and toes. Babies first develop the ability to use their upper arms and upper legs (which are closest to the center of the body), then the forearms and forelegs, then hands and feet, and finally, fingers and toes.

STATES OF AROUSAL: THE BODY'S CYCLES

Babies have an internal "clock," which regulates their daily cycles of eating, sleeping, elimination, and perhaps even their moods. These periodic cycles of wakefulness, sleep, and activity, which govern an infant's *state of arousal*, or degree of alertness, seem to be inborn. All neonates experience the same states of arousal (see Table 3-7); but each baby's pattern is different. Newborn babies average about 16 hours of sleep a day, but one may sleep only 11 hours while another sleeps 21 hours (Parmelee, Wenner, & Schulz, 1964).

Most new babies wake up every 2 to 3 hours, day and night; short stretches of sleep alternate with shorter periods of consciousness. Newborns have about six to eight sleep periods, which alternate between quiet and active sleep. Active sleep is probably the equivalent of rapid eye movement (REM) sleep, which in adults is associated with dreaming. Active sleep appears rhythmically in cycles of about 1 hour and accounts for 50 to 80 percent of a newborn's total sleep time.

At about 3 months, babies grow more wakeful in the late afternoon and early evening and start to sleep through the night. By 6 months, more than half their sleep occurs at night. The place where they do their sleeping may change too, perhaps from the parents' bedroom to a room of their own (see Box 3-2). By this time, active sleep accounts for only 30 percent of sleep time, and the length of the cycle becomes more consistent (Coons & Guilleminault, 1982). The amount of REM sleep continues to decrease steadily throughout life.

Parents and caregivers spend a great deal of time and energy trying to change babies' states, for example, by soothing a fussy infant to sleep. Although crying is usually more distressing than serious, it is particularly important to quiet low-birthweight babies, because quiet babies maintain their weight better. Steady stimulation is the time-proven way to soothe crying babies: by rocking or walking them, wrapping them snugly, letting them hear rhythmic sounds, or allowing them to suck on a pacifier.

Beginning at birth, babies behave in different ways while awake. One baby sticks her tongue in and out, over and over; another makes rhythmic sucking movements. Some babies smile often; others, rarely. Some infant boys have frequent erections; others never do. Some new babies are more

active than others. These activity levels reflect temperamental differences that continue throughout childhood, and often throughout life.

As babies become more awake, alert, and active, they develop according to their own unique patterns, and these patterns elicit varying responses from their caregivers. Adults react very differently to a placid baby than to an excitable one; to an infant they can quiet easily than to one who is often inconsolable; to a baby who is often awake and alert than to one who seems uninterested in the surroundings. Babies, in turn, respond to the way their caregivers treat them. This bidirectional influence can have far-reaching effects on what kind of person a baby turns out to be. Thus, from the start, children affect their own lives by molding the environment in which they grow.

GROWTH

Children grow faster during the first 3 years, especially during the first few months, than they ever will again. At 5 months, the average baby's birthweight has doubled from 7½ pounds to about 15 pounds; by 1 year, the birthweight has

---

BOX 3-2   WINDOW ON THE WORLD

SLEEPING CUSTOMS

Until her first birthday, Maria shared the "family bed" with her parents. At first, Sean slept in a cradle next to his parents' bed but was soon moved into a crib in a separate room. There is considerable cultural variation in newborns' sleeping arrangements. In the United States, the commonest practice, reflecting the prevailing recommendations of child-care experts, is to have a separate bed, and ideally a separate room, for the infant. White and college-educated mothers are less likely to take their babies into bed with them than are African American mothers and mothers whose education ended with high school (Morelli, Rogoff, Oppenheim, & Goldsmith, 1992).

Some experts find health benefits in the shared sleeping pattern. One

research team that has been monitoring sleep patterns of mothers and their 3-month-old infants found that those who sleep together tend to wake each other up during the night and that this may prevent the baby from sleeping too long and too deeply and having long breathing pauses that might be fatal (McKenna & Mosko, 1993).

In many cultures, infants sleep with their mothers for the first few years of life, often in the same bed. In interviews, middle-class American parents and Mayan mothers in rural Guatemala revealed their child-rearing values and goals in their explanations about sleeping arrangements (Morelli et al., 1992).

The American parents, many of whom kept their infants in the same room but not in the same bed

for the first 3 to 6 months, said they moved the babies to separate rooms because they wanted to make them self-reliant and independent. The Mayan mothers kept infants and toddlers in the parental bed until the birth of a new baby, when the older child would sleep with another family member or in a bed in the mother's room. The Mayan mothers valued close parent-child relationships and expressed shock at the idea that anyone would put a baby to sleep in a room all alone.

We see, then, how societal values influence parents' attitudes and behaviors. Throughout the first half of this book we will see many ways in which parents' attitudes and behaviors, often culturally determined, affect their children.

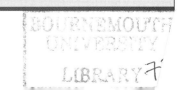

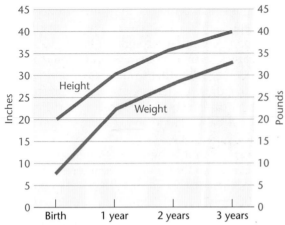

FIGURE 3-5
Growth in height and weight during infancy and toddlerhood. Babies grow most rapidly in both height and weight during the first few months of life, then taper off somewhat by age 3.

tripled to about 22 pounds. This rapid growth tapers off during the second year, when a child gains 5 or 6 pounds, quadrupling the birthweight by the second birthday. During the third year, the gain is somewhat less, about 4 to 5 pounds. Height increases by about 10 to 12 inches during the first year (making the typical 1-year-old about 30 inches tall); by about 5 inches during the second year (so that the average 2-year-old is about 3 feet tall); and by 3 to 4 inches during the third year. (See Figure 3-5.)

Growth seems to occur in spurts, often after long periods of no growth. Parents sometimes worry when an infant's growth seems to have halted; but the child may simply be between growth spurts. In one small-scale study, babies whose measurements had not changed for 2 to 63 days sprang up as much as a full inch in less than 24 hours (Lampl, Veldhuis, & Johnson, 1992).

As a young child grows, body shape and proportions change too. The head becomes proportionately smaller until full adult height is reached (refer back to Figure 3-4). Most children become leaner; a 3-year old is slender, compared with the chubby, potbellied 1-year-old. Black children mature earlier than white children; they tend to be larger, their bones harden earlier, and their permanent teeth appear sooner (AAP, 1973).

The genes a child inherits help determine whether the child will be tall or short, thin or stocky, or somewhere in between (Stunkard et al., 1990; Stunkard, Foch, & Hrubec, 1986). This genetic influence interacts with such environmental influences as nutrition and living conditions, which also affect general health. Well-fed, well-cared-for children grow taller and heavier than less well nourished and nurtured children. They also mature sexually and attain maximum height earlier, and their teeth erupt sooner (AAP, 1973). Today, children are growing taller and maturing sexually at an earlier age than they did a century ago, probably because of better nutrition, improved sanitation, and the decrease in child labor. Better medical care, especially immunization and antibiotics, also plays a part; heart disease, kidney disease, and some infectious illnesses can have grave effects on growth. Children who are ill for a long time may never achieve their genetically programmed stature because they may never make up for the loss of growth time while they were sick.

NOURISHMENT

Most babies in developed countries grow normally and stay healthy under a variety of feeding regimens. (In developing countries, poor sanitation, inadequate medical care, and poverty contribute to health problems for all ages.) Still, some feeding practices seem to be more beneficial than others.

Breast Milk or Formula

Breast milk or formula is the only food most babies need until 4 to 6 months of age. In the United States, more than half of mothers breastfeed their infants (Ryan et al., 1991). White mothers are more inclined to breastfeed than African American and Mexican American mothers, regardless of economic differences (Eiger & Olds, 1987; Ross Products Division of Abbott Laboratories, 1994). Most bottle-fed babies receive a formula based on either cow's milk or soy protein; it closely resembles mother's milk with the addition of supplemental vitamins and minerals. After 4 months or so, infants fed either way need supplemental iron to prevent anemia (Calvo, Galindo, & Aspres, 1992).

Even though many babies thrive on formula, breast milk is almost always the best food for newborns and is recommended to continue for at least 6 months (Lindberg, 1996). It is a complete source of nutrients for the first 4 to 6 months, more digestible than cow's milk and less likely to produce allergic reactions. Because the way babies suck at the breast is different from the way they suck on a bottle, their teeth and jaws tend to develop better when they are breastfed (Labbok & Hender-

Almost any woman can breastfeed with proper information, encouragement, and support. Besides its nutritional advantages, breastfeeding fosters emotional bonding between mother and baby. *(Nancy Durrell McKenna/Photo Researchers)*

shot, 1987). Breastfed babies get varying degrees of protection against diarrhea, respiratory infections (such as pneumonia and bronchitis), and otitis media, an infection of the middle ear (Dewey, Heinig, & Nommsen-Rivers, 1995; Duncan et al., 1993; A. L. Wright, Holberg, Martinez, Morgan, & Taussig, 1989). Breastfeeding also seems to have benefits for visual acuity (Makrides, Neumann, Simmer, Pater, & Gibson, 1995) and neurological development (Lanting, Fidler, Huisman, Touwen, & Boersma, 1994).

Breastfeeding is an emotional as well as a physical act. Warm contact with the mother's body fosters bonding, or emotional linkage, between mother and baby. Of course, such bonding can take place with bottle-feeding as well. Babies who are fed with properly prepared formula and raised with love also grow up healthy. The quality of the relationship between mother and child is more important than the feeding method.

Almost every woman can breastfeed with proper information, encouragement, and support. However, breastfeeding is inadvisable if a mother has AIDS, which can be transmitted through her milk (Hilts, 1991; Van de Perre et al., 1991), or has had a silicone breast implant (J. J. Levine & Ilowite, 1994), or has an infectious illness that she could pass on through close contact. A mother should refrain from nursing when a baby is too ill or if the mother must take a medicine or is using any drug that would not be safe for the baby (AAP Committee on Drugs, 1994; Chasnoff, Lewis, & Squires,

1987). Nursing mothers need to observe the same care as pregnant women regarding what they eat and drink and what drugs they take.

It is ironic that many poor women do not breastfeed (MacGowan et al., 1991), since breast milk is far more economical than formula. The provincial government of Quebec considers breastfeeding so important that it pays low-income women to nurse, as an investment in future health-care savings (Farnsworth, 1994). In the United States, one prenatal educational and counseling program boosted breastfeeding rates among urban black low-income women by explaining the benefits to their babies' health (Kistin, Benton, Rao, & Sullivan, 1990).

Employed mothers tend to stop breastfeeding when they return to work; they are more likely to continue, and to do so longer, if they work part time rather than full time. Government or company policies that provide 6 months of maternity leave and offer options for part-time employment can help women give their babies the healthiest possible start. Facilities in the workplace for breastfeeding and for pumping and storage of mothers' milk, as well as on-site infant care, would encourage working mothers to continue nursing (Lindberg, 1996).

Cow's Milk and Solid Foods

Because infants fed plain cow's milk in the early months of life suffer from iron deficiency (Sadowitz & Oski, 1983), the American Academy of Pediatrics (AAP, 1989; AAP Committee on Nutrition, 1992b) recommends that babies receive breast milk or iron-fortified formula for the first year. At 1 year, babies can switch to cow's milk if they are getting a balanced diet of supplementary solid foods that provide one-third of their caloric intake. The milk should be homogenized whole milk fortified with vitamin D, not skim milk or reduced-fat (1 or 2 percent) milk; babies need the calories in whole milk for proper growth. They do not need specially blended follow-up, or "weaning," formulas (AAP, 1989).

Although the American Academy of Pediatrics strongly recommends waiting to start solid foods and fruit juices until 4 to 6 months of age, many infants begin getting "solids"—usually cereal or strained fruits—by the age of 2 months. This practice often results from aggressive marketing of baby food, as well as from the ill-founded belief that solid food helps babies sleep through the night. Of course, babies cannot eat truly solid foods until they grow teeth. Teething usually begins around 3 or 4 months, when infants begin grabbing almost everything in sight to put into their mouths; but the first tooth may not actually arrive until sometime between 5 and 9 months of age, or even later. By the first birthday, babies generally have 6 to 8 teeth; by age 2½, they have a mouthful of 20 (Behrman, 1992).

Babies usually love fruit juice, and after 4 to 6 months it is fine in moderation. However, a study of toddlers who had failed to grow normally found that large quantities of juice seemed to be interfering with the children's appetite for higher-calorie, more nutritious foods. Also, some got diarrhea (Smith & Lifshitz, 1994). Children 2 or 3 years old should drink no more than 4 to 8 ounces of juice a day, and younger children should have less.

EARLY SENSORY CAPACITIES

"The baby, assailed by eyes, ears, nose, skin, and entrails at once, feels that all is one great blooming, buzzing confusion," wrote the psychologist William James in 1890. We now know that this is far from true. Even newborn infants are able to make some sense of their perceptions of touch, smell, taste, hearing, and sight.

Touch and Pain Sensitivity

Touch seems to be the first sense to develop, and for the first several months it is the most mature sensory system. When a hungry newborn's cheek is stroked near the mouth, the baby responds by trying to find a nipple. Early signs of this rooting reflex show up in the womb, 2 months after conception. By 32 weeks of gestation, all body parts are sensitive to touch, and this sensitivity increases during the first 5 days of life (Haith, 1986).

The sense of touch is what enables people to feel pain. Often physicians performing surgery on newborn babies have shied away from giving anesthesia because of a mistaken belief that neonates cannot feel pain and because of the known side effects of many pain relievers. Most doctors performing circumcision (removal of the foreskin from the penis of male newborns for religious or medical reasons) do not administer analgesics (pain-killing medications); or, if they do, they tend to give pain relievers of questionable effectiveness (Wellington & Reider, 1993). Actually, even on the first day of life, babies can and do feel pain; and they become more sensitive to it during the next few days. Therefore, the American Academy of Pediatrics now recommends the use of pain relievers during most surgery on infants.

Smell

Newborns can tell where odors are coming from. When an ammonium compound is dabbed on one side of a newborn's nose, even a 1-day-old baby will turn the nose to the other side (Rieser, Yonas, & Wilkner, 1976). Newborns also can distinguish odors. They seem to show by their expression that they like the way vanilla and strawberries smell but do not like the smell of rotten eggs or fish (Steiner, 1979). Six-day-old breastfed infants prefer their mother's breast pad over that of another nursing mother, but 2-day-old infants do not, suggesting that babies need a few days' experience to learn how their mothers smell (Macfarlane, 1975).

Taste

Newborns prefer sweet tastes to sour or bitter ones. The sweeter the fluid, the harder they suck and the more they drink (Haith, 1986). This preference for sweet tastes helps the baby adapt to life outside the womb, since human breast milk is quite sweet. Newborns reject bad-tasting food, probably a survival mechanism.

Hearing

Hearing begins in the womb and is acute even before birth. Fetuses respond to sounds and may even learn to recognize them. On the third day after birth, infants respond differently to a story heard while in the womb than to other stories, by sucking more on a nipple that activates a recording of the story heard prenatally (DeCasper & Spence, 1986). Immediately after birth, hearing may be impaired because of fluid that fills the inner ears during the birth process. After a day or two, the fluid disappears and hearing becomes efficient again.

Newborns' ability to distinguish sounds is well established. Three-day-old infants can tell new speech sounds from those they have heard before (L. R. Brody, Zelazo, & Chaika, 1984); at 1 month, babies can discriminate between sounds as close as "ba" and "pa" (Eimas, Siqueland, Jusczyk, & Vigorito, 1971). Babies less than 3 days old can tell their mother's voice from a stranger's. In one study, newborns sucked about 24 percent more on a nipple that turned on a recording of their mother's voice than when the voice was that of a strange woman (DeCasper & Fifer, 1980). Apparently, since they knew their mother's voice, they were more interested in hearing it. Early recognition of voices may be based on having heard these voices while in the womb and may be a mechanism for bonding between parents and child. In another experiment, 2-day-old babies sucked more when they heard their native language than when they heard another language, suggesting that they may have become familiar with their parents' language prenatally (Moon, Cooper, & Fifer, 1993).

Infants' sensitivity to auditory differences may be an early indicator of cognitive abilities. One study found significant correlations between the ability to discriminate between sounds at 4 months of age and IQ scores at 5 years (O'Connor, Cohen, & Parmelee, 1984). In Chapter 4, we look further at the relationship between infants' processing of sensory information and childhood IQ.

Sight

Vision is the least well developed sense at birth. The eyes of newborns are smaller than those of adults, the retinal structures are incomplete, and the optic nerve is underdeveloped. Newborns blink at bright lights. Their peripheral vision is very narrow; it more than doubles between 2 and 10 weeks of age (Tronick, 1972). The ability to shift the gaze to follow a moving target also develops rapidly in the first months. So does color perception. By about 2 months, babies can tell red from green; by about 3 months, they can distinguish

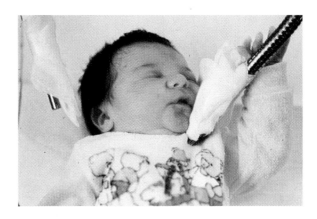

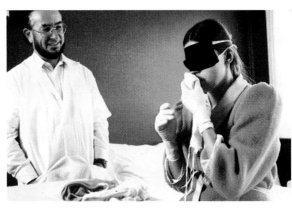

The nose knows. Three-day-old infants, like this one, act more peaceful when they smell pieces of gauze that their mothers have worn than when they smell cloth worn by other women. Also, blindfolded mothers can distinguish by smell between shirts their own babies have worn and shirts worn by other babies. *(J. Guichard/Sygma)*

blue (Haith, 1986). Four-month-old babies can discriminate among red, green, blue, and yellow; like most adults, they prefer red and blue (Bornstein, Kessen, & Weiskopf, 1976; Teller & Bornstein, 1987).

A neonate's eyes focus best from about 1 foot away, the typical distance from the face of a person holding the baby. This may help promote mother-infant bonding. Vision becomes much more acute during the first year, reaching the 20/20 level by about the sixth month (Aslin, 1987). (This measure of vision means that a person can read letters on a specified line on a standard eye chart from 20 feet away.) *Binocular vision*—the use of both eyes to focus, which allows perception of depth and distance—usually does not develop until 4 or 5 months (Bushnell & Boudreau, 1993).

Babies, from birth, can choose what to look at; the amount of time they spend looking at different sights is a measure of their *visual preference.*

No matter how enticing a mother's arms are, this baby is staying away from them. As young as she is, she can perceive depth and wants to avoid falling off what looks like a cliff. *(Innervisions)*

Babies less than 2 days old prefer curved lines to straight, complex patterns to simple, three-dimensional objects to two-dimensional objects, pictures of faces to pictures of other things, and new sights to familiar ones (Fantz, 1963, 1964, 1965; Fantz, Fagen, & Miranda, 1975; Fantz & Nevis, 1967).

Neonatal *pattern vision,* the ability to distinguish between patterns, is related to future cognitive development. In one classic experiment, ratings on a neonatal visual pattern test predicted children's IQ scores at age 3 or 4 better than neonatal ratings on neurological tests (Miranda, Hack, Fantz, Fanaroff, & Klaus, 1977).

A classic contribution to the study of infants' perceptions, and to the nature-nurture controversy, made use of a ***visual cliff*** (Walk & Gibson, 1961). Researchers tested the hypothesis that children are born with no knowledge of space and come to know about height, depth, and distance only through experience. The researchers put babies on a glass tabletop, over a checkerboard pattern. The glass formed a continuous surface; but, to an adult's eye, the pattern underneath made it appear that there was a vertical drop in the center of the table—a "visual cliff." Would infants see the same illusion of depth and feel themselves in danger?

Young infants did see a difference between the "ledge" and the "drop." Six-month-old babies crawled freely on the "ledge" but avoided the "drop," even when they saw their mothers on the far side of the table. When even younger infants, ages 2 and 3 months, were placed face down over the visual cliff, their hearts slowed down, probably in response to the illusion of depth (Campos, Langer, & Krowitz, 1970). However, a slowed heart rate, which indicates interest, does not mean that the younger infants were afraid of falling; fear would be indicated by a *faster* heart rate. The sense of danger generally does not develop until babies can get around by themselves (Bertenthal, Campos, & Kermoian, 1994).

The visual cliff experiments showed that *depth perception,* the ability to perceive objects and surfaces three-dimensionally, is either innate or learned very early. More recent analysis suggests that it may depend, at least in part, on motor development. An infant develops *haptic perception,* the ability to acquire information about objects by handling them rather than just looking at them, only after being able to reach for and grasp objects. In much the same way, depth perception may depend, not only on eye coordination, but also on the ability to control the head enough to move it or hold it still so as to evaluate visual cues (Bushnell & Boudreau, 1993).

The two-way connection between perception and action is currently an important topic of investigation. Perception allows an infant to learn about the environment and navigate in it. At the same time, motor experience sharpens and modifies the infant's sensory perceptions. Infants "perceive in order to move and move in order to perceive" (Thelen, 1995, p. 89). This insight is central to recent research on motor development.

MOTOR DEVELOPMENT

Babies do not have to be taught such basic motor skills as grasping, crawling, and walking. They just need room to move and freedom to see what they can do. When the central nervous system, muscles, and bones are mature enough and the environment offers the right opportunities, babies keep surprising the adults around them with their new abilities. The more babies can do, the more they can explore; and the more they can explore, the more they can learn and do.

How Does Motor Development Occur? Maturation in Context

Newborn babies are busy. They turn their heads, kick their legs, flail their arms, and display an array of reflex behaviors. By about the fourth month, babies begin to make more deliberate movements. Increasing control over body parts is believed to reflect the growing role of the cerebral cortex, which allows infants to do specific motor tasks with growing accuracy. They master these tasks by repeated practice—a fact that can become tiresome for caregivers when the new skill involves dropping an object from the high chair and then crying for it until an adult picks it up so that the baby can drop it again!

Babies develop motor skills in a certain sequence, which is generally believed to be genetically programmed. Children must reach a certain level of physiological maturation before they are ready to exercise an ability; and each newly mastered ability prepares a baby to tackle the next. Skills proceed from simple to complex and follow the two principles of development outlined earlier: head to toe and inner to outer. We can see this progression in the development of two of the most distinctively human motor capacities that develop during infancy: the precision grip, in which thumb and index finger meet at the tips to form a circle, and the ability to walk on two legs. In developing the precision grip, an infant first learns to pick things up with the whole hand, fingers closing against the palm; later the baby begins to use neat little pincer motions with the thumb and forefinger to pick up tiny objects. In learning to walk, an infant first gains control of separate movements of the arms, legs, and feet before putting these movements together to take that momentous first step.

Today, some developmentalists are questioning the traditional view of motor development as a largely automatic, preordained series of stages directed by the maturing brain. Instead, according to Esther Thelen (1995) of Indiana University, it is a continuous, dynamic, multifactorial process of interaction between baby and environment.

As evidence of the shortcomings of traditional maturational theory, Thelen points to what is usually called the walking reflex: stepping movements a neonate makes when held upright with the feet touching a surface. This behavior usually disappears in the second or third month; not until the last part of the first year, when a baby is getting ready to walk, do such movements appear again. The usual explanation is a shift from subcortical to cortical control; an older baby's deliberate walking is seen as a new skill masterminded by the developing brain. But, Thelen observes, a newborn's stepping involves the same kinds of movements neonates make while lying down and kicking. Why should stepping stop, only to reappear months later, while kicking continues? The answer, she suggests, may be that babies' legs become thicker and heavier during the early months, but not yet strong enough to carry the increased weight (Thelen & Fisher, 1982, 1983). In fact, when young infants are held in warm water, which helps support the legs, stepping reappears. The ability to produce the movement has not changed, only the physical and environmental conditions that inhibit or promote it.

Maturation alone cannot adequately explain such observations, says Thelen; a baby must be studied in a physical and social context. Infant and environment form an interconnected system, and development has interacting causes. One is the infant's motivation to do something (say, pick up a toy or get to the other side of the room). The infant's physical characteristics and his or her position in a particular environmental situation (for example, lying in a crib or being held upright in a pool) offer opportunities and constraints that affect whether and how the goal can be achieved. Ultimately, a solution emerges as a result of trying out behaviors and retaining those which most efficiently meet the goal. Babies' ongoing perceptions, including their recognition of what happens when they move in a certain way, may be the impetus for developmental change. Rather than being solely in charge of this process, says Thelen, the brain is only one part of it.

According to Thelen, normal babies develop the same skills in the same order because they are built approximately the same way and have similar physical challenges and needs. Thus they eventually discover (for example) that walking is more efficient than crawling in most situations. The idea that this discovery arises from each particular baby's experience in a particular setting may help explain why some babies learn to walk earlier than others.

Milestones of Motor Development

Motor development, however we explain it, is marked by a definite series of "milestones": achievements a child masters before going on to more difficult ones. The *Denver Developmental Screening Test* was designed to identify children who are not developing normally, but it can also be used to chart normal progress between the ages of 1 month and 6 years (Frankenburg, Dodds, Fan-

Lifting and holding up the head from a prone position, crawling along the floor to reach something enticing, such as a furry cat's tail, and walking well enough to push a doll's carriage are important early milestones of motor development. *(Erika Stone; Elizabeth Crews; Margaret Miller/Photo Researchers)*

dal, Kazuk, & Cohrs, 1975). The test covers such gross motor skills (those using large muscles) as rolling over and catching a ball, and such fine motor skills (using small muscles) as grasping a rattle and copying a circle. It also assesses language development (for example, knowing the definitions of words) and personality and social development (such as smiling spontaneously and dressing without help).

The newest edition, known as the Denver II (Frankenburg et al., 1992), includes revised norms and many new items. The norms are the ages at which 25 percent, 50 percent, 75 percent, and 90 percent of children can perform each skill (see Table 3-8 for examples). A child who cannot yet do

something that 90 percent of children the same age can already do is considered developmentally delayed. A child with two or more delays in two or more categories may need special attention.

In the following discussions, when we talk about what the "average" baby can do, we refer to the 50 percent Denver norms. There is, however, no "average" baby. Normality covers a wide range; about half of all babies master these skills before the ages given, and about half afterward. Also, it's important to remember that the Denver norms were standardized on a western population and are not necessarily valid in assessing children from other cultures. For example, southeast Asian children who were given the Denver test did not play

TABLE 3-8

Milestones of Motor Development

Skill	25 Percent	50 Percent	90 Percent
Rolling over	2.1 months	3.2 months	5.4 months
Grasping rattle	2.6 months	3.3 months	3.9 months
Sitting without support	5.4 months	5.9 months	6.8 months
Standing while holding on	6.5 months	7.2 months	8.5 months
Grasping with thumb and finger	7.2 months	8.2 months	10.2 months
Standing alone well	10.4 months	11.5 months	13.7 months
Walking well	11.1 months	12.3 months	14.9 months
Building tower of two cubes	13.5 months	13.5 months	20.6 months
Walking up steps	14.1 months	16.6 months	21.6 months
Jumping in place	21.4 months	23.8 months	2.4 years
Copying circle	3.1 years	3.4 years	4.0 years

Note: This table shows the approximate ages when 25 percent, 50 percent, and 90 percent of children can perform each skill, according to the Denver Training Manual II.
SOURCE: Adapted from Frankenburg et al., 1992.

pat-a-cake, did not pick up raisins, and did not dress themselves at the expected ages (V. Miller, Onotera, & Deinard, 1984). Yet that did not indicate slow development: in their culture, children do not play pat-a-cake; raisins look like a medicine they are taught to avoid; and their parents continue to help them dress much longer than western parents do.

Head Control At birth, most infants can turn their heads from side to side while lying on their backs. While lying chest down, many can lift their heads enough to turn them. Within the first 2 to 3 months, they lift their heads higher and higher. By 4 months of age, almost all infants can keep their heads erect while being held or supported in a sitting position.

Hand Control Babies are born with a grasping reflex. If the palm of an infant's hand is stroked, the hand closes tightly. At about 3½ months, most infants can grasp an object of moderate size, such as a rattle, but have trouble holding a small object. Next they begin to grasp objects with one hand and transfer them to the other, and then to hold (but not pick up) small objects. Sometime between 7 and 11 months, their hands become coordinated enough to pick up a tiny object, such as a pea, with pincerlike motion. After that, hand control becomes increasingly precise. By 15 months, the average baby can build a tower of two cubes. A few months after the third birthday, the average toddler can copy a circle fairly well.

Locomotion After 3 months, the average infant begins to roll over purposefully, first from front to back and then from back to front. (Before this time, babies sometimes roll over accidentally, and so even the youngest ones should never be left alone on a surface from which they might roll off.)

Babies sit by raising themselves from a prone (face down) position or by plopping down from a standing position. The average baby can sit without support by 6 months and can assume a sitting position without help about 2½ months later.

At about 6 months, most babies begin to get around under their own power. They may wriggle on their bellies and pull their bodies along with their arms, dragging their feet behind. They may hitch or scoot by moving along in a sitting position, pushing forward with their arms and legs. They may bear-walk, with hands and feet touching the ground. They may crawl on hands and knees with their trunks raised, parallel to the floor. By 9 or 10 months, most babies get around quite well by such means, and so parents have to keep a close eye on them. This new ability of self-locomotion also has important psychological implications (see Box 3-3).

By holding onto a helping hand or a piece of furniture, the average baby can stand at a little past 7 months of age, but will only occasionally stand erect. A little more than 4 months later, after dogged practice in pulling themselves to an upright posture, most babies let go and stand alone. The average baby can stand well about 2 weeks or so before the first birthday.

BOX 3-3   FOOD FOR THOUGHT

THE FAR-REACHING EFFECTS OF SELF-LOCOMOTION

Did you ever drive for the first time to a place where you had gone only as a passenger? As a driver, you probably saw landmarks and were aware of turns you had never noticed before. After getting to your destination on your own, you most likely felt more familiar with the route than you had earlier. Something similar seems to happen to babies when they begin to get around on their own, first by crawling and then by walking, after having always been carried or wheeled. The emergence of self-produced locomotion is a turning point in the second half of the first year of life, influencing all domains of development—physical, cognitive, emotional, and social.

Between 7 and 9 months, babies change greatly in many ways. They show an understanding of such concepts as "near" and "far." They imitate more complex behaviors, and they show new fears; but they also show a new sense of security around their parents or other caregivers. Since these changes, and others that occur around this time, involve so many different psychological functions and processes and occur during such a short time span, some observers tie them all in with a reorganization of brain function. This neurological development may be set in motion by a skill that emerges at this time: the ability to crawl, which makes it possi-

ble to get around independently. Crawling has been called a "setting event" because it sets the stage for other changes in the infant and in his or her relationships with the environment and the people in it (Bertenthal & Campos, 1987; Bertenthal, Campos, & Barrett, 1984; Bertenthal et al., 1994).

Crawling exerts a powerful influence on the life of a baby by giving the child a new view of the world. When carried, babies need not pay much attention to their surroundings. When they begin to crawl, they become more sensitive to where objects are, how big they are, whether they can be moved, and how they look. Crawling babies can differentiate similar forms that are unlike in color, size, and location (Campos, Bertenthal, & Benson, 1980). Babies are more successful in finding a toy hidden in a box when they crawl around the box than when they are carried around it (Benson & Uzgiris, 1985); and when they see an object hidden in a new location, they will look for it there again (Bertenthal et al., 1994).

Crawling helps babies learn to judge distances and perceive depth. As they move about, they see that people and objects can look different, depending on how close they are. Crawling babies also develop fear of heights. When babies start to move around by

themselves, they are in danger of falling. To keep them from getting hurt, caregivers often hover over babies, remove them from dangerous locations, or cry out and jump up when a child is about to get into trouble. Babies are sensitive to these actions and emotions, and they learn to be afraid of places from which they might fall.

The ability to move from one place to another also has social implications. Crawling babies are no longer "prisoners" of place. If Milly wants to be close to her mother and far away from a strange dog, she can move toward the one and away from the other. This is an important step in developing a sense of mastery, enhancing self-confidence and self-esteem.

The ability to crawl gets babies into new situations. They learn to look to their parents for clues as to whether a situation is secure or frightening—a skill known as *social referencing* (see Chapter 5). Crawling babies do more social referencing than babies who have not yet begun to crawl. They seem to pick up emotional signals from their parents' faces or gestures, which in turn influence their behavior (J. B. Garland, 1982). Thus the physical milestone of crawling has far-reaching effects in helping babies see and respond to their world in new ways.

All these developments are milestones along the way to the major motor achievement of infancy: walking. Humans begin to walk later than other species, possibly because babies' heavy heads and short legs make balance difficult (Thelen, quoted in Bushnell & Boudreau, 1993). For some months before they can stand without support, babies practice walking while holding onto furniture— sitting down abruptly when they reach table's end

and crawling or lurching from chair to sofa. Soon after they can stand alone well, at about 11½ months, most infants take their first unaided steps, tumble, go back to crawling, and then try again. The average baby is walking regularly, if shakily, within a few days. Within a few weeks, soon after the first birthday, the child is walking well and thus achieves the status of toddler.

During the second year, children begin to climb

stairs one at a time. (Since they can crawl upstairs before that—and tumble down long before—vigilance and baby gates are needed.) At first they put one foot and then the other on the same step before going on to the next higher one; later they will alternate feet. Walking down stairs comes later. In their second year, toddlers run and jump; their parents, trying to keep up with them, run out of energy. By age 3½, most children can balance briefly on one foot and begin to hop.

Contextual Influences on the Pace of Motor Development

From a traditional maturational viewpoint, the role of the environment in motor development is quite limited; but a growing body of research suggests a wider reaction range. Although motor development does not seem to be affected by sex or by parents' education (Bayley, 1965), its pace does seem to respond to certain contextual factors. For example, one study found that babies born in the winter or spring begin to crawl about 3 weeks earlier than those born in summer or fall (Benson, 1993). It may be that with milder weather and more daylight, the winter and spring babies were more active at critical times in their development.

Cross-cultural studies show differences in how and when certain skills are typically acquired. Let's look at this evidence and then at environmental influences on the pace of development.

Cross-cultural Comparisons Even for basic motor behaviors, what is normal in one culture may not be so in another. African babies tend to be more advanced than infants of European origin in standing and walking; Asian infants are apt to develop such gross motor skills more slowly. Some of these differences may be related to temperament. Asian babies, for example, are typically more docile; this may explain why they respond more calmly when a cloth is pressed to their noses, and why they tend to stay closer to their parents (Kaplan & Dove, 1987).

Some differences in the pace of motor development may reflect a culture's child-rearing practices. A study of 288 normal full-term babies from the Yucatan peninsula in Mexico found that although these babies initially were ahead of American babies in motor skills, by 11 months the Mexican babies lagged so far behind in their ability to move about that an American baby at the typical level of these Mexican babies might be considered

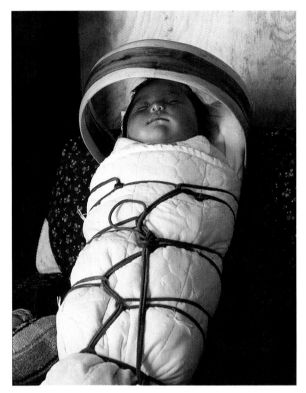

Some observers have suggested that babies from the Yucatan develop motor skills later than American babies because they are swaddled. However, Navajo babies like this one are also swaddled for most of the day, and they begin to walk at about the same time as other American babies, suggesting a hereditary explanation. *(Steve Maines/Stock, Boston)*

neurologically impaired (Solomons, 1978). However, the Mexican babies were *not* slow in developing according to standards and customs of their own culture. As infants, Mexican babies are swaddled, restricting their movement; later they are restrained by being carried more than American babies, by sleeping in hammocks (which become net "cages" compared with the open space of a firm-mattressed crib), and by not being put on the ground to play (because of insects and local beliefs about the dangers of cold floors). On the other hand, Mexican babies may be more advanced in manipulative skills; without toys to play with, they discover and play with their fingers earlier than American babies. Evidence *against* environmental explanations for such differences, however, is that Navajo babies—also swaddled for most of the day—begin to walk at about the same age as other American babies (Chisholm, 1983).

Other research found that children of the Ache in eastern Paraguay do not begin to walk until 18 to 20 months of age, about 9 months later than

American babies (Kaplan & Dove, 1987). Ache mothers pull their babies back to their laps when the infants begin to crawl away. The Ache mothers closely supervise their babies to protect them from the hazards of nomadic life, and also because the women's primary responsibility is child raising rather than subsistence labor. Children whose mothers spend less time with them may become independent sooner because their other caregivers may supervise them less closely. (This may now apply to American babies, who, in an era of prevalent day care, seem to be developing some skills more quickly.)

Slower-developing children often catch up, given a supportive environment. Ache babies show the slowest motor development reported for any human group; but as 8- to 10-year-olds, they climb tall trees, chop branches, and play in ways that enhance their motor skills. Development, then, may be viewed as "a series of immediate adjustments to current conditions as well as a cumulative process in which succeeding stages build upon earlier ones" (Kaplan & Dove, 1987, p. 197).

How Environment Can Slow or Speed Development When children are well fed and well cared for and have physical freedom and the chance to practice motor skills, their motor development is likely to be normal. An environment grossly deficient in any of these areas may retard motor development, as was seen in a classic study of three orphanages in Iran (Dennis, 1960).

In two of the orphanages, overworked attendants hardly ever handled the children. The younger babies spent almost all their time on their backs in cribs. They drank from propped bottles. They were never put in a sitting position or placed stomach down. They had no toys and were not taken out of bed until they could sit without help (often not until 2 years of age). These children were delayed in their motor development, apparently because the deficient environment kept them from moving around and provided little stimulation. The children in the third orphanage were fed in the arms of attendants, were placed on their stomachs and propped up so they could sit, and had many toys. Their motor development was normal.

When the children in the first two orphanages did start to get about, they moved around in a sitting position, pushing their bodies forward with their arms and feet rather than creeping on hands and knees. Having never been placed on their stomachs, they had had no opportunity to practice raising their heads or pulling their arms and legs beneath their bodies, the movements needed for crawling. Also, having never been propped in a sitting position, they had not practiced raising their heads and shoulders to learn how to sit at the usual age. However, older institutionalized children, whose motor development presumably had also been delayed as infants and toddlers, worked and played normally (Dennis, 1960). Thus, although a severely deprived environment can delay maturation, such delays are likely to be temporary.

Can environmental influences speed up motor development? For many years, the answer was thought to be no. In a famous experiment, Arnold Gesell (1929) trained one monozygotic twin, but not the other, in stair climbing, block building, and hand coordination. As the children got older, the untrained twin became just as expert as the trained one, showing, said Gesell, "the powerful influence of maturation." According to Gesell, children perform certain activities when they are ready, and training gives no advantage.

However, later research indicates that early training can influence development. In one study, infants trained in stepping at 8 weeks walked at an average of 10 months, while those in an untrained control group did not begin walking until an average of 12⅓ months (Zelazo, Zelazo, & Kolb, 1972). Why did this happen? Perhaps there is a critical period during which the newborn's repetitive walking response can be translated into a specific later voluntary action. Then again, practice in one such behavior pattern might promote maturation of the brain's ability to control related activities. Another possibility, in line with Thelen's work, is that training strengthened the infants' legs, allowing them to resume stepping at an earlier-than-usual age.

A randomized follow-up experiment was designed to see whether the effects of training are limited to the practiced ability. Six-week-old healthy baby boys who were trained for 7 weeks, either in stepping alone or in stepping and sitting, stepped more than those untrained in stepping movements; and infants trained either in sitting alone or in stepping and sitting sat more. Infants trained in sitting alone did not step more, and infants trained in stepping alone did not sit more (Zelazo, Zelazo, Cohen, & Zelazo, 1993). Apparently early training can accelerate a specific behavior, but the training does not carry over to other abilities. These results do not indicate whether changes in the brain or in muscle strength, or both, are involved; but they do seem to "rule out a strict view of maturation as biological unfolding" and suggest that "the role of learning in early motor development has been underestimated" (p. 690).

In recent years, many parents have put their babies in mobile walkers, partly because the babies like them and also because the parents think the walkers help the babies learn to walk earlier. This belief is mistaken; use of baby walkers may discourage crawling and *delay* walking. Walkers were responsible for an estimated 25,000 injuries in the United States in 1993 and 11 deaths in the previous 5 years. Safety experts recommend not using them (Collins, 1994), and the American Academy of Pediatrics has called for a ban on their manufacture and sale (AAP Committee on Injury and Poison Prevention, 1995).

HOW DIFFERENT ARE BOYS AND GIRLS?

Why was the recent experiment in motor training described above (Zelazo et al., 1993) done only on baby boys, and not girls? The reason presumably was to control for any possible gender differences that might have affected the results.

As we discussed in Chapter 2, males are physically more vulnerable than females from conception throughout the life span. Baby boys are a bit longer and heavier than baby girls, and boys may be slightly stronger. (Boys remain larger throughout adulthood, except for a brief time during puberty, when girls' earlier growth spurt causes them to overtake boys.) Newborn boys and girls also react differently to stress, possibly suggesting genetic, hormonal, or temperamental differences. Much like older children and adult men and women, infant boys salivate more, while infant girls' hearts beat faster. Girls also become more active and irritable (M. Davis & Emory, 1995).

In general, however, infant boys and girls are very similar. Although some research has found baby boys more active than baby girls (Maccoby & Jacklin, 1974), other studies have found the two sexes equally active during the first 2 years, and equally sensitive to touch. Girls and boys tend to teethe, sit up, and walk at about the same ages (Maccoby, 1980). Gender differences in personality and social development are somewhat more pronounced (see Chapter 5).

By the time small children of either sex can run, jump, and play with toys requiring fairly sophisticated coordination, they are very different from the neonates described at the beginning of this chapter. The cognitive changes that have taken place are equally dramatic, as we discuss in Chapter 4.

✔ SUMMARY

BIRTH

■ Birth normally begins when the fetus is ready and occurs in four stages: (1) dilation of the cervix; (2) descent and emergence of the baby; (3) expulsion of the umbilical cord and the placenta; (4) contraction of the uterus and recovery of the mother.

■ Excessive anesthesia in medicated deliveries may have a harmful effect on the newborn. Natural and prepared childbirth can minimize the need for pain-killing drugs and maximize the parents' active involvement.

■ Almost 21 percent of babies born in the United States are delivered by cesarean section. Critics claim that many cesareans, which carry special risks to mother and baby, are unnecessary.

■ Electronic fetal monitoring is widely used during labor and delivery. It is intended to detect signs of fetal distress, especially in high-risk births.

■ Delivery at home or in birth centers attended by midwives are alternatives to hospital delivery for women with normal, low-risk pregnancies.

THE NEWBORN

■ The neonatal period, the first 4 weeks of life, is a time of transition. At birth, the neonate's circulatory, respiratory, gastrointestinal, and temperature regulation systems become independent of the mother's.

■ A newborn baby's brain is one-fourth the weight of an adult's brain and grows to 70 percent of adult weight by the end of the first year. The most rapid growth occurs in the months before and after birth.

■ At 1 minute and 5 minutes after birth, the neonate is assessed medically by the Apgar scale, which measures how well the newborn is adjusting to extrauterine life. The neonate may also be screened for one or more medical conditions and for responsiveness to the environment to predict future development.

SURVIVAL AND HEALTH DURING INFANCY

■ A small minority of infants suffer from injuries sustained at the time of birth. Low birthweight can influence early adjustment to life outside the womb and may even exert an influence on later development. A supportive postnatal environment can often improve the outcome for babies suffering from birth complications.

■ Although the infant mortality rate in the United States has improved, it is still disturbingly high, especially for African American babies. Birth defects are the leading cause of death in the first year. Low birthweight is the second leading cause.

■ Sudden infant death syndrome (SIDS) is the third leading cause of death in the first year in the United States. Although the cause of SIDS has not been fully established; exposure to smoke and sleeping in the prone position seem to be major risk factors.

■ Rates of immunization have improved in the United States, but many preschoolers, especially among the poor and minority groups, are not protected.

EARLY PHYSICAL DEVELOPMENT

■ Normal physical growth and motor development proceed according to two principles:

1 According to the cephalocaudal principle, development proceeds from the head to lower body parts.
2 According to the proximodistal principle, development proceeds from the center of the body to the outer parts.

■ Newborn babies alternate between states of sleep, wakefulness, and activity, with sleep taking up the major (but diminishing) amount of their time.

■ A child's body grows most dramatically during the first year of life; growth proceeds at a rapid but diminishing rate throughout the child's first 3 years.

■ Breastfeeding offers physiological benefits to the infant and facilitates formation of the mother-infant bond. However, the quality of the relationship between parents and the infant is more important than the feeding method in promoting healthy development.

■ Sensory capacities, present from birth, develop rapidly in the first months of life. Very young infants show pronounced abilities to discriminate between stimuli. Auditory and visual discrimination appear to be related to later cognitive functioning. Depth perception seems to be related to motor development.

■ During the first 3 months of life, infants gain control over their body movements. Motor skills develop in a definite sequence. Self-locomotion seems to be a setting event, effecting changes in all domains of development.

■ The Denver Developmental Screening Test is widely used to assess motor, linguistic, and personality and social development.

■ Environmental factors, including cultural patterns, may affect the pace of motor development.

■ Although infant boys are somewhat larger and more vulnerable than girls and seem to react differently to stress, researchers have found few other significant physical or maturational differences between the sexes in infancy.

✔ KEY TERMS

natural childbirth (page 82)
prepared childbirth (82)
cesarean delivery (82)
electronic fetal monitoring (83)
neonatal period (84)
neonate (84)
fontanels (85)
lanugo (85)
vernix caseosa (85)
anoxia (85)
meconium (85)

neonatal jaundice (86)
central nervous system (86)
neurons (86)
reflex behaviors (88)
Apgar scale (88)
Brazelton Neonatal Behavioral
    Assessment Scale (90)
birth trauma (91)
low birthweight (91)
preterm (premature) infants (91)
small-for-date infants (91)

postmature (95)
infant mortality rate (97)
sudden infant death syndrome
    (SIDS) (98)
cephalocaudal principle (99)
proximodistal principle (100)
state of arousal (100)
visual preference (105)
visual cliff (106)
Denver Developmental Screening
    Test (107)

✔ QUESTIONS FOR THOUGHT AND DISCUSSION

1 Given the relatively poor prognosis for very-low-birthweight babies, should they be resuscitated aggressively at birth? Or is this an unwise use of limited health care resources? Who should make such decisions: parents or health care providers? On what basis?

2 "Every mother who is physically able should breastfeed." Do you agree or disagree? Give reasons.

3 Is it advisable to try to teach babies skills such as walking before they develop them on their own?

4 Who should be primarily responsible for ensuring that children are immunized: parents, community agencies, or government?

CHAPTER FOUR

COGNITIVE DEVELOPMENT DURING THE FIRST THREE YEARS

So runs my dream; but what am I?
An infant crying in the night;
An infant crying for the light,
And with no language but a cry.

Alfred, Lord Tennyson,
In Memoriam, Canto 54

ASK YOURSELF

✔ What can the behaviorist, Piagetian, psychometric, and information-processing approaches tell us about infants' and toddlers' cognition?

✔ How do newborns learn, and how well can they remember?

✔ When do babies begin to think?

✔ Is it possible to measure an infant's or a toddler's intelligence?

✔ How do infants and toddlers process information, and how does information-processing ability relate to intelligence?

✔ How do babies develop language?

✔ How do babies develop a sense of competence?

f newborn infants could speak, they might protest that their cognitive abilities have been underestimated for centuries. This underestimation persisted almost to the present because of two major movements toward the end of the nineteenth century. Just as psychologists were beginning to propose theories of human development, doctors were establishing a routine under which babies were born in hospitals, exposed to sedative drugs, and isolated from their mothers—hardly a situation designed to show a newcomer's abilities to advantage! Also, the first tests to study infant intelligence were based on tests for adults or animals, none of which were suited to human infants.

Today our picture of babies' cognitive abilities has changed radically. During the past few decades, there has been more research on this topic than during all previous history. We now know that the normal, healthy human baby is remarkably competent. Infants are born with the ability to learn and remember and with a capacity for acquiring and using speech. Newborns begin sizing up what their senses tell them. They use their cognitive abilities to distinguish between sensory experiences (such as the sounds of different voices), to build on their small inborn repertoire of behaviors (especially sucking), and to exert growing control over their behavior and their world.

■ In this chapter we look at infants' and toddlers' cognitive abilities from four perspectives: the behaviorist, Piagetian, psychometric, and information-processing approaches. We trace the development of language in infancy and toddlerhood. And we discuss how adults can help babies and young children become more competent. ■

✔ STUDYING COGNITIVE DEVELOPMENT: FOUR APPROACHES

Rebecca, at 1 year, loved Cheerios, and she loved to play games. One day her father, Dan, put some Cheerios in his hand, closed it, and put his fist on the tray of Rebecca's high chair. With both hands, she pulled his fingers open, saw the Cheerios, and released his fingers as she tried to get the cereal. His fingers free, Dan again closed them over the Cheerios. After two more tries, Rebecca discovered that she could hold his fingers open with one hand while she retrieved the Cheerios with the other. One day, when one hand held a toy that she did not want to drop, Rebecca came up with another solution. She opened Dan's fingers with her free hand and held them open with her chin, so that she could use the same hand to get the Cheerios.

Rebecca showed intelligent behavior, behavior involving complex, self-initiated learning. *Intelligent behavior* is generally agreed to have two key aspects. First, it is *goal-oriented:* conscious and deliberate rather than accidental. Second, it is *adaptive:* directed at adjusting to the circumstances and conditions of life. As we discussed in Chapter 2, intelligence is influenced by both inherited ability and experience. Intelligence enables people to acquire, remember, and use knowledge; to understand concepts and relationships; and to apply knowledge and understanding to everyday problems.

How and when do babies learn to solve problems? How and when does memory develop? What accounts for individual differences in cognitive abilities? Can we measure a baby's intelligence? Can we predict how smart that baby will be later? Most investigators of cognitive development have taken one of four approaches to the study of such questions:

- The *behaviorist approach* studies the basic mechanics of learning. It is concerned with how behavior changes in response to experience.
- The *Piagetian approach* looks at changes in the quality of cognitive functioning, or what people can do. It is concerned with the evolution of mental structures and how children adapt to their environment, and it maintains that cognition develops in stages.
- The *psychometric approach* tries to measure individual differences in quantity of intelligence— how much intelligence someone has. The higher a person scores on an intelligence test, the more intelligent he or she is presumed to be.
- The *information-processing approach* focuses on individual differences in the ways people use their intelligence. It attempts to discover the processes involved in perceiving and handling information.

All four approaches help us understand intelligent behavior. Let us see what each can tell us about the cognitive development of infants and toddlers.

BEHAVIORIST APPROACH: HOW INFANTS LEARN

Do babies learn to suck on a nipple? They probably do not; sucking is a reflex they are born with. But sucking quickly becomes a learned behavior when it leads to a comfortably full stomach.

Human beings are born with the ability to learn from experience. Babies learn from what they see, hear, smell, taste, and touch. Maturation is essential to this expanding ability to learn. Even if Vanessa was born with the soul of a poet, she will not be able to speak until her mouth and vocal cords have developed sufficiently to form verbal sounds and her brain and nervous system are mature enough to assign meanings to sounds and remember them. Certain neurological, sensory, and motor capacities must be developed before learning can occur. Learning theorists recognize maturation as a limiting factor, but they do not focus on it. Their main interest is in the mechanisms by which people learn.

Types of Learning

Behaviorists study two simple learning processes: classical conditioning and operant conditioning. (Later we will look at *habituation,* another simple form of learning, which information-processing researchers study. Social learning theory and research, discussed in Chapter 1, focus on learning that occurs through observation and imitation. More complex learning can involve combinations of these modes.)

In Chapter 1, we saw how Anna, after her father had taken many pictures of her, eventually blinked *before* the flashbulb on his camera went off. This is an example of **classical conditioning,** in which a person or an animal learns to respond automatically to a stimulus that originally did not provoke the response. In Anna's case, the stimulus was her father's camera. In classical conditioning, a person learns to anticipate an event before it happens.

Babies only 2 hours old have been classically conditioned to turn their heads and suck if their foreheads are stroked, by stroking the forehead at the same time that they are given a bottle of sweetened water (Blass, Ganchrow, & Steiner, 1984, in Rovee-Collier, 1987). Newborn babies have learned to suck when they hear a buzzer or a tone; to show the Babkin reflex (turning their heads and opening their mouths) when their arms are moved (instead of the usual stimulus, pressure on the palm of the hand); to dilate and constrict the pupils of their eyes; to blink; and to show a change in heart rate (Rovee-Collier & Lipsitt, 1982).

One of the earliest demonstrations of classical conditioning in human beings showed that emotions, such as fear, can be conditioned (Watson & Rayner, 1920). An 11-month-old baby known as "Little Albert," who loved furry animals, was brought into a laboratory. Just as he was about to grasp a furry white rat, a loud noise frightened him, and he began to cry. After repeated pairings of the rat with the loud noise, the child whimpered with fear whenever he saw the rat. The fear also generalized to rabbits, dogs, a Santa Claus mask, and other furry white objects. Under today's ethical standards, this research would never be permitted because it would be unethical to arouse fear in the name of science. However, the study did show that a baby could be conditioned to fear things he had not been afraid of before.

Terrell's smiling to get loving attention from his

An Indian snake charmer's baby eagerly plays with a snake the father has trained, showing that fear of snakes is a learned response. Children can be conditioned to fear animals that are associated with unpleasant or frightening experiences, as "Little Albert" was in a classic study by John B. Watson and Rosalie Rayner. *(Mary Ellen Mark)*

parents (described in Chapter 1) is an example of *operant conditioning,* in which a baby learns to make a certain response in order to produce a particular effect. Operant conditioning, in which the learner operates on and influences the environment, can be used to learn voluntary behaviors (as opposed to involuntary behaviors such as blinking).

In one study, 2-day-old infants sucked nipples connected to a music source. The babies kept sucking when their sucking turned on the music but stopped when their sucking turned off the music (Butterfield & Siperstein, 1972). Studies like this, which change what babies do by reinforcing certain behaviors, show that neonates can learn by operant conditioning *if* the conditioning encourages them to perform some kind of behavior they can already do (such as sucking or turning the head).

Classical and operant conditioning together can produce increasingly complex behavior. In studies with 1- to 20-week-old infants, the babies received milk if they turned their heads left at the sound of a bell. The babies who did not learn to turn their heads through this operant conditioning were then classically conditioned. When the bell sounded, the left corner of the baby's mouth was touched, and the baby turned his or her head and received the milk. (The touch was the unconditioned stimulus; turning the head was the unconditioned response. The bell was the conditioned stimulus; turning the head to the bell became the conditioned response.) By 4 to 6 weeks, all the babies

had learned to turn their heads when hearing the bell. Then the babies learned to differentiate the bell from a buzzer (Papousek, 1959, 1960a, 1960b, 1961). When the bell rang, they were fed on the left; when the buzzer rasped, they were fed on the right. At about 3 months of age, the babies had learned to turn to whichever side brought food, as signaled by the bell or buzzer. By 4 months, they even learned to reverse their responses to bell and buzzer—an impressively complex feat.

Infant Memory

If infants did not have at least a short-term ability to remember, they would not be able to learn. Studies using operant conditioning have found that babies 2 to 6 months old can remember to perform an action that brought pleasure—if the testing situation is virtually identical to the one in which the initial training occurred.

In a series of experiments, babies whose left leg was attached to a mobile above the crib quickly learned that kicking would activate the mobile. When they saw the mobiles again a few days later, the babies kicked even though their legs were no longer attached to the mobiles. After 2 weeks, however, infants just under 3 months old showed no retention unless they were reminded by seeing an experimenter move the mobile. Seeing a *stationary* mobile was not enough to cause the babies to kick; nor was it enough to see a *new* mobile rather than the one they had been trained with, nor to see the original mobile stand and ribbon without the mobile (Hayne & Rovee-Collier, 1995). On the other hand, babies trained with different mobiles on different days learned to expect a different one each time (Fagen, Morrongiello, Rovee-Collier, & Gekoski, 1984).

Contextual cues can help retention. Infants as young as 3 to 6 months of age recognize differences in their surroundings, and they seem to encode information about the setting (that is, get the information into memory) along with what they are learning. To test this hypothesis, babies were given the mobile training in playpens hung with patterns of stripes, squares, dots, or triangles. One day, 3 days, 3 weeks, or 6 months later, the babies remembered to kick if retested in a playpen with the same pattern; but if retested in a differently patterned playpen, they did not kick. Furthermore, babies trained and tested in such distinctively patterned settings were more likely to respond differently to a new mobile than to the one they had originally seen (Amabile & Rovee-Collier, 1991; Hayne & Rovee-Collier, 1995; Rovee-Collier, Schecter, Shyi, & Shields, 1992; Shields & Rovee-Collier, 1992).

Thus, even very young infants can remember, and they are likely to do best in situations that are familiar, especially when prompted by a reminder.

PIAGETIAN APPROACH: COGNITIVE STAGES

According to behaviorists, the basic mechanisms of learning are the same for infants as for older children, and even for adults. Jean Piaget's approach was quite different: He explored growth in children's thought processes. To examine how children's thought evolves, Piaget watched his own three children. On the basis of his observations, he described the first of four stages of cognitive development (refer back to Table 1-5 in Chapter 1), the *sensorimotor stage.* His theory has inspired much research on cognition in infancy and early childhood. Some of this research has shown that, as important as Piaget's contributions were, he underestimated young children's abilities.

Piaget's Sensorimotor Stage

During the **sensorimotor stage** (approximately the first 2 years of life), said Piaget, infants learn about themselves and their world through their own developing sensory and motor activity. Babies change from creatures who respond primarily through reflexes and random behavior into goal-oriented toddlers. They learn to organize their activities in relation to their environment, coordinate information they receive from their senses, and progress from trial-and-error learning to the use of rudimentary insights to solve simple problems.

The sensorimotor stage consists of six substages (see Table 4-1), which flow from one to another as the baby's **schemes,** or organized patterns of behavior, become more elaborate. Much of this cog-

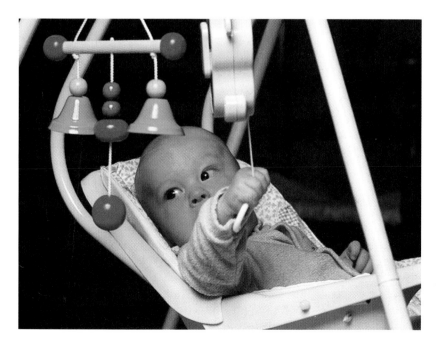

This baby, about 6 months old, has learned by operant conditioning that he can affect his environment. Perhaps he discovered accidentally that by pulling the string on his toy, he can make the bells ring; and this interesting experience reinforced his tendency to pull the string again. *(Joel Gordon)*

TABLE 4-1

Six Substages of Piaget's Sensorimotor Stage of Cognitive Development

Substage	Description
Substage 1 (birth to 1 month)	Infants exercise their inborn reflexes and gain some control over them. They do not coordinate information from their senses. They do not grasp an object they are looking at. They have not developed object permanence.
Substage 2 (1 to 4 months)	Infants repeat pleasurable behaviors that first occur by chance (such as sucking). Activities focus on infant's body rather than the effects of the behavior on the environment. Infants make first acquired adaptations; that is, they suck different objects differently. They begin to coordinate sensory information. They have still not developed object permanence.
Substage 3 (4 to 8 months)	Infants become more interested in the environment and repeat actions that bring interesting results and prolong interesting experiences. Actions are intentional but not initially goal-directed. Infants show partial object permanence: they will search for a partially hidden object.
Substage 4 (8 to 12 months)	Behavior is more deliberate and purposeful as infants coordinate previously learned schemes (such as looking at and grasping a rattle) and use previously learned behaviors to attain their goals (such as crawling across the room to get a desired toy). They can anticipate events. Object permanence is developing, although infants will search for an object in its first hiding place, even if they saw it being moved.
Substage 5 (12 to 18 months)	Toddlers show curiosity as they purposefully vary their actions to see results. They actively explore their world to determine how an object, event, or situation is novel. They try out new activities and use trial and error in solving problems. Concerning object permanence, they will follow a series of object displacements, but since they cannot imagine movement they do not see, they will not search for an object where they have not observed its being hidden.
Substage 6 (18 to 24 months)	Since toddlers can mentally represent events, they are no longer confined to trial and error to solve problems. Symbolic thought allows toddlers to begin to think about events and anticipate their consequences without always resorting to action. Toddlers begin to demonstrate insight. Object permanence is fully developed.

Note: Infants show enormous cognitive growth during Piaget's sensorimotor stage, as they learn about the world through their senses and their motor activities. Note their progress in problem solving, object permanence, and the coordination of sensory information.

nitive growth comes about through what Piaget called *circular reactions,* in which a baby learns to reproduce pleasurable or interesting events originally discovered by chance. The process is based on operant conditioning. Initially, an activity produces a sensation so welcome that the child wants to repeat it. The repetition then feeds on itself in a continuous cycle in which cause and effect keep reversing (see Figure 4-1).

In the *first substage* (birth to 1 month), as neonates exercise their inborn reflexes, they gain some control over them. They begin to engage in a behavior even when the stimulus that elicits it as an automatic reflex is not present. For example, newborns suck reflexively when their lips are touched. They soon learn to find the nipple even when they are not touched, and they suck at times when they are not hungry. Thus infants modify

and extend the scheme for sucking as they begin to initiate activity.

In the *second substage* (1 to 4 months), babies learn to repeat a pleasant bodily sensation first achieved by chance (say, sucking their thumbs). Piaget called this a *primary circular reaction.* Babies also learn to adjust or accommodate their actions by sucking their thumbs differently from the way they suck on a nipple. They begin to turn toward sounds, showing the ability to coordinate different kinds of sensory information (vision and hearing).

The *third substage* (4 to 8 months) coincides with a new interest in manipulating objects. Babies engage in *secondary circular reactions:* intentional actions repeated not merely for their own sake, as in the second substage, but to get results beyond the infant's own body (for example, cooing when a friendly face appears to make the face stay longer).

By the time they reach the *fourth substage* (8 to 12 months), infants have built on the few schemes they were born with and have learned to generalize from past experience to solve new problems. They will crawl to get something they want, grab it, or push away a barrier to it (such as someone else's hand). They try out, modify, and coordinate previous schemes, to find one that works.

In the *fifth substage* (12 to 18 months), babies begin to experiment with new behavior. Once they begin to walk, they can satisfy their curiosity by exploring their environment. They now engage in *tertiary circular reactions,* varying an action to see what will happen rather than merely repeating pleasing behavior they have accidentally discovered. For the first time, children show originality in problem solving. By trial and error, they try out new behaviors until they find the best way to attain a goal, as Rebecca did when she wanted to get the Cheerios from her father's hand.

Representational ability—the ability to mentally represent objects and actions in memory, largely through symbols such as words, numbers, and mental pictures—develops in the *sixth substage* between about 18 months and 2 years. Evidence of this development of symbolic thought can be seen in any bookshop with a good section of children's books. Many books for babies are made of cloth or heavy board or vinyl, reflecting the fact that a baby first reacts to books by banging them, chewing on them, and taking them into the bathtub—in short, using them as objects. Not until the latter part of the sensorimotor stage do children realize that pictures in books stand for objects in the real world, and not until still later do they understand that black marks in books represent ideas as well as things.

Children in the sixth substage can use symbols, such as words, to *think* about actions before taking them. Since they now have some understanding of cause and effect, they no longer have to go through laborious trial and error to solve new problems. Piaget's daughter Lucienne demonstrated this when, in figuring out how to pry open a partially closed matchbox to remove a watch chain, she opened her mouth wider to signify her idea of widening the slit in the box (Piaget, 1952).

The ability to manipulate symbols frees children from immediate experience. They can now engage in *deferred imitation,* imitating actions they no longer see in front of them. They can pretend, as Anna did at 20 months when she was given a tea set and immediately "served tea" to Diane and

Baby sucks thumb   Baby enjoys sucking

(a) Primary circular reaction: action and response both involve infant's own body (1 to 4 months)

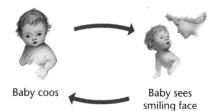

Baby coos   Baby sees smiling face

(b) Secondary circular reaction: action gets a response from another person or object, leading to baby's repeating original action (4 to 8 months)

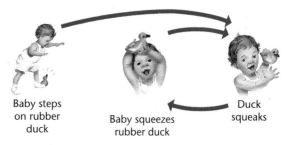

Baby steps on rubber duck   Baby squeezes rubber duck   Duck squeaks

(c) Tertiary circular reaction: action gets one pleasing result, leading baby to perform similiar actions to get similiar results (12 to 18 months)

FIGURE 4-1

Primary, secondary, and tertiary circular reactions. According to Piaget, infants learn to reproduce pleasing events they have discovered accidentally.

(a) Primary circular reaction: A baby happens to suck a thumb, enjoys sucking, and puts the thumb back into the mouth or keeps it there. The stimulus (thumb) elicits the sucking reflex; pleasure then stimulates the baby to keep on sucking.

(b) Secondary circular reaction: This involves something outside the baby's body. The baby coos; the mother smiles; and because the baby likes to see the mother smile, the baby coos again.

(c) Tertiary circular reaction: The baby tries different ways to reproduce an accidentally discovered response. When the baby steps on a rubber duck, the duck squeaks. The baby then tries to produce the squeak in other ways, perhaps by squeezing it or sitting on it.

This baby seems to be showing at least the beginning of the concept of object permanence by searching for an object that is partially hidden. She will probably have the complete concept by 18 months of age, when she will look for objects or people even when she has not seen where they were hidden. *(Doug Goodman/Monkmeyer)*

Jonathan. This simple "pretend" play is the forerunner of the more elaborate dramatic play that occurs at age 3 and older, as children become better able to remember and imagine.

During the sensorimotor stage, children also develop *object permanence:* the realization that an object or person continues to exist even when out of sight (refer back to Table 4-1). At first, infants have no such concept. By the third substage, according to Piaget, they will look for something they have dropped, but if they cannot see any part of it, they act as if it no longer exists. In the fourth substage, they will look for an object in a place where they first saw it hidden, even if they have seen it being moved to another place. In the fifth substage, they will search for an object in the *last* place they saw it being hidden; but they will not search for it in a place where they did not see it being hidden. By the sixth substage, toddlers' imagination allows them to look for an object even if they did not see where it was hidden.

Object permanence is the basis for children's awareness that they exist apart from objects and other people. It also allows a child whose parent has left the room to feel secure in the knowledge that the parent continues to exist and will return. It is essential to the child's understanding of time, space, and a world full of objects and events. The

development of this concept in many cultures can be seen in the game of peekaboo (see Box 4-1).

Post-Piagetian Research: Strengths of Infant Cognition

Piaget's work is highly regarded for its innovative contribution to our understanding of cognitive development; but although research has supported some of his claims, it has refuted others. Studies since the late 1970s challenge some of his ideas about the time that certain abilities appear, particularly his view that babies up to 18 months cannot conceptualize or think about objects not physically present. Research on memory, described later in this chapter, shows that even very young infants have symbolic capabilities and can remember past events. All in all, recent studies build an impressive case for babies' cognitive strengths.

What Abilities Develop Earlier Than Piaget Thought? Initially, research using Piaget's methodology found that *object permanence* seems to progress in the sequence he described (Kramer, Hill, & Cohen, 1975). However, more recent research suggests that Piaget may have underestimated infants' grasp of object permanence because of his testing methods. Babies may fail to search for hidden objects because they are not able to perform the sequence of actions necessary for solving a problem, such as moving a cushion to look for something hidden behind it. Infants as young as $3\frac{1}{2}$ months, when tested by a more age-appropriate procedure, acted as if they remembered an object they could not see (Baillargeon & DeVos, 1991; see Figure 4-2).

Research also refutes Piaget's belief that the *senses are unconnected at birth* and are only gradually integrated through experience. We now know that newborns will look at a source of sound, showing a connection between hearing and sight. One-month-olds will look longer at either a bumpy or a smooth pacifier, depending on which kind they have sucked, suggesting an integration between vision and touch (Mandler, 1990; Meltzoff & Borton, 1979).

How early do babies engage in *invisible imitation*—imitation using parts of the baby's body that the baby cannot see, such as the mouth? Piaget maintained that invisible imitation develops at about 9 months, after *visible imitation*—the use of the hands or feet, for example, which babies can see. Yet in some controversial research, babies less

BOX 4-1   WINDOW ON THE WORLD

PLAYING PEEKABOO

In a mud hut in rural South Africa, a Bantu mother smiles at her 9-month-old son, covers her eyes with her hands, and asks, "Uphi?" (Where?) After 3 seconds, the mother says, "Here!" and uncovers her eyes to the baby's delight. In a Tokyo apartment a Japanese mother, using different language and covering her eyes with a cloth, plays the same game with her 12-month-old daughter, who shows the same joyous response.

"Peekaboo" is played across diverse cultures, using similar routines (Fernald & O'Neill, 1993). In all cultures where the game is played,* the moment when the mother reappears is exhilarating. It is marked by exaggerated gestures and consistent voice tones, high-pitched or low, drawn out or intense.

Why is this game so popular?

Psychoanalysts maintain that it helps babies master anxiety when their mother disappears. Cognitive psychologists see it as a way babies play with developing ideas about the existence, disappearance, and reappearance of objects—the concept of object permanence. It may also be a clue to the development of a sense of humor; a social routine that helps babies learn the kinds of rules that govern language (such as taking turns in conversation); and preparation for developing attention and learning.

Infants' pleasure from the immediate sensory stimulation of the game is heightened by their fascination with faces and voices, especially the high-pitched tones the adult usually uses. As babies develop the cognitive competency to predict future events, expectations

become important and the game takes on new dimensions.

The way the game develops during the first year reflects intertwining changes in the baby's perceptual, cognitive, and motor development (see table). By 1 year, children have gone from being relatively passive observers to actively initiating the game and engaging adults in play—thus showing bidirectional influence. Seeing her father's tee shirt on the floor, Cindy drapes it over her head and toddles over to him. "Where's Cindy?" he asks. She whips the shirt off her face, and as her father exclaims, "Peekaboo!" Cindy laughs.

*The cultures included in this report are those found in Malaysia, Greece, India, Iran, Russia, Brazil, Indonesia, Korea, and South Africa.

Development as Measured by the Game of Peekaboo

Baby's Age	What Adult Does	Who Usually Initiates	What Baby Does
3–5 months	Moves own face in and out of infant's view	Adult	Smiles and laughs; begins to develop expectation of what will happen next.
5–8 months	1. Gets baby's attention 2. Covers eyes or face or hides 3. Uncovers or reappears 4. Uses voice cues throughout 5. Smiles and laughs	Adult	Smiles and laughs; shows anticipatory looking and smiling to adult's "alert call" just before adult's reappearance.
8–15 months	Responds to baby's cues	Baby	Increasingly takes active role in initiating game; if game is discontinued, baby repeats own turn, "talks," looks at or touches adult to resume. In game: 1. Covers eyes or face or hides. 2. Uncovers or reappears. 3. Smiles and laughs.

SOURCE: Fernald & O'Neill, 1993.

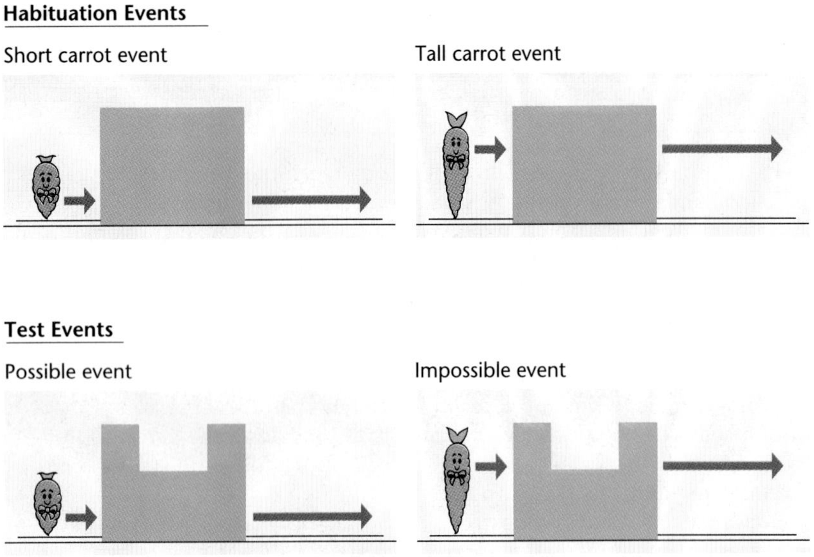

Habituation Events

Short carrot event

Tall carrot event

Test Events

Possible event

Impossible event

FIGURE 4-2

Object permanence in infants. In this experiment, 3½-month-old infants watched a short and then a tall carrot slide along a track, disappear behind a screen, and then reappear. After they became accustomed to seeing these events, the track's center was hidden by a screen with a large window at the top. The short carrot did not appear in the window when passing behind the screen; the tall carrot, which should have appeared in the window, also did not. The babies looked longer at the tall than at the short carrot event, suggesting that they were surprised that the tall carrot did not appear. *(Source: Baillargeon & DeVos, 1991.)*

than 72 hours old (including one who was tested only 42 minutes after birth) appeared to imitate adults by opening their mouths and sticking out their tongues, as well as duplicating adults' head movements (Meltzoff & Moore, 1983, 1989). In another study, which showed a link between cognitive and emotional development, babies at an average age of 36 hours reproduced three different emotional expressions—a smile, a pout, and the wide-opened mouth and eyes that usually denote surprise (T. M. Field, Woodson, Greenberg, & Cohen, 1982).

Neonatal invisible imitation has been explained in two ways. One hypothesis is that a baby imitating an adult's expression is making an automatically triggered, reflexive response to a particular sensory stimulus pattern (Abravanel & Sigafoos, 1984). The other hypothesis is that human beings are born with a primitive tendency to try to match the acts of other human beings, one aspect of an underlying representational system that lets babies perceive and produce human acts (Meltzoff & Moore, 1989).

A related issue is the development of *deferred imitation.* According to Piaget, children under 18 months cannot imitate an action they saw some time before; yet babies have been found to display deferred imitation as early as 6 *weeks* of age (Meltzoff & Moore, 1994), suggesting that very young babies can retain a memory of an event and a mental representation for it, a "picture" in the mind. In one experiment, 6-week-old infants who were randomly assigned to four groups saw adults either open their mouths, stick out their tongues at

the middle of the mouth, stick out their tongues to the side, or make no movement. Not only did the infants in the first three groups tend to immediately reproduce the type of movement they had seen, thus demonstrating invisible imitation, but they also showed deferred imitation by making similar movements 24 hours later in the presence of the same adult, who at that time was expressionless (Meltzoff & Moore, 1994). In successive trials, the infants became more and more accurate in matching the remembered behavior of the adult. Since the infants in each group made a different type of movement—the one they had seen a particular adult make—their actions could not be reflexive. Instead, they had to be based on mental representations triggered by the sight of the person originally seen to make the movement.

Why do very young infants try to match the behavior of people they see? Meltzoff and Moore (1992, 1994) suggest that infants may use imitation as a sort of identity check—to see whether a certain person is someone they have seen before and to distinguish "those like me" (people) from things. Mutual-imitation games between parents and infants may be an important type of early communication that reinforces this interactive aspect of learning (Meltzoff & Gopnik, 1993).

Are Babies Born Thinkers? It appears that babies can think at a much earlier age than Piaget believed; either they are born with the capacity to form concepts or they acquire it very early in life. This conclusion has come from research based on

Babies as young as this 5-month-old can add and subtract small numbers of objects, as shown in this experiment using different numbers of dolls. It has been suggested that the ability to grasp the rudiments of arithmetic may be inborn and that when parents teach their babies numbers, they are only teaching them the names ("one, two, three") for concepts the babies already know. *(David Sanders/Arizona Daily Star)*

infants' tendency to look longer at an unusual sight, showing that the infant recognizes it as surprising.

One series of experiments suggests that an *understanding of number* begins long before Piaget's sixth substage, when he claimed children first begin to use symbols. Karen Wynn (1992) used Mickey Mouse dolls to show that 5-month-old babies may be able to add and subtract small numbers of objects (see Figure 4-3). For the problem "1

Sequence of events 1 + 1 = 1 or 2

1. Object placed in case   2. Screen comes up   3. Second object added   4. Hand leaves empty

Then either: possible outcome   or: impossible outcome

5. Screen drops ... revealing 2 objects   5. Screen drops ... revealing 1 object

Sequence of events 2 − 1 = 1 or 2

1. Two objects placed in case   2. Screen comes up   3. Empty hand enters   4. One object removed

Then either: possible outcome   or: impossible outcome

5. Screen drops ... revealing 1 object   5. Screen drops ... revealing 2 objects

FIGURE 4-3

Can 5-month-old infants count? For the problem "1 plus 1," a researcher showed a baby 1 doll, then hid it behind a screen. The baby saw a hand place another doll behind the screen; then the screen was pulled away, revealing 2 dolls. Sometimes there was a false answer: the baby was shown only 1 doll or 3 dolls. In the "2 minus 1" trials, the researcher showed 2 dolls, then took 1 away, and the baby saw either 1 or 2 dolls. Babies consistently looked longer at the surprising "wrong" answers than at the expected right ones, which suggests that they had "computed" the right answers in their minds. *(Source: Wynn, 1992.)*

Possible Event

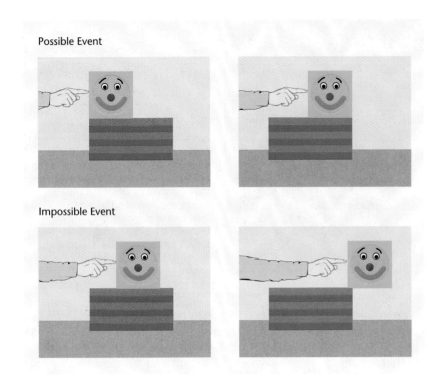

Impossible Event

FIGURE 4-4

Test for infants' understanding of the way objects are supported. A gloved hand pushes a box toward the right edge of a supporting platform. In the possible event, the box stops when its bottom surface is still resting on the platform. In the impossible event, the box is pushed off the edge of the platform until only a small portion of its bottom surface rests on the platform. Infants 6½ months old, but not those 3 months old, look longer at the impossible event than at the possible event, suggesting that they recognize that such a small area of contact cannot support the box. *(Source: Baillargeon, 1994.)*

plus 1," Wynn showed a baby a doll, then hid it behind a screen. The baby saw a hand place another doll behind the screen, and then the screen was pulled away to show two dolls. The length of time that the baby looked at the dolls was measured. Sometimes the screen was pulled away to show a false answer; in the "1 plus 1" situation, a baby might see three dolls or only one. In other experiments the researcher started by showing two dolls, then took one away, and the babies saw either one or two dolls. In all the experiments, the babies looked longer at the surprising "wrong" answers than at the expected "right" ones, suggesting (according to Wynn) that they had mentally "computed" the right answers. This research suggests that the ability to grasp the rudiments of arithmetic may be inborn, and that when parents teach their babies numbers, they may only be teaching them the names ("one, two, three") for concepts the babies already know.

Other studies using similar methodology have explored how infants *learn about the physical world.* How, for example, does a baby come to understand that an unsupported object will fall? Renée Baillargeon (1994) and her colleagues showed infants a box, first resting on a platform and then pushed to the edge of it (see Figure 4-4). Three-month-old babies stared longer at the box when it had lost contact with the platform, apparently realizing

that the box should fall. By 6½ months, infants appeared to recognize the importance of two other factors: where the box touches the platform (on top or on the side) and how much of the box is touching the platform. Baillargeon suggests that in thinking about a physical phenomenon such as this one, infants first form a general, "all-or-nothing" idea about it and later modify this initial concept by considering variables that enable them to make more accurate predictions.

The ability to reason about physical phenomena may well be tied to motor development. Six-month-old babies who can sit up and handle objects learn from experience that an object placed on the edge of a table will fall unless enough of its bottom surface is on the table. This also suggests a second developmental principle: Babies first reason qualitatively and then quantitatively, and their quantitative reasoning continuously improves. Baillargeon tested the latter hypothesis by first repeatedly showing infants a screen rotating through a 180-degree arc (see Figure 4-5). When the infants became accustomed to seeing the rotation, a barrier was introduced in the form of a box. At 4½ months of age, infants showed that they realized the screen could not move through the entire box, but they did not recognize the point at which the screen must stop. Although 6½-month-olds knew that the screen could not rotate through

80 percent of the box, it was not until 8½ months that infants recognized that rotation through 50 percent of the box was also impossible.

Such findings, says Baillargeon, suggest that infants may have *innate learning mechanisms* that help them make sense of the data they encounter in the physical world, mechanisms more complex than simple conditioning. Further research is needed to determine precisely what those mechanisms are and how they operate.

PSYCHOMETRIC APPROACH: INTELLIGENCE TESTS

As we mentioned in Chapter 1, Piaget's curiosity about children's thought processes was initially whetted by his work on early intelligence tests being developed in Paris. At the beginning of the twentieth century, school administrators in that city asked the psychologist Alfred Binet to devise a way of identifying children who could not handle academic work and who should be removed from regular classes and given special training. The test that Binet and his colleague Theodore Simon developed was the forerunner of psychometric tests, used for children of all levels of ability, which try to score intelligence by numbers. One is the Stanford-Binet Intelligence Scale, an American version of the traditional Binet-Simon tests (see Chapter 6).

In contrast with Piaget's concern with qualitative change, the goal of psychometric testing is to measure quantitatively the factors that make up intelligence, such as comprehension and reasoning. *IQ (intelligence quotient) tests* consist of questions or tasks that are supposed to show how much of these abilities a person has, by comparing her or his performance with that of other test-takers. A child's score is compared with **standardized norms**—standards obtained from the scores of a large, representative sample of children of the same age who were given the test while it was being developed.

Test developers devise techniques to try to ensure that tests have high *validity* (that is, that tests measure the abilities they claim to measure) and *reliability* (that is, that test results are reasonably consistent from one time to another). Tests can be meaningful and useful only if they are both valid and reliable. For school-age children, intelligence test scores can predict school performance fairly accurately and reliably. Testing infants' and toddlers' intelligence is another matter.

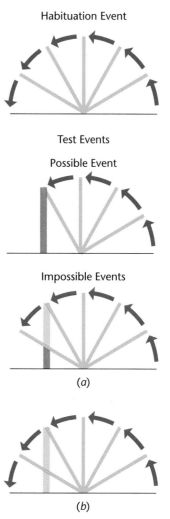

FIGURE 4-5

Test for infants' understanding of how a barrier works. Infants first become accustomed to seeing a screen rotate 180 degrees on one edge. Then a box is placed beside the screen. In the possible event, the screen stops when it reaches the edge of the box. In the impossible events, the screen rotates through part or all of the space occupied by the box. On the basis of how long they stare at each event, 4½-month-old infants seem to know that the screen cannot pass through the entire box (b); but not until 6½ months do infants recognize that the screen cannot pass through 80 percent of the box (a). *(Source: Adapted from Baillargeon, 1994.)*

Testing Infants' and Toddlers' Intelligence

Infants are intelligent from birth, but measuring their intelligence is a problem. For one thing, babies cannot talk. They cannot tell you what they know and how they think. The most obvious way to gauge their intelligence is by assessing what they can do. Experimenters try to catch babies' attention and coax them into a particular behavior; but if they do not grasp a rattle, it is hard to tell whether they do not know how, do not feel like doing it, or do not realize what is expected of them.

Infant test scores are unreliable; they tend to vary widely from one time to another, and they are almost useless for predicting future functioning. Not until the third year of life do the child's scores, along with such factors as the parents' IQ and educational level, help predict later test scores (Kopp & Kaler, 1989; Kopp & McCall, 1982).

Even for toddlers, predictions from psychometric intelligence tests are unreliable. In one longitudinal study, IQs changed markedly, by an average of 28½ points, between ages 2½ and 17, and the IQs of 1 in 7 children shifted by more than 40 points (McCall, Appelbaum, & Hogarty, 1973). As children are tested closer to their fifth birthday, the relationship between current scores and those in later childhood becomes stronger (Bornstein & Sigman, 1986).

Why do early intelligence scores fail to predict later ones? For one thing, the tests traditionally used for babies measure mostly sensory and motor abilities, while tests for older children are heavily verbal and seem to measure different and largely unrelated kinds of intelligence (Bornstein & Sigman, 1986). Even when we look at motor skills alone, children who are good at the large-muscle activities tested at an early age may not be as adept at fine motor, or manipulative, skills considered to be a sign of intelligence later on. A 1-year-old who can build towers with blocks may not, by age 7, be able to copy a design made from colored blocks.

Psychologists are better able to predict the future IQ of infants with disabilities. Yet some children born with mental and motor problems make impressive strides in tested intelligence as they grow older (Kopp & Kaler, 1989; Kopp & McCall, 1982). Human beings have a "strong self-righting tendency"; given a favorable environment, infants will follow normal developmental patterns unless they have suffered severe damage. Sometime between the ages of 18 and 24 months, however, this self-righting tendency diminishes as children begin to acquire skills (such as verbal abilities) in which there will eventually be great variations in proficiency. As these skills develop, individual differences become more pronounced and lasting.

Despite the problems in measuring the intelligence of very young children, sometimes there are reasons to test them. If parents are worried because

a baby is not doing the same things as other babies the same age, developmental testing may reassure them that development is normal or may alert them to abnormal development.

The design of developmental tests is based on observation of large numbers of children. After determining what most infants or toddlers can do at particular ages, the test makers assign a developmental age to each activity, and a child's performance is then evaluated in comparison to these norms.

The **Bayley Scales of Infant Development** (Bayley, 1969; revised Bayley II, 1993) are widely used to measure development (see Table 4-2). The Bayley II is designed to assess the current developmental status of children from 1 to 42 months of age (3½ years). It is used primarily with children suspected of being at risk for abnormal development (B. Thompson et al., 1994). The Bayley II is organized into three categories: a *mental scale,* which measures such abilities as perception, memory, learning, and verbal communication; a *motor scale,* which measures gross (large-muscle) and fine (manipulative) motor skills; and a *behavior rating scale,* a 30-item rating of the child's test-taking behaviors. The separate scores calculated for each scale are most useful for early detection of emotional disturbances and sensory, neurological, and environmental deficits (Anastasi, 1988).

Improving Infants' and Toddlers' Test Scores

Good parenting skills and an enriched day care environment can improve young children's test scores. In Project CARE, one experimental group of babies from disadvantaged homes received home visits and day care, starting before they were 5 months old (Wasik, Ramey, Bryant, & Sparling, 1990). Trained visitors helped the babies' parents solve problems of child rearing and daily life and encouraged them to play educational games with their children. The babies' activities at the day care center were designed to stimulate language and to foster social and cognitive development. Babies in a second experimental group received only the home visits, and a third (control) group got no systematic intervention.

The 65 children were given cognitive tests nine times between ages 6 months and 4½ years. On each occasion after the first (6-month) assessment, the experimental group that received both home

TABLE 4-2

Sample Tasks in the Bayley Scales of Infant Development

Age (in months)	Tasks Most Children This Age Can Do
5.8	Grasp edge of piece of paper held out by examiner
5.9	Vocalize pleasure and displeasure
6.0	Reach persistently for cube placed just out of reach
6.1	Turn head to watch spoon dropped to floor by child's side
6.3	Say several syllables
11.5	Stop doing something (like putting an object into the mouth) when adult says "no, no"
11.7	Try to imitate words like *mama, dada,* and *baby*
12.1	Imitate rattling of spoon in cup with stirring motion to make noise
12.6	Put round block into round hole of form board

SOURCE: Kessen, Haith, & Salapatek, 1970.

and day care intervention did better than the other two groups. The children who received only the home visits did no better than the control group. However, since other studies that reported no intervention effects during the preschool years found such effects later, it is possible that such a "delayed reaction" might emerge for these home-visit-only children, too. In any case, these results suggest that the kind of attention babies get can affect cognitive development.

Measuring the Impact of the Home Environment

To assess the impact of home surroundings on cognitive growth, researchers developed a measure called the *Home Observation for Measurement of the Environment (HOME)* (Bradley, 1989). One factor measured by HOME is parental responsiveness. HOME gives credit to the parent of a toddler for caressing or kissing the child during an examiner's visit; to the parent of a preschooler for spontaneously praising the child at least twice during the visit; and to the parent of an older child for answering the child's questions. Examiners evaluate how parent and child talk to each other, and they give high ratings for a parent's friendly, nonpunitive attitude. A longitudinal study found positive correlations between how responsive parents were to their 6-month-old babies, as measured by HOME, and how well the children did at age 10

on IQ and achievement test scores and teachers' ratings of classroom behavior (Bradley & Caldwell, 1982; Bradley, Caldwell, & Rock, 1988).

The HOME scale also assesses the number of books in the home, the presence of playthings that encourage the development of concepts, and parents' involvement in children's play. High scores on all these factors are fairly reliable in predicting children's IQ; when combined with the parents' level of education, they are even more accurate. In one study, researchers compared HOME scores for low-income 2-year-olds with the children's Stanford-Binet intelligence test scores 2 years later. The single most important factor in predicting high intelligence was the mother's ability to create and structure an environment that fostered learning (Stevens & Bakeman, 1985).

The influence of parents is also seen in a study of 931 African American, Mexican American, and white children up to age 3. In the lives of these children in inner-city neighborhoods, socioeconomic status and other aspects of the wider environment were less closely related to cognitive development than were such aspects of the home environment as how responsive parents were and whether the child had access to stimulating play materials (Bradley et al., 1989). In all three ethnic groups, a favorable home environment could offset problems in infancy; but when early development *and* early home environment were poor, chances for a good outcome were much lower.

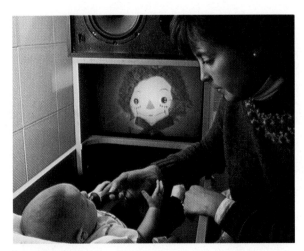

Can this baby tell the difference between Raggedy Ann and Raggedy Andy? This researcher may find out by seeing whether the baby has habituated—gotten used to one face—and then stops sucking on the nipple when a new face appears, showing recognition of the difference. *(James Kilkelly/DOT)*

INFORMATION-PROCESSING APPROACH: PERCEPTIONS AND SYMBOLS

At about 6 weeks, André makes sucking noises and waves his arms excitedly as his mother approaches. Anyone can see that he recognizes her and that the sight and sound of her fill him with joy. But how does recognition take place? What is going on in André's head?

The information-processing approach, the newest way to explain cognitive development, is coming up with answers to such questions. Information-processing researchers focus on memory, problem solving, and learning. They see people as manipulators of perceptions and symbols. Their goal is to discover what infants, children, and adults do with information from the time they perceive it until they use it. Like the psychometric approach, information-processing theory is concerned with individual differences in intelligent behavior; but it concentrates on describing the mental processes involved in acquiring information or solving problems, rather than merely assuming differences in mental functioning from answers given or problems solved.

Because of the poor correlation between scores on developmental tests for infants and later IQ tests, many psychologists believed that the cognitive functioning of infants had little in common with that of older children and adults—in other words, that there was a discontinuity in cognitive development. Today, discoveries about the ability of babies to interpret their perceptions challenge this view. When we assess how infants process information rather than how they perform on psychometric tests, we see that mental development seems to be fairly continuous from birth into childhood (Bornstein & Sigman, 1986; McCall & Carriger, 1993; L. A. Thompson, Fagan, & Fulker, 1991).

Habituation

How do infants process information? Many of the answers come from studies that measure habituation. *Habituation* is a type of learning in which repeated exposure to a stimulus (such as a sound or a sight) results in a reduced response to that stimulus. Habituation allows people to conserve mental energy by remaining alert to things and events in the environment only as long as they seem to merit attention. Cognitive development occurs as infants transform the novel into the familiar, the unknown into the known (Rheingold, 1985).

Researchers study habituation in newborns by repeatedly presenting a stimulus (usually a sound or visual pattern) and then monitoring such responses as heart rate, sucking, eye movements, and brain activity. A baby who has been sucking typically stops when the stimulus is first presented and does not start again until after it has ended. After the same sound or sight has been presented again and again, it loses its novelty and no longer causes the baby to stop sucking. By continuing to suck, the infant shows that he or she has habituated to the stimulus. A new sight or sound, however, will capture the baby's attention and the baby will again stop sucking. This increased response to a new stimulus is called *dishabituation.*

Researchers gauge the efficiency of infants' information processing by measuring how quickly babies habituate to familiar stimuli, how fast their attention recovers when they are exposed to new stimuli, and how much time they spend looking at the new and the old (Bornstein, 1985a; Bornstein & Sigman, 1986; McCall & Carriger, 1993). Efficiency of habituation correlates with other signs of mental development, such as a preference for complexity, rapid exploration of the environment, sophisticated play, fast problem solving, and the ability to match pictures.

Speed of habituation shows promise as a predictor of intelligence, especially of verbal abilities. Infants who are efficient at taking in and interpreting sensory information score well on childhood intelligence tests later. In several longitudinal studies, habituation and attention-recovery abilities during the first 6 months of life were moderately useful in predicting scores on psychometric tests taken between ages 2 and 8 (Bornstein & Sigman, 1986).

Sensory Discrimination

If infants pay more attention to new stimuli than to familiar ones, they can tell the new from the old; therefore, say information-processing theorists, they must be able to remember the old. To compare new information with information they already have, they must be able to form mental images or representations of stimuli; and the efficiency of their information processing depends on the speed with which they form and refer to such images.

Contrary to Piaget's view, habituation studies have found that this representational ability seems to be working very soon after birth, and it quickly becomes more efficient. Newborns can tell sounds they have already heard from those they have not; in one study, infants who heard a certain speech sound one day after birth appeared to remember that sound 24 hours later, as shown by a reduced tendency to turn their heads toward the sound and even a tendency to turn away (Swain, Zelazo, & Clifton, 1993). Early sensitivity to sounds may predict aspects of later cognitive functioning: a high positive correlation was found between the ability of 4-month-old infants to discriminate sounds and their IQ scores at age 5 (O'Connor et al., 1984).

Visual novelty preference, an infant's preference for new rather than familiar sights, seems to predict general intelligence, as well as certain specific abilities. In one study, babies who, at 5 and 7 months, preferred looking at new pictures rather than ones they had seen before tended to score higher on the Bayley Scales at 2 years and the Stanford-Binet at 3 years. They also showed stronger language skills and memory ability at age 3 (L. A. Thompson et al., 1991).

Other research has examined how well infants can identify by sight items they earlier felt with their hands but did not see. This ability, known as *cross-modal transfer,* shows a fairly high level of abstraction; it implies central processing of tactile and visual information. One study compared high-risk, very-low-birthweight babies with normal full-term infants from the same low-income population. The combination of two scores—the infants' *visual recognition memory* (ability to rec-

ognize something previously seen) at 7 months and cross-modal transfer at 1 year—was significantly associated with the children's IQ scores at 3, 4, and 5 years (S. A. Rose, Feldman, Wallace, & McCarton, 1991).

Even more impressive support for the continuity of cognitive abilities comes from a later study, which found that visual recognition memory at 7 months and cross-modal transfer at 1 year predict IQ at age 11 (S. A. Rose & Feldman, 1995). The common core of all these abilities seems to be the speed of processing perceptual information, and the findings suggest that individual differences in speed remain as infants grow into early and middle childhood.

Information Processing and Exploratory Competence

As babies begin to get around on their own, they show curiosity about their world by such behaviors as squeezing, jabbing, rubbing, shaking, and banging objects. The degree to which a baby initiates such activities is related to competence in solving problems and provides clues to early cognitive development (Caruso, 1993).

One longitudinal study found that information-processing skills in early infancy help predict *exploratory competence* at 13 months—a cognitive capacity that seems to underlie the growing variance at that age in the sophistication of toddlers' play and their ability to sustain attention (Tamis-LeMonda & Bornstein, 1993). For example, 5-month-olds who looked longer at novel sights, such as a bull's-eye and a female face projected on a screen, had a longer attention span at 13 months and were more likely to engage in highly symbolic play (such as pretending a block is a spoon). The infants' activity also made a difference: the more the 5-month-olds cooed, looked at their mothers or at an object, or touched an object, the more exploratory competence they showed at 13 months.

Caregivers' Influence

A major influence on cognitive development is how caregivers act toward infants. Studies of the ways American and Japanese mothers respond to their babies' behavior found that the age of 4 to 5 months appears to be a sensitive period for the effect of maternal responsiveness (Bornstein, 1985b; Bornstein & Tamis-LaMonda, 1989).

In one series of experiments, almost all mothers

responded quickly when their babies cried in distress. However, their responsiveness to *nondistress* behavior, such as babbling or looking at the mother, varied greatly, regardless of the mothers' education or socioeconomic status. As toddlers, the children of the most responsive mothers had more advanced representational abilities. As 4-year-olds, they scored higher on a preschool intelligence test and other learning tasks (Bornstein & Tamis-LeMonda, 1989). In a later study, maternal responsiveness to 5-month-olds, together with the mother's IQ and the infant's own early visual discrimination ability (as shown at 2 months of age), was related to the 5-month-olds' habituation, novelty responsiveness, and cross-modal transfer—skills that, as we have seen, predict differences in cognitive abilities later in childhood (Bornstein & Tamis-LeMonda, 1994).

How does an adult's responsiveness help children develop cognitively? It may raise children's self-esteem and make them feel that they have some control over their lives. It may also make them feel secure enough to explore and motivate them to persist. And it may help them regulate themselves to pay attention and learn. Although most of these studies have been done with mothers, their findings may be relevant to fathers and other primary caregivers.

✔ LANGUAGE DEVELOPMENT

At 4½ months, Stefan chuckles out loud. He also says "ngoo-ooo" and "ngaaah." At 7 months he makes more sounds, mostly sounding like "da" or "ga." At 11 months he says "dada," and at 14 months he points to everything, asking "What zis?" or saying "Da" for "I want that." At 17 months he points to the right places when asked "Where is your nose? tongue? belly button?" By 21 months, he says, or tries to say, at least 50 words, and he understands many more. He can now tell you, in his own language, exactly what he does or does not want. If asked "Do you want to go to bed?" he answers "Eh-eh-eh," accompanied by vigorous arm waving—in other words, "No!" He also says his first three-word sentence: "Choo-choo bye-bye da-da," meaning "The train went away, and now it's all gone."

Stefan's growing ability to use *language,* a communication system based on words and grammar, is a crucial element in his cognitive development. Once he knows words, he can use them to repre-

sent objects. He can reflect on people, places, and things; and he can communicate his needs, feelings, and ideas in order to exert control over his life.

The growth of language illustrates the interaction of all aspects of development—physical, cognitive, emotional, and social. As the physical structures needed to produce sounds mature, and the neuronal connections necessary to associate sound and meaning become activated, social interaction with adults introduces babies to the communicative nature of speech. Let's look at the typical sequence of language development (see Table 4-3), at some characteristics of early speech, at the way babies acquire language, and at ways parents and other caregivers help toddlers prepare for *literacy,* the ability to read and write.

SEQUENCE OF EARLY LANGUAGE DEVELOPMENT

The word *infant* is based on the Latin for "without speech." Before babies say their first words, they make sounds that progress from crying to cooing and babbling, then to accidental imitation, and then deliberate imitation. These sounds are known as *prelinguistic speech.* During this period, infants also grow in the ability to recognize and understand speech sounds and to use meaningful gestures. Around the end of the first year, babies typically say their first word, and about eight months to a year later, toddlers begin speaking in sentences.

Early Vocalization

Crying is the newborn's only means of communication. To a stranger, all cries may sound alike, but a baby's parents can often tell the cry for food from the cry of pain. Different pitches, patterns, and intensities signal hunger, sleepiness or anger.

Between 6 weeks and 3 months, babies start to make sounds when they are happy. *Cooing* includes making squeals, gurgles, and vowel sounds like "ahhh." At about 3 months, babies begin to play with speech sounds, matching the sounds they hear from people around them (Bates, O'Connell, & Shore, 1987).

Babbling—repeating consonant-vowel strings, such as "ma-ma-ma-ma"—occurs suddenly between 6 and 10 months of age and is often mistaken for a baby's first word. Babbling is not real

TABLE 4-3

Language Milestones from Birth to 3 Years

Age in Months	Development
Birth	Can perceive speech, cry, make some response to sound.
1½ to 3	Coos and laughs.
3	Plays with speech sounds.
5 to 6	Makes consonant sounds, trying to match what she or he hears.
6 to 10	Babbles in strings of consonants and vowels.
9	Uses gestures to communicate and plays gesture games.
9 to 10	Begins to understand words (usually "no" and baby's own name): imitates sounds.
9 to 10	Loses ability to discriminate sounds not in own language.
9 to 12	Uses a few social gestures.
10 to 14	Says first word (usually a label for something); imitates sounds.
10 to 18	Says single words.
13	Understands symbolic function of naming.
13	Uses more elaborate gestures.
14	Uses symbolic gesturing.
16 to 24	Learns many new words, expanding vocabulary rapidly, going from about 50 words to up to 400; uses verbs and adjectives.
18 to 24	Says first sentence (two words).
20	Uses fewer gestures; names more things.
20 to 22	Has comprehension spurt.
24	Uses many two-word phrases; no longer babbles; wants to talk.
30	Learns new words almost every day; speaks in combinations of three or more words; understands very well; makes some grammatical mistakes.
36	Says up to 1,000 words, 80 percent intelligible; makes mistakes in syntax.

SOURCES: Bates et al., 1987; Capute, Shapiro, & Palmer, 1987; Lenneberg, 1969.

language, since it does not hold meaning for the baby, but it becomes more wordlike. "Word babies" seem to understand words earlier and produce word sounds in their babbling, whereas "intonation babies" babble in sentencelike patterns and tend not to break down their babbling strings into individual "words" (Dore, 1975). Cross-cultural studies, such as one study of babies growing up in families that spoke French, Chinese, or Arabic, found that babies do not, as was once believed, "try out" all speech sounds in all human languages, but instead focus on sounds used in their own language (Boysson-Bardies, Sagart, & Durand, 1984).

The importance of babbling is underscored by its appearance, in the form of gestures, among deaf babies (Petitto & Marentette, 1991; see Box 4-2). Although these babies may also babble vocally, they do so about 5 months later than hearing babies do (Oller & Eilers, 1988).

Language development among babies with normal hearing and speech continues with accidental *imitation of language sounds* they hear and then of themselves making these sounds. At about 9 to 10 months, they deliberately imitate sounds without understanding them. Once they have a repertoire of sounds, they string them together in patterns that sound like language but seem to have no meaning (Eisenson, Auer, & Irwin, 1963; Lenneberg, 1967).

Prelinguistic speech can be rich in emotional expression. Starting at about 2 months with contented cooing, the range of emotional tone increases steadily. Before children can express ideas in words, parents become attuned to babies' feelings through the sounds they make.

Recognizing Language Sounds

Long before babies can utter anything but a cry, they can distinguish between speech sounds as

BOX 4-2   FOOD FOR THOUGHT

WHAT THE BABBLING OF HEARING-IMPAIRED BABIES TELLS US ABOUT THE DEVELOPMENT OF LANGUAGE

A profoundly deaf baby, whose parents are also deaf, makes a series of rhythmic, repetitive motions in front of her torso. Another baby, also the nonhearing child of nonhearing parents, makes similar hand motions around his head and face. What these children are doing is babbling. But instead of repeating syllables with their voices ("ma-ma-ma") as hearing babies do, they are using gestures. The gestures, like the syllables uttered by hearing babblers, do not have any meaning by themselves. But the babies repeat and string together a few motions over and over again (see figure). The hand-babbling begins before 10 months of age, about the time when hearing infants begin voice-babbling.

Apparently, these babies are copying the sign language they see their parents using, just as hearing babies copy vocal utterances. The researchers who described and an-

Example of manual babbling by a nonhearing baby who had been exposed to sign language. The baby repeated this series of hand movements over and over again in sequence. Each motion is comparable to a syllable in a sequence of vocal babbling. *(Source: Petitto & Marentette, 1991.)*

alyzed the hand motions of two nonhearing babies and two hearing babies found that the nonhearing babies' motions were much more systematic and deliberate than the random clenching fists and fluttering fingers of the hearing babies (Petitto & Marentette, 1991). The researchers concluded that babies learn sign language (which is structured very much like spoken languages) in the same way that other babies learn speech. First, they string together meaningless units; then, as parents reinforce the gestures, the babies attach meaning to them. This suggests

that there is an inborn language capacity in the brain that underlies the acquisition of both spoken and signed language and that manual babbling is tied to brain maturation rather than to maturation of the vocal cords.

similar as "ba" and "pa" (Eimas et al., 1971; see Chapter 3). This ability seems to exist in the womb. In one study, two groups of Parisian women in their ninth month of pregnancy each recited a different nursery rhyme, saying it 3 times a day for 4 weeks. A month later, researchers played recordings of both rhymes close to the women's abdomens. The fetuses' heart rates slowed when the rhyme the mother had spoken was played, but not for the other rhyme. Since the voice on the tape was not that of the mother, the fetuses apparently were responding to the linguistic sounds they had heard the mother use. This suggests that hearing the "mother tongue" before birth may "pre-tune" an infant's ears to pick up linguistic sounds (DeCasper, Lecanuet, Busnel, Granier-Deferre, & Maugeais, 1994).

Before 6 months of age, babies have learned the basic sounds of their native language. In one study, 6-month-old Swedish and American babies rou-

tinely ignored variations in sounds common to their own language but noticed variations in an unfamiliar language (Kuhl, Williams, Lacerda, Stevens, & Lindblom, 1992). Recognition of metrical patterns seems to develop as babies become increasingly familiar with their own language. Nine-month-old American babies, but not six-month-olds, listened longer to words with the stress pattern most common in English: strong-weak, as in *butter* (but'-ter) rather than weak-strong as in *restore* (re-store'). This preference may be the beginning of the ability to segment continuous speech into words, an ability needed for acquiring a vocabulary (Jusczyck, Cutler, & Redanz, 1993).

By 9 or 10 months, children lose the ability to differentiate sounds that are not part of the language they hear spoken. For example, Japanese infants lose their initial ability to tell "ra" from "la," a distinction that does not exist in the Japanese language (Bates et al., 1987).

These toddlers are clearly communicating something—maybe saying a word meaning "block" as they point to the structure. The most common first words are names of things. *(Laura Dwight)*

Gestures

At 9 months Antonio *pointed* to an object, sometimes making a noise to show that he wanted it. Between 9 and 12 months, he learned a few *conventional social gestures:* waving bye-bye, nodding his head to mean *yes,* and shaking his head to signify *no.* By about 13 months, he used more elaborate *representational gestures;* for example, he would hold an empty cup to his mouth or hold up his arms to show that he wanted to be picked up.

Symbolic gestures, such as blowing to mean "hot," often emerge just before or at about the same time as babies say their first words; these gestures show that children understand that things and ideas have names and that symbols can refer to specific everyday objects, events, desires, and conditions. Gestures usually appear before children have a vocabulary of 25 words and drop out when children learn the word for the idea they were gesturing and can say it instead (Lock, Young, Service, & Chandler, 1990).

First Words

The average baby says a first word sometime between 10 and 14 months, initiating **linguistic speech**—verbal expression that conveys meaning. Before long, the baby will use many words and will show some understanding of grammar, pronunciation, intonation, and rhythm. For now, an infant's total verbal repertoire is likely to be "mama" or "dada." Or it may be a simple syllable that has more than one meaning. "Da" may mean "I want that," "I want to go out," or "Where's Daddy?" A word like this is called a **holophrase;** it expresses a complete thought in a single word. Its meaning depends on the context in which the child utters it. As children rely more on words to express themselves, the sounds and rhythms of speech grow more elaborate; and even if much of the speech still consists of babbling, even over the age of 1 year, it is quite expressive.

Babies understand many words before they can use them. The first words most babies understand, at about 9 or 10 months, are their own names and the word "no." Babies also learn to recognize words with special meaning for them; Emma's parents may start spelling words in front of her if, for example, it is not time yet to give her a b-a-n-a-n-a. Babies listen especially closely to words they are getting ready to pronounce. In one study, French 11- to 12-month-olds who were just beginning to talk paid more attention to familiar words that French children typically begin to say at 14 to 18 months than to unfamiliar words of equal phonetic complexity (Hallé & de Boysson-Bardies, 1994).

By 13 months, most children understand that a word stands for a specific thing or event, and they can quickly learn the meaning of a new word (Woodward, Markman, & Fitzsimmons, 1994). But the addition of new words to their *expressive* (spoken) vocabulary is slower at first. A typical 15-month-old uses 10 different words or names (K. Nelson, 1973).

Vocabulary continues to grow throughout the single-word stage, which generally lasts until about 18 months of age. The most common early spoken words are *names* of things, either general ("bow-wow" for dog) or specific ("Unga" for one particular dog). Others are *action* words ("bye-bye"), *modifiers* ("hot"), words that express *feelings or relationships* (the ever-popular "no"), and a few *grammatical* words ("for") (K. Nelson, 1973, 1981). Sometime between 16 and 24 months a "naming explosion" occurs. Within a few weeks, a toddler goes from saying about 50 words to saying about 400 (Bates, Bretherton, & Snyder, 1988).

Sentences, Grammar, and Syntax

The next important linguistic breakthrough comes when a toddler puts two words together to express one idea ("Dolly fall"). Generally, children do this between 18 and 24 months—about 8 to 12 months after they say their first word—whether they are learning spoken language or are children of deaf parents and are learning sign language. However, this age range varies greatly. Although prelinguistic speech is fairly closely tied to chronological age, linguistic speech is not. Most children who begin talking fairly late catch up eventually, and many make up for lost time by talking nonstop to anyone who will listen! Furthermore, there does not seem to be a direct relationship between a child's rates of progress in the different aspects of language development. In one study, children who at 20 months of age were early talkers continued to be verbally precocious at age 4½ but did not tend to be early readers (Crain-Thoreson & Dale, 1992.)

A child's first sentence typically deals with everyday events, things, people, or activities (Braine, 1976; Rice, 1989; Slobin, 1973). This early speech is called "telegraphic" because, like most telegrams, it includes only essential words. When Rita says, "Damma deep," she seems to mean "Grandma is sweeping the floor." Telegraphic speech was once thought to be universal, but we now know that children vary in the degree to which they use it (Braine, 1976), and the form varies depending on the language being learned (Slobin, 1983). Word order conforms to some extent to what a child hears: Rita does not say "Deep Damma" when she sees her grandmother pushing a broom.

First sentences generally consist of nouns, verbs, and adjectives. Tense and case endings, articles, and prepositions are missing ("Dolly fall"), and frequently so are subjects or verbs ("Go bye-bye" and "Mommy sock"). As children's speech becomes more complex, they may string two-word couplings together ("Adam hit" and "Hit ball") to form a more complete thought ("Adam hit ball").

Sometime between 20 and 30 months, children acquire the fundamentals of **syntax**—the rules for putting sentences together in their language. They begin to use articles (*a, the*), prepositions (*in, on*), conjunctions (*and, but*), plurals, verb endings, past tense, and forms of the verb *to be* (*am, are, is*). By age 3, speech is fluent, longer, and more complex; although children often omit parts of speech, they get their meaning across well (R. Brown, 1973a, 1973b). At 2 years, 10 months, Maika said clearly and grammatically (despite her frustration), "I can't get this glove on my hand." This simple sentence, which she had never heard before, showed the impressive achievement that command of language represents. Language continues to develop, of course; by late childhood, children have become increasingly proficient in grammar and continue to enlarge their vocabulary and improve their style.

CHARACTERISTICS OF EARLY SPEECH

Young children's speech is not just an immature version of adult speech; it has a character all its own. This is true no matter what language a child is speaking (Slobin, 1971).

As we have already seen, children *simplify*. They use telegraphic speech to say just enough to get their meaning across ("No drink milk!"). Early speech also has several other distinct characteristics.

Children *understand grammatical relationships they cannot yet express*. At first, Erica may understand that a dog is chasing a cat, but she cannot string together enough words to express the complete action. Her sentence comes out as "Puppy chase" rather than "Puppy chase kitty."

Children *underextend word meanings*. Miranda's uncle gave her a toy car, which Miranda, at 13 months, called her "koo-ka." Then her father came home with a gift, saying, "Look, Miranda, here's a little car for you." Miranda shook her head. "Koo-ka," she said, and ran and got the one from her uncle. To her, *that* car—and *only* that car—was a little car, and it took some time before she called any other toy cars by the same name. Miranda was underextending the word *car* by restricting it to a single object.

Children also *overextend word meanings.* At 14 months, Eddie jumped in excitement at the sight of a gray-haired man on the television screen and shouted, "Gampa!" Eddie was overgeneralizing, or *overextending*, a word; he thought that because his grandfather had gray hair, all gray-haired men could be called "Grandpa." As children develop a larger vocabulary and get feedback from adults on the appropriateness of what they say, they overextend less. ("No, honey, that man looks a little like Grandpa, but he's somebody else's grandpa, not yours.")

Children *overregularize rules:* they apply them rigidly, not knowing that some rules have exceptions. When John says "mouses" instead of "mice" or Anna says "I thinked" rather than "I thought," this represents progress. Both children initially used the correct forms of these irregular words, but merely in imitation of what they heard. Once children learn grammatical rules for plurals and past tense (a crucial step in learning language), they apply them universally. The next step is to learn the exceptions to the rules, which they generally do by early school age.

HOW DO CHILDREN ACQUIRE FACILITY WITH LANGUAGE?

How do babies figure out the secrets of verbal communication? Is this ability learned or inborn? What determines how quickly and how well children learn to understand and speak their native language?

Nature Versus Nurture: The Historic Debate

In the 1950s, a debate raged between two schools of thought about language development—one led by B. F. Skinner, the foremost proponent of learning theory, the other by the linguist Noam Chomsky. Skinner (1957) maintained that language learning, like other learning, is based on experience. According to learning theory, children learn language in the same way they learn other kinds of behavior, through operant conditioning. At first, children utter sounds at random. Caregivers reinforce the sounds that resemble adult speech by smiling, paying attention, and talking to a child, and children repeat these reinforced sounds. Children also imitate the sounds they hear

adults making and, again, are reinforced for doing so. As this process continues, children learn to produce meaningful speech by generalizing from their experience.

Reinforcement and imitation probably do contribute to language development; but, as Chomsky (1957) persuasively argued, they cannot fully explain it (Flavell, Miller, & Miller, 1993). For one thing, linguistic rules and nuances of meaning are so many and so complex that they could not all be acquired by specific reinforcement and imitation. Furthermore, learning theory does not account for children's imaginative ways of saying things they have never heard. Anna, for example, described a sprained ankle as a "sprangle" and said she didn't want to go to sleep yet because she wasn't "yawny." The observation that deaf children make up their own sign language when they do not have models to follow strongly suggests that environmental influences alone cannot explain a young child's growing capacity for linguistic expression (H. Feldman, Goldin-Meadow, & Gleitman, 1979; Hoff-Ginsberg & Shatz, 1982).

Chomsky's own view, more widely accepted today, is called *nativism.* Chomsky (1957) proposed that the human brain has an inborn capacity for acquiring language; babies learn to talk as naturally as they learn to walk. This innate capacity allows very young children to figure out the syntax of any language they hear.

In support of this view, nativists point out that almost all children master their native language in the same age-related sequence without formal teaching. Furthermore, human beings, the only animals with spoken language, are the only species whose brain is larger on one side than on the other, suggesting that an inborn mechanism for language may be localized in the larger hemisphere (the left for most people).

Additional support for the nativist position comes from newborns' ability to differentiate similar sounds (Eimas et al., 1971). One researcher suggests that neonates can put sounds into categories because all human beings are "born with perceptual mechanisms that are tuned to the properties of speech." Children in English-speaking countries, for example, learn English rather than another language because contact with the sounds of a particular language leads children to "tune in" the corresponding preset "channels" and "tune out" unused ones (Eimas, 1985, p. 49).

How do babies go from simple sound recognition to the creation of complex utterances that follow the specific rules of their language? Chomsky (1972) proposed that an inborn *language acquisition device (LAD)* programs children's brains to analyze the language they hear and to extract from it the rules of grammar and syntax. Using these rules, they can then make up their own sentences. Still, the nativist approach does not explain why some children acquire language more rapidly and efficiently than others, why children differ in linguistic skill and fluency, how children come to understand the meanings of words, or why (as we'll see in a moment) speech development appears to depend on having someone to talk with.

Most developmentalists today believe that language acquisition, like most other aspects of development, depends on an intertwining of nature and nurture. Children probably do have an inborn capacity to acquire language, which is then activated and enhanced by maturation, cognitive development, and experience. Research during the past two or three decades has focused on specific influences, both within and outside the child, that contribute to this development.

Genetic and Temperamental Influences

A genetic influence is apparent in the moderate positive correlation between parents' intelligence and the rate at which their biological children develop communication skills during the first year of life. In adopted children, this correlation exists with their biological mothers but not with their adoptive parents (Hardy-Brown & Plomin, 1985; Hardy-Brown, Plomin, & DeFries, 1981).

Another influence on language development, which may be inborn, is temperament. According to one study (Slomkowski, Nelson, Dunn, & Plomin, 1992), children who at age 2 are happy, cooperative, and interested in other people are more advanced at ages 2, 3, and 7 in expressing themselves and responding to what other people say. This may be because extroverted children get more practice in speaking; they talk more, and they have the kind of personality that makes other people want to talk to them. As we will see in Chapter 5, the fit between a child's temperament and a parent's style of parenting affects the child's development. This interplay between a child's personality and the conditions parents create shows the bidirectional influence of individual and environment.

Environmental Influences: The Importance of Social Interaction

Many differences in language abilities that surface by the end of the second year reflect differences in environment, including how much and what kind of speech a child hears. Indeed, a highly influential view today is that *social interaction*—how adults talk with an infant or toddler, and how often—is crucial to language acquisition.

Language is a social act, which requires practice: The more parents or other adults talk with babies, the sooner babies can pick up the nuances of speech and correct wrong assumptions. By talking to babies, adults show how to use new words, structure phrases, and carry on a conversation. A review of the research literature concludes, "No child has been observed to speak a human language without having had a communicative partner from whom to learn" (Hoff-Ginsberg & Shatz, 1982, p. 22).

The value of frequent verbal interaction is supported by research on twins, who usually speak later than single-born children. An observational study of 15- and 21-month-olds suggests a reason: Harried mothers who must divide their attention between two babies the same age cannot interact individually with each twin as much as mothers of single babies do (Tomasello, Mannle, & Kruger, 1986). Mothers of twins speak less frequently to each child and have shorter conversations. Although twins have each other to talk to, and often develop a private language between themselves, their interaction is not as influential as the kind they would have with an adult.

How Parents and Caregivers Help Babies Learn to Talk Parents and other caregivers play an important role at each stage of an infant's speech development. At the babbling stage, adults help infants advance toward true speech by repeating the sounds a baby makes; the baby soon joins in the game and repeats the sounds back. Parents' imitation of babies' sounds affects the pace of language learning (Hardy-Brown & Plomin, 1985; Hardy-Brown, Plomin, & DeFries, 1981). It also helps babies experience the social aspect of speech, the sense that a conversation consists of taking turns, an idea most babies seem to grasp at about 7½ to 8 months of age.

Caregivers help babies understand spoken words by, for example, pointing to a doll and saying, "Please give me Kermit." If the baby doesn't respond, the adult may pick up the doll and say, "Kermit." A baby's ability to understand grows by discovering through language what another person is thinking. By 1 year, a baby has some sense of intentional communication, a primitive idea of reference, and a set of signals to communicate with familiar caregivers (Bates et al., 1987).

When babies begin to talk, parents or caregivers often help them by repeating their first words and pronouncing them correctly. The vocabularies of toddlers are related to how much their caregivers talk to them. A strong relationship has appeared between the frequency of various words in mothers' speech and the order in which children learn these words (Huttenlocher, Haight, Bryk, Seltzer, & Lyons, 1991). Vocabularies get a boost when adults seize an appropriate opportunity to teach children new words. If Elijah's mother says, "This is a ball" when Elijah is looking at the ball, he is more likely to remember the word than if he were playing with something else and she tried to divert his attention to the ball (Dunham, Dunham & Curwin, 1993). Adults help a toddler who has begun to put words together by expanding on what the child says. If Christina says "Mommy sock," her mother may reply, "Yes, that is Mommy's sock."

From early in their second year, children talk to their parents about what they see on television. They label objects, repeat slogans and jingles, and ask questions. Parents can build on the children's interest and lead them into exchanges that enhance language development (Lemish & Rice, 1986). These exchanges are crucial. Hearing speech on television is not enough; for example, Dutch children who watch German television every day do not learn German (C. E. Snow et al., 1976).

Socioeconomic status (SES) seems to affect the amount and quality of verbal interaction between parents and children, and also the children's long-range language and cognitive development. In one longitudinal study, 40 midwestern families with 7-month-old babies were initially observed in their homes for an hour each month until the children were 3 years old. The children's language usage was taped and analyzed. The parents with lower incomes and educational and occupational levels tended to spend less time in positive verbal interaction with their children; the children were exposed to less varied language and were given less opportunity to talk, and their own spoken vocabulary was more limited (B. Hart & Risley, 1989). A follow-up study, which repeatedly assessed 32 of the children between ages 5 and 10,

Not only mothers use child-directed speech, popularly known as "motherese." This simplified way of speaking to babies and toddlers also seems to come naturally to fathers, too, as well as to other adults and even to older children. *(Corroon/Monkmeyer)*

found that these differences in language experience and development in early childhood predicted linguistic and academic performance during the elementary school years (D. Walker, Greenwood, Hart, & Carta, 1994).

Child-directed Speech ("Motherese") You do not have to be a mother to speak "motherese." If you pitch your voice high, simplify your speech by using short words and sentences, speak slowly, ask questions, and repeat your words often when you speak to an infant or toddler, you are using *child-directed speech (CDS)*, or *motherese.* Most adults, and even children, do it naturally. Many researchers believe that CDS helps children learn their native language, or at least to pick it up faster; but some have questioned its value.

Those who consider CDS important believe that it serves several social, emotional, and linguistic functions. It helps adults and children develop a relationship. It teaches children how to carry on a conversation: how to introduce a topic, comment on and add to it, and take turns talking. It teaches them how to use new words, structure phrases, and put ideas into language. Because CDS is confined to simple, down-to-earth topics, children can use their own knowledge of familiar things to help them work out the meanings of the words they hear (C. E. Snow, 1972, 1977).

Some research has found positive correlations between the use of CDS and the rate of 2-year-olds' language growth (Hoff-Ginsberg, 1985, 1986). A study of language functioning in 2½-year-olds found modest support for the value of CDS but concluded that "the differences among mothers that predicted rate of language growth in their children were not differences in the use of motherese per se" (Hoff-Ginsberg, 1985, p. 384). Instead, the differences concerned an adult's goals in talking to a child: whether, for example, the adult used scaffolding (see Chapter 1), prodding the child to move up to the next level of language skill (Hoff-Ginsberg, 1986).

Investigators who challenge the value of CDS contend that children speak sooner and better if they hear and can respond to more complex speech from adults. Children can then select from this speech the parts they are interested in and are able to deal with. In fact, some researchers say, children discover the rules of language faster when they hear complex sentences that use these rules more often and in more ways (Gleitman, Newport, & Gleitman, 1984).

Studies in some nonwestern societies, in which CDS is rarely used and young children instead hear normal adult speech, suggest that simplified speech is not necessary to language development. Conversations among older family members may be an important model, for example, for learning the correct usage of personal pronouns such as *you* and *me*, which can refer to different people depending on the situation. Similarly, in a Canadian study, English-speaking second-born 21-month-olds, who experienced less speech directed *to* them than firstborn children and more complex *overheard* conversations between caregivers and older siblings, were more advanced in the use of personal pronouns at age 2 than were firstborns the same age, though the general language development of the two groups was about equal (Oshima-Takane, Goodz, & Derevensky, 1996).

If babies could vote in this debate, there is little doubt which side they would take. Infants prefer simplified speech. This preference is clear before 1 month of age, and it does not seem to depend on any specific experience (R. P. Cooper & Aslin, 1990). Parents usually do not start speaking CDS until babies show by their expressions, actions, and sounds that they have some understanding of what is being said to them. This interactive behavior on the infant's part encourages the use of CDS; in one study, women used it less when asked to make tapes addressed to unseen children (C. E. Snow, 1972).

Infants' preference for CDS is not confined to English. In a Canadian study, 4½- and 9-month-old babies of immigrants from Hong Kong whose native tongue was Cantonese were more attentive, interested, happy, and excited when shown a videotape of a Cantonese-speaking woman using CDS than when the woman used normal adult speech. Babies of English-speaking parents reacted similarly to the same tape, showing that the appeal of CDS extends even to an unfamiliar language (Werker, Pegg, & McLeod, 1994).

In a Japanese study, deaf mothers were videotaped reciting everyday sentences in sign language, first to their deaf 6-month-old infants and then to deaf adult friends. The mothers signed more slowly and with more repetition and exaggerated movements when directing the sentences to the infants, and other deaf infants the same age paid more attention and appeared more responsive when shown these tapes. It may be, then, that infants are equally predisposed to attend to motherese whether it be in spoken or in signed form (Masataka, 1996).

How adults talk to children teaches them the norms of their culture along with the rules of their language. A study of how 30 Japanese and 30 American mothers used CDS with their 6-, 12-, and 19-month-old babies found both universal and culturally specific features (Fernald & Morikawa, 1993). Both the Japanese and the American mothers simplified their language, repeated often, and spoke differently to babies of different ages. Differences appeared in the mothers' styles of interaction with the babies, which reflected cultural values about child rearing. For example, American mothers labeled objects more, attempting to expand the babies' vocabulary ("That's a car. See the car? You like it? It's got nice wheels"). Japanese mothers encouraged politeness by give-and-take routines ("Here! It's a vroom vroom. I give it to you. Now give this to me. Yes! Thank you"). Japanese mothers use CDS longer and more extensively than American mothers, whose culture places a higher value on fostering independence in children.

By reading aloud to his 2-year-old son and asking questions about the pictures in the book, this father is helping the boy build language skills and prepare to become a good reader. *(Anthony Wood/Stock, Boston)*

Directive versus Nondirective Speech *What* adults say to children may be almost as important as how and how often they speak. Too much direction—commands, requests, and instructions—does not help language development. Asking questions and elaborating on what children say is more effective in encouraging fluency (K. Nelson, 1973, 1981). In a study mentioned earlier, one factor in the delayed speech of twins was that when their mothers did speak to them, what they said consisted more of telling the child what to do than of conversational comments and questions; and the mothers were more likely to imitate what children said than to elaborate on it (Tomasello et al., 1986).

Among 2-year-olds in day care centers in Bermuda, children whose caregivers spoke to them often to give or ask for information rather than to control behavior had better language skills than children who did not have such conversations (McCartney, 1984). A possible explanation for the favorable effect of high socioeconomic status on language development may be that upper-middle-class American mothers tend to follow their children's conversational cues by answering questions or pursuing a topic the child has brought up; working-class mothers are more likely to give orders or directions (Hoff-Ginsberg, 1991).

These parental speaking styles influence whether children are *referential*, using their first words (mainly nouns and verbs) to *refer* to objects and events by naming and describing them, or *expressive*, using first words (often pronouns) to *ex-*

press social routines and repeat formulas such as "stop it" (Lieven, 1978; K. Nelson, 1981; Olsen-Fulero, 1982). Referential children, who learn new words faster than expressive children do (E. V. Clark, 1983), tend to be firstborns from better-educated families, whose parents encourage labeling by asking their children many questions. Parents of expressive children use more directive speech (K. Nelson, 1973).

PREPARING FOR LITERACY: THE BENEFITS OF READING ALOUD

From an early age, most children love to be read to, and the way parents or caregivers read to them can influence how well children speak and eventually how well they read. Reading to a child fosters parent-child conversation; when mothers and children play with toys together, the mothers are more likely to issue commands (Hoff-Ginsberg, 1991). Adults help a child's language development most when they paraphrase what the child says, expand on it, talk about what interests the child, remain quiet long enough to give the child a chance to respond, and ask specific questions (Rice, 1989). Read-aloud sessions offer a perfect opportunity for this kind of interaction.

A child will get more out of read-aloud sessions if adults ask challenging, open-ended questions rather than those calling for a simple yes or no ("What is the cat doing?" instead of "Is the cat asleep?"). In one study, 21- to 35-month-old children whose parents asked open-ended questions—and who added to the child's answers, corrected wrong ones, gave alternative possibilities, encouraged the child to tell the story, and bestowed praise—scored 6 months higher in vocabulary and expressive language skills than did a control group whose parents did not use these practices in reading to the children. The experimental group also got a boost in their *preliteracy skills,* the competencies helpful in learning to read, such as learning how letters look and sound (G. J. Whitehurst et al., 1988).

Children who are read to often, especially in this way, when they are 2 years old show better language skills at ages 2½ and 4½ (Crain-Thoreson & Dale, 1992). This may also be true of children with below-normal language abilities, who are at risk of developing reading problems. At a low-quality day care center in Mexico, teachers specially trained in these techniques read to 2-year-olds from low-income homes, where they were not read to frequently. After 6 or 7 weeks of one-on-one read-aloud sessions, these children did significantly better on standardized language tests and in spontaneous language usage than children whose teachers spent time with them individually doing arts and crafts (Valdez-Menchaca & Whitehurst, 1992).

✔ DEVELOPMENT OF COMPETENCE

Why do some children, at an early age, seem better able than others to overcome obstacles, get what they want, and function in their world? In 1965, Burton L. White and his colleagues began the Harvard Preschool Project to test and observe some 400 preschoolers and rate them on their cognitive and social competence (B. L. White, 1971; B. L. White, Kaban, & Attanucci, 1979). The researchers found significant individual differences related to factors in the children's environment.

The most competent children—the researchers called them A's—had such *social skills* as getting and holding the attention of adults in acceptable ways, using adults as resources, and showing both affection and hostility. They got along well with other children, were proud of their accomplishments, and tried to act grown up. They also showed a wide range of *cognitive skills:* they used language well, planned and carried out complicated activities, and could pay attention to a task while being aware of what else was going on. Children classified as B's were less accomplished

in these skills, and children classified as C's were very deficient. Follow-up studies 2 years later showed stability in the classifications.

To find out how the A and C children became the way they were, the researchers looked at their mothers' handling of the children's younger siblings. The researchers assumed that few fathers spent enough time with children of this age to be influential, an assumption they might not make today. They also assumed that the mothers acted the same with their younger children as they had with the older ones, an assumption that could not be tested.

Significant differences in mothering appeared after the younger siblings were about 8 months old. At this age, when babies are getting ready to understand language, the way parents talk to them is important. Then, too, as babies begin to crawl, some parents react with pleasure, some with annoyance. Since babies become attached to the person they spend the most time with, this person's personality is important.

The major differences in mothering revolved around three aspects of child rearing: the ability to "design" a child's world, to serve as a "consultant" for a child, and to provide a balance between freedom and restraint. Mothers from all socioeconomic levels fell into both groups; some welfare mothers raised A children, and some middle-class women raised C's.

The A mothers designed a safe physical environment full of interesting things to see and touch (common household objects as often as expensive toys). They were "on call" for their babies without devoting their entire lives to them. A number of these women had part-time jobs: those who stayed home full time generally spent less than 10 percent of their time interacting with their infants. They went about their daily routine but were available to answer a question, label an object, or share in a discovery. These women generally had positive attitudes toward life, enjoyed being with young children, and gave of themselves. They were energetic, patient, tolerant of messiness, and fairly casual about minor risks. They were firm and consistent, setting reasonable limits while showing love and respect. When they wanted to change an infant's behavior, they used distraction; for children over 1 year old, they used a combination of distraction, physical removal, and firm words.

The C mothers were a diverse group. Some were overwhelmed by life, ran chaotic homes, and were too absorbed in daily struggles to spend much

BOX 4-3   PRACTICALLY SPEAKING

HELPING CHILDREN BECOME MORE COMPETENT

The findings from the Harvard Preschool Project and from studies using the HOME (Home Observation for Measurement of the Environment) scales can be translated into the following guidelines for caregivers of babies and toddlers:

1 The best time for enhancing a child's competence is from the age of 6 to 8 months until about 2 years, but it is never too late.
2 Encourage children to have close social relationships with important people in their lives, especially from the first few months after their first birthday.
3 Give children help when they need it rather than press it on them too soon, ignore them, or see them as a burden to be dealt with quickly.
4 Stay fairly close to young children but do not hover so much that you discourage them from developing attention-seeking skills.
5 Talk to children about whatever they are interested in at the moment and play with them on their level instead of trying to redirect their attention to something else.
6 Speak with them. They will not pick up language from listening to the radio or television or overhearing conversations.

They need interaction with adults.
7 Create an environment that fosters learning—one that includes books, interesting objects, and a place to play.
8 Give them physical freedom to explore. Do not confine them regularly in a playpen, crib, jump seat, or small room.
9 Use punishment sparingly; instead, find opportunities for positive feedback.

SOURCES: Bradley et al., 1989; Bradley & Caldwell, 1982; Bradley et al., 1988; Stevens & Bakeman, 1985; B. L. White, 1971; B. L. White et al., 1979.

time with their children. Others spent *too much* time: hovering, being overprotective, pushing their babies to learn, and making them dependent. Some were physically present but rarely made real contact. They provided for their children materially but confined them in cribs or playpens.

The researchers identified several guidelines for successful parenting (see Box 4-3). However, they did not investigate the children's own contributions to their mothers' child-rearing styles. It is quite possible that the children of the A mothers had personalities that made their mothers

want to respond as they did. Perhaps they showed more curiosity, more independence, and more interest in what their mothers said and did than the C children.

Interaction is a key to much of childhood development: cognitive, emotional, and social. Children call forth responses from the people around them and they, in turn, react to those responses. In Chapter 5, we'll look more closely at these bidirectional influences as we explore early psychosocial development.

✔ SUMMARY

STUDYING COGNITIVE DEVELOPMENT: FOUR APPROACHES

- ■ Four major approaches to studying cognitive development in infants and children are the behaviorist, Piagetian, psychometric, and information-processing approaches.
- ■ The behaviorist approach is concerned with the mechanics of learning. Two simple types of learning that occur early in infancy are classical conditioning and operant conditioning; more complex learning may combine both.

- ■ The Piagetian approach is concerned with qualitative stages of cognitive development. During the sensorimotor stage, infants develop from primarily reflexive creatures to goal-oriented toddlers capable of symbolic thought.
- ■ Recent research suggests that a number of abilities develop earlier than Piaget described. These include object permanence, coordination of the senses, invisible and deferred imitation, the concept of number, and the ability to reason about physical phenomena.

■ The psychometric approach seeks to determine and measure quantitatively the factors that make up intelligence. Psychometric testing for infants emphasizes sensory and motor skills and may not measure the same thing that verbal tests do.

■ Psychometric tests of infant intelligence are generally poor predictors of intelligence in later childhood and adulthood. The Bayley Scales of Infant Development are widely used for the measurement of development in infants and toddlers.

■ The home and day care environments can affect measured intelligence. Parental responsiveness is associated with optimal cognitive development.

■ The information-processing approach is concerned with the processes underlying intelligent behavior: how people manipulate symbols and what they do with the information they perceive.

■ Indicators of the efficiency of infants' information processing include speed of habituation and dishabituation, visual novelty preference, and cross-modal transfer. These abilities also tend to predict later intelligence. Early visual attentiveness is a predictor of a toddler's exploratory competence. Information-processing ability is influenced by the responsiveness of significant adults.

LANGUAGE DEVELOPMENT

■ Prelinguistic speech, which precedes the first word, includes crying, cooing, babbling, and imitating language sounds. Neonates can distinguish speech sounds; by 6 months, babies have learned the basic sounds of their language.

■ Before they say their first word, babies use gestures, including pointing, conventional social gestures, representational gestures, and symbolic gestures.

■ By 9 or 10 months, babies begin to understand meaningful speech. During the second year of life, the typical toddler begins to speak the language of the culture. The first word typically comes sometime between 10 and 14 months, initiating linguistic speech. The first single words may be holophrases, which express a complete thought in a single word.

■ Linguistic speech, unlike prelinguistic speech, is not closely tied to chronological age. A "naming explosion" typically occurs sometime between 16 and 24 months of age. The first two-word sentences, which are called *telegraphic*, generally come between 18 and 24 months.

■ By age 3, grammar and syntax are fairly well developed. Early speech is characterized by simplification, underextending and overextending word meanings, and overregularizing rules.

■ Historically, two opposing views about how children acquire language were learning theory (which emphasizes the roles of reinforcement and imitation) and nativism (which maintains that people have an inborn capacity to acquire language). Today, most developmentalists hold that children have an inborn capacity to learn language and that it is activated and enhanced by maturation, cognitive development, and certain environmental experiences.

■ Specific influences on language development include genetic factors, temperament, and social interaction.

■ Communication between caregivers and children is essential to language development. The value of hearing simple, direct language (child-directed speech, or motherese) is not clear, though infants show a preference for it. Questioning and elaboration are more effective than directive speech, both in conversation and in reading aloud.

DEVELOPMENT OF COMPETENCE

■ Parents' child-rearing styles seem to affect children's cognitive and social competence.

■ Parents of the most competent children are those who know how to "design" a child's environment, serve as "consultants" for a child, and use appropriate controls.

✔ KEY TERMS

intelligent behavior (page 118)
behaviorist approach (119)
Piagetian approach (119)
psychometric approach (119)
information-processing approach (119)
classical conditioning (119)
operant conditioning (120)
sensorimotor stage (121)
schemes (121)

circular reactions (122)
representational ability (123)
deferred imitation (123)
object permanence (124)
invisible imitation (124)
visible imitation (124)
IQ (intelligence quotient) tests (129)
standardized norms (129)
validity (129)
reliability (129)

Bayley Scales of Infant Development (130)
habituation (132)
dishabituation (132)
visual novelty preference (133)
cross-modal transfer (133)
visual recognition memory (133)
exploratory competence (133)
language (134)
literacy (134)

prelinguistic speech (134)   syntax (138)   (140)
linguistic speech (137)   nativism(139)   child-directed speech (CDS), or
holophrase (137)   language acquisition device (LAD)   motherese (141)

✔ QUESTIONS FOR THOUGHT AND DISCUSSION

1 Watson and Rayner's experiment with "Little Albert" would violate today's ethical standards for research, yet it provided valuable information about human behavior. In an experiment such as this, where would you draw the line between society's need to learn and an infant's rights?

2 On the basis of observations by Piaget and others about early cognitive development, what factors would you consider in designing or purchasing a toy or book for an infant or a toddler?

3 What ethical questions should be considered in designing an intervention to enhance the cognitive development of disadvantaged infants and toddlers?

4 The HOME scale assesses the relationship between a toddler's home environment and the child's later cognitive functioning. If you were designing such a measure, what aspects of the home situation, if any, would you add to those mentioned in the text?

5 White and his colleagues tried to measure influences on competence by correlating a preschooler's social and cognitive skills with the way the mother handled an infant sibling. What is a key weakness of this research design? How else could a study be designed to achieve the goal of this research?

CHAPTER FIVE

PSYCHOSOCIAL DEVELOPMENT DURING THE FIRST THREE YEARS

I'm like a child
trying to do everything
say everything
and be everything
all at once

John Hartford,
"Life Prayer," 1971

ASK YOURSELF

✔ How do infants and toddlers develop distinct personalities?

✔ When do emotions develop, and how do babies show them?

✔ What role does temperament play in personality development?

✔ What is the importance of early experiences with parents?

✔ How do infants gain trust in their world and form attachments?

✔ How does the sense of self develop?

✔ How do toddlers develop autonomy and standards for socially acceptable behavior?

✔ How do infants and toddlers interact with other children?

✔ What is the impact of early day care?

At 2 years, 10 months, Anna shouted, "No! Won't go!" running away from Jonathan as soon as she saw him walk over to the sandbox. At this point, getting Anna to do anything her parents suggested had become a challenge. Even though Diane and Jonathan knew that their daughter's frequent negativity was a normal, healthy aspect of this stage of life, it was hard to keep smiling through the "terrible twos."

During the latter part of the first three years, the urge for self-determination often takes the form of resistance. Docile, trusting infants are transformed into strong-willed, sometimes ill-tempered little creatures with minds of their own. Beyond the tears and the tantrums, the "no's" and the noise, toddlers' emphatic expression of what *they* want to do signals the shift from the dependence of infancy to the growing independence of childhood. That shift, which is related to increasing physical and cognitive competence, has roots in personality development during infancy and in relationships with parents and others from the first day of life.

■ In this chapter we first examine the foundations of psychosocial development: emotions, temperament, and early experiences with parents. We consider Erik Erikson's theories about the formation of trust and the growth of autonomy. We look at patterns of attachment and their long-term effects, at early stirrings of the sense of self, and at the way children adopt socially accepted standards of behavior. We explore relationships with siblings and other children. Finally, we consider the increasingly widespread impact of early day care. ■

✔ FOUNDATIONS OF PSYCHOSOCIAL DEVELOPMENT

Although babies share common patterns of development, they also—from the start—show distinct personalities, which reflect both inborn and environmental influences. From infancy on, personality development is intertwined with social relationships (see Table 5-1).

EMOTIONS

Normal human beings have the same basic *emotions:* pleasant or unpleasant subjective feelings, such as sadness, joy, and fear, which motivate behavior. People differ, though, in how often they feel a particular emotion, what kinds of experiences produce it, and how they act as a result. Emotional reactions to events and people, which are tied to cognitive perceptions, are a basic element of personality.

Studying babies' emotions is a challenge. Does a baby's cry express anger, fear, loneliness, or discomfort? It will be a long time before the infant can tell us. Still, parents, caregivers, and researchers learn to recognize subtle cues. Carroll Izard and his colleagues, for example, have sought to identify infants' emotions from their facial expressions. In one study, the researchers videotaped 5-, 7-, and 9-month-olds playing games with their mothers, seeing a jack-in-the-box pop up, being given shots by a doctor, and being approached by a stranger. College students and health professionals who viewed the tapes interpreted the babies' facial expressions as showing joy, sadness, interest, and fear, and to a lesser degree anger, surprise, and disgust (Izard, Huebner, Resser, McGinness, & Dougherty, 1980). We do not know that these babies actually had the feelings they were credited with, but their facial expressions were remarkably similar to adults' expressions of these emotions; so it seems likely that they were experiencing similar feelings.

TABLE 5-1

Highlights of Infants' and Toddlers' Psychosocial Development, Birth to 36 Months

Approximate Age, Months	Characteristics
0–3	Infants are open to stimulation. They begin to show interest and curiosity, and they smile readily at people.
3–6	Infants can anticipate what is about to happen and experience disappointment when it does not. They show this by becoming angry or acting warily. They smile, coo, and laugh often. This is a time of social awakening and early reciprocal exchanges between the baby and the caregiver.
6–9	Infants play "social games" and try to get responses from people. They "talk" to, touch, and cajole other babies to get them to respond. They express more differentiated emotions, showing joy, fear, anger, and surprise.
9–12	Infants are intensely preoccupied with their principal caregiver, may become afraid of strangers, and act subdued in new situations. By 1 year, they communicate emotions more clearly, showing moods, ambivalence, and gradations of feeling.
12–18	Toddlers explore their environment, using the people they are most attached to as a secure base. As they master the environment, they become more confident and more eager to assert themselves.
18–36	Toddlers sometimes become anxious because they now realize how much they are separating from their caregiver. They work out their awareness of their limitations in fantasy and in play and by identifying with adults.

SOURCE: Adapted from Sroufe, 1979.

When Do Emotions Develop?

Very soon after birth, babies show signs of distress, interest, and disgust. Within the next few months these primary emotions differentiate into joy, anger, surprise, sadness, shyness, and fear. The emergence of these emotions seems to be governed by the biological "clock" of the brain's maturation (see Table 5-2). From an ethological perspective, this timetable may have value for survival. Expressions of distress by helpless 2-month-olds may bring the help they need; expressions of anger may mobilize 9-month-olds to help themselves— for example, to push away an offender (Trotter, 1983). The emotional timetable can be altered by extreme environmental influences; abused infants show fear several months earlier than other babies do (Gaensbauer & Hiatt, 1984).

Although the development of certain basic emotions seems to be universal, there may be cultural variations. In one study, 33 Japanese and American babies were videotaped as experimenters gently but firmly restrained the babies' arms for

TABLE 5-2

Timetable of Emotional Development

Emotion	Approximate Age of Emergence
Interest Distress (in response to pain) Disgust (in response to unpleasant taste or smell)	Present at birth or soon after
Anger, surprise, joy, fear, sadness, shyness	First 6 months
Empathy, jealousy, embarrassment	18–24 months
Shame, guilt, pride	30–36 months

SOURCES: Adapted from information in Izard & Malatesta, 1987; and M. Lewis, 1987, 1992.

up to 3 minutes. In both cultures, older babies seemed more distressed than younger ones. At 5 months, the Japanese babies showed a less intense reaction than the American babies did, but by 12 months babies in both cultures showed similar negative expressions (Camras, Oster, Campos, Miyake, & Bradshaw, 1992).

"Self-conscious" emotions, such as empathy, jealousy, embarrassment, shame, guilt, and pride, do not arise until the second and third year, after children have developed *self-awareness:* the understanding that they are separate from other people and things. As we discuss later in this chapter, self-awareness, which has been found to be present by 18 months, is necessary before toddlers can reflect on their actions and measure them against social standards (Izard & Malatesta, 1987; Kopp, 1982; M. Lewis, 1987; Stipek, Gralinski, & Kopp, 1990).

How Do Infants Show Their Emotions?

Newborns plainly show when they are unhappy. They let out piercing cries, flail their arms and legs, and stiffen their bodies. It is harder to tell when they are happy. During the first month, they become quiet at the sound of a human voice or when they are picked up, and they smile when their hands are moved together to play pat-a-cake. As time goes by, infants respond more to people—smiling, cooing, reaching out, and eventually going to them.

These early signals of babies' feelings are important steps in development. When babies want or need something, they cry; when they feel sociable, they smile or laugh. When their messages bring a response, their sense of connection with other people grows. Their sense of control over their world grows, too, as they see that their cries bring help and comfort and that their smiles and laughter elicit smiles and laughter in return.

As time goes by, the meaning of these emotional signals changes. At first, crying signifies physical discomfort; later, it more often expresses psychological distress. An early smile comes spontaneously as an expression of well-being; around 3 to 6 weeks, a smile may show pleasure in social contact (Izard & Malatesta, 1987).

Crying   Crying is the most powerful way—and sometimes the only way—infants can communicate their needs. Babies have four patterns of cry-

ing (P. H. Wolff, 1969): the basic *hunger cry* (a rhythmic cry, which is not always associated with hunger); the *angry cry* (a variation of the rhythmic cry, in which excess air is forced through the vocal cords); the *pain cry* (a sudden onset of loud crying without preliminary moaning, sometimes followed by holding the breath); and the *frustration cry* (two or three drawn-out cries, with no prolonged breath-holding). Babies in distress cry louder, longer, and more irregularly than hungry babies and are more apt to gag and interrupt their crying (Oswald & Peltzman, 1974).

Some parents worry that they will spoil a child by responding too much to crying, but that is not so. Just as parental responsiveness helps cognitive development, it also helps emotional development. Babies whose cries of distress bring relief seem to gain confidence in their power to affect their condition. By the end of the first year, babies whose mothers have regularly responded to their crying with tender, soothing care cry less (Ainsworth & Bell, 1977; S. Bell & Ainsworth, 1972). By 1 year, they are communicating more in other ways—with babbling, gestures, and facial expressions—while babies whose mothers punish or ignore them continue to cry more.

Smiling and Laughing   A baby's smile is irresistible. It sets in motion a cycle of trust and affection: adults smile back, and the infant's smile widens. Some infants smile much more than others do. A happy, cheerful baby who rewards caregiving efforts with smiles and gurgles is likely to form better relationships than one who smiles less often.

The earliest faint smile occurs spontaneously soon after birth, as a result of central nervous system activity. It frequently appears as the infant is falling asleep. In the second week, babies often smile drowsily after a feeding, possibly responding to the caregiver's sounds. After the second week, infants are more likely to smile when they are alert but inactive. At about 1 month, smiles become more frequent and more social. Babies this age smile when their hands are clapped together or when they hear a familiar voice. During the second month, as visual recognition develops, babies smile more at people they know. At about 3 months, their smiles become broader and longer-lasting (Kreutzer & Charlesworth, 1973; Sroufe & Waters, 1976; P. H. Wolff, 1963).

At about the fourth month, infants start to laugh

At 7 months, Daniel's winning smile shows that he enjoys his food—and the person who feeds him. A baby who rewards caregiving with smiles helps create an affectionate, trusting relationship with the caregiver. *(Ruth Duskin Feldman)*

out loud—perhaps at being kissed on the stomach, hearing various sounds, or seeing a parent do something unusual. As babies grow older, they laugh more often and at more things. A 4- to 6-month-old may giggle in response to sounds and touch; a 7- to 9-month-old laughs during a game of peekaboo. This change reflects cognitive development: by laughing at the unexpected, older babies show that they know what to expect. Laughter also helps babies discharge tension, such as fear of a threatening object (Sroufe & Wunsch, 1972).

TEMPERAMENT

Even in the womb, fetuses show unique personalities. They have different activity levels and favorite positions. After birth, these differences become even more apparent. Babies as young as 8 weeks show differences in emotional response (Izard, Hembree, et al., in Trotter, 1987). These patterns often persist, suggesting that temperament, or disposition, is largely inborn. A 2-month-old who screams in outrage when given a shot is likely to become just as infuriated at 19 months when a playmate takes away a toy; another 2-month-old who takes the shot more calmly will probably put up with later indignities without much fuss.

Temperament has been called the *how* of behavior: not *what* people do, but how they go about doing it (A. Thomas & Chess, 1984). Two toddlers, for example, may be equally able to dress themselves and equally motivated, but one may do it more quickly than the other, be more willing to put

on a new outfit, and be less distracted if the cat jumps on the bed.

Components and Patterns of Temperament

The New York Longitudinal Study (NYLS), begun in 1956 by Alexander T. Thomas, Stella C. Chess, and Herbert B. Birch, followed 133 infants into adulthood. Researchers interviewed, tested, and observed the participants and interviewed their parents and teachers.

This pioneering study found nine aspects or components of temperament that show up soon after birth and generally remain stable: (1) *activity level:* how and how much a person moves; (2) *rhythmicity, or regularity:* how predictable the biological cycles of hunger, sleep, and elimination are; (3) *approach or withdrawal:* what response a person initially makes to a new stimulus, such as a new toy, food, or person; (4) *adaptability:* how easily an initial response to a new or an altered situation is modified in a desired direction; (5) *threshold of responsiveness:* how much stimulation is needed to evoke a response; (6) *intensity of reaction:* how energetically a person responds; (7) *quality of mood:* whether a person's behavior is predominantly pleasant, joyful, and friendly or unpleasant, unhappy, and unfriendly; (8) *distractibility:* how easily an irrelevant stimulus can alter or interfere with a person's behavior; and (9) *attention span and persistence:* how long a person pursues an activity and continues in the face of obstacles (A. Thomas, Chess, & Birch, 1968).

TABLE 5-3

Three Temperamental Patterns

Easy Child	Difficult Child	Slow-to-Warm-Up Child
Has moods of mild to moderate intensity, usually positive	Displays intense and frequently negative moods; cries often and loudly; also laughs loudly	Has mildly intense reactions, both positive and negative
Responds well to novelty and change	Responds poorly to novelty and change	Responds slowly to novelty and change
Quickly develops regular sleep and feeding schedules	Sleeps and eats irregularly	Sleeps and eats more regularly than difficult child, less regularly than easy child
Takes to new foods easily	Accepts new foods slowly	Shows mildly negative initial response to new stimuli (like a first encounter with a new person, place, or situation)
Smiles at strangers	Is suspicious of strangers	
Adapts easily to new situations	Adapts slowly to new situations	
Accepts most frustrations with little fuss	Reacts to frustration with tantrums	
Adapts quickly to new routines and rules of new games	Adjusts slowly to new routines	Gradually develops liking for new stimuli after repeated, unpressured exposures

SOURCE: Adapted from A. Thomas & Chess, 1984.

To better appreciate how temperament affects behavior, let's look at three sisters. Aretha, the eldest, was a cheerful, calm baby who ate, slept, and eliminated at regular times. She greeted each day and most people with a smile, and the only sign that she was awake during the night was the tinkle of the musical toy in her crib. When Belinda, the second sister, woke up, she would open her mouth to cry before she even opened her eyes. She slept and ate little and irregularly; she laughed and cried loudly, often bursting into tantrums; and she had to be convinced that new people and new experiences were not threatening before she would have anything to do with them. The youngest sister, Clarissa, was mild in her responses, both positive and negative. She did not like most new situations, but if allowed to proceed at her own slow pace, she would eventually become interested and involved.

Almost two-thirds of the children in the New York Longitudinal Study fell into one of three categories exemplified by these three sisters (see Table 5-3). Forty percent were *easy children* like Aretha: generally happy, rhythmic in their biological functioning, and accepting of new experiences. Ten

percent were *difficult children* like Belinda: more irritable and harder to please, irregular in their biological rhythms, and more intense in expressing emotion. Fifteen percent were *slow-to-warm-up children* like Clarissa: mild but slow to adapt to new people and situations (A. Thomas & Chess, 1977, 1984).

Many children (including 35 percent of the NYLS sample) do not fit neatly into any of these three groups. A baby may have regular eating and sleeping schedules but be afraid of strangers. A child may be easy most of the time, but not always. Another child may warm up slowly to new foods but adapt quickly to new baby-sitters. All these variations are normal (A. Thomas & Chess, 1984).

Influences on Temperament

Temperamental differences seem to be inborn and largely hereditary (Braungart, Plomin, DeFries, & Fulker, 1992; Emde et al., 1992; A. Thomas & Chess, 1977, 1984). They also tend to be stable. In a longitudinal study, infants whose parents rated them as difficult were perceived as negative and relatively unadaptable at every age from 2 through

12. They were seen as intense and irregular in their habits; and the boys, especially, as highly active (Guerin & Gottfried, 1994).

However, environmental factors, such as parental treatment, can bring about considerable change. Among 148 firstborn infants, some, who at 3 months cried a lot and were given negative emotional ratings by their mothers, by 9 months smiled, laughed, and vocalized frequently. This kind of change tended to occur when parents were psychologically healthy and in a good marriage, had high self-esteem, and had harmonious relationships with their babies. Parents of babies who went from generally positive emotional states at 3 months to negative ones 6 months later showed more negative characteristics themselves (Belsky, Fish, & Isabella, 1991).

The way a mother feels about her roles may affect her child's temperament. In one analysis of NYLS data, mothers who were dissatisfied either with their jobs or with being homemakers were more likely to show intolerance, disapproval, or rejection of their 3-year-olds' behavior, and the rejected children were apt to become difficult (J. V. Lerner & Galambos, 1985).

Effects of Temperament on Adjustment: "Goodness of Fit"

About one-third of the NYLS participants developed behavior problems at some time. Most were mild disturbances that showed up between ages 3 and 5 and had cleared up by adolescence, but some remained or had grown worse by adulthood. No temperamental type was immune to trouble. Even easy children had problems when they were expected to act contrary to their temperamental style.

The key to healthy adjustment is a good fit between a child and the environmental demands and constraints parents or caregivers set up. If a very active child is expected to sit still for long periods, if a slow-to-warm-up child is constantly pushed into new situations, or if a persistent child is constantly taken away from absorbing projects, trouble may result. "Goodness of fit" between parent and child—the degree to which parents feel comfortable with their child's temperamental pattern—is an important factor in a child's adjustment. When parents recognize that a child acts in a certain way, not out of willfulness, laziness, or stupidity, but largely because of inborn temperament, they are less likely to feel guilty, anxious, or hostile or to be rigid or impatient. Rather than regard a child's temperament as an impediment, they can help the child make the most of it.

EARLIEST SOCIAL EXPERIENCES: THE CHILD IN THE FAMILY

Right from the start, the family has an enormous influence on a child's development. Was a birth planned and welcomed? How well do the personalities of parent and child mesh? Relationships formed in infancy affect the ability to form intimate relationships throughout life. Influence travels the other way, too. Children affect their parents' moods, priorities, plans, and even their marital relationship.

Family life near the turn of the twenty-first century is quite different from a century ago, and it probably will change even more in the future. A child growing up in the United States today is likely to have an employed mother, a father who is more involved in his children's lives than his own father was, and fewer siblings than in some earlier generations. The child is likely to receive a considerable amount of care from nonrelatives, perhaps outside the home. Today's children have a nearly 50 percent chance of living with only one parent, usually the mother and generally because there has been a divorce (Furukawa, 1994; Glick & Lin, 1986b).

In the past, research on infant psychosocial development focused almost exclusively on mothers and babies, but now researchers are studying relationships between infants and their fathers, siblings, and other caregivers. Another trend is to examine the family as a whole. How old are the parents? Are they healthy? What is their financial status? How many people live at home? Do the parents act differently when either one is alone with the baby than when all three are together? How does the quality of the marital relationship affect the relationship each spouse has with the baby? How does living in a single-parent household, in a stepfamily, or with grandparents or other relatives affect a baby's development? By looking at the family as a functioning unit, we get a fuller picture of the network of relationships among all its members.

Let's look first at the roles of the mother and father—how they care for and play with their babies and how their influence begins to shape differences between boys and girls. Later in this chapter, we look more deeply at children's relationships with parents and at the influence of siblings.

In a series of classic experiments, Harry Harlow and Margaret Harlow showed that food is not the most important way to a baby's heart. When infant rhesus monkeys could choose whether to go to a wire surrogate "mother" or a warm, soft terry-cloth "mother," they spent more time clinging to the cloth mother, even if they were being fed by bottles connected to the wire mother. *(Harry Harlow Primate Laboratory/University of Wisconsin)*

The Mother's Role

In a famous series of experiments, rhesus monkeys were separated from their mothers 6 to 12 hours after birth and raised in a laboratory. The infant monkeys were put into cages with one of two kinds of surrogate "mothers": a plain cylindrical wire-mesh form or a form covered with terry cloth. Some monkeys were fed from bottles connected to the wire "mothers"; others were "nursed" by the warm, cuddly cloth forms. When the monkeys were allowed to spend time with either kind of "mother," they all spent more time clinging to the cloth surrogates, even if they were being fed only by the wire forms. In an unfamiliar room, the babies "raised" by cloth surrogates showed more natural interest in exploring than those "raised" by wire surrogates, even when the appropriate "mothers" were there.

Apparently, the monkeys also remembered the cloth surrogates better. After a year's separation, the "cloth-raised" monkeys eagerly ran to embrace the terry-cloth forms, whereas the "wire-raised" monkeys showed no interest in the wire forms (Harlow & Zimmerman, 1959). None of the monkeys in either group grew up normally, however (Harlow & Harlow, 1962), and none was able to mother its own offspring (Suomi & Harlow, 1972).

It is hardly surprising that a dummy mother would not provide the same kind of stimulation and opportunities for development as a live mother. These experiments show that feeding is not the most important benefit babies get from their mothers. Mothering includes the comfort of close bodily contact and, in monkeys, the satisfaction of an innate need to cling. Human infants also have needs that must be satisfied if they are to grow up normally. A major task of developmental research is to find out what those needs are.

How and when does the special intimacy between mothers and their babies form? In 1976, two researchers concluded that if mother and baby are separated during the first hours after birth, the **mother-infant bond**—the mother's feeling of close, caring connection with her newborn—may not develop normally (Klaus & Kennell, 1976). However, follow-up research has not confirmed a critical time for bonding (Chess & Thomas, 1982; Lamb, 1982a, 1982b; Rutter, 1979b). Some mothers do seem to achieve closer bonding with their babies after early extended contact, but no long-term effects have been shown. This finding has relieved the worry and guilt sometimes felt by adoptive parents and parents who had to be separated from their infants after birth. (In another section of this chapter we discuss *attachment*, a two-way linkage that develops later in infancy.)

Since child-raising practices vary greatly around the world, we should be wary of conclusions drawn from experience in any one culture. For example, unlike American infants, who first have a close relationship with the mother and then pattern other ties after it, infants among the Efe people of the African country of Zaire have intimate interactions with many adults from birth. Efe infants typically receive care from five or more people in a given hour and are routinely breastfed by other women as well as by their mothers. At age 3, they spend about 70 percent of their time with people other than their mothers (Tronick, Morelli, & Ivey, 1992). This social pattern may result in a distinctive set of social skills. Unlike American babies, who spend more time alone or with just one or two family members and may learn to amuse themselves earlier than Efe babies, the Efe may learn to be more sociable at an earlier age. We need to remember, then, that patterns of psychological development we take for granted may be culture-based.

Even in western cultures, the mother-infant bond is not the only meaningful tie that babies form. Mothers may suckle infants, but other people—fathers, other caregivers, siblings, and grand-parents—also comfort and play with them and give them a sense of security. Fathers are especially important.

The Father's Role

The days of ignoring or minimizing a father's contribution to his child's development seem to be over. Developmental researchers are devoting more study to the father's role in an infant's life, and the findings underscore the importance of fathering.

Fathers form close bonds with their babies soon after birth. Proud new fathers admire their babies and pick them up. The babies contribute to the bond simply by doing the things normal babies do: opening their eyes, grasping their fathers' fingers, or moving in their fathers' arms.

Despite a common belief that women are biologically predisposed to care for babies, men can be just as sensitive and responsive (Lamb, 1981). Today, the amount of child care by men in industrialized countries is increasing (Lamb, 1987b). Still, although fathers generally believe they should be involved in their children's lives, most are not nearly as involved as mothers are (Backett, 1987; Boulton, 1983; LaRossa, 1988; LaRossa & LaRossa, 1981). For example, although studies in Jamaican and middle-class African American families show strong paternal involvement, in both groups the mothers are more involved (Roopnarine, Brown, Snell-White, & Riegraft, 1995; Hossain & Roopnarine, 1994). The fathers spend more time playing with their babies than feeding or bathing them—a pattern other studies have found to be characteristic of American fathers (Easterbrooks & Goldberg, 1984). Even mothers who work full time spend more time taking care of their babies than the fathers do (Pedersen, Cain, & Zaslow, 1982).

Fathers who are closely involved with their babies exert a significant influence. One study of 48 working-class Irish fathers, which found a high level of child care, also found a strong relationship between father care and the babies' cognitive development at 1 year. The men most likely to care for their infants were younger, happily married men who had been present at the birth of their children and who had modified their work schedules to share domestic duties (Nugent, 1991). In another study, a group of toddlers, two-thirds of whose mothers worked outside the home, showed benefits of the father's involvement in caring for and playing with them, especially when his attitude was sensitive and positive. The father had a particularly strong influence on competence in problem solving (Easterbrooks & Goldberg, 1984).

American fathers tend to play vigorously with infants and toddlers: throwing them up in the air, wrestling, or—as this father is doing—taking them out for a brisk run. However, this is not true in all cultures. *(Norman Y. Lono/NYT Pictures)*

In the United States, fathers tend to act differently with their babies than mothers do. Fathers "play rough": they toss infants up in the air and wrestle with toddlers, whereas mothers typically play gentler games and sing and read to babies (Lamb, 1977; Parke & Tinsley, 1981; Yogman, 1984; Yogman, Dixon, Tronick, Als, & Brazelton, 1977). Vigorous play with fathers offers an infant excitement and a challenge to conquer fears (Lamb, 1981). However, a highly physical style of play is not typical of fathers in all cultures. Swedish and German fathers usually do not play with their babies this way (Lamb, Frodi, Frodi, & Hwang, 1982; Parke, Grossman, & Tinsley, 1981). African Aka fathers (Hewlett, 1987) and fathers in New Delhi, India, also tend to play gently with their small children (Roopnarine, Hooper, Ahmeduzzaman, & Pollack, 1993; Roopnarine, Talokder, Jain, Josh, & Srivastav, 1992). Such cross-cultural variation casts doubt on the idea that rough play is a function of male biology; instead, it seems to be culturally influenced.

How Parents Shape Gender Differences

In research on infants' temperament—including their activity level, irritability, and interest in exploring their surroundings—findings of gender differences before age 2 have rarely held up when the studies were repeated. However, parental shaping of boys' and girls' personalities, whether conscious or not, begins very early. Parents behave differently toward baby boys than toward baby girls. Boys get more attention; girls are encouraged to smile more and to be more social (Birns, 1976). Mothers' facial expressions show a wider range of emotion with baby daughters than with baby sons; perhaps this explains why girls are better than boys at interpreting emotional expressions (Malatesta, in Trotter, 1983).

Fathers treat boys and girls more differently than mothers do, even during the first year (M. E. Snow, Jacklin, & Maccoby, 1983). During the second year, this difference intensifies: fathers talk more and spend more time with sons than with daughters (Lamb, 1981). Fathers, more than mothers, seem to promote *gender-typing*—the process by which children learn the behavior that their culture considers appropriate for each sex (Bronstein, 1988).

Home observations of 12-month-old, 18-month-old, and 5-year-old children found the biggest gender differences at 18 months, when both mothers and fathers fostered gender-typed play. Parents encouraged girls to communicate but discouraged boys' efforts to do so. Boys received more positive reactions for aggressive behavior and for playing with "boys' toys" and fewer positive responses from their fathers (but not their mothers) for playing with "girls' toys." By the time children were 5 years old, parents treated both sexes about the same—possibly because the children had already become gender-typed and needed no more influence in that direction (Fagot & Hagan, 1991).

✔ DEVELOPMENTAL ISSUES IN INFANCY

How does a dependent newborn, with a limited emotional repertoire and pressing physical needs, become a 3-year-old with complex feelings, a strong will, and the beginnings of a conscience? Much of this development revolves around issues regarding the self in relation to others. In this section, we look at the development of trust and attachment in infancy, at emotional communication between infants and caregivers, and at stranger anxiety and separation anxiety—developments that pave the way for the very different issues of toddlerhood.

DEVELOPING TRUST

For a far longer period than the young of other mammals, human babies are dependent on other people for food, for protection, and for their very lives. How do they come to trust that their needs will be met? According to Erikson (1950), early experiences are the key.

The first of the eight crises, or critical developmental stages, Erikson identified is *basic trust versus basic mistrust* (refer back to Table 1-5). This stage begins in infancy and continues until about 18 months. In these early months, babies develop a sense of how reliable the people and objects in their world are. They need to develop a balance between trust (which lets them form intimate relationships) and mistrust (which enables them to protect themselves). If trust predominates, as it should, children develop the "virtue" of *hope:* the belief that they can fulfill their needs and obtain their desires (Erikson, 1982). If mistrust predominates, children will view the world as unfriendly and unpredictable and will find it difficult to form relationships.

This baby, like most infants, is developing a strong attachment to his mother. Secure attachment thrives when a mother is affectionate, attentive, and responsive to a baby's signals. *(David Young–Wolff/PhotoEdit)*

The critical element in developing trust is sensitive, responsive, consistent caregiving. Erikson saw the feeding situation as the setting for establishing the right mix of trust and mistrust. Can the baby count on being fed when hungry, and can the baby therefore trust the mother as a representative of the world? Trust enables an infant to let the mother out of sight "because she has become an inner certainty as well as an outer predictability" (Erikson, 1950, p. 247).

Mothers or other primary caregivers are not the only important influences on the development of trust or mistrust. A child's own contribution can be substantial.

DEVELOPING ATTACHMENTS

When Ahmed's mother is near, he looks at her, smiles at her, talks to her, and crawls after her. When she leaves, he cries; when she comes back, he squeals with joy. When he is frightened or unhappy, he clings to her. Ahmed has formed his first attachment to another person.

Attachment is an active, affectionate, reciprocal, enduring relationship between two people whose interaction continues to strengthen their bond. It is what is often meant by *love*. As Mary Ainsworth (1979), a pioneering researcher on attachment, has said, it may be "an essential part of the ground plan of the human species for an infant to become attached to a mother figure" (p. 932).

Virtually any activity on a baby's part that leads to a response from an adult can be an attachment-seeking behavior: sucking, crying, smiling, clinging, and looking into the caregiver's eyes. As early as the eighth week of life, babies direct some of these behaviors more to their mothers than to anyone else. These overtures are successful when the mother responds warmly, expresses delight, and gives the baby frequent physical contact and freedom to explore (Ainsworth, 1969).

Ainsworth (1964) described four overlapping stages of attachment behavior during the first year:

1 Before about 2 months, infants respond indiscriminately to anyone.
2 At about 8 to 12 weeks, babies cry, smile, and babble more to the mother than to anyone else but continue to respond to others.
3 At 6 or 7 months, babies show a sharply defined attachment to the mother. Fear of strangers may appear between 6 and 8 months.
4 Meanwhile, babies develop an attachment to one or more other familiar figures, such as the father and siblings.

This sequence seems to be common in western societies but does not necessarily apply to babies in cultures where there are numerous caregivers from birth on.

Studying Patterns of Attachment: The Strange Situation

Ainsworth first studied attachment in the early 1950s with John Bowlby (1951). Both were con-

TABLE 5-4

Summary of Episodes in the Strange Situation

Episode	Persons Present	Duration	Brief Description of Action
1	Mother, baby, and observer	30 sec.	Observer introduces mother and baby to experimental room, then leaves.
2	Mother and baby	3 min.	Mother is nonparticipant while baby explores; if necessary, play is stimulated after 2 minutes.
3	Stranger, mother, and baby	3 min.	Stranger enters. First minute: Stranger silent. Second minute: Stranger converses with mother. Third minute: Stranger approaches baby. After 3 minutes mother leaves unobtrusively.
4	Stranger and baby	3 min. or less*	First separation episode. Stranger's behavior is geared to that of baby.
5	Mother and baby	3 min. or more†*	First reunion episode. Mother greets and comforts baby, then tries to settle him or her again in play. Stranger leaves. Mother then leaves, saying "bye-bye."
6	Baby alone	3 min. or less*	Second separation episode.
7	Stranger and baby	3 min. or less*	Continuation of second separation. Stranger enters and gears behavior to that of baby.
8	Mother and baby	3 min.	Second reunion episode. Mother enters, greets baby, then picks him or her up. Meanwhile stranger leaves unobtrusively.

*Episode is curtailed if the baby is unduly distressed.
†Episode is prolonged if more time is required for the baby to become reinvolved in play.

SOURCE: Adapted from Ainsworth et al., 1978, p. 37.

vinced of the importance of the mother-baby bond (see Chapter 1). After studying attachment in African babies in Uganda through naturalistic observation in their homes (Ainsworth, 1967), Ainsworth changed her approach and devised the *Strange Situation,* a now-classic technique designed to assess attachment patterns between an infant and an adult in the laboratory. Typically, the adult is the mother (though other adults have taken part as well), and the infant is 10 to 24 months old.

The Strange Situation consists of a sequence of eight episodes (see Table 5-4), which take place in less than a half hour. During that time, the mother twice leaves the baby in an unfamiliar room, the first time with a stranger. The second time she leaves the baby alone, and the stranger comes back before the mother does. The mother then encourages the baby to explore and play again and gives comfort if the baby seems to need it (Ainsworth, Blehar, Waters, & Wall, 1978). Of particular con-

cern is the response of the baby each time the mother returns.

When Ainsworth and her colleagues observed 1-year-olds in the Strange Situation and also at home, they found three main patterns of attachment: *secure attachment* (the most common category, into which 66 percent of American babies fell) and two forms of anxious, or insecure, attachment: *avoidant attachment* (20 percent of American babies) and *ambivalent, or resistant, attachment* (12 percent). Later, other research (Main & Solomon, 1986) identified a fourth pattern, *disorganized-disoriented attachment.*

Securely attached babies cry or protest when the mother leaves and greet her happily when she returns. They use her as secure base, leaving her to go off and explore but returning occasionally for reassurance. They are usually cooperative and relatively free of anger.

Avoidant babies rarely cry when the mother leaves, and they avoid her on her return. They tend to be angry and do not reach out in time of need. They dislike being held but dislike being put down even more.

Ambivalent (resistant) babies become anxious even before the mother leaves and are very upset when she goes out. When she returns, they show their ambivalence by seeking contact with her while at the same time resisting it by kicking or squirming. Resistant babies do little exploring and are hard to comfort.

Babies with *disorganized-disoriented* attachment often show inconsistent, contradictory behaviors. They greet the mother brightly when she returns but then turn away or approach without looking at her. They seem confused and afraid. This may be the least secure pattern. It seems to occur in babies whose parents have suffered unresolved trauma, such as loss or abuse (Main & Hesse, 1990).

Almost all research on attachment has been based on the Strange Situation. This research has yielded findings (some of them discussed below) that help us understand attachment, but critics question its conclusions. The Strange Situation *is* strange; it's also artificial. It sets up a series of eight brief, controlled episodes. It asks mothers not to initiate interaction, exposes babies to repeated comings and goings of adults, and expects the infants to pay attention to them. Since attachment influences a wider range of behaviors than are seen in the Strange Situation, some researchers have called for a more comprehensive, sensitive method of measuring it, one that will allow us to see how mother and infant interact during natural, non-stressful situations (T. M. Field, 1987).

It has been suggested that the Strange Situation may be especially inappropriate for studying attachment in children of employed mothers, who are used to routine separations from their mothers and the presence of other caregivers (K. A. Clarke-Stewart, 1989; L. W. Hoffman, 1989). However, a direct comparison of 15-month-old toddlers who had received varying amounts of day care virtually from birth found no difference in attachment, as measured by the Strange Situation, between children who received 30 or more hours of day care per week and those who received fewer than 10 hours. Thus the Strange Situation appears to be equally valid for children with and without early and extensive child care (NICHD Early Child Care Research Network, 1996).

The Strange Situation may, however, be less valid in other cultures. Research on Japanese infants, who are less commonly separated from their mothers than are American babies, showed high rates of resistant attachment, which may reflect the extreme stressfulness of the Strange Situation for these babies (Miyake, Chen, & Campos, 1985). The Strange Situation also seems to be inappropriate for assessing the attachment of children who have disabilities such as Down syndrome (Vaughn et al., 1994).

Some researchers have begun to supplement the Strange Situation with other methods, such as a Q-sorting technique. In this procedure, observers may sort a set of descriptive words or phrases ("cries a lot"; "tends to cling") into categories ranging from most to least characteristic of the child. In the Waters and Deane (1985) Attachment Q-set, raters compare descriptions of a child's actual behavior with descriptions of the "hypothetical most secure child." We will undoubtedly learn more about attachment as researchers develop and use more diversified ways of measuring it.

How Attachment Is Established

Both mother and baby contribute to security of attachment by their personalities and behavior and the way they respond to each other. On the basis of a baby's interactions with the mother, said Ainsworth, the baby builds a "working model" of what can be expected from her. The various patterns of emotional attachment represent different cognitive representations that result in different expectations. As long as the mother continues to act the same way, the model holds up. If her behavior changes—not just once or twice but consistently—the baby may revise the model, and security of attachment may change. In one study, almost half of a group of 43 middle-class babies changed attachment patterns between ages 12 and 19 months, most becoming more securely attached (R. A. Thompson, Lamb, & Estes, 1982). This may happen as new mothers gain experience and skill and feel better about being mothers (Egeland & Farber, 1984).

A baby's working model of attachment is related to Erikson's concept of basic trust. Secure attachment evolves from trust; insecure attachment reflects mistrust. Securely attached babies have learned to trust not only their caregivers but their own ability to get what they need. Thus babies who fuss and cry a lot and whose mothers respond by soothing them tend to be securely attached (Del Carmen, Pederson, Huffman, & Bryan, 1993).

Mothers of securely attached 1-year-olds generally have been sensitive to their infants throughout the first year of life (Isabella, 1993). They take their cues from their babies about when to feed them, and they respond to the babies' signals to stop, slow down, or speed up feeding (Ainsworth, 1979). Mothers who have affectionate, attentive, and responsive interactions with their 5-month-olds tend to have positive personalities, higher levels of education, and supportive husbands (Fish, Stifter, & Belsky, 1993). Attachment does not depend on speech; hearing-impaired toddlers are as likely to be securely attached as children with normal hearing (Lederberg & Mobley, 1990).

The more anxious a mother was while pregnant, the less securely attached her 1-year-old is likely to be (Del Carmen et al., 1993). After birth, a mother's emotional state continues to affect her baby. In one study (Stifter, Coulehan, & Fish, 1993), babies of employed mothers who were highly anxious about being away from home tended to develop avoidant attachments, as measured at 18 months by the Strange Situation. The mothers' anxiety seemed to express itself in overintrusiveness. In a laboratory free-play session when the babies were 10 months old, these mothers had stimulated their babies too much, had taken away objects when the baby was still interested in them, and had not let the baby influence the focus and pace of play. The mother's employment itself does not seem to be at the root of such behaviors but rather her *feelings* about working and the separation it causes. Some employed mothers may be overcontrolling because they feel a need to compensate for their absences.

There has been less study of attachment to the father than of attachment to the mother, but both attachments follow similar patterns. Babies develop attachments to both parents at about the same time, and security of attachment to father and mother is quite similar (N. A. Fox, Kimmerly, & Schafer, 1991). As early as 3 months after birth, it may be possible to predict the security of attachment between father and baby. Fathers who show delight in their 3-month-olds, respond with sensitivity to their needs, place a high priority on spending time with them, and see themselves as important in their babies' development are likely to have infants who are securely attached at 1 year (Cox, Owen, Henderson, & Margand, 1992). Fathers of securely attached infants tend to be more extraverted and agreeable than fathers of insecure infants; they have more loving, communicative marriages and report more positive interaction between their work and family roles (Belsky, 1996).

The similarity of attachment to both parents suggests that the baby's temperament may be an important factor (N. A. Fox et al., 1991); but researchers disagree about how much influence temperament exerts (Vaughn et al., 1992). Some studies have identified frustration levels, amounts of crying, and irritability as temperamental predictors of attachment (Calkins & Fox, 1992; Izard, Haynes, Chisholm, & Baak, 1991). Neurological or physiological conditions may underlie temperamental differences in attachment. For example, variability in heart rate is associated with irritability, and heart rate seems to vary more in insecurely attached infants (Izard, Porges, Simons, Haynes, & Cohen, 1991). In one study of attachment to the father, the infant's temperament did not appear to influence whether attachment was secure or insecure, but *did* seem to affect the type of insecure attachment. Insecure-avoidant babies tended to be seen by their fathers as having more positive temperamental characteristics than did insecure-resistant babies (Belsky, 1996).

A baby's temperament may have an indirect impact on attachment through its effect on the parents. In one study of 114 white middle-class mothers and their 2½- to 13-month-old infants, insecurely attached babies (as measured by the Strange Situation) cried more, demanded more attention, and showed more sadness and anger than securely attached infants. The mothers of the insecurely attached babies also felt more insecure and helpless; they were angrier and sadder but were less open about showing these feelings than the mothers of the securely attached babies, who tended to be more sociable, nurturant, and empathic. The mothers' and babies' emotional states probably fed on each other. The insecure babies' behavior may have made their mothers feel sad, angry, and helpless; and the mothers' behavior, in turn, probably affected the babies (Izard, Haynes et al., 1991).

A recent study of infants from 6 to 12 months and their families (which used frequent home observations, maternal reports, and Q-sorts in addition to the Strange Situation) suggests that both a mother's sensitivity and her baby's temperament are important in establishing attachment patterns. Further research may turn up additional factors.

Both Anna and Diane contribute to the attachment between them by the way they act toward each other. The way the baby molds herself to her mother's body shows her trust and reinforces Diane's feelings for her child, which she then displays through sensitivity to Anna's needs. Again we see how babies actively influence their world. *(Jonathan Finlay)*

As with other issues concerning temperament, "goodness of fit" between parent and child may well be a key to understanding security of attachment (Seifer, Schiller, Sameroff, Resnick, & Riordan, 1996).

Long-Term Effects of Attachment

The more secure a child's attachment to a nurturing adult, the easier it seems to be for the child eventually to become independent of that adult. The relationship between attachment and characteristics that appear years later underscores the continuity of development and the interrelationship of emotional, cognitive, and physical development.

From ages 3 to 5, securely attached children are more curious and more competent, get along better with other children, and are more likely to form close friendships (Arend, Gove, & Sroufe, 1979; J. L. Jacobson & Wille, 1986; Waters, Wippman, & Sroufe, 1979; Youngblade & Belsky, 1992). They are also more independent in preschool, seeking help from teachers only when they need it (Sroufe, Fox, & Pancake, 1983).

Their advantages continue into middle childhood and adolescence (Sroufe, Carlson, & Shulman, 1993). When 10- and 11-year-olds were observed in summer day camp, those with histories of secure attachment were better at making and keeping friends and functioning in a group than

children who had been classified as avoidant and resistant. They were also more self-reliant and adaptable and better physically coordinated. In a reunion of 15-year-olds who had gone to camp together, the adolescents who had been securely attached in infancy were rated higher on emotional health, self-esteem, ego resiliency, and peer competence by their counselors and peers and by the researchers who observed them. They also scored high in "capacity to be vulnerable," or openness to feelings.

If children, on the basis of early experience, have positive expectations about their ability to get along with others, and if they think well of themselves, they may set up social situations that tend to reinforce these beliefs and the gratifying interactions that result from them (Sroufe et al., 1993). Conversely, children with insecure attachment often have other problems: inhibitions at age 2, hostility toward other children at age 5, and dependency during the school years (Calkins & Fox, 1992; Lyons-Ruth, Alpern, & Repacholi, 1993; Sroufe et al., 1993).

However, it may be that the correlations between attachment in infancy and later development stem, not from attachment itself, but from personality characteristics that affect both attachment and parent-child interactions *after* infancy (Lamb, 1987a). Because interaction patterns are often set early and remain consistent over the years, it is hard to tell when they are most influential.

LIFE-SPAN ISSUE
DO ATTACHMENT PATTERNS SPAN GENERATIONS?

Mary Main is a professor of developmental and biological psychology at the University of California, Berkeley. Her research focuses on individual differences in attachment-related behavior and its mental representations during infancy, middle childhood, and adulthood. Together with her students at Berkeley and elsewhere, she has discovered a fourth category of infant attachment, disorganized-disoriented attachment (which we have already discussed), and has devised a method of assessing attachment status in adulthood, called the Adult Attachment Interview. *Her findings have been widely replicated in the United States and Europe.*

Is it possible to predict, before a baby's birth, how securely attached the baby will be? Research suggests that the answer is yes. Parents who can clearly, coherently, and consistently describe their own early experiences with attachment figures—whether those experiences were favorable or unfavorable, secure or insecure—tend to have babies who become securely attached to *them* (Main, 1995; Main, Kaplan, & Cassidy, 1985).

The Adult Attachment Interview (AAI; George, Kaplan, & Main, 1985) is a semi-structured interview that calls for general and specific recollections about childhood relationships with parents or other caregivers. Participants are asked which five adjectives best describe their relationship with each parent, why the adjectives are appropriate, and to which parent they felt closest. They are also asked about childhood experiences of rejection, separation, loss, and abuse, and about incidents of being upset, hurt, or ill. They are asked why they think their parents behaved as they did, how relationships with parents affected their own behavior, and how those relationships have changed.

Most interviewees fall into one of three categories: *autonomous* (secure) or one of two insecure classifications, *dismissing* and *preoccupied. Autonomous* adults are not necessarily those with the most positive childhood memories; they are those who can talk coherently about their memories and assess them accurately. *Dismissing* adults tend to put attachment-related experiences out of their minds. They may claim to be unable to remember such experiences, even though they have no trouble remembering other events of their childhood. Or they may describe their attachment-related experiences in glowing terms that are contradicted by other things they say. *Preoccupied* adults seem to be obsessed with memories about the objects of their attachment but describe them in a confused, angry, or passive way. A fourth group, *unresolved/disorganized* adults,

usually have suffered childhood loss, abuse, or other trauma that was not emotionally resolved. Adults who become disorganized or disoriented in attempting to discuss such events may not show this pattern all the time, so they generally are also placed in one of the other three categories (Main, 1990, 1993; Main & Hesse, 1990). Finally, a fifth group of adults has been identified whose way of speaking about early attachment experiences fails to fit any single category or shifts unpredictably during the interview (Hesse, 1996). Recent studies show that these adults—termed *cannot classify*—are overrepresented in clinical and criminal populations.

An analysis of 18 studies using the AAI found that it reliably predicts the quality of attachment between the parent being interviewed and the infant, as seen during the Strange Situation (van IJzendoorn, 1995). The security of the infant's responses to the parent was predicted by the security of the parent's responses to the AAI about 75 percent of the time. In 4 of these studies, women expecting their first child were given the AAI during pregnancy, and the predictions held up when the infants' attachment was measured (see especially Fonagy, Steele, & Steele, 1991).

How does intergenerational transmission of attachment patterns occur? Apparently, adults' ability to be clear, coherent, and consistent in recalling their early experiences and the consequences of these experiences affects the way they treat their own children. Let's say that Katya, an insecurely attached baby, grows up with a mental working model of her mother as rejecting and of herself as unlovable. Unless this distorted self-image is later revised—perhaps through psychotherapy, through a secure attachment to her husband, or through mature, thoughtful reflection on her childhood experiences—Katya's memory of her relationship with her mother may lead her to misinterpret her baby's attachment behaviors and respond inappropriately. ("How can this child want to love me? How could anybody?") In turn, Katya's insensitivity to the baby's signals misleads the baby, making it difficult for the infant to form a working model of a loving, accepting mother and a lovable self. On the other hand, Katya's husband, who was securely attached to his parents, accurately recognizes the baby's attachment behaviors, responds encouragingly, and helps the baby form a secure attachment to him (Bretherton, 1990).

In a study of infants, their mothers, and their maternal grandmothers using the AAI and the Strange Situation (administered when the infants were 12 months old), attachment categories of 65 percent of the family groups were consistent across all three generations. The mothers' classifications remained stable from pregnancy throughout the child's first year, suggesting that a consistent maternal state of mind is involved in attachment behavior. This state of mind appears to be communicated to the child, especially when the mother is under stress (Benoit & Parker, 1994).

The working model a mother retains from her childhood relationships can affect her relationship with her child well beyond infancy. Forty-five mothers were video-taped helping their 16-month- to 5-year-old children solve a puzzle. Mothers with secure working models (as measured by the AAI) tended to have securely attached children (as measured by the Attachment Q-set) and to show more sensitivity in interacting with them than insecure mothers did. The quality of the mother's marriage made a difference; insecure mothers were more likely to have securely attached children if the marriage was strong (Eiden, Teti, & Corns, 1995).

This line of research shows promise for identifying prospective parents at risk for developing unhealthy attachment patterns with their children. Much more research will have to be done to develop interventions that might change the course of these at-risk relationships.

EMOTIONAL COMMUNICATION WITH CAREGIVERS

If, at a formal dinner party, you have ever cast a sidelong glance to see which fork the person next to you was using, you have read another person's nonverbal signals to get information on how to act. Babies and caregivers do something like this, developing two-way signals that become a precise language of emotional communication. Psychologists observe an infant's responses to a parent's emotional signals during play to assess whether the baby is developing normally.

Mutual Regulation and Social Referencing: "Reading" Signals

Max smiles at his mother. She interprets this signal as an invitation to play and kisses his stomach, sending him into gales of giggles. But the next day,

when she begins to kiss his stomach again, he looks at her glassy-eyed and turns his head away. His mother interprets this as "I want to be quiet now." Following his cue, she tucks him into a baby carrier and lets him rest quietly against her body.

The interaction between infant and adult that determines the quality of attachment depends on the ability of both to respond appropriately to signals about each other's emotional states. This process is called **mutual regulation.** According to the *mutual-regulation model* (Tronick & Gianino, 1986), infants as young as 3 months of age take an active part in regulating their emotional state. They do not just receive caregivers' actions; they affect how caregivers act toward them.

Babies differ in the amount of stimulation they need or want. Too little leaves them uninterested; too much overwhelms them. Healthy interaction occurs when a caregiver "reads" a baby's messages accurately and responds appropriately. When a baby's goals are met, the baby is joyful or at least interested (Tronick, 1989). If a caregiver ignores an invitation to play or insists on playing when the baby has signaled "I don't feel like it," the baby may become angry or sad. When babies do not achieve the desired results, they usually keep on sending signals to repair the interaction. Normally, interaction moves back and forth between poorly regulated and well-regulated states, and babies learn from these shifts how to send signals and what to do when their initial signals do not result in a comfortable emotional balance.

Relationships with parents and other caregivers also help babies learn to "read" others' expectations. The ability to decipher other people's attitudes seems to be inborn; it helps human beings

According to the *mutual regulation* model, this baby's playful attempt to "feed" his mother is more than just a game; it is a way of initiating interaction between them. When the mother "reads" her baby's behaviors accurately and responds appropriately, she helps him learn how to send and receive signals. *(Shackman/Monkmeyer)*

form attachments to others, live in society, and protect themselves.

Even very young infants can perceive emotions expressed by others and can adjust their own behavior accordingly. At 10 weeks of age, they meet anger with anger (Lelwica & Haviland, 1983). At 3 months, infants faced with a stony-faced, unresponsive mother will make faces, sounds, and gestures to get a reaction (J. F. Cohn & Tronick, 1983; Tronick, 1980). Nine-month-olds show more joy, play more, and look at their mothers longer when the mothers seem happy; they look sad and turn away when their mothers seem sad (Termine & Izard, 1988). Toddlers 18 months to 3 years old may respond to signs of a mother's unhappiness or emotional withdrawal by moving away from her, making more negative bids for attention (such as hitting the mother or a toy, or throwing something at the mother), staring vacantly, wandering around the room, or simply doing nothing (Seiner & Gelfand, 1995).

By "reading" caregivers' signals, babies can figure out how to act in ambiguous, puzzling, or confusing situations. Through *social referencing*— seeking out and interpreting an adult's perception of a situation—they gain an understanding of appropriate ways of responding to it. Babies show social referencing when they look at their caregivers upon encountering a new person or toy. They generally learn to do this sometime after 6 months of age, when they begin to judge the possible consequences of events, imitate complex behaviors, and distinguish among and react to various emotional expressions.

In a study using the visual cliff (described in Chapter 3), when the drop looked very shallow or very deep, 1-year-olds did not look to their mothers; they were able to judge for themselves whether to cross over or not. When they were uncertain about the depth of the "cliff," they paused at the "edge," looked down, and then looked up at their mothers. Most of the babies whose mothers showed joy or interest crossed the "drop," but very few whose mothers looked angry or afraid crossed it (Sorce, Emde, Campos, & Klinnert, 1985).

Reading emotional signals, then, lets caregivers assess and meet babies' needs; and it lets babies influence the caregiver's behavior toward them and seek guidance in handling situations they do not understand. What happens if that communication system breaks down?

How a Mother's Depression Affects Mutual Regulation

Depression is more than ordinary sadness; it is an affective disorder (a disorder of mood) in which a person feels unhappy and often has trouble eating, sleeping, or concentrating (APA, 1994). Women of childbearing age are twice as likely as men to develop serious depression, which can last as long as 3 years and then tends to recur within 2 years (Gelfand & Teti, 1995).

Temporary depression may have little effect on the way a mother interacts with her baby; but chronic depression, lasting 6 months or more, can have serious effects (S. B. Campbell, Cohn, & Meyers, 1995; Teti, Gelfand, Messinger, & Isabella, 1995). Severely or chronically depressed mothers may ignore or override their babies' emotional signals, often with grave consequences. These mothers tend to be punitive, to consider their children bothersome and hard to care for, and to feel as if their own lives are out of control (T. M. Field et al., 1985; Whiffen & Gotlib, 1989; B. S. Zuckerman & Beardslee, 1987). Their babies often give up on sending emotional signals and try to comfort themselves by sucking or rocking. If this defensive reaction becomes habitual, babies learn that they have no power to draw responses from other people, that their mothers are unreliable, and that the world is untrustworthy. Both as infants and as preschoolers, they tend to be insecurely attached to their mothers (Gelfand & Teti, 1995; Teti et al., 1995).

Children of chronically depressed mothers are at risk of various emotional and cognitive disturbances (Gelfand & Teti, 1995). As infants, they are more likely than other babies to be drowsy, to show tension by squirming and arching their backs, to cry frequently, to look sad or angry more often, and to show interest less often (Pickens & Field, 1993; T. Field, Morrow, & Adelstein, 1993). They seem less upset when separated from their mothers (G. Dawson, Klinger, Panagiotides, Hill, & Spieker, 1992). They are less motivated to explore and more apt to prefer relatively unchallenging tasks (Redding, Harmon, & Morgan, 1990). As toddlers they are less likely to suppress frustration and tension (Cole, Barrett, & Zahn-Waxler, 1992) and to engage in symbolic play. Later they are likely to grow poorly and to perform poorly on cognitive measures, to have accidents, and to have behavior problems (T. M. Field et al., 1985; Gelfand & Teti, 1995; B. S. Zuckerman & Beardslee, 1987).

They are also more likely to become depressed themselves (Gelfand & Teti, 1995).

Professional or paraprofessional home visitors have helped depressed mothers by putting them in touch with community resources, such as parenting groups, and by modeling and reinforcing positive interaction. In one study, after about 47 home visits over a 13-month period, 18-month-olds scores higher on the Bayley mental scale and were twice as likely to be securely attached to their mothers than a control group of nonvisited babies of depressed mothers (Lyons-Ruth, Connell, & Grunebaum, 1990).

STRANGER ANXIETY AND SEPARATION ANXIETY

Sophie used to be a friendly baby, smiling at strangers and going to them, continuing to coo happily as long as someone—anyone—was around. Now, at 8 months, she turns away when a new person approaches and howls when her parents try to leave her with a babysitter. Sophie is experiencing both *stranger anxiety,* which is wariness of a person she does not know, and *separation anxiety,* which is distress when a familiar caregiver leaves her.

Separation anxiety and stranger anxiety used to be considered emotional and cognitive milestones of the second half of infancy, reflecting attachment to the mother. Babies rarely react negatively to strangers before 6 months of age, commonly do so by 8 or 9 months, and do so more and more throughout the rest of the first year (Sroufe, 1977). Even then, however, a baby may react positively to a new person, especially if the person waits a little while and then approaches the baby gradually, gently, and playfully. Furthermore, more recent research suggests that although Sophie's reactions are fairly typical, they are not universal. Whether a baby cries when a parent leaves or when someone new approaches may say more about the baby's temperament or life circumstances than about security of attachment (R. J. Davidson & Fox, 1989).

Navajo infants, for example, show less fear of strangers during the first year of life than Anglo infants do. Then, there are differences within a culture. Navajo babies who have many opportunities to interact with other people—who have frequent contacts with relatives or live close to a trading post—are less wary of new people than are other Navajo infants (Chisholm, 1983). In one laboratory experiment, infants whose mothers described them as wary of strangers tended to avert their gaze from a strange woman longer than other infants and to cling more closely to their mothers (Mangelsdorf, Shapiro, & Marzolf, 1995).

A baby's reaction to a stranger is likely to be affected by the caregiver's reaction (Dickstein & Parke, 1988; Klinnert, Emde, Butterfield, & Campos, 1986). A baby will often use social referencing to pick up cues. In one study, 10-month-old babies who were approached by an unfamiliar woman acted friendlier to her when their mothers spoke positively to them about the stranger (Feinman & Lewis, 1983).

Separation anxiety may be due less to the separation itself than to the quality of substitute care. Measurements of 9-month-olds' physiological and behavioral responses to brief separations from their mothers showed that when caregivers were warm and responsive and played with the infants *before* they cried, the babies cried much less than when they were with less responsive caregivers (Gunnar, Larson, Hertsgaard, Harris, & Brodersen, 1992). This was especially true of babies temperamentally disposed to be quick to anger in situations in which they seemed to feel a loss of control.

Stability of substitute care is also important. The pioneering work done by René Spitz (1945, 1946) on institutionalized children emphasized the need for care as close as possible to good mothering. Research has underlined the value of continuity and consistency in caregiving so that children can form early emotional bonds to their caregivers.

Today, neither early and intense fear of strangers nor intense protest when the mother leaves is considered to be a sign of secure attachment. Researchers now measure attachment more by what happens when the mother returns than by how many tears the baby sheds at her departure.

✔ DEVELOPMENTAL ISSUES IN TODDLERHOOD

About halfway between their first and second birthdays, babies begin to turn into children. This transformation can be seen not only in such physical and cognitive skills as walking and talking, but in the way toddlers express their personalities and interact with others. Let's look at three psychological issues that toddlers—and their caregivers—have to deal with: the emerging *sense of self*; the growth of *autonomy*, or self-determination; and the *internalization of behavioral standards.*

THE EMERGING SENSE OF SELF

Before children can take responsibility for their own activities, they must have a cognitive sense of themselves as physically distinct persons—separate from the rest of the world—whose characteristics and behavior can be described and evaluated. Self-awareness is the first step toward developing standards of behavior; it lets children understand that a parent's response to something they have done is directed at *them* and not just at the act itself.

How does the **self-concept,** or sense of self, begin to develop? After interviewing the mothers of 123 children 14 to 40 months old, a team of researchers (Stipek et al., 1990) identified this sequence:

1 *Physical self-recognition and self-awareness:* Most toddlers recognize themselves in mirrors or pictures by 18 months, showing awareness of themselves as physically distinct beings. In an earlier study, researchers counted how often 6- to 24-month-old children touched their noses. Then the researchers dabbed rouge on the babies' noses and sat them in front of a mirror. The 18-month-olds touched their red noses much more often than younger babies did, showing that they knew they didn't normally have red noses and that they recognized the image in the mirror as their own (M. Lewis & Brooks, 1974).

2 *Self-description and self-evaluation:* Once they have a concept of themselves as distinct beings, children begin to apply descriptive terms ("big" or "little"; "straight hair" or "curly hair") and evaluative ones ("good," "pretty," or "mean") to themselves. This normally occurs sometime between 19 and 30 months, as representational ability and vocabulary expand.

3 *Emotional response to wrongdoing:* The third stage has arrived when children show that they are upset by a parent's disapproval and will stop doing something they are not supposed to do—at least while they are being watched. This stage, which lays the foundation for moral understanding and development of conscience, comes about more gradually than the second stage, and there is some overlap.

According to the mothers in this study, children as young as 14 months showed an urge for autonomy, refusing help, acting contrary, and resisting attempts to dress or diaper them or pick them up (Stipek et al., 1990). Let's see what Erikson's theory has to say about this important development of toddlerhood.

DEVELOPING AUTONOMY

As children mature—physically, cognitively, and emotionally—they are driven to seek independence from the very adults they are attached to. "Me do!" is the byword as toddlers use their developing muscles and minds to try to do everything on their own: not only to walk, but to feed, dress, and protect themselves, and to expand the boundaries of their world.

Erikson (1950) identified the period from about 18 months to 3 years as the second stage, or crisis, in personality development, **autonomy versus shame and doubt,** which is marked by a shift from external control to self-control. Having come through infancy with a sense of basic trust in the world and an awakening self-awareness, toddlers begin to substitute their own judgment for their caregivers'. The "virtue" that emerges during this stage is *will.* Toilet training is an important step toward autonomy and self-control. So is language; as children are better able to make their wishes understood, they become more powerful and independent.

Since unlimited freedom is neither safe nor healthy, said Erikson, shame and doubt have a necessary place. As in all of Erikson's stages, an appropriate balance is crucial. Self-doubt helps children recognize what they are not yet ready to do, and shame helps them learn to live by reasonable rules. Toddlers need adults to set appropriate limits, and shame and doubt help them recognize the need for those limits.

The "terrible twos" are a normal manifestation of the drive for autonomy. Toddlers have to test the new notion that they are individuals, that they have some control over their world, and that they have new, exciting powers. They are driven to try out their own ideas, exercise their own preferences, and make their own decisions. Parents and other caregivers who view children's expressions of self-will as a normal, healthy striving for independence, not as stubbornness, can help them learn self-control, contribute to their sense of competence, and avoid excessive conflict. (Box 5-1 gives research-based suggestions for dealing with the "terrible twos.")

DEVELOPING SELF-REGULATION

Katy is about to poke her finger into an electric outlet. In her parents' "child-proofed" apartment, the sockets are covered, but not here in her grandmother's home. When Katy hears her father shout "No!" the toddler pulls her arm back. The next time she goes near an outlet, she starts to point her finger, hesitates, and then says "No." She has stopped herself from doing something she remembers she is not supposed to do. She is beginning to show *self-regulation:* control of her own behavior to conform to a caregiver's demands or expectations, even when the caregiver is not present.

Self-regulation links all domains of development: physical, cognitive, and emotional. Until Katy was physically able to get around on her own, electric outlets posed no hazard. To stop herself from poking her finger into an outlet requires that she consciously understand and remember what her father told her. Cognitive awareness, however, is not enough; restraining herself also requires emotional control.

Parents are the most important people in a toddler's life and the ones whose approval matters more than anything else in the world. Through social referencing and by "reading" their parents' emotional responses to their behavior, children continually absorb information about what conduct their parents approve of. As children process, store, and act upon this information, their strong desire to please their parents leads them to do as they know their parents wish, whether or not the parents are there to see. This growth of self-regulation parallels the development of the self-conscious emotions, such as empathy, shame, and guilt. It requires flexibility and the ability to wait for gratification.

When young children want very badly to do something, however, they easily forget the rules; they may run into the street after a ball or take a forbidden cookie. In most children, then, the full development of self-regulation takes about 3 years (Kopp, 1982).

At first, babies cannot generalize from one situation to another; when Katy was 1 year old, she had to be told to stay away from electric outlets each time she approached one. Then she would stay away for only a short time—and only while

This toddler's attempt to dress himself—clumsy as it may be at first—expresses his strong urge for autonomy. *(Kopstein/Monkmeyer)*

her father was around—and she was apt to keep poking her finger into other dangerous places. Now, at 1½ years of age, she can think and remember well enough to connect what she wants to do with what she has been told. By the time she is 2, she probably will know (but not always follow) many rules about what and how to eat, how to dress for sleep or play, and what she is and is not allowed to touch and do. Still, not until age 3 is she likely to stay away from all electric outlets and anything that looks like one.

INTERNALIZATION: DEVELOPING A CONSCIENCE

The shift to self-regulation is the basis for *socialization,* the process by which children develop habits, skills, values, and motives that make a person a responsible, productive member of a society (Kochanska, 1993; Maccoby, 1992). Compliance with parental expectations is a first step toward compliance with societal standards of conduct (Kochanska & Aksan, 1995; Kopp, 1982; Maccoby & Martin, 1983). Socialization rests on *internalization* of these standards. Children who are successfully socialized no longer merely obey rules or commands to get rewards or avoid punishment; they have made society's standards their own

BOX 5-1   PRACTICALLY SPEAKING

DEALING WITH THE "TERRIBLE TWOS"

As almost any parent of a toddler well knows, the "terrible twos" are marked by **negativism,** the tendency to shout "No!" just for the sake of resisting authority. Almost all children show negativism to some degree; it usually begins before 2 years of age, tends to peak at about 3½ to 4, and declines by age 6.

The following research-based guidelines can help parents and toddlers get through the "terrible twos" and can encourage children to learn socially acceptable behavior (Haswell, Hock, & Wenar, 1981; Kochanski & Aksan, 1995; Kopp, 1982; Kuczynski & Kochanska, 1995; Power & Chapieski, 1986):

- *Be flexible.* Learn the child's natural rhythms and special likes and dislikes. The most flexible parents tend to have the least resistant children.
- *Think of yourself as a safe harbor,* with safe limits, from which a child can set out to discover the world and keep coming back for support.
- *Make your home "child-friendly."* Fill it with unbreakable objects that are safe to explore.
- *Avoid physical punishment.* It is

often ineffective and may even lead a toddler to do more damage.
- *Offer a choice,* even a limited one, to give the child some control. For example, "Would you like to have your bath now, or after we read a book?"
- *Be consistent* in enforcing necessary requests. Many children refuse to obey to show their control, but do not really mean what they say and will eventually comply.
- *Don't interrupt an activity unless absolutely necessary.* Try to wait until the child's attention has shifted to something else.
- *If you must interrupt, give warning:* "We have to leave the playground soon." This gives the child time to prepare and either finish an activity or think about resuming it another time.
- *Suggest alternative activities.* When Ashley is throwing sand in Keiko's face, say, "Oh, look! Nobody's on the swings now. Let's go over, and I'll give you a good push!"
- *Suggest; don't command.* Accompany requests with smiles or hugs, not criticism, threats,

or physical restraint.
- *Link requests with pleasurable activities:* "It's time to stop playing, so you can come to the store with me."
- *Remind the child of what you expect:* "When we go to this playground, we *never* go outside the gate."
- *Wait a few moments before repeating a request* when a child doesn't comply immediately.
- *Use "time out"* to end conflicts. In a nonpunitive way, remove either yourself or the child from a situation. Very often this results in a reduction in, or even the disappearance of, resistance.
- *Expect less self-control from the child during times of stress* (illness, a divorce, the birth of a sibling, or a move to a new home).
- *Expect it to be harder for toddlers to comply with "do's" than with "don'ts."* "Clean up your room" takes more effort than "Don't write on the furniture."
- Above all, *keep the atmosphere as positive as possible.* Maintaining a warm, enjoyable relationship is the key to making children *want* to cooperate.

(Grusec & Goodnow, 1994; Kochanska & Aksan, 1995).

Some children internalize societal standards more readily than others. The way parents go about their job, together with a child's temperament and the quality of the parent-child relationship, may help predict how hard or easy it will be to socialize a child (Kochanska, 1993, 1995). Other factors in successful socialization may include secure attachment to responsive parents, observational learning of parents' behavior, and the way parents and child interact (Maccoby, 1992). All these may play a part in a child's motivation to comply.

Internalization of societal standards is essential

to the development of a **conscience,** which includes both emotional discomfort about doing something wrong and the ability to refrain from doing it (Kochanska, 1993; see Box 5-2). Conscience depends on willingness to do the right thing because a child believes it is right, not just because someone else says so.

Origins of Conscience: Committed Compliance

Grazyna Kochanska (1993, 1995) and her colleagues have sought the origins of conscience in a longitudinal study of a socioeconomically and eth-

BOX 5-2   FOOD FOR THOUGHT

EARLY SIGNS OF CONSCIENCE

Matthew, age 18 months, toddles across the living room floor and points to a chipped vase. "Broke?" he asks, with a worried look at his babysitter.

Does toddlers' concern with flawed objects—a concern that typically arises during the second year—have something to do with anxiety about their own wrongdoing, which also emerges around that time? Jerome Kagan (1984) thought so. By age 2, according to Piaget (1952), children understand that some actions are intentional and others are not. As part of their developing self-awareness, they also begin to understand and react emotionally to harm they have caused (Stipek et al., 1990). However, in ambiguous situations, young children's assessment of who caused what may be confused (Zahn-Waxler & Kochanska, 1990).

Grazyna Kochanska and her colleagues (Kochanska, Casey, & Fukumoto, 1995) videotaped 2- and 3-year-olds—participants in a longitudinal study of socialization and conscience development—in laboratory interactions with whole and damaged objects. (Younger children were not used in this study because the design required cooperation during a fairly long, challenging trial.)

First, the experimenter showed a child four pairs of objects: teddy bears, beds, blankets, and cups. One object in each pair was defective—broken, torn, or stained, or missing a part—and the other was intact. The children were asked what they thought of each object, which of each pair they liked better, and why. Then the children were allowed to play with all the objects. The children were more interested in and concerned about the flawed items, even though by age 2½ they clearly preferred the undamaged versions.

The experimenters then set up two scenarios in which the child was led to believe that she or he had damaged the experimenter's doll or shirt. In the "doll mishap," the experimenter invited the child to play a game with two dolls. The experimenter would "walk" one doll, clap its hands, and make it do a somersault, and the child would do the same with the other doll. During the somersault, the head of the doll the child was playing with, which had been rigged, fell off. After the child had put the doll down, the experimenter asked a few questions about what had happened, then left the room briefly, came back with an identical but undamaged doll, and let the child play with it a little longer.

In the "shirt mishap," the experimenter asked the child to bring her a tee shirt from a nearby table. When the child picked up the shirt, a cup of ink, which had been hidden in its folds, spilled on the shirt. After questioning the child, the experimenter claimed responsibility for the mishap, took the shirt out of the room saying she would try to clean it, and came back with an identical, clean shirt.

Everything the child said during each mishap was transcribed. The statements fell into six categories: (1) *objective statements:* "Head fell off" or "There's a mess"; (2) *apologies:* "Sorry" or "Didn't mean to"; (3) *statements about repairing the damage:* "Put head back on" or "Wash this off"; (4) *self-blaming statements:* "I did it"; (5) *denials of blame:* "Nothing happened," "Doll did it," or "Not me"; and (6) *statements of distress or withdrawal:* "I'm done with this doll," "Take this shirt away," or "Can we leave now?" The researchers also observed the children's emotional reactions.

Responses to the mishaps fit three patterns, which seem to correspond to the emotions of guilt, shame, or a combination of the two. "Amenders" accepted responsibility and sought to repair the damage (guilt). "Avoiders" showed distress and a desire to escape (shame). A third group made both apologetic and reparatory comments.

These children's reactions to flawed objects, both in an emotionally neutral situation and in one in which they might conceivably be to blame, suggest a cognitive and emotional concern with violations of standards, which may be an early sign of emerging conscience. A fascination with flaws may develop cognitively as a result of repeated exposure to the way objects are supposed to look, and emotionally as a result of repeated exposure to caregivers' disapproval of damaging actions. As other research has shown, protection of personal property is one of the earliest and most effective demands parents make on young children (Gralinski & Kopp, 1993). Research with younger children might show whether sensitivity to flawed objects is a forerunner of emotional responses to wrongdoing or whether both develop at about the same time.

nically mixed group of toddlers and mothers in urban and rural areas in Iowa. Researchers videotaped 103 children ages 26 to 41 months and their mothers playing together for 2 to 3 hours, both at home and in a homelike laboratory setting (Kochanska & Aksan, 1995). After a free-play period, the mother gave the child 15 minutes to put the toys away. The laboratory also had a special shelf with unusually attractive toys, such as a bubble gum machine, a walkie-talkie, a music box, a fishing set, and a beautiful doll. The child was told not to touch anything on the shelf during the entire session. After about an hour, the experimenter asked the mother to go into an adjoining room, leaving the child with the toys. A few minutes later, a strange woman entered, played with several of the toys on the forbidden shelf, and then left the child alone for 8 minutes.

The researchers assessed each child's compliance with the mother's demands by how willingly the child cleaned up and whether the child made any attempt to touch the forbidden toys while the mother was in the room. Children were judged as showing **committed compliance,** which seems to be an early form of conscience, if they appeared to wholeheartedly accept the mother's orders, following them without reminders or lapses. Children showed **situational compliance** if they needed prompting to obey; their compliance depended on ongoing parental control.

Children whose mothers rated them as having internalized household rules showed the most committed compliance. These children refrained from touching the forbidden toys even when left alone with them, showing that they had internalized the prohibition. By contrast, children whose compliance was only situational tended to yield to temptation when their mothers were out of sight. The oldest children and those who had had positive interchanges with their mothers during play showed more committed compliance than younger children and those whose interactions with their mothers were characterized by irritation, boredom, anger, fear, or sadness.

A follow-up study when the children were 3½ to 4½ years old provides further evidence that internalization grows out of committed, but not situational, compliance. Children who, as toddlers, had shown committed compliance were more likely to continue to show it as they got older; and they were also more likely to internalize adult rules (Kochanska, Aksan, & Koenig, 1995).

A mutually responsive parent-child relationship during the toddler years may foster committed compliance and thus affect socialization. Mothers of committed compliers, as contrasted with mothers of situational compliers, tend to rely on gentle guidance rather than force, threats, or other forms of negative control. Gentle parenting and a warm, affectionate relationship may create a climate that fosters transmission of societal standards. There may also be a bidirectional effect: a mother of a resistant child may tend to become overcontrolling (Kochanska & Aksan, 1995).

Gentle guidance may be particularly suited to fearful or anxious children, who tend to become upset when they misbehave. Such a child will readily internalize parental messages with a minimum of prodding; displays of power would merely make the child more anxious. Something more may be needed with bolder children, but they too are likely to respond better to appeals for cooperation than to threats (Kochanska, 1995).

Effects of Parenting Styles and Demands

In a study that explored effects of parenting styles and parental demands, 70 mothers and their 1½- to 3½-year-olds were videotaped through one-way mirrors in a naturalistic apartment setting. Two-thirds of the mothers and children participated in a follow-up study when the children were 5 years old (Kuczynski & Kochanska, 1995).

The demands the mothers made fell into three categories: (1) *caretaking demands,* which concerned the child's physical care or supervision ("Wash your hands!" or "Careful on the stairs!"), (2) *demands for appropriate behavior,* which dealt with social rules and proper handling of objects ("Sit up straight" or "Don't write on the wall"), and (3) *demands for competent action* that would benefit the child or others, such as doing chores, helping, and engaging in constructive play ("Share your cookies" or "Look, what's this for?"). Demands made on the youngest toddlers had more to do with physical care and protection of objects; older ones were expected to do more helping and to engage in socially appropriate behavior.

Mothers who had an *authoritarian* style of parenting—emphasizing strict supervision, control, and punishment—issued many prohibitions, regardless of content. Mothers with an *authoritative* style—emphasizing rational guidance, encouragement of independence, and open communication of feelings—made demands that promoted competence more than regulation of behavior. Toddlers were more likely to comply with these authoritative demands; and those whose mothers made them had fewer behavior problems at age 5 than those with authoritarian mothers, who concentrated on regulation and restriction. (Authoritarian and authoritative parenting are more fully described in Chapter 7.)

Children who actively resisted their mothers' demands tended to receive more regulatory and restrictive demands and fewer requests for cooperation and competence. Thus a cycle may be created in which parents respond to resistant children by making even less effort to socialize the child in a positive way. Conversely, when parent and child get along well from the start, "a habit of competent and cooperative behavior" may develop (Kuczynski & Kochanska, 1995, p. 625).

✔ CONTACT WITH OTHER CHILDREN

Although parents exert a major influence on children's lives, relationships with other children—both in the home and out of it—are important too, from infancy on.

SIBLINGS

If you have brothers or sisters, your relationships with them are likely to be the longest-lasting you'll ever have. You and your siblings may have fought continually as children, or you may have been each other's best friends. Either way, your siblings share your roots; they "knew you when," they accepted or rejected the same parental values, and they probably deal with you more candidly than almost anyone else you know.

How Children React to the Arrival of a New Baby

Children react in various ways to the arrival of a sibling. Some suck their thumbs, wet their pants, ask to suck from breast or bottle, or use baby talk. Others withdraw, refusing to talk or play. Some suggest taking the baby back to the hospital, giving it away, or flushing it down the toilet. Some take pride in being the "big ones," who can dress themselves, use the potty, eat with the grown-ups, and help care for the baby. Most behavioral problems related to the arrival of a new baby disappear by the time the baby is 8 months old (Dunn, 1985).

The birth of a younger sibling may change the way a mother acts toward her first child. The mother is likely to play less with the older child, to be less sensitive to his or her interests, to give more orders, to have more confrontations, and to initiate fewer conversations and games (Dunn, 1985; Dunn & Kendrick, 1982). The older child's personality makes a difference. Children who take the initiative to start a conversation or play a game with the mother show less sibling rivalry than those who withdraw. Older siblings adjust better if their fathers give them extra time and attention to make up for the mother's involvement with the infant (Lamb, 1978).

Parents are wise to prepare the older child for the birth of a new baby by making any changes in the child's life (such as moving to another bedroom or from a crib to a bed, or starting nursery school) well in advance to minimize feelings of displacement (Spock & Rothenberg, 1985). It is important to accept a child's anxiety and jealousy as normal, while protecting the new baby from any harmful expression of those feelings. Parents can encourage the older child to play and help with the baby and can emphasize how much they value *each* child.

How Siblings Interact

Babies interact more with their older siblings after the first 6 months. One-year-olds spend almost as much time with their siblings as with their mothers and far more time than with their fathers (Dunn & Kendrick, 1982; Lawson & Ingleby, 1974). In many societies, older siblings have considerable responsibility for care of babies, often when the older ones are only about 4 or 5 years old (Dunn, 1985).

Although rivalry is often present, so is affection. Young children usually become attached to their older brothers and sisters. Babies become upset when their siblings go away, greet them when they come back, prefer them as playmates, and go to them when a stranger enters the room (Dunn, 1983; R. B. Stewart, 1983). The more securely attached siblings are to their parents, the better they get along with one another (Teti & Ablard, 1989). When a younger sibling becomes a toddler, the older one tends to initiate both positive and negative behaviors, which the younger one imitates. Older boys tend to be more aggressive; older girls are more likely to share, cooperate, and hug (Abramovitch, Corter, & Lando, 1979).

Babies and toddlers become closely attached to their older brothers and sisters, especially when, as with these Chinese children, the older siblings assume a large measure of care for the younger ones. *(Eastcott/The Image Works)*

The environment siblings create for one another affects not only their future relationship but the personality development of each child. When little girls imitate their big brothers, they may take on some characteristics commonly thought of as masculine (Dunn, 1983). Children teach their younger siblings and thus influence their cognitive development (R. B. Stewart, 1983). (Lack of siblings, too, affects children's lives; we consider the "only child" in Chapter 7.)

SOCIABILITY WITH NONSIBLINGS

Although the family is the center of a baby's social world, infants and—even more so—toddlers show interest in people outside the home, particularly people their own size. Now that more infants and toddlers spend time in day care settings in close contact with other children, researchers are better able to study how they react to one another.

In a hospital nursery, newborns who have been lying quietly in their cribs start to cry when they hear another baby's cries (G. B. Martin & Clark, 1982; Sagi & Hoffman, 1976; Simner, 1971). During the first few months, they show interest in other babies in about the same way they respond to their mothers: by looking, smiling, and cooing (T. M. Field, 1978). Increasingly, during the last half of the first year, they smile at, touch, and babble to another baby, especially when they are not distracted by the presence of adults or toys (Hay, Pedersen, & Nash, 1982).

At about 1 year, when the biggest items on their agenda are learning to walk and to manipulate objects, babies pay more attention to toys and less to other people (T. M. Field & Roopnarine, 1982). This stage does not last long, though; from about 1½ years of age to almost 3, they show more interest in what other children do and increasing understanding of how to deal with them. This insight seems to accompany awareness of themselves as separate individuals. A 10-month-old who holds out a toy to another baby pays no attention to whether the other's back is turned, but an 18-month-old toddler knows when the offer has the best chance of being accepted and how to respond to another child's overtures (Eckerman, Davis, & Didow, 1989; Eckerman & Stein, 1982).

Toddlers learn by imitating one another. In one set of experiments, 14- to 18-month-olds who watched other toddlers play with objects (for example, putting beads in a cup or sounding a buzzer), either in a laboratory or in a day care center, were more likely to do the same thing than a control group who had seen the objects but had not seen another child playing with them. The experimental groups also repeated the behavior when given the same objects at home 2 days later—evidence that toddlers are capable of deferred imitation (see Chapter 4) even in a different context (Hanna & Meltzoff, 1993). Imitative games, such as follow-the-leader, help toddlers connect with other children and pave the way for more complex games during the preschool years (Eckerman et al., 1989).

Conflict, too, can have a purpose: helping children learn how to negotiate and resolve disputes. In one study, groups of three toddlers who had not known one another before were observed playing with toys. Overall, the children got along well—sharing, showing, and demonstrating toys to one another, even just before and after squabbling over the toys. Two-year-olds got into more conflicts than 1-year-olds but also resolved them more, often by sharing toys when there were not enough to go around (Caplan, Vespo, Pedersen, & Hay, 1991).

Some children, of course, are more sociable than others, reflecting such temperamental traits as their usual mood, readiness to accept new people, and ability to adapt to change. Sociability is also influenced by experience: babies who spend time with other babies become sociable earlier than those who spend all their time at home alone. As children grow older and enter more fully into the world beyond the home, social skills become increasingly important. The first step into that wider world for many children is entrance into day care.

THE IMPACT OF EARLY DAY CARE

What happens to the development of children who, from the age of a few weeks or a few months, are cared for by someone other than the parents? Does day care, especially infant day care, help or harm children? Few questions in child development arouse as much controversy. The answers are important: in the United States, more than half of all mothers of children under 1 year of age are working for pay, full or part time, in or out of the home (Bachu, 1993)—a higher proportion than at any time in the nation's history.

The way we break down our questions is important, too. Where does care take place—in a group day care center or in a home? What is high-quality care? By what criteria do we judge harm and benefit? How can we distinguish the effects of the day care experience from the effects of parenting?

Research is seeking answers; but many studies are open to criticism, and their findings are often ambiguous, inconsistent, or contradictory. Furthermore, although most children are cared for either in their own homes or in someone else's, much of what we know about the effects of day care comes from studies of well-funded, university-based centers. We have relatively little information about the effects of the most common kinds of day care that children typically receive.

Currently, the kinds of child-care arrangements that working parents make for young children are changing dramatically. The big shift is from care by relatives, including mothers or fathers, to care in organized centers: day care centers or preschools. In 1993, relatives still cared for almost half (48 percent) of children under age 5 whose mothers were gainfully employed; but this figure was down from 53 percent in 1991, largely because, with the lifting of an economic recession, fewer fathers were serving as primary caregivers. Meanwhile, the proportion of these preschoolers who were in organized centers jumped from 23 percent to 30 percent—an all-time high. Only 18 percent, an all-time low, were in family day care outside their own homes. The rest were in the care of nonrelatives in the children's homes (Casper, 1996; see Figure 5-1). In Sweden, by contrast, parental leave policies and child care subsidies make it possible for a very high percentage of infants and toddlers to be cared for at home before going into group care (see Box 5-3).

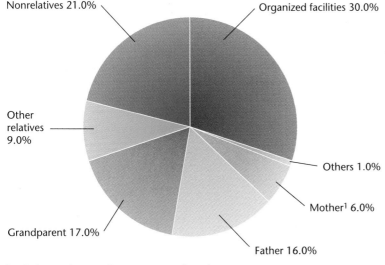

¹Includes mothers working at or away from home

FIGURE 5-1
Primary child-care arrangements used by employed mothers for children under 5. In 1993, about 3 out of 10 of these preschoolers—more than ever before—were in group day care centers.
(Source: Casper, 1996.)

BOX 5-3   WINDOW ON THE WORLD

HOW SWEDEN CARES FOR PARENTS AND CHILDREN

In most societies throughout history other people have helped mothers care for children. Today the issue of nonparental child care in the United States has taken on a new urgency for several reasons: the great numbers of mothers working outside the home, the rise of group day care as a business venture, and the belief that day care should enhance children's development rather than just offer baby-sitting. Sweden is often held up as a model.

Swedish family policy came about because of rapid industrialization and ensuing labor shortages. To enable women to work and also bear and rear future workers, Sweden developed a system that includes good pay, generous parental leaves, and high-quality early child care (Lamb & Sternberg, 1992; Hwang & Broberg, 1992).

Every Swedish family receives an allowance from the state for each child, from birth through age 16. Both mothers and fathers can take parental leave, ranging from 2 weeks at 90 percent of regular salary through 18 months, part paid, part unpaid, for one parent at a time. Thus almost all Swedish babies have one parent home for the first year, and children up to 18 months of age are cared for at home by parents.

In 1989 more than 80 percent of Swedish babies were cared for by parents, and 8 percent were cared for by relatives or private baby-sitters. Only 8 percent under 18 months were in day care operated by local municipalities, but about half of all children over this age received such care. Since the national government sets guidelines for quality, municipal child care is of a very high caliber. Standards are set for the physical facility, staffing and staff training, size of groups, and so forth. Family day care, however, which is common, is almost unregulated; efforts are being made to develop guidelines for "daymothers."

Child care, seen as every family's right, is financed mostly from public funds. Parents pay an average of only 10 to 15 percent of the real cost; the state and the municipality each contribute just under half the remaining costs from revenues received from employers and from business and personal taxes.

Research has shown the positive effects of high-quality infant day care in Sweden (Andersson, 1992). Children ages 8 and 13 who had entered out-of-home care before age 1 (usually during the second half of the first year) were compared with children cared for at home. The day care youngsters generally did better in school and were rated more highly by teachers on such social and emotional variables as school adjustment and social competence. The *type* of care did not affect children's social, emotional, or cognitive development. The most important factors seem to be the quality of care the children receive in their own homes and the health of the emotional climate there. Parents are still children's most important caregivers.

In the United States, family income, ethnicity, and marital status affect the choice of child care. Since organized child care is costly, children of families in lower economic circumstances tend to be under the care of fathers, grandparents, or other relatives. The mothers are more likely to be black or Hispanic than white, and to work evening or night shifts or part time. Care by relatives (but not fathers) is much more common for children in single-parent families than for those living with both parents (Casper, 1996).

As we look at what makes good day care and at its impact on the interrelated areas of cognitive, emotional, and social development, our focus will be on organized centers, in part because their use is growing rapidly and in part because that is where most of the research on day care has been done.

What Is Good Day Care?

Good day care is like good parenting. Children thrive in day care that has small groups, a high adult-to-child ratio, and a stable, competent, highly involved staff. (When groups are too large, adding more adults to the staff does not help.) Children develop best when they have access to educational toys and materials, when they have caregivers who teach and accept them, and when caregivers are neither too controlling nor merely custodial but provide a balance between structured activities and free play (Clarke-Stewart, 1987). The quality of care is particularly important for infants, since stimulating interactions with responsive adults are crucial to a baby's cognitive and linguistic as well as emotional and social development (Burchinal, Roberts, Nabors, & Bryant, 1996).

A licensed day care center must meet minimum state standards for health, fire, and safety (if it is inspected regularly), but many centers and home care facilities are not licensed or regulated. Furthermore, licensing does not tell anything about the program's quality. In choosing a day care facility, what should parents look for?

First, they should note whether the facility is clean and safe. Then, are caregivers trained in child development? Are they warm, affectionate, responsive to all the children, sensitive to their needs, and authoritative but not too restrictive? Does the program promote good health habits? Does it stimulate mastery of cognitive and communicative skills while encouraging children to develop at their own pace? Does it nurture self-confidence, curiosity, creativity, and self-discipline? Does it encourage children to ask questions, solve problems, and make decisions? Does it foster self-esteem, respect for others, and social skills? Finally, does it help parents improve their child-rearing skills and promote cooperation with public and private schools and the community? (AAP, 1986; Belsky, 1984; S. W. Olds, 1989).

By and large, children in good day care programs do at least as well physically, cognitively, and socially as those raised at home. High-quality day care seems to enhance emotional development, too. Let's look more closely at each of these domains.

Day Care and Cognitive Development

The most clear-cut conclusions emerge in the cognitive realm for children ages 2 to 4 who attend day care centers. On a number of cognitive measures, children in adequate or superior group day care seem to do as well as, or better than, children who spend the day at home with parents or babysitters or in day care homes. Where differences appear, children in group day care—regardless of how long they have been in day care or how old they were when they entered—tend to score higher on IQ tests, to show more advanced eye-hand coordination, to play more creatively, to know more about the physical world, to count and measure better, to show better language skills, and to be more advanced in knowing their names and addresses. However, this cognitive edge seems to represent a temporary speedup in acquiring skills rather than a permanent advantage. Some studies show that the differences do not hold up once children leave the center; by the end of first grade, home-reared children have caught up (Clarke-Stewart, 1992).

Children from low-income families or stressful homes benefit the most from good day care. Disadvantaged children in good programs tend not to show the declines in IQ often seen when such children reach school age, and they may be more motivated to learn (AAP, 1986; Belsky, 1984; Bronfenbrenner, Belsky, & Steinberg, 1977).

A study of 79 African American 12-month-olds in poor to mediocre community-based day care centers found that infants' scores on the Bayley Scales of Infant Development, as well as on measures of language and communicative skills, were related to the quality of care (Burchinal et al., 1996). In another study, children who had been in high-quality infant care were more likely to be assigned to gifted programs in elementary school and, as

These children in a high-quality group day care program are likely to do at least as well physically, cognitively, and socially as children cared for full time at home. *(Joseph Schuyler/Stock, Boston)*

sixth graders, to get higher math grades (T. Field, 1991).

The importance of quality of care is underscored by research in nine day care centers in Bermuda, where 84 percent of 2-year-olds spend most of the workweek. As we reported in Chapter 4, when caregivers spoke often to children to give or ask for information and encouraged children to start conversations with them, the children did better on tests of language development (McCartney, 1984). A follow-up study (D. Phillips, McCartney, & Scarr, 1987) found that children who talked often with their caregivers were also more sociable and considerate, showing a link between cognitive influences and psychosocial development. In fact, the quality and amount of verbal stimulation seemed even more important for social development than the children's family background.

Day Care and Emotional Development

A complex issue regarding infant day care is its effect on a baby's attachment to the mother. Evidence suggests that regular, early care outside the home or by someone other than the mother does not in itself harm attachment; the risk lies in a combination of poor-quality care and unresponsive parenting (L. W. Hoffman, 1989; NICHD Early Child Care Research Network, 1996; Scarr, Phillips, & McCartney, 1989).

An ongoing longitudinal study of 1,153 children and their families has been designed to separate the effect of day care from the effects of the personalities of mother and child and of the care the child receives at home (NICHD Early Child Care Research Network, 1996). The study began in 1991 in 10 locations across the United States and will continue until the children are 7 years old. Investigators videotaped mothers and babies in their homes when the babies were 1 month, 6 months, and 15 months old. The mothers filled out questionnaires, and observers rated how they cared for their babies. The observers also noted the infants' temperamental characteristics. At 15 months, the children were placed in the Strange Situation to assess their attachment to their mothers.

The study found no danger to healthy attachment even for infants who enter nonmaternal care before 3 months of age and remain in it for 30 or more hours a week. However, infants whose mothers are insensitive and unresponsive tend to be insecurely attached if they get poor-quality or unstable day care or if they receive outside care for 10 or more hours a week. One gender difference emerged: boys who spent more than 30 hours a week in child care and girls who spent fewer than 10 hours a week were slightly more likely to be insecurely attached, suggesting that boys tend to react more negatively to a mother's prolonged absence.

This research supports an earlier finding that boys who receive more than 35 hours a week of substitute care tend to be insecurely attached to both parents. This earlier research also found that factors other than day care affected attachment. The most vulnerable boys had been "difficult babies" and had mothers who were dissatisfied with their marriages, insensitive to other people, and strongly career-motivated (Belsky & Rovine, 1988).

Day Care and Social Development

Findings about the effects of infant day care on social development are mixed. In general, children who spent much of their first year in day care tend to be as sociable, self-confident, persistent, achieving, and skilled at solving problems as children who were at home—and some more so. Preschoolers raised in day care also tend to be more comfortable in new situations, more outgoing, less timid and fearful, more helpful and cooperative, and more verbally expressive (Clarke-Stewart, 1989, 1992). One study of children who started day care, on average, at just under 7 months found that between 5 and 8 years of age they had more friends and were more physically affectionate with them, took part in more extracurricular activities, and asserted themselves more than children who had been at home as infants (T. Field, 1991). However, day care children also have been found to be more disobedient and less polite to adults, bossier and more aggressive with other children, louder, more boisterous, and more demanding (Clarke-Stewart, 1989, 1992).

Among 36 children in a semirural area who entered day care before the age of 8 months, quality of care was a better predictor of social adjustment than age of entry or the number of hours an infant spent in day care. The study found that temperamentally vulnerable infants may be at risk for social difficulties if placed in poor-quality day care. They are less likely to develop social problems if they have high-quality care, where they get more one-on-one attention (Volling & Feagans, 1995).

The most important element in the quality of care is the caregiver or teacher. How children relate to caregivers can strongly influence their behavior with their peers. In one longitudinal study, 4-year-olds who had formed secure attachments to their earliest and current child-care teachers tended to be more sociable, sensitive, empathic, and better-liked than those who were insecurely attached (Howes, Matheson, & Hamilton, 1994). A relationship with a caregiver has several dimensions, each of which may affect social development in different ways and at different ages. Four-year-olds who as toddlers felt secure with their caregivers tend to be more gregarious and less aggressive. Those who got along well with the early teacher tend to be popular with other children. Children who are overly dependent on their current preschool teachers are more aggressive and socially withdrawn (Howes, Hamilton, & Matheson, 1994).

However infants and toddlers are cared for, the experiences of these important first 3 years lay a foundation for the future. In Part Two, we'll see how young children build on that foundation.

✔ SUMMARY

FOUNDATIONS OF PSYCHOSOCIAL DEVELOPMENT

■ Foundations of psychosocial development include emotions, temperament, and early experiences with parents.

■ The development and expression of various emotions seem to be tied to brain maturation and cognitive development, including development of self-awareness; but unusual environmental factors can affect the timing of their arrival.

■ Infants show their emotions by crying, smiling, and laughing.

■ Temperamental patterns appear to be largely inborn but may be affected by significant environmental changes. "Goodness of fit" between a child's temperament and environmental demands is important for adjustment.

■ Research has failed to support the idea of a critical period for forming the mother-infant bond. However, infants do have strong needs for closeness and warmth as well as physical care.

■ Fathers and babies form close bonds early in a baby's life. Infants' and toddlers' experiences with mothers and fathers generally differ; mothers, even when employed outside the home, spend more time in infant care, and mothers and fathers in some cultures have different styles of interacting with babies.

■ Significant physiological and behavioral differences between the sexes typically do not appear until after infancy. However, parents treat their sons and daughters differently almost from birth, contributing to gender-typing.

DEVELOPMENTAL ISSUES IN INFANCY

■ According to Erik Erikson, infants in the first 18 months of life experience the first in a series of eight crises that influence personality development throughout life. That first critical task is to find a balance between basic trust and mistrust of the world. Successful resolution of this crisis results in the "virtue" of hope.

■ On the basis of the Strange Situation, three main patterns of mother-infant attachment have been found: secure attachment and two types of insecure attachment: avoidant attachment and ambivalent (resistant) attachment. A fourth pattern, disorganized-disoriented, may be the least secure.

■ Attachment patterns may depend on the baby's temperament and other characteristics, as well as on the quality of mothering, and may have long-term implications for development. Some research suggests that attachment patterns are passed on from generation to generation.

■ According to the mutual regulation model, babies play an active part in regulating their emotional states. They "read" the emotions of others and, after about 6 months of age, engage in social referencing.

■ Separation anxiety and stranger anxiety may arise during the second half of the first year and appear to be related to temperament and life circumstances.

DEVELOPMENTAL ISSUES IN TODDLERHOOD

■ The self-concept begins to emerge in the following sequence: (1) physical self-recognition and self-awareness, (2) self-description and self-evaluation, and (3) emotional response to wrongdoing.

■ Erikson's second crisis, which a toddler faces from about 18 months to 3 years, concerns autonomy versus shame and doubt. Successful resolution results in the "virtue" of will.

■ At about age 3 children develop self-regulation,

or control of their behavior to conform to external expectations. Self-regulation is the basis for socialization, the internalization of societally approved standards. Committed compliance to a caregiver's demands—the first step in developing a conscience—leads to internalization.

CONTACT WITH OTHER CHILDREN

- Siblings influence one another both positively and negatively from an early age. Parents' actions and attitudes affect sibling relationships.

- Infants' interest in other children grows during infancy and toddlerhood. Contact with other children, especially during toddlerhood, affects cognitive, and psychosocial development.

- High-quality day care appears to have a generally positive impact on cognitive, emotional, and social development. Although the effect of early day care on attachment is controversial, a new, ongoing study suggests that day care is not harmful unless it is poor-quality, unstable, or extensive and is combined with insensitive mothering.

✔ KEY TERMS

emotions (page 150)
self-awareness (152)
easy children (154)
difficult children (154)
slow-to-warm-up children (154)
mother-infant bond (156)
gender-typing (158)
basic trust versus basic mistrust (158)
attachment (159)
Strange Situation (160)

secure attachment (160)
avoidant attachment (160)
ambivalent (resistant) attachment (160)
disorganized-disoriented attachment (160)
mutual regulation (165)
social referencing (166)
depression (166)
stranger anxiety (167)
separation anxiety (167)

self-concept (168)
autonomy versus shame and doubt (168)
self-regulation (169)
socialization (169)
internalization (169)
negativism (170)
conscience (170)
committed compliance (172)
situational compliance (172)

✔ QUESTIONS FOR THOUGHT AND DISCUSSION

1 Give some examples of ways parents can promote "goodness of fit."
2 "Despite the women's liberation movement and changes in child care, a mother will always be more important to babies and young children than a father." Do you agree or disagree?
3 Should parents try to treat male and female infants and toddlers the same?

4 Critics of the Strange Situation say it has limited relevance to cultures in which children have multiple caregivers from birth. Can you think of ways of studying attachment in such cultures?
5 Would you like to see the United States adopt child-care policies similar to those in Sweden? Why or why not?

PART TWO

Early Childhood

D uring the years from 3 to 6, often called the *preschool years,* children make the transition from toddlerhood to childhood. Their appearance changes, their motor and mental abilities flower, and their personalities become more complex.

All aspects of development—physical, cognitive, emotional, and social—continue to intertwine. As muscles come under more conscious control, children can tend to more of their own personal needs, such as dressing and toileting, and thus gain a greater sense of competence and independence. The neighborhood environment and wider societal influences can have a profound impact—for better or for worse—on physical health and cognitive growth. Even the common cold can have cognitive and emotional implications, as we'll see in Chapter 6. And, as we discuss in Chapter 7, cognitive awareness of gender has far-reaching psychosocial effects. Yet, even as we describe general patterns that apply to many or most children, we need to look at each child as a unique person, setting more and more challenging goals and finding more and more diverse ways to meet them.

CHAPTER SIX

PHYSICAL AND COGNITIVE DEVELOPMENT IN EARLY CHILDHOOD

Children live in a world of imagination and feeling. . . . They invest the most significant object with any form they please, and see in it whatever they wish to see.

Adam G. Oehlenschlager

ASK YOURSELF

✔ How do children's bodies and motor skills grow and develop from ages 3 to 6?

✔ How can young children be kept safe and healthy?

✔ What sleep patterns and problems develop during early childhood, and how can they be handled?

✔ What are some advances and limitations in young children's thinking?

✔ How do language facility and memory improve in early childhood?

✔ How is preschoolers' intelligence measured, and how does the home environment influence it?

✔ What is the impact of early educational experiences?

t is the day before Keisha's third birthday. "Pretty soon," she tells her mother, "I'll be big enough to sleep without sucking my thumb. And maybe tomorrow I'll be big enough to wear pajamas like Daddy's."

The big day dawns. Keisha leaps out of bed at her usual early hour and runs to the mirror. She examines her image closely and then runs to her parents' room. "Mommy, Daddy!" she squeals into sleepy ears. "I'm 3!" Then a note of disappointment creeps into her voice as she acknowledges, "But I don't look different."

Keisha may not have changed noticeably from the day before, but in comparison with a year earlier, she is very different indeed. Children who have celebrated their third birthday are no longer babies. They are capable of bigger and better things, both physically and cognitively. The 3-year-old is a sturdy adventurer, very much at home in the world and eager to explore its possibilities, as well as the developing capabilities of his or her own body. A child of this age has come through the most dangerous time of life—the years of infancy and toddlerhood—to enter a healthier, less threatening phase. The environment is widening now; although formal schooling has not yet begun, many children attend preschools, or nursery schools, starting at age 3, and most go to kindergarten at 5.

■ Youngsters between the ages of 3 and 6 grow more slowly than before, but still at a fast pace; and they make so much progress in muscle development and coordination that they can do much more. Children also make enormous advances in their abilities to think, speak, and remember. In this chapter, we trace all these developing capabilities and consider several important concerns. We also assess the effects of early childhood education. ■

✔ ASPECTS OF PHYSICAL DEVELOPMENT

In early childhood, children slim down and shoot up. They improve in gross motor abilities such as running, hopping, skipping, jumping, and throwing balls. They also become better at fine motor tasks such as tying shoelaces (in bows instead of knots), drawing with crayons (on paper rather than on walls), and pouring cereal (into the bowl, not onto the floor); and they begin to show a preference for either the right or left hand. They need less sleep than before, and sleep problems become more common.

PHYSIOLOGICAL GROWTH AND CHANGE

At about age 3, children begin to lose their babyish roundness and to take on the slender, athletic appearance of childhood. As abdominal muscles develop, the toddler's potbelly tightens. The trunk, arms, and legs grow longer. The head is still relatively large, but the other parts of the body continue to catch up as body proportions steadily become more adultlike.

The pencil mark on the wall that shows Keisha'a height at 3 years is a little more than 37 inches from the floor, and she now weighs more than 31 pounds. Boys at age 3 are slightly taller and heavier than girls and have more muscle per pound of body weight; girls have more fatty tissue. Both boys and girls typically grow 2 to 3 inches a year during early childhood and gain 4 to 6 pounds annually. The boys' slight edge in height and weight then continues until the growth spurt of puberty.

These changes in appearance reflect developments inside the body. Muscular and skeletal growth progresses, making children stronger. Cartilage turns to bone at a faster rate than before, and bones become harder, giving the child a firmer shape and protecting the internal organs. These changes, coordinated by the maturing brain and nervous system, promote the development of a wide range of motor skills. The increased capacities of the respiratory and circulatory systems build physical stamina and, along with the developing immune system, keep children healthier.

By age 3, all the primary, or deciduous, teeth are in place, and children can chew anything they want to. The permanent teeth, which will begin to appear at about age 6, are developing.

NUTRITION

Proper growth and health depend on good nutrition. Preschoolers eat less in proportion to their size than infants do; as growth slows, they need fewer calories per pound of body weight. Parents often worry that their preschool children are not eating enough, but children seem to know how much food they need at a given time. In one study, 15 children ages 2 to 5 took in roughly the same number of calories every day for 6 days, even though they often ate very little at one meal and a great deal at another (Birch, Johnson, Andersen, Peters, & Schulte, 1991). Preschoolers whose mothers let them eat when they are hungry and do not pressure them to eat everything given to them are more likely to regulate their own calorie intake than are children with more controlling mothers (S. L. Johnson & Birch, 1994).

What children eat is a different matter. Children whose diets are heavy in sugared cereal, cake, candy, and other low-nutrient foods will not have enough appetite for the foods they need; so parents should offer only nutritious foods, including snacks. In a study comparing 2- to 5-year-old children of mothers working outside the home with children of nonemployed mothers, both groups of children ate equally well, but both got too little calcium, iron, zinc, and Vitamin E, and too much fat (R. K. Johnson, Smiciklas-Wright, Crouter, & Willits, 1992).

Such dietary deficiencies are especially disturbing because the nutritional demands of early childhood are easily satisfied. The daily protein requirement can be met with two glasses of milk and one serving of meat or an alternative such as fish, cheese, or eggs. Vitamin A can come from carrots, spinach, egg yolk, or whole milk (among other

foods). Vitamin C is in citrus fruits, tomatoes, and leafy dark-green vegetables. Calcium, essential to build bone mass, can come from dairy products, broccoli, and salmon; lactose-intolerant children, who have a bad reaction to milk, can get necessary nutrients from other foods.

Although a fat baby is no cause for concern, a fat child may be. Obese children tend to become obese adults, and excess body mass can be a threat to health. A tendency to overweight in early childhood is partly hereditary, but it also depends on fat intake and exercise (Klesges, Klesges, Eck, & Shelton, 1995). Concern about dietary fat and cholesterol has led to recommendations that children over age 2 should get only about 30 percent of their total calories from fat, and less than 10 percent of the total from saturated fat. Meat and dairy foods should remain in the diet to provide protein, iron, and calcium; but meat should be lean, and milk and other dairy products can now be skim or low-fat (AAP Committee on Nutrition, 1992a). A study that followed a predominantly Hispanic group of 215 healthy 3- to 4-year-olds for 1 to 2 years found no negative effects on height, weight, or body mass from a moderately low-fat diet (Shea et al., 1993).

MOTOR SKILLS

At 3, David could walk a straight line and jump a short distance. At 4, he could hop a few steps on one foot. On his fifth birthday, he could jump nearly 3 feet and hop for 16 feet and was learning to roller-skate.

Children between ages 3 and 6 make great advances in *gross motor skills,* such as running and jumping, which involve the large muscles (see Table 6-1). The sensory and motor areas of the cortex are more developed than before, permitting better coordination between what children want to do and what they can do. Their bones and muscles are stronger, and their lung capacity is greater, making it possible to run, jump, and climb farther, faster, and better.

Children vary in adeptness, depending on their genetic endowment and their opportunities to learn and practice motor skills. Those under age 6 are rarely ready to take part in any organized sport. Only 20 percent of 4-year-olds can throw a ball well, and only 30 percent can catch well (AAP Committee on Sports Medicine and Fitness, 1992). Physical development blossoms best in active, unstructured free play.

Fine motor skills, such as buttoning shirts and

TABLE 6-1

Gross Motor Skills in Early Childhood

3-Year-Olds	4-Year-Olds	5-Year-Olds
Cannot turn or stop suddenly or quickly	Have more effective control of stopping, starting, and turning	Can start, turn, and stop effectively in games
Can jump a distance of 15 to 24 inches	Can jump a distance of 24 to 33 inches	Can make a running jump of 28 to 36 inches
Can ascend a stairway unaided, alternating feet	Can descend a long stairway alternating feet, if supported	Can descend a long stairway unaided, alternating feet
Can hop, using largely an irregular series of jumps with some variations added	Can hop four to six steps on one foot	Can easily hop a distance of 16 feet

SOURCE: Corbin, 1973.

drawing pictures, involve eye-hand and small-muscle coordination. Gains in these skills allow young children to take more responsibility for their personal care. At 3, Winnie can pour milk into her cereal bowl, eat with silverware, and use the toilet alone. She can also draw a circle and a rudimentary person—without arms. At 4, Nelson can dress himself with help. He can cut along a line, draw a fairly complete person, make designs and crude letters, and fold paper into a double triangle. At 5, Juan can dress himself without much help, copy a square or triangle, and draw a more elaborate person than before.

Changes in young children's drawings apparently reflect maturation of the brain as well as of the muscles (Kellogg, 1970). Two-year-olds *scribble,* not randomly but in patterns, such as vertical and zigzag lines. By age 3, children draw *shapes*—circles, squares, rectangles, triangles, crosses, and X's—and then begin combining the shapes into more complex *designs.* The *pictorial* stage begins between ages 4 and 5. This switch from abstract form and design to depicting real objects marks a fundamental change in the purpose of children's drawing, which may reflect cognitive development of representational ability.

HANDEDNESS

Handedness, the preference for using one hand over the other, is usually evident by 3 years of age. About 9 out of 10 children and adults are right-handed. This propensity seems to reflect the usual dominance of the left hemisphere of the brain, which controls the right side of the body. In people whose brains are more symmetrical, the right hemisphere tends to dominate, making them left-handed (Coren, 1992; Porac & Coren, 1981). Boys are more likely to be left-handed than girls. So are children who suffered difficult births and those whose maturation is delayed.

Although some scientists have suggested that handedness is genetic, twin studies indicate otherwise: Identical twins are no more likely to be concordant for handedness than fraternal twins or any two people in the general population. Some research suggests that fetal position in the womb may be a factor (Coren & Halpern, 1991).

Both "lefties" and "righties" have advantages and disadvantages. "Lefties" tend to have a highly developed spatial imagination; this may explain the high proportion of left-handed architects. Left-handed people may be more likely to be academically gifted. Among more than 100,000 twelve- and thirteen-year-olds who took the Scholastic Aptitude Test (SAT), 20 percent of the top-scoring 300 children were left-handed, twice the rate in the general population (Bower, 1985). On the other hand, left-handed children tend to have more accidents (Graham, Dick, Rickert, & Glenn, 1993) and to suffer from allergies, sleep problems, and migraine headaches.

Many cultures have viewed left-handedness as abnormal and have tried to discourage it. In Japan, for example, many parents try to force their children to use the right hand, even going so far as to bind the left hand with tape. In the United States, some older adults who showed an early preference for the left hand were taught to write with the right hand. However, science has found no reason for such practices, and prejudice against left-handedness is waning in western industrial countries.

Children make significant advances in motor skills during the preschool years. As they develop physically, they are better able to make their bodies do what they want. Large-muscle development lets them run or ride a tricycle; increasing eye-hand coordination helps them to use scissors or chopsticks. Children with disabilities can do many normal activities with the aid of special devices. *(Top left, Laura Dwight, top right, Tony Freeman/PhotEdit, bottom left, Miro Vintoniv/Stock, Boston, bottom right, Tom McCarthy/The Image Bank)*

SLEEP PATTERNS AND PROBLEMS

Sleep patterns change throughout life, and early childhood has its own distinct rhythms. Young children usually sleep more deeply at night than they will later in life, but they still need a daytime nap or quiet rest until about age 5.

Going to bed in the evening often becomes an issue. As young children gain in mastery over their environment, it is hard for them to let go of a stimulating world full of people and be alone in bed. They may develop elaborate bedtime routines to put off retiring, and it may take them longer than before to fall asleep. They are likely to want a light left on and to sleep with a favorite toy or blanket (Beltramini & Hertzig, 1983). Such *transitional objects,* used repeatedly as bedtime companions, help a child shift from the dependence of infancy to the independence of later childhood. Parents sometimes worry when their child cannot fall asleep without a tattered blanket or stuffed animal, but such worry seems unfounded. In one longitudinal study, 11-year-olds who at age 4 had insisted on taking cuddly objects to bed were now outgoing, sociable with adults, and self-confident; they enjoyed playing by themselves and tended not to be worriers. At age 16, they were just as well adjusted as children who had not used transitional objects (Newson, Newson, & Mahalski, 1982).

Walking and talking during sleep are fairly common in early childhood and are usually harmless. However, persistent sleep disturbances may indicate an emotional problem that needs to be examined.

Sleep Disturbances

Many children—between 20 and 30 percent of those in their first 4 years, according to one study—engage in bedtime struggles lasting more than an hour and wake their parents frequently at night. Children with these problems tend to sleep in the same bed with the parents. The family is likely to have experienced a stressful accident or illness; or the mother is likely to be depressed or ambivalent about motherhood or to have recently changed her schedule so as to be away for most of the day (Lozoff, Wolf, & Davis, 1985).

About 1 in 4 children ages 3 to 8 have night terrors or nightmares (Hartmann, 1981). A child who experiences a *night terror* awakens abruptly from a deep sleep in a state of panic. The child, generally a boy, may scream and sit up in bed, breathing rapidly and staring. Yet he is not really awake, quiets down quickly, and the next morning remembers nothing about the episode. Night terrors alarm parents more than children and may simply be an effect of very deep sleep; they rarely signify a serious emotional problem and usually go away by age 6. If they are severe and long-lasting and occur once a week or more, some physicians prescribe a short course of therapy with drug treatment (McDaniel, 1986).

A *nightmare* is a frightening dream, often brought on by staying up too late or eating a heavy meal close to bedtime, or by overexcitement. Unlike night terrors, which usually occur within an hour after falling asleep, nightmares come toward morning and are often vividly recalled. An occasional bad dream is no cause for alarm, especially in a child under 6; but frequent or persistent nightmares, especially those which make a child fearful or anxious during waking hours, may signal excessive stress. A repeated theme may point to a specific problem the child cannot solve while awake.

Bed-Wetting

Most children stay dry, day and night, by 3 to 5 years of age; but *enuresis,* repeated urination in clothing or in bed, is common, especially at night. A child may be diagnosed as having primary, or persistent, enuresis if wetting occurs at least twice a week for at least 3 months after age 5, or if the condition is causing significant stress or impairment at school or in other everyday activities. About 7 percent of 5-year-old boys and 3 percent of girls wet the bed regularly, but most outgrow the condition without special help (APA, 1994). Fewer than 1 percent of bed-wetters have a physical disorder, and persistent enuresis is not primarily an emotional problem.

Enuresis runs in families. About 75 percent of bed-wetters have a close relative who also wet the bed, and identical twins are more concordant for the condition than fraternal twins (APA, 1994; Fergusson, Horwood, & Shannon, 1986). The discovery of the approximate site of a gene linked to enuresis (Eiberg, Berendt, & Mohr, 1995) points to heredity as a major factor, possibly in combination with such other factors as slow motor maturation, allergies, and poor behavioral control (Goleman, 1995a). The gene does not appear to account for occasional bed-wetting.

Children and their parents need to be reassured

that enuresis is common and not serious. The child is not to blame and should not be punished. Generally parents need not do anything unless children themselves see bed-wetting as a problem. The most effective treatments include rewarding children for staying dry; waking them when they begin to urinate by using devices that ring bells or buzzers; and teaching children to practice controlling the sphincter muscles and to stretch the bladder (Rappaport, 1993). As a last resort, hormones or antidepressant drugs may be given for a short time (Goleman, 1995a; McDaniel, 1986).

✔ HEALTH AND SAFETY

What used to be a very vulnerable time of life is much safer now. Because of widespread immunization, many of the major diseases of childhood are now fairly rare. Deaths are relatively few compared with deaths in adulthood, and most are caused by injury rather than illness (Starfield, 1991). Still, environmental influences—poverty, homelessness, and stress—make this a less healthy time for some children than for others.

ILLNESSES AND ACCIDENTS

Coughs, sniffles, stomachaches, and runny noses are a part of early childhood. These minor illnesses typically last 2 to 14 days but are seldom serious enough to need a doctor's attention. Because the lungs are not fully developed, respiratory problems are common, though less so than in infancy. Three- to five-year-olds catch an average of seven to eight colds and other respiratory illnesses a year. These illnesses help build natural immunity (resistance to disease). During middle childhood, when the respiratory system is more fully developed, children average fewer than six such illnesses a year (Denny & Clyde, 1983). Minor illnesses may have emotional and cognitive benefits, helping children learn to cope with physical distress and understand its causes (see Box 6- 1).

Children's death rates from all kinds of illness have come down in recent years. Deaths from influenza and pneumonia dropped by 50 percent between 1950 and 1980 and remain at about the 1980 level (USDHHS, 1982, 1996). The 5-year disease-free survival rate for cancer (considered a cure in medical terms) has risen sharply for children under 15 (American Cancer Society, 1993).

Because young children are naturally venture-

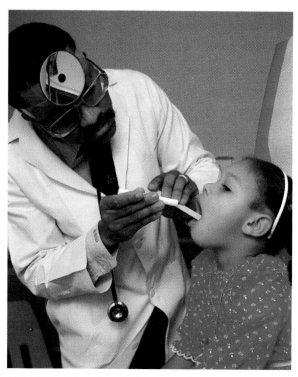

Although sore throats and other minor illnesses are common among 3- to 6-year-olds, they are usually not serious enough to require visits to the doctor. This 5-year-old will probably have fewer colds and sore throats in the next few years, as her respiratory and immune systems mature. *(Elliott Varner Smith/International Stock Photo)*

some and often unaware of danger, it is hard for caregivers to protect them from harm without *over*protecting them. Although most cuts, bumps, and scrapes are "kissed away" and quickly forgotten, some accidental injuries result in lasting damage or death. Accidents are the leading cause of death in childhood in the United States. The most frequent cause is motor vehicle injuries; the next is drowning (Rivara & Grossman, 1996; USDHHS, 1996; Williams & Miller, 1991, 1992). Young children are more likely to be hit *by* cars than to be injured *in* them (B. C. Williams & Miller, 1992).

Still, children's deaths from accidents in the United States declined 26 percent between 1978 and 1991. This improvement is largely due to use of restraining devices in cars and to fewer pedestrian injuries (Rivara & Grossman, 1996). All 50 states and the District of Columbia have laws requiring young children to be restrained in cars, either in specially designed seats or by standard seat belts. In 1991, 63 percent of children under age 5 who died in automobiles were unrestrained (Rivara & Grossman, 1996).

BOX 6-1   FOOD FOR THOUGHT

IS ILLNESS GOOD FOR CHILDREN?

Nobody likes to be sick; but are the frequent minor illnesses of early childhood a blessing in disguise? Their physical benefit in building immunity is well known, and one researcher has identified cognitive and emotional benefits as well (Parmelee, 1986).

Illness helps children learn to cope with physical distress and thus enhance their sense of competence and their understanding of their changing physical states. Repeated experience with minor illness causes children to pay more attention to their bodily sensations. When children feel such familiar symptoms as aches and pains, muscular weakness, lack of energy, and "the blues," they realize from

past experience that they will soon be their usual selves again.

Furthermore, when children see their brothers, sisters, playmates, and parents go through similar bouts with illness, they learn *empathy*, the ability to put themselves in someone else's place and feel what that person is feeling. When Adam's younger sister Jenny catches the flu, Adam knows how she feels and can help give her the comfort and care he gets when *he* is ill.

Dealing with illness also can help advance understanding of language. For example, Adam may have confused two meanings of the word *bad*: the way he feels physically when his throat hurts

("feels bad") and the way he feels emotionally when he has done something he knows is wrong (was a "bad" boy). Such confusion is especially likely to occur when adults use the term *bad* to apply to a child or the child's behavior. Since young children tend to have "magical" explanations for illness and to blame it on something they did (see Box 8-1), Adam may think he got sick because, for example, he hit his sister. Illness gives parents and other caregivers a chance to help children clear up such confusion by reassuring a child: "I know you feel bad because you're sick, but it's not because of anything you did, and you'll soon be well."

Laws requiring car restraints, "child-proof" caps on medicine bottles, and mandatory helmets for bicycle riders have improved child safety. Making playgrounds safer would be another valuable measure. An estimated 3 percent of children in day care are hurt badly enough each year to need medical attention (Briss, Sacks, Aldiss, Kresnow, & O'Neil, 1994), and about half of accidents at day care centers occur on playgrounds (Briss et al., 1994; Sacks et al., 1989). Many of these could be averted by lowering the height of climbing equipment and covering the ground with impact-absorbing materials, such as wood chips, loose sand, or mats.

Children are less likely to be injured in day care, however, than in and around the home (Thacker, Addiss, Goodman, Holloway, & Spencer, 1992), where most fatal nonvehicular accidents occur. Children drown in bathtubs, pools, and buckets containing liquids (as well as in lakes, rivers, and oceans); are burned in fires and explosions; fall from heights; drink or eat poisonous substances; get caught in mechanical contrivances; and suffocate in traps, such as abandoned refrigerators. Another dangerous place is the supermarket; the number of children injured in shopping carts doubled during the 1980s, and more than 12,000 serious head injuries to children under 5 were reported in 1989 (U.S. Consumer Product Safety Commission, 1991).

HEALTH IN CONTEXT: ENVIRONMENTAL INFLUENCES

Why do some children have more illnesses or injuries than others? The genetic heritage contributes: some children seem predisposed toward some medical conditions. In addition, as Bronfenbrenner's ecological model might predict, the home, the day care center, the school, the neighborhood, and the larger society play major roles. In the United States, about 9 million children under age 5 live with a smoker and are exposed daily to secondhand smoke, which can cause pneumonia, bronchitis, and asthma (American Heart Association, 1994; United States Environmental Protection Agency, 1994). Family situations involving stress or economic hardship increase vulnerability to illness and accidents.

Exposure to Illness and Stress

Children in large families are sick more often than those in small families (Loda, 1980). Similarly, children in day care centers, who come in contact daily with many other children, are 2 to 4 times more likely to pick up mild infectious diseases (such as colds, flu, and diarrhea) than are children cared for at home. They also have a higher risk of contracting more serious gastrointestinal diseases and hepatitis A (Thacker et al., 1992). However, children in high-quality day care, where nutrition is well-planned, hygiene is emphasized, and illnesses may be detected and treated early, tend to be healthier than those not in day care programs (AAP, 1986).

Stress is an organism's physiological and psychological response to demands made on it. Some sources of stress are physical: illness, changes in the chemistry of the central nervous system, and effects of drugs. Others are psychological: changes in family structure, shifts in male and female roles, increasing urbanization, and disruption of relationships due to greater geographic mobility (Cross-National Collaborative Group, 1992; Klerman & Weissman, 1989). Although the sources of stress are often environmental, hereditary factors play a part in the way people respond.

Stressful events in the family, such as moves, job changes, divorce, and death, increase the frequency of minor illnesses and home accidents. In one study, children whose families had experienced 12 or more such stressful events were more than twice as likely to have to go into the hospital as children from families that had experienced fewer than 4 traumatic events (Beautrais, Fergusson, & Shannon, 1982). Children can be directly affected by adults' stress: a distraught adult may forget to put away a kitchen knife or a poisonous cleaning fluid, fasten a gate, or make sure that a child washes before eating. Entry into day care is stressful for many children (Craft, Montgomery, & Peters, 1992).

Poverty

Poverty is stressful, unhealthy—and dangerous. Low income is the *chief* factor associated with poor health (J. L. Brown, 1987), and young children are the largest age group living in poverty in the United States (Strawn, 1992). Child poverty rates in the United States are 2 to 9 times higher than those in other major industrialized countries (Children's Defense Fund, 1996; see Figure 6-1). In 1994, more than 1 in 5 children—and 1 in 4 children under age 6—were poor, as defined by the official poverty level ($15,141 a year for a family of four). About 44 percent of black children and 41.5 percent of Latino children were poor, compared with

17 percent of white children (Children's Defense Fund, 1996). Death rates for African American children and teenagers are considerably higher than for whites for every cause except suicide, car injuries, and accidental poisoning and falls (B. C. Williams & Miller, 1992).

The health problems of poor children begin before birth. Poor mothers often do not eat well and do not receive adequate prenatal care, and their babies are likely to be of low birthweight, to be stillborn, or to die soon after birth (see Figure 6-2). Poor children often do not eat properly and do not grow properly, and thus are weak and susceptible to disease. Poor children are also at high risk of injury. Many poor families live in crowded, unsanitary housing, and the children may lack adequate supervision, especially when the parents are at work. They are more likely than other children to suffer lead poisoning, hearing and vision loss, and iron-deficiency anemia, as well as such stress-related conditions as asthma, headaches, insomnia, and irritable bowel. They also tend to have more behavior problems, psychological disturbances, and learning disabilities (J. L. Brown, 1987; Egbuono & Starfield, 1982; Santer & Stocking, 1991; Starfield, 1991).

An estimated 3 million American children under age 6 have lead levels high enough to interfere with cognitive development. Boys in minority groups, living in poverty, are most at risk (Pirkle et al., 1994). Children can get lead in the bloodstream from lead-contaminated food or water, from putting contaminated fingers in their mouths, or from inhaling dust in homes or schools where there is lead-based paint (Baghurst et al., 1992; Bellinger, Stiles, & Needleman, 1992; Dietrich, Berger, & Succop, 1993). The effects of lead poisoning can last for years; it can cause seizures, mental retardation, or death (AAP Committee on Environmental Health, 1993) and is associated with antisocial and delinquent behavior (Needleman, Riess, Tobin, Biesecker, & Greenhouse, 1996). Moderate lead poisoning can be successfully treated (Ruff, Bijur, Markowitz, Ma, & Rosen, 1993). Removal of lead from gasoline and soldered food cans has helped prevention efforts (Pirkle et al., 1994).

Many poor children do not get the medical care they need. In the United States, the number of children whose families lack health insurance is growing, largely due to a decline in employer-provided coverage. About 1 percent of children have lost coverage each year since 1987 (Children's Defense

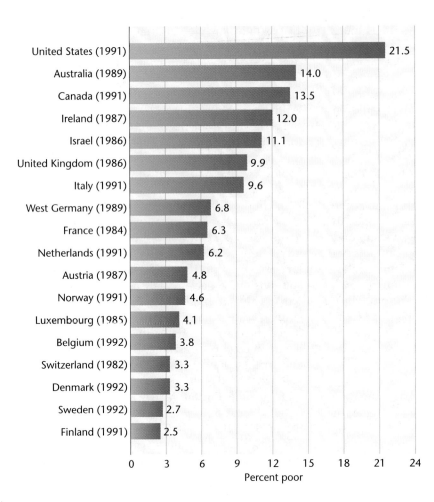

FIGURE 6-1
Child poverty rates in 18 industrialized countries. The poverty rate for children in the United States is higher than that in 17 other industrialized countries; yet upper- and middle-class children in the United States are much better off than their counterparts in the other countries. (*Source: Luxembourg Income Study; reprinted in Children's Defense Fund, 1996, p. 6.*)

Fund, 1996). Children who are uninsured see doctors less often, are in worse health, are less likely to have up-to-date immunizations, and when they get sick are more likely to require long hospital stays than children with health coverage (Children's Defense Fund, 1996; D. L. Wood, Hayward,

Corey, Freeman, & Shapiro, 1990). White children are much more likely to be under a doctor's care; minority children, especially black children, tend to be treated in hospital emergency rooms. Many black and Latino families do not have money to pay private doctors, have no medical insurance,

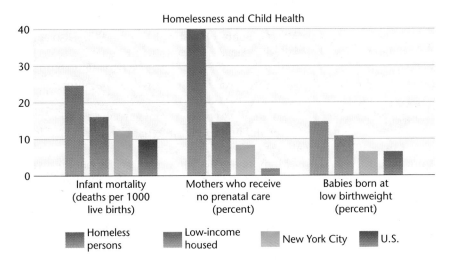

FIGURE 6-2
Homelessness and child health. Homeless children suffer more health problems than do other poor children who have homes. (*Source: Bassuk, 1991, p. 70.*)

This family living in a tent is among the estimated 43 percent of homeless people in the United States made up by families with children. Homeless children are more likely than other poor children to have health problems. *(Mark Richards/PhotoEdit)*

and—especially if they do not speak English—may have less ready access to doctors than white families do (Newacheck, Stoddard, & McManus, 1993).

In European countries, by contrast, no child goes without preventive health services or medical care; the government provides free health care for everyone. Important "safety nets" for poor children in the United States have been federally funded Aid to Families with Dependent Children (AFDC) and Medicaid. However, AFDC has now been eliminated, and responsibility for welfare for needy families has been shifted to the states. Although Medicaid now covers 1 in 4 children, it does not fully offset losses in private, employer-sponsored coverage. In 1994, 1 in 7 children was uninsured (Children's Defense Fund, 1996). A critical issue for the coming decades is whether further tightening of federal and state budgets will be at the expense of the health of poor and minority children.

Homelessness

Poor children who do not have homes have the greatest problems of all. Children need homes if they are to thrive (AAP Committee on Community Health Services, 1996). An estimated 43 percent of the estimated 2½ to 3 million homeless people in the United States are families with children, the fastest-growing segment of this population. More than half (53 percent) of these families are headed by young single women, many of whom have abused alcohol or drugs or have been phys-

ically or sexually abused. In some cities, as many as 75 percent of the homeless are children, and a disproportionate number are black (AAP Committee on Community Health Services, 1996).

Why is the homeless population growing? Reasons include lack of affordable housing; cutbacks in rent subsidies and welfare programs; unemployment, especially among people with marginal skills; divorce and domestic violence; substance abuse; deinstitutionalization of the mentally ill; and growing poverty (AAP Committee on Community Health Services, 1996).

Many homeless children spend their crucial early years in an unstable, insecure, and often unsanitary environment. They sleep in emergency shelters, welfare hotels, abandoned buildings, or cars, or on the street. Homeless children and their parents are cut off from a supportive community, family ties, and institutional resources and from ready access to medical care. The effects are devastating, both physically and psychologically (AAP Committee on Community Health Services, 1996; J. L. Bass, Brennan, Mehta, & Kodzis, 1990; Bassuk, 1991; Bassuk & Rosenberg, 1990; Rafferty & Shinn, 1991).

From birth, these children suffer more health problems than do poor children who have homes (refer back to Figure 6-2). They are 3 times more likely than other children to lack immunizations, and 2 to 3 times more likely to have iron deficiency anemia. They experience high rates of diarrhea; hunger and malnourishment; obesity (from eating excessive carbohydrates and fats); tooth decay;

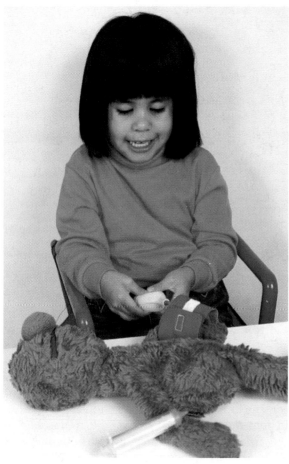

As Anna pretends to take Grover's blood pressure, she is showing a major cognitive achievement: deferred imitation, the ability to act out an action she observed some time before. *(Erika Stone)*

asthma; respiratory, skin, and eye and ear infections: scabies and lice; and elevated levels of lead. Homeless children tend to suffer severe depression and anxiety and to have neurological deficits, developmental delays, behavior problems, and learning difficulties. Uprooted from their neighborhoods, as many as half do not go to school; if they do, they tend to have problems, partly because they miss a lot of it and have no place to do homework. They tend to do poorly on standardized reading and math tests and are more likely to repeat a grade or to be placed in special classes than are children with homes (AAP Committee on Community Health Services, 1996; Bassuk, 1991; Rafferty & Shinn, 1991).

In 1994, a U.S. Court of Appeals in Washington, D.C., guaranteed homeless children in that city access to public education; and Congress directed school districts, wherever possible, to enroll homeless children in the schools their parents request. To prevent homelessness, Virginia has adopted a program of no-interest loans or direct grants to landlords to help families keep their homes during a temporary financial emergency. In 1990, the program's first year, the average family received help for about 3½ months at a cost amounting to about one-third of the cost of temporary shelter. The program has been so successful that it has been expanded each year (Children's Defense Fund, 1995).

✔ THE PREOPERATIONAL CHILD

Jean Piaget named early childhood the *preoperational stage.* In this second major stage of cognitive development, which lasts from approximately ages 2 to 7, children become far more sophisticated in their use of symbolic thought (see Chapter 4). However, according to Piaget, children cannot think logically until the stage of concrete operations in middle childhood (Chapter 8).

Piaget's theory and research form a valuable starting point for understanding young children's cognitive development. However, Piaget seems to have underestimated the capabilities of preoperational children, as he did with sensorimotor children. More recent research, using more age-appropriate techniques, has found that certain abilities seem to develop earlier than he suggested. When given tasks compatible with what they are familiar with and explained in language they understand, many children show greater competence than Piaget thought possible. Let's look at the current status of research on advances and limitations of preoperational thought (summarized in Tables 6-2 and 6-3).

ADVANCES IDENTIFIED BY PIAGET AND OTHERS

Among the cognitive advances of the preoperational stage are the symbolic function, understanding of identities, understanding of cause and effect, ability to classify, and understanding of number. Some of these abilities have roots in infancy and toddlerhood; others develop in early childhood but are not fully achieved until middle childhood.

The Symbolic Function

"I want an ice cream cone!" announces Sharon, age 4, trudging indoors from the hot, dusty backyard.

TABLE 6-2

Cognitive Advances of Early Childhood*

Advance	Significance	Example
Use of symbols	Children can think about something without needing to see it in front of them.	Jeffrey knows the name "Pumpkin" stands for his cat. He can talk or hear about her without having the cat in front of him. Words also stand for objects, people, and events.
Understanding of identities	The world is more orderly and predictable; children are aware that superficial alterations do not change the nature of things.	When Jeffrey cannot find his cat, he says, "Maybe Pumpkin put on a bear suit and went to someone else's house to be their pet bear." But when asked, Jeffrey shows that he knows that Pumpkin would—even if she put on a bear suit—still be his cat.
Understanding of cause and effect	It becomes more evident that the world is orderly; also, children realize that they can cause events to happen.	Marie knows that if she jumps into a puddle, she will get her sneakers dirty. She can choose to jump anyway; she can do it barefoot; or she can resist the temptation.
Understanding of numbers	Children can count and can deal with quantities.	Marie has two carrots on her plate. She leaves the table and comes back to find only one. "Who took my carrot?" she demands.
Ability to classify	It becomes possible to organize objects, people, and events into meaningful categories.	Marie lists which of her classmates are "nice" and which are "mean" and says, "The nice ones are my friends."
Empathy	Relationships with others become possible as children become able to imagine how others might feel.	Jeffrey tells a friend who brought him crayons, "I already have some." Then he quickly adds, "But I wanted more."
Theory of mind	It becomes possible to explain and predict other people's actions by imagining their beliefs, feelings, and thoughts.	Jeffrey wants to play ball with some bigger boys. His mother says no; so Jeffrey asks his father, but he does not tell his father that his mother has already said no. He knows that if his father knew, he would say no, too.

*Although the beginnings of these ways of thought are present in early childhood, their full achievement usually does not take place until middle childhood.

She has not seen anything that triggered this desire—no open freezer door, no television commercial. She no longer needs this kind of sensory cue to think about something. She remembers ice cream, its coldness and taste, and she purposefully seeks it out. This absence of sensory or motor cues characterizes the *symbolic function:* the ability to use symbols, or mental representations—words, numbers, or images to which a person has attached meaning. Having symbols for things helps children to think about them and their qualities, to remember them and talk about them, without having them physically present. The development of symbolic thought makes possible other important advances of the preoperational stage.

Children show the symbolic function through deferred imitation, symbolic play, and language. *Deferred imitation,* which appears to begin in infancy, is the repetition of an observed action after time has passed. In *symbolic play,* children make an object stand for (symbolize) something else; for example, a doll may represent a child. *Language,*

TABLE 6-3

Limitations of Preoperational Thought

Limitation	Description	Example
Centration: Inability to decenter	Child focuses on one aspect of a situation and neglects others.	Jeffrey cries when his father gives him a cookie broken in half. Because each half is smaller than the whole cookie, Jeffrey thinks he is getting less.
Inability to distinguish appearance from reality	Child confuses what is real with outward appearance.	Jeffrey thinks a sponge made to look like a rock really is a rock.
Irreversibility	Child fails to understand that an operation or action can go both ways.	Jeffrey does not realize that both halves of the cookie can be put next to each other to show the whole cookie.
Focus on states rather than transformations	Child fails to understand the significance of the transformation between states.	In the conservation task, Jeffrey does not understand that transforming the liquid (pouring it from one glass into another) does not change the amount.
Transductive reasoning	Child does not use deductive or inductive reasoning; instead, he jumps from one particular to another and sees cause where none exists.	"I had bad thoughts about my brother. My brother got sick. So I made my brother sick." Or "I was bad so mommy and daddy got divorced."
Egocentrism	Child assumes everyone else thinks as she does.	Jenny takes out her game and tells her mother, "This is *your* treat." She assumes her mother likes to play the game as much as she does.
Animism	Child attributes life to objects not alive.	Jenny thinks clouds are alive because they move.

which we discuss more fully later in this chapter, involves the use of a common system of symbols (words) to communicate.

Understanding Identities

The world becomes more orderly and predictable as children develop a better understanding of *identities:* the concept that people and many things are basically the same even if they change in form, size, or appearance. This understanding underlies the emerging self-concept (see Chapters 5 and 7).

Understanding Cause and Effect

Young children's persistent "why" questions show that they are beginning to link cause and effect. Very young children spontaneously use such words as *because* and *so.* "He's crying because he doesn't want to put his pajamas on," said Marie at 27 months, watching her brother cry loudly as he was being dressed for bed.

Researchers asked 3- and 4-year-olds to look at pictures like those on the top line of Figure 6-3 and then to choose the picture on the bottom line that would tell what happened (Gelman, Bullock, & Meck, 1980). The children showed an understanding of causality by telling such stories as: "First you have dry glasses, and then water gets on the glasses, and you end up with wet glasses."

Ability to Classify

Young children develop proficiency at classifying, or grouping objects, people, and events into categories based on similarities and differences. By the age of 4, many children can classify by two criteria, such as color and shape (Denney, 1972).

Understanding Number Concepts

Understanding of basic number concepts seems to begin in infancy (see Chapter 4). By early childhood, children recognize five principles of counting (Gelman & Gallistel, 1978; Sophian, 1988):

1 The *1-to-1 principle:* You say only one number-name for each item being counted ("One, two, three . . .").
2 The *stable-order principle:* You say number-names in a set order ("One, two, three . . ." rather than "Three, one, two . . .").
3 The *order-irrelevance principle:* You can start counting with any item, and the total count will be the same.
4 The *cardinality principle:* The last number-name you use is the total number of items being counted. (If there are 5 items, the last number will be "5.")
5 The *abstraction principle:* You can count all sorts of things.

Children now have words for comparing quantities. They can say one tree is *taller* than another, or one cup holds *more* juice than another. As early as age 3 or 4, they know that if they have one cookie and then get another cookie, they have more cookies than they had before; and then if they give one cookie to another child, they have less. Such quantitative knowledge appears to be universal, though it develops at different rates, depending on how important counting is in a particular family or culture and how much instruction parents, teachers, or educational television programs provide (Resnick, 1989; Saxe, Guberman, & Gearhart, 1987).

LIMITATIONS OF PREOPERATIONAL THOUGHT

Although early childhood is a time of significant cognitive achievement, Piaget found important limitations in preoperational thinking compared with what children can do when they reach the stage of concrete operations in middle childhood. Awareness of these limitations is important for parents, teachers, health professionals, and other adults who need to explain things to children. Let us look at some of these limitations: centration,

Story A

Choices for A

FIGURE 6-3
Examples of sequences to test understanding of causality. A child is asked to look at pictures like those in the top row, to pick the one in the bottom row that would show what happened, and to tell a story about what happened. (*Source: Gelman et al., 1980.*)

confusing appearance with reality, irreversibility, focus on states, transductive reasoning, and egocentrism. We'll also discuss more recent research that has challenged some of Piaget's observations.

Centration

Preoperational children show **centration:** they focus on one aspect of a situation and neglect others. They come to illogical conclusions because they cannot **decenter**—think about several aspects of a situation at one time.

A classic example of centration is Piaget's famous experiment designed to test the development of **conservation,** the awareness that two things which are equal remain so if their appearance is altered, so long as nothing is added or taken away. He found that children do not fully understand this principle until the stage of concrete operations and that they develop different kinds of conservation at different ages. Table 6-4 shows how various dimensions of conservation have been tested.

In one type of conservation task, conservation of liquid, a 5-year-old we'll call Jeffrey is shown two identical clear glasses, each one short and wide and each holding the same amount of water. Jeffrey is asked whether the amount of water in

TABLE 6-4

Tests of Various Kinds of Conservation

Conservation Task	Show Child (and Have Child Acknowledge) That Both Items Are Equal	Perform Transformation	Ask Child	Preoperational Child Usually Answers
Number	Two equal rows of candies	Space one row farther apart.	"Are there the same number of candies in each row or does one row have more?"	"The longer one has more."
Length	Two sticks of the same length	Move one stick.	"Are both sticks the same size or is one longer?"	"The one on the right (or left) is longer."
Liquid	Two glasses holding equal amounts of liquid	Pour liquid from one glass into a taller, narrower glass.	"Do both glasses have the same amount or does one have more?"	"The taller one has more."
Matter (mass)	Two balls of clay of the same size	Roll one ball into a sausage shape.	"Do both pieces have the same amount of clay or does one have more?"	"The sausage has more."
Weight	Two balls of clay of the same weight	Roll one ball into a sausage shape.	"Do both weigh the same or does one weigh more?"	"The sausage weighs more."
Area	Two toy rabbits, two pieces of cardboard (representing grassy fields), with blocks or toys (representing barns on the fields); same number of "barns" on each board	Rearrange the blocks on one piece of board.	"Does each rabbit have the same amount of grass to eat or does one have more?"	"The one with the blocks close together has more to eat."
Volume	Two glasses of water with two equal balls of clay in them	Roll one ball into a sausage shape.	"If we put the sausage back in the glass, will the water be the same height in each glass or will one be higher?"	"The water in the glass with the sausage will be higher."

the two glasses is equal. When he agrees, the water in one glass is poured into a third glass, a tall, thin one. Jeffrey is now asked whether both contain the same amount of water or whether one contains more, and why. In early childhood—even after watching the water poured out of one of the short, fat glasses into a tall, thin glass or even after pouring it himself—Jeffrey will say that either the taller glass or the wider one contains more water. When asked why, he says, "This one is bigger this way," stretching his arms to show the height or width. Preoperational children cannot consider height *and* width at the same time. Since they center on one aspect, they cannot think logically.

Confusing Appearance with Reality

Another way in which Jeffrey's logic is flawed is that his thinking is tied to what he thinks he sees; if one glass *looks* bigger, he thinks it must *be* bigger. In other words, he confuses appearance with reality.

Not until about age 5 or 6, said Piaget, do children understand the distinction between what *seems* to be and what *is*. This flaw in thinking may account for some of children's fears. For example, a young child may be afraid of something that looks scary, such as a witch on a movie screen, failing to understand that the witch is not real.

In one series of experiments (Flavell, Green, Wahl, & Flavell, 1987), children under age 6 or 7 confused appearance and reality in a variety of tests. For example, the experimenters showed preschoolers a red car and then covered it with a filter that made it look black. When the children were asked what color the car really was, they said "black." When the children put on special sunglasses that made milk look green, they said the milk *was* green, even though they had just seen white milk. When an experimenter put on a Halloween mask in front of the children, they thought the experimenter was someone else.

Irreversibility

Preoperational logic is also limited by *irreversibility:* failure to understand that an operation or action can go two or more ways. Children show irreversibility by worrying that a cut will not heal or a broken leg cannot be mended. In the liquid conservation task, once Jeffrey can imagine restoring the original state of the water by pouring it

back into the other glass, he will realize that the amount of water in both glasses is the same.

Focus on States Rather Than on Transformations

Preoperational children commonly think as if they were watching a filmstrip with a series of static frames: they focus on successive states and do not recognize the transformation from one state to another. In the conservation experiment, they focus on the water as it stands in each glass rather than on the water being poured from one glass to another, and so they fail to realize that the amount of water is the same.

Transductive Reasoning

Preoperational children, said Piaget, reason by *transduction:* they view one situation as the basis for another situation, often one occurring at about the same time, whether or not there is logically a causal relationship. For example, they may think that their "bad" thoughts or behavior caused their own or another child's illness (refer back to Box 6-1), or feel guilty about their parents' divorce. ("I was bad today. Mom and Dad don't love each other any more. I made them not love each other.")

Egocentrism

At age 4, Jenny was at the beach. Awed by the constant thundering of the waves, she turned to her father and asked, "But when does it stop?" "It doesn't," he replied. "Not even when I'm *asleep?*" asked Jenny incredulously. Her thinking was so egocentric, so focused on herself as the center of her world, that she could not consider anything—even the mighty ocean—as continuing its motion when she was not there to see it.

Egocentrism is the inability to see things except from one's own point of view. It is not selfishness but self-centered understanding, and, according to Piaget, it is at the heart of much of the limited thinking of young children. Egocentrism is a form of centration: Piaget claimed that young children center so much on their own point of view that they cannot take in another's view. Three-year-olds are not, of course, as egocentric as newborn babies, who cannot distinguish between the universe and their own bodies; but, said Piaget, they still think the universe centers on them. Egocen-

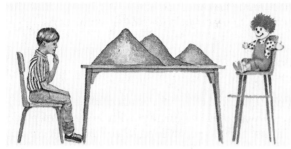

FIGURE 6-4
Piaget's mountain task. A preoperational child is unable to describe the "mountain" from the doll's point of view—an indication of egocentrism, according to Piaget.

trism may help explain why young children have trouble separating reality from what goes on inside their own heads and why they show confusion about what causes what. When Adam believes that his "bad thoughts" have made his sister sick or that he caused his parents' marital troubles, he is thinking egocentrically.

To study egocentrism, Piaget designed the *three-mountain task* (see Figure 6-4). A child sits facing a table that holds three large mounds. A doll is placed on a chair at the opposite side of the table. The investigator asks the child how the "mountains" would look to the doll. Piaget found that young children usually could not answer the question correctly; instead, they described the "mountains" from their own perspective. Piaget saw this as evidence that preoperational children cannot imagine a different point of view (Piaget & Inhelder, 1967).

However, another experimenter who posed a similar problem in a different way got different results (Hughes, 1975). In the *doll and police officer task*, the child sits in front of a square board with dividers that separate it into four sections. A toy police officer is put at the edge of the board; a doll is set in one section and then moved from one section to another. After each move the child is asked, "Can the police officer see the doll?" Then another toy police officer is brought into the action, and the child is told to hide the doll from both officers. In this study, 30 children between the ages of 3½ and 5 were correct 9 out of 10 times.

Why were these children able to take another person's point of view (the police officer's) when those doing the mountain task were not? It may be because the "police officer" task calls for thinking in more familiar, less abstract ways. Most children do not look at mountains and do not think about what other people might see when looking at one, but most 3-year-olds know about dolls and police officers and hiding. Thus, contrary to Piaget's claim, young children may show egocentrism primarily in situations beyond their experience.

Egocentrism and Animism   *Animism* is the tendency to attribute life to objects that are not alive. When Piaget asked young children whether the wind and the clouds were alive, their answers led him to think they were confused about what is alive and what is not. Piaget attributed this to egocentrism; one child, for example, said the moon is alive "because we are."

However, when later researchers questioned 3- and 4-year-olds about differences between a rock, a person, and a doll, the children showed they understood that people are alive and rocks and dolls are not (Gelman, Spelke, & Meck, 1983). They did not attribute thoughts or emotions to rocks, and they cited the fact that dolls cannot move on their own as evidence that dolls are not alive.

The "animism" Piaget saw in young children may have been due to the fact that the things he asked about (such as wind and clouds) show movement—and are very far away. Since children know so little about wind and clouds, they are less certain about them than about familiar things like rocks and dolls.

Egocentrism and Empathy   Research also challenges Piaget's belief that egocentrism delays the development of *empathy*, the ability to understand what another person is feeling. Even 10- to 12-month-old babies cry when they see another child crying; by 13 or 14 months, they pat or hug a crying child; by 18 months they may hold out a new toy to replace a broken one or give a bandage to someone with a cut finger (Yarrow, 1978). In early childhood, empathy, which is important for forming and maintaining relationships, shows itself more and more.

When Anna, at 4, was going home with her parents after a visit to her grandmother, she said, "Don't be sad, Grandma. We'll come see you again, and you can come see us in New York." Anna's grandmother had not cried or talked about feeling sad, but Anna imagined how she must have been feeling. This kind of understanding usually comes earlier to children in families that talk a lot about feelings and causality, underscoring the relationship between the cognitive and the emotional

This young girl is old enough to know that her brother would like a lick of her popsicle. Empathy, the ability to understand another person's feelings, begins at an early age. *(S. Lousada/ Petit Format/Photo Researchers)*

(Dunn, 1991; Dunn, Brown, Slomkowski, Tesla, & Youngblade, 1991).

Empathy is closely related to children's *theory of mind,* their emerging awareness of their own mental state and that of other people.

DO YOUNG CHILDREN HAVE THEORIES OF MIND?

"Why does Pedro look sad?" "What made Mommy mad at me?" The ability to make sense of other people's actions is a major step in cognitive development. How and when do children come to understand what another person is thinking and feeling? For that matter, how and when do they become aware of their own state of mind?

Piaget (1929) was the first scholar to investigate children's conception of their mental life—their theory of mind. He asked children such questions as "Where do dreams come from?" and "What do you think with?" On the basis of the answers, he concluded that children younger than 6 cannot distinguish between thoughts or dreams and real physical entities and have no theory of mind. But more recent research indicates that children do discover their minds sometime between the ages of 2 and 5, when their knowledge about mental states and attitudes grows dramatically (Astington, 1993; Bower, 1993).

Again, methodology appears to have made the difference. Piaget's questions were abstract, and he expected children to be able to put their understanding into words. Contemporary researchers use vocabulary and objects that children are familiar with. Instead of talking in generalities, they observe children in their everyday activities or they give them concrete examples. In this way, we have learned, for example, that 3-year-olds can tell the difference between a boy who has a cookie and a boy who is thinking about a cookie; they know which boy can touch, share, and eat it (Astington, 1993).

Of course, young children's theory of mind is less than fully developed. Let's look at some aspects of it: *knowledge about thinking, distinction between fantasy and reality, awareness of false beliefs,* and *use of deception.*

Knowledge about Thinking

Young children know something about thinking, but they do not seem to be aware that the mind is constantly engaged in thought (Flavell, 1993). At 3, Dylan understands that someone can be thinking of one thing while doing or looking at something else, that a person whose eyes and ears are covered can think about objects, that someone who looks pensive is thinking, and that thinking is different from talking (Flavell, Green, & Flavell, 1992). At 4, he does not consider "thinking about" and "knowing" as the same thing. However, he believes mental activity starts and stops; he assumes that when the mind has nothing pressing to do, it does nothing. Not until middle childhood do children realize that the mind is continuously active (Flavell, 1993).

Distinguishing Fantasy from Reality

Sometime between 18 months and 3 years, children learn to distinguish between real and imagined events. Still, 4- to 6-year-olds are not always sure that what they imagine is not real. In one study (Harris, Brown, Marriott, Whittall, & Harmer, 1991), 40 children ages 3 to almost 7 were shown two cardboard boxes. They were asked to pretend that there was a small, friendly puppy in one and a big, scary monster in the other. Each box had a small hole in it, and the children were asked whether they wanted to put a finger or a stick in the holes. Even though most of the children claimed they were just pretending about both the puppy and the monster, most preferred to touch the box holding the imaginary puppy, and more used their finger in that box and the stick in the monster box. The results of this and other experiments show that young children understand the distinction between fantasy and reality, yet they sometimes act as if the creatures of their imagination could exist.

False Beliefs and Deception

Five-year-old Mariella is shown a candy box and is asked what is in it. "Candy," she says. But when she opens the box, she finds crayons, not candy. "What will a child who hasn't opened the box think is in it?" the researcher asks. "Candy!" shouts Mariella, grinning at the joke. When the researcher repeats the same procedure with 3-year-old Bobby, he too answers the first question with "Candy." But after seeing the crayons in the box, when asked what another child would think was in the box, he says "Crayons." And then he says that he himself originally thought crayons would be in the box (Flavell, 1993). Not until most children are 4 or 5 years old do they understand that they or other people can hold false beliefs (Moses & Flavell, 1990). However, 3- to 5-year-olds with more advanced language development—as well as those from large families, who are likely to experience many interactions with siblings involving teasing, trickery, and the like—tend to be more sophisticated in their understanding of false beliefs (Jenkins & Astington, 1996).

Telling a lie can be a sign of cognitive development. For a child to deceive someone, the child has to be able to imagine what the other person might think. In one study, 3-year-olds who knew their mother had broken a toy lied to a stranger to pro-

tect the mother; but when speaking to the mother they acknowledged that they knew she had broken the toy. However, they also lied to the mother, telling her they had told the stranger that the mother broke the toy (Ceci & Leichtman, 1992). It seems, then, that children this young change their story to accomplish different aims: first to protect the mother from being punished and then, with the mother, to preserve the child's image as a good and truthful person.

CAN ACQUISITION OF COGNITIVE ABILITIES BE SPEEDED UP?

Whether acquisition of cognitive abilities can deliberately be speeded up depends on the ability, the timing, and the way a child is taught. Training does not seem to help young children distinguish appearance from reality (Flavell, Zhang, Zou, Dong, & Qi, 1983); but certain methods of teaching conservation seem to work when a child is already on the verge of acquiring the concept.

In one study (D. Field, 1981), 3- and 4-year-olds were shown sets of checkers, candies, and sticks. A child was asked to pick the two rows that had the same number of items or to show which two objects were the same length. Then the objects were moved or changed, and the child was asked whether they were the same. The child was then given one of three rules explaining *why* they were the same:

1 *Identity* (sameness of materials): "No matter where you put them, they're still the same candies."
2 *Reversibility* (possibility of returning the items to their original arrangement): "We just have to put the sticks back together to see that they are the same length."
3 *Compensation* (showing that a change in one dimension was balanced by a change in the other): "Yes, this stick does go farther in this direction, but at the other end the stick is going farther, and so they balance each other."

The type of training and the children's age affected how well they learned. Children who were told the identity rule made the most progress, and those who learned reversibility also advanced; but those who were taught compensation benefited little from the training. Four-year-olds (who presumably were closer to acquiring conservation on their own) were more apt than three-year-olds to learn the concept and to retain it up to 5 months later. Three-year-olds were not able to conserve as many quantities and tended to lose whatever abilities they did gain. Apparently, when children's cognitive structures are well enough developed to handle the principle of conservation, training can give them a strategy for integrating the principle into their thought processes.

✔ ASPECTS OF COGNITIVE DEVELOPMENT

At the breakfast table, Terry, age 3½, overheard his grandparents discussing the number of square feet of tile needed for their kitchen. "But then," he piped up, "you'd need to have square shoes!"

Young children's growing facility with ideas and speech helps them form their own unique view of the world, in ways that often surprise and amuse adults. As they become more competent in the use of language and memory, children form and use concepts and share them with others. And, as children apply their intelligence to solving problems both at home and in day care, preschool, or kindergarten, individual differences become more apparent and more measurable.

LANGUAGE

During early childhood Anna was full of questions: "How many sleeps until tomorrow?" "Who filled the river with water?" "Do babies have muscles?" "Do smells come from inside my nose?" Young children are interested in the whole wide world. They ask questions about everything, and their linguistic skills progress rapidly.

Vocabulary and Diction

By the age of 6, the average child understands more than 14,000 words, having learned an average of 9 new words a day since about 1½ years of age (Rice, 1982). Apparently children do this by *fast mapping,* which allows them to absorb the meaning of a new word after hearing it only once or twice in conversation. On the basis of the context, children seem to form a quick partial understanding of the word and store it in memory. Linguists do not know how fast mapping occurs, but it seems likely that children draw on what they know—rules for forming words, similar words, grammatical contexts, and the subject under discussion.

Still, young children do not always use a word as adults do (Pease & Gleason, 1985). For example, Anna at about age 4 used *tomorrow* to refer to any time in the future, and *yesterday* for any time in the past. On the other hand, a child may be quite literal in interpreting a word and thus receive a different meaning from the intended one. When Diane told 5-year-old Anna that her shiny red boots were "sharp," Anna said, "No, they aren't— they don't have nails in them!"

The use of *metaphor,* a figure of speech in which a word or phrase that usually designates one thing is applied to another, becomes increasingly common during these years (Vosniadou, 1987). Once Anna, upset by her parents' quarreling, exclaimed, "Why are you two being such grumpy old bears?" Anna's use of metaphor reflected her growing ability to see similarities between (in this case) parents and bears and thus was related to her ability to classify. The use of metaphor shows an ability to use knowledge about one type of thing to better understand another, an ability needed for acquiring many kinds of knowledge.

Grammar and Syntax

At 3, children typically use plurals and past tense and know the difference between *I, you,* and *we.* Between ages 4 and 5, sentences average four to five words. Children now use prepositions such as *over, under, in, on,* and *behind.* In some respects, though, their comprehension may be immature. For example, 4-year-old Noah can carry out a command that includes more than one step ("Pick up your toys and put them in the cupboard"); but if his mother tells him "You may watch TV after you pick up your toys," he may process the words in the order in which he hears them and think he may first watch television and then pick up his toys.

Around ages 5 and 6, children speak in longer and more complicated sentences. They use more conjunctions, prepositions, and articles. Between 6 and 7 years of age, children begin to speak in compound and complex sentences and use all parts of speech.

Although young children speak fluently, understandably, and fairly grammatically, they often make errors because they have not yet learned exceptions to rules. Saying "holded" instead of "held" or "eated" instead of "ate" is a normal sign of linguistic progress. When children discover a rule, such as adding *-ed* to a verb for past tense, they tend to *overregularize*—to use it even with

Although Piaget believed that most of young children's speech is egocentric, research shows that children like these boys playing on the beach communicate, both verbally and through gestures, from an early age. *(Newman Brown/ Monkmeyer)*

words that do not conform to the rule. Eventually, they notice that *-ed* is not always used to form the past tense of a verb.

Pragmatics and Social Speech

The form and function of speech are linked. As children master words, sentences, and grammar, they become more competent at communicating. *Pragmatics,* the practical knowledge needed to use language for communicative purposes, includes learning how to ask for things, how to tell a story or joke, how to begin and continue a conversation, and how to adjust comments to the listener's perspective (Rice, 1982). These are all aspects of *social speech*—speech intended to be understood by a listener.

Although Piaget characterized most of young children's speech as egocentric, research suggests that children use both gestures and verbal speech communicatively from an early age. Two-year-olds show objects to others (Wellman & Lempers, 1977), and 4-year-olds use "motherese" when speaking to 2-year-olds (Shatz & Gelman, 1973). Three- to five-year-olds communicate very differently with a person who can see as opposed to one who cannot; they will point to a toy for a sighted listener but describe it to someone who is blindfolded (Maratsos, 1973).

Private Speech

Anna, age 4, was alone in her room painting. When she finished, she was overheard saying aloud,

"Now I have to put the pictures somewhere to dry. I'll put them by the window. They need to get dry now. I'll paint some more dinosaurs."

Private speech, talking aloud to oneself with no intent to communicate with others, is normal and common in childhood, accounting for 20 to 60 percent of what children say. The youngest children playfully repeat rhythmic sounds. Older children "think out loud" or mutter in barely audible tones.

The purpose and value of private speech have been controversial. Piaget viewed it as egocentric. Also, he maintained, young children talk while they do things because the symbolic function is not fully developed: they do not yet distinguish between words and the actions the words stand for. The Russian psychologist Vygotsky (see Chapter 1), instead of looking upon private speech as immature, saw it as a special form of communication: communication with oneself. Like Piaget, Vygotsky (1962) believed that private speech helps children integrate language with thought. Unlike Piaget, who saw private speech as characteristic of the preoperational stage, Vygotsky suggested that private speech increases during the early school years as children use it to guide and master their actions and then fades away as they become able to do this silently.

Research supports Vygotsky's interpretation. Among nearly 150 middle-class children ages 4 to 10, private speech rose and then fell with age. The most sociable children used it the most, apparently supporting Vygotsky's view that private speech is stimulated by social experience (Berk, 1986; Kohlberg, Yaeger, & Hjertholm, 1968). The brightest children used it earliest; for them, it peaked around age 4, compared with ages 5 to 7 for children of average intelligence. By age 9 it had virtually disappeared in all the children.

Understanding the significance of private speech has practical implications, especially in school (Berk, 1986). Talking or muttering to oneself should not be considered misbehavior; a child may be struggling with a problem and may need to think out loud. Instead of insisting on perfect quiet, teachers can set aside areas where children can talk and learn without disturbing others. Children should also be encouraged to play with others to help them develop the internal thought processes that will eventually displace thinking aloud.

Delayed Language Development

Albert Einstein did not start to speak until he was 3 years old, a fact that may encourage parents of other children whose speech develops later than usual. Language development is delayed in about 3 percent of preschool-age children, though their intelligence is usually average or better (Rice, 1989). Some have a history of otitis media (an inflammation of the middle ear) between 12 and 18 months of age; these children improve when the infection, with its related hearing loss, clears up (Lonigan, Fischel, Whitehurst, Arnold, & Valdez-Menchaca, 1992).

It is unclear why children with no detectable physical or cognitive problems speak late. They do not necessarily lack linguistic input at home. Some of their parents talk to them more in terms of what the children can say rather than what they can understand (Whitehurst, Fischel, Caulfield, DeBaryshe, & Valdez-Menchaca, 1989); but this may be more the result than the cause of their delay. These children may have a cognitive limitation that makes it hard for them to learn the rules of language (Scarborough, 1990).

Some current investigations focus on problems in fast mapping new words heard in conversation. Studies suggest that children with delayed language skills need to hear a word more often than other children do before they can incorporate it into their vocabulary (Rice, 1989; Rice, Oetting, Marquis, Bode, & Pae, 1994).

Delayed language development can have cognitive, social, and emotional consequences. Children who show an unusual tendency to mispronounce words at age 2, who have poor vocabulary at age 3, or who have trouble naming objects at age 5 are apt to have reading disabilities later on

(Rice et al., 1994; Scarborough, 1990). Furthermore, children who do not speak or understand as well as their peers tend to be judged negatively by adults and other children and may be treated accordingly. In one study, kindergarten teachers, college students, laypersons, and specialists in speech problems listened to audiotaped samples of preschool children's speech. All four groups of adults rated children with delayed language skills as less bright, less likable, less socially mature, less likely to succeed in kindergarten, and less likely to be classroom leaders than other children (Rice, Hadley, & Alexander, 1993).

Significant verbal deficits, unless treated (see Chapter 1), can have far-reaching consequences. Children whom adults view as unintelligent or immature may "live down" to these expectations. Also, peers are less likely to want to play with a child who does not readily understand what others are saying (Gertner, Rice, & Hadley, 1993); and children who are not accepted by peers have trouble making friends. In both respects, self-esteem suffers. Social rejection can further impede language development; preschoolers whose language skills are deficient may especially need opportunities to interact verbally with adults and other children (Rice, 1989).

Preparation for Literacy

Social interaction, especially in the home, is a key factor in preparing young children for literacy. Furthermore, the *kind* of interaction matters. Interactive techniques for reading aloud to infants and toddlers, such as those described in Chapter 4, are equally effective for preschoolers.

How adults speak with children is an important predictor of literacy. Children are more likely to become good readers and writers if, during the preschool years, parents provide conversational challenges the children are ready for, using a rich vocabulary and centering dinner-table talk on the day's activities or on questions about why people do things and how things work. Such conversations help young children learn to choose words and put sentences together coherently (C. E. Snow, 1990, 1993). Preschool teachers have helped socioeconomically disadvantaged children expand their vocabularies by using relatively uncommon words. The children in these classes scored higher on vocabulary tests than those whose teachers did not use such words, and the children who heard the unfamiliar words used many of them in play (Dickinson, Cote, & Smith, 1993).

Educational television can help prepare children for literacy, especially if parents talk with children about what they see. In one study, the more time 3- to 5-year-olds spent watching *Sesame Street*, the more their vocabulary skills improved (Rice, Huston, Truglio, & Wright, 1990). The program teaches letters and numbers, as well as problem solving, reasoning, and understanding of the physical and social environments. The format is designed to attract children's attention and to get them to participate actively.

How children play is another factor in preliteracy development. Imaginative play (see Chapter 7), involving pretending or "make-believe," is most closely linked to literacy (Christie, 1991). As children grow older, this kind of play becomes increasingly social, involving other people and a wide variety of objects. Story lines become more complex, evolving into well-coordinated scenarios, and roles and themes become more creative and unusual. All these changes offer children rich opportunities to learn, use, and practice language.

MEMORY

When Anna was 3, she went on an apple-picking trip. Months later, she talked about riding on the bus, visiting a farm, picking apples, bringing them home, and eating them. She had a vivid memory of the event and enjoyed talking about it.

During early childhood, children show significant improvement in attention and in the speed and efficiency with which they process information. These advances allow cognitive strides, particularly in memory.

Before the mid-1960s, there was little research on memory in children younger than 5; and until about the 1980s, most of that research was done in the laboratory. Now, with a surge of interest in information processing and the development of memory, we have a clearer picture of the "remembering child" in the everyday world.

Recognition and Recall

Recognition is the ability to identify something encountered before (for example, to pick out a missing mitten from a lost-and-found box). *Recall* is the ability to reproduce knowledge about memory (for example, to describe the mitten to someone). Preschool children, like all age groups, do better on recognition than on recall; both abilities improve with age (Lange, MacKinnon, & Nida, 1989; N. Myers & Perlmutter, 1978).

The more familiar children are with an item, the better they can recall it. Also, young children can more easily recall items that have an understandable relationship to one another. When 3- and 4-year-olds were shown pairs of pictures, they did much better in recalling related pairs than unrelated ones (Staub, 1973). The type of relationship affects degree of recall. Children are more likely to recall pictures when one member of a pair is a part of the other (say, a tire and a car) than when one item is the usual habitat of the other (say, a lake and a fish). They are least apt to recall pairs in which the two items belong to the same category (say, a hat and a sock).

Recall depends both on motivation to master skills and on the way a child approaches a task. In one study (Lange et al., 1989), ninety-three 3- and 4-year-olds were tested on their knowledge of a variety of objects, assessed on how reflective or impulsive they were, and rated by preschool teachers and parents on such characteristics as initiative, use of problem-solving strategies, and pursuit of difficult tasks. The children were videotaped as they handled two assortments of toys in succession and then tried to name them from memory. The best predictor of success was "mastery motivation"—the tendency to be independent, self-directed, and generally resourceful, as rated by the child's teacher. The only other relevant factor was what the child did while studying the toys. The more children named or grouped the toys or spent time thinking about or repeating their names (in other words, the more they used strategies to help them remember), the better their recall. These two factors did not seem related to each other; that is, "mastery motivation" did not seem to encourage the use of particular study strategies.

Childhood Memories

Can you remember anything that happened to you before you were 3 years old? The chances are you can't. This inability to remember early events is called *infantile amnesia*. One explanation, held by Piaget (1969) and others, is that early events are not stored in memory at all. Freud believed that early memories are repressed because they are emotionally troubling. Some information-processing theorists suggested that early memories become inaccessible because they are not *encoded* (prepared for storage) as later memories are. None of these explanations is supported by recent research (K. Nelson, 1992, 1993). Very young children do

"Remember when we went on the airplane to visit Grandma and Grandpa?" Young children better remember events that are unique and new, and they may recall many details from a special trip for a year or longer. *(Elizabeth Crews/The Image Works)*

seem to remember things that happened to them, much as adults do. Even children younger than 2 can talk about events that occurred a month before, and 4-year-olds remember trips they took at age 2 (K. Nelson, 1992). Why, then, don't these early memories last?

A newer explanation arises from evidence that different *kinds* of memories are encoded in different ways. Memories that people know they have (such as knowledge of facts, names, and events) are encoded in a way that allows for intentional, or *explicit memory.* Other memories (for example, of how to throw a ball) seem to be encoded in a way that can produce behavioral change without intentional recall or even conscious awareness of the memory. This kind of memory is called *implicit memory* (Schacter, 1992), and it may exist before the brain structures necessary for explicit memory have formed (Newcombe & Fox, 1994). Memory in early childhood is rarely deliberate: young children simply remember events that made a strong impression, and most of these early conscious memories seem to be short-lived.

However, implicit (unconscious) memories may persist much longer. In one study of implicit memory (Newcombe & Fox, 1994), 9- and 10-year-olds were shown photos of preschool classmates they had not seen for 5 years, along with photos of children they had never known. The children's *skin conductance* (movement of electrical impulses through the skin) was measured while they viewed the pictures. In a small but significant number of cases, positive responses appeared when the children saw pictures of their former classmates, even when they did not consciously recognize the faces. This finding suggests that people may retain memories from infancy or early childhood of which they are not aware and that these submerged memories may affect their behavior.

How, when, and why do children begin to form permanent conscious memories? One researcher, Katherine Nelson (1993), has proposed three types of explicit childhood memory that serve different functions: generic, episodic, and autobiographical.

Generic memory, which begins at about age 2, produces a *script,* or general outline of a familiar, repeated event without details of time or place. The script contains routines for situations that come up again and again; it helps a child know what to expect and how to act. For example, a child may have scripts for riding the bus to preschool or having lunch at Grandma's house.

Episodic memory refers to a particular incident that happened at a specific time and place. Young children remember more clearly events that are unique or new to them. Three-year-olds may recall details about a trip to the zoo for a year or longer (Fivush, Hudson, & Nelson, 1983), whereas generic memories of frequent events (such as going to the park) tend to blur together. However, given a young child's limited memory capacity, episodic memories are temporary, as they serve no useful purpose in guiding behavior. Unless they recur several times (in which case they are transferred to generic memory), they last for a few weeks or months and then fade. The reliability of children's episodic memory has become an im-

BOX 6-2   PRACTICALLY SPEAKING

CHILDREN'S EYEWITNESS TESTIMONY

In 1984, fourteen children who had attended a California preschool made charges of child abuse against seven teachers, charges that eventually included rape, sodomy, fondling, oral copulation, and drugging and photographing children in the nude. After 17 months of preliminary hearings, charges against five teachers were dropped. In 1990, after a 3-year trial, and after the remaining defendants—a 62-year-old woman and her 30-year-old son—had spent 6 years in jail, they were acquitted on almost all charges, and the jury deadlocked on the others. Both defendants were set free (Ceci & Bruck, 1993).

The key issue was whether the testimony of the children could be believed. Some people said such young children could not have imagined the bizarre events they reported—such events as satanic rituals and animal mutilation. Others claimed the children were responding to suggestions made to them during interviews by parents, therapists, and officials. This and similar cases have sparked research into the reliability of young children's memories.

Child abuse (see Chapter 7) is a crime that often can be proved only by the testimony of preschool children (Doris, 1993). If a child's testimony is not accurate, an innocent adult may be unfairly punished. A series of studies by Stephen J. Ceci and Maggie Bruck demonstrates that children can "remember" events that never occurred. For 11 consecutive weeks, an interviewer told a 4-year-old, "You went to the hospital because your finger got caught in a mousetrap. Did this ever happen to you?" At first the boy said, "No, I've never been to the hospital." In the second interview he said, "Yes, I cried." In the third: "Yes. My mom went to the hospital with me." By the eleventh interview he said, "My daddy, mommy and my brother [took me] in our van. . . . The hospital gave me . . . a little bandage. . . . The mousetrap was in our house . . . down in the basement. . . . I was playing a game. . . . [My brother] pushed me [into the mousetrap]. I caught my finger in it yesterday. I went to the hospital yesterday" (Ceci, in Goleman, 1993).

Many children, given anatomically correct dolls, will insert fingers or sticks into a doll's vagina or anus, reporting that someone did that to them—even when those events have not happened (Ceci & Bruck, 1993). On the other hand, 5- to 7-year-old girls, when questioned about doctors' examinations, were unlikely to falsely report genital contact. They were far more likely to fail to report contact that did occur, unless they were specifically asked about it (Saywitz, Goodman, Nicholas, & Moan, 1991).

Most research has found that young preschoolers are more suggestible than older children. This may be due to younger children's weaker episodic memory and also to their greater vulnerability to bribes, threats, or adult expectations. However, since much of the older research was laboratory-based, it is unclear whether the

---

portant issue in lawsuits involving charges of child abuse (see Box 6-2).

Autobiographical memory refers to memories that form a person's life history. These memories are specific and long-lasting. Although autobiographical memory is a type of episodic memory, not everything in episodic memory becomes part of it—only those memories that have a special, personal meaning. Autobiographical memory serves a social function, letting a person share something of the self with others.

Autobiographical memory begins for most people around age 4, and rarely before age 3. It increases slowly between ages 5 and 8; memories from then on may be recalled for 20, 40, or more years. Individuals differ in the onset of autobiographical memory; some people have vivid memories from the age of 3, whereas others do not remember much before age 8 (K. Nelson, 1992).

These findings suggest that autobiographical memory is dependent on the development of language. Not until children can put memories into words can they hold them in their minds, reflect on them, and compare them with the memories of others. In line with Vygotsky's view of the importance of social interaction with adults, talking about shared events may help children learn how to formulate permanent memories to be called up when desired. Children of a higher social class, especially girls, who tend to show early language development, seem to develop autobiographical memory earlier than other children (K. Nelson, 1992, 1993). So do firstborns, who spend more time interacting with their parents than laterborns can (Mullen, 1994).

Most research on memory has focused on middle-class American or western European children, who have been talking since about age 2. We know

findings apply to a real-life situation such as a trial (Ceci & Bruck, 1993; Leichtman & Ceci, 1995).

To test young children's veracity in circumstances similar to what may occur on the witness stand, researchers had a man called Sam Stone visit a day care center for a few minutes (Leichtman & Ceci, 1995). The visitor commented on a story that was being read, strolled around the room, and then waved goodbye and left. The eight classes that witnessed the event were randomly assigned to one of four groups. All the children were interviewed once a week for 4 weeks. Children in a *control* group were given no information about the visitor in advance and were questioned neutrally afterward. A *stereotype* group was repeatedly told stories about "Sam Stone" before his visit, depicting him as a well-meaning bumbler. A *suggestion* group, when questioned afterward, was given false suggestions that he had ripped a book and

soiled a teddy bear. A *stereotype-plus-suggestion* group received both the stereotyped advance preparation and the misleading questioning.

The results show that preschoolers, especially the youngest, are far more suggestible than was previously thought. In a fifth session with a new interviewer, nearly half the 3- and 4-year-olds and 30 percent of 5- and 6-year-olds in the stereotype-plus-suggestion group spontaneously reported the damage to the book and the soiling of the teddy bear; and when asked probing questions, nearly 3 out of 4 of the younger children claimed the visitor had done one or both. Lesser proportions of the groups that had received *only* stereotyped preparation or suggestive questioning gave false reports, generally in response to probing. Younger children were more suggestible than older ones. By contrast, none of the children in the control group freely made false re-

ports, and very few did so even when probed, showing that young children's testimony *can* be accurate when elicited neutrally. However, when shown videotapes of three final interviews, 119 researchers and clinicians could not tell the true from the false accounts or whether the "events" in question had occurred.

Ceci and Bruck (1993) conclude that (1) preschoolers are more suggestible and therefore can be less reliable than older children; (2) young children may make mistakes, especially after being asked leading questions; (3) children's reports are likely to be more reliable if the children have been interviewed only once, as soon after the event as possible, and if they are interviewed by people who do not have an opinion about what took place, who do not ask leading questions, who ask open-ended rather than yes-or-no questions, who are patient and nonjudgmental, and who do not reward any responses.

little about the relationship between memory and language among children who begin to speak later because of different social and cultural practices, or among deaf children of hearing parents who cannot as easily converse with them (K. Nelson, 1993).

Influences on Children's Memory

Why do some early episodic memories last longer than others? To find out, Nelson (1989) read mothers' diaries, interviewed children, analyzed tape-recordings of a friend's daughter's bedtime "self-talk" from 21 months to age 3, and drew on other studies of early memories.

One factor, as we've seen, is the uniqueness of the event. In addition, preschoolers tend to remember things they *did* better than things they merely *saw* (D. C. Jones, Swift, & Johnson, 1988).

In one study, sixty-five 3- and 4½-year-olds visited a replica of a turn-of-the-century farmhouse, where they did such things as pretend to sew a blanket on a treadle sewing machine and chop ice with a pick and hammer. When interviewed—later the same day, 1 week later, or 8 weeks later—children remembered best the objects they had used to do something, such as the sewing machine.

Drawing can help preschoolers remember. In one series of experiments, children who had visited a fire station where they had seen several unusual staged events were interviewed the next day or 1 month later. Half the children were asked to tell about what they had seen; the other half were asked to draw and describe it. Five- and six-year-olds (but not three- and four-year-olds) who drew pictures reported more verbally than those who did not draw (S. Butler, Gross, & Hayne, 1995).

How adults talk with a child during a shared experience can influence how well the child will remember it. In one field experiment, ten 3-year-olds and their mothers visited a museum (Tessler, 1986, 1991). Half the mothers talked naturally with their children as they walked through the museum; the other half simply responded to the children's comments. A week later, the children recalled *only* those objects they had talked about with their mothers, and the children in the "natural conversation" group remembered them better, supporting the connection between language and memory. Mothers' conversational styles also had an effect. Four mothers had a *narrative* style, reminiscing about shared experiences ("Remember when we went to a museum and saw a dinosaur?"). The other six mothers had a *pragmatic* style, using memory for specific practical purposes, such as helping a child solve a puzzle the child has done before. When asked specific questions about the museum trip, children of "narrative" mothers recalled more than twice as many details as the "practical" group.

Another analysis of how adults talk with children about the past identified two styles among 24 white middle-class two-parent families (Reese & Fivush, 1993). In a *repetitive* conversation, parents repeat either the general thrust or the exact content of their own previous statement or question. In an *elaborative* conversation, parents move on to a new aspect or event or add more information. A repetitive-style parent might ask, "Do you remember how we traveled to Florida?" and then, receiving no answer, ask, "How did we get there? We went in the ———." An elaborative-style parent might instead follow up the first question by saying, "Did we go by car or by plane?" In this study, 3-year-old children—especially daughters—of elaborative-style parents took part in longer conversations and remembered more details. Both fathers and mothers were more likely to use the elaborative style with girls than with boys. However, it is hard to tell whether girls converse more than boys because parents elaborate more with them or whether parents elaborate more because girls talk more. Whatever the case, adults' conversational styles are influential: reminiscing and elaborating on information help children remember.

INTELLIGENCE

One factor that may affect how early children develop both language and memory is intelligence.

Let's look at two ways intelligence is measured—through traditional psychometric tests and through newer tests of cognitive potential—and at how parents influence children's performance.

Traditional Psychometric Measures

As we pointed out in Chapter 4, psychometric tests seek to measure quantitatively the factors that make up intelligence. The tests consist of questions or tasks, usually divided into verbal and performance categories, that indicate cognitive functioning.

Because children of 3, 4, and 5 are more proficient with language than before, intelligence tests can now include verbal items; and these tests produce more reliable results than the largely nonverbal tests used in infancy. As children approach age 5, there is a higher correlation between their scores on intelligence tests and the scores they will achieve later (Bornstein & Sigman, 1986). IQ tests given near the end of kindergarten are among the best predictors of future school success; others are linguistic ability, visual-motor and visual-perceptual performance, and attention span (Tramontana, Hooper, & Selzer, 1988).

Although preschool children are easier to test than infants and toddlers, they still need to be tested individually. The two most commonly used individual tests for preschoolers are the Stanford-Binet Intelligence Scale and the Wechsler Preschool and Primary Scale of Intelligence. The **Stanford-Binet Intelligence Scale**, the first individual childhood intelligence test to be developed, takes 30 to 40 minutes. The child is asked to define words, string beads, build with blocks, identify the missing parts of a picture, trace mazes, and show an understanding of numbers. The child's score is supposed to measure memory, spatial orientation, and practical judgment in real-life situations.

The fourth edition of the Stanford-Binet, revised in 1985, includes an equal balance of verbal and nonverbal, quantitative, and memory items. Instead of providing the IQ as a single overall measure of intelligence, the revised version assesses patterns and levels of cognitive development. The updated standardization sample is well balanced geographically, ethnically, socioeconomically, and by gender and includes children with disabilities.

The **Wechsler Preschool and Primary Scale of Intelligence, Revised (WPPSI- R)**, an hour-long individual test used with children ages 3 to 7, yields separate verbal and performance scores as well as a combined score. Its separate scales are similar to those in the Wechsler Intelligence Scale for Children (WISC-III), discussed in Chapter 8. The 1989 revision includes new subtests and new picture items. It too has been restandardized on a sample of children representing the population of preschool-age children in the United States. Because children of this age tire quickly and are easily distracted, the test may be given in two separate sessions.

Influences on Measured Intelligence: The Home

Many people believe that IQ scores represent a fixed quantity of intelligence that a person is born with. This is not so. The score is simply a measure of how well a child can do certain tasks in comparison with others the same age. On the whole, test-takers have done better in recent years (Anastasi, 1988), forcing test developers to raise previous standardized norms. This improvement may reflect exposure to educational television, preschools, better-educated parents, and a wider variety of experiences, as well as changes in the tests themselves.

How well children do on intelligence tests is influenced by such factors as their temperament, the match between their cognitive style and the tasks they are asked to do, their social and emotional maturity, their ease in the testing situation, their preliteracy or literacy skills, and their socioeconomic status and ethnic background. (We will examine several of these factors in Chapter 8.) Parents are a very important influence because they provide a child's earliest environment for learning.

Parents of children with higher IQs tend to be warm, loving, and sensitive. They tend to use an *authoritative* style of child rearing (described in Chapter 7), which combines respect for the child with firm parental guidance. They accept children's behavior, letting them express themselves and explore. When these parents want to change a child's behavior, they use reasoning or appeals to feelings rather than rigid rules. They encourage independence, creativity, and growth by reading to children, teaching them, and playing with them. They use sophisticated language and teaching strategies. The children respond with curiosity and creativity and do well in school. Parents who provide challenging, pleasurable learning opportunities for a child lay a foundation for optimum cognitive growth (Clarke-Stewart, 1977).

Parents of children with high IQs tend to be warm, loving, and sensitive and to encourage independence and creativity. Even such an ordinary shared activity as baking bread can foster cognitive growth. *(Kerbs/Monkmeyer)*

Family economic circumstances exert a powerful influence on measured intelligence. Poor children tend to have lower IQs at age 5 than more well-to-do children, especially if the family has been poor for a long time. This seems to be true regardless of related factors, such as family structure and the mother's educational level. These conclusions come from an analysis of a longitudinal survey of American households and a study of children originally identified as low birthweight (G. J. Duncan, Brooks-Gunn, & Klebanov, 1994). Poverty affects children not only through their parents' inability to provide educational resources but through the negative psychological effect poverty has on the parents.

An observational study (some of whose findings we reported in Chapter 4) shows how specific aspects of parenting in infancy and toddlerhood, often associated with socioeconomic status, can influence IQ. Once a month for more than 2 years, until the participating children turned 3, researchers visited the homes of 40 well-functioning families (B. Hart & Risley, 1992, 1996). In 32 of the families, both parents were present; 15 families were African American and 25 were white; 13 families were professional or white-collar, 23 were working-class, and 6 were on welfare.

The researchers noted how much attention parents gave a child, the nature of parent-child interaction, and what kinds of speech parents directed to children—prohibitions, questions, or repetitions and elaborations of the children's statements. There were considerable differences on some of these points; for example, one parent addressed 200 words to a child in the course of an hour, while another addressed almost 4,000 words. Parents in higher-income families spent more time with their children, gave them more attention, talked more with them, and showed more interest in what they had to say; and children whose parents did these things tended to do well on IQ tests at age 3 and again at age 9. Much more of the talk of the lower-income parents included such words as "stop," "quit," and "don't"; and the children of parents who talked that way had lower IQs. This study, then, pinpoints differences in parenting that may help account for typical differences in IQ and school performance of children from higher- and lower-income families and shows what kinds of parental practices can help children do better in school.

Testing and Teaching Based on Vygotsky's "Zone of Proximal Development"

A form of testing popular in Russia and now becoming influential in the United States is based on Vygotsky's (1978) sociocultural theory of cognitive development (introduced in Chapter 1). According to Vygotsky, children learn by internalizing the results of their interactions with adults. Adults direct children's learning most effectively in the *zone of proximal development (ZPD)*, that is, with regard to tasks children are almost ready to accomplish on their own.

Tests based on Vygotsky's approach emphasize potential rather than present achievement. These tests contain items up to 2 years above a child's current level of competence. The items a child can answer with help determine the ZPD, or potential level of development. Vygotsky (1956) gives an example of two children, each with a mental age of 7 years (based on ability to do various cognitive tasks). With the help of leading questions, examples, and demonstrations, Natasha can easily solve problems geared to a mental age of 9, two years

beyond her mental age; but Ivan, with the same kind of help, can do tasks at only a 7½-year-old level. If we measure these children by what they can do on their own (as traditional IQ tests do), their intelligence seems about the same; but if we measure them by their immediate potential development (their ZPD), they are quite different.

The ZPD, in combination with the related concept of *scaffolding* (see Chapter 1), can help parents and teachers efficiently guide children's cognitive progress. Scaffolding means that the less able a child is to do a task, the more direction an adult must give. As the child can do more and more, the adult helps less and less. When the child can do the job alone, the adult takes away the "scaffold," which is no longer needed.

In one study of scaffolding, parents worked with their 3-year-old children on three tasks: copying a model made of blocks; classifying by size, color, and shape; and having the children retell a story they had heard. As the experiment progressed, parents became more sensitive to the amount of support their children needed; the more finely tuned a parent's help became, the better the child did (Pratt, Kerig, Cowan, & Cowan, 1988). In another study, Mexican women were videotaped teaching young girls to weave. When working with beginners, the teachers did not give spoken instruction. Instead, when the weaving became too difficult, the teachers simply took over, and the girls learned by watching. None of the 14 students experienced failure; the teachers intervened as soon as they saw the girls having the slightest problem (Greenfield, 1984).

Scaffolding seems to come naturally in so many situations that adults often do not recognize that they are using the method or even that they are teaching. One Mexican woman who was interviewed about how girls learn to weave said, "They learn by themselves." Similarly, many western parents, unaware of their role in teaching toddlers to talk, think that children learn how to talk by themselves rather than through interaction (N. Chomsky, 1965).

✔ EARLY CHILDHOOD EDUCATION

Today more young children than ever spend part of the day in preschool, day care, or kindergarten. Preschools have flourished in the United States since 1919, when the first public nursery schools were established. Preschool enrollment has grown

Not every preschooler wants to do the same thing at the same time. Preschool provides a certain level of individual freedom, while it helps children grow in many ways—physically, intellectually, socially, and emotionally. *(K. B. Kaplan/ The Picture Cube)*

dramatically since 1970 despite a sharp decline in the birthrate. Many privately run preschools serve mainly well-educated, affluent families, but more and more public schools are moving into preschool education. The typical 5-year-old gets a preview of "real school" in kindergarten, a traditional introduction to formal schooling.

Both day care centers (discussed in Chapter 5) and preschools are *learning centers,* places where young children come together and learn. The difference lies in their primary purpose. Day care provides a safe place where children can be cared for, usually all day, while their parents are at work or school. Preschool emphasizes educational experiences geared to children's developmental needs, typically in sessions of only 2 hours or so. However, good day care centers seek to meet children's cognitive, social, and emotional needs, and today many preschools offer longer days. So, as we discuss the educational environment of preschool, much of what we say will also apply to many day care programs.

Goals of preschool education vary according to the values of the culture (see Box 6-3). In the United States, a good preschool is considered to be one that stimulates children's development in all domains—physical, social, emotional, and cognitive—through active interaction with teachers, other children, and carefully chosen materials. It offers an environment in which children can choose from activities tailored to their individual interests, abilities, and learning styles. Through these activities, children experience successes that build confidence and self-esteem. A good preschool

provides experiences that let children learn by doing. It stimulates their senses through art, music, and tactile materials—clay, water, and wood. It encourages children to observe, talk, create, and solve problems. Through storytelling, dramatic play, conversation, and written activities, it helps children develop preliteracy skills. A good preschool helps children learn how to get along with others and to develop social and emotional skills, such as cooperation, negotiation, compromise, and self-control. Perhaps preschool's most important contribution is to make children feel that school is fun, that learning is satisfying, and that they are competent.

COMPENSATORY PRESCHOOL PROGRAMS

Children from deprived socioeconomic backgrounds often enter school at a considerable disadvantage. Since the 1960s, large-scale programs have been developed to help such children compensate for what they have missed and to prepare them for school.

The best-known compensatory preschool program for children of low-income families in the United States is Project Head Start, launched in 1965. A committee of 14 experts in child development, health, and education formulated the initial plan. One of them, Urie Bronfenbrenner, was just beginning to work out his ecological approach to human development (see Chapter 1). He maintained that intervention must address the interrelationships among children, families, and communities (Zigler & Styfco, 1993).

BOX 6-3   WINDOW ON THE WORLD

PRESCHOOLS IN THREE CULTURES

It is morning in a Japanese preschool. After a half-hour workbook session, lively with talk, laughter, and playful fighting among the children, twenty-eight 4-year-olds sing in unison: "As I sit here with my lunch, I think of mom, I bet it's delicious, I wonder what she's made?" The children speak freely, loudly, even vulgarly to each other for much of the day, but then have periods of formal, teacher-directed group recitations of polite expressions of greeting, thanks, and blessings.

In a Chinese preschool, twenty-six 4-year-olds sing a cheerful song about a train, acting out the words by hooking onto each other's backs and chugging around the room. They then sit down and, for the next 20 minutes, follow their teacher's direction to put together blocks, copying pictures she has handed out. They work in an orderly way, and their errors are corrected as the session proceeds. The teacher has taught the children to recite long pieces and sing complicated songs, emphasizing enunciation, diction, and self-confidence, but she discourages spontaneous talk as possible distraction from work.

The eighteen 4-year-olds at an American preschool begin their day with a show-and-tell session in which children speak individually. They sing a song about monkeys and, for the next 45 minutes, separate into different activities—painting, playing with blocks, completing puzzles, playing in the housekeeping corner, and listening to a story. The teacher moves around the room, talking with the children about their activities, mediating fights, and keeping order. She encourages children to express their own feelings and opinions, helps them learn new words to express concepts, and corrects their speech.

What makes a good preschool? Your answer depends on what you regard as the ideal child, the ideal adult, and the ideal society. Some ways in which schools reflect such values showed up in a comparison among preschools in Japan, China, and the United States (Tobin, Wu, & Davidson, 1989). The wide-ranging study involved videotaping preschool activities in all three countries, showing the tapes and discussing them with parents and educators, and asking 750 teachers, administrators, parents, and child development specialists to fill out questionnaires. The classroom activities were consistent with the values expressed by each cultural group.

One big difference was in the importance of teaching subject matter. Over half the Americans listed "to give children a good start academically" as one of the top three reasons for a society to have preschools. Only 2 percent of the Japanese gave this answer: they tended to see preschools as havens from the academic pressure and competition that children would face in the years to come. Japanese preschoolers are encouraged to develop more basic skills such as concentration and the ability to function in a group. Teachers cultivate perseverance, for example, by refusing to help children dress and undress themselves.

The Chinese emphasized academics even more than the Americans, with 67 percent giving this answer. Their emphasis on early learning seems to stem from the Confucian tradition of early, strenuous study; from the Cultural Revolution's discouragement of frivolity and its stress on reading, writing, working with numbers, and clear speaking; and from the desire of parents to compensate for their own disrupted educations. This early stress on academics is controversial, however, and a less academic preschool curriculum is becoming more popular, especially among developmentalists.

In sum, although preschoolers in all three cultures do many of the same activities, China stresses academic instruction, Japan stresses play, and the United States presents a mixed picture. But in all three countries, parents often pressure preschools to give their children a strong educational start so they will achieve prominent positions in the society. It would be interesting to follow today's children to find out whether those who work harder at ages 3 or 4 or 5 do, in fact, achieve more as adults.

SOURCE: Tobin et al., 1989.

Head Start's administrators adopted a "whole child" approach. Their goals were to improve physical health, enhance cognitive skills, and foster self-confidence, relationships with others, social responsibility, and a sense of dignity and self-worth for the child and the family. The program provides medical, dental, and mental health care; nutrition (at least one hot meal a day); cognitive enrichment; social services; and parent involvement. Due to inadequate funding, Head Start serves little more than one-third of eligible children: 752,000 in 1995 (Children's Defense Fund,

1996). More than 13 million have been enrolled since the program's inception (Zigler & Styfco, 1994). Recently, some communities have combined Head Start with all-day child care (Children's Defense Fund, 1996).

Has Head Start lived up to its name? Because it is community-based and community- directed, the program varies around the country. With less funding in recent years, quality has been uneven, and evaluation has not kept current (Zigler & Styfco, 1993, 1994). Still, the program has had considerable success.

Head Start has probably had its strongest impact on physical health and well-being (Zigler & Styfco, 1994). Head Start children have also shown substantial cognitive and language gains, with the neediest children benefiting most. Being healthier, Head Start children are absent less often. They do better on tests of motor control and physical development (R. C. Collins & Deloria, 1983). Head Start has had a positive impact on self-esteem, socialization, and social maturity (McKey et al., 1985). It has also had a favorable effect on families by offering parenting education, social support, and jobs and job training (Zigler & Styfco, 1993, 1994). The most successful Head Start programs have been those with the most parental participation, the best teachers, the smallest groups, and the most extensive services.

A major concern has been that gains in IQ do not last. Although Head Start children do better on IQ tests than children from comparable backgrounds, this advantage disappears after the children start school. Nor have Head Start children equaled the average middle-class child in school achievement or on standardized tests (R. C. Collins & Deloria, 1983; Zigler & Styfco, 1993, 1994). These findings point to a need for earlier and longer-lasting intervention (Zigler & Styfco, 1993, 1994). In another large-scale federally funded compensatory program, the Chicago Child Parent Centers, which extends from preschool through third grade, the added years of academic enrichment significantly increased achievement (Reynolds, 1994). However, we must be wary of unrealistic expectations: "neither Head Start nor any preschool program can inoculate children against the ravages of poverty" (Zigler & Styfco, 1994, p. 129).

Some positive effects of Head Start and other compensatory preschool programs have persisted through elementary or high school or even beyond. Children in 10 early intervention programs assessed by the Consortium for Longitudinal Stud-

ies were less likely than other needy children to be held back or to require special education for slow learners and were more likely to stay in school (L. B. Miller & Bizzel, 1983). A number of other studies have found long-term benefits for children enrolled in high-quality compensatory preschool programs (Darlington, 1991; Haskins, 1989), including less likelihood of delinquency (see Chapter 11). Poor African American children who participated in the Perry Preschool Program of the High/Scope Educational Research Foundation (which predated Head Start) have been followed to age 27. They were much more likely than a comparison group who lacked preschool experience to finish high school, to enroll in college or vocational training, and to be employed. They also did better on tests of competence and were less likely to be on welfare or to have been arrested. The women among them were less likely to have become pregnant in their teens (Berrueta-Clement, Schweinhart, Barnett, Epstein, & Weikart, 1984; Schweinhart, Barnes, & Weikart, 1993). It seems, then, that early childhood education can help compensate for deprivation and that well-planned programs produce long-term benefits that far exceed the original cost (Haskins, 1989; Schweinhart et al., 1993).

HOW ACADEMICALLY ORIENTED SHOULD PRESCHOOL AND KINDERGARTEN BE?

In the United States, most preschools traditionally have followed a "child-centered" philosophy stressing social and emotional growth in line with young children's developmental needs. Some, such as those based on the theories of Piaget or the Italian educator Maria Montessori, have a strong cognitive emphasis. In some other countries, such as China, preschools are expected to provide academic preparation (refer back to Box 6-3).

In recent years, as part of a debate over how to improve education in the United States, pressures have built to offer instruction in basic academic skills in preschool. Some of these pressures have filtered down from kindergarten. Historically a year of transition between the relative freedom of home or preschool and the structure of the primary grades, the kindergarten experience since the 1970s has become more like first grade. Children spend less time on freely chosen activities that stretch their muscles and imaginations and more time on worksheets and learning to read (Egertson, 1987).

Many educators and psychologists maintain that although children may learn more at first, too much teacher-directed instruction in early childhood may stifle their interest and interfere with self-directed learning. Furthermore, such instruction may neglect young children's needs for play, exploration, and freedom from undue demands (Elkind, 1986; Zigler, 1987).

One study compared 227 poor, minority, and middle-class 4- to 6-year-olds in highly academic and child-centered preschool and kindergarten classes. The children in the academic programs did better in recognizing letters and words, though not numbers; but these children had lower motivation, a poorer opinion of their abilities, less pride in their accomplishments, and lower expectations for academic success. They were more dependent on adults for permission and approval, and they worried more about school. This was true of both disadvantaged and middle-class children and of both preschoolers and kindergartners (Stipek, Feiler, Daniels, & Milburn, 1995). In another study, children from both academic and child-centered preschools learned equally well in kindergarten, but the children from the academic preschools were more anxious abut taking tests, less creative, and more negative about school (Hirsch-Pasek, 1991; Hirsh-Pasek, Hyson, & Rescorla, 1989).

What are the long-term effects of differing philosophies of preschool education? One study (Schweinhart, Weikart, & Larner, 1986) compared what happened to low-income children in three high-quality preschool programs: a traditional one that stressed child-initiated activities; a highly structured, teacher-directed one; and the High/Scope program (mentioned in the previous section), which took a middle ground, emphasizing joint planning by teachers and children. Children from all three programs did better in elementary school than children with no preschool experience, but the children from the academic program had more behavior problems. By 15 years of age, many of those children had lost interest in school and had become involved in vandalism or delinquency.

In part because of pressures for academic achievement and in part to meet the needs of working parents, many kindergartners now spend a full day in school rather than the traditional half day—with mixed results (Robertson, 1984; Rust, cited in Connecticut Early Childhood Education Council, 1983). Longer blocks of time permit an unhurried atmosphere and more opportunities for pupil-teacher and parent-teacher contact; afternoon activities tend to be less structured, so as to match childrens' energy levels. However, opponents say some 5-year-olds cannot handle a 6-hour day and the long separation from parents. There is also a danger of overemphasizing academic skills and sedentary activities.

One proposed solution is a half day of kindergarten followed by an optional half day of care by certified child caregivers for those who need it (Zigler, 1987). In any case, some experts warn against sending children to kindergarten too early, since the youngest children in a class tend to do less well than the oldest (Sweetland & DeSimone, 1987).

Many 5-year-olds, and some younger children, can be taught that 2 times 2 equals 4, just as some 9-month-old infants can be taught to recognize words on flash cards. Unless the motivation comes from *them,* however, and the learning arises naturally from their experience, their time might be better spent on play—the "business" of early childhood and one of the topics we turn to in Chapter 7.

✔ SUMMARY

ASPECTS OF PHYSICAL DEVELOPMENT

- Physical growth increases during the years from 3 to 6, but more slowly than during infancy and toddlerhood. Boys on average are slightly taller and heavier than girls.
- The muscular, skeletal, nervous, respiratory, circulatory, and immune systems are maturing, and all primary teeth are present. Children eat less than before and need a balanced diet.

- Motor development advances rapidly; children progress in gross and fine motor skills and eye-hand coordination.
- Handedness is usually evident by age 3. Left-handed and right-handed people tend to differ in a number of other characteristics.
- Sleep patterns change during early childhood. Young children generally sleep through the night and take one daytime nap; they sleep more deeply than later in life.

▪ It is normal for children close to age 5 to develop bedtime rituals that delay going to sleep. However, prolonged bedtime struggles or persistent night terrors or nightmares may indicate emotional disturbances that need attention.

▪ Bed-wetting is common, especially at night, and is usually outgrown without special help.

HEALTH AND SAFETY

▪ Major contagious illnesses are rare due to widespread immunization, and death rates have declined. Minor illnesses help build immunity to disease and may also have cognitive and emotional benefits.

▪ Accidents, the leading cause of death in childhood in the United States, are most common in cars or at home.

▪ Environmental factors such as exposure to illness and stress, poverty, and homelessness increase the risks of illness or injury.

THE PREOPERATIONAL CHILD

▪ According to Piaget, a child is in the preoperational stage of cognitive development from approximately 2 years to 7 years of age. The symbolic function—as shown in deferred imitation, symbolic play, and language—enables children to mentally represent and reflect upon people, objects, and events. However, the child cannot yet think logically. Research shows that, in some ways, Piaget underestimated abilities of the children he described as preoperational.

▪ Preoperational children can understand the concept of identity, are beginning to understand causal relationships, are developing proficiency at classification, and understand principles of counting and quantity. They do not understand conservation. They also tend to confuse reality and fantasy, reason transductively, and do not understand reversibility and the implications of transformations. Preoperational children appear to be less egocentric than Piaget thought and are capable of empathy. They show signs of having a theory of mind, including awareness of their own thought processes, some ability to distinguish real and imagined events, ability to deceive, and understanding that people can hold false beliefs.

ASPECTS OF COGNITIVE DEVELOPMENT

▪ During early childhood, vocabulary increases greatly, and grammar and syntax become fairly sophisticated. Piaget characterized much of early speech as egocentric, but recent research indicates that young children engage in social (communicative) speech more than was previously thought.

▪ Private speech—children's talking aloud to themselves—appears to help children gain control over their actions. It usually disappears by age 9 or 10.

▪ Delayed language development may involve problems in fast mapping (incorporating new words into the vocabulary) and, if untreated, may have serious cognitive, social, and emotional consequences.

▪ Conversations with adults, using relatively challenging vocabulary and subject matter, are important in preparing children for literacy, as is imaginative play.

▪ Studies of memory development indicate that recognition is better than recall, but both increase during early childhood. Recall is influenced by mastery motivation and study strategies.

▪ Inability to remember early childhood events at a later age may be due to the way young children encode memories. Early episodic memories are temporary; they may become part of a generic script to guide behavior in recurring situations.

▪ Formation of permanent autobiographical memories begins at about age 4 and may be related to language development. Children are more likely to remember unusual activities that involve active participation. The way adults talk with children about events influences memory formation.

▪ Since psychometric intelligence tests for young children include verbal items, they are better predictors of later IQ than infant tests. Parenting has a major influence on intelligence test performance.

▪ A newer form of intelligence testing is based on Vygotsky's concept of the zone of proximal development (ZPD). Such tests, when combined with scaffolding (temporary support to do a task), can help parents and teachers guide children's progress.

EARLY CHILDHOOD EDUCATION

▪ Preschools and kindergartens prepare children for formal schooling. Some programs focus more on structured cognitive tasks, others on social and emotional development and child-initiated activities.

▪ Since the 1970s, the academic content of early childhood education programs has increased, causing concern about the effects of academic pressure on young children.

▪ Compensatory preschool programs, such as Project Head Start, have had positive outcomes, but participants generally have not equalled the performance of middle-class children.

✔ KEY TERMS

gross motor skills (page 185)
fine motor skills (185)
handedness (186)
transitional objects (188)
enuresis (188)
empathy (190)
stress (191)
preoperational stage (194)
symbolic function (195)
centration (197)
decenter (197)
conservation (197)

irreversibility (199)
transduction (199)
egocentrism (199)
animism (200)
theory of mind (201)
fast mapping (203)
pragmatics (204)
social speech (204)
private speech (204)
recognition (206)
recall (206)
explicit memory (207)

implicit memory (207)
generic memory (207)
script (207)
episodic memory (207)
autobiographical memory (208)
Stanford-Binet Intelligence Scale (210)
Wechsler Preschool and Primary Scale of Intelligence, Revised (WPPSI-R) (210)

✔ QUESTIONS FOR THOUGHT AND DISCUSSION

1 Who should be responsible for children's well-being when parents cannot provide adequate food, clothing, shelter, and health care: government, religious and community institutions, or the private sector, or a combination of these?

2 Can you suggest strategies for dealing with the problem of homelessness besides those mentioned in this chapter?

3 Is it better to let children develop concepts like conservation naturally, or to teach them?

4 If you were a preschool teacher, how helpful do you think it would be to know a child's IQ? The child's ZPD?

5 Can you think of an effective way in which you have used scaffolding, or seen it used?

6 Is publicly funded compensatory education the best way to help poor children catch up?

7 Should the primary purpose of preschool and kindergarten be to provide a strong academic foundation for elementary school or to foster social and emotional development?

PSYCHOSOCIAL DEVELOPMENT IN EARLY CHILDHOOD

PSYCHOSOCIAL DEVELOPMENT IN EARLY CHILDHOOD

Children's playings are not sports and should be deemed as their most serious actions.

Montaigne, Essays

ASK YOURSELF

- ✔ How does the self-concept develop during early childhood?
- ✔ How do young children advance in understanding their emotions?
- ✔ How do young children develop initiative and self-esteem?
- ✔ How do preschoolers play, and what does their play tell us about their social and cognitive development?
- ✔ How do boys and girls become aware of their gender, and what explains differences in behavior between the sexes?

- ✔ How do child-rearing practices influence personality?
- ✔ What makes young children altruistic or aggressive?
- ✔ What accounts for common fears in early childhood?
- ✔ How do young children choose friends, and why are some children more popular than others?

At 5 years of age, Anna usually got along very well with her friend Danielle as they played with wooden blocks or pretended to fix pizza for lunch. They did fight sometimes; one day Anna took Danielle's pail and shovel, and Danielle threw sand in Anna's face. Then, on another day, when Danielle was crying, Anna said, "Danielle is upset," and kissed her "best friend." Danielle was an important presence in Anna's life. As they played and talked and even as they squabbled, it was apparent that they had changed since infancy and toddlerhood. "They're becoming real people," Anna's father said.

What does it mean to become a real person? It means that Anna was developing a sense of herself as a unique individual with her own traits, her own likes and dislikes, and her own ideas. She was also becoming a more social being. These processes did not begin on her third, fourth, or fifth birthday, nor did they end in early childhood. Anna's self-concept and her relationships with others will continue to develop as part of her singular personality throughout life.

These are pivotal years for psychosocial development. As children's self-concept grows stronger, they learn which sex they are and begin to act accordingly. Their behavior also becomes more socially directed. Social life expands as friends and playmates play a bigger role.

■ In this chapter we discuss preschool children's understanding of themselves and their emotions and the ways children develop initiative and self-

esteem. We describe the activity on which young children spend most of their time: play. We see how children's identification of themselves as male or female affects their behavior. We consider the influence—for good or ill—of what parents do. We then turn to specific developmental issues of this age group: why children help or hurt others and why they develop fears. Finally, we look at relationships with siblings and other children. ■

✔ THE DEVELOPING SELF

"Who in the world am I? Ah, *that's* the great puzzle," said Alice in Wonderland, after her size had abruptly changed—again. Solving Alice's "puzzle" is a lifelong process of getting to know the developing self.

The *self-concept* is our image of ourselves. It is what we believe about who we are—our total picture of our abilities and traits. It is a cognitive structure with emotional overtones and behavioral consequences, a "system of descriptive and evaluative representations about the self," which determines how we feel about ourselves and guides our actions (Harter, 1993, p. 1).

The sense of self might seem to be the most personal thing in the world, but it has social roots. Children incorporate into their self-image a growing understanding of how others see them. The picture of the self comes into focus in toddlerhood and becomes clearer and more compelling as a

A young child's self-concept is based mainly on external characteristics, such as physical features. *(Laura Dwight/ PhotoEdit)*

person gains in cognitive abilities and deals with the developmental tasks of childhood, adolescence, and then of adulthood. Let's look at important aspects of the self-concept in early childhood.

SELF-DEFINITION: A NEO-PIAGETIAN VIEW

As an infant (see Chapter 5), Jason gradually realized he was separate from other people and things. At about 18 months, he had his first moment of *self-recognition,* when he looked in a mirror and realized the image was his. Next came attempts at *self-description* and *self-evaluation* as he began to reflect on himself and his behavior. Now, at age 4, his attempts at **self-definition** are becoming more comprehensive as he begins to identify a cluster of characteristics to describe himself:

My name is Jason and I live in an apartment with my mommy and daddy. I have a kitty and her name is Pumpkin. We have a television and I like to watch cartoons. I know all of my A-B-Cs. Listen: A-B-C-D-F-G-J-L-K-O-M-P-Q-X-Z. I can run faster than anyone! I can climb to the top of the jungle gym, I'm not scared! Just happy. You can't be happy *and* scared, no way! I have black hair. I go to preschool. I'm really strong. I can lift this chair, watch me! (Adapted from Harter, 1993, p. 2*)

*Much of this discussion of children's developing understanding of themselves, including their understanding of their emotions, is indebted to Susan Harter (1990, 1993).

The way Jason describes himself is typical of children his age. He talks mostly about concrete, observable behaviors; external characteristics, such as physical features; preferences; possessions; and members of his household. He mentions particular skills (running and climbing) rather than general abilities (being athletic). His self-descriptions spill over into demonstrations; what he *thinks* about himself is almost inseparable from what he *does.* Not until middle childhood will he describe himself in generalized terms such as *popular, smart,* or *dumb.*

Neo-Piagetian thinkers describe this shift as occurring in three steps, which actually form a continuous progression (Fischer, 1980). At 4, Jason's statements about himself are **single representations,** isolated from one another. His thinking is *transductive;* it jumps from particular to particular, without logical connections. At this stage he cannot image having two emotions at once ("You can't be happy *and* scared"). Because he cannot decenter, he cannot consider different aspects of himself at the same time. His thinking is all-or-nothing. He cannot acknowledge that his **real self,** the person he actually is, is not the same as his **ideal self,** the person he would like to be; so he describes himself as a paragon of virtue and ability.

At about ages 5 to 6, Jason begins to link one aspect of himself to another: "I can run fast, and I can climb high. I'm also strong. I can throw a ball real far, I'm going to be on a team some day!" (Harter, 1993, p. 9) However, these **representational** *mappings*—logical connections between parts of his image of himself—are still expressed in all-or-none terms. Since good and bad are opposites, he cannot see how he might be good at some things and not at others.

The third step, *representational systems*, takes place in middle childhood (see Chapter 9), when children begin to integrate specific features of the self into a general concept. As all-or-none thinking declines, Jason's self-descriptions will become more balanced ("I'm good at hockey but bad at arithmetic").

UNDERSTANDING EMOTIONS

"I hate you!" Maya, age 5, shouts to her mother. "You're a mean mommy!" Angry because her mother sent her to her room for pinching her baby brother, Maya cannot imagine ever loving her mother again. "Aren't you ashamed of yourself for making the baby cry?" her father asks Maya a little later. Maya nods, but only because she knows what response he wants. In truth, she feels a jumble of emotions—not the least of which is being sorry for herself.

Emotions Directed Toward the Self

Maya's confused emotional state is not unusual for her age. Shame—like its opposite, pride—is a complex emotion, which young children rarely understand. Emotions directed toward the self, such as shame and pride, do not seem to develop until at least the second or third year, after children gain self-awareness (see Chapter 5). These emotions are "socially derived" (Harter, 1993, p. 20); they depend on internalization of parental standards of behavior.

Even children a few years older often lack the cognitive sophistication to recognize such emotions and what brings them on. In one study (Harter, 1993), 4- to 8-year-olds were told two stories: one in which a child takes money after being told not to take it, and another in which a child performs a difficult gymnastic feat. Each story was presented in two versions: one in which a parent sees the child doing the act, and one in which the child is not observed. The children were asked how they and their parents would feel in each circumstance.

The answers revealed a progression in understanding of feelings about the self. At ages 4 to 5, children did not say that either they or their parents would feel pride or shame. At 5 to 6, children said their parents would be ashamed or proud of them, but did not mention feeling these emotions

themselves. At 6 to 7, children said they would feel proud or ashamed, but only if they were observed. At 7 to 8, children acknowledged that even if no one saw them, they would feel ashamed or proud of themselves. By this age, the standards that produce pride and shame appear to be fully internalized. Until that happens, children appear to need the prod of parental observation.

Simultaneous Emotions

Part of the confusion in young children's understanding of their feelings is the inability to recognize that they can experience different emotional reactions at the same time. The problem has two dimensions: the quality of the emotion (positive or negative) and the target toward which it is directed. Children gradually acquire an understanding of simultaneous emotions as they move through five levels of development between ages 4 and 12 (Harter & Buddin, 1987):

- *Level 0:* At first children do not understand that *any* two feelings can coexist. At this stage, a child may say, "You can't have two feelings at the same time because you only have one mind!" The child cannot even acknowledge feeling two similar emotions at once (such as happy and glad).
- *Level 1:* Children can be aware of two emotions at the same time, but only if both are either positive or negative and are directed toward the same target ("If my brother hit me, I would be mad and sad"). A child at this level cannot understand the possibility of feeling simultaneous emotions toward two different people or feeling contradictory emotions toward the same person.
- *Level 2:* Children can recognize having two feelings of the same kind directed toward different targets ("I was excited about going to Mexico and glad to see my grandparents"). However, they cannot acknowledge holding contradictory feelings ("I couldn't feel happy and scared at the same time; I would have to be two people at once!").
- *Level 3:* Children can now understand having two opposing feelings at the same time, but only if they are directed toward two different targets. Maya can express a negative feeling toward her baby brother ("I was mad at Tony, so I pinched him") and a positive feeling toward her father ("I was happy my father didn't spank me"); but she cannot recognize that she has positive and negative feelings (anger and love) toward both.

■ *Level 4:* Children can now describe opposite feelings toward the same target ("I'm excited about going to my new school, but I'm a little scared too").

INITIATIVE VERSUS GUILT

The need to deal with conflicting feelings about the self is at the heart of the third crisis of personality development identified by Erik Erikson (1950): *initiative versus guilt.* The conflict arises from the growing sense of purpose, which lets a child plan and carry out activities, and the growing pangs of conscience the child may have about such plans.

In early childhood, children face contradictory pressures. They *can* do—and *want* to do—more and more. At the same time, they are learning that some of the things they want to do (such as singing a cute song) meet social approval, whereas others (such as taking apart Mommy's clock) do not. How do they resolve their desire to *do* with their desire for approval?

This conflict marks a split between two parts of the personality: the part that remains a child, full of exuberance and a desire to try new things and test new powers, and the part that is becoming an adult, constantly examining the propriety of motives and actions. Children who learn how to regulate these opposing drives develop the "virtue" of *purpose,* the courage to envision and pursue goals without being unduly inhibited by guilt or fear of punishment (Erikson, 1982). If this crisis is not resolved adequately, said Erikson, a child may turn into an adult who is constantly striving for success or showing off, or who is inhibited and unspontaneous or self-righteous and intolerant, or who suffers from impotence or psychosomatic illness. With ample opportunities to do things on their own—but under guidance and firm limits—children can attain a healthy balance between the tendency to overdo competition and achievement and the tendency to be repressed and guilt-ridden.

SELF-ESTEEM

Although children cannot articulate a concept of self-worth until about age 8, they show by their behavior that they have one (Harter, 1990, 1993). However, in young children, *self-esteem*—the judgment one makes about one's worth—is not based on a realistic appraisal of abilities or personality traits. In fact, children between 4 and 7 usually overrate their abilities. For one thing, they do not yet have the cognitive and social skills to compare themselves accurately with others. Also, although young children can make judgments about their competence at various activities, they are not yet able to rate them in importance; and they tend to accept the judgments of adults, who often give them positive, uncritical feedback (Harter, 1990).

In one study (Haltiwanger & Harter, 1988), preschool and kindergarten teachers were asked to describe behaviors of children with high or low self-esteem. Another group of teachers was asked to tell which of the 84 items cited by the first group were most typical of children at both extremes of self-esteem. The assessments of the two groups of teachers matched. Self-esteem was *not* related to actual competence, activity level, ability to pay attention, tendency to finish tasks, ability to make friends, or need for encouragement from teachers. Instead, differences in self-esteem seemed to be expressed chiefly in a child's confidence, curiosity, willingness to explore, and adaptability.

Self-esteem at this age tends to be global—"I am good" or "I am bad"—and may depend on adult approval (Burhans & Dweck, 1995). Supportive behavior by loving parents—listening to a child, reading stories, making snacks, kissing away tears—is a major contributor to self-esteem (Haltiwanger & Harter, 1988). Not until middle childhood do personal evaluations of competence and adequacy become critical in shaping and maintaining a sense of self-worth (Harter, 1990).

When self-esteem is high, a child is motivated to achieve (Harter, 1990). On the other hand, children whose self-esteem is contingent on success may view failure as an indictment of their worth and feel helpless to do better. Instead of feeling challenged to try a different way of completing a puzzle—as a child with unconditional self-esteem might do—children who show the "helpless" pattern feel ashamed and give up or go back to an easier puzzle they have already done. They do not expect to succeed, and so, to avoid further damage to self-esteem, they do not try (Burhans & Dweck, 1995).

Between one-third and one-half of preschoolers seem to show elements of this "helpless" pattern. In role-playing with dolls, these children are more likely to punish a doll for failure than to reward effort. They tend to interpret poor performance as a sign of being "bad" and to believe that "badness" cannot be overcome. This sense of being a bad person may persist into adulthood. Parents and teachers can avoid fostering the "helpless" pattern by giving children specific, strategy-focused feedback rather than criticism of the child as a person (Burhans & Dweck, 1995).

✔ PLAY: THE BUSINESS OF EARLY CHILDHOOD

When Carmen, age 3, comes to breakfast, she pretends that the pieces of cereal floating in her bowl are "fishes" swimming in the milk, and she "fishes," spoonful by spoonful. After breakfast, she puts on her mother's old hat, picks up a discarded briefcase, and is a "mommy" going to work. She runs outside to ride her tricycle through the puddles, comes in for an imaginary telephone conversation, turns a wooden block into a truck and makes the appropriate sound effects. Carmen's day is one round of play after another.

An adult might be tempted to dismiss Carmen's activities as no more than "having fun." But that would be a mistake: play is the "work" of the young. Through play, children grow. They stimulate the senses, learn how to use their muscles, coordinate what they see with what they do, and gain mastery over their bodies. They find out about the world and themselves. They acquire new skills. They become more proficient with language, they try out different roles, and—by reenacting real-life situations—they cope with complex emotions.

Preschoolers engage in different types of play at different ages. Particular children have different styles of playing, and they play at different things. One kindergartner might put on dress-up clothes with a friend, while another is absorbed in building a block tower. What can we learn about children by seeing how they play?

TYPES OF PLAY

Researchers categorize children's play in both social and cognitive terms. *Social play* refers to the extent to which children interact with other children. *Cognitive play* reflects a child's level of mental development.

Social and Nonsocial Play

In the 1920s, Mildred B. Parten (1932) observed forty-two 2- to 5-year-olds during free-play periods at nursery school. She identified six types of play, ranging from the least to the most social (see

Table 7-1). She found that as children get older, their play tends to become more social and more cooperative. At first they play alone, then alongside other children, and finally, together.

However, in a similar study done 40 years later, forty-four 3- and 4-year-olds played much less sociably than the children in Parten's group (K. E. Barnes, 1971). The change may have reflected a changed environment. Because these children watched television, they may have become more passive; because they had more elaborate toys and fewer siblings, they may have played alone more.

We might expect children who have spent considerable time in group day care to play more sociably. That expectation has been borne out for children attending day care centers that emphasize social skills, have mixed age groups, and have a high adult-child ratio; but it does not seem applicable to children in small centers with same-age grouping and an emphasis on academic skills (Schindler, Moely, & Frank, 1987).

Is solitary play always less mature than group play? Parten thought so. She and some other observers suggest that young children who play alone may be at risk for developing social, psychological, and educational problems. Actually, though, much nonsocial play consists of constructive or educational activities that further cognitive, physical, and social development. Among children in six kindergartens, about one-third of solitary play consisted of goal-directed activities such as block building and artwork; about one-fourth was large-muscle play; about 15 percent was educational; and only about 10 percent involved just looking (Moore, Evertson, & Brophy, 1974). Thus many types of solitary play seem to reflect independence and maturity, not poor social adjustment.

Another study looked at nonsocial play in relation to the cognitive and social competence of 4-year-olds, as measured by role-taking and problem-solving tests, teacher ratings, and popularity with other children. Some kinds of nonsocial play turned out to be associated with a high level of competence. For example, *parallel constructive play* (such as working on puzzles near another child) is most common among children who are good problem solvers, are popular with other children, and are seen by teachers as socially skilled (K. Rubin, 1982).

Children need some time alone to concentrate on tasks and problems, and some simply enjoy nonsocial activities more than group activities. We

TABLE 7-1

Types of Social and Nonsocial Play in Early Childhood

Category	Description
Unoccupied behavior	The child does not seem to be playing, but watches anything of momentary interest.
Onlooker behavior	The child spends most of the time watching other children play. The onlooker talks to them, asking questions or making suggestions, but does not enter into the play. The onlooker is definitely observing particular groups of children rather than anything that happens to be exciting.
Solitary independent play	The child plays alone with toys that are different from those used by nearby children and makes no effort to get close to them.
Parallel play	The child plays independently, but among the other children, playing with toys like those used by the other children, but not necessarily playing with them in the same way. Playing *beside* rather than *with* the others, the parallel player does not try to influence the other children's play.
Associative play	The child plays with other children. They talk about their play, borrow and lend toys, follow one another, and try to control who may play in the group. All the children play similarly if not identically; there is no division of labor and no organization around any goal. Each child acts as she or he wishes and is interested more in being with the other children than in the activity itself.
Cooperative or organized supplementary play	The child plays in a group organized for some goal—to make something, play a formal game, or dramatize a situation. One or two children control who belongs to the group and direct activities. By a division of labor, children take on different roles and supplement each other's efforts.

SOURCE: Adapted from Parten, 1932, pp. 249–251.

need to look at what children *do* when they play, not just at whether they play alone.

Cognitive Play

Kaia, at 13 months, pushes an imaginary spoon holding imaginary food into her father's mouth. Joseph, at 2 years, "talks" to a doll as if it were a real person. Michael, 3, wears a kitchen towel as a cape and "flies" around as Batman. All these children are engaged in **imaginative play** (also called *fantasy play, dramatic play, symbolic play,* or *pretend play*), which involves make-believe people or situations.

Imaginative play is one of the categories of play identified by Piaget and others as signs of cognitive development (Piaget, 1951; Smilansky, 1968). Young children progress from simple, *repetitive play* involving muscular movements (such as rolling a ball) to three increasingly complex forms: *constructive* play (building a block tower), then *imaginative play* (playing doctor), and then *formal*

games with rules (hopscotch and marbles).

Imaginative play emerges during the second year, when repetitive play is on the wane. It increases during the next 3 to 4 years and then declines as children become more interested in playing games with rules. According to Piaget (1962), the ability to pretend rests on the ability to use and remember symbols, and its emergence approximately coincides with the preoperational stage (see Chapter 6).

About 10 to 17 percent of preschoolers' play is imaginative play, and the proportion rises to about 33 percent among kindergartners (K. Rubin, Maioni, & Hornung, 1976; W. Rubin, Watson, & Jambor, 1978). The social dimension of imaginative play also changes during these years, from solitary pretending to sociodramatic play involving other children (Singer & Singer, 1990). Jessie, who at age 3 would climb inside a box by herself and pretend to be a train conductor, will by age 6 want to have passengers on her train. Many young children have imaginary playmates (see Box 7-1).

BOX 7-1   FOOD FOR THOUGHT

IMAGINARY PLAYMATES

At age 3½, Anna had 23 sisters with such names as Och, Elmo, Zeni, Aggie, and Ankie. She often talked to them on the telephone, since they lived about 100 miles away, in the town where her family used to live. During the next year, most of the sisters disappeared, but Och continued to visit, especially for birthday parties. Och had a cat and a dog (which Anna had begged for in vain), and whenever Anna was denied something she saw advertised on television, she announced that she already had one at her sister's house.

All 23 sisters—and some "boys" and "girls" who have followed them—lived only in Anna's imagination. Like about 15 to 30 percent of children between ages 3 and 10, she created imaginary companions, with whom she talked and played. This normal phenomenon

of childhood is seen most often in bright, creative firstborn and only children (Manosevitz, Prentice, & Wilson, 1973). Girls are more likely than boys to have imaginary playmates (or at least to acknowledge them); girls' imaginary playmates are usually human, whereas boys' are more often animals (D. G. Singer & Singer, 1990).

Children who have imaginary companions can distinguish fantasy from reality, but in free-play sessions they are more likely to engage in pretend play than are children without imaginary companions (Taylor, Cartwright, & Carlson, 1993). They play more happily and more imaginatively than other children and are more cooperative with other children and adults (D. G. Singer & Singer, 1990; J. L. Singer & Singer, 1981). They are more fluent with lan-

guage, watch less television, and show more curiosity, excitement, and persistence during play.

What role do imaginary companions play in a child's life? They are good company for an only child (like Anna). They provide wish-fulfillment mechanisms ("There was a monster in my room, but Elmo scared it off with magic dust"), scapegoats ("I didn't eat those cookies—Och must have done it!"), displacement agents for the child's own fears ("Aggie is afraid she's going to be washed down the drain"), and support in difficult situations. (One 6-year-old "took" her imaginary companion with her to see a scary movie.) In sum, children use imaginary companions to help them get along better in the real world.

Through pretending, children learn how to understand another person's viewpoint, develop skills in solving social problems, and express creativity. Children who frequently play imaginatively tend to cooperate more with other children and tend to be more popular and to be more joyful than those who don't play imaginatively (Singer & Singer, 1990).

Mothers and fathers of children who play imaginatively tend to get along well with each other, expose the children to interesting experiences, engage them in conversation, and do not spank (Fein, 1981). They provide a time and place to play, and they encourage imaginative play by providing such simple props as costumes, blocks, paints, and toy people (Singer & Singer, 1990). Children who watch a great deal of television tend to play less imaginatively, possibly because they get into the habit of passively absorbing images rather than generating their own. Children in high-quality day care play at more cognitively complex levels than children in barely adequate care (Howes & Matheson, 1992).

HOW CULTURE INFLUENCES PLAY

Both social and cognitive categories of play can be seen in many cultures. For example, categories similar to those described by Parten and by Smilansky showed up in the play of children in Taiwan (Pan, 1994). However, the frequency of specific forms of play differs across cultures and may be influenced by the environments adults set up for children, which in turn tend to reflect cultural values (refer back to Box 6-3).

One study compared 48 middle-class Korean American and 48 middle-class Anglo American children in separate full-day, year-round preschools (Farver, Kim, & Lee, 1995). The Anglo American preschools, in keeping with typical American values, encouraged independent thinking, problem solving, and active involvement in learning by letting children select from a wide range of activities. The Korean American preschool, in keeping with traditional Korean values, emphasized academic skills, perseverance in completing tasks, and passive learning. The Anglo

This young "veterinarian" examining his toy dog is showing an important cognitive development of early childhood, which underlies imaginative play: the ability to use symbols to stand for people or things in the real world. (Zabala/Monkmeyer)

American preschools encouraged social interchange among children and collaborative activities with teachers. The Korean American preschool, with its structured schedule, did not: children were allowed to talk and play only during outdoor recess.

Not surprisingly, the Anglo American children engaged in more social play. In contrast, the Korean Americans engaged in more unoccupied or parallel play and less imaginative play. Their lack of make-believe play is also not surprising, since their classroom offered few materials that would stimulate pretending, such as "dress-up" clothes or dolls. In addition, the greater amount of pretend play among the Anglo American children may have been influenced by the greater value American culture places on individuality and self-expression. Korean American children played more cooperatively, often offering toys to other children—very likely a reflection of their culture's emphasis on group harmony. Anglo American children were more aggressive and often responded negatively to other children's suggestions, reflecting the competitiveness of American culture.

Given the Korean American stress on "school-like" learning, it is again not surprising that these children scored higher on a picture vocabulary test, an indication of cognitive functioning. This finding may tie in with other findings (discussed in Chapter 8) of Asian schoolchildren's high academic performance.

✔ GENDER

Being male or female affects how we look, how we move, and, often, how we work, play, and dress. It influences what we think about ourselves and what others think of us. All those characteristics—and more—are included when we use the word *gender:* what it means to be male or female.

GENDER DIFFERENCES

Two 4-year-olds, Kendra and Michael, are neighbors. They were wheeled together in the park as babies. They learned to ride tricycles at about the same time and pedaled up and down the sidewalk, often colliding with each other. They go to preschool together. All in all, Kendra and Michael have followed very similar paths; but there are some definite differences between them. Besides having different sex organs, Kendra and Michael are different in size, strength, appearance, physical and cognitive abilities, and personality.

Which of their differences are due to the fact that Kendra is a girl and Michael is a boy, and which are simply differences between two individual human beings? In discussing this question, we need to distinguish between *sex differences*, the physical differences between males and females, and *gender differences*, the psychological or behavioral differences between the sexes.

How Different Are Girls and Boys in Abilities and Personality?

Differences between baby boys and girls—physical, cognitive, and emotional—are slight (see Chapter 3). Some differences become more pronounced after age 3; but on average, boys and girls are more alike than different (Maccoby, 1980).

A landmark review of more than 2,000 studies found only a few significant differences between boys and girls. Three cognitive differences—girls' superior verbal ability and boys' better mathematical and spatial abilities—did not show up until after age 10 or 11 (Maccoby & Jacklin, 1974). More recent analyses found that gender differences in verbal abilities are so small as to be almost meaningless (Hyde & Linn, 1988). Differences in math and spatial abilities are complex and have been getting smaller in recent years. In the general population, neither sex shows better understanding of mathematical concepts; girls excel in computation (adding, subtracting, and so on), and boys do not show superior problem-solving ability until high school (Hyde, Fennema, & Lamon, 1990). In a meta-analysis of 286 studies of spatial abilities, the male advantage increased with age and emerged at different ages for different abilities, with few significant differences appearing before adolescence (Voyer, Voyer, & Bryden, 1995).

Regarding personality, the clearest finding is that boys tend to be more aggressive than girls (Turner & Gervai, 1995). Some studies suggest that girls are more likely to be empathic and more compliant and cooperative with parents, and to seek adult approval more than boys do (N. Eisenberg, Fabes, Schaller, & Miller, 1989; M. L. Hoffman, 1977; Maccoby, 1980; Turner & Gervai, 1995).

We need to remember, of course, that gender differences are valid for large groups of boys and girls but not necessarily for individuals (Turner & Gervai, 1995). By knowing a child's sex, we cannot predict whether that *particular* boy or girl will be faster, stronger, smarter, more obedient, or more assertive than another child.

How Differently Do Boys and Girls Play?

By age 4, Anna much preferred to play with other girls than with boys. She constantly classified toys, games, and activities as "girls' things" or "boys' things"; when she was not sure how an item should be classified, she asked about it. Her friend Stephen also was more interested in playing with children of his own sex.

One of the earliest gender differences that shows up—as early as age 2 and more consistently from age 3 on—is the choice of toys and play activities and of playmates of the same sex (Turner & Gervai, 1995). A tendency toward sex segregation in play seems to be universal across cultures. It is common among preschoolers and becomes even more so in middle childhood, when boys often play in the streets and other public places, while girls meet in one another's homes or yards (Maccoby, 1988, 1990, 1994).

Boys and girls typically play differently, and neither sex seems to like the other's style (Serbin, Moller, Gulko, Powlishta, & Colburne, 1994). Most boys like rough-and-tumble play (see Chapter 8) in fairly large groups, while girls are inclined to quieter play with one playmate (Benenson, 1993). Boys play more boisterously; girls tend to set up rules, such as taking turns, to avoid clashes (Maccoby, 1980). Another possible reason girls prefer not to play with boys is that boys often do not pay attention to girls' requests but make their own wishes known by direct demands. Even 33-month-old boys tend not to go away when a girl asks them to, but are more likely to do so when a boy tells them to (Maccoby, 1990).

GENDER DEVELOPMENT: THEORETICAL EXPLANATIONS

Gender identity, the awareness of one's gender and all it implies, is an important aspect of the developing self-concept. From early childhood, it affects how boys and girls feel about themselves and how they act. The meaning of gender identity may be strongly influenced, through socialization, by the culture in which a child grows up.

Gender roles are the behaviors, interests, attitudes, skills, and personality traits a culture considers appropriate for males and females. All societies have gender roles. Historically, in most cultures, women have been expected to devote most of their time to caring for the household and children, while men were providers and protectors. Women were expected to be compliant and nurturant; men were expected to be active, aggressive, and competitive. Today, gender roles in western cultures have become more diverse and more flexible.

Gender-typing is a child's learning of his or her

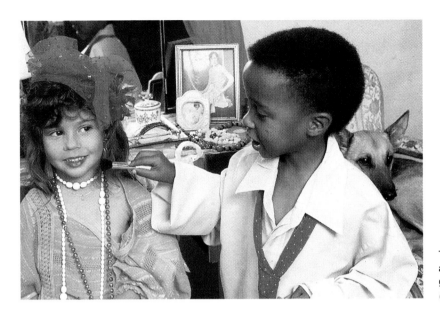

These preschoolers playing dress-up already show a strong awareness of gender identity and gender roles. *(Network Pro/The Image Works)*

gender role. Children learn these roles early through socialization, though people vary in the degree to which they take on gender roles. *Gender stereotypes* are exaggerated generalizations about male or female behavior ("All females are passive and dependent; all males are aggressive and independent"). Gender stereotypes pervade many cultures and are found in children as young as 3 (Haugh, Hoffman, & Cowan, 1980; J. E. Williams & Best, 1982). Gender stereotypes, if incorporated into gender roles, can restrict children's views of themselves and their future. By seeing certain activities as unmasculine or unfeminine, people may deny their natural inclinations and abilities. Gender stereotypes can affect the simplest, most everyday tasks as well as far-reaching life decisions. Children who absorb these stereotypes may become men who are "all thumbs" when it comes to giving a baby a bottle or women who "can't" nail boards together (Bem, 1976).

How do children achieve gender identity and acquire gender roles? Let's look at several theoretical perspectives (see Table 7-2). In the next section, we'll consider research on the relative influences of nature and nurture.

Psychoanalytic Theory: Identification with a Parent

"Dad, where will you live when I grow up and marry Mommy?" asks Timmy, age 4. From the psychoanalytic perspective, Timmy's question is part of his acquisition of gender identity. That process, according to Freud, is one of *identification,* the adoption of the characteristics, beliefs, attitudes, values, and behaviors of the parent of the same sex. Freud and other classical psychoanalytic theorists considered identification an important personality development of early childhood; some social-learning theorists also have used the term.

According to Freud, identification will occur for Timmy when he represses or gives up the wish to possess the parent of the other sex and identifies with the parent of the same sex. Although this explanation for gender identity has been influential, research has found that children's gender-typed behavior is not much like that of their parents and that identification seems to be a result, not a cause, of gender-typing (Maccoby, 1992). Today, most psychologists favor explanations for gender identity advanced by social-learning or cognitive theorists.

Social-Learning Theory: Observing and Imitating Models

Anna, at age 5, insisted on dressing in a new way. She wanted to wear leggings with a skirt over them, and boots—indoors and out. When Diane asked her why, Anna replied, "Because Katie dresses like this—and Katie's the king of the girls!"

In social-learning theory, children learn gender identity and gender roles in the same way that they learn other behavior: by observing and imitating

TABLE 7-2

Four Perspectives on Gender Identity

Theory	Major Theorist	Key Process	Basic Belief
Psychoanalytic	Sigmund Freud	Emotional	Gender identity occurs when child identifies with same-sex parent.
Social-learning	Albert Bandura	Learning	Gender identity is a result of observing and imitating models and being reinforced for gender-appropriate behavior.
Cognitive-developmental	Lawrence Kohlberg	Cognitive	Once child learns she is a girl or he is a boy, child actively sorts information by gender into what girls do and what boys do, and acts accordingly.
Gender-schema	Sandra Bem	Cognitive and learning	Child organizes information about what is considered appropriate for a boy or a girl on the basis of learning what a particular culture dictates, and behaves accordingly. Child sorts by gender because the culture dictates that gender is an important schema.

models. Typically, one model is the parent of the same sex, but children also model themselves after other people.

Reinforcement strengthens the learning of gender roles. A boy sees that he is physically more like his father than his mother. He imitates his father and is rewarded for acting "like a boy." A comparable process takes place for a girl. By the end of early childhood, these lessons are internalized; a child no longer needs praise, punishment, or the model's presence to act in socially appropriate ways. However, since gender identity and gender roles are learned, they can later be modified through selection and imitation of new models or through reinforcement of different kinds of behavior.

Although social-learning theory seems to make sense, it has been hard to prove. Children do imitate adults, but not always those of the same sex. Children are no more like their parents in personality than like other parents chosen at random; and if they *are* like their own parents, they are no more like the same-sex parent than like the other parent (Hetherington, 1965; Mussen & Rutherford, 1963).

An analysis of a large number of studies suggests that parents, especially fathers, do encourage gender-typed activities in play and chores. However, it is not clear whether the behavior being reinforced arises from imitation, from the children's own preferences, or from some other cause (Lyt-

ton & Romney, 1991). Social learning may have something to do with children's acquisition of gender identity and gender roles, but simple imitation and reinforcement do not seem to explain fully how this occurs.

Cognitive-Developmental Theory: Mental Processes

Anna learns she is a girl because people call her a girl. She figures out what things girls are supposed to do and does them. She learns about gender the same way she learns everything else: by thinking about her experience. This is the heart of Lawrence Kohlberg's (1966) cognitive-developmental theory.

To learn their gender identity, Kohlberg says, children do not depend on adults as models or as dispensers of reinforcements and punishments; instead, they classify themselves and others as male or female and then organize their behavior around that classification, adopting behaviors they perceive as consistent with their gender. From this perspective, the reason Anna preferred dolls to trucks was not that she got approval for playing with dolls (as in social-learning theory); instead, the reason was her cognitive awareness that playing with dolls was consistent with her idea of herself as a girl. According to Kohlberg, gender identity typically arrives at about age 2; by 3, most children have a firm idea of which sex they belong to. A girl with a short haircut, for example, will indignantly correct people who mistake her for a boy.

Gender constancy, or *gender conservation,* a child's realization that his or her sex will always be the same, comes at age 4 or 5. At 3, Anna's friend David told his mother, "When I grow up, I want to be a mommy just like you so I can play tennis and drive a car." Anna, who was then 4, said she would always be a girl and David would always be a boy, even if he played with dolls. David had not achieved gender constancy; Anna had. According to Kohlberg, gender constancy precedes acquisition of gender roles. Once children realize they will always be male or female, they adopt what they see as gender-appropriate behaviors.

While research supports a connection between gender concepts and cognitive development, very little evidence directly links acquisition of gender constancy to gender-related behavior—except when it comes to boys' television preferences. Five-year-old boys who have achieved gender constancy pay more attention to male characters on television and watch more sports and action programs than boys who have not yet achieved it (Luecke-Aleksa, Anderson, Collins, & Schmitt, 1995). Even before they attain gender constancy, however, children categorize activities and objects by gender, know a lot about what males and females do, and often acquire gender-appropriate behaviors (G. D. Levy & Carter, 1989; Luecke-Aleksa et al., 1995). It seems reasonable, then, to look for additional factors in gender-role development besides gender constancy.

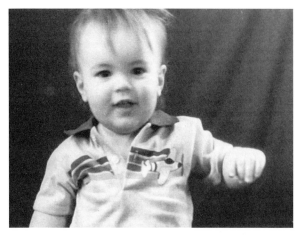

In one study, children saw three photos of this little boy: nude, dressed in boys' clothes, and dressed in girls' clothes. Preschoolers who identified the child's sex by genitals rather than by dress were more likely to show gender constancy— to know that they themselves would remain the sex they were. *(Sandra Lipsitz Bem)*

Gender-Schema Theory: A Cognitive-Social Approach

Why—of all the differences among people—do children pay so much attention to sex in setting up the classifications by which they make sense of their world? To answer that question, Sandra Bem (1983, 1985) developed *gender-schema theory,* a cognitive-social approach that contains elements of both cognitive-developmental theory and social-learning theory. A *schema* (much like the schemes in Piaget's theory) is a mentally organized pattern of behavior that helps a child sort information. A *gender schema* is a pattern of behavior organized around gender.

According to gender-schema theory, children socialize themselves in their gender roles by developing a concept of what it means to be male or female in their culture. They do this by organizing their observations around the schema of gender. They organize information on this basis because they see that their culture classifies people that way: males and females wear different clothes, play with different toys, use separate bathrooms, and line up separately in school. Children then adapt their own attitudes and behavior to their culture's gender schema—what boys and girls are "supposed" to be and do. When they act "gender-appropriate," their self-esteem rises; when they don't, they feel inadequate.

As in social-learning theory, since the gender schema is learned, it can be modified. Thus, Bem (1974, 1976) suggests, adults can teach children to substitute other schemas for a prevailing cultural schema that promotes gender-role stereotypes.

Adults can do this by sharing household tasks, giving nonstereotyped gifts (dolls for boys and trucks for girls), exposing children to men and women in nontraditional occupations, and emphasizing anatomy and reproduction rather than clothing and behavior as the main distinctions between males and females. A child raised in this way may develop an *androgynous* personality, one that integrates positive characteristics normally thought of as masculine with those normally considered feminine. An androgynous person might be assertive, dominant, and self-reliant ("masculine" traits), as well as compassionate, sympathetic, and understanding ("feminine" traits). Androgynous men and women can do what seems best in a particular situation rather than confine themselves to what is considered "manly" or "womanly."

Of course, ingrained cultural attitudes about gender can be highly resistant to change; yet in many places they *are* changing. In the United States and other industrialized countries, women have entered nontraditional occupations and are gaining power in business, in government, and in the family. Egalitarian attitudes and behavior have become more common, especially among younger, better-educated, and higher-income people. Men and women are exploring aspects of their personalities that were suppressed by the old gender stereotypes. If Bem is right, these cultural changes will be reflected in children's gender schemas, which in turn shape their attitudes and behavior.

Each of these theories focuses on a different aspect of gender development. The psychoanalytic perspective emphasizes emotional ties to parents; the social-learning viewpoint stresses what and how children learn in various contexts; and the cognitive approach notes children's growing ability to take in and interpret information about the world and their place in it. Each theory contributes to our understanding, but none fully explains why boys and girls turn out differently in some respects and not in others.

INFLUENCES ON GENDER DEVELOPMENT: NATURE AND NURTURE

Do cultural influences create gender differences, or merely accentuate them? The existence of similar gender roles in many cultures suggests that some gender differences, at least, may be innate. On the other hand, psychological and behavioral differences among people of the same sex are larger than the average differences between the sexes, suggesting that the role of biology, if any, is limited. Research does not yield clear-cut answers to the nature-nurture question; as with other aspects of development, an interaction of factors may be at work.

Hormonal Influences

In animals, hormones circulating in the bloodstream before or about the time of birth seem to influence gender differences. The male hormone testosterone has been linked to aggressive behavior in mice, guinea pigs, rats, and primates, and the female hormone prolactin to motherly behavior in virgin or male animals (Bronson & Desjardins, 1969; D. M. Levy, 1966; R. M. Rose, Gordon, & Bernstein, 1972). Of course, human beings are influenced far more by learning than animals are, so conclusions drawn from animal studies may not apply.

Two small but often-cited studies of people who had unusual prenatal exposure to hormones or who were born with sexual abnormalities suggest that both nature and nurture may play a role in gender differences. In one study (Ehrhardt & Money, 1967), girls whose mothers had taken certain hormones during pregnancy were born with abnormal external sex organs. After surgery, the girls looked normal and had normal female reproductive capability, but they acted "boyish." They played with trucks and guns and competed with boys in sports. Was this behavior due to prenatal hormones or to parental reinforcement of "tomboy" behavior, or to some combination of factors? The answer is unclear. The other study (Money, Ehrhardt, & Masica, 1968) highlights the role of environment. The participants were chromosomally male and had testes instead of ovaries but looked female and had been raised as girls. All were "typically female" in behavior and outlook: all considered marriage and raising a family very important and had played mostly with dolls and other "girls'" toys. Perhaps, then, hormones may predispose people toward certain behaviors, but the environment shapes these behaviors. However, the very small samples in these two studies make their findings inconclusive.

Parental Influences

Even in today's more "liberated" American society, parents treat sons and daughters differently,

A father who encourages his son to engage in traditionally masculine activities, such as woodworking, delivers a powerful message about what kinds of interests are appropriate for a boy. *(Tom McCarthy/The Picture Cube)*

especially in toddlerhood (Fagot & Hagan, 1991; see Chapter 5). Parents accept aggression more in boys and show more warmth to girls. An analysis of 172 studies between 1952 and 1987 (Lytton & Romney, 1991) found that boys are gender-socialized more strongly than girls. Parents pressure boys more to act "like real boys" and avoid acting "like girls" than they pressure girls to avoid "boyish" behavior and to act in "feminine" ways. Parents are more likely to show discomfort if a boy plays with a doll than if a girl plays with a truck. Girls have much more freedom in the clothes they wear, the games they play, and the people they play with (Miedzian, 1991).

Some (but not all) studies find that fathers, in particular, promote gender-typing (Turner & Gervai, 1995). For example, one study found that fathers are apt to be more social with, more approving of, and more affectionate toward their preschool daughters, but more controlling and directive toward their sons. Fathers also tend to be more concerned with their sons' cognitive achievements than with their daughters' (Bronstein, 1988). Still, according to an analysis of 67 studies of single-parent families, the father's absence seems to make little difference in a child's gender development. No differences showed up for girls, and those for boys were quite small (M. R. Stevenson & Black, 1988). Other research suggests that what fathers do has long-range implications: men and women who get along well at work and in relationships are most apt to have had warm ties to fathers who were competent, strong,

secure in their own masculinity, and nurturant toward their children (Biller, 1981).

One reason for these mixed findings may be that researchers were studying different kinds of gender-related behavior and were using different measuring instruments. Gender-typing has many facets, and the particular combination of "masculine" and "feminine" traits and behaviors a child acquires is a very individual matter. Jonathan may play mainly with boys, but not aggressively; Marguerite may insist on wearing dresses instead of jeans but may yell with all her lung power when she doesn't get her way. Furthermore, much may depend on the child's age (Turner & Gervai, 1995).

In one multidimensional study (Turner & Gervai, 1995), researchers talked with 4-year-old children in Cambridge, England, and Budapest, Hungary. The researchers showed the children pictures to determine their play preferences, their knowledge of gender stereotypes, and the adult occupations that appealed to them. The children were observed at preschool to see how they played and with whom, and their parents were interviewed and filled out questionnaires. One goal was to compare parents' and children's gender-typing; another was to find out whether parents' contribution to gender-typing differed for different kinds of behavior.

The findings were complex. Highly gender-typed parents did tend to produce highly gender-typed children, but parents seemed to have more influence on children's *knowledge* of gender stereotypes than on their *behavior*. This was especially true of choice of playmates: children played with others of the same sex regardless of what their parents thought. Indeed, same-sex peer groups may themselves be a major influence on gender-typing. Fathers were a more consistent influence than mothers. Surprisingly, though, they influenced both boys and girls in the same direction: daughters as well as sons of a highly "masculine" father tended to be more self-assertive and less expressive than sons and daughters of less "masculine" men. Less surprisingly, children of fathers who did more housework and child care were less aware of gender stereotypes and engaged in less gender-typed play. More research on the multiple aspects of gender may help sort out the ways parents influence children's gender-related attitudes and behavior.

Cultural Influences

When Derek and his friend Shani play house in preschool, Shani, as the "mommy," is likely to "cook" and "take care of the baby" while Derek puts on a hat and "goes to work." When he comes home, sits at the table, and says "I'm hungry," Shani drops what she is doing to wait on him. This scenario would be less surprising if both children's mothers did not work outside the home and if both their fathers did not do a fair amount of housework. These children have absorbed the gender roles of their culture rather than those of their own households.

One important instrument for the transmission of cultural attitudes about gender is television. The typical American high school graduate has watched more than 25,000 hours of television (Action for Children's Television, undated) and has absorbed highly gender-stereotyped attitudes from it. Although women seen on television are now more likely to be working outside the home and men are sometimes shown caring for children or doing the marketing, life as portrayed on television is, for the most part, more stereotyped than life in the real world.

Social-learning theory predicts that children who watch a lot of television will become more gender-typed by imitating the models they see on the screen. By the same token, young children who watched a series of nontraditional episodes, such as a father and son cooking together, had less stereotyped views than children who had not seen the series (J. Johnston & Ettema, 1982). Of course, children bring their own attitudes to the television set.

Boys turn on more cartoons and action adventure programs than girls do, and both sexes remember television sequences that confirm the stereotypes they already hold better than they remember non-stereotypical sequences (Calvert & Huston, 1987).

Children's books are another source of gender stereotypes, as research in the 1970s pointed out. Today, friendship between boys and girls is portrayed more often, and girls are braver and more resourceful. Still, male characters predominate, females are more likely to need help, and males are more likely to give it (Beal, 1994).

✔ CHILD-REARING PRACTICES

As children gradually become their own persons, their upbringing can be a baffling, complex challenge. Parents must deal with small people who have minds and strong wills of their own, but who still have a lot to learn about what kinds of behavior work well in a civilized society. Parents struggle to make the right decisions in bringing up children. They want to raise human beings who enjoy life, think well of themselves, and fulfill their goals. They also want their children to learn to live harmoniously with other people and to form and maintain close, constructive relationships. To accomplish these ends, parents have to use discipline. How do parents discipline children and teach them self-discipline? Are some way of parenting more effective than others?

FORMS OF DISCIPLINE

Discipline is not a synonym for punishment. The word comes from the Latin for "knowledge" or "instruction"; it refers to methods of teaching children character, self-control, and acceptable behavior. Discipline, then, can be a powerful tool for socialization.

What forms of discipline work best? Social-learning research has compared reinforcement and punishment. Other researchers have looked at forms of discipline in terms of the quality of interaction between parent and child.

Reinforcement and Punishment

"What are we going to do with that child?" Noel's mother says. "The more we punish him, the more he misbehaves!"

Parents sometimes punish children to stop undesirable behavior, but research shows that children usually learn more from being reinforced for good behavior. *External* reinforcements may be tangible (candy, money, toys, or gold stars) or intangible (a smile, a word of praise, a hug, extra attention, or a special privilege). Whatever the reinforcement, the child must see it as rewarding and must receive it fairly consistently after showing the desired behaior. Eventually, the behavior should provide its own *internal* reward: a sense of pleasure or accomplishment. In Noel's case, his parents ignore him most of the time when he behaves well but scold or spank him when he acts up. In other words, they unwittingly reinforce his *misbe-havior* by giving him attention when he does what they do *not* want him to do.

Punishment can have harmful effects. Early and severe physical punishment poses an especial risk of injury to the child. In addition, harsh physical or verbal punishment may encourage children to imitate the punisher's aggressive behavior. Children who are punished harshly may have trouble interpreting other people's actions and words; they may attribute hostile intentions where none exist and may consider violence an effective response to problems (B. Weiss, Dodge, Bates, & Pettit, 1992). On the other hand, such children may become passive because they feel helpless. Children may become frightened if parents lose control and yell, scream, chase, or hit the child. A child may eventually try to avoid a punitive parent, undermining the parent's ability to influence behavior (Grusec & Goodnow, 1994).

Despite the potentially negative effects of punishment, at times it does seem necessary. Children may have to be immediately and forcefully taught not to run out into traffic or bash one another over the head with heavy toys. When punishment must be used, the following factors influence its effectiveness (Parke, 1977): (1) *Timing:* The shorter the time between misbehavior and punishment, the more effective the punishment. When children are punished as they begin to engage in a forbidden act, such as approaching an object they have been told to stay away from, they will go to it less often than if they are not punished until after they have actually touched it. (2) *Explanation:* Punishment is more effective when accompanied by a short, simple explanation (rather than a long, involved one or none at all). (3) *Consistency:* The more consistently a child is punished for the same misbehavior, the more effective the punishment will be. Behavior that brings punishment only

"Young lady, don't get gutsy with me."

Power assertion, consisting of threats, demands, or physical punishment, is usually less effective than other types of discipline. However, the choice and effectiveness of a disciplinary strategy may depend on the personalities of parent and child, the child's age, the quality of their relationship, and the culture. *(Drawing by Bernard Schoenbaum; © 1996 The New Yorker Magazine, Inc.)*

some of the time is likely to continue longer than if punished every time. (4) *The person who punishes:* The better the relationship between the punishing adult and the child, the more effective the punishment.

Power Assertion, Induction, and Withdrawal of Love

From the point of view of a parent's interaction with a child, research has identified three types of discipline: *power assertion, induction,* and temporary *withdrawal of love.*

Power assertion includes demands, threats, withdrawal of privileges, spanking, and other physical punishment. *Inductive techniques* are used to induce desirable behavior; they include setting limits, demonstrating logical consequences of an action, explaining, reasoning, and getting ideas from the child. *Withdrawal of love* may take the form of ignoring, isolating, or showing dislike for a child. Analysis of data from a number of studies suggests that induction is usually the most effective method, and power assertion the least effective, in getting children to internalize parental standards (M. L. Hoffman, 1970a, 1970b).

Most parents call upon more than one of these strategies, depending on the situation. Parents tend to use reasoning in getting a child to show concern for others or in teaching table manners. They use power assertion to stop play that gets too rough, and they use both power assertion and reasoning to deal with lying and stealing. Sometimes parents use power assertion to get a child's attention (by raising their voices or picking up a child who will not move) and then use reasoning to make their position clear. The choice and effectiveness of a strategy may depend in part on the personality of the parent, the personality and age of the child, and the quality of their relationship. Cultural factors also play a role: in a culture in which power assertion is accepted and expected, children may respond to it better (Grusec & Goodnow, 1994).

The 1990 National Longitudinal Survey of Youth found spanking highly prevalent (Giles-Sims, Straus, & Sugarman, 1995). More than 6 out of 10 mothers of 3- to 5-year-olds reported having spanked their children an average of three times during the previous week—a rate that works out to more than 150 spankings a year. Spanking is more prevalent in the south and less so among Catholic mothers. Factors that add to the stress of parenting, such as being young, poor, rural, and unmarried, seem to increase spanking. More boys are spanked than girls, apparently because mothers consider boys more aggressive and more in need of physical discipline. Ironically, as we will discuss later in this chapter, spanking often *stimulates* aggressive behavior.

PARENTING STYLES AND CHILDREN'S COMPETENCE

The effectiveness of any form of discipline may depend on how a child interprets and responds to it in the context of the overall, ongoing relationship with a parent. Instead of focusing on specific forms of discipline, therefore, some researchers have tried to find overall patterns, or styles, by which parents approach their task. Let's look at one influential model.

Baumrind: Three Parenting Styles

Why does Stacy hit and bite the nearest person when she cannot finish a jigsaw puzzle? What makes David sit and sulk when he cannot finish the puzzle, even though his teacher offers to help him? Why does Consuelo work on the puzzle for 20 minutes and then shrug and try another? Why are children so different in their responses to the same situation? Temperament is a major factor, of course; but some research suggests that styles of parenting may affect children's competence in dealing with their world.

In her pioneering research, Diana Baumrind (1971, 1996; Baumrind & Black, 1967) studied 103 preschool children from 95 families. Through interviews, testing, and home studies, she measured how children were functioning, identified three parenting styles, and described typical behavior patterns of children raised according to each.

Authoritarian parents value control and unquestioning obedience. They try to make children conform to a set standard of conduct and punish them arbitrarily and forcefully for violating it. They are more detached and less warm than other parents. Their children tend to be more discontented, withdrawn, and distrustful.

Permissive parents value self-expression and self-regulation. They consider themselves resources, not models. They make few demands and allow children to monitor their own activities as much as possible. When they do have to make rules, they explain the reasons for them. They consult with children about policy decisions and rarely punish. They are warm, noncontrolling, and undemanding. Their preschool children tend to be immature—the least self-controlled and the least exploratory.

Authoritative parents respect a child's individuality but also stress social values. They have confidence in their ability to guide children, but they also respect children's independent decisions, interests, opinions, and personalities. They are loving, consistent, demanding, firm in maintaining standards, and willing to impose limited, judicious punishment—even occasional, mild spanking—when necessary, within the context of a warm, supportive relationship. They explain the reasoning behind their stands and encourage verbal give-and-take. Their children apparently feel secure in knowing both that they are loved and what is expected of them. These preschoolers tend to be the most self-reliant, self-controlled, self-assertive, exploratory, and content.

Why does authoritative parenting seem to enhance children's competence? It may well be because authoritative parents set reasonable expectations and realistic standards. In authoritarian homes, children are so strictly controlled that often they cannot make independent choices about their own behavior. In permissive homes, children receive so *little* guidance that they may become uncertain and anxious about whether they are doing the right thing. In authoritative homes, children know when they are meeting expectations and can decide whether it is worth risking parental displeasure or other unpleasant consequences to pursue a goal. These children are expected to perform well, fulfill commitments, and participate actively in family duties as well as family fun. They know the satisfaction of meeting responsibilities and achieving success.

Evaluating Baumrind's Work

Baumrind's work has inspired much research, and the superiority of authoritative parenting has repeatedly been supported. However, because these findings seem to suggest that there is one "right" way to raise children well, they have caused some controversy. Sandra Scarr, for example, argues that heredity normally exerts a much greater influence than parenting practices (see Box 7-2).

Furthermore, since Baumrind's findings are correlational, they merely establish associations between each parenting style and a particular set of child behaviors; they do not show that styles of child rearing *cause* children to be more or less competent. Also, it is impossible to know whether the children were, in fact, raised in a particular style. It may be, for example, that some of the better-adjusted children were raised inconsistently, but by the time of the study their parents had adopted the authoritative pattern. Furthermore, even if parents *usually* act toward their children in a certain way, they do not respond to *all* situations in that way.

Finally, Baumrind did not consider innate factors, such as temperament, that might have affected children's competence and exerted an influence on the parents. Parents of "easy" children may be more likely to respond to the child in a permissive or authoritative manner, while parents of "difficult" children may become more authoritarian.

INTERNALIZATION AND OTHER GOALS OF PARENTING

The goal of socialization is to help a child internalize parental teachings in the form of self-discipline. From an information-processing perspective, the effectiveness of parental discipline may hinge on how well the child understands and accepts the parent's message, both cognitively and emotionally, in whatever form or style it is conveyed (Grusec & Goodnow, 1994).

For children to *perceive* a message accurately, parents need to get the child's attention. They need to get across their belief that the issue is important and that their intent is to help the child. They need to be clear and consistent (but not overly repetitive!) about their expectations. For the child to *accept* the message, the child has to recognize it as appropriate; so parents need to be fair, truthful, and fit their actions to the misdeed and to the child's temperament and cognitive and emotional level. A child may be more motivated to accept the message as a guide to behavior if the parents are normally warm and responsive, making the child want to identify with or act like them; if they arouse the child's empathy (say, for another child who was the victim of the misdeed); and if they make the child feel less secure in their affections as a result of the misbehavior. It may help if parents respect a child's autonomy by couching the message in humorous or indirect terms (Grusec & Goodnow, 1994).

Important as internalization is, it is not the only goal of parenting. In some situations, other goals—such as encouraging flexibility and initiative or preserving the child's self-esteem and a good parent-child relationship—may take precedence. When a child refuses to do as a parent says, the parent—rather than get into a possibly futile power struggle—may take the opportunity to teach the child positive ways to communicate his or her own point of view and negotiate acceptable alternatives. Internalization of this broader set of skills, not just of specific behavioral demands, may well be a key to the success of authoritative parenting (Grusec & Goodnow, 1994). The outcome is not a child who acts just like the parent, but a unique individual who, while accepting a set of core values necessary for social functioning, is free to vary from those values or to apply them in her or his own way.

In the long run, specific parenting practices may be less important than how parents feel about their children and show their feelings. That is the conclusion of a major study of young adults whose mothers were interviewed about their child-rearing techniques 20 years earlier (McClelland, Constantian, Regalado, & Stone, 1978; Sears, Maccoby, & Levin, 1957). How these adults turned out bore little or no relation to specific parenting practices. The most important influence—dwarfing

BOX 7-2   PRACTICALLY SPEAKING

IS "GOOD-ENOUGH" PARENTING GOOD ENOUGH?

How much difference do parents make in the way their child turns out? Not a great deal under most circumstances, says Sandra Scarr (1992). Scarr argues that being reared in one family rather than in another—as long as the family is not violent, abusive, or neglectful—makes little difference in children's development. Diana Baumrind (1993) strongly disagrees; she maintains that parenting practices can and do influence children's lives. Jacquelyn Faye Jackson (1993) expresses concern that Scarr's view will harm children who need special help, by giving policymakers less reason to support interventions. Let's see how each of these thinkers supports her opinion.

SCARR'S THESIS: "GOOD-ENOUGH" PARENTING IS GOOD ENOUGH (Rhoda Baer)

Most families provide supportive environments for their children, and "superparents" are probably no more effective than "goodenough" parents. It does not matter whether or not parents take children to a ball game or to a museum, since children's inherited characteristics will outweigh environmental differences.

Twin studies and adoption studies have found a strong genetic influence on differences in intelligence and personality. "Parents do not have the power to make their children into whatever they want" (p. 15); children to a great extent create their own environment on the basis of their genetic tendencies. If the environment is varied enough so that children can choose experiences which fit their inborn tendencies, the athletic child will end up playing ball and the artistic child will create, no matter what their parents do. This is not, of course, true of children in "very disadvantaged circumstances and adults with little or no choice about occupations and leisure activities" (Scarr, 1992, p. 9). Among environments that support normal development, however, variations in parenting are not very important in determining outcomes.

One reason developmentalists have overemphasized the role of the family environment is that parents also provide children's genes, and so genetic and environmental influences are correlated. Parents who read well bring books into the house, read to the child, and encourage reading. Parents with reading problems raise children in a less literate environment. When children's reading abilities are correlated with their parents' abilities, the effects of heredity can be confused with the effects of the environment.

Since ordinary parents are good enough, they can take comfort in raising their children in ways that are comfortable for them without feeling guilty when they do not conform to current wisdom about good parenting.

BAUMRIND'S VIEW: EXCELLENT PARENTING IS BETTER THAN "GOOD ENOUGH" (Jane Scherr)

All nonabusive, nonpoor families are not alike in fostering healthy development. The person a child will become in one "normal" environment is different from what

all others—was how much their parents had loved them, enjoyed them, and shown them affection.

The most beloved children grew up to be the most tolerant of other people, the most understanding, and the most likely to show active concern for others. The least mature adults had grown up in homes where they were considered a nuisance and an interference in adults' lives. Their parents had been intolerant of noise, mess, and roughhousing and had reacted unkindly to children's aggressiveness, to normal childhood sex play, and to expressions of dependency. However,

children of easygoing, loving parents had been less well-behaved as they were growing up than children of stricter parents, prompting the researchers to conclude that some childhood misbehavior may be a necessary step in the development of a person's own value system.

MALTREATMENT: CHILD ABUSE AND NEGLECT

Sometimes parent-child relationships go tragically wrong, resulting in serious maltreatment of children. Maltreatment can take several forms. *Child*

the same child would become in another.

Scarr fails to specify what kinds of environment are "good enough" or what constitutes "normal development," making it hard to evaluate her thesis. She also fails to explore cross-cultural differences.

Many American children today—from both poor and well-off families—are growing up at risk of violence, drug abuse, poor reading and math skills, eating disorders, school failure, and sexually transmitted disease. "Thus, the average environment of most young people today is not really good enough" (Baumrind, 1993, p. 1302).

Biology is not destiny. Parents affect children's development by using such techniques as *scaffolding* and *induction* (described in Chapters 6 and 7), monitoring children's activities, and modeling desirable behavior. All these practices take a high level of parental involvement and commitment, not just "good enough" parenting.

Scarr's thesis is dangerous because it may encourage parents to deny responsibility for children's healthy development. Parents who ascribe a child's dysfunctional behavior to the child's genes rather than to anything the parent did or did not do are less likely to try to improve the situation, and the child is less likely to turn out well.

JACKSON'S VIEW: INTERVENTIONS CAN BE EFFECTIVE (Jane Scherr)

 Research based on studies of twins and adopted children, who are atypical in important respects, cannot adequately support a theory about the development of "normal" children raised in "average" family environments. Scarr's theory can harm disadvantaged minority children by discouraging intervention to improve their environment. Research shows that interventions can be beneficial, for example, in boosting IQs of children of mothers with low IQs and in helping children with Down syndrome learn higher-order thinking skills.

SCARR'S RESPONSE

"Both biological and environmental explanations are required to account for human development" (Scarr, 1993, p. 1334). That which is normal for a given culture is not the same as that which is normal for the human species; cultures define what behavior is desirable and provide a range of opportunities for development.

"Genetic does not mean intractable!" (Scarr, 1993, p. 1350). Minority and socially disadvantaged children do benefit from interventions that transmit values of the dominant culture. Still, this does not negate the strong effect of inherited characteristics. Because of their genetic makeup, different people—even siblings within the same household—react differently to the same environment. Biology and culture together shape behavior.

It is important to recognize the power of heredity and not to bend scientific truth to a social agenda. "All children should have opportunities to become species-normal, culturally appropriate and uniquely themselves. . . . But humanitarian concerns should not drive developmental theory" (Scarr, 1993, p. 1350).

abuse involves physical injury, in a pattern often referred to as the **battered child syndrome** (Kempe, Silverman, Steele, Droegemueller, & Silver, 1962). **Sexual abuse** is any kind of sexual contact between a child and an older person. **Child neglect** is failure to provide such necessary care as food, clothing, and supervision. **Emotional abuse** involves verbal or other nonphysical action or failure to act, causing damage to a child's behavioral, cognitive, emotional, or physical functioning. It may include rejection, terrorization, isolation, exploitation, degradation, or ridicule.

Although maltreatment is more widely recognized than in the past, its incidence is hard to determine. Methods for collecting data are flawed and interpretations difficult. The rise in reported cases since 1976, when the first national statistics were compiled, may reflect an increase in maltreatment or better reporting, or both; but many cases are never reported to protective agencies, and many more are not investigated. A 1995 Gallup poll of parents indicated that 1.3 million children are sexually abused every year—10 times as many as the official federal figure (Lewin, 1995).

This adult volunteer uses dolls to help young children realize that they have control over their bodies and need not let anyone—even friends or family members—touch them. Such programs for preventing sexual abuse need to walk a fine line between alerting children to danger and frightening them or discouraging appropriate affection. *(Janet Fries/TIME Magazine)*

Overall, according to the most recent government estimate (based on information from community professionals nationwide), the number of abused and neglected children nearly doubled—from 1.4 million to 2.8 million—between 1986 and 1993, though the number of reported cases in 1993 was just over 1 million. A disproportionate amount of abuse occurs in poor and single-parent families. Children are consistently vulnerable to sexual abuse from age 3 on. Girls are more likely to be sexually abused, but boys are more vulnerable to emotional abuse and serious physical injury (Sedlak & Broadhurst, 1996).

Maltreatment has become a leading cause of death among young children; at least 2,000 die every year and 140,000 are seriously injured (U.S. Advisory Board on Child Abuse and Neglect, 1995). Parents were charged in 57 percent of murders of children under 12 years old in large urban areas in 1988, and in 8 out of 10 cases the parent had previously abused the child (J. M. Dawson & Langan, 1994). Sometimes the killer is the mother's boyfriend, and the mother fails to intervene or tries to cover up. Sometimes the mother is a victim of abuse herself and is too intimidated to protect her child.

Abused children are often caught in a web of conflicting values: protecting children's safety versus preserving families and respecting privacy. Many allegations of abuse are never confirmed, and adults unjustly accused of abuse suffer grievously and unfairly. On the other hand, many children whose precarious situation is known to authorities or neighbors are left in the hands of abusive or neglectful parents, often with fatal results.

Causes of Abuse and Neglect

Why do adults hurt or neglect children? Answers are complex. We can look at the problem using the ecological perspective proposed by Urie Bronfenbrenner (see Chapter 1), which considers the child in the family, the community, and the larger society.*

The Microsystem: The Child in the Family Maltreatment is a symptom of extreme disturbance in child rearing; it usually appears in the context of other family problems, such as alcoholism or antisocial behavior. More than 9 out of 10 abusers are not psychotic and do not have criminal personalities, but many are lonely, unhappy, anxious, depressed, angry, aggressive, and under great stress, and they tend to have low self-esteem and poor impulse control. About one-third of abusing parents were abused themselves as children (B. D. Schmitt & Kempe, 1983; D. A. Wolfe, 1985).

Abusive parents tend to be ignorant of normal child development; they expect children not to cry, or to stay clean and neat at an unrealistically early age. In fact, they may expect their children to take

---

*Unless otherwise referenced, this discussion is indebted to Belsky (1993) and the National Research Council, NRC (1993b).

care of *them* and become enraged when this does not happen. Often deprived of good parenting themselves, they do not know how to be good parents. They tend to be highly stressed by behavior that most parents take in stride. They are less effective in resolving problems and have more confrontations with their children (J. R. Reid, Patterson, & Loeber, 1982; Wolfe, 1985). By contrast, neglectful parents tend to be apathetic, incompetent, irresponsible, and emotionally withdrawn (Wolfe, 1985). Sexual abusers have a wide range of personality disorders.

Abusive parents are more likely than others to have marital problems and to fight physically with each other. They have more children and have them closer together, and their households are more disorganized. They experience more stressful events than other families (J. R. Reid et al., 1982). Abusive parents tend to cut themselves off from others, leaving them with no one to turn to in times of stress—and no one to see what is happening. The arrival of a new man in the home (a stepfather or the mother's boyfriend) often leads to abuse.

When parents who think poorly of themselves, had troubled childhoods, and have problems handling negative emotions have children who seem particularly needy or demanding, the likelihood of abuse may increase. These children's greater needs may stem from poor health, "difficult" personalities, or physical disabilities. It may be that characteristics of the child do not initially provoke abuse but serve to keep it up. Then too, abuse can make children more aggressive and defiant, perpetuating the cycle.

The Exosystem: Jobs, Neighborhood, and Social Support

The outside world can create a climate for family violence. Poverty, unemployment, job dissatisfaction, social isolation, and lack of assistance for the primary caregiver are closely correlated with child and spouse abuse. None of these, however, are determining factors.

What makes one low-income neighborhood a place where children are highly likely to be abused, while another, matched for ethnic population and income levels, is safer? In one inner-city Chicago neighborhood, the proportion of children who died from maltreatment (1 death for every 2,541 children) was about twice the proportion in another inner-city neighborhood. Researchers who interviewed community leaders in both neighborhoods found a depressed atmosphere in the high-abuse community. Criminal activity was rampant, and facilities for community programs were dark and dreary. People had trouble thinking of anything good to say about their neighborhood. Even people who worked in local agencies knew little about community services and resources, had no sense of a social support system, and showed no positive feelings about their political leaders. The research team concluded that this was an environment with "an ecological conspiracy against children" (Garbarino & Kostelny, 1993, p. 213). In the low-abuse neighborhood, people talked readily about their community and, while acknowledging its problems, described it as a poor but decent place to live. They painted a picture of a neighborhood with robust social support networks, well-known community services, and strong political leadership.

The Macrosystem: Cultural Values and Patterns

Two cultural factors associated with child abuse are societal violence and physical punishment of children. In countries where violent crime is infrequent and children are rarely spanked, such as Japan, China, and Tahiti, child abuse is rare (Celis, 1990).

By comparison, the United States is a violent place. Homicide, wife battering, and rape are common, and resistance to gun control is high. A 1977 Supreme Court ruling that school personnel may strike disobedient children is still in effect, with some qualifications. Many states still permit corporal punishment in schools; minority and handicapped children are paddled more often than their classmates. According to a 1995 Gallup poll, more than 5 percent of parents admit to punishing their children so brutally that it amounts to abuse.

Effects of Abuse and Neglect

Abuse or neglect can produce grave consequences—not only physical, but emotional and cognitive as well. The severest emotional trauma generally occurs when a nonabusive parent does not believe a child's account of abuse and does not try to protect the child, when the child is removed from the home, or when the child has suffered more than one type of abuse (Browne & Finkelhor, 1986; Bryer, Nelson, Miller, & Krol, 1987; Burgess, Hartman, & McCormack, 1987; Emery, 1989; Kendall-Tackett, Williams, & Finkelhor, 1993).

Abused children often show delayed speech (Coster, Gersten, Beeghly, & Cicchetti, 1989). They

TABLE 7-3

Developmentally Related Reactions to Sexual Abuse

Age	Most Common Symptoms
Preschoolers	Anxiety Nightmares Inappropriate sexual behavior
School-age children	Fear Mental illness Aggression Nightmares School problems Hyperactivity Regressive behavior
Adolescents	Depression Withdrawn, suicidal, or self-injurious behaviors Physical complaints Illegal acts Running away Substance abuse

SOURCE: Adapted from Kendall-Tackett et al., 1993.

are more likely to repeat a grade, to do poorly on cognitive tests, and to be discipline problems in school (Eckenrode, Laird, & Doris, 1993). They tend to be aggressive and uncooperative and, consequently, less well liked than other children (Haskett & Kistner, 1991; Salzinger, Feldman, Hammer, & Rosario, 1993). Teenagers who were abused when they were younger may react by running away, which may be self-protective, or they may abuse drugs, which is not (National Research Council, NRC, 1993b). Although most abused children do not become delinquent or criminal as adults, abuse makes it likelier that they will (Dodge, Bates, & Pettit, 1990; Widom, 1989).

Consequences of sexual abuse vary with age (see Table 7-3). Sexually abused children are likely to be fearful, to have low self-esteem, to become preoccupied with sex, and to have problems with behavior and school achievement (Einbender & Friedrich, 1989; Kendall-Tackett et al., 1993). Fearfulness and low self-esteem often continue into adulthood. Adults who were sexually abused as children tend to be anxious, depressed, angry, or hostile; not to trust people; to feel isolated and stigmatized; and to be sexually maladjusted (Browne

& Finkelhor, 1986). The effects of sexual abuse are more pronounced when the abuser is someone close to the child, when the sexual contact has been frequent and has persisted for a long period of time, when force has been used, when there has been oral, anal, or vaginal penetration, or when the child has a negative outlook or coping style (Kendall-Tackett et al., 1993).

Still, many maltreated children show remarkable resilience, especially if they have been able to form an attachment to a supportive person (Egeland & Sroufe, 1981). High intelligence, advanced cognitive abilities, and high self-esteem seem to help. Also important is the child's interpretation of the abuse or neglect. Children who see it as coming from a parent's weaknesses or frustrations seem to cope better than those who take it as parental rejection (Garmezy, Masten, & Tellegren, 1984; Zimrin, 1986).

Growing up to be an abuser is far from an inevitable result of being abused as a child. According to one analysis, one-third of abused children grow up to abuse their own children (Kaufman & Zigler, 1987). Abused girls who do *not* become abusers are likely to have had someone to whom they could turn for help, to have received therapy, and to have a good marital or love relationship. They usually are more openly angry about and able to describe their experience of abuse. They are likely to have been abused by only one parent and to have had a loving, supportive relationship with the other (Egeland, Jacobvitz, & Sroufe, 1988; Kaufman & Zigler, 1987).

Emotional maltreatment is more subtle than physical maltreatment, and its effects may be harder to pin down. It has been linked to lying, stealing, low self-esteem, emotional maladjustment, dependency, underachievement, depression, aggression, learning disorders, homicide, and suicide, as well as to psychological distress later in life (Hart & Brassard, 1987).

LIFE-SPAN ISSUE
CAN PARENTAL TEACHING POISON A CHILD FOR LIFE?

 Alice Miller, a Swiss psychotherapist, has studied the long-range effects of psychological deprivation in childhood. In For Your Own Good: Hidden Cruelty in Child Rearing and the Roots of Violence (1983, 1984), she argues—on the basis of her clinical experience and her study of central European child-rearing practices during the past two centuries—that much societal violence, as well as personal suffering, can be traced to parents' treatment of children.

One of the most important aspects of parenting is the way parents teach a child to deal with feelings. According to Alice Miller, much pain in adult life stems from these early "lessons," which are passed on from generation to generation.

Miller (1983, 1984) identified a psychologically injurious cluster of child-rearing practices and attitudes she called *poisonous pedagogy (PP)*. Through ridicule, criticism, teasing, scolding, impatience, and strict, authoritarian discipline, says Miller, parents break a child's will, undermine the child's self-confidence and curiosity, and force the child to suppress authentic feelings and impulses. These suppressed emotions surface in adulthood in the form of rage and violence directed against the self and others. The end results can range from the stifling of empathy and creativity to drug addiction, mental illness, and suicide.

Why do parents do this to children? In Miller's view, they do it both consciously, in the belief that they are helping their children become more competent and self-

sufficient, and unconsciously, in reaction to the emotional harm they themselves suffered as children. Only by breaking this generation-to-generation cycle of transmission, she says, can adults help children grow up to be psychologically healthy.

To test Miller's theory, David Harrington (1993) drew on data from a longitudinal study of 100 mostly middle-class families, begun in the late 1960s, when the children studied were 3 and 4 years old. About two-thirds were white, one-fourth were African American, and one-twelfth were Asian.

Near the outset of the study, the mothers and fathers had each completed a report of their parenting practices. Harrington asked a committee consisting of a psychologist, a graduate student, and four undergraduate psychology majors (who were also parents) to group the practices in the parents' reports according to their similarity to Miller's description of poisonous pedagogy (see Table 7-4). In addition, when the children were about 4½ years old, their mothers and fathers separately had taught them four thinking tasks while researchers observed and described the encounters. Again, Harrington asked his committee to examine these reports and sort the parents' behaviors into those most and least characteristic of PP (see Table 7-5).

Finally, Harrington correlated the parents' self-reported and observed PP ratings with their children's scores on measures of psychological adjustment at ages 18 and 23. Strong correlations appeared between parents' early use of PP-like practices and their adult children's psychological ill health, as indicated by avoidance of close relationships, anxiety, self-pity, distrust, and other negative attributes (see Table 7-6). The correlations were stronger for observed practices than for self-reported ones. Young adults whose mothers had shown high levels of PP were deemed less comfortable with themselves and others and more vulnerable to stress than young adults whose mothers had shown low levels of PP. A mother's use of PP seemed more influential than a father's, probably because the mothers spent more time with their young children than the fathers did.

Of course, as usual in correlational studies, we cannot be sure to what extent poisonous pedagogy itself caused psychological problems. Perhaps a bidirectional influence was at work, with child-raising practices being shaped at least in part by children's characteristics. Then too, aspects of the parents' personalities that led them to engage in PP could have independently contributed to the problems the children experienced as they grew up. We also don't know whether a more socioeconomically diverse sample might have yielded different results.

Still, the study seems to present striking support of one part of Miller's theory: the influence of poisonous pedagogy on adult personality. Within the next decade, as the young adults in this study become parents, it will be possible to test the other part of the theory: Miller's prediction of intergenerational transmission of PP.

TABLE 7-4

Child-rearing Practices Judged Most and Least Descriptive of "Poisonous Pedagogy" (PP)

Most Characteristic of PP

I do not allow my child to get angry with me.

I believe too much affection and tenderness can harm or weaken a child.

I sometimes tease and make fun of my child.

I do not allow my child to question my decisions.

I think children must learn early not to cry.

I teach my child to keep control of his/her feelings at all times.

I believe a child should be seen and not heard.

I believe scolding and criticism make my child improve.

Least Characteristic of PP

I express affection by hugging, kissing, and holding my child.

My child and I have warm, intimate times together

I respect my child's opinions and encourage him/her to express them.

I feel a child should be given comfort and understanding when she/he is scared or upset.

I usually take into account my child's preferences in making plans for the family.

I believe in praising a child when she/he is good and think it gets better results than punishing him/her when she/he is bad.

I encourage my child to be curious, to explore and question things.

SOURCE: Adapted from Harrington, 1993.

TABLE 7-5

Parent-Child Interactions in Preschool Teaching Task: Most and Least Descriptive of "Poisonous Pedagogy" (PP)

Most Characteristic of PP Parent

Was critical of child; rejected child's ideas and suggestions
Tended to control the tasks
Tended toward overcontrol of own needs and impulses
Appeared ashamed of child; lacked pride in child
Pressured child to work at the tasks
Was impatient with the child
Tended to reject inadequate solutions

Least Characteristic of PP Parent

Was supportive and encouraging of child in the situation
Was responsive to child's needs from moment to moment
Was warm and supportive
Praised the child
Reacted to the child in an ego-enhancing manner
Encouraged the child
Surrendered control of the situation to the child
Encouraged the child to proceed independently
Valued the child's originality

SOURCE: Harrington, 1993.

TABLE 7-6

Personality Characteristics at Ages 18–23 Years Associated with Mothers' Poisonous Pedagogy (PP) in the Teaching Situation at 4.5 Years*

Personality Characteristics of Adult Child of PP Mother

Has a brittle ego-defense system; has a small reserve of integration; is disorganized and maladaptive when under stress

Is vulnerable to real or fancied threat; is generally fearful

Keeps people at a distance; avoids close interpersonal relationships

Gives up and withdraws where possible in the face of frustration and adversity

Is basically anxious

Is thin-skinned, sensitive to anything that can be construed as criticism or an interpersonal slight

Is concerned with own adequacy as a person

Tends to be self-defensive

Feels cheated and victimized by life; is self-pitying

Seeks reassurance from others

Is anxious and tense; shows corresponding bodily symptoms

Feels a lack of personal meaning in life

Is basically distrustful of people in general

Is subtly negativistic; tends to undermine and obstruct or sabotage

Characteristics of Adult Child of Non-PP Mother

Is turned to for advice and reassurance

Appears straightforward, forthright, candid

Responds to humor

Is personally charming

Has warmth; has the capacity for close relationships; is compassionate

Has social poise and presence; appears socially at ease

Is socially perceptive of a wide range of interpersonal cues

Tends to arouse liking and acceptance in people

Is able to see to the heart of important problems

Emphasizes being with others; is gregarious

Is cheerful

*Listed characteristics yielded a significant correlation with mothers' observed PP.

SOURCE: Adapted from Harrington, 1993, p. 306.

✔ SPECIFIC DEVELOPMENTAL ISSUES

Three specific issues of especial concern to parents, caregivers, and teachers of preschool children are how to promote altruism, curb aggression, and deal with fears that normally arise at this age.

ALTRUISM, OR PROSOCIAL BEHAVIOR

Anna, at 3½, responded to two fellow preschoolers' complaints that they did not have enough modeling clay, her favorite plaything, by giving them half of hers. Anna was showing *altruism,* or *prosocial behavior*—acting out of concern for another person with no expectation of reward. Prosocial acts like Anna's often entail cost, self-sacrifice, or risk.

Children given responsibilities at home tend to develop prosocial qualities, such as cooperation and helpfulness. This 3-year-old girl, who is learning to care for plants, is likely to have caring relationships with people as well. *(Margaret Miller/Photo Researchers, Inc.)*

Why do some children reach out to comfort a crying friend or stop to help someone who has fallen while crossing a street? What makes them empathic, generous, compassionate, and sensitive to other people's needs? Following Bronfenbrenner's ecological model, we can look at factors contributing to caring behavior within the child and influenced by the social context.

Characteristics of the Prosocial Child

Prosocial behavior appears early. Even before the second birthday, children often help others, share belongings and food, and offer comfort. Such empathic behaviors emerge at a time when children are increasingly able to think representationally. The ability to imagine how another person might feel may enable children to develop a sense of responsibility for others (Zahn-Waxler, Radke-Yarrow, Wagner, & Chapman, 1992). Altruistic children tend to be advanced in reasoning skills and able to take the role of others (Carlo, Knight, Eisenberg, & Rotenberg, 1991). They are also active and self-confident (C. H. Hart, DeWolf, Wozniak, & Burts, 1992).

A tendency toward empathy may be genetic, according to a study of twins (Zahn-Waxler, Robinson, & Emde, 1992). Socioeconomic status is *not* a factor, and in most studies no sex differences turn up.

The Role of the Family

The family is important as a model, as a source of explicit standards, and as a guide to adopting other models. Children who receive empathic, nurturant, responsive care as infants tend to develop those same qualities. Altruistic children generally feel secure in their parents' love and affection. Preschoolers who were securely attached as infants are more likely to respond to other children's distress. They have more friends, and their teachers consider them more socially competent (Kestenbaum, Farber, & Sroufe, 1989; Sroufe, 1983).

Parents of prosocial children typically are altruistic themselves. They point out models of prosocial behavior and steer children toward stories and television programs, such as *Mister Rogers' Neighborhood,* that depict cooperation, sharing, and empathy and encourage sympathy, generosity, and helpfulness (Mussen & Eisenberg-Berg, 1977; National Institute of Mental Health, NIMH, 1982; D. M. Zuckerman & Zuckerman, 1985). Prosocial children are expected to be honest and helpful. They have responsibilities at home and are expected to meet them.

Parents encourage prosocial behavior by using inductive disciplinary methods. When Sara took candy from a store, her father did not lecture her on honesty, spank her, or tell her what a bad girl she had been. Instead, he explained how the owner of the store would be harmed by her failure to pay for the candy, and he took her back to the store to return it. When such incidents occur, Sara's parents ask "How do you think Mr. Jones feels?" or "How would you feel if you were Maria?" In one study of 106 three- to six-year-olds, the most prosocial children were disciplined by such inductive techniques (C. H. Hart et al., 1992).

The Role of the School

Teachers, like parents, can be models. Warm, empathic teachers foster helping and caring behavior (N. Eisenberg, 1992).

In many countries, moral education is part of the curriculum. In China, teachers tell stories about prosocial heroes and encourage children to imitate them. In one program in a suburb of San Francisco, children from kindergarten on hear about prosocial values and read books and see films depicting altruism. Children are encouraged to help other students and to perform community service, as well as classroom chores. After 5 years, children in the program were found to be more helpful, cooperative, and concerned about other people than a comparison group who were not in the program (Battistich, Watson, Solomon, Schaps, & Solomon, 1991).

The Role of Culture

Why are children in some cultures more prosocial than in others? It may be because they experience more love and less rejection. Among the Papago Indians of Arizona, parents are warm, supportive, and nurturant; by contrast, Alorese parents in Java are hostile and neglectful. This, among other differences, may account for the cooperative, peaceful personality typical of Papago children, as compared with the hostile, distrustful, and aggressive behavior of Alorese children (N. Eisenberg, 1992).

Children tend to reflect the prevalent cultural values of the adults who socialize them. The founders of *kibbutzim*, communal settlements in Israel, aimed to create a society of unselfish, cooperative citizens. A measure of their success is that at every age and stage of development, children reared on a kibbutz tend to think more about obligations to others than do children raised in private homes (Snarey, Reimer, & Kohlberg, 1985).

AGGRESSION

A young child who roughly snatches a toy away from another child is usually interested only in getting the toy, not in hurting or dominating the other child. This is *instrumental aggression,* or aggression used as an instrument to reach a goal—the most common type of aggression in early childhood.

Young children often focus single-mindedly on something they want and make threatening gestures against anyone keeping it from them. Between ages 2½ and 5, children commonly struggle over toys and the control of space. Aggression surfaces mostly during social play, and the children who fight the most tend to be the most sociable and competent. In fact, the ability to show *some* aggression may be a necessary step in social development.

As children become better able to express themselves verbally, they typically shift from showing aggression with blows to doing it with words (Maccoby, 1980). Physical aggression generally declines in frequency and average length of episodes. However, individual differences tend to be fairly stable, especially among boys; those who hit or grab toys from other children at age 2 are likely to remain aggressive at age 5 (Cummings, Iannotti, & Zahn-Waxler, 1989). After age 6 or 7, most children become less aggressive as they become more cooperative, less egocentric, and more empathic. They can now put themselves into someone else's place, can understand why the other person may be acting in a certain way, and can develop more positive ways of dealing with that person. They also can communicate better.

Not all aggression is instrumental. *Hostile aggression*—action intended to hurt another person—normally increases during early childhood

The kind of aggression involved in fighting over a toy, without intention to hurt or dominate the other child, is known as *instrumental aggression.* It surfaces mostly during social play and normally declines as children learn to ask for what they want. *(Shackman/Monkmeyer)*

and then declines. However, some children do not learn to control hostile aggression; they become more and more destructive. Such aggression may be a reaction to major problems in a child's life. It may also *cause* major problems by making other children and adults dislike a child. Even normal aggression can sometimes get out of hand and become dangerous.

Triggers of Aggression

The male hormone testosterone may underlie aggressive behavior and may explain why males are more likely to be aggressive than females. Social-learning research points to other contributing factors: imitation of models (real or televised) combined with reinforcement of aggressive behavior, often compounded by frustration.

Aggression may start with ineffective parenting (G. R. Patterson, DeBaryshe, & Ramsey, 1989). Parents of children who later become antisocial often fail to reinforce good behavior and are harsh or inconsistent, or both, in punishing misbehavior. Harsh punishment, especially spanking, may backfire, because children see aggressive behavior in an adult with whom they identify. As one classic study suggested, parents who spank provide a "living example of the use of aggression at the very moment they are trying to teach the child not to be aggressive" (Sears et al., 1957, p. 266). Also, as we've already mentioned, punishment can reinforce aggressive behavior, since some children would rather get negative attention than none at all. The least aggressive children and those with the strongest conscience have parents who deal with misbehavior by reasoning with them, making them feel guilty, or withdrawing approval and affection, rather than by using power-assertive techniques such as spanking, threats, and taking away privileges (Sears et al., 1957).

The frustration, pain, and humiliation that result from physical punishment and insults can be added spurs to violence. A frustrated child is more apt to imitate aggressive models than a contented one. In one classic study, the social-learning theorist Albert Bandura and his colleagues (Bandura, Ross, & Ross, 1961) divided seventy-two 3- to 6-year-olds into two experimental groups and one control group. One by one, each child in the first experimental group went into a playroom. An adult model (male for half of the children, female for the other half) quietly played in a corner with toys. The model for the second experimental group

began to assemble Tinker Toys, but then spent the rest of the 10-minute session punching, throwing, and kicking a life-size inflated doll. The children in the control group saw no model.

After the sessions, all the children were mildly frustrated by seeing toys they were not allowed to play with. They then went into another playroom. The children who had seen the aggressive model acted much more aggressively than those in the other groups, imitating many of the same things they had seen the model say and do. Both boys and girls were more strongly influenced by an aggressive male model than an aggressive female, suggesting that their gender-typing led them to consider aggression more appropriate for males. The children who had been with the quiet model were less aggressive than those who had not seen any model, suggesting that a positive adult model can moderate the effects of frustration.

Effects of poor parenting extend beyond the home. Often parents of aggressive children are not positively involved in their children's lives. The children tend to do poorly in school, to be rejected by peers, and to have poor self-esteem. They may seek out and model themselves after other troubled children who engage in antisocial behavior (G. R. Patterson et al., 1989).

Children who do not see aggressive models in real life often see them on television. Indeed, research suggests that children are influenced more by filmed models of violence than by live ones (Bandura, Ross, & Ross, 1963). A Canadian study found that 28 to 40 percent of children ages 3 to 10 watch violent television programs (Bernard-Bonnin, Gilbert, Rousseau, Masson, & Maheux, 1991).

Research since the 1950s shows that children who see televised violence behave more aggressively themselves (NIMH, 1982). This is true across geographic locations and socioeconomic levels, for both boys and girls, and for normal children as well as for those with emotional problems. These correlations do not, of course, prove that viewing televised violence *causes* aggression, though the findings strongly suggest it. It is possible that children already prone to aggression may watch more violent television and may become more aggressive after seeing violence on-screen. In fact, research suggests that aggressive children do watch more television than nonaggressive children, identify more strongly with aggressive characters, and are more likely to believe that aggression seen on television reflects real life (Eron, 1982). Then, too, some third factor may be involved: perhaps children who watch and react aggressively to televised violence are spanked more than other children.

However, evidence from a wide range of other research, including experimental and longitudinal studies, supports a causal relationship between watching televised violence and acting aggressively (Geen, 1994; Huston et al., 1993). One experimental group of 5- to 9-year-olds watched a 3½-minute segment from a television series that included two fistfights, two shootings, and a knifing. A control group watched 3½ minutes of sports. Afterward, the children were asked to play a "game": They could push a "help" button to help an unseen child win a game or a "hurt" button to make a handle touched by that child so hot it would hurt. (Of course, there was no such child.) Children who had watched the violent program were more willing than those who had watched the sports program to hurt the unseen child and to inflict more severe pain (Liebert, 1972).

The influence of televised violence may endure for years. Among 427 young adults whose viewing habits had been studied at age 8, the best predictor of aggressiveness in 19-year-old men and women was the degree of violence in the shows they had watched as children (Eron, 1980, 1982).

How might watching violence on television make children more aggressive? Two hypotheses involve mechanisms of cognitive processing. One mechanism is the *behavioral script,* which converts televised images into guides for behavior (Huesmann, 1986). When children see a television character shooting someone, they may make a judgment about the reason for the shooting—for example, anger. Once they have learned that being angry is a reason for becoming violent, they may retrieve this script from memory and use it to guide their own behavior when they get angry. The other mechanism is *cognitive priming* (L. Berkowitz, 1984). Seeing televised violence may stimulate associations with aggressive ideas and emotions. These associations are retrieved when a child is frustrated, attacked, in pain, or under stress, and they *prime,* or prepare, the child to respond aggressively.

Another explanation is that when children see televised violence, they absorb the values depicted and come to view aggression and lawbreaking as acceptable behavior (NIMH, 1982). Aggressive acts make a more vivid impression than any punishment the "bad guy" receives (Liebert & Poulos, 1976, in Lickona, 1976). Children who see both heroes and villains on television getting what they want through violence may become less sensitive to the pain that results from real-life aggression. They may, for instance, fail to protect the victim of a bully. They are also more likely to break rules and less likely to cooperate to resolve differences.

Parents can help reduce children's aggression by monitoring television watching—limiting total time and selecting programs that promote prosocial behavior. The American Psychological Association in 1993 called for a major effort to reduce violence on television, including limits on violence shown between 6 A.M. and 10 P.M. and warning labels on videotapes containing violent material. In 1996, Congress enacted a law requiring all new television sets to be equipped with a V chip (the *V* stands for "violence"), an electronic blocking device that parents can use to screen out objectionable programs. The law also prods the networks to devise a violence rating system (Mifflin, 1996).

FEARFULNESS

When Kelly was 3 years old, she was frightened by a neighbor's large, barking dog. The next day, she refused to go out to play. When her mother asked why, she said she had a stomachache; but when dinnertime came, she cleaned her plate. The next day, Kelly again refused to go outside. When her father insisted on taking her to the store, Kelly burst into tears and clung to his arm. Kelly had developed a fear of dogs. Yet by her sixth birthday, this fear had gone away; in fact, she had to be stopped from patting strange dogs in the park.

Passing fears are common in early childhood. Many 2- to 4-year-olds are afraid of animals, especially dogs. By 6 years, children are more likely to be afraid of the dark. Other common fears are of thunderstorms and doctors (DuPont, 1983). Most of these disappear as children grow older and lose their sense of powerlessness.

Young children's fears stem from their intense fantasy life and their tendency to confuse appearance with reality. Sometimes their imaginations get carried away, making them worry about being attacked by a lion or being abandoned. Young children are more likely to be frightened by something that *looks* scary, such as a cartoon monster, than by something capable of doing great harm, such as a nuclear explosion (Cantor, 1994). For the most part, older children's fears tend to be more realistic (see Table 7-7).

TABLE 7-7

Childhood Fears

Age	Fears
0–6 months	Loss of support, loud noises
7–12 months	Strangers; heights; sudden, unexpected, and looming objects
1 year	Separation from parent, toilet, injury, strangers
2 years	A multitude of stimuli, including loud noises (vacuum cleaners, sirens and alarms, trucks, and thunder), animals, dark rooms, separation from parent, large objects or machines, changes in personal environment, unfamiliar peers
3 years	Masks, dark, animals, separation from parent
4 years	Separation from parent, animals, dark, noises (including noises at night)
5 years	Animals, "bad" people, dark, separation from parent, bodily harm
6 years	Supernatural beings (e.g., ghosts, witches), bodily injury, thunder and lightning, dark, sleeping or staying alone, separation from parent
7–8 years	Supernatural beings, dark, media events (e.g., news reports on the threat of nuclear war or child kidnapping), staying alone, bodily injury
9–12 years	Tests and examinations in school, school performances, bodily injury, physical appearance, thunder and lightning, death, dark

SOURCE: Adapted from Morris & Kratochwill, 1983.

Still, experience may underlie some early fears. A preschooler whose mother is sick in bed may become upset by a story about a mother's death, even if it is an animal mother. Often fears come from appraisals of danger, such as the likelihood of being bitten by a dog, or are triggered by events, as when a child who was hit by a car becomes afraid to cross the street. Children who have lived through an earthquake, a kidnapping, or some other frightening event may fear that it will happen again (Kolbert, 1994). Ridicule ("Don't be such a baby!"), coercion ("Pat the nice doggie—it won't hurt you"), and logical persuasion ("The closest bear is 20 miles away, locked in a zoo!") are not helpful in overcoming children's fears; cognitive immaturity cannot be reasoned away. Not until elementary school can children relieve fear by telling themselves that what they fear is not real (Cantor, 1994). However, *modeling*—observing fearlessness in others—can be effective with young children. Preschoolers who feared dogs took part in eight brief sessions in which they watched an unafraid child play happily with a dog. Later, two-thirds of the fearful children were able to climb into a playpen with the dog (Bandura, Grusec, & Menlove, 1967).

Children can also be helped to overcome fears by *systematic desensitization*, gradual exposure to a feared object or situation. In one study, first-through third-graders overcame their fear of snakes through gradually closer, more frequent contact. After an average of two 15- minute sessions, 39 out of 45 children held snakes in their laps for 15 seconds, compared with only 5 of 22 children in a control group, who did not have the treatment (C. M. Murphy & Bootzin, 1973).

✔ RELATIONSHIPS WITH OTHER CHILDREN

Although the most important people in young children's world are the adults who take care of them, relationships with siblings and playmates become more important in early childhood. Almost every characteristic activity and personality issue of this age, such as play, gender identity, and aggressive or prosocial behavior, involves other children.

BROTHERS AND SISTERS

Sibling rivalry is *not* the main pattern between brothers and sisters early in life. While some rivalry exists, so do affection, interest, companionship, and influence. Observations of young sibling pairs (same-sex and mixed-sex) have shown that siblings separated by as little as 1 year or as much as 4 years interact closely with each other in many ways.

Three sets of observations began when the younger siblings were about 1½ years old and the older ones ranged from 3 to 4½. The studies continued until the younger ones were 5 and the older ones, 6½ to 8 (Abramovitch et al., 1979; Abramovitch, Corter, Pepler, & Stanhope, 1986; Abramovitch, Pepler, & Corter, 1982). Older siblings initiated more behavior, both friendly (sharing a toy, smiling, hugging, or starting a game) and unfriendly (hitting, fighting over a toy, teasing, or tattling). The younger children tended to imitate the older ones. As the younger children reached their fifth birthday, the siblings became less physical and more verbal, both in showing aggression (through commands, insults, threats, tattling, put-downs, bribes, and teasing) and in showing care and affection (by compliments and comfort rather than hugs and kisses).

The age difference between siblings had an effect: in closely spaced pairs, older siblings initiated more prosocial behavior. Same-sex siblings were a bit closer and played together more peaceably than boy-girl pairs. Siblings got along better when their mother was not with them. (Squabbling can be a bid for parental attention.) Overall, these researchers found prosocial and play-oriented behaviors to be more common than rivalry and concluded, "It is probably a mistake to think of siblings' relationships, at least during the

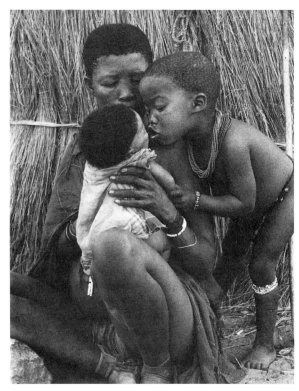

These Kung San children in the Kalahari Desert of southwest Africa show the affection, interest, and companionship typical of early sibling relationships. *(Mel Konner/Anthro Photo)*

preschool years, as primarily competitive or negative" (Abramovitch et al., 1986, p. 229).

Ties between brothers and sisters set the stage for later relationships. What, then, about children who grow up with no siblings?

THE ONLY CHILD

People often think of only children as spoiled, selfish, lonely, or maladjusted, but research does not bear out this negative view. According to an analysis of 115 studies of children of various ages and backgrounds, only children do comparatively well (Falbo & Polit, 1986; Polit & Falbo, 1987). In occupational and educational achievement and intelligence, "onlies" surpass children with siblings, especially those with many siblings or older siblings. Only children also tend to be more mature and motivated to achieve and to have higher self-esteem. They do *not* differ, however, in overall adjustment or sociability. Perhaps these children do better be-

BOX 7-3   WINDOW ON THE WORLD

A NATION OF ONLY CHILDREN

A group of Chinese kindergartners are learning how to fold paper to make toys. When the toys do not come out right, some of the children try again on their own or watch their classmates and copy what they do. Other children become bored and impatient and ask someone to do it for them, or else they give up, bursting into tears. In some research (Jiao, Ji, & Jing, 1986), the children in the second category tended to come from one-child families—a worrisome finding for the People's Republic of China, which in 1979 established an official policy of limiting families to one child each.

The Chinese government is serious about this policy. Without a check on China's exploding population, there will not be enough classroom places for all its children, not enough jobs for adults, and not enough food for everyone. To lower the birthrate, family-planning workers oversee factory workshops and agricultural brigades, and special birth control departments exist in every inhabited area. The policy goes beyond using propaganda campaigns and rewards (housing, money, child care, health care, and preference in school placement) to induce voluntary compliance. There have been millions of involuntary abortions and sterilizations, and people who have children without permission are fined and denied job promotions and bonuses. As a result, more only children live in China than in any other country. By 1985, at least 8 out of 10 young urban couples and half of those in rural areas had only one child (Yang, Ollendick, Dong, Xia, & Lin, 1995). Today in Chinese cities, kindergartens and primary classrooms are almost completely filled with children who have no brothers or sisters.

This situation marks a great change in Chinese society, in which newlyweds were traditionally congratulated with the wish, "May you have a hundred sons and a thousand grandsons." No culture in human history has ever been composed entirely of only children. Critics ask whether the Chinese are sowing the seeds of their own destruction.

Some research has suggested that only children are more egocentric, less persistent, less cooperative, and less well liked than children with siblings. They were more likely to refuse to help another child or to help grudgingly, less likely to share their toys or to enjoy playing or working with other children, less modest, less helpful in group activities, and more irresponsible (Jiao et al., 1986).

However, later research contradicts previous findings that only children are spoiled, overindulged "little emperors." A sample of 4,000 third- and sixth-graders from urban and rural districts were as-

cause their parents spend more time and focus more attention on them, talk to them more, do more with them, and expect more of them. Research in China, which mandates one-child families, also produced findings that bode well for only children (see Box 7-3).

PLAYMATES AND FRIENDS

Toddlers play alongside or near each other, but not until about age 3 do children begin to have friends. Through friendships and interactions with casual playmates, young children learn how to get along with others. They learn that *being* a friend is the way to *have* a friend. They learn how to solve problems in relationships, they learn how to put themselves in another person's place, and they see models of various kinds of behavior. They learn moral values and gender-role norms, and they practice adult roles. Children who have friends talk more than other children and take turns directing and following. Children who do not have friends tend to fight with those who do or to stand on the sidelines and watch them (Roopnarine & Field, 1984).

Having a friend is not only a factor in a child's emotional well-being; it can also affect school achievement, showing a link between social and cognitive development. Children with friends enjoy school more (Ladd & Hart, 1992). A study of 125 kindergartners found that those who had friends in their class when they entered in August liked school better two months later, and those who kept up these friendships continued to like school better the following May. Also, kindergartners who made new friends scored higher on achievement tests, whereas children rejected by their classmates began to dislike school, were absent more, and did only half as well on academic

sessed on academic achievement, physical growth, and personality. In academic achievement and physical growth, only children did about the same or better than those with siblings. They did especially well on verbal achievement; and in two of the four provinces studied, only children were taller or heavier than others. Personality differences, as rated by the children themselves and by parents, teachers, and peers, were few (Falbo & Poston, 1993).

Indeed, only children now seem to be at a distinct advantage in China. When questionnaires were administered to 731 urban children and adolescents, children with siblings reported higher levels of fear, anxiety, and depression than only children, regardless of sex or age. Apparently children with siblings are less well adjusted in a society that favors and rewards the only child (Yang et al., 1995).

Cognitively, a randomized study in Beijing schools (Jiao, Ji, & Jing, 1996) found that only children outperformed first-grade classmates with siblings in memory, language, and mathematics skills. This finding may reflect the greater attention, stimulation, hopes, and expectations that parents shower on a baby they know will be their first and last. Fifth grade only children, who were born before the one-child policy was strongly enforced—and whose parents may have originally planned on a larger family—did not show a pronounced cognitive edge.

Both of these studies had urban samples. Further research may reveal whether the findings hold up in rural areas, where children with siblings are more numerous, and whether only children maintain their cognitive superiority as they move through school.

China's population policy has wider implications. If it succeeds, most Chinese will eventually lack aunts, uncles, nephews, nieces, and cousins, as well as siblings. How this will affect individuals, families, and the social fabric is at present incalculable.

A more sinister question is this: what has happened to the girls? A 1990 census suggests that 5 percent of all infant girls born in China (some half a million infants born alive each year) are unaccounted for. Suspicions are that parents who are permitted only one child have decided to have the baby girls killed or to withhold care from them so that they will die and allow the parents the chance to bear and raise more highly valued sons. A more benign explanation is that these girls are hidden and raised secretly to evade the one-child policy (Kristof, 1991, 1993). In either case, China's one-child policy has ramifications its developers may not have considered.

tests (Ladd, 1990). These findings suggest that school personnel might do well to group new entrants with friends and to help children maintain old friendships and form new ones.

Choosing Friends and Playmates

Young children define a friend as "someone you like." They usually become friendly with other children who like to do the same kinds of things *they* like. Friends generally have similar energy and activity levels and are of the same age and sex (Gamer, Thomas, & Kendall, 1975).

In one study, 4- to 7-year-olds were asked to rate pictured activities that would make children friends. They rated the most important features of friendships as doing things together, liking and caring for each other, sharing and helping one another, and to a lesser degree, living nearby or

going to the same school. Older children rated affection and support higher than did younger ones and rated physical traits, such as appearance and size, lower (Furman & Bierman, 1983).

The traits that make a child desirable or undesirable as a playmate are similar to the traits young children look for in friends. Children prefer prosocial preschoolers as playmates (C. H. Hart et al., 1992). They like to play with peers who smile and offer a toy or a hand; they reject overtures from disruptive or aggressive children and ignore those who are shy or withdrawn (Roopnarine & Honig, 1985).

Well-liked preschoolers and kindergartners generally cope well with anger. They respond in direct, active ways that minimize further conflict and keep relationships going. Boys are more likely to express angry feelings or resist a child who provokes them, whereas girls are more apt to show disapproval of the other child. Unpopular children

Young children learn the importance of *being* a friend in order to *have* a friend. One way of being a friend can involve a sighted child's helping a blind playmate to enjoy the feel of the sand and the sound of the surf. *(Nita Winter)*

tend to hit back or tattle (Asher, Renshaw, Geraci, & Dor, 1979; Fabes & Eisenberg, 1992). Of course, popular children are less likely to be involved in angry conflicts in the first place, since other children are less likely to attack them or try to take their toys. Then too, popular children have a strong coping tool: they can threaten not to play with or not to like the other child (Fabes & Eisenberg, 1992). Still, whether because of inner resources or what they have learned, popular children do seem better able to regulate their anger, and therefore to handle social situations, than unpopular children.

How Family Relationships Affect Peer Relationships

Although the quality of young children's relationships with their brothers and sisters often carries over to relationships with other children, specific patterns established with siblings are not always repeated with friends. A child who is dominated by an elder sibling can easily step into a dominant role with a playmate. Usually children are more prosocial and playful with playmates than with siblings (Abramovitch et al., 1986).

Young children's relationships with their parents may have a more significant influence. Parents of popular children generally have warm, positive relationships with their children. They teach by reasoning more than by punishment (Kochanska, 1992; Roopnarine & Honig, 1985). They are more likely to be authoritative, and their children have learned to be both assertive and cooperative. Parents of rejected or isolated children tend to have a different profile. The mothers do not have confidence in their parenting, rarely praise their children, and do not encourage independence. The fathers pay little attention to their children, dislike being disturbed by them, and consider child rearing women's work (Peery, Jensen, & Adams, 1984, in Roopnarine & Honig, 1985). Children whose parents clearly communicate disapproval (rather than anger), as well as strong positive feelings, are more prosocial, less aggressive, and better-liked (Boyum & Parke, 1995).

The parents' relationship may be a factor. Children whose parents do not get along sometimes respond to the resulting stress by trying to avoid conflict with other children. Consequently, they do not participate fully in play activities and do not learn how to get along with others (Gottman & Katz, 1989).

Peer relationships become even more important during middle childhood (from about age 6 to 12), which we discuss in Chapters 8 and 9.

✔ SUMMARY

THE DEVELOPING SELF

■ The self-concept is one's total picture of one's ability and traits; it develops gradually throughout life.

■ According to neo-Piagetians, self-definition in early childhood shifts from single representations to representational mappings. Development of emotions directed toward the self depends upon socialization and cognitive development. Children gradually develop an understanding of simultaneous emotions between ages 4 and 12.

■ According to Erikson, the chief developmental crisis of early childhood is *initiative versus guilt*. Successful resolution of this conflict results in the "virtue" of purpose and enables a child to plan and carry out activities within appropriate limits.

■ Self-esteem is a judgment about self-worth. An important source of self-esteem in early childhood is social support from parents, teachers, and peers.

PLAY

■ Changes in the type of play children engage in reflect social and cognitive development. Imaginative play becomes increasingly common during early childhood and helps children develop social and cognitive skills.

■ Forms of play vary across cultures and are influenced by the environments adults create for children.

GENDER

■ Sex differences are physical differences between males and females; gender differences are psychological or behavioral differences.

■ There are few behavioral differences between the sexes in early childhood, and these differences are generally quite small. Boys are more aggressive than girls, and girls are more empathic.

■ Gender differences in play show up earlier than other gender differences; between early and middle childhood, children in all cultures increasingly segregate themselves by sex.

■ All societies hold beliefs about appropriate behaviors for the two sexes, and children learn these expectations at an early age. Gender roles are the behaviors and attitudes a culture deems appropriate for males and females. Gender-typing refers to the learning of culturally determined gender roles. Gender stereotypes are exaggerated generalizations that may not be true of individuals.

■ In Freudian theory, a child develops gender identity through identification with the same-sex parent after giving up the wish to possess the other parent. According to social-learning theory, gender identity develops through observation and imitation of models and through reinforcement of gender-appropriate behavior. Cognitive-developmental theory maintains that the development of gender identity is the result of thinking about experience. Gender-schema theory holds that children fit their self-concept to the gender schema for their culture, a socially organized pattern of behavior for males and females.

■ Both biological and environmental factors, such as the influence of parents and the media, appear to have an impact on gender-typing.

CHILD-REARING PRACTICES

■ Parents influence children's behavior through discipline: ways of teaching character, self-control, and acceptable behavior.

■ Reinforcement is generally more effective than punishment. Punishment is most effective when it is immediate, consistent, accompanied by an explanation, and carried out by someone who has a good relationship with the child. Physical punishment can have damaging effects.

■ Discipline based on induction is generally the most effective; temporary withdrawal of love is less effective, and power assertion the least effective.

■ Baumrind has identified three child-rearing styles: authoritarian, permissive, and authoritative. The authoritative style tends to have the most positive outcomes.

■ Internalization of parental teachings depends on how accurately the message is perceived and whether it is accepted or rejected.

■ Maltreatment, including child abuse, sexual abuse, and neglect, often has serious long-range effects. Characteristics of the child, the family, the community, and the larger culture may contribute to maltreatment.

■ Miller's theory of "poisonous pedagogy" suggests that certain parental behaviors can damage a child's future psychological health and may be transmitted to future generations.

SPECIFIC DEVELOPMENTAL ISSUES

- Whether children exhibit prosocial or aggressive behavior is influenced by their parents' treatment of them as well as by their observation of models in real life and in the media.
- Preschool children show many temporary fears of both real and imaginary objects and events. Such fears can sometimes be overcome by modeling or systematic desensitization.

RELATIONSHIPS WITH OTHER CHILDREN

- Most sibling interactions are positive. Older siblings tend to initiate activities, and younger ones to imitate.
- Only children seem to develop at least as well as children with siblings.
- Children who are aggressive or withdrawn tend to be less popular with playmates than children who are friendly.
- The kind of relationship children have with their parents affects the ease with which they find playmates and friends.

✔ KEY TERMS

self-concept (page 222)
self-definition (223)
single representations (223)
real self (223)
ideal self (223)
representational mappings (223)
initiative versus guilt (225)
self-esteem (225)
social play (226)
cognitive play (226)
imaginative play (227)
gender (229)

sex differences (229)
gender differences (229)
gender identity (230)
gender roles (230)
gender-typing (230)
gender stereotypes (231)
identification (231)
gender constancy, or gender conservation (233)
gender-schema theory (233)
gender schema (233)
androgynous (234)

discipline (236)
authoritarian parents (238)
permissive parents (238)
authoritative parents (238)
child abuse (240)
battered child syndrome (241)
sexual abuse (241)
child neglect (241)
emotional abuse (241)
altruism, or prosocial behavior (247)
instrumental aggression (249)
hostile aggression (249)

✔ QUESTIONS FOR THOUGHT AND DISCUSSION

1 Looking back, can you think of ways in which your parents or other adults helped you develop self-esteem?

2 "Males are innately more aggressive, and females more nurturing. Although these traits can be altered to some degree, the basic tendencies will remain." Does research support these statements? Whether true or not, what implications do these widely held beliefs have for personality development?

3 Where would you place your own views on the continuum between the following extremes? Explain.

- Family A thinks girls should wear only ruffly dresses and boys should never wash dishes or cry.
- Family Z treats sons and daughters exactly alike, without making any references to the children's sex.

4 As a parent, what forms of discipline would you favor in what situations? Give specific examples, and tell why.

5 To what extent would you like your children to adopt your values and behavioral standards?

6 Is it wise to teach a child never to be aggressive?

PART THREE

Middle Childhood

The middle years of childhood, from about age 6 to age 12, are often called the *school years* because school is the central experience during this time—a focal point for physical, cognitive, and psychosocial development. Children develop more competence in all realms. As we see in Chapter 8, they grow taller, heavier, and stronger; learn new skills and concepts; and apply their knowledge and skills more effectively. During these years children acquire physical skills needed to participate in organized games and sports. Cognitively, children make major advances in log-

ical and creative thinking, in moral judgments, in memory, and in literacy. Individual differences become more evident and special needs more important, as competencies affect success in school.

Competencies also affect self-esteem and popularity, as we see in Chapter 9. Although parents still have an important impact on personality, as well as on all other aspects of development, the peer group is more influential than before. Children develop physically, cognitively, and emotionally, as well as socially, through contacts with other youngsters.

CHAPTER EIGHT

PHYSICAL AND COGNITIVE DEVELOPMENT IN MIDDLE CHILDHOOD

What we must remember above all in the education of our children is that their love of life should never weaken.

Natalia Ginzburg, The Little Virtues, 1985

✔ **ASPECTS OF PHYSICAL DEVELOPMENT**
Growth
Nutrition and Dentition
Motor Development and Physical Play

✔ **HEALTH, FITNESS, AND SAFETY**
Exercise: Maintaining Health and Fitness
Medical Problems
Accidental Injuries

✔ **THE CONCRETE OPERATIONAL CHILD**
Advances in Cognitive Abilities
Moral Reasoning

✔ **ASPECTS OF COGNITIVE DEVELOPMENT**
Memory
Intelligence
Language

✔ **INFLUENCES ON SCHOOL ACHIEVEMENT**
The Child
The Parents
The Teacher
The Educational System
The Culture

✔ **CHILDREN WITH SPECIAL EDUCATIONAL NEEDS AND STRENGTHS**
Children with Learning Problems
Gifted, Creative, and Talented Children

✔ **BOXES**
8-1 Food for Thought: Children's Understanding of Health and Illness
8-2 Window on the World: How Can Children of Asian Extraction Achieve So Much?
8-3 Practically Speaking: Enhancing Thinking Skills and Creativity

ASK YOURSELF

✔ What gains in growth and motor development occur during middle childhood, and what health hazards do children face?

✔ What are the causes and implications of malnutrition, obesity, and dissatisfaction with body image?

✔ How is schoolchildren's thinking different from that of younger children, and what progress do they make in moral development?

✔ How do memory and communicative abilities expand?

✔ How accurately can schoolchildren's intelligence be measured?

✔ How do schools meet the needs of children with disabilities and special gifts?

✔ What is creativity, and how can it be nurtured?

"What will the teacher be like?" 6-year-old Julia wonders as she walks up the steps to the big red-brick schoolhouse, wearing her new backpack. "Will the kids like me? Will the work be too hard? What games will we play at recess?"

Even today, when many children go to preschool and most go to kindergarten, the start of first grade is often approached with a mixture of eagerness and anxiety. The first day of "regular" school is a milestone—a sign that a child has entered a new stage of development. During the next 6 years, Julia will most likely gain in self-confidence as she reads, thinks, talks, plays, and imagines in ways that were well beyond her only a few years before.

She will also gain in size, speed, and coordination. Compared with its rapid pace in early childhood, growth between the ages of 6 and 12 slows considerably until the spurt toward the end of this period, and motor abilities improve less dramatically than before. Still, although day-by-day changes may not be obvious, they add up to a startling difference between 6-year-olds, who are still small children, and 12-year-olds, who are now beginning to resemble adults. For most children, despite frequent colds and sore throats, middle childhood is a relatively healthy time; but many are not as healthy or as physically fit as they should be, and some have eating problems.

■ In this chapter we look at these physical developments, which also have social and emotional dimensions. Cognitively, we see how entry into Piaget's stage of concrete operations enables children to think logically and to make more mature moral judgments. As children improve in memory and problem solving, intelligence tests become more accurate in predicting school performance.

The abilities to read and write open the door to participation in a wider world. We describe all these changes, and we examine influences on school achievement. Finally, we see how schools try to meet special needs. ■

✔ ASPECTS OF PHYSICAL DEVELOPMENT

If we were to walk by a typical elementary school just after the three o'clock bell, we would see a virtual explosion of children of all shapes and sizes. Tall ones, short ones, husky ones, and skinny ones would be bursting out of the school doors into the open air. We would see that 6- to 12-year-olds look very different from children a few years younger. They are taller, and most are fairly wiry; but more are likely to be overweight than in past decades, and some may be malnourished.

If we were to follow a group of children on their way home from school, we would see some of them running or skipping and some leaping up onto narrow ledges and walking along, balancing till they jump off, trying to break distance records—but occasionally breaking a bone instead. Many of these youngsters will reach home (or a baby-sitter's apartment), get a snack, and dash outside again. There they will jump rope, play ball, skate, cycle, throw snowballs, or splash in front of an open fire hydrant, depending on the season, the community, and the child. Some, especially those with working parents, may stay at school for organized after-school programs. Many children, however, go inside after school, not to emerge for the rest of the day. Instead of practicing new skills that stretch their bodies, they sit in front of the television set. When we talk about physical development in middle childhood, then, we need to look closely at individual children.

GROWTH

During middle childhood, children grow about 1 to 3 inches each year and gain about 5 to 8 pounds or more, doubling their average body weight. African American boys and girls tend to be a bit taller and heavier than white children of the same age and sex. Late in this stage, usually between ages 10 and 12, girls begin a growth spurt, gaining about 10 pounds a year. Suddenly they are taller and heavier than the boys in their class, and they remain so until about age 12 or 13, when the boys begin *their* spurt and overtake the girls (see Chapter 10). Girls retain somewhat more fatty tissue than boys, a characteristic that will persist through adulthood.

Children's growth rates and sizes vary widely. A study of 8-year-old children in different parts of the world (Meredith, 1969) yielded a range of about 9 inches between the average height of the shortest children (mostly from southeast Asia, Oceania, and South America) and the tallest ones (mostly from northern and central Europe, eastern Australia, and the United States). Although genetic differences account for some of this diversity, environmental influences are important too. In general, the tallest children come from parts of the world where malnutrition and infectious diseases are not major problems. For similar reasons, children from affluent homes tend to be larger and more mature than children from poorer homes.

NUTRITION AND DENTITION

Schoolchildren usually have good appetites. To support their steady growth and high level of activity, they need, on average, 2,400 calories every day—more for older children and less for younger ones. Breakfast should supply about one-fourth of total calories; a healthy, balanced breakfast makes children more alert and productive in school. Daily food intake should include high levels of complex carbohydrates, found in such foods as potatoes, pasta, bread, and cereals. Simple carbohydrates, found in sweets, should be kept to a minimum. Most people in the United States eat more protein than they need. The government-recommended daily allowance (RDA) for 7- to 10-year-olds is 28 grams, but the average intake for both boys and girls is 71 grams (Bittman, 1993).

It used to be thought that sugar makes children hyperactive, interferes with learning, or has other negative effects on behavior or mood. However, although sweets are less desirable than nutritious foods in *anyone's* diet because they generally provide nonnutritive or "empty" calories, recent research suggests that neither sugar nor the artificial sweetener aspartame significantly affects most children's behavior, cognitive functioning, or mood (Kinsbourne, 1994; B. A. Shaywitz et al., 1994; Wolraich et al., 1994; Wolraich, Wilson, & White, 1995). Sugar's "bad press" may have resulted from its consumption in large amounts at such occasions as birthday parties, where disruptive behavior probably arises from the excitement of the situation, not the sweets.

Malnutrition

Some 40 to 60 percent of the world's children suffer from mild to moderate malnutrition, and 3 to 7 percent are severely malnourished (Lozoff, 1989). Because undernourished children usually live in poverty and suffer other kinds of environmental deprivation, the specific effects of malnutrition may be hard to isolate. However, taken together, these deprivations may affect not only physical well-being but cognitive abilities and emotional and social development as well (Ricciuti, 1993).

African children in Kenya who suffered mild-to-moderate undernutrition scored lower than well-nourished children on verbal abilities and on selecting a pattern to fit in with a set of other patterns (Sigman, Neumann, Jansen, & Bwibo, 1989). Another Kenyan study found better-nourished children happier, more active, and more likely to be leaders, while poorly nourished children were more anxious (Espinosa, Sigman, Neumann, Bwibo, & McDonald, 1992). When Kenya experienced a severe drought-induced famine, malnourished schoolchildren showed significant declines in rate of weight gain, activity on the playground, and attention in the classroom (McDonald, Sigman, Espinosa, & Neumann, 1994). In Massachusetts, when low-income third- to sixth-graders took part in a school breakfast program, their scores on achievement tests rose (Meyers, Sampson, Weitzman, Rogers, & Kayne, 1989).

Since malnutrition affects several aspects of development, its treatment may need to go beyond physical care. One longitudinal study followed two groups of Jamaican children with low developmental levels who were hospitalized for severe malnourishment in infancy or toddlerhood. One group received only standard medical care, and their developmental levels remained low. Health care paraprofessionals played with a second, experimental group in the hospital and, after discharge, visited them at home every week for 3 years, showing the mothers how to use homemade toys and encouraging them to interact with their children. Three years after the program stopped, the experimental group's IQs were well above those of the group who had not received the intervention (though not as high as those of a non-malnourished control group); and their IQs remained significantly higher 7, 8, 9, and 14 years after leaving the hospital (Grantham-McGregor, Powell, Walker, Chang, & Fletcher, 1994).

Schooling, even when limited in length and quality, can make a difference. One longitudinal study followed approximately 1,400 Guatemalan children in impoverished rural villages, many of whom had stunted growth due to malnutrition and who lived in unsanitary, infection-causing conditions. Those who completed at least 4 years of school did better on tests of cognition during adolescence than those who dropped out earlier. Although schooling did not fully compensate for early biological and environmental risk factors, it did seem to act as a partial buffer against their ill effects (Gorman & Pollitt, 1996).

Obesity

Obesity (extreme overweight) in children has become a major health issue in the United States. The proportion of American children ages 6 to 17 who are obese more than doubled between 1981 and 1991—from 5 percent to nearly 11 percent (CDC, 1994c). A child whose weight, in comparison with height, was in the 95th percentile (that is, higher than that of 95 percent of children of the same age and sex) was considered obese.

What accounts for the increase in obesity? Research findings are most often correlational, and so we cannot draw conclusions about cause and effect. However, there is strong evidence that overweight often results from an inherited tendency (see Chapters 2 and 12), aggravated by too little exercise and too much food. Obese children are less active than other children and tend to watch more television (Dietz & Gortmaker, 1985; Kolata, 1986).

Obese children often suffer emotionally because of taunts from their peers. Furthermore, obese children tend to become obese adults, and obesity puts

adults at risk for such problems as high blood pressure, diabetes, and heart disease. Behavioral therapies, which help children change their eating and exercise habits, have had some effect (L. H. Epstein & Wing, 1987), especially when they involve parents. Parents can be taught not to use food as a reward for good behavior and to stop buying tempting high-calorie treats.

Unfortunately, children who try to lose weight are not always the ones who need to do so. Concern with *body image*—how one believes one looks—begins to be important at this age, especially to girls, and may develop into eating disorders that become more common in adolescence (see Chapter 10). As prepubertal girls begin to fill out and add body fat, some—influenced by the ultra-thin models in the media—see this normal development as undesirable. According to one study done in the United States, about 40 percent of 9- and 10-year-old girls work at trying to lose weight. White girls, although thinner than black girls, are more likely to be dissatisfied with their bodies and are more worried about overweight than African American girls, many of whom try to *gain* weight. Mothers exert a strong influence over their daughters' weight-control efforts. Girls whose mothers have told them they are too fat or too thin are more likely to try to lose or gain weight (Schreiber et al., 1996).

Tooth Development and Dental Care

Most of the adult teeth arrive early in middle childhood. The primary teeth begin to fall out at about age 6 and are replaced by permanent teeth at a rate of about four teeth per year for the next 5 years. The first molars erupt at about age 6; the second molars at about age 13; and the third molars—the wisdom teeth—in the early twenties (Behrman, 1992).

Until recently, the high rate of dental problems among children was a major health concern in the United States. Now, however, the picture is brighter, thanks to better dental care and widespread use of fluoride in toothpaste, mouthwash, and water used for drinking and food preparation. About one-half of 5- to 17-year-olds have no tooth decay (USDHHS, 1988).

MOTOR DEVELOPMENT AND PHYSICAL PLAY

During the middle years, children's motor abilities continue to improve (see Table 8-1). Children get stronger, faster, and better-coordinated; and they

These girls proudly show off a childhood milestone: the normal loss of baby teeth, which will be replaced by permanent ones. American children today have fewer dental cavities than in the past, probably owing to the widespread use of fluoride and to better dental care. *(Mary Kate Denny/ PhotoEdit)*

derive great pleasure from testing their bodies and learning new skills.

About 10 percent of schoolchildren's free play on playgrounds consists of *rough-and-tumble play,* vigorous activity that involves wrestling, hitting, and chasing. Rough-and-tumble play seems to be universal; it takes place from early childhood through adolescence in such diverse places as India, Mexico, Okinawa, the Kalahari Desert in Africa, the Philippines, Great Britain, and the

United States (Humphreys & Smith, 1984). Rough-and-tumble play helps children assess their own strength in relation to that of other children. In the United States, boys engage in it more than girls do (Humphreys & Smith, 1984), but in some cultures this gender difference is slight or nonexistent (Blurton Jones & Konner, 1973). The amount of rough-and-tumble play diminishes between ages 7 and 11 (Humphreys & Smith, 1987) as children move into games with rules—such traditional

TABLE 8-1

Motor Development in Middle Childhood

Age	Selected Behaviors
6	Girls are superior in movement accuracy; boys are superior in forceful, less complex acts. Skipping is possible. Can throw with proper weight shift and step.
7	One-footed balancing without looking becomes possible. Can walk 2-inch-wide balance beams. Can hop and jump accurately into small squares. Can execute accurate jumping-jack exercise.
8	Have 12-pound pressure on grip strength. Number of games participated in by both sexes is greatest at this age. Can engage in alternate rhythmic hopping in a 2-2, 2-3, or 3-3 pattern. Girls can throw a small ball 40 feet.
9	Boys can run 16½ feet per second. Boys can throw a small ball 70 feet.
10	Can judge and intercept pathways of small balls thrown from a distance. Girls can run 17 feet per second.
11	Standing broad jump of 5 feet is possible for boys; 6 inches less for girls.
12	Standing high jump of 3 feet is possible.

SOURCE: Adapted from Cratty, 1986.

games as hopscotch, leapfrog, hide-and-seek, and tag, which are played around the world (Opie & Opie, 1969).

Differences in boys' and girls' motor skills become greater as children approach puberty. Boys tend to run faster, jump higher, throw farther, and display more strength than girls (Cratty, 1986). After age 13, boys' motor abilities improve while girls' stay the same or decline. Some of the gender difference is due to boys' growing strength, but much of it is due to differing cultural expectations and experiences, levels of coaching, and rates of participation. Throwing, catching, and dribbling a ball are skills that have to be learned, and boys are routinely taught these skills, whereas girls generally are not. Since girls' physical needs get more attention these days, the discrepancy between the sexes may narrow in years to come.

✔ HEALTH, FITNESS, AND SAFETY

The development of vaccines for major childhood illnesses has made middle childhood a relatively safe time of life. Since immunizations are required for school admission, children this age are likely to be protected. The death rate in these years is the lowest in the life span. Still, many children get too little exercise to maintain physical fitness; some suffer from *acute* or *chronic* medical conditions; and some are injured in accidents. As children's experience with illness increases, so does their cognitive understanding of the causes of health and illnesses and of the steps people can take to promote their own health (see Box 8-1).

EXERCISE: MAINTAINING HEALTH AND FITNESS

Many schoolchildren are not as physically fit as they should be—and could be. Fewer than half of American youth (ages 6 to 17) can pass a full battery of fitness tests, including the mile run, flexed arm hang, sit and reach, and situps. Twenty to thirty percent fail to meet standards for cardiovascular fitness (Corbin & Pangrazi, 1992). In addition, during the past 50 years children in the United States—and not just those who are obese—seem to have gotten fatter, according to skinfold measurements and average weight. These trends are ominous because research suggests that the more physically fit children are, the lower their risk

of heart disease in adulthood (Kuntzleman & Reiff, 1992).

Children who are not fit are children who are not active enough. With cutbacks in funding, physical education classes are offered less often. Outside of school, the most strenuous exercise many children engage in, particularly in cold weather, is switching television channels (Dietz & Gortmaker, 1985). Children who watch a lot of television tend to have lower metabolic rates and higher cholesterol levels than more active children, putting them at risk of obesity (Klesges, Shelton, & Klesges, 1993; Wong et al., 1992).

Furthermore, most physical activities, in and out of school, are team and competitive sports and games. These activities do not promote fitness, will usually be dropped after leaving school, and are typically aimed at the fittest and most athletic youngsters, not those who need help. Nearly 20 million children under age 14 take part in team sports outside of school, but 3 out of 4 children who start to play a sport at age 6 or 7 quit by age 15 (C. Rubenstein, 1993). Too often, parents and coaches pressure children to practice long hours, focus on winning rather than playing the game, criticize children's efforts, or offer bribes to make them do well (R. Wolff, 1993). All these tactics discourage rather than encourage long-term participation. The American Academy of Pediatrics Committee on Sports Medicine and Committee on School Health (1989) recommend that a sound physical education program include a variety of competitive and recreational sports for all children, emphasizing activities that can be part of a lifetime fitness regimen, such as tennis, bowling, running, swimming, golf, and skating. Organized programs should offer the chance to try a variety of sports and should gear coaching to improving skills, not just winning games.

Since adult hypertension has roots in childhood, blood pressure should be measured once a year from age 3 through adolescence (AAP Task Force on Blood Pressure Control in Children, 1987). Treatment should be given if a child's blood pressure, after three measurements, is above the 95th percentile for age and sex. Taking off excess weight, reducing salt intake, and increasing aerobic exercise are usually beneficial; some children are also given drugs to avoid heart damage.

Programs of education and behavior modification have had excellent results. In one program in Michigan, second-, fifth-, and seventh-graders learned how to analyze the foods they ate; how to

BOX 8-1 FOOD FOR THOUGHT

CHILDREN'S UNDERSTANDING OF HEALTH AND ILLNESS

When Angela was sick, she overheard her doctor refer to *edema* (an accumulation of fluid, which causes swelling), and she thought her problem was "a demon." Being sick is frightening at any age. For young children, who do not understand what is happening, it can be especially distressing and confusing.

From a Piagetian perspective, children's understanding of health and illness is tied to cognitive development. As they mature, their explanations for disease change. Before middle childhood, children are egocentric; they tend to believe that illness is magically produced by human actions, often their own (refer to Box 6-1). Later they explain all diseases—only a little less magically—as the doing of all-powerful germs; the only "protection" is a variety of superstitious behaviors to ward them off. "Watch out for germs," a child may say. As children approach adolescence, they see that there can be multiple causes of disease, that contact with germs does not automatically lead to illness, and that people can do much to keep healthy.

As AIDS (acquired immune deficiency syndrome) has spread, attempts have been made to educate children about it. One study found that preschoolers knew practically nothing about AIDS. Third- and fifth-graders had a fair amount of accurate information about its causes, outcome, and prevention, but did hold mistaken beliefs—for example, that AIDS could be contracted from mosquito bites or that it could be prevented by good nutrition (Schvaneveldt, Lindauer, & Young, 1990).

Children's understanding of AIDS seems to follow the same developmental sequence as their understanding of colds and of cancer, but they understand the cause of colds earlier than they do the causes of the other two illnesses, probably because they are more familiar with colds. Interviews with 361 children in kindergarten through sixth grade (Schonfeld, Johnson, Perrin, O'Hare, & Cicchetti, 1993) found that children often give superficially correct explanations but lack real understanding of the processes involved. For example, although 96 children mentioned drug use as a cause of AIDS, most did not seem to realize that the disease is spread through blood adhering to a needle shared by drug users. One second-grader gave this version of how someone gets AIDS: "Well, by doing drugs and something like that . . . by going by a drug dealer who has AIDS. . . . Well, you go by a person who's a drug dealer and you might catch the AIDS from 'em by standing near 'em" (Schonfeld et al., 1993, p. 393).

From a young child's point of view, such a statement may be a logical extension of the belief that germs cause disease. The child may assume that AIDS can be caught, as colds are, from sharing cups and utensils, from being near someone who is coughing or sneezing, or from hugging and kissing. One AIDS education program (Sigelman et al., 1996) sought to replace such intuitive "theories" with scientifically grounded ones and to test Piaget's idea that if children have not mastered a concept, they are not yet ready to do so. The developers of the program hypothesized that what young children lack is knowledge about disease, not the ability to think about it.

A carefully scripted program was tried on 306 third-, fifth-, and seventh-graders—mostly low-income Mexican Amercans—in Catholic schools in Tucson. Trained health instructors conducted two 50-minute sessions consisting of lectures, video clips, drawings, and discussion, and using vocabulary appropriate for third-graders. Content included an introduction to contagious and noncontagious diseases; specific information about the AIDS virus; an overview of the immune system; the meaning of the letters in "AIDS"; differences between transmission of colds and of AIDS; misconceptions about how the AIDS virus is transmitted; risk factors for AIDS; how the disease develops; and how it can be prevented. The curriculum emphasized that there are only a few ways to get AIDS and that normal contact with people infected with the virus is not one of them. Flip charts summarized key points.

Experimental and control groups were tested before the program began and again about 2 weeks afterward. Students who had received instruction knew more about AIDS and its causes than those who had not, were no more (and no less) worried about it than before, and were more willing to be with people with AIDS. Another test almost a year later found that gains were generally retained. Third-graders gained about as much from the program as seventh-graders. It was somewhat less effective with fifth-graders, perhaps because children that age already know more about AIDS than younger children and find it less relevant to their own lives than older ones do. The success of this program shows that, contrary to Piaget, even relatively young children can grasp complex scientific concepts about disease if properly taught.

measure their own blood pressure, heart rate, and body fat; and how to withstand peer and advertising pressure to smoke and to eat junk food. They also were encouraged to take part in physically demanding games. The children in the program ran faster and lowered their cholesterol level, blood pressure, and body fat (Fitness Finders, 1984).

Indoor play centers, where children run, climb, and crawl through colorful, complex structures, are becoming increasingly popular and may strengthen cardiovascular health. At one such center, 5- to 10-year-olds freely using the apparatus continuously for 20 minutes averaged 77 percent of their maximum heart rate—well above the 60 percent level required for improving cardiorespiratory fitness (Whitehurst, Groo, & Brown, 1996; Whitehurst, Groo, Brown, & Findley, 1995).

MEDICAL PROBLEMS

Richard, age 10, is home in bed with a cold. He sneezes, snoozes, watches television, and enjoys his break from the school routine. He is lucky. He has had no other illnesses this year, while some of his classmates have had six or seven bouts with colds, flus, or viruses. That number of respiratory infections is common during middle childhood, as germs pass freely among youngsters at school or at play (Behrman, 1992).

Illness in middle childhood tends to be brief and transient. A 6-year longitudinal study of mostly white, middle-class children in a health maintenance plan found that almost all the children had *acute medical conditions:* short-term conditions, such as upper-respiratory infections and strep or sore throats (Starfield et al., 1984). However, most school-age children are free of *chronic medical conditions:* illnesses or impairments expected to last 3 months or longer, requiring special medical attention and care, lengthy hospitalization, or health services in the home (Starfield, 1991). Still, a national survey of households of 17,100 children under age 18 found, using a broad definition of chronic illness, that about 3 out of 10 children had chronic conditions (Newacheck et al., 1993; see Table 8-2). White families were more likely than African American or Hispanic families to report mild conditions (such as allergies and repeated ear infections), but the prevalence of severe conditions was about equal.

Children and adolescents with chronic conditions tend to be remarkably resilient (AAP Committee on Children with Disabilities and Committee on Psychosocial Aspects, 1993). Most do not exhibit problems in mental health, behavior, or schooling. However, certain specific conditions—such as vision and hearing problems, asthma, and AIDS—can greatly affect everyday living.

Vision and Hearing Problems

Most youngsters in middle childhood have keener vision than when they were younger. Children under 6 years old tend to be farsighted; their visual apparatus is immature, and their eyes are shaped differently from those of adults. By age 6, vision is more acute; and because the two eyes are better-coordinated, they can focus better. Still, estimates are that almost 13 percent of children under 18 are blind or have impaired vision. Deafness and hearing loss affect an estimated 15.3 percent of children under 18.

Asthma

Asthma, a chronic respiratory disease, seems to have an allergic basis. It is characterized by sudden attacks of coughing, wheezing, and difficulty in breathing; and it can be fatal. Its prevalence increased by one-third between 1981 and 1988, and mortality rates are rising in the United States and several other countries. A reported 4.3 percent of American children under 18 are asthmatic; poor, nonwhite, inner-city children are more likely to be severely affected (Halfon & Newacheck, 1993). Nearly 30 percent of children with asthma have limitations on daily activity (W. R. Taylor & Newacheck, 1992).

The disproportionate impact of asthma on poor and minority children seems to be related to access to health care. Poor children are more likely to receive care in emergency rooms, hospital-based clinics, and neighborhood health centers than in doctors' offices. Poor children with asthma also miss more days of school, must limit their activities more, and spend more days in bed at home or in the hospital than do children from better-off families (Halfon & Newacheck, 1993). The most common barrier to care reported by families in one study was inability to pay for medicine (P. R. Wood, Hidalgo, Prihoda, & Kromer, 1993).

HIV and AIDS

Children infected with the human immunodeficiency virus (HIV) are at a high risk to develop AIDS (acquired immune deficiency syndrome). In

TABLE 8-2

Prevalence of Specified Chronic Conditions among Children Younger Than 18 Years

Condition	Cases/1,000			
	All*	White	Black	Hispanic
Respiratory allergies	96.8	114.7	53.6	47.4
Frequent or repeated ear infections	83.4	94.2	53.8	69.7
Asthma	42.5	42.0	51.3	35.1
Eczema and skin allergies	32.9	36.7	21.7	19.2
Speech defects	26.2	24.0	34.5	35.4
Frequent or severe headaches	25.3	28.4	21.1	14.7
Digestive allergies	22.3	27.0	9.9	8.4[†]
Frequent diarrhea/bowel trouble	17.1	17.7	12.9	18.5
Deafness and hearing loss	15.3	18.0	6.0[†]	15.2
Heart disease	15.2	18.3	7.7[†]	10.0
Musculoskeletal impairments	15.2	15.8	10.6	15.2
Blindness and vision impairment	12.7	13.8	8.7[†]	13.3[†]
Anemia	8.8	8.9	9.2[†]	7.5[†]
Arthritis	4.6	4.8	5.4[†]	2.0[†]
Epilepsy and seizures	2.4	1.9	2.4[†]	6.2[†]
Cerebral palsy	1.8	1.7	0.4[†]	3.2[†]
Sickle-cell disease	1.2[†]	<0.1[†]	7.1[†]	0.3[†]
Diabetes	1.0[†]	1.3[†]	<0.1[†]	0.3[†]
Other	19.8	23.6	10.2	9.2[†]

*Includes white, black, Hispanic, and other races.
[†]Indicates prevalence estimate has a relative standard error in excess of 30%.
SOURCE: Adapted from Newacheck et al., 1993; based on original tabulations of the 1988 National Health Interview Survey.

addition to the devastating physical effects of this almost-always fatal disease (see Chapter 10), the child's entire family may be stigmatized, and the child may be shunned or kept out of school even though there is virtually no risk of infecting classmates. Infected people do not transmit HIV to others except through bodily fluids, even when they share toys, toothbrushes, eating utensils, toilets, or bathtubs (Rogers et al., 1990). According to the American Academy of Pediatrics Task Force on Pediatric AIDS (1991), children who carry the HIV virus but do not show any disease symptoms should be treated like well children at home and in school. They do not need to be isolated, either for their own health or for that of other children. However, children who show symptoms of HIV infection need special care and special education.

Children with AIDS may develop central nervous system dysfunction that can interfere with their ability to learn and can also cause behavior problems (AAP Task Force on Pediatric AIDS, 1991). In one study at a developmental diagnostic and treatment center, most of the children in a sam-

ple of 5- to 14-year-olds who had been diagnosed with HIV infection had cognitive, linguistic, or emotional problems, although the children were living longer and doing better than predicted (Papola, Alvarez, & Cohen, 1994).

ACCIDENTAL INJURIES

Accidental injuries continue to be the leading cause of death in middle childhood (USDHHS, 1996). Injuries increase between ages 5 and 14, as children become involved in more physical activities and are supervised less. The family situation apparently makes a difference. In a longitudinal study of 693 families who sought medical care over a 6-year period, 10 percent of the families accounted for almost 25 percent of the injuries, after adjustment for family size (Schor, 1987). Families with high injury rates may be undergoing stress that interferes with the ability to make the home safe or watch over children. Children with siblings have more injuries than only children. Perhaps parents of more than one child are not as vigilant

Safety-approved helmets protect children of all ages from disabling or fatal head injuries. Bicycle accidents are believed to account for about 300,000 visits to emergency rooms and 600 deaths of children under age 15 each year. *(Bob Daemmrich/Stock, Boston)*

as parents of one child; or younger children may imitate their older siblings and take more risks; or children in larger families may be more active.

The most common cause of serious injury and death in young schoolchildren is being hit by a moving vehicle. Parents tend to overestimate the safety skills of young children; many kindergartners and first-graders walk alone to school, often crossing busy streets without traffic lights (Dunne, Asher, & Rivara, 1992; Rivara, Bergman, & Drake, 1989). However, pedestrian deaths for children under 15 in the United States have decreased 49 percent since 1978, possibly because children today do less walking. Similar decreases have occurred in other countries (Rivara & Grossman, 1996).

Each year about 300,000 visits to emergency rooms and 600 deaths of children under 15 are attributed to bicycle accidents. Head injury, which can be avoided by using safety-approved helmets, is the cause of disability or death in three-fourths of these accidents (AAP Committee on Accident and Poison Prevention, 1990; Cushman, Down, MacMillan, & Waclawik, 1991; Rivara & Grossman, 1996).

✔ THE CONCRETE OPERATIONAL CHILD

At about age 7, according to Piaget, children enter a new stage of cognitive development: *concrete operations.* They are less egocentric and can use thinking (mental operations) to solve concrete (actual) problems. Children can now think logically because they can take multiple aspects of a situation into account rather than focus on only one aspect, as they did in the preoperational stage. Increased ability to understand other people's viewpoints helps them to communicate more effectively and to be more flexible in their moral judgments.

However, according to Piaget, children in this stage are still limited to thinking about situations in the here and now. They cannot yet think in hypothetical terms, about what *could be* rather than what *is.* This ability to think abstractly does not develop until adolescence.

ADVANCES IN COGNITIVE ABILITIES

Children in the stage of concrete operations, roughly between ages 7 and 12, can perform many tasks at a much higher level than they could in the preoperational stage. They have a better understanding of conservation, of the difference between appearance and reality, and of relationships between objects; they are more proficient with numbers; and they are better able to distinguish fantasy from reality.

Conservation

Piaget and other researchers have tested children's grasp of *conservation,* the ability to recognize that the amount of something remains the same even if the material is rearranged, as long as nothing is added or taken away. Tests of conservation deal with such attributes as number, substance, length, area, weight, and volume (refer back to Table 6-4). In solving conservation problems, concrete operational children can work out the answers in their heads; they do not have to measure or weigh the objects.

In a typical test of conservation of substance, an experimenter shows a child two identical clay balls and asks whether the amount of clay in both balls is the same. Once the child agrees that the amount is indeed the same, the experimenter or the child rolls or kneads one of the balls into a different shape, say, a long, thin "sausage." The child is again asked whether the two objects contain the same amount of clay, and why. Felipe, who is still in the preoperational stage, is deceived by appearances. He says the long, thin roll contains more clay because it *looks* longer. Stacy, who has reached the stage of concrete operations, correctly answers that the ball and the "sausage" have the same amount of clay.

When children are asked about the reasoning behind their answers, they show whether they understand the logical principles underlying conservation. Stacy understands the principle of *identity:* she knows the clay is still the same clay, even though it has a different shape. She also understands the principle of *reversibility:* she knows she can reverse the transformation and restore the original shape (change the sausage back into a ball). Felipe, the preoperational child, does not understand either of these principles. Finally, Stacy can *decenter:* she can focus on more than one relevant dimension—in this case, on both length and width. She recognizes that although the ball is shorter than the "sausage," it is also thicker. Felipe centers on one dimension (length) while excluding the other (thickness).

According to Piaget, children's mastery of conservation depends largely on neurological maturation. Typically, children can solve problems involving conservation of *substance* (like the one just described) by about age 7 or 8. But in tasks involving conservation of *weight*—in which they are asked, for example, whether the ball and the "sausage" weigh the same—children typically do not give correct answers until about age 9 or 10. In tasks involving conservation of *volume*—in which children must judge whether the "sausage" and the ball displace an equal amount of liquid when placed in a glass of water—correct answers are rare before age 12.

Piaget's term for this inconsistency in the development of different types of conservation is *horizontal décalage.* Children's thinking at this stage is so concrete, so closely tied to a particular situation, that they cannot readily transfer what they have learned about one type of conservation to another type, even though the underlying principles are the same. Also, children who are just beginning to understand conservation may go through a transitional stage in which they do not always apply it. These children may answer correctly when they see a short "sausage" but fail to conserve if the "sausage" is very long and thin.

This Malaysian newspaper boy must be able to add and subtract—skills based on typical cognitive developments of middle childhood, such as understanding of reversibility, seriation, and the relationship between a whole and its parts. *(David R. Frazier/Photo Researchers, Inc.)*

Classification

Children's ability to *classify,* or sort items into categories, enables them to organize and understand their world. One classification ability that develops in middle childhood is **class inclusion,** the ability to see the relationship between a whole and its parts. If preoperational children are shown a bunch of 10 flowers—7 roses and 3 carnations—and are asked whether there are more roses or more flowers, they are likely to say there are more roses, because they are comparing the roses with the carnations rather than with the whole bunch. Not until the stage of concrete operations do children come to realize that roses are a subclass of flowers and that, therefore, there cannot be more roses than flowers (Flavell, 1963).

Seriation and Transitive Inference

Children show that they understand *seriation* when they can arrange objects in a series by placing them in order according to one or more dimensions, such as weight (lightest to heaviest) or color (lightest to darkest). Piaget (1952) tested this ability by asking children to put sticks in order from shortest to longest. By age 4 or 5, children can pick out the smallest and the largest sticks. Then, by age 5 or 6, they can arrange the rest of the sticks by trial and error. Finally, at age 7 or 8, they can grasp the relationships among the sticks on sight, picking out the shortest, then the next shortest, and so on to the longest.

Transitive inference, the ability to recognize a relationship between two objects by knowing the relationship between each of them and a third, also develops in middle childhood. Stacy is shown three sticks: a yellow one, a green one, and a blue one. She is shown that the yellow stick is longer than the green one, and the green one is longer than the blue. Without physically comparing the yellow and blue sticks, she can say that the yellow one is longer than the blue one. She bases her answer on her knowledge of how each of these sticks compares to the green stick (Chapman & Lindenberger, 1988; Piaget & Inhelder, 1967).

Number and Mathematics

With greater ability to manipulate symbols, to appreciate such concepts as reversibility, and to understand seriation and the idea of part-and-whole, children can now tackle arithmetic. Young children intuitively devise strategies for adding by counting on their fingers or with the help of other objects. For example, to add 5 and 3 they may create one set of 5 pennies and another set of 3 pennies and then combine both sets to get 8 pennies. After they have counted each set, they put all the pennies together and count them over again. By age 6 or 7, they can count in their heads. They also learn to *count on:* to add 5 and 3, they start counting at 5 and then go on to 6, 7, and 8 to add the 3. They can also *reverse* the numbers, starting with 3 and adding 5 to it. It may take 2 or 3 more years for them to perform a comparable operation for subtraction, but by age 9 most children can either count up from the smaller number or down from the larger number to get the answer (Resnick, 1989).

Children also become more adept at solving simple story problems, such as: "Pedro went to the store with $5 and spent $2 on candy. How much did he have left?" However, when the starting amount is the unknown ("Pedro went to the store, spent $2 and had $3 left. How much did he start

out with?"), the problem is harder because the arithmetic operation needed to solve it (addition) is not as clearly indicated. Few children can solve this kind of problem before 8 or 9 years of age (Resnick, 1989).

Distinguishing between Fantasy and Reality

To some extent, preoperational children can tell the difference between what is real and what is imaginary, but this ability becomes more sophisticated during the stage of concrete operations. In one study, when second- and fifth-graders were asked about what nurses and police officers do in real life and on television, both the older and younger children perceived that these occupations were shown on television as offering more glamor, more money, and more drama than in real life. However, the older children were more likely than the younger ones to recognize the television portrayals as unrealistic. Children who watched a lot of television were more likely to believe it was like real life and to want to be nurses and police officers like the ones on the screen (J. C. Wright et al., 1995).

MORAL REASONING

According to Piaget, moral development is linked to cognitive growth. Piaget maintained that children make sounder moral judgments when they achieve enough cognitive maturity to look at things from more than one perspective. He proposed that moral reasoning develops in two stages (summarized in Table 8-3). Children may go through these moral stages at varying ages, but the sequence is the same.

In the first stage, *morality of constraint,* the young child thinks rigidly about moral concepts. In this stage children are quite egocentric; they cannot imagine more than one way of looking at a moral issue. They believe that rules cannot be changed, that behavior is right or wrong, and that any offense deserves punishment (unless they themselves are the offenders!).

The second stage, *morality of cooperation,* is characterized by flexibility. As children mature, they interact with more people and come into contact with an increasingly wide range of viewpoints; some of these contradict what they have learned at home. They conclude that there is not one unchangeable, absolute standard of right and wrong. A combination of experience and maturation helps

TABLE 8-3

Piaget's Two Stages of Moral Development

	Stage I: Morality of Constraint	Stage II: Morality of Cooperation
Point of view	Child views an act as either totally right or totally wrong and thinks everyone sees it the same way. Children cannot put themselves in place of others.	Children put themselves in place of others. They are not absolutist in judgments but see that more than one point of view is possible.
Intention	Child judges acts in terms of actual physical consequences, not the motivation behind them.	Child judges acts by intentions, not consequences.
Rules	Child obeys rules because they are sacred and unalterable.	Child recognizes that rules are made by people and can be changed by people. Children consider themselves just as capable of changing rules as anyone else.
Respect for authority	Unilateral respect leads to feeling of obligation to conform to adult standards and obey adult rules.	Mutual respect for authority and peers allows children to value their own opinions and abilities and to judge other people realistically.
Punishment	Child favors severe punishment. Child feels that punishment itself defines the wrongness of an act; an act is bad if it will elicit punishment.	Child favors milder punishment that compensates the victim and helps the culprit recognize why an act is wrong, thus leading to reform.
Concept of justice	Child confuses moral law with physical law and believes that any physical accident or misfortune that occurs after a misdeed is a punishment willed by God or some other supernatural force.	Child does not confuse natural misfortune with punishment.

SOURCE: Adapted partly from M. L. Hoffman, 1970b; Kohlberg, in M. L. Hoffman & Hoffman, 1964.

children begin to formulate their own moral code. Because they can consider more than one aspect of a situation, they can make more subtle moral judgments, considering the intent behind behavior in deciding whether or how it should be punished.

To draw out children's thinking on this point, Piaget (1932) would tell them a story about two little boys: "One day Augustus noticed that his father's inkpot was empty and decided to help his father by filling it. While he was opening the bottle, he spilled a lot of ink on the tablecloth. The other boy, Julian, played with his father's inkpot and spilled a little ink on the cloth." Then Piaget would ask, "Which boy was naughtier, and why?"

Children under about age 7, in the stage of constraint, usually consider Augustus naughtier, since he made the bigger stain. Older children, in the stage of cooperation, recognize that Augustus meant well and made the large stain by accident, whereas Julian made a small strain while doing something he should not have been doing. Immature moral judgments center only on the degree of offense; more mature judgments consider intent.

Lawrence Kohlberg's influential theory of moral development, which builds on Piaget's, is discussed in Chapter 10.

✔ ASPECTS OF COGNITIVE DEVELOPMENT

Unlike Piaget, who described qualitative changes in the way children think, other researchers focus on gradual improvements in specific aspects of cognitive development. Some of these may come from learning. In fact, some developmentalists suggest that acquisition of knowledge, or expertise—in part through formal schooling—may help explain the advances Piaget observed (Flavell et al., 1993). Like adults, children can think more logically about things they know something about (refer back to Box 8-1). Understanding of conservation, for example, may come not from new patterns of mental organization, but simply from greater experience with the physical world. Similarly, *an-*

imism (see Chapter 6), the tendency of young children to believe that such things as fire and wind are alive, may reflect lack of knowledge about fire and wind and what makes them move.

In addition to acquiring more information than they had before, schoolchildren become able to process it faster. Processing time for such tasks as matching pictures and adding numbers in their heads steadily decreases (Kail, 1991). Furthermore, this improvement seems to hold for all kinds of tasks. In one study, 10-year-olds were nearly twice as slow as 19-year-old college students in identifying, matching, and mentally manipulating computer images; but 15-year-olds did all the tasks as quickly as the college students (Hale, 1990).

More efficient information processing profoundly affects many aspects of cognitive performance. It increases the mind's capacity to hold and handle information, making possible better recall as well as more complex reasoning (Flavell et al., 1993). It makes it easier for children to comprehend what they read, to express themselves verbally, and to do the tasks on intelligence tests. Let's look, then, at memory, intelligence, and language.

MEMORY

Memory improves greatly in middle childhood. For one thing, most school-age youngsters are better able to pay attention. They can concentrate longer and can focus on the information they need and want while screening out irrelevant information. In addition, as processing time decreases, children's short-term memory capacity—the amount of information they can keep in mind at a given time—increases (Flavell et al., 1993). And, as they learn how their own memory works, they devise strategies, or deliberate plans, to help them remember.

How Memory Works: Encoding, Storing, and Retrieving

It is helpful to think of memory as a filing system that involves three steps: encoding, storage, and retrieval. In order to file something in memory, we first must decide which "folder" to put it in—for example, "people I know" or "places I've been." *Encoding* attaches a "code" or "label" to the information to prepare it for storage, so that it will be easier to find when needed. Next, we *store* the material (put the folder away in the filing cabinet). The last step is to *retrieve* the information when we need it (search for the file and take it out). Difficulties in any of these steps may cause memory problems.

Information that is being encoded or retrieved is kept in *working memory,* a short-term "storehouse" for information a person is actively working on, or trying to remember. The capacity of working memory increases rapidly in middle childhood. Researchers may assess working memory by asking children to recall a series of digits in reverse order (for example, "2-8-3-7-5-1" if they heard "1-5-7-3-8-2"). At ages 5 to 6, children usually remember only two digits; the typical adolescent remembers six.

Young children's poor short-term memory may help explain why they have difficulty with conservation. Even if they are able to master the concept, they may not be able to remember all the relevant pieces of information (Siegler & Richards, 1982). They may forget that two differently shaped pieces of clay were equal initially; they can judge only by present appearance. Improved short-term memory may contribute to the ability to solve problems like this in middle childhood.

Metamemory: Understanding Memory

Metamemory is awareness of, and knowledge about, the processes of memory. Even 4-year-olds understand that the passage of time affects memory. They know that if a doll saw two objects, the doll would be more likely to "remember" the one just seen than the one seen a long time before (Lyon & Flavell, 1993).

From kindergarten through fifth grade, children advance steadily in understanding memory (Kreutzer, Leonard, & Flavell, 1975). Kindergartners and first-graders know that people remember better if they study longer, that people forget things with time, and that relearning something is easier than learning it for the first time. By third grade, children typically know that some people remember better than others and that some things are easier to remember than others. And, as children know more about how memory works, they can plan better to remember something.

Mnemonics: Strategies for Remembering

One reason older children can remember better than younger children is that they take deliberate actions to help them remember. Devices to aid memory are called *mnemonic strategies.* Children may discover mnemonic techniques on their own, but they also can be taught to use them. As children get older, they develop better strategies and tailor them to meet specific needs. The most common mnemonic strategy among both children and adults is use of external memory aids. Others are rehearsal, organization, and elaboration.

External Aids   Writing down a telephone number, making a list, setting a timer, and putting a library book by the front door are examples of *external memory aids:* prompting by something outside the person. Even kindergartners recognize the value of external aids, and as children mature, they use them more (Kreutzer et al., 1975). For example, third-graders are more likely than first-graders to think of putting their skates by their schoolbooks if they want to remember to take their skates to school the next day.

Rehearsal   Anna, at age 6, wanted to call her grandmother. As she went to the telephone, she said the number out loud again and again. She was using *rehearsal,* or conscious repetition, a common mnemonic strategy to assist working memory.

Some early research suggested that children do not usually use rehearsal spontaneously until after first grade. When an experimenter pointed to several pictures that children knew they would be asked to recall, first-graders typically sat, waited till they were asked for the information, and then tried to recall the pictures. Second- and fifth-graders moved their lips and muttered almost inaudibly between the time they saw the pictures and the time they were asked to recall them, and these children remembered the material better (Flavell, Beach, & Chinsky, 1966). When experimenters asked first-graders to name the pictures out loud when they first saw them (a form of rehearsal), the children recalled the order better. However, young children who were taught to rehearse applied the technique to the immediate situation but not spontaneously to new situations (Keeney, Canizzo, & Flavell, 1967).

More recent research shows that some children between 3 and 6 years of age do use rehearsal. And although 6-year-olds are more likely than 3-year-olds to rehearse, those 3-year-olds who do rehearse can remember a grocery list just as well as 6-year-olds (Paris & Weissberg-Benchell, in Chance & Fischman, 1987).

Organization   Another way to remember material is by mentally placing it into related groupings

Contestants in a spelling bee can make good use of mnemonic strategies—devices to aid memory—such as rehearsal (repetition), organization, and elaboration. This boy may be trying to remember by putting a word into a mental category with other words that contain similar elements. *(Charles Gupton/Stock, Boston)*

or categories, a mnemonic strategy known as *organization.* Adults tend to organize automatically. Children younger than 10 or 11 tend not to do this, but they can be taught to do it, or they may acquire the skill by imitation (Chance & Fischman, 1987). If they see randomly arranged pictures of, say, animals, furniture, vehicles, and clothing, they do not mentally sort the items into categories spontaneously; but if shown how to organize, they recall the pictures as well as older children. Again, however, the younger children do not generalize this learning to other situations.

Elaboration   In the mnemonic strategy called *elaboration,* children associate items with an imagined scene or story. To remember to buy lemons, ketchup, and napkins, for example, a child might imagine a ketchup bottle balanced on a lemon, with a pile of napkins handy to wipe up spilled ketchup. Older children are more likely than younger ones to use elaboration spontaneously, and they remember better when they make up the elaborations themselves. Younger children remember better when a parent or someone else makes up the elaboration (Paris & Lindauer, 1976; H. W. Reese, 1977).

INTELLIGENCE

Intelligence tests (or IQ tests) are called *aptitude tests:* they claim to measure general intelligence, or the capacity to learn, as contrasted with *achievement tests,* which assess how much children have learned in various subject areas. However, intelligence tests are validated against measures of achievement, such as school performance, and such measures are affected by factors beyond intelligence. For this and other reasons, there is strong disagreement over how accurately IQ tests assess differences among children. Let's see what kinds of intelligence tests schoolchildren take and then consider arguments about their use.

Group and Individual Tests

Most schools give group intelligence tests every few years. In addition, individual tests may be given to help school administrators decide whether to admit particular students, whether they would benefit from an enriched program, or whether they need special help.

One popular group test is the **Otis-Lennon School Ability Test,** which has levels for kindergarten up to twelfth grade. Children are usually tested in groups of 10 to 15. They are asked to classify items, to show an understanding of verbal and numerical concepts, to display general information, and to follow directions.

The most widely used individual test is the **Wechsler Intelligence Scale for Children (WISC-III).** This test measures verbal and performance abilities, yielding separate scores for each, as well as a total score. Separating subtest scores makes it easier to pinpoint a child's strengths and to diagnose specific problems. For example, if a child does well on verbal tests (such as understanding a written passage and knowing vocabulary words) but poorly on performance tests (such as figuring out mazes and copying a block design), the child may have difficulty with perceptual or motor development. A child who does well on performance tests and poorly on verbal tests may have a language problem. Another commonly used individual test is the Stanford-Binet Intelligence Scale, described in Chapter 6.

A nontraditional individual test is the **Kaufman Assessment Battery for Children (K-ABC)** (Kaufman & Kaufman, 1983). Developed during the 1980s, it is administered to test-takers from 2½ to 12½ years of age. It is intended to fairly assess children from cultural minorities and children with disabilities, and members of these groups were included in the standardization sample. There is a nonverbal scale for children with hearing impairments or speech or language disorders and for those whose primary language is not English.

The K-ABC has separate scales for aptitude (mental processing abilities) and achievement. The aptitude scales yield scores for two kinds of information-processing abilities. *Simultaneous processing* requires the integration of a number of stimuli at the same time (such as remembering an array of objects seen briefly). *Sequential processing* demands step-by-step thinking (say, repeating a series of numbers). These scales incorporate Vygotsky's concept of *scaffolding* (see Chapter 6): if a child fails any of the first three items on a subtest, the examiner can clarify what kind of response is expected by using different words or gestures or even a different language. Subtests in the achievement scale measure reading, arithmetic, word knowledge, and general information. Although these subtest items are more like items in a traditional aptitude test than like a standard school achievement test, the developers consider the battery a test of the information a child has absorbed rather than a measure of the child's innate abilities.

Pros and Cons of Intelligence Testing

The use of psychometric intelligence tests is controversial. On the positive side, because IQ tests have been standardized, there is extensive information about their norms, validity, and reliability (see Chapter 4). IQ scores are good predictors of achievement in school, especially for highly verbal children; and they help identify youngsters who are either especially bright or in need of special help.

On the other hand, there is serious concern that the tests may be unfair to many children. For one thing, they may underestimate the intelligence of children who, for one reason or another, do not do well on tests. Knowing how to sit still and pay attention, interest in the tasks, motivation to excel, and awareness of test-taking strategies (such as quickly giving answers one is sure of, and then going back to focus on more difficult questions) all affect the results (Anastasi, 1988; Ceci, 1991).

Because IQ tests are timed, they equate intelligence with speed. A child who works slowly and deliberately is penalized. Furthermore, IQ tests do not cover important aspects of intelligent behavior, such as "street smarts" (common sense and shrewdness in everyday life), social skills (getting along with other people), creative insight, and self-knowledge (Gardner, 1983; Sternberg, 1985a, 1987). According to Howard Gardner's (1983) theory of multiple intelligences, people have not just one but at least seven relatively independent kinds of intelligence, and IQ tests tap only three of them: *linguistic* (reading and writing), *logical-mathematical* (using numbers and solving logical problems), and *spatial* (finding one's way around an environment). The other four, which are not reflected in IQ scores, are: *musical* (perceiving and creating patterns of pitch and rhythm), *bodily-kinesthetic* (moving precisely, as in surgery or dance), *interpersonal* (understanding others), and *intrapersonal* (knowing oneself). Robert Sternberg has also proposed a theory involving more than one kind of intelligence (see Chapter 12).

Critics also claim that test-developers' decisions on which answers to accept sometimes seem arbitrary: answers that may be perfectly reasonable are considered wrong. For example, 4- to 6-year-olds taking the 1973 edition of the Stanford-Binet Intelligence Scale are asked, "What is a house made of?" If a child says "A house is made of walls," the answer will be marked incorrect; the only "correct" answers are materials, such as wood, bricks, or stone (Miller-Jones, 1989).

A more fundamental criticism is that tests cannot assess aptitude directly; instead, they infer it from tasks that tap information and skills. Although some test makers have tried to separate what children have already learned (achievement) from their ability to acquire new knowledge (intelligence), critics maintain that it cannot be done. Experience, especially education, affects test results: scores, especially on verbal tasks, are more closely related to the amount of schooling a child has had than to the child's age (Cahan & Cohen, 1989).

The fact that many people's IQs change is further evidence for the role of experience. According to Vygotsky, intelligence is not a fixed, inborn quantity; it results from the ongoing interaction between child and environment. Thus we should not be surprised if intelligence increases as children mature and grow more knowledgeable and more skillful in using their minds; and assessments should seek to capture this dynamic process. Tests based on Vygotsky's concept of the zone of proximal development (ZPD) offer an alternative to traditional IQ tests (see Chapter 6).

Ethnic and Cultural Differences

Although there is considerable overlap in intelligence test scores among ethnic groups, with some African Americans scoring higher than most whites, on average black Americans tend to score about 15 points lower than white Americans (N. Brody, 1985; Neisser et al., 1995; C. R. Reynolds, 1988). It has been argued that part of the cause for this difference is genetic (Herrnstein & Murray, 1994; Jensen, 1969). However, although there is strong evidence of a genetic influence on differences in intelligence *within* a group (see Chapter 2), there is no direct evidence that differences *between* ethnic, cultural, or racial groups are hereditary (Neisser et al., 1995).

Instead, most scholars attribute such differences to inequalities in *environment*—in income, in nutrition, in living conditions, in intellectual stimulation, in schooling, in culture, or in other circumstances that can affect self-esteem, motivation, and academic performance (Kamin, 1974, 1981; Kottak, 1994; Miller-Jones, 1989) and even, in the first few years of life, the very structure of the brain (see Chapter 3). Indeed, the discrepancy in IQ between white and black Americans appears to be diminishing, perhaps as a result of efforts to improve the education and life circumstances of minority children (Neisser et al., 1995). In one study of 5-year-olds who had been low-birthweight babies, adjusting for economic and social differences between black and white children (including differences in home environment) virtually eliminated intergroup differences in IQ (Brooks-Gunn, Klebanov, & Duncan, 1996).

Other ethnic comparisons suggest that the relationships between environmental factors, IQ, and achievement may be complex. Asian Americans, whose scholastic achievements consistently outstrip those of other ethnic groups, do not seem to have a significant edge in IQ, despite earlier findings to the contrary (Neisser et al., 1995). Instead, Asian American children's strong scholastic achievement seems to be best explained by cultural factors (see Box 8-2). On the other hand, IQ scores do tend to predict the achievement of His-

BOX 8-2   WINDOW ON THE WORLD

HOW CAN CHILDREN OF ASIAN EXTRACTION ACHIEVE SO MUCH?

The striking academic success of many Asian American children, especially those of Chinese and Japanese extraction—as well as the disproportionate success of adults from these ethnic groups in scientific and professional fields—has raised provocative questions. Why do students from Asian families make such a strong showing? Is it because of superior innate ability, or other factors? To help answer these questions, some researchers have looked at differences in cognitive ability, educational practices, and family and cultural attitudes in these children's countries of origin.

COGNITIVE ABILITY

Asian students do not start out with any overall cognitive superiority, according to a cross-cultural study of American, Japanese, and Chinese children. In fact, American first-graders outperform Asians on many tasks, possibly because they are more used to answering adults' questions, whereas Chinese children, for example, are expected to be "seen but not heard" (H. W. Stevenson et al., 1985). In another study, American children did better at ages 4 to 6 in counting and in judging relative quantities; but by age 7

Children from Asian families often do better in school than other American youngsters. The reasons seem to be cultural, not genetic. *(Peter Dublin/Stock, Boston)*

or 8, Korean children had surpassed them (Song & Ginsburg, 1987).

American students' mathematical abilities decline from first to eleventh grade compared with the abilities of Asian students, but their general information scores become increasingly similar (H. W. Stevenson, Chen, & Lee, 1993). Since children learn advanced math skills almost entirely in

school, whereas general information can be learned outside of school, better teaching in Asian schools seems to make the difference.

EDUCATIONAL PRACTICES

Educational practices differ markedly in Asian and American cultures (Song & Ginsburg, 1987; Stigler, Lee, & Stevenson, 1987).

panic children, as well as of African Americans. Average IQ scores of Hispanic children fall between those of black and white children, probably reflecting language difficulties; Latino children tend to do better on performance tasks than on verbal tasks (Neisser et al., 1995).

Language may play a part in the black-white differential as well. Differences between black and white children's test scores do not appear until about 2 or 3 years of age (Golden, Birns, & Bridger, 1973). In fact, some classic research suggests that African American babies are precocious on developmental tests (Bayley, 1965; Geber, 1962; Geber &

Dean, 1957). The disadvantage that shows up later may reflect the switch from predominantly motor to predominantly verbal tasks, which tend to reflect environmental factors, such as the fact that many African American children hear black English rather than standard English around them.

IQ tests are subject to *cultural bias:* a tendency to include questions that use language or call for information or skills more familiar or meaningful to some cultural groups than to others (Sternberg, 1985a, 1987). The contents of a test—the tasks it poses—tend to reflect the test-developers' values and experience; but people from other cultural

Asian children spend more time in school each year and each day, and more time being taught mathematics, in part because the curriculum is set centrally. Asian teachers spend more than three-fourths of their time teaching the whole class; American teachers spend less than half. American children spend more time working alone or in small groups. Although the American approach offers more individual attention, each child ends up with less total instruction.

FAMILY AND CULTURAL ATTITUDES

In Japan, a child's entrance into school is a greater occasion for celebration than is graduation from high school: first-graders receive such expensive gifts as desks, chairs, and leather backpacks. Japanese and Korean parents spend a great deal of time helping children with schoolwork, and Japanese children who fall behind are tutored or go to *jukus*, private remedial and enrichment schools (McKinney, 1987; Song & Ginsburg, 1987).

Chinese and Japanese mothers view academic achievement as a child's most important pursuit and hold high standards for academic achievement (H. W. Stevenson et al., 1993; H. W. Stevenson, Lee, Chen, & Lummis, 1990; H. W. Stevenson, Lee, Chen, Stigler, et al., 1990). American mothers are more satisfied with their children's school performance and their schools than Asian mothers (H. W. Stevenson et al., 1993). Chinese and Japanese children spend more time on homework, get more help from parents, and like doing homework more than do American children (C. Chen & Stevenson, 1989).

Similarly, many Asian American families see education as the best route to upward mobility (Sue & Okazaki, 1990). Whereas other American students are more likely to hold after-school jobs, go out on dates, engage in sports, and do chores, Asian American students are expected to devote themselves almost entirely to study. Among Southeast Asian refugees, parents relieve children of household chores, set daily study goals, and expect equivalent achievements from boys and girls. Older siblings help younger ones, learning as they teach. Most important, perhaps, Asian parents communicate an attitude that learning is valuable, mastery is satisfying, and effort is more important than ability (H. W. Stevenson et al., 1993; N. Caplan et al., 1992). It is apparently culture, then, and not inborn cognitive superiority, that has helped Asian American students achieve so much in school.

A common belief is that high-achieving students in Japan and China suffer psychologically from pressure to achieve. Actually, lower-achieving American students report more frequent feelings of stress, academic anxiety, and aggression; and school is their most commonly identified source of stress (H. W. Stevenson et al., 1993). On the other hand, although 90 percent of Japanese students graduate from high school in comparison with 76 percent of American students, only 29 percent go to college in comparison with 58 percent in the United States (C. Simons, 1987). A growing number of Japanese parents, students, and lawyers are challenging long-established practices, arguing that regimentation stifles individuality (Chira, 1988).

Culture shapes attitudes and encourages some kinds of behaviors rather than others. If cultural standards change, the relative standing of Asian and American students eventually may change too. Such changes ultimately would be likely to affect the academic standing of Asian American students as well.

---

groups may not have the same values or experiences. As a result, the test may underestimate their abilities. Specifically, it has been argued that intelligence tests are built around the dominant thinking style and language of white people of European ancestry, putting African American children at a disadvantage. For example, most tests designate only one right answer to each question—the one that is considered appropriate according to standards of the dominant culture; but being socialized in a minority culture may lead children to see alternative answers, which are then marked wrong (Heath, 1989; Helms, 1992).

Rapport with the examiner and familiarity with the surroundings make a difference. African American and Latino children, disabled children, and children from low socioeconomic levels often make higher scores when tests are given in their own classrooms by their own teachers than in unfamiliar rooms with examiners they do not know (D. Fuchs & Fuchs, 1986; L. S. Fuchs & Fuchs, 1986).

Cross-cultural Testing

As early as 1910, researchers recognized the difficulty of designing intelligence tests for people in diverse cultural groups. Ever since, they have tried to design tests that can measure intelligence without introducing cultural bias, generally by posing tasks that do not require language. Testers use gestures, pantomime, and demonstrations for such tasks as tracing mazes, finding absurdities in pictures, putting the right shapes in the right holes, and completing pictures. However, test designers have not been able to eliminate all cultural influences. For example, when Lucas, an American child, was asked to identify the missing detail in a picture of a face with no mouth, he said, "the mouth." However, Ari, an Asian immigrant child in Israel, said the *body* was missing. Since the art he was used to would not present a head as a complete picture, he thought the absence of a body was more important than the omission of "a mere detail like the mouth" (Anastasi, 1988, p. 360).

It seems impossible to design a *culture-free test*—a test having *no* culture-linked content. Instead, test developers have tried to produce *culture-fair tests,* tests dealing with experiences common to people in various cultures. However, it is almost impossible to screen for culturally determined values and attitudes. On a simple sorting task, a child in a western culture will categorize things by what they *are* (say, putting *bird* and *fish* in the category *animal*). Kpelle tribespeople in Nigeria consider it more intelligent to sort things by what they *do* (grouping *fish* with *swim*, for example) (Sternberg, in Quinby, 1985; Sternberg, 1985a, 1986). In the United States, children in low-income homes, where tasks and roles are less clearly defined than in high-income households, tend to classify more like the Kpelle than like high-income Americans (Miller-Jones, 1989).

Cultural attitudes also can affect how well a child does in a particular testing situation. A child from a culture that stresses sociability and cooperation may be handicapped taking a test alone. A child from a nonindustrial culture that stresses slow, painstaking work may be handicapped in a timed test (Kottak, 1994). A counter-argument is that in order to succeed, children will have to function in the majority culture; and so, shielding children from the need to compete on that culture's terms will not help them in the long run.

LANGUAGE

Language abilities continue to grow during middle childhood. Children are now better able to understand and interpret communications from others, both oral and written, and to make themselves understood.

Vocabulary, Grammar, and Syntax

Six-year-olds use complex grammar and have a vocabulary of several thousand words, but they have yet to master many fine points of language. During the early school years, they rarely use the passive voice (as in "The sidewalk is being shoveled"), verb tenses that include the auxiliary *have* ("I have already shoveled the sidewalk"), and conditional sentence ("If Barbara were home, she would help shovel the sidewalk").

Up to and possibly after age 9, children develop an increasingly sophisticated understanding of *syntax,* how words are organized into phrases and sentences. Carol S. Chomsky (1969) found considerable variation in the ages at which children grasp certain syntactic structures (see Table 8-4). For example, most children under 5 or 6 years old think the sentences "John promised Bill to go shopping" and "John told Bill to go shopping" both mean that Bill is the one to go to the store. Their confusion is understandable, since almost all English verbs other than *promised* that might be used in such a sentence (such as *ordered, wanted,* and *expected*) would have that meaning. Many 6-year-olds have not yet learned how to deal with constructions such as the one in the first sentence, even though they know what a promise is and are able to use and understand the word correctly in other sentences. By age 8, most children can interpret the first sentence correctly.

Pragmatics: Knowledge about Communication

Young children's misinterpretions of what others say often stem from difficulties in *metacommunication:* knowledge of how communication takes place. This knowledge increases during middle childhood.

One aspect of metacommunication is awareness of the connection between instructions and results. In one experiment, kindergartners and second-graders were asked to construct block buildings exactly like those built by another child. They were to do this on the basis of the other child's audio-taped instructions without seeing the buildings themselves (Flavell, Speer, Green, & August, 1981). The instructions were often incomplete, ambiguous, or contradictory. The "builders" were then

TABLE 8-4

Acquisition of Complex Syntactic Structures

Structure	Difficult Concept	Age of Acquisition
John is easy to see.	Who is doing the seeing?	5.6 to 9 years*
John promised Bill to go.	Who is going?	5.6 to 9 years*
John asked Bill what to do.	Who is doing it?	Some 10-year-olds still have not learned this.
He knew that John was going to win the race.	Does the "he" refer to John?	5.6 years.

*All children 9 and over know this.
SOURCE: C. S. Chomsky, 1969.

asked whether they thought their buildings looked like the ones the child on the tape had made and whether they thought the child's instructions were good or bad.

The second-graders were more likely than the younger children to notice when instructions were inadequate and to pause or look puzzled. They were much more likely to know when they did not understand something and to recognize that their buildings might not look exactly like those made by the child on the tape because they had not received good enough instructions. The kindergartners sometimes knew that the instructions were not clear, but they did not seem to realize that this would mean they might not be able to do the job well.

These findings have important implications. Young children often do not understand what they see, hear, or read, but they may not be aware that they do not understand. Adults need to realize that they cannot take children's understanding for granted and need to make sure that children know what the adults want them to know.

Literacy and Social Interaction

School-age children use reading and writing for the same kinds of purposes adults do. They read for enjoyment, for learning facts and discovering ideas, and to stimulate their thinking. They write to express ideas, thoughts, and feelings. As before, the social context can foster the growth of literacy. While parents and teachers are still important, peers now exert a major influence.

According to Vygotsky, words are symbols that enable children to link their mental activity with the collective "mind" of the culture. Literacy is not just a matter of manipulating marks on a page; it becomes an increasingly effective tool for acting in the social world. One researcher, after reading journal entries and stories by 4- to 8-year-old African American children from working-class homes, concluded that other people's responses give social meaning to a child's use of words and pictures (Dyson, 1993). The children used language in particular ways with particular aims that involved their relationships with people and the world around them.

The children initially "wrote" by talking and drawing, and they used stories to strengthen their relationships with other children. They expressed their thoughts and feelings to one another and talked about and acted out one another's stories. They put their friends into stories as characters and included words or actions designed to tease or amuse the other children. The stories influenced and were influenced by the children's ongoing social lives.

As children become literate, they use writing to strengthen their participation in their culture and to make social connections. For example, one third-grader wrote about rap stars on television. Children tried to gain their peers' attention and respect by using rhyme, rhythm, and humor.

Ironically, in the typical classroom children are discouraged from discussing their work with other children. This practice is based on the belief that children, especially friends, will distract one another, turn learning time into playtime, and prevent one another from doing their best work. Research based on Vygotsky's social interaction model suggests that this is not so.

One study of 60 fourth-graders found that children progress more when they write with other

These Inupiat (Eskimo) children in Kotzebue, Alaska, are learning in their native language, Inupiaq, as well as in English, so as to preserve their cultural heritage. Although bilingual education is controversial, research suggests that knowing one language does not interfere with learning a second language, nor does learning a second language rob a child of fluency in the first. Bilingual children usually can switch readily from one language to the other. *(Lawrence Migdale/Stock, Boston)*

children, especially friends (Daiute, Hartup, Sholl, & Zajac, 1993). The children were asked to write pieces for a class publication about the rain forest. Children working in pairs wrote stories with more solutions to problems, more explanations and goals, and fewer errors in syntax and word use than did children working alone. Children working with friends concentrated more intently than those paired with mere acquaintances. The acquaintances tended to stray from the task, joke around, and make less of a joint effort. The friends collaborated in complex ways, elaborating on each other's ideas, working as a team, and posing alternative ideas.

What makes collaboration between friends so fruitful? Since friends know one another well, they may better understand each other's needs, abilities, and likely behaviors. They can expect reciprocal commitment, and they are more comfortable and trusting; thus they may have more courage to take intellectual risks (Hartup, 1996).

Second-language Education

More than 2.5 million school-age children in the United States come from non-English-speaking homes (Hakuta & Garcia, 1989). A goal of the federal Equal Education Opportunity Act of 1974 is for foreign-speaking students to learn English well enough to compete academically with native English-speakers. How this can best be done is a controversial issue. The issue also has psychological and political ramifications, since identity is entwined with language and culture, and competence in school and in society affect self-esteem.

Some schools use an *English-immersion* approach (sometimes called ESL, or English as a Second Language), in which minority children are immersed in English from the beginning, in special all-day or part-time classes. Other schools have adopted programs of *bilingual education,* in which children are taught in two languages, first learning academic subjects in their native language and then switching to English when they become more proficient in it. These programs can encourage children to become *bilingual* (fluent in two languages) and to feel pride in their cultural identity.

Advocates of early English-immersion claim that the sooner children are exposed to English and the more time they spend speaking it, the better they learn it (Rossel & Ross, 1986). Proponents of bilingual programs claim that children progress faster academically in their native languages and later make a smoother transition to all-English classrooms (Padilla et al., 1991). Some educators maintain that the English-only approach stunts children's cognitive growth; because foreign-speaking children can understand only simple English at first, the curriculum must be watered down, and children are less prepared to handle complex material later (Collier, 1995).

Findings on the relative success of these approaches have been mixed; and most studies have focused only on how well children learn English, not on how well they do in school and society

(Hakuta & Garcia, 1989). Now, large-scale research on the long-term academic achievement of children in high-quality bilingual and immersion programs offers strong support for a bilingual approach (Collier, 1995; W. P. Thomas & Collier, 1995).

Researchers examined the elementary and high school records of 42,000 foreign-speaking students in five districts across the United States and compared their standardized achievement test scores and grade-point averages with those of native English-speakers. In the primary grades, the type of language teaching made little difference; but from seventh grade on, differences were dramatic. Children who had remained in bilingual programs at least through sixth grade caught up with or even surpassed their native English-speaking peers, while the relative performance of those who had been in traditional immersion programs began to decline. By the end of high school, those in part-time ESL programs—the least successful type—scored lower than 80 percent of native English-speakers their age. ESL programs that emphasized problem solving, discovery learning, and interactive activities combined with complex academic content were more effective than traditional structured programs.

Most successful was the less common *two-way,* or *dual-language,* approach, in which English-speaking and foreign-speaking children learn together in their own and each other's languages. This approach avoids stigmatizing minority children by placement in segregated classes; instead, by valuing both languages equally, it helps build self-confidence and self-esteem. An added advantage is that English-speakers learn a foreign language at an early age, when they can acquire it most easily (Collier, 1995; W. P. Thomas & Collier, 1995). These findings echo earlier ones: the more bilingually proficient children are, the higher their cognitive achievement—as long as school personnel value bilingualism and the second language is added at no sacrifice to the first (Diaz, 1983; Padilla et al., 1991).

Critics question whether a child with two languages will become really fluent in either one, but this does not seem to be cause for concern. Knowing one language does not interfere with learning a second; and learning the second does not rob a child of fluency in the first (Hakuta, Ferdman, & Diaz, 1987; Hakuta & Garcia, 1989). Bilingual children usually can switch easily from one language to the other (Zentella, 1981). Changing speech to match the situation, or **code switching**, seems to

come naturally to children. They learn very early, for example, to talk differently to their parents than they do to their friends. A common example of code switching occurs among African Americans who speak black English at home but switch to standard English at school or work.

✔ INFLUENCES ON SCHOOL ACHIEVEMENT

Children's experience in school affects and is affected by every aspect of their development—cognitive, physical, emotional, and social. In addition to children's own characteristics, each level of the context of their lives—from the immediate family to what goes on in the classroom to the messages they receive from the larger culture (such as "It's not cool to be smart")—influences how well they do in school. Let's look at this "nest" of influences.

THE CHILD

Most children, by the time they start school, have developed an impressive array of abilities that help them succeed. They can devise and use strategies to learn, remember, and solve problems. They can use language to show what they know, to ask and answer questions, to discuss ideas, and to seek help. They also become increasingly able to allocate their time and to take responsibility for doing their schoolwork. Some children, of course, are better prepared for school than others. Although differences in cognitive ability are important, temperamental and emotional factors also affect children's adjustment to school and their ability to apply themselves.

Temperament

Does a "teacher's pet" make better academic progress than a fidgety child who throws tantrums, cannot sit still, and has a short attention span? To find out, researchers followed 790 first-graders with a range of ethnic, racial, and economic backgrounds through fourth grade (K. L. Alexander, Entwisle, & Dauber, 1993). Children rated by teachers as cooperative and compliant were no more likely to get high scores on achievement tests or high marks in reading and math than children rated lower on those qualities. Interest, attention, and active participation were, however, associated with achievement test scores and, even more so, with teachers' marks. Furthermore, these influences carried over from first grade to later years.

Apparently, to make optimum academic progress, a child need not be polite and helpful but does need to be involved in what is going on in class. A child who tries hard, pays attention, and participates eagerly also tends to make a good impression on the teacher and is more likely to get high marks. A good report card, in turn, reinforces positive behavior and effort. Since patterns of classroom behavior seem to be set in first grade, this first year of formal schooling offers a "window of opportunity" for parents and teachers to help a child form good learning habits.

Emotional State

Children's school performance is also related to their emotional life. This is especially true of girls. In one study of 143 eight- to eleven-year-olds, researchers assessed children's empathy by their reactions to audiovisual vignettes. The researchers also asked the children questions designed to measure emotional states. The children were tested in reading, spelling, and arithmetic and were rated by teachers on tendencies toward aggression and depression. Among girls, particularly, empathy was associated with good scores in reading and spelling, while depression and aggression seemed to interfere with the development of cognitive skills (Feshbach & Feshbach, 1987).

Since the ability to imagine and share another person's feelings has a cognitive basis (see Chapter 6), it is not surprising that empathy is linked with cognitive achievement. The connection is bidirectional. Sensitivity to other people's feelings can help create a positive social environment that contributes to learning; at the same time, cognitive ability helps children learn from dealings with other people and thus become more empathic. We can also see a bidirectional link concerning depression and aggression. A depressed or unusually aggressive child may have trouble concentrating; conversely, problems with schoolwork may make a child depressed or frustrated, and frustration may lead to aggression. Why are these connections stronger in girls than in boys? Perhaps it is because, in American culture, girls are socialized to be more empathic and to seek love and approval. Girls are more affected by other people's reactions, while boys are brought up to master skills for their own sake (Feshbach & Feshbach, 1987).

THE PARENTS

A small but growing number of parents—estimated at 500,000 to 1 million—school their children at home. These parents tend to be more educated than average and better off financially, and to have larger families; 3 out of 4 go to religious services every week, and 9 out of 10 are of white Anglo-Saxon extraction (Menendez, 1995).

However, parents need not be their children's teachers in order to influence their education. Parents have a strong indirect influence through the ways they motivate children to achieve, their involvement in their children's schooling, and the attitudes they transmit.

Motivating Children

How do parents motivate their children to do well? Some use *extrinsic* (external) means—giving children money or treats for good grades or punishing them for bad ones. Others encourage children to develop their own *intrinsic* (internal) motivation by praising them for ability and hard work.

Intrinsic motivation seems more effective. In fact, some educators claim that even praise should be used sparingly, as it shifts the focus from the child's own motivation to the need to please others (Aldort, 1994). In a study of 77 third- and fourth-graders, all of whom scored above the median on achievement tests, those who sought grades or parents' approval did not do as well in school as those who were interested in the work itself. These children got lower grades, lost interest in school activities, and felt angry, anxious, or bored (Miserandino, 1996).

Parenting styles may affect motivation. In one study, fifth-graders who were the highest achievers had *authoritative* parents (see Chapter 7), who encouraged and praised them and fostered autonomy. These children were curious and interested in learning; they liked challenging tasks and enjoyed solving problems by themselves. *Authoritarian* parents, who reminded children to do their homework, supervised closely, and relied on extrinsic motivation, tended to have lower-achieving children, perhaps because such external control undermines children's ability to trust their own judgment about what they need to do to achieve success. Children of *permissive* parents, who are uninvolved and do not seem to care how the children do in school, also tend to be low achievers (G. S. Ginsburg & Bronstein, 1993).

Since this was a correlational study, we cannot draw firm conclusions about causation. Influence between parents and children tends to be bidirectional: parents of poor achievers may resort to bribes and threats and may feel obliged to make sure homework gets done, while parents of children who are motivated and successful may not feel the need to offer rewards or punishments or to take such an active supervisory role.

Some parental supervision is desirable. Parents of achieving children provide a place to study and to keep books and supplies; they set and insist on times for meals, sleep, and homework; they monitor how much television their children watch and what their children do after school; and they show interest in their children's lives at school by talking about school events and about the children's problems and successes (U.S. Department of Education, 1986b) and by being involved in school activities (D. L. Stevenson & Baker, 1987).

Socioeconomic Effects

The family's socioeconomic status, including financial resources and parents' educational background, can have a major influence on children's school achievement. In one study of 90 rural African American families with firstborn children ages 9 to 12, parents with more education were likely to have higher incomes and to be more involved in the child's schooling. Higher-income families also tended to be more supportive and harmonious. Children growing up in a positive family atmosphere, whose mothers were involved in their schooling, tended to develop better self-regulation and to perform better in school (G. H. Brody, Stoneman, & Flor, 1995).

Thus socioeconomic status in itself does not determine school achievement; it is its effects on family life that can make a difference. A longitudinal study of low-income African American children who had attended the Perry Preschool (discussed in Chapters 6 and 11) found that some did much better in school—and in adult life—than others. An important factor in the success of the higher-achieving children was the positive influence of parents who placed a high value on education and helped them overcome obstacles to obtaining it. Children who, in kindergarten, had higher IQs and whom teachers rated as more motivated to learn tended to have mothers who had completed more years of schooling and who were more cooperative with the teacher and more involved. These

children also did better on achievement tests in the first and eighth grades, spent more time on homework at age 15 than less successful students, and were more likely to finish high school. Parents' expectations for their children also seemed to play a role—though it is hard to know whether children did well because their parents expected them to achieve or whether parents expected more of children who showed the potential to succeed (Luster & McAdoo, 1996).

Parental Attitudes and Beliefs

Children are affected not only by what parents do but by what they think. In one study described above (G. S. Ginsburg & Bronstein, 1993), parents who assumed that outside forces were responsible for their fate—and who presumably communicated that belief to their children—had children who were less self-reliant, less self-motivated, less persistent, and less successful in their schoolwork.

Many parental beliefs come down via cultural routes. A California survey related parents' beliefs about child rearing, intelligence, and education to children's school performance (Okagaki & Sternberg, 1993). Of the 359 parents, some were immigrants from Mexico, Cambodia, Vietnam, and the Philippines; others were native-born, either Mexican American or Anglo American. The one belief most clearly related to educational outcomes was approval of conformity to external standards. This value was rated low by American-born parents (who tend to value autonomy and creativity) but high by immigrants (who may consider it important in adapting to a new culture). Children of parents who valued conformity did not do as well in American schools (which, of course, are oriented to American values) as did other children.

THE TEACHER

If you're lucky, you may have had a special teacher who had a major influence on you—who inspired a love of knowledge and spurred you to work and to learn. One study showed the power of a teacher's influence by linking the success of a number of people who had grown up in a poor city neighborhood with a very special first grade teacher. As adults, "Miss A's" former pupils showed greater increases in IQ, held better jobs, lived in better housing, and had a neater personal appearance than did other graduates of the same school (E. Pederson, Faucher, & Eaton, 1978). What

An exceptional teacher's influence can extend far into the future, and an interest she or he inspires may shape a child's entire life. *(Mary Kate Denny/ PhotoEdit)*

did Miss A do? She showed confidence in children's ability and encouraged them to work hard to justify it. She was affectionate and gave extra time to children who needed it.

Miss A's belief in her students probably had much to do with how well they did. According to the principle of the *self-fulfilling prophecy,* children live up to—or down to—other people's expectations for them. In the "Oak School" experiment, teachers were told at the beginning of the term that some students had shown unusual potential for cognitive growth, when these children actually had been chosen at random. Yet several months later, many of them, especially first- and second-graders, showed unusual gains in IQ. Their teachers did not spend more time with these children than with the others, nor did they treat them differently in any obvious way; but subtler influences may have been at work, possibly the teachers' tone of voice, facial expressions, touch, and posture (R. Rosenthal & Jacobson, 1968).

Although this research has been criticized for methodological flaws, other researchers have confirmed the basic principle: that teachers' expectations "can and do function as self-fulfilling prophecies, although not always or automatically" (Brophy & Good, 1974, p. 32). Even first-graders are aware that teachers treat high and low achievers differently. One study found that this awareness did not seem to affect first-graders' opinions of themselves very much, but by fifth grade the effect was marked (Weinstein, Marshall, Sharp, & Botkin, 1987).

This principle has important implications for minority and poor children. Since many middle-class teachers may believe (perhaps subconsciously) that such students are less able than others, they may somehow convey their limited expectations to the children—and get from them the little that they expect.

THE EDUCATIONAL SYSTEM

How can school best enhance children's development? Conflicting views, along with historical events, have brought great swings in educational theory and practice during the twentieth century. The traditional curriculum, centered on the "three R's" (reading, 'riting, and 'rithmetic), gave way first to "child-centered" methods that focused on children's interests and then, during the late 1950s, to an emphasis on science and mathematics to overcome the Soviet Union's lead in the space race. During the turbulent 1960s and early 1970s, rigorous studies were replaced by student-directed learning, electives, and "open classrooms," in which children chose their own activities and teachers served as "facilitators." Then, a decline in high school students' scores on the Scholastic Aptitude Test (SAT) in the mid-1970s sent schools back to the "basics" (Ravitch, 1983). In the 1980s, a series of governmental and educational commissions proposed plans for improvement, ranging from more homework to a longer school day and school year to a total reorganization of schools and curricula.

BOX 8-3   PRACTICALLY SPEAKING

ENHANCING THINKING SKILLS AND CREATIVITY

Parents and teachers can help children think more clearly and solve problems more effectively. Adults can also instill attitudes that encourage rather than discourage creativity. Here are some research-based suggestions.

THINKING AND PROBLEM-SOLVING SKILLS

Children need to learn how to evaluate a situation, focus on its most important aspects, and decide what to do. Adults can teach such skills in the context of everyday activities (Marzano & Hutchins, 1987; Maxwell, 1987):

■ When reading to children, ask open-ended questions (beginning with what, why, and how).

■ Help children find the most important points in what they read, see, or hear.

■ Ask children to compare new information with what they already know. Identifying commonalities and differences can help children organize information, which helps them think as well as remember.

■ Teach children not to accept a statement that contradicts common knowledge without reliable proof.

■ Encourage children to write. Putting thoughts on paper forces them to organize their thoughts. Projects may include

keeping a journal, writing a letter to a famous person, and presenting an argument to parents (say, for an increase in allowance or a special purchase or privilege).

■ Encourage children to think imaginatively about what they have learned. ("How do you think the soldiers in the American Revolution felt at Valley Forge? What do you suppose they wore?")

■ When writing a poem or drawing a picture, encourage children to produce a first version and then to polish or revise it.

■ Show children how to approach a problem by identifying what they do and don't know about it, by designing a plan to solve it, by carrying out the plan, and then by deciding whether it has worked.

■ Ask children to invent a new product, such as a gadget to ease a household chore.

■ Teach children such skills as reading a map and using a microscope, and provide opportunities to practice them.

CREATIVITY

The most important way to avoid stifling children's natural creativity is to refrain from rigid control. Children who are constantly directed and molded lose the confidence and spontaneity essential for creative thinking. The following

positive steps can promote creativity (T. M. Amabile, 1983; B. Miller & Gerard, 1979):

■ Provide an environment tailored to a child's special interests and aptitudes. If a child does not show a special interest, offer a variety of experiences and materials.

■ Set an example by pursuing absorbing, mentally or artistically stimulating occupations or hobbies.

■ Focus on a child's strengths rather than criticize weaknesses.

■ Encourage nonconforming behavior and help children withstand peer pressure. Parents can do this more easily if they themselves feel secure, are uninhibited and unconventional, and do not gear their behavior to what other people think.

■ Open up children's thinking and let them see new possibilities by exposing them to cultural diversity and to creative people and by deemphasizing traditional gender roles.

■ Respect children and show confidence in their ability by giving them both freedom and responsibilities.

■ Give children warm support, but also give them enough space to breathe and think for themselves.

Today, educators who question the "back-to-basics" approach recommend teaching children in the primary grades in a way that integrates subject matter fields and builds on children's natural interests and talents: teaching reading and writing, for example, in the context of a social studies project or teaching math concepts through the study of music. They favor cooperative projects, hands-on experience, use of concrete materials to solve problems, and close parent-teacher cooperation (Rescorla, 1991). Many contemporary educators also emphasize a "fourth R": reasoning. Children who are taught thinking skills in the context of academic subject matter (see Box 8-3) perform better on intelligence tests and in school (R. D. Feldman, 1986; Sternberg, 1984, 1985a, 1985c).

Some big-city school systems, such as New York's, Philadelphia's, and Chicago's, are experimenting with small elementary and high school programs, either freestanding or within larger school buildings—small enough for students, teachers, and parents to form a true learning community united by a common vision of good education. Teachers are usually handpicked and are given free rein to put their ideas into practice. The curriculum may have a special focus, such as ethnic studies. Teaching is flexible, innovative, and personalized; teachers work together more closely and get to know students better than in larger schools (Meier, 1995; R. Rossi, 1996). Results in some cases have been promising; in Central Park East, a complex of four small, ethnically diverse elementary and secondary schools in New York's East Harlem, 90 percent of the students finish high school and 9 out of 10 of those go on to college, as compared with an average citywide graduation rate of 50 percent (Meier, 1995).

THE CULTURE

When a minority culture values different behavioral styles than the majority culture does, minority children may be at a disadvantage, both on intelligence tests and in school performance. In the past, these children were considered to be suffering from a cultural *deficit*; today educators refer to cultural *difference,* with its own cognitive and behavioral strengths (Helms, 1992; Tharp, 1989).

The Kamehameha Early Education Program (KEEP) has produced dramatic improvements in primary-grade Hawaiian children's cognitive performance by designing educational programs to fit cultural patterns. Whereas children in non-KEEP classes score very low on standard achievement tests, children in KEEP classes approach national norms. The principles underlying KEEP have also been applied to, or suggested for, other minorities.

To help teachers teach in a way that helps children learn, KEEP addresses the following issues:

■ *Social organization of the classroom:* Since Hawaiian culture values collaboration, cooperation, and assisted performance, children are placed in small groups of four to five students, who continually teach and learn from one another. For Navajo children, who are trained in self-sufficiency and are separated by sex from about age 8, groupings are most effectively limited to two or three children of the same sex (Tharp, 1989).

■ *Accommodation for language styles:* Hawaiians typically overlap one another's speech, a style of social involvement often interpreted by non-Hawaiian teachers as rude. At the other extreme, Navajos speak slowly, with frequent silent pauses; non-Navajo teachers often interrupt, misinterpreting such pauses as signaling the end of a response. When teachers adjust their styles of speaking to their students', children participate more freely (Tharp, 1989).

■ *Sensitivity to rhythms:* Both in speech and in movement, cultural groups maintain different tempos. When teachers adopt a rhythm children are familiar with, the children participate more in class and learn better. African American children and adults often interact in back-and-forth "challenge games" involving subtle nuances of meaning (Hale, 1982; Heath, 1989). Such patterns can be adapted to classroom teaching.

■ *Adjustment for learning styles:* Most western teaching stresses verbal and analytic thought. This approach favors Japanese, Chinese, and white Americans, but not Native Americans, who tend to think in visual, holistic patterns and learn at home by imitation, with little verbal instruction. Contrary to typical American classroom practice, Native American parents expect children to listen to an entire story without interruption before discussing it. Teachers can help children by acknowledging culturally different learning styles and helping children adjust to an unfamiliar style (Tharp, 1989).

✔ CHILDREN WITH SPECIAL EDUCATIONAL NEEDS AND STRENGTHS

Just as educators have become more sensitive to teaching children from varied cultural backgrounds, they have also sought to meet the needs of children with special abilities and disabilities.

CHILDREN WITH LEARNING PROBLEMS

Three of the most frequent sources of learning problems are mental retardation, attention deficit disorders, and learning disabilities.

Mental Retardation

Mental retardation is significantly subnormal intellectual functioning. It is indicated by an IQ of about 70 or less, coupled with a deficiency in age-appropriate adaptive behavior (such as communication, social skills, and self-care), appearing before age 18. About 1 percent of the population are mentally retarded; about 3 boys are affected for every 2 girls (APA, 1994).

In about 30 to 40 percent of cases, the cause of mental retardation is unknown. Known causes include problems in embryonic development, such as those caused by a mother's alcohol or drug use (30 percent); mental disorders, such as autism, and environmental influences, such as lack of nurturance (15 to 20 percent); problems in pregnancy and childbirth, such as fetal malnutrition or birth trauma (10 percent); hereditary conditions, such as Tay-Sachs disease (5 percent); and medical problems in childhood, such as trauma or lead poisoning (5 percent) (APA, 1994).

With a supportive and stimulating early environment and continued guidance and help, many mentally retarded children can expect a reasonably good outcome. Most mentally retarded children can benefit from schooling.

Hyperactivity and Attention Deficits

Johnny cannot sit still, finish a simple task, or keep a friend, and he is always in trouble. He may be suffering from *attention-deficit/hyperactivity disorder (ADHD).* ADHD is the psychiatric condition most commonly diagnosed in children ("Attention Deficit Disorder—Part II," 1995). It is marked by persistent inattention, impulsivity, low tolerance for frustration, distractibility, and a great deal of activity at the wrong time and the wrong place, such as the classroom. These characteristics appear to some degree in all children; but in about 3 to 5 percent of school-age children, they are so frequent and severe as to interfere with the child's functioning in school and in daily life (AAP Committee on Children with Disabilities and Committee on Drugs, 1996; APA, 1994). Although some symptoms appear earlier, the disorder is often not recognized until the child starts school. However, a new test using computer measures of body movement and attention seems to be a reliable, objective indicator (Teicher et al., 1996). Boys are 4 to 9 times as likely to be diagnosed as girls (APA, 1994), perhaps because girls' behavior may be less disruptive. More than 1 out of 4 learning-disabled children has ADHD (Roush, 1995; Zametkin, 1995).

ADHD seems to be at least partly inherited; in 1 out of 4 diagnosed cases, a biological parent also

has the syndrome (APA, 1994; Zametkin, 1995). Various hypotheses point to neurological, biochemical, and environmental factors, including such toxins as lead (G. Weiss, 1990; Zametkin, 1995). The disorder is now believed to be caused by an irregularity in brain functioning in the region that inhibits impulses (Rosen, 1996). Family conflict, provoked or exacerbated by a hyperactive child, may compound the problem ("Attention Deficit Disorder—Part II," 1995). Research has failed to substantiate any link between ADHD and food additives, such as artificial colorings and flavorings and the sugar substitute aspartame (B. A. Shaywitz et al., 1994; Zametkin, 1995).

If untreated, ADHD can lead to extreme frustration, alienation, failure in school, antisocial behavior, or substance abuse (Zametkin, 1995). By age 15 most hyperactive children continue to show poor cognitive skills and disruptive behavior (McGee, Partridge, Williams, & Silva, 1991). As adults, many have high rates of job changes, marital disruption, traffic accidents, and trouble with the law (B. Henker & Whalen, 1989).

ADHD is generally treated with drugs, combined with behavioral modification (see Chapter 1), counseling, and proper classroom placement. In about 70 to 80 percent of cases, stimulants such as Ritalin can help children concentrate and reduce antisocial behavior, but they do not seem to improve long-range academic achievement; and the effects of drug treatment on a particular child are uncertain. Drugs should not be used in isolation, without other treatments, and should be discontinued if clear improvement does not occur (AAP Committee on Children with Disabilities and Committee on Drugs, 1996; McDaniel, 1986; "Ritalin Improves Behavior," 1995; Zametkin, 1995).

Parents and teachers can help hyperactive children by providing structure and routine; teaching the child to break up work into small, manageable segments; asking repeated, direct questions about the child's behavior and its effects; alternating study with physical activity; avoiding timed tests; and offering alternative ways of demonstrating learning, such as conferences or tape-recorded instead of written reports (AAP Committee on Children with Disabilities and Committee on Drugs, 1996; "Attention Deficit Disorder—Part II," 1995; M. A. Stewart & Olds, 1973).

Learning Disabilities

Nelson Rockefeller, former vice president of the

United States, had so much trouble reading that he ad-libbed speeches instead of using a script. The inventor Thomas Edison never learned how to spell or write grammatically. General George Patton, a World War II hero, read poorly and got through West Point by memorizing entire lectures (Schulman, 1986). All these people apparently suffered from *dyslexia,* a developmental reading disorder in which reading achievement is at least 2 years below the level predicted by IQ.

Dyslexia is the most commonly diagnosed of a large number of **learning disabilities (LDs),** disorders that interfere with specific aspects of school achievement, resulting in performance substantially lower than would be expected given a child's age, intelligence, and amount of schooling (APA, 1994). A growing number of children are identified as learning-disabled—2.3 million in the 1992–1993 school year (Roush, 1995). Learning-disabled (LD) children often have near-average or higher-than-average intelligence and normal vision and hearing, but they seem to have trouble processing sensory information. They tend to be less task-oriented and more easily distracted than other children; they are less organized as learners and less likely to use memory strategies (Feagans, 1983). Because success in school is important for self-esteem, learning disabilities can have devastating effects on the psyche as well as on the report card.

Estimates of the prevalence of dyslexia range from 3 to 20 percent of the school population, and there is disagreement about its definition and causes; some observers claim that what looks like dyslexia is often the result of poor teaching. Dyslexia affects boys and girls equally. It is more common in children from large families and in lower socioeconomic levels and may be at least partly genetic (Barinaga, 1996a; Council on Scientific Affairs of the American Medical Association, 1989; DeFries, Fulker, & LaBuda, 1987; Roush, 1995; S. E. Shaywitz, Shaywitz, Fletcher, & Escobar, 1990; Tallal et al., 1996; Tashman, 1995). Dyslexics seem to have trouble matching written words with speech sounds or breaking down words into sounds. They often confuse up with down and left with right; thus they may read *saw* for *was.* This may be because their brains do not process fast-paced sensory information rapidly enough or because of a defect in the pathway between the eyes and the brain (Barinaga, 1996a; Lehmkuhle, Garzia, Turner, Hash, & Baro, 1993; Roush, 1995).

Dyslexia may be part of a generalized language impairment ("Dyslexia," 1989; Tallal et al., 1996). Language-impaired children are late in starting to talk, have trouble understanding what people say, speak and write unclearly, and have limited memory for verbal material. Some researchers have found subtle variations in brain structure and activity in language-impaired people, but it is not clear what role these differences may play or whether they are the causes or the effects of early learning problems (Hynd & Semrud-Clikeman, 1989; Merzenich et al., 1996; Roush, 1995).

Some children who have difficulty with language learning may be unable to hear differences between certain sounds (Barinaga, 1996b). One research team (Kraus et al., 1996) measured brain-wave activity of 6- to 15-year-old children who had been diagnosed as having learning disabilities or attention deficit disorders, or both, and who had trouble distinguishing such sounds as "da" and "ga." These children's auditory brain waves showed no change—as the brain waves of normal children did—when "ga" was piped into their ears following a string of "da's."

A training technique using computerized games and listening exercises shows promise of helping children who have difficulty distinguishing briefly spoken consonant sounds (such as "ba" in "banana"). In a series of studies, children were asked to recognize or reproduce sound sequences or to follow spoken commands in which short consonant sounds were stretched out and accentuated. The children also listened to taped stories with similarly modified sounds. After 4 weeks of training, 5- to 10-year-old language-impaired children gained 1 to 2 years in ability to make out normal speech, and these gains were maintained 6 weeks later. A control group, trained without the modified speech sounds, showed much less improvement (Merzenich et al., 1996; Tallal et al., 1996). Further research is needed to determine whether such training can help language-impaired children in general—not just those with this particular impairment (Barinaga, 1996a).

Mathematical disabilities may be even more common than reading disabilities, with which they are often associated; yet they have been relatively neglected. Math disabilities involve difficulty in counting, comparing numbers, calculating, and remembering basic arithmetic facts. One cause may be a neurological deficit, which may be partly inherited. Some children, however, have problems with arithmetic because they haven't learned it properly, because they are anxious or have trouble reading or hearing directions, or because of a developmental delay, which eventually disappears (Geary, 1993; Roush, 1995). Other learning disorders affect different aspects of learning. For example, poor coordination of fine motor movements can interfere with the ability to write.

Children generally do not outgrow learning disabilities but can learn to cope with them. Children at high risk of a poor outcome are those who had low birthweight or birth trauma, are malnourished, have difficult temperaments, or grow up in poor, chaotic families (M. D. Levine, 1987). Supportive adults can help these children organize their lives, learn to concentrate, improve basic skills, and use cognitive strategies. Children whose disabilities are discovered and dealt with early do best; if dyslexia, for example, is diagnosed before third grade, the prognosis is better. Certain other factors are also beneficial: temperamental traits that draw other people toward the child, good self-esteem, and opportunities at school, work, or elsewhere to develop competence and confidence ("Dyslexia," 1989; M. D. Levine, 1987; Werner, 1993).

Educating Children with Disabilities

The Individuals with Disabilities Education Act (IDEA) assures a free, appropriate public education for all children with disabilities in the United States. More than half (51 percent) of covered children are learning-disabled, 22 percent are speech-impaired, 11 percent are mentally retarded, and 9 percent have serious emotional disturbances (Terman, Larner, Stevenson, & Behrman, 1996).

Under the law, an individualized program must be designed for each child, with parental involvement. Children must be educated in the "least restrictive environment" appropriate to their needs: that means, whenever possible, the regular classroom. Most of these students can be served by "inclusion" programs, in which they are integrated with nondisabled youngsters for all or part of the day. Inclusion can help children with disabilities learn to get along in society and can let nondisabled children know and understand people with disabilities.

Critics maintain that children with disabilities can be taught better and more humanely in small, separate classes with specially trained teachers. Inclusion requires sophisticated teaching techniques, and not all teachers can meet the challenge. Many, however, have effectively taught mixed classes

This wheelchair-bound third-grader gets computerized instruction along with nondisabled classmates. "Inclusion" programs, in which children with disabilities learn in the regular classroom for all or part of the day, give disabled and nondisabled children an opportunity to learn how to get along with and understand each other. *(Lawrence Migdale/Photo Researchers, Inc.)*

with the help of teachers' aides, individual tutors, and computers (D. Thomas, 1985).

GIFTED, CREATIVE, AND TALENTED CHILDREN

At age 12, Balamurati Krishna Ambati was a third-year premedical student at New York University. He had mastered calculus at age 4, had scored 750 on the math SAT at age 10, and hoped to be a doctor before age 18 (Stanley, 1990). Although his parents encouraged his achievements from the beginning, his teachers urged him to slow down and his peers have not always understood his drive to excel.

Giftedness can be a mixed blessing. Like intelligence, it also is hard to define and measure. Although there is little doubt that some children are gifted, educators disagree on how many qualify and on what basis, and what kinds of educational programs they need. The relationship between giftedness, creativity, and artistic talent is also unclear; creativity and talent are sometimes viewed as aspects or types of giftedness and sometimes as independent qualities (Hunsaker & Callahan, 1995). According to Sternberg (1985a; J. E. Davidson & Sternberg, 1984), gifted children process information with unusual efficiency, especially on novel (creative) tasks requiring insight. Another influential theorist, Joseph Renzulli, sees giftedness as the product of above-average cognitive ability, creativity, and *task commitment,* or motivation (Renzulli, 1978).

The traditional criterion of giftedness is an IQ score of 130 or higher (Horowitz & O'Brien, 1986). This criterion tends to exclude highly creative children (whose unusual answers often lower their test scores), children from minority groups (whose abilities may not be well developed, though the potential is there), and children with aptitudes in specific areas.

Most states have adopted a broader definition presented by a congressional commission in the early 1970s: "Gifted and talented children are those, identified by professionally qualified persons, who by virtue of outstanding abilities are capable of high performance" (Marland, 1972, p. 2). This definition includes children who have shown high potential or achievement in one or more of the following areas: general intellect, specific aptitude (such as in mathematics or science), creative or productive thinking, leadership, talent in the arts (such as painting, writing, or acting), and psychomotor ability.

The Lives of Gifted Children

A classic longitudinal study of gifted children began in the 1920s, when Lewis Terman (who brought the Binet intelligence test to the United States) identified more than 1,500 California children with IQs of 135 or higher. The study demolished the widespread stereotype of the bright child as a puny, pasty-faced bookworm. These children were taller, healthier, better-coordinated, better-adjusted, and more popular than the average child (Wallach & Kogan, 1965); and their cognitive, scholastic, and vocational superiority has held up for more than 70 years. They were 10 times more likely than a comparison group to graduate from college and 3 times more likely to be elected to honorary societies such as Phi Beta Kappa. By midlife, they were highly represented in such listings as *Who's Who in America.* At a time when men were expected to be the family breadwinner, almost 90 percent of the men were in the professions or in higher echelons of business (Terman & Oden, 1959). The lives of these people show that intelligence tests can spot children with promise and that cognitively gifted children tend to fulfill that promise. (In Chapter 17, we discuss

recent findings about the Terman sample in late life.)

Three elements essential to the flowering of gifts and talents seem to be inborn ability, a drive to excel, and recognition and encouragement by adults (B. S. Bloom, 1985). Children identified as gifted tend to have well-educated, well-to-do, emotionally supportive, happily married parents who spend time with them, answer their questions, and encourage their curiosity. The homes of underachieving gifted children are often less harmonious. Gifted children tend to be relatively mature in their social relationships and moral reasoning; but two groups of gifted children tend to have social and emotional problems—those with IQs over 180 and those with high IQs who do not do well in school. The problems of both groups seem to stem in part from unsatisfactory schooling: inflexibility, overemphasis on grades, lack of challenge, and unsupportive teachers (Janos & Robinson, 1985).

Defining, Measuring, and Fostering Creativity

One definition of *creativity* is the ability to see things in a new light—to produce something never seen before or to discern problems others fail to recognize and find new and unusual solutions. IQ does not predict creative achievement: Terman's group never produced a great musician, an exceptional painter, or a Nobel prize winner. Classic research that found only modest correlations between creativity and IQ (Getzels, 1964, 1984; Getzels & Jackson, 1962) suggests that creative thinking requires different abilities from those needed to do well in school (Renzulli & McGreevy, 1984).

IQ tests measure *convergent thinking,* the ability to give a single correct answer. Tests of creativity seek to measure *divergent thinking,* the ability to come up with a wide array of novel possibilities (Guilford, 1967). The *Torrance Tests of Creative Thinking* (Torrance, 1966, 1974; Torrance & Ball, 1984), for example, include such tasks as listing unusual uses for a paper clip, completing a figure, and telling what a sound brings to mind. One problem with these tests is that the score depends partly on speed, which is not a hallmark of creativity. Furthermore, although the tests are fairly reliable (they yield consistent results), there is little evidence that they are valid—that children who do well on them are creative in real life (Anastasi, 1988; Mansfield & Busse, 1981; Simonton,

1990). Divergent thinking may not be the only important factor in creativity. More research needs to be done to identify youngsters who will be creative adults (see Chapter 14).

Very young children are imaginative in their stories, drawings, and play, but many do not remain so. Watching television may hinder creativity (Valkenburg & van der Voort, 1994). Adults may stifle creativity by telling children not to color outside the lines and not to make clouds blue and grass red (Gardner, 1983). Children are more creative when parents and teachers are open to unconventional questions ("Do rocks grow?"), welcome and praise original ideas, and do not grade everything a child does (Torrance in Chance & Fischman, 1987). (Refer back to Box 8-3 for other ways to encourage creativity.)

Educating Gifted, Creative, and Talented Children

In the United States, the achievement of the most promising students lags behind that in other technologically advanced countries (Feldhusen & Moon, 1992). To benefit these children and society as a whole, many parents and educators advocate special education to make the most of gifted children's abilities and to meet their needs for intellectual stimulation. Opponents to devoting extra resources to able youngsters say money and effort should go toward educational improvements for all students.

Most states have officially recognized programs for the gifted and talented, but the economic recession of the early 1990s resulted in cutbacks in many communities (Purcell, 1995). These programs take two main approaches: enrichment and acceleration. *Enrichment* broadens and deepens knowledge and skills through extra classroom activities, research projects, field trips, or coaching by mentors (experts in a child's field of talent or interest). *Acceleration,* often recommended for highly gifted children, speeds up their education, moving them through the curriculum quickly. This may be done by skipping grades, by accelerated classes, by special schools, or by advanced classes in specific subjects, taken by correspondence or at a nearby high school, college, or university. Some educators fear that emphasis on rapid cognitive development may put these children under social and emotional pressure, but research suggests that this concern is largely unfounded (VanTassel-Baska, 1992).

Many school districts use multiple criteria for admission to programs for the gifted, including achievement test scores, grades, classroom performance, creative production, parent and teacher nominations, and student interviews; but IQ remains an important, and sometimes the determining, factor (Reis, 1989). Some educators advocate inclusion of more students—perhaps 25 percent—in flexible programs tailored to individual needs (J. Cox, Daniel, & Boston, 1985; R. D. Feldman, 1985).

There is no firm dividing line between being gifted and not being gifted, creative and not creative. All children benefit from being encouraged in their areas of interest and ability. What we learn about fostering intelligence, creativity, and talent in the most able youngsters may help all children make the most of their potential. The degree to which they do this will affect their self-concept and other aspects of personality, as we discuss in Chapter 9.

✔ SUMMARY

ASPECTS OF PHYSICAL DEVELOPMENT

- ■ Physical development is less rapid in middle childhood than in the earlier years. Boys are slightly larger than girls at the beginning of this period, but girls undergo the growth spurt of adolescence sooner and thus tend to be larger than boys at the end.
- ■ Obesity is increasingly common among American children. It is influenced by genetic and environmental factors and can be treated.
- ■ Motor development enables school-age children to participate in a wider range of motor activities than preschoolers. From ages 7 to 11, rough-and-tumble play diminishes as children engage in games with rules. Differences in boys' and girls' motor abilities increase as puberty approaches, in part due to boys' greater strength and in part due to cultural expectations and experience.

HEALTH, FITNESS, AND SAFETY

- ■ Middle childhood is a relatively healthy period; most children are immunized against major illnesses, and the death rate is lowest in the life span.

■ Children today are less fit than in earlier years. Developing lifetime fitness habits and skills is important.

■ Respiratory infections and other common health problems tend to be of short duration. Most children this age are free of chronic medical conditions, but the prevalence of such maladies has increased.

■ Vision becomes keener in middle childhood; fewer than 16 percent of children have defective vision or hearing.

■ Accidents are the leading cause of death in middle childhood. Most childhood accidents occur in or from automobiles, or at home.

THE CONCRETE OPERATIONAL CHILD

■ The child from about age 7 to age 12 is in the Piagetian stage of concrete operations and can use thinking to solve concrete problems. Children are less egocentric than before and are more proficient at tasks requiring logical reasoning, such as conservation, classification, working with numbers, and distinguishing fantasy from reality.

■ According to Piaget, moral development is linked with cognitive maturation and occurs in two stages. The first, morality of constraint, is characterized by moral rigidity. The second, morality of cooperation, is characterized by moral flexibility.

ASPECTS OF COGNITIVE DEVELOPMENT

■ Memory improves greatly during middle childhood because information-processing time decreases, attention and short-term memory capacity increase, and children become more adept at using mnemonic strategies such as external aids, rehearsal, organization, and elaboration. Metamemory (understanding the way memory works) also improves.

■ The intelligence of school-age children is assessed by group tests (such as the Otis-Lennon School Ability Test) and individual tests (such as the WISC-III, Stanford-Binet, and K-ABC). IQ tests are good predictors of school success but may underestimate the intelligence of some children.

■ Differences in IQ between ethnic groups appear to result primarily from environmental and cultural differences. Attempts to devise "culture-free" or "culture-fair" tests have not been successful.

■ Children's understanding of increasingly complex syntax develops at least up to age 9, and understanding of processes of communication improves. Interaction with peers aids in the development of literacy.

■ The most effective second-language programs appear to be high-quality programs which encourage bilingual fluency.

INFLUENCES OF SCHOOL ACHIEVEMENT

■ Children's characteristics, such as temperament and emotional state, influence school performance.

■ Parents influence children's learning by motivating them to achieve, becoming involved in their schooling, and transmitting attitudes and beliefs about learning.

■ Teachers' attitudes influence children's success in school. Self-fulfilling prophecies may limit the achievement of poor and minority children.

■ Minority children can benefit from educational programs adapted to their cultural styles.

CHILDREN WITH SPECIAL EDUCATIONAL NEEDS AND STRENGTHS

■ Mental retardation has a variety of causes. Most retarded people can benefit from schooling at least up to sixth grade.

■ Learning disabilities, which interfere with learning to read and other school tasks, may be due to problems in processing sensory information.

■ Hyperactivity and attention-deficit disorders are more common in boys than in girls and, unless treated, can lead to serious problems in school and in adult life.

■ In the United States, every child with disabilities is entitled to a free, appropriate education. Children must be educated in the least restrictive environment possible—which often means in the regular classroom.

■ An IQ of 130 or higher is a common standard for identifying gifted children for special programs. Broader definitions of giftedness include creativity, artistic talent, and other abilities and rely on multiple criteria for identification. Creativity is sometimes identified by tests of divergent thinking, but their validity is questionable.

■ Although Terman's study found that gifted children tend to be unusually successful adults, these children may need special educational programs to help them reach their full potential.

✔ KEY TERMS

obesity (page 264)
body image (264)
rough-and-tumble play (265)
acute medical conditions (268)
chronic medical conditions (268)
concrete operations (270)
horizontal décalage (271)
class inclusion (271)
seriation (271)
transitive inference (272)
morality of constraint (272)
morality of cooperation (272)
working memory (274)
metamemory (274)
mnemonic strategies (274)

external memory aids (275)
rehearsal (275)
organization (275)
elaboration (275)
Otis-Lennon School Ability Test
    (276)
Wechsler Intelligence Scale for
    Children (WISC-III) (276)
Kaufman Assessment Battery for
    Children (K-ABC) (276)
cultural bias (278)
culture-free test (280)
culture-fair tests (280)
metacommunication (280)
English-immersion (282)

bilingual education (282)
bilingual (282)
code switching (283)
self-fulfilling prophecy (286)
mental retardation (288)
attention-deficit/hyperactivity
    disorder (ADHD) (289)
dyslexia (290)
learning disabilities (LDs) (290)
creativity (292)
convergent thinking (292)
divergent thinking (292)
Torrance Tests of Creative Thinking
    (292)

✔ QUESTIONS FOR THOUGHT AND DISCUSSION

1   Is intelligence related to how well a person adapts to the dominant culture, or should intelligence tests be designed to take a minority culture into account?

2   Can you think of an example in your own life of a self-fulfilling prophecy?

3   Which approach to education do you consider most successful for children in the primary grades: instruction in the "basics," or a more flexible, child-centered curriculum?

4   How would you define and assess giftedness? Should schools actively seek out gifted students and give them special learning opportunities?

CHAPTER NINE

PSYCHOSOCIAL DEVELOPMENT IN MIDDLE CHILDHOOD

Have you ever felt like nobody?
Just a tiny speck of air.
When everyone's around you,
And you are just not there.

Karen Crawford, age 9

ASK YOURSELF

✔ How do children develop a realistic self-concept?

✔ What are the sources of self-esteem?

✔ What changes in family relationships occur in middle childhood?

✔ What are the effects of parents' work, divorce, remarriage, and sexual orientation?

✔ How do siblings influence one another?

✔ What are the functions of the peer group?

✔ What influences popularity, and how do children develop friendships?

✔ What are some common childhood emotional disturbances, and how are they treated?

✔ What enables "resilient" children to withstand stress?

When a fourth grade teacher put together a collection of her students' verse, the themes reflected the children's reactions to everyday experiences. Laurie's poem told how her mother cared for her when she hurt her knee or got a "D" on her report card or had a nightmare. Billy's poem extolled the pleasures of popcorn; Jennifer's told of running to her room and slamming the door after a family quarrel; Jeff's cheerfully ticked off his parents' complaints about his table manners; and Marcie's recalled how she had cried when her father and mother made her take her pet frog back to the pond. Terry's confessed to an occasional urge to hit his pesty little brother, and Dina's revealed the "funny feeling" she got in her stomach right after a test.

■ In this chapter, we trace the rich and varied emotional and social lives of school-age children, and we look at personality changes that accompany physical and cognitive growth. We see how youngsters develop a more realistic concept of themselves and how they become more independent of parents and more involved with other children. Through being with peers, they make discoveries about their own attitudes, values, and skills. Still, the family remains a vital influence, and children's lives are profoundly affected by such family issues as parental employment, divorce, and remarriage. Although most children are healthy, some suffer emotional disorders; we look at some of these. We also describe resilient children, who emerge from the stresses of childhood healthier and stronger. ■

✔ THE DEVELOPING SELF

At age 6, Anna became a "published author" when she and her fellow first-graders wrote and illustrated their own books. Anna's opinion of herself went up several notches when she saw her book, "Anna in Outer Space," exhibited for all to see. At age 10, Anna's self-concept has expanded to include her proficiency in swimming as well as her reputation as the "class artist."

The self-concept develops continuously from infancy on. The cognitive growth that takes place during middle childhood enables youngsters to develop more realistic and more complex concepts of themselves and of their ability to survive and succeed in their culture. Self-esteem develops as children begin to see themselves as valuable members of society.

REPRESENTATIONAL SYSTEMS: A NEO-PIAGETIAN VIEW

"At school I'm feeling pretty smart in certain subjects, Language Arts and Social Studies," said 8-year-old Lisa. "I got A's in these subjects on my last report card and was really proud of myself. But I'm feeling really dumb in Arithmetic and Science, particularly when I see how well the other kids are doing. . . . I still like myself as a person, because Arithmetic and Science just aren't that important to me. How I look and how popular I am are more important" (Harter, 1993, p. 2).

Around age 7 or 8, children reach the third of the neo-Piagetian stages of self-concept development described in Chapter 7. They now have the cognitive ability to form *representational systems:* broad, inclusive self-concepts that integrate different features of the self (Harter, 1993). Lisa no longer focuses on a single dimension of herself ("I am smart" or "I am popular" or "I am pretty") but on many. She has outgrown an all-or-nothing, black-or-white self-definition; she recognizes that she can be "smart" in certain subjects and "dumb" in others. Her self-descriptions are more balanced; she can verbalize her self-concept better, and she can weigh different aspects of it ("How I look and how popular I am are more important. . . "). She can compare her *real self* with her *ideal self* and can judge how well she measures up to the social standards she has taken into her self-concept. Her view of herself is important to the development of self-esteem, her assessment of her personal worth ("I like myself as a person").

SELF-ESTEEM AND ITS SOURCES

Kendall has high self-esteem. He is confident, curious, and independent. He trusts his own ideas, approaches challenges and initiates new activities with confidence, describes himself positively, and takes pride in his work. He adjusts fairly easily to change, tolerates frustration, perseveres in pursuing a goal, and can handle criticism. Kerry, by contrast, has low self-esteem. He describes himself negatively, does not trust his own ideas, lacks confidence and pride in his work, sits apart from other children, and hangs back and watches instead of exploring on his own. He gives up easily when frustrated and reacts immaturely to stress.

Self-esteem, or *global self-worth,* is an important component of personality. Children with high self-esteem tend to be cheerful; those with low self-esteem are likely to be depressed (Harter, 1990). A depressed mood can lower energy level, which can affect how well a child does in school and elsewhere, leading to a downward spiral in self-esteem. Children with low self-esteem often retain a negative self-image long after childhood has been left behind.

According to Erikson (1982), a major determinant of self-esteem is children's view of their capacity for productive work; the issue to be resolved in the crisis of middle childhood is *industry versus inferiority.* The "virtue" that develops with successful resolution of this crisis is *competence,* a view of the self as able to master skills and complete tasks.

Children have to learn skills valued in their society. Arapesh boys in New Guinea learn to make bows and arrows and to lay traps for rats; Arapesh girls learn to plant, weed, and harvest. Inuit children of Alaska learn to hunt and fish. Children in industrialized countries learn to read, write, count, and use computers. Children compare their abilities with those of their peers; if they feel inadequate, they may retreat to the protective embrace of the family. If, on the other hand, they become *too* industrious, says Erikson, they may neglect social relationships and turn into "workaholics."

Middle childhood, according to Erikson, is a time for learning the skills one's culture considers important. In driving geese to market, this Vietnamese girl is developing a sense of competence and gaining self-esteem. In addition, by taking on responsibilities to match her growing capabilities, she learns about how her society works, her role in it, and what it means to do a job well. *(M. Justice/The Image Works)*

Another view of the sources of self-esteem comes from research by Susan Harter (1985, 1990, 1993). Harter (1985) asked 8- to 12-year olds about their appearance, behavior, school performance, athletic ability, and acceptance by other children. The children rated themselves and assessed how much each of these five domains affected their opinion of themselves. They also answered questions about how much they liked themselves, how happy they were with the way they were, and how parents, teachers, classmates, and close friends treated them.

Among the five domains, the children rated physical appearance most important. Social acceptance came next. Less critical were schoolwork, conduct, and athletics. In contrast, then, to the high value Erikson placed on mastery of skills, Harter's research suggests that school-age children judge themselves (as Lisa did) more by good looks and popularity. The greatest contributor to self-esteem, however, seems to be how much social support a child feels—first, from parents and classmates, then from friends and teachers. Do these important people like and care about the child? Do they treat the child as a person who matters and has valuable things to say? Still, social support will not compensate for a poor self-evaluation. If Juanita thinks sports are important but that she is not athletic, she will lose self-esteem no matter how much praise she gets from family and friends. On the other hand, even if Mike thinks it's important to be handsome and smart and considers himself both, his self-esteem will suffer if he does not feel valued by his family and other important people.

Both emotional and cognitive development contribute to self-esteem. By age 7 or 8, children can fully internalize shame and pride (see Chapter 7); and these complex emotions, which depend on awareness of the implications of their actions and on what kind of socialization children have received, affect their opinion of themselves (Harter, 1993).

✔ THE CHILD IN THE FAMILY

School-age children spend more time away from home than when they were younger; yet home and the people who live there remain the most important part of their world. According to some research, parents in the United States spend only 30 minutes of the average workday interacting with their school-age children (Demo, 1992). Children spend much more time with their peers. Counting minutes and hours, however, can be deceptive. Most parents continue to be highly supportive, loving, and involved with their children.

Among 199 mostly middle-class fifth- and sixth-graders, relationships with parents were the most important ones in their lives. The children looked to their parents for affection, guidance, dependable and lasting bonds, and affirmation of competence or personal value. Most important after parents were grandparents, who were seen as warm and supportive, offering affection and enhancing self-worth (Furman & Buhrmester, 1985).

As children's lives change, so do the issues between them and their parents. Many parents wonder how involved they should be in a child's school life. They wonder what to do about a child who complains about the teacher or misbehaves in school. They worry about where children are, and with whom, when they are not in school. Disagreements often arise over household chores and allowance.

Of course, many of these issues are irrelevant in societies in which children must work to help the family survive. To understand the child in the family we need to look at the family environment—its structure and atmosphere; but these in turn are influenced by what goes on beyond the walls of the home. As Bronfenbrenner points out (see Chapter 1), additional layers of influence—including parents' work and socioeconomic status and societal trends such as divorce and remarriage—help shape the family environment and, thus, children's development. Beyond these influences are overarching cultural values that define rhythms of family life and roles of family members. Let's look first at these.

THE CULTURAL CONTEXT: FAMILY RELATIONSHIPS AND ROLES

Different ethnic groups have distinct adaptive strategies—cultural patterns that promote group survival and well-being and affect how children are socialized. African American, Native American, Asian-Pacific American, and Hispanic families emphasize group values (such as loyalty) more than the individualistic ones (autonomy, competition, and self-reliance) stressed in western cultures. Children in these minority families are encouraged to cooperate, share, and develop interdependence. Social roles tend to be more flexible. Because of economic need, adults more often share bread-

Although school-age children spend less time at home than before, parents continue to be very important in children's lives. Affectionate parents who enjoy being with their children, like Anna's father, Jonathan, tend to raise children who feel good about themselves—and about their parents. *(Erika Stone)*

winning; and children assume more responsibility for younger brothers and sisters. The *extended family* (a multigenerational family consisting, not only of parents and children, but also of more distant relatives—grandparents, aunts, uncles, and cousins) provides close ties and strong support systems. These kinfolk are more likely than in white families to live in a child's household and interact daily with the child (Harrison, Wilson, Pine, Chan, & Buriel, 1990).

These cultural patterns affect developmental ones. In a survey of 333 African American, Latino, and white schoolchildren ages 7 to 14, extended family members became increasingly important to older children as a bridge to the wider social world. African American and Latino children were more likely than white children to include extended family in their inner circle of support (Levitt, Guacci-Franco, & Levitt, 1993). As we look at the child in the family, then, we need to be aware of cultural differences.

PARENTING SCHOOL-AGE CHILDREN: COREGULATION AND DISCIPLINE

During the course of childhood, control of behavior gradually shifts from parents to child. A preschooler's acquisition of self-control and self-regulation reduces the need for constant supervision, but not until adolescence or even later are many young people permitted to decide how late to stay out, who their friends should be, and how to spend their money.

Middle childhood is a transitional stage of *coregulation,* in which parent and child share power: parents oversee, but children make moment-by-moment decisions (Maccoby, 1984). Coregulation reflects social aspects of the child's developing self-concept. As children begin to coordinate what they want with what society demands, they are more likely to anticipate how other people will react to what they do or to accept a reminder from parents that others will think better of them if they behave differently. Children are more likely to follow their parents' wishes when they recognize that the parents are fair and have the family's well-being at heart and that they may "know better" because of experience. It also helps if parents try to defer to children's growing judgment and take strong stands only on important issues.

Coregulation is a cooperative process; it can succeed only if parents and children communicate clearly. If children do not let their parents know where they are, what they are doing, and what their problems are—or if parents become preoccupied with their own activities and do not pay attention to their children's—the parents will not be able to judge when to step in. To make this transitional phase work, parents need to influence their children when the children are with them and to monitor their behavior when they are not, either by phone or through a baby-sitter. Children also must learn to monitor their *own* behavior: to adopt acceptable standards, avoid undue risks, and recognize when they need support or guidance (Maccoby, 1984).

The shift to coregulation affects how parents handle *discipline:* the teaching of acceptable behavior. Most parents use somewhat different methods with older children than with younger ones (Maccoby, 1984; Roberts, Block, & Block, 1984). Parents of school-age children are more likely to use inductive techniques that include reasoning. For example, 8-year-old Jared's father points out how his actions affect others: "Hitting Jermaine hurts him and makes him feel bad." In other situations, Jared's parents may appeal to his self-esteem ("What happened to the helpful boy who was here yesterday?"), sense of humor ("If you go one more day without a bath, we'll know when you're coming without looking!"), moral values ("A big, strong boy like you shouldn't sit on the train and let an old person stand"), or appreciation ("Aren't you glad that your father cares enough to remind you to wear boots so that you won't catch a cold?"). Above all, Jared's parents let him know he must bear the consequences of his behavior ("No wonder you missed the school bus today—you stayed up too late last night! Now you'll have to walk to school").

Still, discipline is usually fairly consistent throughout the child-raising years. In one study, parents filled out a questionnaire when their children were 3 years old and again when they were 12 (Roberts et al., 1984). The questions related to independence, control, handling aggression and sex, early training, emphasis on health and achievement, expression of feelings, protectiveness, supervision, and punishment. Over the 9-year period, the parents' basic approach to child rearing seemed to remain constant. Most of them, all along, emphasized rational guidance and praise while using specific techniques appropriate to a child's level of development.

Some use of corporal (physical) punishment is generally considered acceptable or even desirable in the United States ("Spare the rod and spoil the child"). Although it is used less frequently as children get older, one study found that almost 50 percent of early adolescents are still subjected to it (Straus & Donnelly, 1993). Corporal punishment can be stressful for children. The more often it is given, the more likely it is to lead to distress or depression; but even a spanking or slapping once or twice a year can take a toll, according to survey data from a national random sample of 2,000 girls and boys ages 10 to 16 (Turner & Finkelhor, 1996). Physical punishment was more stressful when it came from parents who were usually supportive,

perhaps because children then saw them as unpredictable or because children were less able to "write off" the parents' behavior as "mean" or "unfair" and were more likely to attribute the punishment to their own lack of worth.

FAMILY ATMOSPHERE, PARENTS' WORK, AND POVERTY

The environment in a child's home has two major components. There is the *family structure:* whether there are two parents or one, or someone else raising the child. Then there is the economic, social, and psychological *atmosphere* (Haurin, 1992). Both factors have been affected by changes in family life.

As we will see in a later section, children generally perform better in school and have fewer emotional and behavior problems when they spend their childhood in an intact family with two parents who have a good relationship with each other. However, structure in itself is not the key; how parents get along and their ability to create a favorable environment affect children's adjustment more than does marital status per se (Bray & Hetherington, 1993; Bronstein, Clauson, Stoll, & Abrams, 1993; D. A. Dawson, 1991; Emery, 1988; Hetherington, 1989). The most important influence of the family environment on children's development is the social and psychological atmosphere within the home: whether it is supportive and loving or conflict-ridden and whether there is economic well-being or lack of it (Demo, 1991). Often these two facets are interrelated.

A significant aspect of the atmosphere in the home is the family's socioeconomic status, which largely reflects the work one or both parents do for pay. Parents' work has other, indirect effects on the family atmosphere and thus on children's development. Much of adults' time, effort, and emotional involvement go into their occupations. How do their work and their feelings about it affect children? What happens when parents cannot adequately support the family?

Effects of Mothers' Work

Today, about 3 out of 4 mothers of school-age children are in the work force (Children's Defense Fund, 1996). With more than half of all new mothers going to work soon after giving birth (Bachu, 1993), many children have never known a time when their mothers were *not* working for pay.

In general, research has shown mostly beneficial effects of mothers' employment. However, the impact of a mother's work depends on many factors: the child's age, sex, temperament, and personality; whether the mother works full time or part time; how she feels about her work; whether she has a supportive mate; the family's social and economic status; and the kind of care the child receives (see Box 9-1).

Despite the guilt many employed mothers feel about being away from their children, these women often feel more competent, more economically secure, and more in charge of their lives than mothers who do not work for pay. Their self-esteem, sense of personal effectiveness, and overall well-being tend to be higher than that of full-time homemakers, whose work is generally undervalued in American society (Demo, 1992). The more satisfied a mother is with her life, the more effective she is as a parent; this may be especially true of lower-income women and single mothers with little education.

The division of labor among dual-income couples tend to be different from that in one-paycheck families. Even though the mother typically does more housework and child care, the father is likely to do more of this work than the husband of a full-time homemaker (Almeida, Maggs, & Galambos, 1993; Demo, 1991). He can spend more time with his children, since he is less likely to have a second job. On weekends, both parents spend more time with their children than in families with at-home mothers (Demo, 1992). The father tends to be most involved when the mother works full time and earns close to what he does, when they have more than one child, and when the children are young (L. W. Hoffman, 1986). Daughters of working women and sons of involved fathers have fewer stereotypes about gender roles than children in breadwinner-father, homemaker-mother families (Carlson, 1984); but this effect depends more on the mother's attitude toward the father's participation in home duties than on how much he actually does (G. K. Baruch & Barnett, 1986).

School-age children of employed mothers tend to live in more structured homes than children of full-time homemakers, with clear-cut rules giving them more household responsibilities. They are also encouraged to be more independent. Independence helps girls to become more competent, to achieve more in school, and to have higher self-esteem (Bronfenbrenner & Crouter, 1982).

For boys, the effects of a mother's working vary with socioeconomic status. Both boys and girls in low-income families tend to benefit academically from the more favorable environment a working mother's income can provide (Vandell & Ramanan, 1992). Sons of middle-class working mothers, however, have done less well in school than sons of homemakers (Heyns & Catsambis, 1986). How well parents keep track of their sons may be more important than whether the mother works for pay; in one study, 9- to 12-year-old boys whose parents did not closely monitor their activities earned poorer grades than more closely monitored children (Crouter, MacDermid, McHale, & Perry-Jenkins, 1990).

During school vacations, monitoring becomes harder. Fathers tend to do more monitoring in summer and to be more knowledgeable about children's activities. Mothers who do not work during the summer become more involved with their children then (Crouter & McHale, 1993).

Families with working mothers fit no single pattern. Problems may "stem mainly from the slow pace with which society has adapted to this new family form" (L. W. Hoffman, 1989, p. 290). When good child care is available and affordable, when men assume a large role in the home, and when employers support workers' family roles, children are more likely to do well.

Effects of Fathers' Work

Most studies of the effects of men's work on their families have focused on the nature of the work and how psychologically fulfilling it is, as well as on how work and family roles interact. A New York Times–CBS poll in 1989 found that nearly as large a proportion of working men (72 percent) as of working women (83 percent) feel conflict between their work and family responsibilities.

According to one study, men's family roles are just as important to them as their work roles. Researchers interviewed 300 husbands, ages 25 to 40, in two-earner couples, asking them to evaluate rewards and concerns related to work, marital, and parental roles (Barnett, Marshall, & Pleck, 1992). For example, rewards of the parent role included "seeing your children mature and change"; concerns included "having too many arguments and conflicts with them." Good relationships with wife and children often made up for a poor job experience; but when both job and family roles were unsatisfactory, men tended to feel distress, which might affect the children.

BOX 9-1   PRACTICALLY SPEAKING

AFTER-SCHOOL CARE: WHAT KIND IS BEST?

When Kim, age 11, comes home from school, she unlocks the front door, throws down her books, and feeds her cat before sitting down for her own snack. Then she calls her mother to check in and to report whether she will be staying home, going outside to play, or visiting a friend's home. She may fold laundry, set the table, or start dinner. If she wants to watch television in the evening, she will do her homework in the afternoon.

Kim is among some 2 million *self-care children,* who regularly care for themselves at home without adult supervision because both parents or a single custodial parent works outside the home (C. Cole & Rodman, 1987). Although most self-care takes place after school, some children spend time alone in the morning or evening, too. However, most self-care children are alone for no more than 2 hours a day. Contrary to the stereotyped picture of the "latchkey child" as a lonely, neglected youngster from a poor, single-parent family in a high-risk inner-city setting, many self-care children are in well-educated, middle- to-upper-class suburban or rural families (Cain & Hofferth, 1989).

Children who are not under self-care may be supervised after school by one or both parents or by baby-sitters or relatives. Some go to structured after-school programs, where they do their homework under adult supervision, take music or art lessons, or engage in other activities.

What difference does it make what kind of after-school care a child gets? As in many other aspects of development, there is no simple answer. Among 150 suburban middle-class children, no differences were found between mother-care and self-care children on a number of dimensions (Vandell & Corasaniti, 1988). Both

groups did about the same in classroom work, standardized tests, and parent and teacher ratings, and they were equally popular with other children. Children who went to after-school programs or stayed with baby-sitters tended to get lower school grades, to do worse on tests, and to be less popular. However, the type of care was not necessarily responsible for these children's poorer showing; it's possible that working parents who think their children are having problems may be more likely to see that they are supervised.

The picture seems to be different in low-income neighborhoods. There, both black and white third-graders from single-parent and two-parent families seem to thrive in formal after-school programs (Posner & Vandell, undated). These children get higher grades, have better work habits, and are better-adjusted than children who stay alone or are cared for by their mothers or baby-sitters. However, another examination of after-school care for 390 third- through fifth-graders found that when family income and parental emotional support are controlled, the type of after-school care is less important than the quality of children's experiences with their families (Vandell & Ramanan, 1991).

How can parents tell whether a child is ready for self-care, and how can they make the situation as comfortable as possible (Cole & Rodman, 1987; S. W. Olds, 1989)? Before children take care of themselves, they should be able to control their bodies well enough to keep from injuring themselves; keep track of keys and handle doors well enough to avoid locking themselves in or out; safely operate necessary household equipment; stay alone without being too afraid or lonely; be resourceful enough to handle the unexpected;

This schoolboy letting himself into his home with his own key typifies some 2 million children of working parents who regularly care for themselves after school. Self-care children should have a regular time to check in with a parent by phone and need to know how to reach a responsible adult in an emergency. *(Jeff Dunn/Stock, Boston)*

be responsible enough to follow important rules; understand and remember spoken and written instructions; and read and write well enough to take telephone messages. They should know what to say and do about visitors and callers; for example, they should not tell strangers that they are alone, and they should not open the door to anyone but family and close friends. They should also know how to get help in an emergency: how to call police and firefighters, which friends and neighbors to call, and what other resources to call upon.

Parents and guardians should stay in touch by phone, preferably by setting up a regular time for check-in calls. They should establish safety procedures and tell children what to do and how to reach a responsible adult in an emergency. It is also advisable to set up a schedule to guide children during their self-care time.

A man who is upset about losing his job may nurture his children less and punish them more; and the children may react with emotional or behavior problems and reduced aspirations (McLoyd, 1989, 1990). Of course, not all unemployed fathers act this way. Indeed, some men find the chance to spend more time with their children a positive aspect of being out of work. A man's reactions are tempered by his wife's relationship with him and his children, as well as by the children's personalities and temperaments (Bronfenbrenner & Crouter, 1982).

Poverty and Parenting

Poverty can inspire people to work hard and make a better life for their children—or it can crush their spirits. Vonnie McLoyd's (1990) ecological analysis of the pervasive effects of poverty traces a typical route that leads to adult psychological distress, to effects on child rearing, and finally to effects on children.

Parents who live in poor housing (or have none), who are worried about their next meal, and who feel a lack of control over their lives are likely to become anxious, depressed, and irritable. Their distress leads them to be less affectionate with, and less supportive of, their children—in some cases, even abusive. They discipline inconsistently and arbitrarily, with physical punishment and authoritarian commands rather than explaining, reasoning, and negotiating. They may ignore good behavior and pay attention only to misbehavior. Their children in turn have social, emotional, and behavior problems. They tend to become depressed themselves, to have trouble getting along with peers, to lack self-confidence, and to engage in antisocial acts. Marital conflict may make fathers, especially, more hostile and punitive, particularly toward unattractive or temperamentally difficult children. Parents who can turn to relatives or community representatives for emotional support, help with child care, and child-rearing information often can parent their children more effectively.

This analysis may help explain why power-assertive discipline, including physical punishment, is more common among black families, who are more likely than white families to be poor. It may also help explain academic and behavioral problems. Families under economic stress are less likely to monitor their children's activities, and lack of monitoring is associated with poorer school performance and social adjustment (Bolger, Patterson, Thompson, & Kupersmidt, 1995).

Aggressive behavior tends to be bred from early childhood by a combination of a stressful and unstimulating home atmosphere; harsh discipline; lack of maternal warmth and social support; exposure to aggressive adults and neighborhood violence; and transient peer groups, which prevent stable friendships. Through such negative socializing experiences, children growing up in poor, high-risk surroundings may absorb antisocial attitudes despite their parents' best efforts (Dodge, Pettit, & Bates, 1994).

Lack of financial resources can make it harder for mothers and fathers to support each other in parenting. One study looked at African American 9- to 12-year-olds and their married parents in the rural south, with annual incomes ranging from $2,500 to $57,500. In many of the poor families, parents worked several fatiguing jobs, some of them at night, to make ends meet. These parents were less optimistic and more depressed than parents in better-off families; they found it harder to communicate and cooperate and often fought over child raising. Contradictory parental messages interfered with development of self-regulation and led to behavioral and scholastic problems (Brody et al., 1994).

Effects of poverty are more damaging when it is persistent. One study followed 534 white and African American children in the Charlottesville, Virginia, public schools for 4 years, from middle childhood into early adolescence. In terms of self-esteem, peer relations, and conduct, children from persistently deprived families—regardless of ethnicity—started out behind and stayed behind; boys, especially, tended to show aggressive or antisocial behavior or to become anxious or shy. Children whose families experienced intermittent hardship showed fewer problems, but more than those with no hardship (Bolger et al., 1995).

FAMILY STRUCTURE: TRADITIONAL AND NONTRADITIONAL

In the United States, most children under 18 live with two parents, though this proportion slipped from 76.6 percent in 1980 to 71.9 percent in 1990 (see Figure 9-1). However, barely half of American children live with both *biological* parents—about 56 percent of white children but only 26 percent of African American children and 38 percent of Hispanic children (Furukawa, 1994). Many two-

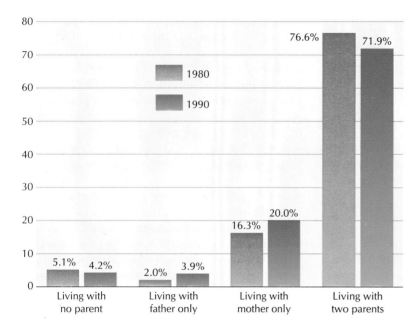

FIGURE 9-1
Living arrangements of children younger than 18 during the decade 1980–1990. Most children under 18 in the United States live with two parents, but this proportion dropped between 1980 and 1990. Many of these two-parent families are stepfamilies. *(Source: Children's Defense Fund, 1994.)*

parent families are stepfamilies, resulting from divorce and remarriage. There also are a growing number of other nontraditional families, including single-parent families and gay and lesbian families.

Intact Families

Much research has found that children tend to do better in traditional, or intact, families—those which include two biological parents or two parents who adopted the child in infancy (Bray & Hetherington, 1993; Bronstein et al., 1993; D. A. Dawson, 1991). In a nationwide study of 17,110 children under 18, those living with single or remarried mothers were more likely than those living with both biological parents to have repeated a grade of school, to have been expelled, to have health problems, or to have been treated for emotional or behavioral troubles in the previous year (D. A. Dawson, 1991). Again, family atmosphere makes a difference. Traditional families do not have to deal with the stress and disruption experienced in families riven by divorce or the death of a parent; with the financial, psychological, and time pressures on single parents; or with the need to adjust to remarriage.

In a smaller study of 136 fifth-graders, those in traditional families were better-adjusted than children in nontraditional families. Traditional parents did more with their children, talked more with them, disciplined them more appropriately and

consistently, and were likely to share parenting responsibilities more cooperatively than nontraditional parents. Deficiencies in family relationships in single-mother households were almost entirely linked to socioeconomic status (Bronstein et al., 1993).

In a traditional family, a father's involvement is usually deeper when there is at least one son. Fathers are more likely to play with, supervise, and discipline sons than daughters. A father's involvement with his children may be a gauge of whether the parents will stay together. When a father is heavily involved, the mother is likely to be more satisfied and to expect the marriage to last (Katzev, Warner, & Acock, 1994).

How couples deal with disagreements is another aspect of family atmosphere; and this, too, influences children's adjustment. In one study, 5-year-olds whose fathers expressed anger by withdrawing emotionally during conflicts with the mother tended to be seen by teachers 3 years later as self-blaming, distressed, and ashamed. Five-year-olds whose parents insulted, mocked, and disparaged each other were likely at age 8 to be disobedient, unwilling to obey rules, and unable to wait their turn. These patterns held true whether or not the parents had separated by then. The children's behavior problems may have been triggered by seeing models of poor conflict resolution or by worry that their parents might break up. Or perhaps these parents behaved negatively with their children as well as with each other (L. F. Katz & Gottman, 1993).

When Parents Divorce

The divorce rate has leveled off since its high point around 1980 (Guyer et al., 1995), but an estimated 50 percent of marriages end in divorce (Bray & Hetherington, 1993). No matter how unhappy a marriage has been, its breakup usually comes as a shock to a child. Children may feel afraid of the future, guilty about their own (usually imaginary) role in causing the divorce, hurt by the parent who moves out, and angry at both parents. Children of divorce tend to have more social, academic, and behavioral problems than children from intact homes; they may become aggressive, hostile, disruptive, disobedient, depressed, or withdrawn and may lose interest in schoolwork and social life (Amato & Keith, 1991a; Hetherington, Stanley-Hagan, & Anderson, 1989).

Different children react differently, of course; reactions are tempered by age and personality, and some children show great resilience (Hetherington, Stanley-Hagan, & Anderson, 1989). This, and the way parents handle the separation and the challenge of raising children alone, may affect children's success in completing six psychological "tasks" of adjusting to divorce (Wallerstein, 1983; Wallerstein & Kelly, 1980). (These are not stages, and may not be completed in order.)

1 *Acknowledging the reality of the marital rupture:* Young children often do not understand what is happening, and many older children initially deny it; but by the end of the first year most children face the facts.
2 *Disengaging from parental conflict and distress and resuming customary pursuits:* At first, children may be so worried that they cannot play, do schoolwork, or take part in other usual activities. After 1 to 1½ years, most children have resumed their own lives.
3 *Resolving loss:* Children need to deal with loss of the parent they are not living with, loss of security in feeling loved and cared for by both parents, loss of familiar daily routines and family traditions—loss of a whole way of life. Some children take years to adjust to these losses. Some never do.
4 *Resolving anger and self-blame:* Some children stay angry at their parents for years. They also may blame themselves, believing the divorce was caused by something they did, or didn't do. When and if they forgive their parents and themselves, they feel more in control of their lives.

5 *Accepting the permanence of divorce:* Some children hold on for years to the fantasy that their parents will be reunited, even after both have remarried. Some children accept the permanence of the breakup only in adolescence or early adulthood.
6 *Achieving realistic hope regarding relationships:* It takes some children many years to risk intimate relationships of their own—to overcome fear of failure. Others never do.

Factors in Children's Adjustment to Divorce

Although divorce is a wrenching experience, the resilience of the human spirit allows many children to come through it with emotional and social skills that serve well in later life. Factors that influence children's adjustment to divorce include how parents handle the separation, custody arrangements, finances, contact with the noncustodial parent, whether and when parents remarry, and the quality of the relationship with a stepparent. A child's age, gender, and temperament also make a difference. Younger children are more anxious at the time of a divorce and have less realistic perceptions of what caused it, but they may adapt more quickly and have fewer bad memories than older children do. Boys and temperamentally difficult children find it especially hard to adjust (Hetherington et al., 1989).

Children's emotional or behavioral problems may stem from conflict between the parents, both before and after divorce, more than from the separation itself (Amato, Kurdek, Demo, & Allen, 1993). When parents argue frequently over child support and custody, children suffer (Donnelly & Finkelhor, 1992). Children whose parents can control their anger, cooperate in parenting, and avoid exposing the children to quarreling are less likely to have problems. Children of authoritative parents usually have fewer problems and do better in school than children of authoritarian or permissive parents (Bray & Hetherington, 1993; Guidubaldi & Perry, 1985; Hetherington, 1987).

Some research suggests that joint custody—custody shared by both parents—does not improve a child's situation in an amicable divorce and may worsen it in a bitter one (Kline, Tschann, Johnston, & Wallerstein, 1988). Children in joint custody seem to have no better relationships with their parents than those in sole custody (Donnelly & Finkelhor, 1992).

Children do better when the custodial parent (typically the mother) provides a stable, struc-

Children of divorce tend to be better adjusted if they have reliable, frequent contact with the noncustodial parent, usually the father. *(C. Boretz/The Image Works)*

tured, and nurturing environment and does not expect the children to act more mature or take on more responsibility than they are ready for (Hetherington et al., 1989). For the first few years following a separation or divorce, the custodial parent may be preoccupied with personal concerns and may be less attentive and responsive to the child (Kline et al., 1991). These effects generally wear off in time, especially if the custodial parent forms a new relationship. Custodial mothers who do not remarry within 6 years tend to have more emotional problems and to be less satisfied with their lives. They may have intense, ambivalent, conflicted relationships with their sons, who tend to show behavior problems. However, these mothers generally have good relationships with their daughters, who are fairly well adjusted (Hetherington, 1987).

Boys, especially, benefit from reliable, frequent contact with the noncustodial parent, typically the father (J. B. Kelly, 1987). The more recent the separation, the closer a divorced father lives to his children, and the higher his socioeconomic status, the more involved he is likely to be (Amato & Keith, 1991a). Fathers who see their children often, help to make child-rearing decisions, and feel that they have some control over their children's upbringing tend to make regular child support payments (Braver et al., 1993).

Friends and family members (especially grandparents and siblings) can offer practical and emotional support to parents and children going through a difficult adjustment to divorce. Schools and day care centers that provide warm, structured environments can be havens of predictability (Hetherington et al., 1989).

Long-Term Effects of Parental Divorce Although most children of divorce adjust reasonably well, some remain troubled after a decade or more. Among thirty-eight 16- to 18-year-olds whose parents had divorced 10 years earlier, three-fourths of the girls and about half of the boys were doing fairly well. Most were in school full time, working part time, law-abiding, and living at home (75 percent with their mothers). The girls were getting along well with their mothers and were likely to be involved in relationships with boys. Boys were more likely to be sad, lonely, emotionally constricted, and inhibited in relationships with girls (Wallerstein, 1987). This study, however, may be of limited validity, since the sample was drawn mostly from white, middle-class families who had expressed interest in psychological counseling and there was no comparison group of nondivorced families.

Effects of divorce can persist beyond childhood. An analysis of 37 studies involving more than 81,000 people found that adult children of divorced parents tend to be slightly more depressed, to have more marital problems, to be in poorer health, and to have lower socioeconomic status than adults who grew up in intact families (Amato & Keith, 1991b). However, the differences were smaller than in earlier studies (perhaps because divorce is more common than it used to be), weaker among African Americans (where one-parent families are more prevalent), and strongest among people who had sought counseling or therapy.

In a nationally representative British study based on data gathered on children from birth on, those whose parents divorced were at greater risk of adjustment problems at age 23. However, the vast majority of these children came through well. The more recent the divorce, the greater the chance of problems carrying over to young adulthood. Divorce seemed to create greater difficulties at first for children whose previous lives had been relatively smooth, but these children eventually made a stronger recovery (Chase-Landale, Cherlin, & Kiernan, 1995).

Living in a One-Parent Family

In 1995, about 31 percent of American families with children under 18—64 percent of African American families, 36 percent of Hispanic families, and 25 percent of white families—were single-parent families, as compared with only 13 percent in 1970 (Bryson, 1996). As of the mid-1980s, the United States had the highest percentage of single-parent families (28.9 percent) among eight industrialized countries (Australia, France, Japan, Sweden, United Kingdom, United States, Soviet Union, and West Germany). Japan had the lowest rate, 4.1 percent (A. Burns, 1992; see Figure 9-2). Although 86 percent of single-parent households in the United States are headed by women, the number of father-only families more than doubled between 1980 and 1992 (U.S. Bureau of the Census, 1993c).

One-parent families most often result from divorce or separation. Children in these families typically spend 5 years in a single-parent home, usually the mother's, before she remarries (Bray & Hetherington, 1993). Other one-parent families are created by death or by a parent who never marries. Between 1940 and 1990, births to unmarried mothers in the United States rose sevenfold—from fewer than 4 percent of all births to 28 percent; and 67 percent of all births to black mothers in 1990 were out of wedlock (National Center for Health Statistics, 1993, 1994b). By 1994 nearly 1 in 3 births was to an unwed mother (Rosenberg et al., 1996). The trend has been especially marked among white and college-educated women but has also occurred among African American and Hispanic women (who still are far more likely to be unwed mothers) and among women of all educational levels (Bachu, 1993; U.S. Bureau of the Census, 1993c). In 1995, the out-of-wedlock birthrate dropped 4 percent, for the first time in two decades, from about 47 births per 1,000 unmarried women ages 15 to 44 in 1994 to about 45 (Rosenberg et al., 1996). Out-of-wedlock births have increased dramatically in other developed countries, but not in Japan, where unwed mothers and their children face economic discrimination and social pressure (Bruce, Lloyd, & Leonard, 1995; Wudunn, 1996).

FIGURE 9-2
Single-parent families as a percentage of all families.

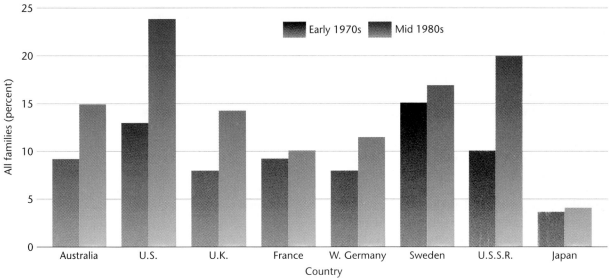

(Source: A. Burns, 1992.)

Children in one-parent families do not have two adults who can share child-rearing responsibilities, take children to activities, and model gender roles and the interplay of personalities. Compared with children in intact families, children in one-parent families are more on their own. They have more household responsibility, more conflict with siblings, less family cohesion, and less support, control, or punishment from fathers (Amato, 1987). Divorce often brings family income down to or near the poverty level, and financial hardship has negative effects on children's health, well-being, and school achievement. Mother-only families often suffer from the mother's low earning capacity and the father's failure to pay child support (McLanahan & Booth, 1989). Nearly three times as many mother-only families as father-only families are poor—35 percent as compared with 13 percent (U.S. Bureau of the Census, 1996a).

Students from one-parent homes tend to have more problems in school (D. A. Dawson, 1991); but what looks like a single-parent effect is often a low-income effect. A study of 18,000 students showed that low income affected school achievement more strongly than did the number of parents at home (Zakariya, 1982).

Some studies report that children with only one parent get into more trouble than those with two parents and that, as adults, they may be at greater risk of marital and parenting problems themselves (Rutter, 1979a). Children from mother-only families are more likely to become poor single parents than are children who live with both parents (McLanahan & Booth, 1989). In general, though, children tend to be better-adjusted when they have had a good relationship with a single parent than when they have grown up in a two-parent home marked by discord and discontent (Bray & Hetherington, 1993; Hetherington et al., 1989; Rutter, 1983). An inaccessible, rejecting, or hostile parent can be more damaging than an absent one (Hetherington, 1980).

Living in a Stepfamily

It generally takes 2 to 3 years for children to adjust to a single-parent household. When the custodial parent remarries, they have to adjust again; and sometimes they have to adjust to the breakup of the new marriage (Hetherington et al., 1989).

Since 75 percent of divorced mothers and 80 percent of divorced fathers remarry, families made up of "yours, mine, and ours" are common. The step-family—also called the *blended,* or *reconstituted,* family—is different from the "natural" family. It has a larger cast, which may include the relatives of up to four adults (the remarried pair, plus one or two former spouses); and it has many stressors. Because of losses from death or divorce, children and adults may be afraid to trust or to love. A child's loyalties to an absent or dead parent may interfere with forming ties to a stepparent. Past emotional and behavior problems often resurface. Adjustment is harder when there are many children, including those from both the man's and the woman's previous marriages, or when a new child is born (Hetherington et al., 1989).

Boys, who have more trouble than girls in adjusting to divorce and single-parent living, generally benefit from a stepfather. A girl, on the other hand, may find the new man in the house a threat to her independence and to her close relationship with her mother and is less likely to accept him (Bray & Hetherington, 1993; Hetherington, 1987; Hetherington et al., 1989; J. B. Kelly, 1987). Early adolescent boys and girls, perhaps because of their emerging concern with sexuality, have more trouble than younger children in adapting to remarriage and bonding with a stepparent (Hetherington et al., 1989).

Stepparents generally take a "hands-off" attitude toward children of the custodial parent, but stepmothers may take a more active role than stepfathers (Hetherington et al., 1989). In one study most of the children of remarried women were doing well and had good feelings about their stepfathers, who had been in the role an average of 3 years. These men, though involved in the children's care, deliberately remained somewhat detached. Nearly one-fourth said that they had tried to assume a parental role too fast and that this had caused problems. By contrast, in stepfamilies in which the father was the natural parent, the stepmothers were much more involved, taking children to and from school and other activities, providing emotional support and comfort, and disciplining them (Santrock, Sitterle, & Warshak, 1988).

Still, a stepchild's most enduring ties are with the custodial parent; and a positive relationship with that parent is "a key ingredient in helping the child. . . as the family [moves] from. . . intact to divorced to becoming a stepfamily" (Santrock et al., 1988, p. 161). In the study just described, the remarried mothers were just as involved, nurturant, and available to their children as mothers in intact

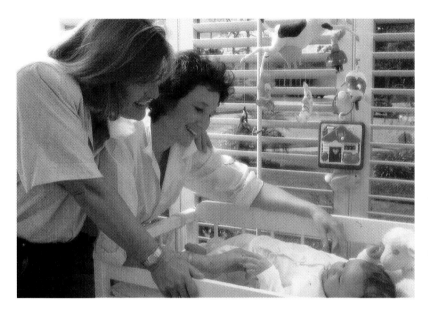

This baby has two mothers—and both obviously dote on the child. Contrary to popular stereotypes, children living with homosexual parents are no more likely than other children to have social or psychological problems or to turn out to be homosexual themselves. *(Deborah Davis/PhotoEdit)*

marriages. These women's renewed satisfaction with life seemed to carry over to their relationships with their children and to increase the likelihood of success in establishing blended families.

Children of Gay and Lesbian Parents

The number of children living with gay and lesbian parents is unknown; conservative estimates range from 6 to 14 million (C. J. Patterson, 1992). These numbers are probably low because many homosexual parents do not openly acknowledge their sexual orientation.

Opposition to homosexuals' raising children is usually based on a belief that homosexuals are more likely to abuse them or that growing up in such a family will cause children to become homosexual or to develop psychological problems. Such beliefs have social policy implications for custody and visitation disputes, foster care, and adoptions.

Several studies have focused on the sexual identity and gender-role behavior of children of homosexuals; on their personal development, including self-concept, moral judgment, and intelligence; and on their social relationships. Although research is still sparse and studies vary in methodology, none has indicated psychological risks (C. J. Patterson, 1992, 1995a, 1995b). Openly homosexual parents usually have positive relationships with their children (Turner et al., 1985), and the children are no more likely than children raised by heterosexual parents to have social or psychological problems (C. J. Patterson, 1992, 1995a). Abuse by homosexual parents is rare (R. L. Barrett & Robinson, 1990; Cramer, 1986).

Children of homosexuals are no more likely to be homosexual themselves than are children of heterosexuals (B. M. King, 1996). In one study, the vast majority of adult sons of gay fathers were heterosexual (Bailey, Bobrow, Wolfe, & Mikach, 1995). Likewise, a longitudinal study of adult children of lesbians found that a large majority identified themselves as heterosexual (Golombok & Tasker, 1996).

SIBLING RELATIONSHIPS

"I fight more with my little brother than I do with my friends," reports Monique, age 10. "But when I fight with Billy, we always make up." The tie between Monique and Billy is deeper and more lasting than ordinary friendships, which may founder on a quarrel or just fade away. It is also ambivalent, marked by special affection as well as by intense competition and resentment.

Sibling relations are a laboratory for learning how to resolve conflicts. Siblings are impelled to make up after quarrels, since they know they will see each other every day. They learn that expressing anger does not end a relationship. Firstborns tend to be bossy and are more likely to attack, interfere with, ignore, or bribe their siblings. Younger siblings plead, reason, and cajole; they often become quite skillful at sensing other people's needs, negotiating, and compromising. Children

This boy in Surinam has an important responsibility: taking care of his younger brother. Siblings in nonindustrialized societies have clear, culturally defined roles throughout life. *(James R. Holland/Stock, Boston)*

are more apt to squabble with same-sex siblings; two brothers quarrel more than any other combination (Cicirelli, 1976a).

Older children often mind younger ones and help them with homework. In one study, older siblings (who were in second or third grade) were better teachers of their younger siblings (in kindergarten or first grade) than were unrelated classmates of the older siblings. The older siblings were more likely to give spontaneous guidance, and the younger ones often prompted explanations and pressured their older siblings into giving them more control of the task (Azmitia & Hesser, 1993).

Help is most likely to be effective (and accepted) when it comes from a sibling, especially a sister, who is at least 4 years older (Cicirelli, 1976a, 1976b). Girls explain more to younger siblings than boys do, and when girls want younger siblings to do something, they are more apt to reason with them or to make them feel obligated. Older brothers tend to attack (Cicirelli, 1976a, 1976b).

LIFE-SPAN ISSUE

HOW DOES CULTURE AFFECT SIBLING RELATIONSHIPS THROUGHOUT LIFE?

Victor G. Cicirelli is director of the developmental psychology program at Purdue University. His areas of research and teaching have ranged from early childhood to aging. Among his best-known work is that on sibling relationships across the life span. In today's interdependent global economy, he believes that it is important to understand cross-cultural differences in family life.

With the growth in dual-earner families and in the older adult population, industrialized societies may have something to learn from the way siblings in the nonindustrialized world care for and depend on one another, says Victor Cicirelli (1994).*

In nonindustrialized societies, such as those in remote rural areas or villages of Asia, Africa, Oceania, and Central and South America, it is common to see a tiny child of 3 rocking a baby. It is also common to see older girls stay home from school to care for three or four younger siblings: to feed, comfort, and toilet-train them; discipline them; assign chores; and generally keep an eye on them. By delegating these responsibilities to a daughter, the mother is free to work; the family's survival is at stake. Sometimes, even when the mother is present, girls or boys share in the care of younger children.

In a poor agricultural or pastoral community, group cooperation is essential to make the most of limited resources. Sibling care is continuous and obligatory; older children have an important, culturally defined role. Parents train children from an early age to teach their younger sisters and brothers skills such as gathering firewood, carrying water, tending animals, and growing food. At the same time, younger siblings absorb intangible values, such as respecting elders and placing the welfare of the group above that of the individual.

In these societies, the solidarity created by early sibling relationships carries over into adult life. Adults cooperate, share with, and care for their brothers and sisters. Younger siblings continue to show older ones respect and obedience. In both childhood and adulthood, siblings may fight and compete, but they do so within the bounds of societally set rules and roles.

In industrialized societies, individual freedom and choice are important for advancement, and sibling ties in adulthood are voluntary. Parents generally try to treat children equally and not to "burden" older children with the care of younger ones (Weisner, 1993). Some care-

*Unless otherwise referenced, this discussion is based on Cicirelli, 1994.

taking does take place, but it is typically sporadic and mainly custodial: providing for basic needs, supervising, protecting, and sometimes entertaining younger children to keep them out of mischief when the parents are busy. Older siblings do teach younger ones, but this usually happens informally, by chance, and not as an established part of the social system. Youngsters grow up knowing that they will leave home and make their own lives, and so will their siblings. As adults, they can be as close or as distant as they choose. They generally stay in touch, but their frequency of contact depends on their feelings about one another and their other commitments.

The number of siblings in a family, as well as their spacing, birth order, and gender, determines roles and relationships more rigidly in nonindustrialized societies. The larger number of siblings in these societies helps the family carry on its work and provide for aging members. The definition of *siblings* may even include cousins, aunts, uncles, grandparents, or same-age peers, who are expected to fulfill the obligations of brothers and sisters. In industrialized societies, the number and spacing of siblings vary from family to family; siblings tend to be fewer and farther apart in age, making it easier for parents to pursue careers or other interests and to focus more resources and attention on each child. This also means, however, that adults have fewer siblings to turn to in time of need.

In industrialized societies, adult sisters tend to hold the family together; they are closer to their siblings and keep in touch more than brothers do. In most nonindustrialized societies, adult brothers have definite family roles, protecting and providing for their sisters and arranging their marriages; and the tie between adult brothers may be an integral part of the community's economic and social structure. Lines of authority depend on both birth order and gender; the eldest brother has the highest status, then the eldest sister, and so on. An older sister may resolve family conflicts; an order brother may parcel out inheritances.

Sibling relationships among some American working families and ethnic minority groups are closer to the pattern of nonindustrialized cultures than to that of the majority culture in the United States. Older siblings are responsible for after-school care of younger ones. Such ethnic variations carry over to adult life. For example, Italian American adults are closer to their siblings and see each other more often than white Protestant siblings of northern European descent (C. L. Johnson, 1985).

We see, then, how economic systems and cultural patterns affect sibling relationships not only in childhood but throughout life.

✔ THE CHILD IN THE PEER GROUP

"Sweep!" Malcolm bellows as he whisks away a wax-filled bottle cap he and a friend have been flicking in the street game known as "skellzies." This game, played on city streets for some 80 years, is part of the culture of the peer group, passed down from generation to generation. Impromptu games of tag, catch, jacks, marbles, and "let's pretend" have historically served the time-honored mandate of childhood: to learn through play. Through play, children are in physical and social contact with others, gain confidence in their abilities, and practice using their imagination. Play offers socially acceptable ways to compete, to expend energy, and to act aggressively. The decline in egocentrism and growth of cognitive skills allow school-age children to interact more meaningfully with peers.

Today we are seeing new social patterns as technology changes the tools and habits of leisure. Television and videocassettes turn many children into "couch potatoes." Computer games demand few social skills. Children engage in more organized sports, which replace children's rules with adult rules and in which adult referees settle disputes so that children do not need to find ways to resolve matters among themselves. Still, children spend more time with others their own age than they did in early childhood.

How does the peer group form, and how is it structured? What functions does it fulfill? How does it influence children? What determines their acceptance by peers and their ability to make friends?

STRUCTURE, FUNCTIONS, AND INFLUENCE OF THE PEER GROUP

Babies are aware of one another, and preschoolers begin to make friends; but not until middle childhood does the peer group come into its own. Groups form naturally among children who live near one another or go to school together. *Peers* means "equals"; children who play together are usually close in age, though a neighborhood play group may include mixed ages. Groups are usually all girls or all boys (Hartup, 1992). Children of the same sex have common interests; girls are generally more mature than boys, and (as we pointed out in Chapter 7) girls and boys play and talk to one another differently. Same-sex groups help children to learn gender-appropriate behav-

These boys playing marbles have found a time-honored, socially acceptable outlet for aggressive energy. Competition with peers helps build the self-concept by giving children a standard against which to measure their own abilities. *(Tony Freeman/PhotoEdit)*

iors and to incorporate gender roles into their self-concept.

Positive Effects of Peer Relationships

Children benefit in several ways from doing things with peers. They develop skills needed for sociability and intimacy, they enhance relationships, and they gain a sense of belonging. They are motivated to achieve, and they attain a sense of identity. They learn leadership, communication skills, cooperation, roles, and rules.

Such conclusions emerged from a study (Zarbatany, Hartmann, & Rankin, 1990) in which 91 Canadian fifth- and sixth-graders kept week-long diaries of what they did with other children and what they liked and disliked about their peers' behavior. Then another group of 81 children the same age rated the importance and prevalence of each activity and which behaviors they would most like or dislike in each (see Table 9-1).

Children benefit from a variety of activities with peers. Noncompetitive activities (such as talking) offer opportunities for enhancing relationships: competitive ones (such as sports) help children develop their self-concept and build self-esteem. By comparing themselves with others their age, children obtain a more realistic gauge of their abilities.

As children begin to move away from parental influence, the peer group opens new perspectives. Testing values they previously accepted unquestioningly against those of their peers helps them decide which to keep and which to discard. The peer group helps children learn how to get along in society—how to adjust their needs and desires to those of others, when to yield, and when to stand firm. The peer group also offers emotional security. It is reassuring for children to find out that they are not alone in harboring thoughts which might offend an adult.

Doing things with other children has cognitive benefits, as well. In Chapter 8, we pointed out the value of peer interaction in language learning. Similarly, when children work on computer tasks with a partner, they may seem to concentrate less on the task and more on the social interaction, but they enjoy the sessions more and learn more from them than children working alone (Perlmutter, Behrend, Kuo, & Muller, 1989).

Negative Effects: Conformity and Segregation

To be part of a peer group, a child must accept its values and behavioral norms; even though these may be undesirable, children may not have the strength to resist. It is usually in the company of peers that children shoplift, begin to use drugs, and act in other antisocial ways. Preadolescent children are especially susceptible to pressure to conform, and this pressure may change a troublesome child into a delinquent one. Children who already have antisocial leanings are the ones most likely to gravitate toward other antisocial youngsters and to be further influenced by them (Hartup, 1992).

Of course, some degree of conformity to group

TABLE 9-1

Important and Prevalent Peer Activities as Rated by Fifth- and Sixth-Graders

Most Common Activities*	Most Important Activities*
Conversation	Noncontact sports
Hanging out	Watching TV or listening to records
Walking around at school	Conversation
Talking on the telephone	Talking on the telephone
Traveling to and from school	Physical games
Watching TV or listening to records	Going to parties
Physical games	Hanging out

Most Liked Behaviors		
Invitations to participate	Sharing	Facilitating achievements
Performing admirably	Loyalty	Being nice or friendly
Physically helping	Humor	Absence of unpleasant behavior
Complimenting or encouraging	Instructing	
Giving permission	Helping	

Most Disliked Behaviors		
Physical aggression	Teasing	Annoying or bothersome behavior
Interfering with achievements	Ignoring	
Verbal aggression	Violating rules	Expressing anger
Dishonesty	Criticizing	Unfaithfulness
		Greed or bossiness

*There were some gender differences. Boys liked sports more than girls did and spent more time in contact sports; girls spent more time shopping, talking on the telephone, and talking about hair styles and clothing than boys did.
SOURCE: Zarbatany et al., 1990.

standards is healthy. It is unhealthy when it becomes destructive or prompts people to act against their own better judgment. A classic study of conformity tested the reactions to group pressure of 90 children ages 7 to 13 (Berenda, 1950). The children were shown cards with two lines of clearly different lengths and were asked to tell which line was shorter or longer. When the children were alone, they answered correctly; but in a room with eight other children who had been told to give wrong answers to 7 of the 12 cards, the children being tested were torn between describing what they actually saw and going along with the group.

In that situation, only 43 percent of 7- to 10-year-olds and 54 percent of 10- to 13-year-olds gave the right answers.

Peer influence is even stronger when issues are unclear. Since the world presents children with many ambiguous issues that call for careful judgment, peer-group influences can have grave consequences.

Another negative effect of the peer group may be a tendency to reinforce *prejudice:* unfavorable attitudes toward "outsiders," especially members of certain racial or ethnic groups. Since children tend to associate with others who are like them and live near them, peer groups usually consist of children of the same racial or ethnic origin and similar socioeconomic status.

Prejudice can corrode the self-esteem of members of disfavored groups. Studies conducted between the 1960s and the mid-1970s found bias against African Americans among both white and black children in northern and southern American cities, from preschool through the early school years (Morland, 1966; J. Williams, Best, & Boswell, 1975).

A study done in Montreal, where tensions exist between French-speaking and English-speaking citizens, found signs of prejudice in a sample of 254 English Canadian children in kindergarten through sixth grade (Powlishta, Serbin, Doyle, & White, 1994). The sample included equal numbers of boys and girls. The children were given brief descriptions of positive and negative traits (such as *helpful, smart, mean,* and *naughty*) and were asked whether one or both of two cartoon children — one English-speaking and the other French-speaking — would be likely to possess each trait. A similar procedure was followed with regard to male and female figures (using gender stereotypes such as *ambitious* and *gentle*) and figures of overweight and normal-weight children. The researchers also assessed prejudice in several other ways—for example, by asking the children which of two pictured children they would like to play with.

In general, children showed biases in favor of children like themselves, but these biases (except for a preference for children of the same sex) diminished with age and cognitive development. Girls were more biased with regard to gender, and boys with regard to ethnicity. However, individual differences were significant, and a child who was highly prejudiced in one respect was not necessarily prejudiced in another.

Prejudice may be lessened or eliminated by modifying children's experience. The most effective programs get children from different groups to work together, as in athletic teams; working toward a common goal produces positive feelings (Gaertner, Mann, Murrell, & Dovidio, 1989).

POPULARITY

Popularity gains importance in middle childhood, when youngsters spend more time with other children and are greatly affected by opinions of peers. Popular children typically have good cognitive abilities, are good at solving social problems, are helpful to other children, and are assertive without being disruptive or aggressive. Their behavior enhances, rather than undermines, other children's goals. They are trustworthy, loyal, and self-disclosing enough to provide emotional support for other children. Their superior social skills make other people enjoy being with them (Newcomb, Bukowski, & Pattee, 1993).

Children can be unpopular for many reasons, some of which may not be fully within their control. Some unpopular youngsters are aggressive, some are hyperactive and inattentive, and some are withdrawn (Dodge, Coie, Pettit, & Price, 1990; Newcomb et al., 1993; A. W. Pope, Bierman, & Mumma, 1991). Others act silly and immature or anxious and uncertain. They are often insensitive to other children's feelings and cannot adapt to new situations (Bierman, Smoot, & Aumiller, 1993). Some show undue interest in being with groups of the other sex (Sroufe, Bennett, Englund, Urban, & Shulman, 1993).

Unpopular children do not have good social skills. Some unpopular children expect not to be liked, and this becomes a self-fulfilling prophecy. In one experiment, unpopular children (third grade boys and fourth and fifth grade girls) were told that certain other children, whom they had met once before, liked them and looked forward to seeing them again. Then they were reunited with these new acquaintances. Children who got this positive "feedback" were liked better by the new acquaintances than were children in a control group who had received no such message. In addition, independent observers rated the girls who had gotten positive messages as more socially competent (Rabiner & Coie, 1989).

Family and Cultural Influences on Popularity

It is often in the family that children acquire behaviors that affect popularity. Authoritative parenting tends to have better outcomes than authoritarian parenting (Dekovic & Janssens, 1992). Children of parents who punish and threaten are likely to threaten or act mean with other children; they are less popular than are children of parents who reason with them and try to help them understand how another person might feel (C. H. Hart, Ladd, & Burleson, 1990). Parents of aggressive children are likely to be either coercive or inept with them, and the children tend to be impulsive, mean, and disruptive. Disliked by other children, they generally seek out friends as antisocial as they are (Hartup, 1989, 1992). Unpopular

BOX 9-2　WINDOW ON THE WORLD

POPULARITY: A CROSS-CULTURAL VIEW

How does culture affect popularity? Would a child who has what it takes to be popular in one culture be equally popular in another? Researchers compared 480 second- and fourth-graders in Shanghai, China, with 296 children the same ages in Ontario, Canada (X. Chen, Rubin, & Sun, 1992). Although the two samples were quite different— for example, none of the Canadian children came from peasant families, but many of the Chinese children did—both samples were representative of school-age children in the two countries.

The researchers assessed the children's popularity by means of two kinds of peer perceptions. First, each child was asked to name up to three classmates whose behavioral characteristics made them most suitable to take certain roles in a class play. Next, the children filled out a sociometric rating telling which three classmates they most and least liked to be with and which three classmates were their best friends.

The results showed that certain traits are valued similarly in both cultures: a sociable, cooperative child is likely to be popular in both China and Canada, and an aggressive child is likely to be rejected in both countries. However, one important difference emerged: shy, sensitive children are well-liked in China, but not in Canada. This is not surprising. Chinese children are encouraged to be cautious, to restrain themselves, and to inhibit their urges; thus a quiet, shy youngster is considered well-behaved. In a western culture, by contrast, such a child is likely to be seen as socially immature, fearful, and lacking in self-confidence.

A follow-up study at ages 8 and 10 (X. Chen, Rubin, & Li, 1995) again found that shy, sensitive Chinese children were popular with peers; they were also rated by teachers as socially competent, as leaders, and as academic achievers. However, by age 12, an interesting twist had occurred: shy, sensitive Chinese children were no

longer popular. In fact, they tended to be rejected by their peers, just as in western cultures.

It may be, then, that shyness and sensitivity take on different social meanings in China in the late part of middle childhood, as peer relationships become more important and adult approval becomes less so. As in the west, a shy preadolescent may lack the assertiveness and communication skills needed to establish and maintain strong peer relationships.

This research suggests that the influence of culture may interact with, and be tempered by, developmental processes that are more or less universal. Even in China, with its strong tradition of obedience to authority, the influence of adult social standards may wane as children's urge to make their own independent judgments of their peers asserts itself.

---

children report the least supportive relationships with their fathers (C. J. Patterson, Kupersmidt, & Griesler, 1990).

Culture helps determine what traits make children popular. For example, in China, where shyness and sensitivity are valued, children who show these traits are more likely to be popular than in the United States—at least in middle childhood (see Box 9-2).

Helping Unpopular Children

Popularity is not a frivolous issue. Unpopular children are deprived of a basic developmental experience—positive interaction with other youngsters—and may suffer sadness, a sense of rejection, and low self-esteem. Unpopularity during the preschool years is not necessarily cause for concern, but by middle childhood peer relationships

are strong predictors of later adjustment. Schoolchildren whose peers like them are likely to be well-adjusted as adolescents. Those who have trouble getting along with peers are more likely to develop psychological problems, drop out of school, and become delinquent (Hartup, 1992; Kupersmidt & Coie, 1990; Morison & Masten, 1991; Newcomb et al., 1993; Parker & Asher, 1987).

It is not clear whether unpopularity is a cause of such disturbances or a symptom. Either way, adults can help. Children who are simply *neglected* or overlooked by classmates and other peers may do better in a different class or a new school, or if they join a new club or go to a new camp. Children who are *rejected* by peers—the ones most at risk for emotional and behavioral difficulties—can be taught or shown how to get other children to like them (Hartup, 1992).

In one experiment, fifth- and sixth-graders were

School-age friends often share secrets—and laughs—as Anna and her friend Cristina are doing. Friendship becomes deeper and more stable in middle childhood, reflecting cognitive and emotional growth. Girls tend to have fewer friends, but more intimate ones, than boys do. *(Erika Stone)*

trained in social skills. They learned how to carry on a conversation: how to share information about themselves, how to show interest in others by asking questions, and how to give help, suggestions, invitations, and advice. When they had a chance to practice their new conversational skills in a group project with other children, they became better liked by the others and interacted more with them (Bierman & Furman, 1984). The experimental group who received the social skills training and took part in the group project showed more general and lasting improvement over a 6-week period (on measures of conversational skills, rates of interaction, peer acceptance, and self-perception) than did three other groups: a control group who received no training, an experimental group who received the training but did not participate in the group project, and another experimental group who took part in the group project but received no social skills teaching.

Apparently, children not only need to learn social skills but also need to be in situations where they can use these skills and where other children can see the changes in them. Otherwise, other children may hold on to their former opinions of these youngsters. Furthermore, since children who expect to be liked *are* better liked (Rabiner & Coie, 1989), positive expectations should be built into programs to increase children's popularity. Findings about the impact of the family suggest that effective interventions should focus on parent-child relations as well as on a child's social skills.

FRIENDSHIP

Jordan and his best friend play ball together and are in the same Scout troop. Melissa and her best friend eat lunch together, play together during recess, walk home together, talk on the phone after school, and play frequently at each other's homes.

Children may spend much of their free time in groups, but only as individuals do they form friendships. Even an unpopular child can make and be a good friend. Popularity is the peer group's opinion of a child, but friendship is a two-way street. The strongest friendships involve equal commitment. They are not based on dominance or control, but on mutual give-and-take (Hartup, 1992; Newcomb & Bagwell, 1995).

Friendship begins with choice. A friend is someone a child feels affection for, is comfortable with, likes to do things with, and can share feelings and secrets with. Children look for friends who are like them: of the same age, sex, and ethnic group and with common interests (Hartup, 1992). Building on these commonalities, friendship becomes a complex pattern woven of the many positive experiences two children have with one another, which nourish and sustain their relationship (Newcomb & Bagwell, 1995).

Children's concepts of friendship, and the ways they act with their friends, change with age, reflecting cognitive and emotional growth (Hartup, 1992; Newcomb & Bagwell, 1995). Preschool friends play together, but friendship among school-age children is deeper and more stable (Hartup, 1992). Friendships become more intimate as children approach adolescence (Sullivan, 1953). School-age children typically have four or five friends with whom they spend most of their free time, but they usually play with only one or two at a time (Hartup, 1992). Girls care less about having many friends than about having a few close friends they can rely on; boys have more friendships, but they tend to be less intimate and affectionate (Furman, 1982; Furman & Buhrmester, 1985).

Through friendships, children learn to communicate and cooperate. They obtain partners for mutually enjoyable and mutually productive activities. They learn about similarities and differences between themselves and others and about how to maintain a relationship. They learn to show and control their emotions. Friendship helps children to feel good about themselves; to become more sensitive and loving, more loyal and faithful, more able to give and receive respect. The bond needs to be sturdy enough to withstand the inevitable quarrels. Friends often disagree and compete; learning to resolve conflict is an important function of friendship (Hartup, 1992; Furman, 1982; Newcomb & Bagwell, 1995; Sullivan, 1953).

✔ MENTAL HEALTH

The mental health of American children seems to have worsened since the mid-1970s. When parent and teacher ratings of 2,466 children ages 7 to 16 who were not under psychological treatment in 1989 were compared with ratings of similar samples of children in 1976 and 1981, it appeared that emotional and behavioral problems had increased during those years (Achenbach & Howell, 1993). In 1976, only 10 percent of the children were judged to have problems that might need clinical treatment; in 1989, the comparable figure was more than 18 percent. Furthermore, nearly 3 times the proportion of children as in 1976 were excluded from the 1989 sample because they had required mental health services during the previous year.

Although poor children had more problems, the decline in mental health occurred across economic levels. When income was taken into account, black and white children were about equally affected. Among the problems showing significant increases, according to parents and teachers, were:

withdrawal or social problems (wanting to be alone or to play with younger children or being secretive, sulky, overly dependent, or lethargic); *attention or thinking problems* (impulsiveness, hyperactivity, or difficulty in concentrating and doing schoolwork); *aggression or delinquency* (being mean, stubborn, hot-tempered, disobedient, destructive, or antisocial); and *anxiety or depression* (feeling sad, unloved, nervous, fearful, or lonely).

The growth in emotional disturbances may reflect the increasing stress of modern life. The trend is no better in several other countries, including France, Australia, Thailand, and Puerto Rico (Achenbach & Howell, 1993). However, different problems are prevalent in different cultures. For example, Embu children of Kenya, whose parents emphasize obedience, tend to be troubled by fears, guilt, and bodily complaints without known medical causes; whereas American children, whose parents value independence, are more likely to argue excessively or to be cruel or disobedient (Weisz, Sigman, Weiss, & Mosk, 1993). Some children, of course, are more resilient than others. Some problems seem to be associated with a particular phase of a child's life and will go away on their own, but others need to be treated to prevent future trouble.

COMMON EMOTIONAL DISTURBANCES

Emotional disturbances can affect all aspects of development: cognitive, social, and even physical. According to one study of 776 children ages 9 to 18, girls who show anxiety disorders grow up to be, on average, one to two inches shorter than other women, apparently because such disorders affect the brain's release of growth hormones (Pine et al., 1996). Let's look at one common type of anxiety disorder involving separation from parents. We'll also describe two other disorders often seen among American schoolchildren: acting-out behavior and childhood depression.

Separation Anxiety Disorder and School Phobia

Nicole wakes up on a school morning complaining of nausea, stomachache, or headache. Soon after she receives permission to stay home, the symptom clears up. This goes on day after day, and the longer she is out of school, the harder it is to get her back.

Nicole's behavior is typical of children with *school phobia,* an unrealistic fear of going to school. School phobia may be a type of *separation anxiety disorder,* a condition involving excessive anxiety for at least 4 weeks concerning separation from home or from people to whom the child is attached. Separation anxiety disorder affects some 4 percent of children and young adolescents and may persist through the college years. These children often come from close-knit, caring families. They may develop the disorder after the death of a pet, an illness, or a move to a new school (APA, 1994).

School phobia seems to have more to do with children's fear of leaving their mothers than with a fear of school. If there *is* a problem at school—a sarcastic teacher, a bully in the schoolyard, or overly demanding work—the child's fears may be realistic; the environment may need changing, not the child. School-phobic children tend to be average or good students, ages 5 to 15, and are equally likely to be boys or girls. They tend to be timid and inhibited away from home, but willful, stubborn, and demanding with their parents. Their parents are more likely than other parents to be depressed, to suffer from anxiety disorders, and to report family dysfunction (G. A. Bernstein & Garfinkel, 1988). The most important element in treatment is an early, gradual return to school. Usually children go back without too much trouble once treatment is begun.

Acting-out Behavior

When children continually fight, lie, steal, and destroy property, they may be showing *acting-out behavior,* misbehavior that is an outward expression of emotional turmoil. Almost all children lie occasionally, but when children past the age of 6 or 7 continue telling tall tales, they are often signaling a sense of insecurity. They may be seeking attention and esteem or showing hostility toward their parents. Similarly, occasional minor stealing, while it needs to be dealt with, is not necessarily a sign of serious trouble; but children who steal repeatedly are often showing hostility. Sometimes the stolen items seem to symbolize the parents' love, power, or authority, of which the child feels deprived (A. H. Chapman, 1974). Any chronic antisocial behavior may be a symptom of deep-seated emotional upset.

Childhood Depression

"Nobody likes me" is a common complaint among school-age children, who tend to be popularity-conscious; but a prolonged sense of friendlessness may be one sign of *childhood depression*—an affective disorder, or disorder of mood, that goes beyond normal, temporary sadness. Other symptoms may include inability to have fun or concentrate, fatigue, extreme activity or apathy, crying, sleep problems, feelings of worthlessness, weight change, physical complaints, or frequent thoughts about death or suicide. Any five of these symptoms, lasting for at least 2 weeks, may point to depression (APA, 1994). If symptoms persist, the child should be given psychological help. Treatment is important, not only for immediate relief, but also because childhood depression may result in attempted suicide and often signals the beginning of a problem that may persist into adulthood.

TREATMENT TECHNIQUES

The choice of treatment depends on many factors: the nature of the problem, the child's personality, the family's willingness to participate and its finances, the facilities available in the community, and often, the orientation of the professional first consulted.

Types of Therapy

Psychological treatment can take several forms. In *individual psychotherapy,* a therapist sees a child one on one, to help the child gain insights into his or her personality and relationships and to interpret feelings and behavior. Such treatment may be helpful at a time of stress, such as the death of a parent, even when a child has not shown signs of disturbance. The therapist may use play materials (for example, dolls representing family members) to help a child express feelings. The therapist accepts the child's feelings and the child's right to them. Child psychotherapy is usually more effective when combined with counseling for the parents.

In *family therapy,* the therapist sees the family together, observes how members act with one another, and points out both growth-producing and growth-inhibiting or destructive patterns of family functioning. Sometimes the child whose problem brings the family into therapy is, ironically, the healthiest member, responding to a troubled family situation. Therapy can help parents confront differences and begin to resolve them. This is often the first step toward solving the child's problems as well.

Behavior therapy, or *behavioral modification,* is a form of psychotherapy that uses principles of learning theory (see Chapter 1) to eliminate undesirable behaviors (such as temper tantrums) or to develop desirable ones (such as putting dirty clothes into a hamper). In the latter example, every time the child uses the hamper, she or he gets a reward, such as praise, a treat, or a token to be exchanged for a new toy.

A statistical analysis of many studies found that, in general, psychotherapy is effective with children and adolescents, especially with adolescent girls. Behavior therapy was more effective than nonbehavioral methods. Results were best when treatment was targeted to specific problems and desired outcomes (Weisz, Weiss, Han, Granger, & Morton, 1995).

During the 1980s, an increase occurred in the use of *drug therapy* to treat childhood emotional disorders (Tuma, 1989). In Chapter 8, we mentioned the use of Ritalin to treat hyperactivity. Antidepressants are commonly prescribed for bed-wetting, and antipsychotics for severe psychological problems. Drugs help sometimes, but they are usually most effective when combined with psychotherapy and should not be used in its place. Giving pills to change children's behavior is a radical step: many medicines have side effects. Furthermore, drugs may produce merely surface changes without getting at underlying causes. Many therapists therefore turn to drugs only as a last resort.

STRESS AND RESILIENCE

Stressful events are part of childhood, and most children learn to cope; but stress that becomes overwhelming can lead to psychological problems. Illness, the birth of a sibling, day-to-day frustration, and parents' temporary absence are common sources of stress for almost every child. Divorce or death of parents, hospitalization, and the day-in, day-out grind of poverty affect many children. Some children survive wars, earthquakes, or kidnapping. Such severe stressors may have long-

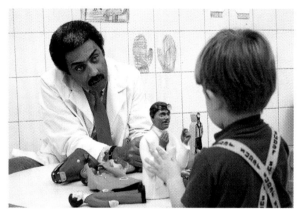

Therapists who work with troubled children often encourage them to express themselves through play, which helps bring out their emotions. *(Michal Heron/Monkmeyer)*

term effects on physical and psychological well-being (Garmezy, 1983; Pynoos et al., 1987).

Stresses of Modern Life

The child psychologist David Elkind (1981, 1984, 1986) has called today's child the "hurried child." He is concerned that the pressures of modern life are forcing children to grow up too soon and are making their childhood too stressful. Today's children are pressured to succeed in school, to compete in sports, and to meet parents' emotional needs. Children are exposed to many adult problems on television and in real life before they have mastered the problems of childhood. They know about sex and violence, and if they live in single-parent homes or dual-earner families, they often must shoulder adult responsibilities. Yet children are not small adults. They feel and think like children, and they need the years of childhood for healthy development.

One contemporary source of stress is the disruption that occurs when families move. Children in some countries, such as the United States, move much more often than in others (see Figure 9-3). Frequent moves tend to be related to low socioeconomic status and parental separation (Long, 1992). Sometimes frequent moving is a symptom, as well as a cause, of stress, chaos, and major emotional problems within the family (G. A. Simpson & Fowler, 1994).

Moving is hard on children. They feel the loss of friends, perhaps of extended family, and of control over their lives. They generally have to change

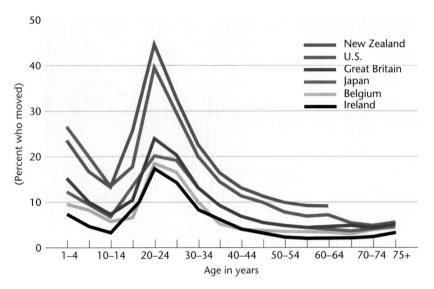

FIGURE 9-3
Percentage of population that changed usual residence in 1 year for six countries, by age, circa 1981. Children in some countries move much more often than those in others. In the United States such moves seem to be due largely to poverty and to parental separation. (*Source: Long, 1992.*)

schools and are less likely to know many adults well. Children who move three or more times have about twice the risk of emotional, behavior, or school problems as children who have never moved, even when income and other social factors are taken into account. They are more at risk for health problems and less likely to have a stable source of medical care. Frequent movers are more likely to be depressed, headstrong, hyperactive, antisocial, or immature; to repeat a school grade or to be suspended or expelled; and to receive psychological help (Fowler, Simpson, & Schoendorf, 1993; G. A. Simpson & Fowler, 1994).

Moving from one home to another can be stressful enough, but moving to no home at all can be devastating. The rise in the number of homeless families in the United States has led to severe psychological difficulties in children (Bassuk & Rubin, 1987; see Chapter 6).

Given how much stress children are exposed to, it should not be surprising that they worry a lot. What they worry *about*, however, may come as a surprise. We might expect that children would worry most about things that are part of their daily lives, such as how they are doing in school. Indeed, in a survey and interviews of 272 ethnically diverse second- through sixth-graders in a large metropolitan area (Silverman, La Greca, & Wasserstein, 1995), school did emerge as one of the children's chief concerns, as it has in previous studies. So did health—their own or someone else's. However, the worry reported by the largest number of children (56 percent of the sample) was personal harm from others: being robbed, stabbed, or shot. Girls had more worries than boys, and African

Americans had more worries than whites or Hispanics.

These children were not in a high-crime area, nor had they personally experienced many attacks. Their intense anxiety about their safety seemed to reflect the high rates of crime and violence in the larger society. A steady diet of violence on television, in comic books and movies, and in the newspapers can make even relatively protected children feel that their world is not as safe as they had thought and that their parents cannot always guard them. How much more stressful life must be, then, for children who are in real, constant danger! (See Box 9-3.)

Adults can help children by respecting their worries and encouraging children to talk about them. Most childhood worries are normal, and overcoming them helps children grow, achieve identity, and master their world.

Coping with Stress: The Resilient Child

If two children of the same age and sex are exposed to the same stressful experience, one may crumble while the other remains emotionally healthy. Why?

Resilient children are those who bounce back from circumstances that would blight most others. They are the children of the ghetto who go on to distinguish themselves in the professions. They are the neglected or abused children who go on to form intimate relationships and be good parents. They are survivors of the Holocaust who went on to lead normal, successful adult lives (Helmreich, 1991). In spite of the bad cards they have been dealt, these children are winners.

BOX 9-3 FOOD FOR THOUGHT

CHILDREN WHO LIVE IN CHRONIC DANGER

A 6-year-old in Washington, D.C., when asked whether she felt safe anywhere, said, "In my basement," because it had no windows where bullets could enter. A 10-year-old ran away in terror after seeing a man shot in the back on the street. A 6-year-old saw her mother punched in the face by a drug addict. These inner-city children are, unfortunately, typical of many who live in the midst of violence and, as a result, are fearful, anxious, distressed, and depressed (Garbarino, Dubrow, Kostelny, & Pardo, 1992).

Possibly because the subject is so painful or because children may not report all that they see or experience, parents tend to underestimate the extent and effects of children's exposure to violence. Even if they are aware, some parents are powerless to shield their children from witnessing violence or becoming victims. Children may become desensitized to brutality; they may come to take it for granted and may not take necessary precautions to protect themselves (Garbarino et al., 1992).

Children who grow up surrounded by violence often have trouble concentrating and remembering because fears keep them from getting enough sleep. They may be afraid that their mothers will abandon them. Some become aggressive in order to hide their fear or protect themselves, or simply in imitation of what they have seen. Many do not allow themselves to become attached to other people, for fear of more hurt and loss (Garbarino et al., 1992).

Children who first see or experience violence before age 11 are 3 times more likely to develop psychiatric symptoms than if first exposed to it as teenagers (Davidson & Smith, 1990). (Table 9-2 gives typical reactions to violence at different ages.) Children with multiple risks—those who live in violent communities, who are poor, and who receive inadequate parenting, education, and health care—are the most likely to suffer permanent developmental damage (Rutter, 1987).

These children need islands of safety in their lives. They need caring relationships with adults outside the family—teachers or community leaders—who can deal with their concerns in the day-to-day context of classroom or group meetings. Play and art activities can help a child express feelings about a traumatic event, restore a sense of inner control, build self-worth, and set the stage for dialogue with an adult whom the child can trust (Garbarino et al., 1992).

To reduce violence, the American Academy of Pediatrics (1992) recommends regulating and restricting ownership of handguns and ammunition; stopping the romanticizing of gun use in television and movies; and targeting adolescents at high risk for becoming violent (chiefly teenage boys and drug and alcohol abusers) for community services. In addition, the American Psychological Association's Commission on Violence and Youth recommends community programs built around the interests and needs of youth, including health care, recreation, and vocational training (Youngstrom, 1992). Positive adult role models, peer-group discussions, and family intervention may help deter drug abuse and violence.

■ TABLE 9-2

Typical Reactions to Violence at Different Ages

Age	Reaction
Early childhood	Passive reactions and regression (such as bed-wetting, clinging, and speaking less); fear of leaving the mother or of sleeping alone; aggressive play; sleep problems
School-age	Aggressiveness, inhibition, somatic complaints (headaches, stomachaches, etc.); learning difficulties (forgetfulness, trouble concentrating); psychological difficulties (anxiety, phobias, withdrawal, denial); grief and loss reactions (hopelessness, despair, depression, inability to play, suicidal thoughts, uncaring behavior, destructiveness); acting tough to hide fears; constricted activities
Adolescence	Some of the same reactions as school-age children, plus acting-out and self-destructive behavior (drug abuse, delinquency, promiscuity, life-threatening reenactments of the trauma); identification with the aggressor (becoming violent, joining a gang)

SOURCE: Garbarino et al., 1992.

Protective factors that seem to contribute to resilience (Anthony & Koupernik, 1974; Garmezy, 1983; M. S. Rosenberg, 1987; Rutter, 1984; E. E. Werner, 1993) include:

- *The child's personality:* Resilient children are adaptable. They try to look for the bright side of a situation. They are friendly, independent, and sensitive to others. They feel competent, have high self-esteem, and tend to be good students. They are creative, resourceful, independent, and pleasant to be with.
- *The family:* Resilient children are likely to have good relationships with one or two supportive parents. If not, they usually are close to at least one other adult who is interested and caring and whom they trust. Resilient abused children are likely to have been abused by only one parent and to have had a loving, supportive relationship with the other parent or a foster parent (Kaufman & Zigler, 1987).
- *Learning experiences:* Resilient children typically have had experience solving social problems. They have seen parents, older siblings, or others deal with frustration and make the best of a bad situation. They have faced challenges themselves, worked out solutions, and learned that they can exert some control over their lives.
- *Reduced risk:* Children who have been exposed to only one of a number of factors strongly related to psychiatric disorder (such as parental discord, low social status, a disturbed mother, a criminal father, and experience in foster care or an institution) are often able to overcome the stress. When two or more factors are present, the risk of developing an emotional disturbance increases fourfold or more (Rutter, quoted in M. Pines, 1979).
- *Compensating experiences:* A supportive school environment and successful experiences in sports, in music, or with other children or interested adults can help make up for a destructive home life. In adulthood, a good marriage can compensate for poor relationships earlier in life.

All this does not mean that bad things which happen in a child's life do not matter. In general, children with unfavorable backgrounds have more problems in adjustment than children with more favorable backgrounds. What is heartening about these findings is that negative childhood experiences do not necessarily determine the outcome of a person's life and that many children have the strength to rise above the most difficult circumstances.

Adolescence, too, is a stressful, risk-filled time— more so than middle childhood. Yet most adolescents develop the skills and competence to deal with the challenges they face, as we'll see in Chapters 10 and 11.

✔ SUMMARY

THE DEVELOPING SELF

- The self-concept develops greatly during middle childhood. Cognitive development allows school-age children to form representational systems that are more balanced and realistic than before.
- Self-esteem links cognitive, emotional, and social aspects of personality. According to Erikson, the chief source of self-esteem is children's view of their own productive competence, the "virtue" that develops through resolution of the crisis of middle childhood: *industry versus inferiority.* According to Susan Harter's research, self-esteem, or global self-worth, arises both from how competent children think they are and from how much social support they receive.

THE CHILD IN THE FAMILY

- Although school-age children spend less time with parents than with peers, relationships with parents continue to be the most important. Culture influences family relationships and roles, including the importance of extended family.
- Coregulation is an intermediate stage in the transfer of control from parent to child. Although disciplinary methods change as children get older, there appears to be an underlying consistency.
- Most mothers are now in the work force. In general, effects on children seem positive. The impact of mothers' working depends on such factors as the child's age, sex, temperament, and personality; whether the mother works full time or part

time; how she feels about her work; whether she has a supportive mate; the family's social and economic status; and the kind of care the child receives. Men's family roles seem to be as important to them as work roles.

■ Parents living in poverty may be less able to offer children effective discipline and emotional support.

■ Many children in the United States today are growing up in a variety of nontraditional family structures. These include families with divorced parents, other one-parent families, stepfamilies, and gay and lesbian families. Children tend to do better in traditional, or intact, families if the family atmosphere is positive.

■ Children's reactions to divorce depend on a number of factors, including age, gender, and resilience; the way the parents handle the situation; the custody arrangement; financial circumstances; contact with the noncustodial parent; and circumstances surrounding a parent's remarriage. Some children show long-term negative effects of parental divorce.

■ Children living with only one parent or in stepfamilies are at risk of lower achievement in school and other problems. In single-parent families, these effects seem to be largely the result of low income. Although boys tend to have more trouble adjusting to divorce, girls have more difficulty with a custodial mother's remarriage.

■ Despite public concern about children living with homosexual parents, studies have found no ill effects.

■ Siblings learn about social relationships from their relationships with one another. The roles and responsibilities of siblings in nonindustrialized societies are more significant and more structured throughout life than in industrialized societies.

THE CHILD IN THE PEER GROUP

■ Peer groups generally consist of children who are similar in age, sex, ethnicity, and socioeconomic status, and who live near one another.

■ The peer group has several positive developmental functions: it helps children develop social skills, gives them a sense of belonging, and fosters the self-concept. One negative effect is encouragement of conformity; another is racial or ethnic segregation, which can reinforce prejudice.

■ Popularity influences self-esteem. Children who are rejected by their peers are at risk for emotional and behavioral problems.

■ Friendship differs from popularity in that it involves mutual commitment and give-and-take. Friends typically are of the same age, sex, and ethnicity and have common interests. The basis of friendship changes with age; intimacy and stability of relationships increases during middle childhood.

MENTAL HEALTH

■ Emotional and behavioral problems among school-age children have increased since the mid-1970s. Common disorders include separation anxiety disorders (such as school phobia), acting-out behavior, and childhood depression.

■ Psychotherapy, especially behavior therapy, is generally effective. Although the use of drug therapy has increased, it should be used with caution, along with psychotherapy.

■ Normal childhood stresses take many forms and can affect emotional development. Unusual stresses, such as natural disasters and wars, also affect many children.

■ As a result of media exposure, pressure to achieve, and family responsibilities, many children today (according to Elkind) are experiencing a shortened and stressful childhood. Another source of stress in modern life is frequent mobility. Children tend to worry about their personal safety, about school, and about health.

■ Factors contributing to children's resilience include the child's personality, supportive family relationships, learning experiences, small number of risk factors, and compensating experiences.

✔ KEY TERMS

representational systems (page 299)
industry versus inferiority (299)
extended family (301)
coregulation (301)
self-care children (304)

prejudice (315)
school phobia (320)
separation anxiety disorder (320)
acting-out behavior (320)
childhood depression (320)

individual psychotherapy (320)
family therapy (320)
behavior therapy (321)
drug therapy (321)
resilient children (322)

✔ QUESTIONS FOR THOUGHT AND DISCUSSION

1 If finances permit, should either the mother or the father stay home to take care of the children instead of going to work?

2 Should parents who want a divorce stay married until their children have grown up? Why or why not?

3 Should older siblings in industrialized societies have regular formal duties in taking care of younger ones?

4 Should parents attempt to steer children to peer groups the parents approve of?

5 How can adults contribute to children's resilience? Give examples from your experience or observation.

PART FOUR

Adolescence

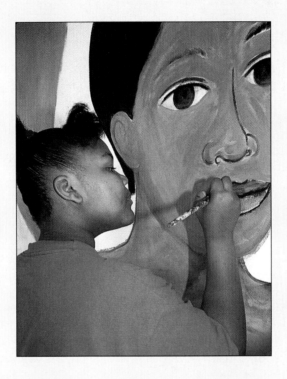

In adolescence, young people's appearance changes as a result of the hormonal events of puberty. Their thinking changes as they develop the ability to deal with abstractions. Their feelings change about almost everything. All areas of development converge as adolescents confront their major task: establishing an identity—including a sexual identity—that will carry over to adulthood. In Chapters 10 and 11, we see how adolescents incorporate their drastically changed appearance, their puzzling physical yearnings, and their new cognitive abilities into their sense of self. We see how the peer group serves as the testing ground for teenagers' ideas about life and about themselves. We look at risks and problems that arise during the teenage years, as well as at characteristic strengths of adolescents.

CHAPTER TEN

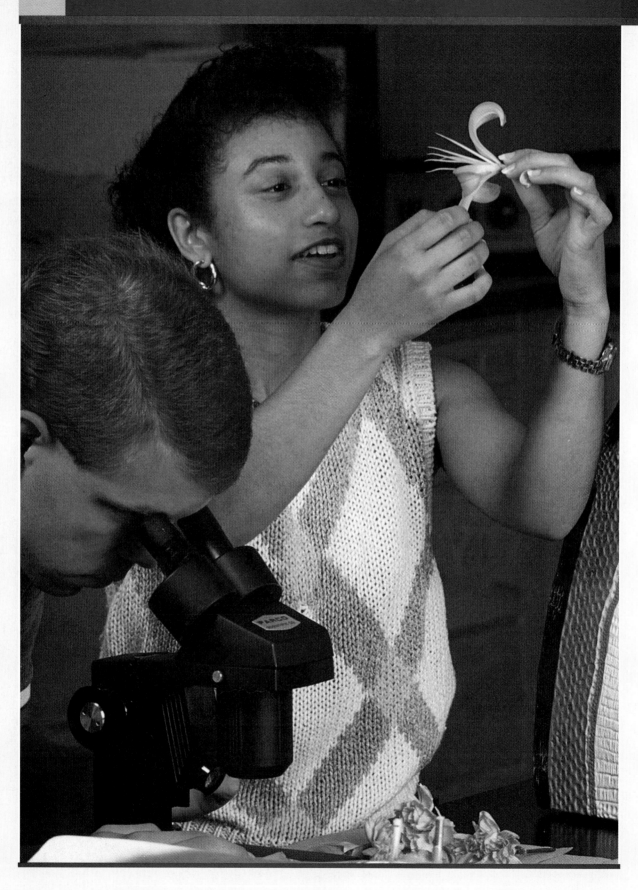

PHYSICAL AND COGNITIVE DEVELOPMENT IN ADOLESCENCE

I think what is happening to me is so wonderful, and not only what can be seen on my body, but all that is taking place inside.

Anne Frank, The Diary of a Young Girl, *1952*
(entry written January 5, 1944)

ASK YOURSELF

✔ What is adolescence, and when does it begin and end? What opportunities and risks does it entail?

✔ What physical changes do adolescents experience, and how do these changes affect them psychologically?

✔ How prevalent are eating disorders, drug abuse, sexually transmitted diseases, depression, and other health problems?

✔ How does adolescent thinking differ from that of younger children?

✔ How do adolescents make moral judgments and life decisions?

✔ What factors affect success in secondary school, and why do some teenagers drop out?

✔ How do gender and parents influence vocational choice?

I n Nepal, a girl marks her transition to womanhood by exchanging the short skirt she wore as a child for the ankle-length wrapped skirt worn by adult women. Rituals to mark a child's "coming of age" are common in many societies. Rites of passage may include religious blessings, separation from the family, severe tests of strength and endurance, marking the body in some way (see Box 10-1), or acts of magic. The ritual may be held at a certain age, as are the bar mitzvah and bat mitzvah ceremonies that mark the assumption by 13-year-old Jewish boys and girls of responsibility for traditional religious observance; or it can be tied to a specific event, such as a girl's first menstruation, which Apache tribes celebrate with a four-day ritual of sunrise-to-sunset chanting.

In modern industrial societies, the passage to adulthood is generally less abrupt and less clearly marked. Instead, these societies recognize a long transitional period known as *adolescence*, a developmental transition between childhood and adulthood that entails major, interrelated physical, cognitive, and psychosocial changes.

■ In this chapter we describe the tremendous physical changes of this period and how they influence young people's feelings about themselves. We consider the impact of early and late maturation, we look at health problems that affect adolescents, and we see how cognitive advances help them consider abstract ideas and moral issues. We discuss practical aspects of cognitive growth having to do with school and work. In Chapter 11, we focus on issues concerning personality and social relationships. ■

✔ ADOLESCENCE: A DEVELOPMENTAL TRANSITION

Adolescence lasts almost a decade, from about age 12 or 13 until the late teens or early twenties. Neither its beginning nor its end point is clearly marked. Adolescence is generally considered to begin with *puberty,* the process that leads to sexual maturity, or fertility—the ability to reproduce.* Before the twentieth century, children in western cultures entered the adult world when they matured physically or when they began a vocational apprenticeship. Today entry into adulthood takes longer and is less clear-cut. Puberty begins earlier than it used to, and entrance into a vocation tends to occur later, since complex societies require longer periods of education or vocational training before a young person can take on adult responsibilities.

Contemporary American society has a variety of markers of entrance into adulthood. There are *legal* definitions: at 17, young people may enlist in the armed forces; at age 18, in most states, they may marry without their parents' permission; at 18 to 21 (depending on the state), they may enter into binding contracts. Using *sociological* definitions, people may call themselves adults when they are self-supporting or have chosen a career, have married or formed a significant relationship, or have founded a family. There are also *psychological* definitions. Cognitive maturity is often considered to coincide with the capacity for abstract thought. Emotional maturity may depend on such

*The term *puberty* is sometimes used to mean the end point of sexual maturation, and the process is called *pubescence;* but our usage conforms to that of most psychologists today.

BOX 10-1   WINDOW ON THE WORLD

FEMALE GENITAL MUTILATION

Many traditional societies have coming-of-age rituals that signal membership in the adult community. These ceremonies often include putting an enduring mark on the body; for example, tattooing or scarring the face, removing the foreskin from the penis, or sharpening the teeth. One custom widely practiced in some parts of Africa, the Middle East, southeastern Asia, and Central and South America is surgery to alter the female genitals (Samad, 1996).

This 4,000-year-old practice, euphemistically called *female circumcision,* is termed *female genital mutilation (FGM)* by the World Health Organization. The operation—which is performed, usually without anesthesia, on girls of varying ages from infancy to puberty—entails *clitoridectomy,* the removal of part or all of the clitoris. Its most extreme form, *infibulation,* includes total clitoridectomy plus removal of parts of the labia (the lips of the vulva), the raw edges of which are then sewn together with catgut or held by thorns, leaving only a tiny opening for menstrual blood and urine. When a woman marries, the scar may be cut open and then enlarged for childbirth (Council on Scientific Affairs, 1995; Samad, 1996). About 80 to 100 million women worldwide have had such surgery, and 2 million girls undergo it each year (MacFarquhar, 1996; Samad, 1996).

The purposes of these procedures include preserving (and proving) virginity before marriage, reducing sexual appetite, maintaining cleanliness, increasing fertility, enhancing beauty, and affirming femininity through removal of the "malelike" clitoris. Some communities believe that the clitoris can poison men during intercourse and babies during childbirth or that an unremoved clitoris will grow to the size of a penis. In such cultures, an uncircumcised girl may not be considered marriageable and may be ostracized. The operation also affirms the stability of established custom and reinforces respect for authority (Council on Scientific Affairs, 1995; Lightfoot-Klein, 1989; Samad, 1996).

Besides loss of sexual fulfillment, the consequences of FGM can include psychological dysfunction and various immediate or long-term medical problems, such as shock, infection, hemorrhaging, damage to the urethra or anus, tetanus, inability to urinate normally, painful intercourse, complications of childbirth, sterility, or even death (Council on Scientific Affairs, 1995; Lightfoot-Klein, 1989; Samad, 1996).

In more than 20 countries where these operations are practiced, government officials, physicians, and women's groups have tried to end them. However, because many women believe in FGM and are often the ones who carry it out (or fear that their daughters will not be able to marry without it) and because it is sanctioned by some religious leaders, the practice continues (MacFarquhar, 1996; Samad, 1996). A ban by the Egyptian Health Ministry in 1996 met widespread local defiance. FGM has been practiced among east African refugees in Europe and North America—an estimated 40,000 procedures each year in the United States alone (MacFarquhar, 1996).

A number of countries, including Britain, France, Sweden, and Switzerland have passed laws banning the practice, and the United States Congress outlawed it in 1996. (Previously some states had made it a crime.)

The World Health Organization, the World Medical Association, and the American Medical Association condemn FGM as medically unnecessary, harmful, and abusive. A British organization, the Foundation for Women's Health Research and Development (FORWARD), which was formed in 1981 to raise awareness of FGM, views it as a violation of human rights. Despite some resistance to interfering with a practice that reflects cultural beliefs (Samad, 1996), these organizations have urged physicians not to participate in such surgery and have supported efforts to abolish it. The AMA's Council on Scientific Affairs (1995) urges that doctors "provide culturally sensitive counseling" to awaken patients and their families to its dangers.

Attitudes are changing in some areas where the surgery has traditionally been performed. Some western-educated African women have modified versions of the surgery done antiseptically, at home or in clinics, using anesthesia. Others have rejected it altogether (Samad, 1996). A survey of 150 third-year high school girls in the Sudan found that even though about 96 percent had undergone FGM, more than 70 percent were strongly opposed to it for their sisters and other young girls (Pugh, 1983).

achievements as discovering one's identity, becoming independent of parents, developing a system of values, and forming relationships. Some people never leave adolescence, no matter what their chronological age.

Early adolescence, the transition out of childhood, may be the most intense segment of the entire life span. It offers opportunities for growth in competence, autonomy, self-esteem, and intimacy. However, it also carries great risks. Some young people have trouble handling so many changes at once and may need help in overcoming dangers along the way. Adolescence is a time of increasing divergence between the majority of young people, who are headed for a fulfilling and productive adulthood, and a sizable minority (about 1 out of 5) who will be dealing with major problems (Offer, 1987; Offer & Schonert-Reichl, 1992).

American adolescents today face greater hazards to their physical and mental well-being than did their counterparts in earlier years (Petersen, 1993; Takanishi, 1993). Some of these hazards are early pregnancy and childbearing (see Chapter 11), shrinking job prospects, and high death rates from accidents, homicide, and suicide (CDC, 1994c; Rivara & Grossman, 1996; USDHHS, 1996). These problems are not typical in other developed countries (Petersen, 1991). Behavior patterns that contribute to these risks, such as heavy drinking, drug abuse, sexual and gang activity, motorcycling without helmets, and use of firearms, are established early in adolescence and need to be changed then (Petersen, 1993; Rivara & Grossman, 1996).

✔ PUBERTY

The biological changes of puberty, which signal the end of childhood, result in rapid growth in height and weight (second only in pace to that in infancy), changes in body proportions and form, and attainment of sexual maturity. These dramatic physical changes are part of a long, complex process of maturation that begins even before birth, and their psychological ramifications continue into adulthood.

Puberty begins when the pituitary gland at the base of the brain sends a message to the sex glands to increase their secretion of hormones. The precise time when this occurs is determined by the interaction of genes, health, and environment; it may be related to reaching a critical weight level. In girls the ovaries sharply step up production of the female hormone estrogen, which stimulates growth of female genitals and development of breasts. In boys, the testes increase the manufacture of androgens, particularly testosterone, which stimulate growth of male genitals and body hair. (Boys and girls have both types of hormones, but girls have higher levels of estrogen and boys have higher levels of androgens.)

Because hormones are associated with aggression in boys and with both aggression and depression in girls (Brooks-Gunn, 1988), some researchers attribute the increased emotionality and moodiness of early adolescence to hormonal changes. However, social influences may combine with hormonal ones and may even predominate. Although there is a relationship between hormone production and sexuality, adolescents may begin sexual activity more in accord with what their friends do than with what their glands secrete (Brooks-Gunn & Reiter, 1990).

TIMING, SEQUENCE, AND SIGNS OF MATURATION

Any eighth or ninth grade class picture presents startling contrasts. Flat-chested little girls stand next to full-bosomed, full-grown young women. Skinny little boys stand next to broad-shouldered, mustached young men.

There is about a 7-year range for the onset of puberty in both boys and girls. The process typically takes about 4 years for both sexes and begins about 2 or 3 years earlier for girls than for boys. Some people move through puberty very quickly and others more slowly. Girls, on average, begin to show pubertal change at 8 to 10 years of age. However, it is normal for girls to show the first signs as early as age 7 or as late as 14. The average age for boys' entry into puberty is 12, but boys may begin to show changes any time between 9 and 16 (Chumlea, 1982; Herman-Giddens et al., 1997).

On the basis of historical sources, developmentalists have found a *secular trend* (a trend that spans several generations) in the onset of puberty: a lowering of the age when puberty begins and when young people reach adult height and sexual maturity. The trend, which also involves increases in adult height and weight, began about 100 years ago and has occurred in the United States, western Europe, and Japan (Chumlea, 1982). The most likely explanation seems to be a higher standard of living. Children who are healthier, better-nourished, and better cared for mature earlier and grow bigger. Thus, the age of sexual maturity is later in less developed countries than in more industrialized ones. For example, Bundi girls of New Guinea do not begin to menstruate until an average age of 18, about five years later than American girls (Tanner, 1989). Although the secular trend is generally thought to have ended in the United States, recent data challenge this view. Girls, on average, appear to be maturing earlier than previous studies showed. African American girls seem to be 1 to 1½ years ahead of white girls (Herman-Giddens et al., 1997).

Physical changes during puberty include the adolescent growth spurt, the beginning of menstruation for girls, the production of sperm in males, the maturation of reproductive organs, the development of pubic hair and a deeper voice, and muscular growth, which peaks at age 12½ for girls and 14½ for boys. These changes unfold in a sequence that is much more consistent than their timing, though it does vary somewhat. One girl, for example, may be developing breasts and body hair at about the same rate; in another, body hair may grow so fast that it shows an adult pattern a year or so before her breasts develop. Similar variations occur among boys (Tobin-Richards, Boxer, McKavrell, & Petersen, 1984). Table 10-1 shows the usual sequence for each sex.

The Adolescent Growth Spurt

The *adolescent growth spurt,* a rapid increase in height and weight, generally begins in girls between ages 9½ and 14½ (usually at about 10) and in boys, between 10½ and 16 (usually at 12 or 13). The growth spurt typically lasts about 2 years; soon after it ends, the young person reaches sexual maturity. Since girls' growth spurt usually occurs earlier than that of boys, girls between ages 11 and 13 are taller, heavier, and stronger than boys the same age. After their growth spurt, boys are again larger, as before. Both boys and girls reach virtually their full height by age 18 (Behrman, 1992).

Boys and girls grow differently, of course. A boy becomes larger overall: his shoulders wider, his legs longer relative to his trunk, and his forearms longer relative to his upper arms and his height. A girl's pelvis widens to make childbearing easier, and layers of fat are laid down just under the skin, giving her a more rounded appearance.

The adolescent growth spurt affects practically all skeletal and muscular dimensions. Even the eye

As this sixth-grade couple illustrates, girls at this age tend to be taller and heavier than their male classmates, who reach their adolescent growth spurt later than girls do. *(Barbara Rios/Photo Researchers)*

grows faster, causing an increase in nearsightedness, a problem that affects about one-fourth of 12- to 17-year-olds (Gans, 1990). The lower jaw becomes longer and thicker, the jaw and nose project more, and the incisor teeth become more upright. Because each of these changes follows its own timetable, parts of the body may be out of proportion for a while. The result is the familiar teenage gawkiness that accompanies unbalanced, accelerated growth.

Primary and Secondary Sex Characteristics

The *primary sex characteristics* are the organs necessary for reproduction. In the female, the sex organs are the ovaries, uterus, and vagina; in the male, the testes, prostate gland, penis, and seminal vesicles (see Figure 2-1 and Table 10-2). During puberty, these organs enlarge and mature. In boys, the first sign of puberty is the growth of the testes and scrotum.

The *secondary sex characteristics* are physiological signs of sexual maturation that do not directly involve the sex organs: for example, the breasts of females and the broad shoulders of males. Other secondary sex characteristics are changes in the voice and skin texture, muscular development, and the growth of pubic, facial, axillary (armpit), and body hair (see Table 10-3).

The first sign of puberty in girls is usually the

TABLE 10-1

Usual Sequence of Physiological Changes in Adolescence

Female Characteristics	Age of First Appearance
Growth of breasts	7–13
Growth of pubic hair	7–14
Body growth	9.5–14.5
Menarche	10–16.5
Underarm hair	About 1 or 2 years after appearance of pubic hair
Increased output of oil- and sweat-producing glands (which may lead to acne)	About the same time as appearance of underarm hair

Male Characteristics	Age of First Appearance
Growth of testes, scrotal sac	10–13.5
Growth of pubic hair	10–15
Body growth	10.5–16
Growth of penis, prostate gland, seminal vesicles	11–14.5
Change in voice	About the same time as growth of penis
First ejaculation of semen	About 1 year after beginning of growth of penis
Facial and underarm hair	About 2 years after appearance of pubic hair
Increased output of oil- and sweat-producing glands (which may lead to acne)	About the same time as appearance of underarm hair

TABLE 10-2

Primary Sex Characteristics: Sex Organs

Female	Male
Ovaries	Testes
Fallopian tubes	Penis
Uterus	Scrotum
Vagina	Seminal vesicles
	Prostate gland

TABLE 10-3

Secondary Sex Characteristics

Girls	Boys
Breasts	Pubic hair
Pubic hair	Axillary (underarm) hair
Axillary (underarm) hair	Muscular development
Changes in voice	Facial hair
Changes in skin	Changes in voice
Increased width and depth of pelvis	Changes in skin
Muscular development	Broadening of shoulders

budding of the breasts. The nipples enlarge and protrude, the *areolae* (the pigmented areas surrounding the nipples) enlarge, and the breasts assume first a conical and then a rounded shape. Some adolescent boys, much to their distress, experience temporary breast enlargement; this is normal and may last up to 18 months.

The voice deepens, partly in response to the growth of the larynx and partly, especially in boys, in response to the production of male hormones. The skin becomes coarser and oilier. Increased activity of the sebaceous glands (which secrete a fatty substance) may give rise to pimples and blackheads. Acne is more common in boys and seems related to increased amounts of testosterone.

Pubic hair—which at first is straight and silky and eventually becomes coarse, dark, and curly—appears in different patterns in males and females. Adolescent boys are usually happy to see hair on the face and chest; but girls are usually dismayed at the appearance of even a slight amount of hair on the face or around the nipples, though this is normal.

Signs of Sexual Maturity: Sperm Production and Menstruation

In males, the principal sign of sexual maturity is the production of sperm. Its timing is highly variable, but nearly one-fourth of 15-year-old boys have sperm in the urine (D. W. Richardson & Short, 1978). A boy may wake up to find a wet spot or a hardened, dried spot on the sheets—the result of a *nocturnal emission,* an involuntary ejaculation of semen (commonly referred to as a *wet dream*). Most adolescent boys have these emissions, sometimes in connection with an erotic dream. There is little research on boys' feelings about the first ejaculation (*spermarche*), which occurs at an average age of 13; most boys in one study reported positive reactions, though about two-thirds were somewhat frightened (Gaddis & Brooks-Gunn, 1985).

The principal sign of sexual maturity in girls is menstruation, a monthly shedding of tissue from the lining of the womb. The first menstruation, called *menarche,* occurs fairly late in the sequence of female development (refer back to Table 10-1). On average, a girl in the United States first menstruates before her thirteenth birthday—about 2 years after her breasts have begun to develop and her uterus has begun to grow, and shortly after her growth spurt has slowed down. However, the normal timing of menarche can vary from ages 10 to 16½.

Strenuous exercise, as in competitive athletics, can delay menarche (Graber, Brooks-Gunn, & Warren, 1995), and nutrition is a factor. One study suggests a combination of genetic, physical, emotional, and environmental influences on its timing (Graber et al., 1995). Seventy-five girls were examined at ages 10 to 14, before starting to menstruate, and again after menarche. Their age of first menstruation turned out to be similar to that of their mothers. Bigger girls and those whose breasts were more developed tended to menstruate ear-

lier. Even when these factors were controlled, girls with early menarche tended to show aggression or depression or reported poor family relationships (conflict with parents, lack of parental approval and warmth, or negative feelings about the home environment). This last finding supports previous suggestions of a link between family conflict and early menarche (Moffitt, Caspi, Belsky, & Silva, 1992; L. Steinberg, 1988). The mechanism by which family problems may affect menarche is not clear, though it may have something to do with hormonal activity.

Menarche is more than a physical event; it is "a concrete symbol of a shift from girl to woman" (Ruble & Brooks-Gunn, 1982, p. 1557). Although in many cultures menarche is taken as the sign that a girl has become a woman, early menstrual periods usually do not include ovulation, and many girls are unable to conceive for 12 to 18 months. However, since ovulation and conception do sometimes occur in these early months, girls who have begun to menstruate should assume that they can become pregnant.

Unfortunately, in the past, the negative side of menstruation—the discomfort and embarrassment that may accompany it—was emphasized. Today, although many girls have mixed feelings about starting to menstruate, most take it in stride. The better-prepared a girl is for menarche, the more positive her feelings and the less her distress (Koff, Rierdan, & Sheingold, 1982; Rierdan, Koff, & Flaherty, 1986; Ruble & Brooks-Gunn, 1982).

A survey of 587 sixth through ninth grade girls in middle-class suburbs of Boston (Stubbs, Rierdan, & Koff, 1989) found both positive and negative attitudes, often in the same girl. Most girls considered menstruation something to be happy about—a sign of normal, healthy womanhood—and felt comfortable talking about it with their mothers or friends. This positive attitude seemed to be well established by sixth grade and held true regardless of age and of whether or not a girl had reached menarche. Still, many girls worried about having an "accident" and about someone knowing they had their period; they were more easily upset at that time of the month; and they envied boys for not having to menstruate. Girls who reached menarche early were more likely to have strong negative feelings, possibly because they were less prepared or felt out of step with their friends. Among those who were not yet menstruating, worries increased with age, perhaps reflecting the experience of peers.

Young girls need information from parents,

The wide range of sizes and body shapes that can be seen among a group of early adolescents results from the 6- to 7-year variation in the onset of puberty. Boys tend to like maturing early, but girls do not. *(Robert Brenner/ PhotoEdit)*

teachers, or health professionals that addresses both the affirmative and negative aspects of menstruation—information geared to their biological, cognitive, and social readiness (Stubbs et al., 1989). They need to understand that menstruation is a normal, universal female experience, different from injury or disease.

PSYCHOLOGICAL EFFECTS OF EARLY AND LATE MATURATION

One of the great paradoxes of adolescence is the conflict between a young person's yearning to assert a unique self and an overwhelming desire to be exactly like his or her friends. Anything that sets an adolescent apart from the crowd can be unsettling, and youngsters may be disturbed if they mature sexually either much earlier or much later than usual. However, the effects of early and late maturing are not clear-cut and differ in boys and girls.

Some research has found early-maturing boys to be more poised, relaxed, good-natured, popular with peers, likely to be leaders, and less impulsive than late maturers. Other studies have found them to be more worried about being liked, more cautious, and more bound by rules and routines. Some studies suggest that early maturers retain a head start in cognitive performance into late adolescence and adulthood (R. T. Gross & Duke, 1980; M. C. Jones, 1957; Tanner, 1978). Late maturers have been found to feel more inadequate, rejected, and dominated; to be more dependent, aggressive,

and insecure; to rebel more against their parents; and to think less of themselves (Mussen & Jones, 1957; Peskin, 1967, 1973; Siegel, 1982).

Apparently there are pluses and minuses in both situations. Boys like to mature early, and those who do so seem to gain in self-esteem (Alsaker, 1992; Clausen, 1975). Being more muscular than late maturers, they are stronger and better in sports and have a more favorable body image. They also have an edge in dating (Blyth et al., 1981). However, an early maturer sometimes has trouble living up to expectations that he should act as mature as he looks.

Unlike most boys, girls tend *not* to like maturing early; they are generally happier if their timing is about the same as that of their peers. Early-maturing girls tend to be less sociable, less expressive, and less poised; more introverted and shy; and more negative about menarche (M. C. Jones, 1958; Livson & Peskin, 1980; Ruble & Brooks-Gunn, 1982; Stubbs et al., 1989). Some research suggests that they are apt to have a poor body image and lower self-esteem than later-maturing girls (Alsaker, 1992; Simmons, Blyth, Van Cleave, & Bush, 1979). However, other research has found that maturational status in itself does not affect self-esteem, which depends more on the overall context of the girl's social surroundings (Brooks-Gunn, 1988).

An early-maturing girl may feel less attractive if her new curviness clashes with cultural standards equating beauty with thinness (Crockett & Petersen, 1987). She may feel dismayed if she sees herself as changing for the worse, not for the better (Simmons, Blyth, & McKinney, 1983).

Early-maturing girls may also react to other people's concerns about their sexuality. Parents and teachers sometimes assume that girls who look mature are sexually active and may treat an early-maturing girl more strictly or disapprovingly. Other adolescents may put pressures on her that she is ill-equipped to handle. She may "hang out" with older boys and young men and may be faced with sexual demands appropriate to her appearance but not to her age (Petersen, 1993). This may help explain why some research has found early-maturing girls likely to reach lower levels of educational and occupational achievement (Stattin & Magnusson, 1990). These effects were not found, however, with upper-middle-class girls, who may be less vulnerable to manipulation (Dubas, 1992).

It is hard to generalize about the psychological effects of timing of puberty, because they depend so much on how the adolescent and other people in his or her world interpret the accompanying changes. Effects of early or late maturation are most likely to be negative when adolescents are *much* more or less developed than their peers; when they do not see the changes as advantageous; and when several stressful events occur at about the same time (Petersen, 1993; Simmons et al., 1983). As we'll see in the next section, early maturation is associated with a tendency toward risky behavior. Adults need to be sensitive to the potential impact of pubertal changes so as to help young people experience these changes as positively as possible.

✔ HEALTH CONCERNS

These years are healthy ones for most adolescents; they have low rates of disability and chronic disease. Only 27 percent of deaths of 10- to 19-year-olds are from natural causes (Gans, 1990). Still, a report to the U.S. Congress suggests that about one-fifth of the nation's 10- to 18-year-olds have at least one serious health problem, often related to mental health, and that many more young people need counseling or other health services (Dougherty, 1993).

Health problems often stem from lifestyle or poverty. Across ethnic and social-class lines, many young adolescents (ages 12 to 14) use drugs, drive while intoxicated, and become sexually active, and these behaviors increase throughout the teenage years (see Figure 10-1). Adolescents whose families have been disrupted by parental separation or death are more likely to start these activities early and to engage in them more frequently over the next few years (Millstein et al., 1992). White boys are especially prone to risky behavior; so are boys and girls who enter puberty early or whose cognitive maturation is delayed (D. P. Orr & Ingersoll, 1995).

Exercise—or lack of it—affects both mental and physical health. In a British study, 16-year-olds who participated in team or individual sports had

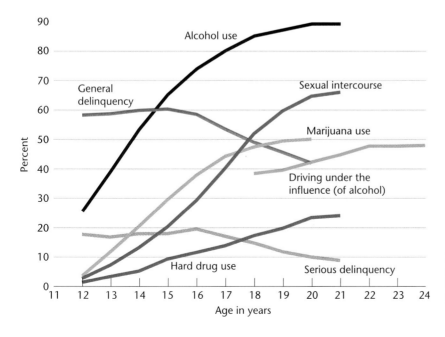

FIGURE 10-1

Age-specific rates for prevalence of high-risk behaviors, averaged over 3 years. (*Source: Adapted from Elliott, 1993.*)

fewer physical or emotional problems and felt better about themselves than less active classmates (Steptoe & Butler, 1996). A sedentary lifestyle that carries over into adulthood may result in increased risk of obesity, diabetes, osteoporosis, and heart disease. Only 35 percent of ninth grade girls and 53 percent of ninth grade boys participate in 20 minutes of vigorous activity 3 times a week, and participation rates drop to only 25 to 50 percent, respectively, for high school seniors (CDC, 1994b). On the other hand, high school students are most often injured in sports. Some of these injuries could be avoided by grouping players by size, skill, and maturational level rather than by age (AAP Committee on Sports Medicine and Committee on School Health, 1989).

The health status of adolescents is expected to worsen during the next few decades, largely because more young people will be poor. Adolescents from poor families are 3 times as likely to be in fair or poor health and 1½ times as likely to have disabling chronic illnesses as adolescents from families above the poverty line (Newacheck, 1989).

Adolescents are less likely than younger children to see a physician regularly. An estimated 14 percent of young people under age 18 do not receive the medical care they need (Gans, 1990). Adolescents with mental health problems are more likely to turn to family or friends (if anyone) than to professionals (Offer & Schonert-Reichl, 1992).

When adolescents die, it is usually from violence. The leading causes of death among 15- to 24-year-olds in the United States are accidents, homicide, and suicide (USDHHS, 1996). For African American males ages 15 to 24, homicide is the number one killer, at a rate 7 times greater than that for white males (McGinnis, Richmond, Brandt, Windom, & Mason, 1992). Still, firearms are the leading cause of death among both African American and white adolescent boys (M. Singer, Anglin, Song, & Lunghofer, 1995). Between 1985 and 1991, killings of 15- to 19-year-old boys— nearly 9 out of 10 firearm-related—increased 154 percent (CDC, 1994c). Homicide has declined since then among 15- to 24-year-olds but still claimed nearly 6,800 lives in 1994 (National Center for Health Statistics, 1995a).

Many teenagers grow up with violence as a fact of daily life. In an anonymous survey, 62 percent of the boys and 49 percent of the girls in one Cleveland high school reported having seen someone shot at, and one-third of the boys had been victims

of shootings (Singer et al., 1995). The American Academy of Pediatrics and the Center for the Prevention of Handgun Violence have developed a program to help doctors educate parents about the dangers of guns in the home, which increase the risk of teenage homicide more than threefold and suicide more than tenfold (Rivara & Grossman, 1996). (Teenage suicide is discussed further in Chapter 18.)

Let's look now at several major health concerns of adolescence: depression, eating disorders, drug abuse, and sexually transmitted diseases.

DEPRESSION

Most young people negotiate adolescence without major emotional problems, but some undergo mild to severe bouts of depression, which may lead to thoughts of, or attempts at, suicide. Research among adolescents who have *not* sought psychotherapy suggests that somewhere between 10 and 35 percent of boys and 15 to 40 percent of girls experience depressed moods (Petersen, Compas, Brooks-Gunn, Stemmler, Ey, & Grant, 1993). Before puberty, rates for depression are the same in boys and girls; but after age 15, females are about twice as likely to be depressed as males. Possibly girls have less assertive ways of coping with challenge and change, and this, coupled with the greater challenges and changes girls face during early adolescence, puts them at more risk. A girl who tends to be passive or compliant may have trouble dealing with sexual pressure from male dating partners or with competition for college entrance and career opportunities (Nolen-Hoeksema & Girgus, 1994).

Girls are more likely than boys to experience several stressful life changes at about the same time. One such change is the move from elementary to secondary school. A young person who makes this move either at or just after puberty runs a higher risk of depression, and since girls enter puberty earlier, they are more likely than boys to experience these two events simultaneously (Petersen, Sarigiani, & Kennedy, 1991). Then, because parents of daughters have a higher divorce rate than parents of sons, adolescent girls are more likely to experience their parents' divorce (Petersen et al., 1993). Still another factor is worry about appearance. Adolescent girls tend to be unhappier about their looks than adolescent boys, perhaps because of a greater cultural emphasis on women's physical attributes (Tobin-Richards, Boxer, & Petersen, 1983). In addition, males may have more effective ways of coping with a depressed mood: they typically distract themselves until the mood lifts, whereas females tend to look for reasons for their depression. These patterns may begin in adolescence (Petersen, Kennedy, & Sullivan, 1991).

Drug treatment, which often works well with depressed adults, has not proved effective for adolescent depression, for reasons that are not clear. However, psychotherapy has achieved improvement (Petersen et al., 1993).

NUTRITION AND EATING DISORDERS

The average teenage girl needs about 2,200 calories per day; the average teenage boy needs about 2,800. Teenagers (like everyone else) should avoid "junk foods" such as french fries, soft drinks, ice cream, and snack chips and dips, which are high in cholesterol, fat, and calories, and low in nutrients.

Adolescents' most common mineral deficiencies are of calcium, zinc, and iron. The need for calcium, which supports bone growth, is best met by drinking enough milk; young people who suffer from lactose intolerance (the inability to digest milk) may obtain calcium from other foods. Calcium supplements can increase bone density and may protect against osteoporosis (thinning of the bones), a condition common among middle-aged and older women (Lloyd et al., 1993; see Chapter 14). Regular weight-bearing exercise, such as walking or running, also protects against osteoporosis.

Iron-deficiency anemia is common among American adolescents because their diet tends to be iron-poor. Teenagers need a steady source of iron-fortified breads, dried fruits, and green leafy vegetables. Foods containing zinc—meats, eggs, seafood, and whole-grain cereal products—belong in the diet; even a mild zinc deficiency can delay sexual maturity (E. R. Williams & Caliendo, 1984).

Obesity

Many adolescents eat more calories than they expend and thus put on weight. Obesity is the most common eating disorder in the United States. About 5 percent of adolescents are obese (defined as weighing more than 20 percent above the recommended maximum for their height), and 15 percent are seriously overweight (Gans, 1990).

Some causes of obesity—too little physical activity and poor eating habits—are within a per-

son's control, and weight-loss programs using behavioral modification to help adolescents make changes in diet and exercise have had some success. However, genetic and other factors having nothing to do with willpower or lifestyle choices seem to make some people susceptible to obesity. Among these factors are faulty regulation of metabolism, inability to recognize body clues about hunger and satiation, and development of an abnormally large number of fat cells (see Chapter 12).

Obese teenagers tend to become obese adults, subject to physical, social, and possibly psychological risks. One 60-year longitudinal study found that overweight in adolescence can lead to life-threatening chronic conditions in adulthood, even if the excess weight is lost. The effects are particularly strong for heavy boys, who as adults have death rates nearly double those of men who were more slender as teenagers (Must, Jacques, Dallal, Bajema, & Dietz, 1992).

In another longitudinal study, 370 people, ages 16 to 24, who were above the 95th percentile of weight for their age and sex, were compared with normal-weight people, some of whom had chronic health conditions. After 7 years, the women in the overweight group had completed fewer years of school and were more likely to be poor; and both the overweight women and the overweight men were less likely to be married. These differences held even when original socioeconomic circumstances were taken into account (Gortmaker, Must, Perrin, Sobol, & Dietz, 1993). These social and economic consequences may in part be attributable to discrimination against, or social disapproval of, heavy people. Although this study found no effect of overweight on self-esteem or psychological disturbance (Gortmaker et al., 1993), other research did find an association between overweight and poor psychological adjustment (Alsakar, 1992).

Anorexia Nervosa and Bulimia Nervosa

Sometimes a determination *not* to become obese can result in even graver problems than obesity itself. For the sake of health and beauty, some adolescents—especially girls—embark on a lifelong struggle to reduce, which in some cases becomes pathological. White girls tend to be more weight- and diet-conscious than black girls. Among 497 urban and suburban high school seniors, about 66 percent of the girls were preoccupied with weight and dieting, compared with only 15 percent of the

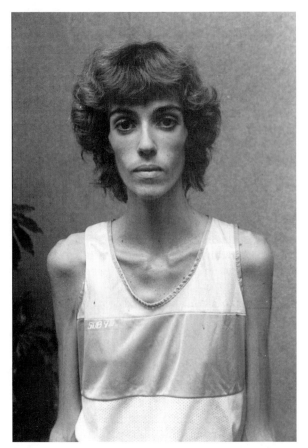 

Before this girl received therapy for anorexia nervosa, she probably had a grossly distorted body image, which prevented her from seeing how shockingly thin she was. Treatment for anorexia is sometimes successful, as these before-and-after photos show. *(William Thompson/The Picture Cube (2))*

boys (Casper & Offer, 1990). Another study found that more than half of female high school seniors have dieted seriously. Some never stop (J. D. Brown, Childers, & Waszak, 1988), and some adopt abnormal eating habits. Some young female athletes, driven to excel, try so hard to keep their weight down that they develop eating disorders, which can lead to severe bone loss and delayed menstruation (Skolnick, 1993). In recent years, two eating disorders—*anorexia nervosa* and *bulimia nervosa*—have become increasingly common.

Anorexia Someone suggests to Susanna, 14, that she would perform better in gymnastics if she lost a few pounds. She loses them—and then continues to diet obsessively. Her body weight becomes less than 85 percent of what is considered normal for her height and age (APA, 1994). Meanwhile, she stops menstruating, thick soft hair spreads over her body, and she becomes overactive. She is

preoccupied with food—cooking it, talking about it, and urging others to eat—but she eats very little herself. She brags that she exists on only three apples a day. Yet she has a distorted body image: she thinks she is too fat. She is a good student, described by her parents as a "model" child, and is compulsive about exercising. She is also withdrawn and depressed and engages in repetitive, perfectionist behavior (Garner, 1993).

This is a typical scenario for **anorexia nervosa,** or self-starvation, an eating disorder seen mostly in young white women, though it may affect both sexes. The disorder occurs across socioeconomic levels, typically during adolescence; the average age of onset is 17. The incidence of anorexia has increased in recent years; it is estimated to affect from 0.5 to 1 percent of late adolescent females and an unknown, but growing, percentage of males (APA, 1994; Garner, 1993).

The cause of anorexia is unknown. Some authorities suggest that it may be a physical disorder caused by a deficiency of a crucial chemical in the brain or by a disturbance of the hypothalamus. Others believe that it may develop because of inadequate coping skills; an anorexic may feel that controlling her weight is the only way to control any part of her life (Garner, 1993). Still others see anorexia as a psychological disturbance related to fear of growing up or fear of sexuality or to a malfunctioning family that seems harmonious while members are actually overdependent, overly involved in each other's lives, and unable to deal with conflict (Dove, undated). Anorexia may in part be a reaction to extreme societal pressure to be slender—a cultural standard more extreme than at any time since the 1920s, when the last epidemic of similar eating disorders occurred (Silverstein, Perdue, Peterson, et al., 1986; Silverstein, Peterson, & Perdue, 1986). The disorder is most prevalent in industrialized societies, such as the United States, Canada, Europe, Australia, Japan, New Zealand, and South Africa, where food is abundant and attractiveness is equated with thinness (APA, 1994). It is especially common among female competitors in figure skating and gymnastics, in which scoring can be influenced by appearance (Skolnick, 1993).

Early warning signs include determined, secret dieting; dissatisfaction after losing weight; setting new, lower weight goals after reaching an initial desired weight; excessive exercising; and interruption of regular menstruation. Diagnosis and treatment (discussed below) should occur as soon as such symptoms appear.

Bulimia   In *bulimia nervosa,* a person—usually an adolescent girl or a young woman—regularly goes on huge eating binges within a short time, usually 2 hours or less, and then tries to undo the high caloric intake by self-induced vomiting, strict dieting or fasting, engaging in excessively vigorous exercise, or taking laxatives, enemas, or diuretics to purge the body. These episodes occur at least twice a week for at least 3 months (APA, 1994). (Binge eating without purging is a separate disorder associated with obesity.)

Most people with bulimia are females; an estimated 1 to 3 percent of adolescent girls and young women suffer from the disorder. People with bulimia are obsessed with their weight and shape. They do not become abnormally thin, but they become overwhelmed with shame, self-contempt, and depression over their abnormal eating habits. They also suffer extensive tooth decay (caused by

repeated vomiting of stomach acid), gastric irritation, skin problems, and loss of hair. There is some overlap between anorexia and bulimia; some victims of anorexia have bulimic episodes, and some people with bulimia lose weight. However, the two are separate disorders.

Bulimia may be intermittent or chronic, and the long-term outcome is unknown. It is about equally common in each of the industrialized countries with high rates of anorexia, noted above (APA, 1994). One theory attributes the prevalence of bulimia in these countries to the same pressures that create a social climate for anorexia. However, bulimia may also have a biological basis; it seems to be related to low levels of the brain chemical serotonin. Then there is a psychoanalytic explanation: bulimic people use food to satisfy their hunger for love and attention. This interpretation rests on reports by some bulimic patients that they felt abused, neglected, and deprived of parental nurturing (Humphrey, 1986).

Treatment for Anorexia and Bulimia   Anorexia and bulimia can be treated, but the relapse rate for anorexia is very high. Up to 25 percent of anorexic patients progress to chronic invalidism, and between 2 and 10 percent die prematurely of starvation, suicide, electrolyte imbalance, or related causes (APA, 1994; Beumont, Russell, & Touyz, 1993; D. B. Herzog, Keller, & Lavori, 1988).

The immediate goal of treatment for anorexia is to get patients to eat and gain weight. They are likely to be admitted to a hospital, where they may be given 24-hour nursing, drugs to encourage eating and inhibit vomiting, and behavior therapy, which rewards eating with such privileges as being allowed to get out of bed and leave the room (Beumont et al., 1993). Both anorexia and bulimia are also treated by psychotherapy that helps patients understand their feelings. Since these patients are at risk for depression and suicide, antidepressant drugs can be helpful (Fluoxetine-Bulimia Collaborative Study Group, 1992; Hudson & Pope, 1990; Kaye, Weltzin, Hsu, & Bulik, 1991).

People with anorexia seem to need long-term support even after they have stopped starving themselves. Some 27 months after completion of treatment, most of the 63 females in one study were gaining weight, had resumed menstruating, and were functioning in school or at work. Still, they continued to have problems with body image. Even though they averaged 8 percent below ideal weight, most thought of themselves as being overweight and as having excessive appetites, and many felt depressed and lonely (Nussbaum, Shenker, Baird, & Saravay, 1985). Similarly, a Canadian study that followed anorexic patients for 9 years, starting 5 years after treatment, found a tendency toward depression or anxiety disorders (Toner, Garfinkel, & Garner, 1986).

USE AND ABUSE OF DRUGS

Although the great majority of adolescents do not abuse drugs, a significant minority do. They turn to drugs out of curiosity or a desire for sensation, because of peer pressure, or as an escape from overwhelming problems, and thereby endanger their present and future physical and psychological health.

Substance abuse means harmful use of alcohol or other drugs. It is a poorly adaptive behavior pattern, lasting more than 1 month, in which a person continues to use a substance after knowingly being harmed by it or uses it repeatedly in a hazardous situation, such as driving while intoxicated (APA, 1994). Abuse can lead to *substance dependence,* or addiction, which may be physiological or psychological, or both, and is likely to continue into adulthood. In one longitudinal study, more than 1,000 high school sophomores and juniors were interviewed and then reinterviewed at age 24 or 25. Those who had begun using a certain drug in their teens tended to continue to use it. Users of illicit drugs, including marijuana, were in poorer health than nonusers, had more unstable job and marital histories, and were more likely to have been delinquent (Kandel, Davies, Karus, & Yamaguchi, 1986).

Drug use among American adolescents has been on the upswing during the 1990s, though it is not as prevalent as during the late 1970s and early 1980s and considerably less so than at its peak in the 1960s. Marijuana has shown the sharpest increase, but other illicit drugs are also becoming more popular (see Table 10-4). These findings come from a series of annual surveys of a nationally representative sample of approximately 50,000 eighth-, tenth-, and twelfth-graders in more than 400 schools around the United States (National Institute on Drug Abuse, NIDA, 1995). The proportion of eighth-graders who admit to having taken illicit drugs during the previous year has almost doubled since 1991, from 11 to 21 percent. Since 1992, illicit drug use among tenth-graders has risen from 20 to 33 percent, and among twelfth-graders,

from 27 to 39 percent. These surveys probably underestimate drug use since they do not reach high school dropouts, who are likely to have higher rates.

The rise in drug use has accompanied a decline in perception of its dangers and a softening of peer disapproval. Today's teenagers have had less opportunity to observe the harm drugs can do; and their parents, many of whom were heavy users in the 1960s and 1970s, may be more complacent or less effective in warning about it. A revival of popular music and culture of the sixties and seventies has brought a flood of pro-drug messages. Arguments in favor of legalizing drugs have had an effect. Still, the great majority of young people disapprove of trying illicit drugs other than marijuana; and even for marijuana, disapproval rates range from 71 percent of eighth-graders to 57 percent of twelfth-graders (NIDA, 1995).

Legal restrictions, social norms, and economic factors such as price and taxation affect the availability and desirability of drugs and thus the extent of their use; but what makes it likely that a particular young person will abuse them? Research has pinpointed a number of characteristics of the individual and the environment: (1) poor impulse control and a tendency to seek out sensation rather than avoid harm (which may have a biochemical basis), (2) family influences (such as a genetic predisposition to alcoholism, parental use or acceptance of drugs, poor or inconsistent parenting practices, family conflict, and troubled or distant family relationships), (3) difficult temperament, (4) early and persistent behavior problems, particularly aggression, (5) academic failure and lack of commitment to education, (6) peer rejection, (7) associating with drug users, (8) alienation and rebelliousness, (9) favorable attitudes toward drug use, and (10) early initiation into drug use. The earlier young people start using a drug, the more frequently they are likely to use it and the greater the tendency to abuse it. Contrary to popular belief, poverty is not linked with drug abuse unless deprivation is extreme (Hawkins, Catalano, & Miller, 1992).

Of course, these characteristics do not necessarily *cause* drug abuse, but they are fairly reliable predictors of it. The more risk factors that are present, the greater the chance that an adolescent or young adult will abuse drugs.

Alcohol, marijuana, and tobacco are the three drugs most popular with adolescents. These are sometimes called *gateway drugs,* because their use

TABLE 10-4

Percentage of Students Who Have Ever Used Drugs, 1991–1995

Drug	Eighth-Graders, %	Tenth-Graders, %	Twelfth-Graders, %
Marijuana	1991: 10.2 1992: 11.2 1993: 12.6 1994: 16.7 1995: 19.9	1991: 23.4 1992: 21.4 1993: 24.4 1994: 30.4 1995: 34.1	1991: 36.0 1992: 32.6 1993: 35.3 1994: 38.2 1995: 41.7
Cocaine	1991: 2.3 1992: 2.9 1993: 2.9 1994: 3.6 1995: 4.2	1991: 4.1 1992: 3.3 1993: 3.6 1994: 4.3 1995: 5.0	1991: 7.8 1992: 6.1 1993: 6.1 1994: 5.9 1995: 6.0
Crack cocaine	1991: 1.3 1992: 1.6 1993: 1.7 1994: 2.4 1995: 2.7	1991: 1.7 1992: 1.5 1993: 1.8 1994: 2.1 1995: 2.8	1991: 3.1 1992: 2.6 1993: 2.6 1994: 3.0 1995: 3.0
Inhalants	1991: 17.6 1992: 17.4 1993: 19.4 1994: 19.9 1995: 21.6	1991: 15.7 1992: 16.6 1993: 17.5 1994: 18.0 1995: 19.0	1991: 17.6 1992: 16.6 1993: 17.4 1994: 17.7 1995: 17.4
LSD	1991: 2.7 1992: 3.2 1993: 3.5 1994: 3.7 1995: 4.4	1991: 5.6 1992: 5.8 1993: 6.2 1994: 7.2 1995: 8.4	1991: 8.8 1992: 8.6 1993: 10.3 1994: 10.5 1995: 11.7
Alcohol*	1991: 70.1 1992: 69.3 1993: 67.1 (55.7) 1994: 55.8 1995: 54.5	1991: 83.8 1992: 82.3 1993: 80.8 (71.6) 1994: 71.7 1995: 70.5	1991: 88.0 1992: 87.5 1993: 87.0 (80.0) 1994: 80.4 1995: 80.7
Cigarettes	1991: 44.0 1992: 45.2 1993: 45.3 1994: 46.1 1995: 46.4	1991: 55.1 1992: 53.5 1993: 56.3 1994: 56.9 1995: 57.6	1991: 63.1 1992: 61.8 1993: 61.9 1994: 62.0 1995: 64.2
All illicit drugs	1991: 18.7 1992: 20.6 1993: 22.5 1994: 25.7 1995: 28.5	1991: 30.6 1992: 29.8 1993: 32.8 1994: 37.4 1995: 40.9	1991: 44.1 1992: 40.7 1993: 42.9 1994: 45.6 1995: 48.4

*Note: In 1993, the question was reworded on half the forms to indicate that a "drink" meant "more than a few sips." The data in parentheses came from forms using the revised wording, which was then used on all forms in 1994 and 1995.
SOURCE: Adapted from NIDA, 1995.

To prevent alcohol-related motor vehicle accidents involving teenagers, educational campaigns stress the importance of naming a "designated driver," one person in a group who will take the wheel and will agree not to drink on a specific night. *(Louis Fernandez/Black Star)*

often leads to use of more addictive substances, such as cocaine and heroin.

Alcohol

Many of the same people who worry about the illegal use of marijuana forget that alcohol too is a potent, mind-altering drug, that it is illegal for

FIGURE 10-2

A sharp increase in marijuana use during the 1990s among eighth-, tenth-, and twelfth-graders accounts for most of the increase in use of illicit drugs in these age groups. The rise in use of marijuana accompanied an increase in ease of availability and a decrease in young people's perception of risk of harm from using the drug. (*Source: NIDA, 1995, Figure 7.*)

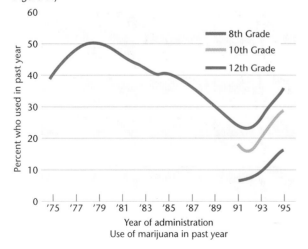

Year of administration
Use of marijuana in past year

most high school students and for college students younger than 21, and that it is a much more serious problem nationwide. High school students do seem to be drinking less than they used to; college students and young adults, slightly less. Although 4 out of 5 high school seniors report having taken "more than a few sips" of alcoholic beverages, only about 51 percent say they have had a drink during the previous month, down from the peak of 72 percent in 1980. Still, many students drink heavily; about 30 percent of twelfth-graders, 24 percent of tenth-graders, and 15 percent of eighth-graders report having had five or more drinks in a row during the previous 2 weeks. Thirty-three percent of seniors, 21 percent of tenth-graders, and about 8 percent of eighth-graders admit to having been drunk during the past month (NIDA, 1995).

Marijuana

Marijuana has been used all over the world for centuries, but only since the 1960s has it become popular among the American middle class. Despite a decline in use since 1979 (when more than 50 percent of high school seniors had smoked marijuana during the previous year), it is still by far the most widely used illicit drug in the United States; and usage has increased dramatically since the low point in the early 1990s. In 1995, 35 percent of twelfth-graders had smoked marijuana during the previous year—an increase of more than half from the 22 percent who reported using it in 1992. Increases for younger students were even greater: usage among tenth-graders nearly doubled, from 15 percent to 29 percent; and among eighth-graders, it rose to 16 percent, 2½ times as high as in 1991 (NIDA, 1995; see Figure 10-2).

Adolescents try marijuana for many of the same reasons they try alcohol: they are curious, they want to do what their friends do, and they want to be like adults. Marijuana also can be a symbol of rebellion against parental values, but this attraction may be waning, since today's teenagers are much more likely to have parents who have smoked (or now smoke) it themselves.

Heavy use of marijuana can lead to heart and lung disease; contribute to traffic accidents, nutritional deficiencies, respiratory infections, and other physical problems; and impede memory and learning. It may also lessen motivation, interfere with schoolwork, and cause family problems (AAP Committee on Drugs, 1980; Farrow, Rees, & Worthington-Roberts, 1987).

Tobacco

A U.S. Surgeon General's report in 1964 linked smoking to lung cancer, heart disease, emphysema, and several other illnesses. Many adolescents eventually got the message, and the percentage of high school seniors who were daily smokers dropped by 34 percent between 1976 and 1993. Most of that drop reflected a nearly 84 percent decline among black teenagers (H. McIntosh, 1995). Smoking, both frequent and occasional, is far less prevalent among black teenagers, especially girls, than among white and Hispanic youth. Only about 12 percent of black girls smoke at all, and only about 1 percent smoke heavily (CDC, 1996d). This may be because black girls are less concerned about weight control than white girls, who may use smoking as a way to keep from overeating (Center on Addiction and Substance Abuse at Columbia University, CASA, 1996). Black teenagers also may regard smoking as a "white thing."

Unfortunately, smoking among adolescents has taken a recent upturn; by 1995, one-third of high school seniors and 19 percent of eighth-graders were smoking regularly, up from 28 percent and 14 percent, respectively, in 1991 (NIDA, 1995). The average age of starting a smoking habit has dropped to 14½; about 9 out of 10 smokers begin before age 18 (Bartecchi, MacKenzie, & Schrier, 1995; CDC, 1996d).

Peer influence on smoking has been documented extensively (CASA, 1996), but recent research points to the influence of family factors. One 6-year longitudinal study followed 312 adolescents—most of them from white, college-educated, two-parent families—who were not smoking at ages 11 and 13. Those whose families were not close and whose parents smoked were more than twice as likely as others in the sample to smoke by ages 17 to 19 (Doherty & Allen, 1994). Tobacco advertising may be an even stronger factor (N. Evans, Farkas, Gilpin, Berry, & Pierce, 1995). National Health Interview Surveys found a sudden, marked increase in cigarette smoking by girls under 18 after the launching in 1967 of advertising campaigns specifically targeted to women (Pierce, Lee, & Gilpin, 1994).

SEXUALLY TRANSMITTED DISEASES (STDs)

Sexually transmitted diseases (STDs), also referred to as *venereal diseases,* are diseases spread by sexual contact. The prevalence of STDs has soared since the 1960s. Rates in the United States are among the highest in the industrialized world; 1 out of 4 Americans is likely to contract such a disease (Alan Guttmacher Institute, 1994).

The most prevalent STD, according to some estimates, is human papilloma virus (HPV), which sometimes produces warts on the genitals (AAP Committee on Adolescence, 1994). Next is genital herpes simplex, a chronic, recurring, often painful, and highly contagious disease caused by a virus (Alan Guttmacher Institute, 1994). The condition can be fatal to a person with a deficiency of the immune system or to the newborn infant of a mother who has an outbreak at the time of delivery. There is no cure, but the antiviral drug acyclovir can prevent active outbreaks. Both diseases have been associated, in women, with increased incidence of cervical cancer.

The most common *curable* STD is chlamydia, which causes infections of the urinary tract, rectum, and cervix and can lead, in women, to pelvic inflammatory disease (PID), a serious abdominal infection. In 1995, chlamydia was the infectious disease most frequently reported to the Centers for Disease Control (1996c), followed by gonorrhea and AIDS, which was 4 times as common among men as among women. Also among the 10 most commonly reported diseases were hepatitis A, syphilis, and hepatitis B. (Not all diseases are reported, and reports are believed to vastly underestimate true incidence.) Gonorrhea was the infectious disease most commonly reported among 15- to 24-year-olds. (Table 10-5 summarizes some common STDs: their causes, most frequent symptoms, treatment, and consequences.)

HIV and AIDS

Although AIDS is not as prevalent as some other STDs, it has reached epidemic proportions since 1980. AIDS results from the human immunodeficiency virus (HIV), which attacks the body's immune system, leaving affected persons vulnerable to a variety of fatal diseases. HIV is transmitted through bodily fluids (mainly blood and semen) and is believed to stay in the body for life, even though the person carrying it may show no signs of illness. Symptoms of AIDS—which include extreme fatigue, fever, swollen lymph nodes, weight loss, diarrhea, and night sweats—may not appear until 6 months to 10 or more years after initial infection. As of now, AIDS is incurable; but in many

TABLE 10-5

Common Sexually Transmitted Diseases

Disease	Cause	Symptoms: Male	Symptoms: Female	Treatment	Consequences If Untreated
Chlamydia	Bacterial infection	Pain during urination, discharge from penis.	Vaginal discharge, abdominal discomfort.†	Tetracycline or erythromycin.	Can cause pelvic inflammatory disease or eventual sterility.
Tricho-moniasis	Parasitic infection, sometimes passed on in moist objects such as towels and bathing suits	Often absent.	May be absent, or may include vaginal discharge, discomfort during intercourse, odor, painful urination.	Oral antibiotic.	May lead to abnormal growth of cervical cells.
Gonorrhea	Bacterial Infection	Discharge from penis, pain during urination.*	Discomfort when urinating, vaginal discharge, abnormal menses.†	Penicillin or other antibiotics.	Can cause pelvic inflammatory disease or eventual sterility; can also cause arthritis, dermatitis, and meningitis.
HPV (genital warts)	Human papilloma virus	Painless growths that usually appear on penis, but may also appear on urethra or in rectal area.*	Small, painless growths on genitals and anus; may also occur inside the vagina without external symptoms.*	Removal of warts; but infection often reappears.	May be associated with cervical cancer. In pregnancy, warts enlarge and may obstruct birth canal.
Herpes	Herpes simplex virus	Painful blisters anywhere on the genitalia, usually on the penis.*	Painful blisters on the genitalia, sometimes with fever and aching muscles; women with sores on cervix may be unaware of outbreaks.*	No known cure, but controlled with antiviral drug acyclovir.	Possible increased risk of cervical cancer.
Hepatitis B	Hepatitis B virus	Skin and eyes become yellow.	Skin and eyes become yellow.	No specific treatment; no alcohol.	Can cause liver damage, chronic hepatitis.

(Continued)

Disease	Cause	Symptoms: Male	Symptoms: Female	Treatment	Consequences If Untreated
Syphillis	Bacterial infection	In first stage, reddish-brown sores on the mouth or genitalia, or both, which may disappear, though the bacteria remain; in the second, more infectious stage, a widespread skin rash.*	Same as in men.	Penicillin or other antibiotics.	Paralysis, convulsions, brain damage, and sometimes death.
AIDS (acquired immune deficiency syndrome)	Human immunodeficiency virus (HIV)	Extreme fatigue, fever, swollen lymph nodes, weight loss, diarrhea, night sweats, susceptibility to other diseases.*	Same as in men.	No known cure; AZT and other drugs appear to extend life.	Death, usually due to other diseases, such as cancer.

*May be asymptomatic.
†Often asymptomatic.

cases the related infections that kill people can be stopped with antibiotics. Many HIV-infected people live active lives for years.

The average time from HIV infection to death is about 10 years, with clinical and immunological decline evident much earlier; but about 5 percent of HIV-infected people are characterized as having "nonprogressive disease" because they remain healthy and do not show declining blood counts, as do those whose disease progresses. The eventual fate of these "nonprogressors" is not known, but many seem to be healthy 10 or more years after being infected (Baltimore, 1995).

Worldwide, most HIV-infected adults are heterosexual. In the United States, HIV is most prevalent among drug abusers who share contaminated hypodermic needles, homosexual and bisexual men, people who have received transfusions of infected blood or blood products, people who have had sexual contact with someone in one of these high-risk groups, and infants who have been infected in the womb or during birth. Unprotected heterosexual activity with multiple partners (for example, among users of crack cocaine selling sex to support their drug habit) is an increasingly high-risk factor for contracting HIV (Edlin et al., 1994). Heterosexual transmission was responsible for

AIDS education stressing safer sexual practices—as exemplified by this poster—has reduced promiscuity and encouraged consistent use of condoms among sexually active teenagers. *(CDC National AIDS Clearing House)*

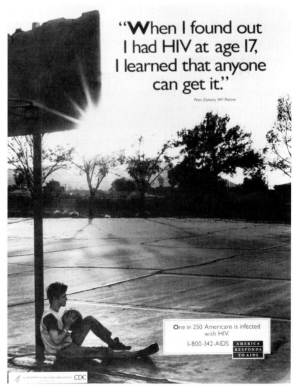

"When I found out I had HIV at age 17, I learned that anyone can get it."

Pedro Zamora, HIV Positive

One in 250 Americans is infected with HIV.
1-800-342-AIDS

9 percent of new AIDS cases in the United States in 1993—up from about 2 percent in 1985—and for more than half of all new cases among women (B. M. King, 1996).

AIDS can be avoided by changes in behavior. Prevention efforts focus on education about safer sex practices (such as using condoms, which offer some protection, and avoiding promiscuity) and screening of blood used in transfusions. Among 15- to 19-year-old boys, those who receive AIDS education and sex education have fewer sex partners and less frequent intercourse and use condoms more consistently (Ku, Sonenstein, & Pleck, 1992). More controversial are proposals to reduce sharing of hypodermic needles by distributing clean ones to drug users.

STDs and Adolescents

One out of three cases of STDs occurs among adolescents; the younger the teenager, the greater the chance of infection. The chief reasons for the spread of STDs among adolescents are early sexual activity, which increases the likelihood of having multiple high-risk partners, and failure to use condoms or to use them regularly and correctly. Half of all young people are sexually active by age 17, and an estimated 25 percent may develop an STD before high school graduation (AAP Committee on Adolescence, 1994).

Adolescents at high risk for contracting STDs—besides those who engage in unprotected sex—are those who experiment with alcohol and drugs, which can impair judgment; homosexual males; young people who "hang out" on the streets, are in jail, or engage in prostitution; and pregnant girls (AAP Committee on Adolescence, 1994).

STDs are more likely to develop undetected in women than in men, and in adolescents as compared with adults; symptoms may not show up until the disease has progressed to the point of causing serious long-term complications. Programs that promote abstaining from or postponing sexual activity, responsible decision making, and ready availability of condoms for those who are sexually active may have some effect in controlling the spread of STDs. It is important to target programs to women and teenagers, since they are disproportionately affected by many STDs (AAP Committee on Adolescence, 1994; Alan Guttmacher Institute, 1994). Box 10-2 lists steps that people can take to protect themselves from STDs.

✔ ASPECTS OF COGNITIVE MATURATION

Despite the perils of adolescence, most young people emerge from the teenage years with mature, healthy bodies and a zest for life. Their cognitive development has continued too. Adolescents not only look different from younger children; they also think differently. They are capable of abstract reasoning and sophisticated moral judgments, and they can plan more realistically for the future.

PIAGET'S STAGE OF FORMAL OPERATIONS

What differentiates adolescent thinking from the thought processes of younger children is the awareness of the concept "What if . . . ?" Much of childhood appears to be a struggle to come to grips with the world as it *is*. Teenagers become aware of the world as it *could be*.

According to Piaget, adolescents enter the highest level of cognitive development—*formal operations*—when they develop the capacity for abstract thought. This development, which usually occurs around age 12, gives them a new way to manipulate (or operate on) information. No longer limited to thinking about the here and now, they can think in terms of what *might* be true, rather than just in terms of what *is* true. They can imagine possibilities, test hypotheses, and form theories.

Evidence of Cognitive Maturity

To appreciate the advance in thinking that the stage of formal operations brings, let's follow the progress of a typical child in dealing with a classic Piagetian problem, the pendulum problem.* The child, Adam, is shown the pendulum—an object hanging from a string. He is then shown how he can change any of four factors: the length of the string, the weight of the object, the height from which the object is released, and the amount of force he may use to push the object. He is asked to figure out which factor or combination of factors determines how fast the pendulum swings.

When Adam first sees the pendulum, he is not yet 7 years old and is in the preoperational stage. Unable to formulate a plan for attacking the problem, he tries one thing after another in a hit-or-

*This description of age-related differences in approach to the pendulum problem is adapted from Ginsburg and Opper (1979).

BOX 10-2　　PRACTICALLY SPEAKING

PROTECTING AGAINST SEXUALLY TRANSMITTED DISEASES

How can people protect themselves against sexually transmitted diseases (STDs)? Abstinence is safest, of course. For those who are sexually active, the following guidelines minimize the possibility of acquiring an STD and maximize the chances of getting good treatment if one is acquired.

■ Have regular medical checkups. All sexually active persons should request tests specifically aimed at diagnosing STDs.

■ Know your partner. The more discriminating you are, the less likely you are to be exposed to STDs. Partners with whom you develop a relationship are more likely than partners you do not know well to inform you of any medical problems they have.

■ Avoid having sexual intercourse with many partners, promiscuous persons, and drug abusers.

■ Practice "safer sex": avoid sexual activity involving exchange of bodily fluids. Use a latex condom during intercourse and oral sex. Avoid anal intercourse.

■ Use a contraceptive foam, cream, or jelly; it will kill many germs and help to prevent certain STDs.

■ Learn the symptoms of STDs: vaginal or penile discharge; inflammation, itching, or pain in the genital or anal area; burning during urination; pain during intercourse; genital, body, or mouth sores, blisters, bumps, or rashes; pain in the lower abdomen or in the testicles; discharge from or itching of eyes; and fever or swollen glands.

■ Inspect your partner for any visible symptoms.

■ If you develop any symptoms yourself, get immediate medical attention.

■ Just before and just after sexual contact, wash genital and rectal areas with soap and water; males should urinate after washing.

■ Do not have any sexual contact if you suspect that you or your partner may be infected. Abstinence is the most reliable preventive measure.

■ Avoid exposing any cut or break in the skin to anyone else's blood (including menstrual blood), body fluids, or secretions.

■ Practice good hygiene routinely: frequent, thorough hand washing and daily brushing under fingernails.

■ Make sure needles used for ear piercing, tattooing, acupuncture, or any kind of injection are either sterile or disposable. Never share a needle.

■ If you contract any STD, notify all recent sexual partners immediately so that they can obtain treatment and avoid passing the infection back to you or on to someone else. Inform your doctor or dentist of your condition so that precautions can be taken to prevent transmission. Do not donate blood, plasma, sperm, body organs, or other body tissue.

SOURCE: Adapted from American Foundation for the Prevention of Venereal Disease, AFPVD, 1988; Upjohn Company, 1984.

---

miss manner. First he puts a light weight on a long string and pushes it; then he tries swinging a heavy weight on a short string; then he removes the weight entirely. Not only is his method random; he also cannot understand or report what has happened.

Adam next encounters the pendulum at age 11, when he is in the stage of concrete operations. This time, he discovers that varying the length of the string and the weight of the object affect the speed of the swing. However, because he varies both factors at the same time, he cannot tell which is critical or whether both are.

Adam is confronted with the pendulum for a third time at age 15, and this time he goes at the problem systematically. He designs an experiment to test all the possible hypotheses, varying one factor at a time—first, the length of the string; next, the weight of the object; then the height from which it is released; and finally, the amount of force used—each time holding the other three factors constant. In this way, he is able to determine that only one factor—the length of the string—determines how fast the pendulum swings.

Adam's solution of the pendulum problem shows that he has arrived at the stage of formal operations. Since he can imagine a variety of possibilities, he is now capable of *hypothetical-*

What determines how fast the pendulum swings: the length of the string? the weight of the object suspended from it? the height from which the object is released? the amount of force used to push the object? According to Piaget, an adolescent who has achieved the stage of formal operations can form a hypothesis and figure out a logical way to test it. However, many people never figure out how to solve this problem. *(Mimi Forsyth/Monkmeyer)*

deductive reasoning. He can develop a hypothesis and can design an experiment to test it. He considers all the relationships he can imagine and goes through them one by one, to eliminate the false and arrive at the true.

Adolescents can apply this new-found ability to consider and test possibilities to all sorts of problems: fixing the family car, planning a career, constructing political theories, or interpreting social situations (Offer & Schonert-Reichl, 1992). The ability to think abstractly has emotional implications too. Earlier, a child could love a parent or hate a classmate. Now "the adolescent can love freedom or hate exploitation. . . . The possible and the ideal captivate both mind and feeling" (H. Ginsburg & Opper, 1979, p. 201).

What Brings about Cognitive Maturity?

According to Piaget, neurological and environmental influences combine to bring about cogni-

tive maturity. The adolescent's brain has matured, and the wider social environment offers more opportunities for experimentation and cognitive growth. Interaction between the two kinds of change is essential: even if young people's neurological development has advanced enough to allow them to reach the stage of formal reasoning, they may never attain it without environmental stimulation. One way this happens is through peer interaction.

In one study, researchers gave college students (average age, 18½ years) a chemistry problem, asked them questions about it, and told them to set up their own experiments (Dimant & Bearison, 1991). Students were randomly assigned to work alone or with a partner. Those working in twosomes were told to discuss their answers with each other. Their videotaped statements were categorized as (1) disagreement, (2) explanation, (3) question, (4) agreement, or (5) extraneous. The researchers coded one dialogue as follows (Dimant & Bearison, 1991, p. 280):

Student A: "What you said can't be. It's no sense." (*disagreement*)

Student B: "I'm right. I know it." (*disagreement*)

Student A: "Look here, see B [a container in the experiment] didn't work with D and E, so it can't be B." (*explanation*)

Student B: "Oh, you're right." (*agreement*)

Students who worked in pairs solved more problems than those who worked alone. Quality as well as frequency of feedback was important. The more disagreeing, explaining, and questioning a student received—that is, the more a partner challenged his or her reasoning—the greater were the advances in thinking.

Limitations of Piaget's Theory

Does Piaget's stage of formal operations represent the highest reaches of cognitive development? Some critics say no.

Perhaps one-third to one-half of American adults never attain the stage of formal operations as measured by the pendulum problem and conservation of volume (Kohlberg & Gilligan, 1971; Papalia, 1972). Even by late adolescence or adulthood not everyone seems to be capable of abstract thought as Piaget defined it, and those who are capable do not always use it. Are these people cognitively immature? Or are there other aspects of mature thought not captured by Piaget's theory?

According to Piaget's critics, formal reasoning is not the only, and perhaps not even the most important, aspect of mature thinking. Such Piagetian measures as the pendulum problem and conservation of volume seem to imply that cognition is bounded by mathematical and scientific thinking—a narrow view of a person as "living in a timeless world of abstract rules" (Gilligan, 1987a, p. 67). Formal logic may be less important in such nonscientific fields as history, languages, writing, and the arts. And, as we discuss in Chapter 14, Piaget's theory may not give enough weight to such aspects of mature intelligence as practical problem solving and the wisdom that helps adults cope with an often chaotic world.

IMMATURE ASPECTS OF ADOLESCENT THOUGHT

By adolescence, those totally egocentric beings whose interest extended not much farther than the nipple have developed into people who can solve complex problems, make moral judgments, and envision ideal societies. Yet sometimes, as any parent of a teenager will attest, adolescents' thought seems immature. On the basis of clinical work with adolescents, the psychologist David Elkind (1984) described typical behaviors and attitudes that may stem from young people's inexperienced ventures into abstract thought:

- *Finding fault with authority figures:* Adolescents now realize that the adults they once worshipped fall far short of their ideals, and they feel compelled to say so—loudly and often. Parents who look at this criticism as a typical part of teenagers' cognitive and social development can deal with such remarks matter-of-factly, acknowledging that nothing and nobody (not even a teenager!) is perfect.
- *Argumentativeness:* Adolescents often become argumentative as they practice their new abilities to explore the nuances of a problem and to build a case for their viewpoint. If adults encourage and take part in debates about principles while avoiding personality issues, they can help young people stretch their reasoning powers without becoming embroiled in family feuds.
- *Indecisiveness:* Many teenagers have trouble making up their minds even about simple things

because they are now more aware of how many choices life offers. Should Rosalie go to the mall with her girlfriend on a Saturday, or to a movie with her mother, or to the library to work on a school assignment? She may ponder such dilemmas at length, even though the decision will not substantially change her life.

- *Apparent hypocrisy:* Young adolescents often do not recognize the difference between expressing an ideal and living up to it. Bill marches against pollution while littering along the way, and Beth aggressively protests for peace. Part of growing up is the realization that for values to be meaningful, they have to be acted upon.
- *Self-consciousness:* Adolescents can now put themselves in someone else's place and think about what someone else is thinking. However, since they have trouble distinguishing what is interesting to them from what is interesting to someone else, they often assume that everyone else is thinking about the same thing they are thinking about: themselves. The extreme self-consciousness of young adolescents has a great deal to do with the *imaginary audience,* a conceptualized "observer" who is as concerned

According to the psychologist David Elkind, indecisiveness—illustrated by this girl's difficulty in choosing what to wear—is a common immature aspect of adolescent thought. *(Spencer Grant/Stock, Boston)*

with their thoughts and behavior as they are. Because self-consciousness can be especially painful in adolescence, it is important to avoid public criticism or ridicule of young teenagers.

■ *Assumption of invulnerability:* Elkind uses the term **personal fable** to denote a belief by adolescents that they are special, that their experience is unique, and that they are not subject to the rules that govern the rest of the world ("These things happen only to other people, not to me"). According to Elkind, this special form of egocentrism shows up strongly in early adolescence and underlies much risky, self-destructive behavior. A girl thinks *she* cannot become pregnant; a boy thinks *he* cannot get killed by fooling around with guns; teenagers think *they* cannot get hooked on drugs.

Although the "personal fable" has been widely accepted, its validity as an earmark of adolescence has little support. Some research has found that most people of *any* age are unrealistically optimistic in assessing danger (S. E. Taylor, 1989). One study compared three groups: 86 mostly white, middle-class teenagers, their parents, and 95 mostly male, nonwhite teenagers in homes for adolescents with legal and substance abuse problems. Participants were asked to estimate their risk, compared with other people they knew, of being in a car accident, having an unwanted pregnancy, becoming alcoholic, being mugged, or becoming sick from air pollution. All three groups saw themselves as facing less risk than others; this attitude was no more pronounced in teenagers than in adults. In fact, for some risks adolescents considered themselves *more* vulnerable than their parents considered themselves (Quadrel, Fischoff, & Davis, 1993). Similarly, in another study, college students and adults were more likely than adolescents to see themselves as invulnerable to alcohol and other drug problems (Millstein, in press).

The importance of this research goes beyond questioning the "personal fable." If this frequently cited concept is invalid, perhaps other beliefs about "immature" adolescent thinking patterns are equally so.

MORAL REASONING: KOHLBERG'S THEORY

A woman is near death from cancer. A druggist has discovered a drug that doctors believe might save her. The druggist is charging $2,000 for a small dose—10 times what the drug costs him to make. The sick woman's husband, Heinz, borrows from everyone he knows but can scrape together only $1,000. He begs the druggist to sell him the drug for $1,000 or let him pay the rest later. The druggist refuses, saying "I discovered the drug and I'm going to make money from it." Heinz, desperate, breaks into the man's store and steals the drug. Should Heinz have done that? Why or why not? (Kohlberg, 1969).

Heinz's problem is the most famous example of Lawrence Kohlberg's approach to studying moral development. Starting in the 1950s, Kohlberg and his colleagues posed hypothetical dilemmas like this one to 75 boys ages 10, 13, and 16, and continued to question them periodically for more than 30 years. At the heart of each dilemma was the concept of justice. By asking respondents how they arrived at their answers, Kohlberg concluded that how people think about moral issues reflects cognitive development and that people arrive at moral judgments on their own, rather than merely internalizing standards of parents, teachers, or peers.

Kohlberg's Levels and Stages

Moral development in Kohlberg's theory bears some similarity to Piaget's (see Chapter 8), but his model is more complex. On the basis of thought processes shown by responses to his dilemmas, Kohlberg (1969) described three levels of moral reasoning, each divided into two stages (see Table 10-6):

■ *Level I:* **Preconventional morality.** People, under external controls, obey rules to avoid punishment or reap rewards, or act out of self-interest. This level is typical of children ages 4 to 10.
■ *Level II:* **Morality of conventional role conformity.** People have internalized the standards of authority figures. They are concerned about being "good," pleasing others, and maintaining the social order. This level is typically reached after age 10; many people never move beyond it, even in adulthood.
■ *Level III:* **Morality of autonomous moral principles.** People now recognize conflicts between moral standards and make their own judgments on the basis of principles of right, fairness, and justice. People generally do not reach this level of moral reasoning until at least age 13, or more commonly in young adulthood, if ever.

TABLE 10-6

Kohlberg's Six Stages of Moral Reasoning

Levels	Stages of Reasoning	Typical Answers to Heinz's Dilemma
Level 1: Preconventional (ages 4 to 10) Emphasis in this level is on external control. The standards are those of others, and they are observed either to avoid punishment or to reap rewards.	*Stage 1: Orientation toward punishment and obedience.* "What will happen to me?" Children obey the rules of others to avoid punishment. They ignore the motives of an act and focus on its physical form (such as the size of a lie) or its consequences (for example, the amount of physical damage).	*Pro:* "He should steal the drug. It isn't really bad to take it. It isn't as if he hadn't asked to pay for it first. The drug he'd take is worth only $200: he's not really taking a $2,000 drug." *Con:* "He shouldn't steal the drug. It's a big crime. He didn't get permission; he used force and broke and entered. He did a lot of damage, stealing a very expensive drug and breaking up the store, too."
	Stage 2: Instrumental purpose and exchange. "You scratch my back, I'll scratch yours." Children conform to rules out of self-interest and consideration for what others can do for them in return. They look at an act in terms of the human needs it meets and differentiate this value from the act's physical form and consequences.	*Pro:* "It's all right to steal the drug, because his wife needs it and he wants her to live. It isn't that he wants to steal, but that's what he has to do to get the drug to save her." *Con:* "He shouldn't steal it. The druggist isn't wrong or bad; he just wants to make a profit. That's what you're in business for—to make money."
Level II: Morality of conventional role conformity (ages 10 to 13 or beyond) Children now want to please other people. They still observe the standards of others, but they have internalized these standards to some extent. Now they want to be considered "good" by those persons whose opinions are important to them. They are now able to take the roles of authority figures well enough to decide whether an action is good by their standards.	*Stage 3: Maintaining mutual relations, approval of others, the golden rule.* "Am I a good boy or girl?" Children want to please and help others, can judge the intentions of others, and develop their own ideas of what a good person is. They evaluate an act according to the motive behind it or the person performing it, and they take circumstances into account.	*Pro:* "He should steal the drug. He is only doing something that is natural for a good husband to do. You can't blame him for doing something out of love for his wife. You'd blame him if he didn't love his wife enough to save her." *Con:* "He shouldn't steal. If his wife dies, he can't be blamed. It isn't because he's heartless or that he doesn't love her enough to do everything that he legally can. The druggist is the selfish or heartless one."
	Stage 4: Social concern and conscience. "What if everybody did it?" People are concerned with doing their duty, showing respect for higher authority, and maintaining the social order. They consider an act always wrong, regardless of motive or circumstances, if it violates a rule and harms others.	*Pro:* "You should steal it. If you did nothing, you'd be letting your wife die. It's your responsibility if she dies. You have to take it with the idea of paying the druggist." *Con:* "It is a natural thing for Heinz to want to save his wife, but it's still always wrong to steal. He still knows that he's stealing and taking a valuable drug from the man who made it."

(Continued)

Levels	Stages of Reasoning	Typical Answers to Heinz's Dilemma
Level III: Morality of autonomous moral principles (age 13, or not until young adulthood, or never) This level marks the attainment of true morality. For the first time, the person acknowledges the possibility of conflict between two socially accepted standards and tries to decide between them. The control of conduct is now internal, both in the standards observed and in the reasoning about right and wrong. Stages 5 and 6 may be alternative expressions of the highest level of moral reasoning.	*Stage 5: Morality of contract, of individual rights, and of democratically accepted law.* People think in rational terms, valuing the will of the majority and the welfare of society. They generally see these values as best supported by adherence to the law. While they recognize that there are times when human need and the law conflict, they believe that it is better for society in the long run if they obey the law.	*Pro:* "The law wasn't set up for these circumstances. Taking the drug in this situation isn't really right, but it's justified." *Con:* "You can't completely blame someone for stealing, but extreme circumstances don't really justify taking the law into your own hands. You can't have people stealing whenever they are desperate. The end may be good, but the ends don't justify the means."
	Stage 6: Morality of universal ethical principles. People do what they as individuals think right, regardless of legal restrictions or the opinions of others. They act in accordance with internalized standards, knowing that they would condemn themselves if they did not.	*Pro:* "This is a situation that forces him to choose between stealing and letting his wife die. In a situation where the choice must be made, it is morally right to steal. He has to act in terms of the principle of preserving and respecting life." *Con:* "Heinz is faced with the decision of whether to consider the other people who need the drug just as badly as his wife. Heinz ought to act not according to his particular feelings toward his wife, but considering the value of all the lives involved."

SOURCE: Adapted from Kohlberg, 1969; Lickona, 1976.

Kohlberg later added a transitional level between levels II and III, when people no longer feel bound by society's moral standards but have not yet developed rationally derived principles of justice. Instead, they base their moral decisions on personal feelings.

In Kohlberg's theory, it is the reasoning underlying a person's response to a moral dilemma, not the answer itself, which indicates the stage of moral development. As illustrated in Table 10-6, two people who give opposite answers may be at the same stage if their reasoning is based on similar factors.

One reason the ages attached to Kohlberg's levels are so variable is that factors besides cognition, such as emotional development and life experience, affect moral judgments. Some adolescents, and even some adults, remain at Kohlberg's level

I. Like young children, they seek to avoid punishment or satisfy their own needs. Most adolescents, and most adults, seem to be at level II. They conform to social conventions, support the status quo, and do the "right" thing to please others or to obey the law. Very few people reach level III; in fact, at one point Kohlberg questioned the validity of stage 6, since so few people seem to attain it (Muuss, 1988). Later, however, he proposed a seventh, "cosmic" stage (see Chapter 12), in which adults consider the effect of their actions not only on other people but on the universe as a whole (Kohlberg, 1981; Kohlberg & Ryncarz, 1990).

Family Influences on Moral Development

Neither Piaget nor Kohlberg considered parents important to children's moral development. Recent research, however, emphasizes parents' contribution in both the cognitive and the emotional realms. In one study, parents of 63 students in grades 1, 4, 7, and 10 were asked to talk with their children about two dilemmas: a hypothetical one and an actual one the child described (L. J. Walker & Taylor, 1991). The children and adolescents who, during the next two years, showed the greatest progress through Kohlberg's stages were those whose parents had used humor and praise, listened to them, and asked their opinions. These parents had asked clarifying questions, reworded answers, and checked to be sure the children understood the issues. They reasoned with their children at a slightly higher level than the children were currently at, much as in Vygotsky's method of scaffolding. The children who advanced the least were those whose parents had lectured them or challenged or contradicted their opinions.

Evaluating Kohlberg's Theory

Kohlberg's work and that of his colleagues and followers has had a major impact. His theory has enriched our thinking about how morality develops, has supported an association between cognitive maturation and moral maturation, and has stimulated much research and other theories of moral development.

Research has supported some aspects of Kohlberg's theory but has left others in question. The American boys that Kohlberg and his colleagues followed through adulthood progressed through Kohlberg's stages in sequence, and none skipped a stage. Their moral judgments correlated positively with age, education, IQ, and socioeconomic status (Colby, Kohlberg, Gibbs, & Lieberman, 1983). However, as we'll see, Kohlberg's stages may be limited in their applicability to women and girls and to people in nonwestern cultures.

Another serious criticism is the lack of a clear relationship between moral reasoning and behavior. Recent studies suggest that people at postconventional levels of reasoning do not necessarily *act* more morally than those at lower levels (Colby & Damon, 1992; Kupfersmid & Wonderly, 1980; see Box 14-3).

One practical problem in evaluating Kohlberg's system is its time-consuming testing procedures. The standard dilemmas need to be presented to each person individually and then scored by trained judges. One alternative is the Defining Is-

sues Test (DIT), which can be given quickly to a group and scored objectively (Rest, 1975). The DIT has 12 questions about each of 6 moral dilemmas; its results correlate moderately well with scores on Kohlberg's traditional tasks.

Validity for Women and Girls Carol Gilligan (1982), on the basis of research on women, argued that Kohlberg's theory is oriented toward values more important to men than to women. According to Gilligan, women see morality not so much in terms of justice and fairness as of responsibility to show care and avoid harm. Although Gilligan has since modified her position on gender differences in moral judgments (see Chapter 12), some research has found such differences in early adolescence.

Researchers interviewed forty-six 11- and 12-year-old girls and boys, asking, for example, what a hypothetical young person should do if she or he has accepted a friend's dinner invitation and then receives an invitation from another friend to see a favorite rock band on the same evening (Skoe & Gooden, 1993). The researchers assessed the responses according to five "ethic-of-care" levels based on Gilligan's work: survival, responsibility, goodness, truth in relationships, and caring for self and others. Girls scored higher than boys: girls were more concerned about maintaining friendships and not hurting others, whereas boys tended to be concerned mainly about avoiding trouble. When participants were asked to talk about a real dilemma they had experienced, girls described problems involving people they knew well, whereas boys brought up moral conflicts involving distant acquaintances or institutions.

More recent research found a developmental progression in the ethic of care: older people scored higher than younger ones (Skoe & Diessner, 1994). This may help explain girls' higher scores, since girls generally mature earlier than boys.

Cross-cultural Validity Kohlberg maintained that the developmental pattern of moral reasoning is universal, transcending cultural boundaries. Cross-cultural studies support his sequence of stages—up to a point. Older people from countries other than the United States do tend to score at higher stages than younger people, but people from nonwestern cultures rarely score above stage 4 (Edwards, 1977; Nisan & Kohlberg, 1982; Snarey, 1985). It is possible that these cultures do not foster higher moral development, but it seems more

Moving up to junior high school can be exciting but also stressful, especially for girls, many of whom enter puberty at about the same time. *(Bob Daemmrich/ Stock, Boston)*

likely that some aspects of Kohlberg's definition of morality may not fit the cultural values of some societies (see Box 12-2 for examples).

Kohlberg himself observed that people, before they can develop a fully principled morality, must recognize the relativity of moral standards. Adolescents begin to understand that every society evolves its own definitions of right and wrong; in some cases, the values of one culture may even seem shocking to members of another (see Box 2-3 and Box 10-1). Many young people question their earlier views about morality when they enter high school or college and encounter people whose values, culture, and ethnic background are different from their own.

✔ EDUCATIONAL AND VOCATIONAL ISSUES

School is the central organizing experience in most adolescents' lives. It offers opportunities to learn information, master new skills, and sharpen old ones; to participate in sports, the arts, and other activities; to explore vocational choices; and to be with friends. It widens intellectual and social horizons. Some adolescents, however, experience school not as an opportunity but as one more hindrance on the road to adulthood.

The move from elementary school to secondary school sets the stage for the high school experience, and the way that transition takes place can have a profound effect on psychological adjust-

ment, as well as on educational attainment. Let's look first at that transition. Then we'll examine contextual influences on school achievement: the school, the neighborhood, the family, and the peer group. Next, we'll look at why some students drop out of school and what can be done about it. Finally, we'll consider planning for college and careers.

LEAVING ELEMENTARY SCHOOL

At the end of sixth grade, most American children leave the familiar surroundings of elementary school to enter a junior high school or middle school with many more students and a more impersonal setting in which teachers, classrooms, and classmates change constantly throughout the day. In 3 more years they move again, to an even larger high school. This typical sequence is known as the *6-3-3 pattern*. A minority of children follow the *8-4 pattern*, staying in elementary school through eighth grade and then going directly to high school.

Research has found a number of stresses associated with the typical sequence. For example, junior high school students have less personal, less positive relationships with their teachers; and their teachers tend to judge them by higher standards than elementary school teachers do, often resulting in lowered grades and a drop in self-esteem (Eccles et al., 1993).

One 5-year study followed 594 white students in the Milwaukee public schools from sixth through tenth grade, comparing students in the 6-3-3 pattern with those in the 8-4 pattern (Blyth, Simmons, & Carlton-Ford, 1983). Students in the 6-3-3 group had more problems than those in the 8-4 group. Both boys and girls in the 6-3-3 pattern had a decrease in grade-point averages, took less part in extracurricular activities, and saw their schools as more anonymous. Girls were especially vulnerable; their self-esteem dropped, an effect that persisted into tenth grade (Blyth et al., 1983).

Why did the girls have more problems? As we mentioned earlier, girls who enter puberty at the same time they change schools are likely candidates for depression (Petersen et al., 1991). The more major changes that take place at once, the greater the likelihood that grade-point averages, extracurricular participation, and self-esteem will decline (Simmons, Burgeson, Carlton-Ford, & Blyth, 1987). Since girls usually enter puberty sooner than boys and begin to date earlier, they are more likely to experience "life-change overload" (Petersen, 1993). Also, there is more emphasis on girls' looks and popularity at this age, and they may miss the security of being with old friends.

As Bronfenbrenner's model suggests, a change in parents' work status can affect a child's adjustment to a new school. A 2-year study found that when parents had been demoted or laid off at about the same time their children were moving into junior high school, the youngsters had a hard time adjusting. They had more trouble getting along with other students and were more disruptive than children of parents with stable employment or those whose parents had just been rehired or promoted (Flanagan & Eccles, 1993).

SCHOOL ACHIEVEMENT: CONTEXTUAL INFLUENCES

Historically in the United States, education has been the ticket to economic and social advancement and to a successful adult life. However, for many students today, especially those from low-income families and neighborhoods, school does not perform this vital function.

During the 1970s, high school seniors' standardized test scores fell, most dramatically in vocabulary and reading—in part, apparently, due to a decreased academic emphasis in the schools (Rock, Ekstrom, Goertz, Hilton, & Pollack, 1985). Another reason was the broader base of students going to high school. The National Commission on

Excellence in Education (1983) found that the average high school or college graduate is not as well educated as the average graduate of previous generations, when fewer people finished high school or college. However, the average *citizen* is better-educated than the average citizen of the past.

Today, nearly 82 percent of Americans age 25 or older—more than ever before—have graduated from high school or the equivalent. Furthermore, the proportion is growing. Among 25- to 29-year-olds, it is approximately 86 percent, including—again for the first time—statistically equal percentages of blacks and whites (J. Day & Curry, 1996). The 1980s and 1990s have seen a greater emphasis on academics, though English skills have scarcely improved. College entrance test scores have risen somewhat, especially for minorities; but for most minorities, an achievement gap remains (American College Testing Program, 1995; National Center for Education Statistics, NCES, 1995a).

Let's see how parents, peers, neighborhoods, and schools influence achievement.

Parents, Peers, and Neighborhood

Even though adolescents are more independent than elementary school children, the atmosphere in the home influences how well they do in school. Students whose parents are closely involved in their lives and monitor their progress fare best, according to a survey of more than 30,000 high school seniors in more than 1,000 schools (NCES, 1985; see Table 10-7). This is particularly true of fathers, whose involvement varies more than that of mothers. In this survey, 85 percent of the A students but only 64 percent of the D students had fathers who kept close track of how they were doing. The father's importance is also evident from the fact that students who live with both parents earn better grades.

Parents of high-achieving adolescents make time to talk to them and know what is going on in their lives. They go to PTA meetings (NCES, 1985). They take the children seriously, and the children reward that interest.

Parents' involvement may depend on their style of child rearing (see Chapter 7). *Authoritative parents* urge adolescents to look at both sides of issues, admit that children sometimes know more than parents, and welcome their participation in family decisions. These students receive praise and privileges for good grades; poor grades bring encouragement to try harder, offers of help, and loss

TABLE 10-7

Parents' Involvement and High School Students' Grades

Survey Item	Self-reported Grades			
	Mostly A's	Mostly B's	Mostly C's	Mostly D's
Mother keeps close track of how well child does in school.	92%	89%	84%	80%
Father keeps close track of how well child does in school.	85%	79%	69%	64%
Parents almost always know child's whereabouts.	88%	81%	72%	61%
Child talks with mother or father almost every day.	75%	67%	59%	45%
Parents attend PTA meetings at least once in a while.	25%	22%	20%	15%
Child lives in household with both parents.	80%	71%	64%	60%

Note: This table, based on a survey of more than 30,000 high school seniors, shows the percentage of students with various grade averages who gave positive answers to each survey item. In each instance, the higher the grades were, the more likely the parents were to be involved with the child.
SOURCE: NCES, 1985.

of freedom. *Authoritarian parents* tell adolescents not to argue with or question adults and tell them they will "know better when they are grown up." Good grades bring admonitions to do even better; poor grades upset the parents, who may punish by reducing allowances or "grounding." *Permissive parents* do not care about grades, make no rules about watching television, do not attend school functions, and neither help with nor check their children's homework. These parents may not be

neglectful or uncaring, but simply convinced that teenagers should be responsible for their own lives.

Studies of about 6,400 California high school students found that children of authoritative parents tend to do better in school than children of authoritarian and permissive parents (Dornbusch, Ritter, Leiderman, Roberts, & Fraleigh, 1987; Steinberg & Darling, 1994; Steinberg, Lamborn, Dornbusch, & Darling, 1992). Inconsistency is associated

Even though adolescents are more independent than younger children, the home atmosphere continues to influence school achievement. Parents help not only by monitoring homework but by taking an active interest in other aspects of teenagers' lives. Children of authoritative parents, who discuss issues openly and offer praise and encouragement, tend to do best in school. *(Erika Stone)*

with the lowest grades, possibly because children who do not know what to expect from their parents become anxious and distracted.

However, although these conclusions hold for white teenagers, Latino and African American students—even those with authoritative parents—do not do as well, apparently because of lack of peer support for academic achievement. On the other hand, Asian American students, whose parents tend to be authoritarian, get high grades, apparently because both parents and peers prize achievement (Steinberg, Dornbusch, & Brown, 1992). Asian American students score higher than white students on math achievement tests, though less well than students in China and Japan (C. Chen & Stevenson, 1995). In addition to having parents and peers with high academic standards, who value hard work, Asian American students tend to go to good schools, to take challenging courses, and to like math. They also spend more time studying than white students and less time socializing with friends, and they are less likely to hold outside jobs (see Box 10-3). Parenting styles, then, may be less important than other factors that affect motivation. Young people who are interested in what they are learning and whose parents and peers esteem education are more motivated to succeed.

Socioeconomic status is a powerful factor in educational achievement through its influence on family atmosphere, on choice of neighborhood, and on parents' way of rearing children (NRC, 1993a). Is the family stable and harmonious, or conflict-ridden? Do the parents talk to their children? What goals do they have for their children, and how do they help them reach those goals? Do parents show interest in schoolwork and expect children to go to college? Whether a family is rich or poor, the answers to questions like these are important, but the answers are more likely to be positive in a higher-income, better-educated family (K. R. White, 1982). Children of poor, uneducated parents are more likely to experience negative family and school atmospheres and more stressful events (Felner et al., 1995). The neighborhood a family can afford generally determines the quality of schooling available, as well as opportunities for higher education; and the availability of such opportunities, together with attitudes in the neighborhood peer group, affect motivation.

Still, some young people from poor families and disadvantaged neighborhoods do well in school and improve their condition in life. What may

TABLE 10-8

Factors Contributing to Social Capital

Within family

Family cohesion

Mother's support to and from own mother

Parents see siblings or grandparents weekly

Father in home:
  Biological father or
  long-term stepfather

Parents' help with homework

Child's activities with parents

Parents' expectations for school
performance

Parents' educational aspirations for child

Mother's encouragement of child

Mother's attendance at school meetings

Number of child's friends mother
knows

Family links to community

Religious involvement

Strong help network

Mother sees close friend weekly

Child ever changed schools due
to move

Child's friends' educational expectations

School quality

Neighborhood as a place to
grow up

SOURCE: Adapted from Furstenberg & Hughes, 1995.

make the difference, according to one model, is *social capital:* the family and community resources children can draw upon to enhance their opportunities. Parents who invest time and effort in their children and who have a strong network of community support build the family's social capital (J. S. Coleman, 1988). In a 20-year study of 252 children born to mostly poor and African American teenage mothers in Baltimore, those who—regardless of parents' income, education, and employment—had more social capital (according to such measures as those listed in Table 10-8) were more likely by the end of adolescence to have completed high school and in some cases to have gone to college or to have entered the labor force and to enjoy stable incomes (Furstenberg & Hughes, 1995).

BOX 10-3 FOOD FOR THOUGHT

SHOULD TEENAGERS WORK PART TIME?

Many teenage students today hold part-time jobs. This trend conforms to the American belief in the moral benefits derived from working. However, some research challenges the value of part-time work for high school students who do not have to work to help support their families. Let's look at both sides of the issue.

On the *positive* side, paid work is generally believed to teach young people to handle money responsibly. It helps them develop good work habits, such as promptness, reliability, and efficient management of time (National Commission on Youth, 1980).

A good part-time job helps a teenager assume responsibility and work with people of different ages and backgrounds. It enables an adolescent to learn workplace skills, such as how to find a job and how to get along with employers, coworkers, and sometimes the public. By helping a young person learn more about a particular field of work, it may guide her or him in choosing a career (National Commission on Youth, 1980). Furthermore, by showing adolescents

how demanding and difficult the world of work is and how unprepared they are for it, part-time jobs, especially menial ones, sometimes motivate young people to continue their education.

On the *negative* side, research has questioned the benefits of part-time work and has identified serious costs. Most high school students who work part time have low-level, repetitive jobs in which they do not learn skills useful later in life (Hamilton & Crouter, 1980). Teenagers who work are no more independent in making financial decisions and are not likely to earn any more money as adults than those who do not hold jobs during high school (Greenberger & Steinberg, 1986).

Outside work seems to undermine performance in school, especially for teenagers who work more than 15 to 20 hours per week. Grades, involvement in school, and attendance decline. Students who work more than 15 hours a week are more likely to drop out of school (NCES, 1987) and thus to be less prepared for careers and for life.

Paid work has other hidden costs. Young people who work long hours are less likely to eat breakfast, exercise, get enough sleep, or have enough leisure time (J. G. Bachman & Schulenberg, 1993). They spend less time with their families and may feel less close to them. They have little contact with adults on the job, and their jobs usually reinforce gender stereotypes. Some teenagers spend their earnings on alcohol or drugs, develop cynical attitudes toward work, and cheat or steal from their employers (Greenberger & Steinberg, 1986; Steinberg, Fegley, & Dornbusch, 1993).

However, some of these undesirable effects may result, not from working itself, but from the factors that motivate some teenagers to take jobs. Some may want to work because they are already uninterested in school or feel alienated from their families or because they want money to buy drugs and liquor. Jobs may actually help keep such young people out of trouble by providing legal ways for them to earn money.

The School

An important factor in students' achievement is the quality of the schools they attend. A good high school has an orderly, unoppressive atmosphere, an active, energetic principal, and teachers who take part in making decisions. Principal and teachers should have high expectations for students, place greater emphasis on academics than on extracurricular activities, and closely monitor student performance (Linney & Seidman, 1989). Schools largely populated by students from low-income families often fall far short of these conditions and generally have the fewest material resources. Despite the efforts of some dedicated educators and parents, such schools often fail to

help students build the skills they need for successful adult lives (NRC, 1993a).

The educational practice known as *tracking*, or grouping students by abilities, may contribute to failure. Students placed in low-track classes lack the stimulation of higher-ability peers and often get poorer teaching. They rarely move up to higher tracks, and many lose interest in trying to do better (NRC, 1993a). Furthermore, since school failure and contact with antisocial peers are often related to antisocial behavior, grouping poor achievers together may solidify problem behaviors (Dishion, Patterson, Stoolmiller, & Skinner, 1991). Some research suggests that mixed-ability classes have cognitive, social, and psychological benefits for these young people while not holding back more competent students (Oakes, Gamoran, & Page, 1992; Rutter, 1983). However, other research has found that gifted students achieve better and are more motivated when grouped with their intellectual peers (Feldhusen & Moon, 1992).

DROPPING OUT OF HIGH SCHOOL

Students who leave school before receiving a diploma reduce their opportunities. Dropping out does not guarantee poverty, but dropouts do have to scramble harder to start a career—if they ever have one. Many employers require a high school diploma, and many jobs require skills based on a solid education.

Dropouts have trouble getting and keeping jobs, and the jobs they do get tend to be low-level and poorly paying. In one national study of high school dropouts, 27 percent of the males and 31 percent of the females were looking for work; 32 percent of the women were full-time homemakers. Of those who were working, only about 14 percent of the men and 3 percent of the women had jobs that required technical skills. More than half the dropouts soon regretted leaving school, but only a small percentage took part in educational programs (NCES, 1987).

Why do people drop out? When asked 2 years later, one group of young men mentioned poor grades, not liking school, being expelled or suspended, or having to support a family. Women attributed dropping out to marriage or plans to marry, poor grades, pregnancy, jobs, or a feeling that "school is not for me" (NCES, 1983). However,

these explanations probably do not tell the whole story. Dropping out may be related to lack of motivation and self-esteem, lack of parental encouragement, low expectations by teachers, inappropriate skill training for non-college-bound youth, and disciplinary problems (Hamilton, 1990; Rule, 1981).

Fewer students are dropping out these days, and some eventually go back to school to earn a high school equivalency certificate. The dropout rate declined from 13.9 percent in 1982 to 11 percent in 1993. Latino students are about twice as likely to drop out as African Americans (27.5 percent as compared with 13.6 percent), and African Americans are nearly twice as likely to drop out as non-Latino whites (7.9 percent). However, rates for all three groups have improved (NCES, 1995a). In all three groups, low-income students are more likely to drop out than middle- or high-income students (Children's Defense Fund, 1995; see Figure 10-3). The high dropout rates among minority groups living in poverty may stem in part from the poor quality of their schools as compared with those attended by more advantaged children. Among the possible reasons for the high Latino rates are language difficulties, financial pressures, and a culture that puts family first, since these students often leave school to help support their families (U.S. Department of Education, 1992).

Students whose parents are poorly educated and in low-level jobs and those in large, single-parent families are 3 to 5 times more likely to drop out than other teenagers (NCES, 1987). Even those from relatively affluent single-parent and remarried families are more likely to drop out than those living with both parents (Zimiles & Lee, 1991). An

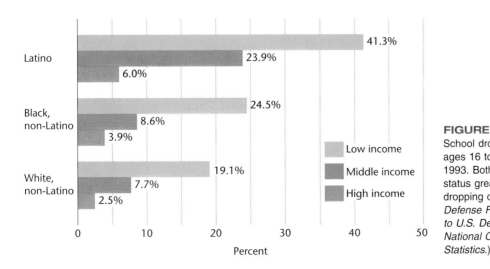

FIGURE 10-3

School dropout rates among youths ages 16 to 24, by income and ethnicity, 1993. Both family income and minority status greatly affect the likelihood of dropping out. (*Source: Children's Defense Fund, 1995, p. 94; attributed to U.S. Department of Education, National Center for Education Statistics.*)

adolescent living with a single parent of the same sex is more likely to drop out when the custodial parent marries, perhaps because the marriage disrupts the strong attachment that often develops between child and parent in such families. Other factors associated with dropping out include having repeated a grade in elementary school, working more than 15 hours a week while in high school, being married, having a child, being alienated from family and community, and displaying such signs of antisocial behavior as suspension, probation, or trouble with the law (NCES, 1987; S. B. Williams, 1987). Dropouts tend to be risk takers; they are less likely to use safety belts in a car and more likely to ride with a drinking driver, carry a weapon, use drugs, or have sexual intercourse than youngsters who stay in school (CDC, 1994b).

COLLEGE AND CAREER PLANNING

How do young people develop career goals? How do they decide whether or not to go to college and, if not, how to enter the world of work? Many factors enter in, including individual ability and personality, education, socioeconomic and ethnic background, the advice of school counselors, life experiences, and societal values. Let's look at two important influences: gender and the role of parents. Then we'll examine what happens to young people who do not go to college.

Influences of Gender and Parents

A woman who entered engineering school at Ohio State University in 1945 was one of six females in her class. Some 35 years later, women made up about 30 percent of the incoming class (R. D. Feldman, 1982). Similar increases have occurred in the number of women studying law, medicine, and other traditionally male fields, but women are still underrepresented in these occupations (Reis, 1991; see Chapter 12).

Despite the greater flexibility in career goals today, gender—and gender-stereotyping—often influence vocational choice. Although there is little or no difference between boys and girls in mathematical or verbal ability and although girls' grades are on average better than boys', many girls are not encouraged to continue in gifted programs, to take advanced science and math courses, or to pursue demanding careers. Many parents, teachers, and counselors still steer young people into gen-

der-typed roles, even though there is no real basis for doing so (Hyde & Linn, 1988; Maccoby & Jacklin, 1974; McCormick & Wolf, 1993; Read, 1991; Reis, 1991).

For both girls and boys, parents' encouragement and financial support influence aspiration and achievement; in fact, parental encouragement predicts high ambition better than social class does. When 2,622 sixth, eighth, tenth, and twelfth grade students, black and white and from all social strata, were asked to describe their own expectations for their education and their fathers' and mothers' expectations for them, more than half the students agreed with the perceived goals of each parent (T. E. Smith, 1981). By encouraging their children to pursue higher education and helping to foot the bill, many parents make it easier for their children to go to college. With or without parental assistance, however, many students manage to get a college education through loans or scholarships or by working their way through school.

Guiding Students Not Bound for College

About half the high school graduates in the United States do not go on to college; of those who do, fewer than half earn 4-year degrees. Still, although some 75 percent of high school students will not finish college, most vocational counseling in high schools is oriented toward college-bound youth (NRC, 1993a).

Most other industrialized countries offer some kind of structured guidance to non-college-bound students, but the United States relies almost entirely on market forces to help these youths find work. Many young people, ignorant about the job market, do not obtain the skills they need. Others take jobs beneath their abilities. Some do not find work at all. For people under age 20, being raised in a low-income family is the strongest predictor of joblessness (NRC, 1993a). In a few communities, demonstration programs help in the school-to-work transition. The most successful ones offer instruction in basic skills, counseling, peer support, mentoring, apprenticeship, and job placement (NRC, 1993a)

Vocational planning is closely tied to an adolescent's search for identity. The question "What shall I do?" is very close to "Who shall I be?" People who feel they are doing something worthwhile, and doing it well, feel good about themselves.

Those who feel that their work does not matter— or that they are not good at it—may wonder about the meaning of their lives. A prime personality is-sue in adolescence, which we discuss in Chapter 11, is the effort to define the self.

✔ SUMMARY

ADOLESCENCE: A DEVELOPMENTAL TRANSITION

- Adolescence is a developmental transition between childhood and adulthood. It begins with puberty, a process that leads to sexual maturity.
- The end of adolescence is not clear-cut in western societies; no single sign indicates that adulthood has been reached. In some nonwestern cultures, adulthood is regarded as beginning at puberty and is signified by puberty rites.

PUBERTY

- Puberty is triggered by hormonal changes. A secular trend toward earlier attainment of adult height and sexual maturity began about 100 years ago, probably because of improvements in living standards.
- During puberty, both boys and girls undergo an adolescent growth spurt: sharp growth in height, weight, and muscular and skeletal development.
- Primary sex characteristics (the female and male reproductive organs) enlarge and mature during puberty. Secondary sex characteristics also appear.
- The principal signs of sexual maturity, or fertility, are menstruation (for females) and production of sperm (for males). Menarche, the first menstruation, occurs, on average, between the ages of 12 and 13 in the United States. Girls who mature early tend to adjust less easily than early maturing boys.

HEALTH CONCERNS

- For the most part, the adolescent years are relatively healthy. Health problems often result from poverty, a risk-taking lifestyle, or a sedentary one. The three leading causes of death among adolescents are accidents, homicide, and suicide.
- Between 10 and 40 percent of adolescents experience depressed moods, with higher rates for females after age 15. Depression is often associated with concern about appearance and the occurrence of several life changes at about the same time.

- Three common eating disorders in adolescence are obesity, anorexia nervosa, and bulimia nervosa.
- Drug abuse by adolescents is less common today than during the 1960s, late 1970s, and early 1980s, but it has increased during the 1990s. The three drugs most popular with adolescents are alcohol, marijuana, and tobacco.
- Sexually transmitted diseases (STDs) are contracted through sexual contact; 1 out of 3 cases occurs among adolescents.

ASPECTS OF COGNITIVE MATURATION

- Many adolescents attain Piaget's stage of formal operations, which is characterized by the ability to think abstractly. People in the stage of formal operations can engage in hypothetical-deductive reasoning. They can think in terms of possibilities, deal flexibly with problems, and test hypotheses.
- According to Elkind, immature thought patterns characteristic of adolescence include finding fault with authority figures, argumentativeness, indecisiveness, apparent hypocrisy, self-consciousness, and an assumption of invulnerability, which he calls the *personal fable*.
- According to Kohlberg, moral reasoning involves the development of a sense of justice and occurs on three main levels: preconventional, conventional role conformity, and autonomous moral principles. The applicability of Kohlberg's system to women and girls and to people in nonwestern cultures has been questioned.

EDUCATIONAL AND VOCATIONAL ISSUES

- Stress is associated with the transition to secondary school, especially in the 6-3-3 pattern and especially for girls.
- Parents, peers, the neighborhood, and quality of schooling all influence educational achievement. Socioeconomic status is a powerful factor; it affects home atmosphere (including parents' involvement and family relationships), quality of schooling, opportunities for higher education, and peer attitudes, which in turn influence motivation to achieve. Poor families whose children

do well in school tend to have more social capital on which to draw.

■ Although most Americans graduate from high school, the dropout rate is particularly high among poor Latino and African American students.

■ Vocational choice is influenced by several factors, including gender and parental support. About half of American high school graduates do not go to college, but there is little vocational counseling or preparation for non-college-bound youth.

✔ KEY TERMS

adolescence (page 330)
puberty (330)
secular trend (332)
adolescent growth spurt (333)
primary sex characteristics (333)
secondary sex characteristics (333)
spermarche (335)
menarche (335)
anorexia nervosa (340)

bulimia nervosa (341)
substance abuse (342)
substance dependence (342)
gateway drugs (342)
sexually transmitted diseases (STDs) (345)
formal operations (348)
hypothetical-deductive reasoning (349)

imaginary audience (351)
personal fable (352)
preconventional morality (352)
morality of conventional role conformity (352)
morality of autonomous moral principles (352)
social capital (359)

✔ QUESTIONS FOR THOUGHT AND DISCUSSION

1 Do you think adolescents in western societies miss something by not having a specific rite of passage from childhood? If so, what kind of observance do you think would be appropriate?

2 What are some implications of attaining sexual maturity years before the customary age of marriage and attaining physical maturity years before attaining independence from parents?

3 Should marijuana be legal, like alcohol? Why or why not?

4 Should there be tighter restrictions on cigarette advertising targeted at minors? If so, what kinds of restrictions would you favor?

5 In view of the prevalence of sexually risky behavior, do you think sex education should aim at encouraging "safe sex" or at promoting abstinence, or both?

6 How would you define the highest level of cognition: as (1) formal reasoning, (2) the ability to solve practical problems, (3) attainment of wisdom, or (4) something else?

7 In what ways can parents and teachers help students with the transition to junior high, middle school, or high school?

CHAPTER ELEVEN

PSYCHOSOCIAL DEVELOPMENT IN ADOLESCENCE

*This face in the mirror
stares at me
demanding Who are you? What will you become?
And taunting, You don't even know.
Chastened, I cringe and agree
and then
because I'm still young,
I stick out my tongue.*

Eve Merriam, "Conversation with Myself," 1964

ASK YOURSELF

✔ How do adolescents form an identity?
✔ What influences sexual orientation?
✔ What are the prevailing sexual practices and attitudes among adolescents, and what leads some to engage in high-risk sexual behavior?
✔ How typical is "adolescent rebellion"?

✔ How are adolescents' attitudes and behavior influenced by parents, siblings, and peers?
✔ What are the causes and consequences of teenage pregnancy and juvenile delinquency, and what can be done to reduce these and other risks of adolescence?

Adolescence is an exciting time—when all things seem possible. Teenagers are on the threshold of love, of life's work, and of participation in adult society. They are getting to know the most interesting people in the world: themselves. Yet adolescence is also a time of risk, when some young people engage in behavior that closes off their options and limits their possibilities.

At the age of 15, Carmen, for example, has the body of a woman. Now capable of sexual attraction and rational thinking, she has yet to attain emotional maturity. She knows that she will soon be responsible for her own life. How will she choose to live it? What kind of work will she do? What decisions will she make about sexual and other relationships? What principles will she live by?

Adolescents need to embrace values and make commitments. They need to discover what they can do and take pride in their accomplishments. They need to form close ties with boys and girls their own age and to be liked and loved and respected for who they are and what they stand for. This means they have to *find out* what they stand for.

These tasks are not easy, nor are they performed in a vacuum. Today, research is increasingly focusing on how to help young people whose environments are not optimal avoid hazards that can keep them from fulfilling their potential.

These years are not easy for parents, either. Adolescents trying their wings can be as erratic and unpredictable as birds taking flight from the nest, and they may see adults as more inhibiting than helpful. Yet while teenagers look to peers as comrades in the struggle for independence, they still turn to parents for guidance and support.

■   A central theme in the drama of adolescence—and a continuing theme for years to come—is "Who am I?" This question encompasses all aspects of development. In Chapter 10 we looked at some important factors that contribute to an adolescent's sense of self: appearance and other physical attributes, cognitive abilities, moral reasoning, school achievement, and preparation for the world of work. In this chapter, we turn to psychosocial aspects of the quest for identity. We discuss how adolescents come to terms with their sexuality and what factors increase the risk of early sexual activity and teenage pregnancy. We consider how teenagers' burgeoning individuality expresses itself in relationships with parents, siblings, and peers. We examine sources of antisocial behavior and ways of reducing the risks of adolescence so as to make it a time of positive growth and expanding possibilities.   ■

✔ THE SEARCH FOR IDENTITY

The search for identity comes into focus during the teenage years. As Erikson (1950) emphasized, the teenager's effort to make sense of the self is not "a kind of maturational malaise." It is part of a healthy, vital process that builds on the achievements of earlier stages—on trust, autonomy, initiative, and industry—and lays the groundwork for coping with the crises of adult life. Let's look at Erikson's view of identity formation and at research that has tested and extended it.

IDENTITY VERSUS IDENTITY (ROLE) CONFUSION

Erikson's concept of the identity crisis was based on his own life and his research on adolescents in various societies (see Chapter 1). The chief task of adolescence, said Erikson (1968), is to confront the crisis of *identity versus identity (or role) confusion* so as to become a unique adult with a coherent sense of self and a valued role in society. The identity crisis is seldom fully resolved in adolescence; issues concerning identity may crop up again and again throughout adult life.

According to Erikson, adolescents form their identity not by modeling themselves after other people, as younger children do, but by modifying and synthesizing earlier identifications into "a new psychological structure, greater than the sum of its parts" (Kroger, 1993, p. 3). To form an identity, adolescents must ascertain and organize their abilities, needs, interests, and desires so they can be expressed in a social context.

Erikson saw the prime danger of this stage as identity (or role) confusion, which can greatly delay reaching psychological adulthood—even until after age 30. (He himself did not resolve his own identity crisis until his mid-twenties.) Some degree of identity confusion is normal. It accounts for both the seemingly chaotic nature of much adolescent behavior and teenagers' painful self-consciousness. Cliquishness and intolerance of differences—both hallmarks of the adolescent social scene—are defenses against identity confusion. Adolescents may also show confusion by regressing into childishness to avoid resolving conflicts or by committing themselves impulsively to poorly thought-out courses of action.

Identity forms as young people resolve three major issues: the choice of an occupation, the adoption of values to believe in and live by, and the development of a satisfying sexual identity. During the crisis of middle childhood, that of *industry versus inferiority,* children acquire skills needed for success in their culture. Now, as adolescents, they need to find ways of using these skills. When young people have trouble settling on an occupational identity, they are at risk of behavior with serious negative consequences, such as early pregnancy or criminal activity.

During the *psychosocial moratorium*—the "time out" period that adolescence provides—many young people search for commitments to which they can be faithful. Naomi commits herself to working for racial harmony in her community, Raul becomes a vegetarian, and Michelle studies the violin. These youthful commitments, both ideological and personal, may shape a person's life for years to come. The extent to which young peo-

"Who am I?" is a major question of adolescence, as young people search for identity and ponder their life choices. *(Dario Perla/International Stock Photo)*

ple remain faithful to commitments influences their ability to resolve the identity crisis. Adolescents who satisfactorily resolve that crisis develop the "virtue" of *fidelity:* sustained loyalty, faith, or a sense of belonging to a loved one or to friends and companions. Fidelity can also mean identification with a set of values, an ideology, a religion, a political movement, a creative pursuit, or an ethnic group (Erikson, 1982). Self-identification emerges when young people *choose* values and people to be loyal to, rather than simply accepting their parents' choices.

Fidelity is an extension of trust. In infancy, it is important to trust others, especially parents; in adolescence, it becomes important to be trustworthy oneself. In addition, adolescents now transfer their trust from parents to mentors or loved ones. In sharing thoughts and feelings, an adolescent clarifies a tentative identity by seeing it reflected in the eyes of the beloved. However, these adolescent "intimacies" differ from mature intimacy (see Chapter 13), which involves greater commitment, sacrifice, and compromise.

Erikson's theory, which was based largely on interviews with men, describes male development as the norm. According to Erikson, a man is not capable of real intimacy until after he has achieved a stable identity, whereas women define themselves through marriage and motherhood (something that may have been truer when Erikson developed his theory than it is today). Thus, said Erikson, women (unlike men) develop identity through intimacy, not before it. As we'll see, the male orientation of Erikson's theory has prompted criticism. Still, Erikson's concept of the identity crisis has inspired much valuable research.

IDENTITY STATUS: CRISIS AND COMMITMENT

Kate, Andrea, Nick, and Mark are all about to graduate from high school. Kate has considered her interests and her talents and plans to become a social worker. She has narrowed her college choices to three schools that offer good programs in this field. She knows that college will either confirm her interest in social work or lead her in another direction. She is open to both possibilities.

Andrea knows exactly what she is going to do with her life. Her mother, a union leader at a plastics factory, has arranged for Andrea to enter an apprenticeship program there. Andrea has never considered doing anything else.

Nick, on the other hand, is agonizing over his future. Should he attend a community college or join the army? He cannot decide what to do now or what he wants to do eventually.

Mark still has no idea of what he wants to do, but he is not worried. He figures he can get some sort of a job—maybe at a supermarket or fast-food restaurant—and make up his mind about the future when he is ready.

These four young people are involved in identity formation. What accounts for the differences in the way they go about it, and how will these differences affect the outcome? According to research by the psychologist James E. Marcia, these students are in four different states of ego (self) development, or *identity statuses,* which seem to be related to certain aspects of personality.

Marcia's definition of *identity* is similar to Erikson's: "an internal, self-constructed, dynamic organization of drives, abilities, beliefs, and individual history" (Marcia, 1980, p. 159). Through 30-minute, semistructured identity-status interviews (see Table 11-1), Marcia found four types of identity status: *identity achievement, foreclosure, moratorium,* and *identity diffusion.* The four categories

differ according to the presence or absence of *crisis* and *commitment,* the two elements Erikson saw as crucial to forming identity (see Table 11-2). Marcia defines *crisis* as a period of conscious decision making, and *commitment* as a personal investment in an occupation or system of beliefs (ideology). He found relationships between identity status and such characteristics as anxiety, self-esteem, moral reasoning, and patterns of behavior. Building on Marcia's theory, other researchers have identified other personality and family variables related to identity status (see Table 11-3.) Marcia and other researchers have also studied differences in identity formation between males and females and among ethnic groups. Here is a thumbnail sketch of people in each of the four identity statuses:

1 *Identity achievement* (*crisis leading to commitment*). Kate has resolved her identity crisis. During the crisis period, she devoted much thought and some emotional struggle to major issues in her life; she has made choices and expresses strong commitment to them. Her parents have encouraged her to make her own decisions; they have listened to her ideas and given their opinions without pressuring her to adopt them. Kate has *flexible strength:* She is thoughtful but not so introspective as to be unable to act. She has a sense of humor, functions well under stress, is capable of intimate relationships, and holds to her standards while being open to new ideas. Research in a number of cultures has found people in this category to be more mature and more competent in relationships than people in the other three (Marcia, 1993).

2 *Foreclosure* (*commitment without crisis*). Andrea has made commitments, not as a result of a crisis, which would involve questioning and exploring possible choices, but by accepting someone else's plans for her life. She has *rigid strength:* she is happy and self-assured, perhaps even smug and self-satisfied, and she becomes dogmatic when her opinions are questioned. She has close family ties, is obedient, and tends to follow a powerful leader (like her mother), who accepts no disagreement.

3 *Moratorium* (*crisis with no commitment yet*). Nick is in crisis, struggling with decisions. He is lively, talkative, self-confident, and scrupulous, but also anxious and fearful. He is close to his mother but also resists her authority. He

TABLE 11-1

Identity-Status Interview

Sample Questions	Typical Answers for the Four Statuses
About occupational commitment: "How willing do you think you'd be to give up going into _____ if something better came along?"	*Identity achievement.* "Well, I might, but I doubt it. I can't see what 'something better' would be for me." *Foreclosure.* "Not very willing. It's what I've always wanted to do. The folks are happy with it and so am I." *Moratorium.* "I guess that if I knew for sure, I could answer that better. It would have to be something in the general area—something related. . . " *Identity diffusion.* "Oh, sure. If something better came along, I'd change just like that."
About ideological commitment: "Have you ever had any doubts about your religious beliefs?"	*Identity achievement.* "Yes, I even started wondering whether there is a God. I've pretty much resolved that now, though. The way it seems to me is. . . ." *Foreclosure.* "No, not really; our family is pretty much in agreement on these things." *Moratorium.* "Yes, I guess I'm going through that now. I just don't see how there can be a God and still so much evil in the world or. . . ." *Identity diffusion.* "Oh, I don't know. I guess so. Everyone goes through some sort of stage like that. But it really doesn't bother me much. I figure that one religion is about as good as another!"

SOURCE: Adapted from Marcia, 1966.

wants to have a girlfriend but has not yet developed a close relationship. He will probably come out of his crisis eventually with the ability to make commitments and achieve identity.

4 **Identity diffusion** (*no commitment, no crisis*). Mark has not seriously considered options and has avoided commitments. He is unsure of himself and tends to be uncooperative. His parents do not discuss his future with him; they say it's up to him. Some people in this category

become aimless drifters without goals. They tend to be unhappy, and they are often lonely because they have only superficial relationships.

These categories are not permanent, of course; they may change as people continue to develop (Marcia, 1979). From late adolescence on, more and more people are in moratorium or achievement: seeking or finding their own identity. Still, many

TABLE 11-2

Criteria for Identity Statuses

Identity Status	Crisis (Period of Considering Alternatives)	Commitment (Adherence to a Path of Action)
Identity achievement	Resolved	Present
Foreclosure	Absent	Present
Moratorium	In crisis	Absent
Identity diffusion	Absent	Absent

SOURCE: Adapted from Marcia, 1980.

TABLE 11-3

Family and Personality Factors Associated with Adolescents in Four Identity Statuses*

Factor	Identity Achievement	Foreclosure	Moratorium	Identity Diffusion
Family	Parents encourage autonomy and connection with teachers; differences are explored within a context of mutuality.	Parents are overly involved with their children; families avoid expressing differences; parents use denial and repression to avoid dealing with unwelcome thoughts and events.	Adolescents are often involved in an ambivalent struggle with parental authority.	Parents are laissez-faire in child-rearing attitudes; are rejecting or not available to children.
Personality	High levels of ego development, moral reasoning, internal locus of control, self-certainty, self-esteem, performance under stress, and intimacy.	Highest levels of authoritarianism and stereotypical thinking, obedience to authority, external locus of control, dependent relationships, low levels of anxiety.	Most anxious and fearful of success; high levels of ego development, moral reasoning, and self-esteem.	Mixed results, with low levels of ego development, moral reasoning, cognitive complexity, and self-certainty; poor cooperative abilities.

*These associations have emerged from a number of separate studies. Since the studies have all been correlational, rather than longitudinal, it is impossible to say that any factor caused placement in any identity status.
SOURCE: Kroger, 1993.

people, even as young adults, remain in foreclosure or diffusion (Kroger, 1993). Although people in foreclosure seem to have made final decisions, that is often not so; when adults in midlife look back on their lives, they most commonly trace a path from foreclosure to moratorium to achievement (Kroger & Haslett, 1991).

GENDER DIFFERENCES IN IDENTITY FORMATION

Freud's statement "Biology is destiny" suggests that the differing patterns of male and female development in almost all cultures are an inevitable result of anatomical differences. Today, many people believe that most gender differences arise from societal attitudes and practices (see Chapter 7). Whatever the reasons, the sexes (at least in the United States) seem to differ somewhat in rates of emotional and social maturation (see Box 11-1) and perhaps also in routes to identity.

To explore female identity, Marcia (1979) asked questions about attitudes toward premarital intercourse, views on women's roles, and concerns re-

lated to lifestyle. His findings were surprising. In their answers to his questions, men in moratorium (in crisis) most closely resembled men who had achieved identity. But the women whose answers most closely resembled those of male identity achievers were in foreclosure: they had made commitments without undergoing a crisis. Marcia's explanation was that society expects women to carry on social values from one generation to the next, and therefore stability of identity is extremely important for them. He suggested that, for women, early foreclosure of identity may be just as adaptive as a struggle to achieve identity. (This may no longer be true in light of the changes in women's roles that have taken place since the 1970s.)

Much research supports Erikson's view that, for women, identity and intimacy develop together. Indeed, intimacy matters more to girls than to boys even in grade school friendships (Blyth & Foster-Clarke, 1987). Rather than view this pattern as a departure from a male norm, however, some researchers who have studied girls and women see it as pointing to a weakness in Erikson's theory, which, they claim, is based on male-centered western concepts of individuality, autonomy, and competitiveness. According to Carol Gilligan (1982, 1987a, b; L. M. Brown & Gilligan, 1990), the female sense of self develops not so much through achieving a separate identity as through establishing relationships. Girls and women, says Gilligan, judge themselves on their handling of their responsibilities and on their ability to care for others as well as for themselves. Even highly achieving women attain identity more through cooperation than through competition.

Some developmentalists, however, have begun to question how different the male and female paths to identity really are—especially today—and whether individual differences may be more important than gender differences (S. L. Archer, 1993; Marcia, 1993). Indeed, Marcia (1993) argues that relationships and an ongoing tension between independence and connectedness are at the heart of all of Erikson's psychosocial stages for *both* men and women.

Self-esteem is an important aspect of identity. Interviews with 99 girls from kindergarten through twelfth grade suggest that girls' confidence in themselves and in their observations of their en-

vironment stays fairly high until age 11 or 12. Until then, they tend to be perceptive about relationships and assertive about expressing feelings. As adolescents, however, they often accept stereotyped notions of the way they should act and repress their true feelings for the sake of being "nice" (L. M. Brown & Gilligan, 1990). As they recognize that they are burying parts of themselves and thus can no longer have authentic relationships, says Gilligan, girls' confidence falters. Only those who continue to acknowledge their true feelings and express them appropriately stay in healthy relationship with themselves, with others, and with the society they are entering. These girls, unlike their peers, retain high self-esteem. They see themselves as competent and are more apt than other girls to choose nontraditional careers.

ETHNIC FACTORS IN IDENTITY FORMATION

What happens to young people's identity when the values of their own ethnic community conflict with those of the larger society—for example, when Native Americans are expected to partici-

---

BOX 11-1 FOOD FOR THOUGHT

GENDER DIFFERENCES IN PERSONALITY DEVELOPMENT

Popular wisdom holds that boys and girls develop differently, that girls mature earlier and are more empathic, and that boys are more aggressive. But in 80 years of research about development, this belief has rarely been investigated scientifically. Now a statistical analysis of 65 studies of personality growth, involving about 9,000 participants, has found that adolescent girls apparently do mature earlier in some ways (L. D. Cohn, 1991).

The analysis was based on research using the Washington University Sentence Completion Test, which consists of 36 sentence stems for respondents to complete. Examples include: "At times she (he) worried about . . ." and "A woman (man) should always. . . ."

Overall, girls tended to give answers showing more advanced personality development. However, these gender differences were generally small. They arose by late childhood, increased at about age 13, and remained fairly large throughout adolescence. When boys were still egocentric, girls had moved toward social conformity; when boys began to be conformists, girls were becoming more self-aware. (Ironically, teenage boys are often granted earlier dating privileges, independence, and freedom from adult supervision, even though it's the girls who are more mature!)

These differences in rates of development seem to stem from differences in social experiences, such

as in play. The looser structure of girls' games, which are less rule-bound than those played by boys, may foster the development of moral reasoning. The small groups in which girls play provide more opportunities for conversation and for mimicking adult relationships than do the large groups common in boys' play. Furthermore, the competitiveness encouraged in boys may reinforce a tendency toward impulsiveness, which is discouraged in girls.

The female edge in developmental status declines markedly among college-age adults and disappears entirely among older men and women. Perhaps maturation enables men to "catch up."

pate in a tribal ceremony on a day when they are also supposed to be in school? Or when young people face and perhaps internalize (take into their own value system) prejudice against their group? Or when discrimination limits their occupational choice? All these situations can lead to identity confusion.

Identity formation is especially complicated for young people in minority groups, who need to integrate multiple identities. In fact, for some adolescents ethnicity may be central to identity formation (Phinney, 1993). Skin color and other physical features, language differences, and stereotyped social standing are extremely influential in molding minority adolescents' self-concept (Spencer & Markstrom-Adams, 1990).

Some research using Marcia's (1966) identity-status measures has shown a disproportionately large number of minority teenagers in foreclosure (Spencer & Markstrom-Adams, 1990). However, for them, this status may be adaptive. For example, Latino adolescents living in predominantly Latino communities may find social recognition, strength, and a robust sense of identity through following the customs and values of their culture. In a survey sponsored by the American Association of University Women, many more black girls than white and Hispanic girls remained self-confident in high school; white girls lost their self-assurance the earliest. African American girls may feel more self-confident because they often see strong women around them. They seem less dependent on school achievement for their self-esteem, drawing their sense of themselves more from family and community (Daley, 1991).

✔ SEXUALITY

Seeing oneself as a sexual being, coming to terms with sexual stirrings, and forming romantic attachments are all parts of achieving sexual identity. This urgent awareness of sexuality is an important aspect of identity formation, profoundly affecting self-image and relationships. This process, which begins in adolescence and continues in adulthood, is biologically driven, but its expression is in part culturally defined.

What influences sexual orientation? How have sexual attitudes and behavior changed in recent decades? What factors affect the likelihood, risks, and consequences of sexual activity during the teenage years?

SEXUAL ORIENTATION

Although present in younger children, it is in adolescence that a person's *sexual orientation* is usually expressed: whether that person will consistently be sexually, romantically, and affectionately interested in members of the other sex *(heterosexual)* or in persons of the same sex *(homosexual)*.

The incidence of homosexuality seems to be similar in a number of cultures (Hyde, 1986). In one study of 38,000 American students in grades 7 through 12, about 88 percent described themselves as predominantly heterosexual and only 1 percent as predominantly homosexual or bisexual (interested in members of both sexes). About 11 percent, mostly younger students, were unsure of their sexual orientation. Those who were unsure were more likely to report homosexual fantasies and attractions and were less likely to have had heterosexual experiences (Remafedi, Resnick, Blum, & Harris, 1992).

Much research on sexual orientation has been spurred by efforts to explain homosexuality. Although it was once considered a mental illness, several decades of research have found no association between homosexuality and emotional or social problems (American Psychological Association, undated; C. J. Patterson, 1992, 1995a, 1995b; see Chapter 9). These findings (along with political lobbying and changes in public attitudes) eventually led the psychiatric profession to stop classifying homosexuality as a mental disorder. The most recent edition of the American Psychiatric Association's *Diagnostic and Statistical Manual of Mental Disorders* contains no references to it at all (APA, 1994).

Other theories of the sources of homosexuality— all of which lack convincing scientific support— point to disturbed relationships with parents; parental encouragement of unconventional, cross-gender behavior; imitation of homosexual parents; or chance learning through seduction by a homosexual. Many young people have one or more homosexual experiences as they are growing up, usually before age 15. However, isolated experiences, or even homosexual attractions or fantasies, do not determine sexual orientation.

According to one newer theory, sexual orientation may be influenced by a complex prenatal process involving both hormonal and neurological factors (Ellis & Ames, 1987). If the levels of sex hormones in a fetus of either sex are in the typical female range between the second and fifth months of gestation, the person is likely to be attracted to males after puberty. If the hormone levels are in the male range, the person is likely to be attracted to females. Whether and how hormonal activity may affect brain development, and whether and how differences in brain structure may affect sexual orientation have not been established (Golombok & Tasker, 1996); but an anatomical difference between homosexual and heterosexual men in an area of the brain that governs sexual behavior has been reported (LeVay, 1991).

There also is growing evidence that sexual orientation may be at least partly genetic. One series of studies links male homosexuality to a small region of the X chromosome inherited from the mother; no such effect was found for women (Hamer, Hu, Magnuson, Hu, & Pattatucci, 1993, Hu et al., 1995). An identical twin of a homosexual has about a 50 percent probability of being homosexual himself or herself, while a fraternal twin has only about a 20 percent likelihood and an adopted sibling 10 percent or less (Gladue, 1994).

Controversy remains as to whether or not sexual orientation is decisively shaped either before birth or at an early age and as to the relative contributions of biological, psychological, and social influences (Baumrind, 1995; C. J. Patterson, 1995b). Indeed, these influences may well be "impossible to untangle," and their relative strength may differ among individuals (Baumrind, 1995, p. 132).

Many people have sought treatment to change their own sexual orientation or that of a child, but there is no good evidence that such therapy works. Furthermore, many mental health providers question the ethics of trying to alter a trait which is not a disorder and which is important to a person's identity (American Psychological Association, undated).

SEXUAL ATTITUDES AND BEHAVIOR

Sexual activity—which may range from casual kissing to genital contact—can fulfill a number of needs, only one of which is physical pleasure. Teenagers may become sexually active for any of a variety of reasons: to achieve closeness, to seek new experience, to prove their maturity, to keep up with peers, to find relief from pressures, or to investigate the mysteries of love.

It is difficult to do research on sexual expression. Virtually all studies about sex—from Kinsey's surveys in the 1940s to those being done now—have been criticized on the grounds that people willing

Attitudes toward sexuality have liberalized during the past 50 years. This "sexual evolution" includes more open acceptance of sexual activity and a decline in the double standard by which males are freer sexually than females. Teenagers become sexually active for a number of reasons besides physical pleasure: to achieve closeness, seek new experience, prove their maturity, keep up with peers, find relief from pressures, and investigate the mysteries of love. *(Ellen Skye/Monkmeyer)*

to answer questions about sex tend to be sexually active and liberal in their attitudes toward sex and thus are not representative of the population. Also, there is often a discrepancy between what people *say* about sex and what they *do*, and there is no way to corroborate what people say. Some may conceal sexual activity; others may exaggerate. Problems multiply in surveying young people. For one thing, parental consent is often required, and parents who grant permission may not be typical. Still, even if we cannot generalize findings to the population as a whole, within the groups that take part in surveys we can see trends that reveal changes in sexual mores.

The "Sexual Evolution"

The early 1920s through the late 1970s witnessed an evolution in sexual attitudes and behavior. One change has been greater approval of and indulgence in premarital sex, especially in a committed relationship. Another is a decline in the *double standard:* the code that gives males more sexual freedom than females. This wave of sexual liberation may have crested and may even be ebbing; but meanwhile, like the rest of the population, today's teenagers are more sexually active and more accepting of sexual activity. This is especially true of girls.

In 1965, at a large southern university, 33 percent of male students and 70 percent of female students called premarital sexual intercourse immoral. By 1985, only about 16 percent of the men and 17 percent of the women thought so (I. Robinson, Ziss, Ganza, Katz, & Robinson, 1991). Rates of premarital sexual activity have risen accordingly, especially for girls. In the mid-1950s, 1 out of 4 girls had sexual experience by age 18. Today, more than 1 out of 2 girls and nearly 3 out of 4 boys have had intercourse by that age. Fewer than 1 out of 5 young people refrain from intercourse during their teens (Alan Guttmacher Institute, AGI, 1994).

The double standard is not dead, however. In a telephone survey of 500 high school students, more boys said that sex was pleasurable and that they felt good about their sexual experiences, whereas more girls said that they were in love with their last sexual partner and that they should have waited until they were older before having sex (G. Lewin, 1994). A girl is likely to experience her first sexual relations with a steady boyfriend; a boy is likely to have his with someone he knows casually (Dreyer, 1982; Zelnik, Kantner, & Ford, 1981; Zelnik & Shah, 1983). In a study of 1,880 fifteen-to-nineteen-year-old males, the average sexually active boy had had sexual relationships with two girls at different times during the previous year, each one lasting a few months (Sonenstein, Pleck, & Ku, 1991).

The sexual evolution has brought more acceptance of homosexuality. In 1995, 31 percent of 240,082 college freshmen in a major survey said homosexual relations should be prohibited, down from 53 percent in 1987 (Sax, Astin, Korn, & Mahoney, 1996). Still, teenagers who openly identify as gay or lesbian often feel isolated in a hostile environment and may be subject to prejudice and even violence. In high school they generally keep their sexual activity private, do not discuss their sexuality, and may become depressed or suicidal (C. J. Patterson, 1995b).

SEXUAL RISK TAKING

Two major concerns about teenage sexual activity are the risks of sexually transmitted disease (see

Chapter 10) and of pregnancy. Delinquency may also be a danger. In a survey of 1,167 mostly white, Catholic, middle-class, suburban high school sophomores and juniors, those who began sexual activity early, and continued it frequently, were more likely to show antisocial behavior than those who abstained. The sexually active group may have been less mature than those who waited to engage in sex, or they may have been influenced toward both sexual activity and delinquency by rebellion against authority and by the influence of antisocial peers. They were also more likely to be depressed, to have alcohol problems, and to have low grades (Tubman, Windle, & Windle, 1996).

Let's look at several factors in sexual risk taking: when sexual activity begins; who takes (or fails to take) protective measures, and why; and where youngsters get information about sex. In the next section, we'll focus on the problem of teenage pregnancy.

When and Why Do Adolescents Become Sexually Active?

American adolescents are becoming sexually active at earlier ages than in previous generations, and many apparently become active earlier than they say they should. In one poll during the 1980s, teenagers gave a median age of 18 as the "right age" to start having intercourse, even though most of the 17-year-olds and nearly half of the 16-year-olds had already done so (Louis Harris & Associates, 1986).

Teenage girls (and, to a lesser extent, boys) often feel under pressure to engage in activities they do not feel ready for. Social pressure was the chief reason given by 73 percent of the girls and 50 percent of the boys in the Harris poll when asked why many teenagers do not wait to engage in sex until they are older. Both boys and girls also mentioned curiosity as a reason for early sexual intimacy. More boys than girls cited sexual feelings and desires. Only 6 percent of the boys and 11 percent of the girls gave love as a reason (Louis Harris & Associates, 1986). Often, girls who begin having sexual relations early are coerced into it (AGI, 1994).

Various factors—including timing of puberty, personality style, drug use, education, family structure, socioeconomic status, age, ethnicity, and gender—influence the likelihood of early sexual activity (see Table 11-4). In general, girls are more influenced by such psychological factors as self-

TABLE 11-4

Factors Associated with Timing of First Intercourse

	Factors Associated with Early Age	Factors Associated with Later Age
Timing of puberty	Early	Late
Personality style and behavior	Risk taking, impulsive	Traditional values, religious orientation
	Depressive symptoms	Prosocial or conventional behavior
	Antisocial or delinquent	
Substance use	Use of drugs, alcohol, tobacco	Nonuse
Education	Fewer years of schooling	More years of schooling; valuing academic achievement
Family structure	Single-parent family	Two-parent family
Socioeconomic status	Disadvantaged	Advantaged
Race	African American	White, Latino

SOURCES: B. C. Miller & Moore, 1990; Sonnenstein et al., 1991.

esteem, religiosity, desire for a career, and perceived control of their lives, whereas boys are more affected by factors having to do with family and community, such as the presence of a father in the home, the father's educational level, and living in a rural or urban setting. Rural teens are more likely to have intercourse, and among younger (but not older) adolescents, those with lower self-esteem and less autonomy are more likely to do so (Day, 1992).

Girls who move frequently are more likely to engage in premarital sex. Among a national sample of 1,287 fifteen- to nineteen-year-olds, this was true in all geographic regions regardless of age, race, father's education, and such other factors as family disruption, religiosity, opportunity for sexual activity, and peer attitudes and behavior (Stack, 1994). Girls who move repeatedly may be lonely and may use sexuality as a means of forming friendships in a new neighborhood. Their bonds with family and community may be weakened: they may be less closely supervised by parents, they may be removed from extended family, and they may have come to regard relationships as casual and temporary.

A national longitudinal survey of 11,725 white, African American, and Hispanic adolescents showed more ethnic variation among boys than among girls (R. D. Day, 1992). On average, girls in all ethnic groups had their sexual initiation around age 17, though for black girls it took place a few months before that. Black boys became sexually active the earliest—at about 14. White, Mexican, and Mexican American boys began having intercourse at 16, but Cuban and Puerto Rican boys started at 15. Still, differences in sexual activity based on gender, race, religion, and socioeconomic status have narrowed considerably (AGI, 1994).

Who Is Most at Risk from Sexual Activity?

Premarital sexual activity is always risky, but some patterns of sexual behavior are especially so. Most in danger are teenagers who start sexual activity early, who have multiple partners, and who do not use contraceptives, or use them improperly. The best safeguard for sexually active teens is regular use of condoms, which gives some protection against sexually transmitted diseases (STDs) as well as against pregnancy.

Most sexually active adolescents do take protective measures. About two-thirds use some method of protection, usually a condom, the first time they engage in sex, and between 72 percent and 84 percent of teenage girls use contraceptives regularly (AGI, 1994). Adolescents who do not use contraceptives, or who use them irregularly or ineffectively, tend to be in their early teens. They tend to have low educational and career aspirations, to be uninvolved in sports or other activities, and to use alcohol or drugs. They are relatively inexperienced with sex, ignorant about it, and ashamed of engaging in it, and typically they are not in committed relationships. African American and Latina girls, girls who live with a single parent, girls from impoverished families, and girls whose parents are relatively uneducated tend to use no birth control or to use less effective methods (AGI, 1994; Ford, Zelnick, & Kantner, 1979; Louis Harris & Associates, 1986; Luster & Small, 1994; B. C. Miller & Moore, 1990).

In one national survey, the most common reason teenagers gave for not using birth control was that they did not expect to have intercourse and therefore did not prepare for it. Yet when asked why their *peers* did not use contraceptives, many told a different story. Nearly 40 percent said that young people either prefer not to use birth control, do not think about it, do not care, enjoy sex more without it, or want to get pregnant. Other often-mentioned reasons were lack of knowledge about or access to birth control, embarrassment about seeking it, and fear that parents would find out they were having sex (Louis Harris & Associates, 1986).

Many teenagers with multiple sex partners do not use reliable protection (Luster & Small, 1994). Among 1,091 tenth-graders from urban working-class and welfare families and middle-class suburban families, at least one-third of sexually active students had had two or more partners, and more than two-thirds reported inconsistent or no use of condoms (Walter, Vaughan, & Cohall, 1991). Nationally, among high school seniors, 38.5 percent of all boys and 17 percent of girls have had four or more sex partners. Teenagers in this high-risk group tend to have low grades, to be frequent drinkers, and to have little parental supervision or support; they are more likely to have been abused by parents than teenagers who abstain from sex or use contraceptives responsibly (Luster & Small, 1994).

Where Do Teenagers Get Information about Sex?

Most parents do not give their children enough information about sex, and youngsters still get much of their information (and much misinformation) from friends (Conger, 1988). For example, some girls mistakenly believe that they cannot get pregnant during the first intercourse, or in certain positions, or at certain times in the menstrual cycle (Quadrel et al., 1993). Thirty-one percent of the teenagers in the Harris poll, including 28 percent of those who were sexually active, had never talked with their parents about sex, and 42 percent said they were too nervous or afraid to bring it up. Furthermore, nearly two-thirds (64 percent) had never discussed birth control at home (Louis Harris & Associates, 1986). This is important because teenagers, especially girls, who *have* had discussions with parents about sexual matters and who are knowledgeable about sex are more likely to use contraceptives and to use them consistently (Louis Harris & Associates, 1986; Luster & Small, 1994). They are also more likely to postpone sexual intimacy—the most effective means of birth control (Conger, 1988; Jaslow, 1982). Teenagers who can go to their parents or other adults with questions about sex and those who get sex education from school or community programs (see Box 11-2) have a better chance of avoiding pregnancy and other risks connected with sexual activity.

The media exert a powerful influence on adolescents' sexual attitudes and behavior. Unfortunately, that influence is negative. The media present a distorted view of sexual activity. It is often associated with fun, excitement, danger, or violence, but the risks of unprotected sexual relations are seldom shown (AAP Committee on Communications, 1995). Between 1975 and 1988, the amount of sexual behavior on prime time television doubled. An American adolescent is typically exposed to nearly 14,000 sexually suggestive references or jokes each year, and only 165 of these deal with birth control, self-control, abstinence (which is rarely portrayed positively), or STDs (Louis Harris & Associates, 1988). On soap operas, unmarried couples have sex 24 times more often than married couples, and contraceptives are almost never mentioned; but women seldom get pregnant, and nobody seems to worry about STDs (Lowry & Towles, 1989).

Not surprisingly, then, adolescents who get their information about sex from television and who lack well-formed value systems, critical viewing skills, and strong family influence may accept the idea of premarital and extramarital intercourse with multiple partners and without protection against pregnancy and disease. Furthermore, tele-

BOX 11-2   PRACTICALLY SPEAKING

PREVENTING TEENAGE PREGNANCY

Rates of early intercourse are similar in the United States and the Netherlands, yet pregnancy and abortion rates for girls ages 15 to 19 are about 7 times higher in the United States. In Sweden, where girls become sexually active even earlier, rates of pregnancy and abortion are less than half the American rates. Although many people believe that welfare programs encourage pregnancy, industrial countries that are more generous than the United States in their support of poor mothers have much lower teenage pregnancy rates. Even white American teenagers, who tend to be socioeconomically advantaged, have far higher rates of pregnancy and abortion than those in European countries (E. F. Jones et al., 1985). Why?

For one thing, Europe's industrialized countries provide comprehensive sex education. Sweden's compulsory curriculum covers all grade levels. Dutch schools have no special sex education programs, but the mass media and many private groups provide extensive information about contraceptive techniques, so that nearly all Dutch teenagers are well informed about birth control.

Contrary to some critics, community- and school-based sex education does *not* lead to more sexual activity (M. Eisen & Zellman, 1987). Realistic programs to prevent early pregnancy have two aims: to encourage young teenagers to delay intercourse and to improve contraceptive use among adolescents who are already sexually active. Such programs include education about sexuality and acquisition of skills for sexual decision making and communication with partners. They provide information about risks and consequences of teenage pregnancy, about birth control methods, and about where to get medical and contraceptive help

(AGI, 1994; I. C. Stewart, 1994).

Of course, parents are young people's first and often best teachers. Teenagers whose parents have talked with them about sex from an early age, have communicated healthy attitudes, and have been available to answer questions tend to wait longer for sexual activity (J. J. Conger, 1988; Jaslow, 1982). Parents and other adults who serve as positive role models can encourage teenagers to make responsible decisions (Children's Defense Fund, 1995, 1996). However, adolescents are often uncomfortable talking about sex with their parents. Many parents need community support to prevent their children from becoming pregnant while they are still children themselves.

Community programs can help young people stand up against peer pressure to be more sexually active than they want to be, can teach them how to say no gracefully, and can offer guidance in problem solving (J. Gross, 1994; Howard, 1983). The two arguments for delaying sex that teenagers find most convincing are the risk of STDs and the danger that pregnancy will ruin their lives (Louis Harris & Associates, 1986). Programs that include peer counseling can be effective; teenagers often heed peers when they might not pay attention to the same advice from an older person. Teenage girls tend to respond especially well to counseling by other girls close to their own age (Jay, DuRant, Shoffitt, Linder, & Litt, 1984).

Since almost 1 out of 3 pregnancies is preceded by a negative test result, girls who have had negative pregnancy tests should be especially targeted for preventive efforts (Zabin, Emerson, Ringers, & Sedivy, 1996). And, because the media are a strong influence on adolescent behavior, radio and television executives should present sexual situations responsibly

and should permit advertising of contraceptives (AAP Committee on Communications, 1995).

Another important factor in preventing pregnancy is access to reproductive services. Contraceptives are provided free to adolescents in Britain, France, Sweden, and, in many cases, the Netherlands. In Sweden, parents cannot be told that their children have sought contraceptives if the teenagers request privacy. A desire to keep the abortion rate among teenagers from rising has helped persuade conservatives in those countries to support such policies. When similar programs are proposed in the United States, they generally are not adopted for fear that they might seem to endorse sexual activity among teenagers— even though our teenage pregnancy rate is already one of the highest in the world (E. F. Jones et al., 1985). American teenagers say that making birth control services free, readily accessible (close to schools), and confidential are the three most effective ways to encourage contraception (Louis Harris & Associates, 1986; Zabin & Clark, 1983). Many say they would not go to a clinic that insisted on notifying their parents or obtaining parental consent (Jaslow, 1982).

In the long run, preventing teenage pregnancy requires attention to underlying factors that put teenagers and families at risk: improving education for disadvantaged youth, expanding employment and social and recreational opportunities, and reducing poverty (AGI, 1994; Children's Defense Fund, 1995, 1996). Adolescents who have high aspirations for the future are less likely to become pregnant. Programs that focus on motivating young people to achieve and raising self-esteem, rather than merely on the mechanics of contraception, have achieved some success (Carrera, 1986).

About half of the 1 in 10 teenage girls who become pregnant each year have and keep their babies, often drastically limiting the mother's career opportunities. Talking with a sympathetic, knowledgeable school counselor, as this pregnant high school student is doing, may help a prospective teenage mother sort out her options. *(Richard Hutchings/ PhotoEdit)*

vision tends to reinforce a stereotypical double standard, in which women, but not men, consider marriage important. Movies and rock music lyrics also have become more and more sexually explicit; music videos are full of sexual images and violence against women (AAP Committee on Communications, 1995).

In ironic contrast to the blatantly irresponsible portrayals of sexuality in television programming, network executives have almost universally refused to show contraceptive advertisements, claiming that they would be controversial and offensive and might encourage sexual activity. However, there is no evidence for the latter claim, and trial advertisements in limited markets have brought mostly commendations instead of complaints (AAP Committee on Communications, 1995).

TEENAGE PREGNANCY AND CHILDBEARING

In the United States, about 1 in 10 girls age 15 to 19 becomes pregnant each year (Ventura, Taffel, Mosher, Wilson, & Henshaw, 1995). During the past two decades, the estimated pregnancy rate among sexually active teenage girls fell 19 percent, from about 1 out of 4 in 1972 to 1 out of 5 in 1990 (AGI, 1994). This rate change may reflect gains in contraceptive use due to fear of AIDS. However, because the number of sexually active teenagers doubled during this period, the number of teenage pregnancies remains about 1 million each year; and 4 out of 5 of these pregnancies are unplanned

(AGI, 1994; Children's Defense Fund, 1995, 1996). The younger a girl is at first intercourse, the longer she is likely to wait before seeking help with contraception and the more likely she is to become pregnant (Tanfer & Horn, 1985).

About half of pregnant teenagers have their babies and plan to raise them themselves; very few place their children for adoption. Slightly more than a third have abortions, and the rest miscarry (AGI, 1994). The teenage birth rate has dropped steadily since 1991, from about 62 births per 1,000 to fewer than 57 in 1995, a modest reversal of the sharp increase of 5 percent or more per year during the 1980s (Children's Defense Fund, 1996; National Center for Health Statistics, 1995b; H. M. Rosenberg et al., 1996). A greater proportion of these births than ever—nearly 3 out of 4—are to unmarried mothers (Children's Defense Fund, 1996; see Figure 11-1). The decline in the birth rate has occurred entirely among black teenagers, and the greatest increase in out-of-wedlock births is among white teens; but black girls are still far more likely to have babies than are white girls (Children's Defense Fund, 1996). More than 8 out of 10 adolescent mothers are from low-income families (AGI, 1994); pregnant girls from advantaged families are more likely to have abortions.

Teenage Parenthood: Problems and Outcomes

Teenage pregnancies often have poor outcomes. Many of the mothers are impoverished and poorly educated, do not eat properly, and get inadequate prenatal care or none at all; and their babies are likely to be dangerously small. Nearly 1 out of 10 babies born to 15- to 19-year-olds, and more than 1 out of 8 born to black mothers in that age group, have low birth weight (S. S. Brown, 1985; Children's Defense Fund, 1995).

Regardless of socioeconomic factors, however, babies of teenage mothers are at risk. Among more than 134,000 white, largely middle-class girls and women in Utah who had their first babies between 1970 and 1990, 13- to 19-year-olds were more likely than 20- to 24-year-olds to have low-birthweight babies, even when the mothers were married, well-educated, and had adequate prenatal care. Thirteen- to seventeen-year-old girls were nearly twice as likely to have premature deliveries as older teenage mothers. Although prenatal care is a factor in prematurity, good prenatal care apparently cannot overcome the biological disadvantage inherent in being born to a still-growing girl whose own body may be competing with the developing fetus for vital nutrients (Fraser, Brockert, & Ward, 1995).

Birth complications are just the beginning of the problems that may beset a teenage mother and her child. Teenage mothers are 3 times as likely to drop out of high school as age-mates who do not have babies until their twenties (Children's Defense Fund, 1995). However, many do finish later on. In one large study, 5 years after giving birth, only half of urban black adolescent mothers had graduated from high school; but 10 years later, two-thirds had graduated (Furstenberg, Brooks-Gunn, & Morgan, 1987).

Teenage mothers are likely to have financial troubles. It is true that many states require fathers to pay child support for the first 18 years of a child's life, sometimes through payroll deductions. However, these laws are spottily enforced, and court-ordered payments are often inadequate. Even though paternity can be clearly established through biological testing, many men assume little or no responsibility for their children. Many of the mothers must go on public assistance, at least for a while. About one-fourth of women in their twenties and thirties who became mothers in adolescence are poor. Most of them were poor before becoming mothers and probably would have remained poor even without having had a baby. Still, early childbearing does restrict opportunity for both mothers and children (AGI, 1994). Furthermore, teenage mothers are at high risk of repeat pregnancies; the risk is highest for those who drop out of school and do not use reliable birth control (McAnarney & Hendee, 1989).

Some children of teenage mothers do better than others. In one follow-up study of disadvantaged teenage mothers enrolled at an adolescent health center in New York City, 13 percent of the children at 28 to 36 months of age had behavior problems severe enough to need clinical treatment, according to a checklist filled out by the mothers. These were most likely to be African American boys whose mothers had shown symptoms of depression or had experienced stressful events during the first year after giving birth. Problems were less likely if the mothers received emotional support from friends or family, and particularly if they were living with their grandmothers, who may have been more supportive than their own mothers (Leadbeater & Bishop, 1994). Similarly, in another study, the prognosis for low-birthweight infants of teenage mothers was better when mother and baby lived with the infant's grandmother, who could help with caregiving (S. K. Pope et al., 1993).

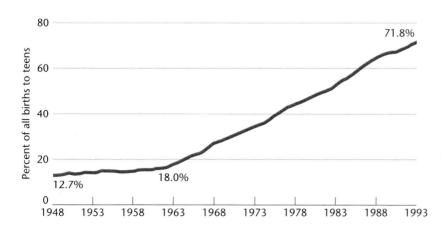

FIGURE 11-1

Proportion of teenage mothers who were unmarried when giving birth, 1948 to 1993. Although the number of births to teenage girls has declined considerably since 1970, the proportion of these births to unmarried girls has risen. This is largely because fewer teenagers are marrying today, and fewer married teenagers are having babies. *(Source: Children's Defense Fund, 1996, p. 47. Based on data from U.S. Department of Health and Human Services and National Center for Health Statistics.)*

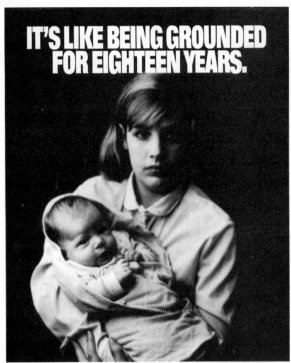

IT'S LIKE BEING GROUNDED FOR EIGHTEEN YEARS.

Having a baby when you're a teenager can do more than just
take away your freedom, it can take away your dreams.

THE CHILDREN'S DEFENSE FUND

To many teenagers, one of the most persuasive arguments
against sexual risk-taking is the danger that pregnancy will
ruin their lives. Teenage girls respond better when the advice
comes from other girls close to their own age. *(Children's
Defense Fund)*

Sometimes teenage pregnancy sets in motion a
cycle that spans generations. However, this may
happen less often than is generally believed. A 20-
year study of more than 400 teenage mothers in
Baltimore found that two-thirds of their daughters
did not become teenage mothers themselves, and
most graduated from high school (Furstenberg,
Levine, & Brooks-Gunn, 1990).

Helping Pregnant Teenagers and
Teenage Parents

An unmarried pregnant teenager is especially vulnerable to emotional upheaval. However she
handles her pregnancy, she is likely to have conflicting feelings. Just when she needs the most
emotional support, she may get the least: her
boyfriend may be frightened by the responsibility
and turn away, her family may be angry, and she
may be isolated from her school friends. If a young
mother and her baby need additional support, an

interested, sympathetic, and knowledgeable counselor may be of great help.

Pregnant girls need to learn both job and parenting skills. In one program, 80 low-income
teenage mothers learned such skills either from bi-
weekly home visits by a graduate student and a
teenage aide or through paid training as teachers'
aides in the nursery of a medical school. The infants of trained mothers developed better than babies of untrained mothers. They weighed more,
displayed more advanced motor skills, and interacted better with their mothers. The mothers who
worked as teachers' aides and their children
showed the most gains: more mothers returned to
work or school, fewer became pregnant again, and
their babies made the most progress (T. M. Field,
Widmayer, Greenberg, & Stoller, 1982).

The mother usually bears the major impact of
teenage parenthood, but a young father's life is often affected as well. A boy who feels committed to
the girl he has impregnated has decisions to make.
At a time when his financial resources may be mea-
ger and his prospects uncertain, he may pay for an
abortion or become obligated to continuing child
support; or he may marry the girl, a move that may
drastically affect his educational and career plans.
The father, too, needs someone to talk to, to help
him sort out his own feelings so that he and the
mother can make the best decisions for themselves
and their child.

✔ RELATIONSHIPS WITH FAMILY, PEERS, AND ADULT SOCIETY

The teenage years have been called a time of ***adolescent rebellion,*** involving emotional turmoil,
conflict within the family, alienation from adult society, and hostility toward adults' values. Yet research on adolescents in the United States and
other countries the world over (see Box 11-3) suggests that fewer than 1 out of 5 teenagers—at least
among those who remain in school—fit this pattern of tumult, alienation, and disturbance
(Brooks-Gunn, 1988; Offer, 1987; Offer, Ostrov, &
Howard, 1989; Offer, Ostrov, Howard, & Atkinson,
1988; Offer & Schonert-Riechl, 1992). Adolescence
does not typically bring wide emotional swings,
though negative moods do increase as boys and
girls move through these years (R. Larson &
Lampman-Petraitis, 1989). Furthermore, although
adolescents defy parental authority with some reg-

BOX 11-3 WINDOW ON THE WORLD

IS THERE A "UNIVERSAL ADOLESCENT"?

Do teenagers growing up in Hungary go through more or fewer "growing pains" than adolescents in the United States? Do adolescents in Taiwan and Japan, whose cultures traditionally show great respect to parents, have any special advantages or difficulties in navigating the transition to adulthood? How much does the psychological world of adolescence vary in cultures as diverse as those of Australia and Bangladesh? Is the communication revolution making the world a "global village" and breaking down cultural differences among the young people who inhabit it?

To answer questions like these, Daniel Offer and his colleagues (Offer et al., 1988) administered the Offer Self-Image Questionnaire to 5,938 adolescents in 10 countries: Australia, Bangladesh, Hungary, Israel, Italy, Japan, Taiwan, Turkey, the United States, and West Germany. The young people answered questions about five aspects of themselves: (1) the *psychological self:* impulse control, fluctuations in mood and emotions, and feelings about their bodies, (2) the *social self:* peer relations, moral attitudes, and educational and vocational goals, (3) the *sexual self:* attitudes toward sexuality and sexual behavior, (4) the *familial self:* feelings about parents and the atmosphere in the home, and (5) the *coping self:* ability to deal with the world.

The researchers found cross-cultural commonalities in each of the five "selves," particularly familial, social, and coping. For example, about 9 out of 10 adolescents in each country had positive feelings toward their parents, valued work and friendship, and tried to learn from failure. There was less consistency in the psychologi-

cal and sexual areas; here socioeconomic circumstances and local customs were more crucial. In general, however, these "universal adolescents" described themselves as happy; felt able to cope with life, make decisions, and use self-control; cared about others and liked being with and learning from them; enjoyed a job well done; were confident about their sexuality; did not harbor grudges against their parents; saw their mothers and fathers as getting along well most of the time; and expected to be able to take responsibility for themselves as they grew older. All in all, the researchers judged at least 73 percent of the total sample as having "a healthy adolescent self-image" (p. 124).

Teenagers in each country showed strengths and weaknesses; in no country were adolescents better- or worse-adjusted in all respects. In Bangladesh, the third poorest country in the world, even middle-class teenagers were low in impulse control; felt lonely, sad, and vulnerable; and had a poor body image. They also reported the most problems with peers and the highest rate of depression (48 percent). In Taiwan, where traditional sexual taboos still operate, large numbers of young people seemed to be afraid of sex or inhibited about it. On the other hand, Bengali and Taiwanese youths seemed superior in enjoyment of solving difficult problems and in willingness to find out how to deal with new situations.

The lower a country's economic output and the higher the proportion of adolescents who must compete for educational and work opportunities, the less positive were the teenagers' emotional tone and peer relationships: "very positive peer relationships seem to

be a luxury of relatively well-advantaged adolescents" (p. 105). This finding echoes earlier surveys of American adolescents in the 1960s, 1970s, and 1980s. Although most young people in all three cohorts had no major problems, teenagers in the 1960s seemed to be the best-adjusted and those in the 1970s the worst (Offer et al., 1989). Adolescents in the 1960s were at the end of a "baby bust" generation; those in the 1970s were in the middle of a "baby boom," which ran its course by the 1980s. In "boom" periods, competition for jobs and college admission is keener, and this pressure may help explain the greater unease of teenagers in the 1970s, as well as in less developed countries today.

Some consistent gender and age differences emerged in the cross-cultural study. Boys felt more sure of themselves, less afraid of competition, more in control of their emotions, and more interested in sex. Boys were also prouder of their bodies; girls in both early and late adolescence were more likely to feel unattractive. Girls were more empathic, caring, and socially responsible—more likely to help a friend and to refrain from actions that harm others. Girls were also more committed to work and study.

Generally speaking, older adolescents were less self-conscious than younger ones, more willing to learn from others, and better able to take criticism without resentment. These findings point to normal developmental growth in self-confidence and self-esteem and a smooth transition toward adulthood. Older adolescents were also more comfortable with their sexuality and more realistic in their view of family relationships.

(Continued)

BOX 11-3   (Continued)

IS THERE A "UNIVERSAL ADOLESCENT"?

The researchers attributed the "surprising unity of adolescent experience" across cultures largely to the media, which give young people a "collective consciousness" of what is going on in one another's lives all over the world (p. 114). Through the eye of television, adolescents see themselves as part of a world culture.

We do need to be careful about drawing overly broad generalizations from these findings. The samples included only young people in school—urban and mostly middle-class. Also, some of the questionnaire items may have taken on slightly different meanings in translation. Nevertheless, this study draws a fascinating picture of the universal and not-so-universal aspects of adolescence and raises many questions for future research.

---

ularity, the emotions attending this transition do not normally lead to family conflict of major proportions or to a "generation gap"—a sharp break with parental or societal standards (Offer & Church, 1991; Offer et al., 1989).

Age does become a powerful bonding agent in adolescence—more powerful than race, religion, community, or sex. Between ages 9 and 15, the amount of time young people spend with parents and siblings declines dramatically (R. Larson & Richards, 1991). Adolescents spend much of their free time with peers, with whom they identify and feel comfortable. They sometimes seem to believe that most other adolescents share their values and that most older people do not. Actually, though, most teenagers' fundamental values remain closer to those of their parents than is generally realized (Offer & Church, 1991). "Adolescent rebellion" frequently amounts to little more than a series of minor skirmishes.

The biggest danger in assuming that adolescent turmoil is normal and necessary is that parents, teachers, community leaders, and makers of social policy may erroneously assume that teenagers will "outgrow" problems and may fail to recognize when a young person needs help. In addition to spotting individual characteristics of troubled adolescents, we need to pay attention to the influence of the environment—the family, the peer group, and the community—to find ways of reducing young people's exposure to high-risk settings (NRC, 1993a).

THE ADOLESCENT IN THE FAMILY

The idea that parents and teenagers do not get along may have been born in the first formal theory of adolescence, that of the psychologist G. Stanley Hall. Hall (1904/1916) believed that young people's efforts to adjust to their changing bodies and to the imminent demands of adulthood usher in a period of "storm and stress," which inevitably leads to conflict between the generations. Sigmund Freud (1935/1953) and his daughter, Anna Freud (1946), also described parent-child friction as inevitable, growing out of adolescents' need to free themselves from dependency on their parents. However, the anthropologist Margaret Mead (1928, 1935), who studied adolescence in nonwestern cultures, concluded that when a culture provides a gradual, serene transition from childhood to adulthood, adolescent rebellion is not typical.

It now appears that full-fledged rebellion is uncommon even in western societies, at least among middle-class youngsters who are in school, and that teenagers who are very rebellious may well need special help. In his classic studies of midwestern American boys, Daniel Offer (1969) found a high level of bickering over unimportant issues between 12- and 14-year-olds and their parents, but little turmoil. A follow-up study (Offer & Offer, 1974) found that most of the participants—now out of their teens—were happy, had a realistic self-image, and were reasonably well-adjusted. Less than one-fifth had experienced a tumultuous adolescence. More recent research has found that most young people feel close to and positive about their parents, share similar opinions on major issues, and value their parents' approval (J. P. Hill, 1987; Offer et al., 1989; Offer et al., 1988). Significant conflict is reported in only 15 to 25 percent of families; and these families often had problems before the children approached adolescence (W. A. Collins, 1990; J. P. Hill, 1987; Offer et al., 1989).

Some conflict between teenagers and parents is

normal, of course. Let's look at its levels and sources, what forms it takes, and what kind of parenting is most effective. We'll also look at the impact of mothers' employment, divorce and single parenting, and economic stress. Then we'll consider adolescents' relationships with siblings.

Family Conflict and Parenting Styles

Many arguments between teenagers and their parents focus on "how much" or "how soon": how much freedom teenagers should have to plan their own activities or how soon they can take the family car. Family conflict generally rises during early adolescence, stabilizes in middle adolescence, and then decreases in late adolescence. The increased strife in early adolescence may be related to the strains of puberty and the need to assert independence. The calmer climate in late adolescence may reflect adjustment to the momentous changes of the teenage years and a renegotiation of the balance of power between parent and child (Fuligni & Eccles, 1993; L. Steinberg, 1988).

Conflict is more likely with mothers than with fathers, perhaps because most mothers have been more closely involved with their children and may be more ambivalent about giving up that involvement (L. Steinberg, 1981, 1987). Just as adolescents feel tension between dependency on their parents and the need to break away, parents often have mixed feelings too. They want their children to be independent, yet they find it hard to let go. Parents have to walk a fine line between giving adolescents enough independence and protecting them from immature lapses in judgment.

Parents and teenagers rarely clash over economic, religious, social, or political values or even about sexual activity and drug use. Most arguments concern day-to-day matters: chores, family relations, schoolwork, dress, money, curfews, and friends (B. K. Barber, 1994). Subjects of conflict are similar in married and divorced families (Smetana, Yau, Restrepo, & Braeges, 1991) and across ethnic lines. However, white parents report more frequent clashes with teenagers than black or Hispanic parents, who tend to enforce higher behavioral expectations as a means of survival in the majority culture (B. K. Barber, 1994).

Regardless of ethnicity, the level of family discord seems to hinge primarily on teenagers' personalities and on their parents' treatment of them. These factors may explain why disagreements in some families tend to blow over, whereas in other families they escalate into major confrontations. Dissension is most likely when parents see a teenager as having negative personality characteristics (such as a hot temper, meanness, or anxiety) and a history of problem behavior, and when parents use coercive discipline (B. K. Barber, 1994). Among 335 two-parent rural midwestern families with teenagers, conflict declined in warm, supportive families during early to middle adolescence but worsened in a hostile, coercive, or critical family atmosphere (Rueter & Conger, 1995).

In looking at teenagers' adjustment, then, we need to consider the emotional "fit" between the adolescent and the family. Young people may react to a negative family atmosphere by distancing themselves emotionally from the parents; and this can be an effective adaptive strategy, according to a study of 96 white and African American 10- to 18-year-olds from two-parent, single-parent, and stepfamilies. When the family atmosphere was stressful and conflict-ridden, youngsters who were emotionally independent of their parents tended to be relatively well-adjusted. However, emotional distance did *not* indicate good adjustment when mothers were warm and supportive and when conflict levels were low (Fuhrman & Holmbeck, 1995).

Warmth and acceptance are characteristic of an authoritative parenting style. Although adolescents need to be treated differently from younger children, authoritative parenting still works best. Authoritative parents insist on important rules, norms, and values but are willing to listen, explain, and negotiate. They encourage teenagers to form their own opinions (Lamborn, Mounts, Steinberg, & Dornbusch, 1991). They exercise appropriate control over the child's conduct but not the child's sense of self (L. Steinberg & Darling, 1994).

Overly strict, authoritarian parenting may be counterproductive as children enter adolescence and feel a need to be treated more as adults. When parents do not adjust to this need, their children may reject parental influence and seek peer support and approval at all costs. Among 1,771 predominantly white, middle-class sixth- and seventh-graders, those who saw their parents as giving them little opportunity to be involved in decisions affecting them were apt to do virtually anything to gain popularity with peers, even if it meant breaking family rules and neglecting schoolwork and their own talents. This was *not* true of students whose parents simply monitored their activities. Apparently it is power assertion,

Communication between parents and adolescents may flow more naturally when they are engaged in a shared pursuit. Grinding corn in the traditional manner strengthens the bond between this Navajo mother and daughter. Most adolescents feel close to and positive about their parents, appreciate their approval, and have similar values on major issues. *(Ruth Duskin Feldman)*

not appropriate supervision, that evokes negative reactions (Fuligni & Eccles, 1993).

Effects of Parents' Life Situation

Many adolescents today live in families that are very different from families of a few decades ago. Most mothers work outside the home, and teenage children often care for themselves after school. Many youngsters live with single parents or step-parents. Many families must cope with severe economic stress.

How do these family situations affect adolescents? A combination of factors may be involved. The impact of a mother's employment, for example, may depend upon whether there are two parents or only one in the home. Often a single mother must work to stave off economic disaster; how her working affects her teenage children may hinge on how much time and energy she has left over to spend with them and what sort of role model she provides. These factors, in turn, may be influenced by others: what kind of work she does, how many hours she works, how much she earns, and how much she likes her work (B. L. Barber & Eccles, 1992).

Parents' Employment Most research about how parents' work affects adolescents deals with mothers' employment. Some research has found that adolescent children of working mothers tend to be better-adjusted socially than other teenagers; they feel better about themselves, have more of a sense of belonging, and get along better with families and friends. On the negative side, they tend to spend less time on homework and leisure reading and more time watching television (Gold & Andres, 1978; Milne, Myers, Rosenthal, & Ginsburg, 1986).

Teenagers may like being freer to direct their own activities when their mothers are out of the house. However, with less supervision adolescents are more susceptible to peer pressure. A survey of 3,993 ninth-graders in six school districts in southern California, who came from a wide range of ethnic and socioeconomic backgrounds, found that students who are unsupervised after school tend to smoke, drink, use marijuana, or engage in other risky behavior; to be depressed; and to have low grades (Richardson, Radziszewska, Dent, & Flay, 1993). Being unsupervised does not in itself significantly increase the risk of problems as long as parents know where their son or daughter is; the less consistently parents monitor their child's activities and the more hours the young person is unsupervised, the greater the risk. Lack of supervision seems to have the most detrimental effect on girls, who otherwise are less prone to problems than boys. Although other research has found that children in divorced families are less likely to be closely supervised and more likely to engage in deviant behavior (B. L. Barber & Eccles, 1992), this survey found no such pattern (Richardson et al., 1993).

Parents' work stress seems to affect early adolescents differently, depending on which parent is under stress. Mothers who experience work overload tend to become less caring and accepting, and their children often show behavior problems. When fathers are overloaded at work—and especially when both parents are overworked—parent-child conflict tends to rise (Galambos, Sears, Almeida, & Kolaric, 1995).

In the 1950s, 1960s, and 1970s, when most mothers who could afford to stay home did so, adolescent sons of working women held less stereotyped attitudes about female roles than did sons of at-home mothers. Also, daughters of employed women had higher and less gender-stereotyped career aspirations, were more outgoing, scored higher on several academic measures, and seemed better-adjusted on social and personality measures (L. W. Hoffman, 1979). Today, however, a mother's work status seems to be just one of many factors that shape attitudes toward women's roles (Galambos, Petersen, & Lenerz, 1988). In fact, maternal employment in itself does not seem to affect teenagers much; whatever effect it has is filtered through other factors, such as the warmth in a relationship (Galambos et al., 1995) or a woman's satisfaction with her dual roles as mother and worker. Teenage sons of working mothers tend to have more flexible attitudes toward gender roles when they have warm relationships with their mothers, and teenage daughters show unstereotyped attitudes when their mothers are happy with their roles (Galambos et al., 1988).

Divorce and Single Parenting Divorce and single parenting do not necessarily produce problem adolescents. Indeed, a review of the literature suggests that some of the detrimental effects of living in a "broken home" may have been overgeneralized (B. L. Barber & Eccles, 1992). For example, a number of studies suggest that children of divorce do worse in school than those in two-parent families. However, in younger children, the differences depend on such factors as age, gender, the type of skill tested, and the length of time since the marriage ended. In adolescents, the differences are

usually minor and may be nonexistent when other factors, such as socioeconomic status and parental conflict, are held constant. Similarly, findings of lower self-esteem and differences in attitudes toward gender roles are small, inconsistent, or inconclusive. Furthermore, most of these studies are cross-sectional and thus do not show changes in the same young person before and after a divorce.

In evaluating the effects of divorce and single parenting, then, we need to look at particular circumstances. Divorce affects different children differently. Sometimes divorce can improve the situation by reducing the amount of conflict within the home. And, while the immediate effects of a marital breakup may be traumatic, in the long run some adolescents may benefit from having learned new coping skills that make them more competent and independent (B. L. Barber & Eccles, 1992).

Parental support may be more important than family structure, especially in some minority cultures. In one study of 254 urban African American adolescent boys, those living with a single mother were no more likely than those in two-parent, step-parent, or extended family households to use alcohol or drugs, to become delinquent, to drop out of school, or to have psychological problems. The only difference was a positive one: sons in single-mother households experienced more parental support than other youths. It may be that the mothers provided extra support to compensate for the fathers' absence. However, many fathers also continued to be involved in their sons' lives, and this involvement was related to positive outcomes. Almost 2 out of 3 boys not living with their fathers considered them role models. In addition, African American parents and children may be more able than white families to draw on support from extended family (M. A. Zimmerman, Salem, & Maton, 1995).

Economic Stress The major problem in many single-parent families is economic stress. Poverty can complicate family relationships and harm children's development through its impact on parents' emotional state (see Chapter 9). Such indirect effects of economic hardship may be felt by adolescents too. On the other hand, some adolescents may benefit from the *social capital* their families have accumulated—the support of kin and community (see Chapter 10).

One study looked at single African American mothers of seventh- and eighth-graders in a midwestern city that was experiencing widespread manufacturing layoffs. Unemployed mothers, especially those without outside help and support, tended to become depressed; and depressed mothers tended to be negative in their perception of their maternal role and punitive with their children. Young people who saw their relationships with their mothers deteriorate tended to be depressed themselves and to have trouble in school (McLoyd, Jayaratne, Ceballo, & Borquez, 1994).

Another study looked at 51 poor, urban African American families, in which teenagers were living with their mothers, grandmothers, or aunts. The women who had strong kinship networks to rely on tended to be psychologically healthy, and so were the youngsters. The more social support the women received, the greater their self-esteem and acceptance of the children. The women with stronger support exercised firmer control and closer monitoring while granting appropriate autonomy, and teenagers in these families were more self-reliant and had fewer behavior problems (R. D. Taylor & Roberts, 1995).

Of course, economic distress can strike two-parent families as well. Among 378 intact white families in an economically declining area of rural Iowa, arguments over money were worsened by the parents' tendency to be depressed and to fight with each other. Conflict within the family led to parental hostility and coercion, which in turn increased the risk of teenage behavior problems (R. C. Conger, Ge, Elder, Lorenz, & Simons, 1994).

Sibling Relationships

As teenagers begin to separate from their families and spend more time with peers, they have less time and less need for the emotional gratification they used to get from the sibling bond.* Changes in sibling relationships may well precede similar changes in the relationship between adolescents and parents: more independence on the part of the younger person and less authority exerted by the older person over the younger. As children reach high school, their relationships with their siblings become progressively more equal and more distant (Buhrmester & Furman, 1990). Adolescents still show intimacy, affection, and admiration for their brothers and sisters, but they spend less time with them (Raffaelli & Larson, 1987), and their re-

lationships are less intense. Older siblings exercise less power over younger ones, fight with them less, are not as close to them, and are less likely to look to them for companionship.

These changes seem to be fairly complete by the time the younger sibling is about 12 years old. By this time, the younger child no longer needs as much supervision and differences in competence and independence between older and younger siblings are shrinking. (A 6-year-old is vastly more competent than a 3-year-old, but a 15-year-old and a 12-year-old are more nearly equal.)

Older and younger siblings tend to have different feelings about their changing relationship. As the younger sibling grows up, the older one has to give up some of his or her accustomed power and status and may look on a newly assertive younger brother or sister as a pesky annoyance. On the other hand, younger siblings still tend to look up to older ones and try to feel more "grown up" by identifying with them.

Siblings born farther apart tend to be more affectionate toward each other and to get along better than those who are closer in age. The quarreling and antagonism between closely spaced brothers and sisters may reflect more intense rivalry, since their capabilities are similar enough to be frequently compared—by themselves and others. Same-sex siblings are usually closer than a brother and sister.

These effects of birth order, spacing, and gender have held up across several studies. Still, these factors are less important in the quality of sibling relationships than the youngsters' ages and temperaments and the parents' treatment of them (Stocker, Dunn, & Plomin, 1989).

THE ADOLESCENT IN THE PEER GROUP

An important source of emotional support during the complex transition of adolescence, as well as a source of pressure for behavior that parents may deplore, is young people's growing involvement with their peers.

Adolescents going through rapid physical changes take comfort from being with others going through like changes. Young people challenging adult standards and the need for parental guidance find it reassuring to turn for advice to friends who can understand and sympathize because they are in the same position themselves. Adolescents questioning their parents' adequacy as models of behavior, but not yet sure enough of themselves to

---

*Unless otherwise noted, this discussion is indebted to the work of Buhrmester and Furman, 1990.

The peer group is an important source of emotional support during adolescence. Young people going through rapid physical changes feel more comfortable with peers who are experiencing similar changes. *(Tom McCarthy/PhotoEdit)*

stand alone, look to peers to show them what's "in" and what's "out." The peer group is a source of affection, sympathy, and understanding; a place for experimentation; and a setting for achieving autonomy and independence from parents. It is also a place to form intimate relationships that serve as "rehearsals" for adult intimacy (J. S. Coleman, 1980; Gecas & Seff, 1990; Newman, 1982).

How Adolescents Spend Their Time—and with Whom

What do teenagers do on a typical day? With whom do they do it, and how do they feel about what they are doing? To answer these questions, 75 high school students in a suburb of Chicago carried beepers that rang at random once in every 2 waking hours for 1 week. Each student was asked to report what she or he was doing when the beeper sounded, and where and with whom. From the 4,489 self-reports, the researchers put together a picture of the everyday life of a teenager today (Csikszentmihalyi & Larson, 1984).

These adolescents spent more than half their waking hours with peers: 29 percent with friends and 23 percent with classmates. By contrast, they spent only 5 percent of their time alone with one or both parents and 8 percent with parents and siblings together. They felt happiest when with friends—free, open, involved, excited, and motivated. They had more fun with friends—joking, gossiping, and fooling around—than at home, where the atmosphere tended to be more serious

and humdrum. Friends were the people they most wanted to be with. Being with the family ranked second; next came being alone; and last, being with classmates.

However, newer research has found dramatic cultural differences in the role of the peer group in adolescents' lives. Interviews with a representative cross section of 942 adolescents in Toledo, Ohio, found that African American teenagers maintain more intimate family relationships and less intense peer relations than white teenagers. Black teenagers also tend to be more flexible in their choice of friends and less dependent on peer approval. Black adolescents may look upon their families as havens in a hostile world and thus may be less likely to distance themselves from parents (Giordano, Cernkovich, & DeMaris, 1993).

In another study, researchers asked a representative sample of eleventh-graders in Minneapolis how they spent their time at and after school. The investigators then compared the results with similar interviews of teenagers in Taiwanese and Japanese cities (Fuligni & Stevenson, 1995). The American students spent much more time socializing with friends, whereas the Chinese and Japanese students spent more time in school, studying, and reading for pleasure. Not surprisingly, the Asian teens were better academic performers than the Americans, as measured by math achievement tests. Also, young people in the three cultures did different kinds of things with friends. American students were more likely to go to parties, dances, movies, concerts, or sporting events or to engage

Friendships are likely to be closer and more intense in adolescence than at any other time in the life span. Adolescents have the most fun when they are doing something with their friends, with whom they feel free, open, involved, excited, and motivated. *(Erika Stone)*

in athletics or watch television together; Chinese and Japanese students spent more time studying with friends or just "hanging out."

Friendships

The intensity of friendships is greater in adolescence than at any other time in the life span. As in middle childhood, adolescents see mutual help, mutual interaction, and mutual liking as the core of friendship. Friendships seem to last about as long in both age groups and to involve about the same level of conflict, but there are important differences. In early adolescence, friendships become more intimate and supportive than at earlier ages. Teenage friends regard loyalty as more critical, and they compete less and share more than do younger friends (Berndt & Perry, 1990). These are features of adult friendship; their appearance in adolescence marks a transition to adultlike relationships.

These changes are due in part to cognitive development. Adolescents confiding in friends are now better able to express their private thoughts and feelings. They can also more readily consider another person's point of view, and so it is easier for them to understand a friend's thoughts and feelings.

Increased intimacy also ties in with psychological adjustment and social competence—a link that becomes stronger and more consistent during adolescence. Adolescents who have close friends are high in self-esteem; consider themselves competent; are unlikely to be hostile, anxious, or de-

pressed; and do well in school. Those whose friendships have a high degree of conflict score lower on these measures (Berndt & Perry, 1990; Buhrmester, 1990). It seems likely that a bidirectional process is at work: intimate friendships foster adjustment, which in turn helps young people form intimate friendships. Friendships also tend to become more reciprocal in adolescence: there is a greater likelihood that both friends will perceive the closeness of their friendship in the same way (Buhrmester, 1990).

Adolescents tend to choose friends who are like them, and friends influence each other to become even more alike (Berndt, 1982; Berndt & Perry, 1990). Friends usually are of the same race (Giordano et al., 1993); and have similar status within the peer group (Berndt & Perry, 1990). Boys and men typically have more friends than girls and women, but male friendships are rarely as close: emotional support and sharing of confidences are more vital to female friendships throughout life (Blyth & Foster-Clark, 1987; Bukowski & Kramer, 1986).

How Parents Affect Choice and Influence of Friends

Parents often worry about the influence of peers and feel powerless against it. Actually, peer influence can be either positive or negative, and parents have considerable indirect influence on their children's choice of friends. Parents help shape prosocial or antisocial behavior, which leads children to gravitate toward particular crowds. In a study of 3,781 high school students (B. B. Brown, Mounts, Lamborn, & Steinberg, 1993), the extent to which parents monitored adolescents' behavior and schoolwork, encouraged achievement, and allowed joint decision making were related to academic achievement, drug use, and self-reliance. These behaviors, in turn, were linked with membership in such peer groups as "populars, jocks, brains, normals, druggies, and outcasts" (p. 471).

Furthermore, parental influence can temper an adolescent's susceptibility to peer influences, as a 1-year study of 500 ninth- through eleventh-graders found. By their own reports, students whose close friends were drug users tended to increase their own drug use, but that was less true of those who saw their parents as highly authoritative. By the same token, adolescents whose close friends were academic achievers tended to improve their grades, but that was less true of students whose parents were *not* authoritative. Thus authoritative parenting can help young people internalize standards that insulate them against negative peer influences and open them to positive ones (Mounts & Steinberg, 1995).

Teenagers' behavior can also be indirectly influenced by the upbringing of their friends. Researchers asked 4,431 high school students of varied ethnic backgrounds about their parents' practices (Fletcher, Darling, Steinberg, & Dornbusch, 1995). The students were also asked to list three close friends. Students whose friends described their parents as authoritative were more likely to do well in school and less likely to use drugs or get in trouble with the law than other students; this was true over and above the effect of a youngster's own parenting. Boys whose friends had authoritative parents were less likely to misbehave in school and less susceptible to antisocial peer pressure; girls were more self-reliant and work-oriented, had higher self-esteem, and were less likely to be anxious or depressed. Apparently, authoritative parents tend to raise well-adjusted teenagers, who seek out other well-adjusted teenagers as friends. Thus the peer group reinforces and enhances the beneficial effects of effective parenting.

ADOLESCENTS IN TROUBLE: JUVENILE DELINQUENCY

Teenagers, especially boys, are responsible for more than their share of crimes. In 1990, 30 per-

cent of all arrests in the United States, and 43 percent of arrests for serious crimes, were of persons under age 21; and 28 percent of those arrested for serious crimes were under 18 (Federal Bureau of Investigation, FBI, 1991). Teenagers are also disproportionately likely to be victims of crime. Twelve- to seventeen-year-olds account for less than 10 percent of the American population but 23 percent of the victims of assault, rape, and robbery (Office of Juvenile Justice and Delinquency Prevention, 1994).

What influences young people to engage in—or refrain from—antisocial acts? What determines whether or not a juvenile delinquent will grow up to be a hardened criminal?

Influences on Delinquency

Delinquency is often attributed to the influence of the peer group; parents worry about a child's "falling in with the wrong crowd." Peers do exert a strong influence; young people who take drugs, drop out of school, and commit delinquent acts usually do all these in the company of friends. However, children do not usually "fall in" with a group; they seek out their friends or, when rejected by one group of peers, accept the overtures of others. Of all the groups in a school or neighborhood, what makes a youngster go with the "wrong" one? The implication of the studies discussed in the previous section is that parents play more of a role than they may realize.

As we examine the roots of delinquency, we need to keep in mind an important distinction. Some adolescents are guilty of isolated or occasional antisocial behavior. Then there is a smaller group of chronic (repeat) offenders, who habitually commit a variety of antisocial acts, such as stealing, setting fires, breaking into houses or cars, destroying property, physical cruelty, frequent fighting, and rape. Chronic offenders are responsible for most juvenile crime and are most likely to continue their criminal activity in adulthood (Yoshikawa, 1994). Adolescents who were aggressive or got in trouble when they were younger— lying, being truant, stealing, or doing poorly in school—are more likely than other youngsters to become chronic delinquents (Loeber & Dishion, 1983; Yoshikawa, 1994).

How do "problem behaviors" escalate into chronic delinquency? Research points to early patterns of parent-child interaction that lead to negative peer influence. Parents of chronic delinquents often failed to reinforce good behavior in early childhood and were harsh or inconsistent, or both, in punishing misbehavior. Through the years these parents have not had close, positive involvement in their children's lives (G. R. Patterson, De-Baryshe, & Ramsey, 1989). The children may get payoffs for antisocial behavior: when they act up, they may gain attention or get their own way. Antisocial behavior interferes with schoolwork and with the ability to get along with well-behaved classmates. Unpopular and low-achieving children tend to seek out others like themselves, and the friends influence one another toward further misconduct (G. R. Patterson, Reid, & Dishion, 1992).

Ineffective parenting tends to continue in adolescence. Antisocial behavior at this age is closely related to parents' inability to keep track of what their children do and with whom. Parents of delinquents tend to punish rule breaking with nothing more severe than a lecture or a threat (G. R. Patterson & Stouthamer-Loeber, 1984).

Some studies suggest a genetic influence, but this is relatively small in comparison with parenting style, family atmosphere, and socioeconomic status. However, the risk is far greater when genetic and environmental influences combine. A comprehensive review of the literature suggests that chronic delinquency may be predictable from a network of interacting early risk factors (Yoshikawa, 1994). Children at genetic risk—whose biological parents are antisocial or alcoholic, or both—are more likely to become chronic delinquents if exposed to family conflict at an early age. Those who had complications at birth, such as prematurity, low birthweight, anoxia, or other trauma, are at greater risk if they grow up in poor, unstable families. Infants who are insecurely attached or whose parents are constantly arguing and fighting are more at risk if the parents are hostile, rejecting, insensitive, or neglectful. Young people in impoverished circumstances are more at risk if they come from large, quarrelsome families, if they had birth complications, or if their parents are poorly educated or mentally ill. On the other hand, low-income youngsters are at less risk if they have been raised with a mixture of discipline and affection and if their verbal ability is normal for their age; and young people who suffer from poor parenting are at less risk if their parents get effective community support (Yoshikawa, 1994). The more we learn, then, about factors that contribute to delinquency, the less satisfactory such a simplistic answer as "peer influence" becomes.

Long-Term Prospects

Most delinquents do not grow up to become criminals; many who are not hard-core offenders simply outgrow their "wild oats" (L. W. Shannon, 1982). Delinquency peaks at about age 15 and then declines, unlike alcohol use and sexual activity, which become more prevalent with age (refer back to Figure 10-1). Since alcohol and sexual activity are accepted parts of adult life, it is not surprising that as teenagers grow older they increasingly want to engage in them (Petersen, 1993). Antisocial behavior that is *not* accepted in adulthood may diminish as most adolescents and their families come to terms with young people's need to assert independence.

Middle- and high-income adolescents may experiment with problem behaviors and then drop them, but low-income teenagers who do not see positive alternatives are more likely to adopt a permanently antisocial lifestyle (Elliott, 1993). Both delinquency and crime tend to be concentrated in poor, overcrowded urban neighborhoods with dilapidated housing, high unemployment rates, and predominantly minority populations (NRC, 1993a; Yoshikawa, 1994). A youth who sees that the only rich people in the neighborhood are drug dealers may be seduced into a life of crime.

How can we help young people stuck in a morass of delinquency and alienation to become productive and law-abiding? How can we protect society? The answers to these questions are not easy, and the two goals sometimes seem to conflict. Some programs have helped delinquents by teaching them social and vocational skills (NRC, 1993a). Even more promising are efforts to *prevent* delinquency. Let's look at some.

LIFE-SPAN ISSUE

CAN JUVENILE DELINQUENCY BE NIPPED IN THE BUD?

Edward F. Zigler is former chair of the psychology department at Yale University and now heads the psychology section of the university's Child Study Center and

directs its Bush Center in Child Development and Social Policy. He was one of the planners of Project Head Start and the first director of the U.S. Office of Child Development. He has received numerous professional and governmental awards for his work, which covers both normal child development and pathology. Zigler and others have pulled together strands of research that may point the way to preventing juvenile delinquency.

Since juvenile delinquency has roots early in childhood, so must preventive efforts. Effective programs are directed toward both children and families and attack multiple risk factors that lead to delinquency (Yoshikawa, 1994; Zigler, Taussig, & Black, 1992).*

Four early childhood programs that have achieved impressive long-term reductions in antisocial behavior and delinquency, as measured 5 to 12 years later, are the Syracuse Family Development Research Project, the Yale Child Welfare Project, the Houston Parent Child Development Center, and the Perry Preschool Project (see Chapters 6 and 8). These programs did not specifically aim to head off delinquency; instead, that outcome was a byproduct of efforts to overcome the negative developmental effects of economic and social deprivation. Children in these programs, particularly boys, proved much less likely than their equally disadvantaged peers to become aggressive or get in trouble with the law. For example, by early adulthood, only 31 percent of the Perry preschool graduates (still a large proportion) had been arrested or charged with an offense, compared with 51 percent of the control group (Berrueta-Clement, Schweinhart, Barnett, & Weikart, 1987).

Each program had a different character and focus. In the Syracuse program, paraprofessionals met weekly with low-income women—mostly young, single mothers with erratic work histories, no high school diplomas, and (in many cases) brushes with the law. Beginning in the last trimester of pregnancy, the mothers received information about nutrition and learned effective ways of interacting with their children. The children received day care half time from 6 months to 15 months and then full time until 5 years of age. The Yale program provided home visits to 17 poor expectant mothers, continuing until their firstborn children were 2½ years old. The children got pediatric examinations, developmental assessments, and child care.

In the Houston program, 100 low-income Mexican American mothers were visited at home starting when their children were 1 year old. The mothers learned how to care for their babies, what to expect developmentally, and how to create a stimulating home environment. The entire family attended weekend workshops. In the sec-

ond year of the two-year program, the children went to morning nursery school at the center while their mothers took classes on homemaking and child management. The Perry preschool offered early childhood education to low-income African American 3- and 4-year-olds. Through monthly meetings and frequent home visits from teachers, parents learned how to discipline and motivate their children and to build relationships with the teachers.

What did these programs have in common? All targeted high-risk urban children who normally are denied the "extensive support and early education that middle- and upper-class families often obtain as a matter of course" (Yoshikawa, 1994, p. 42). All lasted for at least 2 years during the child's first 5 years of life, an important period for establishing parent-child relationships. All embraced a comprehensive view of child development, influencing children directly, through high-quality day care or education, and at the same time indirectly, by offering families assistance and support geared to their needs. In terms of Bronfenbrenner's ecological model (see Chapter 1), these programs operated on the mesosystem by affecting interactions between two or more settings (the home and the educational or child-care center) of which a child was a part. The programs also went one step further to the exosystem, by creating supportive parent networks and linking parents with community providers of prenatal and postnatal health care, vocational training, and other services. Through their multipronged approach, these programs made an impact on several early risk factors for delinquency. Children's cognitive development and social-emotional competence benefited, as did parents' behavior toward their children.

How did these effects come about? The sponsors of the Perry project, which focused on preparing children for school, suggest that the program may have produced a snowball effect on cognitive development by catching youngsters "at a critical time when their identities within the education system were being established" (Woodhead, 1988, p. 488). Teachers had a more positive attitude toward better-prepared kindergartners, the children liked school better, and they achieved more in later grades. This in turn led to higher self-esteem and aspirations for the future, both of which tend to deter antisocial behavior (Berrueta-Clement et al., 1987). The Houston and Yale programs may have enhanced school achievement by giving children early positive experiences with peers, with a similar snowball effect. At the same time, by offering parents practical and social support, all these programs helped them do a better job of parenting, which may have helped the children's school performance and lowered the chance of delinquency. In the Perry and Yale projects, parents even improved their socioeconomic status—in the Yale program, probably as a result of educational and vocational counseling.

Even though the early benefits to school performance

---

*This discussion is indebted to Yoshikawa, 1994, and Zigler, Taussig, and Black, 1992.

did not always hold up, young people who had taken part in these programs did, on the whole, show less antisocial behavior than peers who had not been in the programs. These, of course, were small, quality programs with ample staff, but the results suggest that simply in terms of the savings realized by keeping young people out of the criminal justice system, such programs can more than repay their cost. Furthermore, since risk factors for delinquency overlap with risk factors for schizophrenia, depression, child abuse, and drug abuse, programs that can reduce these risk factors may have multiple benefits. A first step toward broader application of the lessons learned from these successful programs would be to improve Head Start—currently the only nationwide early intervention program—by offering it even earlier, during infancy or toddlerhood, and expanding family outreach.

Still, effective as such early preventive efforts may be, they cannot buffer a child against years of negative influences during middle childhood and adolescence. To further reduce the likelihood that at-risk youngsters will become delinquents, programs need to be designed for older children as well, focusing on such factors as peer rejection, chronic poverty, media influences, and availability of drugs and guns.

Fortunately, the great majority of adolescents do not get into serious trouble. Those who do show disturbed behavior can—and should—be helped. With love, guidance, and support, adolescents can avoid risks, build on their strengths, and explore their possibilities as they approach adult life.

✔ SUMMARY

THE SEARCH FOR IDENTITY

- A central concern during adolescence is the search for identity, which has occupational, sexual, and values components. Erik Erikson described the psychosocial crisis of adolescence as the conflict between identity and identity (or role) confusion. The "virtue" that should arise from this crisis is *fidelity*.
- James Marcia, in research based on Erikson's theory, described four identity statuses: identity achievement (crisis leading to commitment), foreclosure (commitment without crisis), moratorium (crisis with no commitment yet), and diffusion (no commitment, no crisis).
- Researchers have found differences in male and female identity formation. Ethnic differences also seem to exist.

SEXUALITY

- Adolescents' sexuality strongly influences their developing identity. Sexual orientation appears to be influenced by an interaction of biological and environmental factors.
- Sexual attitudes and behaviors are more liberal than in the past. There is more acceptance of premarital sexual activity, and there has been a decline in the double standard. This more liberal sexual climate involves increased risks.
- The teenage pregnancy rate in the United States is one of the highest in the world; about half of pregnant teenagers have their babies and keep them. Teenage pregnancy often has negative consequences for mother, father, child, and society. Teenagers at greatest risk for pregnancy and sexually transmitted diseases are those who begin

sexual activity early, have multiple partners, and do not use contraceptives.

RELATIONSHIPS WITH FAMILY, PEERS, AND ADULT SOCIETY

- Although relationships between adolescents and their parents are not always smooth, full rebellion does not seem usual, and parents and their teenage children often hold similar values. Authoritative parenting appears to be associated with the most positive outcomes.
- The effect of maternal employment on adolescents' development is filtered through other factors, such as mothers' warmth and role satisfaction. Although adolescents not living with biological fathers are at greater risk of trouble, the effects of divorce and single parenting may be less severe than has been believed and may depend on individual circumstances. Economic stress affects relationships in both single-parent and two-parent families.
- Relationships with siblings tend to become more equal and more distant during adolescence.
- Adolescents spend most of their time with their peers, who play an important role in their development. Friendships become more intimate.
- Peer pressure influences some adolescents toward antisocial behavior, but effective parenting can insulate teenagers from negative peer influences.
- Adolescents account for more than their share of crimes, but most juvenile delinquents grow up to be law-abiding. Chronic delinquency is associated with multiple early risk factors, including ineffective parenting, school failure, and low socioeconomic status.

✔ KEY TERMS

identity versus identity (or role) confusion (page 369)
identity status (370)
crisis (370)
commitment (370)

identity achievement (370)
foreclosure (370)
moratorium (370)
identity diffusion (371)

sexual orientation (374)
heterosexual (374)
homosexual (374)
adolescent rebellion (382)

✔ QUESTIONS FOR THOUGHT AND DISCUSSION

1 Can you think of values you hold that are different from those of your parents? How did you come to develop these values?

2 Which of Marcia's identity statuses do you think you fit into? Has your identity status changed since adolescence?

3 Since girls generally bear the burdens of adolescent pregnancy, should teenage girls be urged to follow a stricter standard of sexual behavior than teenage boys? Should more emphasis be placed on encouraging teenage boys to be more responsible sexually? Or both?

4 Under what circumstances do you think each of the following choices might be best for a teenage girl who discovers that she is pregnant: marry the father and raise the child, stay single and raise the child, give the baby to adoptive parents, or have an abortion?

5 When teenagers complain that their parents "don't understand" them, what do you think they mean?

6 When faced with a first-time juvenile offender who has committed a felony, do you think the judge should: let the offender off with a warning, investigate the offender's family background and socioeconomic status before deciding, sentence the offender to a term in a penal institution, or take some other action? What circumstances might affect your answer?

PART FIVE

Young Adulthood

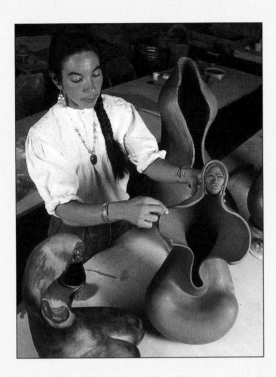

Contrary to what was once widely believed, development does not screech to a halt after adolescence. Changes during adulthood may be more gradual and less dramatic than in childhood, and they are not all positive, but they are no less real. Important advances, as well as some declines, occur during young adulthood (which we define approximately as the span between ages 20 and 40), middle age (from age 40 to age 65), and late adulthood (age 65 and over).

During the two decades of young adulthood, human beings build a foundation for much of their later development. At this time most people leave their parents' home, take their first job, get married or establish other intimate relationships, and have and raise children. They make decisions that will affect the rest of their lives: their health, their happiness, and their success.

During young adulthood, as throughout life, all aspects of development—physical, cognitive, and psychosocial—intertwine. In Chapters 12 and 13 we see, for example, how income, education, and lifestyle—even marital status—influence health, how emotions play a role in intelligence, and how pressures at work can affect family life. Development, as in childhood and adolescence, is a seamless web.

CHAPTER TWELVE

PHYSICAL AND COGNITIVE DEVELOPMENT IN YOUNG ADULTHOOD

If ... happiness is the absence of fever then I will never know happiness. For I am possessed by a fever for knowledge, experience, and creation.

Diary of Anaïs Nin (1931–1934),
written when she was between 28 and 31

ASK YOURSELF

✔ How do lifestyle and behavior in young adulthood affect future health and well-being?

✔ What is distinctive about adult intelligence?

✔ How do moral reasoning and faith develop?

✔ Who goes to college, and who is likely to drop out?

✔ How do gender and ethnicity affect occupational choice and opportunity?

✔ Does age influence work performance and satisfaction with work?

Young adulthood is a "can-do" period. Most people at this age are on their own for the first time, setting up and running households and proving themselves in college or on the job. Every day, they test and expand their physical and cognitive abilities. They encounter the "real world" and find their way through or around the problems of everyday living. They make decisions that help determine their health, their careers, and the kinds of people they wish to be.

At one time, developmentalists considered the years from the end of adolescence to the onset of old age a relatively uneventful plateau, but research has confirmed what personal experience tells us: that this is not so. The life-span developmental approach of Paul B. Baltes (see Chapter 1) suggests that growth and decline go on throughout life in a shifting balance that differs for each individual. Choices made during young adulthood have much to do with how that balance is struck.

▪ In this chapter, we look at young adults' physical functioning, which is usually at its height; and we note factors that affect health in young adulthood and in later life. How adults eat, how much they drink, whether they smoke, how much exercise they get, how they handle stress—all these factors influence present and future physical functioning. We discuss aspects of intelligence that come to the fore in adulthood and ways in which education can stimulate cognitive growth. We examine routes to moral maturity and the development of faith. Finally, we discuss one of the most important tasks during this period: entering the world of work. ▪

✔ ASPECTS OF PHYSICAL DEVELOPMENT

Your favorite professional spectator sport may be tennis, basketball, figure skating, or football. Whatever it is, most of the athletes you root for are young adults, people in prime physical condition. Besides being at the peak of sensory and motor functioning, young adults are the healthiest age group in the United States.

SENSORY AND PSYCHOMOTOR FUNCTIONING

Young adults typically are at the peak of their strength, energy, and endurance. By the middle twenties, most body functions are fully developed. Most of the senses are sharpest during young adulthood. Visual acuity is keenest from about age 20 to age 40; and taste, smell, and sensitivity to pain and temperature generally remain undiminished until at least 45. However, a gradual hearing loss, which typically begins during adolescence, becomes more apparent after 25, especially for very high-pitched sounds.

HEALTH STATUS

More than 93 percent of Americans ages 15 to 44 consider their health good, very good, or excellent (USDHHS, 1996). Many young adults are never seriously ill or incapacitated; and the vast majority have no chronic conditions or impairments. When young adults do get sick, it is usually from a cold or other respiratory illness, which they easily shake off.

On the basis of provisional data for 1993, AIDS

is now the leading cause of death for 25- to 44-year-olds in the United States (CDC, 1995c; see Figure 12-1). The rate of new HIV infections has leveled off among white men, especially those older than 30, but not among women and minorities. However, men are still about 5 times as likely as women to be infected (P. S. Rosenberg, 1995). The infection rate for women is rising worldwide, particularly in developing countries, often through sexual contact with infected men. The World Health Organization predicts that by the year 2000 most new infections will be in females (Altman, 1992). The epidemic is especially virulent in India, which is expected to have more than 5 million infected people by the turn of the century—more than any other country (Bollinger, Tripathy, & Quinn, 1995).

Since most young adults are healthy, it is not surprising that accidents are the second leading cause of death for Americans ages 25 to 44. Next comes cancer, followed by heart disease, suicide, and homicide (CDC, 1995c). Men this age are more than twice as likely to die as women (USDHHS, 1996). Young American men are slain at rates 4 to 73 times higher than in other industrial nations. Three-fourths of the killings in this country involve guns, compared with only one-fourth of those in nations with more stringent gun control (Fingerhut & Kleinman, 1990).

INFLUENCES ON HEALTH AND FITNESS

Health, as defined by the World Health Organization, is "a state of complete physical, mental, and social well-being and is not merely the absence of

Although few young adults are in as superb physical condition as Jackie Joyner-Kersee, an Olympic champion who won a bronze medal in the long jump in 1996, young adulthood is the time when most people are at their peak of strength, energy, and endurance. *(Gamma-Liaison)*

disease and infirmity" (Danish, 1983). Good health is not just a matter of luck; it usually reflects a way of life, a series of choices. People can seek health by pursuing some activities and refraining from others.

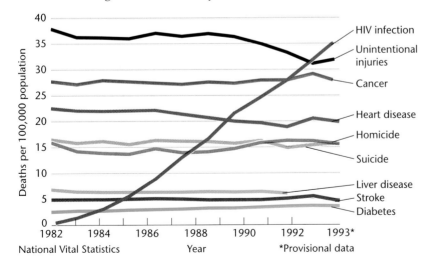

FIGURE 12-1

Death rates from leading causes of death among 25- to 44-year-olds in the United States, 1982–1993. Deaths from HIV infection, the virus that causes AIDS, have increased dramatically in comparison with all other leading causes of death in this age group. *(Source: CDC, 1995c.)*

TABLE 12-1

Progress toward Health Goals for the Year 2000

Goal	Baseline*	Update*	Target*	Improvement?
More people exercising regularly	22%	24%	30%	Yes
Fewer people overweight	26%	34%	20%	No
Fewer people eating high-fat diets	36%	34%	30%	Yes
Fewer cigarette smokers	29%	25%	15%	Yes
Fewer homicides (per 100,000 people)	8.5	10.3	7.2	No
Lower average cholesterol (mg/dL)	213	205	200	Yes
Fewer cancer deaths (per 100,000 people)	134	133	130	Yes

*Note: Baseline figures are for the period 1976–1987; update figures, 1988–1993; target figures, for the year 2000.

SOURCE: Adapted from McGinnis & Lee, 1995, pp. 1126–1127; from U.S. Public Health Service, 1995.

In a study of 7,000 adults, ages 20 to 70, health was directly related to several common habits: eating regular meals, including breakfast, and not snacking; eating and exercising moderately; sleeping regularly 7 to 8 hours each night; not smoking; and drinking in moderation. People who followed all these habits were the healthiest; those who followed the fewest of these habits were unhealthiest (Belloc & Breslow, 1972). Ten or more years later, people who did not follow these health habits were twice as likely to be disabled as people who followed most or all of them (Breslow & Breslow, 1993).

The link between behavior and health points up the interrelationships among physical, cognitive, and emotional aspects of development. What people know about health affects what they do, and what they do affects how they feel. Knowing about good health habits is not enough, however. Personality, emotions, and social surroundings often outweigh what people know they should do and, if these factors do not have a positive influence, can lead them into unhealthy behavior. (Table 12-1 summarizes progress by the American public in meeting goals set by the United States Public Health Service in 1990.)

Let's look at several behaviors that are strongly and directly linked with health and fitness: diet, exercise, and use of tobacco and alcohol. Then we'll consider indirect influences: socioeconomic status, ethnicity, and gender.

Diet

The saying "You are what you eat" sums up the importance of diet for physical and mental health.

What people eat affects how they look, how they feel, and how likely they are to get sick. For example, people who eat plenty of fruits and vegetables lessen their chance of stroke (Gillman et al., 1995) and of cancer (Voelker, 1995). Stomach and esophageal cancers, which are more common among people in Japan than among Americans of Japanese descent, are associated with eating pickled, smoked, and salted fish, which is more common in Japan than in the United States (Gorbach, Zimmerman, & Woods, 1984).

A diet high in animal fat has been linked with colon cancer (Willett, Stampfer, Colditz, Rosner, & Speizer, 1990). However, some studies point only to the fat in red meat—or to other components of red meat, such as protein, iron, or substances that become cancer-producing when cooked—as likely culprits (Willett, 1994). A high-fiber diet can reduce the chance of colon cancer.

Fat consumption is not clearly related to breast cancer but does seem implicated in coronary heart disease (Matthews et al., 1997) and prostate cancer (Willett, 1994; Willett et al., 1992). A diet high in red meat, butter, and chicken with the skin left on seems to advance prostate cancer to a lethal stage (Giovannucci et al., 1993). A 6-year study of nearly 48,000 men found that eating tomato-based sauces reduces the risk of prostate cancer by as much as 45 percent. Tomatoes are rich in lycopene, an antioxidant that may protect against the disease (Giovannucci et al., 1995).

Diet and Cholesterol   A waxy substance called **cholesterol**, found in human and animal tissue, is essential to life; but excess cholesterol deposited in blood vessels can narrow them so much as to cut off the blood supply to the heart, causing a heart attack. In a 25-year study of more than 12,000 men in five European countries, the United States, and Japan, cholesterol levels were directly related to the risk of death from coronary heart disease (Verschuren et al., 1995). Controlling cholesterol through diet and drugs can significantly lower this risk (Lipid Research Clinics Program, 1984a, 1984b; Scandinavian Simvastatin Survival Study Group, 1994; Shepherd, Cobbe, Ford, et al., 1995).

Cholesterol—in combination with proteins and triglycerides (fatty acids)—circulates through the bloodstream, carried by low-density lipoprotein (LDL), commonly called "bad" cholesterol. More than 1 out of 2 American men age 35 or older and American women 45 or older have undesirably high LDL levels (Liebman, 1995). High-density lipoprotein (HDL)—commonly called "good" cholesterol—flushes cholesterol out of the system (American Heart Association, AHA, 1995). Since HDL is protective, a key to preventing heart disease is the ratio between total cholesterol and HDL (Willett, 1994). If total cholesterol and HDL are both high, the risk may be acceptable or even low; but low HDL can be dangerous even if total cholesterol levels are acceptable (Liebman, 1995). In general, total cholesterol should be no more than 4 or 5 times as high as HDL ("Cholesterol: New Advice," 1993). Since estrogen seems to raise HDL and lower LDL, premenopausal women are at relatively low risk; after menopause, hormone replacement therapy can cut the risk by one-third to one-half (Adult Treatment Panel II, 1994; AHA, 1995).

Adults should be tested for cholesterol at least every 5 years. The tests should be repeated in 1 or 2 years if the results are in the undesirable range and if other risk factors, such as advanced age (45 for men, 55 for women), a family history of early heart disease, smoking, and high blood pressure, are present (Adult Treatment Panel II, 1994; Liebman, 1995). New evidence that high LDL levels carry over from childhood suggests a need for periodic screening of children as well (Bao, Srinivasan, Wattigney, Bao, & Berenson, 1996).

One way to lower total cholesterol and LDL while raising HDL is to eat fewer egg yolks, which are high in cholesterol. Even more important is to replace saturated fats (as in meat, cheese, and milk) and trans-fats (as in margarine, cakes, pies, frostings, and processed foods made with partially hydrogenated oil) with polyunsaturated fats (sunflower or safflower oil), which lower LDL and total cholesterol, or monounsaturated fats (olive oil and canola oil), which have little effect on cholesterol. It is also helpful to eat more soluble fiber (in oats, beans, fruits, and vegetables), lose excess weight, exercise, drink alcohol only in moderation, and stop smoking ("Cholesterol: New Advice," 1993; Liebman, 1995). Drug treatment may be advisable for people whose LDL remains very high even after adjusting the diet (Adult Treatment Panel II, 1994).

Diet and Obesity   In a society that values slenderness, being overweight can lead to emotional problems. It also carries risks of high blood pressure, heart disease, stroke, diabetes, gallstones, and certain cancers (National Task Force on the Prevention and Treatment of Obesity, 1993). An estimated 300,000 deaths a year are attributable to being overweight, second only to the 400,000 deaths a year believed to be caused by cigarette smoking. A 16-year study of 115,195 female nurses found that even a moderate gain of 22 pounds after age 18 increases the risk of death in middle age (Manson et al., 1995).

Nearly 7 in 10 Americans age 25 and over weigh more than they should for their age, sex, height, and body type; this includes 49 percent of those in their mid- to late twenties and 66 percent of 30- to 49-year-olds (*Prevention Index*, 1995). About one-third of adults are considered obese, weighing at least 20 percent more than recommended guidelines—which have become more lenient in recent years. Adults' average weight has increased by nearly 8 pounds since 1980 (Kuczmarski, Flegal, Campbell, & Johnson, 1994; Manson et al., 1995). The problem is worse among lower socioeconomic groups, especially women and minorities: close to 50 percent of Native American, African American, and Mexican American women are overweight (AHA, 1995; National Task Force, 1993). Overweight becomes more prevalent with age, as metabolism slows down (*Prevention Index*, 1995); thus young adults are a prime target for prevention (Williamson, Kahn, Remington, & Anda, 1990).

New hope for help with weight control may have come from identification of a genetic mutation in mice that may disrupt the appetite control center in the brain (Zhang et al., 1994). Mice with a flawed *ob*-gene become obese, apparently because their bodies fail to produce a protein called *leptin*, which tells the brain when the body has consumed enough. When injected with leptin, the mice lose weight (Campfield, Smith, Guisez, De-

Not everyone has to run a marathon to get the benefits of regular physical activity. Even moderate exercise can help people feel and look good, builds muscles, strengthens heart and lungs, keeps weight down, and protects against various disorders. *(Frank Siteman/The Picture Cube)*

vos, & Burn, 1995; Halaas et al., 1995; Pelleymounter et al., 1995). A similar protein is produced by human fat cells. However, since obese people have *higher*-than-normal leptin levels, perhaps their brains simply fail to respond to the protein's signals (Travis, 1996). In mice, a receptor for leptin seems to be located in the hypothalamus, a brain structure that regulates metabolism (G.-H. Lee et al., 1996; Tartaglia et al., 1995). Researchers have also found a natural hormone that stimulates the production of fat cells (Forman et al., 1995; Kliewer et al., 1995).

Eventually such research may lead to identification and treatment of people predisposed to obesity. Meanwhile, the healthiest course for overweight people—which is usually the most difficult—is to lose weight slowly and then maintain the loss. Very low calorie diets are recommended only for people who are severely obese or have medical problems stemming from overweight. The most effective ways of losing weight are to eat less, decrease the amount of fat in the diet, use behavior modification techniques to change eating pat-

terns, and exercise more (National Task Force, 1993).

Exercise

Adults who exercise regularly reap many benefits. Physical activity helps maintain desirable body weight; build muscles; strengthen heart and lungs; lower blood pressure; protect against heart attacks, stroke, diabetes, cancer, and osteoporosis (a thinning of the bones that tends to affect middle-aged and older women, causing fractures); relieve anxiety and depression; and lengthen life (AHA, 1995; P. R. Lee, Franks, Thomas, & Paffenbarger, 1981; I.-M. Lee & Paffenbarger, 1992; McCann & Holmes, 1984; Notelovitz & Ware, 1983).

According to a nationwide survey, 78 percent of American adults engage in regular physical activity. However, only 37 percent (46 percent of those under age 40) exercise strenuously 3 or more times a week. The proportions of women and of all people in their forties who get regular strenuous exercise (both 30 percent) are on the decline (*Prevention Index*, 1995).

These figures may be important because in a study of more than 17,000 alumni of Harvard University who had filled out questionnaires about their physical activity during the 1960s, only vigorous exercise (which speeds up metabolism sixfold or more) turned out to protect against death in middle age. Healthy men who expended 1,500 calories a week—the equivalent of 3 hours of playing singles tennis, swimming laps, or jogging 6 to 7 miles an hour—had a 25 percent lower death rate than those who burned less than 150 calories weekly (I.-M. Lee, Hsieh, & Paffenbarger, 1995).

On the other hand, there is evidence for a correlation between moderate exercise and decreased mortality. In an 8-year longitudinal study of more than 13,000 healthy men and women, those who walked ½ hour to 1 hour every day at a fast but comfortable pace cut their health risks by half or more (Blair et al., 1989). And a 5-year follow-up of nearly 10,000 men found a 44 percent reduction in mortality risk among those who had been sedentary and became moderately fit (Blair et al., 1995).

Apparently, moderate exercise does have health benefits, and even nonvigorous exercise is better than none (I.-M. Lee et al., 1995; NIH Consensus Development Panel on Physical Activity and Cardiovascular Health, 1996). Experts recommend that adults—and children as well—do at least 30 minutes of moderate physical activity daily (NIH

Consensus Development Panel, 1996; Pate, Pratt, Blair, Haskell, et al., 1995). It has been estimated that this would avoid 250,000 deaths a year, most of them from cardiovascular disease. The total time spent exercising is more important than the type, intensity, or continuity of activity. Even brief periods of moderate exercise throughout the day can add up to lifesaving protection. (See Table 12-2 for examples of light, moderate, and vigorous exercise.)

Pushing to the limit of endurance is not necessarily beneficial; overexertion does not seem to confer extra benefits and may even be harmful (I.-M. Lee et al., 1995). Exercising to the point of exhaustion, especially when a person has a respiratory illness, can weaken the immune system and increase susceptibility to infection ("Does Exercise Boost Immunity," 1995).

Smoking

Smoking is the leading preventable cause of death (AHA, 1995). It kills about 400,000 Americans yearly and disables millions. When victims of passive smoking—inhaling other people's smoke—are added, the death toll reaches more than 450,000 (Bartecchi et al., 1995). Worldwide, 3 million peo-

---

TABLE 12-2

Levels of Exercise

Light Exercise	Moderate Exercise	Hard or Vigorous Exercise
Activities that increase oxygen consumption to less than 3 times the level burned by the body at rest. Some health benefits can be expected.	Activities that increase oxygen consumption to 3 to 6 times the level burned by the body at rest. The Centers for Disease Control and the American College of Sports Medicine recommend that every adult do 30 minutes or more of activities like these on most days, and preferably every day. Many studies suggest that these activities have life-prolonging value.	Activities that raise oxygen consumption to more than 6 times the level burned by the body at rest, with examples of the duration and frequency that may be associated with the biggest reduction in death rates.
Walking slowly (strolling)		
Stationary cycling (low to moderate pedaling, low resistance)	Walking briskly (3 to 4 miles an hour)	Walking briskly uphill or with a load; 4 to 5 miles an hour for 45 minutes a day, 5 times a week
Swimming (slowly treading water)	Cycling for pleasure or transportation (up to 10 miles an hour)	Fast cycling or racing (more than 10 miles an hour); 1 hour, 4 times a week
Golf, using a powered cart	Swimming, using moderate effort	Swimming (fast treading or crawl); swimming laps 3 hours a week
Bowling	Conditioning exercises and general calisthenics	Cardiovascular exercise (stair-climbing machine or ski machine); 2 to 3 hours a week
Fishing while sitting	Racket sports (like table tennis)	
Power boating	Fishing (standing and casting)	Racket sports (singles tennis or racquetball); an hour of singles tennis 3 days a week
Home care (like carpet sweeping)	Canoeing (leisurely, 2 to 3.9 miles an hour)	Fishing (wading in a rushing stream)
Mowing the lawn (using a riding mower)	Home care (like general cleaning)	Canoeing (more than 4 miles an hour)
Home repair (like carpentry)	Mowing the lawn (using a power mower)	Moving furniture (picking up heavy furniture)
	Home repair (like painting)	Mowing the lawn (using a hand mower)

SOURCE: J. E. Brody, 1995b; adapted from *The Journal of the American Medical Association.*

ple die each year as a result of smoking. That number may well climb to 12 million by 2050, largely as a result of tobacco exports from the United States. These exports grew by 275 percent between 1985 and 1993 and again by 20 percent between 1993 and 1994, leading the American Medical Association to call for a ban on such exports (American Cancer Society, 1994; Peto, quoted in Bartecchi et al., 1995; Powelson, 1995).

The link between smoking and lung cancer is well established. Since 1977, deaths from lung cancer for 25- to 64-year-olds have risen 250 percent. Smoking is estimated to be responsible for more than 80 percent of these deaths and for at least one-third of all cancer deaths in the United States ("Are We 'in the Middle,'" 1994; USDHHS, 1990). Lung cancer is now the leading cause of cancer deaths in women as well as in men, claiming the lives of 59,000 women in 1994 (Kessler, 1995; "Research Shows," 1992). Smoking is also linked to cancer of the larynx, mouth, esophagus, bladder, kidney, pancreas, and cervix; to gastrointestinal problems, such as ulcers; to respiratory illnesses, such as bronchitis and emphysema; and to heart disease (National Institute on Aging, NIA, 1993; USDHHS, 1987).

Smoking strains the heart. By constricting the blood vessels, it makes the heart beat faster, raises blood pressure, and reduces the oxygen supply (AHA, 1995). A British study found that smokers are 5 times as likely as nonsmokers to have heart attacks in their thirties or forties (Parish et al., 1995). A woman who smokes may increase her risk if she uses high-dose oral contraceptives. A smoker who has a heart attack is more likely than a nonsmoker to die from it; nearly one-fifth of deaths from cardiovascular disease are attributable to smoking (AHA, 1994, 1995). Cigar and pipe smokers are in less danger of heart attack than cigarette smokers, but still at higher risk than nonsmokers; and they are more likely to get cancer of the lips, tongue, and mouth (Katchadourian, 1987). Because smoking damages cells and tissues, smokers tend to develop wrinkles and blotches, as well as skin cancer, psoriasis, and a variety of other skin conditions (J. B. Smith & Fenske, 1996).

A woman who smokes one pack of cigarettes each day throughout adulthood is likely to have 5 to 10 percent less bone density than a nonsmoking identical twin by the time she reaches menopause (Hopper & Seeman, 1994). Smokers enter menopause earlier and lose bone more rapidly afterward, increasing the risk of fractures. Male smokers also tend to lose bone mass more rapidly (Slemenda, 1994).

People exposed to secondhand smoke in the workplace increase their risk of lung cancer by 39 percent ("Environmental Tobacco Smoke," 1994). A nonsmoker who lives with a moderate smoker runs a 30 percent higher risk of lung cancer and of death from heart disease than otherwise; the increased risk of lung cancer jumps to 80 percent if the other person has been smoking four packs a day for 20 years (Bartecchi et al., 1995). Seventeen percent of lung cancer among nonsmokers can be traced to heavy smoke exposure during childhood and adolescence (Bartecchi et al., 1995).

As the risks became known, smoking in the United States declined by more than 37 percent since 1965—but only 27 percent among women (AHA, 1995). Unfortunately, the trend has leveled off. One out of four Americans age 18 and over smoke: nearly 28 percent of men and 23 percent of women in 1993 (USDHHS, 1996). About one-third of adults in their thirties smoke—more than in any other age group (*Prevention Index*, 1995). And smoking is on the rise in developing countries. A survey near Shanghai, China, found that two-thirds of men and boys age 15 and older smoke an average of 16.5 cigarettes a day, starting at earlier and earlier ages, and although most are aware of the dangers, only 14 percent want to quit (Gong et al., 1995).

Given the known risks of smoking, why do many people still do it? One reason is that smoking is addictive. Also, many women are afraid that if they stop smoking, they will gain weight; women who quit gain more, on average, than those who continue to smoke. However, weight gain can be minimized with a moderate increase in exercise (Flegal, Troiano, Pamuk, Kuczmarskia, & Campbell, 1995; Kawachi, Troisi, Rotnitzky, Coakley, & Colditz, 1996). People with higher income and education are less likely to continue smoking (Center on Addiction and Substance Abuse at Columbia University, CASA, 1996).

At least 9 out of 10 people who stop smoking do it on their own (Fiore, Novotny, Pierce, et al., 1990; J. S. Rose, Chassin, Presson, & Sherman, 1996). Others turn to support groups. The U.S. Food and Drug Administration has approved nicotine chewing gum and nicotine patches (which are free of damaging substances) as safe and effective in helping addicted persons taper off, especially in combination with counseling (J. E. Brody, 1995a; NIA, 1993). People who successfully stop smoking are likely to have smoked less than a pack a day, to have

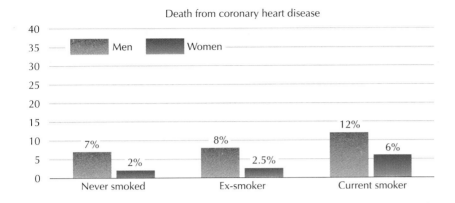

Death from coronary heart disease

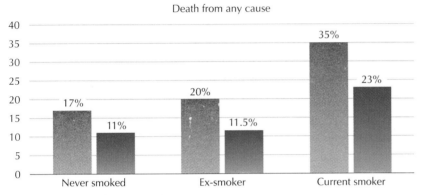

Death from any cause

Person ages 40–59 when screened.

FIGURE 12-2

Death rates in 20 years for smokers, ex-smokers, and those who never smoked. Among 40,000 adults ages 18 to 74 screened during the years 1968–1973 to identify high risk factors for coronary heart disease, those who had quit smoking were only slightly more likely to die within the next 20 years than those who had never smoked. Smokers had much higher death rates from heart disease and all other causes than the other two groups. *(Source: Adapted from Stamler, Stamler, & Garside, undated, chart 6, p. 6.)*

relatively few friends who smoke (and thus less social pressure to do so), to be employed, and not to have children at home (Rose et al., 1996). It generally takes three or four attempts to stop for good. Women are less likely than men to succeed on their first try (J. E. Brody, 1995a; "Research Shows," 1992).

Whenever and however people stop smoking, their health is likely to improve immediately. Giving up smoking reduces the risks of heart disease and stroke, even after an initial heart attack (Katchadourian, 1987; Kawachi et al., 1993; NIA, 1993; Wannamethee, Shaper, Whincup, & Walker, 1995). Men and women who give up smoking have virtually no greater risk of suffering a heart attack, or of dying from heart disease within 3 to 20 years, than those who have never smoked (L. Rosenberg, Palmer, & Shapiro, 1990; Stamler, Dyer, Shekelle, Neaton, & Stamler, 1993; see Figure 12-2). The risk of cancer takes longer to decline but within 10 years is no greater than for a nonsmoker (NIA, 1993).

Alcohol

The United States is a drinking society. Advertising equates liquor, beer, and wine with the good life. According to a national survey, 60 percent of adults say they sometimes drink. Of these, 47 percent (as compared with 53 percent in 1983) consume three drinks or fewer each day. However, the proportion who are heavy drinkers, consuming four or more drinks a day, remains about 12 percent (*Prevention Index*, 1995).

Long-term heavy drinking may lead to cirrhosis of the liver, other gastrointestinal disorders (including ulcers), pancreatic disease, certain cancers, heart failure, stroke, damage to the nervous system, psychoses, and other medical problems (AHA, 1995; Fuchs et al., 1995; National Institute on Alcohol Abuse and Alcoholism, NIAA, 1981). Alcohol is a major cause of deaths from automobile accidents; 17 percent of drivers in one survey admitted that they sometimes drive after drinking (*Prevention Index*, 1995). Alcohol is also implicated in deaths from drowning, suicide, fire, and falls; and it is often a factor in family violence (NIAAA, 1981). It is estimated that a majority of homicides involve alcohol (APA, 1994).

Although moderate consumption of alcohol seems to reduce the risk of fatal heart disease, the definition of *moderate* is becoming more restricted. Men who take more than one drink a day have much higher death rates. Apparently, increased risk of cancer of the throat, gastric system, urinary tract, and brain outweighs any benefits to the heart (Camargo, Gaziano, Hennekens, Manson, & Stampfer, 1994). Women can safely drink only about half as much as men. Although light-to-moderate alcohol consumption decreases women's risk of cardiovascular disease, especially among women age 50 and older who have one or more coronary risk factors (Fuchs et al., 1995), women seem to be more sensitive than men to toxic effects of heavy alcohol use on heart muscles (Urbano-Marquez et al., 1995).

Despite the damage alcohol can do, many drinkers deny—or do not realize—that it prevents them from functioning well on the job, at home, and in society. In a randomized clinical study by the World Health Organization in Kenya, Mexico, Norway, the United Kingdom, Russia, the United States, and Zimbabwe, five minutes of simple advice about abstaining or setting sensible limits prompted men who were heavy drinkers to cut down on their daily consumption by 17 percent (WHO Brief Intervention Study Group, 1996).

Alcoholism, on the other hand, is not cured by willpower; it is a chronic disease, which may involve periods of remission and relapse. More than 7 percent of Americans abuse alcohol or are dependent on it (Grant et al., 1994); an estimated one-third of alcoholics are women (Urbano-Marquez et al., 1995).

Alcoholism runs in families; close relatives of people who are addicted to alcohol are 3 to 4 times as likely to become dependent on it as people whose relatives are not addicted (APA, 1994; McGue, 1993). Sons of alcoholic men are 4 times as likely as sons of nonalcoholic men to develop alcoholism, even when they are adopted at birth, and regardless of whether their adoptive parents are alcoholic. Children whose adoptive parents, but not their biological parents, are alcoholic have no special risk (Schuckit, 1985, 1987). Most studies have found monozygotic twins significantly more concordant for alcoholism than dizygotic twins (APA, 1994). However, newer twin studies suggest that genes may play only a minor role, especially in women (Plomin et al., 1994).

Alcoholism is also influenced by environmental factors, such as the price and availability of liquor, cultural attitudes toward its use and abuse, and the way drinking makes a person feel (APA, 1994). No one is predestined to develop alcoholism; but

since genetic factors seem to make some people more vulnerable, people whose parents were alcoholic may not be able to handle liquor as their peers do.

Depending on the severity of the condition, treatment for alcoholism may include detoxification (removing all alcohol from the body), hospitalization, medicine and vitamins, individual and group psychotherapy, avoidance of all mood-altering drugs, involvement of the family, and referral to a support organization, such as Alcoholics Anonymous. Although not a cure, treatment can give alcoholics new tools for coping with their addiction and leading productive lives. Among 199 alcoholic men, those who stopped drinking lived as long as casual drinkers or teetotalers (Bullock, Reed, & Grant, 1992).

Socioeconomic Status and Ethnicity

Apart from the things people do, or refrain from doing, which affect their health directly, there are indirect influences on health. Among the most important are income, education, and ethnicity. Wealthier, college-educated, and white people rate their health better than less educated, lower-income, and minority-group people (USDHHS, 1982, 1985, 1990, 1992, 1995, 1996). Although death rates have declined overall in the United States since 1960, the disparity between the high death rates of poor and poorly educated people and the lower death rates of more affluent, better-educated people has increased (Pappas, Queen, Hadden, & Fisher, 1993).

Poverty results in poor nutrition, substandard housing, inadequate prenatal care, and limited access to health care (Otten, Teutsch, Williamson, & Marks, 1990). People without health insurance tend to receive substandard medical care, putting them at risk for a variety of medical problems (Burstin, Lipsitz, & Brennan, 1992). Education is important, too. The less schooling people have had, the greater the chance that they will develop and die from such chronic ailments as hypertension and heart disease (Pincus, Callahan, & Burkhauser, 1987).

This does not mean that good income and education actually *cause* good health; instead, they are related to lifestyle factors that are likely to be causative. Better-educated and more affluent people can afford a healthier diet and better preventive health care and medical treatment. They also

Income is a major influence on health. This homeless family may not be getting the nutrition and medical care needed for good health. *(Mark Ludak/ Impact Visuals)*

tend to have sensible personal habits. They exercise more strenuously and smoke less. (Only 13 percent of college graduates smoke, as compared with 30 percent of adults who have not gone past high school.) They are more likely to use alcohol, but to use it in moderation. College-educated women are more likely to get routine screening for cervical cancer (*Prevention Index*, 1995).

The associations between income, education, living conditions, and health help explain the deplorable state of health in some minority populations. Black men under age 65 in New York's Harlem have a lower life expectancy than men in underdeveloped Bangladesh (see Figure 12-3). Death rates are considerably higher in inner-city African American communities than in some places that have been designated as "natural disaster areas" (C. McCord & Freeman, 1990). African Americans ages 25 to 44 are more than twice as likely as white people to die in young adulthood, in part because young black men are at high risk of being victims of homicide (U.S. Department of Justice, 1995; USDHHS, 1996).

Young black adults are 20 times more likely to have high blood pressure than young white adults (Agoda, 1995). Chronic hypertension among pregnant black women may lead to complications, including hemorrhaging, convulsions, and coma, and may contribute to the high incidence of low birthweight and infant mortality among black babies (Samadi et al., 1996). Black women are more than 3 times as likely as white women to die during pregnancy, in part because they are less likely

to get early prenatal care (CDC, 1995a).

Gender

Which are healthier: women or men? One difficulty in answering this question is that until recently women have been excluded from many important studies of health problems that affect both sexes (Healy, 1991; Rodin & Ickovics, 1990). As a result, much of what we know applies only to men. Of course, certain health problems—those affecting the female reproductive system—are limited to women; others, such as prostate and testicular cancer, affect only men. Some diseases, such as lung cancer, are more common among men, though this difference is decreasing. Others, such as heart disease, tend to strike women later in life. Still others, such as eating disorders (see Chapter 10), rheumatoid arthritis, and osteoporosis (see Chapter 16), are more common among women.

To remedy the unevenness of information about women's health, the National Institutes of Health has launched a multidisciplinary study to gather data about causes of death and disability among women. Medical experts are debating how best to treat women: by developing a new specialty in women's health or by giving it more attention in standard medical school curricula (T. Lewin, 1992).

Patterns of Longevity and Illness We do know that women have a higher life expectancy than

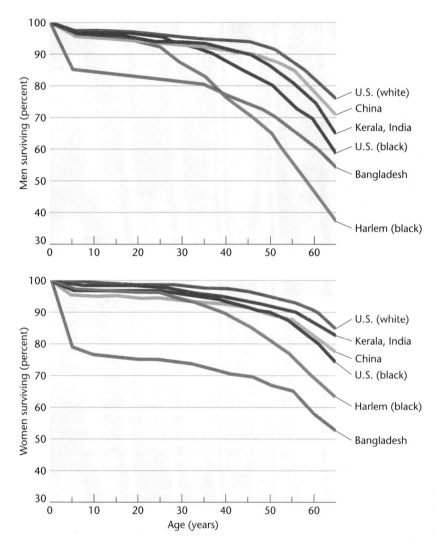

FIGURE 12-3
Variations in survival rates by sex, race, and region. *(Source: Sen, 1993, p. 45.)*

men and lower death rates throughout life (U.S. Bureau of the Census, 1995a; USDHHS, 1996; see Chapter 16). Women's greater longevity has been attributed to genetic protection given by the second X chromosome (which men do not have) and, before menopause, to beneficial effects of the female hormone estrogen, particularly on cardiovascular health (Rodin & Ickovics, 1990; USDHHS, 1992). However, 1 out of 4 women age 20 and over has high blood pressure; and within a decade after menopause, as estrogen levels drop, women's risk of heart disease nearly catches up with men's. This happens faster after a hysterectomy (AHA, 1995).

Despite their longer life, women of all ages report being ill more often than men, use health services more often, and take more medications. Women are more likely to be hospitalized than men (most often for surgery related to the reproductive system). On the other hand, when men go

to the hospital, they tend to stay longer; and their health problems are more likely to be chronic and life-threatening (Rodin & Ickovics, 1990; USDHHS, 1996).

Women's greater tendency to say they are sick and to seek treatment does not necessarily mean that women are in worse health than men nor that they are imaging ailments or are preoccupied with illness. They may simply be more health-conscious. Menstruation and childbearing make women aware of the body and its functioning, and cultural standards encourage medical management of those processes. Many women see doctors, not only during pregnancy, but for routine gynecological tests. Women generally know more than men about health, think and do more about preventing illness, are more aware of symptoms and susceptibility, and are more likely to talk about their medical worries (Nathanson & Lorenz, 1982).

Men may feel that illness is not "masculine" and thus may be less likely to admit that they do not feel well. It may be that the better care women take of themselves helps them live longer than men.

Differences in medical treatment complicate the picture. Two out of three surgeries in the United States are performed on women—most frequently hysterectomies, many of which, according to some experts, are of dubious benefit. On the other hand, women are less likely to receive lifesaving coronary bypass surgery. The fact that 70 percent of tranquilizers and antidepressants are prescribed for women may reflect "the stereotype that women's health complaints are more emotionally laden and psychosomatic than men's" (Rodin & Ickovics, 1990, p. 1018). Furthermore, women are more likely than men to be poor and to lack health insurance and adequate health care.

As women's lifestyles have become more like men's, so—in some ways—have their health patterns. Women were slower to stop smoking than men, and in recent years many have taken up the habit, resulting in a 182 percent increase in female deaths from lung cancer between 1970 and 1993, more than 7 times the increase for men (USDHHS, 1996). The gap between men and women in use of tobacco, alcohol, and illicit drugs has narrowed; and women become addicted more easily and develop substance-related diseases earlier than men (CASA, 1996).

On the other hand, as women enter the work force, their health seems to improve. Employed women are less likely to be ill than homemakers; and women are no more likely than men to stay home from work because of illness. It is not clear whether employment itself promotes health or whether healthier women are more likely to get and keep jobs (Rodin & Ickovics, 1990). Or it may be that employed people of both sexes are reluctant to call in sick because they need to protect their jobs, their salaries, and their image as healthy producers (Nathanson & Lorenz, 1982).

Problems Related to Menstruation   Although women enjoy important protection due to hormonal activity during the reproductive years, the menstrual cycle can produce health problems. *Premenstrual syndrome (PMS)* is a disorder involving physical discomfort and emotional tension during the 1 to 2 weeks before a menstrual period. Symptoms may include fatigue, food cravings, headaches, swelling and tenderness of the breasts, swollen hands or feet, abdominal bloating, nausea,

constipation, weight gain, anxiety, depression, irritability, mood swings, tearfulness, and difficulty concentrating or remembering ("PMS: It's Real," 1994; R. L. Reid & Yen, 1981). These symptoms are not distinctive in themselves; it is their timing that identifies PMS. Unlike *dysmenorrhea,* or menstrual cramps, which tend to afflict adolescents and younger women, PMS typically affects women in their thirties or older.

Up to 70 percent of menstruating women may have some symptoms, but in fewer than 10 percent do they create significant health problems ("PMS: It's Real," 1994; Freeman, Rickels, Sondheimer, & Polansky, 1995). An estimated 3 to 5 percent have **premenstrual dysphoric disorder (PMDD),** a mood disorder akin to clinical depression (APA, 1994).

The causes of PMS and PMDD are not known. The conditions may be related to cyclical depletion of neurotransmitters in the brain that affect well-being or relaxation or stimulate the central nervous system. There may also be psychological and cultural factors. Most cases are diagnosed on the basis of self-reports, and women's interpretation of the severity and normality of symptoms varies. One study found bigger differences in self-esteem, guilt, anger, and coping patterns than in physical symptoms among women who did and did not report having PMS (Gallant, Popiel, & Hoffman et al., 1992a, 1992b). Studies in the United States, Italy, and Bahrain found some differences in premenstrual symptoms. At least 30 percent of the women in all three cultures reported swelling, irritability, breast pain, mood swings, and fatigue, but such reports were more common among American and Italian women than among Bahraini women (Dan & Monagle, 1994).

How to treat PMS is controversial. One widely used treatment—administration of the female hormone progesterone in the form of a pill or suppository—proved in a large, randomized, controlled study to be no more beneficial than a placebo, which has no active ingredients (Freeman, Rickels, Sondheimer, & Polansky, 1990). In a follow-up study, antianxiety pills proved more effective (Freeman et al., 1995). For milder symptoms, some doctors recommend exercise and dietary changes, such as avoiding fat, sodium, caffeine, and alcohol ("PMS: It's Real," 1994).

Another complication of menstruation, which occurs in less than 3 percent of women, is *endometriosis.* In this condition, living cells from the uterine lining are flushed backward through the fallopian tubes into the abdominal cavity and attach themselves to the ovaries, bladder, bowels, or other organs. Hormonal activity just before menstruation may cause the endometrial tissue to swell painfully, sometimes leading to discomfort during intercourse, intestinal blockage, or infertility. Symptoms usually end by menopause but can be reactivated by hormone replacement therapy unless doses are low (Cabe-McGill, 1991).

✔ ADULT COGNITION

Common sense tells us that adults think differently from children or adolescents. They engage in different kinds of conversations, understand more complicated material, and use their broader experience to solve practical problems. Is common sense correct? Let's see what research has found. Then we'll examine two current theories that seek to redefine the way we look at adult intelligence. As we do, we may gain insight into a puzzling phenomenon: the frequent mismatch between apparent intellectual promise and mature achievement.

THE SHIFT TO POSTFORMAL THOUGHT

The early adult years are often a time of self-discovery. For young people in transition from adolescence to adulthood, the exposure to a new educational or work environment, sometimes far away from one's childhood home, offers a chance to question long-held assumptions.

William Perry (1970) interviewed 67 Harvard and Radcliffe students throughout their undergraduate years and found that their thinking progressed from *rigidity* to *flexibility* and ultimately to *freely chosen commitments.* Students come to college with rigid ideas about truth; they cannot conceive of any answer but the "right" one. As they encounter a wide variety of ideas, they recognize the existence of many different points of view. They also accept their own uncertainty. They consider this stage temporary, however, and expect to learn the "one right answer" eventually. Next, they come to see all knowledge and values as relative. They recognize that different societies and different individuals have their own value systems. They now realize that their opinions on many issues are as valid as anyone else's, even those of a parent or teacher; but they cannot find meaning or value in this maze of systems and beliefs. Chaos has re-

placed order. Finally, they achieve *commitment within relativism:* they make their own judgments and choose their own beliefs and values despite uncertainty and the recognition of other valid possibilities.

Relativistic thinking is similar to what is sometimes called **postformal thought,** a development that may occur with or without higher education. Research and theoretical work since the 1970s suggest that mature thinking may be far richer and more complex than the abstract intellectual manipulations described by Piaget's highest stage, formal operations. Thought in adulthood (as we discuss further in Chapter 14) often appears to be flexible, open, adaptive, and individualistic. It relies on intuition as well as logic. It applies the fruits of experience to ambiguous situations. It is characterized by the ability to deal with uncertainty, inconsistency, contradiction, imperfection, and compromise (Arlin, 1984; Labouvie-Vief, 1985, 1990a; Labouvie-Vief & Hakim-Larson, 1989; Sinnott, 1984, 1989a, 1989b, 1991).

One prominent researcher (Sinnott, 1984) proposed several criteria of postformal thought:

■ *Shifting gears:* Ability to shift back and forth from abstract reasoning to practical, real-world considerations. ("This might work on paper but not in real life.")
■ *Multiple causality, multiple solutions:* Awareness that most problems have more than one cause and more than one solution and that some solutions are more likely to work than others.
■ *Pragmatism:* Ability to choose the best of several possible solutions and to recognize criteria for choosing. ("If you want the most practical solution, do this; if you want the quickest solution, do that.")
■ *Awareness of paradox:* Recognition that a problem or solution involves inherent conflict. ("Doing this will give him what he wants, but it will only make him unhappy in the end.")

Is this kind of thinking more characteristic of young men or young women? One group of researchers (Belenky, Clinchy, Goldberger, & Tarule, 1986) identified five ways of knowing (or perceiving reality): silent, received, subjective, procedural, and constructed. *Silent knowing* shows passive acceptance of what someone else knows. *Received knowing,* most common in childhood, means accepting the teachings of authorities; it is usually concrete, absolute, and black-or-white. *Subjective knowing* is based on intuition. *Procedural knowing*, the dominant style in colleges and universities, takes a systematic, analytical approach, such as the scientific method. *Constructed knowing* integrates two or more of the other ways of knowing (for example, intuition with procedural knowledge); it is similar to postformal thought.

To test gender differences in ways of knowing, another research team gave 30 female and 30 male students at an Australian university two practical problems to solve (R. Orr & Luszcz, 1994). The researchers also interviewed the students about how they generally arrived at knowledge and gave them personality tests to measure traits typically seen as "masculine" or "feminine." Women favored subjective knowing (intuition); men were more likely to prefer procedural methods. Men and women were equally likely to use constructed knowing and relativistic problem solving, but students of *either* sex who scored high on "femininity" were more likely to do both.

A number of studies support the existence of postformal thought (Berg & Klaczynski, 1996; Sinnott, 1996). This literature challenges the basis for psychometric assessment of intelligence in adulthood. If the postformal theorists are right, adults may do poorly on questions or tasks that are not meaningful to them or do not reflect their experience.

Critics say the idea of postformal thought has a thin research base. Because qualitative change does not readily lend itself to quantitative measurement, much of the supporting research has taken the form of extensive, time-consuming interviews, which are not easy to replicate; thus the validity of the conclusions cannot easily be tested. Future research may determine whether reliable, objective measures of postformal thinking can be developed.

STERNBERG: INSIGHT AND KNOWHOW

Each of us knows individuals who succeed in school but fail in their careers, or conversely, who fail in school but succeed in their careers. We have watched as graduate students, at the top of their class in the initial years of structured coursework, fall by the wayside when they must work independently on research and a dissertation. Most of us know of colleagues whose brilliance in their academic fields is matched only by their incompetence in social interactions. (Sternberg, Wagner, Williams, & Horvath, 1995, p. 912)

Alix, Barbara, and Courtney applied to graduate programs at Yale University. Alix had earned almost straight A's in college, scored high on the Graduate Record Examination (GRE), and had excellent recommendations. Barbara's grades were only fair, and her GRE scores were low by Yale's standards, but her letters of recommendation enthusiastically praised her exceptional research and creative ideas. Courtney's grades, GRE scores, and recommendations were good but not among the best.

Alix and Courtney were admitted to the graduate program. Barbara was not admitted but was hired as a research associate and took graduate classes on the side. Alix did very well for the first year or so, but less well after that. Barbara confounded the admissions committee by doing outstanding work. Courtney's performance in graduate school was only fair, but she had the easiest time getting a good job afterward (Trotter, 1986).

According to Robert Sternberg (1985a, 1987), Barbara and Courtney were strong in two aspects of intelligence that psychometric IQ tests do not measure: creative insight and practical intelligence. Sternberg's *triarchic* (three-part) theory of intelligence embraces three elements of intelligence, which everyone has to a greater or lesser extent and which are useful in different kinds of situations:

1 *Componential element: how efficiently people process information.* This is the *analytic* aspect of intelligence. It tells people how to solve problems, how to monitor solutions, and how to evaluate the results. Alix was strong in this area; she was good at taking intelligence tests and finding holes in arguments.

2 *Experiential element: how people approach novel or familiar tasks.* This is the *insightful* aspect of intelligence. It allows people to compare new information with what they already know and to come up with new ways of putting facts together—in other words, to think originally. Automatic performance of familiar operations (such as recognizing words) facilitates insight because it leaves the mind free to tackle unfamiliar material. Barbara was strong in this area.

3 *Contextual element: how people deal with their environment.* This is the *practical* aspect of intelligence. It is the ability to size up a situation and decide what to do: adapt to it, change it, or find a new, more suitable setting. Courtney was strong in this area.

These corporate colleagues in San Juan, Puerto Rico, trading stories about their work, will be helped to achieve professional success by their tacit knowledge—the practical, "inside" information about how things are done, which is not formally taught but must be gained from experience. *(R. Lord/ The Image Works)*

Since experiential (insightful) and contextual (practical) intelligence are very important in adult life, psychometric tests are much less useful in gauging adults' intelligence and predicting their life success than in measuring children's intelligence and predicting their school success. As an undergraduate, Alix's componential ability helped her sail through examinations. However, in graduate school, where original thinking is expected, Barbara's superior experiential intelligence—her fresh insights and innovative ideas—began to shine. So did Courtney's practical, contextual intelligence—her "street smarts." She knew her way around. She chose "hot" research topics, submitted papers to the "right" journals, and knew where and how to apply for jobs.

Studies suggest that both creative production and the ability to solve practical problems grow at least until midlife (see Chapter 14), while the ability to solve academic problems generally declines (Sternberg et al., 1995). Practical problems emerge from personal experience, as does the information needed to solve them. Thus they are usually far more interesting to the solver than academic problems, which are made up by someone else, provide all relevant information, and are disconnected from everyday life. Unlike academic problems, which generally have a definite answer and one right way to find it, practical problems are often ill-defined and have a variety of possible solutions and ways of reaching them, each with its advantages and disadvantages (Neisser, 1976; Wagner &

Sternberg, 1985). Life experience equips adults to solve such problems.

An important aspect of practical intelligence is ***tacit knowledge:*** "inside information," "knowhow," or "savvy" that is not formally taught or openly expressed (Sternberg & Wagner, 1993; Sternberg et al., 1995; Wagner & Sternberg, 1986). Tacit knowledge, acquired largely on one's own, is useful knowledge of how to act to achieve personal goals. It is "commonsense" knowledge of how to get ahead—how to win a promotion or cut through red tape. Tacit knowledge may include *self-management* (knowing how to motivate oneself and organize time and energy), *management of tasks* (knowing, for example, how to write a grant proposal), and *management of others* (knowing when to reward or criticize subordinates).

Sternberg's method of testing tacit knowledge (see Table 12-3) is to compare a person's chosen course of action in hypothetical, work-related situations with the choices of experts in the field and with accepted "rules of thumb." Tacit knowledge, measured in this way, seems to be unrelated to IQ and predicts job performance better than psychometric tests, which by themselves account for only 4 to 25 percent of the variation in how well people do in real-life situations. Also, tests of tacit knowledge may better identify managerial potential in women and minorities, who often do better in practical situations than traditional intelligence test scores would predict (Sternberg et al., 1995; see Box 12-1).

Of course, tacit knowledge is not all that is

needed to succeed; other aspects of intelligence count, too. In studies of business managers, tests of tacit knowledge together with IQ and personality tests predicted virtually *all* the variance in performance, as measured by such criteria as salary, years of management experience, and the company's success (Sternberg et al., 1995). In a more recent study, tacit knowledge was related to the salaries managers earned at a given age and to the level of their advancement, independent of family background and education. Interestingly, the most knowledgeable managers were not those who had spent many years with a company or many years as managers, but those who had worked for the most companies, perhaps gaining a greater breadth of experience (W. M. Williams & Sternberg, in press).

Further research is needed to determine how and when tacit knowledge is acquired, why some people acquire it more efficiently than others, and how it can best be measured. In the meantime, tests of practical intelligence, such as these, can be a valuable supplement to the aptitude tests now widely used in hiring and promotion.

EMOTIONAL INTELLIGENCE

In the mid-1980s, half of Metropolitan Life Insurance Company's sales force quit during their first year on the job, and 4 out of 5—unable to take the constant frustration of being turned down during cold calls—stayed less than four years. To protect its investment in training, the company asked the psychologist Martin Seligman to design a test to

TABLE 12-3

Sample Test Items for Tacit Knowledge in Work-related Situations*

Academic Psychology	Business Management
It is your second year as an assistant professor in a prestigious psychology department. This past year you published two unrelated empirical articles in established journals. You don't believe, however, that there is a research area that can be identified as your own. You believe yourself to be about as productive as others. The feedback about your first year of teaching has been generally good. You have yet to serve on a university committee. There is one graduate student who has chosen to work with you. You have no external source of funding, nor have you applied for funding. Your goals are to become one of the top people in your field and to get tenure in your department. The following is a list of things you are considering doing during the next two months. You obviously cannot do them all. Rate the importance of each by its priority as a means of reaching your goals. ——a. Improve the quality of your teaching ——b. Write a grant proposal ——c. Begin long-term research that may lead to a major theoretical article ——d. Concentrate on recruiting more students ——e. Serve on a committee studying university–community relations ——f. Begin several related short-term research projects, each of which may lead to an empirical article ——g. Volunteer to be chairperson of the undergraduate curriculum committee	It is your second year as a midlevel manager in a company in the communications industry. You head a department of about thirty people. The evaluation of your first year on the job has been generally favorable. Performance ratings for your department are at least as good as they were before you took over, and perhaps even a little better. You have two assistants. One is quite capable. The other just seems to go through the motions but to be of little real help. You believe that although you are well liked, there is little that would distinguish you in the eyes of your superiors from the nine other managers at a comparable level in the company. Your goal is rapid promotion to the top of the company. The following is a list of things you are considering doing during the next two months. You obviously cannot do them all. Rate the importance of each by its priority as a means of reaching your goal. ——a. Find a way to get rid of the "dead wood" (e.g., the less helpful assistant and three or four others) ——b. Participate in a series of panel discussions to be shown on the local public television station ——c. Find ways to make sure your superiors are aware of your important accomplishments ——d. Make an effort to better match the work to be done with the strengths and weaknesses of individual employees ——e. Write an article on productivity for the company newsletter

Note: Respondents' answers are scored in comparison with the average answers of an expert group.

SOURCE: Adapted from Sternberg et al., 1995, p. 927.

BOX 12-1 FOOD FOR THOUGHT

HOW WELL DO INTELLIGENCE TESTS PREDICT JOB PERFORMANCE?

Today, tests to screen prospective employees are common. But can the same kind of test accurately predict success in such varied kinds of work as bricklaying and data processing?

Two Texans—Malcolm James Ree, a psychologist at St. Mary's University; and James A. Earles, a mathematician in San Antonio—say yes. Ree and Earles (1992) touched off a controversy with their claim that tests of general intelligence (*g*, as researchers call it) are the best predictors of performance on any job and that measures of specific aptitudes—verbal, quantitative, spatial, or mechanical—add little. The claim was based on a statistical review of a number of large-scale studies, many done in the armed services.

The article, published in *Current Directions in Psychological Science*, a journal of the American Psychological Society, provoked so much reaction that the journal devoted a special section to the subject. Robert Sternberg (whose theory of intelligence we discuss in this chapter) and his colleague Richard K. Wagner (1993) wrote one rebuttal, entitled "The *g*-ocentric View of Intelligence and Job Performance Is Wrong." They compared the idea that all abilities revolve around general intelligence to the discredited belief that the earth is the center of the universe. Sternberg and Wagner argued that intelligence tests predict job performance less reliably than they predict school performance because real-life and academic problems require different kinds of intelligence.

Other contenders weighed in on both sides. Arthur Jensen (1993) argued that *g* is not limited to academic intelligence and that such factors as personality, motivation, interests, and values are more likely than specific abilities to account for the difference between actual job performance and what the tests predict. David McClelland (1993) criticized the omission of such factors as gender, race, education, and social class: "Being white, male, better educated, and from an advantaged background often correlate with better job performance, particularly as measured by a supervisor's ratings. Any of these correlations . . . may predict job performance better than intelligence" (p. 6).

Ree and Earles (1993) replied to their critics by pointing to well-documented relationships between *g* and other job qualifications, such as motivation, leadership, and social skills. An applicant selected for general intelligence, they maintained, is likely to show these other characteristics as well.

The heated exchange skirted a troubling aspect of the modest relationship between test scores and job performance: white adults referred for jobs on the basis of a battery of tests used by state employment agencies tend to perform less well after being hired than their scores would predict, while African Americans do better on the job than on the tests. This situation led to the controversial practice—later outlawed—of "race-norming," ranking scores within racial categories to avoid screening out capable minority applicants. It also

led to calls for revising the tests to eliminate cultural bias, and to pleas to employers to rely less on the tests in hiring. Ree and Earles (1992) gave passing recognition to this problem, suggesting the substitution of "content-free" tests designed to measure *g* through such basic cognitive indicators as speed of information processing; but there is dispute over whether such tests could legitimately be related to job performance.

One question we need to ask in weighing findings about job performance is just what they are measuring. Ree and Earles (1992) used occupational level—the difficulty or complexity of a job—as one index of job performance. It would hardly be surprising if an engineer had a higher IQ than a lumberjack; but is a mediocre engineer a better performer than a competent, industrious lumberjack? How would a finding that engineers have (and presumably need) higher measured intelligence than lumberjacks support the conclusion that intelligence tests can select the best performers in any field?

Much more thought and study need to go into the issue of how much weight should be given to "intelligence" (however measured) in employment decisions and what other factors, if any, should be taken into consideration to make predictions of performance more reliable for employers and fairer to applicants.

predict which prospective salespeople would stick it out. Job applicants were asked to choose between two responses to a series of hypothetical problems, such as this one (A. Park, 1995, p. 65):

> You fall down a great deal while skiing.
>
> A. Skiing is difficult.
>
> B. The trails were icy.

The answer Seligman was looking for was *B*. Success, he reasoned, is related to self-esteem; he expected optimistic people, who view failure as a temporary setback rather than a permanent obstacle, to be better able to handle rejection. Sure enough, "superoptimists"—who did exceptionally well on Seligman's test but failed the company's usual screening test—outperformed those who did well on the regular test by 21 percent in the first year and 57 percent in the second (Gibbs, 1995).

The observation that emotional qualities such as optimism influence success is not new, of course, nor does it apply only to adults. However, it is in adult life, with its "make-or-break" challenges, that we can perhaps see most clearly the role of the emotions in determining how effectively people use their minds.

In 1990, two psychologists, Peter Salovey and John Mayer, coined the term *emotional intelligence* (sometimes called *EQ*). It refers to the ability to understand and regulate emotions: to recognize and deal with one's own feelings and the feelings of others. Daniel Goleman (1995b), the psychologist and science writer who popularized the term, speculates that emotional intelligence may be largely set by midadolescence, when the parts of the brain that control how people act on their emotions mature.

Perhaps the most essential ingredient of emotional intelligence is self-awareness, which permits self-control and the ability to cope with rejection and discouragement. Empathy, impulse control, and the capacity to delay gratification are other elements. These abilities may be more important to success, on the job and elsewhere, than is IQ.

Emotional intelligence is not the opposite of cognitive intelligence; some people are high in both, whereas others have little of either. Emotional intelligence may play a part in the ability to acquire tacit knowledge. As some corporate personnel executives have noted, "IQ gets you hired, but EQ gets you promoted" (Gibbs, 1995, p. 66). It also, of course, affects how well people navigate intimate relationships. Emotional intelligence and tacit knowledge, as much as or more than "purely" cognitive abilities, seem to be important to life success.

Although the role of the emotions in intelligent behavior has been confirmed by much research, the concept of emotional intelligence is controversial. Hard as it is to assess cognitive intelligence, emotional intelligence may be even harder to measure. For one thing, lumping the emotions together can be misleading. How do we assess someone who can handle fear but not guilt, or who can face stress better than boredom? Then too, the usefulness of a certain emotion may depend on the circumstances. Anger, for example, can lead to either destructive or constructive behavior. Anxiety may alert a person to danger but also may block effective action (Goleman, 1995b).

Ultimately, acting on emotions comes down to a value judgment: When is it "intelligent" to laugh? to cry? to show pride or distress? Is it smarter to obey or to disobey authority? to inspire others or to exploit them? "Emotional skills, like intellectual ones, are morally neutral. . . . Without a moral compass to guide people in how to employ their gifts, emotional intelligence can be used for good or evil" (Gibbs, 1995, p. 68). Let's look next at moral development in adulthood.

✔ MORAL DEVELOPMENT

Moral development of children and adolescents, in Lawrence Kohlberg's influential theory, is a rational process accompanying cognitive maturation. Youngsters advance in moral judgment as they shed egocentric thought and become capable of abstract thought. In adulthood, however, moral judgments often seem more complex; experience and emotion play an increasingly important role. For many adults, religious faith is a guide to moral decisions, and faith itself may develop throughout life. Let's look at how Kohlberg dealt with these issues. Then we'll examine James Fowler's stages of faith. Finally, we'll turn to the work of Carol Gilligan, who investigated moral development in women and challenged the values at the heart of Kohlberg's theory.

LIVE AND LEARN: THE ROLE OF EXPERIENCE IN KOHLBERG'S THEORY

According to Kohlberg, advancement to the third level of moral reasoning—fully principled, postconventional morality—is chiefly a function of experience (see Chapter 10). Most people do not reach this level until their twenties—if ever. Although cognitive awareness of higher moral principles often develops in adolescence, most people do not commit themselves to such principles until adulthood (Kohlberg, 1973). Two experiences that spur moral development in young adults are encountering conflicting values away from home (as happens in college or the armed services or sometimes in foreign travel) and being responsible for the welfare of others (as in parenthood).

Experience leads adults to reevaluate their criteria for what is right and fair. Some adults spontaneously offer personal experiences as reasons for their answers to moral dilemmas. For example, people who have had cancer, or whose relatives or friends have had cancer, are more likely to condone a man's stealing an expensive drug to save his dying wife and to explain this view in terms of their own experience (Bielby & Papalia, 1975). Such experiences, strongly colored by emotion, trigger rethinking in a way that hypothetical, impersonal discussions cannot, and are more likely to help people see other points of view.

With regard to moral judgments, then, cognitive stages do not tell the whole story. Of course, someone whose thinking is still egocentric is unlikely to make moral decisions at a postconventional level; but even someone who can think abstractly may not reach the highest level of moral development unless experience catches up with cognition. Many adults who are capable of thinking for themselves do not break out of a conventional mold unless their experiences have prepared them for the shift. Furthermore, experience is interpreted within a cultural context (see Box 12-2).

Kohlberg, shortly before his death, proposed a seventh stage of moral reasoning, which moves beyond considerations of justice and has much in common with the concept of self-transcendence in the eastern philosophical tradition. In the seventh stage, adults reflect on the question *"Why* be moral?" (Kohlberg & Ryncarz, 1990, p. 192; emphasis added). The answer, said Kohlberg, lies in achieving a cosmic perspective: "a sense of unity with the cosmos, nature, or God," which enables a person to see moral issues "from the standpoint of the universe as a whole" (Kohlberg & Ryncarz, 1990, pp. 191, 207). In experiencing oneness with the universe, people come to see that everything is connected; each person's actions affect everything and everyone else, and the consequences

rebound on the doer. This idea was eloquently expressed in a letter written in the mid-nineteenth century by the Native American chief Seattle when the United States government sought to buy his tribe's lands:

> We are part of the earth and it is part of us.... Man did not weave the web of life, he is merely a strand in it. Whatever he does to the web, he does to himself.... So, if we sell you our land, love it as we have loved it. Care for it as we have cared for it.... As we are part of the land, you too are part of the land. We are brothers after all. (Chief Seattle, quoted in Campbell & Moyers, 1988, pp. 34–35)

Stage 7 may or may not involve religious belief, but Kohlberg recognized that it parallels the most mature stage of faith that the theologian James Fowler (1981) identified, in which "one experiences a oneness with the ultimate conditions of one's life and being" (Kohlberg & Ryncarz, 1990, p. 202).

LIFE-SPAN ISSUE
HOW DOES FAITH CHANGE ACROSS THE LIFE SPAN?

 In the 1970s, James Fowler, an ordained minister and faculty member of the Harvard Divinity School, began questioning his students about their faith and how it had evolved. From their responses emerged a stage theory of faith development.

Can faith be studied from a developmental perspective? Yes, according to James Fowler (1981, 1989). Influenced by Piaget and Kohlberg, as well as by other developmental theorists, Fowler defined faith as a way of seeing or knowing the world. To find out how people arrive at this knowledge, Fowler and his divinity students eventually interviewed more than 400 people of all ages and of various ethnic, educational, and socioeconomic backgrounds and various religious or secular identifications and affiliations.

Fowler's theory focuses on the *form* of faith, not its content or object; it is not limited to any particular belief system. Faith, said Fowler, can be not only "a sense of relatedness to an ultimate being or an ultimate reality," but also "a sense of relatedness to the world, the neighbor, the self." It is "a dynamic, evolving pattern for the making and maintenance of meaning in our lives" (1989, p. 3). Faith can be religious or nonreligious: a person may have faith in a god, in science, in humanity, or in a cause to which he or she attaches ultimate worth.

BOX 12-2 WINDOW ON THE WORLD

CROSS-CULTURAL PERSPECTIVES ON MORAL DEVELOPMENT

Kohlberg claimed that his stages of moral development are universal. How well has this claim held up? Let's look at the results of studies of Kohlberg's dilemmas in three cultures: China, Israel, and India.

ISRAEL

People born and raised on a kibbutz (collective farming or industrial settlement) in Israel are imbued with a socialist perspective. How do such people score on a problem such as Heinz's dilemma, which weighs the value of human life against a druggist's right to charge what the traffic will bear?

Interviewers using Kohlberg's standardized scoring manual ran into trouble trying to classify such responses as the following:

The medicine should be made available to all in need; the druggist should not have the right to decide on his own. . . . The whole community or society should have control of the drug.

I believe everyone has the right . . . to reach happiness. . . . People are not born equal genetically and it is not fair that one who is stronger physically should reach his happiness by whatever means at the expense of one who is weaker because the right to happiness is a basic human right of everyone, equal to all. (Snarey, 1985, p. 222)

These responses were coupled with statements about the importance of obeying the law and thus were confusing to the interviewers, who estimated them as fitting in with conventional stage 4 reasoning or as being in transition between stages 4 and 5. However, from the perspective of an Israeli

kibbutz, such responses may represent a postconventional moral principle missing from Kohlberg's description of stage 5. If membership in a kibbutz is viewed as a commitment to certain social values, including cooperation and an equal right to happiness for all members of a society, then concern about upholding the system may function not merely for its own sake, but to protect those principles (Snarey, 1985).

INDIA

When asked whether Heinz should steal a drug to save his pet's life (instead of his wife's), a 50-year-old Indian found such an action commendable because it recognized the oneness of all life (Vasudev, 1983, pp. 7–8). This principle, characteristic of Indian philosophical, spiritual, and religious thought, was missing from Kohlberg's system until his preliminary exploration of stage 7.

When Kohlberg's dilemmas were tested in India, participants displayed all of Kohlberg's modes of moral reasoning, but not all Indian modes of moral reasoning were reflected in Kohlberg's scheme (Snarey, 1985). Thus, Buddhist monks from Ladakh, a Tibetan enclave in India, scored lower than laypeople. Apparently Kohlberg's model, while capturing the preconventional and conventional elements of Buddhist thinking, was inadequate for understanding postconventional Buddhist principles of cooperation and nonviolence (Gielen & Kelly, 1983). Kohlberg's scoring methods also broke down when Indian participants responded to probing questions by telling stories from which the listener was supposed to draw a lesson—a common form of moral discourse in that country

(Shweder, personal communication, 1984, as cited in Snarey, 1985).

CHINA

The dilemma of Heinz, who could not afford a drug for his sick wife, was revised for use in Taiwan. In the revision, a shopkeeper will not give a man food for his sick wife.

This version would seem unbelievable to Chinese villagers, who in real life are more accustomed to hearing a shopkeeper in such a situation say, "You have to let people have things whether they have money or not" (Wolf, 1968, p. 21).

Other cultural differences are involved as well (Dien, 1982). In Kohlberg's format, respondents make an either-or decision based on their own value systems. In Chinese society, people faced with such a dilemma discuss it openly, are guided by community standards, and try to find a way of resolving the problem to please as many parties as possible. The Chinese view is that human beings are born with moral tendencies whose development has to do with intuitive, spontaneous feelings supported by society, rather than with analytical thinking, individual choice, or personal responsibility. In the west, even good people may be harshly punished if, under the force of circumstances, they break a law. The Chinese are unaccustomed to universally applied laws; they prefer to abide by the sound decisions of a wise judge. Whereas Kohlberg's philosophy is based on justice, the Chinese ethos leans toward conciliation and harmony.

How, then, can Kohlberg's theory, rooted in western values and reflecting western ideals, be applied to moral development in a society that works along very different lines?

According to Fowler, faith develops—as do other aspects of cognition—through interaction between the maturing person and the environment. As in other stage theories, Fowler's stages of faith progress in an unvarying sequence, each building on those which went before. New experiences—crises, problems, or revelations—that challenge or upset a person's equilibrium may prompt a leap from one stage to the next. The ages at which these transitions occur are variable, and some people never leave a particular stage. However, Fowler proposed that his sequence of stages is generalizable and can be tested across cultures.

The beginnings of faith, he said, come at about 18 to 24 months of age, after children become self-aware, begin to use language and symbolic thought, and have developed what Erikson called *basic trust:* the sense that their needs will be met by powerful others. "Pre-images" of God, formed during infancy and toddlerhood through interactions with parents, lay the foundation for the stages that follow. These stages roughly correspond to those described by Piaget, Kohlberg, and Erikson and to the "eras" of adult psychosocial development described by Daniel Levinson (see Chapter 13).

Stage 1: ***Intuitive-projective faith*** *(ages 18–24 months to 7 years).* As young children struggle to understand the forces that control their world, they form powerful, imaginative, often terrifying, and sometimes lasting images of God, heaven, and hell. These images—drawn from the stories adults read to them—are often irrational, since preoperational children tend to be confused about cause and effect and may have trouble distinguishing between reality and fantasy. Still egocentric, they have difficulty distinguishing God's point of view from their own or their parents'. They think of God mainly in terms of obedience and punishment.

Stage 2: ***Mythic-literal faith*** *(ages 7 to 12 years).* Children are now more logical; through their fascination with stories and myths, they begin to develop a more coherent view of the universe. Not yet capable of abstract thought, they tend to take religious stories and symbols literally, as they adopt their family's and community's beliefs and observances. They can now see God as having a perspective beyond their own, which takes into account people's effort and intent. They believe that God is fair and that people get what they deserve.

Stage 3: ***Synthetic-conventional faith*** *(adolescence or beyond).* Adolescents, now capable of abstract thought, begin to form ideologies (belief systems) and commitments to ideals. As they search for identity, they seek a more personal relationship with God. However, their identity is not yet on firm ground; they look to others (usually peers) for moral authority. Their faith is unquestioning and conforms to community standards. This stage is typical of followers of organized religion; about 50 percent of adults may never move beyond it.

Stage 4: ***Individuative-reflective faith*** *(early to middle twenties or beyond).* Adults who reach this postconventional stage examine their faith critically and think out their own beliefs, independent of external authority and group norms. Since young adults are deeply concerned with intimacy, movement into this stage is often triggered by divorce, the death of a friend, or some other stressful event.

Stage 5: ***Conjunctive faith*** *(midlife or beyond).* Middle-aged people become more aware of the limits of reason. They recognize life's paradoxes and contradictions, and they often struggle with conflicts between fulfilling their own needs and sacrificing for others. As they begin to anticipate death, they may achieve a deeper understanding and acceptance by integrating into their faith aspects of their earlier beliefs.

Stage 6: ***Universalizing faith*** *(late life).* In this rare, ultimate category Fowler placed such moral and spiritual leaders as Mahatma Gandhi, Martin Luther King, and Mother Teresa, whose breadth of vision and commitment to the well-being of all humanity profoundly inspire others. Consumed with a sense of "participation in a power that unifies and transforms the world," they seem "more lucid, more simple, and yet somehow more fully human than the rest of us" (J. Fowler, 1981, p. 201). Because they threaten the established order, they often become martyrs; and though they love life, they do not cling to it. This stage parallels Kohlberg's proposed seventh stage of moral development.

As one of the first researchers to systematically study how faith develops. Fowler has had great impact; his work has become required reading in many divinity schools. It also has been criticized on several counts (Koenig, 1994).

First, critics say, Fowler's concept of faith is at odds with conventional definitions, which involve acceptance, not introspection. They challenge his emphasis on cognitive knowledge and claim that he underestimates the maturity of a simple, solid, unquestioning faith (Koenig, 1994). Second, critics question whether faith develops in universal stages—at least in those Fowler identified. Fowler himself has cautioned that his advanced stages should not be seen as better or truer than others, though he does portray people at his highest stage as moral and spiritual exemplars.

There are methodological problems. Fowler's sample was not randomly selected; it consisted of paid volunteers who lived in or near North American cities with major colleges or universities. Thus the findings may be more representative of people with above-average intelligence and education (Koenig, 1994) and may not apply to people in rural areas or nonwestern cultures. Also, the initial sample included few people over age 60. To remedy this weakness, Richard N. Shulik (1988) interviewed 40 older adults and found a strong relationship between their stages of faith and their Kohlbergian levels of moral development. However, he also found that older people at intermediate levels of faith development were less likely to be depressed than older people at higher or lower stages; perhaps those with more advanced cognition were more aware of changes associated with aging. Thus Fowler's theory may overlook the adaptive value of conventional religious belief for many older adults (Koenig, 1994; see Box 17-1).

Some of these criticisms resemble those made against other models of life-span development. Piaget's, Kohlberg's, and Erikson's initial samples were not randomly selected either. More and wider research is needed to support, modify, or extend Fowler's theory.

GILLIGAN'S THEORY: WOMEN'S MORAL DEVELOPMENT

Since Kohlberg's original studies were done on boys and men, Carol Gilligan (1982, 1987a, b) has argued that his system gives a higher place to "masculine" values (justice and fairness) than to "feminine" values (compassion, responsibility, and caring). According to Gilligan, a woman's central moral dilemma is the conflict between her own needs and those of others. Although most societies typically expect assertiveness and independent judgment from men, they expect from women self-sacrifice and concern for others.

To find out how women make moral choices, Gilligan (1982) interviewed 29 pregnant women about their decisions to continue or end their pregnancies. These women saw morality in terms of selfishness versus responsibility, defined as an obligation to exercise care and to avoid hurting others. Gilligan concluded that women think less about abstract justice and fairness than men do and more about their responsibilities to specific people. (Table 12-4 lists Gilligan's proposed levels of moral development in women.)

Does other research bear out gender differences in moral reasoning? Some studies based on Kohlberg's dilemmas have shown differences in the levels achieved by men and women—differences that consistently favored men. However, a large-scale analysis comparing results from many studies found no significant differences in men's and women's responses to Kohlberg's dilemmas across the life span (L. J. Walker, 1984). In the few studies in which men scored slightly higher, the

The psychologist Carol Gilligan studied moral development in women and concluded that they are more concerned about responsibilities to others than about abstract justice. Her later research suggests that for *both* women and men, concern for others is at the highest level of moral thought. *(Richard E. Schultz)*

findings were not clearly gender-related, since the men generally were better-educated and had better jobs than the women. A more recent study of male and female college and university students found no evidence that men's thinking is more principled and women's more relationship-oriented (Orr & Luszcz, 1994). Thus the weight of evidence does not appear to back up either of Gilligan's original contentions: a male bias in Kohlberg's theory or a distinct female perspective on morality.

In her own later research, Gilligan has described moral development in *both* men and women as evolving beyond abstract reasoning. In studies using real-life moral dilemmas (rather than hypothetical ones, as Kohlberg did), Gilligan and her colleagues found that many people in their twenties become dissatisfied with the limitations of a narrow moral logic and become more able to live with moral contradictions, such as not telling a truth that may hurt someone (Gilligan, Murphy, & Tappan, 1990). It seems, then, that if the "different voice" in Gilligan's earlier research reflected an alternative value system, it was not gender-based. At the same time, with the inclusion of his seventh stage, Kohlberg's theory has evolved to a point of greater agreement with Gilligan's. Both theories now place responsibility to others at the highest

TABLE 12-4

Gilligan's Levels of Moral Development in Women

Stage	Description
Level 1: Orientation of individual survival	The woman concentrates on herself—on what is practical and what is best for her.
Transition 1: From selfishness to responsibility	The woman realizes her connection to others and thinks about what the responsible choice would be in terms of other people (including her unborn baby), as well as herself.
Level 2: Goodness as self-sacrifice	This conventional feminine wisdom dictates sacrificing the woman's own wishes to what other people want—and will think of her. She considers herself responsible for the actions of others, while holding others responsible for her own choices. She is in a dependent position, one in which her indirect efforts to exert control often turn into manipulation, sometimes through the use of guilt.
Transition 2: From goodness to truth	The woman assesses her decisions not on the basis of how others will react to them but on her intentions and the consequences of her actions. She develops a new judgment that takes into account her own needs, along with those of others. She wants to be "good" by being responsible to others, but also wants to be "honest" by being responsible to herself. Survival returns as a major concern.
Level 3: Morality of nonviolence	By elevating the injunction against hurting anyone (including herself) to a principle that governs all moral judgment and action, the woman establishes a "moral equality" between herself and others and is then able to assume the responsibility for choice in moral dilemmas.

SOURCE: Based on Gilligan, 1982.

level of moral thought. Both recognize the importance for both sexes of connections with other people and of compassion and care.

✔ EDUCATION

Education after high school can mean anything from a basic literacy program to a 2-year community college stressing vocational training to a large university with graduate divisions.

ADULT LITERACY

Ed is a 29-year-old silk-screen printer, a trade he learned in high school. Because he's quick-witted, personable, and determined, his employers and coworkers do not realize, at first, that he cannot read beyond a fourth or fifth grade level. "I've lost lots of jobs because of my reading problem," he says (R. D. Feldman, 1985).

Ed is one of an estimated 40 to 44 million adults in the United States who are functionally illiter-

ate—who cannot read, write, or do arithmetic well enough to handle many everyday tasks. Another 50 million are only marginally literate (Kirsch, Jenkins, Jungeblut, & Kolstad, 1993). The estimates come from the National Adult Literacy Survey, which was given to more than 26,000 people age 16 or older in 1992. Participants were rated on their ability to do such tasks as finding information in a newspaper article and filling out a bank deposit slip. More than 20 percent showed limited skills. More than 40 percent at the lowest level of skills were poor, 25 percent were immigrants, 62 percent had not completed high school, and 19 percent had visual problems. Adults over 65 did worse than other age groups, and young adults did worse than in a 1985 survey (Kirsch et al., 1993).

Literacy is a fundamental requisite for participation in a modern, information-driven society. According to Madeleine M. Kunin, deputy secretary of education, "We simply are not keeping pace with the kinds of skills required in today's economy" (Ludmer-Gliebe, 1994, p. 19). At the turn of the century, a fourth grade education was considered enough to be literate; today, a high school diploma is barely adequate. Even a college degree does not guarantee a high level of literacy: about half of college graduates can't decipher a bus schedule, and only 13 percent can do math problems involving several steps (Barton & Lapointe, 1995).

Globally, illiteracy is more common among women than among men, largely because in many cultures education is not considered important for girls and women. In 1985, an estimated 889 million adults throughout the world—1 in 4—were illiterate, and nearly two-thirds of them were women. More than 50 percent of adult Africans are illiterate, as compared with 36 percent of Asians and only 17 percent of Latin Americans (Sticht & McDonald, 1990; United Nations Educational, Scientific, and Cultural Organization, UNESCO, 1989).

In 1990, the United Nations launched literacy programs in such places as Bangladesh, Nepal, and Somalia (Linder, 1990). In 1991 the United States Congress passed the National Literacy Act, which requires the states to establish literacy centers with federal funding assistance.

HIGHER EDUCATION

Today's college students are a diverse group. Of the 14.3 million students enrolled in colleges and universities in the United States, about 8.7 million go to 4-year colleges and 5.6 million to 2-year community colleges. About 23 percent are from minority groups, and about 40 percent are age 25 and over (NCES, 1995b). White people age 25 and over are nearly twice as likely as African Americans in that age group to have completed college: 24 percent versus 13.2 percent (Day & Curry, 1996). Despite the availability of financial aid, family income still makes a big difference: only 44 percent of unmarried high school graduates of traditional age from families making less than $20,000 a year go to college, compared with almost 80 percent from families earning more than $60,000. This gap has changed little since 1970 (Mortenson, 1992). The most popular undergraduate majors are business administration and management, psychology (which has shown a dramatic increase), engineering, education, English literature, and accounting, in that order (Murray, 1996).

Women in College

In the 1970s, women were less likely than men to go to college and less likely to finish. Today, 55 percent of college and university enrollees, more than half of the recipients of bachelor's and master's degrees, and about 38 percent of those who earn doctoral and professional degrees are women (NCES, 1995b). Most colleges and universities now are coeducational, though a few are still all-male or all-female. However, women still tend to be concentrated in traditionally "feminine" fields: the great majority of engineering, architecture, and physical science students are male, whereas most students in home economics, education, and foreign languages are female (NCES, 1995b).

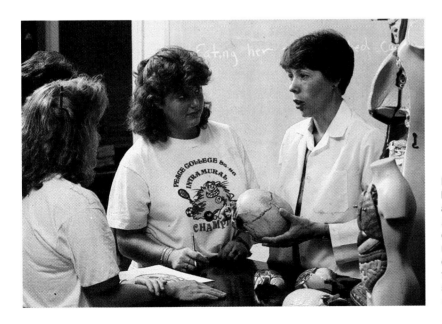

In the 1970s, high school girls were less likely than boys to go to college and less likely to finish. Today girls are *more* likely than boys to pursue higher education. Female college students may develop more interest and confidence in studying anatomy when taught by a female instructor who serves as a role model. *(Charles Gupton/Stock, Boston)*

Some observers attribute such differences to lingering sexism—textbooks showing women in stereotyped occupations, parents and counselors who urge girls to prepare for "women's work," and disproportionately male professors who treat male and female students differently. American society gives teenage girls and young women messages that emphasize the roles of wife and mother and stress the often-real difficulties of combining personal achievement with love and family. Young men are given no reason to believe that their roles as future husbands and fathers might interfere with developing their career potential.

These may be among the reasons that explain why even highly gifted girls are at risk of underachievement, particularly in math and science (McCormick & Wolf, 1993), why they have tended to go to less selective colleges than men and have been less likely to go on to prestigious graduate schools and high-status occupations (Kerr, 1985), and why many of those who did go to graduate school ended up in careers that did not make the most of their talents (Reis, 1995). Although these patterns are changing, they have not been eradicated. In one study, 126 gifted women who had been enrolled in a career development program in high school were surveyed at ages 27 to 29. Although their attainments compared favorably with those of earlier cohorts of gifted women, one-third to one-half had yet to achieve their original educational and occupational aspirations (Hollinger & Fleming, 1992).

Dropping Out of College

College dropouts may take time off before resuming studies or end their studies altogether. Those in the latter category severely limit their vocational opportunities.

There is no "typical" college dropout. Students leave school for many reasons—marriage, the desire to be close to a loved one, a change in occupational status, or dissatisfaction with the school. Although most dropouts have lower average aptitude scores than those who stay in school, their work is usually satisfactory.

African American students are much more likely to drop out than other students. It has been suggested that this is because of the stress of coping with minority status, inadequate preparation, or self-fulfilling racial stereotypes, which can damage self-esteem. One study found that *stereotype threat*—fear of fulfilling racial stereotypes—can

have a dramatic impact on black students' performance. Those who were told that a test was intended to determine their intellectual ability performed much more poorly than those who were simply told that the test was a problem-solving task (Steele & Aronson, 1995). However, in a study of 301 high-risk students, coping resources were less predictive of who would drop out than were such factors as an expressed intent to leave, employment status, financial support, living arrangements, and the amount of encouragement a student received to pursue higher education (Ryland, Riordan, & Brack, 1994). In a survey of 46 African Americans who dropped out of a large, predominantly white midwestern university, the primary reason was academic failure, followed by financial problems, an uncomfortable social environment, and a desire for full-time work experience (Sailes, 1993). Among 679 minority students who were underprepared for college, tutoring resulted in lower attrition rates (J. D. House & Wohlt, 1991).

Leaving college temporarily can be a positive step. Some students gain by working for a while, enrolling at a more compatible institution, or just allowing themselves time to mature. Many colleges make it easy for students to take leaves of absence or to earn credit for independent study, life experience, and work done at other institutions. Some colleges actively seek students who have dropped out, even for many years.

Education, formal or otherwise, need not—and often does not—end in the early twenties. It can continue throughout adulthood, as we'll see in Chapters 14 and 16.

✔ ENTERING THE WORLD OF WORK

Finding the first adult job can be an exciting challenge, but it also can be a source of frustration. Job opportunities in some sectors of the United States economy are shrinking. For the first time, during the 1980s, there were more people in executive, professional, and technical jobs (nearly 1 out of 3 workers) than in manufacture or transport of goods (1 in 5). The number of white-collar jobs jumped 38 percent from 1980 to 1990, while the number of skilled blue-collar jobs declined. Only 4 percent of the work force held unskilled jobs (U.S. Bureau of the Census, 1990). One result was a sharp decline in job opportunities and wages for less educated workers (L. Eisenberg, 1995).

During the 1990s, technology and global com-

BOX 12-3   PRACTICALLY SPEAKING

DEALING WITH UNDEREMPLOYMENT

When Judd received his Ph.D. in literature from an elite eastern university, he applied for a teaching job but couldn't land one. He ended up selling washing machines at Sears. Renata has an M.B.A. (master's degree in business administration) from a medium-ranked state university and couldn't get an interview at a major corporation. She is now waiting tables in a restaurant. Judd and Renata are two of the growing army of college graduates who are dealing with *underemployment.* People who are underemployed have preparation or skills beyond the normal requirements of their jobs, or feel that their abilities are not fully utilized, or are doing work unrelated to their training and goals (Forteza & Prieto, 1994; Khan & Morrow, 1991).

In 1990, according to the Bureau of Labor Statistics, 18 percent of college graduates in the labor force were in jobs not requiring college degrees, nearly twice as many as in 1969 ("A Waste of Talent," 1993). Much of the reason lies in a weak job market. Then, there is a mismatch between the number of young people who prepare for particular careers and the shifting demand for workers in those fields. For example, in 1992 about 16 percent of people graduating with bachelor's degrees in journalism failed to find jobs, nearly twice as many as in 1988. This phenomenon was very likely related to the increasing number of newspapers and magazines that have folded, merged, or downsized. As demand for entry-level workers shrinks,

employers often insist on higher credentials (such as a master's degree) for work that formerly required only a bachelor's degree.

Underemployment also occurs when longtime employees are laid off. Highly educated managerial and technical personnel often fail to find replacement positions comparable to their previous ones and are forced to take lower-paying, lower-skilled jobs to support their families (McClenahen, 1993). However, not all underemployed people are college-educated; a carpenter working as a ditch digger would meet the criteria. Nevertheless, most of the research on underemployment has been done on college graduates.

A survey of 256 nonacademic university employees suggests that defining and measuring underemployment may not be as simple as it seems. Reassigning employees who felt overqualified for their jobs to positions requiring more education did not eliminate their dissatisfaction. Thus, underemployment may be based more on subjective perceptions, such as a sense of being in a dead-end job, than on objective factors, such as educational background relative to the demands of the work. If so, underemployment might be reduced by giving employees opportunities to learn and grow in their jobs (Khan & Morrow, 1991). College graduates are often more productive than less educated workers, even in slots not traditionally filled by degree holders. If employers upgrade job descriptions to better utilize their employees' education

and skills, underemployment may become less of a problem (Alsalam, 1993).

Former U.S. Secretary of Labor Robert Reich (quoted in Brazaitis, 1996) has these insights and advice for teenagers and young adults facing a crowded, competitive job market:

- In today's changing economy, predictable career paths have disappeared. Large corporations no longer "finger" promising college graduates and move them immediately into executive training programs. Graduates—even those with advanced degrees—must find their own way through ingenuity, networking, and entrepreneurial skills.
- Increasingly, experience will count for more than degrees. College graduates should expect to spend 3 to 5 years in jobs they may feel overqualified for but actually are not, since they haven't handled "real responsibility." Eventually, if they perform well, they will get a chance to move up to a better job.
- The line between formal education and on-the-job training will become blurred as people take time off before or during college for internships or work experience.
- Young people who are not college-bound can take community college courses to equip them for highly skilled technical jobs that employers have trouble filling.

petition have produced corporate downsizing and falling wages (Kuttner, 1994). Most of the new jobs being created are either low-paid retail or service jobs; others require skills that large numbers of

prospective workers do not have. At the same time, many people just out of college are forced to take jobs for which they feel overqualified (see Box 12-3). In the future, less work (only 20 percent, ac-

Justice Leah J. Sears was appointed to the Georgia Supreme Court in 1992, the first African American woman to serve on the court. Vocational opportunities for women and minorities have greatly expanded but, overall, are not yet equal to opportunities for white men. *(Frank Niemeir/The Atlanta Constitution)*

cording to one knowledgeable prediction) will be done by full-time salaried employees and more by outside contractors, specialized consultants, and part-time or temporary help. More and more adults will be self-employed, working at home, or spreading their services among several employers (Handy, 1991).

Laws mandating equal opportunity in employment are designed to give people equal rights in hiring, pay, and promotion, regardless of gender or ethnicity; but reality still falls short of this ideal. Women and minorities are more likely to be unemployed and are likely to be paid less than white males. Between now and the year 2000, five-sixths of the net additions to the labor force (people who are working full or part time or who are actively looking for work) will be nonwhites, women, and immigrants (W. B. Johnston & Packer, 1987; Wharton, 1993). Will there be enough good jobs for them?

Let's look at how ethnicity and gender affect work opportunities and how young adults differ from older ones in attitudes toward work and job performance. In later chapters we'll discuss other work-related issues, including work-family conflicts, occupational stress, unemployment, career changes, and preparation for retirement.

WORK AND ETHNICITY

Despite great strides in education of African Americans since 1940, their employment rates and wages have fallen in comparison with those of white people. About 80 percent of young adults of both races have finished high school, and differences in standardized test scores have narrowed; but more white people still go to college and qualify for better-paying jobs. The shrinkage of well-paid manufacturing jobs and the shift to lower-paid service positions has been particularly disastrous for young African American men (J. Bernstein, 1995); 46 percent of them held good blue-collar jobs in 1974, but only half as many did by 1986 (L. Eisenberg, 1995). Unemployment is epidemic among black urban youth who have dropped out of school—higher than during the great depression of the 1930s. Nationally, unemployment for African Americans ages 16 to 19 has reached 38 percent (U.S. Department of Labor, 1996b). Many more are not counted as unemployed because they have dropped out of the system; they are not even trying to find jobs and probably never will.

The wage difference between white people and African Americans with high school diplomas has widened from $2,200 a year in 1979 to more than $4,300 in 1995 (U.S. Department of Labor, 1996c). The gap is even wider for male college graduates (J. Bernstein, 1995). The median salary of American-born black professionals is only a little more than $26,000. Only 2 percent of African American professionals earn more than $100,000, compared with 44 percent of white, 41 percent of Asian, and 13 percent of Hispanic professionals (Bouvier & Simcox, 1994). Black professional men earn only 79 percent, and black professional women only 60 percent, of what white men in similar positions earn (Federal Glass Ceiling Commission, 1995).

WORK AND GENDER

Like men, women work to earn money, to achieve recognition, and to fulfill personal needs. The increase in women's employment is a global phenomenon (see Figure 12-4). A longer life span means that women no longer spend most or all of their adult lives raising children (L. Eisenberg, 1995). Worldwide, 40 percent of women are involved in remunerative work (United Nations, 1991), and the proportion is expected to reach 60

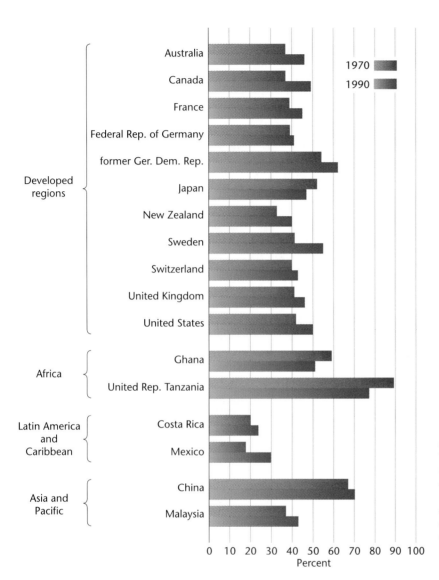

FIGURE 12-4
Economic activity rates of women in selected countries, 1970 and 1990. Women's participation in the work force has increased in developed regions, except for Japan. The dramatic increase in Mexico is due to greater opportunities for employment. The decline in Africa is due to poor economic growth. *(Source: United Nations, 1991, table 8, reprinted in O'Grady-LeShane, 1993, p. 28.)*

percent by the year 2000 (Nuss, Denti, & Viry, 1989). Trends toward later marriage, later childbearing, and smaller families, as well as flexible schedules and job sharing, have made it easier for women in some countries to pursue occupational goals. However, especially during the child-rearing years, women the world over tend to work in part-time or low-status clerical and service jobs, where they earn less than men (Bruce et al., 1995; O'Grady-LeShane, 1993; United Nations, 1991).

In the United States, more women are in the labor force than ever before: about 59 percent in 1994, including more than 70 percent of 20- to 54-year-olds (Schick & Schick, 1994), 66 percent of mothers of children under age 18, and about 58 percent of mothers with children under 6 (H. Hayghe of the U.S. Department of Labor, personal communication, March 1992). According to the U.S. Department of Labor (1994), 99 percent of women will work for pay sometime during their lives. In addition, most mothers continue to be primary caregivers for their children.

Women's occupational choices are far more varied than in the past. Women now hold about half of all managerial, executive, and professional positions (U.S. Department of Labor, 1995). Today, 50 percent of accountants, 34 percent of journalists, and 24 percent of doctors—though only 15 percent of scientists, mathematicians, and engineers—are women. The number of female psychologists grew

4 times as fast as the number of male psychologists between 1973 and 1991 ("Report Explains," 1995; U.S. Department of Labor, 1992). However, the top echelons of business, government, and the professions are still male-dominated, and many younger women at middle levels complain of a "glass ceiling" (Federal Glass Ceiling Commission, 1995). Women now constitute 23 percent of the legal profession—up from 3 percent in 1971—and 44 percent of first-year law students. Yet an American Bar Association panel found that they still face barriers to high earnings and advancement ("Women in Legal Profession," 1996).

Women's relative earnings have improved somewhat: more women have moved into traditionally male fields, and men's earnings have dropped with the disappearance of many highly paid manufacturing jobs. Still, for every dollar men earn, women in the United States who work full time earn only 76.4 cents (U.S. Department of Labor, 1995), and in some Latin American and Caribbean countries, as little as 50 cents (Lim, 1996). Women in the United States earn less than men even in jobs that are traditionally "women's work," such as nursing, teaching, cashiering, and general office work; and 36 percent of families headed by women live in poverty (U.S. Department of Labor, 1995). In high executive positions, the gap between women's earnings and those of their male counterparts has widened during the past decade, from 21 to 35 percent (C. Scott, 1993). However, the differential has narrowed for college-educated women as a whole; their earnings (adjusted for inflation) have risen 15 percent since 1979, while college-educated men's real earnings declined 3 percent (Mishel & Bernstein, 1994).

Despite some progress, then, women and minorities have yet to achieve equal opportunity in the workplace.

WORK AND AGE

Does age affect how people feel about their work and how they perform on the job? Overall, workers under age 40 tend to be less satisfied than older workers (Salthouse & Maurer, 1996). They are less involved with their work, less committed to their employers, less highly paid, and more likely to change jobs. Young adults may have higher goals and expectations and may look at their jobs more critically, since they are still establishing careers, are generally more attractive to employers, and can change companies or career directions more

easily than can older workers. It's also possible that younger employees tend to have more unpleasant, stressful work or that older employees are more likely to have already left a job they didn't like (Forteza & Prieto, 1994; Rhodes, 1983; Warr, 1994).

Again, we have to be careful about differences that show up in cross-sectional studies. For example, older people's commitment to the "work ethic"—the idea that hard work develops character—may be a cohort effect; it may reflect a generational difference, not the length of time someone has lived (Warr, 1994). There may be more of a developmental difference in the relative importance of specific aspects of work. Younger workers tend to be more satisfied if they receive recognition and get along well with supervisors and colleagues, whereas older workers are more concerned about pay and the type of work they do (Forteza & Prieto, 1994).

In general, absenteeism declines with age (Salthouse & Maurer, 1996). It is highest during the late teens, when jobs are usually menial and relatively unimportant in people's lives. Women have higher absentee rates than men, particularly during the child-raising years and beyond (Klein, 1986, cited in Rhodes & Steers, 1990). Analyses of large numbers of studies found that younger men (but not women) have more *avoidable* absences than older ones, possibly because of a lower level of commitment. Although older workers are widely believed to have longer *unavoidable* absences (because of poorer health and slower recovery rates), this has not proved to be so (Hackett, 1990; Martocchio, 1989). Absenteeism tends to drop sharply during economic recessions, when workers with high absence rates are likely to be the first laid off (Rhodes & Steers, 1990).

When we look at how well people do their work, findings are mixed. In general, performance improves with age, at least until midlife; and some workers, depending in part on the type of work they do, continue to increase their productivity late in life. Even manual laborers lose only 8 to 10 percent of their efficiency between ages 40 and 65 (Forteza & Prieto, 1994). A key factor may be experience rather than age: when older people perform better, it may be because they have been on a job or have done similar work longer (Warr, 1994); and people in older cohorts may have changed jobs less than younger people.

Older workers do tend to be more dependable, careful, responsible, and frugal with time and materials than younger workers; and their suggestions are more likely to be accepted. However, age differences may depend on how performance is measured and on the demands of a specific kind of work. A job requiring quick responses is likely to be done better by a young person; a job that depends on precision, a steady pace, and mature judgment may be better-handled by an older person (Forteza & Prieto, 1994; Warr, 1994).

Work affects day-to-day life, not only on the job but at home, and it brings both satisfaction and stress. In Chapter 13, we'll explore the effects of work on relationships as we look at psychosocial development of young adults.

✔ SUMMARY

ASPECTS OF PHYSICAL DEVELOPMENT

■ The typical young adult is in good condition; physical and sensory abilities are usually excellent. More than 93 percent of 15- to 44-year-olds rate their health as good, very good, or excellent.

■ AIDS is the leading cause of death for 25- to 44-year-olds, followed by accidents, cancer, heart disease, suicide, and homicide.

■ Health is a state of physical, mental, and social well-being, not just the absence of illness or impairment. Behavior patterns such as diet, exercise, smoking, and drinking alcohol can affect health.

■ Good health is related to higher income and education. Members of some minority groups tend to be less healthy than white people.

■ Women are usually more likely than men to report being ill, to use health services, and to be hospitalized. Men's illnesses tend to be more serious. Women tend to live longer than men, in part for biological reasons, but perhaps also because they are more health-conscious.

■ Hormones of the menstrual cycle have protective effects but also can cause health problems. Disorders related to menstruation include premenstrual syndrome (PMS), its more severe form, premenstrual dysphoric disorder (PMDD), and endometriosis.

ADULT COGNITION

■ New experiences may evoke new, distinctively adult thinking patterns, as young adults question long-held assumptions and values. College students tend to develop from rigid to relativist thinking, sometimes called *postformal thought.*

■ Robert Sternberg has proposed three aspects of intelligence: componential (analytic), experiential (insightful), and contextual (practical). The experiential and contextual aspects become particularly important during adulthood. Tests that measure tacit knowledge, an aspect of practical intelligence, are useful complements to traditional intelligence tests in predicting job performance.

■ Emotional intelligence includes self-understanding, understanding of others, and the ability to regulate feelings. These abilities may play an important part in life success.

MORAL DEVELOPMENT

■ According to Lawrence Kohlberg, moral development in adulthood depends primarily on experience, though it cannot exceed the limits set by cognitive development. However, experience may be interpreted differently in various cultural contexts.

■ Kohlberg, shortly before his death, proposed a seventh stage of moral development, which involves seeing moral issues from a cosmic perspective. This is similar to the highest stage of faith, the universalizing stage, proposed by James Fowler.

■ Carol Gilligan proposed that women have moral concerns and perspectives that are not tapped in Kohlberg's theory and research. However, research has not generally supported a distinction between men's and women's moral outlook.

■ More recently, Gilligan has proposed that caring, compassion, and the ability to live with moral contradictions are characteristic of advanced moral thinking in both sexes.

EDUCATION

■ Adults who lack basic literacy skills are at a severe disadvantage in a modern economy. In the United States, literacy levels are not keeping pace with societal change. Worldwide, illiteracy is more common among women than among men.

■ College enrollment is more diverse than in the past and includes more women and minorities and more students of nontraditional age.

■ Although more women now are going to college and are earning advanced degrees, the fields that men and women choose still differ markedly.

■ The high dropout rate among black college students has been attributed to a variety of causes, including the stress of coping with minority status, inadequate preparation, stereotype threat, academic failure, financial problems, discomfort with the social environment, and a need or desire to work.

■ Some students benefit from dropping out temporarily to gain life experience and then returning to complete their course work.

ENTERING THE WORLD OF WORK

■ Occupational development is important during young adulthood. Downsizing, technological change, and other trends are producing underemployment and unemployment. The changing workplace poses special challenges for African Americans, whose employment and earnings rates have worsened in relation to those of white people.

■ Women tend to earn less than men, and although more women are getting better jobs than in previous decades, most are still doing low-paid work. An increasing number of women are pursuing careers in traditionally male-dominated fields.

■ Younger workers tend to be less committed to their present jobs than older workers. In general, job performance improves with age and experience; however, younger workers may do better in work requiring quick responses.

✔ KEY TERMS

cholesterol (page 402)
premenstrual syndrome (PMS) (411)
premenstrual dysphoric disorder (PMDD) (411)
endometriosis (411)
postformal thought (412)

componential element (413)
experiential element (413)
contextual element (413)
tacit knowledge (414)
emotional intelligence (417)
intuitive-projective faith (420)
mythic-literal faith (420)

synthetic-conventional faith (420)
individuative-reflective faith (420)
conjunctive faith (420)
universalizing faith (420)
stereotype threat (424)
underemployment (425)

✔ QUESTIONS FOR THOUGHT AND DISCUSSION

1 What specific things could you do to have a healthier lifestyle?

2 From your observation, does college students' thinking typically seem to follow the stages Perry outlined?

3 In what kinds of situations would postformal thought be most useful? Give specific examples.

4 Who is the most intelligent person you know? Would you ask this person for advice about a personal problem? Why or why not?

5 Which do you consider to be higher moral priorities: justice and fairness, or compassion and care?

6 In your opinion, is faith in a divine being required in order to live a moral life?

7 If you were competing for a job, would you rather compete against someone your own age or someone younger or older than you? Would the type of job affect your answer?

CHAPTER THIRTEEN

PSYCHOSOCIAL DEVELOPMENT IN YOUNG ADULTHOOD

In most of us, by the age of thirty, the character has set like plaster, and will never soften again.

William James,
The Principles of Psychology, *1890*

Human beings are not born once and for all on the day their mothers give birth to them. . . . Life obliges them over and over again to give birth to themselves.

Gabriel García Márquez,
Love in the Time of Cholera, *1988*

✔ Does personality change during adulthood? If so, does it develop in definite, predictable patterns, or does the course of development depend on what happens in people's lives?

✔ What are some similarities and differences between young men's and young women's personality development?

✔ How do young adults get along with their parents?

✔ What do friendship, sexuality, and love have in common, and how do they differ?

✔ Why do some people prefer to remain single?

✔ How likely is a marriage to end in divorce? Are people who cohabit before marriage more likely to divorce than those who don't?

✔ Why do people choose to have children? to remain childless?

D oes personality stop growing when the body does, or does it keep developing throughout life? The two quotations at the beginning of this chapter represent the extremes of this debate. Some developmentalists maintain that personality is virtually "set like plaster" by the middle of young adulthood; others see adults as periodically "giving birth" to themselves as long as they live.

■ In this chapter, we look at theories and research on adult personality—how and how much it changes during young adulthood—and at the effects of cultural attitudes and social change. We also examine issues that frame personal and social life beginning in young adulthood, issues that revolve around core choices: adopting a sexual lifestyle; marrying, cohabiting, or remaining single; having children or not; and establishing and maintaining friendships. ■

✔ PERSONALITY DEVELOPMENT: FOUR MODELS

Four major approaches to adult personality development are represented by trait models, normative-crisis models, the timing-of-events model, and humanistic models. *Trait models* focus on mental, emotional, temperamental, and behavioral traits, or attributes, which influence behavior. Trait-based studies find that adult personality changes very little. *Normative-crisis models* portray a typical sequence of age-related development that continues throughout the adult life span, much as in childhood and adolescence. Normative-crisis research

has found major, predictable changes in adult personality. The *timing-of-events model* emphasizes individual and contextual differences. Researchers who take this approach find that change is related not so much to age as to the varied circumstances and events of life. *Humanistic models* emphasize adults' control of their own development. In these models, change is related neither to age nor, primarily, to external events, but to progress in realizing a person's potential.

TRAIT MODELS: COSTA AND MCCRAE'S FIVE FACTORS

Are you cheerful? Are you easily irritated? Are you persistent? Cheerfulness, irritability, and persistence are personality traits related to temperament. Longitudinal studies find that bubbly junior high schoolers grow up to be cheerful 40-year-olds, complaining adolescents turn into querulous adults, assertive 20-year-olds become outspoken 30-year-olds, and people who cope well with the problems of youth are equally able to handle the problems of later life (Block, 1981; Costa & McCrae, 1980; Eichorn, Clausen, Haan, Honzik, & Mussen, 1981).

Paul T. Costa and Robert R. McCrae, gerontology researchers with the National Institute on Aging, have developed and tested a *five-factor model* (see Figure 13-1) based on five groupings of associated personality traits: (1) neuroticism, (2) extraversion, (3) openness to experience, (4) conscientiousness, and (5) agreeableness. (Early research on this model included only the first three categories and measured personality by the *NEO Scale*.)

Costa and McCrae (1980, 1988, 1994a, 1994b;

Costa et al., 1986; McCrae & Costa, 1984; McCrae, Costa, & Busch, 1986) analyzed cross-sectional, longitudinal, and sequential data from their Baltimore Longitudinal Study of Aging and several other large samples of men and women in their twenties to their nineties and found remarkable stability in all five domains. Because the Baltimore study consisted of predominantly white, college-educated volunteers, Costa and McCrae compared their findings on neuroticism, extraversion, and openness with those in a nationwide cross-sectional sample of more than 10,000 people ages 32 to 88. The differences between the two studies were small, confirming the stability of all three domains. By contrast, Costa and McCrae (1994b) did find age-related differences in cross-sectional comparisons of college students with young and middle-aged adults. "Somewhere between age 21 and age 30 personality appears to take its final, fully developed form," Costa and McCrae (1994a) conclude.

Costa and McCrae's influential work has made a powerful case for the stability of personality traits (though, as we'll see in Chapter 15, there is contrary evidence). Still, some theorists say, personality is more than a collection of traits. It is the sum total of a person's ways of thinking, feeling, and behaving, and although it does show continuity, there also seem to be definite patterns of change.

NORMATIVE-CRISIS MODELS

Looking back, many people at midlife would say that they are very different from the people they were at age 20, when they entered young adulthood, and by age 60 or 70 they may feel they have changed even more. Furthermore, when they compare notes, adults often find that their friends have gone through similar changes.

Normative-crisis models hold that everyone follows the same basic, built-in "ground plan" for development, though the details vary. This "ground plan" consists of a sequence of age-related social and emotional changes. The changes are *normative* in that they seem to be common to most members of a population, and they emerge in successive periods, phases, or stages, often marked by emotional *crises* that must be satisfactorily resolved, or else further development may be impeded.

Erik Erikson broke with Freud in part because of his conviction that personality is not frozen at puberty—that people grow and change throughout adult life. Variations on Erikson's theory grew out of pioneering studies by George Vaillant and Daniel Levinson. In this section we describe how these three classic normative-crisis theorists explain the changes of young adulthood (see Table 13-1), and we introduce the work of Ravenna Helson on normative changes in women. In Chapters 15 and 17 we discuss changes later in life.

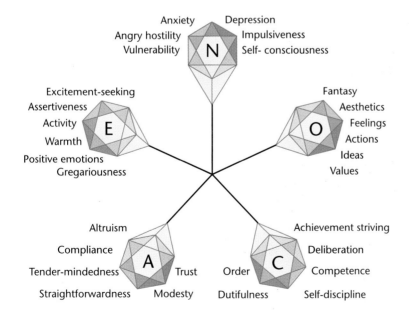

FIGURE 13-1
Costa and McCrae's five-factor model. Each factor, or domain of personality, represents a cluster of related traits or facets. N = neuroticism, E = extraversion, O = openness to experience, A = agreeableness, C = conscientiousness. *(Source: Adapted from Costa & McCrae, 1980.)*

TABLE 13-1

Three Normative-Crisis Views of Phases or Crises in Young Adults' Development

Erikson	Vaillant	Levinson*

Intimacy versus isolation (ages 20 to 40): Resolving conflicting demands of intimacy, competitiveness, and distance so as to enter into a loving heterosexual relationship with the ultimate aim of providing a nurturing environment for children.	*Age of establishment (ages 20 to 30):* Moving from under the parents' dominance to autonomy; finding a spouse; raising children; developing and deepening friendships.
	
	Age of consolidation (twenties to forties): Consolidating career; strengthening marriage; not questioning goals.
		Entry phase of early adulthood (ages 17 to 33): Building a provisional life structure.
		1 *Early adult transition (ages 17 to 22):* Moving out of the parents' home; becoming more independent.
		2 *Entry life structure for early adulthood (ages 22 to 28):* Choosing an occupation; marrying; establishing a home and a family; following a "dream" and finding a mentor.
		3 *Age-30 transition (ages 28 to 33):* Reassessing work and family patterns; creating the basis for the next life structure.
		
		Culminating phase of early adulthood (ages 33 to 45): Building a second adult life structure.
		1 *Culminating life structure for early adulthood (ages 33 to 40):*
		  a "Settling down": Making deeper commitments to work and family; setting timetables for specific life goals; establishing a niche in society; realizing youthful aspirations.
		  b "Becoming one's own man": Getting out from under other people's power and authority; seeking independence and respect; discarding the mentor.

	Age of transition (around age 40): Leaving the compulsive busywork of occupational apprenticeships to examine the "world within."	2 *Midlife transition (age 40 to age 45):* Reassessing the second adult life structure; moving into middle adulthood.

Note: This outline summarizes Levinson's findings for men. According to Levinson (1996), women go through similar age-related phases and transitions, but the content of their life structures is more variable.

SOURCES: Erikson, 1950; Levinson, 1978, 1986; Vaillant, 1977.

Erik Erikson: Intimacy versus Isolation

Erikson's sixth crisis of psychosocial development, ***intimacy versus isolation,*** is the major issue of young adulthood. Young adults need to make deep personal commitments to others. If they are unable or afraid to do this, said Erikson, they may become isolated and self-absorbed. However, they do need a certain amount of isolation to think about their lives. As they work to resolve conflicting demands of intimacy, competitiveness, and distance, they develop an ethical sense, which Erikson considered the mark of the adult.

Intimate relationships demand sacrifice and compromise. Young adults who have developed a strong sense of self—the chief task of adolescence, according to Erikson—are ready to fuse their identity with that of another person. They are willing to risk temporary loss of self in coitus and orgasm and very close friendships.

Erikson distinguished sexual *intimacies,* which may take place in casual encounters, from mature *intimacy with a capital "I,"* which goes beyond mere sexuality (E. Hall, 1983). Not until a person is ready for this kind of intimacy can "true genitality" occur—mutual orgasm in a loving heterosexual relationship, in which trust is shared and cycles of work, procreation, and recreation are regulated.

Resolution of this crisis results in the "virtue" of *love:* mutual devotion between partners who have chosen to share their lives, have children, and help those children achieve their own healthy development. A decision not to fulfill the natural procreative urge has serious consequences for development, according to Erikson.

Erikson's exclusion of single, celibate, homosexual, and childless lifestyles from his blueprint for healthy development has brought criticism. Furthermore, the focus on a male pattern of development as normative (see Chapter 11) limits the validity of his theory. However, Erikson's work has inspired much important research, including that of Vaillant and Levinson.

George Vaillant: Adaptation to Life

In 1938, 268 eighteen-year-old Harvard undergraduates—self-reliant and emotionally and physically healthy—were selected for the Grant Study. Retesting them in middle age, Vaillant (1977; Vaillant & Vaillant, 1990) concluded that lives are shaped primarily by adaptation to circumstances and by the quality of sustained relationships. Of

Intimacy, the major achievement of young adulthood in Erikson's theory of personality development, comes about through commitment to a relationship that may demand sacrifice and compromise. According to Erikson, intimacy is possible for a man only after he has achieved his own identity, but women achieve identity through intimacy. Gilligan and other researchers propose a different sequence for women, who, they say, often achieve intimacy first and then go on to find identity later, sometimes years later. *(Jeffrey Dunn/Stock, Boston)*

the men who at age 47 were considered best-adjusted, 93 percent had had stable marriages before age 30 and were still married at 50.

With some variations, Vaillant (1977) saw a typical pattern. At age 20, many of the men were still dominated by their parents—a finding that has appeared again in later research (Frank, Avery, & Laman, 1988; see Box 13-1). During their twenties, and sometimes their thirties, they established themselves: achieved autonomy, married, had children, and deepened friendships. Somewhere between the twenties and the forties, these men entered a stage of *career consolidation.* They worked hard at strengthening their careers and devoted themselves to their families. They followed the rules, strove for promotions, and accepted "the system," rarely questioning whether they had chosen the right woman or the right occupation. The excitement, charm, and promise they had radiated as students disappeared; now they were described as "colorless, hardworking, bland young men in gray flannel suits" (Vaillant, 1977, p. 217).

In comparing how the young men in the Grant Study adapted to the circumstances of their lives, Vaillant identified four characteristic patterns, or ***adaptive mechanisms:*** (1) *mature* (such as using

BOX 13-1   FOOD FOR THOUGHT

ESTABLISHING MATURE RELATIONSHIPS WITH PARENTS

When does a person become an adult psychologically? Research suggests that the transition to adulthood usually does not occur until the mid- to late twenties. Interviews with 78 women and 72 men between 22 and 32 years of age found a dramatic shift toward maturity between ages 24 and 28 (Frank et al., 1988).

These white middle-class high school graduates from a midwestern suburb were assessed on autonomy (how well they could make decisions and take responsibility for their own lives) and on their relationships with their parents (how close they were, how they communicated, and how the young people felt about their parents). About half of those over 28 years of age felt that they could cope with most aspects of life without asking their parents for help, and only 1 in 5 had serious doubts that they could manage on their own. For people under 24, however, these proportions were reversed: only 1 in 5 felt that they could cope with most aspects of life independently, and half had serious doubts that they could manage on their own. Whether a person was married or unmarried did not seem to matter.

The researchers described six patterns of adjustment:

1 *Individuated:* Young adult (YA) feels respected by parents, freely seeks their advice and help, acknowledges their strengths, enjoys being with them, and has

few conflicts with them. Yet YA feels separate from parents and is aware of (and untroubled by) a lack of intensity and depth in the relationship.

2 *Competent-connected:* YA is strongly independent, with life views that differ radically from parents' beliefs, but feels more empathic toward parents than individuated YA and often helps parents resolve their own problems of health, drinking, or relationships. The mother may be seen as demanding and critical, but YA understands her limitations, keeps conflicts within limits, and stays close to her.

3 *Pseudoautonomous:* YA pretends not to care about conflicts with parents and disengages rather than confronting parents openly. Fathers are often seen as uninterested and mothers as intrusive; both are seen as unable to accept YA for himself or herself.

4 *Identified:* In this unusually open and intimate relationship, YA accepts parents' values and outlook on life, seeks advice on most major decisions, and feels secure in the parents' availability. There is little tension, and parents are seen as nonjudgmental and supportive.

5 *Dependent:* YA cannot cope with ordinary life situations without parents' help, feels troubled by this but unable to change, and sees parents as overbearing and judgmental or emotionally

detached and preoccupied with themselves. YA either goes along with parents' wishes or gets into childish power struggles. (This pattern is equivalent to insecure or avoidant attachment.)

6 *Conflicted:* This profile emerged only with fathers. YA sees the father as hot-tempered and incapable of a close relationship, feels constantly under attack, is ashamed of the father's inadequacies, and longs to be closer to him.

Young women were most likely to be "competent-connected" with their mothers and "identified" or "conflicted" with their fathers. Men were most often "individuated" with both parents or "pseudoautonomous" with their fathers. Women were more likely than men to be "dependent" on their mothers.

Once again, though, we have to guard against drawing sweeping conclusions from relatively small, limited samples; and we need to be alert to possible cohort effects. This delayed schedule for achieving adulthood may reflect the fact that middle-class young people remain dependent on their parents for support longer today than in the past. Less affluent young people and those who grow up in stepfamilies and single-parent families, especially when they have many siblings, are likely to leave home at younger ages (B. A. Mitchell et al., 1989).

humor or helping others), (2) *immature* (such as developing aches and pains with no physical basis), (3) *psychotic* (distorting or denying reality), and (4) *neurotic* (repressing anxiety or developing irrational fears). Men who used mature mechanisms were mentally and physically healthier, as well as happier, than others; they got more satisfaction

from work, enjoyed richer friendships, made more money, and seemed better-adjusted.

Daniel Levinson: Life Structure

Levinson (1978, 1980, 1986) and his colleagues at Yale University conducted in-depth interviews and personality tests with 40 men ages 35 to 45, equally divided among industrial workers, business executives, biologists, and novelists. From this study, as well as from biographical sources and other research, Levinson formed a theory of personality development in adulthood. Shortly before his death, Levinson (1996) completed a companion study of 45 women.

At the heart of Levinson's theory is an evolving *life structure:* "the underlying pattern or design of a person's life at a given time" (1986, p. 6). This structure is built around whatever a person finds most important—people, places, things, institutions, and causes—as well as the values, dreams, and emotions that make them so. Most people build a life structure around work and family.

People shape their life structures during overlapping eras of about 20 to 25 years each. The eras are divided into entry and culminating phases. Each phase has its own tasks, whose accomplishment becomes the foundation for the next life structure. The eras and phases are linked by transitional periods, when people reappraise, and think about restructuring, their lives. Indeed, according to Levinson, people spend nearly half their adult lives in transitions, which may involve crises.

Men and women go through the same eras, phases, and transitions, according to Levinson (1996), but their life structures differ. Let's look first at Levinson's male model for early adulthood (refer back to Table 13-1) and then at his more recent findings about women.

Men's Life Structures in Early Adulthood

In the entry phase of early adulthood, a man builds his first provisional life structure. During the early adult transition, from about ages 17 to 22, he moves out of his parents' home and becomes financially and emotionally independent. Entering an institutional framework, such as college or the armed services, can ease the transition to full adult status. During his twenties, he forms relationships, usually leading to marriage and parenthood, and chooses an occupation.

Two important tasks of this phase are forming a dream and finding a mentor. A dream usually has to do with a career: a vision of, say, winning a Nobel Prize. A mentor is a slightly older man who offers guidance and inspiration and passes on wisdom, moral support, and practical help in career and personal matters. The mentor can give helpful advice when realities clash with a man's dream.

In the age-30 transition, from about ages 28 to 33, a man reevaluates his entry life structure and

seeks to improve it. Then, in the culminating phase of early adulthood, he settles down. He sets goals (a professorship, for instance, or a certain level of income) and a time for achieving them (say, by age 40). He anchors his life in family, occupation, and community. As time goes on, he chafes under authority; he wants to become his own man. He may discard his mentor and be at odds with his wife, children, lover, boss, friends, or coworkers. How he deals with the issues of this phase will affect the midlife transition.

Women's Life Structures in Early Adulthood

From 1980 to 1982, Levinson (1996) and his staff conducted biographical interviews with 15 homemakers, 15 corporate businesswomen, and 15 female academicians, ages 35 to 45, in northeastern cities. The results suggest that women go through the same eras, phases, and transitions as men do; but the timetable may differ, and their life structures are more varied than men's.

Due to *gender splitting*—rigid divisions that, according to Levinson, have existed in all cultures between masculine and feminine roles—women bring different resources to bear on the task of forming a life structure, and they face different psychological and environmental constraints. Gender splitting takes four interrelated forms: (1) allocation of the "domestic sphere" to women and the "public sphere" (economy, government, and other societal institutions and occupations) to men, (2) in marriage, a split between the female homemaker and the male provider, (3) a division between "women's work" and "men's work," and (4) a split between "feminine" and "masculine" personality characteristics.

The gender revolution—driven by the advent of reasonably reliable birth control, the increase in life expectancy beyond the child-rearing years, and the rise in divorce and nontraditional lifestyles—is breaking down these divisions. As a result, "the lives and personalities of women and men are becoming more similar" (Levinson, 1996, p. 414). However, the young women in Levinson's study came of age when this revolution was just gathering steam. For them, the early adult transition took as long as 10 years, as they struggled to define their life goals, give up the care and protection they had had as children, and establish new, mature relationships with parents. They had varying degrees of difficulty forming a dream, finding a mentor, and establishing an occupation and a love relationship, and their life structures tended to be more tentative and temporary than men's.

These women were torn between two "selves" with conflicting dreams. The Traditional Homemaker Figure finds fulfillment by subordinating herself to her family; her dream is to nurture and support her husband's and children's achievements. The Anti-Traditional Figure aspires to be her own person and seeks a more fulfilling life outside the home; her dream, which can be realized only by "killing off" the traditional dream, is to be independent and equal to a man. Whichever dream these women followed at first, the other tended to surface during transitional periods, forcing them to pay attention to suppressed parts of themselves.

Most of the 15 women whose lives centered on homemaking came from poor, working-class, or lower-middle-class homes; neither they nor their parents were college graduates. Their family backgrounds often included abuse, alcoholism, and divorce or discord. Among this group, the traditional dream predominated. They tended to marry early and to become pregnant almost immediately, but most of these marriages failed or proved disappointing. If these women were employed, it was generally in unskilled or semiskilled jobs or in typically female fields such as nursing and teaching, where they were subordinate to men. The antitraditional dream often asserted itself during the midlife transition, when children were leaving the nest.

"The homemakers' lives," Levinson concludes, "give evidence that the traditional pattern is hard to sustain. Most women who tried to maintain this pattern formed life structures that were relatively unsatisfactory—not viable in the world, not suitable for the self. The few who were more or less contented paid a considerable price in restriction of self-development" (p. 415).

Most of the 30 career women, by contrast, grew up in well-educated middle-class or upper-middle-class families, but their family life had been less smooth than it appeared. Most went to elite colleges away from home and experienced recurrent tension between the traditional and antitraditional dreams as they slowly forged their way into formerly male, high-status occupations. At first, these women's dreams were limited and vague; they entered graduate school or the world of work without clear goals and only gradually developed the desire for a serious career. Their mentors, if any, were almost invariably men. By their late twenties, most of these women were or had been married; nearly half had children, and most of the others still wanted them.

The problem of combining commitments to work and family became a major theme of the age-30 transition, which involved a moderate or severe crisis for 90 percent of the career women, leading to a markedly altered life structure. Some tried to emphasize both work and family, struggling to "do it all" or experimenting with a more equal division of rights and responsibilities in the home. Some, as they approached midlife, had suppressed one dream or the other, limiting their career goals or their family involvement.

Ravenna Helson: The Struggle for Independent Identity

One of the most comprehensive longitudinal studies of women's personality development is that of Ravenna Helson, who for nearly four decades has followed 140 women from the classes of 1958 and 1960 at Mills College in Oakland, California. Helson (1992) asked these women, then in their early fifties, to write about "the most unstable, confusing, troubled, or discouraged time in your life since college—the one with the most impact on your values, self-concept, and the way you look at the world" (p. 336).

Since each woman was asked to describe only the single time of greatest turmoil, the 88 responses do not constitute a fully fleshed-out model of development; but they do reveal a succession of transforming experiences typical of certain ages. The timing of these critical periods was related to identity status (Marcia, 1966; see Chapter 11). Women who had *achieved* identity or were *in moratorium* (active exploration) tended to experience their most critical times between ages 36 and 46. Women with the less developed statuses of *diffused* and *foreclosed* identity tended to report their critical times as earlier or later. Motherhood also tended to delay the critical times.

Typical themes during the early to middle twenties were *bad self* and *bad partner*. The "bad self" theme was characterized by feeling lonely, isolated, unattractive, inferior, and often passive until the woman did something to change herself or her situation. The "bad partner" theme often revolved around a husband who developed, or turned out to have, a serious flaw: for example, being inconsiderate, exploitive, suicidal, or a substance abuser. The woman either resented (but accepted) her subordinate status, endeavored to protect and cover up for her partner, or, eventually, divorced him.

Common enough to be considered a stage in women's development was a struggle for independent identity and control over one's life. This was a major theme around both ages 30 and 40, often leading to graduate training, a career, or a love affair (heterosexual or lesbian). Then, between ages 36 and 46, many women suffered unpleasant consequences of independence and assertiveness: rebuffs at work, for instance, or abandonment by husbands. Separate personality ratings taken at ages 21, 27, and 43 suggest that the search for independent identity came at a time, beginning in the late twenties, of growing confidence and decreasing vulnerability, which may have led to marital conflict. However, an increase in independence as women approached midlife occurred regardless of whether they were married or had children.

Evaluating the Normative-crisis Approach*

The idea of a predictable sequence of age-related changes throughout adult life has been influential, but its validity is questionable. Although age may be fairly indicative of children's development, environmental circumstances or life events may be more significant for adults. As young people enter the adult world, choose differing lifestyles, and have different experiences, the uniqueness of individual personality is accentuated and reinforced, and this diversity becomes more striking with the passing years.

Furthermore, it is risky to generalize from studies with such limited samples. Both the Grant Study and Levinson's early work were based on small groups of mostly white middle-class to upper-middle-class men, all born in the 1920s or 1930s. Likewise, the women in Helson's sample were born in the late 1930s and were mostly white and upper-middle-class. Levinson's small sample of women born between about 1935 and 1945, although more diverse, was not representative. These men's and women's development was most likely influenced by societal events that did not affect earlier or later cohorts, as well as by their socioeconomic status, race, and gender. Still, despite such limitations, these studies may help identify developmental threads that run through the lives of many people.

TIMING-OF-EVENTS MODEL

Instead of looking at adults' development as a function of age, the *timing-of-events model*, sup-

*We offer a more complete critique of the normative-crisis approach in Chapter 15.

ported by Bernice Neugarten and others (Neugarten, Moore, & Lowe, 1965; Neugarten & Neugarten, 1987), views *life events* as markers of development. In childhood and adolescence, internal maturational events signal the transition from one developmental stage to another. A baby says the first word, takes the first step, loses the first tooth; the body changes at the onset of puberty. In adulthood, people move from "a biological to a social clocking" of development (Danish & D'Augelli, 1980, p. 111). Physiological and cognitive maturation are now less important to growth than the effects of such events as marriage, parenthood, divorce, widowhood, and retirement. Menopause is usually less important in a woman's life than a job change.

According to this model, adults develop in response to the times in their lives when key events do or do not occur. Events that occur when they are expected, such as graduating from high school at age 18, are *on time;* events that occur at unexpected times, such as becoming a widow at age 25, are *off time.*

Normative and Nonnormative Events

Life events are of two types: normative and nonnormative. *Normative life events* are those which happen to most adults, such as parenthood and retirement. *Nonnormative life events* are unusual events that cannot be expected, such as a traumatic accident, an unanticipated promotion, or a lottery prize. Unlike these *individual events*, which happen to one person or one family, a *cultural event* (such as an economic depression or boom, an earthquake, a war, a famine, the computer revolution, or an accident at a nuclear reactor) influences the context in which all individuals develop at a particular time and place.

Whether or not a life event is normative, and therefore expected, often depends on its timing. Events that are normative when they are "on time" become nonnormative when they are "off time," that is, earlier or later than usual. Marrying at age 14 or, for the first time, at 41 would be a nonnormative event. So would retiring at 41 or 91. People are usually keenly aware of their own timing and describe themselves as "early," "late," or "on time" in marrying, having children, settling on careers, or retiring.

Normative events that come "on time" are generally taken in stride; "it is the events that upset the expected sequence and rhythm of the life cycle that cause problems" (Neugarten & Neugarten,

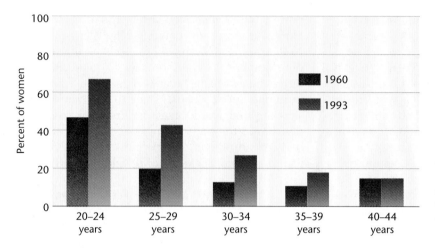

FIGURE 13-2
Proportion of women ages 20 to 44 who had not yet given birth, 1960 and 1993. Today, women tend to have children later in life than their mothers did. More women now have a first child after age 30. *(Source: Adapted from USDHHS, 1996, figure 26.)*

1987, p. 33). Crises result not from changes typical at certain ages (as in normative-crisis models), but from the unexpected occurrence and timing of life events. If events occur as expected, development proceeds smoothly. If not, stress can result. Stress may come from an unexpected event (such as losing a job), an event that happens earlier or later than expected (being widowed at age 35, having a first child at 45, being forced to retire at 55), or the failure of an expected event to occur at all (never being married or being unable to have a child).

Cultural and Cohort Variations

Cultural attitudes affect the *social clock,* the societal norms or expectations for the proper timing of life events. The typical timing of some events varies from culture to culture and from generation to generation; a timetable that seems right to people in one cohort may not seem so to those in the next. One illustration is the rise in the average age when adults first marry in the United States (U.S. Bureau of the Census, 1996b); another is the trend toward delayed first childbirth (see Figure 13-2). When Neugarten's original research was repeated with 214 Australian university students, the perceived "best" ages for such transitions as leaving school, marriage, parenthood, grandparenthood, and retirement differed widely from those Neugarten had found among American adults three decades earlier (C. C. Peterson, 1996).

Since the mid-twentieth century, western societies have become less age-conscious; the feeling that there is a "right time" to do certain things is less rigid (Neugarten & Hagestad, 1976; Neugarten & Neugarten, 1987), and the acceptable range of age norms is much wider (Peterson, 1996). Today people are more accepting of 40-year-old first-time parents and 40-year-old grandparents, 50-year-old retirees and 75-year-old workers, 60-year-olds in blue jeans and 30-year-old college presidents.

Such rapid social change undermines the predictability on which the timing-of-events model is based. Consider this: American couples who delay becoming parents until ages 28 to 37 seem to adjust no better and no worse than younger parents with similar demographic characteristics (Roosa, 1988). Does this finding suggest that the timing-of-events model is wrong about the stressful effects of not being "on time"? Or does it reflect the current "blurring of traditional life periods" (Neugarten & Neugarten, 1987, p. 32), which gives the social clock less meaning?

The timing-of-events model has made an important contribution to our understanding of adult personality by emphasizing the importance of the individual life course and challenging the idea of universal, age-related change. However, its usefulness may well be limited to cultures and historical periods in which norms of behavior are stable and widespread.

HUMANISTIC MODELS: MASLOW'S HIERARCHY OF NEEDS

The *humanistic perspective* developed in the 1950s and 1960s in response to what some psychologists saw as negative beliefs about human nature underlying psychoanalytic and behavioral theories. Humanistic psychologists stress the potential for positive, healthy development; negative characteristics, they say, are the result of damage inflicted on the developing person. Unlike trait theorists (who view personality as set early in adulthood) or normative-crisis theorists (who see change as a function of age) or the timing-of-events model (which sees people as reactors to events), humanistic psychologists emphasize people's ability, regardless of age or circumstances, to take charge of their lives and foster their own development through the distinctively human capacities of choice, creativity, and self-realization.

One influential humanistic psychologist is Abraham Maslow (1954), who identified a *hierarchy of needs,* a rank order of the needs that motivate human behavior (see Figure 13-3). According to Maslow, only when people have satisfied basic needs can they strive to meet higher needs. The most basic need is physiological survival. Starving persons will take great risks to get food; only when they have obtained it can they focus on the next level of needs, those concerning personal security. These needs, in turn, must be substantially met before people can freely seek love and acceptance, esteem and achievement, and finally *self-actualization,* the full realization of potential.

Self-actualized people, says Maslow (1968) have a keen perception of reality, accept themselves and others, and appreciate nature. They are sponta-

neous, highly creative, and self-directed; they are good problem solvers. They identify with others and establish satisfying, evolving relationships, but they also have a certain detachment, a desire for privacy. They have a strong sense of values and a nonauthoritarian character structure. They respond to experience with fresh appreciation and rich emotion, and many have what Maslow calls *peak experiences.* Only about 1 person in 100 is said to attain this ideal (R. Thomas, 1979). No one is ever completely self-actualized; a healthy person is continually moving up to more fulfilling levels.

On first impression, Maslow's hierarchy of needs seems to be grounded in human experience, but it does not invariably hold true. History is full of accounts of self-sacrifice, in which people gave up what they needed for survival so that someone else (a loved one or even a stranger) might live.

Maslow and other humanistic theorists offer optimistic models of development that give special attention to internal factors in personality: feelings, values, and hopes. Humanistic theories have made a valuable contribution by promoting approaches, both to child rearing and to adult self-improvement, that respect the individual's uniqueness. Their limitations as scientific theories have to do largely with subjectiveness; their concepts are not

FIGURE 13-3
Maslow's hierarchy of needs. According to Maslow, human needs have different priorities. As each level of needs is met, a person can look to the needs of the next higher level. *(Source: Maslow, 1954.)*

clearly defined and so are hard to use as a basis for research. Furthermore, the humanistic approach is not truly developmental: its proponents generally make a broad distinction only between childhood and adulthood and do not see common patterns in particular periods across the life span.

✔ FOUNDATIONS OF INTIMATE RELATIONSHIPS

According to Erikson, developing intimate relationships is the crucial task of young adulthood. Traditionally, this is when people establish relationships that may continue for most of their adult lives—relationships based on friendship, love, and sexuality. In today's highly mobile society, friendships may come and go. In a freer society, so may lovers and sexual partners. Still, for most young adults, relationships remain pivotal as they decide to marry, cohabit, live alone, or form homosexual unions, and to have or not to have children.

Intimacy is a "close, warm, communicative experience" (Rosenbluth & Steil, 1995), which may or may not include sexual contact. An important element of intimacy is *self-disclosure:* "revealing important information about oneself to another" (Collins & Miller, 1994, p. 457). People tend to like those who confide in them. Also, not surprisingly, people tend to confide more in someone they like, and having shared a confidence cements the bond.

Intimacy includes a sense of belonging. The need to belong to someone—to form strong, stable, close, caring relationships—is a powerful motivator of human behavior, with effects on mind, body, and morale. The strongest emotions, both positive and negative, are evoked by intimate attachments. People think more, and more favorably, about friends and lovers than about others. And people deprived of friendship and love tend to be less healthy, physically and mentally, than others (Baumeister & Leary, 1995). Let's look at friendship, sexuality, and love, and then at the link between relationships and health.

FRIENDSHIP

Friendships are usually based on mutual interests and values and develop among people of the same generation or at the same stage of family life. Friends tend to validate each other's beliefs and behavior (Dykstra, 1995).

Young adults who are building careers and per-

haps caring for babies may have limited time to spend with friends. Friendships do, however, play an important role during these years. According to 150 adults—two-thirds of whom were college students and one-third no longer in school—friendship involves trust, respect, understanding, and acceptance; enjoyment of each other's company; willingness to help and confide in one another; and spontaneity, or feeling free to be oneself. Romantic bonds have these aspects too—plus sexual passion and extreme caring. The participants saw "best friendships" as more stable than ties to a spouse or lover. Most people's close and best friends were of the same sex, but 27 percent listed members of the other sex as best friends (K. E. Davis, 1985).

Women tend to have more intimate friendships than men do. They confide more in their friends—especially women friends, who usually share their values. They find friendships with other women more satisfying than those with men, which are usually less intimate. Men tend to share information and activities, not confidences, with friends. They are less motivated to engage in intimacy and tend to pull back from conversations that get into very intimate subjects (Rosenbluth & Steil, 1995).

SEXUALITY

People entering their twenties need to achieve independence, competence, responsibility, and equality—all in relation to sexuality. During the next few years, most people—heterosexual, homosexual, or bisexual—make major decisions about sexual lifestyles and about the kinds of relationships they will establish: whether they will engage in casual, recreational sex or be monogamous or have a series of intimate sexual relationships. Many of the issues young adults face have a sexual aspect: the decision to marry or enter a homosexual union, the decision to have a child, the foray into extramarital sex that is said to come with the "seven-year itch," and changes in sexual patterns following divorce.

Surveys of sexual behavior have found that by age 20 or 22, about 9 out of 10 young adults have had intercourse (Michael, Gagnon, Laumann, & Kolata, 1994; Seidman & Rieder, 1994); most have had several partners, often in succession (Seidman & Rieder, 1994). According to a major, nationally representative survey of 3,432 randomly selected 18- to 59-year-olds, fewer than 3 percent of men and 1½ percent of women consider themselves homosexual or bisexual, though 5 percent of men and 4 percent of women report at least one homosexual encounter in adulthood. Homosexual identification is more prevalent in big cities: 9 percent for men and 3 percent for women (Laumann, Gagnon, Michael, & Michaels, 1994; Michael et al., 1994). In another survey by the National Opinion Research Center, fewer than 2 percent of sexually active men and women said they had had homosexual relations within the previous year, and fewer than 1 percent reported bisexual activity during that period (T. W. Smith, 1994).

Gender differences in sexual behavior have diminished with the decline in the double standard. More women are engaging in sex before marriage. In one survey, 61 percent of men but only 12 percent of women born before 1910 admitted to premarital sex. By 1988, unmarried teenage girls had nearly as much sexual experience as boys did: 51.5 percent as compared with 60 percent (T. W. Smith, 1994). Among women born between 1933 and 1942, 84 percent were virgins when they turned 20 or had had only one sex partner (generally the man they married); this was true for only about half of women born after 1953 (Michael et al., 1994).

Men are still much more likely to masturbate and to approve of casual premarital sex than are women, but in other areas of sexuality the differences are smaller. These findings come from an overview of 177 studies done from 1966 through 1990, which included nearly 59,000 males and 70,000 females of all ages, largely young adults. There were *no* gender differences in attitudes about masturbation, homosexuality, and civil liberties for homosexuals. Nor were there differences in sexual satisfaction or participation in kissing or oral sex. Between adolescence and young adulthood, women and men tended to become more alike in their attitudes toward sexual permissiveness, but differences in frequency of intercourse and incidence of masturbation increased (Oliver & Hyde, 1993). Men are more likely to fantasize about sex during masturbation or throughout the day, but women are equally likely to fantasize during sexual activity with a partner (Leitenberg & Henning, 1995).

Neither men nor women appear to be as promiscuous as is sometimes thought. One major survey found that half of adult Americans had had fewer than four sex partners during their entire lifetime; 67 percent of men and 75 percent of women said they had had only one partner during the past year,

and the comparable proportions are even higher in several European countries (Michael et al., 1994).

The threat of AIDS appears to have affected sexual attitudes and behavior somewhat. A 1995 survey of more than 240,000 entering freshman at American colleges and universities found that 43 percent approved of casual sex, down from 52 percent in 1987 (Sax et al., 1996). Many adults say they have modified their sexual behavior by having fewer partners (see Figure 13-4), selecting partners more carefully, or using condoms. Fourteen percent of men and ten percent of women ages 18 to 59, including 23 percent of single men and 32 percent of single women who are not living with a partner, say they are abstaining from sex altogether. Safer sex practices have become more prevalent among homosexuals (Laumann et al., 1994; Michael et al., 1994).

However, the proportion of adults—approximately 1 in 10—who have had large numbers of partners (21 or more) since they turned 18 and thus are most at risk for infection has declined very little among the generation now in their late twenties, who reached sexual maturity in the age of AIDS (Michael et al., 1994). A telephone survey of more than 10,000 married and unmarried Americans ages 18 to 75 found that many adults, including those especially at risk, do not take precautions against AIDS and other sexually transmitted diseases. Only 17 percent of heterosexuals with multiple partners, and only 13 percent of those with high-risk partners, use condoms whenever they have sex (Catania, Coates, Stall, Turner, et al., 1992). A small study of women who sought HIV testing and counseling (but tested negative) found that only one-fourth adopted safer sex practices afterward (Ickovics et al., 1994). There is still a widespread, but false, impression that AIDS is primarily a "homosexual disease," and this may lull many heterosexuals into complacency.

LOVE

Most people like love stories, including their own. In a sense, says Robert J. Sternberg (1995), love *is* a story. The lovers are its authors, and the kind of story they make up reflects their personalities and interests and affects their feelings about the relationship. Love "stories" also differ across cultures (see Box 13-2).

The idea of love as a story suggests that people do not fall in love; they create it. A couple's love

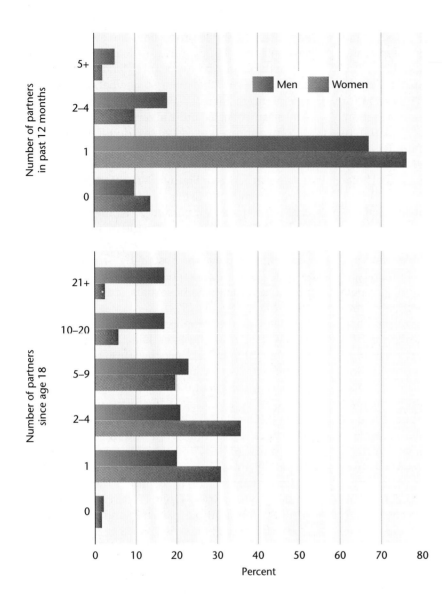

FIGURE 13-4
Number of sex partners during the past 12 months and since age 18. *(Source: Data from Laumann et al., 1994; Michael et al., 1994.)*

story may be based on a familiar "script," which they modify to fit their situation. Love, to some people, is an addiction—a strong, anxious, clinging attachment. Others think of it as a fantasy, in which one party (usually the woman) expects to be saved by a "knight in shining armor" (usually the man). Still others think of love as a game, a war, or a power relationship, with a winner and loser or governor and governed. Love can be a horror story (with abuser and victim), a mystery, or a detective story, in which one partner constantly tries to keep tabs on the other. Or it can be the story of a garden that needs to be tended and nurtured.

Whatever the nature of the story, it takes on its own momentum. The lovers look at whatever happens between them in terms of the story line they have "written." Stories, once begun, are hard to

change because that would involve reinterpreting and reorganizing everything the couple have understood about the relationship. When something occurs that conflicts with that understanding (such as an extramarital affair), people resist changing their story and instead try to interpret the new information to fit it ("It was my fault—I wasn't giving him enough attention"). In Piaget's terms (see Chapter 1), people prefer to assimilate the new information into the existing story rather than accommodate the story to it.

Thinking of love as a story may help us understand how people select and mix the elements of the "plot." According to Sternberg's *triangular theory of love* (1985b; Sternberg & Barnes, 1985; Sternberg & Grajek, 1984), the three elements of love are intimacy, passion, and commitment. *Inti-*

BOX 13-2   WINDOW ON THE WORLD

CROSS-CULTURAL CONCEPTIONS OF LOVE

In William Shakespeare's *A Midsummer Night's Dream*, a fairy king who wants to play a trick on his queen squeezes the juice of a magic flower into her sleeping eyes so that she will fall in love with the first person she sees upon awakening—who turns out to be an actor wearing a donkey's head. That tale is one source of the old saying, "Love is blind."

Actually, students of love find that chance plays a much smaller role than the cultural context. Although love—"an intense attraction and longing to be with the loved one"—seems to be virtually universal (Goleman, 1992), its meaning and expression vary across time and space.

According to Anne E. Beall and Robert Sternberg* (1995), people in different cultures define love differently, and the way they think about love affects what they feel. Love, say these investigators, is a *social construction*, a concept people create out of their culturally influenced perceptions of reality. This concept influences what is considered normal, acceptable, or ideal. Culture influences not only the definition of love, but the features considered desirable in choosing a beloved, the feelings and thoughts expected to accompany love, and the way lovers act toward each other. Social approval and support from family and friends reinforce

satisfaction with and commitment to a relationship.

In many cultures, love has been considered a dangerous distraction, disruptive of a social order based on arranged marriages. During the past two centuries, in western societies and in some non-western ones as well (Goleman, 1992), marriage has come to be built on love—a trend accelerated by women's increasing economic self-sufficiency. Romantic love is more commonly accepted in individualistic societies than in collectivist ones. In Communist China, for example, such love is frowned upon. Chinese see themselves in terms of social roles and relationships, and self-indulgent emotional displays are viewed as weakening the social fabric.

Within western civilization, ideas about love have changed radically. In ancient Greece, homosexual love was prized above heterosexual relationships. Greek men fell in love with teenage boys and inscribed ardent notes to them on urns; the poet Sappho wrote graphically of her physical arousal when she saw the woman she loved. In some cultures, love has been separated from sexuality. In King Arthur's court, love involved a nonsexual chivalry rather than intimacy; knights undertook feats of bravery to impress fair ladies but didn't seek to marry them. In

the Roman Catholic Church, love of God is considered superior to love of a human being, and priests remain celibate so as to devote themselves completely to their calling. In Victorian England, love was viewed as a noble emotion, but sexual intimacy was considered a necessary evil, required only for producing children. The Victorian poets placed the beloved on a pedestal. A more modern view is that of loving someone for the person he or she is, warts and all.

Ideas about love are influenced by how a culture looks at human nature. For example, during the eighteenth-century European Enlightenment, love—like other aspects of human experience—was thought to be subject to scientific understanding and rational control, and people were expected to hold their passions in check. By the nineteenth century, disillusionment with the power of science and reason had set in. People were seen as creatures of sensation, prejudice, and irrational emotion, and love was described as an uncontrollable passion. Today, the popularity of marriage counseling suggests a reassertion of the possibility of consciously affecting the course of love.

*Unless otherwise noted, this discussion is indebted to Beall & Sternberg, 1995.

---

macy, the emotional element, involves self-disclosure, which leads to connection, warmth, and trust. *Passion*, the motivational element, is based on inner drives that translate physiological arousal into sexual desire. *Commitment*, the cognitive element, is the decision to love and to stay with the beloved. The degree to which each of the three elements is present or absent determines what kind of love the couple share (see Table 13-2). Mismatches can lead to problems in relationships.

Some research suggests that trust, which is essential to intimacy, depends on the security of earlier attachments to parents or caregivers (DeAngelis, 1994). Commitment may be influenced by the rewards and costs of being in a relationship; how well it meets each partner's expectations; their investment in it; the availability of desirable alternatives; and barriers to leaving. A psychometric measurement of these factors found that homosexual partners living together tend to

TABLE 13-2

Patterns of Loving

Type	Description
Nonlove	All three components of love—intimacy, passion, and commitment—are absent. This describes most personal relationships, which are simply casual interactions.
Liking	Intimacy is the only component present. There is closeness, understanding, emotional support, affection, bondedness, and warmth. Neither passion nor commitment is present.
Infatuation	Passion is the only component present. This is "love at first sight," a strong physical attraction and sexual arousal, without intimacy or commitment. This can flare up suddenly and die just as fast—or, given certain circumstances, can sometimes last for a long time.
Empty love	Commitment is the only component present. This is often found in long-term relationships that have lost both intimacy and passion, or in arranged marriages.
Romantic love	Intimacy and passion are both present. Romantic lovers are drawn to each other physically and bonded emotionally. They are not, however, committed to each other.
Companionate love	Intimacy and commitment are both present. This is a long-term, committed friendship, often occurring in marriages in which physical attraction has died down but in which the partners feel close to each other and have made the decision to stay together.
Fatuous love	Passion and commitment are present, without intimacy. This is the kind of love that leads to a whirlwind courtship, in which a couple make a commitment on the basis of passion without allowing themselves the time to develop intimacy. This kind of love usually does not last, despite the initial intent to commit.
Consummate love	All three components are present in this "complete" love, which many people strive for, especially in romantic relationships. It is easier to reach it than to hold onto it. Either partner may change what he or she wants from the relationship. If the other partner changes, too, the relationship may endure in a different form. If the other partner does not change, the relationship may dissolve.

SOURCE: Sternberg, 1985b.

be as committed to their relationships as married couples (Kurdek, 1995a).

Do opposites attract? Not as a rule. Just as people choose friends with whom they have something in common, they tend to choose life partners much like themselves (E. Epstein & Gutmann, 1984). Lovers often resemble each other in physical appearance and attractiveness, mental and physical health, intelligence, popularity, and warmth. They are likely to be similar in the degree to which their parents are happy as individuals and as couples, and in such factors as socioeconomic status, race, religion, education, and income (Murstein, 1980). Couples often have similar temperaments, too; risk takers tend to marry other risk takers, though they may be risking early divorce (M. Zuckerman, 1994)! Gay male partners tend to be less like each other in age, income, and education than are heterosexual and lesbian partners (Kurdek & Schmitt, 1987).

Of course, love doesn't always last. Among college students who were asked to recall how or why they fell in and out of love with a previous partner, those who could explain why their earlier relationships ended were more satisfied with their current partners than those whose earlier relationships appeared to be unresolved (Clark & Collins, 1993).

RELATIONSHIPS AND HEALTH

Personal relationships are vital to health. Adults without friends or loved ones are susceptible to a wide range of troubles, including traffic accidents, eating disorders, and suicide (Baumeister & Leary, 1995). People isolated from friends and family are twice as likely to fall ill and die as people who maintain social ties. The 10 to 20 percent of people who have close contact with others less than once a week and have no one with whom to share feelings are most at risk. The effect is greater for men; even if a woman has few social ties, those she has are more likely to be intimate and nurturing (House, Landis, & Umberson, 1988).

What is it about relationships that fosters health, or about their absence that undermines it? Social ties may foster a sense of meaning or coherence in life. Emotional support may help minimize stress. People who are in touch with others may be more likely to eat and sleep sensibly, get enough exercise, avoid substance abuse, and get necessary medical care (House et al., 1988).

✔ NONMARITAL AND MARITAL LIFESTYLES

Today's rules for acceptable behavior are more elastic than they were during the first half of the twentieth century. Current norms no longer dictate that people must get married, stay married, or have children (Thornton, 1989), and at what ages. Lifestyle options include staying single, living with a partner of either sex, divorce, remarriage, and childlessness; and people's choices may change. In this section, we look at marriage and its alternatives. In the next section we examine family life.

SINGLE LIFE

The percentage of young adults who have not yet married has increased dramatically during the past few decades in every age bracket from 20 to 39, and a growing number never marry at all. Between 1970 and 1994, the proportion of 30- to 34-year-olds who had never married more than tripled, from 6 to 20 percent of women and from 9 to 30 percent of men (U.S. Bureau of the Census, 1993b, 1996a). More women today are self-supporting, and there is less social pressure to marry. Widespread unemployment makes marriage less practical and less attractive to both sexes.

Some young adults stay single so they can be freer to take risks, experiment, and make changes—move across the country or across the world, shift careers, further their education, or do creative work—without worrying about how their quest for self-fulfillment affects another person. Some enjoy sexual freedom; the later people marry, the less likely they are to be virgins on the wedding day. Some find the lifestyle exciting. Some just like being alone. And some postpone or avoid mar-

Lovers often resemble each other in appearance and personality. These military cadets, for instance, have common career goals. According to Sternberg, love has three elements: intimacy, passion, and commitment. *(Robert Kristofik/The Image Bank)*

riage for fear it will end in divorce (P. C. Glick & Lin, 1986b). Postponement makes sense, since, as we'll see, the younger people are when they first marry, the likelier they are to split up.

By and large, singles like their status. Most are not lonely (Cargan, 1981; Spurlock, 1990); they are busy and active and feel secure about themselves.

HOMOSEXUAL RELATIONSHIPS

The small minority of the population who are homosexual—fewer than 3 percent of men and 1½ percent of women, as we mentioned earlier—face strong societal disapproval. Negative attitudes toward homosexuality have declined somewhat since 1976, when 70 percent of a national sample of 2,904 Americans thought homosexual relations are always wrong; but 61 percent still thought so in 1996 (National Opinion Research Center, 1996). As a result, *coming out*—the process of openly disclosing one's homosexual orientation—is often slow and painful. Coming out generally occurs in four stages, which may never be fully achieved (B. M. King, 1996):

1 *Recognition of being homosexual.* This may happen as early as age 4 or not until adolescence or later. It can be a lonely, painful, confusing experience.
2 *Getting to know other homosexuals* and establishing sexual and romantic relationships with them. This may not happen until adulthood.

Although homosexual relationships take many forms, most homosexuals—like most heterosexuals—seek love, companionship, and sexual fulfillment in a stable relationship with one person. *(Amy Etra/PhotoEdit)*

Contact with other homosexuals can diminish feelings of isolation and improve self-image.

3 *Telling family and friends.* Many homosexuals cannot bring themselves to do this at all, or not for a long time. The revelation can bring disapproval, rejection, and conflict.

4 *Complete openness.* This includes telling colleagues, employers, and anyone else a person comes in contact with. Homosexuals who reach this stage have achieved healthy acceptance of their sexuality as part of who they are.

Homosexual relationships take many forms, including anonymous contacts, nonexclusive group living, "open" couples, and roommates who may or may not be lovers. However, most homosexuals (like most heterosexuals) seek love, companionship, and sexual fulfillment through a relationship with one person. The ingredients of long-term satisfaction are very similar in homosexual and heterosexual relationships (C. J. Patterson, 1995b). Lesbians are more likely to have stable, monogamous relationships; gay men (like heterosexual men) are more likely to "cruise," looking for multiple partners. Since the AIDS epidemic, however, gay men have become more interested in long-term relationships. The notion that partners in homosexual relationships typically play "masculine" and "feminine" roles has been thoroughly discredited by research (Berger, 1984; Berger & Kelly, 1986; B. M. King, 1996).

Homosexual men in the early stages of coming out tend to be more competitive and independent and less intimate than lesbians are. Gay male relationships during this period tend to have a clearly sexual rather than emotional focus, and couples may have problems unless they learn to control the struggle for dominance. By contrast, women in lesbian relationships may eventually need to develop more autonomy and individuality (Gonsiorek, 1995).

Lesbian couples may be more intimate than heterosexual couples, for reasons that may have to do with the ways men and women are socialized. One study looked at 90 mostly white, highly educated women with an average age of 34; half were in lesbian relationships and half in heterosexual ones—virtually all monogamous. Women with high self-esteem and a large capacity for intimacy were more likely to *show* intimacy in lesbian relationships than in heterosexual ones, perhaps because lesbian couples tend to act more like best friends than like marriage partners. Men may restrict intimacy, as they are generally less interested in it than women are (Rosenbluth & Steil, 1995). Another reason for greater intimacy in lesbian relationships may be a more egalitarian balance of power and sharing of everyday chores than in most heterosexual relationships (C. J. Patterson, 1995b; Rosenbluth & Steil, 1995).

A national survey taken by a newsletter for gay and lesbian couples gave a detailed picture of what life was like for 1,749 couples involved in homosexual relationships. The respondents were predominantly white and college-educated, and their average age was in the midthirties (Bryant &

Demian, 1990). Seventy-five percent of the female couples and eighty-two percent of the male couples had been living together during the previous year, and the same proportions shared all or part of their incomes. For 38 percent of the men and 32 percent of the women, the current relationship was their first major homosexual one; 27 percent of the women and 19 percent of the men had been married to someone of the other sex. Twenty-one percent of the women and nine percent of the men were caring for children, usually from a previous marriage. Fifty-seven percent of the women and thirty-six percent of the men wore rings or other symbols of their relationship, and 19 percent of the women and 11 percent of the men had celebrated it with a ceremony. Couples received social support mainly from friendships with other homosexuals, but also from siblings, mothers, and fathers, in that order.

Today, homosexuals in the United States are seeking the legal recognition of their unions that already exists in some countries (Kottak, 1994), and the right to adopt children or raise their own. (Many homosexuals who have been married and had children before coming out have been unable to gain or keep custody.) They also are pressing for an end to discrimination in employment and housing. A recent trend is the inclusion of unmarried domestic partners—homosexual or heterosexual—in health insurance, pension plans, and bereavement leave.

COHABITATION

Cohabitation is a lifestyle in which an unmarried couple involved in a sexual relationship live together in what is sometimes called a *consensual*, or *informal, union*. Such unions are common among homosexual couples and have become common among heterosexual couples in many countries (United Nations, 1991). In Sweden, in 1992, there were twice as many new consensual unions as new marriages (L. Eisenberg, 1995). In the United States that same year, 3.3 million unmarried, unrelated couples—more than 6 times as many as in 1970 and about twice as many as in 1980—were in the census category of "POSSLQ" (people of opposite sex sharing living quarters). About two-thirds were 25 to 44 years old, and about one-third had children under 15 living in the household (U.S. Bureau of the Census, 1993b).

Of course, not all POSSLQs have sexual relationships, but data from a major national survey confirm that cohabitation is becoming more prevalent. Among women born between 1933 and 1942 (and now in late middle age), 93 percent got married without first living with their future husbands; only 36 percent of women born between 1963 and 1974 (and now in their twenties to early thirties) did. Furthermore, many cohabiting couples do *not* marry; they break up fairly quickly, and each party looks for a new partner. As a result, adults today tend to have more live-in partners before marriage (Michael et al., 1994).

One of the main reasons for the rise in cohabitation is the secular trend toward earlier sexual maturation (see Chapter 10). This, together with the increased number of young people pursuing advanced education, creates a longer span between physiological maturity and social maturity. Many young adults want close romantic and sexual relationships but are not ready for marriage—and may never be. The average age at which young adults form their first live-in partnership is about the same as in 1970: 22 for men and 20 for women. The difference is that about two-thirds of young adults' first partnerships are now cohabitations rather than marriages (Michael et al., 1994; see Table 13-3).

Couples who live together before marrying tend to have lower-quality marriages, less commitment to marriage, and greater likelihood of divorce (Bumpass & Sweet, 1988; Hall & Zhao, 1995; Thomson & Colella, 1992). These findings may reflect the kinds of people who choose cohabitation rather than the effects of cohabitation itself (Schoen, 1992). Cohabitants tend to be unconventional in their attitudes about family, and they are less likely than most other people to select partners like themselves in age and previous marital status. They are more likely to have divorced parents and to have stepchildren. All these factors tend to predict unstable marriages (Hall & Zhao,

TABLE 13-3

Percentage of First Partnerships That Were Marriages in Cohorts Born 1933–1974

Birth Dates	Men	Women
1933–1942	84.5	93.8
1943–1952	66.7	75.7
1953–1962	46.6	57.3
1963–1974	33.9	35.3

SOURCE: Michael et al., 1994.

1995). Cohabitants who have children together may be more likely to stay together. A Canadian survey of 3,015 cohabiting couples who had never been married showed that the presence of children had a stabilizing effect. This was true regardless of the number of children and their age and sex (Wu, 1995).

It may be misleading, however, to generalize about cohabitation without considering ethnic differences, which reflect socioeconomic pressures and cultural influences (Manning & Landale, 1996). For white couples, cohabitation is often a modern version of "going steady," a brief prelude to marriage; and they are relatively unlikely to start a family before the wedding. National survey data show that 44 percent of white women who are cohabiting expect to marry within the next year. Most of those involved in a first cohabitation do eventually marry—if they do become pregnant, before the child is born.

Young black women are more likely to cohabit than are young white women, but most never marry their partners. Despite the high out-of-wedlock black birthrate, African American women are unlikely to have their first baby while cohabiting. If they do become pregnant, they are unlikely to marry before giving birth; they tend to rely on extended family rather than on a male partner (Manning & Landale, 1996).

Puerto Ricans traditionally view cohabitation as an alternative to marriage. Almost half of their first unions are cohabitations, which tend to be unstable and usually do not lead to marriage. When these unions produce children, which they often do, they are considered informal marriages; the woman is *less* likely to marry during her pregnancy than if she were not cohabiting. About half of Puerto Rican babies born out of wedlock have cohabiting parents (Manning & Landale, 1996).

Mexican Americans are even more pro-marriage than non-Hispanic whites, but they are more tolerant of cohabitation—*if* the couple intend to marry. Cohabitation occurs mainly among the less educated and less affluent. About 25 percent of first unions of Mexican American women ages 20 to 49, and 16 percent of current ones, are informal unions (Oropesa, 1996).

MARRIAGE

In Tibet, a man and his father have the same wife. In Zaire, it's just the opposite: a woman shares her husband with her mother. In Cameroon, husbands are not supposed to be faithful (World Features Syndicate, 1996). In some Himalayan cultures a woman may marry a set of brothers (Kottak, 1994). In west Africa, a working woman who is married to a man may also take a "wife" to care for her home and children (Amadiume, 1987).

Marriage customs differ widely, but the universality of some form of marriage throughout history and around the world shows that it meets a variety of fundamental needs. Marriage is usually considered the best way to ensure orderly raising of children. One of its most important economic benefits is the provision for a division of labor within a consuming and working unit. Ideally, it offers intimacy, friendship, affection, sexual fulfillment, companionship, and an opportunity for emotional growth. The high divorce rates show how hard it is to attain these ideals, but the high remarriage rates show that people keep trying.

The typical "marrying age" varies across cultures. In eastern Europe, people tend to marry in or before their early twenties. Industrialized nations, such as the United States, Japan, and the Scandinavian countries, are seeing a trend toward later marriage as young adults take time to pursue educational and career goals or to explore relationships (Bianchi & Spain, 1986).

In the United States in 1994, the median age of first-time bridegrooms was 26.7, and of first-time brides, 24.5 years—a rise of 3 years since 1975 (U.S. Bureau of the Census, 1996a). Ninety percent of American women, but only 75 percent of African American women, eventually marry. Until the late 1970s, 95 percent of American women married during their lifetime, and rates for black and white women were similar (Norton & Miller, 1992). The lower marriage rate among African Americans since then is attributed to high unemployment among black men and greater economic independence among black working women (Manning & Landale, 1996; Tucker, Taylor, & Mitchell-Kiernan, 1993).

Marriage and Health

A large-scale Canadian survey found single people to be healthier than their married counterparts (J. M. White, 1992), but most studies go the other way. Married people, especially married men, tend to be healthier physically (and, in some reported research, psychologically) than those who never married or who are widowed, separated, or divorced (C. E. Ross, Mirowsky, & Goldsteen, 1990). Married people have fewer disabilities or chronic

Married people tend to be healthier and happier than unmarried people. Couples who are satisfied with their marriage are more likely to sustain sexual intimacy, which can be shown not only in genital contact but in casual moments of physical closeness. *(David Young-Wolff/PhotoEdit)*

conditions that limit their activities, and when they go to the hospital, their stays are generally short. Married people live longer, too, according to a study going back to 1940 in 16 industrial countries (Hu & Goldman, 1990). Married people, especially men, seem to lead healthier, safer lives, taking fewer risks and encouraging each other to pay more attention to their health (R. G. Rogers, 1995).

Married people also tend to be better off financially, a factor that contributes to physical and mental health (C. E. Ross et al., 1990). In 1986, among more than 36,000 men and women ages 25 to 64, married people were less likely to die than unmarrieds. However, people with high incomes, married or single, were more likely to survive than were married people with low incomes; the highest mortality was among low-income singles.

Marriage and Happiness

Marriage makes people happy, and not only in romance novels—even though, today, some of the benefits of marriage, such as sex, intimacy, and economic security, are not confined to wedlock. Among a national sample of more than 2,000 adults ages 18 to 90, married people tended to be happier than unmarried people, though not much happier than people who cohabit. However, "unhappy relationships are worse than none" (C. Ross, 1995, p. 129). Contrary to earlier studies, men and women were found to benefit equally from a marital attachment and the economic and emotional support it entails. The difference is that women

who are single, divorced, or widowed are more likely to lack economic support, whereas men in those circumstances tend to lack emotional support.

The two sexes do have different expectations about marriage, stemming from different definitions of intimacy. To many women, marital intimacy entails sharing of feelings and confidences. Men tend to express intimacy through sex, practical help, companionship, and doing things together (A. J. Thompson & Walker, 1989).

Marital and Extramarital Sexual Activity

Americans apparently engage in sexual activity less often than images in the media suggest, and married people do so more often than singles, though not as often as cohabitors. Face-to-face interviews with a random sample of 3,432 men and women ages 18 to 59 found that, overall, only about one-third have intercourse 2 or more times a week; this includes 40 percent of married couples and more than 50 percent of cohabiting couples, but fewer than 25 percent of those who do not live with a sex partner. On average, married couples have sex 7 times a month (Laumann et al., 1994; Michael et al., 1994). Couples who cohabited before marriage or who had previous marriages tend to have sex more often (Call, Sprecher, & Schwartz, 1995).

Frequency of sexual relations in marriage drops sharply after the early months, apparently due to loss of novelty, and then declines gradually as time goes on. Satisfaction with the marriage is the second most important factor after age, though it is unclear whether satisfaction influences frequency of sex or the other way around. Pregnancy, sterilization, and the presence of young children reduce sexual activity (Call et al., 1995).

Some married people seek sexual intimacy outside of marriage, especially after the first few years, when the excitement of sex with the spouse wears off or problems in the relationship surface. It is hard to know just how common extramarital sex is, because there is no way to tell how truthful people are about their sexual practices, but recent surveys suggest that it is much less common than is often assumed. In one survey, only about 21 percent of men and 11.5 percent of women who were ever married reported having had extramarital relations. Extramarital activity was more prevalent among younger cohorts than among those born before 1940 (T. W. Smith, 1994). Even today, however, more than 75 percent of the population say extramarital affairs are always wrong, and an additional 14 percent say they are almost always wrong (Laumann et al., 1994; Michael et al., 1994).

Fear of AIDS and other sexually transmitted diseases may well have curtailed extramarital sex since its reported peak in the late 1960s and early 1970s. In one nationwide survey, only about 2 percent of married respondents admitted to having been unfaithful during the previous year. Infidelity was more common among younger adults (ages 18 to 29), city dwellers, men, minorities, and people with low income and education. People who still engage in extramarital sex seem to be risk takers; only about 10 percent say they always use condoms (Choi, Catania, & Dolcini, 1994).

A legacy of the double standard is that women are more willing to accept a partner's infidelity than men are, perhaps because of men's greater economic independence. Researchers asked 250 Dutch couples, 79 percent of whom were married and the rest cohabiting, to imagine their reaction upon learning of a partner's adultery. The responses suggest that men and women are equally likely to be jealous in such a situation, but women tend to adapt more readily. The more often a man has previously strayed, the less anger and disappointment the woman is likely to express. Instead, women, especially those with low self-esteem, tend to express self-doubt—to wonder whether something they did might have driven the man to look elsewhere for satisfaction (Buunk, 1995). Of course, we can't be sure that people would actu-

ally respond to such a situation the way they imagine they would.

Domestic Violence

Partner abuse—violence against a spouse, a former spouse, or an intimate partner—typically begins with shoving or hitting and then escalates into beating. Some victims are critically injured, some die, and others live in constant terror.

The full extent of partner abuse is unknown. It generally occurs in private, and victims often do not report it because they are ashamed or afraid (R. Bachman, 1994). More than 9 out of 10 victims are women, and they are more likely than men to be seriously harmed. Once a woman has been abused, she is likely to be abused again—in about 1 in 5 cases, at least twice more within 6 months (Holtzworth-Munroe & Stuart, 1994; U. S. Bureau of Justice Statistics, 1994).

More than 570,000 women each year are reported to suffer domestic violence, and more than 1,400 women are killed by intimate partners (U.S. Bureau of Justice Statistics, 1994). Twenty-nine percent of murders of women are committed by a husband, ex-husband, or suitor (Reiss & Roth, 1994). Partner abuse occurs at every level of society, in all income groups; but the women at greatest risk are young, poor, uneducated, and divorced or separated (U.S. Bureau of Justice Statistics, 1994). Men who abuse women tend to have low incomes and alcohol problems (Heyman, O'Leary, & Jouriles, 1995; McKenry, Julian, & Gavazzi, 1995). There is no appreciable difference in domestic violence against black and white women (R. Bachman, 1994).

Pushing, shoving, and slapping often begin even before marriage; among 625 newlywed couples, 36 percent reported premarital violence (McLaughlin, Leonard, & Senchak, 1992). If nothing is done about it, the violence tends to increase (Holtzworth-Munroe, 1995; O'Leary et al., 1989). Men who are seriously aggressive before marriage generally continue to be aggressive after marriage, and such marriages are likely to deteriorate and fail (Heyman et al., 1995). Spousal abuse is more frequent in marriages in which the man seeks to control or dominate (Yllo, 1984, 1993). Such relationships may be products of a socialization process in which boys are taught by example to prevail by means of aggression and physical force. Eight out of ten men who physically assault their wives saw their fathers beat their mothers (Reiss & Roth, 1994). Men brought up in violent homes tend not to have learned to deal with conflict, frustration, and anger (Holtzworth-Munroe, 1995).

Why do women stay with men who abuse them? Some have low self-esteem and feel they deserve to be beaten. Constant ridicule, criticism, threats, punishment, and psychological manipulation may destroy their self-confidence (NOW Legal Defense and Education Fund & Chernow-O'Leary, 1987). Some women feel they have nowhere to turn. Their abusive partners isolate them from family and friends. They are often financially dependent and lack outside social support (Kalmuss & Straus, 1982; McKenry et al., 1995; Strube & Barbour, 1984). If they try to end the relationship or call the police, they get more abuse (Geller, 1992). Some women are afraid to leave—a realistic fear, since some abusive husbands later track down and beat or even kill their estranged wives (Reiss & Roth, 1994). Women who are victims of severe violence they did not initiate or of coercive sex are the most fearful, perhaps because they feel the least control over what happens to them (DeMaris & Swinford, 1996).

The effects of domestic violence extend beyond the couple. The children, especially sons, are likely to be abused by both parents (Jouriles & Norwood, 1995), and they may grow up to be abusers themselves.

In some cases, marital or family therapy may stop mild-to-moderate abuse before it escalates (Gelles & Maynard, 1987; Holtzworth-Munroe, 1995). Evidence suggests that men who are arrested for family violence are less likely to repeat the abuse, and communities are increasingly adopting this approach (Bouza, 1990; L. W. Sherman & Berk, 1984; L. W. Sherman & Cohn, 1989). The federal Violence against Women Act, adopted in 1994, provides for tougher law enforcement, funding for shelters, a national domestic violence hotline, and educating judges and court personnel—as well as young people—about domestic violence.

What Makes Marriage Work?

Although marriage has both economic and psychic benefits, the latter seem to be more important. Among a national sample of 2,331 married people, the partners' dependence on each other to provide income and do household chores played a part in commitment to marriage, but the strongest factor was a feeling of obligation to the spouse (Nock, 1995). Success in marriage is closely associated with the way partners communicate, make decisions, and deal with conflict (Brubaker, 1983, 1993). Arguing and openly expressing anger seem to be good for a marriage (Gottman & Krokoff, 1989). Among 150 couples who were followed through the first 10 years of marriage, those who learned to "fight fair" were 50 percent less likely to divorce (Markman, Renick, Floyd, Stanley, & Clements, 1993).

Marriages change as partners mature and deal with new issues, needs, desires, expectations, and problems. Still, patterns set in young adulthood affect the quality of marriage at midlife. A major study identified four patterns: (1) the *traditional* marriage, with women as homemakers and men as providers, (2) the *romantic* marriage, built around sexual passion, (3) the *rescue* marriage, which makes up for previous painful experiences, and (4) the *companionate* marriage (most common among young couples today), based on friendship and an equal division of work and family roles. Regardless of the type of marriage, partners have to master nine psychological tasks: to redefine the connection with each spouse's original family, to build intimacy without sacrificing autonomy, to adjust to parenthood while preserving privacy, to cope with crises without weakening the marital bond, to allow safe expression of conflict, to establish a fulfilling sexual relationship insulated from the demands of work and family, to share laughter and fun, to provide nurturance and emotional support, and to sustain romance while facing reality (Wallerstein & Blakeslee, 1995).

DIVORCE AND REMARRIAGE

The United States has one of the highest divorce rates in the world: in 1994, 46 divorces a year per 10,000 people, more than twice the rate in 1960 (Bruce et al., 1995; Singh, Mathews, Clarke, Yannicos, & Smith, 1995; U.S. Bureau of the Census, 1996b). The rate peaked in 1979–1980 and since then has declined and then leveled off (Singh et al., 1995). Among African Americans, the divorce rate—more than twice the rate for whites—is rising as the marriage rate declines (E. J. Lawson & Thompson, 1995).

Divorce has doubled since 1970 in many other developed countries (see Figure 13-5). This increase has accompanied the passage in most western countries, mainly in the 1960s and 1970s, of more liberal divorce laws, which eliminate the need to find one partner at fault. Countries such as Italy and Ireland, where religious opposition to

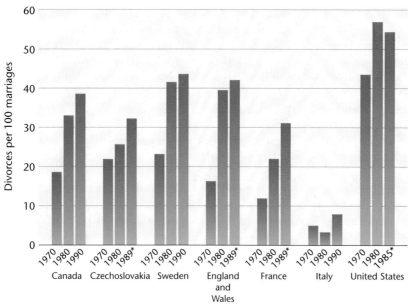

*Latest year a comparable figure was calculated

FIGURE 13-5
Divorce rates before and after the passage of more lenient divorce laws in the United States and many European countries. Divorce has risen since 1970 in many industrial societies, but rates remain relatively low in Italy, where religious opposition has prevented liberalization of divorce. *(Source: A. Burns, 1992.)*

divorce is strong, have not experienced appreciably higher rates. This may change in Ireland, where, by a close vote, a November 1995 referendum eliminated a constitutional prohibition on divorce (Montalbano, 1995).

In the United States, as in other countries, the no-fault laws that led to higher divorce rates were a response to societal developments that prompted a greater demand for divorce (Nakonezny, Shull, & Rodgers, 1995). A woman who is financially independent is less likely to remain in a bad marriage; women today, according to one study, are 24 percent more likely than men to plan and initiate a divorce (Crane et al., 1995). Instead of staying together "for the sake of the children," many embattled spouses conclude that exposing children to continued parental conflict does greater damage. And, for the increasing number of childless couples, it's easier to return to a single state (Berscheid & Campbell, 1981; L. Eisenberg, 1995). Perhaps most important, while most people today hope their marriages will endure, fewer expect it.

On the other hand, in some ways young people expect more from marriage than ever. Young adults who live far from their families of origin may expect a spouse to take the place of parents and friends, as well as to be a confidante and lover—an impossibly tall order. Conflicts between men's and women's expectations may produce tension.

Age at marriage is a major predictor of whether it will last. Teenagers have high divorce rates; peo-

ple who wait until their late twenties or later to marry have the best chances for success. Also more likely to divorce are women who drop out of high school or college (Norton & Miller, 1992). When there are children, the likelihood of a breakup increases if the husband is unemployed or under age 30, if the family is living in poverty, or if both parents work full time (U.S. Bureau of the Census, 1992c). Table 13-4 summarizes other factors influencing the likelihood of divorce.

Adjusting to Divorce

Divorce is not a single event. It is a *process* with an indefinite beginning and ending—"a sequence of potentially stressful experiences that begin before physical separation and continue after it" (Morrison & Cherlin, 1995, p. 801). Ending even an unhappy marriage can be extremely painful, especially when there are children. Divorce can bring feelings of failure, blame, hostility, and self-recrimination, as well as high rates of illness and death (Kitson & Morgan, 1990). Some divorced women (even more than widows) have difficulty performing ordinary social activities (Kitson & Roach, 1989). Depression and disorganized thinking and functioning are common after divorce; so are relief and hope for a fresh start (J. B. Kelly, 1982).

Adjustment depends partly on how people feel about themselves and their ex-partners and on how the divorce is handled. The person who takes the first step to end a marriage often feels a mixture of relief, sadness, guilt, apprehension, and anger. Nonetheless, the initiating partner is usually in better emotional shape in the early months of separation than the other partner, who has the additional pain of rejection, loss of control, and feelings of powerlessness (J. B. Kelly, 1982; Pettit & Bloom, 1984).

An important factor in adjustment is emotional detachment from the former spouse. An active social life helps cut the emotional ties. People who argue with their ex-mates or have not found a new lover or spouse experience more distress (Tschann, Johnston, & Wallerstein, 1989).

Among 290 divorced parents—most of them white and well educated—those who made the best adjustment had more personal resources before the separation: higher socioeconomic status for men and better psychological functioning for women. Those whose income underwent a less dramatic drop adjusted better (Tschann et al., 1989). Divorced people in less advantaged circumstances tend to have more difficulties: a lower standard of living, increased work hours, and continued struggles with an ex-spouse who may default on child support (Kitson & Morgan, 1990). Only about half (52 percent) of custodial mothers and 43 percent of custodial fathers receive full

child support payments; about one-fourth of women (24 percent) and more than one-third (37 percent) of men with support awards receive no payments at all (U.S. Bureau of the Census, 1996a). The lower a man's income, the less likely he is to come up with support money (D. R. Meyer & Bartfeld, 1996).

Remarriage after Divorce

Remarriage, said the essayist Samuel Johnson, "is the triumph of hope over experience." A high divorce rate is not a sign that people do not want to be married. Instead, it generally reflects a desire to be *happily* married and a belief that divorce is like surgery—painful and traumatic, but necessary for a better life.

An estimated three-quarters of divorced women in the United States remarry, and men are even likelier to remarry than women. A woman is more likely to remarry if her first marriage was brief, if she was young when it ended, if she has no children, if she is non-Hispanic white, if she has a high school education, and if she lives in the west. Remarriages tend to be less stable than first marriages; 37 percent of remarriages fail within 10 years, compared with 30 percent of first marriages (Bumpass, Sweet, & Martin, 1990).

TABLE 13-4

Personal Factors Associated with Probability of Divorce

Factor	Remarks
Premarital cohabitation	This factor has been explained as a result of the fact that people who live together before marriage are less conventional. As this lifestyle becomes more common, it should exert less influence; and in fact, for recent cohorts the effect is weaker.
Young age at marriage	This is the strongest predictor of divorce in the first 5 years of marriage.
Bearing a child before marriage	Premarital pregnancy of itself does not seem to increase the risk of divorce.
Having no children	Having at least one child reduces the risk of divorce, especially if that child is a boy. Fathers tend to be more involved with sons than with daughters, and greater involvement of the father in child care reduces the risk of divorce.
Stepchildren in the home	The presence of children from a previous marriage brings additional stresses and divided loyalties.
Divorce of own parents	This is still an important risk factor, even now that it is more common to have divorced parents.
Being African American	This difference still exists when socioeconomic status, fertility, sex ratios, and age at marriage are controlled.

SOURCES: Schoen, 1992; L. K. White, 1990.

✔ FAMILY LIFE

Although the desire for children is almost universal, the "traditional" family—a husband, a wife, and their biological children—is not. In Brazil, for example, the man and woman continue to belong to their families of origin, and their children belong to both (Kottak, 1994). In western countries, family size, composition, structure, and living arrangements have changed dramatically (L. Eisenberg, 1995; Gilliand, 1989). People are having smaller families and starting them later. More single women are having children and raising them. Infertile couples are acquiring children by technological means unheard of a generation ago. Most mothers now work for pay, in or outside the home, and a small but growing number of fathers are primary caregivers. Divorce and remarriage have produced an increasing number of blended families, and millions of children live with homosexual parents (see Chapter 9).

When and how do adults become parents, and why do some people choose not to become parents? How does parenthood influence young adults' development?

BECOMING PARENTS

At one time, a blessing offered to newlyweds in the Asian country of Nepal was "May you have enough sons to cover the hillsides!" Today, Nepali couples are wished "May you have a very bright son" (B. P. Arjyal, personal communication, February 12, 1993). Although sons still are preferred over daughters, even boys are not wished for in such numbers as in the past.

In preindustrial societies, large families were a necessity: children helped with the family's work and would eventually care for aging parents. The death rate in childhood was high, and having many children made it more likely that some of them would reach maturity. Today, in technologically advanced societies, fewer workers are needed; because of modern medical care, more children survive; and through government programs, some care of the aged is provided. Overpopulation and hunger are major problems in some parts of the world, and large families are no longer an economic asset. In developing countries, as well as in industrial countries such as the United States, there is greater interest in limiting family size and in spacing children farther apart. In 1955, the average American woman was likely to have

Today many women, especially educated women, are delaying childbirth until their thirties or forties, but most births are still to women in their twenties. The risks of delayed childbearing seem to be less than was previously thought, and babies of older women may benefit from the mother's greater maturity. *(Erika Stone)*

3.6 children; by 1994, she was likely to have 2.1 (National Center for Health Statistics, 1996b; U.S. Bureau of the Census, 1995b).

When People Have Children

By and large, people today have children later in life than before (refer back to Figure 13-2). In England and Wales, the birthrate among women ages 35 to 39 increased by 44 percent in the 1980s, while births to women in their twenties declined by 19 percent (P. Brown, 1993). In the United States, between 1970 and 1987, the percentage of women who had a first child after age 30 quadrupled, though most births were still to women in their twenties (National Center for Health Statistics, 1990). The birthrate for women ages 40 to 44 rose nearly 50 percent between 1974 and 1994, reaching almost 10 out of every 1,000 births (Clay, 1996). However, the trend toward motherhood after 30 appears to have peaked, in part because more women who wait that long are choosing to remain childless (National Center for Health Statistics, 1994b).

More educated women have babies later; educational level is the most important predictor of the age at which a woman will bear her first child (Rindfuss, Morgan, & Swicegood, 1988; Rindfuss & St. John, 1983). Among 1,438 Flemish and Dutch couples, those with higher education and less commitment to religion were more likely to delay childbearing. So were couples who were cohabiting or had done so. In these couples, more than in those who had married without cohabiting first, the timing of parenthood tended to be a mutual decision (Corijn, Liefbroer, & Gierveld, 1996).

The risks of delayed childbearing appear to be less than previously believed. After age 35 there is a greater chance of miscarriage and more likelihood of chromosomal abnormalities (such as Down syndrome), birth-related complications, or fetal death; but most risks to the baby's health are not much higher (G. S. Berkowitz, Skovron, Lapinski, & Berkowitz, 1990; P. Brown, 1993). On the positive side, babies of older mothers may benefit from their mothers' greater ease with parenthood. When 105 new mothers ages 16 to 38 were interviewed and observed with their infants, the older mothers reported more satisfaction with parenting and spent more time at it. They were more affectionate and sensitive to their babies and more effective in encouraging desired behavior (Ragozin, Basham, Crnic, Greenberg, & Robinson, 1982).

Coping with Infertility

One risk in waiting to have children is failure to conceive. About 8 percent of American couples experience *infertility:* inability to conceive after 12 to 18 months of trying (Mosher & Pratt, 1991). Infertility can occur before or after having a first child. In young adulthood either partner is equally likely to be infertile (R. B. Glass, 1986).

The most common cause in men is production of too few sperm. Although only one sperm is needed to fertilize an ovum, a sperm count lower than 60 to 200 million per ejaculation makes conception unlikely. There is disputed evidence that sperm counts, as well as quality of sperm (see Chapter 2), in males worldwide have begun to decline, possibly due to drugs, tobacco, alcohol, gasoline fumes, industrial pollutants, stress, and other hazards of modern life (B. M. King, 1996; L. Wright, 1996). Sometimes a passageway is blocked, making sperm unable to exit; or sperm may be unable to "swim" well enough to reach the cervix. Some cases of male infertility seem to have a genetic basis (Reijo, Alagappan, Patrizio, & Page, 1996).

If the problem is with the woman, she may not be producing ova, the ova may be abnormal, mucus in the cervix may prevent sperm from penetrating it, or a disease of the uterine lining may prevent implantation of the fertilized ovum. The most common female cause, however, is blockage of the fallopian tubes, preventing ova from reaching the uterus. In about half these cases, the tubes are blocked as a result of scar tissue from sexually transmitted diseases (STDs), which results in pelvic inflammatory disease (B. M. King, 1996). The marked increase in adolescent sexual activity and in STDs is likely to lead to sharp rises in infertility as today's teenagers enter adulthood (Shafer & Moscicki, 1991).

According to one study, women with a history of depression are twice as likely to be infertile as other women. Use of antidepressant medications and drinking alcohol at least twice a week are associated with infertility (Lapane et al., 1995). Smoking and heavy coffee consumption seem to delay conception (Stanton & Gray, 1995).

About 50 percent of infertile couples eventually conceive, with or without help; an increasing proportion get treatment (H. W. Jones & Toner, 1993). Sometimes drug therapy or surgery can correct the problem. Hormone treatment may raise a man's sperm count or increase a woman's ability to ovulate. However, fertility drugs increase the likelihood of multiple, and very likely premature, births (B. M. King, 1996).

Infertility burdens a marriage emotionally. Women, especially, often have trouble accepting the fact that they cannot do what comes so naturally and easily to others. Partners may become frustrated and angry with themselves and each other, and they may feel empty, worthless, and depressed (Abbey, Andrews, & Halman, 1992; H. W. Jones & Toner, 1993). Their sexual relationship may suffer as intimacy becomes a matter of "making babies, not love" (Sabatelli, Meth, & Gavazzi, 1988).

Some infertile adults remain childless, but others adopt children or try new "high-tech" solutions.

Adoption

Diane's daughter, Anna, is among the fewer than 2 percent of children in the United States who have been adopted ("Effects of Open Adoption Vary," 1995). Not only married couples (like Diane and Jonathan) but single people, older people, and homosexual couples have become adoptive parents. Among African Americans, adoption is related less to infertility than to a wish to provide a family for a known child, often a relative (Bachrach,

Anna, the adopted daughter of Diane Papalia (one of the authors of this book) and her husband, Jonathan, was born in Chile. Because of a decrease in the number of adoptable American babies, many children adopted today are of foreign birth. Adoptive parents face special challenges, such as the need to explain the adoption to the child. But most adoptive children view their adoption positively and see it as playing only a minor role in their identity. *(Erika Stone)*

London, & Maza, 1991), and many of these adoptions are informal (L. Richardson, 1993). Advances in contraception and legalization of abortion have reduced the number of adoptable, healthy white American babies; thus many of the children available for adoption are disabled, are beyond infancy, or are of foreign birth.

Although adoption is widely accepted in the United States, there are still prejudices and mistaken ideas about it. One seriously mistaken belief is that adopted children are bound to have problems because they have been deprived of their biological parents. Actually, a study of 715 families with teenagers who had been adopted in infancy found that nearly 3 out of 4 saw their adoption as playing only a minor role in their identity (Bemon & Sharma, 1994). In another study of 85 adopted children, most viewed their adoption positively—though teenagers saw it less positively than younger children (D. W. Smith & Brodzinsky, 1994).

Adopting a child does carry special risks and challenges. Besides the usual issues of parenthood, adoptive parents need to deal with acceptance of their infertility (if this is why they adopted), the need to explain the adoption to the child, and possible discomfort about the child's interest in the biological parents.

New Ways to Parenthood: Assisted Conception

Many couples yearn to have children who carry on their hereditary legacy—to see in future generations the almond-shaped eyes of one ancestor or the artistic talent of another. Technology now enables many people to have children who are genetically at least half their own.

Artificial insemination—injection of sperm into a woman's cervix—can be done when a man has a low sperm count. Sperm from several ejaculations can be combined for one injection. If the man is infertile, a couple may choose *artificial insemination by a donor (AID)*. The donor may be matched with the prospective father for physical characteristics, and the two men's sperm may be mixed so that no one knows which one is the biological father.

An increasing number of couples are attempting *in vitro fertilization (IVF)*, fertilization outside the mother's body. It is most effective in women whose fallopian tubes are blocked or damaged. First, fertility drugs, such as Clomid or Pergonal, are given to increase production of ova. Then a mature ovum is surgically removed, fertilized in a laboratory dish, and implanted in the mother's uterus. This method can also address male infertility, since a single sperm can be injected into the ovum. Usually several ova are fertilized and implanted to increase the chance of success. Many couples conceive only after several tries, if at all; estimates of success rates range from 12 to 20 percent (de Lafuente, 1994; Gabriel, 1996). When successful, the procedure often results in multiple births (P. Brown, 1993). Two newer techniques with higher success rates are *gamete intrafallopian transfer (GIFT)* and *zygote intrafallopian transfer (ZIFT)*, in which the egg and sperm or the fertilized egg are inserted in the fallopian tube (Society for Assisted Reproductive Technology, 1993). Although children conceived through IVF tend to be small, their head circumference and mental development are normal (Brandes et al., 1992). In vitro fertilization costs thousands of dollars and may or may not be covered by insurance.

A major cause of declining fertility in women after age 30 is deterioration in the quality of their ova (van Noord-Zaadstra et al., 1991). A woman who is producing poor-quality ova or who has had her ovaries removed may try **ovum transfer.** In this procedure (the female counterpart of AID), an unfertilized ovum, or *donor egg*—provided, usually anonymously, by a fertile young woman—is fertilized in the laboratory and implanted in the prospective mother's uterus (Lutjen et al., 1984). Alternatively, the ovum can be fertilized in the donor's body by artificial insemination. The donor's uterus is flushed out a few days later, and the embryo is retrieved and inserted into the recipient's uterus. Ovum transfer has been used by women 40 to 44 years old and even past menopause (Sauer, Paulson, & Lobo, 1990, 1993). The cost of the procedure may be up to $20,000, only a relatively small portion of which is the donor's fee.

In *surrogate motherhood,* a fertile woman is impregnated by the prospective father, usually by artificial insemination. She carries the baby to term and gives the child to the father and his mate. Surrogate motherhood is in legal limbo, partly as a result of the "Baby M" case, in which a surrogate changed her mind and wanted to keep the baby (Hanley, 1988a, 1988b; Shipp, 1988). Although not granted custody, she did receive visitation rights. Today, courts in most states view surrogacy contracts as unenforceable (A. Toback, personal communication, January 23, 1997), and some states have banned the practice or placed strict conditions upon it. The American Academy of Pediatrics

Committee on Bioethics (1992) recommends that surrogacy be considered a tentative, preconception adoption agreement in which the surrogate is the sole decision maker before the birth. The AAP also recommends a prebirth agreement on the period of time in which the surrogate may assert her parental rights.

Perhaps the most objectionable aspect of surrogacy, aside from the possibility of forcing the surrogate to relinquish the baby, is the payment of money (up to $30,000, including fees to a "matchmaker"). Payment for adoption is forbidden in about 25 states; but surrogate motherhood is not adoption, since the biological father is the legal father. Still, the creation of a "breeder class" of poor and disadvantaged women who carry the babies of the well-to-do strikes many people as wrong. Similar concerns have been raised about payment for donor eggs. Exploitation of the would-be parents is an issue, too: some observers worry about the rapid growth of fertility clinics that may prey on desperate couples through misleading claims driven by the profit motive (Gabriel, 1996).

New and unorthodox means of conception raise other serious questions. Must people who use them be infertile, or should people be free to make such arrangements simply for convenience? Should single people and cohabiting and homosexual couples have access to these methods? What about older people, who may become frail or die before the child grows up? Should the children know about their parentage? Should chromosome tests be performed on prospective donors and surrogates? What happens if a couple who have contracted with a surrogate divorce before the birth?

One concern is the psychological risk to children conceived with donated eggs or sperm. Will the lack of a genetic bond with one or both parents, together with strains created by the usual secrecy of such procedures and lingering disappointment about infertility, color the family atmosphere? One study suggests that the answer is no and that a strong desire for parenthood is more important than genetic ties. The quality of parenting was *better* when a child was conceived by in vitro fertilization or donor insemination than in the usual way, and no overall differences appeared in the children's feelings, behavior, or relationships with their parents. Parents of adopted children scored similarly to parents who had used assisted conception (Golombok, Cook, Bish, & Murray, 1995).

One thing seems certain: as long as there are people who want children but are unable to conceive or bear them, human ingenuity and technology will come up with new ways of satisfying their need.

REMAINING CHILD-FREE BY CHOICE

"When are you going to have a baby?" This question is heard less often these days, as societal attitudes have moved away from the belief that all married couples who *can* have children *should* have them (Thornton, 1989). According to a projection by the U.S. Bureau of the Census, 16 percent of "baby boom" women will not become mothers—about twice as many as in their mothers' generation (O'Connell, 1991).

Some couples decide before marriage never to have children. Others keep postponing conception, waiting for the "right time," until they decide that the right time will never come. Some of these couples want to concentrate on careers or social causes. Some feel more comfortable with adults or think they would not make good parents. Some want to retain the intimacy of the honeymoon. Some enjoy the freedom to travel or to make spur-of-the-moment decisions.

Some do not want the considerable financial burdens of parenthood (F. L. Campbell, Townes, & Beach, 1982). For a child born in 1992, it was estimated that an average middle-class family would spend a total of $128,670 for food, clothing, and shelter by the time the child was 17 years old (U.S. Department of Agriculture, 1992). On the other hand, some people may want children but may be discouraged by the costs and the difficulty of combining parenthood with employment. Better child care and other support services might help such couples make truly voluntary decisions (Bloom & Pebley, 1982).

PARENTHOOD AS A DEVELOPMENTAL EXPERIENCE

A first baby marks a major transition in parents' lives. This totally dependent new person changes individuals and changes relationships. Whether a child is a biological offspring or is adopted and whether or not the parents are married, parenthood can be a developmental experience. As children develop, parents do too.

Both women and men often feel ambivalent about becoming parents. Along with excitement, they may feel anxiety about the responsibility of caring for a child and the commitment of time and energy it entails. Among couples who do not have children, husbands consider having them more important and are more apt to want them than wives do (Seccombe, 1991), but once children come, fathers enjoy looking after them less than mothers do. Although fathers generally believe they should be involved in their children's lives, most are not nearly as involved as the mothers (Backett, 1987; Boulton, 1983; LaRossa, 1988).

A study of parents of 4-year-olds in 10 European, Asian, and African countries and the United States found that fathers think they are contributing more than they actually are. Internationally, fathers average less than 1 hour a day in sole charge of their children during the work week, and when men do supervise their children, it is usually with the mother. American fathers spend only 1 hour a day in such shared child care, while American mothers spend an average of nearly 11 hours each weekday caring for preschoolers—more than mothers in any of the other 10 countries (Olmsted & Weikart, 1994).

Still, family roles are very important to men—as important as what goes on at work. Working men and women seem equally affected by physical and psychological stress, whether due to work interfering with family life or the other way around (Frone, Russell, & Barnes, 1996). Among 300 fathers, ages 25 to 40, in two-earner couples, a man's good relationships with his wife and children often made up for a poor experience on the job; distress tended to occur when both job and family roles were unsatisfactory. For working women, merely being a parent often offsets job concerns; for men the important thing is not parenthood itself, but how rewarding the parental role is (Barnett et al., 1992).

Marital satisfaction typically declines during the child-raising years (see Chapter 15). One research team followed 128 middle- and working-class couples in their late twenties from the first pregnancy until the child's third birthday. Although some marriages improved, many suffered overall, especially in the eyes of the wives. Many spouses reported that they loved each other less, became more ambivalent about their relationship, argued more, and communicated less. This was true no matter what the sex of the child and whether or not the couple had a second child by the time the first was 3 years old (Belsky & Rovine, 1990).

What distinguished marriages that got stronger from those which deteriorated? In weaker marriages, the partners were likely to be younger and less well educated, to earn less money, and to have been married a shorter time. One or both partners tended to have low self-esteem, and husbands were likely to be less sensitive. The mothers who had the hardest time were those whose babies had difficult temperaments. Surprisingly, couples who were most romantic "pre-baby" had more problems "post-baby," perhaps because they had unrealistic expectations. Also, women who had planned their pregnancies were unhappier, possibly because they had expected life with a baby to be better than it turned out to be (Belsky & Rovine, 1990). In another study, mothers of firstborn 1-year-olds reported that their relationships with their husbands, their own physical well-being, and their maternal competence and satisfaction were not as good as they had expected, and they had trouble adjusting (Kalmuss, Davidson, & Cushman, 1992).

If a couple share household tasks fairly equally before becoming parents, and then after the birth the burden shifts to the wife, marital happiness tends to decline, especially for nontraditional wives (Belsky, Lang, & Huston, 1986). Since most mothers now work for pay, the fact that most husbands do not share equally in the burdens of homemaking and child care can be a source of stress (see Box 13-3). Among young Israeli first-time parents, fathers who saw themselves as caring, nurturing, and protecting experienced less decline in marital satisfaction than other fathers, and they felt better about parenthood. Men who were less involved with their babies, and whose wives were more involved, tended to be more dissatisfied. The mothers who became most dissatisfied with their marriages were those who saw themselves as disorganized and unable to cope with the demands of motherhood (Levy-Shiff, 1994).

STEPPARENTHOOD

Divorce and remarriage often bring a different kind of transition: a transition to stepparenthood. Becoming a stepparent presents special problems and concerns, and this may be especially true for stepmothers (see Chapter 9). Interviews with 138 married or cohabiting stepparents who also had biological children in the home found that women have more trouble than men do in raising stepchildren, as compared with raising biological children. This may be because women generally spend more time with the children than men do. It does not seem to matter whether the biological children are from a previous marriage or the present one. The more recent the current marriage and the older the stepchildren, the harder stepparenting seems to be. Nonwhite stepparents and those with higher education tend to derive more satisfaction from their stepchildren (MacDonald & DeMaris, 1996).

This "blended" family consists of a couple and three sets of children: a teenager from the husband's first marriage, two children from the wife's first marriage, and a toddler from the present marriage. Life is more complex in such families and presents special problems for stepparents, but most children in blended families adjust and thrive. *(Erika Stone)*

BOX 13-3   PRACTICALLY SPEAKING

HOW DUAL-EARNER COUPLES COPE

The growing number of marriages in which both husband and wife are gainfully employed presents both opportunities and challenges. A second income raises some families from poverty to middle-income status and makes others affluent. It makes women more independent and gives them a greater share of economic power, and it reduces the pressure on men to be providers; 47 percent of working wives contribute half or more of family income (Louis Harris & Associates, 1995). Less tangible benefits may include a more equal relationship between husband and wife, better health for both, greater self-esteem for the woman, and a closer relationship between a father and his children (Gilbert, 1994).

However, this way of life also creates stress. Working couples face extra demands on time and energy, conflicts between work and family, possible rivalry between spouses, and anxiety and guilt about meeting children's needs. Each role makes greater or lesser demands at different times, and partners have to decide which should take priority when. The

family is most demanding, especially for women, when there are young children (Warren & Johnson, 1995). Careers are especially demanding when a worker is getting established or being promoted. Both kinds of demands frequently occur in young adulthood.

Men and women tend to be stressed by different aspects of the work-family situation. Among 314 spouses with relatively high income and education, husbands were more likely to suffer from overload (perhaps because they had not been socialized to deal with domestic as well as occupational responsibilities), whereas women were more likely to feel the strain of conflicting role expectations—for example, the need to be aggressive and competitive at work but compassionate and nurturing at home (Paden & Buehler, 1995). Temporary withdrawal from social interaction after a busy workday helped settle men down and softened the effects of overload. "Talking things over" seemed to worsen their stress, perhaps because they were uncomfortable expressing feelings or

because the outcome of such discussions might be even greater demands. For both men and women, the most successful way of coping was rethinking the way they looked at the situation.

The effects of a dual-earner lifestyle may depend largely on how husband and wife view their relationship. Dual-income couples fall into three patterns: *conventional, modern,* and *role sharing.* In a *conventional* marriage, both partners consider household chores and child care "women's work." The husband may "help," but his career comes first; he earns more than his wife and sees it as "her choice" to add outside employment to her primary domestic role. In *modern* couples, the wife does most of the housework, but the husband shares parenting and wants to be involved with his children. In the *role-sharing* pattern, characteristic of at least one-third of dual-income marriages, both husband and wife are actively involved in household and family responsibilities as well as careers (Gilbert, 1994). However, even among such couples, tasks tend to be gender-typed: wives buy the

Stepparents seem to have difficulty separating their feelings about their marriage from their feelings about their success as stepparents, as they more easily can with regard to their relationships with their biological children (Fine & Kurdek, 1995). The connection between satisfaction with stepparenting and with the marriage may have to do with the fact that both begin at the same time and are inextricably linked. When problems arise in raising stepchildren, the stepparent is likely to blame the biological parent (for example, for taking the child's side in an argument). The biological parent, whose relationship with the child is

more secure, is less likely to blame the stepparent for trouble involving the child.

Challenging as stepparenting can be, one study found that blended families are no more likely than intact families to experience marital conflict. Findings differ as to whether a new baby increases or decreases tension in a blended family. Some researchers suggest that the impact of the birth may depend on what progress the reconstituted family has made toward becoming a real family unit (MacDonald & DeMaris, 1995).

For people who have been bruised by loss, the blended family has the potential to provide a

---

HOW DUAL-EARNER COUPLES COPE

groceries and husbands mow the lawn (Apostol et al., 1993).

In general, the burdens of the dual-earner lifestyle fall most heavily on the woman. While men, on average, earn more and have more powerful positions, women tend to work more hours—20 percent more in industrialized countries and 30 percent more in less developed countries (Bruce et al., 1995). Women put in a longer "second shift" at home, as well. Although men's participation has been increasing, even husbands in nontraditional marriages still do only one-third of the domestic work (Greenstein, 1995). A Swedish study found that working women with three or more children put in 1½ times as many hours as men at home and on the job (Clay, 1995b). A father is most likely to take on child care when his work schedule is different from his wife's (Brayfield, 1995).

Women's personal activities tend to suffer more than men's, probably due to the disproportionate time they put into domestic work, and in the long run the compromises women make to keep the dual-earner lifestyle afloat may

weaken the marriage (Apostol et al., 1993). An unequal division of work may have contributed to the higher degree of marital distress reported by wives in a study of 300 mostly managerial and professional dual-earner couples (Barnett et al., 1994). On the other hand, unequal roles are not necessarily seen as inequitable; it may be a *perception* of unfairness that contributes most to marital instability. A national longitudinal survey of 3,284 women in two-income families found greater likelihood of divorce the more hours the woman worked, but only when the wife had a nontraditional view of marriage. Nontraditional wives who work full time may feel more resentment of their husbands' failure to share equally in household tasks, whereas traditional wives may be more willing to accept additional burdens (Greenstein, 1995).

What spouses perceive as fair may depend on how much money the wife's earnings contribute, whether she thinks of herself as a coprovider or merely as someone who supplements her husband's income, and what meaning and

importance she and her husband place on her work. Whatever the actual division of labor, couples who agree on their assessment of it and who enjoy a harmonious, caring, involved family life are more satisfied than those who don't (Gilbert, 1994).

Family-friendly policies in the workplace can help alleviate the strains experienced by dual-earner families. Parents in a supportive, flexible work environment with family-oriented benefits tend to feel less stress (Warren & Johnson, 1995). Such benefits might include more part-time, flex-time, and shared jobs, more at-home work (without loss of fringe benefits), more affordable high-quality child care, and tax credits or other assistance to let new parents postpone returning to work (L. Eisenberg, 1995). One encouraging change is the Family and Medical Leave Act of 1993, which requires businesses with 50 or more workers to offer 12 weeks of unpaid leave for the birth or adoption of a child—though this still falls far short of (for example) the 6-month paid leave offered to new parents in Sweden.

---

warm, nurturing atmosphere, as does any family that cares about all its members. Successful, research-based strategies for building a blended family include the following (Visher & Visher, 1983, 1989, 1991):

■ *Have realistic expectations:* Stepparents need to remember that a blended family is different from a biological family. Children may act out feelings of loss and insecurity. It takes time for new, loving relationships to develop.
■ *Recognize divided loyalties:* A child who rejects a warm, loving stepparent may feel caught in a

conflict of loyalties. Such conflict can be diminished by maintaining a courteous relationship with the absent parent. Children adjust best when they have close ties with both parents, when they are not used as weapons by angry parents to hurt each other, and when they do not have to hear a parent or stepparent insult the other parent.
■ *Develop new customs and relationships within the stepfamily:* Blended families need to build new traditions and develop new ways of doing things. They need to see what is positive about their differences and how to make the most of

diverse resources and experiences. Children need time alone with the biological parent, time alone with the stepparent, and time with both parents. The couple also need time alone.

■ *Seek social support:* Sharing feelings, frustrations, and triumphs with other stepparents and children can help the whole family see their own situation more realistically and benefit from the experiences of others.

The bonds forged in young adulthood with friends, lovers, spouses, and children often endure throughout life and influence development in middle and late adulthood. The changes people experience in their more mature years also affect their relationships, as we'll see in Parts Six and Seven.

✔ SUMMARY

PERSONALITY DEVELOPMENT: FOUR MODELS

■ Whether and how personality changes during adulthood are important issues among developmental theorists. Four important perspectives on adult personality are offered by trait models, normative-crisis models, the timing-of-events model, and humanistic models.

■ The five-factor model of Costa and McCrae is organized around five groupings of traits: neuroticism, extraversion, openness to experience, conscientiousness, and agreeableness. Studies find that people change very little in these respects after age 30.

■ Normative-crisis models—exemplified by Erikson, Vaillant, Levinson, and Helson—hold that there is a built-in plan for human development and that during each part of the life span people face a particular crisis or task.

■ The timing-of-events model proposes that adult development is influenced by important events in a person's life and that the timing of an event affects the reaction to it. Events perceived as nonnormative, or "off time," are generally more stressful than those that occur "on time." As society becomes less age-conscious, the "social clock" has less meaning.

■ Humanistic models, exemplified by Maslow, view people as fostering their own development through choice, creativity, and self-realization.

FOUNDATIONS OF INTIMATE RELATIONSHIPS

■ Friendship is similar to love, but without sexual passion. Self-disclosure and a sense of belonging are important aspects of intimacy. Women's friendships tend to be more intimate than men's.

■ The vast majority of American adults are sexually active and are heterosexual. Gender differences in sexual attitudes and behavior have diminished. More women, as well as men, are having sexual experiences before marriage, but AIDS is exerting an inhibiting effect.

■ According to Robert Sternberg's triangular theory, love consists of three components: intimacy, passion, and commitment. These combine into eight types of love relationships.

■ Social ties are valuable for health and well-being.

NONMARITAL AND MARITAL LIFESTYLES

■ Today more people feel free to remain single until a late age or never to marry. Advantages of being single include career opportunities, travel, sexual freedom, and self-sufficiency.

■ For homosexuals, the process of "coming out" may last well into adulthood, and complete openness about their sexual orientation may never be fully achieved. Both gay men and women form enduring sexual and romantic relationships. Lesbians tend to have more stable and more intimate relationships than young gay men or heterosexual couples.

■ Cohabitation is common among both homosexuals and heterosexuals. Couples who cohabit before marriage tend to have weaker marriages. Among white and Mexican American couples, but not African Americans and Puerto Ricans, cohabitation tends to lead to marriage.

■ Marriage is universal, but customs differ widely. People in industrialized nations have been marrying later than in past generations, and the marriage rate of African Americans has declined significantly.

■ Marriage is related to health and happiness. Success in marriage often depends on patterns of interaction set in young adulthood. Age at marriage is a major predictor of whether a marriage will last.

■ Frequency of sexual relations declines with age and loss of novelty. Fewer married people appear to be having sexual relationships outside of marriage than in the past.

■ Women are most likely to be victims of domestic violence. Partner abuse that begins before marriage tends to escalate afterward.

■ The United States has one of the highest divorce

rates in the world. No-fault laws, which led to more divorce, were a response to societal pressures for it. Divorce usually entails a painful period of adjustment. Most divorced people remarry, but remarriages tend to be less stable than first marriages.

FAMILY LIFE

■ Family patterns vary across cultures and have changed greatly in western societies. Today women, especially educated ones, are having fewer children and having them later in life.

■ Infertile couples now have several options in addition to adoption. More couples are trying methods of assisted conception, such as artificial insemination, in vitro fertilization, ovum transfer, and surrogate motherhood.

■ An increasing number of couples remain childless by choice.

■ Marital satisfaction typically declines during the childbearing years. Expectations and sharing of tasks can contribute to a marriage's deterioration or improvement. Dual-earner couples have a particularly difficult challenge coping with conflict between work and family.

■ Stepmothers, who are usually more involved in the raising of stepchildren than are stepfathers, tend to have more difficulty being stepparents.

✔ KEY TERMS

five-factor model (page 434)
normative-crisis models (435)
intimacy versus isolation (437)
adaptive mechanisms (437)
life structure (439)
gender splitting (439)
timing-of-events model (441)
normative life events (441)

nonnormative life events (441)
social clock (442)
humanistic perspective (442)
hierarchy of needs (443)
self-actualization (443)
triangular theory of love (446)
coming out (449)

cohabitation (451)
partner abuse (454)
infertility (459)
artificial insemination (460)
in vitro fertilization (IVF) (460)
ovum transfer (461)
surrogate motherhood (461)

✔ QUESTIONS FOR THOUGHT AND DISCUSSION

1 Which of the models presented in this chapter seems to you to most accurately describe personality development in adulthood? Which model seems to have the most solid research support?

2 Other than sexual attraction, what difference—if any—do you see between a friend and a lover?

3 Is there a best age to leave one's parents' home? get married? have a child? start a new career? take time off to travel? become a grandparent? retire? If so, what are those ages?

4 Is it a good idea to live with a lover before marriage? Why or why not? Does it make a difference whether children are involved?

5 Should homosexuals be allowed to marry? adopt children? be covered by a partner's health care plan?

6 Has divorce become too easy to obtain in the United States?

7 What advice would you give a dual-career couple on handling family responsibilities?

8 Should surrogate parenthood be made illegal? If not, under what conditions should it be allowed?

PART SIX

Middle Adulthood

When does middle age begin? Is it at the birthday party when you see your cake ablaze with 40 candles? Is it the day your "baby" leaves home and you now have time to pursue those activities you've put on hold for so long? Is it the day when you notice that police officers seem to be getting younger?

Middle adulthood, in chronological terms, is usually defined as the years between ages 40 and 65; but it can also be defined contextually, and the two definitions may differ. One context is the family: a middle-aged person is sometimes described as one with grown children or elderly parents. Yet today some people in their forties and beyond are still raising young children; and some adults at any age have no children at all. Those with grown children may find the nest emptying—or filling up again. Age also has a biological aspect: a 50-year-old who has exercised regularly is likely to be biologically younger than a 35-year-old whose most strenuous exercise is clicking the remote control.

As in earlier years, all aspects of development are interrelated. In Chapters 14 and 15, we note (for example) the psychological impact of menopause (and debunk some myths about it!). We see how mature thinkers combine logic with intuition, and we consider how responsibility for aging parents can affect physical and mental health.

CHAPTER FOURTEEN

PHYSICAL AND COGNITIVE DEVELOPMENT IN MIDDLE ADULTHOOD

The primitive, physical, functional pattern of the morning of life, the active years before forty or fifty, is outlived. But there is still the afternoon opening up, which one can spend not in the feverish pace of the morning but in having time at last for those intellectual, cultural, and spiritual activities that were pushed aside in the heat of the race.

Anne Morrow Lindbergh,
Gift from the Sea, 1955

ASK YOURSELF

✔ Why do many adults consider middle age the best years of their lives?

✔ What physical changes occur during these years?

✔ How do lifestyle choices and attitudes about aging affect physical and mental health?

✔ Do mature adults think differently from younger people?

✔ Is there a relationship between creativity and age?

✔ What does it take to be a moral leader?

✔ Why do some people change careers at midlife?

The Spanish toast *Salud, amor, y pesetas—y el tiempo para gustarlos* ("Health, love, and money—and the time to enjoy them") seems to sum up what middle age has to offer (B. Hunt & Hunt, 1974). For many people the middle years are the most challenging and fulfilling part of the life span. It's a busy, sometimes stressful time, one filled with heavy responsibilities, but a time when most adults feel at their peak of competence, productivity, and control—able to handle whatever may come (Gallagher, 1993; M. E. Lachman, Lewkowicz, Marcus, & Peng, 1994).

Although the body may not be quite what it once was, most middle-aged people in the United States today are in good physical, cognitive, and emotional shape—more so than in any previous generation. Unlike most young adults, they tend to feel younger than they are (Montepare & Lachman, 1989). Medical advances and preventive care keep them in good health. They are relatively serene: the anxieties of youth, of starting families and careers, are behind them. Now they can "turn [their] attention to being rather than becoming" (Gallagher, 1993, p. 51). They are likely to be in their top earning period and—once their children achieve independence—in the most secure financial position of their lives. They are experienced enough to have acquired sound judgment and a mature acceptance of life's ups and downs; and they are less likely to be depressed than at any other time in adult life (Gallagher, 1993). Known as the *command generation*, they wield authority in societal institutions.

These richly textured years are marked by growing individual differences. Some middle-aged people can run a marathon; others get winded climbing a steep stairway. Some have sharper memory than ever; others feel their memory beginning to slip. Some are at the height of creativity and careers; others have gotten a slow start or have reached dead ends. Still others dust off mothballed dreams or pursue new goals. This can be a time of taking stock, of reevaluating vocational aspirations and how well they have been fulfilled, and deciding how best to use the remaining part of the life span.

■ In this chapter, we examine physiological changes in middle adulthood, including changes in appearance and in sensory, psychomotor, and sexual and reproductive functioning. We describe prevalent health problems, which may be worsened by poverty, racial discrimination, and other stresses. We consider how intelligence changes, how thought processes mature, and what underlies creative performance and moral leadership. We examine why adults return to the classroom and how careers develop, we describe the effects of burnout and unemployment, and we explore the complex connections between work and other aspects of cognitive development. ■

✔ PHYSICAL CHANGES

"Use it or lose it" is the motto of many middle-aged people, who have taken up jogging, racquetball, tennis, aerobic dancing, and other forms of physical exercise. Research bears out the wisdom of that creed. Some physiological changes are direct results of aging, but behavioral factors and lifestyle, dating from youth, often affect their timing and extent. Large proportions of middle-aged and even older adults show little or no decline in organ functioning. Furthermore, the mind and the body have ways of compensating for changes that do occur. Most people are realistic enough to take in stride changes in sensory and motor abilities, in

Many middle-aged people find that their improved ability to use strategies in a sport, as a result of experience and better judgment, outweigh the changes in strength, coordination, and reaction time that are common in midlife. A consistent exercise program beginning in young adulthood, such as playing tennis regularly, can help build muscles and maintain stamina and resilience in middle and old age. *(David Lawrence/ The Stock Market)*

reproductive and sexual capacities, and in appearance (Gallagher, 1993); and some experience a kind of sexual renaissance.

SENSORY AND PSYCHOMOTOR FUNCTIONING

From young adulthood through the middle years, sensory and motor changes are small and gradual—almost imperceptible—until one day a 45-year-old man realizes that he cannot read the telephone directory without eyeglasses or a 60-year-old woman has to admit that she is not as quick on her feet as she was.

Most age-related visual problems occur in five areas: *near vision, dynamic vision* (reading moving signs), *sensitivity to light, visual search* (for example, locating a sign), and *speed of processing* visual information (D. W. Kline et al., 1992; D. W. Kline & Scialfa, 1996; Kosnik, Winslow, Kline, Rasinski, & Sekuler, 1988). Because the lens of the eye becomes progressively less flexible, its ability to focus diminishes; this change usually becomes noticeable in early middle age and is practically complete by age 60 (D. W. Kline & Scialfa, 1996). Many people age 40 and older need reading glasses for *presbyopia,* a form of farsightedness associated with aging. (The prefix *presby-* means "with age.") Bifocals— eyeglasses in which lenses for reading are combined with lenses for distant vision—aid the eye in adjusting between near and far objects. Middle-

aged people commonly experience a slight loss in *visual acuity,* or sharpness of vision. Because of changes in the pupil of the eye, they need about one-third more brightness to compensate for the loss of light reaching the retina (Belbin, 1967; Troll, 1985).

Although it is rarely noticed, a gradual hearing loss that begins during adolescence speeds up after age 55. This condition, *presbycusis,* is normally limited to higher-pitched sounds than those used in speech (D. W. Kline & Scialfa, 1996). In some men, however, a decline in sensitivity to high-frequency sounds may be detected as early as age 30; and hearing loss proceeds twice as quickly as in women, even among men who do not work in noisy places (Pearson et al., 1995).

Sensitivity to taste and smell generally begins to decline in midlife (Cain, Reid, & Stevens, 1990; J. C. Stevens, Cain, Demarque, & Ruthruff, 1991), especially in people who take medication or undergo medical treatment (Ship & Weiffenbach, 1993). Since the taste buds become less sensitive, foods may seem blander (Troll, 1985). Women tend to retain these senses longer than men. People begin to lose sensitivity to touch after age 45, and to pain after age 50. However, pain's protective function remains: although people feel pain less acutely, they become less able to tolerate it (Katchadourian, 1987).

Strength and coordination decline gradually from their peak during the twenties, but muscles in the upper body keep their strength better than those in the lower body (Spirduso & MacRae, 1990). Most people notice a weakening first in the back muscles, by the early fifties, and then in the arm and shoulder, but not until well into the sixties. The reason for this loss of strength is a loss of muscle mass, which is replaced by fat. Between ages 30 and 80, as much as 30 percent of muscle fiber can atrophy, depending on heredity, on nutrition, and especially on the amount of use a muscle gets. By age 65, a man's body is typically 30 percent fat—the same as a woman's—but nearly 3 times the percentage he had at 20, even if his weight remains the same (Katchadourian, 1987; Spence, 1989).

An exercise program, together with good nutrition, can increase muscular bulk and density (Katchadourian, 1987; M. E. Nelson et al., 1994). The more people do, the more they *can* do. People who become active early in life reap the benefits of more stamina and more resilience after age 60 (Spirduso & MacRae, 1990). People who lead sedentary lives lose muscle tone and energy, and so they become even less inclined to exert themselves physically. A sedentary lifestyle is the major correlate of deaths from heart attacks (J. Brody, 1990).

Endurance—how long a person can continue to exert maximum force before fatigue sets in—often holds up much better than strength. Many competitive runners, swimmers, and cyclists switch from short to longer races as they get older; they can do better in an endurance event, such as running a marathon, than in an event that depends on strength, such as the shot put (Spirduso & MacRae, 1990). "Overpracticed" skills are more resistant to the effects of age than those which are used less; thus athletes show a smaller-than-average loss in endurance (Stones & Kozma, 1996).

Simple reaction time, which involves a single response to a single stimulus (such as pressing a button when a light flashes) slows by about 20 percent, on average, between ages 20 and 60 (Birren, Woods, & Williams, 1980), depending on the amount and kind of information to be processed and the kind of response required. When a vocal rather than a manual response is called for, age differences in simple reaction time are substantially smaller (S. J. Johnson & Rybash, 1993).

Tasks that involve a choice of responses (such as hitting one button when a light flashes and another button when a tone is heard) and complex motor skills involving many stimuli, responses, and decisions (as in playing a video game or driving a car) decline more, but the decline does not neces-

sarily result in poorer performance. Typically, middle-aged adults are better drivers than younger ones (McFarland, Tune, & Welford, 1964), and 60-year-old typists are as efficient as 20-year-olds (Spirduso & MacRae, 1990), apparently because they anticipate the keystrokes that are coming up (Salthouse, 1984).

In these and other activities, knowledge based on experience may more than make up for physical changes. Skilled industrial workers in their forties and fifties are often more productive than ever, partly because they tend to be more conscientious and careful. Middle-aged workers are less likely than younger workers to suffer disabling injuries on the job (Salthouse & Maurer, 1996)—a likely result of experience and good judgment, which compensate for any lessening of coordination and motor skills.

SEXUAL AND REPRODUCTIVE FUNCTIONING

Many people view sexuality as a hallmark of youth. Actually, despite changes in the male and female reproductive systems (summarized in Table 14-1), sexual enjoyment can continue throughout adult life.

One fundamental change of middle age—the decline of reproductive capacity—affects men and women differently. Sometime during this period, women's ability to bear children comes to an end. Although men can continue to father children, they begin to experience reduced fertility and, in some cases, a decrease in the ability to achieve and maintain an erection.

Menopause

Menopause takes place when a woman stops ovulating and menstruating and can no longer conceive a child; it is generally considered to have occurred 1 year after the last menstrual period. For American women, this typically happens between ages 45 and 55, at an average age of 51. Some women, however, experience menstrual changes in their thirties; others, not until their sixties. The period of 2 to 5 years during which a woman's body undergoes physiological changes that bring on menopause is the *climacteric,* popularly known as the "change of life." The ovaries and adrenal glands begin to produce less of the female hormone estrogen, and menstruation usually becomes irregular, with less flow than before and a longer time between menstrual periods.

TABLE 14-1

Changes in Human Reproductive Systems during Middle Age

	Female	Male
Hormonal change	Drop in estrogen and progesterone	Drop in testosterone
Symptoms	Hot flashes, vaginal dryness, urinary dysfunction	Undetermined
Sexual changes	Less intense arousal, less frequent and quicker orgasms	Loss of psychological arousal, less frequent erections, slower orgasms, longer recovery between ejaculations, increased risk of erectile dysfunction
Reproductive capacity	Ends	Continues; some decrease in fertility may occur

At one time, in rural Ireland, women who no longer menstruated would retire to their beds and stay there, often for years, until they died (U.S. Office of Technology Assessment, 1992). This traditional custom may seem extreme, but the attitude it expressed—that a woman's usefulness ends with her ability to reproduce—was typical in western societies until fairly recently (Crowley, 1994a). By contrast, some studies of less developed societies in Africa and India found that women's status and freedom of movement increased once they were free of taboos connected with menstruation and fertility (Lock, 1994). For many women in the United States today, menopause is a positive transition, a time of new possibilities for the second half of adult life (Matthews, quoted in Gallagher, 1993).

In the past, such problems as irritability, nervousness, anxiety, depression, and even insanity were blamed on the climacteric, but research shows no reason to attribute mental illness to this normal change. In fact, clinical depression is more common in younger women juggling work and family roles. Only about 10 percent of healthy women develop symptoms of depression as they enter menopause, and those symptoms tend to be slight; the vast majority do not become depressed (Matthews, 1992). Women who do become depressed tend to be those who are anxious, pessimistic, or under chronic stress (Bromberger & Matthews, 1996).

The myth that menopause produces depression may derive from the fact that women at this time are undergoing changes in roles, relationships, and

responsibilities. These changes may be either stressful or exciting, and how a woman perceives them can affect her view of menopause. In one study, most women reported less stress after menopause than before (K. A. Matthews, 1992). Psychological problems at midlife are more likely to be caused by attitude than by anatomy, and especially by negative societal views of aging. In cultures that value older women, few problems seem to be associated with menopause (Dan & Bernhard, 1989; see Box 14-1).

Also contrary to myth, most women experience little or no physical discomfort during the climacteric (NIA, 1993). About 85 percent have "hot flashes" (sudden sensations of heat that flash through the body) due to expansion and contraction of blood vessels, but only 30 percent call them severe (Oldenhave, Jaszman, Haspels, & Everaerd, 1993). Other possible symptoms, which affect a small minority of women, include vaginal dryness, burning, and itching; vaginal and urinary infections; and urinary dysfunction caused by tissue shrinkage. Some women do not become sexually aroused as readily as before, and some find intercourse painful because of thinning vaginal tissues and inadequate lubrication. Small doses of the male hormone testosterone may solve the first problem, and use of water-soluble gels can prevent or relieve the second. The more sexually active a woman is, the less likely she is to experience such changes (Katchadourian, 1987; Spence, 1989). Other physical problems reported by menopausal women include joint or muscle pain, headache, insomnia, and fatigue (te Velde & van Leusden, 1994).

BOX 14-1 WINDOW ON THE WORLD

JAPANESE WOMEN'S EXPERIENCE OF MENOPAUSE

Many American women accept hot flashes and night sweats as normal accompaniments of menopause. However, that apparently is not true everywhere.

Margaret Lock (1994)* surveyed Japanese women ages 45 to 55 and compared the results with information from women in Massachusetts and Manitoba, Canada. A total of 1,316 Japanese factory workers, farm workers, and homemakers answered questionnaires, and 105 were interviewed, as were Japanese physicians and counselors.

Japanese women's experience of menopause turned out to be quite different from the experience of western women. Fewer than 10 percent of Japanese women whose menstruation was becoming irregular reported having had hot flashes during the previous 2 weeks, compared with about 40 percent of the Canadian sample and 35 percent of the American sample. In fact, fewer than 20 percent of Japanese women had *ever* experienced hot flashes, compared with

65 percent of Canadian women, and most of the Japanese women reported little or no physical or psychological discomfort.

There is no specific Japanese term for "hot flash," though the Japanese language makes many subtle distinctions about body states. This linguistic evidence supports the finding that what most western women report as the most bothersome symptom of menopause has a low incidence in Japan and is rarely perceived as troublesome. The Japanese women in the study were more likely to report stiffness in the shoulders, headaches, lumbago, constipation, and other complaints that, in western eyes, are not necessarily related to the hormonal changes of menopause. Only about 3 percent of the Japanese women said they experienced night sweats, and Japanese women were far less likely than western women to suffer from insomnia, depression, irritability, or lack of energy.

The symptoms physicians noted were quite similar to those the

women reported. Hot flashes were not at the top of the doctors' lists and in some cases did not appear at all. However, very few Japanese women consult doctors about menopause or its symptoms; in Japan, menopause is regarded as a normal event in women's lives, not as a medical condition requiring treatment.

Hot flashes also have been found to be rare or infrequent among Mayan women, North African women in Israel, Navajo women, and some Indonesian women (Beyene, 1986; Flint & Samil, 1990; Walfish, Antonovsky, & Maoz, 1984; A. L. Wright, 1983). It has been suggested that cultural attitudes may affect how women interpret their physical sensations, and these interpretations may be linked to their feelings about menopause itself. For example, Mayan women, who are constantly pregnant or nursing babies, tend to regard childbearing as a burden and look forward to its end (Beyene, 1986, 1989). In Japan the end of menstruation seems to have far less sig-

*Unless otherwise noted, this discussion is based on Lock, 1994.

Since the most troublesome physical effects of menopause, as well as a higher risk of osteoporosis and heart disease (discussed later in this chapter), are linked to reduced levels of estrogen, artificial estrogen is often prescribed, but this treatment is controversial ("Hormone Therapy," 1995; see Box 14-2).

The Male Climacteric

Men have no experience comparable to menopause. They do not undergo a sudden drop in hormone production at midlife, as women do; instead, testosterone levels gradually decline from the late teens onward, adding up to a 30 to 40 percent reduction by age 70 (B. M. King, 1996).

The term *male climacteric* is sometimes used to refer to a supposed period of physiological, emotional, and psychological change involving a man's reproductive system and other body systems, which is thought to begin about 10 years later than a woman's climacteric (Weg, 1989). About 5 percent of middle-aged men experience depression, fatigue, lower sexual drive, occasional erectile failure, and vaguely defined physical complaints (Henker, 1981; Weg, 1989), but it is not clear that these conditions are related to hormonal changes. Researchers have found no relationship between hormone levels and mood changes (Doering, Kraemer, Brodie, & Hamburg, 1975). Instead, men's psychological adjustments, like women's, probably stem from such events as illness,

BOX 14-1   WINDOW ON THE WORLD

JAPANESE WOMEN'S EXPERIENCE OF MENOPAUSE

nificance than it does for western women. In fact, the closest term for it, *kônenki*, refers not specifically to what westerners call menopause, but to a considerably longer period comparable to the climacteric.

An intriguing new hypothesis is that nutritional practices in different cultures may influence the experience of menopause. Some plants, such as soybeans—a staple of Far Eastern diets—contain relatively high amounts of estrogen-like compounds known as *phyto-estrogens*. A diet high in foods made with these plants, such as tofu and soy flour, may influence hormone levels in the blood. In premenopausal women, it is believed, phytoestrogens may *reduce* the effects of estrogen, and indeed, Japanese women have been reported to have lower levels of serum estrogen than western women. However, when natural estrogen levels fall during the climacteric, phytoestrogens may act like estrogen in inhibiting symptoms of menopause. This, then, might explain why middle-aged

Japanese women do not experience the dramatic effects of a precipitous decline in estrogen levels, as many western women do (Margo N. Woods, M.D., Department of Family Medicine and Community Health, Tufts University School of Medicine, personal communication, November 1996).

Interestingly, Japanese women, who, as a group, are the longest-lived in the world, have a much lower incidence of osteoporosis than American white women (despite lower average bone mass) and are about one-fourth as likely as American women to die of coronary heart disease and breast cancer. These ailments (at least in North America) become more common after menopause, and their lower incidence before menopause has been attributed to estrogen's protective effect. Might phytoestrogens mimic this effect in postmenopausal Japanese women? In addition, several other protective factors may be working in favor of middle-aged Japanese women: they tend to eat well-

balanced diets, exercise throughout life, and seldom smoke or drink.

It might be tempting to test the nutritional hypothesis by switching to a high-soy diet to see whether hot flashes go away. However, research of this kind is easily distorted by placebo effects, since a woman's discomfort is a subjective experience, hard to measure except by self-report. Final conclusions about the influence of diet on symptoms of menopause must await the conclusion of controlled longitudinal studies now in progress, using both a soy product and a placebo (Margo N. Woods, personal communication, November 1996).

Meanwhile, the findings about Japanese women's experience of menopause emphasize once again the importance of cross-cultural research with tools appropriate to a particular culture. It would not be useful, for example, to assess women in Japan by means of a list of menopausal symptoms drawn up in Canada, or vice versa.

---

worries about work, children's leaving home, or the death of parents, as well as from negative cultural attitudes toward aging (B. M. King, 1996).

Men do show some changes in sexual functioning. Although they can continue to reproduce until quite late in life, their sperm count tends to decline after age 40, and they may experience decreases in fertility. Erections tend to become slower and less firm, orgasms less frequent, and ejaculations less forceful; and it takes longer to recover and ejaculate again (Bremner, Vitiello, & Prinz, 1983; Katchadourian, 1987; B. M. King, 1996; Masters & Johnson, 1966). Still, sexual excitation and sexual activity remain a normal, vital part of life.

A minority of middle-aged and older men—about 5 percent of 40-year-olds and 15 to 25 per-

cent of those age 65 or older—experience "impotence," more appropriately called *erectile dysfunction:* inability to achieve or maintain an erection sufficient for satisfactory sexual performance. Late-onset diabetes, hypertension, high cholesterol, endocrine problems, depression, neurological disorders, and many chronic diseases, especially kidney failure, can lead to erectile dysfunction. Alcohol, drugs, smoking, poor sexual techniques, lack of knowledge, unsatisfying relationships, anxiety, and stress can be contributing factors.

About 35 percent of men suffering erectile dysfunction can be helped by treating the underlying causes or by adjusting medications ("Effective Solutions for Impotence," 1994; National Institutes of

BOX 14-2   PRACTICALLY SPEAKING

THE ESTROGEN DECISION

Artificial estrogen, which can make up for the loss of natural estrogen, is the most widely prescribed drug in the United States (Crowley, 1994b), alone or in combination with progestin, a form of the female hormone progesterone. There is strong evidence that estrogen can help prevent osteoporosis and cardiovascular disease, and it may also help protect against stroke, colorectal cancer, and Alzheimer's disease (N. E. Davidson, 1995; "Hormone Therapy," 1995; Mayeux, 1996; Paganini-Hill & Henderson, 1994; Tang et al, 1996). Estrogen appears to improve skin tone and memory, help maintain the vitality of the sex organs, help prevent vaginal and urinary infection, and relieve "hot flashes" and other symptoms of menopause. However, estrogen has been linked to higher rates of cancer of the lining of the uterus (endometrial cancer) and possibly to breast cancer.

The safety of long-term hormone treatment is still under study, and alternative treatments are being tested. Meanwhile, women need to weigh potential risks and benefits.

REASONS TO CONSIDER ESTROGEN THERAPY

1 Currently, estrogen therapy, with or without progestin, is the best way to combat bone loss during the first 5 to 7 post-menopausal years. It has proved effective in preventing fractures, especially when started before symptoms of osteoporosis appear (N. E. Davidson, 1995; "Should You Take," 1994). Estrogen therapy can promote bone formation even in women over 70 (Felson et al., 1993; Prestwood et al., 1994).

2 In a number of observational studies, estrogen—or estrogen combined with progestin—cut the risk of heart disease about in half (N. E. Davidson, 1995; Grodstein, 1996; Stampfer et al., 1991). In a large, controlled, randomized double-blind trial, estrogen improved the balance

between HDL ("good") and LDL ("bad") cholesterol; the estrogen-progestin combination had a less protective effect (The Writing Group, 1995). One study of older women enrolled in a health plan in the San Francisco Bay area found that long-term estrogen users cut their mortality risk by more than 40 percent, primarily due to lower rates of cardiovascular disease (Ettinger, Friedman, Bush, & Quesenberry, 1996).

3 Evidence is growing of a protective effect against Alzheimer's disease. Among 1,124 women with an average age of 74, estrogen users were less likely to develop the disease. The longer the estrogen use, the greater the benefit (Tang et al., 1996).

REASONS TO BE WARY OF ESTROGEN THERAPY

1 Estrogen taken alone increases the risk of uterine cancer. However, when it is taken with progesterone, this risk is minimal. Therefore, women whose uterus has not been surgically removed are usually given the estrogen-progestin combination (N. E. Davidson, 1995). Progestin is normally unnecessary if a woman has had a hysterectomy (te Velde & van Leusden, 1994).

2 Concerns about the possible role of estrogen in breast cancer have yet to be resolved. A statistical analysis of many studies found that women who used estrogen after menopause had no special risk of breast cancer (Henrich, 1992). Another overview suggests a 15 to 30 percent increase in risk after 10 years of use (K. K. Steinberg, Smith, Thacker, & Stroup, 1994). A long-term study of more than 120,000 female nurses suggests that use of estrogen, with or without progestin, for more than 5 years does increase risk, especially for women over age 55 (Colditz et al., 1995). How-

ever, this was not a randomized study; a randomized study is planned, but results will not be available for several years.

3 About 10 percent of women taking hormones experience such side effects as headaches, nausea, fluid retention, swollen breasts, and vaginal discharge. There is also some risk of abnormal vaginal bleeding. Women who experience such bleeding should be especially cautious about taking estrogen. So should those who are obese, those who have high blood pressure, migraine headaches, seizures, large uterine fibroids, diabetes, or endometriosis, those with kidney, pancreatic, or gallbladder disease, and those with a history of breast or uterine cancer, heart attack, stroke, liver disease, thrombophlebitis, or thromboembolism ("Alternatives," 1994; NIA, 1993).

Many physicians maintain that estrogen's protective effect against osteoporosis, which results in as many as 50,000 premature deaths annually due to hip fractures, and against heart disease, which kills more women each year than all cancers combined, outweighs any small increase in deaths from cancer (Cobleigh et al., 1994; Goldman & Toteson, 1991; B. M. King, 1996; The Writing Group, 1995). A study of 40,000 postmenopausal women found that those who took estrogen were slightly less likely to die from any cause during a 6-year period (Folsom et al., 1995).

Medical research may not fully resolve this issue. Critics argue that estrogen therapy is predicated on a view of menopause as a disease that needs to be treated with daily medication, rather than as a natural process that should be allowed to take its course (te Velde & van Leusden, 1994). Women need to examine their own situation, their own feelings, and their family health history and, if they do take estrogen, to stay in close touch with their physicians.

Health, NIH, 1992). Other treatments, each of which has both benefits and drawbacks, include a wraparound vacuum constrictive device, which draws blood into the penis, injections of prostaglandin E1 (a drug found in semen, which widens the arteries), and penile implant surgery. Still being tested are a topical cream and a suppository, both based on prostaglandin E1 ("Effective Solutions for Impotence," 1994; NIH, 1992). If there is no apparent physical problem, psychotherapy or sex therapy (with the support and involvement of the partner) may help (NIH, 1992). Therapeutic exercises are often more successful with homosexuals than with heterosexuals, perhaps because partners of the same sex may better understand each other's needs (B. M. King, Camp, & Downey, 1991).

Sexual Activity

My parents don't have sex. They have other things to do. (B. M. King, 1996, p. 258)

Many children of middle-aged parents are vastly ignorant of their parents' sexual activity. Myths about sexuality in midlife—for example, the idea that satisfying sex ends at menopause—have even been believed by middle-aged people themselves and have sometimes become self-fulfilling prophecies. Now, advances in health care and more liberal attitudes toward sexuality are making people more aware that sexual intimacy can be a vital part of life during these—and even later—years.

Surveys suggest that sexual activity diminishes only slightly and gradually during the forties and fifties (B. M. King, 1996). A larger decline in frequency is likely to be due to nonphysiological causes: monotony in a relationship, preoccupation with business or financial worries, mental or physical fatigue, depression, failure to make sexual intimacy a high priority, fear of failure to attain an erection, or lack of a partner. Possible physical causes include chronic disease, surgery, medications, and too much food or alcohol (B. M. King, 1996; Masters & Johnson, 1966; Weg, 1989).

Freed from worries about pregnancy, and having more uninterrupted time to spend with their partners, many people find their sexual relationship better than it has been in years (Reichman, quoted in J. E. Brody, 1993). Women may know their own sexual needs and desires better, feel freer to take the initiative, and experience an increased interest in sexual activity (L. B. Rubin, 1982). Because of men's slowed response, middle-aged

lovers may enjoy longer, more leisurely periods of sexual activity. Women may find their partner's longer period of arousal helpful in reaching their own orgasm—often by means other than intercourse. Homosexual as well as heterosexual couples who hold and caress each other, with or without genital sex, can experience heightened sexuality as part of an intimate relationship (Weg, 1989).

APPEARANCE: THE DOUBLE STANDARD OF AGING

In a youth-oriented society, wrinkles and sags are unwelcome signs of aging and may be more distressing than reproductive changes (Gallagher, 1993). Many middle-aged people spend much time, effort, and money trying to look young.

Both sexes suffer from the premium placed on youth, particularly in the job market and in the business world; it's no coincidence that "antiaging" treatments for men have boomed in an era of corporate downsizing (Spindler, 1996). Women, though, are especially harmed. In men, gray hair, coarsened skin, and "crow's feet" are often seen as indicators of experience and mastery; in women, they are signs of being "over the hill." Such changes in a wife are more likely to affect a husband's sexual responsiveness to her than vice versa (Margolin & White, 1987). Once the appearance of youth is gone, so (in many men's eyes) is a woman's value as a sexual and romantic partner.

According to evolutionary psychology, this double standard of aging goes back to the universal drive to perpetuate the species. Since women lose their reproductive capacity earlier than men, loss of youthful appearance may have warned a man that a woman was no longer desirable as a mate (Katchadourian, 1987). Today, when the value of relationships is not measured only by the biological mandate to reproduce, a societal standard

that regards beauty as the exclusive preserve of the young . . . makes women especially vulnerable to the fear of aging. . . . The relentless social pressures to retain a slim 'girlish' figure make women self-conscious about their bodies . . . [and] can be detrimental to the midlife woman's personal growth and sense of self-worth. (Lenz, 1993, pp. 26, 28)

Self-esteem suffers when people devalue their physical being. However, an effort to maintain youth and vigor can be positive if it reflects concern with health and fitness and is not obsessive

Wrinkles and graying hair often imply that a woman is "over the hill" but that a man is "in the prime of life." This double standard of aging, which downgrades the attractiveness of middle-aged women but not of their husbands, can affect a couple's sexual adjustment. *(Brian Yarvin/The Image Works)*

(Gallagher, 1993). In the face of powerful social forces that reinforce a worship of youth, most middle-aged adults can and do learn to accept realistically the changes taking place in themselves. Men and women who can do this while staying as fit as possible, and who can appreciate maturity as a positive achievement for both sexes, are better able to make the most of middle age—a time when both physical and cognitive functioning are likely to be at an impressively high level.

✔ HEALTH

"Good health is a duty to yourself, to your contemporaries, to your inheritors, to the progress of the world," wrote the poet Gwendolyn Brooks (1972) while in her fifties. Healthy people can more confidently face challenges, surmount hurdles, and achieve goals that benefit themselves and others.

HEALTH STATUS

The typical middle-aged American is quite healthy. About 83 percent of people 45 to 64 years old report their health to be good, very good, or excellent; only 17 percent consider themselves in fair or poor health. Only about 9 percent of people in this age range are unable to carry out important activities for health reasons (USDHHS, 1996).

The most common chronic ailments of middle age are asthma, bronchitis, diabetes, nervous and mental disorders, arthritis and rheumatism, impaired sight or hearing, and malfunctions of the circulatory, digestive, and genitourinary systems. These conditions are not necessarily problems of middle age, however; while three-fifths of 45- to 64-year-olds have one or more of them, so do two-fifths of people between ages 15 and 44 (Metropolitan Life Insurance Company, in B. Hunt & Hunt, 1974; USDHHS, 1992).

People over 40 account for nearly one-third of recorded cases of AIDS (USDHHS, 1996). Although most cases occur in drug abusers or in homosexual or bisexual men who contracted the virus through sexual activity, many patients in this age group contracted it through contaminated blood transfusions before routine screening began in 1985. The disease seems to be more severe and to progress more rapidly in older people, whose immune systems may be weakened (Brozan, 1990; USDHHS, 1992).

One major health problem that increases from midlife on is *hypertension* (high blood pressure), which can lead to heart attack or stroke or to cognitive impairment in late life (Launer, Masaki, Petrovitch, Foley, & Havlik, 1995). Blood pressure screening, low-salt diets, and medication have reduced the prevalence of hypertension, but it still affects more than one-third of men and nearly one-fourth of women ages 45 to 54, and nearly half of both men and women ages 55 to 64. It is more common among African Americans of all ages (USDHHS, 1996).

The leading causes of death between ages 45 and

64 are cancer, heart disease, and stroke, followed by unintentional injuries and conditions related to chronic obstruction of the lungs. Between 1970 and 1993, mortality declined by 37 percent for people ages 45 to 54 and by 30 percent for 55- to 64-year-olds (USDHHS, 1996), largely due to changes in lifestyle. Because many people have lowered their cholesterol—by changing their diets or taking medicine, or both—and have sought medical care for high blood pressure, middle-aged people now are much less likely to die of heart disease or stroke. Middle-aged men and women who stop smoking decrease their risk of both heart disease and stroke (AHA, 1995; Kawachi et al., 1993; Stamler et al., 1993; Wannamethee et al., 1995). Deaths from car crashes have also declined, largely because fewer people drink and drive and more use seatbelts.

However, cancer fatalities are increasing among 55- to 64-year-olds. Although death rates from some cancers have fallen, they have risen even more dramatically for lung cancer, the biggest killer—apparently because of smoking (American Cancer Society, 1994). Between the 1960s and 1980s, lung cancer deaths almost doubled among male smokers and jumped sixfold among female smokers, while rates for nonsmokers remained constant (Thun, Day-Lally, Calle, Flanders, & Heath, 1995).

INFLUENCES ON HEALTH: GENDER, ETHNICITY, AND STRESS

Not only smoking (see Figure 14-1), but diet, alcohol and drug use, exercise, and other influences discussed in Chapter 12 continue to affect health in middle age. Gender and ethnicity make a difference: as in young adulthood, death rates in middle age are higher for men than for women and higher for African Americans than for Hispanic, Asian American, Native American, and white people (USDHHS, 1996). However, women are at increased risk after menopause, particularly for heart disease and osteoporosis. Let's look more closely at women's health and then at health hazards for African Americans. Finally, we'll look at stress, whose cumulative effects often show up in middle age.

Women's Health After Menopause

Women's risk of heart disease rises after menopause, becoming nearly equal to men's

within 10 years. One in eight women age 45 and above has had a heart attack or stroke. Furthermore, women have less chance than men of surviving a heart attack (AHA, 1995). A 3-year study of 500 women between ages 42 and 50 found that moderate daily exercise—or even as little as three brisk 20-minute walks each week—can lower the risk of heart disease (J. F. Owens, Matthews, Wing, & Kuller, 1992).

In a minority of postmenopausal women (1 in 4 over age 60), the decrease in estrogen contributes to *osteoporosis* ("porous bones"), a condition in which the bones become extremely thin and brittle as a result of rapid calcium depletion. Four out of five cases of osteoporosis occur in women ("Should You Take," 1994), most often in white women with fair skin or a small frame, those with a family history of the condition, and those whose ovaries were surgically removed before menopause (NIA, 1993). Affected women may lose up to 50 percent of their bone mass between ages 40 and 60 or 70 (Spence, 1989). Frequent signs of osteoporosis are loss in height and a "hunchbacked" posture that results from compression and collapse of weakened bones. Osteoporosis is a major cause of broken bones in old age.

Proper nutrition and exercise, along with avoidance of smoking, can slow bone loss and prevent osteoporosis (Dawson-Hughes et al., 1990; Hopper & Seeman, 1994; NIA, 1993). Women over age 40 should get 1,000 to 1,500 milligrams of dietary calcium a day, along with recommended daily amounts of vitamin D, which helps the body absorb calcium (NIA, 1993). Some studies have found value in calcium supplements for women over ages 50 or 55 (Dawson-Hughes et al., 1990; Reid, 1993; "Should You Take," 1994). Weight-bearing exercise, such as walking, jogging, aerobic dancing, and bicycling, can increase bone density (Krall & Dawson-Hughes, 1994; NIA, 1993). Weight lifting is particularly valuable, since it also improves muscle mass, strength, and balance, which help protect against falling (M. E. Nelson et al., 1994; see Chapter 16). Estrogen treatment can be effective; but since this treatment is not appropriate for all women (refer back to Box 14-2), nonhormonal drugs (bisphosponates and fluorides) have been developed to increase bone density.

After menopause, many women gain both in weight and girth. They tend to have lower metabolism and a higher ratio of fat to lean tissue, particularly in the abdomen. Significant weight gain

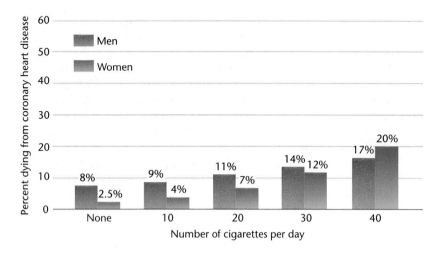

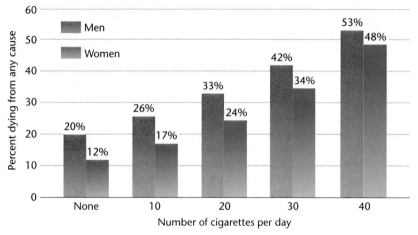

FIGURE 14-1
Effect of cigarette smoking on percentage of people ages 40 to 59 dying within 20 years. Among 40- to 59-year-old men and women screened during the period 1967–1973 to determine risk of dying of coronary heart disease, the percentage who did die of heart disease—or any other cause—within the next 20 years increased with the number of cigarettes smoked per day. *(Source: Stamler et al., undated chart 5, p. 5.)*

can increase the risk of dying early from heart disease, diabetes, or cancer ("The New Weight Guidelines," 1995). Some studies suggest that "middle-age spread" is related to low estrogen levels ("Middle-Age Spread," 1995), but a 15-year follow-up study of 671 Southern California women age 65 and older found no relationship between estrogen use and weight gain or middle-aged spread (Kritz-Silverstein & Barrett-Connor, 1996).

Race, Poverty, and Health

The death rate for middle-aged African Americans is about twice that for white people. About twice as many black people as white people ages 35 to 64 die of heart disease, 1½ times as many of cancer, and 3 times as many of stroke (USDHHS, 1996).

Almost one-third (31 percent) of the excessive mortality of black people ages 35 to 54 can be accounted for by six risk factors: high blood pressure, high cholesterol, excess weight, diabetes, smoking, and alcohol intake. The first four may be partly attributable to heredity, which also predisposes black people to sickle cell disease; but lifestyle plays a part in all six. Probably the largest single underlying factor is poverty, which results in poor nutrition, substandard housing, inadequate prenatal care, and poor access to health care throughout life (Otten et al., 1990).

Even when black people do have access to health care, they are less likely than white people to receive coronary bypass surgery, kidney transplants, and certain other treatments (Council on Ethical and Judicial Affairs, 1990). In one study, African Americans with little education tended not to recognize a heart attack and waited too long before going to the hospital—an average of 23 hours, as compared with 8 hours for white patients (R. Simpson et al., 1991). A delay that long can be life-threatening; treatment must begin within 6 to 8 hours after the initial chest pain to keep heart muscle cells alive.

Some observers attribute the health gap between

black and white Americans in part to stress caused by prejudice (Chissell, 1989; Lawler, 1990, in Goleman, 1990). Constant suppression of anger aroused by racial discrimination, together with a tendency of many black people to retain sodium in the kidneys when under emotional stress, may raise blood pressure (Goleman, 1990).

Black women have been called "a minority within a minority" (Miller, quoted in Eastman, 1995). They are more than twice as likely as white women to die of breast cancer within 5 years of diagnosis, probably because they are less likely to go for mammograms and their cancers tend to be diagnosed later (Eley et al., 1994). Besides being at higher risk for hypertension, black women are more likely than white women to be overweight. They get less exercise and see doctors less often (Eastman, 1995).

Health education, access to basic health care, employment that provides adequate income and decent housing, and eradication of racism might halt or reverse these trends.

Stress and Health

The more stressful the changes that take place in a person's life, the greater the likelihood of illness within the next year or two. That was the finding of a classic study in which two psychiatrists, on the basis of interviews with 5,000 hospital patients, ranked the stressfulness of life events that had preceded illness (Holmes & Rahe, 1976; see Table 14-2). About half the people whose total "life change units" (LCUs) were between 150 and 300 in a single year, and about 70 percent of those with 300 or more LCUs, became ill. Change—even positive change—can be stressful, and some people react to stress by getting sick. However, these findings do not tell us *how* stress produces illness or why some people's bodies handle stress better than others.

Today, stress is under increasing scrutiny as a factor in such diseases as hypertension, heart ailments, stroke, and ulcers (Sapolsky, 1992). According to one survey, 64 percent of Americans feel great stress at least once or twice a week, up from 55 percent in 1983. Some of this stress is work-related, as we'll discuss later in this chapter. However, intense stress becomes less prevalent after age 50 (*Prevention Index*, 1995). The most frequently reported physical symptoms of stress are headaches, stomachaches, muscle aches or muscle tension, and fatigue. The most common psychological symptoms are nervousness, anxiety, tenseness, anger, irritability, and depression.

Such psychological reactions may increase vulnerability to illness. So, it seems, can the effort to cope with stress itself. People who experience stressful events are more likely to catch colds, whether or not they see themselves as under stress and regardless of their emotional reactions to it (S. Cohen, 1996; S. Cohen, Tyrrell, & Smith, 1991, 1993). Intense or prolonged stress seems to weaken

TABLE 14-2

Some Typical Life Events and Weighted Values

Life Event	Value in Life Change Units (LCUs)
Death of spouse	100
Divorce	73
Marital separation	65
Jail term	63
Death of close family member	63
Injury or illness	53
Marriage	50
Being fired at work	47
Marital reconciliation	45
Retirement	45
Change in health of family member	44
Pregnancy	40
Sex difficulties	39
Gain of new family member	39
Change in financial state	38

SOURCE: Adapted from T. H. Holmes & Rahe, 1976.

the immune system. Medical students at examination time, couples who are fighting with each other, and people caring for spouses with Alzheimer's disease all show reduced immune functioning (Kiecolt-Glaser et al., 1984; Kiecolt-Glaser, Fisher, et al., 1987; Kiecolt-Glaser, Glaser, et al., 1987; Kiecolt-Glaser & Glaser, 1995).

Stress also seems to cause blockage of the arteries, which leads to cardiovascular disease (Baum, Cacioppo, Melamed, Gallant, & Travis, 1995). Middle-aged men with high levels of anxiety or tension are more likely to develop high blood pressure later in life (Markovitz, Matthews, Kannel, Cobb, & D'Agostino, 1993) and are 4 to 6 times more likely than less anxious men to die of sudden heart failure (Kawachi, Colditz, et al., 1994; Kawachi, Sparrow, Vokonas, & Weiss, 1994). Female nurses who work rotating night shifts (which tend to upset the body's natural rhythms) for more than 6 years are much more likely than coworkers to have heart attacks (Kawachi et al., 1995).

In some people, response to stress becomes impaired with age. Long-term oversecretion of stress hormones may play a part in a number of age-related disorders, from mature-onset diabetes to osteoporosis (Krieger, 1982; Munck, Guyre, & Holbrook, 1984).

Stress can also harm health indirectly, through lifestyle. People under stress may sleep less, smoke and drink more, eat poorly, and pay too little attention to their health (Baum et al., 1995). Conversely, regular exercise, good nutrition, at least 7 hours of sleep a night, and frequent socializing are associated with lower stress.

One reason stress leads to illness may have to do with loss of a sense of mastery or control. When people feel they can control stressful events, they are less likely to get sick. When expectations of control are violated, as in disasters caused by human error, chronic stress-related problems tend to compound the physiological effects. Many years after the nuclear accident at Three Mile Island, for example, people who lived near the site had elevated blood pressure as compared with a control group who did not live nearby. Stress is shorter-lived in natural disasters, such as earthquakes or floods, which people do not expect to be able to prevent (Baum & Fleming, 1993).

Research on human beings and animals has found links between stressful events perceived as uncontrollable and various illnesses, including cancer (Laudenslager, Ryan, Drugan, Hyson, & Maier, 1983; Matheny & Cupp, 1983; Sklar & Anis-

man, 1981). Belief in external, rather than personal, control may cause health problems by suppressing immune functioning (Rodin, Timko, & Harris, 1985). Or such a belief may lead people to take less care of their health.

Among 2,428 Finnish men ages 42 to 60, those who had little hope for the future were more than twice as likely as more hopeful men to die of heart disease, cancer, or other causes within the next 4 to 10 years. Highly hopeless men who were healthy at the outset were 5 times as likely to die as other healthy men (Everson, Kaplan, Goldberg, & Salonen, 1996). The effect seems to vary with age. Among 238 cancer patients age 30 and over, those under 60 who expressed a pessimistic view of life ("If something can go wrong for me, it will"; "Things never work out the way I want them to") were more likely to die within 8 months than more optimistic men. No link between pessimistic statements and mortality appeared among older patients, for whom such statements may represent a more realistic coping strategy (Schulz, Bookwala, Knapp, Scheier, & Williamson, 1996).

More than two-thirds of American adults say they take active steps to minimize or control stress (*Prevention Index*, 1995). Stress management workshops teach people to control their reactions through relaxation, meditation, and biofeedback. Men infected with the AIDS virus who learn such techniques are slower in developing symptoms of the disease; and women with breast cancer who participate in group therapy live longer than those who do not participate (Sleek, 1995). Some research suggests that optimism can be learned. Children and adolescents can be "inoculated" against pessimism in adulthood by training them in positive beliefs and coping skills (Seligman, 1991, 1996).

✔ INTELLIGENCE

What happens to cognitive abilities in middle age? Does age affect the ability to solve problems, to create, to learn, and to perform on the job? As we discuss these questions, we need to look more closely at issues raised in Chapter 12 about the nature of intelligence and the ways it can be measured in adults. What can standardized tests tell—or not tell—about adult intelligence? What kinds of cognitive abilities improve or decline? Do people develop distinctive forms of intelligence at this time of life? As we will see, cognitive development is multidirectional, involving both gains and losses.

MEASURING ADULT INTELLIGENCE

The *Wechsler Adult Intelligence Scale (WAIS),* like the Wechsler tests for children, has subtests that yield separate scores. Items are not graduated by age. An emphasis on nonverbal performance (identifying the missing part of a picture, copying a design, or mastering a maze) gives the test less bias toward verbal abilities than some other psychometric tests (see Figure 14-2). The eleven subtest scores are combined into a verbal IQ and a performance IQ, and finally, a total IQ.

When adults take psychometric tests like this one, those who had high scores as children generally do best; they also tend to be healthier, better-educated, and at higher socioeconomic levels than adults who score lower. These individual differences persist into midlife. When it comes to how intelligence changes with age, however, the picture is less clear.

In cross-sectional studies, in which people of different ages were tested at the same time, young adults have done better than older ones (Botwinick, 1984; Doppelt & Wallace, 1955; H. Jones & Conrad, 1933; Miles & Miles, 1932). However, this may be a cohort effect. IQ scores have been rising steadily worldwide—an average of 15 points in 50 years (Neisser et al., 1995). People in more recently born cohorts may score higher, not because they are younger but because they have had better or longer schooling, because they have learned more from television, because they are healthier, because they have had more experience with testing, because of better prenatal nutrition, or because of some other factor unrelated to aging.

By contrast, longitudinal studies, in which the same people are tested periodically over the years, have shown an *increase* in intelligence at least until the fifties (Bayley & Oden, 1955; Botwinick, 1984; W. A. Owens, 1966; Kangas & Bradway, 1971). However, longitudinal research may favor older participants because of "practice effects" (feeling more comfortable in the testing situation or remembering how similar problems were solved on earlier tests) and because of attrition (a tendency of poorer scorers to drop out along the way).

A further complication is that cognitive performance seems to be uneven during adulthood, with different abilities peaking at different times. On the basis of results from the WAIS and other psychometric tests, John L. Horn (1967, 1968, 1970, 1982a, 1982b; Horn & Hofer, 1992) and Raymond B. Cattell (1965) proposed a distinction between *fluid* and *crystallized* intelligence—between those aspects of intelligence largely determined by neurological status, which tend to decline with age, and those aspects of intelligence largely affected by cultural experience, which hold their own or even improve.

Fluid intelligence is the ability to apply mental powers to novel problems that require little or no previous knowledge. It involves perceiving relations, forming concepts, and drawing inferences. Psychologists measure fluid intelligence by such tests as the Raven Progressive Matrices, in which a person may be asked to select the pattern that best completes a larger one (see Figure 14-3), to group letters and numbers, to pair related words, or to repeat a series of digits. *Crystallized intelligence* is the ability to remember and use information acquired over a lifetime. It depends on education and cultural background and is measured by tests of vocabulary, general information, and responses to social situations and dilemmas. Whereas fluid intelligence is used to actively process *new* information, crystallized intelligence depends on the use of *stored* information and on how *automatic* information processing has become.

Fluid intelligence peaks and then begins to decline during young adulthood, perhaps because of changes in the brain, but crystallized intelligence typically improves through middle age and often until near the end of life (see Figure 14-4). In fact, up to ages 55 to 65, the improvement in crystallized intelligence is about equal to the decline in fluid intelligence (J. L. Horn, 1982a, 1982b; J. L. Horn & Donaldson, 1980). However, much of the research on fluid and crystallized intelligence has been cross-sectional; thus the results may at least partly reflect generational differences rather than changes with age.

The *sequential approach* (introduced in Chapter 1) is an attempt to overcome the drawbacks of both cross-sectional and longitudinal research. The sequential studies of K. Warner Schaie and his colleagues (discussed in more detail in Chapter 16) found "no uniform pattern of age-related changes . . . [for] all intellectual abilities" (Schaie, 1994, p. 306). In general, cognitive gains continued until the late thirties or early forties, followed by stability until the midfifties or early sixties and then only minor losses until the seventies. However,

VERBAL SCALE

Information	On what continent is the Taj Mahal?
Comprehension	Explain the meaning of this saying: "A journey of 1,000 miles begins with a single step."
Arithmetic	A pair of shoes that normally sells for $70 has been reduced 20 percent. How much do the shoes cost now?
Similarities	In what way are a radio and a television alike?

PERFORMANCE SCALE

1	2	3	4
<	)	:	~

1	4	2	3	4	3	1	2	3	1

Digit symbol (match symbols to numbers using the key)

Picture completion (identify what is missing)

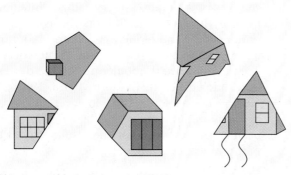

Object assembly (put pieces together)

FIGURE 14-2
Examples of items like those on the verbal and performance sections of the Wechsler Adult Intelligence Scale, revised version (WAIS-R). *(Source: Adapted from R. S. Feldman, 1993.)*

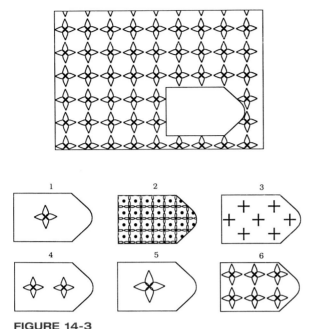

FIGURE 14-3

Item from the Raven Progressive Matrices Test. This task is a measure of fluid intelligence, not dependent on previous knowledge. *(Source: Figure A5 from the latest edition of Raven's Standard Progressive Matrices, © J. C. Raven Ltd. Figure used with permission.)*

there were wide individual differences and different patterns for different abilities. Most participants showed no significant reduction in most abilities until after age 60, and then not in all or even most areas. Virtually no one declined on all fronts, and many people improved in some areas. Much as in Horn and Cattell's studies, fluid abilities generally began to diminish in young adulthood, but crystallized abilities remained stable or increased into middle age and then showed grad-

ual, moderate declines (Schaie, 1990, 1994, 1996).

These findings suggest that no single measure, such as IQ, can adequately describe either age changes in individuals or age differences among groups (Schaie, 1990, 1994). Furthermore, we should ask whether IQ tests tap the abilities that are most central to what intelligence means in adulthood. Timed tests, modeled after those developed to measure knowledge and skills in children, may not be suitable for measuring cognitive competence in adults, who use knowledge and skills to solve practical problems and achieve goals they set for themselves (Schaie, 1977–1978). If conventional tests fail to tap abilities central to adult intelligence, we may need measures that have what Schaie (1978) calls *ecological validity:* tests that show competence in dealing with real-life problems, such as balancing a checkbook or making informed decisions about medical problems. The challenge of developing new strategies to measure adult intelligence may be "no less than that faced by Binet in initially measuring the intelligence of school children" (Schaie, 1977–1978, p. 135).

THE DISTINCTIVENESS OF ADULT INTELLIGENCE

Rather than focus on quantitative changes in intelligence, some developmentalists have described distinctive qualities in the thinking of mature adults. Some, working within the psychometric tradition, claim that accumulated knowledge changes the way fluid intelligence operates. Others (see Chapter 12) maintain that mature, or

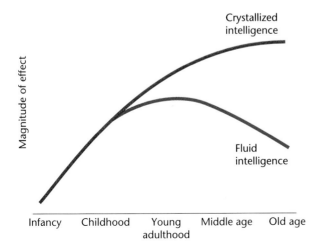

FIGURE 14-4

Changes in fluid intelligence and crystallized intelligence over the life span. Although fluid abilities (largely biologically determined) decline after young adulthood, crystallized abilities (largely culturally influenced) increase until late adulthood. *(Source: J. L. Horn & Donaldson, 1980.)*

Expertise in interpreting x-rays, as in many other fields, depends on accumulated, specialized knowledge, which continues to increase with age. Experts often appear to be guided by intuition and cannot explain how they arrive at conclusions. *(Tim Davis/Photo Researchers)*

postformal, thought represents a new stage of cognitive development. This "special form of intelligence" (Sinnott, 1996, p. 361), which emerges for the first time during adulthood, is said to integrate emotion with intellect, and experience with learning, and it may contribute to practical problem solving.

The Role of Expertise

Two young resident physicians in a hospital radiology laboratory examine a chest x-ray. They study an unusual white blotch on the left side. "Looks like a large tumor," one of them says finally. The other nods. Just then, a longtime staff radiologist walks by and looks over their shoulders at the x-ray. "That patient has a collapsed lung and needs immediate surgery," he declares (Lesgold, 1983).

If fluid intelligence diminishes in mature adults, why do they show increasing competence in solving problems in their chosen fields? The answer, according to William Hoyer and his colleagues (Hoyer & Rybash, 1994; Rybash, Hoyer, & Roodin, 1986), lies in specialized knowledge, a form of crystallized intelligence. This expertise seems relatively independent of any declines in general intelligence and in the brain's information-processing machinery.

In one study (Ceci & Liker, 1986), researchers identified 30 middle-aged and older men who were avid horse racing fans. On the basis of skill in picking winners, the investigators divided the men into two groups: "expert" and "nonexpert."

The experts used a more sophisticated method of reasoning, incorporating interpretations of much interrelated information, whereas nonexperts used simpler, less successful methods. This difference was not related to IQ; there was no significant difference in average measured intelligence between the two groups, and experts with low IQs used more complex reasoning than nonexperts with higher IQs.

Hoyer explains this seeming paradox through the concept of *encapsulation.* With experience, Hoyer suggests, information processing and fluid abilities become *encapsulated,* or dedicated to specific kinds of knowledge, making that knowledge easier to access, add to, and use. In other words, encapsulation "captures" or salvages fluid abilities for expert problem solving. At the same time, these abilities become *less* available for problems outside the specialized field. In a study of food service workers, job-related know-how, or tacit knowledge (see Chapter 12), improved with age, even though general cognitive abilities declined (Perlmutter, Kaplan, & Nyquist, 1990).

Advances in expertise, according to Hoyer, continue at least through middle adulthood. Thus, although middle-aged people may take somewhat longer than younger people to do certain tasks and may not be as adept at solving unfamiliar problems, they more than compensate when solving problems in their own fields with judgment developed from experience.

Expert thinking, like that of the experienced radiologist in our opening example, often seems automatic and intuitive. Experts generally are not aware of the thought processes that lie behind their decisions (Dreyfus, 1993–1994; Rybash et al., 1986). They cannot readily explain how they arrive at a conclusion or where a nonexpert has gone wrong: the experienced radiologist could not see why the residents would even consider diagnosing a collapsed lung as a tumor. Some theorists describe such intuitive, experience-based thinking as characteristic of postformal thought.

Postformal Thought

According to its proponents, postformal thought (introduced in Chapter 12) goes beyond abstract, formal reasoning, which Piaget considered the supreme achievement of adolescence. It relies on subjective feelings and intuition, as well as logic (Labouvie-Vief, 1985, 1990a; Labouvie-Vief & Hakim-Larson, 1989). It personalizes thinking by drawing on concrete experience.

Postformal thought is relativistic. Immature thinking sees black and white (right versus wrong, logic versus emotion, mind versus body); postformal thinking sees shades of gray. It seems to develop in response to events and social interactions that open up unaccustomed ways of looking at things and challenge a simple, polarized view of the world. It enables adults to transcend a logical system (such as a particular theory of human development) and reconcile or choose among conflicting views of reality (Labouvie-Vief, 1990a, 1990b; Sinnott, 1996).

Unlike the problems Piaget studied, which involve physical phenomena and require dispassionate, objective observation and analysis, adults often face social dilemmas, which are less clearly structured and often fraught with emotion. In such situations, one person's view of reality may affect another's and color the situation as a whole (Sinnott, 1984). In these kinds of situations mature adults may call upon postformal thought (Berg & Klaczynski, 1996; Sinnott, 1996).

One study (Labouvie-Vief, Adams, Hakim-Larson, Hayden, & DeVoe, 1987) asked people from preadolescence through middle age to consider the following problem:

> John is a heavy drinker, especially at parties. His wife, Mary, warns him that if he gets drunk once more, she will take the children and leave him. John does come home drunk after an office party. Does Mary leave John?

Children and most young adolescents answered "yes": Mary would leave John because she had said she would. Older adolescents saw that the problem was not so simple, but most of them still tried to approach it logically. More mature adolescents and adults took into account the problem's human dimensions; they realized that Mary might not go through with her threat. The *most* mature thinkers recognized that there are a number of ways of interpreting the same problem and that the way people look at such questions often depends on their life experience. The ability to see many possible outcomes was only partly age-related; although it did not appear until late adolescence or early adulthood, adults in their forties did not necessarily think more maturely than adults in their twenties.

Other studies, however, have found a general, age-related progression toward postformal thought through middle age, especially regarding emotion-laden situations (Blanchard-Fields, 1986). In one study, participants were asked to judge what caused the outcomes of a series of hypothetical situations, such as a marital conflict. Was the main character responsible, or the situation, or a combination of the two? Adolescents and young adults tended to blame the individual, whereas middle-aged people were more likely to attribute behavior to the interplay between person and environment. The more ambiguous the situation, the greater the age differences in interpretation (Blanchard-Fields & Norris, 1994).

An important feature of postformal thought is its integrative nature. Mature adults integrate logic with intuition and emotion, integrate conflicting facts and ideas, and integrate new information with what they already know. They interpret what they read, see, or hear in terms of its meaning for them. Instead of accepting something at face value, they filter it through their life experience and previous learning.

In one study (C. Adams, 1991), early and late adolescents and middle-aged and older adults were asked to summarize a Sufi teaching tale. In the story, a stream was unable to cross a desert until a voice told it to let the wind carry it; the stream was dubious but finally agreed and was blown across. Adolescents recalled more details of the story than adults did, but their summaries were largely limited to repeating the story line. Adults, especially women, gave summaries that were rich in interpretation, integrating what was in the text with its psychological and metaphorical meaning for them, as in this response of a 39-year-old:

I believe what this story was trying to say was that there are times when everyone needs help and must sometimes make changes to reach their goals. Some people may resist change for a long time until they realize that certain things are beyond their control and they need assistance. When this is finally achieved and they can accept help and trust from someone, they can master things even as large as a desert. (p. 333)

Society benefits from this integrative feature of adult thought. Generally it is mature adults who become moral and spiritual leaders (see Box 14-3) and who translate their knowledge about the human condition into inspirational myths and legends, to which younger generations can turn for guidance (Gutmann, 1977).

Practical Problem Solving

Does deciding what to do about a flooded basement take the same kind of intelligence as playing word games? Is the ability to solve practical problems affected by age? Most research on practical problem solving has not found the sharp declines often seen in measures of fluid intelligence, and some research has found marked improvement, at least through middle age (Berg & Klaczynski, 1996).

In a number of studies, the quality of practical decisions (such as what car to buy, what kind of treatment to get for breast cancer, how much money to put away in a pension plan, or how to compare insurance policies) bore only a modest relationship, if any, to performance on tasks like those on intelligence tests (M. M. S. Johnson, Schmitt, & Everard, 1994; Meyer, Russo, & Talbot, 1995) and often no relationship to age (Capon, Kuhn, & Carretero, 1989; T. E. Johnson, 1990; Meyer et al., 1995; Walsh & Hershey, 1993). In other studies, problem solving improved with age (Cornelius & Caspi, 1987; Perlmutter et al., 1990).

In one study (Denney & Palmer, 1981), 84 adults ages 20 to 79 were given two kinds of problems. One kind was like the game Twenty Questions. Participants were shown pictures of common objects and were told to figure out which one the examiner was thinking of, by asking questions that could be answered "yes" or "no." The older the participants were, the worse they did on this part of the test. The second kind of problem involved situations like the following: *Your basement is flooding,* or *You are stranded in a car during a blizzard,* or *Your 8-year-old child is 1½ hours late coming home*

from school. High scores were given for responses that showed self-reliance and recognition of a number of possible causes and solutions. According to these criteria, the best practical problem solvers were people in their forties and fifties, who based their answers on everyday experience.

In a follow-up study, which posed problems with which elderly people would be especially familiar (concerning retirement, widowhood, and ill health), people in their forties still came up with better solutions than either younger or older adults (Denney & Pearce, 1989). However, in other studies—in which problems were real rather than hypothetical and were brought up by the participants themselves, and in which solutions were rated by quality rather than quantity—practical problem-solving ability did *not* seem to decline after middle age (Camp, Doherty, Moody-Thomas, & Denney, 1989; Cornelius & Caspi, 1987).

What explains such inconsistent findings? For one thing, there are differences in the kinds of problems studied, in their relevance to real life, and in the criteria used to rate the solutions. Some of these differences may reflect the perspectives that researchers bring to their work. Then, differences in gender or educational level may affect how people perceive and solve problems (Berg & Klaczynski, 1996).

One thing seems clear: middle-aged people tend to be effective problem solvers. If the function of intelligence is to deal with real-life problems, the strengths of mature thought may compensate for—and even outweigh—any deficiencies.

✔ CREATIVITY

At about age 40, Frank Lloyd Wright designed Robie House in Chicago, Agnes deMille choreographed the Broadway musical *Carousel,* and Louis Pasteur developed the germ theory of disease. At 48 the jazz singer Ella Fitzgerald began to record a 19-album series of nearly 250 popular classics; at 59 she finished it. Charles Darwin was 50 when he presented his theory of evolution, Leonardo da Vinci was 52 when he painted the *Mona Lisa,* and Leonard Bernstein was 53 when he composed his *Mass* in honor of John F. Kennedy. The novelist Toni Morrison, 1993 winner of the Nobel Prize in Literature, won the Pulitzer Price for *Beloved,* a novel she wrote when she was about 55.

Creativity is not, of course, limited to the Darwins and deMilles; we can see it, for example, in

BOX 14-3   FOOD FOR THOUGHT

MORAL LEADERSHIP IN MIDDLE AND LATE ADULTHOOD

What makes a single mother of four young children, with no money and a tenth grade education, dedicate her life to religious missionary work on behalf of her equally poor neighbors? What leads a pediatrician to devote much of his practice to poor children instead of to patients whose parents could provide him with a lucrative income?

In the mid 1980s, two psychologists, Anne Colby and William Damon, sought answers to questions like these. They embarked on a 2-year search for people who showed unusual moral excellence in their day-to-day lives. The researchers eventually identified 23 "moral exemplars," interviewed them in depth, and studied how they had become moral leaders (Colby & Damon, 1992).

To find moral exemplars, Colby and Damon worked with a panel of 22 "expert nominators," people who in their professional lives regularly think about moral ideas—philosophers, historians, religious thinkers, and so forth. The researchers drew up five criteria: sustained commitment to principles that show respect for humanity; behavior consistent with one's ideals; willingness to risk self-interest; inspiring others to moral action; and humility, or lack of concern for one's ego.

The chosen exemplars varied widely in age, education, occupation, and ethnicity. There were 10 men and 13 women, ages 35 to 86, of white, African American, and Hispanic backgrounds. Education ranged from eighth grade up through M.D.s, Ph.D.s, and law degrees; and occupations included religious callings, business, teaching, and social leadership. Areas of concern included poverty, civil rights,

education, ethics, the environment, peace, and religious freedom.

The research yielded a number of surprises, not least of which was this group's showing on Kohlberg's classic measure of moral judgment. Each exemplar was asked about "Heinz's dilemma" (see Chapter 10) and about a follow-up dilemma: how the man should be punished if he does steal the drug. Of 22 exemplars (one response was not scorable), only half scored at the postconventional level; the other half scored at the conventional level. The major difference between the two groups was level of education: those with college and advanced degrees were much more likely to score at the higher level, and no one who had only a high school diploma scored above the conventional level. Clearly, it is not necessary to score at Kohlberg's highest stages to live an exemplary moral life.

How does a person become morally committed? The 23 moral exemplars did not develop in isolation, but responded to social influences. Some of these influences, such as those of parents, were important from childhood on. But many other influences became significant in later years, helping these people evaluate their capacities, form moral goals, and develop strategies to achieve them.

These moral exemplars had a lifelong commitment to change: they focused their energy on changing society and people's lives for the better. But they remained stable in their moral commitments, in what they felt was important in determining their actions. At the same time, they kept growing throughout life, remained open to new ideas, and continued to learn from others.

The processes responsible for stability in moral commitments were gradual, taking many years to build up. They were also collaborative: leaders took advice from supporters, and people noted for independent judgment drew heavily on feedback from those close to them—both those people who shared their goals and those who had different perspectives.

Along with their enduring moral commitments, certain personality characteristics seemed to remain with the moral exemplars throughout middle and late adulthood: enjoyment of life, ability to make the best of a bad situation, solidarity with others, absorption in work, a sense of humor, and humility. They tended to believe that change was possible, and this optimism helped them battle what often seemed like overwhelming odds and to persist in the face of defeat.

While their actions often meant risk and hardship, these people did not see themselves as courageous. Nor did they agonize over decisions. Since their personal and moral goals coincided, they just did what they believed needed to be done, not calculating personal consequences to themselves or their families and not feeling that they were sacrificing or martyring themselves.

Of course, there is no "blueprint" for creating a moral giant, just as it does not seem possible to write directions to produce a genius in any field. What studying the lives of such people can bring is the knowledge that ordinary people can rise to greatness and that openness to change and new ideas can persist throughout adulthood.

Creativity begins with talent, but talent is not enough. The author Toni Morrison, 1993 winner of the Nobel Prize in Literature, worked long, hard hours throughout her prolific career. Her achievements are examples of the creative productivity possible in middle age. *(Ulf Andersen/Gamma-Liaison)*

an inventor who comes up with a better mousetrap or a promoter who finds an innovative way to sell it. Some researchers argue that we can best learn about creativity by studying the lives of notable creative achievers. Others have looked at links between creativity and intelligence and between creativity and age.

STUDYING CREATIVE ACHIEVERS

Children may show *creative potential*, but in adults what counts is *creative performance:* what, and how much, a creative mind produces (Sternberg & Lubart, 1995). Creative performance, says Howard Gardner (1986, 1988), is the product of a web of biological, personal, social, and cultural forces, including the state of development of a person's field of endeavor. Creativity begins with talent, but talent is not enough. Sigmund Freud, for example, attributed his accomplishments more to personality than to intellect. His strengths, he felt, were compulsive curiosity, a bold and adventurous nature, and a passion to conquer, combined with strong self-discipline, tenacity, perseverance, and an ability to withstand hostile detractors. He was a workaholic, often seeing patients until late at night and then writing into the early morning hours—a schedule he maintained almost until his death.

Other creative achievers have similar qualities. Highly creative people are self-starters: their projects and ideas are self-generated or self-discovered (Torrance, 1988). They are usually motivated by love of what they do, a desire to solve a problem for its own sake rather than for external rewards (Getzels, 1964, 1984). They are often painstaking workers, with a strong sense of purpose and direction; and they can juggle several ideas or projects at a time (Gardner, 1981). They have the courage to defy the crowd and the emotional stamina to persist—sometimes for years—despite frustration, rejection, and repeated failure (Shaw, 1989, 1992a, 1992b; Sternberg & Lubart, 1995).

The cognitive abilities and processes that lead to creative performance are hard to pin down. We can observe *what* creative achievers do, but just *how* they do it remains largely a mystery. Freud was able to see in an isolated fact (such as his discovery of his previously submerged feelings toward his parents) a key to the forces motivating human behavior (E. Jones, 1961). Darwin constantly visualized ideas. He drew one image—a branching tree—over and over, as he refined his theory of how more complex, highly developed species evolve on the "tree" of nature (Gruber, quoted in Gardner, 1981).

CREATIVITY AND INTELLIGENCE

According to Robert Sternberg (Sternberg & Lubart, 1995), each of three aspects of intelligence (see Chapter 12) plays an important role in creative performance. The *insightful* component helps to define a problem or to see it in a new light. A classic longitudinal study of art students (Getzels & Csikszentmihalyi, 1968, 1975, 1976) found that those who, by selection and arrangement of objects for a still life, set up the most unusual and complex artistic problems for themselves to solve were the ones whose works were judged by art experts as best and most original and who later proved most successful in the field.

The *analytical* component of intelligence can evaluate an idea and decide whether it is worth pursuing. The molecular biologist James D. Watson, one of the scientists who discovered the structure of DNA, was described by one of his graduate students at Harvard University as having "an uncanny instinct for the important problem, the thing that leads to big-time results. He seems to . . . pluck it out of thin air" (Edson, 1968, pp. 29–31).

The *practical* aspect of intelligence comes into play in "selling" an idea—in getting it accepted. Thomas Edison, for example, held more than 1,000 patents for his inventions, created several companies to market them, and had a knack for getting his name and picture in the newspapers. This practical aspect may well be strongest in middle age.

CREATIVITY AND AGE

Creative growth in adults may be a developmental process that spans a period of years (Gruber, quoted in Gardner, 1981). If so, it should be possible to test the relationship between creative performance and age. One researcher (Simonton, 1990) did just that.*

What did he find? On psychometric tests of divergent thinking (see Chapter 8), age differences consistently show up. Whether data are cross-sectional or longitudinal, scores peak, on average, around the late thirties. A similar age curve emerges when creativity is measured by variations in output (number of publications, paintings, or compositions). A person in the last decade of a creative career typically produces only about half as much as during the late thirties or early forties, though somewhat more than in the twenties.

However, the age curve varies, depending on the field. Poets, mathematicians, and theoretical physicists tend to be most prolific in their late twenties or early thirties. Psychologists reach a peak around age 40, followed by a moderate decline. Novelists, historians, philosophers, and scholars become increasingly productive through their late forties or fifties and then level off. These patterns hold true across cultures and historical periods.

There are three ways of achieving a large lifetime output: (1) start early, (2) keep going, and (3) be unusually prolific. Not only are all three factors associated with high total production, but the three factors are linked. Creative people who start producing early and maintain a large output generally continue to be highly productive in later life. Pablo Picasso, considered by many to be the greatest artist of the twentieth century, began painting in childhood and, up to his death in 1973 at the age of 91, produced more than 200 paintings and sculptures a year.

Of course, not everything a person creates is equally notable; even a Picasso is bound to produce some minor material. The *quality ratio*—the proportion of major works to total output—bears no relationship to age. The periods in which a person creates the largest number of memorable works also tend to be the ones in which he or she produces the largest number of forgettable ones. Thus the likelihood that a particular work will be a masterpiece has nothing to do with age. Irving Berlin, in a life that spanned 101 years, wrote more than 1,500 songs and 17 musical revues; some of his top hits were written in his fifties, sixties, seventies, and eighties. Songs he wrote in his sixties proved no more or less immortal than songs he wrote in his early twenties.

Still, if we assess creativity in terms of sheer quantity of high-quality performance, the picture looks much like the general age curve. The more a creative person produces in, say, a 10-year period, the greater the chance that a large *number* (though not necessarily a large *proportion*) of those works will be major ones. Thus a person is likely to produce the greatest number of major works at peak periods of productivity (midlife or earlier, depending on the field). The Japanese filmmaker Akira Kurosawa, for example, released three of his greatest films—*Rashomon, Ikiru,* and *Seven Samurai*—during a 3-year period within a decade when he was making about one film a year. For the same reason, if we compare two equally creative people, the one who produces more work throughout an entire career is also likely to produce more noteworthy work.

Losses in productivity may be offset by gains in quality as maturity changes the tone and content of creative work. Age-related analyses of themes of ancient Greek and Shakespearean plays show a shift from youthful preoccupation with love and romance to more spiritual concerns (Simonton, 1983, 1986). And a study of the "swan songs" of 172 composers found that their last works—usually fairly short and melodically simple—were among their richest, most important, and most successful (Simonton, 1989).

A classic theory (Beard, 1874) offers a simple explanation for this phenomenon and for the late peak which occurs in such fields as philosophy and history. According to this theory, two factors fuel creativity: enthusiasm and experience. In fields such as poetry, in which enthusiasm plays the dominant role, enthusiasm peaks early and hence so does output, which may thereafter wane. Experience, however, continues to build, infusing

*Unless otherwise noted, this discussion is indebted to Simonton, 1990.

later works, especially those requiring seasoned re-flection, with mature insight and wisdom missing from the products of youth.

✔ EDUCATION, WORK, AND LEISURE

Work plays an important role in development throughout life. Many careers are born in child-hood dreams. Adolescents debate their future; young adults struggle to get ahead; people in midlife often change careers (sometimes voluntar-ily, sometimes not); and as they approach old age, mature adults face issues of whether, when, and how to retire. Furthermore, work is entwined with all aspects of development. Cognitive factors, physical factors, social factors, and emotional fac-tors affect the kind of work people do, and peo-ple's work can affect every other area of their lives, including what they choose to do when they are *not* working.

Education is central in childhood, and it is be-coming more important in adulthood as profound economic shifts call for new vocational skills. Learning is also an increasingly popular leisure pursuit. Let's see how education and work are changing and how both affect the quality of leisure.

LIFE-SPAN ISSUE
ARE AGE-BASED ROLES OBSOLETE?

 Early in her career as a gerontologist, Matilda White Riley became interested in the interaction between the changing age structure of society and the role of aging in the lives of individuals. As a senior so-cial scientist at the National Institute on Aging, she presented her ideas on that subject in the Kent Award Lecture at the 46th Annual Scientific Meeting of the Gerontological Society of America in New Orleans on November 18, 1993. Those ideas form the basis for much of the following discussion. (Photo: Courtesy of Matilda White Riley)

Early theories of career development reflected a stable, mostly middle-class pattern. Donald Super's (1957, 1985) influential theory described an orderly progression of stages: (1) considering vague, general ideas in ado-lescence, (2) focusing on a specific career track in col-lege, (3) trying out one or more entry-level jobs in the early twenties, (4) making a commitment to a career goal in the mid-twenties, (5) striving forward and consolidat-ing gains in the thirties, (6) maintaining one's position in

the forties, (7) slowing down and preparing for retirement in the fifties, and (8) entering retirement in the sixties.

Super developed his theory at a time when relatively few women worked outside the home, and decisions made in the late teens or twenties often shaped a man's entire working life. Today, most women are in the labor force, and technological change and economic disloca-tions have resulted in layoffs, job obsolescence, and fre-quent job or career changes. Occupations that employed millions of people no longer exist; occupations that may employ millions of people in the future have yet to be imagined. In Japan, where a worker used to be guar-anteed the same job for life, only 1 out of 5 is now cov-ered by such a guarantee (Desmond, 1996).

The endpoint of a person's working life, too, is less predictable than in the past. With increased longevity, the retirement years can stretch into the seventies or eighties or beyond. Mandatory retirement has been vir-tually eliminated, but there has been a trend toward early retirement, stimulated by downsizing, company pension plans, and other incentives (Quinn, 1993). However, this may soon change. Members of the bulging post-World War II "baby boom" generation are entering their fifties with too little savings to continue their accustomed lifestyle during retirement, and the social security sys-tem is straining at the seams (C. Farrell, Palmer, Atchi-son, & Andelman, 1994; Rix, 1994). Rather than accept a sharply reduced standard of living, many baby boomers may choose to continue working.

Changes in work and leisure bring parallel changes in education. Many workers and retirees go back to school. Expanding technology and shifting job markets require a life-span approach to learning. Finishing one's education with a college degree earned in the early twenties will not be adequate for most people in the fu-ture (Willis, 1985).

All of this may bring about fundamental shifts in so-cial roles. The traditional life structure in industrialized societies is **age-differentiated,** that is, roles are based on age (as in the left side of Figure 14-5). Young peo-ple are students; young and middle-aged adults are workers; older adults organize their lives around retire-ment and leisure. Yet, as Matilda Riley (1994) has ob-served,

> These structures fail to accommodate many of the changes in people's lives. After all, does it make sense to spend nearly one-third of adult lifetime in retirement? Or to crowd most work into the har-ried middle years? Or to label as "too old" those as young as 55 who want to work? Does it make sense to assume that . . . physically capable older people—an estimated 40 million of them in the next century—should expect greater support from society than they contribute to society? . . . Surely, something will have to change! (p. 445)

Age-differentiated roles are a holdover from a time when

life was shorter and social institutions less diverse. The result is a structural lag: increasing numbers of older adults are able to contribute to society, but opportunities to use and reward their abilities are inadequate. Also, by devoting themselves to one aspect of life at a time, people do not enjoy each period as much as they might and may not prepare adequately for the next phase. By concentrating on work, adults may forget how to play; then, when they retire, they may not know what to do with a sudden abundance of leisure time.

In an *age-integrated* society (as in the right side of Figure 14-5), all kinds of roles—learning, working, and playing—would be open to adults of all ages (Riley, 1994). They could intersperse periods of education, work, and leisure throughout the life span. Things seem to be moving in that direction. College students take work-study programs or "stop out" for a while before resuming their education. Mature adults take evening classes or take time off work to pursue a special interest. A person may have several careers in succession, each requiring additional education or training. People retire earlier or later than in the past, or not at all. Retirees devote time to study or to a new line of work.

Much of the research on education, work, leisure, and retirement reflects the old, age-differentiated model of social roles and the cohorts whose lives it describes. As "age integration" emerges, future cohorts may have very different experiences and attitudes.

THE ADULT LEARNER

A woman marries at age 17, raises six children, and goes to college at 41 and to law school at 48; at 51 she is on the legal staff of a major city. A 49-year-old realtor takes a seminar about the latest forms of home financing. A 56-year-old automotive mechanic enrolls in a night course in philosophy. A 63-year-old retiree signs up for a computer class. Today about half of all adults participate in continuing education, the fastest-growing part of the American educational system (Schaefer & Lamm, 1995).

Why do mature adults go to school? Almost two-thirds who take part-time classes do so for job-related reasons (U.S. Department of Education, 1986a). Some seek training to update their knowledge and skills: to keep up with new developments in their fields and to understand and cope with technological change. Some train for new occupations when their old ones become obsolete or when their needs and interests change. Some want to move up the career ladder or go into business for themselves. Some women who have devoted their young adult years to homemaking and par-

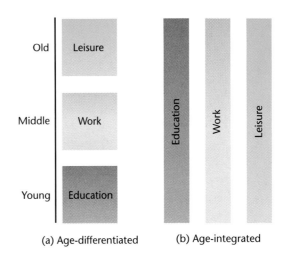

(a) Age-differentiated (b) Age-integrated

FIGURE 14-5
Contrasting social structures.
(a) Traditional age-differentiated structure, typical of industrialized societies. Education, work, and leisure roles are largely "assigned" to different phases of life.
(b) Age-integrated structure, which would spread all three kinds of roles throughout the adult life span and help break down social barriers between generations. *(Source: Riley, 1994, p. 445.)*

enting are taking the first steps toward reentering the job market. People close to retirement often want to expand their minds and skills to make more productive and interesting use of leisure time. Some adults simply enjoy learning and want to keep on doing it throughout life (Willis, 1985).

More than 18 percent of college students today are age 35 and older, including about 78,000 who are 65 and above (NCES, 1995b). These mature learners tend to be more motivated than those of traditional age. What they may lack in academic skills, they make up for in richness and variety of life experience (Datan, Rodeheaver, & Hughes, 1987; Haas, 1989).

To accommodate the practical needs of students of nontraditional age, most colleges grant credit for life experience and previous learning. They also offer part-time matriculation, Saturday and night classes, independent study, child care, financial aid, free or reduced-tuition courses, and "distance learning" via computers or closed-circuit broadcasts.

In today's complex society, education is never finished. For more and more adults, formal learning is an important way to develop their potential, as well as to keep up with the changing world of work.

These government workers improving their computer skills are among the approximately 50 percent of adults in the United States who participate in continuing education. Most mature adults who take part-time classes do so for job-related reasons, and they tend to be more motivated than younger students. *(Bob Daemmrich/The Image Works)*

OCCUPATIONAL PATTERNS: TWO THEORIES

In a society undergoing dramatic change, occupational patterns are in flux. Let's look at two theories that attempt to capture the dynamic character of vocational development.

Ginzberg: Stable and Shifting Career Patterns

In the 1950s, Eli Ginzberg proposed a three-stage model based on research with predominantly white male college students. In 1972, Ginzberg revised his model. After examining occupational histories of women, and of men from a wider variety of backgrounds, he saw that career decisions are often open-ended. Rather than settle for their initial vocational choice, many people try to achieve a better match between what they can do, what they want and expect from their work, and what they are getting out of it. This constant reevaluation can lead to career change. Women's paths tend to be particularly discontinuous: they may start work, take time out for motherhood, and then resume employment, possibly in a new field.

Career paths, said Ginzberg, fall into one of two patterns: stable or shifting. By midlife, people with stable career patterns often reach positions of power and responsibility. Middle-aged men with stable careers tend to be either "workaholics" or "mellowed" (Tamir, 1989). Workaholics work at a frenzied pace, either in a last-ditch effort to reach financial security before they retire or because they find it hard to relinquish authority. Mellowed people have come to terms with their level of achievement, even if they have not gone as far as they had hoped. The best adjusted among them have a sense of relaxation rather than failure. They are often happier, less cynical, and steadier in temperament than their more successful counterparts. Although these men want to do challenging work, they do not pin their emotional well-being on their jobs as much as they used to (D. W. Bray & Howard, 1983).

Because fewer middle-aged and older women have worked throughout adulthood, they are less likely to exhibit this stable pattern, and today that pattern is less common among men as well. Although people may change careers anytime during adulthood, middle age is a common time to do it. With the children now grown or almost grown, a woman's orientation may shift from family to career. People who have paid off the mortgage or put the last child through college may look for an easier workload, a job that pays less but is more satisfying, or a business venture that is risky but exciting. Others realize that they are ill-prepared for retirement and focus on accumulating a nest egg. Divorce or widowhood may create a need for more income. Some men and women are forced by unemployment or technological change to seek new careers. Some, thwarted in the desire to move up the career ladder, strike out in new directions, seeking more personal and intellectual challenge or more opportunity for advancement. People who choose to make a change are often considered particularly valuable employees, since they tend to be highly motivated and ambitious (Schultz & Schultz, 1986).

Raynor: Motivation and Career Paths

Why do some people stay on the same career path while others switch? Why do some people keep striving to advance, while others hit a dead end?

According to Raynor's *achievement motivation* theory (Atkinson & Raynor, 1974; Raynor & Rubin, 1971), the motivation to strive for success is influenced by the perception of what kind of ca-

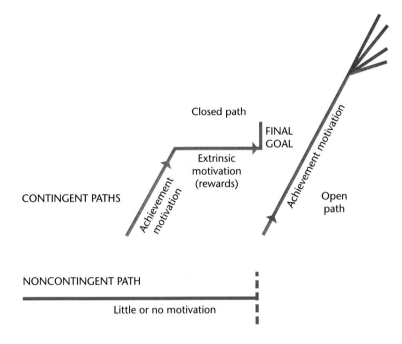

FIGURE 14-6
Raynor's model of career paths. Adults who perceive advancement as contingent on their own efforts are more highly motivated to strive for success than those who do not. On closed paths leading to a fixed goal (such as retirement), motivation shifts from intrinsic to extrinsic rewards (such as bonuses and pensions) as the goal comes within reach. On open paths, where new opportunities keep appearing, people continue to be intrinsically motivated to achieve.

reer path a person is on (see Figure 14-6). People on *contingent paths* believe that their future job status and income will be largely determined by their own actions. People on *noncontingent paths* lack motivation to achieve because they see themselves in dead-end jobs. Eventually they either quit or resign themselves to a hopeless situation.

A worker may perceive a contingent career path as either closed or open. A *closed* path has specific steps leading to a final goal, such as becoming a top-level executive or reaching retirement. The closer people get to the goal, the less they are motivated toward achievement for its own sake and the more they look to external rewards, such as bonuses and retirement benefits. In an *open* career path, there is no fixed end point. New opportunities appear along the way, sustaining the motivation to achieve. Adults on an open career path have incentives to keep updating their skills and acquiring new ones.

Raynor's theory may help explain why performance on a job tends to improve, but only up to a point. In studies of firefighters and military personnel, performance ratings rose for the first 5 years of service but not thereafter (Jacobs, Hofmann, & Kriska, 1990; Schmidt, Hunter, & Outerbridge, 1986). It's possible, of course, that the benefits of experience peak at a certain point. However, it seems likely that workers who remain

in the same job for several years may begin to feel that they are on a noncontingent path and may be less motivated to do their best (Warr, 1994).

No single theory fully explains how people choose vocations and how careers develop. For one thing, none of the theories we have discussed has considered career development in nonwestern societies. Still, each can offer insights as we further explore today's world of work. Let's look at problems that create stress on the job, at how people cope with loss of a job, and at a growing trend: work at home. Then we'll see what kinds of work are most conducive to personal and cognitive growth.

OCCUPATIONAL STRESS

The Japanese have a word for it: *karoshi*, "death from overwork." Occupational stress has become a worldwide epidemic. It affects waitresses in Sweden and bus drivers in continental Europe. It strikes in developing countries, where assembly-line workers must cope with the unfamiliar demands of industrialization (United Nations International Labor Organization, UNILO, 1993). One survey found that 40 percent of Japanese workers are afraid of literally working themselves to death.

Workplaces are generally designed for efficiency and profit, not workers' well-being, but human

TABLE 14-3

Sources of Women's Stress on the Job

Rank	Stressor
1	Lack of promotions or raises
2	Low pay
3	Monotonous, repetitive work
4	No input into decision making
5	Heavy work load or overtime
6	Supervision problems
7	Unclear job descriptions
8	Unsupportive boss
9	Inability or reluctance to express frustration or anger
10	Production quotas
11	Difficulty juggling home and family responsibilities
12	Inadequate breaks
13	Sexual harassment

Note: Working conditions are listed in the order of frequency with which they were reported by 915 female office workers. In most cases the stressors are similar to those reported by workers in general, but there are some differences. Whereas these women rank low pay as the second greatest source of stress, this item is generally eighth or ninth in importance to men. Sexual harassment is almost always a woman's problem. One surprise is the low stress value given to "juggling work schedule with home and family responsibilities," which rates below elements of work life itself.

SOURCE: Adapted from Working Women Education Fund, 1981, p. 9.

costs can hurt the bottom line. When people feel they are in the wrong jobs or when efforts to meet job demands are out of proportion to job satisfaction and other rewards (such as salary, esteem, opportunity for advancement, and a sense of control), stress can result. And, as we have seen, stress—intense, frequent, and prolonged—can play havoc with mental and physical health (Levi, 1990; Siegrist, 1996). In the United States, estimated costs of stress-related injuries and diseases have reached $200 billion a year in workers' compensation claims, medical expenses, health insurance, absenteeism, and loss of productivity (UNILO, 1993).

A combination of high-pressure demands with little autonomy or control and little pride in the product is a common stress-producing pattern (UNILO, 1993; G. Williams, 1991), which increases the risk of heart disease (Siegrist, 1996). Studies of 30- to 60-year-old men in a range of occupations found that those experiencing these conditions were 3 times more likely than other men to have high blood pressure and to show changes in heart

muscles that often precede heart attacks (Schnall et al., 1990).

Another major cause of stress on the job is conflict with supervisors, subordinates, and coworkers. Dissension at work may be especially trying because workers tend to suppress anger (N. Bolger, DeLongis, Kessler, & Schilling, 1989), though violence in the workplace is becoming an increasing problem (Clay, 1995a).

In addition to juggling work and family (see Box 13-3), many women are under special pressure in the workplace, especially in corporations, where their superiors often are men. One of the major sources of stress reported by working women (see Table 14-3) is *sexual harassment:* psychological pressure created by unwelcome sexual overtures, particularly from a superior, which create a hostile or abusive environment. Sexual harassment is a violation of Title VII of the federal Civil Rights Act; complaints can be filed with the Equal Employment Opportunity Commission.

Many companies have programs to help women cope with occupational stress. One high-technology firm established special training opportunities and support groups for women (A. Kaplan, personal communication, 1993). Another approach is to train female workers to become more assertive and task-oriented, to behave more impersonally, and to think more analytically. A third approach, based on qualities commonly thought to be women's strengths, is to offer workshops for both male and female employees focusing on ways people can work together more effectively (I. Stiver, personal communication, 1993).

Burnout may result from occupational stress; it involves emotional exhaustion, a feeling of being unable to accomplish anything on the job, and a sense of helplessness and loss of control. It is especially common among people in the helping professions (such as teaching, medicine, therapy, social work, and police work) who feel frustrated by their inability to help people as much as they would like to. Burnout is usually a response to continuous stress rather than to an immediate crisis. Its symptoms include fatigue, insomnia, headaches, persistent colds, stomach disorders, abuse of alcohol or drugs, and trouble getting along with people. A burned-out worker may quit suddenly, pull away from family and friends, and sink into depression (Briley, 1980; Maslach & Jackson, 1985). Measures that seem to help burned-out workers include cutting down on working hours and taking breaks, including long weekends and vacations. Other standard stress-reducing techniques—exercise, music, and meditation—also help. However, the most effective way of relieving stress and burnout may be to change the conditions that cause it by seeing that employees have opportunities to do work that is meaningful to them, uses their skills and knowledge, and gives them a sense of achievement and esteem (Knoop, 1995).

UNEMPLOYMENT

Perhaps the greatest work-related stressor is sudden, unexpected, permanent loss of a job; it happened to 1.7 million Americans in 1995 alone. The usual official unemployment rate in the United States is about 7 percent of the work force, but unemployment is much higher among certain minorities. About twice as many African Americans as white people are unemployed—10.4 percent versus 4.9 percent (U.S. Department of Labor, 1996a). Furthermore, official unemployment figures count only people who are registered with government agencies as actively seeking work. We do not know how many millions of people have simply given up.

Corporate downsizing has added a growing number of formerly well-paid middle-aged middle management executives to the unemployment rolls (Kuttner, 1994). Many of these longtime employees cannot find work and are forced into early retirement. In the 1970s, 9 out of 10 laid-off white-collar workers quickly found comparable jobs; in 1992, only 1 in 4 did so (Cowan & Barron, 1992). Those who do find new jobs tend to be younger adults. Prospective employers generally prefer not to hire older people, whose skills they often do not view as transferable. When older workers do find work, it is usually at substantially lower pay (Forteza & Prieto, 1994).

Research on unemployment since the 1930s, chiefly among men, has linked it to physical and mental illness, including heart attack, stroke, anxiety, and depression; to marital and family problems; to health, psychological, and behavior problems in children; and to suicide, homicide, and other crimes (Brenner, 1991; Merva & Fowles, 1992; Voydanoff, 1990). Women, too, suffer from loss of a job. Among former employees of a plant in Indiana that closed in 1982, the unemployed of both sexes reported headaches, stomach trouble,

Corporate downsizing has forced many formerly well-paid middle-aged executives into the ranks of the unemployed. These members of the Jobs for All Coalition are demonstrating for full employment and decent benefits. Both men and women cope with unemployment better when they can draw on financial, psychological, and social resources and can see this forced change as an opportunity to do something new or as a challenge for growth. *(Michael Kaufman/Impact Visuals)*

and high blood pressure and felt less in control of their lives (Perrucci, Perrucci, & Targ, 1988).

Stress comes not only from loss of income and the resulting financial hardships, but also from the effect of this loss on the self-concept and on family relationships (Price, quoted in Burnette, 1996). Men who define manhood as supporting a family, and workers of both sexes who derive their identity from their work and define their worth in terms of its dollar value, lose more than their paychecks when they lose their jobs. They lose a piece of themselves and their self-esteem (Forteza & Prieto, 1994; Voydanoff, 1987, 1990).

Those who cope best with unemployment have financial resources (savings or earnings of other family members). Rather than blame themselves for losing their jobs or see themselves as failures, they assess their situation objectively. They have the support of understanding, adaptable families and friends (Voydanoff, 1990). A sense of control is crucial. Among 190 unemployed workers, those who believed they had some influence on their circumstances were less anxious and depressed, had fewer physical symptoms, and had higher self-esteem and life satisfaction than those who believed external forces were in control (Cvetanovski & Jex, 1994). People who can look at loss of a job as a challenge for growth may develop emotionally and professionally. They may change not only their jobs but the direction of their lives.

WORKING AT HOME

For an estimated 40 million Americans, going to work in the morning—at least part of the time—means rolling out of bed and walking down the hall to a home office, perhaps linked by computer, fax machine, and modem with an employer's place of business. This rapidly growing contingent who work at home one or more days a week make up about one-third of the work force. They include about 9½ million telecommuters, 15 million self-employed persons, and more than 15½ million "moonlighters" running part-time home businesses in addition to regular full-time jobs. Some observers estimate that tens of millions of men and women will work at home in years to come (R. Lewis, 1996).

More than one-third of people who do paid work at home are 45 to 64 years old; the likelihood of working at home increases with age (Deming, 1994). According to one survey, the average home business owner is almost 49 (R. Lewis, 1996). Some of these people have lost previous jobs and have taken the opportunity to start home businesses. Men and women are about equally likely to work at home, but more than 9 out of 10 home workers are white. More than half are in service occupations, such as the professions, business services, or repair services (Deming, 1994).

Working at home is convenient and flexible and can be less stressful than daily commuting. It can benefit employers (who need less space), employees (who save on clothing and transportation), and entrepreneurs (who save on office expenses). However, it is not for everyone: it requires enough initiative, independence, and self-confidence to work without supervision. Some home workers feel isolated or have trouble concentrating in the presence of such distractions as television, the refrigerator, and young children. Also, employees who work at home may lose fringe benefits, such as health insurance, and the protection of laws guaranteeing fair labor standards and working conditions (R. Lewis, 1996).

WORK, LEISURE, AND COGNITIVE GROWTH

Do people change as a result of the kind of work they do? Some research says yes. People seem to grow in challenging jobs.

A combination of cross-sectional and longitudinal studies (Kohn, 1980) revealed a reciprocal relationship between the *substantive complexity* of work—the degree of thought and independent judgment it requires—and a person's flexibility in coping with cognitive demands. People doing more complex work tend to become more flexible thinkers, and flexible thinkers are likely to do more complex work.

This circular relationship may begin early, when "children from culturally advantaged families develop skills and other qualities that result in their being placed in classroom situations and tracks that are relatively complex and demanding, which in turn contribute to further development of intellectual flexibility" (Smelser, 1980, p. 16). The circle continues in adulthood; the gap between flexible and inflexible thinkers widens, as flexible thinkers go into increasingly complex work, whereas people who show less flexibility do less complex work, and their cognitive abilities grow more slowly or not at all (Kohn, 1980).

Why is the complexity of work tied so closely to cognitive growth? In a society in which work plays a central role in people's lives, mastery of complex tasks may give workers confidence in their ability to handle problems. It also may open their minds to new experience and stimulate them to become more self-directed.

Nor does growth stop at the end of the workday. People with substantively complex work tend to pursue more cognitively demanding leisure activities (Kohn, 1980). A follow-up study supported a *spillover hypothesis:* the idea that cognitive gains from work carry over to nonworking hours. Substantive complexity of work—more than any other aspect of a job situation—strongly influences the intellectual level of leisure activities of both men and women, regardless of income and educational background (K. Miller & Kohn, 1983).

For many adults, it seems, work and leisure are two sides of the same coin; choices in one facet of life affect the other. If so, then the kind of work people do should make a difference in how they spend their time after retirement. And, in a society in which work is increasingly complex and leisure options are more sophisticated, we may expect to see continuing cognitive gains in late life.

Research about work and leisure—as well as about problem solving, creativity, education, and moral choices—confirms that people's minds continue to develop during adulthood. Such research also confirms the links between the cognitive side of development and its social and emotional aspects, to which we turn again in Chapter 15.

✔ SUMMARY

- Most middle-aged people are in good physical, cognitive, and emotional condition, and some consider this period the best of their lives. The middle years are marked by growing individual differences.

PHYSICAL CHANGES

- Although some physiological changes result from aging, behavior and lifestyle affect their timing and extent. Middle-aged adults compensate well for gradual, minor declines in sensory and psychomotor abilities.

- Menopause, the cessation of menstruation and reproductive ability in women, typically occurs at about age 50. Most women take menopause in stride and have no serious psychological or physical problems.

- Men experience a gradual decline in testosterone levels from the late teens on. Although men can continue to father children until late in life, some experience a decline in fertility and in frequency of orgasm after age 40 and an increase in erectile failure.

- Sexual activity generally diminishes only slightly and gradually in middle age. Declines in frequency of sexual relations are often due to non-physical causes.

- The "double standard of aging" causes women more than men to seem less desirable as they lose their youthful looks. For both sexes, the problems of getting older are often amplified by living in a society that places a premium on youth.

HEALTH

- Most middle-aged people rate their health as good or better. Hypertension is a major health problem of midlife. Leading causes of death are cancer, heart disease, and stroke.

- As in younger age groups, death rates are higher for males than for females and higher for black people than for white people. Postmenopausal women become more susceptible to heart disease and osteoporosis. African Americans have elevated health risks, probably due to a combination of hereditary factors, lifestyle factors, poverty, and the psychosomatic effects of racism.

- Stress, particularly when associated with lack of control, is related to a variety of physical and psychological problems.

INTELLIGENCE

- Performance on measures of fluid intelligence (based on neurological status) declines starting in young adulthood, but crystallized intelligence (based on learning) increases through or beyond middle age. Sequential research has found wide individual differences in cognitive status and variations among abilities.

- Some developmentalists maintain that intelligence takes distinctive forms at midlife. Hoyer and his colleagues proposed that fluid abilities become encapsulated, or dedicated to use in fields of expertise. Postformal theorists describe a shift to relativistic thinking, integration of emotion and intuition with logic, and interpretation of information in the light of experience. The ability to solve practical problems is strong, and may even peak, at midlife.

CREATIVITY

- According to Gardner, creative performance depends on personal attributes and environmental forces, as well as cognitive abilities.

- According to Sternberg, the insightful, analytical, and practical aspects of intelligence all play a part in creative performance.

- An age-related decline in creativity shows up in both psychometric tests and actual output, but peak ages vary by occupation. Individuals tend to produce the greatest number, though not necessarily the greatest proportion, of major works at peak periods of productivity.

EDUCATION, WORK, AND LEISURE

- A shift from age-differentiated to age-integrated roles appears to be occurring in response to greater longevity and economic and social change.

- About half of all American adults participate in continuing education. Adults go to school for many reasons, but chiefly to improve their work-related skills and knowledge or to prepare for a change of career.

■ Ginzberg's theory describes two basic career paths: stability and change. Raynor's theory emphasizes interaction between achievement motivation and people's perception of its effect on their career paths.

■ Causes of occupational stress and burnout include a combination of high pressure and low autonomy, interpersonal conflict, and work overload. Women may experience special sources of tension, including sexual harassment.

■ In the United States, African Americans have the highest rates of unemployment. Unemployment has physical and psychological effects on men and women.

■ A growing proportion of the work force are people working at home, and a large proportion of these are middle-aged.

■ The kind of work adults do affects their cognitive growth. People who do more complex work tend to engage in more intellectually demanding leisure activities.

✔ KEY TERMS

presbyopia (page 473)
presbycusis (473)
menopause (474)
climacteric (474)
erectile dysfunction (477)
hypertension (480)
osteoporosis (481)

Wechsler Adult Intelligence Scale (WAIS) (485)
fluid intelligence (485)
crystallized intelligence (485)
ecological validity (487)
encapsulation (488)
age-differentiated (494)

age-integrated (495)
sexual harassment (498)
burnout (498)
substantive complexity (500)
spillover hypothesis (500)

✔ QUESTIONS FOR THOUGHT AND DISCUSSION

1 Think of people you know who call themselves middle-aged. How old are they? Do they seem to be in good health?

2 How often, and in what ways, do you imagine your parents express their sexuality? When you are their age, do you expect to be more or less sexually active than they seem to be?

3 How do you handle stress? What methods have you found most successful?

4 If you needed surgery, would you rather go to a doctor who is a young adult or one who is considerably older? Why?

5 Think of an adult you know who is extremely creative. To what combination of personal qualities and environmental forces would you attribute her or his creative performance?

6 In what specific ways, in addition to those mentioned in the text, would an age-integrated society be different from an age-differentiated one?

7 From what you have seen, do older students seem to do better or worse in college than younger students? How would you explain your observation?

8 What would you do if you were told that the job you had been doing for 10 years was obsolete and that you were being let go because of corporate downsizing?

CHAPTER FIFTEEN

PSYCHOSOCIAL DEVELOPMENT IN MIDDLE ADULTHOOD

What happens to a dream deferred?
Does it dry up
Like a raisin in the sun?
Maybe it just sags
Like a heavy load.
Or does it explode?

Langston Hughes,
"Montage of a Dream Deferred," 1951

ASK YOURSELF

✔ How common is the "midlife crisis"?
✔ How much does personality change during middle adulthood? How similar are women's and men's development?
✔ Do most marriages become happier or unhappier in the middle years? How likely is divorce at this time?
✔ How do homosexuals adjust at midlife?

✔ How do friendships change?
✔ How do middle-aged people get along with their children, parents, and siblings? How do they cope with the "empty nest" (and sometimes its refilling) and with responsibilities for aging parents?
✔ How is the role of grandparent different from what it used to be?

Changes in personality and lifestyle during the early to middle forties are often attributed to the *midlife crisis,* a supposedly stressful period triggered by review and reevaluation of one's life, which may herald the onset of middle age. The term was coined by the psychoanalyst Elliott Jacques (1967) and burst into public consciousness in the 1970s with the popularization of the normative-crisis theories of Erik Erikson, Carl Jung, and Daniel Levinson. It has become a trendy catchphrase, which may pop up as an explanation for an episode of depression, an extramarital affair, or a career change.

What brings on the midlife crisis, said Jacques, is awareness of mortality. Time has become shorter; many people now realize that they will not be able to fulfill the dreams of their youth or that fulfillment of their dreams has not brought the satisfaction they expected. They know that if they want to change direction, they have to act quickly.

Today, the existence of a universal, psychologically necessary midlife crisis is in doubt. The work of Costa and McCrae provides strong evidence for stability of personality in middle age, and the timing-of-events model holds that personality development is influenced less by age than by the time when important events occur.

Still, midlife is a special time, a time of stock taking with regard to both careers and relationships. It may bring to the surface unresolved issues of identity or role confusion, which, according to Erikson, crop up again and again throughout life. Middle-aged people are not only in the middle of the adult life span, in a position to look back and ahead in their own lives; they also bridge older and younger generations. Very often, they are the ones who hold families together and run societal institutions and enterprises. Much can happen in the lives of an individual and a family during the 25-year span we call *middle adulthood;* and these experiences affect the way people look, feel, and act as they enter old age.

▪ In this chapter we look at psychosocial development in middle age through a normative-crisis prism and then at trait and timing-of-events research. We go on to describe changes in intimate relationships, which often shape the occurrence and timing of life events. As we examine marriage and divorce, homosexual relationships, and friendships, as well as relationships with maturing children, aging parents, siblings, and grandchildren, we see how richly textured are these middle years. ▪

✔ PERSONALITY AT MIDLIFE: NORMATIVE-CRISIS MODELS

Much theory and research on adult development has come from a normative-crisis perspective. Let's see how five classic models—those of Carl Jung, Erik Erikson, Robert Peck, George Vaillant, and Daniel Levinson—conceptualized midlife. Then we'll turn to the work of Levinson, Ravenna Helson, and others on women's development, a topic that until recently has received less attention than men's development. (Table 15-1 summarizes critical developments of middle age in each of the classic models; all but Jung and Peck were introduced in Chapter 13.)

TABLE 15-1

Five Views of Development in Middle Adulthood

Jung	Erikson	Peck	Vaillant	Levinson
Midlife transition (about age 40): After child-rearing obligations have diminished, women and men can balance their personalities by expressing characteristics that had previously been suppressed. Women become more assertive and men become more emotionally expressive. People become more inner-oriented and preoccupied with their inner world. They now need to give up the image of youth, adopt a more appropriate lifestyle, and acknowledge that their lives are finite. This inner work creates stress but is necessary for healthy adjustment.	*Crisis 7—Generativity versus stagnation:* The impulse to foster the development of the next generation leads middle-aged persons to become mentors to young adults. The wish to have children is instinctual, and so childless people must acknowledge their sense of loss and express their generative impulses in other ways, helping to care for other people's children directly or as protégés in the workplace. Some stagnation can provide a rest that leads to greater future creativity. Too much stagnation can lead to physical or psychological invalidism.	1 *Valuing wisdom versus valuing physical powers:* People realize that the wisdom they have gained through the years makes up for declining physical powers and youthful attractiveness. 2 *Socializing versus sexualizing in human relationships:* People appreciate the personalities of others as they value them as friends rather than sex objects. 3 *Emotional flexibility versus emotional impoverishment:* Deaths of parents and friends end relationships. People must shift emotional investments to others. Physical limitations may require a change in activities. 4 *Mental flexibility versus mental rigidity:* People use their past experiences as guides to solving new issues.	*Midlife transition (age 40—"give or take a decade"):* Midlife is stressful, as adolescence is stressful, because of the demands of entrance into a new stage of life. Much of the pain comes from having the maturity to face pain that was suppressed for years. Many men reassess their past, reorder their attitudes toward sexuality, and seize one more chance to find new solutions to old needs. The best-adjusted men are the most generative and find these years (from 35 to 49) the happiest of their lives. *Tranquil fifties:* Males become more nurturant and expressive. Sexual differentiation lessens. The fifties are a generally mellower time of life.	*Midlife transition (age 40 to age 45):* Questioning one's life—values, desires, talents, goals; looking back over past choices and priorities; deciding where to go now; coming to terms with youthful dreams; developing a realistic view of self. *Entry life structure for middle adulthood (age 45 to age 50):** Reappraisal leads to a new life structure involving new choices. Some men retreat into a constricted—or well-organized, overly busy—middle age. *Age 50 transition* (age 50 to age 55):* Men who have not gone through their midlife crisis earlier may do so now. Others may modify the life structures they have formed in their midforties. *Culminating life structure for middle adulthood* (age 55 to age 60):* Men complete middle adulthood; a time of fulfillment. *Late adult transition* (age 60 to age 65):* Middle age ends; preparation for late adulthood.

*Levinson's studies of men did not go beyond the entry period of middle adulthood; subsequent stages were projected. His studies of women did not go beyond the midlife transition.
SOURCES: Erikson, 1950; Jung, 1953; Levinson, 1978, 1986, 1996; Peck, 1955; Vaillant, 1977, 1989.

Coaching a Little League baseball team is one form of what Erikson called *generativity.* Many middle-aged people fulfill this need to establish and guide the next generation by helping other people's children, in addition to or instead of their own. *(Bob Daemmrich/Stock, Boston)*

CLASSIC THEORIES AND RESEARCH

Carl Jung: Balancing the Personality

The Swiss psychologist Carl Jung, like Erikson, departed from Freudian theory in his belief that people grow and change throughout life. Jung (1953, 1969) held that healthy development calls for a balance or integration of conflicting parts of the personality.

Until about age 40, said Jung, adults concentrate on obligations to family and society and develop those aspects of personality that will help them reach these external goals. Women emphasize expressiveness and nurturance; men are primarily oriented toward achievement. Men suppress their feminine aspects; women suppress their masculine aspects. At midlife, when careers are established and children are grown, men and women seek a "union of opposites" by expressing their previously "disowned" aspects. As people do this, they often become preoccupied with their inner selves.

Two necessary tasks of midlife, said Jung, are giving up the image of youth and acknowledging mortality. These are threatening concepts; thus this period is often stressful. However, people who avoid the transition and do not reorient their lives appropriately will not make a good psychological adjustment. According to Jung (1966), the need to acknowledge mortality requires a gradual shift from an outward orientation, a concern with finding a place in society, to an inward orientation, a search for meaning within the self. This inward turn may be unsettling; as people question their goals, they may temporarily lose their moorings.

Adults may emerge from this time of questioning with deeper understanding of themselves and of others, with more wisdom, strength, and courage, and with a greater capacity for love and enjoyment.

Erik Erikson: Generativity Versus Stagnation

Erikson saw the years around age 40 as the time when people go through their seventh normative crisis, *generativity versus stagnation. Generativity* is the concern of mature adults for establishing and guiding the next generation. Looking ahead to the waning of their own lives, people feel a need to participate in life's continuation.

The generative impulse is not necessarily limited to a person's own children and grandchildren; although Erikson (1985) believed that it is difficult for people who have not been parents to fulfill it, this view is now considered narrow. Erikson did say that generativity can be expressed through teaching or mentorship, through productivity or creativity, and through "self-generation," or self-development. The "virtue" of this period is *care:* "a widening commitment to *take care of* the persons, the products, and the ideas one has learned *to care for*" (1985, p. 67). People who do not find an outlet for generativity become self-absorbed, self-indulgent, or stagnant (inactive or lifeless). As in all of Erikson's stages, it is the balance that is important; even the most generative person goes through fallow periods.

Robert Peck: Four Adjustments of Middle Age

Peck (1955), extending Erikson's work, identified four psychological developments as necessary to successful adaptation in middle age. They represent a shift from physical prowess to mental and emotional flexibility.

1 *Valuing wisdom versus valuing physical powers.* Wisdom, defined as the ability to make the best choices in life, depends on a broad range of experience and more than compensates for diminished strength and stamina and the loss of youthful appearance.
2 *Socializing versus sexualizing in human relationships.* People come to value the men and women in their lives as unique individuals, as friends, and as companions rather than primarily as sex objects.
3 *Emotional flexibility versus emotional impov-*

erishment. As children grow up and become independent, and as loved ones die, the ability to shift emotional investment from one person to another and (if physical limitations develop) from one activity to another becomes crucial.

4 *Mental flexibility versus mental rigidity.* Unless people continue to seek new answers to life's important questions, they can become set in their ways and closed to new ideas.

None of these developments need wait until middle age, but, said Peck, if they do not take place by then, successful adjustment is doubtful.

George Vaillant: Introspection and Transition

The Grant Study, reported by Vaillant, followed male Harvard undergraduates into adulthood and identified a midlife transition at about age 40. After the stage of career consolidation, which usually occurred during the thirties, many of the men abandoned the "compulsive, unreflective busy-work of their occupational apprenticeships and once more [became] explorers of the world within" (Vaillant, 1977, p. 220). This introspective shift echoes Jung's concept of turning inward. Bernice Neugarten (1977), a prominent advocate of the timing-of-events model, observed a similar tendency, which she called *interiority.*

According to Vaillant, the midlife transition may be stressful because of the demands made by a new stage of life, such as changing the parenting role to meet the needs of teenage children. Many men reassess their past, come to terms with long-suppressed feelings about their parents, and reorder their attitudes toward sexuality. However, for the men in the Grant Study, the transition rarely assumed crisis proportions. These men were no more likely to become depressed, divorced, or disenchanted with their jobs at midlife than at any other time. In fact, by their fifties, the best-adjusted men looked back on the years from 35 to 49 as the happiest in their lives. The best-adjusted men were also the most generative, as measured by their responsibility for other people at work, their gifts to charity, and their children, whose academic achievements equaled those of their fathers. These men were 4 times more likely to use mature ways of coping, such as altruism and humor, than to use immature ways, such as drinking or becoming hypochondriacs (Vaillant, 1989).

The fifties were a generally mellower and more tranquil time of life than the forties. Vaillant noted the same development seen by Jung: a lessening of gender differentiation and a tendency for men to become more nurturant and expressive.

Daniel Levinson: Changing Life Structures

The concept of a midlife crisis found one of its strongest champions in Levinson (1978, 1980, 1986). In 32 of the 40 men in his sample, the period between ages 40 and 45 was a time of crisis, when they often felt upset and acted irrationally. Levinson maintained that such turmoil is inevitable as people question previously held values. Reevaluation helps them come to terms with youthful dreams, construct a more realistic self-image, and substitute more attainable goals.

Between ages 45 and 50, men carve out new life structures, possibly by taking a new job or a new wife. Those who make no changes lead constricted lives, though they may be busy and well organized. Often those who do change their life structures find middle age the most fulfilling and creative time of life. Levinson and his colleagues (1978) did not follow their sample into the fifties and sixties, but they did make projections about those years (refer back to Table 15-1).

WOMEN'S DEVELOPMENT

The classic normative-crisis models were largely male-oriented in theory or in research samples, or both. More recently, efforts have been made to test their application to women or to formulate separate models of women's development.

Research on Erikson's Theory

In a study of more than one hundred 48-year-old Radcliffe College alumnae (part of a group who had been followed since age 18), researchers assessed generativity by analyzing themes of stories the women made up in response to pictures. Among the women who scored highest on generativity, those on high-status career tracks (a little more than half of the sample) found the most gratification through productivity and helping others at work; those in traditionally female occupations, such as teacher, nurse, or secretary, found the most gratification through parenting (Peterson & Stewart, 1996). Generativity was related to a desire to improve society: the most generative women were, or had been, involved in political and social action. Having had an influential mentor in young adulthood—an inspiring teacher or a supportive employer—increased the motivation to play a similar role in someone else's life.

Other research based on Erikson's theory found a connection between identity and generativity linked to particular roles such as spouse and parent (DeHaan & MacDermid, 1994). Using measures of James Marcia's four identity statuses (see Chapter 11), the researchers tested 40 middle-class female bank employees in their early forties, who were married or cohabiting and had school-age children. Those women who had achieved identity after a period of conscious decision making and had come out with strong commitments were the most satisfied and the most psychologically healthy and felt the most in control of their lives. They also expressed the greatest degree of generativity, bearing out Erikson's view that successful achievement of identity paves the way for other tasks. However, few of the women were in this category. In fact, as a group, these middle-aged women were no more likely to have achieved identity (as Marcia defined it) than a comparison group of college women, and they were less likely to be currently struggling with identity issues. Instead, they were more likely to have *foreclosed* identity—to have made commitments that others expected of them without actively exploring other options.

Levinson's Study of Women

In Levinson's (1996) study of 45 female homemakers and career women, both groups made major changes at midlife. For most of the 8 homemakers who had reached their early forties by the time they were interviewed between 1980 and 1982, both marriage and quality of life hit "rock bottom" during the midlife transition. These women had expected to live out their lives in traditional marriages; they had tried to fulfill their side of the marital bargain, and they felt cheated. As their children prepared to leave the nest, these mothers yearned for the chance to fulfill their own needs and make their own choices, but often didn't know where to start. By age 45, half of these women were divorced (some had remarried), and the others were renegotiating the terms of their marriages. Four out of five were in the work force.

Many of the 13 career women who had reached their early forties by the time of the study also hit rock bottom at midlife. As members of the first sizable cohort to pursue an antitraditional path, they had thought they could "have it all": a full-time career, a more or less egalitarian marriage, and motherhood. Now they saw a wide gap between this goal and the reality of their lives. Gender discrimination often blocked their career advancement, while at home they struggled with overwhelming responsibilities alone or with husbands who did not pull equal weight. None of the career women had been able to achieve and maintain all three components of their dream. One was ending her marriage; others had remained single, or were married but childless, or were divorced (with or without children), or had become full-time homemakers. Nearly all went through moderate or serious crises at midlife, and about half went into psychotherapy, exploring ways to modify their life structures so as to obtain greater personal fulfillment through work and more equality in love and marriage.

Ravenna Helson: The Mills Studies

Among Helson's (1992) Mills College graduates, who had been part of a longitudinal study since their student days in the late 1950s (see Chapter 13), the early forties turned out to be the time of greatest turmoil for the most women, perhaps suggesting a midlife crisis. Often the outcome was a "revision of the life story," giving "the plot of their lives a self-chosen new direction" (p. 343).

The main issue (as it had been for many women in the thirties) was a quest for independence and assertiveness, and this quest often led to problems on the job and at home. The women ran into roadblocks at work, or their husbands left them after the wives became absorbed in careers or community activities, forcing them to reorganize their lives to support themselves and their children. Later midlife themes, between ages 47 and 53, often focused on destructive relationships with partners, parents, or children. Another common theme in later midlife was overload, sometimes caused by the demands of other people, sometimes by economic strain or heavy responsibilities at work.

Role and lifestyle choices made during the twenties affected midlife development. Women who had followed the expected pattern for their generation, marrying and starting families in young adulthood, and who, by age 43, continued to maintain their traditional roles, did not exhibit as strong a gain in both dominance and independence as did less traditional women (Helson & Picano, 1990). Still, more than one kind of lifestyle seemed to foster positive development. Women who had committed themselves during their twenties to career or family, or both, developed more fully than women who had no children and who chose work beneath their capabilities. Between age 27 and the early forties, women who had faced the challenges of career or parenthood became more disciplined, independent, hard-working, and confident, and improved their "people skills." Compared with women who had made neither commitment, they were more dominant, more motivated to achieve, more emotionally stable, more goal-oriented, and more interested in what was going on in the world (Helson & Moane, 1987).

Similar findings by another research team emerged from a study of nearly 300 women between ages 35 and 55 with diverse incomes and lifestyles (Barnett, 1985; Baruch, Barnett, & Rivers, 1983). The two key factors in healthy adjustment, regardless of age, were a sense of mastery over one's life and the amount of pleasure derived from living. Paid work was the single best predictor of mastery; a positive experience with marriage and family, including a good sex life, was the best predictor of pleasure. The single best key to general well-being was a challenging job that paid well and offered opportunities to use skills and make decisions. The women who scored highest overall on both mastery and pleasure were employed married women with children; the lowest scorers were unemployed, childless married women. This research suggests that women's well-being may flourish best in multiple roles, despite the accompanying stress. It may be more distressing for a woman to be underinvolved—to have too little to do, to have a job that is not challenging enough, or to have too few personal and occupational demands.

By the early fifties, most of the Mills women rated their quality of life as high. By this time they were more self-confident, independent, decisive, dominant, and self-affirming and less self-critical than they had been earlier in life (see Table 15-2). They became more comfortable with themselves, partly because they were adhering to their own standards. And they increased on four measures of coping, suggesting that they had grown in the ability to analyze issues, to accept complexity and uncertainty in situations, and to be flexible in their thinking. This normative personality change was unrelated to such typical events as children leaving home, menopause, and caring for aging parents (Helson & Wink, 1992).

Similarly, among another group of nearly 700 Mills alumnae ages 26 to 80, women in their early fifties most often described their lives as "first-rate" (Mitchell & Helson, 1990). They were young enough to be in good health and old enough to have launched their children and to be financially secure. Life at home was simpler; the energy that had gone into child rearing was redirected to partners, work, community, or themselves. They had developed greater confidence, involvement, security, and breadth of personality. The women with the most positive outlook were optimistic; they had good relationships, a favorable self-concept, a feeling of control over their lives, and active interests; and they were managing their lives sensibly.

These women's responses confirm some aspects of normative-crisis theory. They were, as Jung and Erikson observed, more aware of the fleeting of time, though they showed little of the spiritual interest sometimes identified as typical of midlife. They tended to be caring for others, showing generativity. The highest quality of life was associated with a balance of "masculine" autonomy and "feminine" involvement in an intimate relationship, bearing out Jung's idea "that young adult roles increase women's femininity but that women become more confident and assertive around midlife" (Helson, 1993, pp. 101–102).

EVALUATING NORMATIVE-CRISIS MODELS

We need to ask several questions about normative-crisis models of adult personality development. Are the findings limited to the populations studied, or do they establish universal, age-linked stages? How healthy is the male model of development portrayed in this research? How common is the midlife crisis?

Are the Findings Generalizable?

The men and women in these studies were not representative of the United States population. The classic research, for the most part, dealt with privileged white men. Vaillant's sample of Harvard graduates included no African Americans. In Levinson's small sample of 40 men, 30 were middle- or upper-class, and only 5 were black; his more recent sample of 45 women was more diverse but still unrepresentative. Helson's Mills women are educated, mostly white, and upper-middle-class. The findings of these studies may not apply to people of other backgrounds or socioeconomic levels.

TABLE 15-2

Selected Feelings about Life Reported by Women in Their Early Fifties

	More True Now	Less True Now
Identity questioning and turmoil:		
Excitement, turmoil about my impulses and potential	21	56
Searching for a sense of who I am	28	47
Anxious that I won't live up to my potential	25	47
Coming near the end of one road and not finding another	27	45
Assurance of status:		
Feeling established	78	11
Influence in my community or field of interest	63	24
A new level of productivity	70	11
Feeling selective in what I do	91	2
A sense of being my own person	90	3
Cognitive breadth and complexity:		
Bringing both feeling and rationality into decisions	76	1
Realizing larger patterns of meaning and relationship	72	7
Appreciating my complexity	69	10
Discovering new parts of myself	72	11
Present rather than future orientation:		
Focus on reality—meeting the needs of the day and not being too emotional about them	76	6
More satisfied with what I have; less worried about what I won't get	76	11
Feeling the importance of time's passing	76	10
Adjustment and relational smoothness:		
Feeling secure and committed	71	12
Feeling my life is moving well	74	15
Feeling optimistic about the future	58	20
A new level of intimacy	53	30
Doing things for others and then feeling exploited	14	56
Feeling very much alone	26	45
Feelings of competition with other women	7	63
Feeling angry at men and masculinity	14	52
Awareness of aging and reduced vitality:		
Looking old	70	15
Being treated as an older person	64	14
Reducing the intensity of my achievement efforts	44	26
Liking an active social life	27	52
Being very interested in sex	19	64

Note: The women judged whether each item was more applicable to them now than in their early forties, less applicable now than then, or about the same.

SOURCE: Helson & Wink, 1992.

Then there is the issue of cohort. Many of the men in Vaillant's and Levinson's studies grew up during the economic depression of the 1930s. They benefited from an expanding economy after World War II and may have succeeded at work far beyond their early expectations, but then burned out early. Levinson's and Helson's women lived through a time of great change in women's roles brought about by the women's movement, economic trends, changing patterns of family life, and new patterns in the workplace. Cohorts with different experiences may develop differently. For example, these studies do not reflect such recent trends as flexible career patterns, dual-earner marriages, and cohabitation.

Today men's and women's roles are becoming more alike. Women now spend more time in paid work and less in housework than in the past, whereas for men the reverse is true. As their middle-aged wives—who stayed home to raise chil-

BOX 15-1   WINDOW ON THE WORLD

A SOCIETY WITHOUT MIDDLE AGE

The universality of the midlife crisis is questionable even in the United States. What, then, happens in nonwestern cultures, some of which do not even have a clear concept of middle age? One such culture is that of the Gusii in Africa, a society of 1 million people in western Kenya, in which people believe in witchcraft and men take several wives (R. Levine, 1980). The Gusii have a "life plan" with well-defined expectations for each stage, but this plan is very different from that in most western societies.

The Gusii have no words for "adolescent," "young adult," or "middle-aged." Childbearing is not confined to young adulthood; people continue to reproduce as long as they are physiologically able. A man is circumcised sometime between ages 9 and 11 and becomes an elder when his first child marries. Between these two events, he goes through only one recognized stage of life: *omomura*, or "warrior." The *omomura* phase may last anywhere from 25 to 40 years, or even longer.

Many Gusii in western Kenya become ritual practitioners after their children are grown, seeking spiritual powers to compensate for their waning physical strength. For women like the diviner shown here, ritual practice may be a way to wield power in a male-dominated society. *(Levine/Anthro-Photo)*

Because of the greater importance of marriage in a woman's life, women have an additional stage: *omosubaati*, or "married woman."

In Gusii society, then, transitions depend on life events. Status is linked to circumcision, marriage (for women), having children, and becoming a parent of a married child and thus a prospective grandparent. The Gusii have a "social clock," a set of expectations for the ages at which these events should normally occur. People who marry late or do not marry at all and people who have their first child late or have no children are ridiculed and ostracized.

Although the Gusii have no recognized midlife transition, some of them do reassess their lives around the time they are old enough to be grandparents. Awareness of mortality and of waning physical powers can bring on something resembling a midlife crisis, from which a man or woman may emerge as a ritual healer. The quest for spiritual powers has a generative purpose, too: elders are responsible for ritually protecting their children and grandchildren from death or illness. Many older women who become ritual practitioners or witches seek power either to help people or to harm them, perhaps to compensate for their lack of personal and economic power in a male-dominated society.

dren—enter the workplace, the husbands take up part of the slack by doing more household chores (Verbrugge, Gruber-Baldini, & Fozard, 1996). As gender roles continue to change, both women's and men's personality development will be affected. In addition, the findings of normative crisis research may not apply to other cultures, some of which have very different patterns of life course development (see Box 15-1).

Cohort differences challenge the very heart of normative-crisis theory: the idea that development follows a universal, age-linked sequence. Levinson responds that the stages of life building are universal, though their content may vary. Helson readily admits that the normative changes found in the Mills research are not necessarily the same as maturational changes, which would occur regardless of class, cohort, and culture. For example, the

Mills women at age 52 were less dependent on their husbands than their mothers had been at the same age (Wink & Helson, 1993). In the future, as Helson and Moane (1987) observe, "If a substantial number of women continue to launch careers in their 20s and have children in their 30s, the pattern of normative change may take a different form" (p. 185).

Finally, these studies dealt exclusively with heterosexuals. Gay men who do not come out until midlife may experience delayed development and a long, sometimes tumultuous search for identity. For many, midlife is marked by issues similar to those Vaillant found for heterosexual men in young adulthood: the effort to consolidate a career and establish or maintain intimate relationships (Kimmel & Sang, 1995).

Aspects of the midlife transition typical of many heterosexual women, such as a search for an independent identity, a return to the workplace, acknowledgment of the end of fertility, and acceptance of children's leaving home, may be irrelevant to lesbians who have been working throughout adulthood, have never married or had children, and have been fighting all their lives for an identity independent of others' opinions. Furthermore, lesbians tend to be less concerned about signs of aging than are heterosexual women (Kimmel & Sang, 1995). One survey of 110 mostly well-educated, white lesbians, ages 40 to 59, found that achievement was becoming less important to them (as it does to some heterosexual men at this age). Many were seeking and finding a new freedom to relax, enjoy life, and be themselves (Sang, 1991). Still, some normative-crisis findings did seem to apply to these women. Nearly half reported undergoing or having undergone a midlife crisis, trying to balance work, relationships, and time for their own interests. As in the Mills studies, three-fourths called middle age the best time of their lives, a time when they felt freer, wiser, stronger, and more self-directed and self-confident than ever before. This may well be in part a cohort effect, a result of both the women's movement and the greater openness about homosexuality in American society.

How Healthy Is the Male Model?

Despite Levinson's recent publication of a study of women, his model and those of Erikson and Vaillant were built on research on men, whose experiences were taken as norms. These models suggest that the way men resolve developmental tasks tells us about their psychological health. In Erikson's model, a man must achieve identity before intimacy, whereas a woman achieves identity *through* intimacy. Levinson stresses a young man's pursuit of his dream; relationships with a mentor and a "special woman" are mainly means to that end. In his model, healthy development in young adulthood is based on personal achievement and separation from early relationships. Not until middle age does a man even begin to concern himself with attachment. The men in the Grant Study followed a similar pattern, becoming more nurturant in the middle years.

Such a model may not only be inapplicable to women, who typically cultivate a rich network of relationships throughout the life span, but also may offer a dubious view of healthy male development (Bergman, 1991; Gilligan, 1982). Proponents of *relational theory* (introduced in Chapter 1) suggest that men, like women, have a primary desire for connection with other people, that their greatest source of happiness lies in mutually empowering relationships (Bergman, 1991; Miller, 1991). When boys are taught to disconnect from primary attachments, they turn away from the process of intimate connection. In midlife, men may sense "a loss of meaning, an emptiness, loneliness, failure, rage, sadness, leading to further isolation, stagnation and stasis, and depression" (Bergman, 1991, p. 10). Such men often try hard to develop connection with others. Ironically, this increased interest in intimate relationships often comes at a time when children are about to leave home or have already done so and when wives may have adapted to a lack of intimacy in marriage by investing their emotions in other relationships.

Relational theory seems to echo Jung's idea that men at midlife need to express their previously disowned feminine aspects. Unlike Jung, however, relational theory does not seem to see a corresponding need for midlife women to express masculine aspects of their personalities. Indeed, much as the classic normative-crisis theories take male patterns as the norm, relational theory seems to take a female pattern as the standard of healthy development.

A more balanced view is that both the masculine tendency toward *agency* or focus on self, and the feminine tendency toward *communion*, or focus on others, can be unhealthy if taken to extremes. A person who focuses on self to the exclusion of others is likely to engage in antisocial behavior and to lack social support; a person who focuses on others to the exclusion of self is likely to be unhappy and to have low self-esteem (Helgeson, 1994). This is similar to Bem's (1974, 1976) position that an androgynous personality, which balances both "masculine" and "feminine" characteristics (see Chapter 7), is the healthiest.

How Common Is the Midlife Crisis?

Much research fails to support the inevitability of a midlife crisis (Brim, 1977; Chiriboga, 1989; Costa & McCrae, 1980; Costa et al., 1986; Farrell & Rosenberg, 1981; Haan, 1990; Lacy & Hendricks, 1980; Rossi, 1980). Indeed, even the classic normative-crisis researchers do not agree on this point. The transition to middle age may be stressful, but such stress does not necessarily amount to a crisis (Vaillant, 1977). In the Mills studies, women's most critical times appeared at various ages between 21 and 53, and women reported no greater turmoil in their early forties than in their early thirties.

For many people, midlife is just one of life's transitions, often involving a revisiting of unresolved identity issues. Whether a transition turns into a crisis may depend less on age than on the circumstances of a person's life and her or his resources for dealing with them: "One person may go from crisis to crisis while another . . . experience[s] relatively few strains" (Schlossberg, 1987, p. 74). Timing of events may be a factor. One group of men in their thirties who had achieved success quite young were already struggling with the kinds of issues commonly associated with middle age. They were asking themselves questions like "Was it worth it?" "What next?" and "What shall I do with the rest of my life?" (Taguiri & Davis, 1982, in Baruch et al., 1983).

Normative-crisis research has captured both the professional and the public imagination, largely because of its central message: that adults continue to change, develop, and grow—often in similar ways. Whether or not adults develop in the specific ways suggested by normative-crisis models, this research has challenged the idea that nothing important happens to personality in midlife or later.

✔ PERSONALITY AT MIDLIFE: NONNORMATIVE MODELS

Although trait and timing-of-events models of personality development are not tied to age, some research inspired by these models does shed light on what happens in middle adulthood.

TRAIT RESEARCH: STABILITY OR CHANGE?

"I'm a completely different person now from the one I was 20 years ago," said a 47-year-old architect as six friends, all in their forties and fifties, nodded vigorously in agreement. Many people feel and observe personality change occurring at midlife (see Box 15-2), but how deep-seated are such changes? Is there a basic core of personality that remains stable?

Extensive research using both cross-sectional and longitudinal measures has found that five broad dimensions of personality—neuroticism, extraversion, openness to experience, conscientiousness, and agreeableness—change very little after age 30 (see Chapter 13). According to Costa and McCrae (1994a), what may seem to be drastic changes actually reflect continuing tendencies: people who make dramatic lifestyle changes in midlife are likely to have scored high on openness to experience during young adulthood. McCrae and Costa (1994) maintain that impulsiveness and spontaneity are stable traits, more likely to be shown by certain people at any stage of life than by others. Of course, people do not always act the same: personality traits are merely *dispositions* that may be expressed differently in different situations. A person who is inclined to take risks may try rock climbing but not stunt flying, and may or may not accept an offer to invest in a gold mine. A person who is inclined to be conscientious will not be equally conscientious about every task.

However, other research, using different methodology and a somewhat different classification of traits, found change in most domains of personality during some parts of adulthood (Jones & Meredith, 1996). Ironically, the period characterized by the *least* change was the decade from 40 to 50—"midlife crisis" time in normative-crisis models.

The data came from two longitudinal studies, the Berkeley Guidance Study and the Oakland Growth Study. Both studies began around 1930, when the Berkeley participants were infants and those in Oakland were about 11 years old. At intervals from age 18 through middle adulthood, psychologists rated the participants on 100 personality traits. The traits fell into six groupings: (1) self-confidence, (2) cognitive commitment, (3) dependability, (4) outgoingness, (5) warmth, and (6) assertiveness.

Whereas standard longitudinal methods track changes in a *group* of people and thus may obscure individual differences, this research focused on patterns of development in individuals. The researchers graphed each person's development in each of the six domains and compared the resulting patterns. Fairly uniform trends emerged for all clusters except warmth. Dependability and cognitive commitment rose from ages 18 to 30, typically the time for establishing career and family. Thereafter, dependability remained stable, but cognitive commitment shifted downward after age 50, possibly in anticipation of retirement. Outgoingness increased in both sexes between ages 30 and 40, perhaps reflecting men's increasing power in the

BOX 15-2   FOOD FOR THOUGHT

VIEWS ABOUT PERSONALITY AT MIDLIFE

When do you think middle age begins and ends? When is the prime of life? Do you think there is such a thing as a midlife crisis? What are some of the most important events and experiences of midlife?

Researchers posed questions like these to 59 mostly white college students (average age, 20) and their same-sex parents (average age, 48) and grandparents (average age, 75). They also asked all three groups to rate the applicability of certain attributes (such as "wise" and "productive"), the stressfulness of certain experiences (such as relationships with parents and fulfilling responsibilities) and the importance of certain concerns (such as physical fitness and a sense of competence) in young, middle, and late adulthood (Lachman, Lewkowicz, Marcus, & Peng, 1994).

Perceived boundaries of middle age ranged greatly, with entry as early as age 30 and as late as 55 and exit as early as 45 and as late as 75. On average, college students saw middle age as earlier than did their parents and grandparents (between ages 35 and 55, as compared with 40 to 60 for the middle-aged and older groups). The young people defined the prime of life as earlier, too (ages 20 to 40), whereas middle-aged and older adults defined it as 31 to 52. In other words, both the students and their parents defined the prime of life as *their* time of life.

The strongest affirmation of the midlife crisis (86 percent) came from the students, who, of course, were too young to have gone

through one. By contrast, 73 percent of the parents and only 50 percent of the grandparents said such a crisis exists. Nearly half the people who rejected the validity of the midlife crisis said a crisis can occur at any time of life. Some called the midlife crisis a myth or an excuse.

Those who believed in the existence of a midlife crisis described it differently, depending on age. The students and almost half of the mothers associated it with fear of aging; but a majority of the mothers called it a time of adjustment to changing goals. Fathers saw the crisis as a time of reappraisal and self-questioning—a time of recognizing diminishing options and of maladjustment, stress, unhappiness, or loss of control. Grandparents described it as a time of pressure to accomplish unrealized goals before it is too late.

Work and parenting were equally important at midlife in the eyes of both men and women. However, by a margin of approximately 3 to 1, women considered work more important to men, and men viewed parenting as more important to women.

These respondents drew a picture of middle age as a time of gains (mostly psychological and social) and losses (mostly physical). They saw it as a period of increased stress and responsibility, with little free time. However, they also described middle-aged people as possessing the resources to deal with pressure: competence, assertiveness, self-reliance, produc-

tivity, and a sense of purpose and control.

Similarly, in a German study that probed people's views about personality change across the adult life span, midlife came through as a time of strength (Krueger & Heckhausen, 1993). The 180 participants, evenly distributed by age and sex, rated themselves on 91 traits. They also indicated how much they believed each trait increases or decreases during each decade from the twenties through the eighties. The traits were classified by five dimensions (some of which are the same as Costa and McCrae's): extraversion, agreeableness, conscientiousness, emotional stability, and intellect.

As in other cross-sectional trait research, young, middle-aged, and older adults showed little difference in current self-ratings. However, when asked about personality change, the respondents, regardless of gender or education, described modest improvement (increases in desirable traits and decreases in undesirable ones) through middle adulthood. Older adults were more optimistic than younger ones about the direction of change in late life.

Apparently, adults of different ages have remarkably similar "theories" about personality development. These findings suggest that people may "expect and experience similar kinds of change" (Krueger & Heckhausen, 1993, p. 106), which may not be captured by standard trait research.

---

workplace and women's increasing recognition of their strengths. Self-confidence increased, except for cohort differences. Only assertiveness was stable throughout adulthood.

At all ages, men were more assertive and women

more outgoing—a finding that seems to contradict the bulk of cross-sectional and longitudinal research, in which people at midlife tend to show characteristics usually associated with the other sex. In many studies, middle-aged men were more open about feelings, more interested in intimate relationships, and more nurturing than at earlier ages, whereas women were more assertive, self-confident, and achievement-oriented than in young adulthood (Cooper & Gutmann, 1987; Cytrynbaum et al., 1980; Helson & Moane, 1987; Huyck, 1990; Neugarten, 1968). In the Mills women, for example, traits typically associated with femininity—sympathy and compassion combined with vulnerability, self-criticism, and lack of confidence and initiative—increased during the twenties and then declined during middle age (Helson, 1993).

Some social scientists attribute such developments to hormonal changes at midlife (Rossi, 1980), but the psychologist David Gutmann (1975, 1977, 1985) offers a cultural explanation. Traditional gender roles in all cultures, says Gutmann, may have evolved to ensure the security and well-being of growing children. After child raising is over, there is often not just a balancing but a reversal of roles. Men are now free to explore their previously repressed "feminine" side and thus become more passive; women become more dominant and independent.

These changes may be most characteristic of societies or cohorts with relatively conventional gender roles. At a time when most women in western societies combine paid work with child rearing, when some men take a more active part in parenting, and when childbearing may not even begin until close to midlife (or beyond), we may no longer see such dramatic switches in middle age.

Personality development, then, may be more complex than some trait research has suggested.

Cohort-related patterns of life events may play an important role.

TIMING OF EVENTS: THE SOCIAL CLOCK

According to the timing-of-events model, adult personality development hinges on important life events. Twenty or thirty years ago, the occurrence and timing of such major events as marriage, retirement, and the birth of children and grandchildren were fairly predictable. Today lifestyles are more diverse, people's "social clocks" tick at different rates, and a "fluid life cycle" has blurred the boundaries between periods of the life span (Neugarten & Neugarten, 1987).

When women's lives revolved around bearing and rearing children, the end of the reproductive years meant something different from what it means now, when so many middle-aged women enter the work force. When occupational patterns were more stable and retirement at age 65 was almost universal, the meaning of work at midlife may have been different from its current meaning in a period of frequent job changes, downsizing, and early or delayed retirement. When people died earlier, middle-aged survivors felt old, realizing that they too were nearing the end of their lives. Many middle-aged people now find themselves busier and more involved than ever—some still raising young children, while others redefine their roles as parents to adolescents and young adults. The care of the burgeoning older generation is becoming a proportionately greater burden as the teenage population shrinks (see Figure 15-1). In 1900, a middle-aged couple had only a 10 percent

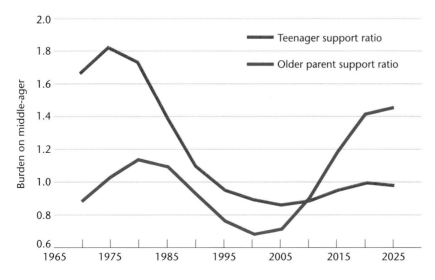

FIGURE 15-1

The changing burden of support on middle-aged people. In the United States, the gap between the teenage support ratio (the number of teenagers for each 40- to 49-year-old) and the older parent support ratio (the number of 60- to 74-year-olds for each 40- to 49-year old) is shrinking, and by 2010 will reverse, so that middle-aged people will have a greater burden of supporting older parents than teenage children. *(Source: Cutler & Devlin, 1996, p. 26. From Boettner Center of Financial Gerontology.)*

chance of having at least two parents alive; by 1976, the probability had risen to 47 percent (Cutler & Devlin, 1996).

Still, the social clock hasn't stopped altogether. In one study done in Berlin (Krueger, Heckhausen, & Hundertmark, 1995) adults of all ages were asked their impressions of hypothetical 45-year-old adults of their own sex whose family or work situations violated normal expectations for that age. Participants, regardless of their own age, expressed surprise about these "off-time" conditions and called them atypical. Reactions were stronger and more negative when development seemed late (as, for example, when a 45-year-old woman was described as having a 1-year-old child). Reactions were positive when development seemed early (as, for example, when a 45-year-old man was said to be branch director of a bank). Expectations seemed to be stronger for family situations than for work situations, and for women than for men. Society, apparently, is not yet age-blind; "people are sensitive to social clocks and . . . use them to understand and judge others" (p. P91).

Many of the markers on the social clock concern personal relationships. In the remaining sections of this chapter, let's look at how intimate relationships develop during the middle years. We'll look first at relationships with spouses, homosexual partners, and friends, next at relationships with maturing children, and then at ties with aging parents, siblings, and grandchildren.

✔ CONSENSUAL RELATIONSHIPS

Marriages, homosexual unions, and friendships typically involve two people of the same generation and involve mutual choice. How do these relationships fare in middle age?

MARRIAGE AND DIVORCE

Midlife is usually not the happiest time in a marriage. In almost all studies, marital satisfaction seems to follow a U-shaped curve. It declines during the child-raising years and until late middle age, and then rises again through the first part of late adulthood (S. A. Anderson, Russell, & Schumm, 1983; Gilford, 1984; Glenn, 1991; Gruber & Schaie, 1986; Lavee, Sharlin, & Katz, 1996). It is typically the positive aspects of marriage (such as cooperation, discussion, and shared laughter) that follow this U-shaped pattern; negative aspects

(such as sarcasm, anger, and disagreement over important issues) decline from young adulthood through age 69 (Gilford, 1984; Gilford & Bengtson, 1979), perhaps because many conflict-ridden marriages end along the way.

Although the U-shaped pattern is well-established, the research has been criticized for its methodology. Many of the early studies dealt with only the husband's or wife's satisfaction, not with both. Also, most studies are cross-sectional; they show differences among couples of different cohorts rather than changes in the *same* couples; and they focus on a couple's age, not the length of their marriage. Furthermore, samples typically include only couples in intact marriages; thus reports of high marital satisfaction in young adulthood do not reflect the experience of couples who have divorced. Then, the midlife portion of the curve may be dragged down by unhappily married couples who stay together because of the children (Blieszner, 1986; Lavee et al., 1966).

One longitudinal study of 175 couples does support the U-shaped curve (Gruber & Schaie, 1986). In a smaller longitudinal study of 17 marriages that lasted 50 or more years, nearly three-fourths followed one of two patterns: either the U-shaped curve or a fairly consistent level of satisfaction. None showed a continuous increase or decline (Weishaus & Field, 1988).

The dip in satisfaction shown by the U-shaped curve is generally attributed to stresses of parenting. These may be of three kinds: (1) stress associated with normative events, such as the first child's reaching puberty or leaving home, (2) stress associated with nonnormative events that create family emergencies, such as economic reverses, earthquakes or floods, or a child's death, and (3) stress that results not from a single event, but from accumulated demands (Lavee et al., 1996).

One study that focused on the third type of stress surveyed 287 socioeconomically diverse couples around age 40, all in their first marriages, in four urban and rural communities in Israel (Lavee et al., 1996). Two-thirds of the mothers were employed outside the home. Strains of parenting strongly affected these men's and women's well-being and the quality of their marriages. One partner's stress affected the other, and each partner's satisfaction with the marriage was influenced by how well the other seemed to be handling his or her role.

Two important factors in the demands on parents are family finances and the number of children still at home. The pressure of too little income and too many mouths to feed burdens a relationship. Overload from multiple roles was not a problem for the Israeli couples, so long as responsibilities were fairly equally shared. Working mothers tended to feel better about themselves and about their marriage than did homemakers, unless their husbands expected them to do most of the housework.

The U-shaped curve generally hits bottom during midlife, when many couples have teenage children and are heavily involved in careers. Some women become less satisfied with marriage as child rearing requires less attention and their feelings of power and autonomy grow (Steinberg & Silverberg, 1987). The husband of a middle-aged woman who goes to work for the first time may have trouble accepting her new assertiveness and her involvement in an outside life that does not include him (Zube, 1982). On the other hand, a man's increased interest in intimate relationships may help the marriage (Bergman, 1991).

In a good marriage, the departure of grown children may usher in a second honeymoon. Hard times draw many couples closer. Communication between partners can mitigate stress caused by aging, diminished sex drive, changes in work status or satisfaction, or the death of parents, siblings, or close friends (Robinson & Blanton, 1993). In a shaky marriage, the departure of the youngest child may spark a personal and marital crisis. A couple may realize that they no longer have much in common and may ask themselves whether they want to spend the rest of their lives together.

Divorce is largely a phenomenon of young adulthood; the divorce rate drops sharply and continuously from age 20 through late life. Furthermore, most divorces occur during the first 10 years of marriage (Clarke, 1995). Longstanding marriages are less likely to break up than more recent ones because as couples stay together they build up *marital capital,* financial and emotional benefits of marriage that become difficult to give up (Becker, 1991; Jones, Tepperman, & Wilson, 1995). However, midlife divorce is more common than it used to be; although divorce rates in general peaked in 1979 and 1980, rates have continued to increase for long-term marriages (Clarke, 1995; National Center for Health Statistics, 1992). For people who do go through a divorce at midlife, when they may have assumed their lives were settled, the breakup can be traumatic. People who divorce after age 50, particularly women, tend to

have more trouble adjusting and less hope for the future than younger divorced people (Chiriboga, 1982). This sense of violated expectations may be decreasing as midlife divorce becomes more normative (A. J. Norton & Moorman, 1987).

How a marriage fares in midlife may depend largely on its quality until then. Among 300 couples who had been happily married for at least 15 years, both men and women tended to credit a positive attitude toward the spouse as a friend and as a person, commitment to marriage and belief in its sanctity, and agreement on aims and goals. Happily married couples spent much time together and shared many activities (Lauer & Lauer, 1985). Similarly, in an in-depth study of 15 couples who had been married more than 30 years (Robinson & Blanton, 1993), the factors that emerged most consistently were enjoyable relationships and commitment, both to the idea of marriage and to the partner. Another key factor was intimacy balanced with autonomy, which in turn affected or was affected by good communication, similar perceptions of the relationship, and religious orientation.

What role does passion play? In a survey of 100 men and women who had been married up to 28 years, both sexes reported similar levels of passionate love, or intense longing; but only in women was this longing related to marital satisfaction. This may be because women are socialized to expect romance, or passion, in marriage, whereas men tend to believe that romance fades over time (Aron & Henkemeyer, 1995).

HOMOSEXUAL RELATIONSHIPS*

Since many homosexuals do not come out until well into adulthood (Chapter 13), the timing of this crucial event can affect other aspects of development. Middle-aged gays and lesbians may be associating openly for the first time and establishing relationships. Many are still working out conflicts with parents and other family members or hiding their homosexuality from them.

Because of the secrecy and stigma that have surrounded homosexuality, studies of homosexuals tend to have sampling problems. What little research exists on gay men has focused mostly on urban white men with above-average income and education. Yet, according to a 1985 American Broadcasting Company–Washington Post poll, 42 percent of self-identified homosexual and bisexual

*Unless otherwise noted, this discussion is indebted to Kimmel & Sang, 1995.

men were in heterosexual marriages (and thus easily overlooked); a disproportionate number were low-income African Americans or Hispanic Americans, and more than half lived in small towns.

Lesbians studied so far also tend to be mostly white, professional, and middle- or upper-class. In one study, more than 25 percent of middle-aged lesbians lived alone, even if they were in intimate relationships (Bradford & Ryan, 1991). This may in part be a cohort effect; lesbians who grew up in the 1950s may be uncomfortable about living openly with a partner, as many younger women do now. According to several studies, only 2 out of 3 middle-aged lesbians are in committed relationships; some may have broken off earlier ones.

Gay and lesbian couples tend to be more egalitarian than heterosexual couples and generally try to balance commitments to careers and relationships (see Chapter 13). This balancing act can be difficult. What happens, for example, if one partner has an opportunity for advancement that requires relocating to another city? Couples in which one partner is less career-oriented than the other may have an easier time.

FRIENDSHIPS

Many middle-aged people have little time and energy to devote to friends; they are too busy with family and work and with building up security for retirement. Still, friendships do persist and are a strong source of emotional support and well-being (Baruch et al., 1983; House, Landis, & Umberson, 1988). Many midlife friends are old friends. Age is less a factor in making new friends than are such commonalities as length of marriage, age of children, and occupational status (Troll, 1975).

The quality of midlife friendships often makes up for what they lack in quantity. Adults turn to friends for emotional support and practical guidance (Suitor & Pillemer, 1993). Friendships are especially important to homosexuals. Lesbians are more likely to get emotional support from lesbian friends, lovers, and even ex-lovers than from relatives. Gay men, too, rely on friendship networks, which they actively create and maintain. Friendship networks provide solidarity and contact with younger people, which middle-aged heterosexuals normally get through family. Loss of friends to the scourge of AIDS has been traumatic for many gay men (Kimmel & Sang, 1995).

✔ RELATIONSHIPS WITH MATURING CHILDREN

Parenthood is a process of letting go. From the moment of birth, children's normal course of development leads toward independence. This process usually reaches its climax during the parents' middle age. It is true that, with modern trends toward delaying marriage and parenthood, an increasing number of middle-aged people now face such issues as finding a good day care or kindergarten program and screening Saturday morning cartoons for appropriateness of content. Still, the majority of parents in the early part of middle age must cope with a different set of issues, which arise from living with children who will soon be leaving the nest. If things go well, parents can celebrate their success. However, even parents with the best of intentions and with optimal parenting skills often find this midlife transition difficult. Once children become adults, parent-child ties usually recede in importance, but these ties normally last as long as parent and child live.

ADOLESCENT CHILDREN: ISSUES FOR PARENTS

It is ironic that the people at the two times of life popularly linked with emotional crisis—adolescence and midlife—often live in the same household. It is usually middle-aged adults who are the parents of adolescent children. While dealing with their own special concerns, parents have to deal daily with young people who are undergoing great physical, emotional, and social changes. Sometimes parents' own long-buried adolescent fantasies resurface as they see their children turning into sexual beings. Living with children on the brink of adulthood, parents may become resentful as they realize how much of their own life is behind them (H. Meyers, 1989).

Although research contradicts the stereotype of adolescence as a time of inevitable turmoil and rebellion, some rejection of parental authority is necessary for the maturing youngster. An important task for parents is to accept children as they are, not as what the parents had hoped they would be. As children become independent, they may choose directions very different from those the parents want them to follow.

WHEN CHILDREN LEAVE: THE "EMPTY NEST"

Research is also challenging popular ideas about the *empty nest*—a supposedly difficult transition, especially for women, when the last child leaves home. Although some women, heavily invested in mothering, do have problems at this time, they are far outnumbered by those who find the departure liberating (Barnett, 1985; Mitchell & Helson, 1990).

For many women, the empty nest is a relief from the "chronic emergency of parenthood" (Cooper & Gutmann, 1987, p. 347). They can now express assertiveness and self-determination—qualities they may have repressed for the sake of harmony during the years of active mothering. When 50 mothers were asked to tell stories about ambiguous pictures, the 25 "pre-empty nesters" tended to tell tales of emotionally conflicted leave takings, of maternal warmth and nurturance, and of rescuing others. The 25 "post-empty nesters" told of leaving home joyfully to realize a personal goal, of a mother as mentor more than nurturer, and of their own achievements (Cooper & Gutmann, 1987).

The empty nest does appear to be hard on women who have not prepared for it by reorganizing their lives (Targ, 1979). The empty nest also may be hard on fathers who regret that they did not spend more time with their children when they had the chance (L. B. Rubin, 1979). Many middle-aged men have become more interested in intimacy at a time when women have been entering the workplace or exploring other facets of their personalities. This mismatch between men's and women's needs may help explain why midlife is usually the low point in marital satisfaction and why many men regret the empty nest while many women welcome it.

The empty nest does not signal the end of parenthood. It is a transition to a new stage: the relationship between parents and adult children.

PARENTING GROWN CHILDREN

Elliott Roosevelt, a son of President Franklin Delano Roosevelt, used to tell this story about his mother, Eleanor Roosevelt. At a state dinner, Eleanor, who was seated next to him, leaned over and whispered in his ear. A friend later asked Elliott, then in his forties, what she had said. "She told me to eat my peas," he answered.

Even after the years of active parenting are over and children have left home, parents are still parents. The midlife role of parent to young adults raises new issues and calls for new attitudes and behaviors on the part of both generations (refer back to Box 13-1). Some parents have difficulty treating their offspring as adults, and many young adults have difficulty accepting their parents' continuing concern about them.

Still, young adults and their parents generally enjoy each other's company and get along well. Most parents of grown children age 16 and over express satisfaction with their parenting role—85 percent, in fact, in one nationwide survey of more than 3,000 people. Eighty percent are generally happy with how their children turned out, though more than 75 percent are bothered or upset about them at times (Umberson, 1992). Sore points include conflicts in values and parents' desire for their children to be like them. Some families maintain harmony by avoiding touchy issues and making certain topics off limits.

Young newlyweds (especially women) tend to maintain close ties with their parents, who often help them with money, baby-sitting, and setting up their first homes. Parents and adult children visit frequently, and young couples spend a great deal of time talking with and about their parents. Parents generally give their children more than they get from them (Troll, 1989). Their continuing support probably reflects the relative strength of middle-aged adults and the continuing needs of young adults, who are experiencing stress as they establish careers and families (Pearlin, 1980).

When Children Stay or Return: The Revolving Door Syndrome

What happens if the nest does not empty when it normally should, or when it unexpectedly refills? In recent decades, more and more adult children are delaying leaving home. In addition, the *revolving door syndrome* has become more common, as increasing numbers of young adults return to their parents' home, sometimes more than once, after completing their education or in times of financial, marital, or other trouble. Jobs are harder to get, housing costs are high, and wages have not kept pace. Many couples have postponed marriage, and divorce and unwed parenthood have climbed (Clemens & Axelson, 1985; Glick & Lin,

1986a; Ward & Spitze, 1996). The family home can be a convenient, supportive, and affordable place to stay while young adults are getting on their feet or regaining their balance. Sometimes they stay permanently.

At any given moment, an estimated 30 to 40 percent of 40- to 60-year-old parents and 15 percent of those over 60 share a household with adult children, and 15 to 20 percent of adult children in their twenties, as well as nearly 10 percent of those over 30, live with their parents. (These figures include aging parents who live with caregiving children, a topic we discuss in Chapter 17; however, the majority are believed to represent families in which young adult children stay in or return to the nest.) About half of these grown children, including one-third of those 25 and over, never left home at all (Ward & Spitze, 1996). Furthermore, these figures are cross-sectional; a much larger percentage of adult children—40 percent in recent cohorts, according to one estimate—reenter the revolving door at some time (Goldscheider & Goldscheider, 1994). Parents who open their homes to adult children tend to be relatively youthful—"healthy, wealthy, and married" (Lee & Dwyer, 1996, p. 57).

Most likely to stay or come home are sons and daughters who never married and, to a lesser extent, those who are divorced or separated (Aquilino, 1990; Ward, Logan, & Spitze, 1992; Ward & Spitze, 1996). As compared with those who never left home, returning children tend to be older and more likely to have gone to college and to have been married; and the sons, especially, tend to plan on shorter stays (Ward & Spitze, 1996).

As the timing-of-events model would predict, this unanticipated situation may lead to tension (Harkins, 1978; Lindsey, 1984). Although most parents like to see their grown children frequently, they generally prefer not to live with them (L. White & Edwards, 1990). Serious conflicts may arise, especially when a young adult child is unemployed and financially dependent. Disagreements may center on household responsibilities and the child's lifestyle. The young adult is likely to feel isolated from peers and to have trouble establishing intimacy, while the parents may be hampered in renewing their own intimacy, exploring personal interests, and resolving marital issues. The most difficult situation for parents seems to be the return of divorced or separated

"Your mother and I think it's time you got a place of your own. We'd like a little time alone before we die."

Financial or marital problems induce an increasing number of adult children to return to the "nest," or not to leave at all. This nonnormative situation can create stress for middle-aged parents, especially when it is not temporary. *(Drawing by Koren; © 1995 The New Yorker Magazine, Inc.)*

children who also bring their own children (Aquilino & Supple, 1991).

Still, most parents express satisfaction with the arrangement, especially when it is temporary and when the child is under age 22 (Clemens & Axelson, 1985). Parents appreciate help with household chores and caring for younger children, and they enjoy sharing leisure activities. Most adult children, especially those who never left, are also quite satisfied (Ward & Spitze, 1996). The return of an adult child works best when parent and child negotiate roles and responsibilities, acknowledging the child's adult status and the parents' right to privacy.

How Parents' Divorce Affects Grown Children

Many couples who divorce at midlife have intentionally waited until the children were grown, hoping to spare them pain. Ironically, grown children are often even more deeply troubled by their parents' divorce than younger children, who do not fully understand what is happening. The litigation can be upsetting, and a daughter or son may be called upon to help resolve disputes, carry messages from one parent to the other, or even to choose sides. Then, a child's own future may be affected if financial support for college education is endangered (Cooney, Hutchinson, & Leather, 1995).

As with divorce that occurs earlier in a marriage, fathers are the ones whose relationships with their children are most likely to suffer. Young adult children who have been involved in court hearings for their parents' divorce are less likely to maintain intimate relationships with their fathers afterward. Remarriage can create additional strains, particularly on sons. When a father remarries, a son is likely to draw closer to the mother (perhaps out of protectiveness), but when a mother remarries and becomes involved with a new family, her son tends to cut down on contact with both parents (Cooney et al., 1995).

✔ OTHER KINSHIP TIES

Except in times of need, ties with the family of origin—parents and siblings—recede in importance during young adulthood, when work, spouses or partners, and children take precedence. At midlife, these earliest kinship ties often reassert themselves in a new way, as the responsibility for care and

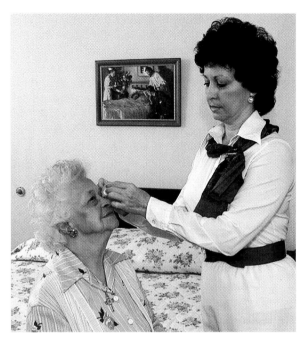

By middle age, many people can look at their parents objectively, neither idealizing them nor exaggerating their shortcomings. This middle-aged daughter putting drops in her mother's eyes realizes that her mother is no longer a tower of strength but instead is beginning to lean on *her*. Mothers and daughters usually remain closer than any other combination of family members. *(Parke/Gamma Liaison)*

support of aging parents shifts to middle-aged children. In addition, a new relationship and role typically begins at this time of life: grandparenthood.

RELATIONSHIPS WITH AGING PARENTS

"My mother is my best friend," says a 45-year-old woman. "I can tell her anything." A 50-year-old man visits his retired father every evening, bringing him news and asking his opinions about problems in the family business. A 40-year-old divorced mother sees her parents more often now than she did during her 15 years of marriage and needs their help more now than at any time since her teens. A couple in their early sixties find that the time they had hoped to spend traveling and playing with their grandchildren is being spent instead caring for their widowed mothers.

The bond between middle-aged children and their elderly parents is strong, growing out of earlier attachment and continuing as long as both generations live (Cicirelli, 1980, 1989b; Rossi & Rossi, 1990). Seven out of ten people enter middle age with two living parents and leave middle age with none (Bumpass & Aquilino, 1993). The years in between often bring dramatic, though gradual, changes in filial relationships. Many middle-aged people look at their parents more objectively than before, neither idealizing them nor blaming them for mistakes and inadequacies. It becomes possible to see parents as individuals with both strengths and weaknesses. Something else happens during these years: one day a son or daughter looks at a mother or father and sees an old person. The middle-aged child realizes that he or she rather than the parent must now be the pillar of strength.

Contact and Mutual Help

Middle-aged adults and their parents often live near each other, and most see each other once a week or more (AARP, 1995; Lin & Rogerson, 1995; Umberson, 1992). In one study, 91 percent of adult children felt close or very close to their mothers, and 87 percent to their fathers (Cicirelli, 1981). Mothers and daughters are especially likely to stay in close contact (G. R. Lee, Dwyer, & Coward, 1993; Troll, 1986), particularly in African American families (Spitze & Miner, 1992). Daughters who have a good relationship with their parents are more likely than those with poor relationships to have a sense of well-being and are less likely to be anxious or depressed (Barnett, Kibria, Baruch, & Pleck, 1991).

Older parents help their children in various ways, and when they themselves need help, their children are the first people they turn to and the ones likely to do the most (Field & Minkler, 1988). Many older adults resume a more active parenting role when a child needs help. Single adult children receive more financial assistance from elderly parents than married ones do; divorced children are more likely to get emotional support and help with child care and housework (Aldous, 1987). Unhappily married, divorced, and widowed adults often become closer to their parents, getting from them the support they do not get from spouses.

Although most older adults are physically fit, vigorous, and independent, some seek their children's assistance in making decisions and may depend on them for daily tasks and financial help. Most middle-aged people are conscious of their obligations to their parents and often expect more of themselves than the parents do of them. Among 144 parent-child pairs, both generations gave top ranking to the same three filial responsibilities:

helping parents understand their resources, providing emotional support, and talking over matters of importance (see Table 15-3). Both generations gave less weight to adjusting work or family schedules to help parents. The children felt that they should give money to their parents, but most of the parents did not. More children than parents considered it important to make room for a parent in their homes in an emergency, to care for parents when they were sick, and to sacrifice personal freedom (Hamon & Blieszner, 1990).

In providing support to parents, most daughters are motivated by affection. For sons, affection plays an indirect role by stimulating them to see their parents more often, which in turn motivates them to help. In addition, regardless of the quality of the relationship, sons are likely to be motivated by a sense of obligation or by the expectation of an inheritance (Silverstein, Parrott, & Bengtson, 1995).

Becoming a Caregiver for Aging Parents

The generations get along best while parents are healthy and vigorous. When older people become infirm—especially if they undergo mental deterioration or personality changes—the burden of caring for them may strain the relationship (Cicirelli, 1983; Marcoen, 1995). This is especially so if the relationship is already tenuous, as with some homosexuals whose parents are unaware of, or have never accepted, their sexual orientation (Kimmel & Sang, 1995).

Only 1 out of 5 older people who need care are in institutions (Center on Elderly People Living Alone, 1995c). With the high cost of nursing homes and the reluctance of most older people to enter and stay in them, many dependent elders receive care in their own home or in a caregiver's. Middle-aged daughters are the ones most likely to take on this responsibility—usually for aging, ailing mothers (Matthews, 1996; Troll, 1986). Often the need arises when a mother is widowed; because women tend to marry older men and to outlive them, they are more likely to end up in need of care. Or a woman may have been divorced years before but can no longer manage alone. Only or older children, or those who live nearby, are most likely to become caregivers (Marks, 1996).

Cultural assumptions that caregiving is a female function make it likely that a daughter will assume the role (Matthews, 1996). Also, perhaps because of the intimate nature of the contact and the

TABLE 15-3

Expectations of Adult Children and Their Parents Regarding Filial Responsibility

Item	Adult Children		Parents	
	Percent	Rank*	Percent	Rank*
Help understand resources	99.3	1	97.2	2
Give emotional support	97.2	2	95.7	3
Talk over matters of importance	96.5	3	98.6	1
Make room in home in emergency†	94.4	4	73.0	7
Sacrifice personal freedom†	93.7	5	81.0	6
Give care when sick†	92.4	6	64.3	9
Be together on special occasions	86.0	7	86.7	5
Give financial help†	84.6	8	41.1	13
Give parent advice	84.0	9	88.7	4
Adjust family schedule to help†	80.6	10	57.4	10
Feel responsible for parent†	78.2	11	66.4	8
Adjust work schedule to help†	63.2	12	42.1	12
Parent should live with child†	60.8	13	36.7	15
Visit once a week	51.4	14	55.6	11
Live close to parent	32.2	15	25.7	16
Write once a week	30.8	16	39.4	14

*Ranking reflects percentage of respondents who "strongly agreed" or "agreed" with each item on the Hamon Filial Responsibility Scale.
†Dagger indicates significant differences in proportion of endorsement for children and parents.
SOURCE: Adapted from Hamon & Blieszner, 1990, p. P111.

strength of the mother-daughter bond, mothers may prefer a daughter's care (Lee et al., 1993). Sons do contribute, more than is often recognized, but they are less likely to provide primary, personal care (Marks, 1995; Matthews, 1996). Often, when a son is in charge, his wife will take over much of the day-to-day care, perhaps because women are socialized to know how to do it and because many daughters-in-law see this as part of their "kin-keeping" function (Globerman, 1996).

The average caregiver is about 55 years old and lives with the person she cares for. About 20 to 25 percent of caregivers are African American, Hispanic, or Asian American (Noelker & Whitlatch, 1995). Caregiving may range from running errands, chauffeuring, and help with finances or housework to complete physical care (Lund, 1993a). The work is often confining and distressing and usually continuous. Most caregivers provide care for 1 to 4 years, 4 to 8 hours a day (Noelker & Whitlatch, 1995).

The chances of becoming a caregiver are greater than ever before, and the likelihood increases through middle age. Longer life means more risk of chronic diseases and disabilities; and families are smaller than in the past, with fewer siblings to share in a parent's care. The *parent-support*

ratio—the number of people 85 and over for every 100 people ages 50 to 64—tripled (from 3 to 10) between 1950 and 1993; it may triple again by 2053 (U.S. Bureau of the Census, 1995a). At the same time, with more women working outside the home, it is harder for them to assume this added role (Marks, 1996). Highly educated women are less likely to become caregivers than women with less education (Marcoen, 1995).

Strains and Rewards of Caregiving: The Sandwich Generation

Many caregivers find the task a physical, emotional, and financial burden. Caregivers who feel the burden most keenly are those who work full time, are raising young children, lack support and assistance, and have limited financial resources. The burden is heavier if the caregiver does not feel close to the person who is receiving the care and if that person is aggressive or violent (Lund, 1993a).

Caregivers tend to have below-average income, to be in relatively poor health, and to be depressed; nearly 1 out of 3 get no help with caregiving duties (Biegel, 1995; Franks & Stephens, 1996; Marks, 1996; Stephens & Franks, 1995). Caring for a person with physical impairments is hard, but it can be harder to care for someone with dementia, who, in addition to being unable to carry on basic functions of daily living, may be incontinent, suspicious, agitated, subject to hallucinations, likely to wander about at night, dangerous to self and others, and in need of constant supervision (Biegel, 1995). If the eventual decision is to place a parent in a nursing home—as does happen in 1 out of 4 cases—the caregiver's role and stress may diminish but not end. The burden now involves finding a good facility, working out financing, dealing with the staff, monitoring care, and facing anxiety, guilt, or other emotional consequences of the decision (Noelker & Whitlatch, 1995).

Strain comes not only from caregiving itself but from its interference with other aspects of a caregiver's life. The need to care for elderly parents often comes at a time when middle-aged adults are trying to launch their own children or, if parenthood was delayed, to raise them. Members of this "generation in the middle," sometimes called the *sandwich generation,* are caught in a squeeze between these competing needs and their limited resources of time, money, and energy. About one-third of caregivers also work for pay, and more than one-fourth have had to quit jobs to meet caregiving obligations (Noelker & Whitlatch, 1995). Flexible work schedules can help alleviate this problem. The Family and Medical Leave Act, adopted in 1993, guarantees family caregivers some unpaid leave, and some large corporations provide time off for caregiving.

Also troubling are conflicts between caregiving duties and personal interests, social activities, or travel plans (Mui, 1992). One of the hardest aspects of caregiving is a sense of being tied down—a loss of control over one's life (J. Evans, 1994; Robinson & Thurnher, 1981). Caregiving can put strains on a marriage and may even lead to divorce (Lund, 1993a). On the other hand, it can enhance a woman's self-esteem and make her husband think more highly of her (Stephens & Franks, 1995).

Caregiving can be an opportunity for growth if a caregiver feels deeply about a parent and about family solidarity, looks at caregiving as a challenge, and has adequate personal, family, and community resources to meet that challenge (Bengtson, Rosenthal, & Burton, 1996; Biegel, 1995; Lund, 1993a). Some caregivers say they feel good about being able to repay the parent's care. Others find satisfaction in gaining inner strength or learning new skills (Archer & MacLean, 1993; Gerstel &

Gallagher, 1993; Motenko, 1989). Some feel closer to the parent they care for and feel better about themselves for meeting their responsibilities. Many become more patient and more appreciative of their own good health. Some learn "to value life more and to take one day at a time" (Lund, 1993a, p. 61).

Rewards, however, may be tempered by stresses. Among 29 pairs of elderly widows and their caregiving daughters, relationships were characterized by either mutual enjoyment, ambivalence, or conflict (A. J. Walker & Allen, 1991). The daughters with the most rewarding ties to their mothers tended to have fewer children, not to be employed, and to have cared for their mothers for a shorter time than the ambivalent or conflicted daughters.

The objective demands of caregiving may be complicated by subjective perceptions and reactions, which make those demands harder or easier to deal with (Biegel, 1995). Some adult children who provide very little care feel overburdened by worry, whereas some who devote a great deal of time and energy to a parent's care take it more or less in stride (Bengtson et al., 1996).

For many adults, the needs of aging parents seem to represent nonnormative, unanticipated demands. Adults expect to assume the physical, financial, and emotional care of their children. Most do *not* expect to have to care for their parents; they ignore the possibility of their parents' infirmity and rarely plan ahead for it. When parents' dependency becomes undeniable, many adult children have trouble coping (Barnhart, 1992). Adults who have been looking forward to the waning of responsibility for their children and who sense keenly that their own remaining years are limited may fear that caring for their parents will deprive them of any chance to fulfill their dreams.

Adult children may be torn between love and resentment, between duty to parents and duty to spouses and children, and between wanting to do the right thing and not wanting to change their lives. Such children may feel disappointment, anger, or guilt. Anxiety over the anticipated end of a parent's life may be tinged with worry about one's own mortality (Cicirelli, 1980; Troll, 1986). When caregiving ends with a parent's death, adult children must come to terms with their ambivalent feelings.

Still, 95 percent of caregivers stick with the job; they do not abandon their parents (Noelker & Whitlatch, 1995). A number of programs have been developed to reduce the strains and burdens of caregiving (see Box 15-3).

Achieving Filial Maturity

The need to care for elderly parents is becoming so widespread that some developmentalists have proposed a new life stage called *filial maturity,* when middle-aged children "learn to accept and to meet their parents' dependency needs" (Marcoen, 1995, p. 125). This normative development is seen as the healthy outcome of a *filial crisis,* in which adults learn to balance love and duty to their parents with autonomy within a two-way relationship. Filial maturity complements the parent's growth toward *parental maturity,* which includes distancing from the child as well as love and understanding.

One study attempted to measure components of filial maturity in 298 mostly middle-class, middle-aged, married adults in Flanders, Belgium (Marcoen, 1995). Women, in keeping with their traditional caregiving role, scored higher than men on items that measured *filial obligation* ("I think every child has the duty to help his or her parents when they need to be taken care of") and *filial help* ("I do what I can to help my parents"). Men scored higher on *filial autonomy* ("I help my father or mother if he or she asks me to"). Interestingly, sons who saw a parent as needing help were more likely to express love and helpfulness, whereas daughters were less likely to do so. It may be that the perception of a parent's need for help causes more anxiety in daughters, who are the ones most likely to be called upon to provide care.

RELATIONSHIPS WITH SIBLINGS

Relationships with siblings are the longest-lasting in most people's lives and become more important as people grow older. Sibling relationships over the life span generally take the form of an hourglass, with the most contact at the two ends: childhood and middle to late adulthood. Marriage often means less contact (the slim neck of the hourglass), though it rarely affects the emotional quality of the relationship. The arrival of children may tighten the sibling bond, as do such unhappy events as divorce, widowhood, and the death of a family member (Connidis, 1992).

After establishing careers and families, siblings often make special efforts to renew ties. Some 85 percent of middle-aged Americans have living siblings. More than two-thirds of those feel close or very close to their siblings, and more than three-fourths say they get along well or very well (Cicirelli, 1980). Many (especially sisters) stay in touch and stand ready to help each other (Cicirelli, 1980; H. G. Ross, Dalton, & Milgram, 1980; J. P. Scott & Roberto, 1981).

Closeness—both emotional and geographic—and a sense of responsibility for each other's welfare are the most important influences on frequency of contact (T. R. Lee, Mancini, & Maxwell, 1990). Siblings usually get together at least several times a year; in many cases, once a month or more. It is unusual for them to lose touch completely (Cicirelli, 1980).

Dealing with the care of aging parents brings some siblings closer together but causes resentment among others (Bengtson et al., 1996). Conflicts sometimes arise over the division of care (Strawbridge & Wallhagen, 1991) or over an inheritance, especially if the sibling relationship has not been good. Among 140 sibling pairs caring for one or both parents, many felt they were doing more for their parents than their siblings were. The closer the siblings, the more they agreed in assessing their respective contributions (Lerner, Somers, Reid, Chiriboga, & Tierney, 1991). Among 95 married daughters caring for parents with dementia, siblings were a strong source of support, but also the most important source of interpersonal stress (Suitor & Pillemer, 1993).

GRANDPARENTHOOD

In some African communities, grandparents are called "noble." In Japan, grandmothers wear red as a sign of their status (Kornhaber, 1986). In western societies, too, becoming a grandparent is an important event in a person's life, but its timing and meaning vary.

Adults in the United States usually become grandparents in middle age, generally around 45. Some grandparents are as young as 30, others as old as 110 (Pruchno & Johnson, 1996). According to a Commonwealth Fund survey, 3 out of 4 adults age 55 and over are grandparents (Coleman, 1995). African Americans generally acquire grandchildren earlier than white Americans (Strom, Collinsworth, Strom, & Griswold, 1992–1993).

Most new grandparents are still in the work force and are in the prime of life. They are likely to be designing rocking chairs rather than sitting

---

BOX 15-3 PRACTICALLY SPEAKING

PREVENTING CAREGIVER BURNOUT

He or she grows weaker, you take over, nobody sees. Whatever he can no longer do, you do. . . . The loss of control over his body frustrates him and he tries to exert control over yours. His wish is your command. . . . Most everybody identifies with him. "How is he doing?" At first, that's all you cared about, too. Now you sometimes wonder why no one asks about you. . . . You start to feel that you don't exist. (Strong, 1988, p. 75)

Despite the emotional rewards of caring for an aging parent, even the most patient, loving caregiver may become frustrated, anxious, or resentful under the constant strain of meeting an older person's seemingly endless needs. *Caregiver burnout* is physical, mental, and emotional exhaustion that affects many adults who care for aged relatives (Barnhart, 1992), especially if they have nowhere else to turn. Almost one-third of caregivers get no help with caregiving

duties (Biegel, 1995). Sometimes the strains created by incessant, heavy demands are so great as to lead to abuse, neglect, or even abandonment of the dependent elderly person (see Chapter 17).

Often families and friends fail to recognize that caregivers have a right to feel discouraged, frustrated, and put upon. Caregivers need a life of their own, beyond the loved one's disability or disease (J. Evans, 1994).

Community support programs are intended to reduce the strains of caregiving, prevent burnout, and postpone the need for institutionalization of the dependent person. Such support services may include meals and housekeeping; transportation and escort services; adult day care centers, which provide supervised activities and care while caregivers are at work or attending to personal needs; and *respite care*, substitute supervision and care by visiting nurses or home health aides, which gives regular caregivers some time off, whether for a few hours, a day, a weekend, or a week. Temporary

admission to a nursing home is another alternative.

Although there is some dispute about their effectiveness, some research suggests that such programs do improve caregivers' morale and reduce stress (Gallagher-Thompson, 1995). Researchers at the University of Utah have developed a series of videotapes for use by caregivers, as well as in adult day care centers and nursing homes. The tapes are designed to engage the attention of patients with Alzheimer's disease, giving the caregiver or professional staff an uninterrupted respite of 20 to 60 minutes (D. Lund, Hill, Caserta, & Wright, 1995).

Behavioral training and psychotherapy can help caregivers deal with a patient's difficult behavior and their own tendency toward depression (Gallagher-Thompson, 1995). One behavioral training program at the University of Chicago had considerable success in getting patients to handle some self-care and to be more sociable and less verbally abusive.

---

in them, marketing cookies rather than baking them, and wearing jogging suits instead of aprons. Now a new role is added to their busy, active lives. Some will spend more than forty years—half a lifetime—as grandparents (Pruchno & Johnson, 1996).

With smaller families and the growing number of childless couples, most middle-aged and older adults have fewer grandchildren than in the past, and a sizable minority have none. The average 60-year-old grandparent has only 3 grandchildren, compared with 12 to 15 around the turn of the century (Uhlenberg, 1988). Grandparenthood is also affected by other societal changes—by stresses that tear at the fabric of families.

What does it mean to be a grandparent today? What part do grandparents play in family life?

The Grandparent's Changing Role

Grandparents can have an important influence on a child's development. They are a link to the *extended family*, the multigenerational kinship network beyond a couple and their children. Grandparent and grandchild may know each other intimately. A grandparent can serve as teacher, caregiver, role model, and sometimes negotiator between child and parent.

In many traditional societies, such as those in Latin America and Asia, extended-family households, including grandparents, uncles, aunts, and cousins, are common. Families are large, and grandparenthood is a natural extension of parenthood. The youngest child may be an infant when the el-

BOX 15-3 PRACTICALLY SPEAKING

PREVENTING CAREGIVER BURNOUT *(continued)*

Caregivers learned such techniques as contingency contracting ("If you do this, the consequence will be . . .), modeling desired behaviors, rehearsal, and giving feedback (Gallagher-Thompson, 1995).

Through counseling, support, and self-help groups, caregivers can share problems, gain information about community resources, and improve skills. One such program helped daughters recognize the limits of their ability to meet their mothers' needs, and the value of encouraging their mothers' self-reliance. This understanding lightened the daughters' burden and improved their relationship with their mothers, and the mothers became less lonely (Scharlach, 1987). In one longitudinal study, caregivers with adequate community support reported many dimensions of personal growth. Some had become more empathic, caring, understanding, patient, and compassionate, closer to the person they were caring for, and more appreciative of their own good health. Others felt good about hav-

ing fulfilled their responsibilities. Some had "learned to value life more and to take one day at a time," and a few had learned to "laugh at situations and events" (Lund, 1993a).

A "Caregiver's Bill of Rights" (Home, 1985, p. 299) can help caregivers keep a positive perspective and remind them that their needs count too:

A CAREGIVER'S BILL OF RIGHTS

I have the right

- to take care of myself. This is not an act of selfishness. It will give me the capability of taking better care of my relative.
- to seek help from others even though my relative may object. I recognize the limits of my own endurance and strength.
- to maintain facets of my own life that do not include the person I care for, just as I would if he or she were healthy. I know that I do everything that I reasonably can for this person, and I have the right to do some things just for myself.

- to get angry, be depressed and express other difficult feelings occasionally.
- to reject any attempt by my relative (either conscious or unconscious) to manipulate me through guilt, anger or depression.
- to receive consideration, affection, forgiveness and acceptance for what I do from my loved ones for as long as I offer these qualities in return.
- to take pride in what I am accomplishing and to applaud the courage it has sometimes taken to meet the needs of my relative.
- to protect my individuality and my right to make a life for myself that will sustain me in the time when my relative no longer needs my full-time help.
- to expect and demand that as new strides are made in finding resources to aid physically and mentally impaired older persons in our country, similar strides will be made toward aiding and supporting caregivers.
- to (add your own statements of rights to this list. Read this list to yourself every day).

dest begins having babies. Grandparents play an integral role in child raising and family decisions.

In the United States today, the extended family remains important in Hispanic, African American, and some other minority communities; but the dominant household pattern is the *nuclear family,* an economic, kinship, and living unit consisting of parents and their growing children. When children grow up, they typically leave home and establish new, autonomous nuclear families wherever their inclinations and aspirations take them—sometimes across the country. Because families are smaller than they used to be, there is often a gap between the emptying of one generation's nest and the filling of the next. This is a time when many middle-aged parents spread their own wings and

make important life changes or begin planning for retirement (Cherlin & Furstenberg, 1986b; Kornhaber & Woodward, 1981). Mobility and rising living standards, as well as social security and pension plans, have intensified this pattern of separation by making the generations less financially dependent on one another.

Thus, according to one study of 300 grandparents and an equal number of grandchildren ages 5 to 18, only 15 percent of children have a "vital connection" with one or more grandparents. Many grandparents feel that they have raised their children and now are entitled to pursue other interests. Yet some are uneasy about what they are missing: intimacy with their grandchildren (Kornhaber, 1986; Kornhaber & Woodward, 1981).

Other research puts contemporary grandparenthood in a more positive light. A major study of a nationally representative three-generation sample found that "grandparents play a limited but important role in family dynamics," and many have strong emotional ties to their grandchildren (Cherlin & Furstenberg, 1986a, p. 26). This research found three styles of grandparenting: remote, companionate (the predominant style), and involved. *Remote* grandparents (29 percent) see their grandchildren so infrequently that the relationship is more symbolic than real. *Companionate* grandparents (55 percent) do not intervene directly in the children's upbringing but enjoy frequent, casual companionship. Only 16 percent of grandparents are *involved* to the extent of disciplining or correcting grandchildren, giving advice, discussing the child's problems, being consulted on important decisions concerning the child, and exchanging help with errands, chores, and projects. (Figure 15-2 shows the most frequent grandparent-

grandchild activities.) Younger grandparents, those who see their grandchildren almost every day, and those who have a close relationship with the child's mother are more likely to be involved.

Grandparenting styles may differ with different grandchildren and at different times in a child's life. Grandparents tend to be more involved during a child's preadolescent years (Cherlin & Furstenberg, 1986b). Still, even though the generations see each other less often as the children grow up, satisfaction with grandchildren remains high (Field & Minkler, 1988).

One prominent researcher (Troll, 1980, 1983) sees grandparents as family "watchdogs." They stay on the fringes of their children's and grandchildren's lives, watching to make sure things are going well, but rarely play a strong role unless needed. In a crisis—after a divorce, for example, or during an illness or a financial emergency—they may step in and become more active (Cherlin & Furstenberg, 1986a, 1986b).

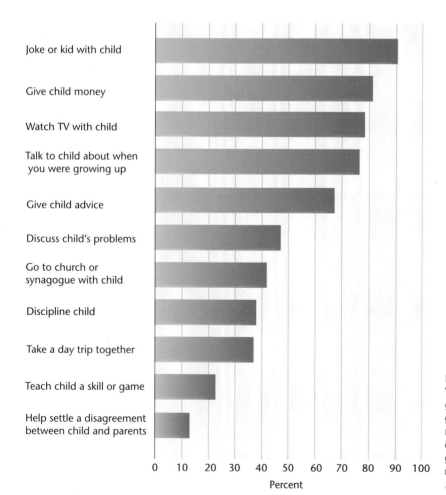

FIGURE 15-2
What grandparents do with their grandchildren: proportions of grandparents in a nationally representative sample who had engaged in various activities with their grandchildren in the previous 12 months. *(Source: Cherlin & Furstenberg, 1986b, p. 74.)*

Grandparents, like this grandmother teaching her granddaughter to make a quilt, can have an important influence on their grandchildren's development. Grandmothers tend to have closer, warmer relationships with their grandchildren than grandfathers. Black grandparents, although often less educated than white grandparents, tend to be especially successful in teaching their grandchildren values, perhaps because they generally spend more time with them. *(Tom McCarthy/The Picture Cube)*

Today, economic insecurity, divorce, and other threats to the stability of the nuclear family are causing many grandparents to play a more central role. Some grandparents provide child care for working parents; in 1993, 16.5 percent of preschool children of employed mothers were under a grandparent's care (Casper, 1996). One survey found that 32 percent of grandparents had provided child care or supervision for at least 1 hour during the previous week, and 9 percent had done it for 20 or more hours (Bass & Caro, 1996). If need be, some grandparents take adult children and grandchildren into their homes. And, as we'll see, some grandparents raise a grandchild when the parents cannot or will not do it.

Gender and Racial Differences

Grandmothers tend to have closer, warmer relationships with their grandchildren than grandfathers and often serve as surrogate parents. The mother's parents are likely to be closer to the children than the father's parents and are more likely to become involved during a crisis (Cherlin & Furstenberg, 1986a, 1986b; Hagestad, 1978, 1982; B. Kahana & Kahana, 1970). Grandmothers tend to be more satisfied with grandparenting than grandfathers (J. L. Thomas, 1986). However, grandfathers may be more nurturing and more physically demonstrative with their grandchildren than they were with their own children; they may regard grandparenthood as a "second chance" to make up

for any failings as parents (Kivnick, 1982). Grandfatherhood may be more central for black men than for white men (Kivett, 1991).

African American grandparents are more likely to become involved in raising their grandchildren, even when there is no crisis (Cherlin & Furstenberg, 1986a, 1986b; Strom et al., 1992–1993). In one study, 2 out of 3 black teenage mothers named their own mothers as their children's primary caregivers. In another study, 3 out of 4 children of teenage mothers lived in a grandmother's household during their first 3 years (Bengtson et al., 1996).

One study (Strom et al., 1992–1993) compared 204 black and 204 white grandparents. The researchers also compared how 295 black and 175 white grandchildren, ages 7 to 18, assessed their own grandparents, who were not the ones in the study. Both groups of grandparents rated their performance favorably, but black grandparents scored themselves significantly higher. Black children also rated their grandparents higher in overall success and specifically in teaching about right and wrong, good manners, the importance of learning, and caring about the feelings of others. (Black grandparents, too, saw teaching as a special strength, even though they had less formal education than white grandparents.) White children gave their grandparents higher ratings in coping with difficulty, managing frustration, and understanding what it is like to grow up today.

One factor in the success of black grandparents

is their investment of time. Black grandparents are more than twice as likely as their white counterparts to spend at least 5 hours a month with grandchildren. Grandparents of both races who spent more time with grandchildren considered themselves more effective, and the children agreed. However, the races had different perspectives on the effect of a grandparent's age. Black grandparents age 60 and over rated themselves as more effective than did younger ones; again, the children agreed. The opposite was true for white grandparents: younger ones considered themselves, and were considered, more effective. Black children said older grandparents had more of an influence on them; white children found younger grandparents more supportive. All in all, black grandparents' strengths—teaching, willingness to spend time with grandchildren of all ages, acceptance of family responsibilities regardless of distance, and effectiveness during old age—make them "a powerful influence in the lives of grandchildren," the study concluded (p. 266).

Grandparenting after Divorce and Remarriage

Divorce changes relationships, not only among a father, mother, and children, but with grandparents as well. One result of the growing number of divorces and remarriages is a growing number of grandparents and grandchildren whose relationships are endangered or severed. Another result is the creation of large numbers of stepgrandparents.

In intact families, both sets of grandparents generally have about the same access and involvement. After a divorce, since the mother usually has custody, her parents tend to have more contact and stronger relationships with their grandchildren; the paternal grandparents tend to have less, leaving them grief-stricken, disappointed, and angry (Cherlin & Furstenberg, 1986b; Myers & Perrin, 1993). A divorced mother's remarriage typically reduces her need for support from her parents, but not their contact with their grandchildren. For paternal grandparents, however, the new marriage increases the likelihood that they will be displaced or that the family will move away, making contact more difficult. Even if the mother does not break off the relationship, it may be awkward for the father's parents to keep it up if their son has dropped out of his children's lives (Cherlin & Furstenberg, 1986b). Some grandparents, afraid of being cut off from their grandchildren, try to gain custody, creating more conflict (Visher & Visher, 1991).

Because ties with grandparents are important to children's development, every state in the Union now gives grandparents (and in some states, great-grandparents, siblings, and others) the right to visitation after a divorce or the death of a parent—if a judge finds it in the best interest of the child. The decision may depend on what sort of relationship the grandparents and grandchild have had and on whether the visits seem likely to interfere with the parent-child relationship or to upset the child (Edelstein, 1990–1991; Lake, 1989).

The remarriage of either parent often brings a new set of grandparents into the picture, and often stepgrandchildren as well. Middle-aged and older adults may also become stepgrandparents after their own divorce and remarriage. One-third of the grandparents in the national three-generational survey discussed above (Cherlin & Furstenberg, 1986b) had at least one stepgrandchild.

When families "multiply by dividing," the web of connections becomes complex and there are no clear guidelines for establishing relationships (T. S. Kaufman, 1993, p. 226). Stepgrandparents may find it hard to become close to their new stepgrandchildren, especially older children and those who do not live with the grandparent's adult child (Cherlin & Furstenberg, 1986b; Longino & Earle, 1996; Myers & Perrin, 1993). Such issues as whether or what kinds of birthday and Christmas presents should be given to a "real" grandchild's half- or stepsiblings, or which grandparents should be visited or included at holidays, can generate tension.

Still, a combined family can offer expanded opportunities for love and nurturing. Because an additional set of grandparents generally does not present the conflict in loyalty that a stepparent may pose, stepgrandparents may be able to smooth the way for a child to become more comfortable with the stepparent. Creating new family traditions; including *all* the grandchildren, step and otherwise, in trips, outings, and other activities; offering a safe haven for the children when they are unhappy or upset; and being understanding and supportive of all members of the new stepfamily are ways in which stepgrandparents can build bridges instead of walls (T. S. Kaufman, 1993; Visher & Visher, 1991).

June Sands of Los Angeles hugs her 5-year-old daughter, Victoria, as her mother—Victoria's guardian, Elaine Sands—smiles fondly. Elaine and her husband, Don Sands, are among a growing number of grandparents raising grandchildren, temporarily or parmanently. Elaine and Don took over Victoria's care while June was overcoming a 20-year drug addiction. June Sands had been in jail and in withdrawal when her daughter was born, but she had been drug-free for a year when this picture was taken. She lived near her parents, worked as a baby-sitter in a health club, and visited her daughter regularly. *(Eugene Richards/Magnum Photos)*

Raising Grandchildren

"We hadn't had children in our home for years; suddenly they were there almost 24 hours a day," said Mary Etta Johnson (Larsen, 1990–1991, p. 32). Johnson and her husband, Albert, took their two preschool-age grandchildren into their home after the divorce of their daughter and son-in-law, who had become involved with drugs. About 1 year later, the Johnsons obtained permanent custody.

An increasing number of grandparents from their late thirties to their late seventies are serving as "parents by default" for children whose parents are addicted to drugs or alcohol, divorced, dead, physically or mentally ill, unwed, underage, unemployed, abusive, neglectful, or in jail, or who have simply abandoned them (Chalfie, 1994; Minkler & Roe, 1996). In 1991, nearly 1.1 million children under 18, including more than 5 percent of black children and about 1 percent of white and Hispanic children, lived with grandparents without a parent in the home (Furukawa, 1994). In some low-income urban areas, an estimated 30 to 50 percent of children are in *kinship care,* living in homes of grandparents or other relatives without their parents (Minkler & Roe, 1996).

Unplanned surrogate parenthood can be a physical, emotional, and financial drain on middle-aged or older adults. They may have to quit their jobs, shelve their retirement plans, drastically reduce their leisure pursuits and social life, and endanger their health (Burton, 1992; Chalfie, 1994; Minkler & Roe, 1992, 1996). Most grandparents do not have as much energy, patience, or stamina as they once had, and respite care is generally unavailable (Crowley, 1993). Financial ruin may become a real threat. More than 40 percent of grandparent caregivers are poor or nearly poor. Their median annual income is $18,000, half that of a parent-headed household. Some states have discriminated against eligible grandparent caregivers who applied for Aid to Families with Dependent Children (AFDC) or for payments comparable to those for licensed foster care (Chalfie, 1994). How welfare reform, which shifts responsibility for welfare to the states, will affect grandparent caregivers remains to be seen.

Most grandparents who take on the responsibility to raise their grandchildren do it because they love the children and do not want them placed in a stranger's foster home. According to one study, two-thirds of custodial grandparents report a greater sense of purpose in life (Jendrek, 1994). However, the age difference between grandparent and grandchild can become a barrier, and both generations may feel cheated out of their traditional roles. At the same time, grandparents often have to deal not only with a sense of guilt because the adult child they raised has failed his or her own offspring, but with the rancor they feel toward this adult child. For some caregiver couples, the strains produce tension in their own relationship. If one or both of the child's parents later resume their normal roles, it may be emotionally wrenching to return the child (Crowley, 1993; Larsen, 1990–1991).

Grandparents who do not become foster parents or gain custody have no legal status and no more rights than unpaid baby-sitters. They may face many practical problems, from enrolling the child in school and gaining access to academic records to obtaining medical insurance for the child. Grandchildren are usually not eligible for coverage under employer-provided health insurance even if the grandparent has custody (Chalfie, 1994; Simon-Rusinowitz et al., 1996). Becoming a foster parent is a long, intrusive process and can be risky, since the state has custody and can later decide to place the child elsewhere. Gaining custody can be difficult, time-consuming, and expensive, and grandparents may lose custody if a parent later challenges it (Chalfie, 1994).

Since custody laws vary from state to state, grandparents' rights activists are urging national standards, as well as other legal and financial remedies (Crowley, 1993; Landers, 1992). Like working parents, working grandparents need good, affordable child care and family-friendly workplace policies, such as time off to care for a sick child or to attend a school conference (Simon-Rusinowitz, Krach, Marks, Piktialis, & Wilson, 1996). The federal Family and Medical Leave Act of 1993 (refer back to Box 13-3) does cover grandparents who are raising grandchildren, but many do not realize it (H. Dabelko, intergenerational coordinator, Generations United, personal communication, November 4, 1996).

Grandparents can be sources of guidance, companions in play, links to the past, and symbols of the continuity of family life. As Erikson has observed, they express generativity, a longing to transcend mortality by investing themselves in the lives of future generations. Men and women who do not become grandparents may fulfill generative needs by becoming foster grandparents or volunteering in schools or hospitals (Porcino, 1983, 1991). By finding a way to develop the "virtue" of care, adults prepare themselves to enter the culminating period of adult development and to discover the wisdom of old age.

✔ SUMMARY

PERSONALITY AT MIDLIFE: NORMATIVE-CRISIS MODELS

- Carl Jung held that men and women at midlife, freed from much of the obligation of child rearing, express previously suppressed aspects of personality. The need to acknowledge mortality prompts introspection and questioning of goals.
- Erikson's seventh psychosocial crisis is *generativity versus stagnation*. The generative person is concerned with establishing and guiding the next generation. A person who fails to develop generativity suffers from self-absorption, self-indulgence, or stagnation.
- Expanding on Erikson's concepts, Peck specified four psychological developments critical to successful adjustment during middle age: valuing wisdom versus valuing physical powers, socializing versus sexualizing, emotional flexibility versus emotional impoverishment, and mental flexibility versus mental rigidity.
- Vaillant's and Levinson's studies suggest that the early forties are a potentially stressful time of transition for men, during which a crisis may occur.

- Normative research suggests that women go through midlife changes, which may involve crises. Mastery or control of one's life is an important issue for women this age. In Helson's research, the early forties were a particularly stressful time for women; the fifties were a "prime time" of life.
- The findings of normative-crisis research may not be generalizable to nonwhite people, people of different socioeconomic levels, homosexuals, and members of other cohorts and other cultures.
- Proponents of relational theory have questioned the psychological health of the male model depicted in much of the classic normative-crisis research. Other research suggests that entering middle age does not necessarily result in a crisis; for many people this is just one of life's many transitions.

PERSONALITY AT MIDLIFE: NONNORMATIVE MODELS

- Costa and McCrae found that personality remains stable after age 30; other trait-based research has found more change, though not during midlife. Nevertheless, much research has found that middle-aged people tend to take on characteristics associated with the other sex: women become more assertive and men more emotionally expressive.

■ Despite the greater fluidity of the life cycle today, people still expect and assess important events in their lives by a "social clock." However, greater longevity and changes in lifestyle have given different meaning to such midlife events as menopause and retirement.

CONSENSUAL RELATIONSHIPS

■ Research on the quality of marriage suggests a dip in marital satisfaction during the years of child rearing, followed by an improved relationship after the children leave home.

■ Divorce at midlife is increasing. The most important factors in marital longevity seem to include positive feelings about the spouse, a commitment to long-term marriage, shared goals, and intimacy balanced with autonomy.

■ Because many homosexuals delay coming out, at midlife they are often just establishing intimate relationships.

■ Middle-aged people tend to invest less time and energy in friendships than younger adults do, but depend on friends for emotional support and practical guidance.

RELATIONSHIPS WITH MATURING CHILDREN

■ Parents of adolescents have to come to terms with a loss of control over their children's lives. The postparental years, when children have left, are often among the happiest. The "emptying of the nest" may be stressful for fathers who have not been involved with child rearing, for parents whose children have not become independent when expected, and for mothers who have failed to prepare for the event.

■ Middle-aged parents tend to remain involved with their young adult children and continue giving them more than they get from them.

■ Today, more young adults are living with their parents, often for economic reasons or after a divorce. Most parents and children seem satisfied with the arrangement, but serious conflict can arise if the child's adult status and the parents' right to privacy are not fully acknowledged.

■ Grown children may be deeply troubled by their parents' divorce, and sons especially tend to become alienated from their fathers.

OTHER KINSHIP TIES

■ Relationships between middle-aged adults and their parents are usually characterized by a strong bond of affection. The two generations generally maintain frequent contact and offer and receive assistance.

■ Middle-aged people, especially daughters, often become caregivers to ailing, aging parents, usually mothers. This can be a source of considerable stress, especially when the caregiver is "sandwiched" between the needs of growing children and infirm parents. Filial maturity occurs when middle-aged children accept and meet their parents' dependency needs while maintaining autonomy within a two-way relationship.

■ Bonds with siblings often become closer during middle age.

■ Although most American grandparents today are less intimately involved in grandchildren's lives than in the past, they often play a more active role when problems arise. Women tend to be closer to their grandchildren than men are, but men may be more attentive to their grandchildren than they were to their children. African American grandparents tend to be more involved in their grandchildren's lives, and are perceived as more successful grandparents overall, than white grandparents.

■ Divorce and remarriage of an adult child often affect grandparent-grandchild relationships and create new stepgrandparenting roles.

■ An increasing number of children are being raised by grandparents. This unplanned role can create physical, emotional, and financial strains.

✔ KEY TERMS

midlife crisis (page 506)
generativity versus stagnation (508)
valuing wisdom versus valuing physical powers (508)
socializing versus sexualizing in human relationships (508)

emotional flexibility versus emotional impoverishment (508)
mental flexibility versus mental rigidity (509)
interiority (509)
marital capital (509)

empty nest (521)
revolving door syndrome (521)
parent-support ratio (525)
sandwich generation (526)
filial maturity (527)
filial crisis (527)

caregiver burnout (528)   extended family (528)   kinship care (533)
respite care (528)   nuclear family (529)

✔ QUESTIONS FOR THOUGHT AND DISCUSSION

1 Did one or both of your parents go through what appeared to be a midlife crisis? If you are middle-aged, did you go through such a crisis? If so, what issues made it a crisis? Did it seem more serious than crises that may have occurred at other times of life?

2 On the basis of your own observations, as well as what you have read in the text, do you believe that personality can change significantly during middle age? Do such changes seem to accompany important events, such as divorce, loss of a job, or grandparenthood?

3 What similarities and differences do you see between the challenges that face men and women at midlife?

4 How many longtime happily married couples do you know? Are the qualities that seem to charac-terize these marriages similar to those mentioned in the text?

5 In what ways could a lasting, monogamous homosexual relationship be like a marriage? In what ways is it likely to be different?

6 Do you think it is a good idea for adult children to live with their parents? If so, under what circumstances? What "house rules" do you think should apply?

7 What would you do if one or both of your parents required long-term care? To what extent should children or other relatives be responsible for such care? To what extent, and in what ways, should society help?

8 Have you had a close relationship with a grandparent? If so, in what specific ways did that relationship influence your development?

PART SEVEN

Late Adulthood and the End of Life

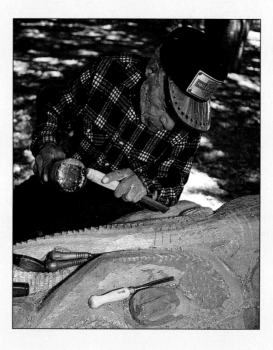

A ge 65 is the traditional entrance point for late adulthood, the last phase of life. Yet many adults at 65—or even 75 or 85—do not feel or act "old." Nor, with the ending of universal mandatory retirement, do they necessarily stop working at 65.

Individual differences become more pronounced in the later years. "Use it or lose it" becomes an urgent mandate in both the physical and cognitive realms. Most older adults enjoy good physical and mental health, and although some abilities may diminish, people who keep physically and intellectually active can hold their own in most respects and even grow in competence. Physical and cognitive functioning have psychosocial effects, often determining an older person's emotional state and the ability to live independently.

Death becomes an inescapable concern in this late chapter of life. As we examine how people of different ages face death and bereavement, we see that death is an integral element of the life span and that understanding the end of life helps us understand the whole of life.

CHAPTER SIXTEEN

PHYSICAL AND COGNITIVE DEVELOPMENT IN LATE ADULTHOOD

Why not look at these new years of life in terms of continued or new roles in society, another stage in personal or even spiritual growth and development?

Betty Friedan,
The Fountain of Age, *1993*

ASK YOURSELF

✔ How is today's older population changing?
✔ What causes aging? How far can the human life span be extended?
✔ What physical changes can people expect as they get older, and what changes vary with individuals?

✔ What influences health in late adulthood?
✔ What mental disorders do some people experience with age?
✔ Are there ways to improve cognitive performance in late adulthood?

I n Japan, old age is a mark of status. There—in sharp contrast to most western countries, where it is considered rude to ask a person's age—travelers checking into hotels are often asked their age to ensure that they will receive proper deference. At a man's sixtieth birthday celebration, he wears a red vest symbolizing rebirth into an advanced phase of life (Kimmel, 1988). Despite this respect for the aged, however, problems of caring for a mushrooming elderly population have brought challenges to Japan, as well as to other Asian nations (see Box 16-1) and other parts of the developing world (Holden, 1996).

In the United States, which also has a rapidly growing older population, aging is generally seen as undesirable—unless one considers the alternative. Although everybody wants to live long, hardly anybody wants to be *old,* a word that connotes physical frailty, narrow-mindedness, incompetence, and loss of attractiveness. Such euphemisms as "senior citizens" and "golden-agers" are responses to *ageism*—prejudice or discrimination, usually against older persons, based on age.

The media often reinforce myths about aging. An article in *Time* magazine on detective programs built around aging stars was titled "Murder, They Wheezed." The central characters of "these arthritic whodunits" were described as "old codgers" or as "easygoing dilettantes [who] would rather be napping." The illustration accompanying the article depicted these crime fighters as doddering and decrepit (Zoglin, 1994).

Such stereotypes reflect widespread misconceptions: that older people are usually tired, poorly coordinated, and prone to infections and accidents, that most of them live in institutions or spend most of their time in bed, that they can neither remember nor learn, that they have no interest in sexual relationships, that they are isolated from others

and depend on television or radio, that they do not use their time productively, and that they are grouchy, self-pitying, touchy, and cranky. These negative stereotypes do real harm. A physician who does not bring up sexual issues with a 75-year-old heart patient may deny the patient an important source of fulfillment. An overprotective adult child may encourage an aging parent to become childlike. A social worker who considers depression "to be expected" in old age may in effect abandon an elderly client.

Negative stereotypes about aging can have effects as subtle as a younger person's unwillingness to listen to an older person's opinions and as serious as loss of a job. Positive stereotypes, which picture a golden age of peace and relaxation when people harvest the fruits of their lifelong labors or enjoy a carefree second childhood spent idly on the golf course or at the card table, are no more accurate or helpful.

Efforts to combat ageism are making headway, thanks to the visibility of a growing cadre of active, healthy older adults. Articles with such titles as "Achievers after the Age of 90" (1993) appear in newspapers and magazines. On television, older people are less often portrayed as "comical, stubborn, eccentric, and foolish" and more often as "powerful, affluent, healthy, active, admired, and sexy" (J. Bell, 1992, p. 305). However, older women still are rarely shown, and then almost invariably as subordinate to men. Meanwhile, "the media continue to bombard us with advertising for cosmetic surgery, hair coloring, anti-wrinkle creams, pills, potions, tonics and diet programs that, they assure us, will make it possible to maintain our youthful attractiveness forever" (Lenz, 1993, p. 26).

We need to look beyond distorted images of age to its true, multifaceted reality, gazing neither with rose-colored glasses nor with dark ones. Late adulthood is a normal period of the life span, with its own challenges and opportunities for growth.

◼ In this chapter we begin by sketching trends in today's older population. We look at the increasing length and quality of life in late adulthood and at theories about causes of biological aging. Next we examine physical changes and health. We then turn to changes in intelligence and memory, the growth of wisdom, and the prevalence of continuing education in late life. In Chapter 17, we look at adjustment to aging and changes in lifestyles and relationships. What emerges is a picture not of "the elderly" but of individual human beings—some needy and frail, but most of them independent, healthy, and involved. ◼

✔ OLD AGE TODAY

Older people are a diverse lot, and they are becoming more so as they grow more numerous.

THE GRAYING OF THE POPULATION

In 1994, more than 33 million people had passed their sixty-fifth birthday—11 times as many as in 1900—and they had grown from 4 percent to 12½ percent of the population. By 2050, 1 in 5 Americans—80 million in all, more than twice the present number—may be 65 or older (U.S. Bureau of the Census, 1995a; see Figure 16-1).

Furthermore, the aged population is aging. About 3 million Americans are 85 or older. This

fastest-growing segment of the United States population increased by a whopping 274 percent between 1960 and 1994, a period in which the elderly population as a whole doubled and the total population grew by only 45 percent (U.S. Bureau of the Census, 1995a). After 2030, more than half of older Americans are expected to be 75 and above; and by 2050, the 85-plus group could be nearly one-fourth of the elderly population and 5 percent of all Americans (Treas, 1995; U.S. Bureau of the Census, 1995a). Ethnic diversity is also increasing: today only 1 in 10 older Americans is nonwhite; by 2050, 1 in 5 will be. Older Hispanics are likely to quadruple from 4 to 16 percent, surpassing the older black population (Treas, 1995; U.S. Bureau of the Census, 1995a).

The graying of the population has several causes: chiefly, high birth rates and high immigration rates during the early to mid-twentieth century and longer life due to medical progress and healthier lifestyles. At the same time, the trend toward smaller families has reduced the relative size of younger age groups. Currently, the rate of growth of the older population has slowed; but it will surge during the first third of the twenty-first century, as the "baby boom" generation (born between 1946 and the early 1960s) enters old age, after which it will subside again (U.S. Bureau of the Census, 1995a).

This "aging avalanche" will change the physical, social, economic, and political environment (see Box 16-2), as the older population becomes more influential at the polls and in the marketplace. Leaders of almost all industrialized nations,

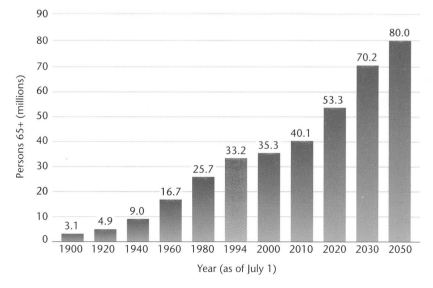

FIGURE 16-1
Population of the United States age 65 and over, 1900–2050 (projected). Since the beginning of this century, the number of people age 65 and over has continued to increase, both absolutely and relative to the rest of the population. This trend is expected to continue through the aging of the "baby boom" generation. The *percentage* of the population age 65 and older is growing, too—from 4 percent at the turn of the twentieth century to about 13 percent at the turn of the twenty-first—and may reach 20 percent between 2030 and 2050. (*Note:* Increments in years on the horizontal scale are uneven.) (*Source: Adapted from AARP, 1995, including data from U.S. Bureau of the Census, 1995a.*)

BOX 16-1   WINDOW ON THE WORLD

AGING IN ASIA

Asians often ask why American families put their parents into institutions and why a country as rich as the United States does not do more for its elderly people. In keeping with Asians' traditional respect for elders, when older people can no longer care for themselves, their families care for them. In recent years, however, Asian countries have encountered some of the same problems as western nations in helping a growing population of older citizens.

Since the 1940s, Asia has been the most successful region of the world in reducing fertility. At the same time, higher standards of living, better sanitation, and immunization programs have extended the adult life span (Martin, 1988). In China, where government policy limits families to one child, it soon may not be unusual to see a young adult couple who are the sole support of four aging parents (Adamchak, quoted in Holden, 1996). By 2025, elderly people in

China, Hong Kong, Singapore, and Sri Lanka are likely to constitute more than 10 percent of the population (Martin, 1988). In Japan, which is growing faster than any other industrial country, the aged are now 14 percent of the population, a proportion that has doubled in the past 25 years. They will reach nearly 24 percent by 2020, straining that nation's universal health insurance system. Furthermore, those older than 75, who are most likely to need long-term care, will amount to more than 11 percent (Nishio, 1994; Oshima, 1996).

Although a large proportion of elderly Asians live with their children, they are less likely to do so than older people were in the past. In Japan, 55 percent of the aged lived with adult children in 1994, as compared with more than 80 percent in 1957. Along with the shifting balance between old and young, such trends as urbanization, migration, and a larger proportion of women in the work

Elderly Chinese people, like this woman, used to take for granted their place in their children's households. But today, although most elderly Asians still live with their children, they are less likely to want to do so than people were in the past, and their children are less prone to urge them to. China is one of several Asian countries that have passed laws obliging people to care for elderly relatives. *(Eastcott/Momatiuk/Woodfin Camp & Associates)*

force—38 percent in Japan, compared with 22 percent in 1960—make home care of elderly relatives less feasible. In Korea, a survey taken in 1981 found that

---

which are experiencing a similar trend, as well as many developing ones, worry about the cost of supporting a growing contingent of older people. In the United States, the cost of medical care, particularly for the growing number of adults over 85, threatens to bankrupt the health care system and reduce the quality of care. By 2040 Medicare costs may increase sixfold (Schneider & Guralnik, 1990) and may consume about 8 percent of the gross domestic product (GDP) (Quinn, 1996). Successful cost containment will depend on discovering how to prevent or cure disorders that require long-term care and on finding more creative ways to fund these services.

A key question may be whether the economy can grow fast enough to meet the challenge without placing an insupportable burden on a shrinking number of working adults (Binstock, 1993;

Crown, 1993). According to one estimate, for every year that is added to the average life span, productivity must rise by nearly 1 percent or consumption must drop by the same amount to pay for added benefits to retirees (Lee, quoted in Roush, 1996).

"YOUNG OLD," "OLD OLD," AND "OLDEST OLD"

An important factor in the economic impact of a graying population is the proportion of that population which is healthy and able-bodied. Here the trend is encouraging. Many problems that used to be considered part of old age are now understood to be due, not to aging itself, but to lifestyle factors or diseases that may or may not accompany getting older. ***Primary aging*** is a gradual, in-

BOX 16-1   WINDOW ON THE WORLD

AGING IN ASIA (continued)

only 7 percent of adults thought their children would care for them in old age; 64 percent expected to care for themselves. To halt the erosion in family care, China, Japan, and Singapore passed laws obliging people to care for elderly relatives, and Japan and Singapore have provided tax relief to those who give older relatives financial help (Martin, 1988; Oshima, 1996).

Throughout Asia, institutionalization is seen as a last resort for those who are destitute or without families. Few nursing homes exist, and limited access to institutional care places severe strains on the traditional family (Martin, 1988).

Many families with feeble, dependent elderly members keep up the tradition of three-generational households. In Japan, when one elderly spouse becomes bedridden, both typically move in with the family of the eldest married son. Thus, in contrast with American custom, daughters-in-law rather than daughters are most likely to

become primary caregivers (Nishio, 1994). An indication of the resulting strain is that suicide among older Japanese women is more prevalent than anywhere else in the world (MacAdam, 1993). Older adults living in three-generation households are more likely to take their lives than those living alone.

Eventually, Japan's exploding older population will outgrow family-based care. Already, since 1990, there has been a tenfold rise in nursing homes, infirmaries, and other institutions serving remote areas. However, the official strategy is to limit the need for hospitalization and institutionalization by broadening and professionalizing home care (Nishio, 1994). The nation's 3,000 nursing homes take only the bedridden or people with dementia, and 60,000 people are on waiting lists. At the same time, a program to expand home services and institutional care through local governments is foundering for lack of funds (Oshima, 1996).

A major controversy in Asia, as in the west, is whether older people should get preference in access to housing, health care, and other social services. Young adults with small children worry that, in order to fund services for the old, governments may have to cut back what little social welfare exists for the young. In Japan, Korea, Indonesia, the Philippines, Singapore, and Thailand, older adults join senior citizens' clubs to strengthen their political clout. The establishment of Respect for the Aged Day (September 15) in Japan and National Aging Day (April 13) in Thailand reflects this growing "gray power" but also underlines the decline in the formerly unquestioned tradition of reverence for age (Martin, 1988).

Most Asians want to help elderly people remain independent and productive as long as possible and, when they do need assistance, to help their families care for them. Meeting these goals, however, is a difficult challenge.

evitable process of bodily deterioration that begins early in life and continues through the years. *Secondary aging* consists of results of disease, abuse, and disuse—factors that are often avoidable and within people's control (Busse, 1987; J. C. Horn & Meer, 1987). By eating sensibly and keeping physically fit, many older adults can and do stave off secondary effects of aging. With improved health habits and medical care, it is becoming harder to draw the line between the end of middle adulthood and the beginning of late adulthood. Many 70-year-olds act, think, and feel much as 50-year-olds did a decade or two ago.

Today, social scientists who specialize in *gerontology,* the study of the aged and aging processes, refer to three groups of older adults: the "young old," "old old," and "oldest old." Chronologically, *young old* generally refers to

people ages 65 to 74, who are usually active, vital, and vigorous. The *old old,* ages 75 to 84, and the *oldest old,* age 85 and above, are more likely to be frail and infirm and to have difficulty managing some activities of daily living. Although only about 5 percent of elderly people are in nursing homes, the proportion rises steeply with age (AARP, 1995). Research in gerontology and *geriatrics,* the branch of medicine concerned with aging, has underlined the need for support services, especially for the oldest old, many of whom have outlived their savings and cannot pay for their own care.

A more meaningful classification is by *functional age:* how well a person functions in a physical and social environment in comparison with others of the same chronological age. A person of 90 who is still in good health may be functionally

BOX 16-2   PRACTICALLY SPEAKING

NEW ENVIRONMENTS FOR AN AGING POPULATION

Have you ever watched a left-handed person try to turn a doorknob designed for right-handers, or have you experienced this challenge yourself? It's not easy—and many everyday tasks can be equally exasperating, or more so, for an older person who has to live and work in an environment designed for young adults. Such simple, everyday activities as reading product labels, reaching high shelves, getting dressed, cleaning house, driving a car, and taking a bath can be annoying or even hazardous.

As the population ages, we can expect many changes in our physical environment and in the products we use. Already, pain relievers, previously packaged in childproof bottles that stymied arthritic adults, are being repackaged in easier-to-open containers.

The gerontologist Ken Dychtwald, in *Age Wave* (Dychtwald & Flower, 1990), predicts ways in which the environment of the twenty-first century will be redesigned to accommodate physical changes that often accompany aging. Here are examples, some already in place:

AIDS TO VISION

Signals now given visually will be spoken as well. There will be talking exit signs, talking clocks, talking appliances that tell you when they get hot, talking cameras that warn you when the light is too low,

and talking automobiles that caution you when you're about to collide with something. Windshields will adjust their tint automatically to varying weather and light conditions and will be equipped with large, liquid-crystal displays of speed and other information (so that older drivers need not take their eyes off the road and readjust their focus). Reading lights will be brighter, and books will have larger print. Floors will be carpeted or textured, not waxed to a smooth, glaring gloss.

AIDS TO HEARING

Public address systems and recordings will be engineered to an older adult's auditory range. Telephones will have adjustable volume and tone controls and extra-loud ringers. Park benches and couches will be replaced by angled or clustered seating so that older adults can communicate face to face.

AIDS TO MANUAL DEXTERITY

To compensate for stiff, aging fingers and joints, it will become increasingly common to find such items as comb and brush extenders, stretchable shoelaces, Velcro tabs instead of buttons, lightweight motorized pot-and-pan scrubbers and garden tools, tap turners on faucets and stove handles, foot mops that will eliminate bending, voice-activated tele-

phone dialers, long-handled easy-grip zippers, and contoured eating utensils.

AIDS TO MOBILITY AND SAFETY

Ramps will become more common, levers will replace knobs, streetlights will change more slowly, and traffic islands will let slow walkers pause and rest. Closet shelves and bus platforms will be lower, as will windows, for people who sit a lot. Bathtubs and showers will have built-in seats and grab bars; regulators will keep tap water from scalding; and "soft tubs" will prevent slips, add comfort, and keep bath water from cooling too fast. Automobiles will be programmed to operate windows, radio, heater, lights, wipers, and even the ignition by verbal commands.

TEMPERATURE ADJUSTMENTS

Because older bodies take longer to adjust to temperature changes and have more trouble keeping warm, homes and hotels will have heated furniture and thermostats in each room. Some people will wear heated clothing and eat heat-producing foods.

Such innovations will make life easier and more convenient for everyone. An environment designed for older rather than younger adults can be more user-friendly for all age groups.

younger than a person of 65 who is not. Some gerontologists, therefore, prefer to use the term *young old* for the healthy, active majority of older adults, and *old old* for the frail, infirm minority, regardless of chronological age (Neugarten & Neugarten, 1987).

As we will see in this chapter and the next, older adults are a varied group in terms of health, education, income, occupation, and living arrangements. Like people of all ages, they are individuals with differing needs, desires, abilities, lifestyles, and cultural backgrounds. Even the group sometimes called the *oldest old*, those 85 and older, are amazingly diverse (Longino, 1994). As our society ages, meeting the needs of the older population will require knowledge, sophistication, and flexibility.

✔ LONGEVITY AND AGING

How long will you live? Why do you have to grow old? Would you want to live forever? Human beings have been wondering about these questions for thousands of years.

The first question involves two different but related concepts: *life expectancy,* the age to which a person born at a certain time and place is statistically likely to live given his or her current age and health status, and *longevity,* how long a person actually does live. Life expectancy is based on the average longevity of members of a population. The second question expresses an age-old theme: a yearning for a fountain or potion of youth. Behind this yearning is a fear, not so much of chronolog-

ical age, as of biological aging: loss of health and physical powers. The third question expresses a concern not just with length but with quality of life.

TRENDS AND FACTORS IN LIFE EXPECTANCY AND MORTALITY

Today, most people can expect to grow old, sometimes very old. A baby born in the United States in 1995 could expect to live 75.8 years, about 28 years longer than a baby born in 1900 (AARP, 1995; H. M. Rosenberg et al., 1996). Such a long life expectancy is unprecedented in the history of humankind (see Figure 16-2). It results largely from a dramatic reduction in deaths during infancy and childhood, fewer deaths in young adulthood (particularly in childbirth), new treatments for many once-fatal illnesses, and a better-educated, more health-conscious population.

The longer people live, the longer they are likely to live. Americans who make it to age 65 today can expect to reach 82—about 6½ years more than the

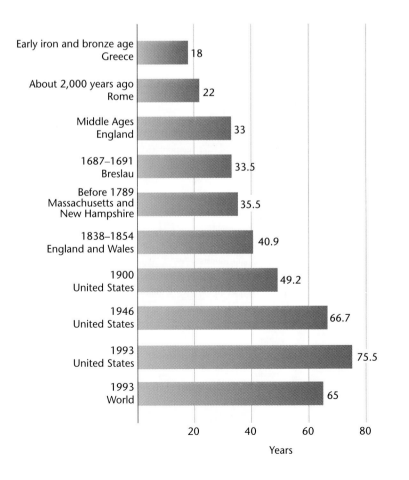

FIGURE 16-2

Changes in life expectancy from ancient to modern times. *(Source: Adapted from Katchadourian, 1987; 1993 data from AARP, 1995, and Worldwatch Institute, 1994.)*

TABLE 16-1

Life Expectancy at Birth in Years, by Sex and Race, 1995, in the United States

	All Races	White	Black
Males	72.6	73.4	65.4
Females	78.9	79.6	74.0

SOURCE: H. M. Rosenberg et al., 1996 (provisional statistics).

life expectancy of people *born* today (U.S. Bureau of the Census, 1995a). Education adds to life expectancy; older Americans with at least a high school diploma, regardless of race or gender, can expect to live about 3 to 4 years longer than those with fewer than 12 years of schooling (Kaplan, 1994).

Worldwide, life expectancy has risen 41 percent since 1950, from 46 years to 65, with the largest increases in developing countries (Worldwatch Institute, 1994). Average life expectancies in industrialized countries hover between 75 and 79 (Zarate, 1994). In Japan, people live longer than anywhere else in the world: on average, 82.5 years for women and 76 for men (Treas, 1995). Life expectancy at birth is lower in the United States than in many other industrialized countries that have lower infant mortality rates, but the gap closes by very old age. At 80, white Americans have life expectancies a year or two longer than 80-year-olds in Sweden, France, England, and Japan—possibly because of more education or greater expenditures on health care (Manton & Vaupel, 1995). (Minorities were not included in this study.)

The dramatic increase in life expectancy since the turn of the century reflects a sharp decline in *mortality,* or death rates (the proportions of people of specific ages who die in a given year). In the United States, deaths from infectious disease are decreasing, but deaths from chronic conditions related to age have risen. Despite progress in treating heart disease, it remains by far the most common killer of people over 65, accounting for about 38 percent of deaths. Furthermore, as more older people survive heart attacks, more die of cancer (23 percent). It is true that deaths from some cancers, such as stomach and uterine cancer, have decreased, thanks to healthier diets, earlier detection, and improved treatment; but lung cancer has taken a rising toll among older women, who are more likely to have smoked than women in previous

generations. Other major causes of death in late life are stroke (8 percent), followed (on the basis of preliminary figures for 1995) by lung disease, pneumonia and influenza, diabetes, accidents, kidney disease, Alzheimer's disease, and septicemia (blood poisoning from bacterial infection) (H. M. Rosenberg et al., 1996; Treas, 1995; USDHHS, 1996).

On average, white Americans live about 6 to 8 years longer than African Americans, and women live about 6 years longer than men (H. M. Rosenberg et al., 1996; see Table 16-1). The racial difference in life expectancy has persisted since the 1970s and may be increasing because of deaths from AIDS and homicide. As discussed in previous chapters, African Americans, especially men, are more vulnerable than white people to illness and death from infancy through middle adulthood, in large part because of socioeconomic and lifestyle factors. However, the picture changes in late life. At 65, a white man or woman can expect to live only 2 years longer than a black man or woman the same age. By 85, the pattern has reversed: African Americans can expect more remaining years than whites, perhaps because those who have managed to live that long are especially fit. However, it also has been suggested that this statistical "black-white crossover" effect may be due to inaccurate data on ages of older black adults, many of whom do not have birth certificates (Treas, 1995).

Women's longer life has been attributed to several factors: their greater tendency to take care of themselves and to seek medical care (see Chapter 12), the greater level of social support that women—particularly older women—enjoy (see Chapter 17), and the greater biological vulnerability of males throughout life (see Chapter 12). Boys are more likely than girls to die in infancy, teenage boys and young men are more likely to die from AIDS or accidents, and middle-aged and older men are more likely than women to die of heart disease or other ailments. The health problems of older women are likely to be long-term, chronic, disabling conditions; men tend to develop short-term, fatal diseases.

Women benefited more than men from the gains in life expectancy during the twentieth century, particularly the reduction in deaths from childbirth. In 1900, there was only a 2-year difference in life expectancy between the sexes. The gap widened to nearly 8 years in 1979; since then, it has narrowed by 1 year, largely because more men than before are surviving heart attacks (Treas,

1995). Older women in the United States currently outnumber older men by 3 to 2 (as compared with 4 to 3 worldwide), and the difference in numbers increases with advancing age (U.S. Bureau of the Census, 1996c; see Figure 16-3).

As a result, older women are more likely than older men to be widowed, to remain unmarried afterward, and to have more years of poor health and fewer years of active life and independence (Katz et al., 1983; Longino, 1987; O'Bryant, 1991; U.S. Bureau of the Census, 1992b, 1995a). They are much more likely to be poor and to live alone, but they are also more likely, at some point, to need help with eating, dressing, bathing, preparing meals, managing money, and going outside. Ultimately, they are more likely to live in nursing homes (AARP, 1995; Treas, 1995; U.S. Bureau of the Census, 1995a, 1996c). The major reason for older women's impoverishment is the death of a husband and the resulting loss of financial support (U.S. Bureau of the Census, 1996c). Older widowers tend to remarry quickly, an option rarely available to older widows because there are fewer elderly men and the ones who are around tend to marry younger women.

With continued medical progress and healthier lifestyles, especially among poor and minority populations, life expectancy in the United States may well equal or even surpass that in Japan (Treas, 1995). According to one prediction, a baby born in the United States in 2040 can expect to live three to four years longer than one born in 1993: a girl to age 83, and a boy to 75 (Schneider & Guralnik, 1990). We are talking, of course, about averages; some people live much longer. Death rates

among the "oldest old" have decreased and probably will continue to do so as better-educated cohorts, who tend to stay healthier, grow older (U.S. Bureau of the Census, 1995a). The number of *centenarians*—people past their one-hundredth birthday—more than tripled between 1980 and 1995 and may double again to 1 million by 2050 (Treas, 1995).

HOW FAR CAN THE LIFE SPAN BE EXTENDED?

There are at least two documented cases of people living to 120, one in Japan and the other in France (Treas, 1995). Is it possible for human beings to live to 130, 150, or even 200? Is there any limit to how long people could live?

Many gerontologists have maintained that 110 to 120 years is the upper limit of the human life span—the potential length of life for members of the human species—just as the upper limit for dogs is about 20 and for tortoises, 150 (NIA, 1993). Leonard Hayflick (1974) found that human cells will divide in the laboratory no more than 50 times; this is called the *Hayflick limit,* and it has since been shown to be genetically controlled (Schneider, 1992). This suggests that there may be a biological limit to the life span of human cells and therefore of human life. According to Hayflick, if all diseases and causes of death were eliminated, humans would remain healthy until about 110 years of age; then the cellular clock would run out and they would die. Historical changes in *survival curves*—percentages of people who live to various ages—support the idea of a limit to human life. Although

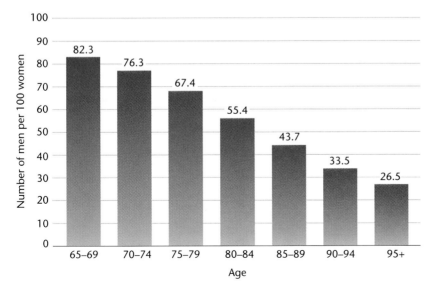

FIGURE 16-3
Number of men per 100 women by age: 1994. With age, the ratio of men to women declines. Because there are more older women, they are more likely than older men to live alone and to need help from their families and from society. *(Source: U.S. Bureau of the Census, 1996c, figure 2-10.)*

Jeanne Calment of Arles, France, is one of the only two human beings known to have lived to age 120, believed by some scientists to be the limit of the human lifespan. (The other was Shigechiyo Izumi of Japan, who died in 1986.) Calment is shown here shortly before her 120th birthday in March 1995, holding up her family photo album open to a picture of herself at age 40. *(Robert Ricci/ Gamma-Liaison)*

many people are living longer than in the past, the curves still end around age 100; this suggests that, regardless of health and fitness, the maximum life span is not much higher than that (see Figure 16-4).

Today, however, animal research is challenging the idea of a fixed limit for each species. A mutant gene has been identified that extends the life span of roundworms by 60 percent, from 26 days to 60, while they remain biologically young (T. E. Johnson, 1990). Perhaps the most promising line of research is on dietary restriction. Rats fed 35 to 40 percent fewer calories than usual, with all necessary nutrients, live as much as 50 percent longer than other laboratory rodents (about 1,500 days as

compared with 1,000 days). The reduction in caloric intake seems to delay age-related decline in the ability to fight disease. A spartan diet has also been found to extend life in worms and fish—in fact, in virtually all species on which it has been tried (Weindruch & Walford, 1988). Studies of caloric restriction in monkeys and other nonhuman primates are not yet complete, but already it has been found to slow the aging process (Sohal & Weindruch, 1996). So far, there has been no similar, systematic research on humans, though one investigator, Roy Walford, is trying such a diet on himself and hopes to live to 140 (Walford, 1983, 1986; Weindruch & Walford, 1988).

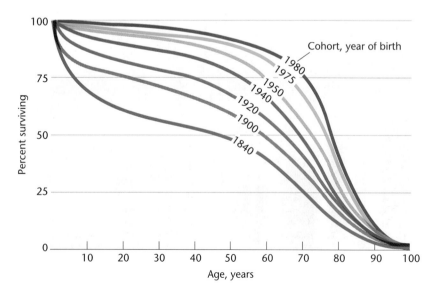

FIGURE 16-4
Survival curves show the percentage of persons born in the United States in selected years who survived, or are expected to survive, to each age. Survival curves have become increasingly "rectangularized" as life expectancy has increased owing to medical advances. Still, although a larger percentage of the population is surviving to more advanced ages, the curves drop to zero by about age 100, suggesting that there may be a genetically determined limit to human life. *(Source: Katchadourian, 1987.)*

It seems unlikely that people will ever live forever, or even well into the hundreds. Still, the new life-extension research does suggest that deaths even in the oldest old are postponable and that we cannot yet tell how far life expectancy and longevity may continue to rise.

QUALITY VERSUS QUANTITY OF LIFE

Eos, a mythological goddess, asked Zeus to allow Tithonus, the mortal she loved, to live forever. Zeus granted Tithonus immortality, and the lovers lived happily for a while. But Tithonus grew older and older until he became so infirm that he could not move; yet he was denied the gift of death. Eos had made a grievous error: she had forgotten to ask Zeus to grant Tithonus eternal youth along with eternal life.

The motto of the Gerontological Society of America is "To add life to years, not just years to life." Some gerontologists fear that eradication of the biggest killers, cancer and heart disease, would merely increase the number of people living long enough to cope with disabling infirmities, such as arthritis and dementia (Cassel, 1992; Treas, 1995).

What if science conquered *all* disease, and all adults stayed healthy throughout a vastly extended life span? The social changes necessary to accommodate a massive population of centenari-

ans would be equally massive. These "oldest old" would have to keep working, so as not to put an impossible burden on younger generations. To encourage them to do so, we might need to reduce pensions, create flexible work times, and change attitudes toward older people in the workplace. Only a thriving economy could absorb such a vast expansion of the work force. Such a social change might be a greater challenge than "unlocking the biological mysteries" of longevity and aging (Cassel, 1992, p. 63).

WHY PEOPLE AGE

The issue of quality versus quantity of life hinges largely on what happens to our bodies as we age. Early in adulthood, physical losses are typically so small and so gradual as to be barely noticed. With age, however, individual differences increase. One 80-year-old man can hear every word of a whispered conversation; another cannot hear the doorbell. One 70-year-old woman runs marathons; another cannot walk around the block. The onset of *senescence,* a period marked by obvious declines in body functioning sometimes associated with aging, varies greatly. Why? In fact, why do people age at all? Most biological aging theories fall into two categories: *genetic-programming theories* and *variable-rate theories* (summarized in Table 16-2).

TABLE 16-2

Theories of Biological Aging

Genetic-Programming Theories	Variable-Rate Theories
Programmed senescence theory. Aging is the result of the sequential switching on and off of certain genes, with senescence being defined as the time when age-associated deficits are manifested.	*Wear-and-tear theory.* Cells and tissues have vital parts that wear out.
Endocrine theory. Biological clocks act through hormones to control the pace of aging.	*Free-radical theory.* Accumulated damage from oxygen radicals causes cells and eventually organs to stop functioning.
Immunological theory. A programmed decline in immune system functions leads to increased vulnerability to infectious disease and thus to aging and death.	*Rate-of-living theory.* The greater an organism's rate of metabolism, the shorter its life span.
	Error-catastrophe theory. Faulty proteins accumulate to a level that causes catastrophic damage to cells, tissues, and organs.
	Somatic-mutation theory. Genetic mutations occur and accumulate with increasing age, causing cells to deteriorate and malfunction.
	Autoimmune theory. Immune system becomes confused and attacks own body cells.

SOURCE: Adapted from NIH/NIA, 1993, p. 2.

Genetic-Programming Theories

Genetic-programming theories hold that bodies age according to a normal developmental timetable built into the genes. Since each species has its own life expectancy and pattern of aging, this pattern must be predetermined and inborn, subject to only minor modifications.

Genetic-programming theory is consistent with the idea of a genetically decreed maximum life span. If, as Hayflick (1981) suggested, human cells go through the same aging process in the body as in a laboratory culture, then environmental influences should play little or no role in aging (Gerhard & Cristofalo, 1992). The human body, like a machine, would be biologically programmed to fail at a certain point, even if kept in tiptop condition.

Failure might come through *programmed senescence:* specific genes "switching off" when age-related losses (for example, in vision, hearing, and motor control) become evident. Or the biological clock might act through genes that control *hormonal changes* or cause problems in the *immune system,* such as a decline in production of antibodies, which leaves the body vulnerable to infectious disease. Researchers have reversed some effects of aging by administering human growth hormone to 21 men ages 61 to 81, suggesting that a decline in this hormone may cause fat to collect, muscles to wither, and organs to atrophy (Rudman et al., 1990). Indices of immune cell production can predict 2-year survival rates among the oldest old (R. A. Miller, 1996).

A variant of genetic-programming theory holds that humans are programmed to live long enough to reproduce. Like a booster stage, which has no further function after putting a satellite into orbit and eventually burns out, adults may continue to live past the childbearing years, but the genetic program no longer helps and may even hurt.

If genes control aging, could modification of the genetic program extend life? Genetic control of a biological process can be extremely complex and can raise ethical questions about tinkering with human life. Approximately 200 genes seem to be involved in regulating human aging (Schneider, 1992), with specific genes controlling different processes, such as those in the endocrine and immune systems. Gene therapy (see Chapter 2) seems unlikely to change the maximum life span, though it may increase average longevity (Gerhard & Cristofalo, 1992).

Variable-Rate Theories

Variable-rate theories, sometimes called *error theories,* view aging as a result of processes that vary from person to person. These processes may be influenced by both internal and external factors. In most variable-rate theories, aging involves damage due to chance errors in, or environmental assaults on, people's biological systems. Other variable-rate theories focus on internal processes such as metabolism (the process by which the body turns food and oxygen into energy), which may more directly and continuously influence the rate of aging (NIA, 1993; Schneider, 1992).

Wear-and-tear theory holds that the body ages as a result of accumulated damage to the system, like a car that develops one problem after another as its parts wear out. A human being (unlike a car) is capable of self-repair and can compensate for damage to the system. However, the cells of the heart and brain do not replace themselves: when damaged, even early in life, they die. Later in life, other cells seem to undergo a similar process: as they grow older, they are less able to repair or replace damaged components. According to wear-and-tear theory, internal and external stressors (including the accumulation of harmful materials, such as chemical by-products of metabolism) may aggravate the wearing-down process.

Free-radical theory focuses on harmful effects of *free radicals:* highly unstable atoms or molecules formed during metabolism, which react with and can damage cell membranes, cell proteins, fats, carbohydrates, and even DNA. Damage from free radicals accumulates with age; it has been associated with arthritis, muscular dystrophy, cataracts, cancer, late-onset diabetes, and neurological disorders such as Parkinson's disease (Stadtman, 1992; Wallace, 1992). Dramatic support for this theory comes from research in which fruit flies were given extra copies of genes that eliminate free radicals. Their life spans were extended by as much as one-third (W. C. Orr & Sohal, 1994). "Antioxidant" supplements of vitamins C and E and beta-carotene are popularly believed to stop free-radical activity. Research on their effects is inconclusive; but in one study, high intake of vitamin C (though not of vitamin E) and of vegetables high in beta-carotene did seem to protect against early death, particularly from heart disease (Sahyoun, Jacques, & Russell, 1996).

Rate-of-living theory suggests that the body can do just so much work, and that's all; the faster it works, the faster it wears out. According to this theory, speed of metabolism determines length of life. Fish whose metabolism is lowered by putting them in cooler water live longer than they would in warm water (Schneider, 1992). The research on dietary restriction in rodents and monkeys appears to support this theory (Masoro, 1985, 1988, 1992; Sohal & Weindruch, 1996).

Error-catastrophe theory and *somatic-mutation theory* are based on the fact that as body cells divide, errors (destruction or changes in cellular structure) occur. External and internal stressors, such as exposure to toxic substances and ultraviolet light, may alter the composition of cells and tissues in the brain, liver, and other organs. Eventually, according to this theory, an accumulation of these errors causes deterioration of body parts, malfunctioning, and death.

Autoimmune theory suggests that the immune system becomes "confused" in old age and releases antibodies that attack the body's own cells. This malfunction, called **autoimmunity,** is thought to be responsible for some aspects of aging (Spence, 1989). One form of arthritis, in which joint tissue is progressively destroyed, is believed to be caused by an autoimmune reaction.

Genetic-programming and variable-rate theories have important practical consequences. If human beings are programmed to age at a certain rate, they can do little to retard the process except, perhaps, look for controlling genes and attempt to alter them. If aging is variable, as evidence presented in the following sections seems to suggest, then lifestyle and health practices may influence it. For example, people who limit their exposure to the sun may be able to minimize wrinkling and avoid skin cancer.

It may be that each of these perspectives offers part of the truth. Genetic programming may limit the maximum length of life, but environmental and lifestyle factors may affect how closely a person approaches the maximum and in what condition.

✔ PHYSICAL CHANGES

How does aging affect physical functioning and health? Until recently, the widely accepted answer was that body systems and organs deteriorate, becoming more susceptible to problems; tissues and structures tend to become less elastic and less efficient, sometimes leading to more serious dys-

functions or disorders. Newer research however, shows that physiological changes in late adulthood are highly variable. Many of the declines commonly associated with aging may actually be *effects* of disease rather than causes (T. F. Williams, 1992).

Findings of age-related physical loss come mainly from cross-sectional studies. For example, one study of healthy adults ages 20 to 80 found a general drop in kidney functioning with age (Rowe et al., 1976). By contrast, in the Baltimore Longitudinal Study of Aging, which measured kidney functioning repeatedly in the same people, many showed only a slight decline with advancing age, and 35 percent showed no decline (Lindeman, Tobin, & Shock, 1985). In addition, some body systems decline more rapidly than others (see Figure 16-5).

As Baltes's life-span developmental approach (see Chapter 1) suggests, gains may compensate for losses. For example, the Baltimore study found that although a healthy heart's ability to pump more rapidly during exercise tends to lessen with age, blood flow diminishes very little because the heart pumps more blood with each stroke (NIH/NIA, 1993; Rodehoffer et al., 1984).

Nutrition, exercise, sanitation, and environmental pollution help determine patterns of health and disease. Obesity, for example, affects the circulatory system, the kidneys, and sugar metabolism, contributes to degenerative disorders, and tends to shorten life. Healthier lifestyles may enable an increasing number of today's young and middle-aged adults to maintain a high level of physical functioning well into old age.

THE AGING BRAIN

Changes in the brain vary considerably from one person to another (Selkoe, 1991, 1992). In normal, healthy older people, changes are generally modest and make little difference in functioning (Kemper, 1994).

After age 30, the brain loses weight, at first slightly, then more and more rapidly. By age 90, the brain may have lost up to 10 percent of its adult weight. It has been believed that this may happen because of a general loss or shrinkage of *neurons* (nerve cells) in the *cerebral cortex*, the part of the brain known as the gray matter, which handles most cognitive tasks. Some research now suggests that it is not a widespread loss of neurons that normally causes the decrease in weight, but rather a

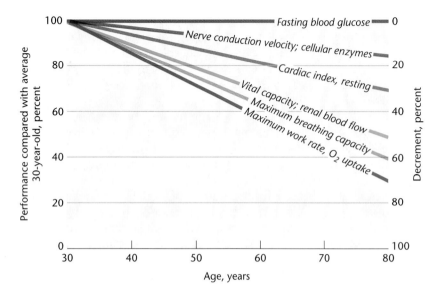

FIGURE 16-5
Declines in organ functioning. Differences in functional efficiency of various internal body systems are typically very slight in young adulthood but widen by old age. *(Source: Katchadourian, 1987.)*

loss of the brain's white matter, which contains *axons,* long projections from nerve cell bodies (Wickelgren, 1996). In addition, the *cerebellum,* which handles balance and fine motor coordination, may lose as much as 25 percent of its cells (Spence, 1989).

Along with loss of brain matter may come a gradual slowing of responses, beginning in middle age. Many adults over 70 no longer show the knee jerk; by 90, all such reflexes are typically gone (Spence, 1989). A slowdown of the central nervous system can affect not only physical coordination, but cognition as well. It can worsen performance on intelligence tests, especially timed tests, and can interfere with the ability to learn and remember (Birren et al., 1980; Salthouse, 1985; Spence, 1989). Slowed information processing may cause older people to ask others to repeat information that has been presented too quickly or not clearly enough.

Not all changes in the brain are destructive. Additional *dendrites,* branches of neurons that carry messages between them, sprout between middle age and early old age. This "resprouting" may compensate for any loss or shrinkage of neurons by increasing the number of *synapses,* or connections among nerve cells (NIH/NIA, 1993; Sapolsky, 1992; Selkoe, 1992). Even though this growth stops in late old age, its occurrence suggests that throughout most of life the brain is capable of some regeneration (Selkoe, 1992).

SENSORY AND PSYCHOMOTOR FUNCTIONING

Although some older people experience sharp declines in sensory and psychomotor functioning,

others find their daily lives virtually unchanged. Among the "old old," impairments tend to be more severe and may deprive them of activities, social life, and independence. New technologies, such as corrective surgery for cataracts and hearing aids or cochlear implants to correct hearing loss, help many older adults avoid these limitations.

Vision

With the help of glasses or contact lenses, most older people can see fairly well. Farsightedness (difficulty seeing things up close) usually stabilizes at about age 60. However, many older adults have no better than 20/70 vision and have trouble perceiving depth or color or doing such things as reading, sewing, shopping, and cooking. Losses in visual contrast sensitivity can cause difficulty reading very small or very light print (Akutsu, Legge, Ross, & Schuebel, 1991; D. W. Kline & Scialfa, 1996). Large print, with thick, dark letters on a light or white background, is more readable for both older and younger adults.

Vision problems can cause accidents both in and outside the home. Driving may be seriously affected, especially at night. Older eyes do not adapt as well to dim light; they are more sensitive to glare and have trouble locating and reading signs (D. W. Kline et al., 1992; Kline & Scialfa, 1996; Kosnik, Winslow, Kline, Rasinski, & Sekuler, 1988). Drivers age 75 and older have a higher accident rate than any other age group except those under 26. The most common causes of accidents involving older drivers are improper left turns, failure to yield the right of way, and collisions in intersections (Wiseman & Souder, 1996). These may be related not so much to loss of visual acuity (sharpness of vision) as to lack of visual attentiveness and reduced cognitive functioning (Owsley, Ball, Sloane, Roenker, & Bruni, 1991).

More than half of people over 65 develop *cataracts,* cloudy or opaque areas in the lens of the eye that cause blurred vision (USDHHS, 1993). Surgery to remove cataracts is usually very successful and is one of the most common operations among older Americans (NIA, 1995a). *Age-related macular degeneration,* in which the center of the retina gradually loses the ability to sharply distinguish fine details, is the leading cause of functional blindness in older adults (Research to Prevent Blindness, 1994). Smokers are about 2½ times as likely as nonsmokers to develop this condition (Christen, Glynn, Manson, Ajani, & Buring, 1996; Seddon, Willett, Speizer, & Hankinson, 1996). More moderate visual problems can often be helped by corrective lenses, medical or surgical treatment, or changes in the environment (refer back to Box 16-2). A complete examination by a specialist every 1 to 2 years can detect most eye diseases early enough for effective treatment (NIA, 1995a).

Hearing

About 1 out of 3 people ages 65 to 74, and about half of those 85 and older, have hearing loss that interferes with daily life (NIA, 1995c). Men, especially, lose sensitivity to high frequencies (D. W. Kline & Scialfa, 1996). Difficulty in hearing high-pitched sounds makes it hard to hear what other people are saying, especially when there is competing noise from radio or television or a buzz of several people talking at once.

Hearing aids can help; but no more than 1 out of 5 older adults who need a hearing aid own one, and fewer than half of those over 75 who do own one use it regularly (Jerger, Chmiel, Wilson, & Luchi, 1995). Conventional hearing aids magnify background noises as well as the sounds a person wants to hear. Newer, more expensive microchip technology can filter out distortion, and volume can be individually adjusted.

People should have their hearing checked if they find it hard to understand words, if they complain that other people are "mumbling," especially when there is background noise, if they find certain sounds overly loud or annoying, or if they do not enjoy parties, television, or concerts because they miss much of what goes on (NIA, 1995c).

Taste and Smell

What you taste very often depends on what you can smell, and losses in these senses are a normal part of aging. When older people complain that their food does not taste good anymore, it may be because they have fewer taste buds in the tongue and also because the olfactory bulb—the organ in the brain that is responsible for the sense of smell—has withered. Sensitivity to sour, salty, and bitter flavors may be affected more than sensitivity to sweetness (Spitzer, 1988).

Many older people compensate for loss of taste by eating more highly seasoned foods. Some over-salt their food, possibly contributing to high blood

The hearing aid in this man's ear makes it easier for him to understand his young granddaughter's high-pitched speech. About one-third of 65- to 74-year-olds and one-half of those 85 and older have some degree of hearing loss that interferes with everyday activities, but only about 1 in 5 has a hearing aid, and many of those who do own one do not use it regularly. *(Barbara Kirk/The Stock Market)*

pressure. Others eat less and become undernourished. One study found a significant correlation between poor nutrition and lack of odor perception in older adults, but it is not clear which causes which (Griep et al., 1995). Women seem to retain the senses of taste and smell better than men (Ship & Weiffenbach, 1993).

Strength, Coordination, and Reaction Time

Older people can do most of the things younger ones can, but more slowly (Birren, Woods, & Williams, 1980; Salthouse, 1985). They have less strength than they once had and are limited in activities requiring endurance or the ability to carry heavy loads. Adults generally lose about 10 to 20 percent of their strength up to age 70, especially in the muscles of the lower body, and more after that; some people in their seventies or eighties have only half the strength they had at 30 (Spence, 1989; Spirduso & MacRae, 1990).

New research has found that such losses may be reversible, even very late in life. High-resistance weight training led to significant gains in muscular strength, size, and functional mobility in 10 nursing home residents in their nineties (Fiatarone et al., 1990). After 8 weeks of weight lifting, they increased their muscle strength by an average of 174 percent. Preliminary findings from an expanded study show unprecedented evidence of new muscle fiber growth (Fiatarone et al., 1994). This finding of *plasticity* or modifiability of performance, in the very old is important because people whose muscles have atrophied are more likely to suffer falls and fractures and to need help with tasks of day-to-day living.

Even response time, which is generally related to neurological changes, can respond to training. Older people who played videogames for 11 weeks, using joysticks and "trigger buttons," had faster reaction times after the training than did a sedentary control group (Dustman, Emmerson, Steinhaus, Shearer, & Dustman, 1992). Although training may not make older adults as quick as young ones who receive the same training, it can enable older adults to work and do everyday activities faster than they otherwise would (D. C. Park, 1992). Perhaps, with many young people today playing rapid-response computer games, we will not see such extensive declines in motor skills when this young adult generation gets older.

Slowed reaction time and less efficient coordination, when combined with visual deficits, can make driving risky; and, especially in rural and suburban areas, driving can make the difference between active participation in society and enforced isolation (Wiseman & Souder, 1996). In many communities, defensive driving courses and regular retesting of older drivers' vision and motor responsiveness help keep them behind the wheel as long as possible. Most older people recognize the slowdown in their functioning and are sensibly cautious. They drive more slowly, for shorter distances, along easier routes, and only in daylight (Sterns et al., 1985). Meanwhile, highway engineers explore ways of making signs easier to read and intersections safer (refer back to Box 16-2). With increasing numbers of older drivers on the road, communities will need to review driver education programs and safety regulations.

SEXUAL FUNCTIONING

Do you expect to give up interest in sex when you get old? Probably not, and neither do most older adults. Yet the physical aspect of sex was not scientifically recognized as a normal element of the lives of older people until the 1960s, with the pioneering research of William H. Masters and Virginia E. Johnson (1966, 1981) and the findings of the Duke University Longitudinal Study. More recent reports also indicate a rich diversity of sexual experience well into late adulthood (B. M. King, 1996; Shiavi, 1990; Shiavi, Mandeli, & Schreiner-Engel, 1994; Starr, 1995).

People who had active sexual lives during their younger years are likely to remain sexually active in later life. The most important factor in maintaining sexual functioning is consistent sexual activity over the years. A healthy man who has been sexually active can usually continue some form of active sexual expression into his seventies or eighties. Women are physiologically able to be sexually active as long as they live; the main barrier to a fulfilling sexual life for them is likely to be lack of a partner (Masters & Johnson, 1966, 1981; NIA, 1994).

Sexual activity is, of course, different in late adulthood from what it was earlier. Older people tend to feel less sexual tension, usually have less frequent sexual relations, and experience less physical intensity. The sexual flush and increased muscle tone that accompany arousal are still present, but to a lesser degree. Men have lower levels of the male sex hormone testosterone; they normally take longer to develop an erection and to ejaculate, may need more manual stimulation, and may experience longer intervals between erections. Erections may be smaller and less firm and may subside more quickly after ejaculation. Erectile dysfunction may increase, especially in men with heart disease, hypertension, or diabetes, but it is often treatable (Bremner, Vitiello, & Prinz, 1983; NIA, 1994; see Chapter 14). Women's breast engorgement, nipple erection, clitoral and labial engorgement, and other signs of sexual arousal are less intense than before. The vagina may become less flexible and may need artificial lubrication. Overindulgence in alcohol may reduce men's potency and delay women's orgasms; and arthritis may limit sexual activity (NIA, 1994). Still, most older men and women can reach orgasm and can enjoy sexual expression.

Human beings are sexual beings. Even if illness or frailty prevents an older person from acting on sexual feelings, the feelings persist. More than two-thirds of 118 older men and women who attended a series of instructional programs on sexuality and aging at a California senior center had active sex partners but engaged in sexual activity less frequently than 10 years before—in most cases, because of erectile difficulties, health problems, or problems with relationships. Still, 9 out of 10, even of those over age 70, said they would like to enjoy sexual intimacy at least once a week (Wiley & Bortz, 1996).

Sexual expression can be more satisfying for older people if both young and old recognize it as normal and healthy. Older people need to accept their own sexuality without shame or embarrassment, and younger ones should avoid ridiculing or patronizing older persons who show signs of healthy sexuality. Housing arrangements should give older men and women chances to socialize, with ample privacy. Medical and social workers should consider the sexual needs of elderly people. Professionals should discuss sexual activity matter-of-factly, for example, with a heart patient who may be embarrassed to ask about it. When possible, they should avoid prescribing drugs that interfere with sexual functioning, and when such a drug must be taken, the patient should be alerted to its effects.

OTHER PHYSICAL CHANGES

Some changes typically associated with aging are obvious even to the most casual observer. Older skin tends to become paler, splotchier, and less elastic; as some fat and muscle disappear, the skin may wrinkle. Varicose veins of the legs become more common. The hair on the head turns white and becomes thinner.

Height shrinks from young adulthood to old age—on average, slightly more than 1 inch for men and as much as 2 inches for women (Whitbourne, 1985). Older adults become shorter as the disks between their spinal vertebrae atrophy; they may look even smaller because of stooped posture. In a minority of women, most of whom show symptoms of osteoporosis, the chemical composition of the bones changes, creating a greater risk of fractures; a woman over 65 has a 1-in-5 chance of breaking a hip (J. E. Brody, 1992). Thinning of the bones may cause a "widow's hump" at the back of the neck.

Although estrogen therapy can protect against osteoporosis, as well as against heart disease and some other conditions, older women tend to be skeptical about its benefits. This skepticism seems to be related not only to concern about harmful effects (refer back to Box 14-1), but to the belief that they don't need it. In one survey of 7,667 older women, more than half (55 percent) had never taken estrogen pills, and more than one-fourth (27 percent) had stopped taking them (Salamone, Pressman, Seeley, & Cauley, 1996). (Black women were excluded from this survey because they tend to have fewer hip fractures.)

As people age, body systems and organs may become more susceptible to disease. The most serious changes affect the heart. Its rhythm tends to become slower and more irregular, deposits of fat accumulate around it and may interfere with functioning, and blood pressure often rises. The digestive system, including the liver and gallbladder, remains relatively efficient. People sleep less in their later years, dream less, and have less deep sleep. Men, especially, tend to wake up during the night to urinate and have trouble going back to sleep (Webb, 1987; Woodruff, 1985).

One important change that may affect health is a decline in *reserve capacity* (or *organ reserve*), a backup capacity that helps body systems function in times of stress. Reserve capacity is like savings for a rainy day. Normally, people do not use their organs and body systems to the limit. Extra capacity is available for extraordinary circumstances, allowing each organ to put forth 4 to 10 times normal effort. Reserve capacity helps preserve *homeostasis*, the maintenance of vital functions within their optimum range (Fries & Crapo, 1981).

With age, reserve levels tend to drop. Although the decline is not usually noticeable in everyday life, older people generally cannot respond to the physical demands of stressful situations as quickly or efficiently as before. Someone who used to be able to shovel snow and then go skiing afterward may now exhaust the heart's capacity just by shoveling. Young people can almost always survive pneumonia; older people often succumb to it. As reserve capacity diminishes, people may become less able to care for themselves and more dependent on others.

However, many normal, healthy older adults barely notice changes in systemic functioning. Many activities do not require peak performance levels to be enjoyable and productive. By pacing themselves, most older adults can do just about anything they need and want to do (Katchadourian, 1987).

✔ PHYSICAL AND MENTAL HEALTH

People in the United States and many other industrialized countries have a higher standard of living and more knowledge about their bodies than ever before. Better sanitation and the widespread use of antibiotics have contributed to better health. However, along with these positive changes have come negative ones: more cancer-causing agents in foods, in the workplace, and in the air we breathe; and a faster pace of life, which contributes to hypertension and heart disease. Also, longer life increases the likelihood of physical and mental disorders that tend to occur in old age. The chances of being reasonably healthy and fit in late life often depend on lifestyle, especially exercise and diet.

HEALTH STATUS AND HEALTH CARE

Most older adults are in good general health. About three-fourths of noninstitutionalized people 65 to 74 years old and two-thirds of those 75 and older rate their own health as good (U.S. Bureau of the Census, 1995a). In fact, people over 65 have fewer colds, flu infections, and acute digestive problems than younger adults. Nevertheless, as people get older they can expect more persistent and potentially incapacitating health problems.

Most older people have one or more chronic physical conditions. Nearly half (49 percent) have arthritis; 35 percent have hypertension, and 31 percent have heart disease. Other common conditions are cataracts, sinusitis, diabetes, tinnitus (buzzing or ringing in the ears), and visual, hearing, and orthopedic impairments (AARP, 1995). Such conditions become more frequent with age, but when a condition is not severe, it can usually be managed so that it does not interfere with daily life.

Most older adults are not limited in any major activity because of health (USDHHS, 1996). About 77 percent of those who are not in institutions can handle such everyday activities as walking, eating, dressing, bathing, and toileting; and 72 percent have no health-related problems with cooking, shopping, telephoning, managing money, or housework (AARP, 1995). Limitations on what people can do increase sharply with age (see Figure 16-6) and are more common among women, minority groups, and people with low incomes (U.S. Bureau of the Census, 1992c, 1995a). Fur-

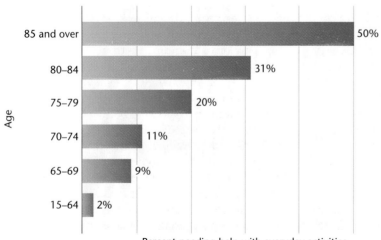

FIGURE 16-6

Percentage (as of 1990–1991) of older adults (noninstitutionalized civilians) of varying ages who needed help with daily activities. Most older adults do not need help with such everyday activities as eating, dressing, bathing, using the toilet, cooking, shopping, or housework, but the proportions who do need help rise steeply with age. *(Source: U.S. Bureau of the Census, 1995a.)*

These enthusiastic cross-country skiiers are deriving the benefits of regular physical exercise in old age, along with having fun. Exercise may well help them extend their lives and avoid some of the physical changes commonly— and apparently mistakenly—associated with "normal aging." *(Boiffin-Viviere/ Explorer/Photo Researchers)*

thermore, in the presence of chronic conditions and loss of reserve capacity, even a minor illness or injury may have serious repercussions.

Older people need more medical care than younger ones. They go to the doctor more often, are hospitalized more frequently, stay in the hospital longer, and spend more than 4 times as much money (an average of $5,360 a year) on health care. Medicare, Medicaid, and other government programs cover only about two-thirds of this cost; about 3 out of 4 people on Medicare buy additional private insurance (AARP, 1995; Treas, 1995).

Far more elderly African Americans (44 percent) than white people (27 percent) rate their health as fair or poor (AARP, 1995). The health status of elderly Hispanic Americans may fall between that of African Americans and whites (Markides, Coreil, & Rogers, 1989). Many aging members of minority groups are at high risk because of poverty, spotty histories of work and education, and inadequate health care; older African Americans and Hispanics tend to be less educated and to have lower incomes than older white people (AARP, 1995). Although their need for social and medical services is greater, they often live in areas where services are least available; and experience with segregated medical care may have taught them not to trust the health care system (Harper, 1996). Older people born in other countries often lack information about community and government services, are too proud to accept help, or feel uncomfortable dealing with agency staff members who do not understand their way of life (D. E. Gelfand, 1982).

A surprisingly large number of the "oldest old"—those over 85—need little medical care, but 50 percent need assistance with everyday self-care activities (U.S. Bureau of the Census, 1995a; refer back to Figure 16-6). Nearly one-fourth (24 percent) are in nursing homes (AARP, 1995), and in 1990 almost 18 percent were homebound. At least 25 percent of those in selected studies were hospitalized during the previous year (Longino, 1987, 1988, 1994). (We discuss issues relating to living arrangements and long-term care in Chapter 17.)

INFLUENCES ON HEALTH: EXERCISE AND DIET

No one is too old to exercise. Physical activity— walking, jogging, bicycling, or weight lifting—is just as valuable in late adulthood as earlier in the life span. Unfortunately, only about 1 out of 4 older adults reaps the benefits of regular exercise (NIA, 1995b).

A lifelong program of exercise may prevent many physical changes formerly associated with "normal aging." People who exercise tend to live longer (Rakowski & Mor, 1992). Regular exercise can strengthen the heart and lungs and decrease stress. It can protect against hypertension, hardening of the arteries, heart disease, osteoporosis, and adult-onset diabetes. It seems to help maintain speed, stamina, and strength and such basic functions as circulation and breathing. It reduces the chance of injuries by making joints and muscles stronger and more flexible, and it helps prevent or relieve lower-back pain and symptoms of arthritis. It may improve mental alertness and cognitive performance, may help relieve anxiety and mild depression, and often improves morale (Blumenthal et al., 1991; Clarkson-Smith & Hartley, 1989; Hawkins, Kramer, & Capaldi, 1992; Hill, Storandt, & Malley, 1993; NIA, 1995b; Rall, Meydani, Kehayias, Dawson-Hughes, & Roubenoff, 1996; Shay & Roth, 1992).

Of course, older people need to be realistic about what they can do. People who have been inactive should begin with small amounts of mild daily exercise, either alone or with friends, and should stop and contact a doctor if they feel ill or short of breath or experience sudden pain (NIA, 1995b).

Many older people do not eat as well as they should, whether because of diminished senses of taste and smell, dental problems, difficulty in shopping and preparing food, or inadequate income. Then too, many older people live by themselves and may not feel like fixing nourishing meals for one. One study of 474 people between 65 and 98 years of age found that most did not get enough nutrients and lacked energy. About 20 percent skipped lunch. The most common deficiencies were in calcium, zinc, and vitamins A and E (Ryan, Craig, & Finn, 1992). Vitamin deficiencies have been implicated in some mental illnesses. One study found that taking vitamin B6 can improve memory performance (Riggs, Spiro, Tucker, & Rush, 1996).

Loss of teeth due to decay or *periodontitis* (gum disease) can have serious implications for nutrition. Because people with poor or missing teeth find many foods hard to chew, they tend to eat less and to choose softer, sometimes less nutritious, foods (Wayler, Kapur, Feldman, & Chauncey, 1982). Extensive loss of teeth, especially among the poor, may reflect inadequate dental care. Although frequency of dental care has increased, in 1993 nearly half (48 percent) of Americans 65 and over reported that they had not seen a dentist during the past year (USDHHS, 1996).

MENTAL AND BEHAVIORAL DISORDERS

Decline in mental health is not typical in late life; in fact, mental illness is less common among older adults than among younger ones. In a 1-year study of 1,300 older adults, about 7 out of 10 maintained or improved their mental health (Haug, Belkgrave, & Gratton, 1984). In the United States, fewer than 14 percent of older women and fewer than 11 percent of older men have any mental disorders

(Wykle & Musil, 1993). However, mental disorders that do occur in older adults are likely to have devastating consequences.

Dementia

Confusion, forgetfulness, and personality changes sometimes associated with old age may or may not have physiological causes. The general term for physiologically based cognitive and behavioral deterioration is *dementia.* Contrary to stereotype, dementia is not an inevitable part of aging. Most dementias are irreversible, but some can be reversed with proper diagnosis and treatment (American Psychiatric Association, APA, 1994; NIA, 1993).

About 80 percent of cases of dementia among older people are caused either by cardiovascular problems, such as hypertension or a series of small strokes, by Parkinson's disease, a progressive neurological disorder characterized by tremor, stiffness, slowed movement, and unstable posture, or by Alzheimer's disease (Selkoe, 1992). When symptoms come on in several sudden steps, rather than gradually, stroke is the likeliest explanation. Small strokes can often be prevented by controlling hypertension through screening, a low-salt diet, and drugs (NIA, 1984). Brain implants of fetal tissue have improved the condition of some patients with Parkinson's disease (L. Thompson, 1992), though this method is controversial and is not widely used. Once dementia has appeared in persons with cardiovascular problems or Parkinson's disease, it is considered irreversible. So is Alzheimer's disease.

Alzheimer's Disease

Alzheimer's disease is a progressive, degenerative brain disorder that gradually robs people of intelligence, awareness, and even the ability to control their bodily functions—and finally kills them. Although the great majority of elderly people do not suffer from this malady, it is the most prevalent, and most feared, irreversible dementia.

Alzheimer's disease rarely strikes before age 50, and the risk rises dramatically with age. Estimates of its prevalence vary from 2 to 10 percent of adults over 65 and from about 13 to 50 percent of those 85 and older. Women, since they are longer-lived than men, are more at risk (D. A. Evans et al., 1989; Folstein, Bassett, Anthony, Romanoski, & Nestadt, 1991; Skoog, Nilsson, Palmertz, Andreasson, & Svanborg, 1993; "Testing for Alzheimer's Disease,"

TABLE 16-3

Alzheimer's Disease versus Normal Behavior

Normal Behavior	Symptoms of Disease
Temporarily forgetting things	Permanently forgetting recent events; asking the same questions repeatedly
Inability to do some challenging tasks	Inability to do routine tasks with many steps, such as making and serving a meal
Forgetting unusual or complex words	Forgetting simple words
Getting lost in a strange city	Getting lost on one's own block
Becoming momentarily distracted and failing to watch a child	Forgetting that a child is in one's care and leaving the house
Making mistakes in balancing a checkbook	Forgetting what the numbers in a checkbook mean and what to do with them
Misplacing everyday items	Putting things in inappropriate places where one cannot usefully retrieve them (e.g., a wristwatch in a fishbowl)
Occasional mood changes	Rapid, dramatic mood swings and personality changes; loss of initiative

SOURCE: Adapted from Alzheimer's Association (undated).

1995). The main reason so many more cases are diagnosed now than in the past, aside from increased knowledge about the disease, is that far more people now reach an age when they are likely to show signs of it. The number of patients with Alzheimer's disease is expected to rise to at least 14 million by the year 2040, as the baby boomers grow old (Friend, 1994). A 10-year delay in the average age of onset of the disease could mean a 75 percent reduction in the number of cases (Banner, 1992).

So far, the cause of most cases of Alzheimer's disease is unknown. An early-appearing form, which shows up in middle age, is thought to be inherited and seems to be related to mutant genes on chromosomes 1, 14, or 21 (Corliss, 1996; Karlinsky, Lennox, & Rossor, 1994; St. George-Hyslop et al., 1987; Schellenberg et al., 1992). A variant of a gene pair on chromosome 19, called *apoE-4*, appears to be a risk factor for some cases of the late-onset type, which appears after age 65 (Corder et al., 1993; Lennox et al., 1994; Reiman et al., 1996; Roses, 1994). Other genetic influences are being discovered at a rapid rate. Environmental influences also may play a part in late-onset Alzheimer's disease (Corliss, 1996).

First signs of the disease are often overlooked: a tendency to garble telephone messages, trouble in using words, inability to play a game of cards or tennis, or sudden episodes of extravagance. The most prominent early symptom is loss of memory, especially for recent events. More symptoms follow: confusion, irritability, restlessness, agitation, and delirium. Judgment, concentration, orientation, and speech all become impaired. (Table 16-3 compares early warning signs of Alzheimer's disease with normal mental lapses.) By the end, the patient cannot understand or use language, does not recognize family members, and cannot eat without help.

So far, the only sure diagnosis depends on analysis of brain tissue, which can be done only by autopsy after death. The brain of a person with Alzheimer's disease shows such abnormalities as loss of nerve cells and tangled masses within nerve cells. Between nerve cells, large chunks of *amyloid plaque* may appear; these are formed by a protein called *beta-amyloid* along with fragments of dead dendrites. These changes are far more pronounced in people suffering from Alzheimer's disease than in other elderly people (Hyman, Van Hoesen, Damasio, & Barnes, 1984).

Doctors usually diagnose Alzheimer's disease in a living person through neurological or memory tests and by ruling out other conditions. Diagnoses made in this way are 80 to 90 percent accurate, as confirmed by autopsy (Banner, 1992). More accurate diagnosis would allow treatment of ailments that are sometimes misdiagnosed as Alzheimer's disease.

Although no cure for Alzheimer's disease has

been discovered, drugs to improve memory and behavior are being tested (G. D. Cohen, 1987; K. L. Davis et al., 1992; Farlow et al., 1992). In the early stages, memory training and memory aids may improve functioning (Camp, Markley, & Kramer, 1983; Camp & McKitrick, 1992; McKitrick, Camp, & Black, 1992). Drugs can relieve agitation, lighten depression, and help patients sleep. Proper nourishment and fluid intake, together with exercise and physical therapy, may be helpful.

Tacrine (sold under the name Cognex) was the first medication for Alzheimer's disease approved by the U.S. Food and Drug Administration. A second drug, sold under the name Aricept, was recently approved. These drugs are generally prescribed at early stages to maintain or raise brain levels of the neurotransmitter acetylcholine, a chemical involved in communication between nerve cells. Although some patients respond well to these drugs, others show little effect, and any gains are lost when their use is discontinued. Tacrine, which must be taken 4 times a day, can have harmful side effects, such as nausea, gastrointestinal distress, and liver damage. Aricept, taken once a day, seems to produce fewer side effects.

These drugs merely control symptoms; they do not stop the underlying deterioration. Clinical trials are under way to see whether antioxidants, such as vitamin E, can slow the progress of the disease (Marx, 1996). Preventive therapies under study include drugs that could reduce concentrations of apoE-4 or deactivate enzymes involved in formation of amyloid plaque (Marx, 1996; Sisodia, Koo, Beyreuther, Unterbeck, & Price, 1990; Whitson, Selkoe, & Cotman, 1989; Cai, Golde, & Younkin, 1993). There is evidence that estrogen or anti-inflammatory drugs, such as ibuprofen, can greatly diminish the likelihood of developing Alzheimer's (W. Stewart, Kawas, Corrada, & Metler, in press; Tang et al., 1996; see Chapter 14). If a preventive treatment is developed in the future, brain scans might identify people genetically at risk, who could then receive the treatment.

The whole family suffers from Alzheimer's disease (Fisher & Lieberman, 1994). The patient's inability to reciprocate expressions of affection and caring may rob relationships of intimacy while imposing a major burden on caregivers. The uncertainty of the diagnosis may be even more stressful than the disease itself (Garwick et al., 1994). Caregivers may be under more stress than the patient, who may become verbally abusive, violent, and dangerous to self and others. Some caregivers go to such lengths to provide care that they jeopardize their own well-being, giving up career opportunities and neglecting their families (Barnhart, 1992; Lund, 1993a; see Chapter 15).

Which Mental Health Conditions Are Reversible?

When the television personality Hugh Downs brought his aging father to live with him and his family, they suspected that the elderly man was developing Alzheimer's disease. Actually, his lapses of memory and his tendency to get lost turned out to be combined effects of several prescription drugs. With a change of medications, his behavior returned to normal; he even began to look younger. For the next 10 years, until he died at 83, he worked in his son's and daughter-in-law's companies and built up a small estate by investing the income (Downs, 1993).

Many older people and their families mistakenly believe that they can do nothing about mental and behavioral problems, even though close to 100 such conditions, including about 10 percent of dementia cases, can be cured or alleviated. Although an estimated 8 percent of noninstitutionalized older adults need psychiatric services, only about 5 percent get treatment (B. Burns & Taub, 1990). Many older adults, especially those in minority groups and those who live in rural areas, are too proud or too fearful to admit they need treatment, think they cannot afford it, or do not realize their symptoms are treatable (Fellin & Powell, 1988; Roybal, 1988). Private treatment can be expensive; not every community offers low-cost mental health services, and not enough programs reach out to find those in need.

Sometimes, as in the case of Hugh Down's father, apparent dementia turns out to be a side effect of drug intoxication. An older person may take as many as a dozen different medicines. Because physicians do not always ask what other medicines a patient is taking, they may prescribe drugs that interact harmfully. Also, because of age-related changes in the body's metabolism, a dosage that would be right for a 40-year-old may be an overdose for an 80-year-old.

Besides drug intoxication, other common reversible conditions include delirium, metabolic or infectious disorders, malnutrition, anemia, alcoholism, low thyroid functioning, minor head injuries, and depression (NIA, 1980, 1993; Wykle & Musil, 1993). Let's look at depression.

Depression

Art Buchwald is a Pulitzer prize–winning author whose humorous columns appear in some 550 newspapers; for four decades he has made millions of Americans laugh. In private life, however, Buchwald has struggled for years with depression so serious that twice he came close to suicide (Buchwald, 1994).

The serious clinical syndrome called a *major depressive disorder* is different from "the blues." It lasts at least 2 weeks, during which time a person shows extreme sadness and loss of interest or pleasure in life. Other symptoms include weight changes, sleeplessness, feelings of worthlessness or inappropriate guilt, loss of memory, inability to concentrate, and thoughts of death or suicide (APA, 1994; American Association for Geriatric Psychiatry, AAGP, 1996). Other forms of clinical depression are either more transient or milder ("Depression," 1995).

About 16 percent of American adults have suffered clinical depression, 10 percent within a given year (Blazer et al., 1994; "Depression," 1995; Kessler et al., 1994). Women are 2 to 3 times as likely as men to be depressed (Wolfe et al., 1996), perhaps because women are more likely to see doctors and to report physical problems which often accompany depression (Wykle & Musil, 1993).

Contrary to popular belief, depression is diagnosed less often in late life. According to one survey, only 1 percent of older adults experience major depressive disorders in a given year, as compared with 4 to 5 percent of young and middle-aged adults (Wolfe, Morrow, & Fredrickson, 1996).

However, *symptoms* of depression are *more* common among older adults than among younger ones. Many older people suffer from aches and pains or chronic illness, have lost spouses, siblings, friends, and sometimes children, take mood-altering medicines, and feel that they have no control over their lives. Any of these conditions can make a person depressed. An estimated 10 to 15 percent of older people living in the community, and a much larger percentage of those in hospitals and nursing homes, show signs of depression (AAGP, 1996; Blazer, 1989; Jefferson & Griest, 1993; Wolfe et al., 1996).

It seems likely, then, that depression is underdiagnosed in older adults. It may be mistaken for dementia, or it may be seen as a natural accompaniment of aging (AAGP, 1996; George, 1993;

Some older people become depressed as a result of physical and emotional losses, and some apparent "dementia" is actually due to depression. Correct diagnosis is important because depression can often be relieved if older people seek help. *(Bill Gillette/Stock, Boston)*

Jefferson & Griest, 1993). It may be masked by physical illness, or older people may simply be less likely to *say* they feel depressed—perhaps because of a belief that depression is a sign of weakness or that it will lift by itself (Gallo, Anthony, & Muthen, 1994; Wolfe et al., 1996). Elderly black adults are particularly likely to be misdiagnosed; their symptoms are often mistaken for schizophrenia (Harper, 1996). Unfortunately, depression that is not properly diagnosed and treated may worsen. One indication that depression is often overlooked in older adults is the high prevalence of suicide in this age group (see Chapter 18).

Depression can have various causes, which may act together. Some people may be genetically predisposed to it through a biochemical imbalance in the brain. Depression is 1½ to 3 times more common in close relatives of depressed people than in the general population (APA, 1994), and a twin study found a modest genetic influence (Kendler, Walters, Truett, et al., 1994). Failure to maintain a healthful lifestyle with adequate exercise can contribute to depression. Stressful events or loneliness may trigger it. It can be a side effect of certain medications (Jefferson & Greist, 1993; "Listening to Depression," 1995). Nearly half of all caregivers of patients with Alzheimer's disease suffer from depression ("Alzheimer's and Stress," 1994).

A strong network of family and friends can help older people ward off depression or find help for it. Cognitive-behavioral psychotherapy, which teaches patients to recognize and correct negative thinking and also uses positive and negative reinforcement, seems to work best and most quickly for older adults (Koenig & Blazer, 1992). Antidepressant drugs can restore the chemical balance in the brain, but they may have unwanted side effects, including inhibition of sexual functioning (Jefferson & Greist, 1993; "Listening to Depression," 1995; "Sexual Side Effects," 1994). Electroconvulsive therapy (ECT), also called shock therapy, may be necessary in severe cases.

✔ ASPECTS OF COGNITIVE DEVELOPMENT

The adage "You can't teach an old dog new tricks" does not apply to human beings. Older people can and do continue to learn new information and skills, and they can remember and use those they already know well. Age often brings changes in cognitive functioning, but not all are detrimental. Let's look first at intelligence, then at wisdom, which is popularly associated with the later years, then at memory, and finally at education in late life.

INTELLIGENCE: DOES IT GROW OR DECLINE?

Does intelligence diminish in late adulthood? During the 1970s, that question became a major issue among psychologists. In one camp were those who challenged the "myth" of general cognitive decline in late life (Baltes & Schaie, 1974, 1976; Schaie & Baltes, 1977). In the other camp were those who dismissed this view as too rosy (J. L. Horn & Donaldson, 1976, 1977). However, the findings of these two groups of investigators were not truly contradictory. Their differences lay mainly in emphasis, and their positions have drawn closer with time. It is becoming clearer, in examining results of intelligence tests given to adults of various ages, that although some abilities—chiefly in nonverbal tasks and in solving unfamiliar problems—may decline, others remain stable or even improve throughout most of adult life. Furthermore, there is much individual variation, suggesting that declines are not inevitable and may be preventable.

A number of physical and psychological factors that tend to lower older people's test scores may lead to underestimation of their intelligence:

■ *Physical health.* Older adults, like younger ones, do their best when they are physically fit and well rested. Neurophysiological problems, high blood pressure, or other cardiovascular problems, which can affect blood flow to the brain, can interfere with cognitive performance (Sands & Meredith, 1992; Schaie, 1990).
■ *Vision, hearing, and coordination.* Older adults may have trouble understanding test instructions and doing certain tasks.
■ *Speed.* The time limits on most intelligence tests are particularly hard on older people. Because both physical and psychological processes, including perceptual abilities (Schaie, 1994), tend to slow with age, older adults do better when they are allowed as much time as they need (Hertzog, 1989; J. L. Horn & Cattell, 1966; Schaie & Hertzog, 1983). However, some psychologists argue that because speed is a function of the central nervous system, it is a true indicator of cognitive functioning. And some studies suggest that even when tests are not timed, older people do not do as well as younger ones (Botwinick, 1984; Salthouse, 1991).
■ *Attitudes toward a testing situation.* Test anxiety is common among older adults, particularly if they are unfamiliar with the testing situation and have not taken tests for a long time. They may lack confidence in their ability to solve test problems, and their expectation that they will do poorly may become a self-fulfilling prophecy. Fear of failing memory may make them skip questions when they are not sure they know the answers (Cavanaugh & Morton, 1989). They may lack interest and motivation: doing well may not mean much to them unless they are taking the test to qualify for a job or for some other important purpose. Finally, tests developed for children may be inappropriate for older people.

Many of the early findings that showed declines in certain aspects of intelligence were based on cross-sectional data that may confound cohort with age. Younger adults may have done better than older adults because they were healthier and better-nourished, had more or better schooling, had gained more information from television, had jobs that depended on thinking rather than on physical labor, or had more—and more recent—

experience taking tests. An analysis of adult IQ scores more than three decades ago (Birren & Morrison, 1961) found that educational level was a more significant influence than age; thus differences between older and younger cohorts should flatten out as young adults who have had the benefit of greater educational opportunity grow older.

Longitudinal studies do not show the marked declines reported in cross-sectional studies. However, this research design may favor an older sample because of attrition and practice effects. People who score poorly are more likely to drop out of a study, and those who remain benefit from having taken the tests before.

Sequential Testing: The Seattle Longitudinal Study

The Seattle Longitudinal Study of Adult Intelligence, conducted by K. Warner Schaie and his colleagues (Schaie, 1979, 1983, 1988a, 1988b, 1990, 1994, 1996; Schaie & Herzog, 1983, 1986; Schaie & Strother, 1968), sought to overcome drawbacks of both cross-sectional and longitudinal research. Although this ongoing study is called longitudinal, it uses sequential testing (see Chapter 1), a combination of cross-sectional, longitudinal, and time-lag methods.

The study (introduced in Chapter 14) began in 1956 with 500 randomly chosen participants: 25 men and 25 women in each 5-year age bracket from 20 to 70. Participants took a battery of timed tests of five primary mental abilities (Thurstone, 1938; see Table 16-4). Additional measures of cognitive abilities were added as the study progressed. Every 7 years, the original participants were retested and new participants were added; by 1994, about 5,000 people, forming a broadly diverse socioeconomic sample, had been tested. The researchers also took personal and health histories and administered psychological tests.

What does the study tell us about intelligence in older adults? One encouraging finding is that cognitive decline is not across-the-board. If people live long enough, their functioning usually will flag at some point; but very few weaken in all or even most abilities, and many improve in some areas. Most fairly healthy adults do not show any significant drop until the early sixties, and then only small losses until the seventies. Losses in the eighties and nineties show up mainly in unfamiliar, highly complex, challenging, or stressful circumstances.

As in other research, the Seattle study found that *fluid* abilities tend to decline early, but *crystallized* intelligence remains stable or even increases into the seventies. After that, performance on tests of crystallized intelligence also dips, but this may be

TABLE 16-4

Tests of Primary Mental Abilities Given in Seattle Longitudinal Study of Adult Intelligence

Test	Ability Measured	Task	Type of Intelligence
Verbal meaning	Recognition and understanding of words	Find synonym by matching stimulus word with another word from multiple-choice list	Crystallized
Number	Applying numerical concepts	Check simple addition problems	Crystallized
Word fluency	Retrieving words from long-term memory	Think of as many words as possible beginning with a given letter, in a set time period	Part crystallized, part fluid
Spatial orientation	Rotating objects mentally in two-dimensional space	Select rotated examples of figure to match stimulus figure	Fluid
Inductive reasoning	Identifying regularities and inferring principles and rules	Complete a letter series	Fluid

SOURCE: Schaie, 1989.

due to older people's slower response time. Women show earlier losses in fluid abilities, men in crystallized abilities.

The most striking feature of the Seattle findings is the tremendous variation among individuals. Some participants showed declines during their thirties, some not until their seventies; and about one-third of those over 70 did better than the average young adult. Fewer than one-third at age 74, and fewer than half at age 81, had deteriorated significantly during the previous 7 years. Even in their eighties, more than half were maintaining their competence in at least four of the five primary abilities. Some people remained relatively strong in one area, others in another. There was far more variability among older adults than among younger ones.

People with higher scores tended to be healthier and better-educated and to have higher incomes. Of course, these factors are related. People with higher incomes tend to be better-educated than poorer people and have access to better medical care. High scorers were also more likely to have stable marriages, intelligent spouses, and active, stimulating lives (Gruber-Baldini, 1991; Schaie, 1990, 1994; Schaie & Willis, 1996).

More recent cohorts scored higher in inductive reasoning, verbal meaning, and spatial orientation. However, this trend is leveling off for inductive reasoning and verbal meaning; and performance in numerical skills has actually declined among the most recent cohorts (see Figure 16-7). Thus we may

be reaching a point where older adults are no longer at much of a competitive disadvantage and, at least in numerical skills, may even outperform younger ones. At the same time, we may be approaching a limit on the improvement possible for successive older cohorts as a result of education and healthy lifestyles (Schaie, 1990).

Cognitive Competence and Everyday Tasks

One purpose of intelligence is to adapt to the problems of daily life. Research has found a strong relationship between fluid intelligence and certain practical skills, such as the ability of older adults to read a map or a newspaper and to perform everyday tasks (Diehl, Willis, & Schaie, 1994; Willis & Schaie, 1986a).

As people get older, an important test of cognitive competence is the ability to live independently, as measured by seven *instrumental activities of daily living (IADLs):* managing finances, shopping for necessities, using the telephone, obtaining transportation, preparing meals, taking medication, and housekeeping (Fillenbaum, 1985). Schaie and his colleagues gave older adults tasks in each of these seven areas: for example, filling out a Medicare form, reading a medicine bottle label, filling out a mail-order catalog form, reading a nutrition label on a food package, looking up an emergency telephone number, figuring out a bus schedule, and reading instructions for using a household appliance. Fluid intelligence and, to a

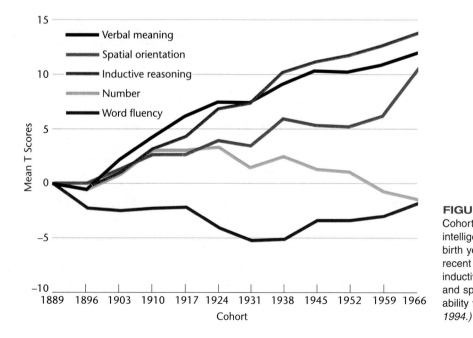

FIGURE 16-7
Cohort differences in scores on intelligence tests. In a group with mean birth years from 1889 to 1966, more recent cohorts scored higher on inductive reasoning, verbal meaning, and spatial orientation, but lower in ability with numbers. *(Source: Schaie, 1994.)*

Many older people are joining the computer age and learning new skills. "Use it or lose it" applies to mental as well as physical capacity. In fact, research has found that older people can expand their cognitive performance with training and practice. *(David Lissy/The Picture Cube)*

lesser extent, crystallized intelligence accounted for more than half of the variance in performance. Follow-up observations of older people at home—putting medicine capsules in a reminder device, completing a health insurance form, activating call forwarding on the telephone, and following instructions for use of a microwave oven—produced similar correlations (Schaie & Willis, 1996).

Again, health and educational background affected the results through their effects on cognitive ability. This relationship may be reciprocal. Not only can poor health and lack of education limit cognition, but people with higher cognitive ability tend to get better educations and take care of their health (Schaie & Willis, 1996).

Can Older People Improve Their Cognitive Performance?

A key issue separating psychologists with a relatively optimistic view of cognitive development in late adulthood from those with a less positive view is plasticity, or modifiability: whether cognitive performance in older adults can be improved with training and practice.

Plasticity is a key feature of Baltes's life-span developmental approach (see Chapter 1), and he and his colleagues have been in the forefront of research on effects of training. Several of these studies have been based on the Adult Development and Enrichment Project (ADEPT), originated at Pennsylvania State University (Baltes & Willis, 1982; Blieszner, Willis, & Baltes, 1981; Plemons,

Willis, & Baltes, 1978; Willis, Blieszner, & Baltes, 1981). A 7-year follow-up of ADEPT found that participants who received training declined significantly less than a control group (Willis, 1990; Willis & Nesselroade, 1990). In one study based on ADEPT, adults with an average age of 70 who received training in figural relations (rules for determining the next figure in a series), a measure of fluid intelligence, improved more than a control group who received no training. A third group who worked with the same training materials and problems without formal instruction also did better than the control group, and this self-taught group maintained their gains better after 1 month (Blackburn, Papalia-Finlay, Foye, & Serlin, 1988). Apparently the opportunity to work out their own solutions fostered more lasting learning.

In *individual* training connected with the Seattle Longitudinal Study (Schaie, 1990, 1994; Schaie & Willis, 1986; Willis & Schaie, 1986b), older people who had already shown declines in intelligence gained significantly in two fluid abilities: spatial orientation and, especially, inductive reasoning. In fact, about 4 out of 10 participants regained levels of proficiency they had shown 14 years earlier. Men improved more from training in inductive reasoning and women from training in spatial orientation, to the point of closing an earlier gender gap in the latter ability. Gains measured in the laboratory showed substantial correlations with objective measures of everyday functioning (Willis, Jay, Diehl, & Marsiske, 1992; Schaie, 1994).

In both the ADEPT and Seattle studies, trained

participants retained an edge over an untrained control group, even after 7 years (Schaie, 1994, 1996). Longitudinal findings suggest that training may enable older adults not only to recover lost competence but even to surpass their previous attainments (Schaie & Willis, 1996). (Later in this chapter, we discuss the results of memory training.)

Cognitive deterioration, then, may often be related to disuse (Schaie, 1994). Much as many aging athletes can call on physical reserves, older people who get training, practice, and social support seem to be able to draw on mental reserves. Adults may be able to maintain or expand this reserve capacity and avoid cognitive decline by engaging in a lifelong program of mental exercise (Dixon & Baltes, 1986).

Mechanics and Pragmatics of Intelligence

Old age "adds as it takes away," said the poet William Carlos Williams in one of three books of verse written between his first stroke at the age of 68 and his death at 79. This comment seems to sum up current findings about cognitive functioning in late adulthood.

Baltes and his colleagues (Baltes, 1993; Dixon and Baltes, 1986; Dixon, 1992) have proposed a *dual-process model,* which includes aspects of intelligence that may continue to advance, as well as aspects that are more likely to deteriorate. This model identifies and seeks to measure two dimensions of intelligence: *mechanics* and *pragmatics.*

Mechanics of intelligence consist of content-free functions of information processing and problem solving. This dimension, like fluid intelligence, is physiologically based and often declines with age. For example, in adults over 70, age-related losses in sharpness of vision and hearing are predictors of cognitive functioning (Lindenberger & Baltes, 1994).

Pragmatics of intelligence include such potential growth areas as practical thinking, application of accumulated knowledge and skills, specialized expertise, professional productivity, and wisdom. This domain, which often continues to develop in late adulthood, is similar to, but broader than, crystallized intelligence.

Older adults are likely to improve in the "pragmatic" use of the information and know-how they have garnered from education, work, and life experience. And, through *selective optimization*

with compensation, older people can often use their pragmatic strengths to compensate for weakened mechanical abilities. For example, the pianist Vladimir Horowitz, in his eighties, slowed his tempos and chose a less technically demanding repertoire, but his interpretations now showed extraordinary ripeness and finesse. A critic for *The New York Times* wrote of him: "Power does not necessarily diminish with age but simply changes its shape" (Schonberg, 1992, p. 288).

WISDOM: A PROVINCE OF OLD AGE?

The wise person is a familiar figure in folklore; King Solomon in the Bible is one example. Many cultural traditions regard wisdom as the province of old age. Today, with the graying of the planet, wisdom has become an important topic of psychological research. Erikson (as we'll see in Chapter 17) saw wisdom as an aspect of late-life personality development. Other investigators, such as Gisela Labouvie-Vief (1990a, 1990b), define wisdom as an extension of postformal thought, a synthesis of reason and emotion. Another approach, which has roots in eastern philosophy, focuses on the spiritual domain.

Baltes, in contrast, classifies wisdom as a *cognitive* ability, a component of intelligence that can be studied and tested (Blanchard-Fields, Brannan, & Camp, 1987). Wisdom, in Baltes's dual-process model, is a part of the pragmatics of intelligence, which may emerge or grow in late adulthood (Baltes, 1993; Dittmann-Kohli & Baltes, 1990). Baltes (1993) defines wisdom as expert knowledge of the fundamental pragmatics of life, "permitting excellent judgment and advice about important and uncertain matters" (p. 586). These "fundamental pragmatics" consist of knowledge and skills having to do with the conduct, interpretation, and meaning of life. In other words, wisdom is knowing how to live well.

Not everyone becomes wise, just as not everyone becomes an expert in chess or computers. In fact, Baltes suggests, wisdom may be fairly rare. Although it may develop at any period of life, aging would seem to provide favorable conditions for its growth. Besides general mental ability, these conditions, according to Baltes, include education or training, practice in using the requisite skills, guidance from mentors, leadership experience, and professional specialization.

BOX 16-3   FOOD FOR THOUGHT

ARE OLDER PEOPLE WISER?

Do people get wiser as they get older? To answer that question, Jacqui Smith and Paul B. Baltes (1990) asked 60 well-educated German professionals ages 25 to 81 to think aloud and come up with plans for resolving the following normative or nonnormative problems encountered by four fictitious characters: (1) Elizabeth, a 33-year-old professional woman, is trying to decide whether to accept a major promotion or start a family. (2) Jack, a 63-year-old man whose company is closing the branch office where he works, has been offered a choice between early retirement and a move to the main office for 2 or 3 years. (3) Michael, a 28-year-old laid-off mechanic, can either move to another city to look for work or stay home with his preschool children while his wife continues the nursing career she has just gone back to. (4) Joyce, a 60-year-old widow who has just finished a business course and opened her own firm, now learns that her son has been left with two young children and wants her to help care for them.

A panel of experienced human-services professionals rated the responses according to criteria drawn up by the researchers. To be considered wise, an answer had to show "expert knowledge in life planning, life management, and life review" (p. 495). Such knowledge would include insight into human development and the ability to offer good judgment, advice, and commentary about difficult life problems. A wise response would also show awareness that life is unpredictable, that its conditions vary greatly, and that people differ in values, goals, and priorities, so that no one solution is best for everyone.

Of the 240 solutions, only 5 percent were rated wise—hardly surprising, since wisdom is extraordinary and rare. What may seem more surprising is that older participants showed no more wisdom than younger adults; the 11 "wise" responses were distributed nearly evenly among young, middle-aged, and older adults. The young and middle-aged participants gave wiser responses to the problems of young people ("Elizabeth" and "Michael") and the normative problem of an older person ("Jack"), while the oldest group gave its best answers to the nonnormative problem of an older person ("Joyce"). In looking at the problems of young adults, older adults tended to be more dogmatic than younger and middle-aged adults and to show less insight and knowledge about strategies and decision making.

Wisdom is not, then, confined to any one age group; it seems to emerge when people are faced with issues from current, everyday life. To see whether certain kinds of life experience lend themselves to the development of wisdom, the researchers set up a similar study of a group of distinguished middle-aged and older adults (average age, 67) who had been identified by others as wise (Baltes, Staudinger, Maercker, & Smith, 1993). Nearly 60 percent of these people had published autobiographies, and more than 40 percent of them had been in the German resistance movement against the Nazis. When presented with two dilemmas—the one described above about the 60-year-old widow and another about a phone call from a friend who intends to commit suicide—these "wisdom nominees" outdid older clinical psychologists (who had previously performed best on such tasks), as well as control groups of older and younger adults with similar education and professional standing.

Of course, the researchers who conducted these studies had drawn up their own definition and criteria of wisdom, which affected their findings. Other definitions and criteria might have produced different results.

To test the relationship between age and wisdom, Baltes and his colleagues compared the responses given by adults of various ages and professional backgrounds who were presented with hypothetical dilemmas. The researchers found that wisdom, though not exclusively the province of old age, is one area in which older people, especially those who have had certain kinds of experiences, can hold their own or better (see Box 16-3).

MEMORY: HOW DOES IT CHANGE?

Failing memory is often considered a sign of aging. The man who always kept his schedule in his head now has to write it in a calendar; the woman who takes several medicines now measures out each day's dosages and puts them where she is sure to see them. Yet in memory, as in intelligence, older people's functioning varies greatly. To understand why, we need to look more closely than in earlier chapters at how memory works.*

Short-Term Memory

Researchers assess short-term memory by asking a person to repeat a sequence of numbers, either in the order in which they were presented (*digit span forward*) or in reverse order (*digit span backward*). Digit span forward ability holds up well with advancing age (Craik & Jennings, 1992; Poon, 1985; Wingfield & Stine, 1989), but digit span backward performance is typically better in young adults than in older ones (Craik & Jennings, 1992; Lovelace, 1990). What accounts for this difference? A widely accepted explanation is that short-term memory has two components, primary memory and working memory, one of which retains its efficiency with age while the other does not.

Primary memory is a passive "holding tank" for small amounts of recently experienced information. If you do nothing to help you remember a telephone number you have just looked up, it will stay in primary memory for about 30 seconds. Age differences on tasks requiring only primary memory are very small; thus, an older adult is about as good as a younger adult at remembering a series of numbers in the order presented.

Working memory (see Chapter 8) not only holds information but manipulates it, and its capacity to do so is believed to shrink with age. A key factor seems to be the complexity of the task (Kausler, 1990; Wingfield & Stine, 1989). Tasks that require only *rehearsal*, or repetition, show very little decline. Tasks that require *reorganization* or *elaboration* show greater falloff (Craik & Jennings, 1992). For example, if you are asked to verbally rearrange a series of items (such as "Band-Aid, elephant, newspaper") in order of increasing size ("Band-Aid, newspaper, elephant"), you must call to mind your previous knowledge of Band-Aids, newspapers, and elephants (Cherry & Park, 1993). More mental effort is needed to keep this additional information in mind, using more of the limited capacity of working memory.

Long-Term Memory

Long-term memory has three main components: episodic memory, semantic memory, and procedural memory.

*This discussion is largely indebted to Smith and Earles, 1996.

Do you remember what you had for breakfast this morning? Did you lock your car when you parked it? Such information is stored in *episodic memory* (see Chapter 6), the component of long-term memory most likely to deteriorate with age. The ability to recall newly encountered information, especially, seems to drop off (Poon, 1985; A. D. Smith & Earles, 1996).

Because episodic memory is linked to specific events, you retrieve an item from this mental "diary" by reconstructing the original experience in your mind. Older adults are less able to do this, perhaps because they focus less on context (where something happened, who was there) and so have fewer connections to jog their memory (Kausler, 1990; Lovelace, 1990). Also, older people have had many similar experiences that tend to run together. When older people perceive an event as distinctive, they can remember it as well as younger ones (Camp, 1989; Cavanaugh, Kramer, Sinnott, Camp, & Markley, 1985; Kausler, 1990).

Semantic memory is like a mental encyclopedia; it holds knowledge of historical facts, geographic locations, social customs, meanings of words, and the like. Semantic memory does not depend on remembering when and where something was learned; it shows little decline with age (Camp, 1989; Horn, 1982b; Lachman & Lachman, 1980). In fact, vocabulary and knowledge of rules of language may even increase (Camp, 1989; Horn, 1982b). On a test that calls for definitions of words, older adults often do better than younger ones, but they have more trouble coming up with a word when given its meaning (Smith & Earles, 1996). Such "tip-of-the-tongue" experiences may relate to problems in working memory (Heller & Dobbs, 1993; Light, 1990; Schonfield, 1974; Schonfield & Robertson, 1960, cited in Horn, 1982b).

Remembering how to ride a bicycle is an example of the third component of long-term memory: *procedural memory*, sometimes called *implicit memory* (Squire, 1992, 1994; see Chapter 6). This includes motor skills, habits, and ways of doing things that can often be recalled without conscious effort. The brilliant pianist Arthur Rubinstein gave his farewell recital at 89, having put off his retirement for almost a year after he began to go blind (Rubinstein, 1980). This is but one of many examples of the persistence of motor learning into very old age.

A special use of unconscious memory that holds up with age is *priming*, which makes it easier to solve a puzzle, answer a question, or do a previously encountered task (Smith & Earles, 1996). For example, if you were asked to fill in the blanks in the word g_z_b_, you would be more likely to come up with the answer ("gazebo") if you had seen the problem before. Much as priming a surface prepares it for paint, perceptual priming prepares you to answer a test question you have seen in a list for review or to do a math problem involving the same process as one you did for a class assignment. Priming explains why older adults are about as likely as younger ones to recall a familiar word association (for example, "dragon" and "fire") but not an unfamiliar one (for example, "dragon" and "fudge").

Why Do Some Aspects of Memory Decline?

What explains older adults' losses in working memory and episodic memory? Investigators have offered several hypotheses. One approach focuses on problems with the three steps required to process information in memory: encoding, storage, and retrieval (see Chapter 8). Another approach focuses on the biological structures that make memory work.

In general, older adults seem less efficient than younger ones at *encoding* new information to make it easier to remember (for example, by arranging material alphabetically or creating mental associations). Also, older people's encoding seems less precise (Craik & Byrd, 1982). Older adults can be taught to encode better; how much they benefit depends on the task (Craik & Jennings, 1992).

Another plausible explanation for memory problems is that material in *storage* may deteriorate to the point where retrieval becomes difficult or impossible. Some research suggests that a small increase in "storage failure" may occur with age (Camp & McKitrick, 1989; Giambra & Arenberg, 1993). However, traces of decayed memories are likely to remain, and it may be possible to reconstruct them, or at least to relearn the material speedily (Camp & McKitrick, 1989; Chafetz, 1992).

Recalling something puts more demands on the *retrieval* system than recognizing something seen before. It's not surprising, then, that older adults have more trouble with recall than younger adults but do about as well with recognition (Hultsch, 1971; Lovelace, 1990). Even then, it takes older people longer than younger ones to search their memories (Anders, Fozard, & Lillyquist, 1972; Lovelace, 1990). Age differences are minimized when older adults are familiar with the material, can practice,

and can work at their own pace (Lovelace, 1990; Poon, 1985).

Biological hypotheses point to neurological changes: the more the brain deteriorates physically, the more loss of memory will take place. The *hippocampus,* a seahorse-shaped structure deep in the central part of the brain (the medial temporal lobe), seems critical to the ability to store new information in long-term memory (Squire, 1992). The hippocampus loses an estimated 20 percent of its nerve cells with advancing age (Ivy, MacLeod, Petit, & Markus, 1992) and is vulnerable to injury as blood pressure rises (Horn, 1982b). High levels of stress hormones in the bloodstream may reduce its performance (Sapolsky, 1992). Unconscious learning, which apparently is independent of the hippocampus, is less affected (Moscovitch & Winocur, 1992). So is recall of prior learning, which may improve as a result of the growing complexity of neural connections in the cortex (Squire, 1992). Extensive loss of nerve cells in the hippocampus is an early sign of Alzheimer's disease.

A neurologically based decline in perceptual speed, which affects efficiency of processing, seems to be associated with most aspects of memory loss, including changes in the capacity of working memory. In a number of studies, controlling for perceptual speed eliminated virtually the entire age-related drop in performance (A. D. Smith & Earles, 1996).

Metamemory: The View from Within

"I'm less efficient at remembering things now than I used to be."

"I have little control over my memory."

"I am just as good at remembering as I ever was."

When adults answer a questionnaire that asks them to agree or disagree with a list of statements like these, they are tapping *metamemory,* beliefs or knowledge about how memory works (see Chapter 8). These questions come from **Metamemory in Adulthood (MIA),** a questionnaire designed to measure metamemory in adults of all ages. The questions deal with several aspects of metamemory, including beliefs about one's own memory and selection and use of memory strategies.

Older adults taking the MIA report more perceived change in memory, less memory capacity, and less control over their memory than young adults (Dixon, Hultsch, & Hertzog, 1988). However, stereotyped expectations may lead older people to assume that minor lapses in memory are signs of age-related decline (Hertzog, Dixon, & Hultsch, 1990; Poon, 1985). When asked for a blanket assessment of their own memory, older adults claim that it has deteriorated, but when it comes to specific items or tasks, older adults are about as accurate as younger adults in judging their "feeling of knowing" (Hertzog & Dixon, 1994; Salthouse, 1991). One series of experiments found no age differences in participants' ability to estimate how well they had done on word-recall tasks, though younger adults showed greater improvement in predicting how well they would do as they became more familiar with a task (Hertzog, Saylor, Fleece, & Dixon, 1994).

Most studies have found that older and younger adults are about equally knowledgeable as to effective encoding strategies and kinds of information that are easiest to remember (Salthouse, 1991). Yet, in laboratory experiments, older adults are less likely to use such strategies as organization and elaboration unless trained—or at least prompted or reminded—to do so (Craik & Jennings, 1992; Salthouse, 1991). One proposed explanation is that older adults are less aware that such strategies are needed and less likely to monitor their use (Hertzog et al., 1990). Then, they may prefer a familiar strategy to one that is more effective but unfamiliar (Brigham & Pressley, 1988). It's also possible that the type of task makes a difference. Metamemory may function better for older adults in the real world than in an artificial laboratory situation.

Can Older Adults Benefit from Memory Training?

Some investigators have offered training programs in *mnemonics:* techniques designed to help people remember (see Chapter 8), such as visualizing a list of items or making associations between a face and a name. The programs also may include training in attention and relaxation, as well as information about memory and aging. An analysis of 33 studies found that older people do benefit from memory training. The particular kind of mnemonic made little difference. Gains were largest for the young old, for those who received pretraining, and for those who were trained in groups and in short sessions (Verhaeghen, Marcoen, & Goossens, 1992). Other studies have reported specific gains in remembering names, in episodic memory, in memory span, and in perceptual speed (Schaie & Willis, 1996).

There is, then, considerable plasticity of memory performance for older people, but it may diminish with advancing age. Some research found that long-term effects of memory training for older adults are minimal (Anschutz et al., 1987). More recent studies suggest, however, that such training can be transferred to everyday tasks and can be maintained (Neeley & Bäckman, 1993, 1995).

✔ EDUCATION

Today's older adults are better-educated than their predecessors, and this trend will continue as younger cohorts age. Furthermore, an increasing number of older adults are choosing to continue their studies.

EDUCATIONAL BACKGROUND

The percentage of noninstitutionalized older adults who had finished high school more than doubled between 1970 (28 percent) and 1994 (62 percent), and about 13 percent had completed college (AARP, 1995). Two out of three of the young old (ages 65 to 74) had high school diplomas, as compared with 55 percent of those 75 and over (Treas, 1995). In 1990, for the first time on record, more than half (56 percent) of the oldest old, those 85 and above, had at least some high school experience; 38 percent were high school graduates—nearly a fivefold rise since 1980—and about 20 percent had attended college (Longino, 1994). However, there are huge ethnic variations: the proportion of high school graduates among white older adults (65 percent) is nearly twice as great as among blacks (37 percent) and more than double the proportion among Hispanics (30 percent). Furthermore, older adults did less well than any other age group on the 1992 National Adult Literacy Survey (AARP, 1995).

LIFELONG LEARNING: EDUCATION IN LATE LIFE

Qian Likun, a star student who walks to his classes on health care and ancient Chinese poetry, took part in a 2.3-mile foot race. This might not seem unusual until you learn that Qian is 102 years old, one of thousands of students in China's network of "universities for the aged." More than 800 of these schools have been founded since the 1980s, showing China's commitment to its elderly population and demonstrating older people's willingness and ability to learn everything from basic skills to esoteric subjects (Kristof, 1990). China's program exemplifies a trend toward *lifelong learning:* organized, sustained study by adults of all ages.

As we've seen, "use it or lose it" applies as much to cognitive ability as to physical functioning. Continuing mental activity helps keep performance high, whether this activity involves reading, conversation, crossword puzzles, bridge, or chess, or going back to school, as more and more older adults are doing. Educational programs specifically designed for mature adults are booming in many parts of the world; many of the students are retired and have more time to earmark for learning than at any other period of life since their youth.

In one category are free or low-cost classes, taught by professionals or volunteers, at neighborhood senior centers, community centers, religious institutions, or storefronts; these classes generally have a practical or social focus (Moskow-McKenzie & Manheimer, 1994). In the mid-1960s, Japan, for example, instituted a system of continuing education for its growing population of older adults (Nojima, 1994). *Kominkans* (community educational centers) offer classes in child care, health, traditional arts and crafts, hobbies, exercise, and sports. A 2-year advanced studies program is designed to train community leaders who have studied 1 year at a *kominkan* or have done extensive community work.

A second category consists of college- and university-based programs with education as the primary goal (Moskow-McKenzie & Manheimer, 1994). *Elderhostel* is an international network of 1,800 colleges and other educational institutions in 47 countries. It offers college-level, noncredit, weeklong residential courses in Shakespeare, geography, early American music, and other subjects for adults age 55 and over and their spouses. For most classes, there are no entrance requirements, no homework, and no examinations or grades. In 1995, about 250,000 people participated. Although costs are relatively low ($340 on average, including tuition, meals, and lodging), the program tends to appeal mostly to the well-to-do (Antczak, 1996).

In the United States, educational opportunities for older adults have mushroomed since the mid-1970s (Moskow-McKenzie & Manheimer, 1994). Many regional community colleges and state universities, as well as a few private universities, offer special programs. Some vocational programs

Ruth Michael of Weslaco, Texas, graduated from college with honors at the age of 83, and now, as a volunteer, administers psychology tests to hospitalized patients. Educational opportunities for older adults have greatly expanded, enabling many older people to obtain the education they couldn't afford or didn't have time for earlier in life. *(Dennis Wells)*

give special attention to the needs of older women who have never worked for pay but now must do so. At a college in New Orleans that offers free minicourses for people age 65 and up, by far the most popular offering, with the longest waiting list, is computer training. Similarly, work training programs of the American Association of Retired Persons (AARP) cannot begin to accommodate all the requests for introductory or advanced courses in computers and word processing.

Why do so many older adults want to learn to use computers? Some are just curious. Some need to acquire new job skills or update old ones. Some want to keep up with the latest technology: to communicate with children and grandchildren who are computer-literate or to emulate friends who are on the Internet.

Older people can learn new skills and information, especially when the materials and methods take into account the physiological, psychological, and cognitive changes they may be experiencing. They do best when material is presented slowly over a fairly long period of time with intervals in between, rather than in concentrated doses. Students with visual or hearing problems benefit from clear, easily understandable audiovisual materials.

The trend toward continuing education in late life illustrates how each stage of life could be made more satisfying by restructuring the course of life (see Chapter 14). Today, young adults usually plunge into education and careers, middle-aged people use most of their energy earning money, and some older people who have retired from work cast about for ways to fill time. If people wove work, leisure, and study into their lives in a more balanced way at all ages, young adults would feel less pressure to establish themselves early, middle-aged people would feel less burdened, and older people would be more stimulated and would feel—and be—more useful. Such a pattern might make an important contribution to emotional well-being in old age, as we discuss in Chapter 17.

✔ SUMMARY

OLD AGE TODAY

- The number and proportion of older people in the United States population are greater than ever before and are expected to continue to grow. People over 85 are the fastest-growing age group.
- Although the effects of primary aging may be beyond people's control, they can often avoid the effects of secondary aging, which result from disease, disuse, and abuse of the body.
- Only about 5 percent of elderly people are in institutions; the proportion rises steeply with age.
- Today, many older people are healthy, vigorous, and active. These people, generally between ages 65 and 74, are sometimes referred to as the *young old*, the frail and infirm (often those over 75) as the *old old*, and those over 85 as the *oldest old*.

LONGEVITY AND AGING

- Life expectancy has increased dramatically since 1900. White people tend to live longer than black people, and women longer than men; thus older women outnumber older men 3 to 2.
- Mortality rates for older adults have declined. Heart disease, cancer, and stroke are the three leading causes of death for people over age 65.
- Research on extension of the life span in several species, especially through caloric restriction, has challenged the idea of a genetically determined limit to human life.
- Senescence, the period of the life span marked by physical changes associated with aging, begins at different ages for different people.
- Theories of biological aging fall into two categories: genetic-programming theories, which hold that the body is programmed to fail at a certain point, and variable-rate theories, which suggest that environment and lifestyle play an important role.

PHYSICAL CHANGES

- Longitudinal studies suggest that changes in body systems and organs with age are highly variable and may be the results of disease, which in turn is affected by lifestyle.
- Although the brain changes with age, the changes vary considerably and are usually modest. They include changes in nerve cells and a general slowing down of responses and of information processing.
- Changes in sensory and psychomotor abilities also vary. Visual problems, combined with slowed coordination and reaction time, may affect certain abilities. Training can improve muscular strength and reaction time.
- Many older people are sexually active, though the degree of sexual tension and the frequency and intensity of sexual experience are generally lower than for younger adults.
- Other physical changes that may occur with advancing age include some loss of skin coloring, texture, and elasticity; thinning and whitening of hair; shrinkage of body size; thinning of bones; and a tendency to sleep less.
- Most body systems generally continue to function fairly well, but the heart, in particular, becomes more susceptible to disease because of its decreased efficiency. The reserve capacity of the heart and other organs declines.

PHYSICAL AND MENTAL HEALTH

- Most older people are reasonably healthy, especially if they follow a lifestyle incorporating exercise and sound nutrition. Most older people have chronic conditions, but these usually do not limit activities or interfere with daily life.
- Most older people are in good mental health. Depression and many other conditions, including some forms of dementia, can be reversed with proper treatment; others, such as those brought on by Alzheimer's disease, Parkinson's disease, or multiple strokes, are irreversible.
- Alzheimer's disease is prolonged, progressively debilitating, and more prevalent with age. Its causes have not been definitively established, though research has found genetic factors in some cases.

■ Depression is more frequently diagnosed in younger than in older adults, and more often in women than in men. Many older adults show symptoms of depression, and it may be under-diagnosed.

ASPECTS OF COGNITIVE DEVELOPMENT

■ Physical and psychological factors and test conditions can influence performance on intelligence tests. Cross-sectional research showing declines may reflect cohort differences more than aging.

■ Schaie's sequential studies show that cognitive functioning in late adulthood is highly variable. Few people decline in all or most areas, and many people improve in some.

■ Fluid and (to a lesser extent) crystallized intelligence account for more than half of the variance in ability to perform tasks of daily living.

■ Older people show considerable plasticity (modifiability) in cognitive performance and can benefit from training.

■ Baltes proposes a dual-process model: the mechanics of intelligence often decline, but the pragmatics of intelligence (practical thinking, specialized knowledge and skills, and wisdom) may continue to grow.

■ Some aspects of memory appear nearly as efficient in older adults as in younger people, but other aspects (mainly the capacity of working memory and the ability to recall specific events or recently learned information) are often less efficient—possibly because of problems with encoding, storage, and retrieval.

■ Neurological changes, especially in the hippocampus, as well as declines in perceptual speed, may account for much of the decline in memory functioning in older adults.

■ Older adults' view of their memory functioning may be colored by stereotyped expectations. In laboratory studies, older adults are less likely than younger adults to use encoding strategies spontaneously. Older people can benefit from memory training.

EDUCATION

■ Today's older adults have had more formal education than their predecessors, and this trend is continuing.

■ Ongoing mental activity, as in adult education programs, can keep older people mentally alert.

✔ KEY TERMS

ageism (page 540)
primary aging (542)
secondary aging (543)
gerontology (543)
geriatrics (543)
functional age (543)
life expectancy (545)
longevity (545)
survival curves (547)
senescence (549)
genetic-programming theories (550)
variable-rate theories (550)

free radicals (550)
autoimmunity (551)
plasticity (554)
reserve capacity (555)
dementia (558)
Alzheimer's disease (558)
major depressive disorder (561)
instrumental activities of daily
   living (IADLs) (564)
dual-process model (566)
mechanics of intelligence (566)
pragmatics of intelligence (566)

selective optimization with
   compensation (566)
primary memory (568)
working memory (568)
episodic memory (568)
semantic memory (568)
procedural memory (568)
priming (568)
Metamemory in Adulthood (MIA)
   (569)
lifelong learning (571)
Elderhostel (571)

✔ QUESTIONS FOR THOUGHT AND DISCUSSION

1 If you could live as long as you wanted to, how long would you choose to live? What factors would affect your answer?

2 Think of the older adults in your life: grandparents or great-grandparents. Do you imagine they are still sexually active? How long do you think you will be able to continue sexual activity?

3 Do you engage regularly in physical exercise? How many of the older people you know do so? What kinds of physical activity do you think you can maintain as you get older?

4 Do your observations of older adults' cognitive

functioning agree with the results of the Seattle Longitudinal Study and the memory research reported in this chapter?

5 Given the importance of sustaining a high level of intellectual activity, what do you think are some good ways to do this? Do you think you need to develop new or broader interests that you will want to pursue as you age?

6 Think of the wisest person you know. Do the criteria Baltes and his colleagues established for wisdom seem to describe this person? If not, how would you define and measure wisdom?

CHAPTER SEVENTEEN

PSYCHOSOCIAL DEVELOPMENT IN LATE ADULTHOOD

There is still today
And tomorrow fresh with dreams:
Life never grows old

Rita Duskin,
"Haiku," Sound and Light, *1987*

ASK YOURSELF

✔ Is there such a thing as "successful aging"? If so, how can it be defined?

✔ Does personality change in old age?

✔ What special issues and tasks do older people have to deal with?

✔ How do older adults cope with physical and emotional losses?

✔ How do older people handle work and retirement, financial resources, and living arrangements?

✔ How do relationships with family and friends provide emotional support in old age?

In the early 1980s, the writer Betty Friedan—then just past 60 and beginning the research that culminated in *The Fountain of Age* (1993)—was asked to organize a seminar at Harvard University on "Growth in Aging." Several gerontologists and behavioral scientists, including the distinguished behaviorist B. F. Skinner, declined to participate. Skinner put his reason bluntly: Age and growth, he said, were "a contradiction in terms" (Friedan, 1993, p. 23).

At the time, Skinner was far from alone in that belief. Yet, little more than a decade later, late adulthood is increasingly recognized as a time of gains as well as losses, growth as well as decline.

Today, such terms as "successful aging" and "optimal aging" appear more frequently in the theoretical and research literature. These terms are controversial because they seem to imply that there is a "right" or "best" way to age. "Successful aging," in particular, suggests some sort of competition for achievement, whereas many older adults are satisfied to simply take each day as it comes and try to live that day to its fullest. Still, some older adults do seem to get more out of life than others, and one of the goals of gerontology is to find out how and why. Research suggests that older people can adapt to the challenge of aging if they are flexible and realistic—if they can conserve their strength, adjust to change and loss, and use time wisely. "Growth in aging" *is* possible, and many older adults who feel healthy and competent and in control of their lives experience this last stage of life as a positive one.

▪ In this chapter, we look at theory and research on psychosocial development in late adulthood. We discuss such late-life options as work, retirement, and living arrangements and their impact on society's ability to support an aging population and to care for the frail and infirm. Finally, we look at relationships with families and friends, which greatly affect the quality of these late years. ▪

✔ THEORY AND RESEARCH ON PERSONALITY DEVELOPMENT

On his seventieth birthday, five years after his retirement as editor of *The New York Times*, A. M. Rosenthal celebrated his bar mitzvah (the coming-of-age ceremony that normally occurs on a Jewish boy's thirteenth birthday). Rosenthal explained that he had felt something missing in his life because his father had given him no religious training in his youth. With age, he said, "the desire to learn more, be more, intensifies." Referring to the column he had begun writing for the *Times* editorial page after his retirement, he added:

> It's an adventure for me now to speak my own mind and my own thoughts, after twenty years as a reporter and foreign correspondent, and twenty years as an editor. . . . What happens if you're lucky when you get older . . . [is that] you get rid of all the things that aren't important, and do the work and spend your time with the friends that you're really interested in. (Friedan, 1993, pp. 578–579)

How much do adults change in personality in late life? Not much, according to some research. Still, the experience of people like A. M. Rosenthal leads some theorists to view late adulthood as a developmental stage with its own special issues and tasks. Many older people reexamine their lives, complete unfinished business, and decide how best to channel their energies and spend their remaining days, months, or years. Acutely aware of the passage of time, some wish to leave a legacy to their children or to the world, pass on the fruits of their experience, and validate the meaning of their lives. Others simply want to take this last chance to enjoy favorite pastimes or to do things they never had enough time for when they were younger.

Let's see what various models of personality development can tell us about this final phase of the life span. We'll also look at ways older people cope with stress and loss and at views of "successful," or "optimal," aging.

TRAIT MODELS

Does personality become more rigid in old age? Early cross-sectional research seemed to say so. Since the 1970s, however, Robert R. McCrae and Paul T. Costa, Jr. (1994), in large longitudinal studies using a variety of samples and measures, have shown that this is not true for most people and that older adults, unless they have dementia, also do not become withdrawn or depressed.

A sophisticated cross-sequential analysis of personality tests of 3,442 participants in the Seattle Longitudinal Study found only modest longitudinal declines in flexibility between ages 60 and 81 but much larger cohort differences (Schaie & Willis, 1991). As a group, people in more recent cohorts seem to be more flexible (that is, less rigid) than previous cohorts. These findings suggest that "increases" in rigidity found in early cross-sectional studies may actually have been tied, not to age, but to the unique, culturally influenced "baggage" of life experience that each generation carries throughout adulthood. If flexibility is becoming more characteristic of today's young adults, and if they carry that flexibility into late life, then future generations of older adults may be able to adapt more readily than their predecessors to the challenges of aging.

Although some research has found late-life change in certain personality dimensions, such as increases in agreeableness and decreases in extraversion (D. Field & Millsap, 1991), Costa and McCrae's work has made an impressive case for the essential stability of personality (see Chapters 13 and 15). Indeed, there is evidence that the persistence of certain traits may even contribute to longevity (see Box 17-1).

Stability of personality, say McCrae and Costa (1994), makes life more manageable and predictable: "our traits characterize us; they are our

very selves; we act most freely when we express our enduring dispositions" (p. 175). These basic tendencies, interacting with life experience, help shape the self-concept, which some theorists view as the core of personality.

SELF-CONCEPT MODELS

Self-concept models deal with the cognitive side of personality: what people think about themselves. The self-concept (see Chapters 7 and 9) is made up of *schemas:* working models of reality around which behavior is organized (for instance, "I am a good mother"). Schemas are only tentative; people continually revise them to conform with experience. Interpretations of experience, however, are subjective; a person may filter out information that challenges beliefs about the self (Caspi, 1993; S. Epstein, 1990; M. Snyder, 1987; Swann, 1983, 1987). Thus, the self-concept's essential stability limits the possibilities for change.

One current self-concept model is that of Susan Krauss Whitbourne (1987, 1996). It focuses on the development of **identity styles:** characteristic ways of confronting, interpreting, and responding to experience. According to Whitbourne, identity is made up of accumulated images of the self, both conscious and unconscious. Perceived personality traits, such as sensitivity and stubbornness, form part of that identity. These self-images normally do not change unless contradicted by new circumstances.

In Whitbourne's model, self-perceptions are confirmed or revised through two ongoing processes of interaction with the social environment (similar to those Piaget described for children's cognitive development): *identity assimilation* and *identity accommodation*. **Identity assimilation** is an attempt to fit new experience into an existing self-concept; **identity accommodation** is adjustment of the self-concept to fit new experience. Many people go to great lengths to assimilate new information in a way that confirms their view of themselves. If a woman thinks of herself as a proud and loving mother and her relationship with one of her children begins to sour, she will probably dismiss the problem as a temporary "phase" or find a specific reason for an upsetting encounter. However, if something happens that she cannot satisfactorily explain to herself (for example, if her child is constantly stealing from her), she may be forced to accommodate her self-image to this fact.

Overuse of either assimilation or accommoda-

BOX 17-1   FOOD FOR THOUGHT

DO PSYCHOSOCIAL FACTORS PREDICT LENGTH OF LIFE?

The Terman study of gifted children (see Chapter 8), which began in 1921, found that childhood personality characteristics and family environment played an important part in adult success. Now it appears that such factors, identified in childhood and at midlife, may influence how long people live.

Most of the approximately 1,500 California schoolchildren chosen for the study on the basis of high IQ have been followed at 5- to 10-year intervals throughout their lives. In 1986, when the survivors were all past age 70, a group of researchers (Friedman et al., 1993; Friedman, Tucker, Schwartz, Martin et al., 1995; Friedman, Tucker, Schwartz, Tomlinson-Keasey et al., 1995) decided to find out how many had died and at what ages, so as to spot predictors of longevity. The very fact that this sample was *not* typical of the general population may have made it easier to identify nonphysiological factors that affect length of life. Since the "Termites" as a group were bright and well-educated, the results were not likely to be confounded by poor nutrition, poverty, or inadequate medical care.

The researchers were able to account for all but 10 percent of the approximately 1,200 Termites who had lived to enter adulthood and for whom childhood personality measures and other relevant data were substantially complete. A little more than one-third were known to have died by 1986.

At first glance, some findings were surprising. Neither childhood self-confidence, energy, nor sociability turned out to be related to longevity. Nor was optimism or a sense of humor in childhood associated with long life. In fact, the reverse was true: cheerful children were more likely to die young. Optimism and good humor may be effective coping mechanisms under certain circumstances—for example, in recovering from surgery—but a carefree approach to life may be unhealthy if it leads a person to ignore dangers and engage in risky, health-threatening behaviors.

What *did* predict longevity in both men and women was the personality dimension called *conscientiousness*, or dependability—sometimes described as orderliness, prudence, or self-control—which has been found in many studies to be stable from early adolescence through old age. Why should conscientiousness lead to long life?

One possibility is that just as optimistic people may be more inclined to be risk takers, conscientious people may be less so. They may be less likely to suffer injuries, to smoke, to drink, and to overeat and become obese. This was, indeed, true of the conscientious Termites—but not enough to fully explain their longevity. Nor does there seem to be a connection between conscientiousness and any genetic, neonatal, or other biological factors that might affect health and length of life.

Subtle psychosocial factors may be at work. Conscientious people may be more likely to cultivate good health habits, to follow sound advice, and to cooperate with doctors. They may avoid stress by thinking ahead, steeling themselves for the worst that might happen, staying out of situations they can't handle, and preparing for contingencies—for example, by carrying extra car keys and plenty of insurance. Then again, their qualities may enable them to achieve career success and to have greater financial, informational, and social resources to deal with medical and other problems. They may also be more likely to have stable marriages and reliable, supportive friendship networks.

Apparently it is not marriage itself but marital *stability* that leads to long life. "Termites" who, at age 40, were in their first marriages tended to live significantly longer than those who were divorced and remarried. Those who were separated or who were divorced or widowed and had *not* remarried had even shorter remaining life spans. Thus, "there seems to be a detrimental effect of previous divorce that is not eliminated when the individuals remarry" (Friedman, Tucker, Schwartz, Tomlinson-Keasey et al., 1995, p. 71). By contrast, "Termites" who had *never* married had only slightly increased risk of early death.

Marital instability apparently has ill effects not only when it occurs in one's own marriage but in the marriage of one's parents. People who, before the age of 21, had experienced the divorce of their parents—13 percent of the sample—lived, on average, 4 years less than those whose parents had stayed together. Death of a parent, on the other hand, made little difference.

The findings about marital stability and personality are interrelated. Children who were rated as impulsive were more likely to grow into adults who had unstable marital histories and were more likely to die young. Also, children of divorce were more likely to go through divorce themselves, explaining part, but not all, of the effect of parental divorce on longevity. Finally, men who, in midlife, were rated as maladjusted were more likely to die early from all causes—and were also least likely to stay married.

It seems, then, that people who are dependable, trustworthy, and diligent both in taking good care of themselves and in preserving their marriages—and who are fortunate enough to have had parents who stayed married—may be rewarded with more years of life.

tion is unhealthy, says Whitbourne. People who constantly assimilate are blind to reality; they see only what they are looking for. People who constantly accommodate are weak and easily swayed. The balance a person customarily strikes between assimilation and accommodation determines his or her identity style.

According to Whitbourne, people cope with the physical, mental, and emotional changes associated with aging much as they cope with other challenges to the self-concept. Those whose identity style is predominantly assimilative seek to maintain a youthful self-image; they may deplete their psychological energy trying to keep up an optimistic outlook and may fail to take measures that might help compensate for losses. People whose style is predominantly accommodative may see themselves—perhaps prematurely—as old and may become overly preoccupied with symptoms of aging and disease. People with a more evenly balanced identity style may be able to make a more realistic adjustment, taking steps to control what can be controlled and striving to accept what cannot.

Whitbourne's model, then, incorporates into an essentially stable personality structure a mechanism for dealing flexibly with new experience in a way unique to the individual. However, this model does not as yet have a strong research base.

NORMATIVE-CRISIS MODELS

According to the classic normative-crisis theorists, adults need to carry out the psychological tasks of each stage of life in an emotionally healthy way. Let's see how Erikson, Peck, and Vaillant described the tasks or issues of late adulthood.

Erik Erikson: Ego Integrity versus Despair

For Erikson, the crowning achievement of late adulthood is a sense of *ego integrity*, or integrity of the self, based on reflection about one's life. In the eighth and final crisis of the life span, *ego integrity versus despair,* older adults need to evaluate, sum up, and accept their lives so as to accept the approach of death. Building on the outcomes of the seven previous crises, they struggle to achieve a sense of coherence and wholeness, rather than give way to despair over an inability to live life differently (Erikson, Erikson, & Kivnick, 1986). People who succeed in this final, integrative task gain a sense of the order and meaning of their lives

within the larger social order: past, present, and future. The "virtue" that may develop during this stage is *wisdom,* an "informed and detached concern with life itself in the face of death itself" (Erikson, 1985, p. 61).

Wisdom, said Erikson, means accepting the life one has lived, without major regrets: without dwelling on "should-have-dones" or "might-have-beens." It involves accepting one's parents as people who did the best they could and thus deserve love, even though they were not perfect. It implies accepting one's death as the inevitable end of a life lived as well as one knew how to live it. In sum, it means accepting imperfection in the self, in parents, and in life. (This definition of *wisdom* as an important psychological resource differs from Baltes's cognitive definition, given in Chapter 16.)

People who do not achieve acceptance are overwhelmed by despair, realizing that time is too short to seek other roads to ego integrity. Although integrity must outweigh despair if this crisis is to be resolved successfully, Erikson maintained that some despair is inevitable. People need to mourn—not only for their own misfortunes and lost chances but for the vulnerability and transience of the human condition.

Yet, Erikson believed, even as the body's functions weaken, people must maintain a "vital involvement" in society. On the basis of studies of life histories of people in their eighties, he concluded that ego integrity comes not just from reflecting on the past but from continued stimulation and challenge—whether through political activity, fitness programs, creative work, or relationships with grandchildren (Erikson, Erikson, & Kivnick, 1986). Studies by other researchers confirm that men and women in late adulthood are most concerned with issues of ego integrity (Ryff, 1982; Ryff & Baltes, 1976; Ryff & Heincke, 1983).

Robert Peck: Three Adjustments of Late Adulthood

Peck (1955), expanding on Erikson's theory, described three psychological adjustments important in late adulthood:

1 *Broader self-definition versus preoccupation with work roles.* People who have defined themselves by their work need to redefine their worth and give new structure and direction to their lives by exploring other interests and taking pride in personal attributes.

Older people, according to Robert Peck, need to find new interests and new sources of self-esteem to take the place of their former work roles and to make up for physical losses. An elderly person like the artist shown here, who can focus on relationships and absorbing activities, can often overcome physical discomforts. *(Nilo Lima/Photo Researchers)*

2   *Transcendence of the body versus preoccupation with the body.* As physical abilities decline, people adjust better if they focus on relationships and activities that do not demand perfect health. People for whom physical well-being is crucial to happiness may be plunged into despair when faced with diminishing faculties or aches and pains. Throughout life, people need to cultivate mental and social powers that can grow with age.

3   *Transcendence of the ego versus preoccupation with the ego.* Probably the hardest, and possibly the most important, adjustment for older people is to move beyond concern with themselves and their present lives to an acceptance of the certainty of death. They can gain this acceptance by recognizing the lasting significance of all they have done, and they can transcend concern with self by continuing to contribute to the well-being of others.

These adjustments, then, allow people to move beyond concerns with work, physical well-being, and mere existence to a deeper understanding of the self and of life's purpose.

George Vaillant: Factors in Emotional Health

In a follow-up to the Grant Study of Harvard men (Vaillant, 1993; Vaillant & Vaillant, 1990; see Chapters 13 and 15), researchers examined 173 of the men at age 65 to identify personality attributes that make for healthy adaptation to aging. *Emotional health* at this age was defined as the "clear ability to play and to work and to love" (p. 31) and as having been happy during the previous decade.

Surprisingly, a satisfying marriage, a successful career, and a childhood free of major problems (such as poverty or the death or divorce of parents) were unimportant in predicting good adjustment late in life. More influential was closeness to siblings at college age, suggesting a long-lasting source of emotional support. Factors predictive of poor adjustment at age 65 included major emotional problems in childhood and, before age 50, poor physical health, severe depression, alcoholism, and heavy use of tranquilizers.

Probably the most significant factor in good adjustment was the ability to handle problems without blame, bitterness, or passivity—to use what the researchers called *mature adaptive mechanisms* (see Chapter 13). The men who, over the years, had not collected injustices, had not complained, had not pretended nothing was wrong, and had not become bitter or prejudiced—and could thus respond appropriately to crises—were the best-adjusted at age 65.

Erikson, Peck, and Vaillant all offer valuable perspectives on adjustment to the later years. Vaillant's research, in particular, suggests that people adapt in old age much as they have all along. Let's look more closely at how people do this.

MODELS OF COPING

Their health may not be what it was, they have lost old friends and family members—often spouses—and they probably don't earn the money they once did. Their lives keep changing in countless stressful ways. Yet in general, older adults have fewer mental disorders and are more satisfied with life than younger adults (Wykle & Musil, 1993). What accounts for this remarkable ability to cope?

Coping is adaptive thinking or behavior aimed at reducing or relieving stress that arises from harmful, threatening, or challenging conditions. It is an important aspect of mental health, especially in old age. Let's examine two approaches to the study of coping: environmental and cognitive-appraisal models. Then we'll discuss one support system to which many older adults turn: religion.

Environmental Models

Two classic models of coping—the congruence model and the environmental-press model—focus on interaction between characteristics of the individual and of the environment.

According to the *congruence model* (Kahana, 1982), people's needs differ, and environments dif-fer in the extent to which they meet those needs. The fit between person and environment determines the amount of satisfaction or stress in a person's life. For example, placing an older adult who has a strong need for independence in a nursing home would probably increase stress, but an older person who enjoyed being taken care of might find such an environment supportive and nonstressful. Successful coping, according to this model, is more likely to take place when there is a good match between a person's perceived needs and the environment's support of those needs.

The *environmental-press model* (Lawton, 1982; Lawton & Nahemow, 1973) emphasizes differences in demands that environments make (environmental press) and in individuals' competence, or ability to meet those demands (see Figure 17-1). When both press and competence are relatively high or low, people are comfortable in their environment and tend to take it for granted; they are at their normal adaptation level. When moderately pressed by the environment, people reach their maximum potential; when environmental press is too low or high in relation to competence, they become uncomfortably aware of the environment and perceive it as either boring or overwhelming.

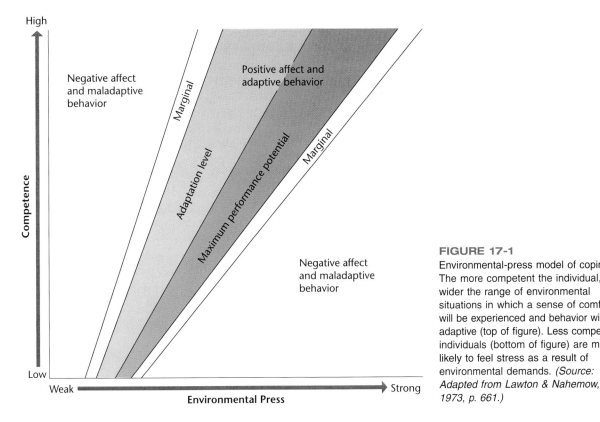

FIGURE 17-1
Environmental-press model of coping. The more competent the individual, the wider the range of environmental situations in which a sense of comfort will be experienced and behavior will be adaptive (top of figure). Less competent individuals (bottom of figure) are more likely to feel stress as a result of environmental demands. *(Source: Adapted from Lawton & Nahemow, 1973, p. 661.)*

The environmental-press model has implications for aging. If environmental press increases (for example, when an older person's city neighborhood becomes unsafe) or competence diminishes (for example, when someone living in a suburb can no longer drive), that person will fall below the adaptation level and feel stress. To restore an adaptive fit, ways must be found to reduce environmental demands or to increase competence.

These two models offer reasons to explain why different situations may cause more or less stress, but they do not tell us *how* people cope with stress. Let's look next at a model which seeks to answer that question.

Cognitive-Appraisal Model

In the *cognitive-appraisal model* (Lazarus & Folkman, 1984), people choose coping strategies on the basis of their cognitive appraisal of a situation. Coping occurs when a person perceives a situation as taxing or exceeding his or her resources and thus demanding unusual effort. Coping includes anything an individual thinks or does in trying to adapt to stress, regardless of how well it works. Because the situation is constantly changing, coping is a dynamic, evolving process; choosing the most appropriate strategy requires continuous reappraisal of the relationship between person and environment (see Figure 17-2).

Coping strategies may be either *problem-focused* or *emotion-focused*. **Problem-focused coping** aims at eliminating, managing, or improving a stressful condition. It generally predominates when a person sees a realistic chance of changing the situation. **Emotion-focused coping**, sometimes called *palliative coping*, is directed toward "feeling better": managing, or regulating, the emotional response to a stressful situation to relieve its physical or psychological impact. This form of coping is likely to predominate when a person concludes that little or nothing can be done about the situation itself. One emotion-focused strategy is to divert attention away from a problem, another is to give in, and still another is to deny that the problem exists. Problem-focused responses to a series of harsh reprimands from an employer might be to work harder, seek ways to improve one's work skills, or look for another job. Emotion-focused responses might be to refuse to think about the reprimands, to throw one's energy into a volunteer activity, or to convince oneself that the boss didn't really mean to be so critical.

In general, older adults do more emotion-focused coping than younger people (Folkman, Lazarus, Pimley, & Novacek, 1987; Prohaska, Leventhal, Leventhal, & Keller, 1985). Is that because they are less able to focus on problems? In one study (Blanchard-Fields, Jahnke, & Camp, 1995), 70 adolescents, 69 young adults, 74 middle-aged adults, and 74 older adults wrote essays on how to handle each of 15 problems. The participants, regardless of age, most often picked problem-focused strategies (either direct action or analyzing the problem so as to understand it better). This was especially true in situations that were not highly emotional, such as what to do about defective merchandise. The largest age differences showed up in problems with highly emotional implications, such as that of a divorced man who is allowed to see his child only on weekends but wants to see the child more often. Both young and old were more likely to use emotion regulation in such situations, but older adults chose emotion-regulating strategies (such as doing nothing, waiting until the child is older, or trying not to worry about it) more often than younger adults did. These findings, along with those of several other studies, suggest that, with age, people develop a more flexible repertoire of coping strategies. Older people *can* do problem-focused coping, but they may also be more able than younger people to use emotion regulation when a situation seems to call for it, that is, when problem-focused action might be futile or counterproductive (Blanchard-Fields & Camp, 1990; Blanchard-Fields & Irion, 1987; Folkman & Lazarus, 1980; Labouvie-Vief, Hakim-Larson, & Hobart, 1987).

Emotion-focused coping can be quite adaptive, and its flexible use in appropriate situations can be a mature coping strategy. In one study that compared coping strategies from early adolescence through old age (Diehl, Coyle, & Labouvie-Vief, 1996), adolescents and young adults tended to respond aggressively to conflict, whereas older adults were less confrontational and less impulsive. Older people were also more likely to withdraw from a conflict or to see its bright side. Perhaps experience had taught them to accept what they could not change—a lesson often reinforced by religion.

Religion and Emotional Well-being in Late Life

Interviewers asked 100 well-educated white men and women—ages 55 to 80, about evenly divided between working class and upper middle class,

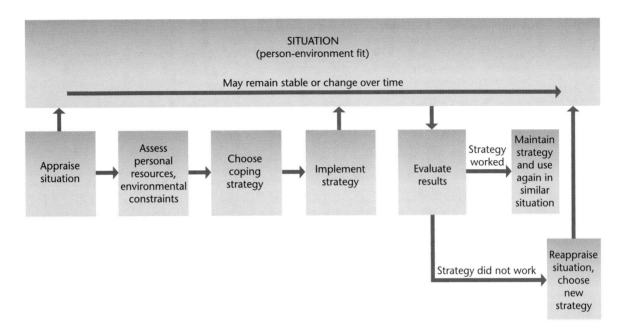

FIGURE 17-2
Cognitive-appraisal model of coping. *(Source: Based on Lazarus & Folkman, 1984.)*

and 90 percent Protestant—to describe how they had dealt with the worst events in their lives. The top strategies, cited by 58 percent of the women and 32 percent of the men, were behaviors associated with religion (Koenig, George, & Siegler, 1988; see Table 17-1 for a ranked listing of all strategies chosen). Other research has confirmed the supportive role of religion for the elderly, especially for women, African Americans, and the oldest old. Possible explanations include social support, the perception of a measure of control over life through prayer, and faith in God as a way of interpreting misfortunes.

In a study of 836 older adults from two secular and three religiously oriented groups, morale was positively associated with three kinds of religious activity: *organized* (church or synagogue attendance and participation), *informal* (praying or reading the Bible), and *spiritual* (personal commitment to religious beliefs). People who were higher on any of these dimensions had higher morale and a better attitude toward aging and were more satisfied and less lonely. Those over 75 showed the strongest correlations between religiosity and well-being (Koenig, Kvale, & Ferrel, 1988).

An analysis of data from four national surveys showed that elderly African Americans are more involved in religious activity than elderly white people, and women are more involved than men

(Levin, Taylor, & Chatters, 1994). The church has always been important to African Americans. At all ages, black women are more active than black men, but involvement is high among the men too, and the gender difference narrows or even reverses in the oldest groups (Levin & Taylor, 1993). For all ages and both sexes, the most common religious activity is personal prayer (Chatters & Taylor, 1989). Elderly black people who feel supported by their church tend to report high levels of well-being, and the more actively religious they are, the more satisfied they are with their lives (Coke, 1992; Walls & Zarit, 1991). Those who are involved in organized religion tend to have higher self-esteem, whereas those whose religious feelings and activity are purely personal have a stronger sense of control (Krause & Van Tran, 1989).

However, the relationship between religiosity and self-esteem seems to be complex. Interviews with a nationwide sample of more than 1,100 people eligible for Medicare found that neither organized nor nonorganizational religiosity (such as reading the Bible or listening to religious radio programs) had any effect on self-esteem. It was only people who turned to religion to cope with problems (by praying or seeking guidance and support from God) who gained a stronger sense of self-worth. Older adults with the most education were least likely to use religion to help them cope.

■ **TABLE 17-1**

Spontaneously Reported Emotion-regulating Coping Strategies Used by Older Adults

Rank Order	Frequency of Mention	
	Number	%
Religious	97	(17.4)
Kept busy	84	(15.1)
Accepted it	63	(11.3)
Support from family or friends	62	(11.1)
Help from professional	34	(6.1)
Positive attitude	31	(5.6)
Took one day at a time	29	(5.2)
Became involved in social activities	19	(3.4)
Planning and preparing beforehand	15	(2.7)
Optimized communication	13	(2.3)
Limited activities; didn't overcommit	11	(2.0)
Sought information	8	(1.4)
Exercised	8	(1.4)
Helped others more needy	7	(1.3)
Realized that time heals all wounds	7	(1.3)
Avoided situation	6	(1.1)
Experience of prior hardships	5	(.9)
Carried on for others' sake	5	(.9)
Ingested alcohol, tranquilizers	5	(.9)
Carried on as usual	4	(.7)
Took a vacation	3	(.5)
Realized others in same situation or worse	3	(.5)
Released emotion (cried or cursed)	3	(.5)
Lowered expectations or devalued	3	(.5)
Miscellaneous	31	(5.6)
Totals	556	(100.6)

Note: 100 older adults reported 556 coping behaviors for 289 stressful experiences. Percentages add up to more than 100 because of rounding.

SOURCE: Koenig, George, & Siegler, 1988, p. 306.

Religiosity apparently boosts self-esteem in the less educated, who are less likely to get self-validation from high-status jobs or other activities (Krause, 1995).

Furthermore, people with the most *or the least* religious commitment had the *highest* self-esteem, whereas those with only a modest degree of religious involvement tended to think less of themselves (Krause, 1995). Similarly, an earlier study found that adults of all ages with either strong religious commitments *or none* have less psycho-logical distress than those with moderate commitments (Ross, 1990). It may be, as Fowler (1981) suggested (see Chapter 12), that the emotional benefits nonreligious people derive from strong commitment to secular values are similar to the benefits religious people derive from a strong faith in God. Or it may be that people's self-esteem is highest when their behavior is consistent with their beliefs, whatever those beliefs may be.

Since almost all research on religion in the lives of older Americans has been cross-sectional and since today's older adults grew up at a time when higher education was less common than it is now, the inverse relationship between religious coping and education suggests that turning toward religion in old age may be a cohort effect and that older adults in the future may be less likely to use religion as a coping strategy. On the other hand, it also seems plausible that as people think about the meaning of their lives and about death as the inevitable end, they may focus more on spiritual matters. Future research may clarify the role of religion in the emotional well-being of older adults.

MODELS OF "SUCCESSFUL," OR "OPTIMAL," AGING

"Successful aging"—what the heck does that mean? . . . Is our society so achievement-oriented that it is now possible to fail at growing old? By encouraging the definition of a right and a wrong way to age, you are discouraging attempts to treat ourselves with kindness. (D. King, 1993, p. 14)

This letter to a magazine from an indignant reader challenges a concept that gerontologists have been studying and arguing about for nearly half a century. Are some adaptations to aging more successful, optimal, or psychologically healthier than others? Is "successful aging" the same for everyone? Or is the only relevant definition a personal one?

Researchers disagree on how to define *successful*, or *optimal, aging*. Some investigators focus on measures of physical, cognitive, or psychological functioning, such as tests of cardiovascular functioning, intellectual abilities, and mental health, which are applicable to people of any age and about which there is considerable consensus as to desirable outcomes. However, in using such measures we need to keep in mind that the whole is sometimes not the same as the sum of its parts: having a strong heart or lungs and normal mental functioning does not necessarily add up to success in living. Other researchers therefore look at subjective experience: how well individuals attain their personal goals and how satisfied they are with their lives. However, these criteria are hard to measure accurately, and people may rationalize about their success in meeting them. Furthermore, such research tells us little that can be generalized beyond the individual. One model emphasizes the degree of control people retain: their ability, within genetic and environmental constraints, to shape their lives to fit their needs and optimize their development (Schulz & Heckhausen, 1996). Still other researchers talk about *productive* or *robust aging;* they view fruitful activity, economic or otherwise, as at least one important criterion for a meaningful or healthful life.

All these definitions, of course, are value-laden—unavoidably so. Keeping this problem in mind, then, let's look at theory and research about aging well.

Disengagement Theory versus Activity Theory

Who is making a healthier adjustment: a person who tranquilly watches the world go by from a rocking chair or one who keeps busy from morning till night? According to **disengagement theory**, aging normally brings a gradual reduction in social involvement and greater preoccupation with the self. According to **activity theory**, the more active people remain, the better they age.

Disengagement theory was one of the first influential theories in gerontology. Its proponents (Cumming & Henry, 1961) saw disengagement as a universal condition of aging. They maintained that declines in physical functioning and awareness of the approach of death result in a gradual, inevitable withdrawal from social roles (worker, spouse, parent) and that since society stops providing useful roles for the older adult, the disengagement is mutual. Disengagement is thought to be accompanied (as Jung suggested) by introspection and a quieting of the emotions.

Disengagement theory, after more than three decades, has received little independent research support, and as a result it has "largely disappeared from the empirical literature" (Achenbaum & Bengtson, 1994, p. 756). David Gutmann (1974, 1977, 1992) has argued that what looks like disengagement in traditional cultures is only a transition between the active roles of middle age and the more passive, spiritual roles of late adulthood and that true disengagement occurs only in societies in which elderly people are left without established roles appropriate to their stage of life. Thus disengagement, rather than mutual and inevitable, may be imposed by some societies, resulting in less-than-optimal satisfaction with life and use of human potential.

Activity theory has been far more influential. According to its proponents, chiefly Bernice Neugarten and her associates (Neugarten, Havighurst, & Tobin, 1968), an adult's roles are major sources

The author Betty Friedan, whose 1963 book, *The Feminine Mystique*, is credited with launching the women's movement in the United States, exemplifies successful aging as described by activity theory. At age 60, she went on the first Outward Bound survival expedition for people over 55. Now in her 70s, she teaches at universities in California and New York, and, in 1993, published her newest best-seller, *The Fountain of Age. (Joyce Ravid)*

of satisfaction; the greater the loss of roles through retirement, widowhood, distance from children, or infirmity, the less satisfied a person will be. People who are aging well keep up as many activities as possible and find substitutes for lost roles. According to this theory, inactivity results chiefly from ageism and from social policies that discourage older people from remaining active and involved.

When Neugarten and her colleagues looked at the personalities, activity, and satisfaction of 159 men and women ages 50 to 90 (Neugarten et al., 1968), they found four major styles of aging: (1) *Integrated* people were functioning well, with a complex inner life, intact cognitive abilities, and a high level of satisfaction. (2) *Armor-defended* people were achievement-oriented, striving, and tightly controlled. (3) *Passive-dependent* people were apathetic or sought comfort from others. (4) *Unintegrated* people were disorganized, had little control over their emotions, showed poor cognitive and psychological functioning, and had problems coping. For the most part, integrated and armor-

defended people were more active than the other two groups, and more activity was generally associated with more satisfaction. However, some disengaged people were well-adjusted, perhaps (as congruence theory suggests) because of a match between their desire to disengage and their environment's permitting them to do so. This finding suggests that although activity may work best for most people, disengagement may be appropriate for some and that generalizations about a particular pattern of "successful aging" may be risky.

Some research suggests that the *kind* of activity matters: informal activities with friends and family are more satisfying than formal, structured, group activities or solitary activities such as reading, watching television, and hobbies (Longino & Kart, 1982). However, a subsequent analysis indicated that people's attitude about life is affected only slightly, if at all, by any kind of activity (Okun, Stick, Haring, & Witter, 1984). Further, a study of mortality among 508 older Mexican Americans and Anglos over an 8-year period found that the age at which death occurred was totally unrelated to activity levels, once other factors such as age, health, and gender were taken into account (D. J. Lee & Markides, 1990). Other studies have found that healthy older people do tend to cut down on social contacts and that activity in and of itself bears little relationship to psychological well-being or satisfaction with life (Carstensen, 1995; Lemon, Bengtson, & Peterson, 1972). Thus although activity theory has not, so far, been discarded (Marshall, 1994), some gerontologists have come to view it as simplistic. Some current theory and research focuses on the degree of continuity between past and present activity levels. Other current research looks at the productive content of activity.

LIFE-SPAN ISSUE
WHAT EXPLAINS AGE-RELATED CHANGES IN SOCIAL CONTACT?

Laura L. Carstensen is associate professor of psychology at Stanford University and an award-winning innovator, researcher, and writer in the field of gerontology. Her chief research interest has been to understand "how normal older people actively construct their social worlds" (1996, p. 254). Rather than focus only on old age, however, she has proposed and tested a theory

of social behavior with implications for the entire life span.

A drop in social contact in old age is "considered to be the most reliable finding in social gerontology" (Carstensen, 1996, p. 255). As people age, they tend to spend less time with others. Why is this so? And since social contact is an important source of enjoyment and of emotional and practical support for older adults, what does the lessening of contact mean for their well-being?

Cross-sectional comparisons show that long-time retirees have fewer social contacts than more recent retirees or those who continue to work at least part time. This is not surprising, since for most adults work is a convenient source of social contact; coworkers may become friends and confidants. For some older adults, infirmities create physical obstacles to getting out and seeing people. However, a 3-year longitudinal study of 1,311 relatively healthy older men found that, while the extent of the social network and the frequency of contacts declines, the quality of social support apparently does not (Bossé, Aldwin, Levenson, Spiro, & Mroczek, 1993).

One proposed explanation is that of **social convoy theory.** According to this theory, changes in social contact affect only a person's outer, less intimate social circles. After retirement, as coworkers and other relatively casual friends drop away, they may be replaced by new leisure friends or by more time spent with old friends and acquaintances. Regardless of what happens to these relationships, however, older adults still have a stable inner circle of *social convoys:* close friends and family members on whom they can rely for continued social support and well-being (Kahn & Antonucci, 1980).

A newer, life-span-based explanation, which builds in part on the concept of social convoys, is Laura Carstensen's (1991, 1995, 1996) **socioemotional selectivity theory.** Its central idea is that people select social contacts to meet changing needs and goals. According to this theory, social interaction, in addition to its role in assuring basic physical survival, has three main psychological functions: (1) it is a source of information, (2) it helps people develop and maintain a sense of self, and (3) it is a source of pleasure and comfort, or emotional well-being. All three goals exist throughout life, but their importance shifts.

In infancy, the need for emotional support is paramount, and babies are often highly selective about who can meet that need. From childhood through young adulthood, information seeking comes to the fore. As young people strive to learn about their society and their place in it, strangers may well be the best sources of knowledge. During adolescence and young adulthood, people strike out on their own and forge new relationships.

From middle adulthood through old age, the importance of information seeking declines. As adults gain experience and expertise, fewer people can give them new,

useful information, and other methods of information gathering (such as reading) become more efficient. Meanwhile, the emotion-regulating function of social contacts once again becomes central. As in infancy, people become more selective about their social interactions, choosing to spend time with family members and close friends—the "social convoys" who can be counted on to deliver dependable support in time of need.

This shift is influenced by the perception of how much time is left to live. When time is short, immediate emotional needs take precedence over long-range goals. A college student may be willing to put up with a disliked teacher for the sake of gaining knowledge to get into graduate school; an older adult may be less willing to spend precious time in emotionally unrewarding situations. Although this shift is largely age-related, it is not determined by biological changes of aging, but by the contextual relevance of a particular goal at a given time. Studies show, for example, that in choosing partners for social interaction, people facing a limited future—whether because of age, disease, or other reasons—give more weight to emotional satisfaction, whereas people who see more time ahead of them prefer novelty in their social lives. Young adults who have a free half hour and no urgent commitments are more likely to spend the time with someone they would like to get to know better; older adults tend to choose a familiar partner. However, when young adults are asked to imagine that they are moving across the country in a few weeks, they—like the older adults—want to be with someone they know well. Similarly, young people who are terminally ill and young gay men who have AIDS generally choose familiar social partners. Conversely, when older adults are asked to imagine that medical progress assures them twenty more years of healthy living, they say they would choose to get to know someone new.

Perhaps the greatest contribution of socioemotional selectivity theory is not just the idea that greater selectivity of social partners in late life can be positive and adaptive, but its suggestion that changes in social behavior are not unique to old age. Its underlying premise is that people of all ages help mold their social environments.

Atchley: Continuity Theory

Whereas Carstensen emphasizes changes in social behavior across the life span, *continuity theory,* as described by the gerontologist Robert Atchley (1989), emphasizes people's need to maintain some continuity, or connection with the past, in both internal and external structures of their lives. *Internal structures* include knowledge, self-esteem, and a sense of personal history, or ego integrity. *External structures* include roles, relationships, activities, and sources of social support, as well as the physical environment.

It is normal, Atchley suggests, for aging adults to seek a satisfactory balance between continuity and change in their life structures. Too much change makes life too unpredictable; too little change makes life too dull. Although some change is both desirable and inevitable, there is an internal drive for consistency, a need to avoid a total break with the past.

In this view, then, activity is important not for its own sake, but to the extent that it represents a continuation of a person's lifestyle. For older adults who always have been active and involved, it may be important to continue a high level of activity. Others, who have been less active, may be happier in the proverbial rocking chair. Many retired people are happiest pursuing work or leisure activities similar to those they have enjoyed in the past (Kelly, 1994).

When aging brings marked physical or cognitive changes, however, a person may become dependent on caregivers or may have to make new living arrangements. Support from family, friends, or social institutions can help compensate for these losses and minimize discontinuity. Thus, as we'll discuss later in this chapter, a growing trend is to try to keep older adults out of institutions and in the community and to help them live as independently as possible.

The Role of Productivity

Some current studies focus on productive activity, either paid or unpaid, as a key to aging well. One research team (Glass, Seeman, Herzog, Kahn, & Berkman, 1995) compared nearly 1,200 men and women ages 70 to 79, who showed high physical and cognitive functioning ("successful agers"), with 162 medium- and low-functioning adults in the same age group ("usual agers"). The high-functioning group tended to be more educated and affluent, to exercise more and to be in better cardiovascular condition, and to have fewer psychiatric problems and a greater sense of self-mastery.

Nearly all "successful" agers and more than 9 out of 10 "usual" agers engaged in some form of productive activity, most commonly housework. However, "successful" agers were far more productive than "usual" agers; on average, they did one-third more housework, more than twice as much yard work, more than 3 times as much paid work, and almost 4 times as much volunteer work. Although there was no significant difference in the total amount of child care done by the two groups, nearly 25 percent of "successful" agers—men as well as women—reported doing *some* child care, as compared with only 17 percent of "usual" agers.

Three years later, the researchers interviewed the "successful" agers again. While 15 percent had become less productive, 13 percent had become more so. People who originally had been more satisfied with their lives were more likely to have increased in productivity; so were people who at the follow-up interview scored higher than before on personal mastery. Married people were less likely to lose productivity than unmarried people. African Americans were nearly twice as likely as white people to gain in productivity, mostly in yard word and housework, and they were also more likely to continue to do some paid or volunteer work. This research supports the idea that productive activity plays an important part in "successful" aging and that older people not only can continue to be productive but can become even more so.

A study of a nationwide sample of more than 1,600 mostly white adults age 60 and older used four measures of "robust aging": the number of hours spent in productive activity each week, frequency of physical exercise, absence of cognitive impairment, and freedom from depression (Garfein & Herzog, 1995). Although fewer than 5 percent of the sample met the most stringent standards the researchers set in three or all four domains, about 4 out of 10 reached the highest level of robustness in one of the four areas. With advancing age, people were less likely to meet these strict criteria. Still, a substantial portion of those age 80 and above did qualify, showing that many people retain top levels of functioning well into old age. Predictors of "robust aging" included self-rated health and vision, frequent personal or telephone contact with family and friends, and absence of stressful life events.

The argument about what constitutes "successful" or "optimal" aging is far from settled, and may never be. One thing is clear: people differ greatly in the ways they can and do live—and want to live—the later years of life.

✔ LIFESTYLE AND SOCIAL ISSUES RELATED TO AGING

"I—will—never—retire!" wrote the comedian George Burns (1983, p. 138) at age 87. Burns, who continued performing until two years before his death at the age of 100, is one of many late-life achievers who have kept their minds and bodies active doing the work they love. Jonas Salk, during the ten years before his death at 80, was working on an AIDS vaccine (Bronte, 1993; Schmeck, 1995). Many other older people without famous names quietly go to work each day as typists, lawyers, nurses, or cashiers.

Whether and when to retire are perhaps the most crucial lifestyle decisions people make as they approach late adulthood. These decisions affect their financial situation and emotional state, as well as the ways they spend their waking hours and the ways they relate to family and friends. Furthermore, as we mentioned in Chapters 14 and 16, the problem of providing financial support for large numbers of retired older people has serious implications for society, especially as the "baby boom" generation nears old age. A related problem is the need for appropriate living arrangements and care for older people who can no longer manage on their own.

WORK, RETIREMENT, AND LEISURE

Retirement is a relatively new idea; it took hold in many industrialized countries during the late nineteenth and early twentieth centuries as life expectancy increased. In the United States, the economic depression of the 1930s was the impetus for the social security system, which, together with company-sponsored pension plans negotiated by labor unions, made it possible for many older workers to retire with financial security. Eventually, mandatory retirement at age 65 became almost universal.

Today compulsory retirement has been virtually outlawed as a form of age discrimination. Adults have many choices: early retirement, retiring from one career or job to start another, working part-time to keep busy or to supplement income, going back to school, doing volunteer work, pursuing other leisure interests—or not retiring at all.

Does Age Affect Job Performance?

Older workers, as we noted in Chapter 12, are often more productive than younger workers. Many older workers are not only experienced and skilled, but dependable, loyal, and respectful of authority (AARP, 1989; Barth, McNaught, & Rizzi, 1993; Rix, 1994). Although they may work more slowly than younger people, they are more accurate and less likely to be absent or to quit (Treas, 1995). Yet managers often assume that older workers are less energetic, less efficient, less flexible, and unwilling or unable to adapt to change ("Negative Stereotypes," 1995; "Older Workers," 1993).

The Age Discrimination in Employment Act (ADEA) protects most workers age 40 and older from being denied a job and from being fired, paid less, or forced to retire because of age. (Commercial airline pilots are still required to retire at age 60 under the Federal Aviation Act.) The ADEA, which applies to firms with 20 or more employees, has eliminated some blatant practices, such as help-wanted ads that specify "ages 25 to 35." Still, many employers exert subtle pressures on older employees (Landy, 1994). In hard times older workers tend to be the first to be laid off or pushed into retirement, often because they are the most highly paid. Complaints of unfair terminations and of unequal pay, promotional, and training policies are increasing, and the backlog of cases filed with the Equal Employment Opportunity Commission is growing. Furthermore, age discrimination can be very difficult to prove. A worker has to establish that it was age, not some other reason the employer may come up with, which actually motivated an action. In almost 700 cases filed between 1970 and the mid-1980s, the employer won about two-thirds of the time (C. J. Snyder & G. V. Barrett, 1988).

Powerful ammunition for older workers has come from a comprehensive study by an interdisciplinary task force commissioned by Congress and chaired by Frank Landy (1992, 1994), professor of psychology and director of the Center for Applied Behavioral Sciences at Pennsylvania State University. The study found that—even in such highly demanding, dangerous work as policing and firefighting—age, in and of itself, does not predict job performance.

When Congress in 1986 outlawed mandatory re-

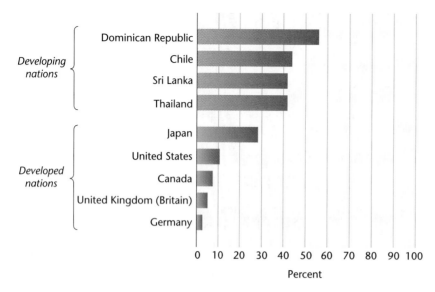

FIGURE 17-3
Percentage of older adults in the work force, selected countries. Note that percentages for developing nations are for people age 60 and over and that percentages for developed nations are for those age 65 and older. *(Sources: Commonwealth Fund, 1992; Kaiser, 1993.)*

tirement under the ADEA, it left a temporary exception for public safety officers, pending the task force's report. The task force spent almost two years combing more than 5,000 research articles and collecting data from more than 500 cities. The chief findings were (1) that physical fitness and mental abilities vary increasingly with age and differ more within age groups than between age groups and (2) that tests of specific psychological, physical, and perceptual-motor abilities can predict job performance far better than age can.

Even though the task force found no grounds for the idea that older workers as a group endanger public safety, Congress in 1996, under conflicting political pressures, reinstated forced retirement of public safety officers. Still, the task force established a benchmark that is likely to have an influence beyond this specific legislation. Already its findings and recommendations have been cited in court cases. As Landy (1994, p. 10) has pointed out, "Although psychologists have made substantial progress in dispelling age stereotypes, it is abundantly clear that there is work left to do."

Trends in Late-Life Work and Retirement

Even when not forced to do so, most adults who *can* retire *do* retire, and, with increasing longevity, they spend more time in retirement than in the past (Kinsella & Gist, 1995). In industrialized countries, the working elderly range from only 3 percent of all older adults in Germany to 28 percent in Japan (Commonwealth Fund, 1992; see Figure 17-3). The pattern is quite different in most of the develop-

ing world, where large numbers of older adults continue to work for income: more than 40 percent in Sri Lanka, Thailand, and Chile and 57 percent in the Dominican Republic, according to a United Nations study (Kaiser, 1993). However, their main means of support is not work but aid from their children, except in Chile, where pensions are sizable. (Box 17-2 describes retirement and pension policies in another developing nation: China.)

Despite a general decline in work force participation by older people in industrialized societies, older women's participation has remained stable or has even expanded. Thus, although older men still form a much larger proportion of the labor force, the proportion of older workers who are women is growing, and this is happening in many developing countries as well. Since many older women throughout the world serve as caregivers for frail, old-old parents, this trend has serious social consequences (Kinsella & Gist, 1995).

In the United States, work force participation by older men has fallen steadily. In 1900, 2 out of 3 men age 65 and over were working: in 1950, fewer than 1 in 2; and today, only about 1 in 6, or 17 percent (AARP, 1995; Quinn, 1993). Older women's participation increased slightly from about 8 percent to 11 percent during the first half of the twentieth century, then fell again, and has now stabilized at around 9 percent (AARP, 1995; Schick & Schick, 1994). As today's middle-aged and younger women, who are accustomed to paid employment, enter old age, the female share of the older labor force may grow again, unless these women follow retirement patterns similar to men's.

BOX 17-2   WINDOW ON THE WORLD

WORK, RETIREMENT, AND HEALTH CARE IN CHINA

Karl Marx, the father of communism, hoped to dignify workers and end exploitation of the working class through communal ownership of property and means of production. Today the People's Republic of China is the last major communist power in the world, but its economy is partly privatized. How do its workers fare when they reach retirement age?

The answer hinges in part on demographic change. As in other Asian countries (refer back to Box 16-1), fertility is declining while longevity is increasing due to rising living standards and better sanitation. In China this effect is particularly pronounced due to a switch in family planning policies. Until the 1970s, the government encouraged the traditional goal of large families to support people in their old age. Faced with rampant population growth, the government then did an about-face and in 1980 imposed penalties for having more than one child (MacAdam, 1993; Mufson, 1995). As a result, "the family structure has been turned around. Instead of many children supporting their parents, a couple must support up to four parents and a child" (Mufson, 1995, p. 31). The burden will become heavier by 2025, when the proportion of the population over age 60 is expected to double from about 9 percent to about 19 percent (Mufson, 1995).

Retirement policies in cities such as Shanghai, where nearly 8 out of 10 people work for large state-owned enterprises, complicate the picture. To combat chronic unemployment among youth, employers can require workers to retire, generally at age 60 for men and age 50 for women. Under a special provision, as many as 80 percent of new retirees have been replaced by their own children (Davis-Friedmann, 1983; Hayward & Wang, 1993).

The swelling ratio of retirees to workers is putting many enterprises in the red. Pension benefits range from 60 to 75 percent of a worker's latest income. Pensions are not automatic, however; they are granted by a government agency, which reviews the applicant's work history, health, finances, and political record. Thus the state, as well as the employer, is directly involved in individual retirement decisions. Some workers are not allowed to retire, others are called back to work after retirement, and some are required to do neighborhood maintenance or public service work, paid or unpaid.

Retirees can continue to work and earn money—supposedly, no more than before retirement, but this restriction is often ignored. Skilled older urban workers, who tend to be better-educated and better-trained than younger workers, are often at an advantage in the job market, especially since the rise of small, privately owned businesses. In fact, healthy older adults can earn more after retirement than before. Their pension funds together with their potential earning power make them central to the economic life of the multigenerational family, reversing the traditional pattern of kinship obligation, in which adult children supported their parents (Davis-Friedmann, 1985).

However, primary responsibility for the frail and infirm remains with the family, community, and work unit; the role of the central government in health care is minimal. Although health insurance for most urban workers extends into retirement, it generally does not cover long-term care. Local committees identify older people who need in-home care and assign a trained person to visit them, run errands, prepare meals, and contact doctors when needed. Child-

less people may be able to live in one of the few government-operated social welfare institutes (Olson, 1994).

In rural areas, whose residents make up almost 80 percent of the Chinese labor force, production is controlled mostly by family households, which contract with state grain production offices (Gui, 1989). Few farm workers receive government pensions; for those who do, the income may amount to one-fourth or less of what urban workers get. Retirement in rural communities typically means, not stopping work, but a shift in the type of work a person does. Older men turn over the most laborious aspects of farm work to their sons but continue to do less strenuous tasks into their seventies. Older women confine themselves to household chores. Parents usually live in the home of the oldest married son. Lacking adequate pensions, they must depend on their children (Davis-Friedman, 1983). However, smaller families and the exodus of young adults to urban areas are eroding this tradition.

Most medical care in rural communities is in the home. Families can hire nursemaids to care for bedridden patients; otherwise, family members are expected to stay at the bedside. For people with no children to care for them, village committees may arrange for someone to deliver groceries, medicine, and coal. The central government has begun to prod rural townships to establish homes for the aged. A town committee decides when it is time for a childless elderly person to enter such a home (Olson, 1994).

As rural areas develop, the state may take a more active role in providing for elderly workers. Until then, family and community support must somehow serve the needs of older adults.

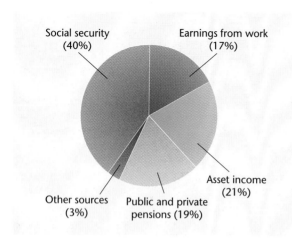

FIGURE 17-4
Sources of income of older Americans. *(Source: Based on data from AARP, 1995.)*

Public and private pension programs, sometimes offered as an inducement to older workers to make way for younger workers, have contributed to a trend toward early retirement in the United States, as in many industrialized countries (Kinsella & Gist, 1995). Downsizing companies offer strong incentives to early retirement; private pension plans often penalize employees who continue to work past their early sixties. About 3 out of 4 American workers now retire before age 65, many in their late fifties (Monk, 1994). However, the trend toward early retirement among men appears to have leveled off, and among women it has been offset by the rise in midlife careers (Quinn, 1993).

Men who continue to work after age 65 tend to be better-educated than those who retire. They are more likely to be in good health, and they may have wives who are still working. Usually they strongly want to work, in contrast to retired men, who generally do not view paid work as necessary to self-fulfillment (Parnes & Sommers, 1994). Older black men are less likely to remain in the work force than older white men. Health problems force many African American men to stop working before normal retirement age (Gendell & Siegel, 1996; Hayward, Friedman, & Chen, 1996). Black men also tend to die young. However, those who do remain healthy tend to continue working longer than white men. Thus voluntary retirement is "more a white experience than a black experience" (Hayward, Friedman, & Chen, 1996, p. S9).

The line between work and retirement is not as clear as it used to be. Some retirees find part-time or new full-time jobs; some (who may call themselves "semiretired") keep doing what they were doing before but cut down on their hours and responsibilities. About half of the older adults in the labor force work part time, in part because earnings above a certain amount cause those under age 70 to lose social security benefits (Treas, 1995). Self-employed men are less likely than wage earners to make an abrupt switch from full-time work to complete retirement (Burkhauser & Quinn, 1989). A longitudinal study of men originally identified as gifted in childhood found that those who had been self-employed at any time before retirement were more likely to do some type of part-time work after retirement (Elder & Pavalko, 1993).

How Do Older Adults Fare Financially?

Social security is the largest single source of income for older people in the United States. More than 90 percent of older Americans receive social security benefits, and 61 percent get at least half their total income from this source. Other sources of income include pensions, earnings from work, and earnings from assets (AARP, 1995; U.S. Bureau of the Census, 1992b; see Figure 17-4).

Social security and other government programs, such as Medicare, have allowed today's older adults, as a group, to be at least as well off financially as younger people. In fact, the poverty rate is slightly lower for noninstitutionalized adults age 65 and over than for those ages 18 to 64 (AARP, 1995). Between 1968 and 1994, partly because of cost-of-living adjustments and increases in social security benefits, the proportion of older Americans living in poverty dropped from 28.5 to 11.7 percent (AARP, 1995; Monk, 1994), and between 1957 and 1992 the median income of older adults (controlling for inflation) more than doubled (U.S. Bureau of the Census, 1995a).

Older men are generally better off than older women, who are less likely to have pension and social security benefits in their own names. In 1994, the median income of older men ($15,250) was nearly twice as high as that of older women ($8,950). White people are generally better off than minorities. In 1994, elderly white people had median incomes one-third to one-half again as high as those of elderly blacks and Hispanics. People who head family households are better off than those who live alone or with nonrelatives. Median income for households headed by older adults in 1994 was $26,512, compared with $11,504 for older persons living in nonfamily households; 42 percent of the latter had incomes of less than $10,000, compared with only 7 percent of those heading family households (AARP, 1995).

Despite the marked improvement in older Americans' financial status, 3.7 million—nearly one-fifth—were classified as poor or near-poor in 1994. (An older person living alone with an income of $7,108, or an older couple with an income of $8,967, was considered to be at the poverty level.) The poverty rate rises with age. Women, minorities, and people living alone are likeliest to be poor; so are people who have not finished high school, who live in the south, or who are too ill or disabled to work. About one-fourth of African Americans (27 percent) and Hispanic Americans (23 percent), who together make up about 12 percent of the elderly population, have incomes below the poverty line (AARP, 1995; U.S. Bureau of the Census, 1995a). Since many minority workers' jobs are not covered by social security, minority elderly are more likely than others to be on Old Age Assistance.

Although fewer older people live in poverty today, many face poverty for the first time in old age. Older women who are single, widowed, or divorced are at greater risk of becoming poor during retirement than married women, who often can rely on a husband's pension (Burkhauser, Holden, & Feaster, 1988; Kinsella & Gist, 1995; Treas, 1995). Once poor, older adults are likely to stay poor (Treas, 1995). They may no longer be able to work, and inflation may have eroded their savings and pensions. Infirm or disabled people often outlive their savings at a time when their medical bills are soaring. Some get help from such public assistance programs as Supplemental Security Income, subsidized housing, Medicaid, and food stamps. Others either are not eligible or do not take part in these programs, often because they do not know what the programs offer or how to apply.

Preparing for Retirement

How well are today's middle-aged adults planning for retirement? Forty percent of 45- to 59-year-olds say they have saved too little or nothing at all, and 2 out of 3 expect to have serious problems living on a retirement income (Rix, 1994). It has been estimated that the "baby boom" generation, who will start retiring early in the twenty-first century, would need to triple their current savings rate to maintain their present standard of living after retirement (Farrell et al., 1994). With a growing el-

derly population and proportionately fewer workers contributing to the social security system, it seems likely that benefits (in real dollars) will not continue to rise and may even decline. As for private pensions, a shift from defined benefit plans that guarantee a fixed retirement income to riskier defined contribution plans, in which benefits depend on returns from invested funds, is making the financial future less certain for many workers (Rix, 1994; Treas, 1995).

Since more middle-aged women are employed than in the past, and because wives tend to be younger than their husbands, many women probably will continue working after their husbands retire. Their earnings will augment family income, and they will be more likely than in the past to be eligible for pensions when they do retire—though still not as likely as men. However, because most women have worked less regularly and for lower pay than men, their pension and social security benefits will be lower (Kinsella & Gist, 1995).

Planning for retirement should include not only providing for financial needs, but structuring life after retirement to make it enjoyable and meaningful, anticipating physical or emotional problems, and discussing how retirement will affect a spouse. Assistance can come from preretirement workshops, self-help books, and company-sponsored programs.

How Do Retired People Use Their Time?

Two common lifestyle patterns after retirement are *family-focused* and *balanced investment*. One researcher found the **family-focused lifestyle** to be typical of a group of retired midwestern factory workers. This lifestyle consists largely of accessible, low-cost activities that revolve around family, home, and companions: conversation, watching television, visiting with family and friends, informal entertaining, going to inexpensive restaurants, playing cards, or just doing "what comes along." The second pattern, **balanced investment,** is typical of more educated people, who allocate their time more equally among family, work, and leisure (J. R. Kelly, 1987, 1994). These patterns may change with age. In one study, younger retirees who were most satisfied with their quality of life were those who traveled regularly and went to cultural events, but after age 75, family- and home-based activity yielded the most satisfaction (J. R. Kelly, Steinkamp, & Kelly, 1986).

Sunday painters, amateur carpenters, and oth-

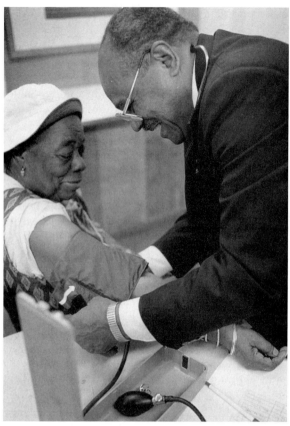

By using his leisure time to work as a volunteer in the field of health care, this retiree is helping not only the community but also himself. The self-esteem gained from using hard-won skills and from continuing to be a useful, contributing member of society is a valuable by-product of volunteer service. *(Joel Gordon)*

yield something useful, such as sewing, gardening, and fishing. Perhaps because poverty and racial discrimination have shut them out of many leisure activities throughout their lives, they may not think of doing things just for fun or they may lack the resources to do so (M. B. Brown & Tedrick, 1993).

Since the late 1960s, the proportion of older adults doing volunteer work has increased greatly. Most older volunteers work alongside adults of all ages, more than half in churches or synagogues. Countless community-based programs are built specifically around older volunteers. Retired executives advise small businesses, retired accountants help fill out tax returns, senior companions visit frail elderly people in their homes, and foster grandparents, for a small stipend, provide social and emotional support to neglected children, teenage parents, or substance abusers. One reason for the increase in volunteerism is a changing public image of older adults and their capabilities—a recognition that older people can be active, healthy, contributing members of a community. Volunteer work itself has taken on higher status, and today's better-educated older population has more to contribute and more interest in contributing (Chambre, 1993).

The many paths to a meaningful, enjoyable retirement have two things in common: doing satisfying things and having satisfying relationships. For most older people, both "are an extension of histories that have developed throughout the life course" (J. R. Kelly, 1994, p. 501).

ers who have made an effort to master a beloved craft or hobby often make that passion central to their lives during retirement (Mannell, 1993). This third lifestyle pattern, *serious leisure,* is dominated by activity that "demands skill, attention, and commitment" (J. R. Kelly, 1994, p. 502), and retirees who engage in it tend to be extraordinarily satisfied with their lives. One divorced woman, within a year after her retirement from operating a clothing boutique, proudly invited friends to a gallery exhibit of her paintings.

African Americans are more likely than white people to engage in productive activity after retirement. According to a nationwide survey of nearly 1,700 older Americans, fewer than 1 in 4 older African Americans participate in outdoor sports, compared with 85 percent or more of older whites, Hispanics, and Native Americans. Instead, most African American retirees do things that

LIVING ARRANGEMENTS

In 1994, about 95 percent of Americans age 65 and older lived in the community, not in institutions; 68 percent of this group—including about 81 percent of men and 58 percent of women—lived with family members. Most lived with a spouse; about 13 percent, with children or other relatives; and about 2 percent of the women and 3 percent of the men, with nonrelatives. Because women live longer than men and are more likely to be widowed, elderly men are more likely to live with a spouse, whereas elderly women are more likely to live alone (AARP, 1995; see Figure 17-5 for a more detailed breakdown by age groups).

Nine out of ten older men and eight out of ten older women live in their own homes, and most prefer to do so; many stay in their homes after they are widowed (Treas, 1995). The likelihood of living alone or in a nursing home increases with age (AARP, 1995; U.S. Bureau of the Census, 1995a). Among the oldest old (those over 85), about 25 percent are in nursing homes or other care facilities; but 60 percent live in their own homes, and a growing proportion—about 37 percent in 1990—live alone (Longino, 1994).

Living arrangements can become a problem in old age. Three flights of stairs may be too much to manage. A neighborhood may deteriorate, and helpless-looking older people may become prey to young thugs. Mental or physical disability may make living alone impractical. Older people in suburban areas, if they can no longer drive, may be isolated and unable to obtain necessities on their own.

Most older people do not need much help, and those who do can often remain in the community if they have at least one person to depend on. The single most important factor keeping people out of institutions is being married. As long as a couple are in relatively good health, they can usually live fairly independently and care for each other. The issue of living arrangements becomes more pressing when one or both become frail, infirm, or disabled, or when one spouse dies.

People who are not living with a spouse most often get help from a child, usually a daughter. Those who cannot call on a spouse or a child usually get help from friends (Chappell, 1991). Social activities—such as going to church or temple or a senior center, or doing volunteer work—help people stay connected to their community (Steinbach, 1992). An emerging array of housing options and community support programs make it easier for older people to live with some degree of independence (see Box 17-3).

Although physical limitations and other practical considerations affect the choice of living arrangements, cultural patterns also play an important part. Elderly white people are more likely than elderly members of minority groups to live with a spouse; minority elders, in keeping with their traditions, are much more likely to live with other relatives as well, often in extended-family households. More than 1 in 4 older Hispanic Americans and 1 in 3 older Asian Americans live with a spouse and other relatives. Far fewer older Hispanics and Asians live alone, but 1 in 4 older white people, black people, and Native Americans do. Institutionalization is twice as common among whites and blacks as among Hispanics and Asians (Himes, Hogan, & Eggebeen, 1996). However, the most vulnerable older African Americans—those with functional impairments and those age 85 and over—are less likely to be institutionalized than white people and more likely to live with a child or someone else and to rely on informal caregiving (Longino, 1994; Soldo, Wolf, & Agree, 1990; Worobey & Angel, 1990).

Let's look more closely at the two most common living arrangements for older adults without spouses—living alone and living with adult children—and then at living in institutions. Finally, we'll discuss a serious problem for dependent older adults: abuse by caregivers.

Living Alone

A growing number of older Americans live alone

FIGURE 17-5
Living arrangements of noninstitutionalized persons age 65 and over, 1994. As compared with men and women ages 65 to 74, fewer of those age 75 and over live with spouses, and more live alone or with children or other relatives. In both age groups, women are more likely than men to live alone; men are more likely to live with spouses. (*Source: Treas, 1995, figure 10, p. 30. Based on Population Reference Bureau analysis of the March 1994 Current Population Survey, U.S. Bureau of the Census.*)

BOX 17-3   PRACTICALLY SPEAKING

CHOOSING LIVING ARRANGEMENTS

Three friends in their late sixties bought a big old house and turned it into a "geriatric commune" with shared kitchen and dining room. "It takes a lot of the stress out of aging to know you have a place that's yours and people who will care," they say (Porcino, 1993, pp. 28, 30). Living with roommates or housemates is but one of an almost bewildering range of choices in living arrangements available to older adults today. Let's see how various options match specific lifestyles and needs.

A growing number of aging Americans—more than 80 percent of those in their fifties or older, according to surveys—say they want to stay in their own homes or apartments indefinitely (AARP, 1993b, 1996). *Aging in place* makes sense for those who can manage on their own or with minimal help, have an adequate income or a paid-up mortgage, can handle the upkeep, are happy in the neighborhood, and want to be independent, to have privacy, and to be near friends, adult children, or grandchildren (Gonyea, Hudson, & Seltzer, 1990). For older people with impairments that make it hard to get along entirely on their own, minor support—such as meals, transportation, and home health aides—can often help them stay put (E. M. Brody, 1978; Lawton, 1981). So can ramps, grab bars, and other modifications within the home.

For many homeowners, a reverse mortgage can make aging in place financially attractive. A reverse mortgage allows older people to live off their home's equity by collecting monthly payments from a lender as long they live there. When the house is sold, or the owner dies, the lender recoups the loan with interest.

Older adults who cannot or do not want to maintain a house, do not have family nearby, or prefer a different locale or climate may move into low-maintenance or maintenance-free townhouses, con-

dominiums, or cooperative or rental apartments. Or they may buy mobile homes so that they can travel and visit far-flung family members.

If and when they cannot manage on their own, nearly 60 percent of adults over 50 would prefer to move to a residential facility that would provide some care and assistance; only 26 percent would prefer to move in with relatives or friends (AARP, 1996). Older adults who want or need varying levels of amenities, services, or care without sacrificing independence and dignity may consider the following options (Porcino, 1993):

- *Retirement hotel.* Hotel or apartment building remodeled to meet the needs of independent older adults. Typical hotel services (switchboard, maid service, message center) are provided.
- *Retirement community.* Large, self-contained development with owned or rental units, or both. Support services and recreational facilities are often available.
- *Shared housing.* Housing can be shared informally by adult parents and children or by friends. Sometimes social agencies match people who need a place to live with people who have houses or apartments with extra rooms. The older person usually has a private room but shares living, eating, and cooking areas and may exchange services such as light housekeeping for rent.
- *Accessory apartment* or *ECHO (elder cottage housing opportunity) housing.* An independent unit created so that an older person can live in a remodeled single-family home or in a portable unit on the grounds of a single-family home—often, but not necessarily, that of an adult child. These units offer privacy, proximity to caregivers, and security.

- *Congregate housing.* Private or government-subsidized rental apartment complexes or mobile home parks designed for older adults. They provide meals, housekeeping, transportation, social and recreational activities, and sometimes health care. One type of congregate housing is called a group home. A social agency that owns or rents a house brings together a small number of elderly residents and hires helpers to shop, cook, do heavy cleaning, drive, and give counseling. Residents take care of their own personal needs and take some responsibility for day-to-day tasks.
- *Assisted-living facility.* Semi-independent living in one's own room or apartment. Similar to congregate housing, but residents receive personal care (bathing, dressing, and grooming) and protective supervision according to their needs and desires. Board-and-care homes are similar but smaller and offer more personal care and supervision.
- *Foster-care home.* Owners of a single-family residence take in an unrelated older adult and provide meals, housekeeping, and personal care.
- *Continuing care retirement community.* Long-term housing planned to provide a full range of accommodations and services for affluent elderly people as their needs change. A resident may start out in an independent apartment and then move into congregate housing with such services as cleaning, laundry, and meals; then the person advances to an assisted-living facility and finally moves into a nursing home. Life-care communities are similar but guarantee housing and medical or nursing care for a specified period or for life; they require a substantial entry fee in addition to monthly payments.

and like it. Between 1980 and 1993, the number of older people who lived alone increased by nearly one-third (AARP, 1994). By 1994, about 30 percent of older adults lived alone: 40 percent of the women and 16 percent of the men (AARP, 1995). Even among the oldest old, the proportion living alone jumped from about 30 percent in 1980 to 37 percent in 1990 (Longino, 1994).

Of the 9.3 million older people who live alone, 7.2 million are women (AARP, 1995). About 80 percent are widowed, and almost 50 percent have no children or none living nearby. They are older and poorer on the average than elderly people who live with someone else. Yet almost 90 percent value their independence and prefer to be on their own (Commonwealth Fund, 1986; U.S. Bureau of the Census, 1992a).

As black women age, they are increasingly less likely than black men to be married, romantically involved, or interested in a romantic relationship—perhaps for practical reasons, as unmarried black women tend to be better off financially than married ones (Tucker, Taylor, & Mitchell-Kernan, 1993). Yet a single state entails risk: a black woman living alone in late life is 3 times as likely to be poor as a white woman in that situation (U.S. Bureau of the Census, 1991b). Furthermore, women living alone are more likely to end up in institutions (Tucker et al., 1993).

Living with Adult Children

Most people in American society do not fall into a pattern common in many other societies, in which older people expect to live and be cared for in their children's homes. Most older people in the United States, even those in difficult circumstances, are reluctant to burden their families and to give up their own freedom. It can be inconvenient to absorb an extra person into a household, and everyone's privacy—and relationships—may suffer. The elderly parent may feel useless, bored, and isolated from friends. If the adult child is married and parent and spouse do not get along well or if caregiving duties become too burdensome, the marriage may be threatened (Lund, 1993a; Shapiro, 1994).

Despite these concerns, many older Americans do live with adult children, and the proportion increases with age. The success of such an arrangement depends largely on the quality of the relationship that has existed in the past and on the ability of both generations to communicate fully and frankly. The decision to move an adult parent into a child's home should be mutual and needs to be thought through carefully and thoroughly. Parents and children need to respect one another's dignity and autonomy and accept their differences (Shapiro, 1994).

Living in Institutions

Although at any given time only 5 percent of people over 65 in the United States live in institutions, the lifetime probability of spending time in a nursing home, even if only briefly to convalesce, is much higher. That probability increases markedly with age: 1 percent at ages 65 to 74, 6 percent at 75 to 84, and 24 percent at 85 and over (AARP, 1995; U.S. Bureau of the Census, 1995a). About half of the women and one-third of the men who were 60 years old in 1990 will eventually stay in a nursing home at least once (Center on Elderly People Living Alone, 1995b; Treas, 1995), and with the aging of the "baby boomers" the need for such care is likely to greatly increase.

Most older people do not want to live in institutions, and most family members do not want them to. Older people often feel that placement in an institution is a sign of rejection, and children usually place their parents reluctantly, apologetically, and with great guilt. Sometimes, though, because of an older person's needs or a family's circumstances, such placement seems to be the only solution. At highest risk of institutionalization are those living alone, those who do not take part in social activities, those whose daily activities are limited by poor health or disability, and those whose caregivers are overburdened (McFall & Miller, 1992; Steinbach, 1992). Nearly three-fourths of the 1.5 million nursing home residents are women; most are white widows in their eighties. About 60 percent are mentally impaired, and nearly 90 percent need help with at least one aspect of personal care, such as dressing, eating, or bathing (AARP, 1995; Center on Elderly People Living Alone, 1995b; Strahan, 1997).

The difference between good and inferior nursing home care can be very great. A good nursing home has an experienced professional staff, an adequate government insurance program, and a coordinated structure that can provide various levels of care (Kayser-Jones, 1982). It is lively, safe, clean, and attractive. It offers stimulating activities and opportunities to spend time with people of both sexes and all ages. It provides privacy, in part so that residents can be sexually active and can visit undisturbed with family members. A good nursing home also offers a full range of social, therapeutic, and rehabilitative services. The best-quality care seems to exist in larger, nonprofit facilities with a high ratio of nurses to nursing aides (Pillemer & Moore, 1989). One essential element of good care is the opportunity for residents to make decisions and exert some control over their lives (E. Langer & Rodin, 1976).

Federal law (Omnibus Budget Reconciliation Act, OBRA, 1987, 1990) sets tough requirements for nursing homes and gives residents the right to choose their own doctors, to be fully informed about their care and treatment, and to be free from physical or mental abuse, corporal punishment, involuntary seclusion, and physical or chemical restraints. Some states train volunteer ombudsmen to act as advocates for nursing home residents, to explain their rights, and to resolve their complaints about such matters as privacy, treatment, food, and financial issues.

In 1993, the cost of institutional care averaged $39,000 a year; because of gaps in private and governmental health insurance, about one-third of this cost fell directly on patients and their families. Medicare paid for less than 9 percent of all expenditures on nursing home care. Although Medicaid covers more than half of such expenditures, it is available only to people who have virtually exhausted their own resources (Center on Elderly People Living Alone, 1995a, 1995c).

With the emergence of less costly home health care services and other alternatives, utilization of nursing home beds fell from nearly 93 percent in 1977 to 87.4 percent in 1995 (Strahan, 1997). However, as the population ages and women's life expectancy continues to increase faster than men's, the number of nursing home residents is expected to grow rapidly. By the time the "baby boomers" reach their eighties and nineties in about 2040, the proportion of older adults needing long-term care may well be 2 to 3 times greater than in 1986 (Kunkel & Applebaum, 1992). This trend is likely to require more nursing homes and new ways to finance care.

Mistreatment of the Elderly

A middle-aged woman drives up to a hospital emergency room in a middle-sized American city. She lifts a frail, elderly woman (who appears somewhat confused) out of the car and into a wheelchair, wheels her into the emergency room, and quietly walks out and drives away, leaving no identification (Barnhart, 1992).

"Granny dumping" is one form of *elder abuse:* maltreatment or neglect of dependent older persons or violation of their personal rights. Each year, an estimated 100,000 to 200,000 geriatric patients are abandoned in emergency rooms throughout the United States by caregivers who feel that they have reached the end of their rope (Lund, 1993a).

A randomized study in the Boston area suggested that about 3 percent of older people are mistreated, but only 1 case in 14 gets public attention (Pillemer & Finkelhor, 1988). Studies in Canada and Great Britain found similar rates of maltreatment, and the number of reported cases appears to be rising (Lachs & Pillemer, 1995). There may be 2 million victims in the United States each year, according to one estimate (AARP, 1993b).

Mistreatment of the elderly may fall under any of four categories: (1) *physical violence* intended to cause injury, (2) *psychological or emotional abuse,* which may include insults and threats (such as the threat of abandonment or institutionalization), (3) *material exploitation,* or misappropriation of money or property, and (4) *neglect*—intentional or unintentional failure to meet a dependent older person's needs (Lachs & Pillemer, 1995). The first three categories represent active abuse; the last is a form of passive abuse. Physical violence may be less common than is generally believed; financial exploitation is probably more so (Bengtson, Rosenthal, & Burton, 1996). The American Medical Association (1992) has added a fifth category: *violating personal rights,* for example, the older person's right to privacy and to make her or his own personal and health decisions.

Elder abuse most often happens to frail or demented elderly people living with spouses or children. The abuser is more likely to be a spouse, since more older people live with spouses (Lachs & Pillemer, 1995; Paveza et al., 1992; Pillemer & Finkelhor, 1988). An estimated 500,000 women age 65 and older are abused by husbands or male partners (Older Women's League, 1994). Often, abuse of an elderly wife is a continuation of abuse that went on throughout the marriage (Bengtson, Rosenthal, & Burton, 1996).

Few studies have looked directly at the incidence of elder abuse among minorities; and among those which have, results are inconsistent. Elderly people in various ethnic groups may have different ideas of what constitutes abuse or may, for cultural reasons, be less likely to complain about it (Moon & Williams, 1993).

Elder abuse should be recognized as a type of domestic violence. Usually both abused and abuser need treatment (Hooyman, Rathbone-McCuan, & Klingbeil, 1982; Pillemer & Finkelhor, 1988). Neglect by family caregivers is usually unintentional; many do not know how to give proper care or are in poor health themselves. Most physical abuse problems can be quickly resolved by counseling or other services (AARP, 1993a). Abusers need treatment to recognize what they are doing and assistance to reduce the stress of caregiving (see Chapter 15). Self-help groups may help victims acknowledge what is happening, recognize that they do not have to put up with mistreatment, and find out how to stop it or get away from it.

✔ PERSONAL RELATIONSHIPS IN LATE LIFE

Most older people's lives are enriched by the presence of people who care about them and to whom they feel close. Although they may see people less often, personal relationships, especially with family members, continue to be important into very old age—perhaps even more so than before (Carstensen, 1995; Johnson & Troll, 1992).

In keeping with socioemotional selectivity theory, the family is the primary source of emotional support in late life, and the late-life family has special characteristics (Brubaker, 1983, 1990). First and foremost, it is likely to be multigenerational. Today, when a family often spans four or five generations, a person may have one or more living grandparents and grandchildren at the same time. For the first time in history, most adults live long enough to see their grandchildren grow up, and most grandchildren know at least two and often three or all four grandparents (Cherlin & Furstenberg, 1986b).

The presence of so many family members can be enriching but can also create special pressures. Many "young-old" people have at least one parent who has lived long enough to have several chronic illnesses and whose care may be physically and emotionally draining. Many women today spend more of their lives caring for parents than for children (Abel, 1991). Now that the fastest-growing group in the population is age 85 and over, many people in their late sixties or beyond, whose own health and energy may be faltering, find themselves in this position.

Let's look at the relationships older people have with spouses, siblings, and adult children. We'll also examine the lives of those who are divorced, remarried, single, or in homosexual relationships and those who are childless. (We discuss widowhood in Chapter 18.) Finally, we'll consider the importance of friendship in late life and of a new role: that of great-grandparent.

LONG-TERM MARRIAGES

The long-term marriage is a relatively new phenomenon; most marriages, like most people, used to have a shorter life span. Many men lost one or more wives in childbirth, and both wives and husbands often succumbed to disease early in adulthood. Today, about 1 marriage in 5 lasts 50 years (Brubaker, 1983, 1993). Because women usually marry older men and outlive them and because men are more likely to remarry after divorce or widowhood, many more men than women are married in late life (AARP, 1995; see Figure 17-6). At ages 65 to 74, 79 percent of men, but only 53 percent of women, are married. Among those age 75 and older, 70 percent of men still have spouses, but the proportion among women has dropped to 26 percent (U.S. Bureau of the Census, 1993b). The imbalance is especially striking among African Americans, since black men have lower life expectancy than white men, and older black men, when they marry, tend to choose much younger women (Tucker, Taylor, & Mitchell-Kernan, 1993).

Socioemotional selectivity theory predicts that intimate relationships, such as marriage, become more emotionally important in old age and that couples in longtime marriages will use strategies to minimize conflict. Research seems to confirm this hypothesis. Married couples who are still together in their sixties are more likely than middle-aged couples to report their marriage as satisfying—and many would call it improved (Gilford, 1986). Since divorce has been easier to obtain for some years, spouses who are still together late in life are likely to have worked out their differences and to have arrived at mutually satisfying accommodations. On the other hand, some people may say that their marriage is happy as a conscious or unconscious justification for having stayed in it so long.

Another possible reason older people report more satisfaction with marriage is that people of this age are more satisfied with life in general. This satisfaction may stem from factors outside the

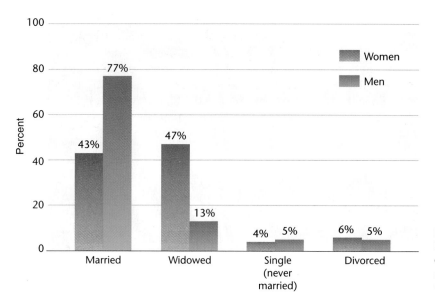

FIGURE 17-6
Marital status of people age 65 and over, 1994. *(Source: AARP, 1995; based on data from U.S. Bureau of the Census.)*

marriage: work, the end of child rearing, or more money in the bank. The ability of married people to handle the ups and downs of late adulthood with relative serenity may well result from mutual supportiveness, which reflects three important benefits of marriage: intimacy (sexual and emotional), interdependence (sharing of tasks and resources), and the partners' sense of belonging to each other (Atchley, 1985; Gilford, 1986).

In one study of 317 older couples, interviewers probed husbands' and wives' perceptions of the closeness of their relationship. If a husband had a confidant, it was likely to be his wife, whereas women (who generally have more intimate friendships) were more likely to confide in someone outside the marriage. Equal proportions (40 percent) of men and women acknowledged receiving emotional support from their spouses—though husbands, in keeping with the traditional male value of self-reliance, were more likely to claim that they did not need such support (Tower & Kasl, 1996).

Marital satisfaction may depend largely on how couples adjust to the freedom that results from shedding the roles of breadwinner and childrearer (Zube, 1982). Some couples find more interest and enjoyment in each other's company. Many couples enjoy retirement because it offers leisure for traveling, spending time with children and grandchildren, and pursuing other interests together or separately. As roles change, however, some may argue over who does what.

In dual-career couples, when employment and retirement patterns conflict with role expectations, trouble may ensue (Szinovacz, 1996). Problems are likely to arise when the husband retires and the wife is still working (G. R. Lee & Shehan, 1989). Because many middle-aged divorced men marry much younger women, a second wife may be at the peak of her career when her husband retires. This situation is more likely to be a problem when the husband has traditional attitudes about gender roles; the husband may object to the wife's continuing to work and may feel threatened by loss of his own status as provider. Arguments may arise if the wife expects him, as the at-home partner, to do more housework. A traditional husband's marital satisfaction tends to improve when his wife retires while he is still working, though initially there may be some conflict, perhaps over his having pressured her to retire. A retired wife is likely to feel better about the marriage if her husband is willing to participate in household chores, whether he is retired or not; her satisfaction seems to depend more on his attitude toward doing housework than on the amount of housework he actually does (Szinovacz, 1996).

Late-life marriage can be severely tested by advancing age and physical ills. People who have to care for disabled partners may feel isolated, angry, and frustrated, especially when they are in poor health themselves (Gilford, 1986). Such couples may be caught in a vicious circle: the illness puts strains on the marriage, and these strains may aggravate the illness, stretching coping capacity to the breaking point (Karney & Bradbury, 1995). Caregiving spouses who are optimistic and well-adjusted to begin with, and who stay in touch with friends, usually cope best (Hooker, Monahan, Shifren, & Hutchinson, 1992; Skaff & Pearlin, 1992).

DIVORCE AND REMARRIAGE

Divorce in late life is rare; couples who take this step usually do so much earlier. Very few people over age 65—6 percent of women and 5 percent of men—are divorced and not remarried (refer back to Figure 17-6). However, since 1990 their numbers have increased 4 times as fast as the older population as a whole (AARP, 1995). Given the high divorce rates among younger cohorts—particularly the "baby boom" generation, who are now middle-aged—the proportion of older people who are divorced is likely to rise in the future. Furthermore, given the greater opportunities for men to remarry, the gap between the sexes will probably widen (Norton & Miller, 1992; Uhlenberg, Cooney, & Boyd, 1990). This is likely to be especially true of African Americans; the proportion of black women ages 55 to 64 who are divorced is about 15 times as high as for those age 85 and over (U.S. Bureau of the Census, 1991b).

Divorce can be traumatic for older people and for members of their families (see Chapter 15). Older divorced and separated men are less satisfied with friendships and leisure activities than married men. For both sexes, rates of mental illness and death are higher than average, perhaps in part because of inadequate social support networks for older divorced people (Uhlenberg & Meyers, 1981).

Remarriage in late life may have a special character. Among 125 well-educated, fairly affluent people, those in late-life remarriages seemed more trusting and accepting, and less in need of deep sharing of personal feelings. Men, but not women, tended to be more satisfied in late-life remarriages than in midlife ones (Bograd & Spilka, 1996).

Remarriage, besides enhancing individual lives, has societal benefits, since older married people are less likely than those living alone to need help from the community. Remarriage could be encouraged by letting people keep pension and social security benefits derived from a previous marriage and by greater availability of shared living quarters, such as group housing.

Many couples who are still together late in life, especially in the middle to late sixties, say that they are happier in marriage now than they were in their younger years. Important benefits of marriage, which may help older couples face the ups and downs of late life, include intimacy, sharing, and a sense of belonging to one another. Romance, fun, and sensuality have their place, too, as this couple in a hot tub demonstrate. *(Paul Fusco/Magnum)*

SINGLE LIFE

About 4 percent of women and 5 percent of men 65 years and older have never married (AARP, 1995; refer back to Figure 17-6). The percentage of never-marrieds in the elderly population is likely to increase as today's middle-aged adults grow old, since larger proportions of that cohort, especially African Americans, have remained single. Black men and women ages 55 to 64 are twice as likely to have remained unmarried as white people of the same age, and 1.5 times as likely as black people older than 84 (U.S. Bureau of the Census, 1991a, 1991b, 1992a, 1993a). The percentage of never-married women has increased worldwide since 1970 (United Nations, 1991).

Older never-married people are more likely than older divorced or widowed people to prefer single life and less likely to be lonely (Dykstra, 1995). However, women who have remained single do feel lonely if they lose their health. Poor health undermines their sense of self-reliance and may force them into dependence on relatives they would rather not be with (Essex & Nam, 1987).

Never-married, childless women in one study rated three kinds of roles or relationships as important: bonds with blood relatives, such as sib-

Bessie and Sadie Delany, daughters of a freed slave, were best friends all their lives—more than 100 years—and wrote two books together about the values they grew up with and the story of their long, active lives. Elderly siblings are an important part of each other's support network, and sisters are especially vital in maintaining family relationships. *(Matthew Jordan Smith/Gamma-Liaison)*

lings and aunts; parent-surrogate ties with younger people: and same-generation, same-sex friendships and companions. Few had close relationships with men (Rubinstein, Alexander, Goodman, & Luborsky, 1991).

A national survey of more than 1,400 previously married single adults ages 55 to over 75 (R. A. Bulcroft & Bulcroft, 1991) found that older men are much more likely to date than older women, perhaps because of the greater availability of women in this age group. Nearly half the daters of both sexes call their relationships "steady." Most elderly daters are sexually active but do not expect to marry. Among both whites and African Americans, men are more interested in romantic involvement; women may fear getting "locked into" traditional gender roles (K. Bulcroft & O'Connor, 1986; Tucker, Taylor, & Mitchell-Kernan, 1993).

HOMOSEXUAL RELATIONSHIPS

Older homosexual adults, like older heterosexual adults, have strong needs for intimacy, social con-

tact, and generativity. Contrary to stereotypes about the lonely, isolated aging homosexual, gays' and lesbians' relationships in late life are often strong, supportive, and diverse. Many homosexuals have children from earlier heterosexual marriages; others have adopted children. Friendship networks or support groups may substitute for the traditional family (Reid, 1995).

Older homosexual couples, like heterosexual couples, place importance on a good sex life. In one study, homosexual couples reported having sex anywhere from daily to every other month. When asked how their sex lives had changed since their youth, men referred to frequency of sex; women responded in terms of the quality of the relationship (Berger, 1984).

Again contrary to widespread belief, many homosexuals—especially those who have maintained close relationships and strong involvement in the homosexual community—adapt to aging with relative ease. Their main problems grow out of societal attitudes: strained relationships with the family of origin, discrimination, lack of medical or social services and social support, and insensitive policies of social agencies (Reid, 1995). Having had practice in dealing with one kind of stigma, gays and lesbians who have achieved a comfortable identity as homosexuals may be better prepared to cope with the stigma of aging. Also, their sexual orientation may make them at home in the flexible, androgynous roles often characteristic of men and women in later life (Berger & Kelly, 1986).

Positive resolution of a homosexual's identity crisis by living openly as a gay man or lesbian may ease the adjustment to aging (R. A. Friend, 1991). Coming out—whenever it occurs—is an important developmental transition, producing an expanded sense of self and new or altered relationships. It can enhance mental health, life satisfaction, self-acceptance, and self-respect (Reid, 1995). Homosexuals who are best-adjusted in the later years—most satisfied with their lives, least self-critical, and least prone to psychosomatic problems—tend to be highly satisfied with their sexual orientation; many of them went through a period of sexual experimentation earlier in life, which may have helped them adjust to the implications of being homosexual (Adelman, 1991).

On the other hand, a study of 47 elderly Canadian gay men suggests that avoidance of stress, including the stress of coming out, can contribute to well-being in old age (J. A. Lee, 1987). Because of the greater stigma attached to homosexuality when these men were younger, many did not acknowledge their homosexuality publicly until late life, if at all; and such a course may well have been quite adaptive, given the circumstances (Reid, 1995).

RELATIONSHIPS WITH SIBLINGS

Elizabeth ("Bessie") and Sarah ("Sadie") Delany both lived to be over 100. Their father was a freed slave who became an Episcopal bishop. Bessie overcame racial and gender discrimination to become a dentist, and Sadie was a high school teacher. The sisters never married; for three decades they lived together in Mount Vernon, New York. Although their personalities were as different as sugar and spice, the two women were best friends, sharing a sense of fun and the values their parents instilled in them (Delany, Delany, & Hearth, 1993).

More than 75 percent of Americans age 65 and older have at least one living sibling, and brothers and sisters play important roles in the support networks of older people (Scott & Roberto, 1981). Elderly siblings see one another as often as in middle age and are just as involved (Field & Minkler, 1988). The nearer people live to their siblings and the more siblings they have, the more likely they are to confide in them (Connidis & Davies, 1992). For people who have only one or two children, or none, relationships with siblings in late life may be increasingly important as a source of emotional support and practical help (Cicirelli, 1980; Rubinstein, Alexander, Goodman, & Luborsky, 1991; Scott & Roberto, 1981). Brothers and sisters, and their children as well, are important sources of support for never-married women (Rubinstein et al., 1991).

Sisters are especially vital in maintaining family relationships (Cicirelli, 1989a). Older people who are close to their sisters feel better about life and worry less about aging than those without sisters or without close ties to them (Cicirelli, 1977, 1989a). Being close to a sister lifts the morale of older widows (O'Bryant, 1988). Among a national sample of bereaved adults in the Netherlands, those coping with the death of a sister experienced more difficulty than those who had lost a spouse or a parent (Cleiren, Diekstra, Kerkhof, & van der Wal, 1994).

Sibling rivalry generally decreases by old age, and some siblings try to resolve earlier conflicts. However, memories of parental favoritism may put a damper on sibling relationships. In one study 8 out of 10 older siblings had positive relationships: either intimate (17 percent), congenial (28 percent), or loyal (35 percent). Ten percent were apathetic and 10 percent were hostile (Gold, 1987). In another study, however, 35 percent of brothers in late life were "disaffiliated": they considered themselves not at all close, disagreed on important issues, and felt that their siblings did not understand them. Some saw each other only because of their parents (Matthews, Delaney, & Adameck, 1989).

Older people who feel close to their brothers or sisters express a sense of peace with life and with themselves, whereas those who are estranged from siblings often feel upset, as if they have failed to live up to expectations. Siblings who have reestablished ties generally feel that they have accomplished something important (H. G. Ross et al., 1980).

RELATIONSHIPS WITH ADULT CHILDREN

Most older people have close relationships with their adult children. Four out of 5 have living children, 6 out of 10 see their children at least once a week, and 3 out of 4 talk on the phone that often (AARP, 1995). Most older people live within 10 miles of at least one adult child, and (if they have more than one child) within 30 miles of another. Despite the greater contact between mothers and daughters (see Chapter 15), daughters live no closer to their parents than sons do (Lin & Rogerson, 1995).

Children provide a link with other family members, especially with grandchildren. In one group of 150 "old-old" people in diverse socioeconomic circumstances, those who were parents were more actively in touch with other relatives than were childless people (Johnson & Troll, 1992). Older people in better health have more contact with their families than those in poorer health and report feeling closer to them (Field, Minkler, Falk, & Leino, 1993).

The mutual help and support that flow between older parents and their adult children has been extensively documented (Bengtson et al., 1990, 1996). Institutional supports such as social security, Medicare, and Medicaid have lifted some responsibilities for the elderly from family members, but many adult children do provide significant assistance and care to aged parents (see Chapter 15). Older adults are likely to be depressed if they need help from their children, whether or not they actually get it. In a society in which both generations value their independence, the prospect of dependency can be demoralizing. Parents do not want to be a burden on their children or to deplete their children's resources. Yet parents may also be depressed if they fear that their children will *not* take care of them when necessary (G. R. Lee, Netzer, & Coward, 1995).

Although the balance of mutual aid tends to shift as parents age, with children providing a greater share of support, older parents continue to show strong concern about their children and help them when needed. Adult children who left their childhood home many years before remain "psychologically present in their parents' thoughts and conversations" (Greenberg & Becker, 1988, p. 789). Aging parents of divorced children see them more often than before and may even take them into their homes. Many people whose adult children are mentally ill, moderately retarded, physically disabled, or stricken with AIDS or other serious illnesses serve as primary caregivers for as long as both parent and child live (Brabant, 1994; Greenberg & Becker, 1988).

Especially in minority communities beset by unemployment, poverty, homelessness, unwed pregnancy, and drug abuse, family networks represent not only sources of help *for* elderly members but also, potentially, demands for help *from* them (Bengtson et al., 1996). Parents of alcoholics and drug abusers often support them financially as well as emotionally. A growing number of grandparents, and even great-grandparents, particularly African Americans, raise or help to raise children. As we discussed in Chapter 15, nonnormative caregivers, who are pressed into an active parenting role at a time in their lives when such a role is unexpected, frequently feel strain, and this may be even truer of elderly caregivers than of middle-aged ones. Often ill-prepared physically, emotionally, and financially for the task, they may not know where to turn for help and support. They worry about who will take over their caregiving role when they become sick or die, as well as who will take care of *them* (Abramson, 1995).

Elderly parents tend to be depressed if their children have serious problems, even when the parents do not provide help (G. R. Lee et al., 1995; Pillemer & Suitor, 1991). In one study, more than half of the elderly mothers and one-third of the fathers experienced significant stress because of their children's problems—in the fathers' case, more because of their wives' reactions than because of the problems themselves. For mothers, the most stressful relationships were those in which a daughter had broken off contact with the family; for fathers, the most stressful relationships were with sons who continued to depend on their parents emotionally or financially (Greenberg & Becker, 1988).

Still, when an adult child moves into the home of elderly parents, the parents report that the generations get along well (Suitor & Pillemer, 1987, 1988). Conflict is lower in households in which parents and children have the same or similar marital status. Of course, parents and children who get along well are those most likely to choose to live together. Then too, older parents' reports of harmony may represent an attempt to make reality match their wishes.

CHILDLESSNESS

Older people without children are no lonelier, no more negative about their lives, and no more afraid of death than those with children (C. L. Johnson & Catalano, 1981; Keith, 1983; Rempel, 1985). Some older women do express regret over not having had children; the older they are, the more intense the regret (Alexander, Rubinstein, Goodman, & Luborsky, 1992).

Widows without grown children may lack an important source of solace (O'Bryant, 1988). Childless people also may lack a ready source of care and support if they become infirm. In 1990, 1 in 4 white women and 1 in 3 black women age 85 and older had no surviving children. Since almost 16 percent of the baby-boom women who were in their early forties in 1992 had not yet had children—and most of them probably will not do so—providing for their care may become a growing problem (Treas, 1995).

FRIENDSHIPS

Friendship is a unique relationship because people *choose* their friends. The element of choice may be especially important to older people, who may feel their control over their lives slipping away (R. G. Adams, 1986). Intimacy is another important benefit of friendship for older adults, who need to know that they are still valued and wanted despite physical and other losses (Essex & Nam, 1987). Most older people have close friends, and those with an active circle of friends are happier and healthier (Steinbach, 1992; Babchuk, 1978–1979; Lemon et al., 1972).

Older people often enjoy the time they spend with friends more than the time they spend with family members. The openness and excitement of relationships with friends help older men and women rise above worries and problems. Intimate friendships give older people a sense of being valued and wanted and help them deal with the changes and crises of aging. *(Cary Wolinsky/Stock, Boston)*

Friends soften the impact of stress on physical and mental health (Cutrona, Russell, & Rose, 1986). People who can confide their feelings and thoughts and can talk about their worries and pain with friends deal better with the changes and crises of aging (Genevay, 1986; Lowenthal & Haven, 1968). They also seem to extend their lives (Steinbach, 1992). It may be that women's greater comfort with self-disclosure and expression of feelings contributes to their greater life expectancy (Weg, 1987).

Most older people's morale depends more on how often they see their friends than on how often they see their children (Glenn & McLanahan, 1981). Although family members provide more reliable emotional support, older people enjoy time spent with their friends more than time spent with their families. In one study, 92 retired adults between ages 55 and 88 wore beepers for 1 week. At about 2-hour intervals, when paged, they filled out reports on what they were doing, with whom, and on what they were thinking and feeling (Larson, Mannell, & Zuzanek, 1986). These people were generally more alert, excited, and emotionally aroused with friends than with family members, including their spouses. One reason may be that older people spend more active, enjoyable leisure time with friends but do household tasks or watch television with family. Older people feel a reciprocal sense of openness with their friends, and the lightheartedness and spontaneity of friendships help them rise above daily concerns.

Still, spending time with friends does not result in higher overall life satisfaction, whereas spending more time with a spouse does. It may be the very brevity and infrequency of the time spent with friends that give it its special flavor. Friends are a powerful source of *immediate* enjoyment; the family provides greater emotional security and support.

People usually rely on neighbors in emergencies and on relatives for tasks requiring long-term commitment, such as caregiving, but friends may, on occasion, fulfill both these functions. Friends and neighbors often take the place of family members who are far away, and although friends cannot replace a spouse or partner, they can help compensate for the lack of one. Interviews with 131 older adults in the Netherlands who were never-married, divorced, or widowed found that those who received high levels of emotional and practical support from friends were less likely to be lonely (Dykstra, 1995).

GRANDPARENTHOOD AND GREAT-GRANDPARENTHOOD

More than 75 percent of older Americans are grandparents, and more than 40 percent are great-grandparents (Menninger Foundation, 1994). As grandchildren grow up, grandparents generally see them less often (see the discussion of grandparenthood in Chapter 15). Then, when grandchildren become parents, grandparents move into a new role: great-grandparenthood. Because of age, declining health, and the scattering of fami-

Grandparents and great-grandparents are an important source of wisdom and companionship, a link to the past, and a symbol of the continuity of family life. This African American great-grandfather points out to his great-granddaughter where her ancestors came from. *(CLEO, The Picture Cube)*

lies, great-grandparents tend to be less involved than grandparents in a child's life. And because four- or five-generation families are relatively new, there are few generally accepted guidelines for what great-grandparents are supposed to do (Cherlin & Furstenberg, 1986b).

Still, most great-grandparents find the role fulfilling (Pruchno & Johnson, 1996). Great-grandparenthood offers a sense of personal and family renewal, a source of diversion, and a mark of longevity. When 40 great-grandfathers and great-grandmothers, ages 71 to 90, were interviewed, 93 percent made such comments as "Life is starting again in my family," "Seeing them grow keeps me young," and "I never thought I'd live to see it"

(Doka & Mertz, 1988, pp. 193–194). More than one-third of the sample (mostly women) were close to their great-grandchildren; the others had less contact. The ones with the most intimate connections were likely to live nearby and to be close to the children's parents and grandparents as well, often helping out with loans, gifts, and baby-sitting.

Grandparents and great-grandparents are important to their families. They are sources of wisdom, companions in play, links to the past, and symbols of the continuity of family life. They are engaged in the ultimate generative function: expressing the human longing to transcend mortality by investing themselves in the lives of future generations.

✔ SUMMARY

THEORY AND RESEARCH ON PERSONALITY DEVELOPMENT

■ Personality traits tend to remain stable in late adulthood, but cohort differences have been found.

■ According to Whitbourne's model of personality development, identity style (either assimilative or adaptive or balanced) can predict adaptation to aging.

■ Erik Erikson's final crisis is integrity versus despair, culminating in the virtue of wisdom, or acceptance of one's life and impending death.

■ Robert Peck specified three adjustments involved

in successful aging: broader self-definition versus preoccupation with work roles, transcendence of the body versus preoccupation with the body, and transcendence of the ego versus preoccupation with the ego.

■ George Vaillant found that people who were able to handle life's problems without bitterness, blame, or passivity were best adjusted at age 65.

■ Two approaches to the study of coping are environmental models and the cognitive-appraisal model. Environmental models emphasize the interaction between characteristics of the individual and the environment. The cognitive-appraisal model views the choice of appropriate coping strategies as the result of constant reappraisal of a situation.

- Two contrasting early models of "successful," or "optimal," aging are disengagement theory and activity theory. According to disengagement theory, aging is characterized by mutual withdrawal between the older person and society. Activity theory, which has been more influential, holds that the more active an older person remains, the better she or he ages.
- According to social convoy theory, reductions or changes in social contact in late life do not impair well-being because a stable inner circle of social support is maintained.
- According to Laura Carstensen's socioemotional selectivity theory, people select social contacts that meet changing needs; older people spend time with people who enhance their emotional well-being.
- According to continuity theory, aging adults seek a balance between continuity and change.
- Some current research emphasizes the role of productive activity in successful aging.

LIFESTYLE AND SOCIAL ISSUES RELATED TO AGING

- Some older people continue to work for pay, but the vast majority are retired. There is a trend toward retirement before age 65. Many retired people do part-time paid or volunteer work.
- The financial situation of older people has improved, but still nearly 1 out of 5 live in poverty or near-poverty. Many, especially widows and the infirm, become poor for the first time after retirement.
- Common lifestyles after retirement include family-focused, balanced investment, and serious leisure patterns.
- Most older people live with family members, usually a spouse. About 30 percent of those who are not institutionalized live alone. Most of those who live alone are widowed women.
- Most older people do not want to live with their children, but 13 percent live with children or other relatives. Hispanic Americans and Asian Americans are more likely than white Americans to live with extended family members.
- Most older people prefer to remain in their own homes. Only 5 percent are institutionalized at a given time, but the proportion increases greatly

with age. Alternatives to institutionalization include retirement and life-care communities, shared housing, group homes, accessory housing, assisted-living facilities, and foster-care homes.
- Elder abuse is most often suffered by a frail or demented older person living with a spouse or child.

PERSONAL RELATIONSHIPS IN LATE LIFE

- Relationships are very important to older people, even though frequency of social contact declines in old age.
- As life expectancy increases, so does the potential longevity of marriage. Marriages that last into late adulthood tend to be relatively satisfying, but strains that arise from personality, health, and role changes may require adjustment by both partners.
- Divorce is relatively uncommon among older people, and few divorced older adults have not remarried, but this proportion is increasing.
- An increasing percentage of adults, especially African Americans, now reach late life without marrying. Never-married adults are less likely to be lonely than those who are divorced or widowed.
- Older homosexuals, like heterosexuals, have needs for intimacy, social contact, and generativity. Many homosexuals adapt to aging with relative ease.
- Often relationships between siblings become closer in later life than they were earlier in adulthood. Sisters in particular maintain these ties.
- Although elderly parents and their adult children do not typically live together, they frequently see or contact one another and offer needed assistance. An increasing number of elderly parents are caregivers for adult children, grandchildren, or great-grandchildren.
- In some respects, childlessness does not seem to be an important disadvantage in old age, but providing for care of infirm elderly people without children can be a problem.
- Friendships are important for enjoyment, for intimacy, and for support in meeting the problems of aging.
- Great-grandparents are less involved in children's lives than grandparents, but most find the role fulfilling.

✔ KEY TERMS

identity styles (page 577)
identity assimilation (577)
identity accommodation (577)
ego integrity versus despair (579)
broader self-definition versus
    preoccupation with work roles
    (579)
transcendence of the body versus
    preoccupation with the body
    (580)

transcendence of the ego versus
    preoccupation with the ego (580)
coping (581)
congruence model (581)
environmental-press model (581)
cognitive-appraisal model (582)
problem-focused coping (582)
emotion-focused coping (582)
disengagement theory (585)
activity theory (585)

social convoy theory (587)
socioemotional selectivity theory
    (587)
continuity theory (587)
family-focused lifestyle (593)
balanced investment (593)
serious leisure (594)
aging in place (596)
elder abuse (598)

✔ QUESTIONS FOR THOUGHT AND DISCUSSION

1 Which theories of personality development in late life seem to be best supported by the facts presented in the sections of this chapter on work, retirement, living arrangements, and relationships? Why?

2 Which kind of coping do you tend to use more, problem-focused or emotion-focused? What kind do your parents use more? your grandparents?

3 Are you satisfied with any of the definitions of "successful" (or "optimal") aging presented in this chapter? If so, why? If not, why not? Do you think this is a valuable subject for study?

4 At what age, if ever, do you expect to retire? Why? Which of the three patterns of use of time during retirement—family-focused, balanced investment, and serious leisure—will most likely describe your lifestyle if and when you retire?

5 Were you surprised to read that a large number of older adults like living alone, and that few want to live with their children? Why do you think this is so?

6 Have you ever lived in a multigenerational household? Do you think you ever will? What aspects of this lifestyle do or do not appeal to you?

CHAPTER EIGHTEEN

DEALING WITH DEATH AND BEREAVEMENT

The key to the question of death unlocks the door of life.

Elisabeth Kübler-Ross
Death: The Final Stage of Growth, *1975*

All the while I thought I was learning how to live, I have been learning how to die.

Notebooks of Leonardo da Vinci

ASK YOURSELF

✔ How do people face their own death and the loss of their loved ones?

✔ What societal perspectives and customs concerning death and mourning have existed in various times and places?

✔ How do feelings about death and dying change across the life span?

✔ Do children and adults cope differently with loss?

✔ Why is suicide increasing, and in what age groups? What can be done to prevent it?

✔ Why are attitudes toward euthanasia ("mercy killing") and assisted suicide changing, and what concerns do these practices raise?

✔ How can people overcome fear of dying?

Human beings are individuals; they undergo different experiences and react to them in different ways. Yet one unavoidable part of everyone's life is its end. The better we understand this inevitable event and the more wisely we approach it, the more fully we can live until it comes.

Death is, of course, a *biological* fact, but it also has *legal, medical, social,* and *psychological* aspects. Although the legal definition varies from state to state, death is generally considered to be the cessation of bodily processes. A person may be pronounced dead when breathing and heartbeat stop for a significant time or when all electrical activity in the brain ceases. Criteria for death have become more complex with the development of medical apparatus that can prolong basic signs of life, sometimes indefinitely. People in a deep coma can be kept alive for years. A person whose brain has completely stopped functioning—and who, therefore, is by definition dead—can be maintained by mechanical devices that artificially sustain heartbeat and respiration. These medical developments have raised agonizing questions about whether or when life supports, such as respirators and feeding tubes, may be withheld or removed, and whose judgment should prevail. Sometimes humanitarian or practical considerations conflict with religious beliefs or professional standards. Many of these issues have ended up in court, and some are still unresolved.

Biological, legal, and medical aspects of death are entangled with its social aspects: cultural attitudes toward death, care of and behavior toward the dying, the place where death occurs, and efforts to postpone or hasten it. Other social aspects of death include disposing of the dead, mourning customs and rituals, and the transfer of posses-

sions and roles. Such social conventions are, in turn, closely linked with psychological aspects of death: how people feel about their own death and about the deaths of those close to them.

The stark biological fact of death, then, is far from the whole story. Its meaning and impact are profoundly influenced by what people feel and do, and people's feelings and behavior are shaped by the time and place in which they live.

■ In this chapter, we look at these intertwined aspects of death (the state) and dying (the process) and at changing societal views and customs. We describe how people of different ages think and feel about dying, and we examine physical and psychological changes people undergo in the face of death. We compare mourning patterns in different cultures, the various forms grief can take, and the ways people deal with the loss of a spouse, parent, or child. We discuss suicide and controversial issues that revolve around a "right to die." Finally, we see how confronting death can give deeper meaning and purpose to life. ■

✔ FACING DEATH

All deaths are different, just as all lives are different. The experience of dying is not the same for an accident victim, someone with terminal cancer, someone who commits suicide, and someone who dies instantaneously of a heart attack; nor is the experience of loss the same for their survivors. As the timing-of-events model suggests, death does not mean the same thing to an 85-year-old man with excruciatingly painful arthritis, a 56-year-old woman at the height of a brilliant legal career who discovers she has breast cancer, and a 15-year-old who dies of an overdose of drugs. Death is not the same for a Brahman in India as for a homeless person in New York. Nor is it the same for a first-generation Japanese American, imbued with Buddhist teachings of accepting the inevitable, as for a third-generation Japanese American who has grown up with a belief in control of one's own destiny.

Yet, just as there are commonalities in people's lives, there are similarities—often based on culture, cohort, and age—in the ways people face death. Let's look first at societal perspectives and practices. Then we'll consider how attitudes toward death develop across the life span. Finally, we'll describe physical and psychological changes that occur as death approaches.

CHANGING SOCIETAL PERSPECTIVES AND PRACTICES

Before modern times, in a typical year, some 50 people out of every 1,000 died, and during plagues or natural disasters the death rate might reach 40 percent. More than one-third of all babies died in infancy, and half of all children died before their tenth birthday. People saw relatives and friends succumb to fatal illnesses at an early age, and they expected some of their own children to die young (Lofland, 1986). Death was a normal, expected event, sometimes even welcomed as a peaceful end to suffering. Caring for a dying family member at home, as Louisa May Alcott described in *Little Women*, was a common experience for adults and children in the nineteenth-century United States, as it still is in many contemporary rural cultures. Looking death in the eye, bit by bit, day by day, people absorbed an important truth: that dying is a natural part of living.

Such experience and understanding is far less common in western societies today. Advances in medicine and sanitation during the twentieth century brought about a "mortality revolution" in developed countries: annual death rates fell below 9 percent (Lofland, 1986, p. 60). Today, as compared with a century ago, women are less likely to die in childbirth, infants are more likely to survive their first year, children are more likely to reach adulthood, adults are more likely to reach old age, and older people can overcome illnesses they grew up regarding as fatal. In the United States, only AIDS is an exception to the general pattern of declining mortality (Centers for Disease Control and Prevention, 1994a).

The urbanized "baby boom" generation born after World War II was the first to reach adulthood with only a 5 percent chance of having experienced the death of an immediate family member. As death increasingly became a phenomenon of late adulthood, it became "invisible and abstract" (Fulton & Owen, 1987–1988, p. 380). Many older people lived and died in retirement communities, and most deaths occurred somewhere other than at home. Care of the dying and the dead, including preparation of bodies for burial, became largely a task for professionals. Many people went through most of their lives without thinking much about their own death (Fulton & Owen, 1987–1988; Lofland, 1986). Avoidance and denial were fostered by such social conventions as isolation of the dying person in a hospital or nursing home, refusal to openly discuss his or her condition, and reluctance to visit, thus leaving the person to cope with dying alone. As medical advances kept people alive longer, death—even of the very old— came to be regarded as a failure of medical treatment rather than as a natural end to life (McCue, 1995).

Today, the picture is changing again. Violence, drug abuse, poverty, and the spread of AIDS make it harder to deny the reality of death. Issues of quality versus quantity of life, and the "right to die" (discussed later in this chapter), are constantly in the news. *Thanatology,* the study of death and dying, is arousing interest, and educational programs have been established to help people deal with death. Because of the prohibitive cost of extended hospital care that cannot save the terminally ill, many more deaths are occurring at home (Techner, 1994). Indeed, a 1992 Gallup poll found that, given 6 months to live, nearly 9 out of 10 people would choose to be cared for and die in their own home or that of a family member. Hospice care is helping some patients and their families to do just that, as well as to face death more openly and supportively wherever and whenever it occurs.

Death Education

How can people prepare for their own death, or the death of those they love? How much should terminally ill patients be told about their situation? These are among the topics covered in *death education* programs intended to teach people about death and to help them deal with it personally and professionally. Such programs are offered to students, social workers, doctors, nurses, and other professionals who work with dying people and

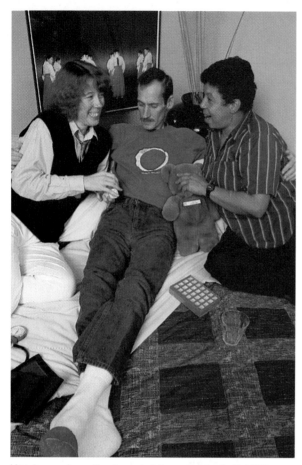

Hospice workers, like these helping a terminally ill AIDS patient, work together to ease patients' pain and treat their symptoms, to keep them as comfortable and alert as possible, to show both interest and kindness to them and their families, and to help the families deal with the patients' illness and death. *(James D. Wilson/Woodfin Camp & Associates)*

survivors, and to the community at large. Goals include allaying death-related anxieties; helping people to develop their own belief systems, to see death as a natural end to life, and to prepare for their own death and the death of those close to them; teaching humane ways to treat the dying; providing a realistic view of health care workers and their obligations to the dying and their families; offering an understanding of the dynamics of grief; counseling suicidal people and those around them; and helping people decide what kinds of funeral services they want.

The Association for Death Education and Counseling is an international, nonprofit organization of professionals who work with any aspect of death and dying. The Hartford-based organization certifies death educators and grief counselors and publishes research journals and a code of ethics. A current project is to integrate death education into elementary and secondary school curricula (Lund, D. A., personal communication, August 1996).

Hospice Care and Self-Help Groups

Along with the growing tendency to face death more honestly, movements have arisen to make dying more humane. These include hospice care and support groups for dying people and their families.

Hospice care is warm, personal, patient- and family-centered care for the terminally ill, focused on relief of pain, control of symptoms, and quality of life. More than 90 percent of hospice care takes place at home, but such care can be given in a hospital or another institution, at a hospice center, or through a combination of home and institutional care.

The hospice movement began in London in 1968 in response to a need for special facilities and special care for dying patients. A typical hospital is set up to treat acute illness, with the goal of curing patients and sending them home well. As a result, dying patients in a hospital often receive needless tests and useless treatments, are given less attention than patients with better chances of recovery, and are constrained by rules that are not relevant to them. Furthermore, hospital care for an extended terminal illness has become enormously expensive, typically $500 to $1,000 a day.

In 1996 there were at least 2,200 hospice programs nationwide; about 1 out of 7 dying patients, an estimated 390,000 in all, used their services in 1995. Nearly 8 out of 10 hospice patients have cancer; most of the rest have heart disease or AIDS. About 7 out of 10 are older adults (National Hospice Organization, 1996).

The hospice philosophy is summed up in the words of its founder, Cicely Saunders: "You matter to the last moment of your life, and we will do all we can, not only to help you die peacefully, but to live until you die" (National Hospice Organization, undated, p. 6). The emphasis is on *palliative care:* relieving pain and suffering and allowing people to die in peace and dignity. Doctors, nurses, social workers, psychologists, aides, clergy, friends, and volunteers work together to keep patients as comfortable and alert as possible, to show interest in and kindness to them and their families, and to help families deal with the illness and ultimately with bereavement. Family members often take an active part in a patient's care.

In a study in which terminally ill cancer patients were randomly assigned either to standard hospital care or to hospice care, the hospice patients and the family members most involved with their day-to-day care were more satisfied than the hospital patients and their relatives. The difference in satisfaction seemed to reflect the greater time spent by the hospice teams in helping patients and their families cope with impending death (Kane, Wales, Bernstein, Leibowitz, & Kaplan, 1984). As a leading thanatologist has written, "The most profound social value actualized by successful hospice programs is perhaps the simplest: the community has not retreated from death and loss" (Kastenbaum, 1993, p. 81).

Self-help groups consist of people who have banded together for treatment, for social support, to solve a problem, or to meet some other mutual need. The World Health Organization lists more than half a million self-help groups, many of which bring together people who are facing a terminal illness (their own or that of a loved one) or who have been widowed. Participants often benefit from a sense of shared pain and mutual understanding; they may gain hope, information, and new ideas. The effectiveness of such groups depends largely on recruiting, screening, training, and supervising qualified leaders (Lund, Redburn, Juretich, & Caserta, 1989).

ATTITUDES TOWARD DEATH AND DYING ACROSS THE LIFE SPAN

Do you ever think about your own death? Do you think about it as much as your parents or grandparents seem to do? How do people of different ages cope with the knowledge that they must die? There is no single way of viewing death at any age, and people's attitudes toward it reflect their personality and experience, as well as how close they believe they are to dying. Still, we can trace typical changes in attitudes toward death across the life span, which depend both on cognitive development and on the normative or nonnormative timing of the event.

Childhood and Adolescence

A first-grader, grieving for a classmate who had died after a violent beating, said, "I'll make a picture of Lisa and put it on her coffin and she'll sit up and become alive again" (Neuffer, 1987). Not until sometime between the ages of 5 and 7 do most

children understand that death is *irreversible*—that a dead person, animal, or flower cannot come to life again. At about the same age, children realize two other important concepts about death: first, that it is *universal* (all living things die), and second, that a dead person is *nonfunctional* (all life functions end at death). Before then, children may believe that certain groups of people (say, teachers, parents, and children) do not die, that a person who is smart enough or lucky enough can avoid death, and that they themselves will be able to live forever. They may also believe that a dead person can still think and feel.

According to a review of 40 studies since the 1930s, most of them based on interviews with children (Speece & Brent, 1984), the concepts of irreversibility, universality, and cessation of functions usually develop at the time when, according to Piaget, children move from preoperational to concrete operational thinking. It seems likely that this cognitive leap allows a mature understanding of death.

Children who are still thinking egocentrically usually cannot understand death because it is beyond their personal experience. However, preschool-age children who are terminally ill commonly do realize the imminence of their own death. One child, not quite 4 years old and suffer-

Sometime between ages 5 and 7, most children come to realize that death is permanent and that a dead animal, person, or flower will not come back to life. This girl, putting flowers on the grave of her pet kitten, has a natural opportunity to develop a realistic understanding of death. *(J. Moore/The Image Works)*

ing from a brain tumor, told hospital workers, "The Great Pumpkin is going to take me away, but I'm not ready." The following week, he woke up one morning and said, "The Great Pumpkin is coming to take me away—and now I'm ready to go with him." He died shortly thereafter (J. Finlay, personal communication, 1991).

Cultural experience influences attitudes toward death. Children from poor families are more likely to associate death with violence, whereas middle-class children associate it with disease and old age (Bluebond-Langner, 1977).

Children can be helped to understand death if they are introduced to the concept at an early age in the context of their own experience and are encouraged to talk about it. The death of a pet or of flowers may provide a natural opportunity. If another child dies, teachers and parents need to try to allay the surviving children's anxieties. (Later in this chapter we discuss ways to help children deal with bereavement.)

Death is not something adolescents normally think much about. On the threshold of making their own lives, they look forward "to becoming, not ceasing to be" (Offer et al., 1988, p. 122). Nor do they worry much about such larger issues as nuclear destruction; optimism is typical of this time of life (Offer, Ostrov, & Howard, 1986). Still, in many high schools and many communities in which adolescents live today, violence and the threat of death are inescapable facts of daily life.

Although Elkind's (1984) concept of the *personal fable*—adolescents' tendency to believe they are invulnerable—has been questioned (see Chapter 10), many adolescents do take heedless risks. They hitchhike, they drive recklessly, and they experiment with drugs and sex—often with tragic results. In their urge to discover and express their identity, they may be more concerned with *how* they live than with how *long* they will live. This may partially explain the appeal of suicide to adolescents.

When teenagers are terminally ill, they may deny their condition and talk as if they are going to recover when they know they are not. Denial, and the accompanying repression of emotions, helps them deal with this crushing blow to their expectations and with their anger at the unfairness of their fate (Feifel, 1977).

Adulthood

Young adults who have finished their education or training and have embarked on careers, mar-

riage, or parenthood are generally eager to live the lives they have been preparing for. If they are suddenly struck by a potentially fatal illness or injury, they are likely to be extremely frustrated. They have worked hard—for nothing. Frustration may turn to rage, which can make them difficult hospital patients (Pattison, 1977).

Today, many homosexuals (and others) who develop AIDS in their twenties or thirties must face issues of death and dying at an age when they would normally be dealing with such issues of young adulthood as establishing an intimate relationship. Rather than having a long lifetime of losses as gradual preparation for the final loss of life, "the gay man may find his own health, the health of his friends, and the fabric of his community all collapsing at once" (Cadwell, 1994, p. 4).

In middle age, most people realize more keenly than before that they are indeed going to die. As they read the obituary pages, which they are likely to do more regularly now, they find more and more familiar names, and they may compare the ages with their own. Their bodies send them signals that they are not so young, agile, and hearty as they once were. As Jung and others have suggested, middle-aged people may become more introspective. Often, especially after the death of both parents, there is a new awareness of being the "older generation" next in line to die (Scharlach & Fredriksen, 1993).

Middle-aged people may perceive time in a new way. Previously, they thought in terms of how many years they had been alive; now they think of how many years are left until death and of how to make the most of those years (Neugarten, 1967). The realization that death is certain and that the time remaining is limited may be an impetus for a major life change. Even people who outwardly continue their previous patterns of living often make subtle shifts and more conscious choices, taking stock of careers, marriages, relationships with children, friendships, values, and the ways they spend their time and energy (see Chapter 15).

According to Erikson, older adults who resolve the final crisis of *integrity versus despair* (see Chapter 17) achieve acceptance both of what they have done with their lives and of their impending death. Peck's psychological adjustments of late life (also in Chapter 17) may help older people cope with dying. People who feel that their lives have been meaningful may be better able to face death. Through the years, as they lose friends and relatives, they gradually accept their own mortality.

Physical losses and other problems of old age may diminish their pleasure in living and their will to live (McCue, 1995).

Nevertheless, even in very old age, acknowledgment of imminent death may be mixed with affirmation of the preciousness of the life that is slipping away. Rita Duskin, the mother of one of the authors of this book, wrote the following lines at 82, shortly before her second, fatal heart attack:

> I refuse to believe I am a piece of dust scuttering through uncaring space. I believe I count—that I have work to do—that there is need of me. I have a place. I want to live. The moment is Now—Now is my forever. I am still somebody—somebody on whom nothing is lost. With my last breath, I sing a psalm. (R. Duskin, personal communication, February 1986)

CONFRONTING ONE'S OWN DEATH

At any time of life, confronting one's own death is a painful, complex process. What kinds of physical and psychological changes do people undergo shortly before death? How do they come to terms with its imminence?

Physical and Psychological Changes

In the absence of any identifiable illness, people around the age of 100—close to the present limit of the human life span—usually suffer cognitive and other functional declines, lose interest in eating and drinking, and die a natural death (McCue, 1995). Changes also have been noted in younger people whose death is near.

Psychological changes often begin to take place even before there are overt physiological signs of dying. A *terminal drop,* a sudden decrease in cognitive functioning shortly before death, affects older people's average performance on intelligence tests (Botwinick, 1984; Kleemeier, 1962; K. F. Riegel & Riegel, 1972). Terminal drop is sometimes attributed to chronic ailments that sap mental energy and motivation. It affects abilities that are relatively unaffected by age, such as vocabulary (N. White & Cunningham, 1988), and it is seen in people who die young as well as in those who die at a more advanced age.

Terminal drop may predict which individuals are within a few years of death. One research team (Siegler, McCarty, & Logue, 1982), using data from the Duke Longitudinal Study, compared scores on intelligence and memory tests of people who died within 1 year of testing with scores of people who

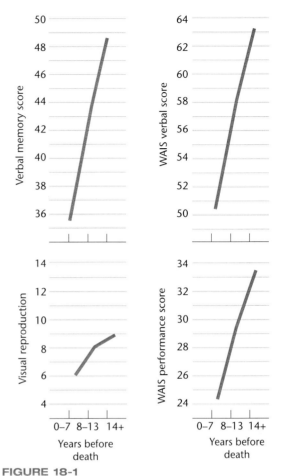

FIGURE 18-1
Effects of terminal drop on memory and intelligence. People closer to death performed more poorly on verbal and visual memory tests and on the verbal and nonverbal performance sections of the Wechsler Adult Intelligence Scale (WAIS). *(Source: Siegler et al., 1982, fig. 2.)*

died 8 to 13 years afterward and people who died 14 or more years afterward or were still alive. Those who survived the longest, regardless of age, tended to have had the highest scores on both verbal and nonverbal items (see Figure 18-1).

Personality changes also can occur during the terminal period. In one study, 80 people ages 65 to 91 were given psychological tests. Afterward, the researchers compared the scores of those who had died within 1 year after testing with the scores of those who had lived an average of 3 years. The people who died within 1 year had lower scores on cognitive tests, indicating terminal drop, and on the whole they were less introspective and more docile. Those who were dealing with a crisis and were close to death at the time of testing were more afraid of death, and more preoccupied with it, than those facing similar crises who were not close to death; those close to death whose lives were relatively stable at the time showed neither special fear of death nor preoccupation with it (Lieberman & Coplan, 1970).

Some people who have come close to death have had visions or other experiences that are sometimes interpreted to be the result of physiological or psychological changes on the brink of death (see Box 18-1).

Kübler-Ross: Stages of Dying

The psychiatrist Elisabeth Kübler-Ross is widely credited with having inspired the current interest in the psychology of death and dying. In her work with dying people, she found that most of them welcomed an opportunity to speak openly about their condition and were aware of being close to death, even when they had not been told.

After speaking with some 500 terminally ill patients, Kübler-Ross (1969, 1970) outlined five stages in coming to terms with death: (1) *denial* (refusal to accept the reality of what is happening), (2) *anger*, (3) *bargaining* for extra time (see Box 18-2), (4) *depression*, and ultimately (5) *acceptance*. She also proposed a similar progression in the feelings of people facing imminent bereavement (Kübler-Ross, 1975).

Kübler-Ross's model has been criticized and modified by other professionals who work with dying patients. Although the emotions she described are common, not everyone goes through all five stages, and people may go through them in different sequences. A person may go back and forth between anger and depression, for example, or may feel both at once. Unfortunately, some health professionals assume that these stages are inevitable and universal, and others feel that they have failed if they cannot bring a patient to the final stage of acceptance. Dying, like living, is an individual experience. For some people, denial or anger may be a healthier way to face death than calm acceptance. Kübler-Ross's description, useful as it may be in helping us understand the feelings of those who are facing the end of life, should not be considered a model or a criterion for a "good death."

✔ FACING BEREAVEMENT

Bereavement is the loss of someone to whom a person feels close and the process of adjustment to it.

Bereavement can affect practically all aspects of a survivor's life, often starting with a change in status and role (for example, from a wife to a widow or from a son or daughter to an orphan). *Grief* is the emotional response experienced in the early phases of bereavement; it can take many forms, from numbness to rage.

Although bereavement and grief are universal experiences, they have a cultural context. **Mourning** refers to the ways, usually culturally accepted, in which the bereaved and the community act while adjusting to a death: the all-night Irish wake, at which friends and family toast the memory of the dead person, or the flying of a flag at half-mast after the death of a public figure. Let's look at some mourning customs before turning to psychological and practical aspects of coping with bereavement.

MOURNING CUSTOMS

Societies help people deal with bereavement through customs with well-understood meanings that provide a reassuring anchor amid the turbulence of loss. These social customs vary greatly from culture to culture and are often governed by religious or legal prescriptions that reflect a society's view of what death is and what happens afterward.

The ancient Egyptian *Book of the Dead* gave instructions for sacrifices and rituals to help a dying or deceased person achieve a rightful place in the community of the dead. In Malayan society, as in many other preliterate societies, death was seen as a gradual transition. A body was at first given only provisional burial. Survivors continued to perform mourning rites until the body decayed to the point where the soul was believed to have left it and to have been admitted into the spiritual realm.

Some modern social customs have evolved from ancient beliefs and practices. Embalming goes back to a practice common in ancient Egypt and China: *mummification*, preserving a body so that the soul can return to it. A traditional Jewish custom is never to leave a dying person alone, even for an instant. Anthropologists suggest that the original reason for this may have been a belief (widespread among ancient peoples) that evil spirits hover around a dying person, trying to enter the body (Ausubel, 1964). Such rituals give people facing a loss something predictable and important to do at a time when they otherwise would feel confused and helpless. The Jewish deathbed vigil

BOX 18-1   FOOD FOR THOUGHT

NEAR-DEATH EXPERIENCES

After the psychoanalyst Carl Jung suffered a heart attack in 1944, he had a vision in which he entered the antechamber of a gigantic stone temple floating in space. A Hindu clothed in white robes sat silently on a stone bench before the gate to the temple, which was surrounded by burning candles, "and," Jung (1961) later wrote, "I knew that he expected me." Before Jung could enter the temple, however, the figure of his doctor floated up from the earth below. Mutely, the doctor informed him that he had been sent to say that Jung must return. "I was profoundly disappointed," Jung's report continues, "for now . . . I was not to be allowed to enter the temple, to join the people in whose company I belonged. . . . Suddenly the terrifying thought came to me that Dr. H. would have to die in my stead." On the day Jung was able to sit up for the first time since his attack, "Dr. H. took to his bed and did not leave it again. . . . Soon afterward he died of septicemia [blood poisoning]" (pp. 289–293).

Many people who have come close to death from drowning, cardiac arrest, or other causes have described **near-death experiences:** profound, subjective events that sometimes result in dramatic changes in values, beliefs, behavior, and attitudes toward life and death (Greyson, 1993). These experiences often include a new clarity of thinking, a feeling of well-being, a sense of being out of the body, and visions of bright lights or mys-

tical encounters. Such experiences are reported by about 5 percent of adult Americans (Gallup & Proctor, 1982), including an estimated 30 to 40 percent of hospital patients who have been revived after coming close to death (Ring, 1980; Sabom, 1982).

Near-death experiences may be classified as cognitive, affective, paranormal, or transcendental, depending on which elements appear to predominate (Grayson, 1993). *Cognitive* elements are changes in thought processes. Time seems to slow down, thoughts speed up, and people may feel a sudden sense of understanding as their whole life seems to pass before them in instantaneous, panoramic review. *Affective* elements are changes in emotional state: overwhelming feelings of peace, painlessness, joy, love, and oneness with the universe, often emanating from an encounter with a mysterious being composed of diffuse light. *Paranormal*, or psychic, elements include heightened sensations, extrasensory perception, visions of the future, and observation of one's body from an outside vantage point. *Transcendental* elements may include journeys to a higher realm (such as Jung experienced), encounters with angels or spirits of the dead, and a barrier, or point of no return to the material world.

Near-death experiences have been explained as a response to a perceived threat of death (a *psychological* theory), as a result of biological states that accompany the

process of dying (a *physiological* theory), or as a foretaste of an actual state of bliss after death (a *transcendental* theory). One study found some support for all three theories (J. E. Owens, Cook, & Stevenson, 1990). Researchers studied the medical records and personal accounts of 28 hospital patients who would have died if doctors had not saved them and of 30 who mistakenly thought they were close to death. The two groups of patients had very similar sensations, a finding that lends support to the psychological theory. Still, those who had actually been near death were more likely to report certain aspects of the near-death experience—evidence for the physiological theory. The researchers saw support for the transcendental theory in the fact that the near-dying patients reported clearer thinking, despite the likelihood that their brain functioning was in fact diminished.

Near-death experiences are sometimes said to offer a reassuring, even romanticized, preview of death. If so, such experiences might be expected to encourage ideas of suicide; yet studies show a decrease in suicidal thoughts. One suggested explanation for this apparent paradox is that near-death experiences enhance the "sense of meaning and purpose in life, a view of problems that transcends the individual, and a sense of belonging to something greater than the self" (Grayson, 1992–1993, p. 87).

not only provides spiritual solace to the dying but helps alleviate any guilt survivors might feel. It allows for extended interaction with the dying person and affirms the strength and efficacy of the community.

A traditional Jewish funeral is designed to help

the bereaved confront the reality of death. The coffin (often a plain pine box) is kept closed. At the cemetery, mourners shovel dirt into the grave. After the funeral, all who attend are invited to the home of the nearest relative, where, throughout the week of *shiva*—a period of intense mourning

BOX 18-2   WINDOW ON THE WORLD

POSTPONING DEATH

President Thomas Jefferson died on the Fourth of July, the anniversary of the Declaration of Independence, of which he had been the principal author. Jefferson's last words were "Is it the Fourth?"

Is there such a thing as a will to live? Can people postpone their own death so that they can celebrate a birthday, an anniversary, a grandchild's wedding, or another significant event?

To test that possibility, researchers have examined death rates around two important holidays, each identified with, and meaningful to, a certain ethnic group. On the Jewish feast of Passover, more than 75 percent of American Jews attend a seder (a ceremonial dinner), usually at home with close family members (Phillips & King, 1988). During the Chinese Harvest Moon festival, the senior woman of the house directs a ceremonial meal (Phillips & Smith, 1990), symbolizing the importance of older women. Passover usually falls near Easter (the last supper of Jesus and the disciples is said to have been a seder), and the Harvest Moon festival takes place

in autumn; but the date of these festivals on our solar calendar changes from year to year by as much as 4 weeks.

In two California studies, death rates from natural causes for people of Jewish extraction were found to be lower just before Passover and higher just afterward. The same was true of the Harvest Moon festival for people of Chinese heritage. The "Passover effect" was strongest if the festival fell on a weekend, when more people tend to be able to celebrate it, but was not affected by the specific date. The effect was especially strong among Jewish men, who usually lead the seder. It was not found in African Americans, in Asians, or in Jewish infants, none of whom celebrate Passover (Phillips & King, 1988). Similarly, the "Harvest Moon effect" did not appear among Jewish people or the general population, or among elderly Chinese men or younger Chinese women. It appeared only among Chinese women over age 75, the group to whom this holiday means the most. The pattern of fewer deaths before the Harvest

Moon festival and more deaths afterward held for the three leading causes of death in the elderly: heart disease, cancer, and stroke (Phillips & Smith, 1990).

How might such effects work? It is not likely that stress or overeating causes high death rates after these holidays; these factors would not explain the much lower death rates before the holidays. Perhaps psychosomatic processes allow some people to postpone death until they have reached an occasion important to them. They may will themselves to live just a little while longer, putting forth every ounce of psychological and physical strength so as to experience the celebration.

A dual effect based on gender showed up in a study of more than 2 million deaths from natural causes. A woman was more likely to die in the week after her birthday than at any other time, but a man was more likely to die just before his birthday (Phillips, 1992). It may be that birthdays serve as an anticipated social event for women, but a discouraging stock taking for men.

---

following a death—mourners vent their feelings and share memories of the deceased. During the following year, the bereaved are gradually drawn back into the life of the community.

Cremation is prohibited under Orthodox Jewish law; in ancient Greece, however, bodies of heroes were publicly burned as a sign of honor. In Japan, religious rituals encourage survivors to maintain contact with the deceased. Families keep an altar in the home dedicated to their ancestors; they talk to their dead loved ones and offer them food or cigars (Stroebe, Gergen, Gergen, & Stroebe, 1992). Alex Haley, in *Roots* (1976), observed that in Gambia the dead were still considered part of the community. Ten-year-old Kunta Kinte, at his grad-

uation, felt proud not only of his family sitting in the front row but of his ancestors buried beyond the village, especially his beloved grandmother. By contrast, among Native Americans, the Hopi try to forget a dead person as quickly as possible. They believe that death brings pollution and that the spirits of the dead are to be feared; they therefore do not keep photos or other reminders of someone who has died. Muslims in Egypt show grief through expressions of deep sorrow; Muslims in Bali are encouraged to suppress sadness, to laugh, and to be joyful (Stroebe et al., 1992).

There is no one "best" way to cope with loss. What works for one culture or one family may not work for another. In helping people handle grief,

An Orthodox Jewish funeral is simple and realistic; it is meant to help the bereaved face their loss. The community provides emotional support and helps mourners begin the process of recovery by serving a meal at their home. Traditional cultures, like the Hasidic sect these mourners belong to, help people deal with death and grief through rituals that have culturally accepted meanings. *(Nathan Benn/ Woodfin Camp & Associates)*

counselors need to take into account both ethnic traditions and individual differences. Let's look now at forms and patterns grief may take and at ways children cope with bereavement. Finally, we'll focus on three particularly difficult losses: those of a spouse, a parent, and a child.

FORMS AND PATTERNS OF GRIEF

Grief is a highly personal experience. Recent research has challenged earlier notions of a single, "normal" pattern of grieving and a "normal" timetable for recovery. A widow talking to her late husband might once have been considered emotionally disturbed; now this is recognized as a common and helpful behavior (Lund, 1993b). Although some people recover fairly quickly after bereavement, others never do.

Anticipatory Grief

The family and friends of a person who has been ill for a long time often prepare themselves for the loss through *anticipatory grief,* symptoms of grief experienced while the person is still alive. Anticipatory grief may help survivors handle the actual death more easily (J. T. Brown & Stoudemire, 1983). Women who can prepare themselves for widowhood psychologically and in practical terms—for example, by discussing pensions and insurance with their husbands—may make a more positive adjustment, though they may be no less distressed after the loss (O'Bryant, 1990–1991). In

one study, however, elderly widows who had expected their husbands' deaths and "rehearsed" for widowhood by thinking and talking about the future were no better or worse adjusted than women whose husbands had died unexpectedly (Hill, Thompson, & Gallagher, 1988).

Grief Work: A Three-Stage Pattern

Perhaps the most common and most widely studied pattern of grief is one that has three stages, in which the bereaved person accepts the painful reality of the loss, gradually lets go of the bond with the dead person, and finally readjusts to life by developing new interests and relationships. This process of *grief work,* the working out of psychological issues connected with grief, generally takes the following path—though, as with Kübler-Ross's stages, it may vary (J. T. Brown & Stoudemire, 1983; R. Schulz, 1978).

1   *Shock and disbelief.* This first stage may last several weeks, especially after a sudden or unexpected death. Immediately following a death, survivors often feel lost and confused. Shock and inability to believe in the death may protect them from more intense reactions. Physical reactions, such as shortness of breath, tightness in the chest or throat, nausea, and a feeling of emptiness in the abdomen are common. As awareness of the loss sinks in, the initial numbness gives way to overwhelming feelings of sadness and frequent crying.

2 *Preoccupation with the memory of the dead person.* In the second stage, which may last 6 months or longer, the survivor tries to come to terms with the death but cannot yet accept it. Crying continues, often accompanied by insomnia, fatigue, and loss of appetite. A widow may relive her husband's death and their entire relationship. From time to time, she may be seized by a feeling that her dead husband is present: she will hear his voice, sense his presence in the room, even see his face before her. She may have vivid dreams of him. These experiences diminish with time, though they may recur—perhaps for years—on such occasions as the anniversary of the marriage or of the death.

3 *Resolution.* The final stage has arrived when the bereaved person renews interest in everyday activities. Memories of the dead person bring fond feelings mingled with sadness, rather than sharp pain and longing. A widower may still miss his dead wife, but he knows that life must go on, and he becomes more active socially. He gets out more, sees people, picks up old interests, and perhaps discovers new ones.

Most bereaved people eventually are able, with the help of family and friends, to come to terms with their loss and resume normal lives. For some, however, *grief therapy*—treatment to help the bereaved cope with their loss—is indicated. Professional grief therapists help survivors express sorrow, guilt, hostility, and anger. They encourage clients to review the relationship with the deceased and to integrate the fact of the death into their lives so that they can be free to develop new relationships and new ways of behaving toward friends and relatives. Self-help groups can help reduce depression, but a person's own inner resources seem to be more influential (Caserta & Lund, 1993).

Varied Reactions to Loss

Although the pattern of grief work described above is common, grieving does not necessarily follow a straight line from shock to resolution. Instead, it may produce a succession of emotional ups and downs of varying lengths, which may eventually subside but never completely flatten out (Lund, 1993b). Furthermore, there are considerable differences in reactions to bereavement. Some people mourn intensely for a very long time:

Queen Victoria of England wore black and mourned her husband, Prince Albert, for the last 40 years of her life. Others, apparently, hardly mourn at all.

One team of psychologists (Wortman & Silver, 1989) reviewed studies of reactions to major losses: in some cases, the death of a loved one; in other cases, loss of a person's own mobility as a result of spinal injury. These researchers found some common assumptions to be more myth than fact.

First, depression is far from universal. From 3 weeks to 2 years after their loss, only 15 to 35 percent of widows, widowers, and victims of spinal cord injury showed signs of depression. *Second,* failure to show distress at the outset does not necessarily lead to problems; the people who were most upset immediately after a loss or injury were likely to be most troubled up to 2 years later. *Third,* not everyone needs to "work through" a loss or will benefit from doing so; some of the people who did the most intense grief work had more problems later. *Fourth,* not everyone returns to normal quickly. Parents of children killed by drunk drivers are likely to be functioning poorly up to 7 years later, and more than 40 percent of widows and widowers show moderate to severe anxiety up to 4 years after the spouse's death, especially if it was sudden. *Fifth,* people cannot always resolve their grief and accept their loss. Parents and spouses of people who die in car accidents often have painful memories of the loved one even after many years (Wortman & Silver, 1989).

Rather than a single three-stage pattern, this research found three main patterns of grieving. In the generally expected pattern, the mourner goes from high to low distress. In a second pattern, the mourner does not experience intense distress immediately or later. In a third pattern, the mourner remains distressed for a long time (Wortman & Silver, 1989).

The finding that grief takes varied forms and patterns has important implications for helping people deal with loss. It may be unnecessary and even harmful to urge or lead mourners to "work through" a loss or to expect them to follow a set pattern of emotional reactions—just as it may be unnecessary and harmful to expect all dying patients to experience Kübler-Ross's stages. Respect for differing patterns of grief can help bereaved people deal with loss without making them feel that their reactions are abnormal.

HOW CHILDREN AND ADOLESCENTS COPE WITH LOSS

Six percent of American children under age 10 have lost at least one parent. More have lost grandparents, many of whom played an important role in their lives. Some mourn the deaths of siblings, other relatives, or friends (American Academy of Pediatrics [AAP] Committee on Psychosocial Aspects of Child and Family Health, 1992).

Among those most grievously affected by the AIDS epidemic are children of stricken mothers. By the year 2000, an estimated 125,000 children and 21,000 adolescents will have lost their mothers to AIDS; 4 out of 5 of these orphans will come from African American and Hispanic families (Callan, 1995). Some of these children will probably be taken in by grandparents or other relatives, perhaps already overburdened by their own health problems or their own families. Some will go into foster care or adoptive homes. Most will face periods of uncertainty and instability in which their grief at losing their mothers will be aggravated by their fears about the future.

Children and adolescents experience grief much as adults do, but they often show it in special ways, depending on cognitive and emotional development (see Table 18-1). Children sometimes express grief through anger, acting out, or refusal to acknowledge a death, as if the pretense that a person is still alive will make it so. They may be confused by adults' euphemisms: that someone "expired" or that the family "lost" someone or that someone is "asleep" and will never awaken. Adolescents mourning the death of a family member sometimes feel embarrassed talking to outsiders; they may feel more comfortable grieving with their peers.

A loss is usually hardest to accept in early childhood or early adolescence. A loss is also more difficult if the child had a troubled relationship with the person who died, if a troubled surviving parent depends too much on the child, if the death was unexpected, especially if it was a murder or suicide, if the child has had previous behavioral or emotional problems, or if family and community support are lacking (AAP Committee on Psychosocial Aspects of Child and Family Health, 1992).

Parents or other caregivers can help children deal with bereavement by helping them under-

TABLE 18-1

Manifestations of Grief in Children

Under 3 years	3 to 5 years	School-Age Children	Adolescents
Regression	Increased activity	Deterioration of school performance caused by loss of concentration, disinterest, lack of motivation, failure to complete assignments, and daydreaming in class	Depression
Sadness	Constipation		Somatic complaints
Fearfulness	Soiling		Delinquent behavior
Loss of appetite	Bed-wetting		Promiscuity
Failure to thrive	Anger and temper tantrums		Suicide attempts
Sleep disturbance	"Out-of-control" behavior	Resistance to attending school	Dropping out of school
Social withdrawal	Nightmares		
Developmental delay	Crying spells	Crying spells	
Irritability		Lying	
Excessive crying		Stealing	
Increased dependency		Nervousness	
Loss of speech		Abdominal pain	
		Headaches	
		Listlessness	
		Fatigue	

SOURCE: Adapted from AAP Committee on Psychosocial Aspects of Child and Family Health, 1992.

Widowhood is one of the most stressful losses that can affect a human being. It takes time for the pain of loss to heal, but most widowed people do rebuild their lives. Friends who have gone through a similar bereavement can offer social support. *(Amy Etra/PhotoEdit)*

stand that death is final and that they did not cause the death by their misbehavior or thoughts. Children need reassurance that they will continue to receive care from loving adults. It is usually helpful to make as few changes as possible in a child's environment, relationships, and daily activities, to answer questions simply and honestly, and to encourage the child to talk about the person who died.

SURVIVING A SPOUSE

Because women tend to live longer than men and tend to be younger than their husbands, they are more likely to be widowed (O'Bryant, 1990–1991; Treas, 1995; U.S. Bureau of the Census, 1995a). They are also more likely to be stronger for the experience (Umberson, Wortman, & Kessler, 1992), though worse off economically. In the United States, 47 percent of women over age 65 are widowed and have not remarried, as compared with 13 percent of men over 65 (AARP, 1995; refer back to Figure 17-6).

Adjusting to Widowhood

Widowhood is one of the greatest emotional challenges that a human being can face. It means not only the loss of a partner but the disruption of virtually every aspect of the survivor's life. In a classic ranking of stressful events, the one requiring the most adjustment was the death of a spouse (refer back to Table 14-2).

Indeed there is a strong likelihood that a widowed person, especially a widower, will follow the spouse to the grave. That finding emerged from a study of all deaths in Finland between 1986 and 1991 of people who, as of the 1985 census, had been 35 to 84 years old and married. The surviving partner was highly likely to also die by the end of the study period. The risk was greatest for young adults and those whose loss was still fresh, suggesting that the stress of unexpected or recent bereavement was a major factor (Martikainen & Valkonen, 1996).

Many studies have found older adults to be better-adjusted to widowhood than younger adults. One interpretation is that loss of a spouse is more traumatic in young adulthood, when it is less expected (DiGiulio, 1992). However, the reason may be that younger widowed people in these studies were more recently bereaved; people who have recently lost a partner to death or divorce tend to be lonelier and more likely to wish for a partner than those whose loss occurred long ago (Dykstra, 1995). One study that controlled for how long people had been widowed found that the age at which bereavement occurs has little long-term effect on morale: losing a husband or wife is no easier or harder at an earlier or a later age. Older widows and widowers did tend to have somewhat higher morale than younger ones, perhaps because of greater availability of companions, especially widowed peers (Balkwell, 1985).

In the short term, younger widows do have more psychological problems. Burdened with full responsibility for breadwinning and parenthood, and often with a drastically reduced standard of living, they may lack the time or energy to develop a new social life. They may find themselves resenting their children and feeling guilty about their resentment (DiGiulio, 1992).

In general, though, age is not a major factor in the grieving process; coping skills are. People who have had practice in coping with loss and have developed effective coping resources—self-esteem and competence in meeting the demands of everyday life—are better able to deal with bereavement (Lund, 1993b).

The survivor of a long marriage is likely to face many emotional and practical problems. A good marriage can leave a gaping emotional void: the loss of a lover, a confidant, a good friend, and a steady companion. Even with a troubled marriage, a loss may be felt. For one thing, the survivor no longer has the *role* of spouse. This loss may be especially hard for a woman who has structured her life and her identity around caring for her husband (Saunders, 1981). It also affects working people of both sexes, who no longer have a partner to come home to, and retirees who have no one to talk to—or argue with.

Social life changes, too. Friends and family usually rally to the mourner's side immediately after the death, but then they go back to their own lives. Married friends, uncomfortable with the thought that bereavement could happen to them too, may avoid the widowed person. Widowed men and women often feel like a "fifth wheel" with couples who have been longtime friends (Brubaker, 1990). However, widows and widowers see friends more often than married people do, perhaps because they have more time and more need for social contact, and although most widowed people make new friends, most of their friends continue to be old ones (Field & Minkler, 1988). Widowed men are more likely than widowed women to seek the companionship of the other sex. Women, especially middle-aged and older women, usually make friends with other widows but find it hard to meet and form relationships with men, since men in their age group are in short supply and tend to be interested in younger women (Brecher & Editors of Consumer Reports Books, 1984).

Economic hardship can be a major problem. When the husband has been the main breadwinner, his widow is deprived of his income; when the husband is widowed, he has to buy many of the services his wife provided. When both spouses have been employed, the loss of one income can be a blow.

Not surprisingly, widowed people of both sexes have higher rates of depression than married people (Balkwell, 1981). Widowed men tend to be more vulnerable to depression than widowed women, perhaps because they are less likely than women to have formed other intimate relationships. Among women, a primary factor in depression seems to be financial strain; among men, it is the stress of managing a household (Umberson et al., 1992).

Despite all its stresses, widowhood can be a developmental experience. Although it takes time for the pain of loss to heal, most bereaved spouses eventually rebuild their lives. They may not get over the loss, but they get used to it. Loneliness and sadness give way to confidence in the ability to manage on their own. The people who adjust best are those who keep busy, take on new roles (such as new paid or volunteer work), or become more deeply involved in ongoing activities. They see friends often (which helps more than frequent visits with their children), and they may join support groups. Social support—including being encouraged to express feelings without being given unsolicited advice—is especially important in the first few months; survivors who cope well during that period usually do better than others in the long run. Quality of relationships may be more important than frequency of contact (T. B. Anderson, 1984; Balkwell, 1981; C. J. Barrett, 1978; Lund, 1989, 1993b; Vachon, Lyall, Rogers, Freedmen-Letofky, & Freeman, 1980).

Remarriage after Widowhood

Elderly widowers are more likely to remarry than elderly widows, much as men of any age are more likely than women to remarry after divorce (P. C. Glick & Lin, 1986b). Because of the greater number of unattached women their age, as well as the tendency to marry younger women, men have more potential partners. Also, men may have more incentive to remarry; women more frequently can handle their own household needs, are sometimes reluctant to give up survivors' pension benefits, or do not want to end up caring for an infirm husband.

In one study of 24 older couples who had remarried when both partners were over 60, most had been widowed. Most of them had known each other during their first marriages or had been in-

The actress Lynn Redgrave came to terms with the death of her father, the celebrated actor Michael Redgrave, through her one-woman show, *Shakespeare for My Father.* The loss of a parent can affect a middle-aged person's sense of self, as well as relationships with others, and it is a poignant reminder of one's own mortality. *(Joan Marcus)*

troduced by friends or relatives (Vinick, 1978). Why had they decided to marry again? Men tended to mention companionship and relief from loneliness; women tended to mention their feelings toward the new husband or his personal qualities. Almost all these people, who had been remarried for 2 to 6 years, were happy. Their new marriages were calmer than marriages earlier in life; the partners had a "live and let live" attitude.

LOSING A PARENT

Little attention has been paid to the impact of the death of a parent on an adult child. Yet that loss too can be hard to bear: "Not only is there the loss of the oldest and one of the most important (yet ambivalent) relationships in one's life, but there [may be] the trauma of breaking up a household in which one may have grown up and of losing the older buffer between oneself and death" (Dainoff, 1989, p. 64). Today this loss often occurs in middle age. With longer life expectancies, it is not unusual for a parent to remain alive during the

first 50 years or more of a child's life (Umberson & Chen, 1994). Half of all people become orphaned by their midfifties and 3 out of 4 by their early sixties (Winsborough, Bumpass, & Aquilino, 1991). Psychological distress generally surfaces quickly; health problems may show up considerably later (Umberson & Chen, 1994).

A survey of 220 bereaved adult children found that 1 out of 4 still suffered social and emotional problems up to 5 years after the parent's death (Scharlach, 1991). In-depth interviews with 83 volunteers ages 35 to 60 found a majority still experiencing emotional distress—ranging from sadness and crying to depression and thoughts of suicide—after 1 to 5 years, especially following loss of a mother. Furthermore, close to half of those who had lost either parent reported physical reactions, such as illness, fatigue, and a general decline in health (Scharlach & Fredriksen, 1993).

Still, the death of a parent can be a maturing experience. It can push adults into resolving important developmental issues: achieving a stronger sense of self and a more pressing, realistic awareness of their own mortality, along with a greater sense of responsibility, commitment, and attachment to others (M. S. Moss & Moss, 1989; Scharlach & Fredriksen, 1993).*

Changes in the Self

Eight years after the distinguished actor Michael Redgrave died, his daughter, the actress Lynn Redgrave (then 50), wrote and performed a one-woman show, *Shakespeare for My Father.* In it, she finally came to terms with the hurt and frustration her father's coldness had caused her as a child. "It was a privilege to be my father's daughter," she told an interviewer. "But with it went a great price. I paid that price, and I'm stronger for it" (Ryan, 1993).

Many middle-aged adults who lose a parent experience some effect on their sense of self (see Table 18-2). They often feel strengthened as they review the parent's life in relation to their own. For the first time they may be able to accept and forgive the parent's failings. They also may be prompted to review their own lives and revise goals and priorities. Many feel themselves becoming more self-assertive, autonomous, self-confident, and re-

*The discussion in the remainder of this section is largely indebted to M. S. Moss and Moss (1989) and Scharlach and Fredriksen (1993).

TABLE 18-2

Self-reported Psychological Impacts of a Parent's Death

Impacts	Death of Mother (Percent)	Death of Father (Percent)
Self-concept		
More "adult"	29	43
More self-confident	19	20
More responsible	11	4
Less mature	14	3
Other	8	17
No impact	19	12
Feelings about mortality		
Increased awareness of own mortality	30	29
More accepting of own death	19	10
Made concrete plans regarding own death	10	4
Increased fear of own death	10	18
Other	14	16
No impact	17	23
Religiosity		
More religious	26	29
Less religious	11	2
Other	3	10
No impact	60	59
Personal priorities		
Personal relationships more important	35	28
Simple pleasures more important	16	13
Personal happiness more important	10	7
Material possessions less important	5	8
Other	20	8
No impact	14	36
Work or career plans		
Left job	29	16
Adjusted goals	15	10
Changed plans due to family needs	5	6
Moved	4	10
Other	13	19
No impact	34	39

SOURCE: Scharlach & Fredriksen, 1993, table 1, p. 311.

sponsible. As one adult who had lost a mother said, "I can't call her up if I need advice anymore" (Scharlach & Fredriksen, 1993, p. 310). Some, though, who overly identified with the dead parent, may feel unable to manage their own lives. They may worry about the future and despair of achieving self-fulfillment.

A parent's death is a reminder of one's own mortality. It may leave the adult child feeling older and unprotected. Yet it also may bring a less anxious acceptance of death, along with a greater sense of purpose about the time remaining. Often the loss of a parent leads people to prepare for death in concrete ways, such as making funeral arrangements or a will.

Changes in Relationships

The death of a parent often brings changes in other relationships, either more intimacy or more conflict. A bereaved adult child may assume more responsibility for the surviving parent and for keeping the family together. The intense emotions of bereavement may draw siblings closer, or they may become alienated over differences that arose during the parent's final illness.

A parent's death may free an adult child to spend more time and energy on relationships that were temporarily neglected to meet demands of caregiving—relationships with a spouse or partner, children, or grandchildren. Or the death may free an adult child to shed a relationship that was being maintained to meet the parent's expectations.

Recognition of the finality of death and the impossibility of saying anything more to the deceased parent motivates some people to resolve disturbances in their ties to the living while there is still time. Some people are moved to reconcile with their own adult children. Sometimes estranged siblings, realizing that the parent who provided a link between them is no longer there, try to mend the rift.

LOSING A CHILD

There is no English word for a parent who has lost a child. A person who has lost a spouse is a widow or widower; a person who has lost both parents is an orphan; but a person whose child has died is bereft even of an identity. A parent is rarely prepared emotionally for the death of a child.

In earlier times, it was more common for a parent to bury a child. Today, with medical advances and the increase in life expectancy in industrialized countries, infant mortality has reached record lows, and a child who survives the first year of life is far more likely to live to old age. The death of a child, no matter at what age, comes as a cruel, unnatural shock, an untimely event that, in the normal course of things, should not have happened. The parents may feel they have failed, no matter how much they loved and cared for the child, and they may find it hard to let go.

If a marriage is strong, the couple may draw closer together, supporting each other in their shared loss. In other cases, the loss weakens and destroys the marriage. One spouse may blame the other, or husband and wife may simply have different ways of grieving and of rebuilding their lives. Unresolved issues stemming from a child's death can lead to divorce, even years later (Brandt, 1989).

Although each bereaved parent must cope with grief in his or her own way, some have found that plunging into work, interests, and other relationships or joining a support group eases the pain. Some well-meaning friends tell parents not to dwell on their loss, but remembering the child in a meaningful way may be exactly what they need to do. At the 1992 Democratic National Convention, Elizabeth Glaser, the wife of the television actor and director Paul Michael Glaser, told how, in 1981, she had contracted the HIV virus from a blood transfusion and unknowingly passed it on to her infant daughter, Ariel, in her breast milk. After Ariel died of AIDS at age 7, Elizabeth Glaser launched a crusade to increase public awareness of pediatric AIDS. By the time of her own death in 1994 at the age of 47, the foundation she established had raised more than $30 million for research and education (Kennedy, 1994).

✔ CONTROVERSIAL ISSUES

A 45-year-old Israeli filmmaker shot a video in which his 83-year-old father and 82-year-old mother said they planned to kill themselves while they were still healthy, to avoid deterioration, suffering, or becoming a burden on their children. Four days later, the couple took an overdose of sleeping pills. At the funeral, the son read a letter from his parents, in which they stated that they hoped their act would help "break the taboo" against suicide (D. Perry, 1995, p. 10).

Although suicide is no longer a crime in modern societies, there is still a stigma against it, based in part on religious prohibitions and on society's interest in preserving life. A person who expresses suicidal thoughts may be considered, often with good reason, mentally ill. On the other hand, as longevity increases—and with it the risk of debilitating long-term illness and of the unwanted prolongation of life, often by extraordinary means—a growing number of people consider a mature adult's deliberate choice of a time to end his or her life a rational decision and a right to be defended.

Do people have a right to die? If so, under what circumstances? Who should decide that a life is not worth sustaining? Should a terminally ill person who wants to commit suicide be prevented from, or helped in, doing so? Should a doctor prescribe medicine that will relieve pain but may also shorten the patient's life? What about giving a lethal injection to end a patient's suffering? What abuses may such decisions entail? These are some of the thorny moral, ethical, and legal questions that face individuals, families, physicians, and society—questions involving the quality of life and the nature and circumstances of death.

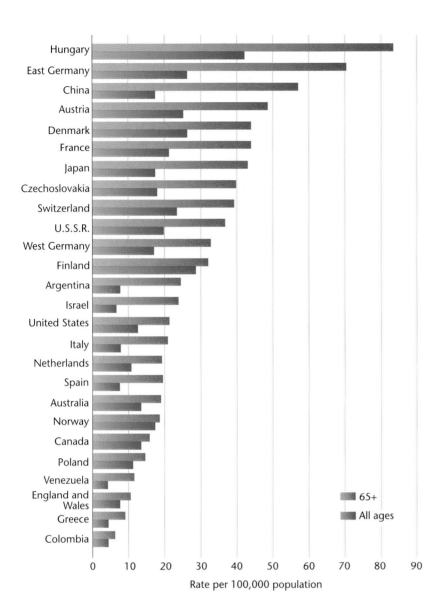

FIGURE 18-2

Suicide rates for all ages and for older adults in selected countries. *(Source: McIntosh, 1992, fig. 5, p. 30; based on data from World Health Organization, 1991.)*

Let's look first at suicide, or self-inflicted death: who is likely to commit it and why, and what some common warning signs are. Then we'll consider two related topics that involve the issue of a "right to die": euthanasia and assisted suicide.

SUICIDE

Many people find life so precious that they cannot understand why anyone would voluntarily end it. Yet in 1995, according to provisional figures, almost 31,000 people in the United States committed suicide, making it the ninth leading cause of death in the nation (H. M. Rosenberg et al., 1996). Furthermore, the yearly suicide rate in the United States—11.8 deaths per 100,000 population (H. M.

Rosenberg et al., 1996)—is moderate compared with rates in some other industrial countries ("Suicide—Part I," 1996; see Figure 18-2). American men end their own lives in far greater proportions than women, and white Americans do so almost twice as often as African Americans. Most other minority groups also have lower suicide rates than whites (USDHHS, 1996), perhaps due to strong extended family support and traditional religious observance. Suicide rates rose between 1980 and 1992 in two age groups: children and adolescents ages 5 to 19 and older adults (Centers for Disease Control and Prevention, 1996b).

Statistics probably understate the number of suicides, since many go unreported and some are not recognized as such. Some suicides look like traffic

"Why?" is what grieving school friends of 15-year-old Alicia Hayes and 14-year-old Amber Hernandez asked themselves after the two ninth-graders at San Pedro High School in Los Angeles killed themselves May 22, 1996, by tying their wrists together and jumping off a rocky cliff beside the Pacific Ocean. It was the second such double-suicide by teenagers at that spot in two months. Suicide is the third leading cause of death among adolescents, and the leading cause is accidents, some of which may actually be suicides. Classmates of young suicide victims need guidance to alleviate their anxiety and to prevent more young people from taking their own lives. *(Susan Sterner/AP/Wide World Photos)*

accidents, accidental overdoses of drugs, or forgetfulness—unintentional failure to take life-preserving medicine. Also, the figures do not include suicide *attempts;* 10 to 40 percent of people who commit suicide have tried before (Meehan, 1990; "Suicide—Part II," 1996). Firearms are used in most completed suicides today (USDHHS, 1992). The increased use of guns instead of less certain methods, such as poison, may indicate that more people who commit suicide are determined to succeed—or that guns are more available than they used to be (Centers for Disease Control, 1985; Rivara & Grossman, 1996; "Suicide—Part I," 1996). Nearly all of the 17 percent increase in suicide among children and teenagers between 1978 and 1991 represented deaths from firearms (Rivara & Grossman, 1996).

Suicide among Children

"It wasn't an accident. I figured if I died it wouldn't hurt as much as if I lived." These were the words of a dying 5-year-old child (Turkington, 1983).

It is painfully hard to believe that young children can be so unhappy as to try to take their lives, but preliminary 1995 data report 329 suicides among 5- to 14-year-old children, making suicide the fifth leading cause of death in this age group (H. M. Rosenberg et al., 1996). Suicidal children tend to have experienced early, frequent, and stressful losses, such as the divorce or death of par-

ents. They tend to be depressed, hopeless, impulsive, and angry (Wilson, 1991).

Some "accidents" among preschoolers may actually be deliberate attempts at suicide. In one study, 16 children ages 2½ to 5 were diagnosed as suicidal; they had seriously injured themselves or had tried to do so, 13 of them more than once. These children were compared with 16 children in the same age group who had serious behavioral problems but were not considered suicidal. The children diagnosed as suicidal were more aggressive, seemed more depressed, harbored more morbid ideas, ran away more, and cried less often after being hurt than the other children. Most of the suicidal children had parents who did not want them and who abused or neglected them; six had been separated from their parents by divorce, foster placement, adoption, or death; and all showed disturbed attachment behavior. Play therapy brought out the children's reasons for trying to kill themselves: to punish themselves, to escape or remedy their painful situations, or to be reunited with a loved, nurturing person, such as a dead father. Half of them apparently believed that death is reversible (P. A. Rosenthal & Rosenthal, 1984).

Suicide among Adolescents

A 16-year-old girl, constantly at odds with her parents because they disapprove of her boyfriend, breaks up with the boy. The next morning, her sister discovers her body next to an empty bottle of sleeping pills. An 18-year-old boy, despondent after a traffic accident that has resulted in the "totaling" of his car, the revocation of his driver's license, and a forthcoming trial, jumps off an icy bridge to his death.

These two teenagers are among a growing number of young people who see no way out of bad times in their life other than ending it. In a 1990 Gallup poll, more than 60 percent of teenagers said they knew someone who had attempted suicide, and 6 percent said they had attempted to kill themselves (Ackerman, 1993). Far fewer completed suicides are reported—13.3 per 100,000 15- to 24-year-olds in 1995, according to preliminary data—but that rate has tripled since 1950. Suicide is the third leading cause of death in this age group; the leading cause is accidents, but some of these may actually be suicides (H. M. Rosenberg et al., 1996; USDHHS, 1996). The suicide rate for 15- to 24-year-old males in 1993—22.4 per 100,000—was almost twice the rate for the population as a whole and 3 times the rate for young males in the 1950s. The rate for females the same age was only 4.1 per 100,000 (NCHS, 1996a).

A suicide attempt may be precipitated by a fight with a boyfriend or girlfriend or a parent, or by a shameful or humiliating experience, such as bad grades, an arrest, or being fired from a job. Still, many young people have such painful experiences, and most do not try to kill themselves. Those who do attempt suicide tend to have histories of emotional illness: commonly depression, substance abuse, antisocial or aggressive behavior, or unstable personality. They also tend to have attempted suicide before or to have friends and family members who did (Garland & Zigler, 1993; Slap, Vorters, Chaudhuri, & Centor, 1989; "Suicide—Part I," 1996). Drugs and alcohol play a part in one-third or more of teenage suicides and probably account for much of the rise in incidence (Garland & Zigler, 1993).

Suicidal teenagers tend to think poorly of themselves, to feel hopeless, and to have poor impulse control and low tolerance for frustration and stress. Feelings of depression may be masked as boredom, apathy, hyperactivity, or physical problems. These young people are often alienated from their parents and have no one outside the family to turn to. Many come from troubled or broken families, often with a history of unemployment, imprisonment, or suicidal behavior. A high proportion of these young people have been abused or neglected (Deykin, Alpert, & McNamara, 1985; Garland & Zigler, 1993; Slap et al., 1989; "Suicide—Part I," 1996; Swedo et al., 1991). School problems—academic or behavioral—are common among would-be suicides, though not universal (National Committee for Citizens in Education, NCCE, 1986).

Ready availability of guns in the home is a major factor in the increase in teenage suicide (Rivara & Grossman, 1996). Although most young people who *attempt* suicide do it by taking pills or ingesting other substances, those who succeed are most likely to use firearms (Garland & Zigler, 1993).

Telephone hotlines are the most prevalent type of suicide intervention for adolescents, but their effectiveness appears to be minimal. The few studies that have been done of school suicide prevention programs found them of limited value. In fact, some may do harm by exaggerating the extent of teenage suicide and painting it as a reaction to the normal stresses of adolescence rather than a pathological act. A review of the research on adolescent suicide suggests that prevention programs should instead seek to carefully identify and treat young people at particular risk of suicide, including those who have already attempted it. Equally important is to attack the risk factors through programs, for example, to reduce substance abuse and strengthen families (Garland & Zigler, 1993).

Suicide among Older Adults

Audience members at a Metropolitan Opera performance of Verdi's *Macbeth* were horrified when, during the intermission, an elderly man plunged to his death from a balcony. Bantcho Bantchevsky was an 82-year-old vocal coach who had lived for his music and his friends. He had been lively and gregarious, but when his health began to deteriorate, he became depressed. His depression grew until he took his life, dying as theatrically as he had lived (Okun, 1988).

Statistically, Bantcho Bantchevsky, as an elderly white man, was a highly likely candidate for suicide. In most nations, suicide is most prevalent among older men (McIntosh, 1992; based on data from World Health Organization, 1991). In the United States, in absolute numbers, more suicides occur among young white males, but by far the highest *rate* of suicide is among older white men (NCHS, 1996a; USDHHS, 1996; see Figure 18-3). Furthermore, this rate, which had been declining

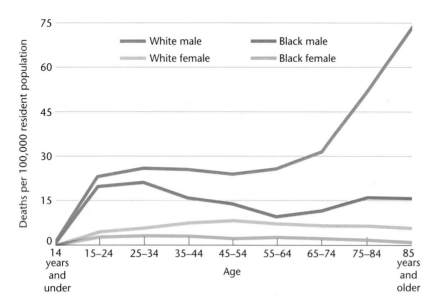

FIGURE 18-3
Suicide rates in the United States in 1993, by sex, race, and age. Where figures for 1993 were not available, because of too few cases, figures for the period 1991–1993 have been used. *(Source: U.S. Department of Health and Human Services, USDHHS, 1996.)*

since the 1940s, rose 10 percent between 1980 and 1992. When we look more closely, however, we see that suicide rates actually *decreased* among the young old but increased among those 75 and older, particularly (by 35 percent) among 80- to 84-year-olds, who are more likely to be frail and infirm (Centers for Disease Control and Prevention, 1996b).

Elderly white men, after the sometimes high achievements of youth, may find it especially hard to face deprivation in old age. They may despair over a progression of losses that they cannot stop: losses of work, of friends, perhaps of a spouse, of children who may have moved away, of memory, of health, and finally of self-esteem and hope. Older African Americans are much less likely to commit suicide (USDHHS, 1996), perhaps in part because of their religious convictions and in part because they are used to coping with hard knocks.

As with Bantcho Bantchevsky, suicide often occurs in conjunction with depression or debilitating physical ailments. Older people who commit suicide are more likely than younger ones to be depressed, to abuse alcohol, and to be socially isolated. They are more likely to be physically or emotionally ill and to have seen a doctor shortly before taking their lives. Older adults who attempt suicide are more likely to succeed, perhaps because they tend to use more lethal methods, especially firearms (Centers for Disease Control and Prevention, 1996b).

Older people who commit suicide are likely to be divorced, widowed, or unemployed or to have experienced other stressful events; they tend to show antisocial behavior, to suffer from schizo-phrenia or panic attacks, to have undergone psychiatric treatment, to have relatives who attempted or committed suicide, and to keep a handgun in the home. They tend to be dependent, helpless (or unable to accept help), hopeless, and extremely anxious or irritable. They often have difficulty concentrating or solving problems (especially under stress) and forming close relationships (Boyer & Guthrie, 1985; Centers for Disease Control and Prevention, 1985; Kellerman et al., 1992; Meehan, 1990; "Suicide," 1986; USDHHS, 1990, 1992; Weissman, Klerman, Markowitz, & Ouelette, 1989).

Preventing Suicide

Even some supporters of a "right to die" hold that family, friends, medical professionals, and others should try to thwart a suicide. According to this view, suicide is often not so much a wish for death as a desire to avoid pain, either physical or emotional. Finding ways to reduce pain, perhaps through hospice care or psychiatric treatment, may avoid an irrevocable action with tragic consequences for self and loved ones.

Sometimes a suicide attempt is a call for help. Some people who attempt suicide do not really want to end their lives; they want to *change* their lives, and the attempt to kill themselves may be a desperate plea for attention and assistance ("Suicide—Part II," 1996). Unfortunately, they may die before aid can reach them. Many suicides are attempted on impulse: if a convenient means is not at hand, a person may desist or defer action long enough to get help.

Although some people intent on suicide carefully conceal their plans, there are often warning signs: withdrawing from family or friends; talking about death, the hereafter, or suicide; giving away prized possessions; abusing drugs or alcohol; and personality changes, such as unusual anger, boredom, or apathy. People who are about to kill themselves may neglect their appearance, stay away from work or other customary activities, complain of physical problems when nothing is organically wrong, or sleep or eat much more or much less than usual. They often show signs of depression, such as unusual difficulty concentrating, loss of self-esteem, and feelings of helplessness, hopelessness, extreme anxiety, or panic. Psychotherapy, medication, or increased social contact may lessen feelings of isolation, lift depression, and restore interest in life. Sometimes, though, all efforts fail. A person who is truly determined to die will probably find a way of doing it.

Survivors of people who take their own lives have been called "suicide's other victims." Many of them blame themselves for failing to recognize the signs. They "obsessively replay the events leading up to the death, imagining how they could have prevented it and berating themselves for their failure to do so" (L. L. Goldman & Rothschild, in press). Because of the stigma attached to suicide, they often struggle with their emotions alone rather than share them with others who might understand. At the same time, many families struggle with a different, but equally excruciating, issue:

what to do about a suffering loved one, with no hope of recovery, who seeks aid in dying.

EUTHANASIA AND ASSISTED SUICIDE

In traditional Inuit (Eskimo) society, where the personality is believed to survive death, an older man who feels his usefulness is over may ask his sons to help him strangle himself, and an older woman who cannot complete an arduous journey may ask her children to leave her behind on the trail. Children usually attempt to change their parents' minds but soon grant this last wish (Guemple, 1983).

In Milwaukee, Wisconsin, in 1983, a 79-year-old man visited his 62-year-old wife in a nursing home. Once a successful businesswoman, the wife, now suffering from advanced Alzheimer's disease, screamed constantly and was unable or unwilling to speak. The man pushed his wife's wheelchair into a stairwell, where he killed her with a pistol shot. The district attorney who prosecuted the husband called his action "classic first-degree murder," but the grand jury refused to indict, and he went free (Malcolm, 1984).

This husband claimed to be practicing euthanasia ("good death"). If so, his act was an example of ***active euthanasia*** (sometimes called *mercy killing*)—direct action taken deliberately to shorten a life in order to end suffering or allow a terminally ill person to die with dignity. ***Passive euthanasia*** is deliberately withholding or discon-

Physician-assisted suicide for the terminally ill has become a controversial issue. Jack Kevorkian, a retired pathologist, has defied Michigan's law banning the practice by attending the suicides of more than 40 people since 1990 and has been acquitted in three jury trials. The two women shown here, Marcella Lawrence (left) and Marguerite Tate (right), took their lives in Kevorkian's presence a few hours before the governor signed the bill into law. *(C. Hillary/Reuters/ Bettmann-Corbis)*

tinuing treatment, such as medication, life-support systems, or feeding tubes, that might extend the life, or postpone the natural death, of a terminally ill patient. Active euthanasia is generally illegal; passive euthanasia, in some circumstances and in some places, is not. An important question regarding either form of euthanasia is whether it is *voluntary,* that is, whether it is done at the direct request, or to carry out the expressed wishes, of the person whose death results. *Assisted suicide*—in which a physician or someone else helps a person bring about a self-inflicted death by, for example, prescribing or obtaining drugs or enabling a patient to inhale a deadly gas—is illegal in most states but recently has come to the forefront of public debate. Assisted suicide is similar in principle to voluntary active euthanasia, in which, for example, a patient asks for, and receives, a lethal injection. The main difference is that in assisted suicide the person who wants to die performs the actual deed (Brock, 1992). All of these are varying forms of what is sometimes called *aid in dying.*

Changing attitudes toward aid in dying can be attributed largely to revulsion against technologies that keep people alive against their will despite intense suffering, and sometimes even after the brain has, for all practical purposes, stopped functioning. The President's Commission for the Study of Ethical Problems in Medicine and Biomedical and Behavioral Research proposed that mentally competent patients, and families acting on behalf of incompetent patients, be allowed to halt medical treatment that keeps the patient alive without any hope of cure or improvement. The commission recommended that ending a life intentionally be forbidden, but that doctors should be allowed to give drugs that are likely to shorten life if the reason for administering the drugs is to relieve pain (Schmeck, 1983).

A 1994 Harris poll found that 70 percent of adults would go further, allowing doctors "to comply with the wishes of a dying patient in severe distress who asks to have his or her life ended" (H. Taylor, 1995). A poll of 352 doctors found that 73 percent believed they should be allowed to help terminally ill patients die with dignity (Larson, 1996). Of these, more than 95 percent favored withholding life support (passive euthanasia), but only 37 percent approved of providing patients with the means to take their own lives (assisted suicide) and fewer than 13 percent would personally administer a lethal medication (active euthanasia).

Advance Directives

The United States Supreme Court has held that a person whose wishes are clearly known has a constitutional right to have life-sustaining treatment discontinued (*Cruzan v. Director, Missouri Department of Health,* 1990). Since that decision, more people have specified in writing what measures they want—or do not want—taken if they become terminally ill or mentally incompetent.

A person's wishes can be spelled out in advance in a document called a ***living will.*** A person who signs a living will must be legally competent at the time, and the document generally cannot be witnessed by anyone who stands to gain. The living will may contain specific provisions with regard to, for example, relief of pain, cardiac resuscitation, mechanical respiration, antibiotics, and artificial nutrition and hydration.

Some "living will" legislation applies only to terminally ill patients, not to those who are incapacitated by illness or injury but may live many years in severe pain, or to those in a coma or in a ***persistent vegetative state,*** a state in which, while technically alive, they have no awareness and only rudimentary brain functioning. Therefore, it may be advisable to draw up a ***durable power of attorney,*** which appoints another person to make decisions if someone becomes incompetent to do so. A number of states have enacted statutes expressly for decisions about health care, which provide for a simple form known as a *medical durable power of attorney.*

Even with advance directives, however, many people die in pain after protracted, fruitless treatment. In a survey of 1,400 doctors and nurses in five major hospitals around the United States, nearly half of attending doctors and nurses and 70 percent of resident doctors reported prolonging life support for terminally ill patients—even though they knew the patients would not want it—while failing to give them enough pain medication (M. Solomon, 1993).

A 5-year study of care given to some 9,000 critically ill patients at five teaching hospitals made similar findings. In almost half (49 percent) of the cases in which patients had asked not to be resuscitated in the event of cardiac arrest, their doctors did not know of the request, and 70 percent of patients were never asked their wishes. Close to 40 percent of dying patients spent more than a week in intensive care, in a coma or hooked up to a respirator, and half of those who were conscious were said by family members to have been in moderate to severe pain. Even when doctors were given daily reports of patients' wishes and computer-generated projections of their chances for recovery, the picture did not change appreciably. Apparently concern about peer review, the press of a perceived medical emergency, or sheer habit sometimes leads physicians to ignore patients' directives and continue "heroic" measures (The SUPPORT Principal Investigators, 1995). Follow-up interviews with family members of patients who died found that many patients did want aggressive treatment, even at the risk of discomfort; only 1 out of 10 patients disagreed with the care they received. Even 10 percent, though, represents a large number of cases in which aggressive life-sustaining treatments may have been used contrary to patients' preferences. Clear doctor-patient communication was found to be uncommon (Lynn et al., 1997).

Such findings have led the American Medical Association to form a Task Force on Quality Care at the End of Life. Many hospitals now have ethics committees that create guidelines, review cases, and help doctors, patients, and their families with decisions about end-of-life care (K. H. Simpson, 1996).

Physician Aid in Dying: Legal and Ethical Issues

In September 1996, an Australian man in his sixties with advanced prostate cancer was the first person to die legally by assisted suicide. Under a law passed in the Northern Territory (but later overturned by the Federal Parliament), he pressed a computer key that administered a lethal dose of barbiturates ("Australian Man," 1996).

In the United States, sentiment is growing for similar action. Dr. Jack Kevorkian, a retired pathologist who has defied Michigan law by attending more than 40 suicides since 1990, has been acquitted in three jury trials (Kolata, 1996). A nationwide Harris poll found 58 percent support for Kevorkian and 2-to-1 support for legislation permitting assisted suicide (H. Taylor, 1995). With other polls favoring doctor-assisted suicide by as much as 3 to 1, an increasing number of physicians, moved by the plight of suffering patients and encouraged by the reluctance of juries to convict, are acceding to such requests (Castaneda, 1996; A. M. Lee et al., 1996; Quill, 1991). According to one report, 25 percent of American physicians say they have helped someone die ("Suicide—Part II," 1996).

The United States Supreme Court in 1997 was expected to rule on two appellate court decisions that overturned California and New York statutes prohibiting physician-assisted suicide for the terminally ill. The Court may also ultimately be asked to rule on a law adopted in Oregon in 1994 through voter initiative, authorizing physician-assisted suicide under controlled conditions. The measure, immediately suspended by a legal challenge, would permit terminally ill patients with less than 6 months to live to ask a doctor for a lethal prescription, with safeguards to make sure that the request is serious and truly voluntary and that all other alternatives have been considered.

Regardless of whether the courts uphold a constitutional right to die, public opinion and public policy appear to be moving toward legalizing physician aid in dying. Some legal scholars question the meaningfulness of a distinction between withholding life-sustaining treatment in response to a patient's request and assisting in suicide (Orentlicher, 1996). Although active euthanasia remains highly controversial, some observers predict that it too will become increasingly common (W. McCord, 1993).

Both supporters and opponents of aid in dying point to the example of the Netherlands. There, although active euthanasia remains technically illegal, a law passed in 1993 permits physicians who engage in it to avoid prosecution under strict conditions. The patient must be suffering unbearably, without hope of recovery. The request must be made freely and repeatedly, unpressured by others. Another physician must agree on the advisability and method of euthanasia, and a complete report must be written (Simons, 1993).

The change in Dutch law reflects a gradual but dramatic change in public opinion. Opposition to physician-administered lethal injection in the Netherlands dropped from 47 percent in 1966 to only 9 percent in 1991. Among doctors interviewed in 1990 and 1991, 49 percent had engaged in active euthanasia at a patient's request, and another 38 percent said they conceivably might do so. Among the responding physicians 1 out of 4 said their opinions on euthanasia had become more permissive, often because of their experience with dying patients. A government study estimated that in 1990, before the revision of the law, voluntary active euthanasia accounted for 2,300 deaths and doctor-assisted suicide for 400 deaths—a total of about 2 percent of all deaths in that year—compared with 9,000 requests for termination of life. Since establishment of a notification procedure in 1994, doctors have become increasingly willing to report engaging in euthanasia (Bishop, 1996; van der Maas, Pijnenborg, & van Delden, 1995). Nevertheless, there are persistent reports that large numbers of patients in the Netherlands have been euthanized without their consent (Butler, 1996; P. A. Singer & Siegler, 1990).

The American Medical Association has consistently opposed participation in aid in dying as contrary to a physician's role as healer. The Hippocratic Oath, taken by all doctors, requires them to "do no harm." However, "harm" can be interpreted in more than one way. Some legal scholars and ethicists advocate legalizing all forms of voluntary euthanasia and assisted suicide (Brock, 1992; R. A. Epstein, 1989). They argue that the key issue is not how death occurs but who makes the decision, that there is no difference in principle between pulling the plug on a respirator and giving a lethal injection or prescribing an overdose of pills, and that a person sufficiently competent to control his or her own life should have the right to exercise that control through consent given either in advance or at the time.

Some opponents acknowledge that open availability of aid in dying would reduce fear and helplessness and improve quality of life by giving patients control of their fate. The question is whether these benefits would be worth the risks. Opponents maintain that there is an important distinction between passive euthanasia, in which nature is simply allowed to take its course, and directly bringing about or facilitating a death. They contend that voluntary active euthanasia and assisted suicide might lead to involuntary euthanasia, especially when patients are physically or mentally unable to express their wishes. They warn that, with mounting medical costs and scarce resources, death may become almost a routine answer to terminal illness or chronic disabilities and that vulnerable patients would be encouraged or pressured into a decision to die so as to spare their families financial and emotional burdens. They cite evidence that people who consider life not worth living are often temporarily depressed and might change their minds with treatment. They further argue that focusing on aid in dying might deter physicians from trying to improve palliative care, which would better serve most patients (Hendin, 1994; Latimer, 1992; K. H. Simpson, 1996; P. A. Singer, 1988; P. A. Singer & Siegler, 1990).

The issue will become more pressing as the population ages. Much of the debate turns on whether it is possible to write laws that contain adequate protections against abuse (Baron et al., 1996; Callahan & White, 1996). In years to come, both the courts and the general public will be forced to come to terms with that question, as increasing numbers of people claim the right to die with dignity and with help.

✔ FINDING MEANING AND PURPOSE IN LIFE AND DEATH

The central character in Leo Tolstoy's "The Death of Ivan Ilyich" is wracked by a fatal illness. Even greater than his physical suffering is his mental torment. He asks himself over and over what meaning there is to his agony, and he becomes convinced that his life has been without purpose and that his death will be equally pointless. At the last minute, though, he experiences a spiritual revelation: a concern for his wife and son, which gives him a final moment of integrity and enables him to conquer his terror.

What Tolstoy dramatized in literature is being confirmed by research. In one study of 39 women whose average age was 76, those who saw the most purpose in life had the least fear of death (Durlak, 1973). Conversely, according to Kübler-Ross (1975), facing the reality of death is a key to living a meaningful life:

> It is the denial of death that is partially responsible for [people's] living empty, purposeless lives; for when you live as if you'll live forever, it becomes too easy to postpone the things you know that you must do. In contrast, when you fully understand that each day you awaken could be the last you have, you take the time that day to grow, to become more of who you really are, to reach out to other human beings. (p. 164)

REVIEWING A LIFE

In Ingmar Bergman's film *Wild Strawberries*, an elderly doctor dreams and thinks about his past and his coming death. Realizing how cold and unaffectionate he has been, he becomes warmer and more open in his last days. In Charles Dickens's *A Christmas Carol*, Scrooge changes his greedy, heartless ways after seeing ghostly visions of his past, his present, and his future—his death. In Akira Kurosawa's film *Ikiru* ("To Live"), a petty bureau-

BOX 18-3 PRACTICALLY SPEAKING

EVOKING MEMORIES FOR A LIFE REVIEW

The following methods for uncovering memories (adapted from M. I. Lewis & Butler, 1974) are often used in life review therapy and can also be used fruitfully outside a therapeutic situation. By engaging in such projects with younger family members or friends, older adults can creatively order their lives, build a bridge between generations, and give younger people insights that may help them in their own old age.

■ *Written or taped autobiographies.* What a person includes or does not include in an autobiography may be significant. One successful professional man put together an extensive record of his life, with practically no mention of his two middle-aged children. When the therapist explored this omission, the man revealed that he was estranged from both children. He was then able to use therapy to examine his feelings about them.

■ *Pilgrimages.* When possible, older people can make trips back to scenes of their birth, childhood, and young adulthood, taking photographs and notes to put their thoughts together. If they cannot do this in reality, they may be able to contact people still living in these places. Such pilgrimages can reawaken memories and provide new understanding.

■ *Reunions.* Getting together with high school and college classmates, distant family members, or members of a religious or civic organization can give older adults a new view of themselves in relation to their peers and other important people in their lives.

■ *Constructing a genealogy.* Developing a family tree can provide a sense of continuity. The search may include putting advertisements in newspapers, visiting cemeteries, and poring over family documents, town records, and records of churches, synagogues, or other religious institutions.

■ *Scrapbooks, photo albums, old letters, and other memorabilia.* By talking about such items, older people can savor their meaning and may recall forgotten events, acquaintances, and experiences.

■ *Focus on ethnic identity.* By describing special ethnic traditions they have enjoyed and valued, older persons can enhance their appreciation of their heritage and pass it on.

■ *Summation of a life's work.* By summing up what they regard

Participating in a class reunion—sharing memories with people who played a part in formative experiences—is one way to review a life. Life review can help people see important events in a new light and can motivate them to seek a sense of closure by rebuilding damaged relationships or completing unfinished tasks. *(William Strode/Woodfin Camp & Associates)*

as their contributions to the world, older people can gain a sense of their meaningful participation in it. Some of these summations have grown into published books, poems, and music.

crai who discovers that he is dying of cancer looks back over the emptiness of his life and, in a final burst of energy, creates a meaningful legacy by pushing through a project for a children's park, which he had previously blocked. These three fictional characters make their remaining time more purposeful through *life review,* a process of reminiscence that enables a person to see the significance of his or her life.

Life review can, of course, occur at any time; but it may have special meaning in old age. It can foster ego integrity—according to Erikson, the final critical task of the life span (see Chapter 17). As the end of their journey approaches, people may look back over their accomplishments and failures and ask themselves what their lives have meant. Awareness of mortality may be an impetus for re-examining values and seeing one's experiences and actions in a new light. Some people find the will to complete unfinished tasks, such as reconciling with estranged family members or friends, and thus to achieve a satisfying sense of closure.

Not all memories are equally conducive to mental health and growth. One research team (E. Sherman, 1991, 1993; E. Sherman & Peak, 1991) identified three common types of reminiscing: (1) *reminiscing for pleasure* (the most frequent kind), which enhances mood and self-image, (2) *reminiscing for self-understanding* (done by about 25 percent of older adults), which helps people resolve past problems and find meaning in life, and (3) *reminiscing to solve present problems and cope with losses* (predominant among about 10 percent of older adults, who show more negative moods).

In a related study, older people who used reminiscence for self-understanding showed the strongest ego integrity, though morale was lower for those currently in the process of life review. Those who entertained only pleasurable memories had high spirits but less ego integrity. The most poorly adjusted were those who kept recalling negative events and were obsessed with regret, hopelessness, and fear of death. From Erikson's perspective, their ego integrity had given way to despair (E. Sherman, 1993; Walasky, Whitbourne, & Nehrke, 1983–1984).

Still another research team distinguished between (1) *integrative* reminiscences, which help people accept their lives, resolve old conflicts, and reconcile their sometimes-idealized view of the past with reality; (2) *instrumental* reminiscences, which draw on proven coping strategies to deal with current problems; (3) *escapist* reminiscences, which glorify the past; and (4) *obsessive* reminiscences, which are colored by guilt, bitterness, or despair. People who were "aging successfully" had more integrative or instrumental reminiscences and relatively few obsessive or escapist ones (P. T. P. Wong & Watt, 1991).

Life-review therapy can help focus the natural process of life review and make it more conscious, purposeful, and efficient (Butler, 1961; M. I. Lewis & Butler, 1974). Box 18-3 describes methods often used for uncovering memories in a life review.

DEVELOPMENT: A LIFELONG PROCESS

In his late seventies, the artist Pierre-Auguste Renoir had crippling arthritis and chronic bronchitis and had lost his wife. He was confined to a wheelchair, and his pain was so great that he could not sleep through the night. He was unable to hold a palette or grip a brush: his brush had to be tied to his right hand. Yet he continued to produce brilliant paintings, full of color and vibrant life. Finally, stricken by pneumonia, he lay in bed, gazing at some anemones his attendant had picked. He gathered enough strength to sketch the form of these beautiful flowers, and then—just before he died—lay back and whispered, "I think I am beginning to understand something about it" (L. Hanson, 1968).

Within a limited life span, no person can realize all capabilities, gratify all desires, explore all interests, or experience all the richness that life has to offer. The tension between virtually infinite possibilities for growth and a finite time in which to do the growing defines human life, particularly during late adulthood. By choosing which possibilities to pursue and by continuing to follow them as far as possible, even up to the very end, each person contributes to the unfinished story of human development.

✔ SUMMARY

■ Dying has at least five interrelated aspects: biological, legal, medical, social, and psychological.

FACING DEATH

■ Although denial of death has been characteristic of modern American society, there is now an upsurge of interest in understanding and dealing realistically and compassionately with death.

■ Attitudes toward death and dying vary at different periods of life.

■ People often undergo physical, cognitive, and personality changes shortly before death.

■ Elisabeth Kübler-Ross proposed five stages in coming to terms with dying: denial, anger, bargaining, depression, and acceptance. These stages, and their sequence, are not universal.

FACING BEREAVEMENT

■ Mourning customs vary greatly from one culture to another.

■ Anticipatory grief may or may not help survivors handle actual bereavement.

■ The most widely studied pattern of grief after a death moves from shock and disbelief to preoccupation with the memory of the dead person and finally to resolution. Research has found several variations: high to low distress, no intense distress, and prolonged distress.

■ Although children experience grief, as adults do, there are age-related reactions based on cognitive and emotional development.

■ Being widowed has been found to be the most stressful life event. Women are more likely to be widowed than men, but men are more likely to remarry.

■ Today, loss of parents often occurs in middle age. Death of a parent can precipitate changes in the self and in relationships with others.

■ The loss of a child can be especially difficult because with advances in medicine it is no longer normative.

CONTROVERSIAL ISSUES

■ Suicide is the ninth leading cause of death in the United States; it is prevalent worldwide and is often associated with depression or debilitating illness. Suicide is increasing among children and teenagers and among the old old. The highest suicide rate in the United States is among elderly white men.

■ The "right to die," including assisted suicide and euthanasia, involves controversial issues. Assisted suicide is illegal in most states, but public support for physician aid-in-dying is increasing; it has been legalized in the Northern Territories of Australia. Passive euthanasia is generally permitted with the patient's consent or with advance directives. Active euthanasia is generally illegal, but voluntary active euthanasia is permitted in the Netherlands under strict conditions.

FINDING MEANING AND PURPOSE IN LIFE AND DEATH

■ The more meaning and purpose people find in their lives, the less they tend to fear death.

■ Life review helps people prepare for death and gives them a last chance to complete unfinished tasks.

■ Development can continue up to the moment of death.

✔ KEY TERMS

thanatology (page 613)
death education (613)
hospice care (614)
palliative care (614)
self-help groups (615)
terminal drop (617)
bereavement (618)

grief (618)
mourning (618)
near-death experiences (619)
anticipatory grief (621)
grief work (621)
grief therapy (622)
active euthanasia (633)

passive euthanasia (633)
assisted suicide (634)
living will (634)
persistent vegetative state (634)
durable power of attorney (634)
life review (638)

✔ QUESTIONS FOR THOUGHT AND DISCUSSION

1 Try to imagine that you are terminally ill. What do you imagine your feelings would be? Would they be similar to or different from those described in the text with reference to your age group?

2 Have you ever had a near-death experience, or do you know someone who has? Which of the three theories (psychological, physiological, or transcendental) discussed in the text seems to you the most likely explanation for such experiences? Can you offer another explanation?

3 Have you lost a parent? a sibling? a spouse? a child? a friend? If not, which of these losses do you imagine would be hardest to bear, and why?

If you have experienced more than one of these kinds of loss, how did your reactions differ?

4 Can you learn anything from practices in other cultures that might help you face bereavement?

5 In your opinion, is the intentional ending of one's own life ever justified? Would you ever consider this option? If so, under what circumstances?

6 Do you think assisted suicide should be legalized? If so, who should be permitted to participate—physicians only, or others as well? What safeguards should be provided? Would your answers be the same or different for voluntary active euthanasia?

GLOSSARY

accommodation In Piaget's terminology, change in an existing cognitive structure to include new information. (30)

acting-out behavior Misbehavior (such as lying or stealing) spurred by emotional turmoil. (320)

active euthanasia Deliberate action taken to shorten the life of a terminally ill person in order to end suffering or to allow death with dignity; also called *mercy killing*. Compare *passive euthanasia*. (633)

activity theory Theory of aging, proposed by Neugarten and others, which holds that in order to age successfully a person must remain as active as possible. Compare *disengagement theory*. (585)

acute medical conditions Illnesses that last a short time. (268)

adaptation Piagetian term for adjustment to new information about the environment through the complementary processes of assimilation and accommodation. (30)

adaptive mechanisms Vaillant's term to describe four characteristic ways people adapt to life circumstances: mature, immature, psychotic, and neurotic. (437)

adolescence Developmental transition between childhood and adulthood entailing major physical, cognitive, and psychosocial changes. (330)

adolescent growth spurt Sharp increase in height and weight that precedes sexual maturity. (333)

adolescent rebellion Pattern of emotional turmoil, characteristic of a minority of adolescents, which may involve conflict with family, alienation from adult society, and hostility toward adults' values. (382)

age-differentiated Life structure in which primary roles—learning, working, and leisure—are based on age; typical in industrialized societies. Compare *age-integrated*. (494)

age-integrated Life structure in which primary roles—learning, working, and leisure—are open to adults of all ages and can be interspersed throughout the life span. Compare *age-differentiated*. (495)

ageism Prejudice or discrimination against a person (most commonly an older person) based on age. (540)

aging in place Remaining in one's own home, with or without assistance, during late life. (596)

alleles Pair of inherited genes (alike or different) that affect a particular trait. (44)

altruism, or **prosocial behavior** Behavior intended to help others without external reward. (247)

Alzheimer's disease Progressive, degenerative brain disorder characterized by irreversible deterioration in memory, intelligence, awareness, and control of bodily functions, eventually leading to death. (558)

ambivalent (resistant) attachment Pattern of attachment in which an infant becomes anxious before the primary caregiver leaves, is extremely upset during his or her absence, and both seeks and resists contact upon his or her return. (160)

amniocentesis Prenatal medical procedure in which a sample of amniotic fluid is withdrawn and analyzed to determine whether any of certain genetic defects are present. (71)

androgynous Personality type integrating positive characteristics typically thought of as masculine with positive characteristics typically thought of as feminine. (234)

animism Tendency to attribute life to objects that are not alive. (200)

anorexia nervosa Eating disorder characterized by self-starvation. (340)

anoxia Lack of oxygen, which may cause brain damage. (85)

anticipatory grief Grief that begins before an expected death in preparation for bereavement. (621)

Apgar scale Standard measurement of a newborn's condition; it assesses appearance, pulse, grimace, activity, and respiration. (88)

artificial insemination Injection of sperm into a woman's cervix in order to enable her to conceive. (460)

assimilation In Piaget's terminology, incorporation of new information into an existing cognitive structure. (30)

assisted suicide Death in which a physician or someone else helps a person take his or her own life. (634)

attachment Active, affectionate reciprocal relationship between two persons (usually infant and parent), in which interaction reinforces and strengthens the link. (159)

attention deficit/hyperactivity disorder (ADHD) Syndrome characterized by persistent inattention, impulsivity, low tolerance for frustration, distractibility, and considerable activity at inappropriate times and places. (289)

authoritarian parents In Baumrind's terminology, parents whose child-rearing style emphasizes the values of control and obedience. Compare *authoritative parents* and *permissive parents*. (238)

authoritative parents In Baumrind's terminology, parents whose child-rearing style blends respect for a child's individuality with an effort to instill social values in the child. Compare *authoritarian parents* and *permissive parents*. (238)

autobiographical memory Memory of specific events in one's own life. (208)

autoimmunity Tendency of an aging body to mistake its own tissues for foreign invaders and to attack and destroy these tissues. (551)

autonomy versus shame and doubt In Erikson's theory, the second crisis in psychosocial development, occurring between about 18 months and 3 years, in which children achieve a balance between self-determination and control by others. (168)

autosomes The 22 pairs of chromosomes not related to sexual expression. (43)

avoidant attachment Pattern of attachment in which an infant rarely cries when separated from the primary caregiver and avoids contact upon his or her return. (160)

balanced investment Pattern of retirement activity allocated among family, work, and leisure. Compare *family-focused lifestyle*. (593)

basic trust versus basic mistrust In Erikson's theory, the first crisis in psychosocial development, occurring between birth and about 18 months, in which infants develop a sense of the reliability of people and objects in their world. (158)

battered child syndrome Condition showing symptoms of physical abuse of a child. (241)

Bayley Scales of Infant Development Standardized test of infants' mental and motor development. (130)

behavior therapy Therapeutic approach using principles of learning theory to encourage desired behaviors or eliminate undesired ones; also called *behavioral modification*. (321)

behaviorism Learning theory that emphasizes the study of observable behaviors and events and the predictable role of environment in causing behavior. (26)

behaviorist approach Approach to the study of cognitive development, based on learning theory, which is concerned with the basic mechanics of learning. (119)

bereavement Loss, due to death, of someone to whom one feels close and the process of adjustment to the loss. (618)

bilingual Fluent in two languages. (282)

bilingual education System of teaching foreign-speaking children in two languages—their native language and English—and later switching to all-English instruction after the children develop enough fluency in English. (282)

birth trauma Injury sustained at time of birth due to oxygen deprivation, mechanical injury, infection, or disease. (91)

body image Descriptive and evaluative beliefs about one's appearance. (264)

Brazelton Neonatal Behavioral Assessment Scale Neurological and behavioral test to measure neonates' response to the environment; it assesses interactive behaviors, motor behaviors, physiological control, and response to stress. (90)

broader self-definition versus preoccupation with work roles One of three adjustments to late adulthood described by Peck, in which people come to define themselves by interests and attributes other than work. (579)

bulimia nervosa Eating disorder in which a person regularly eats huge quantities of food and then purges the body by laxatives, induced vomiting, fasting, or excessive exercise. (341)

burnout Syndrome of emotional exhaustion and a sense that one can no longer accomplish anything on the job. (498)

canalization Limitation on variance of expression of certain inherited characteristics. (56)

caregiver burnout Condition of physical, mental, and emotional exhaustion affecting adults who care for aged persons. (528)

case study Scientific study covering a single case or life, based on notes taken by observers or on published biographical materials. (14)

central nervous system Brain and spinal cord. (86)

centration In Piaget's theory, a limitation of preoperational thought that leads the child to focus on one aspect of a situation and neglect others, often leading to illogical conclusions. (197)

cephalocaudal principle Principle that development proceeds in a head-to-toe direction, that is, that upper parts of the body develop before lower parts. (99)

cesarean delivery Delivery of a baby by surgical removal from the uterus. (82)

child abuse Maltreatment of a child involving physical injury. (240)

child-directed speech (CDS), or **motherese** Form of speech often used in talking to babies or toddlers; includes slow, simplified speech, a high-pitched voice, and much use of repetition and questions. (141)

child neglect Withholding of necessary care from a child, such as food, clothing, and supervision. (241)

childhood depression Affective disorder characterized by such symptoms as a prolonged sense of friendlessness, inability to have fun or concentrate, fatigue, extreme activity or apathy, feelings of worthlessness, weight change, physical complaints, and thoughts of death or suicide. (320)

cholesterol Waxy substance in human and animal tissue, excess deposits of which can narrow blood vessels, leading to heart disease. (402)

chorionic villus sampling Prenatal diagnostic procedure in which tissue from villi (hairlike projections of the membrane surrounding the embryo) is analyzed for birth defects. (72)

chromosome Rod-shaped structure that carries the genes, the transmitters of heredity; in the normal human being, there are 46 chromosomes. (42)

chronic medical conditions Illnesses or impairments that persist for at least 3 months. (268)

circular reactions In Piaget's terminology, processes by which an infant learns to reproduce desired occurrences originally discovered by chance. (122)

class inclusion Understanding of the relationship between the whole and the parts. (271)

classical conditioning Kind of learning in which a previously neutral stimulus (one that does not originally elicit a particular response) acquires the power to elicit the response after the stimulus is repeatedly associated with another stimulus that ordinarily does elicit the response. (26, 119)

climacteric Period of 2 to 5 years during which a woman's body undergoes physiological changes that bring on menopause. (474)

code switching Process of changing one's speech to match the situation, as with people who are bilingual. (283)

cognitive-appraisal model Model of coping, proposed by Lazarus and Folkman, which holds that on the basis of continuous appraisal of their relationship with the environment, people choose appropriate coping strategies to deal with situations that tax their normal resources. (582)

cognitive perspective View of human development which is con-

cerned with qualitative changes in thought processes that affect behavior and which sees people as actively shaping their adaptation to the environment. (29)

cognitive play Forms of play that reveal children's mental development. (226)

cohabitation Status of a couple who live together and maintain a sexual relationship without being legally married. (451)

cohort Group of people who share a similar experience, such as growing up in the same place at the same time. (7)

coming out Process of openly disclosing one's homosexual orientation. (449)

commitment In Marcia's terminology, personal investment in an occupation or system of beliefs. (370)

committed compliance In Kochanska's terminology, a toddler's wholehearted obedience to a parent's orders without reminders or lapses. (172)

componential element In Sternberg's triarchic theory, the analytical aspect of intelligence, which determines how efficiently people process information and solve problems. (413)

concordant Statistically similar in the incidence of certain genetically influenced traits or predispositions; characteristic of monozygotic twins. (56)

concrete operations In Piaget's theory, the third stage of cognitive development (approximately from ages 7 to 12), during which children develop logical but not abstract thinking. (270)

congruence model Model of coping, proposed by Kahana, which holds that life satisfaction or stress depends on the match between an individual's needs and an environment's ability to meet those needs. (581)

conjunctive faith Fifth of Fowler's stages of faith development, in which adults (usually in midlife or beyond) struggle with life's conflicts and contradictions, recognize the limitations of reason,

and seek a deeper understanding and acceptance of mortality. (420)

conscience Internal standards of behavior, which usually control conduct and produce emotional discomfort when violated. (170)

conservation In Piaget's terminology, awareness that two objects which are equal according to a certain measure (such as length, weight, or quantity) remain equal in the face of perceptual alteration (for example, a change in shape) so long as nothing has been added to or taken away from either object. (197)

contextual element In Sternberg's triarchic theory, the practical aspect of intelligence, which determines how effectively people deal with their environment. (413)

contextual perspective View of human development that sees the individual as inseparable from the social context. (32)

continuity theory Theory of aging, described by Atchley, which holds that in order to age successfully people must maintain a balance of continuity and change in both the internal and external structures of their lives. (587)

control group In an experiment, a group of people who are similar to the people in the experimental group but who do not receive the treatment whose effects are to be measured. The results obtained with the control group are compared with the results obtained with the experimental group. (17)

convergent thinking Thinking aimed at finding the one "right" answer to a problem. Compare *divergent thinking*. (292)

coping Adaptive thinking or behavior aimed at reducing or relieving stress that arises from harmful, threatening, or challenging conditions. (581)

coregulation Transitional stage in the control of behavior during middle childhood, in which parent and child share power over the child's behavior, the parent exercising general supervision and the child exercising moment-by-moment self-regulation. (301)

correlational study Research design intended to discover whether a statistical relationship between variables exists, both in direction and in magnitude. (15)

creativity Ability to see things in a new light, resulting in a novel product, the identification of a previously unrecognized problem, or the formulation of new and unusual solutions. (292)

crisis In Marcia's terminology, a period of conscious decision making related to identity formation. (370)

critical period Specific time during development when a given event will have the greatest impact. (7)

cross-modal transfer Ability to identify by sight an item earlier felt but not seen. (133)

cross-sectional study Study design in which people of different ages are assessed on one occasion, providing comparative information about different age cohorts. Compare *longitudinal study*. (19)

cross-sequential study Study design that combines cross-sectional and longitudinal techniques by assessing people in a cross-sectional sample more than once. (20)

crystallized intelligence Type of intelligence, proposed by Horn and Cattell, involving the ability to remember and use learned information; it is relatively dependent on education and cultural background. Compare *fluid intelligence*. (485)

cultural bias Tendency of intelligence tests to include items calling for knowledge or skills more familiar or meaningful to some cultural groups than to others, thus placing some test-takers at an advantage or disadvantage due to their cultural background. (278)

culture-fair test Intelligence test that deals with experiences common to various cultures, in an attempt to avoid cultural bias. Compare *culture-free test*. (280)

culture-free test Intelligence test that, if it were possible to design, would have no culturally linked content. Compare *culture-fair test*. (280)

data Information obtained through research. (12)

death education Programs to educate people about death and dying and to help them deal with related issues in their personal and professional lives. (613)

decenter In Piaget's terminology, to think simultaneously about several aspects of a situation; characteristic of operational thought. (197)

deferred imitation In Piaget's terminology, reproduction of an observed behavior after the passage of time by calling up a stored symbol of it. (123)

dementia Deterioration in cognitive and behavioral functioning due to physiological causes. (558)

Denver Developmental Screening Test Test given to children 1 month to 6 years old to determine whether they are developing normally; it assesses gross motor skills, fine motor skills, language development, and psychosocial development. (107)

deoxyribonucleic acid (DNA) Chemical of which genes are composed, which controls the functions of body cells. (42)

dependent variable In an experiment, the condition that may or may not change as a result of manipulation of the independent variable. Compare *independent variable*. (18)

depression Affective disorder in which a person feels unhappy and often has trouble eating, sleeping, or concentrating. (166)

difficult children Children with irritable temperament, irregular biological rhythms, and intense emotional responses. (154)

discipline Tool of socialization, which includes methods of molding children's character and of teaching them to exercise self-control and engage in acceptable behavior. (236)

disengagement theory Theory of aging, proposed by Cumming and Henry, which holds that successful aging is characterized by mutual withdrawal between the older person and society. Compare *activity theory*. (585)

dishabituation Increase in responsiveness after presentation of a new stimulus. Compare *habituation*. (132)

disorganized-disoriented attachment Pattern of attachment in which an infant, after being separated from the primary caregiver, shows contradictory behaviors upon his or her return. (160)

divergent thinking Thinking that produces a variety of fresh, diverse possibilities. Compare *convergent thinking*. (292)

dizygotic twins Twins conceived by the union of two different ova (or a single ovum that has split) with two different sperm cells within a brief period of time; also called *fraternal twins*. (41)

dominant inheritance Pattern of inheritance in which, when an individual receives contradictory alleles for a trait, only the dominant allele is expressed. (44)

Down syndrome Chromosomal disorder characterized by moderate-to-severe mental retardation and by such physical signs as a downward-sloping skinfold at the inner corners of the eyes. (51)

drug therapy Administration of drugs to treat emotional disorders. (321)

dual-process model Model of cognitive functioning in late adulthood, proposed by Baltes, which identifies and seeks to measure two dimensions of intelligence: mechanics and pragmatics. (566)

durable power of attorney Legal instrument that appoints an individual to make decisions in the event of another person's incapacitation. (634)

dyslexia Developmental disorder in learning to read. (290)

easy children Children with a generally happy temperament, regular biological rhythms, and a readiness to accept new experiences. (154)

ecological approach Bronfenbrenner's system of understanding development, which identifies five levels of environmental influence: the microsystem, mesosystem, exosystem, macrosystem, and chronosystem. (8)

ecological validity Characteristic of adult intelligence tests that indicate competence in dealing with real problems faced by adults. (487)

ego In Freudian theory, an aspect of personality that develops during infancy and operates on the reality principle, seeking acceptable means of gratification in dealing with the real world. (24)

ego integrity versus despair In Erikson's theory, the eighth and final crisis in psychosocial development, in which people in late adulthood either achieve a sense of integrity by accepting the lives they have lived, and thus accept death, or yield to despair that their lives cannot be relived. (579)

egocentrism In Piaget's terminology, inability to consider another person's point of view; a characteristic of preoperational thought. (199)

elaboration Mnemonic strategy of making mental associations involving items to be remembered, sometimes with an imagined scene or story. (275)

elder abuse Maltreatment or neglect of dependent older persons, or violation of their personal rights. (598)

Elderhostel International network of colleges and other educational institutions offering short, non-credit, residential courses for adults age 55 and over and their spouses. (571)

electronic fetal monitoring Mechanical monitoring of fetal heartbeat during labor and delivery. (83)

embryonic stage Second stage of gestation (2 to 8–12 weeks), characterized by rapid growth and development of major body systems and organs. (63)

embryoscopy Prenatal medical procedure in which a scope is inserted in the abdomen of a pregnant woman to permit viewing of the embryo for diagnosis and treatment of abnormalities. (73)

emotion-focused coping In the cognitive-appraisal model, coping strategy directed toward managing or regulating the emotional response to a stressful situation so as to lessen its physical or psychological impact; sometimes called *palliative coping.* Compare *problem-focused coping.* (582)

emotional abuse Nonphysical action or failure to act that damages a child's behavioral, cognitive, emotional, or physical functioning. (241)

emotional flexibility versus emotional impoverishment One of four adjustments of middle age described by Peck, in which the ability to shift emotional investment permits adaptation to losses. (508)

emotional intelligence In Salovey and Mayer's terminology, ability to understand and regulate emotions; an important component of effective, intelligent behavior. (417)

emotions Subjective feelings, such as sadness, joy, and fear, which arise in response to situations and experiences and are expressed through some kind of altered behavior. (150)

empathy Ability to put oneself in another person's place and feel what that person feels. (190)

empty nest Transitional phase of parenting following the last child's leaving the parents' home. (521)

encapsulation In Hoyer's terminology, progressive dedication of information processing and fluid thinking to specific knowledge systems, making knowledge more readily accessible and compensating for declines in cognitive machinery. (488)

endometriosis Complication of menstruation, in which cells from the uterine lining, which have entered the abdominal cavity and have become attached to reproductive or other organs, swell due to hormonal stimulation, causing pain, discomfort, intestinal blockage, or infertility. (411)

English-immersion Approach to teaching English as a second language in which instruction is presented only in English from the outset of formal education. (282)

enuresis Bed-wetting. (188)

environment Totality of nongenetic influences on development, external to the self. (6)

environmental press model Model of coping, proposed by Lawton, which holds that stress and adaptation depend on the fit between environmental demands and an individual's competence to meet them. (581)

episodic memory Long-term memory of specific experiences or events, linked to time and place. (207, 568)

equilibration In Piaget's terminology, the tendency to strive for equilibrium (balance) among cognitive elements within the organism and between it and the outside world. (30)

erectile dysfunction Inability of a man to achieve or maintain a sufficiently erect penis for satisfactory sexual performance. (477)

ethological perspective View of human development that focuses on the biological and evolutionary bases of behavior. (31)

experiential element In Sternberg's triarchic theory, the insightful aspect of intelligence, which determines how effectively people approach both novel and familiar tasks. (413)

experiment Rigorously controlled, replicable (that is, repeatable) procedure in which the researcher manipulates variables to assess the effect of one on the other. (17)

experimental group In an experiment, the group receiving the treatment under study; any changes in these people are compared with changes in the control group. (17)

explicit memory Memory that is intentional and conscious. Compare *implicit memory.* (207)

exploratory competence Cognitive capacity underlying the variance in toddlers' ability to sustain attention and engage in sophisticated symbolic play. (133)

extended family Multigenerational kinship network of parents, children, and more distant relatives, sometimes living together in an *extended-family household*. (301, 528)

external memory aids Mnemonic strategies using something outside the person, such as a list. (275)

extinction In operant conditioning, return of a response to the baseline level when the response is no longer reinforced. (28)

family-focused lifestyle Pattern of retirement activity that revolves around family, home, and companions. Compare *balanced investment*. (593)

family therapy Psychological treatment in which a therapist sees the whole family together to analyze patterns of family functioning. (320)

fast mapping Process by which a child absorbs the meaning of a new word after hearing it only once or twice in conversation. (203)

fertilization Union of sperm and ovum to produce a zygote; also called *conception*. (40)

fetal alcohol syndrome (FAS) Combination of mental, motor, and developmental abnormalities affecting the offspring of some women who drink heavily during pregnancy. (66)

fetal stage Final stage of gestation (from 8–12 weeks to birth), characterized by increased detail of body parts and greatly enlarged body size. (64)

filial crisis In Marcoen's terminology, normative development of middle age, in which adults learn to balance love and duty to their parents with autonomy within a two-way relationship. (527)

filial maturity Stage of life, proposed by Marcoen and others, in which middle-aged children, as the outcome of a filial crisis, learn to accept and meet their parents' need to depend on them. (527)

fine motor skills Abilities such as buttoning and copying figures, which involve the small muscles and eye-hand coordination. (185)

five-factor model Costa and McCrae's model of personality, consisting of five groupings of associated traits: neuroticism, extraversion, openness to experience, conscientiousness, and agreeableness. (434)

fluid intelligence Type of intelligence, proposed by Horn and Cattell, which is applied to novel problems and is relatively independent of educational and cultural influences. Compare *crystallized intelligence*. (485)

fontanels Soft spots on head of young infant. (85)

foreclosure Identity status, described by Marcia, in which a person who has not spent time considering alternatives (that is, has not been in crisis) is committed to other people's plans for his or her life. (370)

formal operations In Piaget's theory, the final stage of cognitive development, characterized by the ability to think abstractly. (348)

free radicals Unstable, highly reactive atoms or molecules formed during metabolism, which can cause bodily damage. (550)

functional age Measure of a person's ability to function effectively in his or her physical and social environment in comparison with others of the same chronological age. (543)

gametes Sex cells (sperm or ova). (42)

gateway drugs Drugs (such as alcohol, marijuana, and tobacco) whose use often leads to the use of more addictive substances (such as cocaine and heroin). (342)

gender Significance of being male or female. (229)

gender constancy, or **gender conservation** Awareness that one will always be male or female. (233)

gender differences Psychological or behavioral differences between males and females. (229)

gender identity Awareness, developed in early childhood, that one is male or female. (230)

gender roles Behaviors, interests, attitudes, skills, and traits that a culture considers appropriate for males and for females. (230)

gender schema In Bem's theory, a pattern of behavior organized around gender. (233)

gender-schema theory Theory, proposed by Bem, that children socialize themselves in their gender roles by developing a concept of what it means to be male or female in a particular culture. (233)

gender splitting In Levinson's terminology, rigid divisions between masculine and feminine roles. (439)

gender stereotypes Exaggerated generalizations about male or female role behavior. (231)

gender-typing Socialization process by which children, at an early age, learn appropriate gender roles. (158, 230)

gene Basic functional unit of heredity, which contains all inherited material passed from biological parents to children. (42)

generativity versus stagnation In Erikson's theory, the seventh crisis in psychosocial development, in which the middle-aged adult develops a concern with establishing and guiding the next generation or else experiences stagnation (a sense of inactivity or lifelessness). (508)

generic memory Memory that produces a script of familiar routines to guide behavior. (207)

genetic counseling Clinical service that advises couples of their probable risk of having children with particular hereditary defects. (53)

genetic-programming theories Theories that explain biological aging as resulting from a genetically determined developmental timetable. Compare *variable-rate theories*. (550)

genetics Study of hereditary factors affecting development. (40)

genotype Genetic makeup of an individual, containing both expressed and unexpressed characteristics. (44)

geriatrics Branch of medicine concerned with processes of aging and age-related medical conditions. (543)

germinal stage First 2 weeks of prenatal development, characterized by rapid cell division and increasing complexity; the stage ends when the conceptus attaches itself to the wall of the uterus. (60)

gerontology Study of the aged and the process of aging. (543)

gestation The approximately 266-day period of development between fertilization and birth. (40)

grief Emotional response experienced in the early phases of bereavement. (618)

grief therapy Treatment to help the bereaved cope with loss. (622)

grief work Common pattern of working out of psychological issues connected with grief, in which the bereaved person accepts the loss, releases the bond with the deceased, and rebuilds a life without that person. (621)

gross motor skills Physical skills such as jumping and running, which involve the large muscles. (185)

habituation Simple type of learning in which familiarity with a stimulus reduces, slows, or stops a response. Compare *dishabituation*. (132)

handedness Preference for using a particular hand. (186)

heredity Inborn influences on development, carried on the genes inherited from the parents. (6)

heritability Statistical estimate of contribution of heredity to individual differences in a trait within a given population. (52)

heterosexual Describing a person whose sexual orientation is toward the other sex. (374)

heterozygous Possessing two differing alleles for a trait. (44)

holophrase Single word that conveys a complete thought. (137)

hierarchy of needs Maslow's rank order of needs that motivate human behavior. (443)

homosexual Describing a person whose sexual orientation is toward the same sex. (374)

homozygous Possessing two identical alleles for a trait. (44)

horizontal décalage In Piaget's terminology, a child's inability to transfer learning about one type of conservation to other types, because of which the child masters different types of conservation tasks at different ages. (271)

hospice care Warm, personal patient- and family-centered care for a person with a terminal illness. (614)

hostile aggression Aggressive behavior intended to hurt another person. (249)

human development Scientific study of quantitative and qualitative ways in which people change and stay the same over time. (3)

humanistic perspective View of personality development that sees people as having the ability to foster their own positive, healthy development through the distinctively human capacities for choice, creativity, and self-realization. (442)

hypertension High blood pressure. (480)

hypotheses Possible explanations for phenomena, used to predict the outcome of research. (12)

hypothetical-deductive reasoning Ability to develop, consider, and test hypotheses; believed by Piaget to accompany the stage of formal operations. (349)

id In Freudian theory, the instinctual aspect of personality, present at birth, which operates on the pleasure principle, seeking immediate gratification. (24)

ideal self The self one would like to be. Compare *real self*. (223)

identification In Freudian theory, the process by which a young child adopts characteristics, beliefs, attitudes, values, and behaviors of the parent of the same sex. (231)

identity accommodation In Whitbourne's terminology, adjusting the self-concept to fit new experience. Compare *identity assimilation*. (577)

identity achievement Identity status, described by Marcia, which is characterized by commitment to choices made following a crisis, a period spent in exploring alternatives. (370)

identity assimilation In Whitbourne's terminology, the effort to fit new experience into an existing self-concept. Compare *identity accommodation*. (577)

identity diffusion Identity status, described by Marcia, which is characterized by absence of commitment and lack of serious consideration of alternatives. (371)

identity status In Marcia's terminology, a person's state of ego development, dependent on the presence or absence of crisis and commitment. (370)

identity styles In Whitbourne's terminology, individuals' characteristic ways of confronting, interpreting, and responding to experience. (577)

identity versus identity (or role) confusion In Erikson's theory, the fifth crisis in psychosocial development, in which an adolescent seeks to develop a coherent sense of self, including the role she or he is to play in society. (369)

imaginary audience In Elkind's terminology, an observer who exists only in an adolescent's mind and is as concerned with the adolescent's thoughts and actions as the adolescent is. (351)

imaginative play Play involving imaginary people or situations; also called *fantasy play, dramatic play,* or *pretend play*. (227)

implicit memory Long-term memory, generally of motor skills, habits, and procedures, that does not require conscious recall; sometimes called *procedural memory*. Compare *explicit memory*. (207)

imprinting Instinctive form of learning in which, during a critical period in early development, a young animal forms an attachment to the first moving object it sees, usually the mother. (31)

in vitro fertilization Fertilization of an ovum outside the mother's body. (460)

independent variable In an experiment, the condition over which the experimenter has direct control. Compare *dependent variable*. (18)

individual psychotherapy Psychological treatment in which a therapist sees a troubled person one on one, to help the patient gain insight into his or her personality, relationships, feelings, and behavior. (320)

individuative-reflective faith The fourth of Fowler's stages of faith development, in which adults examine their faith critically and formulate their own beliefs, independent of external authority or group norms. (420)

industry versus inferiority In Erikson's theory, the fourth crisis in psychosocial development, occurring during middle childhood, in which children must learn the productive skills their culture requires or else face feelings of inferiority. (299)

infant mortality rate Proportion of babies born who die in the first year of life. (97)

infertility Inability to conceive after 12 to 18 months of trying. (459)

information-processing approach Approach to the study of cognitive development by observing and analyzing the mental processes involved in perceiving and handling information, which underlie intelligent behavior. (31, 119)

initiative versus guilt In Erikson's theory, the third crisis in psychosocial development, occurring between the ages of 3 and 6, in which children must balance the urge to pursue goals with the moral reservations that may prevent carrying them out. (225)

instrumental activities of daily living Everyday activities, competence in which is considered a measure of the ability to live independently; these activities include managing finances, shopping for necessities, using the telephone, obtaining transportation, preparing meals, taking medication, and housekeeping. (564)

instrumental aggression Aggressive behavior used as a means of achieving a goal. (249)

intelligent behavior Behavior that is goal-oriented (conscious and deliberate) and adaptive to circumstances and conditions of life. (118)

interiority In Neugarten's terminology, concern with inner life (introversion or introspection), which usually appears in middle age. (509)

internalization Process by which children accept societal standards of conduct as their own; fundamental to socialization. (169)

intimacy versus isolation In Erikson's theory, the sixth crisis in psychosocial development, in which young adults either make commitments to others or face a possible sense of isolation and consequent self-absorption. (437)

intuitive-projective faith First of Fowler's stages of faith development, in which young children (ages 18–24 months to 7 years) form powerful, often terrifying images of supernatural forces drawn from stories adults read to them. (420)

invisible imitation Imitation with parts of one's body that one cannot see, such as the mouth. (124)

IQ (intelligence quotient) tests Psychometric tests that seek to measure how much intelligence a person has by comparing her or his performance with standardized norms. (129)

irreversibility In Piaget's terminology, a limitation on preoperational thought, consisting of failure to understand that an operation can go in two or more directions. (199)

karyotype Chart in which photographs of a person's chromosomes, made through a microscope, are arranged according to size and structure to reveal any chromosomal abnormalities. (53)

Kaufman Assessment Battery for Children (K-ABC) Nontraditional individual intelligence test for children ages 2½ to 12½, which

seeks to provide fair assessments of minority children and children with disabilities. (276)

kinship care Care of children living without parents in the home of grandparents or other relatives, with or without a change of legal custody. (533)

laboratory observation Research method in which the behavior of all participants is noted and recorded in the same situation, under controlled conditions. Compare *naturalistic observation*. (13)

language Communication system based on words and grammar. (134)

language acquisition device (LAD) In Chomsky's terminology, an inborn mechanism that enables children to infer linguistic rules from the language they hear. (140)

lanugo Fuzzy prenatal body hair, which drops off within a few days after birth. (85)

learning Long-lasting change in behavior that occurs as a result of experience. (26)

learning disabilities (LDs) Disorders that interfere with specific aspects of learning and school achievement. (290)

learning perspective View of human development which holds that changes in behavior result from experience, or adaptation to the environment; the two major branches are behaviorism and social-learning theory. (26)

life expectancy Age to which a person in a particular cohort is statistically likely to live (given his or her current age and health status), on the basis of average longevity of a population. (545)

life review Reminiscence about one's life in order to see its significance. (638)

life-span development Concept of development as a lifelong process, which can be studied scientifically. (10)

life structure In Levinson's theory, the underlying pattern of a person's life at a given time, built on whatever aspects of life the person finds most important. (439)

lifelong learning Organized, sustained study by adults of all ages. (571)

linguistic speech Verbal expression designed to convey meaning. (137)

literacy Ability to read and write. (134)

living will Document specifying the type of care wanted by the maker in the event of terminal illness. (634)

longevity Length of an individual's life. (545)

longitudinal study Study design in which data are collected about the same people over a period of time, to assess developmental changes that occur with age. Compare *cross-sectional study*. (19)

low birthweight Weight of less than 5½ pounds at birth because of prematurity or being small for date. (91)

major depressive disorder Mental disorder lasting at least 2 weeks, in which a person shows extreme sadness, loss of pleasure or interest in life, and such other symptoms as weight changes, insomnia, feelings of worthlessness or inappropriate guilt, loss of memory, inability to concentrate, and thoughts of death or suicide. (561)

marital capital Financial and emotional benefits built up during a long-standing marriage, which tend to hold a couple together. (519)

maternal blood test Prenatal diagnostic procedure to detect the presence of fetal abnormalities, used particularly when the fetus is at risk for defects in the central nervous system. (72)

maturation Unfolding of an often age-related sequence of physical changes and behavior patterns, including the readiness to master new abilities. (6)

mechanics of intelligence In Baltes's dual-process model, the abilities to process information and solve problems, irrespective of content; the area of cognition in

which there is often an age-related decline. Compare *pragmatics of intelligence*. (566)

meconium Fetal waste matter, excreted during the first few days after birth. (85)

menarche Girl's first menstruation. (335)

menopause Cessation of menstruation and of ability to bear children, typically around age 50. (474)

mental flexibility versus mental rigidity One of four adjustments of middle age described by Peck, in which people either continue to seek answers to life's important questions or become closed-minded and set in their ways. (509)

mental retardation Significantly subnormal cognitive functioning. (288)

metacommunication Understanding of the processes involved in communication. (280)

metamemory Understanding of processes of memory. (274)

Metamemory in Adulthood (MIA) Questionnaire designed to measure various aspects of adults' metamemory, including beliefs about their own memory and selection and use of strategies for remembering. (569)

midlife crisis In some normative-crisis models, stressful life period precipitated by the review and reevaluation of one's past, typically occurring in the early to middle forties. (506)

mnemonic strategies Techniques to aid memory. (274)

monozygotic twins Twins resulting from the division of a single zygote after fertilization; also called *identical twins*. (41)

morality of autonomous moral principles Third level in Kohlberg's theory of moral reasoning, in which people follow internally held moral principles of right, fairness, and justice, and can decide among conflicting moral standards. (352)

morality of constraint First of Piaget's two stages of moral development, characterized by rigid, simplistic judgments. (272)

morality of conventional role conformity Second level in Kohlberg's theory of moral reasoning, in which the standards of authority figures are internalized. (352)

morality of cooperation Second of Piaget's two stages of moral development, characterized by flexible, subtle judgments and formulation of one's own moral code. (272)

moratorium Identity status, described by Marcia, in which a person is currently considering alternatives (in crisis) and seems headed for commitment. (370)

mother-infant bond Mother's feeling of close, caring connection with her newborn. (156)

mourning Behavior of the bereaved and the community after a death, including culturally accepted customs and rituals. (618)

multifactorial transmission Interaction of genetic and environmental factors to produce certain complex traits. (44)

mutual regulation Process by which infant and caregiver communicate emotional states to each other and respond appropriately. (165)

mythic-literal faith Second of Fowler's stages of faith development, in which children (ages 7 to 12 years) develop a logically coherent view of the universe based on literal acceptance of religious stories and symbols. (420)

nativism Theory that human beings have an inborn capacity for language acquisition. (139)

natural childbirth Method of childbirth, developed by Dr. Grantly Dick-Read, that seeks to prevent pain by eliminating the mother's fear of childbirth through education about the physiology of reproduction and training in methods of breathing and relaxation during delivery. (82)

naturalistic observation Method of research in which people's behavior is studied in natural settings without the observer's intervention or manipulation. Compare *laboratory observation*. (13)

near-death experiences Profound, subjective experiences reported by people who have come close to death; these may include a feeling of well-being, enhanced clarity of thinking, out-of-body sensations, and visions of bright lights or mystical encounters. (619)

negativism Behavior characteristic of toddlers, in which they express their desire for independence by resisting authority. (170)

neonatal jaundice Condition in many newborn babies caused by immaturity of liver and evidenced by yellowish appearance; can lead to brain damage if not treated promptly. (86)

neonatal period First 4 weeks of life, a time of transition from intrauterine dependency to independent existence. (84)

neonate Newborn baby, up to 4 weeks old. (84)

neurons Nerve cells. (86)

nonnormative life events In the timing-of-events model, life experiences which are unusual and thus not normally anticipated—or which are ordinary but come at unexpected times—and which may have a major impact on development. Compare *normative life events*. (441)

nonshared environmental effects The unique environment in which each sibling grows up, consisting of dissimilar influences or influences that affect each child differently. (56)

normative-crisis models Theoretical models that describe psychosocial development in terms of a definite sequence of age-related changes. (435)

normative life events In the timing-of-events model, commonly expected life experiences that occur at customary times. Compare *nonnormative life events*. (441)

nuclear family Two-generational economic, kinship, and living unit made up of parents and their biological or adopted children. (529)

obesity Extreme overweight in relation to age, sex, height, and body type; sometimes defined as having a weight-for-height in the 95th percentile of children the same age and sex or weighing at least 20 percent more than recommended maximum guidelines. (264)

object permanence In Piaget's terminology, the understanding that a person or object still exists when out of sight. (124)

observational learning In social-learning theory, learning that occurs through watching the behavior of others. (28)

observer bias Tendency of an observer to misinterpret or distort data to fit his or her expectations. (14)

operant conditioning Form of learning in which a person tends to repeat a behavior that has been reinforced or to cease a behavior that has been punished. (27, 120)

organization (1) In Piaget's terminology, integration of knowledge into a system to make sense of the environment. (30) (2) Mnemonic strategy consisting of categorizing material to be remembered. (275)

osteoporosis Condition affecting 1 in 4 postmenopausal women, in which the bones become thin and brittle as a result of calcium depletion. (481)

Otis-Lennon School Ability Test Group intelligence test for kindergarten to twelfth grade. (276)

ovulation Expulsion of ovum from ovary, which occurs about once every 28 days in a mature woman until menopause. (40)

ovum transfer Method of fertilization in which a woman who cannot produce normal ova receives an ovum donated by a fertile woman. (461)

palliative care Care aimed at relieving pain and suffering and allowing the terminally ill to die in peace, comfort, and dignity. (614)

parent-support ratio In a given population, number of people age 85 and over for every 100 people ages 50 to 64, who may need to provide care and support for them. (525)

partner abuse Violence directed against a current or former spouse or intimate partner. (454)

passive euthanasia Deliberate withholding or discontinuation of life-prolonging treatment of a terminally ill person in order to end suffering or allow death with dignity. Compare *active euthanasia*. (633)

permissive parents In Baumrind's terminology, parents whose child-rearing style emphasizes the values of self-expression and self-regulation. Compare *authoritarian parents* and *authoritative parents*. (238)

persistent vegetative state State in which a patient, though technically alive, has only rudimentary brain functioning. (634)

personal fable In Elkind's terminology, conviction that one is special, unique, and not subject to the rules that govern the rest of the world. (352)

personality Person's unique and relatively consistent way of feeling, reacting, and behaving. (6)

phenotype Observable characteristic of a person. (44)

Piagetian approach Approach to the study of cognitive development based on Piaget's theory, which describes qualitative stages, or typical changes, in children's and adolescents' cognitive functioning. (119)

plasticity Modifiability of a person's performance. (554)

polygenic inheritance Interaction of several sets of genes to produce a complex trait, such as skin color or intelligence. (44)

postformal thought Mature type of thinking, which relies on subjective experience and intuition as well as logic and is useful in dealing with ambiguity, uncertainty, inconsistency, contradiction, imperfection, and compromise. (412)

postmature Referring to a fetus not yet born 2 weeks after the due date or 42 weeks after the mother's last menstrual period. (95)

pragmatics The practical knowledge needed to use language for communicative purposes. (204)

pragmatics of intelligence In Baltes's dual-process model, the dimension of intelligence that tends to grow with age and includes practical thinking, application of accumulated knowledge and skills, specialized expertise, professional productivity, and wisdom. Compare *mechanics of intelligence*. (566)

preconventional morality First level in Kohlberg's theory of moral reasoning, in which control is external and rules are obeyed in order to gain rewards or avoid punishment. (352)

preimplantation genetic diagnosis Medical procedure in which cells from an embryo conceived by in vitro fertilization are analyzed for genetic defects prior to implantation of the embryo in the mother's uterus. (73)

prejudice Unfavorable attitude toward members of certain groups outside one's own, especially racial or ethnic groups. (315)

prelinguistic speech Forerunner of linguistic speech; utterance of sounds that are not words. Includes crying, cooing, babbling, and accidental and deliberate imitation of sounds without understanding their meaning. (134)

premenstrual dysphoric disorder (PMDD) Mood disorder similar to clinical depression, occurring before a menstrual period. (411)

premenstrual syndrome (PMS) Disorder producing symptoms of physical discomfort and emotional tension during the 1 to 2 weeks before a menstrual period. (411)

preoperational stage In Piaget's theory, the second major stage of cognitive development (approximately from age 2 to age 7), in which children become more sophisticated in their use of symbolic thought but are not yet able to use logic. (194)

prepared childbirth Method of childbirth, developed by Dr. Ferdinand Lamaze, that uses instruction, breathing exercises, and social support to induce controlled physical responses to uterine contractions, reducing fear and pain. (82)

presbycusis Gradual loss of hearing, which accelerates after age 55, especially with regard to sounds at the upper frequencies. (473)

presbyopia Farsightedness associated with aging, resulting when the lens of the eye becomes less elastic. (473)

preterm (premature) infants Infants born before thirty-seventh week of gestation. (91)

primary aging Gradual, inevitable process of bodily deterioration throughout the life span. Compare *secondary aging*. (542)

primary memory Brief initial storage for small amounts of recently acquired information. (568)

primary sex characteristics Organs directly related to reproduction, which enlarge and mature during adolescence. Compare *secondary sex characteristics*. (333)

priming Increase in ease of doing a task or remembering information as a result of a previous encounter with the task or information. (568)

private speech Talking aloud to oneself with no intent to communicate. (204)

problem-focused coping In the cognitive-appraisal model, coping strategy directed toward eliminating, managing, or improving a stressful situation. Compare *emotion-focused coping*. (582)

procedural memory Long-term memory of motor skills, habits, and ways of doing things, which often can be recalled without conscious effort; sometimes called *implicit memory*. (568)

proximodistal principle Principle that development proceeds from within to without—that parts of the body near the center develop before the extremities. (100)

psychoanalytic perspective View of human development concerned with unconscious forces motivating behavior. (21)

psychometric approach Approach to the study of cognitive development that seeks to measure the quantity of intelligence a person possesses. (119)

psychosexual development In Freudian theory, an unvarying sequence of stages of personality development during infancy, childhood, and adolescence, in which gratification shifts from the mouth to the anus and then to the genitals. (21)

psychosocial development In Erikson's theory, the socially and culturally influenced process of development of the ego, or self; it consists of eight maturationally determined stages throughout the life span, each revolving around a particular crisis or turning point in which the person is faced with achieving a healthy balance between alternative positive and negative traits. (24)

puberty Process by which a person attains sexual maturity and the ability to reproduce. (330)

punishment In operant conditioning, a stimulus, experienced following a behavior, which decreases the probability that the behavior will be repeated. (27)

qualitative change Change in kind, structure, or organization, such as the change from nonverbal to verbal communication. (3)

quantitative change Change in number or amount of something, such as height, weight, or vocabulary. (3)

quasi experiment Study which resembles an experiment in that it attempts to measure change or to find differences among groups, but which lacks control based on random assignment. (19)

random selection Method of sampling that ensures representativeness because each member of the population has an equal chance to be selected. (12)

reaction range Potential variability, depending on environmental conditions, in the expression of a hereditary trait. (55)

real self The self one actually is. Compare *ideal self*. (223)

recall Ability to reproduce material from memory. Compare *recognition*. (206)

recessive inheritance Expression of a recessive (nondominant) trait, which occurs only if the offspring receives identical recessive alleles from both parents. (44)

recognition Ability to identify a previously encountered stimulus. Compare *recall*. (206)

reflex behaviors Automatic, involuntary responses to stimulation. (88)

rehearsal Mnemonic strategy to keep an item in working memory through conscious repetition. (275)

reinforcement In operant conditioning, a stimulus, experienced following a behavior, which increases the probability that the behavior will be repeated. (27)

relational theory Theory, proposed by Miller, that all personality growth occurs within emotional connections, not separate from them. (25)

reliability Consistency of a test in measuring performance. (129)

representational ability In Piaget's terminology, capacity to mentally represent objects and experiences, largely through the use of symbols. (123)

representational mappings In neo-Piagetian terminology, the second stage in development of self-definition, in which a child makes logical connections between aspects of the self but still sees these characteristics in all-or-nothing terms. (223)

representational systems In neo-Piagetian terminology, the third stage in development of self-definition, characterized by breadth, balance, and the integration and assessment of various aspects of the self. (299)

reserve capacity Ability of body organs and systems to put forth 4 to 10 times as much effort as usual under stress; also called *organ reserve*. (555)

resilient children Children who bounce back from circumstances that would have a highly negative impact on the emotional development of most children. (322)

respite care Substitute supervision and care for a dependent person, to allow time off for the regular caregiver. (528)

revolving door syndrome Tendency for young adults to return to their parents' home after completing their education or in times of financial, marital, or other trouble. (521)

rough-and-tumble-play Vigorous play involving wrestling, hitting, and chasing. (265)

sample Group of participants chosen to represent the entire population under study. (12)

sandwich generation Middle-aged adults squeezed by competing needs to raise or launch children and to care for elderly parents. (526)

scaffolding Temporary support given to a child who is mastering a task. (33)

schemes In Piaget's terminology, basic cognitive structures consisting of organized patterns of behavior used in different kinds of situations. (30, 121)

school phobia Unrealistic fear of going to school; may be a form of separation anxiety disorder. (320)

scientific method System of established principles and processes of scientific inquiry, including identification of a problem to be studied, formulation and testing of alternative hypotheses, collection and analysis of data, and public dissemination of findings so that other scientists can check, learn from, analyze, repeat, and build on the results. (12)

script General remembered outline of a familiar, repeated event, used to guide behavior. (207)

secondary aging Aging processes which result from disease and bodily abuse and disuse and which are often preventable. Compare *primary aging*. (543)

secondary sex characteristics Physiological signs of sexual maturation (such as breast development and growth of body hair) that do not involve the sex organs. Compare *primary sex characteristics*. (333)

secular trend Trend that can be seen only by observing several generations, such as the trend toward earlier attainment of adult height and sexual maturity, which began a century ago. (332)

secure attachment Attachment pattern in which an infant can separate readily from the primary caregiver and actively seeks out the caregiver upon the caregiver's return. (160)

selective optimization with compensation In Baltes's dual-process model, strategy for maintaining or enhancing overall cognitive functioning by using stronger abilities to compensate for those which have weakened. (566)

self-actualization In Maslow's terminology, the highest in the hierarchy of human needs, the need to realize one's potential; can be achieved only after lower needs are met. (443)

self-awareness Realization that one's existence is separate from that of other people and things. (152)

self-care children Children who regularly care for themselves at home without adult supervision. (304)

self-concept Sense of self; descriptive and evaluative mental picture of one's abilities and traits. (168, 222)

self-definition Cluster of characteristics used to describe oneself. (223)

self-esteem The judgment a person makes about his or her self-worth. (225)

self-fulfilling prophecy Expectation or prediction of behavior that tends to come true because it leads people to act as if it were already true. (286)

self-help groups Groups of people who band together to meet a mutual need, usually for treatment, social support, or the solution of a problem. (615)

self-regulation Child's independent control of behavior to conform to understood social expectations. (169)

semantic memory Long-term memory of general factual knowledge, social customs, and language. (568)

senescence Period of the life span marked by changes in physical functioning associated with aging; begins at different ages for different people. (549)

sensorimotor stage In Piaget's theory, the first stage of cognitive development, during which infants (from birth to approximately 2 years) learn through their developing senses and motor activities. (121)

separation anxiety Distress shown by an infant when a familiar caregiver leaves. (167)

separation anxiety disorder Condition involving excessive, prolonged anxiety concerning separation from home or from people to whom a child is attached. (320)

seriation Ability to order items along a dimension. (271)

serious leisure Leisure activity requiring skill, attention, and commitment. (594)

sex chromosomes Pair of chromosomes that determines sex: XX in the normal female, XY in the normal male. (43)

sex differences Physical differences between males and females. (229)

sex-linked inheritance Pattern of inheritance in which certain characteristics carried on the X chromosome inherited from the mother are transmitted differently to her male and female offspring. (49)

sexual abuse Any kind of sexual contact between a child and an older person. (241)

sexual harassment Unwelcome sexual overtures, particularly from a superior at work, which create a hostile or abusive environment, causing psychological pressure. (498)

sexual orientation Focus of consistent sexual, romantic, and affectionate interest, either heterosexual or homosexual. (374)

sexually transmitted diseases (STDs) Diseases transmitted by sexual contact; also called *venereal diseases*. (345)

shaping In operant conditioning, a method of bringing about a new response by reinforcing responses that are progressively more like it. (28)

single representations In neo-Piagetian terminology, first stage in development of self-definition, in which children describe themselves in terms of individual, unconnected characteristics and in all-or-nothing terms. (223)

situational compliance In Kochanska's terminology, a toddler's obedience to a parent's orders only in the presence of prompting or other signs of ongoing parental control. (172)

slow-to-warm-up children Children whose temperament is generally mild but who are hesitant about accepting new experiences. (154)

small-for-date infants Infants whose birthweight, as a result of slow fetal growth, is less than that of 90 percent of babies of the same gestational age. (91)

social capital Family and community resources upon which a person can draw. (359)

social clock Set of cultural norms or expectations for the times of life when certain important events, such as marriage, parenthood, work, and retirement, should occur. (442)

social convoy theory Theory of aging, proposed by Kahn and Antonucci, which holds that reduction of social contacts in outer circles after retirement may be offset by new contacts within those circles, as well as by maintenance of an inner circle of relationships that provides dependable social support. (587)

social-learning theory Theory, proposed chiefly by Bandura, that behaviors are learned by observing and imitating models; also called *social-cognitive theory*. (28)

social play Play in which children, to varying degrees, interact with other children. (226)

social referencing Understanding an ambiguous situation by seeking out another person's perception of it. (166)

social speech Speech intended to be understood by a listener. (204)

socialization Process of developing the habits, skills, values, and motives shared by responsible, productive members of a particular society. (169)

socializing versus sexualizing in human relationships One of four adjustments of middle age described by Peck, in which other people are valued more as friends and companions than as sex objects. (508)

sociocultural theory Vygotsky's theory, which analyzes how specific cultural practices, particularly social interaction with adults, affect children's development. (32)

socioemotional selectivity theory Theory, proposed by Carstensen, that people select social contacts throughout life on the basis of the changing relative importance of social interaction as a source of information, as an aid in developing and maintaining a self-concept, and as a source of emotional well-being. (587)

spermarche Boy's first ejaculation. (335)

spillover hypothesis Hypothesis that there is a positive correlation between intellectuality of work and of leisure activities because of a carryover of learning from work to leisure. (500)

spontaneous abortion Natural expulsion from the uterus of a conceptus that cannot survive outside the womb; also called *miscarriage*. (63)

standardized norms Standards for evaluating performance of persons who take an intelligence test, obtained from scores of a large, representative sample who took the test while it was in preparation. (129)

Stanford-Binet Intelligence Scale Individual intelligence test used with children to measure memory, spatial orientation, and practical judgment. (210)

state of arousal An infant's degree of alertness; his or her condition, at a given moment, in the periodic daily cycle of wakefulness, sleep, and activity. (100)

stereotype threat Minority-group members' fear of fulfilling racial stereotypes, which may, as a result of this fear, become self-fulfilling. (424)

Strange Situation Laboratory technique used to study attachment. (160)

stranger anxiety Wariness of strange people and places, shown by some infants during the second half of the first year. (167)

stress Organism's physiological and psychological reaction to demands made on it. (191)

substance abuse Repeated, harmful use of a substance, usually alcohol or other drugs. (342)

substance dependence Addiction (physical or psychological, or both) to a harmful substance. (342)

substantive complexity Degree to which a person's work requires thought and independent judgment. (500)

sudden infant death syndrome (SIDS) Sudden and unexplained death of an apparently healthy infant. (98)

superego According to Freudian theory, the aspect of personality that represents socially approved values; it develops around the age of 5 or 6 as a result of identification with the parent of the same sex. (24)

surrogate motherhood Method of conception in which a woman who is not married to a man agrees to bear his baby and then give the child to the father and his mate. (461)

survival curves Curves, plotted on a graph, showing percentages of a population that survive at each age level. (547)

symbolic function In Piaget's terminology, ability to use mental representations (words, numbers, or images) to which a child has attached meaning; this ability,

characteristic of preoperational thought, is shown in deferred imitation, symbolic play, and language. (195)

syntax Rules for forming sentences in a particular language. (138)

synthetic-conventional faith Third of Fowler's stages of faith development, in which adolescents or young adults form abstract belief systems, commit themselves to ideals, and seek a personal relationship with God but look to peers or community standards (as expressed in organized religions) for moral authority; many adults never move beyond this stage. (420)

tacit knowledge In Sternberg's terminology, information that is not formally taught or openly expressed but is necessary to get ahead; includes self-management and management of tasks and of others. (414)

temperament Person's characteristic disposition, or style of approaching and reacting to situations. (41)

teratogenic Capable of causing birth defects. (64)

terminal drop Sudden decrease in cognitive functioning shortly before death. (617)

thanatology Study of death and dying. (613)

theory Coherent set of related concepts that seeks to organize and explain data and to generate hypotheses to be tested by research. (20)

theory of mind Awareness and understanding of mental states and processes. (201)

timing-of-events model Theoretical model, advocated by Neugarten and others, which describes adult psychosocial development as a response to the expected or unexpected occurrence and timing of important life events. (441)

Torrance Tests of Creative Thinking Tests designed to measure divergent thinking. (292)

transcendence of the body versus

preoccupation with the body One of three adjustments to late adulthood described by Peck, in which people focus on mental and social activities not impeded by physical decline. (580)

transcendence of the ego versus preoccupation with the ego One of three adjustments to late adulthood described by Peck, in which people move beyond concern with self and accept death by focusing on contributions of lasting social value. (580)

transduction In Piaget's terminology, a preoperational child's tendency to mentally link particular experiences, whether or not there is logically a causal relationship. (199)

transitional objects Objects used repeatedly by a child as bedtime companions. (188)

transitive inference Understanding of the relationship between two objects by knowing the relationship of each to a third object. (272)

triangular theory of love Sternberg's theory that patterns of love hinge on the balance among three elements: intimacy, passion, and commitment. (446)

ultrasound Prenatal medical procedure using high-frequency sound waves to detect the outline of a fetus, judge gestational age, detect multiple pregnancies, detect abnormalities or death of the fetus, and determine whether the pregnancy is progressing normally. (73)

umbilical cord sampling Prenatal medical procedure in which samples of a fetus's blood are taken from the umbilical cord to assess body functioning. (73)

underemployment Condition in which a person's work is unrelated to, or does not fully utilize, his or her training, abilities, and skills. (425)

universalizing faith Sixth and last of Fowler's stages of faith development, in which a few adults in late life achieve a transcendent vision and commitment to human welfare so broad, unifying, transformative, and inspiring that they become moral and spiritual leaders or even martyrs. (420)

validity Capacity of a test to measure what it is intended to measure. (129)

valuing wisdom versus valuing physical powers One of four adjustments of middle age described by Peck, in which the ability to make choices informed by experience becomes more important than declining physical abilities. (508)

variable-rate theories Theories explaining biological aging as a result of processes that vary from person to person and are influenced by both internal and external factors; sometimes called *error theories.* Compare *genetic-programming theories.* (550)

vernix caseosa Oily substance on a neonate's skin that protects against infection. (85)

visible imitation Imitation with parts of one's body that one can see, such as the hands and the feet. (124)

visual cliff Apparatus designed to give an illusion of depth and used to assess depth perception in infants. (106)

visual novelty preference Infant's preference for new rather than familiar sights. (133)

visual preference An infant's tendency to look longer at certain stimuli than at others. (105)

visual recognition memory Ability to remember and recognize a visual stimulus. (133)

Wechsler Adult Intelligence Scale (WAIS) Intelligence test for adults, which yields verbal and performance scores as well as a combined score. (485)

Wechsler Intelligence Scale for Children (WISC-III) Individual intelligence test for schoolchildren, which yields verbal and performance scores as well as a combined score. (276)

Wechsler Preschool and Primary Scale of Intelligence—Revised (WPPSI-R) Individual intelligence test for children ages 3 to 7, which yields verbal and performance scores as well as a combined score. (210)

working memory Short-term storage of information being actively processed. (274, 568)

zone of proximal development (ZPD) Vygotsky's term for the level at which children can *almost* perform a task on their own and, with appropriate teaching, *can* perform it. (32)

zygote One-celled organism resulting from fertilization. (40)

Abbey, A., Andrews, F. M., & Halman, J. (1992). Infertility and subjective well being: The mediating roles of self-esteem, internal control, and interpersonal conflict. *Journal of Marriage and the Family, 54,* 408–417.

Abel, E. K. (1991). *Who cares for the elderly?* Philadelphia: Temple University Press.

Abramovitch, R., Corter, C., & Lando, B. (1979). Sibling interaction in the home. *Child Development, 50,* 997–1003.

Abramovitch, R., Corter, C., Pepler, D., & Stanhope, L. (1986). Sibling and peer interactions: A final follow-up and comparison. *Child Development, 57,* 217–229.

Abramovitch, R., Pepler, D., & Corter, C. (1982). Patterns of sibling interaction among preschool-age children. In M.E. Lamb (Ed.), *Sibling relationships: Their nature and significance across the lifespan.* Hillsdale, NJ: Erlbaum.

Abrams, B., & Parker, J. D. (1990). Maternal weight gain in women with good pregnancy outcome. *Obstetrics and Gynecology, 76*(1), 1–7.

Abramson, T. A. (1995, Fall). From non-normative to normative caregiving. *Dimensions* (Newsletter of American Society on Aging), pp. 1–2.

Abravanel, E., & Sigafoos, A. D. (1984). Exploring the presence of imitation during early infancy. *Child Development, 55,* 381–392.

Abroms, K., & Bennett, J. (1981). Changing etiological perspectives in Down's syndrome: Implications for early intervention. *Journal of the Division for Early Childhood, 2,* 109–112.

Achenbach, T. M., & Howell, C. T. (1993). Are American children's problems getting worse? A 13-year comparison. *Journal of the American Academy of Child and Adolescent Psychiatry, 32,* 1145–1154.

Achenbaum, W. A., & Bengtson, V. L. (1994). Re-engaging the disengagement theory of aging: On the history and assessment of theory development in gerontology. *The Gerontologist, 34,* 756–763.

Achievers after the age of 90. (1993, September 26). *Parade,* p. 17.

Ackerman, G. L. (1993). A congressional view of youth suicide. *American Psychologist, 48*(2), 183–184.

Action for Children's Television. (undated). *Treat T.V. with T.L.C.* [One-page flyer]. Newtonville, MA: Author.

Adams, C. (1991). Qualitative age differences in memory for text: A life-span developmental perspective. *Psychology and Aging, 6,* 323–336.

Adams, R. G. (1986). Friendship and aging. *Generations, 10*(4), 40–43.

Adelman, M. (1991). Stigma, gay lifestyles, and adjustment to aging: A study of later-life gay men and lesbians. *Gay Midlife and Maturity, 4,* 7–32.

Adult Treatment Panel II. (1994). Detection, evaluation, and treatment of high blood cholesterol in adults. *Circulation, 89,* 1329–1432.

Agoda, L. (1995). Minorities and ESRD. Review: African American study of kidney disease and hypertension clinical trials. *Nephrology News & Issues, 9,* 18–19.

Ainsworth, M. D. (1964). Patterns of attachment behavior shown by the infant in interaction with his mother. *Merrill-Palmer Quarterly, 10,* 51–58.

Ainsworth, M. D. S. (1967). *Infancy in Uganda; infant care and the growth of love.* Baltimore: Johns Hopkins Press.

Ainsworth, M. D. S. (1969). Object relations, dependency, and attachment: A theoretical review of the infant-mother relationship. *Child Development, 40,* 969–1025.

Ainsworth, M. D. S. (1979). Infant-mother attachment. *American Psychologist, 34*(10), 932–937.

Ainsworth, M. D. S., & Bell, S. (1977). Infant crying and maternal responsiveness: A rejoinder to Gerwitz and Boyd. *Child Development, 48,* 1208–1216.

Ainsworth, M. D. S., Blehar, M. C., Waters, E., & Wall, S. (1978). *Patterns of attachment: A psychological study of the strange situation.* Hillsdale, NJ: Erlbaum.

Akutsu, H., Legge, G. E., Ross, J. A., & Schuebel, K. J. (1991). Psychophysics of reading: Effects of age-related changes in vision. *Journal of Gerontology: Psychological Sciences, 46*(6), P325–331.

Alan Guttmacher Institute (AGI). (1994). *Sex & America's teenagers.* New York: Author.

Aldort, N. (1994, Summer). Getting out of the way. *Mothering,* pp. 38–43.

Aldous, J. J. (1987). Family life of the elderly and near-elderly. *Journal of Marriage and the Family, 49*(2), 227–234.

Alemi, B., Hamosh, M., Scanlon, J. W., Salzman-Mann, C., & Hamosh, P. (1981). Fat digestion in very low-birth-weight infants: Effects of addition of human milk to low-birth-weight formula. *Pediatrics, 68*(4), 484–489.

Alessandri, S. M., Sullivan, M. W., Imaizumi, S., & Lewis, M. (1993). Learning and emotional responsivity in cocaine-exposed infants. *Developmental Psychology, 29,* 989–997.

Alexander, B. B., Rubinstein, R. L., Goodman, M., & Luborsky, M. (1992). A path not taken: A cultural analysis of regrets and childlessness in the lives of older women. *The Gerontologist, 32*(5), 618–626.

Alexander, K. L., Entwisle, D. R., & Dauber, S. L. (1993). First-grade classroom behavior: Its short- and long-term consequences for school performance. *Child Development, 64,* 801–814.

Allore, R., O'Hanlon, D., Price, R., Neilson, K., Willard, H. F., Cox, D. R., Marks, A., & Dun, R. J. (1988). Gene encoding the B subunit of S100 protein is on chromosome 21: Implications for Down syndrome. *Science, 239,* 1311–1313.

Almeida, D. M., Maggs, J. L., & Galambos, N. L. (1993). Wives' employment hours and spousal participation in family work. *Journal of Family Psychology, 7,* 233–244.

Alsaker, F. D. (1992). Pubertal timing, overweight, and psychological adjustment. *Journal of Early Adolescence, 12*(4), 396–419.

Alsalam, N. (1993). Interpreting conditions in the job market for college graduates. *Monthly Labor Review, 116*(2), 51–53.

Alternatives to hormone replacement (1994, August). *Harvard Women's Health Watch,* pp. 2–3.

Altman, L. K. (1992, July 21). Women worldwide nearing higher rate for

AIDS than men. *The New York Times*, pp. C1, C3.

Alzheimer's and stress: Caregivers at risk. (1994, Fall). *Alzheimer's Association Newsletter*, pp. 1,9.

Alzheimer's Association. (undated). *Is it Alzheimer's? Warning signs you should know.* Chicago: Author.

Amabile, T. A., & Rovee-Collier, C. (1991). Contextual variation and memory retrieval at six months. *Child Development, 62* 1155–1166.

Amabile, T. M. (1983). *The social psychology of creativity.* New York: Springer-Verlag.

Amadiume, I. (1987). *Male daughters, female husbands.* Atlantic Highlands, NJ: Zed.

Amato, P. R. (1987). Family processes in one-parent, stepparent, and intact families: The child's point of view. *Journal of Marriage and the Family, 49* 327–337.

Amato, P. R., & Keith, B. (1991a). Parental divorce and adult well-being: A meta-analysis. *Journal of Marriage and the Family, 53,* 43–58.

Amato, P. R., & Keith, B. (1991b). Parental divorce and the well-being of children: A meta-analysis. *Psychological Bulletin, 110,* 26–46.

Amato, P. R., Kurdek, L. A., Demo, D. H., & Allen, K. R. (1993). Children's adjustment to divorce: Theories, hypotheses, and empirical support. *Journal of Marriage and the Family, 55,* 23–54.

American Academy of Pediatrics (AAP). (1973). The ten-state nutrition survey: A pediatric perspective. *Pediatrics, 51*(6), 1095–1099.

American Academy of Pediatrics (AAP). (1986). *Positive approaches to day care dilemmas: How to make it work.* Elk Grove Village, IL: Author.

American Academy of Pediatrics (AAP). (1989). Follow-up on weaning formulas. *Pediatrics, 83*(6), 1067.

American Academy of Pediatrics (AAP). (1992, January 15). *APA proposes handgun ban, other measures to curb firearm deaths, injuries.* News release. Elk Grove Village, IL: Author.

American Academy of Pediatrics (AAP) Committee on Accident and Poison Prevention. (1990). Bicycle helmets. *Pediatrics, 85*(1), 229–230.

American Academy of Pediatrics (AAP) Committee on Adolescence. (1987). Alcohol use and abuse: A pediatric concern. *Pediatrics, 79*(3), 450–453.

American Academy of Pediatrics (AAP) Committee on Adolescence. (1994). Sexually transmitted diseases. *Pediatrics, 94*(4), 568–572.

American Academy of Pediatrics (AAP) Committee on Bioethics. (1992). Infants with anencephaly as organ sources: Ethical considerations. *Pediatrics, 89*(6), 1116–1119.

American Academy of Pediatrics (AAP) Committee on Children with Dis-

abilities and Committee on Drugs. **(1996).** Medication for children with attentional disorders. *Pediatrics, 98,* 301–304.

American Academy of Pediatrics (AAP) Committee on Children with Disabilities and Committee on Psychosocial Aspects of Child and Family Health. (1993). Psychosocial risks of chronic health conditions in childhood and adolescence. *Pediatrics, 92,* 876–877.

American Academy of Pediatrics (AAP) Committee on Communications. (1995). Sexuality, contraception, and the media. *Pediatrics, 95*(2), 298–300.

American Academy of Pediatrics (AAP) Committee on Community Health Services. (1996). Health needs of homeless children and families. *Pediatrics, 88,* 789–791.

American Academy of Pediatrics (AAP) Committee on Drugs. (1980). Marijuana. *Pediatrics, 65,* 652–656.

American Academy of Pediatrics (AAP) Committee on Drugs. (1994). The transfer of drugs and other chemicals into human milk. *Pediatrics, 93,* 137–150.

American Academy of Pediatrics (AAP) Committee on Environmental Health. (1993). Lead poisoning: From screening to primary prevention. *Pediatrics, 92,* 176–183.

American Academy of Pediatrics (AAP) Committee on Fetus and Newborn. (1986). Use and abuse of the Apgar scale. *Pediatrics, 78*(6), 1148–1149.

American Academy of Pediatrics (AAP) Committee on Fetus and Newborn and American College of Obstetricians and Gynecologists Committee on Obstetric Practice. (1996). Use and abuse of the Apgar score. *Pediatrics, 98*(1), 141–142.

American Academy of Pediatrics (AAP) Committee on Genetics. (1992). Issues in newborn screening. *Pediatrics, 89*(2), 345–349.

American Academy of Pediatrics (AAP) Committee on Genetics. (1993). Folic acid for the prevention of neural tube defects. *Pediatrics, 92,* 493–494.

American Academy of Pediatrics (AAP) Committee on Infectious Diseases. (1996). Recommended childhood immunization schedule. *Pediatrics, 98*(1), 158–159.

American Academy of Pediatrics (AAP) Committee on Injury and Poison Prevention. (1995). Injuries associated with infant walkers. *Pediatrics, 95*(5), 778–780.

American Academy of Pediatrics (AAP) Committee on Nutrition. (1992a). Statement on cholesterol. *Pediatrics, 90*(3), 469–473.

American Academy of Pediatrics (AAP) Committee on Nutrition. (1992b). The use of whole cow's milk in infancy. *Pediatrics, 89*(6), 1105–1109.

American Academy of Pediatrics (AAP) Committee on Psychosocial Aspects of Child and Family Health. (1992). The pediatrician and childhood bereavement. *Pediatrics, 89*(3), 516–518.

American Academy of Pediatrics (AAP) Committee on Sports Medicine and Committee on School Health. (1989). Organized athletics for preadolescent children. *Pediatrics, 84*(3), 583–584.

American Academy of Pediatrics (AAP) Committee on Sports Medicine and Fitness. (1992). Fitness, activity, and sports participation in the preschool child. *Pediatrics, 90*(6), 1002–1004.

American Academy of Pediatrics (AAP) Committee on Substance Abuse and Committee on Children with Disabilities. (1993). Fetal alcohol syndrome and fetal alcohol effects. *Pediatrics, 91*(5), 1004–1006.

American Academy of Pediatrics (AAP) Provisional Committee on Pediatric AIDS. (1995). Perinatal human immunodeficiency virus testing. *Pediatrics, 95,* 303–307.

American Academy of Pediatrics (AAP) Task Force on Blood Pressure Control in Children. (1987). Report of the second Task Force on Blood Pressure Control in Children. *Pediatrics, 79*(1), 1–25.

American Academy of Pediatrics (AAP) Task Force on Infant Positioning and SIDS. (1992). Positioning and SIDS. *Pediatrics, 89*(6), 1120–1126.

American Academy of Pediatrics (AAP) Task Force on Pediatric AIDS. (1991). Education of children with human immunodeficiency virus infection. *Pediatrics, 88*(3), 645–648.

American Association for Geriatric Psychiatry. (1996). *Brief fact sheet on late-life depression.* Bethesda, MD: Author.

American Association of Retired Persons (AARP). (1989). *Business and older workers: Current perceptions and new directions for the 1990s.* Washington, DC: Author.

American Association of Retired Persons (AARP). (1993a). *Abused elders or battered women?* Washington, DC: Author.

American Association of Retired Persons (AARP). (1993b). *Understanding senior housing.* Washington, DC: Author.

American Association of Retired Persons (AARP). (1994). *A profile of older Americans.* Washington, DC: Author.

American Association of Retired Persons (AARP). (1996, September). *Understanding senior housing into the next century: Survey of consumer preferences, concerns, and needs.* Washington, DC: Author.

American Association of Retired Persons (AARP). (1995). *A profile of older Americans.* Washington, DC: Author.

American Cancer Society. (1993). Cancer statistics, 1993. *Cancer Journal for Clinicians, 43*(1), 7–26.

American Cancer Society. (1994). *Cancer facts and figures—1994*. Atlanta: Author.

American College of Obstetrics and Gynecology. (1994). *Exercise during pregnancy and the postpartum pregnancy* (Technical Bulletin No. 189). Washington, DC: Author.

American College Testing Program. (1995). *ACT high school profile report, 1995*. Iowa City: Author.

American Foundation for the Prevention of Venereal Disease, Inc. (AFPVD). (1986). *Sexually transmitted disease [venereal disease]: Prevention for everyone* (13th rev. ed.). New York: Author.

American Heart Association (AHA). (1994). *Fact sheet: Risk factors–cigarette/tobacco smoke*. Dallas: Author.

American Heart Association (AHA). (1995). *Silent epidemic: The truth about women and heart disease*. Dallas: Author.

American Medical Association (AMA). (1992). *Diagnosis and treatment guidelines on elder abuse and neglect*. Chicago: Author.

American Psychiatric Association (APA). (1987). *Diagnostic and statistical manual of mental disorders* (3d ed., rev.) (*DSM-III-R*). Washington, DC: Author.

American Psychiatric Association (APA). (1994). *Diagnostic and statistical manual of mental disorders* (4th ed.) (*DSM-IV*). Washington, DC: Author.

American Psychological Association. (undated). *Answers to your questions about sexual orientation and homosexuality* [brochure]. Washington, DC: Author.

Anastasi, A. (1988). *Psychological testing* (6th ed.). New York: Macmillan.

Anders, T. R., Fozard, J. L., & Lillyquist, T. D. (1972). Effects of age upon retrieval from short-term memory. *Developmental Psychology, 6*(2), 214–217.

Anderson, S. A., Russell, C. S., & Schumm, W. R. (1983). Perceived marital quality and family life-cycle categories: A further analysis. *Journal of Marriage and the Family, 45*, 127–139.

Anderson, T. B. (1984). Widowhood as a life transition: Its impact on kinship ties. *Journal of Marriage and the Family, 46*, 105–114.

Andersson, B. E. (1992). Effects of daycare on cognitive and socioemotional competence of thirteen-year-old Swedish children. *Child Development, 63*, 20–36.

Anschutz, L., Camp, C. J., Markley, R. P., & Kramer, J. J. (1987). Remembering mnemonics: A 3-year follow-up on the effects of mnemonics training in elderly adults. *Experimental Aging Research, 13*, 141–143.

Antczak, C. A. G. (1996). *Creating a successful Elderhostel program: A social gerontologist's perspective*. Unpublished master's project, University of Utah, College of Nursing.

Anthony, E. J., & Koupernik, C. (Eds.). (1974). *The child in his family: Children at psychiatric risk* (Vol. 3). New York: Wiley.

Antonarakis, S. E., & Down Syndrome Collaborative Group. (1991). Parental origin of the extra chromosome in trisomy 21 as indicated by analysis of DNA polymorphisms. *New England Journal of Medicine, 324*, 872–876.

Apgar, B. S., & Churgay, C. A. (1993). Spontaneous abortion. *Primary Care, 20*, 621–627.

Apgar, V. (1953). A proposal for a new method of evaluation of the newborn infant. *Current Research in Anesthesia and Analgesia, 32*, 260–267.

Apostol, R. A., et al. (1993). Commitment to and role changes in dual career families. *Journal of Career Development, 20*(2), 121–129.

Aquilino, W. S. (1990). The likelihood of parent-adult child coresidence: Effects of family structure and parental characteristics. *Journal of Marriage and the Family, 52*, 405–419.

Aquilino, W. S., & Supple, K. R. (1991). Parent-child relations and parent's satisfaction with living arrangements when adult children live at home. *Journal of Marriage and the Family, 53*, 13–27.

Archer, C. K., & MacLean, M. J. (1993). Husbands and sons as caregivers of chronically ill elderly women. *Journal of Gerontological Social Work, 21*(1–2), 5–23.

Archer, S. L. (1993). Identity in relational contexts: A methodological proposal. In J. Kroger (Ed.), *Discussions on ego identity* (pp. 75–99). Hillsdale, NJ: Erlbaum.

Are we "in the middle of a cancer epidemic"? (1994, September). *University of California at Berkeley Wellness Letter*, pp. 4–5.

Arend, R., Gove, F., & Sroufe, L. A. (1979). Continuity of individual adaptation from infancy to kindergarten: A predictive study of ego-resiliency and curiosity in preschoolers. *Child Development, 50*, 950–959.

Ariès, P. (1962). *Centuries of childhood*. New York: Vintage.

Arlin, P. K. (1984). Adolescent and adult thought: A structural interpretation. In M. L. Commons, F. A. Richards, & C. Armon (Eds.), *Beyond formal operations* (pp. 258–271). New York: Praeger.

Armstrong, B. G., McDonald, A. D., & Sloan, M. (1992). Cigarette, alcohol, and coffee consumption and spontaneous abortion. *American Journal of Public Health, 81*, 85.

Aron, A., & Henkemeyer, L. (1995). Marital satisfaction and passionate love. *Journal of Social and Personal Relationships, 12*(1), 139–146.

Asher, S., Renshaw, P., Geraci, K., & Dor, A. (1979, March). *Peer acceptance and social skill training: The selection of program content*. Paper presented at the meeting of the Society for Research in Child Development, San Francisco.

Aslin, R. N. (1987). Visual and auditory development in infancy. In J. D. Osofsky (Ed.), *Handbook of infant development* (2d ed.). New York: Wiley.

Astington, J. W. (1993). *The child's discovery of the mind*. Cambridge, MA: Harvard University Press.

Atchley, R. C. (1985). *Social forces and aging* (4th ed.). Belmont, CA: Wadsworth.

Atchley, R. C. (1989). A continuity theory of normal aging. *The Gerontologist, 29*, 183–190.

Atkinson, J. N., & Raynor, J. O. (1974). *Motivation and achievement*. New York: Halstead.

Attention deficit disorder—Part II. (1995, May). *The Harvard Mental Health Letter*, pp. 1–3.

Australian man first in world to die with legal euthanasia. (1996, September 26). *The New York Times* (International Ed.), p. A5.

Ausubel, N. (1964). *The book of Jewish knowledge*. New York: Crown.

Aylward, G. P., Pfeiffer, S. I., Wright, A., & Verhulst, S. J. (1989). Outcome studies of low birth weight infants published in the last decade: A meta-analysis. *Journal of Pediatrics, 115*, 515–520.

Azmitia, M., & Hesser, J. (1993). Why siblings are important agents of cognitive development: A comparison of siblings and peers. *Child Development, 64*(2), 430–444.

Azuma, S. D., & Chasnoff, I. J. (1993). Outcome of children prenatally exposed to cocaine and other drugs: A path analysis of three-year data. *Pediatrics, 92*, 396–402.

Babchuk, N. (1978–1979). Aging and primary relations. *International Journal of Aging and Human Development, 9*(2), 137–151.

Babson, S. G., & Clarke, N. G. (1983). Relationship between infant death and maternal age. *Journal of Pediatrics, 103*(3), 391–393.

Babu, A., & Hirschhorn, K. (1992). *A guide to human chromosome defects*. Birth Defects: Original Article Series, *28*(2). White Plains, NY: March of Dimes Birth Defects Foundation.

Bachman, J. G., & Schulenberg, J. (1993). How part-time work intensity relates to drug use, problem behavior, time use, and satisfaction among high school seniors: Are these consequences or merely correlates? *Developmental Psychology, 29*(2), 220–235.

Bachman, R. (1994, January). *Violence against women: A national crime victimization report* (NCJ-145325). Washington, DC: Bureau of Justice Statistics Clearinghouse.

Bachrach, C. A., London, K. A., & Maza, P. L. (1991). On the path to adoption:

Adoption seeking in the United States, 1988. *Journal of Marriage and the Family, 53,* 705–718.

Bachu, A. (1993). *Fertility of American women: June 1992* (Current Population Report P24–470). Washington, DC: U.S. Government Printing Office.

Backett, K. (1987). The negotiation of fatherhood. In C. Lewis & M. O'Brien (Eds.), *Reassessing fatherhood: New observations on fathers and the modern family.* London: Sage.

Baghurst, P. A., et al. (1992). Environmental exposure to lead and children's intelligence at the age of seven years. *New England Journal of Medicine, 327,* 1279–1284.

Bailey, J. M., Bobrow, D., Wolfe, M., & Mikach, S. (1995). Sexual orientation of adult sons of gay fathers. *Developmental Psychology, 31*(1), 124–129.

Baillargeon, R. (1994). How do infants learn about the physical world? *Current Directions in Psychological Science, 3*(5), 133–139.

Baillargeon, R., & De Vos, J. (1991). Object permanence in young infants: Further evidence. *Child Development, 62,* 1227–1246.

Balkwell, C. (1981). Transition to widowhood: A review of the literature. *Family Relations, 30,* 117–127.

Balkwell, C. (1985). An attitudinal correlate of the timing of a major life event: The case of morale in widowhood. *Family Relations, 34,* 577–581.

Baltes, P. B. (1987). Theoretical propositions of life-span development psychology: On the dynamics between growth and decline. *Developmental Psychology, 23*(5), 611–626.

Baltes, P. B., & Schaie, K. W. (1974). Aging and IQ: The myth of the twilight years. *Psychology Today, 7*(10), 35–38.

Baltes, P. B., & Schaie, K. W. (1976). On the plasticity of intelligence in adulthood and old age: Where Horn and Donaldson fail. *American Psychologist, 31,* 720–725.

Baltes, P. B., Reese, H. W., & Lipsitt, L. (1980). Life-span developmental psychology. *Annual Review of Psychology, 31,* 65–110.

Baltes, P. B., Staudinger, U. M., Maercker, A., & Smith, J. (1993). People nominated as wise: A comparative study of wisdom-related knowledge. *Psychology and Aging, 10,* 155–166.

Baltes, P. B., & Willis, S. L. (1982). Enhancement (plasticity) of intellectual functioning in old age: Penn State's Adult Development and Enrichment Project (ADEPT). In F. I. M. Craik & S. Trehub (Eds.), *Aging and cognitive processes* (pp. 353–389). New York: Plenum.

Baltimore, D. (1995). Lessons from people with nonprogressive HIV infection. *New England Journal of Medicine, 332,* 259–260.

Bandura, A. (1977). *Social learning theory.*

Englewood Cliffs, NJ: Prentice-Hall.

Bandura, A. (1989). Social cognitive theory. In R. Vasta (Ed.), *Annals of child development.* Greenwich, CT: JAI.

Bandura, A., Grusec, J. E., & Menlove, F. L. (1967). Vicarious extinction of avoidance behavior. *Journal of Personality and Social Psychology, 5,* 16–23.

Bandura, A., Ross, D., & Ross, S. A. (1961). Transmission of aggression through imitation of aggressive models. *Journal of Abnormal and Social Psychology, 63,* 575–582.

Bandura, A., Ross, D., & Ross, S. A. (1963). Imitation of film-mediated aggressive models. *Journal of Abnormal and Social Psychology, 66*(1), 3–11.

Banner, C. (1992). Recent insights into the biology of Alzheimer's disease. *Generations, 16*(4), 31–35.

Bao, W., Srinivasan, S. R., Wattigney, W. A., Bao, W., & Berenson, G. S. (1996). Usefulness of childhood low-density lipoprotein cholesterol level in predicting adult dyslipidemia and other cardiovascular risks. *Archives of Internal Medicine, 156,* 1315–1320.

Barber, B. K. (1994). Cultural, family, and personal contexts of parent-adolescent conflict. *Journal of Marriage and the Family, 56,* 375–386.

Barber, B. L., & Eccles, J. S. (1992). Long-term influence of divorce and single parenting on adolescent family- and work-related values, behaviors, and aspirations. *Psychological Bulletin, 111*(1), 108–126.

Bardoni, B., Zanaria, E., Guioli, S., Floridia, G., Worley, K. C., Tonini, G., Ferrante, E., Chiumell, G., McCabe, E., & Fraccardo, M. (1994). A dosage sensitive locus at chromosome XP21 is involved in male to female sex reversal. *Nature Genetics, 7,* 497–501.

Bardouille-Crema, A., Black, K. N., & Feldhusen, J. (1986). Performance on Piagetian tasks of black children of differing socioeconomic levels. *Developmental Psychology, 22*(6), 841–844.

Barinaga, M. (1996a). Giving language skills a boost. *Science, 271,* 27–28.

Barinaga, M. (1996b). Learning defect identified in brain. *Science, 273,* 867–868.

Barnes, A., Colton, T., Gunderson, J., Noller, K., Tilley, B., Strama, T., Townsend, D., Hatab, P., & O'Brien, P. (1980). Fertility and outcome of pregnancy in women exposed in utero to diethylstilbestrol. *New England Journal of Medicine, 302*(11), 609–613.

Barnes, K. E. (1971). Preschool play norms: A replication. *Developmental Psychology, 5*(1), 99–103.

Barnett, R. (1985, March). *We've come a long way—but where are we and what are the rewards?* Paper presented at the conference on Women in Transition, New York University School of Continuing Education, Center for Career and Life Planning, New York.

Barnett, R. C., et al. (1994). Gender and the relationship between marital-role quality and psychological distress. *Psychology of Women Quarterly, 18*(1), 105–127.

Barnett, R. C., Kibria, M., Baruch, G. K., & Pleck, J. H. (1991). Adult daughter-parent relationships and their association with daughters' subjective well-being and psychological distress. *Journal of Marriage and the Family, 53,* 29–42.

Barnett, R. C., Marshall, N. L., & Pleck, J. H. (1992). Men's multiple roles and their relationship to men's psychological distress. *Journal of Marriage and the Family, 54,* 358–367.

Barnhart, M. A. (1992, Fall). Coping with the Methuselah syndrome. *Free Inquiry,* pp. 19–22.

Baron, C. H., Bergstresser, C., Brock, D. W., Cole, G. F., Dorfman, N. S., Johnson, J. A., Schnipper, L. E., Vorenberg, J., & Wanzer, S. (1996). A model state act to authorize and regulate physician-assisted suicide. *Harvard Journal on Legislation, 33*(1), 1–34.

Barrett, C. J. (1978). Effectiveness of widows' group in facilitating change. *Journal of Counseling and Clinical Psychology, 46*(1), 20–31.

Barrett, R. L., & Robinson, B. E. (1990). *Gay fathers.* Lexington, MA: Lexington.

Bartecchi, C. E., MacKenzie, T. D., & Schrier, R. W. (1995, May). The global tobacco epidemic. *Scientific American,* pp. 44–51.

Barth, M. C., McNaught, W., & Rizzi, P. (1993). Corporations and the aging workforce. In P. H. Mirvis (Ed.), *Building the competitive workforce.* NY: Wiley.

Barton, P., & Lapointe, A. (1995). *Learning by degrees: Indicators of performance in higher education.* Princeton, NJ: ETS Policy Information Center.

Baruch, G. K., & Barnett, R. C. (1986). Father's participation in family work and children's sex role attitudes. *Child Development, 57,* 1210–1223.

Baruch, G., Barnett, R., & Rivers, C. (1983). *Lifeprints.* New York: McGraw-Hill.

Bass, J. L., Brennan, P., Mehta, K. A., & Kodzis, S. (1990). Pediatric problems in a suburban shelter for homeless families. *Pediatrics, 85,* 33–38.

Bass, M., Kravath, R. E., & Glass, L. (1986). Death-scene investigation in sudden infant death. *New England Journal of Medicine, 315,* 100–105.

Bass, S. A., & Caro, F. G. (1996). The economic value of grandparent assistance. *Generations, 20*(1), 29–33.

Bassuk, E. L. (1991). Homeless families. *Scientific American, 265*(6), 66–74.

Bassuk, E. L., & Rosenberg, L. (1990). Psychosocial characteristics of homeless children and children with homes. *Pediatrics, 85*(30), 257–261.

Bassuk, E. L., & Rubin, L. (1987). Homeless children: A neglected population.

American Journal of Orthopsychiatry, 57(2), 279–286.

Bates, E., Bretherton, I., & Snyder, L. (1988). *From first words to grammar: Individual differences and dissociable mechanisms.* New York: Cambridge University Press.

Bates, E., O'Connell, B., & Shore, C. (1987). Language and communication in infancy. In J. D. Osofsky (Ed.), *Handbook of infant development* (2d ed.). New York: Wiley.

Battistich, V., Watson, M., Solomon, D., Schaps, E., & Solomon, J. (1991). The Child Development Project: A comprehensive program for the development of prosocial character. In W. M. Kurtines & J. L. Gewirtz (Eds.), *Handbook of moral behavior and development: Vol 3. Application* (pp. 1–34). Hillsdale, NJ: Erlbaum.

Baum, A., Cacioppo, J. T., Melamed, B. G., Gallant, S. J., & Travis, C. (1995). *Doing the right thing: A research plan for healthy living.* Washington, DC: American Psychological Association Science Directorate.

Baum, A., & Fleming, I. (1993). Implications of psychological research on stress and technological accidents. *American Psychologist, 48,* 665–672.

Baumeister, R. F., & Leary, M. R. (1995). The need to belong: Desire for interpersonal attachments as a fundamental human motivation. *Psychological Bulletin, 117*(3), 497–529.

Baumrind, D. (1971). Harmonious parents and their preschool children. *Developmental Psychology, 41,* 92–102.

Baumrind, D. (1993). The average expectable environment is not good enough: A response to Scarr. *Child Development, 38,* 1299–1317.

Baumrind, D. (1995). Commentary on sexual orientation: Research and social policy implications. *Developmental Psychology, 31*(1), 130–136.

Baumrind, D. (1996). The discipline controversy revisited. *Family Relations, 45,* 405–414.

Baumrind, D., & Black, A. E. (1967). Socialization practices associated with dimensions of competence in preschool boys and girls. *Child Development, 38,* 291–327.

Bayley, N. (1965). Comparisons of mental and motor test scores for age 1–15 months by sex, birth order, race, geographic location, and education of parents. *Child Development, 36,* 379–411.

Bayley, N. (1969). *Bayley Scales of Infant Development.* New York: Psychological Corporation.

Bayley, N. (1993). *Bayley Scales of Infant Development: II.* New York: Psychological Corporation.

Bayley, N., & Oden, M. (1955). The maintenance of intellectual ability in gifted adults. *Journal of Gerontology, 10,* 91–107.

Beal, C. R. (1994). *Boys and girls: The development of gender roles.* New York: McGraw-Hill.

Beall, A. E., & Sternberg, R. J. (1995). The social construction of love. *Journal of Social and Personal Relationships, 12*(3), 417–438.

Beard, G. M. (1874). *Legal responsibility in old age.* New York: Russell.

Beaty, L. A. (1995). Effects of paternal absence in male adolescents' peer relations and self image. *Adolescence, 30*(120), 873–880.

Beautrais, A. L., Fergusson, D. M., & Shannon, F. T. (1982). Life events and childhood morbidity: A prospective study. *Pediatrics, 70*(6), 935–940.

Becker, G. S. (1991). *A treatise on the family* (enlarged ed.). Cambridge, MA: Harvard University Press.

Behrman, R. E. (1992). *Nelson textbook of pediatrics* (13th ed.). Philadelphia: Saunders.

Behrman, R. E., & Vaughan, V. C. (Eds.). (1983). *Nelson textbook of pediatrics.* Philadelphia: Saunders.

Belbin, R. M. (1967). Middle age: What happens to ability? In R. Owen (Ed.), *Middle age.* London: BBC.

Belenky, M. F., Clinchy, B. M., Goldberger, N. R., & Tarule, J. M. (1986). *Women's ways of knowing: The development of self, voice, and mind.* New York: Basic Books.

Bell, J. (1992). In search of a discourse on aging: The elderly on television. *The Gerontologist, 32*(3), 305–311.

Bell, S., & Ainsworth, M. D. S. (1972). Infant crying and maternal responsiveness. *Child Development, 43,* 1171–1190.

Bellinger, D., Leviton, A., Watermaux, C., Needleman, H., & Rabinowitz, M. (1987). Longitudinal analyses of prenatal and postnatal lead exposure and early cognitive development. *New England Journal of Medicine, 316*(17), 1037–1043.

Bellinger, D. C., Stiles, K. M., & Needleman, H. L. (1992). Low-level lead exposure, intelligence, and academic achievement: A long-term follow-up study. *Pediatrics, 90,* 855–861.

Belloc, N. B., & Breslow, L. (1972). Relationship of physical health status and health practices. *Preventive Medicine, 1*(3), 409–421.

Belsky, J. (1984). Two waves of day care research: Developmental effects and conditions of quality. In R. Ainslie (Ed.), *The child and the day care setting.* New York: Praeger.

Belsky, J. (1993). Etiology of child maltreatment: A developmental-ecological analysis. *Psychological Bulletin, 114,* 413–434.

Belsky, J. (1996). Parent, infant, and social-contextual antecedents of father-son attachment security. *Developmental Psychology, 32,* 905–913.

Belsky, J., Fish, M., & Isabella, R. (1991). Continuity and discontinuity in infant negative and positive emotionality: Family antecedents and attachment consequences. *Developmental Psychology, 27,* 421–431.

Belsky, J., Lang, M., & Huston, T. L. (1986). Sex typing and division of labor as determinants of marital change across the transition to parenthood. *Journal of Personality and Social Psychology, 50,* 517–522.

Belsky, J., & Rovine, M. (1990). Patterns of marital change across the transition to parenthood: Pregnancy to three years postpartum. *Journal of Marriage and the Family, 52,* 5–19.

Belsky, J., & Rovine, M. J. (1988). Nonmaternal care in the first year of life and the security of infant-parent attachment. *Child Development, 59,* 157–167.

Beltramini, A. U., & Hertzig, M. E. (1983). Sleep and bedtime behavior in preschool-aged children. *Pediatrics, 71*(2), 153–158.

Bem, S. L. (1974). The measurement of psychological androgyny. *Journal of Consulting and Clinical Psychology, 42,* 155–162.

Bem, S. L. (1976). Probing the promise of androgyny. In A. G. Kaplan & J. P. Bean (Eds.), *Beyond sex-role stereotypes: Readings toward a psychology of androgyny.* Boston: Little, Brown.

Bem, S. L. (1983). Gender schema theory and its implications for child development: Raising gender-aschematic children in a gender-schematic society. *Signs, 8,* 598–616.

Bem, S. L. (1985). Androgyny and gender schema theory: A conceptual and empirical integration. In T. B. Sondregger (Ed.), *Nebraska Symposium on Motivation, 1984. Psychology and gender.* Lincoln: University of Nebraska Press.

Bemon, P., & Sharma, A. S. (1994). *Growing up adopted: A portrait of adolescents and their families.* Minneapolis: Research Institute of Minnesota.

Benenson, J. F. (1993). Greater preference among females than males for dyadic interaction in early childhood. *Child Development, 64,* 544–555.

Bengtson, V., Rosenthal, C., & Burton, L. (1996). Paradoxes of families and aging. In R. H. Binstock & L. K. George (Eds.), *Handbook of aging and the social sciences* (pp. 253–282). San Diego: Academic Press.

Bengtson, V. L., Rosenthal, C. J., & Burton, L. M. (1990). Families and aging: Diversity and heterogeneity. In R. Binstock & L. George (Eds.), *Handbook of aging and the social sciences* (pp. 263–287). San Diego: Academic Press.

Benoit, D., & Parker, K. C. H. (1994). Stability and transmission of attachment across three generations. *Child Development, 65,* 1444–1456.

Benson, J. B. (1993). Season of birth and

onset of locomotion: Theoretical and methodological implications. *Infant Behavior and Development, 16,* 69–81.

Benson, J. B., & Uzgiris, I. C. (1985). Effect of self-inflicted locomotion on infant search activity. *Developmental Psychology, 21,* 923–931.

Berenda, R. W. (1950). *The influence of the group on the judgments of children.* New York: King's Crown.

Berg, C. A., & Klaczynski, P. A. (1996). Practical intelligence and problem solving: Search for perspectives. In F. Blanchard-Fields & T. M. Hess (Eds.), *Perspectives on cognitive change in adulthood and aging* (pp. 323–357). New York: McGraw-Hill.

Berger, R. M. (1984, January–February). Realities of gay and lesbian aging. *Social Work,* pp. 57–62.

Berger, R. M., & Kelly, J. J. (1986). Working with homosexuals of the older population. *Social Casework, 67,* 203–210.

Bergman, S. J. (1991). *Men's psychological development: A relational perspective* (Work in Progress No. 48). Wellesley, MA: Wellesley College, Stone Center.

Berk, L. E. (1986). Private speech: Learning out loud. *Psychology Today, 20*(5), 34–42.

Berk, L. E., & Garvin, R. A. (1984). Development of private speech among low-income Appalachian children. *Developmental Psychology, 20*(2), 271–286.

Berkowitz, G. S., Skovron, M. L., Lapinski, R. H., & Berkowitz, R. L. (1990). Delayed childbearing and the outcome of pregnancy. *New England Journal of Medicine, 322,* 659–664.

Berkowitz, L. (1984). Some effects of thoughts on anti- and prosocial influences of media events: A cognitive-neoassociation analysis. *Psychological Bulletin, 95,* 410–427.

Bernard, J., & Sontag, L. W. (1947). Fetal reactivity to sound. *Journal of Genetic Psychology, 70,* 205–210.

Bernard-Bonnin, A.–C., Gilbert, S., Rousseau, E., Masson, P., & Maheux, B. (1991). Television and the 3- to 10-year-old child. *Pediatrics, 88,* 48–54.

Berndt, T. J. (1982). The features and effects of friendship in early adolescence. *Child Development, 53,* 1447–1460.

Berndt, T. J., & Perry, T. B. (1990). Distinctive features and effects of early adolescent friendships. In R. Montemayor, G. R. Adams, & T. P. Gullotta (Eds.), *From childhood to adolescence: A transitional period?* Newbury Park, CA: Sage.

Bernstein, G. A., & Garfinkel, B. D. (1988). Pedigrees, functioning, and psychopathology in families of school phobic children. *American Journal of Psychiatry, 145,* 70–74.

Bernstein, J. (1995). *Where's the payoff?* Washington, DC: Economic Policy Institute.

Berrueta-Clement, J. R., Schweinhart, L.

J., Barnett, W. S., Epstein, A. S., & Weikart, D. P. (1984). *Changed lives: The effects of the Perry Preschool program on youths through age 19.* Ypsilanti, MI: High/Scope.

Berrueta-Clement, J. R., Schweinhart, L. J., Barnett, W. S., & Weikart, D. P. (1987). The effects of early educational intervention on crime and delinquency in adolescence and early adulthood. In J. D. Burchard & S. N. Burchard (Eds.), *Primary prevention of psychopathology: Vol. 10. Prevention of delinquent behavior* (pp. 220–240). Newbury Park, CA: Sage.

Berscheid, E., & Campbell, B. (1981). The changing longevity of heterosexual close relationships. In M. J. Lerner & S. C. Lerner (Eds.), *The justice motive in social behavior.* New York: Plenum.

Bertenthal, B. I., & Campos, J. J. (1987). New directions in the study of early experience. *Child Development, 58,* 560–567.

Bertenthal, B. I., Campos, J. J., & Barrett, K. C. (1984). Self-produced locomotion: An organizer of emotional, cognitive, and social development in infancy. In R. N. Emde & R. J. Harmon (Eds.), *Continuities and discontinuities in development.* New York: Plenum.

Bertenthal, B. I., Campos, J. J., & Kermoian, R. (1994). An epigenetic perspective on the development of self-produced locomotion and its consequences. *Current Directions in Psychological Science, 3*(5), 140–145.

Beumont, P. J. V., Russell, J. D., & Touyz, S. W. (1993). Treatment of anorexia nervosa. *The Lancet, 341,* 1635–1640.

Beyene, Y. (1986). Cultural significance and physiological manifestations of menopause: A biocultural analysis. *Culture, Medicine, and Psychiatry, 10,* 47–71.

Beyene, Y. (1989). *From menarche to menopause: Reproductive lives of peasant women in two cultures.* Albany: State University of New York Press.

Bianchi, S. M., & Spain, D. (1986). *American women in transition.* New York: Russell Sage Foundation.

Biegel, D. E. (1995). Caregiver burden. In G. E. Maddox (Ed.), *The encyclopedia of aging* (2d ed., pp. 138–141). New York: Springer.

Bielby, D., & Papalia, D. (1975). Moral development and perceptual role-taking egocentrism: Their development and interrelationship across the lifespan. *International Journal of Aging and Human Development, 6*(4), 293–308.

Bierman, K. L., & Furman, W. (1984). The effects of social skills training and peer involvement on the social adjustment of preadolescents. *Child Development, 55,* 151–162.

Bierman, K. L., Smoot, D. L., & Aumiller, K. (1993). Characteristics of aggressive-rejected, aggressive (non-re-

jected), and rejected (non-aggressive) boys. *Child Development, 64,* 139–151.

Biller, H. B. (1981). The father and sex role development. In M. E. Lamb (Ed.), *The role of the father in child development.* New York: Wiley.

Binstock, R. H. (1993). Healthcare costs around the world: Is aging a fiscal "black hole"? *Generations, 17*(4), 37–42.

Birch, L. L., Johnson, S. L., Andersen, G., Peters, J. C., & Schulte, M. C. (1991). The variability of young children's energy intake. *New England Journal of Medicine, 324,* 232–235.

Birns, B. (1976). The emergence and socialization of sex differences in the earliest years. *Merrill-Palmer Quarterly, 22,* 229–254.

Birren, J. E., & Morrison, D. F. (1961). Analysis of the WAIS subtests in relation to age and education. *Journal of Gerontology, 16,* 363–369.

Birren, J. E., Woods, A. M., & Williams, M. V. (1980). Behavioral slowing with age: Causes, organization, and consequences. In L. W. Poon (Ed.), *Aging in the 1980s.* Washington, DC: American Psychological Association.

Bishop, R. C. (1996). Physician aid in dying: Murder or compassionate care? *Humanistic Judaism, 24*(4), 10–13.

Bittman, M. (1993, October 27). Eating well: Need more protein? Probably not. *The New York Times,* p. C11.

Blackburn, J. A., Papalia-Finlay, D., Foye, B. F., & Serlin, R. C. (1988). Modifiability of figural relations performance among elderly adults. *Journal of Gerontology: Psychological Sciences, 43*(3), P87–89.

Blair, S. N., Kohl, H. W., Barlow, C. E., Paffenbarger, R. S., Gibbons, L. W., & Macera, C. A. (1995). Changes in physical fitness and all-cause mortality: A prospective study of healthy and unhealthy men. *Journal of the American Medical Association, 273,* 1093–1098.

Blair, S. N., Kohl, H. W., Paffenbarger, R. S., Clark, D. G., Cooper, K. H., & Gibbons, L. W. (1989). Physical fitness and all-cause mortality: A prospective study of healthy men and women. *Journal of the American Medical Association, 262,* 2395–2401.

Blanchard-Fields, F. (1986). Reasoning on social dilemmas varying in emotional saliency: An adult developmental perspective. *Psychology and Aging, 1,* 325–333.

Blanchard-Fields, F., Brannan, J. R., & Camp, C. J. (1987). Alternative conceptions of wisdom: An onion-peeling exercise. *Educational Gerontology, 13,* 497–503.

Blanchard-Fields, F., & Camp, C. J. (1990). Affect, individual differences, and real world problem solving across the adult life span. In T. Hess (Ed.), *Aging and cognition: Knowledge organiza-*

tion and utilization (pp. 461–498). Amsterdam: North-Holland, Elsevier.

Blanchard-Fields, F., & Irion, J. (1987). Coping strategies from the perspective of two developmental markers: Age and social reasoning. *Journal of Genetic Psychology, 149,* 141–151.

Blanchard-Fields, F., Jahnke, H. C., & Camp, C. J. (1995). Age differences in problem solving style: The role of emotional salience. *Psychology and Aging, 10,* 173–180.

Blanchard-Fields, F., & Norris, L. (1994). Causal attributions from adolescence through adulthood: Age differences, ego level, and generalized response style. *Aging and Cognition, 1,* 67–86.

Blass, E. M., Ganchrow, J. R., & Steiner, J. E. (1984). Classical conditioning in newborn humans 2–24 hours of age. *Infant Behavior and Development, 7,* 223–235.

Blazer, D. G. (1989). Depression in the elderly. *New England Journal of Medicine,* 320, 164–166.

Blazer, D. G., Kessler, R. C., McGonagle, K. A., & Swartz, M. S. (1994). The prevalence and distribution of major depression in a national community sample: The National Comorbidity Survey. *American Journal of Psychiatry, 151,* 979–986.

Blieszner, R. (1986). Trends in family gerontology research. *Family Relations, 35,* 555–562.

Blieszner, R., Willis, S. L., & Baltes, P. B. (1981). Training research on induction ability: A short-term longitudinal study. *Journal of Applied Developmental Psychology, 2,* 247–265.

Block, J. (1981). Some enduring and consequential structures of personality. In A. I. Rubin et al. (Eds.), *Further explorations in personality.* New York: Wiley.

Bloom, B. S. (1985). *Developing talent in young people.* New York: Ballantine.

Bloom, D. E., & Pebley, A. R. (1982). Voluntary childlessness: A review of the evidence and its implications. *Population Research and Policy Review, 1,* 203–234.

Bluebond-Langner, M. (1977). Meanings of death to children. In H. Feifel (Ed.), *New meanings of death* (pp. 47–66). New York: McGraw-Hill.

Blumenthal, J. A., Emery, C. F., Madden, D. J., Schniebolk, S., Walsh-Riddle, M., George, L. K., McKee, D. C., Higginbotham, M. B., Cobb, F. R., & Coleman, R. E. (1991). Long-term effects of exercise on psychological functioning in older men and women. *Journal of Gerontology, 46*(6), P352–361.

Blurton Jones, N. G., & Konner, M. J. (1973). Sex differences in behavior of London and Bushman children. In R. P. Michael & J. H. Crook (Eds.), *Comparative ecology and behavior of primates.* London: Academic Press.

Blyth, D. A., et al. (1981). The effects of physical development on self-image and satisfaction with body-image for early adolescent males. In R. G. Simmons (Ed.), *Research on community and mental health* (Vol. 2). Greenwich, CT: JAI.

Blyth, D. A., & Foster-Clark, F. S. (1987). Gender differences in perceived intimacy with different members of adolescents' social networks. *Sex Roles, 17,* 689–718.

Blyth, D. A., Simmons, R. G., & Carlton-Ford, S. (1983). The adjustment of early adolescents to school transitions. *Journal of Early Adolescence, 3*(1–2), 105–120.

Bograd, R., & Spilka, B. (1996). Self-disclosure and marital satisfaction in midlife and late-life remarriages. *International Journal of Aging and Human Development, 42*(3), 161–172.

Bolger, K. E., Patterson, C. J., Thompson, W. W., & Kupersmidt, J. B. (1995). Psychosocial adjustment among children experiencing persistent and intermittent family economic hardship. *Child Development, 66,* 1107–1129.

Bolger, N., DeLongis, A., Kessler, R. C., & Schilling, E. A. (1989). Effects of daily stress on negative mood. *Journal of Personality and Social Psychology, 57,* 808–818.

Bollinger, R. C., Tripathy, S. P., & Quinn, T. C. (1995). The human immunodeficiency virus epidemic in India: Current magnitude and future projections. *Medicine, 72,* 97–106.

Bornstein, M., Kessen, W., & Weiskopf, S. (1976). The categories of hue in infancy. *Science, 191,* 201–202.

Bornstein, M. H. (1985a). Habituation of attention as a measure of visual information processing in human infants. In G. Gottleib & N. A. Krasnegor (Eds.), *Development of audition and vision in the first year of post-natal life: A methodological overview.* Norwood, NJ: Ablex.

Bornstein, M. H. (1985b). How infant and mother jointly contribute to developing cognitive competence in the child. *Proceedings of the National Academy of Science, 82,* 7470–7473.

Bornstein, M. H., & Sigman, M. D. (1986). Continuity in mental development from infancy. *Child Development, 57,* 251–274.

Bornstein, M. H., Tal, J., & Tamis-LeMonda, C. S. (1991). Parenting in cross-cultural perspective: The United States, France, and Japan. In M. H. Bornstein (Ed.), *Cultural approaches to parenting.* Hillsdale, NJ: Erlbaum.

Bornstein, M. H., & Tamis-LeMonda, C. S. (1989). Maternal responsiveness and cognitive development in children. In M. H. Bornstein (Ed.), Maternal responsiveness: Characteristics and consequences. *New Directions for Child Development,* No. 43. San Francisco: Jossey-Bass.

Bornstein, M. H., & Tamis-LeMonda, C. S. (1994). Antecedents of information processing skills in infants: Habituation, novelty responsiveness, and cross-modal transfer. *Infant Behavior and Development, 17,* 371–380.

Bossé, R., Aldwin, C. M., Levenson, M. R., Spiro, A., & Mroczek, D. K. (1993). Change in social support after retirement: Longitudinal findings from the normative aging study. *Journal of Gerontology: Psychological Sciences, 48,* P210–217.

Botwinick, J. (1984). *Aging and behavior* (3d ed.). New York: Springer.

Bouchard, T. J. (1994). Genes, environment, and personality. *Science, 264,* 1700–1701.

Boulton, M. G. (1983). *On being a mother: A study of women with pre-school children.* London: Tavistock.

Bouvier, L. F., & Simcox, D. (1994). *Foreign born professionals in the U.S.* Washington, DC: Center for Immigration Studies.

Bouza, A. V. (1990). *The police mystique: An insider's look at cops, crime, and the criminal justice system.* New York: Plenum.

Bower, B. (1985). The left hand of math and verbal talent. *Science News, 127,* 263.

Bower, B. (1993). A child's theory of mind. *Science News, 144,* 40–42.

Bowlby, J. (1951). Maternal care and mental health. *Bulletin of the World Health Organization, 3,* 355–534.

Boyer, J. L., & Guthrie, L. (1985). Assessment and treatment of the suicidal patient. In E. E. Beckham & W. R. Leber (Eds.), *Handbook of depression.* Homewood, IL: Dorsey.

Boysson-Bardies, B., Sagart, L., & Durand, C. (1984). Discernible differences in the babbling of infants according to target language. *Journal of Child Language, 11,* 1–15.

Boyum, L. A., & Parke, R. D. (1995). The role of family emotional expressiveness in the development of children's social competence. *Journal of Marriage and the Family, 57,* 593–608.

Brabant, S. (1994). An overlooked AIDS affected population: The elderly parent as caregiver. *Journal of Gerontological Social Work, 22,* 131–145.

Brackbill, Y., & Broman, S. H. (1979). *Obstetrical medication and development in the first year of life.* Unpublished manuscript.

Bradford, J., & Ryan, C. (1991). Who are we: Health concerns of middle-aged lesbians. In J. W. B. Sang & A. Smith (Eds.), *Lesbians at midlife: The creative transition* (pp. 147–163). San Francisco: Spinsters.

Bradley, R., & Caldwell, B. (1982). The consistency of the home environment and its relation to child development. *International Journal of Behavioral Development, 5,* 445–465.

Bradley, R., Caldwell, B., & Rock, S. (1988). HOME environment and school performance: A ten-year follow-up and examination of three models of environmental action. *Child Development, 59,* 852–867.

Bradley, R. H. (1989). Home measurement of maternal responsiveness. In M. H. Bornstein (Ed.), Maternal responsiveness: Characteristics and consequences. *New Directions for Child Development,* No. 43. San Francisco: Jossey-Bass.

Bradley, R. H., et al. (1989). Home environment and cognitive development in the first 3 years of life: A collaborative study involving six sites and three ethnic groups in North America. *Developmental Psychology, 25*(2), 217–235.

Braine, M. (1976). Children's first word combinations. *Monographs of the Society for Research in Child Development, 41*(1, Serial No. 164).

Branch, L. G., Horowitz, A., & Carr, C. (1989). The implications for everyday life of incident of self-reported visual decline among people over age 65 living in the community. *The Gerontologist, 29*(3), 359–365.

Brandes, J. M., Scher, A., Itzkovits, J., Thaler, I., Sarid, M., & Gershoni-Baruch, R. (1992). Growth and development of children conceived by in vitro fertilization. *Pediatrics, 90*(3), 424–429.

Brandt, B. (1989). A place for her death. *Humanistic Judaism, 17*(3), 83–85.

Brass, L. M., Isaacsohn, J. L., Merikangas, K. R., & Robinette, C. D. (1992). A study of twins and stroke. *Stroke, 23*(2), 221–223.

Braungart, J. M., Plomin, R., DeFries, J. C., & Fulker, D. W. (1992). Genetic influence on tester-rated infant temperament as assessed by Bayley's Infant Behavior Record: Nonadoptive and adoptive siblings and twins. *Developmental Psychology, 28*(1), 40–47.

Braver, S. L., Wolchik, S. A., Sandler, I. N., Sheets, V. L., Fogas, B., & Bay, R. C. (1993). A longitudinal study of noncustodial parents: Parents without children. *Journal of Family Psychology, 7,* 9–23.

Bray, D. W., & Howard, A. (1983). The AT&T longitudinal study of managers. In K. W. Schaie (Ed.), *Longitudinal studies of adult psychological development* (pp. 266–312). New York: Guilford.

Bray, J. H., & Hetherington, E. M. (1993). Families in transition: Introduction and overview. *Journal of Family Psychology, 7,* 3–8.

Brayfield, A. (1995). Juggling jobs and kids: The impact of employment schedules on fathers' caring for children. *Journal of Marriage and the Family, 57,* 321–332.

Brazaitis, T. (1996, March 10). Career paths are gone. *Cleveland Plain Dealer,* p. 3C.

Brazelton, T. B. (1973). *Neonatal behavioral assessment scale.* Philadelphia: Lippincott.

Brecher, E., & the Editors of Consumer Reports Books. (1984). *Love, sex, and aging: A Consumers Union report.* Boston: Little, Brown.

Bremner, W. J., Vitiello, M. V., & Prinz, P. N. (1983). Loss of circadian rhythmicity in blood testosterone levels with aging in normal men. *Journal of Clinical Endocrinology and Metabolism, 56,* 1278–1281.

Brenner, M. H. (1991). Health, productivity, and the economic environment: Dynamic role of socio-economic status. In G. Green & F. Baker (Eds.), *Work, health, and productivity* (pp. 241–255). New York: Oxford University Press.

Breslow, L., & Breslow, N. (1993). Health practices and disability: Some evidence from Alameda County. *Preventive Medicine, 22*(1), 86–95.

Bretherton, I. (1990). Communication patterns, internal working models, and the intergenerational transmission of attachment relationships. *Infant Mental Health Journal, 11*(3), 237–252.

Brigham, M. C., & Pressley, M. (1988). Cognitive monitoring and strategy choice in younger and older adults. *Psychology and Aging, 3,* 249–257.

Briley, M. (1980, July–August). Burnout stress and the human energy crisis. *Dynamic Years,* pp. 36–39.

Brim, O. G. (1977). Theories of male midlife crisis. In N. Schlossberg & A. Entine (Eds.), *Counseling adults.* Monterey, CA: Brooks/Cole.

Briss, P. A., Sacks, J. J., Addiss, D. G., Kresnow, M., & O'Neil, J. (1994). A nationwide study of the risk of injury associated with day care center attendance. *Pediatrics, 93*(3), 364–368.

Brock, D. W. (1992, March–April). Voluntary active euthanasia. *Hastings Center Report,* pp. 10–22.

Brody, E. M. (1978). Community housing for the elderly. *The Gerontologist, 18*(2), 121–128.

Brody, G. H., Stoneman, Z., & Flor, D. (1995). Linking family processes and academic competence among rural African American youths. *Journal of Marriage and the Family, 57,* 567–579.

Brody, G. H., Stoneman, Z., Flor, D., McCrary, C., Hastings, L., & Conyers, O. (1994). Financial resources, parent psychological functioning, parent co-caregiving, and early adolescent competence in rural two-parent African-American families. *Child Development, 65,* 590–605.

Brody, J. E. (1990, October 11). Sedentary living, not cholesterol, is the nation's leading culprit in fatal heart attacks. *The New York Times,* p. B12.

Brody, J. E. (1992, December 9). Hip fracture: A potential killer that can be avoided. *The New York Times,* p. C16.

Brody, J. E. (1993, December 1). Liberated at last from the myths about menopause. *The New York Times,* p. C15.

Brody, J. E. (1995a, April 19). Fighting the nicotine habit with nicotine. *The New York Times,* p. C10.

Brody, J. E. (1995b, April 23). Trying to reconcile exercise findings. *The New York Times,* p. 22L.

Brody, J. E. (1995c, June 28). Preventing birth defects even before pregnancy. *The New York Times,* p. C10.

Brody, L. R., Zelazo, P. R., & Chaika, H. (1984). Habituation-dishabituation to speech in the neonate. *Developmental Psychology, 20,* 114–119.

Brody, N. (1985). The validity of tests of intelligence. In B. B. Wolman (Ed.), *Handbook of intelligence* (pp. 353–389). New York: Wiley.

Bromberger, J. T., & Matthews, K. A. (1996). Longitudinal study of the effects of pessimism, trait anxiety, and life stress on depressive symptoms in middle-aged women. *Psychology and Aging, 11,* 207–213.

Bronfenbrenner, U. (1979). *The ecology of human development.* Cambridge, MA: Harvard University Press.

Bronfenbrenner, U. (1986). Ecology of the family as a context for human development: Research perspectives. *Developmental Psychology, 22,* 723–742.

Bronfenbrenner, U. (1994). Ecological models of human development. In T. Husen & T. N. Postlethwaite (Eds.), *International encyclopedia of education* (2d ed., Vol. 3). Oxford: Pergamon Press/Elsevier Science.

Bronfenbrenner, U., Belsky, J., & Steinberg, L. (1977). *Daycare in context: An ecological perspective on research and public policy.* Review prepared for Office of the Assistant Secretary for Planning and Evaluation, U.S. Department of Health, Education, and Welfare.

Bronfenbrenner, U., & Crouter, A. (1982). Work and family through time and space. In S. B. Kamerman & C. D. Hayes (Eds.), *Families that work: Children in a changing world.* Washington, DC: National Academy of Science.

Bronson, F. H., & Desjardins, C. (1969). Aggressive behavior and seminal vesicle function in mice: Differential sensitivity to androgen given neonatally. *Endocrinology, 85,* 871–975.

Bronstein, P. (1988). Father-child interaction: Implications for gender role socialization. In P. Bronstein & C. P. Cowan (Eds.), *Fatherhood today: Men's changing role in the family.* New York: Wiley.

Bronstein, P., Clauson, J., Stoll, M. F., & Abrams, C. L. (1993). Parenting behavior and children's social, psychological, and academic adjustment in diverse family structures. *Family Relations, 42,* 268–276.

Bronte, L. (1993). *The longevity factor: The new reality of long careers and how it can lead to richer lives.* New York: Harper-Collins.

Brooks, G. (1972). *Report from part one.* Detroit: Broadside Press.

Brooks-Gunn, J. (1988). Pubertal processes and the early adolescent transition. In W. Damon (Ed.), *Child development today and tomorrow.* San Francisco: Jossey-Bass.

Brooks-Gunn, J., Klebanov, P. K., & Duncan, G. J. (1996). Ethnic differences in children's intelligence test scores: Role of economic deprivation, home environment, and maternal characteristics. *Child Development, 67,* 396–408.

Brooks-Gunn, J., Klebanov, P. K., Liaw, F., & Spiker, D. (1993). Enhancing the development of low-birthweight, premature infants: Changes in cognition and behavior over the first three years. *Child Development, 64,* 736–753.

Brooks-Gunn, J., McCarton, C. M., Casey, P. H., et al. (1994). Early intervention in low-birthweight premature infants: Results through age 5 years from the Infant Health Development Program. *Journal of the American Medical Association, 272,* 1257–1262.

Brooks-Gunn, J., & Reiter, E. O. (1990). The role of pubertal processes. In S. S. Feldman & G. R. Elliott (Eds.), *At the threshold: The developing adolescent.* Cambridge, MA: Harvard University Press.

Brophy, J. E., & Good, T. L. (1974). *Teacher-student relationships.* New York: Holt.

Brown, B. B., Mounts, N., Lamborn, S. D., & Steinberg, L. (1993). Parenting practices and peer group affiliation in adolescence. *Child Development, 64,* 467–482.

Brown, J. D., Childers, K. W., & Waszak, C. S. (1988, June). *Television and adolescent sexuality.* Paper presented at the conference on "Television and Teens: Health Implications," Manhattan Beach, CA.

Brown, J. E. (1983). *Nutrition for your pregnancy.* Minneapolis: University of Minnesota Press.

Brown, J. L. (1987). Hunger in the U.S. *Scientific American, 256*(2), 37–41.

Brown, J. T., & Stoudemire, A. (1983). Normal and pathological grief. *Journal of the American Medical Association, 250,* 378–382.

Brown, L. M., & Gilligan, C. (1990, April). *The psychology of women and the development of girls.* Paper presented at the Laurel-Harvard Conference on the Psychology of Women and the Education of Girls, Cleveland.

Brown, L. M., & Gilligan, C. (1992). *Meeting at the crossroads: Women's psychology and girls' development.* Cambridge, MA: Harvard University Press.

Brown, M. B., & Tedrick, T. (1993). Outdoor leisure involvements of black older Americans: An exploration of ethnicity and marginality. In *Activities, adaptation, and aging* (pp. 55–65). New York: Haworth.

Brown, P. (1993, April 17). Motherhood past midnight. *New Scientist,* pp. 4–8.

Brown, R. (1973a). Development of the first language in the human species. *American Psychologist, 28,* 97–106.

Brown, R. (1973b). *A first language: The early stage.* Cambridge, MA: Harvard University Press.

Brown, S. S. (1985). Can low birth weight be prevented? *Family Planning Perspectives, 17*(3), 112–118.

Browne, A., & Finkelhor, D. (1986). Impact of child sexual abuse: A review of research. *Psychological Bulletin, 99*(1), 66–77.

Brozan, N. (1990, November 29). Less visible but heavier burdens as AIDS attacks people over 50. *The New York Times,* pp. A1, A16.

Brubaker, T. H. (1983). Introduction. In T. H. Brubaker (Ed.), *Family relationships in later life.* Beverly Hills, CA: Sage.

Brubaker, T. H. (1990). Families in later life: A burgeoning research area. *Journal of Marriage and the Family, 52,* 959–981.

Brubaker, T. H. (Ed.). (1993). *Family relationships: Current and future directions.* Newbury Park, CA: Sage.

Bruce, J., Lloyd, C. B., & Leonard, A. (1995). *Families in focus: New perspectives on mothers, fathers, and children.* New York: Population Council.

Brumfield, C. G., Lin, S., Conner, W., Cosper, P., Davis, R. O., & Owen, J. (1996). Pregnancy outcome following genetic amniocentesis at 11–14 versus 16–19 weeks' gestation. *Obstetrics and Gynecology, 88,* 114–118.

Bryant, S., & Demian, C. (Eds.). (1990, May/June). *Partners: Newsletter for gay and lesbian couples.* (Available from Partners, Box 9685, Seattle, WA 98109).

Bryer, J. B., Nelson, B. A., Miller, J. J., & Krol, P. A. (1987). Childhood sexual and physical abuse as factors in adult psychiatric illness. *American Journal of Psychiatry, 144*(11), 1426–1430.

Bryson, K. (1996, October). *Household and family characteristics: March 1995* (Current Population Report P20-488; PPL-46). Washington, DC: U.S. Bureau of the Census.

Buchwald, A. (1994). *Leaving home.* New York: Putnam.

Buhrmester, D. (1990). Intimacy of friendship, interpersonal competence, and adjustment during preadolescence and adolescence. *Child Development, 61,* 1101–1111.

Buhrmester, D., & Furman, W. (1990). Perceptions of sibling relationships during middle childhood and adolescence. *Child Development, 61,* 138–139.

Bukowski, W. M., & Kramer, T. L. (1986). Judgments of the features of friendship among early adolescent boys and girls. *Journal of Early Adolescence, 6,* 331–338.

Bulcroft, K., & O'Conner, M. (1986). The importance of dating relationships on quality of life for older persons. *Family Relations, 35,* 397–401.

Bulcroft, R. A., & Bulcroft, K. A. (1991). The nature and function of dating in later life. *Research on Aging, 13,* 244–260.

Bullock, K. D., Reed, R. J., & Grant, I. (1992). Reduced mortality risk in alcoholics who achieve long-term abstinence. *Journal of the American Medical Association, 267*(5), 668–672.

Bumpass, L., & Aquilino, W. (1993). *Mapping the social terrain of midlife in the U.S.* Unpublished manuscript, University of Wisconsin.

Bumpass, L., Sweet, J., & Martin, T. C. (1990). Changing patterns of remarriage. *Journal of Marriage and the Family, 52,* 747–756.

Bumpass, L. L., & Sweet, J. A. (1988). *Preliminary evidence on cohabitation* (NSFH Working Paper No. 2). Madison: University of Wisconsin, Center for Demography and Ecology.

Burchinal, M. R., Roberts, J. E., Nabors, L. A., & Bryant, D. M. (1996). Quality of center child care and infant cognitive and language development. *Child Development, 67,* 606–620.

Bureau of Justice Statistics. See U.S. Bureau of Justice Statistics.

Burgess, A. W., Hartman, C. R., & McCormack, A. (1987). Abused to abuser: Antecedents of socially deviant behaviors. *American Journal of Psychiatry, 144*(11), 1431–1436.

Burhans, K. K., & Dweck, C. S. (1995). Helplessness in early childhood: The role of contingent worth. *Child Development, 66,* 1719–1738.

Burkhauser, R. V., Holden, K. C., & Feaster, D. (1988). Incidence, timing, and events associated with poverty: A dynamic view of poverty in retirement. *Journal of Gerontology: Social Sciences, 43,* S46–52.

Burkhauser, R. V., & Quinn, J. (1989). Work and retirement: The American experience. In W. Schmahl (Ed.), *Redefining the process of retirement: An international perspective.* Berlin: Springer-Verlag.

Burnette, E. (1996, January). Researchers work to prevent social ills: Psychologists are focusing more on preventing stressors that lead to family discord and mental health problems. *APA Monitor,* p. 32.

Burns, A. (1992). Mother-headed families: An international perspective and the case of Australia. *Social Policy Report of the Society for Research in Child Development, 6*(1).

Burns, B., & Taub, C. (1990). Mental health services in general medical care and nursing homes. In B. Fogel, A. Furino, & G. Gottlieb (Eds.), *Mental health policy for older Americans: Protecting minds at risk* (pp. 63–83). Washington, DC: American Psychiatric Press.

Burns, G. (1983). *How to live to be 100— or more: The ultimate diet, sex, and exercise book.* New York: Putnam.

Burns, J. F. (1994, August 27). India fights abortion of female fetuses. *The New York Times,* p. A5.

Burstin, H. R., Lipsitz, S. R., & Brennan, T. A. (1992). Socioeconomic status and risk for substandard medical care. *Journal of the American Medical Association, 268,* 2383–2387.

Burton, L. M. (1992). Black grandparents rearing children of drug-addicted parents: Stressors, outcomes, and social service needs. *The Gerontologist, 32,* 744–751.

Bushnell, E. W., & Boudreau, J. P. (1993). Motor development and the mind: The potential role of motor abilities as a determinant of aspects of perceptual development. *Child Development, 64,* 1005–1021.

Busse, E. W. (1987). Primary and secondary aging. In G. L. Maddox (Ed.), *The encyclopedia of aging* (p. 534). New York: Springer.

Butler, R. (1961). Re-awakening interests. *Nursing Homes: Journal of the American Nursing Home Association, 10,* 8–19.

Butler, R. (1996). The dangers of physician-assisted suicide. *Geriatrics, 51,* 7.

Butler, S., Gross, J., & Hayne, H. (1995). The effect of drawing on memory performance in young children. *Developmental Psychology, 31*(4), 597–608.

Butterfield, E., & Siperstein, G. (1972). Influence of contingent auditory stimulation upon nonnutritional suckle. In J. Bosma (Ed.), *Oral sensation and perception: The mouth of the infant.* Springfield, IL: Thomas.

Buunk, B. P. (1995). Sex, self-esteem, dependency, and extradyadic sexual experience as related to jealousy responses. *Journal of Social and Personal Relationships, 12,* 147–153.

Cabe-McGill, D. (1991, June). Endometriosis: Foreign lesions. *Harvard Health Letter,* pp. 4–7.

Cadwell, S. (1994, August). The psychological impact of HIV on gay men. *The Menninger Letter,* pp. 4–5.

Cahan, S., & Cohen, M. (1989). Age versus schooling effects on intelligence development. *Child Development, 60,* 1239–1249.

Cai, X., Golde, T. E., & Younkin, S. C. (1993). Release of excess amyloid B protein from a mutant amyloid B protein precursor. *Science, 259,* 514–516.

Cain, V. S., & Hofferth, S. L. (1989). Parental choice of self-care for school-age children. *Journal of Marriage and the Family, 51,* 65–77.

Cain, W. S., Reid, F., & Stevens, J. C. (1990). Missing ingredients: Aging and the discrimination of flavor. *Journal of Nutrition for the Elderly, 9,* 3–15.

Cairns, R. B., Cairns, B. D., & Neckerman, H. J. (1989). Early school dropout: Configurations and determinants. *Child Development, 60,* 1437–1452.

Calkins, S. D., & Fox, N. A. (1992). The relations among infant temperament, security of attachment, and behavioral inhibition at twenty-four months. *Child Development, 63,* 1456–1472.

Call, V., Sprecher, S., & Schwartz, P. (1995). The incidence and frequency of marital sex in a national sample. *Journal of Marriage and the Family, 57,* 639–652.

Callahan, D., & White, M. (1996). The legalization of physician-assisted suicide: Creating a regulatory Potemkin village. *University of Richmond Law Review, 30*(1), 1–83.

Callan, M. B. (1995). AIDS orphans. Review of AIDS and the new orphans: Coping with death. *Journal of the American Medical Association, 273*(24), 1960.

Calvert, S. L., & Huston, A. C. (1987). Television and children's gender schemata. In L. S. Liben & M. S. Signorella (Eds.), *Children's gender schemata.* San Francisco: Jossey-Bass.

Calvo, E. B., Galindo, A. C., & Aspres, N. B. (1992). Iron status in exclusively breast-fed infants. *Pediatrics, 90,* 375–379.

Camargo, C. A., Gaziano, M., Hennekens, C. H., Manson, J. E., & Stampfer, M. J. (1994, November). *Prospective study of moderate alcohol consumption and mortality in male physicians.* Paper presented at the 67th Annual Scientific Sessions of the American Heart Association, Dallas.

Camp, C. J. (1989). World-knowledge systems. In L. W. Poon, D. C. Rubin, & B. A. Wilson (Eds.), *Everyday cognition in adulthood and late life.* Cambridge: Cambridge University Press.

Camp, C. J., Doherty, K., Moody-Thomas, S., & Denney, N. W. (1989). Practical problem solving in adults: A comparison of problem types and scoring methods. In J. D. Sinnott (Ed.), *Everyday problem solving: Theory and applications* (pp. 211–228). New York: Praeger.

Camp, C. J., Foss, J. W., Stevens, A. B., Reichard, C. C., McKitrick, L. A., & O'Hanlon, A. M. (1993). Memory training in normal and demented populations: The E-I-E-I-O model. *Experimental Aging Research, 19,* 277–290.

Camp, C. J., Martley, R. P., & Kramer, J. J. (1983). Spontaneous use of mnemonics

by elderly individuals. *Educational Gerontology, 9,* 57–71.

Camp, C. J., & McKitrick, L. A. (1989). The dialectics of remembering and forgetting across the adult lifespan. In D. Kramer & M. Bopp (Eds.), *Dialectics and contextualism in clinical and developmental psychology: Change, transformation, and the social context* (pp. 169–187). New York: Springer.

Camp, C. J., & McKitrick, L. A. (1992). Memory interventions in Alzheimer's-type dementia populations: Methodological and theoretical issues. In R. L. West & J. D. Sinnott (Eds.), *Everyday memory and aging: Current research and methodology* (pp. 155–172). New York: Springer-Verlag.

Campbell, F. L., Townes, B. D., & Beach, L. R. (1982). Motivational bases of childbearing decisions. In G. L. Fox (Ed.), *The childbearing decision: Fertility, attitudes, and behavior.* Beverly Hills, CA: Sage.

Campbell, J., & Moyers, W. (1988). *The power of myth with Bill Moyers.* New York: Doubleday.

Campbell, S. B., Cohn, J. F., & Meyers, T. (1995). Depression in first-time mothers: Mother-infant interaction and depression chronicity. *Developmental Psychology, 31*(3), 349–357.

Campfield, L. A., Smith, F. J., Guisez, Y., Devos, R., & Burn, P. (1995). Recombinant mouse OB protein: Evidence for a peripheral signal linking adiposity and central neural networks. *Science, 269,* 546–549.

Campos, J., Bertenthal, B., & Benson, N. (1980, April). *Self-produced locomotion and the extraction of form invariance.* Paper presented at the meeting of the International Conference on Infant Studies, New Haven, CT.

Campos, J. J., Langer, A., & Krowitz, A. (1970). Cardiac responses on the visual cliff in prelocomotor human infants. *Science, 170,* 196–197.

Camras, L. A., Oster, H., Campos, J. J., Miyake, K., & Bradshaw, D. (1992). Japanese and American infants' responses to arm restraint. *Developmental Psychology, 28,* 578–583.

Cantor, J. (1994). Confronting children's fright responses to mass media. In D. Zillman, J. Bryant, & A. C. Huston (Eds.), *Media, children, and the family: Social scientific, psychoanalytic, and clinical perspectives.* Hillsdale, NJ: Erlbaum.

Caplan, M., Vespo, J., Pedersen, J., & Hay, D. F. (1991). Conflict and its resolution in small groups of one- and two-year olds. *Child Development, 62,* 1513–1524.

Caplan, N., Choy, M. H., & Whitmore, J. K. (1992, February). Indochinese refugee families and academic achievement. *Scientific American,* pp. 36–42.

Capon, N., Kuhn, D., & Carretero, M.

(1989). Consumer reasoning. In J. D. Sinnott (Ed.), *Everyday problem solving: Theory and application* (pp. 153–174). New York: Praeger.

Capute, A. J., Shapiro, B. K., & Palmer, F. B. (1987). Marking the milestones of language development. *Contemporary Pediatrics, 4*(4), 24.

Cargan, L. (1981). Singles: An examination of two stereotypes. *Family Relations, 30,* 377–385.

Carlo, G., Knight, G. P., Eisenberg, N., & Rotenberg, K. J. (1991). Cognitive processes and prosocial behaviors among children: The role of affective attributions and reconciliations. *Developmental Psychology, 27,* 456–461.

Carlson, B. E. (1984). The father's contribution to child care: Effects on children's perception of parental roles. *American Journal of Orthopsychiatry, 54*(1), 123–136.

Carnegie Corporation Task Force on Meeting the Needs of Young Children. (1994). *Starting points: Meeting the needs of our youngest children.* New York: Carnegie Corporation of New York.

Carpenter, M. W., Sady, S. P., Hoegsberg, B., Sady, M. A., Haydon, B., Cullinane, E. M., Coustan, D. R., & Thompson, P. D. (1988). Fetal heart rate response to maternal exertion. *Journal of the American Medical Association, 259*(20), 3006–3009.

Carrera, M. A. (1986, April). *Future directions in teen pregnancy prevention.* Talk presented to the annual meeting of the Society for the Scientific Study of Sex, Eastern Region.

Carstensen, L. L. (1991). Selectivity theory: Social activity in life-span context. In *Annual review of gerontology and geriatrics* (Vol. 11, pp. 195–217). New York: Springer.

Carstensen, L. L. (1995). Evidence for a life-span theory of socioemotional selectivity. *Current Directions in Psychological Science, 4,* 150–156.

Carstensen, L. L. (1996). Socioemotional selectivity: A life span developmental account of social behavior. In M. R. Merrens & G. G. Brannigan (Eds.), *The developmental psychologists: Research adventures across the life span* (pp. 251–272). New York: McGraw-Hill.

Caruso, D. (1993). Dimensions of quality in infants' exploratory competence at one year. *Infant Behavior and Development, 16*(4), 441–454.

Casaer, P. (1993). Old and new facts about perinatal brain development. *Journal of Child Psychology and Psychiatry, 34*(1), 101–109.

Case, R. (1985). *Intellectual development: Birth to adulthood.* Orlando, FL: Academic Press.

Case, R. (1992). Neo-Piagetian theories of child development. In R. Sternberg & C. Berg (Eds.), *Intellectual development.*

New York: Cambridge University Press.

Caserta, M. S., & Lund, D. A. (1993). Intrapersonal resources and the effectiveness of self-help groups for bereaved older adults. *The Gerontologist, 33,* 619–629.

Casper, L. M. (1996). *Who's minding our preschoolers?* (Current Population Reports, P-70-53). Washington, DC: U.S. Bureau of the Census.

Casper, R. C., & Offer, D. (1990). Weight and dieting concerns in adolescents, fashion or symptom? *Pediatrics, 86*(3), 384–390.

Caspi, A. (1993). Why maladaptive behaviors persist: Sources of continuity and change across the life course. In D. C. Funder, R. D. Parke, C. Tomlinson-Keasey, & K. Widaman (Eds.), *Studying lives through time: Personality and development* (pp. 343–376). Washington, DC: American Psychological Association.

Cassel, C. (1992). Ethics and the future of aging research: Promises and problems. *Generations, 16*(4), 61–65.

Castaneda, C. J. (1996, June 16). Right-to-die debate rages on. *Chicago Sun-Times,* p. 57.

Catania, J. A., Coates, T. J., Stall, R., Turner, H., et al. (1992). Prevalence of AIDS-related risk factors and condom use in the United States. *Science, 258,* 1101–1106.

Cattell, R. B. (1965). *The scientific analysis of personality.* Baltimore: Penguin.

Cavanaugh, J. C., Kramer, D. A., Sinnott, J. D., Camp, C. J., & Markley, R. P. (1985). On missing links and such: Interfaces between cognitive research and everyday problem solving. *Human Development, 28,* 146–168.

Cavanaugh, J. C., & Morton, K. R. (1989). Contextualism, naturalistic inquiry, and the need for new science: A rethinking of everyday memory aging and childhood sexual abuse. In D. A. Kramer & M. Bopp (Eds.), *Transformation in clinical and developmental psychology* (pp. 89–114). New York: Springer-Verlag.

Ceci, S., & Liker, J. (1986). A day at the races: A study of IQ, expertise, and cognitive complexity. *Journal of Experimental Psychology: General, 114,* 255–266.

Ceci, S. J. (1991). How much does schooling influence general intelligence and its cognitive components? A reassessment of the evidence. *Developmental Psychology, 27*(5), 703–722.

Ceci, S. J., & Bruck, M. (1993). Child witnesses: Translating research into policy. *Social Policy Report of the Society for Research in Child Development, VII,* 3.

Ceci, S. J., & Leichtman, M. DeS. (1992). "I know that you know that I know that you broke the toy": A brief report of recursive awareness among 3-year-

olds. In S. J. Ceci, M. DeS. Leichtman, & M. E. Putnick (Eds.), *Cognitive and social factors in early deception.* Hillsdale, NJ: Erlbaum.

Celis, W. (1990). More states are laying school paddle to rest. *The New York Times,* pp. A1, B12.

Center on Addiction and Substance Abuse at Columbia University (CASA). (1996, June). *Substance abuse and the American woman.* New York: Author.

Center on Elderly People Living Alone. (1995a, January). *Medicaid and long-term care for older people* (Public Policy Institute Fact Sheet FS18R). Washington, DC: American Association of Retired Persons.

Center on Elderly People Living Alone. (1995b, January). *Nursing homes* (Public Policy Institute Fact Sheet FS10R). Washington, DC: American Association of Retired Persons.

Center on Elderly People Living Alone. (1995c, April). *Long-term care* (Public Policy Institute Fact Sheet FS27-R). Washington, DC: American Association of Retired Persons.

Centers for Disease Control and Prevention (CDC). (1985, June 21). Suicide—United States, 1970–1980. *Morbidity and Mortality Weekly Report.*

Centers for Disease Control and Prevention (CDC). (1993). Rates of cesarean delivery—United States, 1991. *Morbidity and Mortality Weekly Report, 42,* 285–289.

Centers for Disease Control and Prevention (CDC). (1994a). Annual summary of births, marriages, divorces and deaths: United States, 1993. *Monthly Vital Statistics Report, 42*(13), 18–20. Hyattsville, MD: National Center for Health Statistics.

Centers for Disease Control and Prevention (CDC). (1994b). Health risk behaviors among adolescents who do and do not attend school—United States, 1992. *Journal of the American Medical Association, 271,* 1068–1070.

Centers for Disease Control and Prevention (CDC). (1994c). Homicides among 15- 19-year-old males—United States, 1963–1991. *Morbidity and Mortality Weekly Report, 43,* 725–727.

Centers for Disease Control and Prevention (CDC). (1994d, November 11). Prevalence of overweight among adolescents, United States, 1988–1991. *Morbidity and Mortality Weekly Report.*

Centers for Disease Control and Prevention (CDC). (1995a). Differences in maternal mortality among black and white women: United States, 1990. *Morbidity and Mortality Weekly Report, 44*(1), 6–7, 13–14.

Centers for Disease Control and Prevention (CDC). (1995b). Sociodemographic and behavioral characteristics associated with alcohol consumption during pregnancy—United States, 1988. *Morbidity and Mortality Weekly Report, 44,* 261–264.

Centers for Disease Control and Prevention (CDC). (1995c). Unpublished data.

Centers for Disease Control and Prevention (CDC). (1995d). Update: Trends in fetal alcohol syndrome—United States, 1979–1993. *Morbidity and Mortality Weekly Report, 44,* 249–251.

Centers for Disease Control and Prevention (CDC). (1996a, January). Recommendations for childhood immunization. Atlanta: Author.

Centers for Disease Control and Prevention (CDC). (1996b). Suicide among older persons—United States, 1980–1992. *Journal of the American Medical Association, 275,* 509.

Centers for Disease Control and Prevention (CDC). (1996c). Summary of notifiable diseases, United States, 1995. *Morbidity and Mortality Weekly Report, 44*(53), 1–13.

Centers for Disease Control and Prevention (CDC). (1996d, May 24). Tobacco use and usual source of cigarettes among high school students—United States, 1995. *Morbidity and Mortality Weekly Report, 45*(20), 413–418.

Chafetz, M. D. (1992). *Smart for life.* New York: Penguin.

Chalfie, D. (1994). *Going it alone: A closer look at grandparents parenting grandchildren.* Washington, DC: AARP Women's Initiative.

Chambre, S. M. (1993). Volunteerism by elders: Past trends and future prospects. *The Gerontologist, 33,* 221–227.

Chance, P., & Fischman, J. (1987). The magic of childhood. *Psychology Today, 21*(5), 48–58.

Chapman, A. H. (1974). *Management of emotional problems of children and adolescents* (2d ed.). Philadelphia: Lippincott.

Chapman, M., & Lindenberger, U. (1988). Functions, operations, and décalage in the development of transitivity. *Developmental Psychology, 24,* 542–551.

Chappell, N. L. (1991). Living arrangements and sources of caregiving. *Journal of Gerontology: Social Sciences, 46*(1), S1–8.

Chase-Lansdale, P. L., Cherlin, A. J., & Kiernan, K. E. (1995). The long-term effects of parental divorce on the mental health of young adults: A developmental perspective. *Child Development, 66,* 1614–1634.

Chasnoff, I. J., Griffith, D. R., Freier, C., & Murray, J. (1992). Cocaine/polydrug use in pregnancy: Two-year follow-up. *Pediatrics, 89*(2), 284–289.

Chasnoff, I. J., Griffith, D. R., MacGregor, S., Dirkes, K., & Burns, K. A. (1989). Temporal patterns of cocaine use in pregnancy: Perinatal outcomes. *Journal of the American Medical Association, 261*(12), 1741–1744.

Chasnoff, I. J., Lewis, D. E., & Squires, L. (1987). Cocaine intoxification in a breast-fed infant. *Pediatrics, 80,* 836–838.

Chatters, L. M., & Taylor, R. J. (1989). Age differences in religious participation among black adults. *Journal of Gerontology: Social Sciences, 44*(5), S183–189.

Chen, C., & Stevenson, H. W. (1989). Homework: A cross-cultural examination. *Child Development, 60,* 551–561.

Chen, C., & Stevenson, H. W. (1995). Motivation and mathematics achievement: A comparative study of Asian-American, Caucasian-American, and East Asian high school students. *Child Development, 66,* 1215–1234.

Chen, X., Rubin, K. H., & Li, Z. (1995). Social functioning and adjustment in Chinese children: A longitudinal study. *Developmental Psychology, 31*(4), 531–539.

Chen, X., Rubin, K. H., & Sun, Y. (1992). Social reputation and peer relationships in Chinese and Canadian children: A cross-cultural study. *Child Development, 63,* 1336–1343.

Cherlin, A., & Furstenberg, F. F. (1986a). Grandparents and family crisis. *Generations, 10*(4), 26–28.

Cherlin, A., & Furstenberg, F. F., Jr. (1986b). *The new American grandparent.* New York: Basic Books.

Cherry, K. E., & Park, D. C. (1993). Individual differences and contextual variables influence spatial memory in younger and older adults. *Psychology and Aging, 8,* 517–526.

Chervenak, F. A., Isaacson, G., & Mahoney, M. J. (1986). Advances in the diagnosis of fetal defects. *New England Journal of Medicine, 315*(5), 305–307.

Chess, S., & Thomas, A. (1982). Infant bonding: Mystique and reality. *American Journal of Orthopsychiatry, 52*(2), 213–222.

Children's Defense Fund. (1994). *The state of America's children yearbook, 1994.* Washington, DC: Author.

Children's Defense Fund. (1995). *The state of America's children yearbook, 1995.* Washington, DC: Author.

Children's Defense Fund. (1996). *The state of America's children yearbook, 1996.* Washington, DC: Author.

Chira, S. (1988, July 27). In Japan, the land of the rod, an appeal to spare the child. *The New York Times,* pp. A1, A10.

Chiriboga, D. (1982). Adaptation to marital separation in later and earlier life. *Journal of Gerontology, 37,* 109–114.

Chiriboga, D. (1989). Mental health at the midpoint: Crisis, challenge, or relief? In S. Hunter & M. Sundel (Eds.), *Midlife myths.* Newbury Park, CA: Sage.

Chisholm, J. S. (1983). *Navajo infancy: An ethological study of child development.* New York: Aldine.

Chissell, J. T. (1989, July). Paper presented at symposium on race, racism, and health at the 94th annual convention of the National Medical Association, Orlando, FL.

Choi, K.-H., Catania, J. A., & Dolcini, M. M. (1994). Extramarital sex and HIV risk behavior among US adults: Results from the national AIDS behavior survey. *American Journal of Public Health, 84,* 2003–2007.

Cholesterol: New advice. (1993, December). *University of California at Berkeley Wellness Letter,* pp. 4–6.

Chomitz, V. R., Cheung, L. W. Y., & Lieberman, E. (1995). The role of lifestyle in preventing low birth weight. *The Future of Children, 5*(1), 121–138.

Chomsky, C. S. (1969). *The acquisition of syntax in children from five to ten.* Cambridge, MA: MIT Press.

Chomsky, N. (1957). *Syntactic structures.* The Hague: Mouton.

Chomsky, N. (1965). *Aspects of a theory of syntax.* Cambridge, MA: MIT Press.

Chomsky, N. (1972). *Language and mind* (2d ed.). New York: Harcourt Brace Jovanovich.

Christen, W. G., Glynn, R. J., Manson, J. E., Ajani, U. A., & Buring, M. A. (1996). A prospective study of cigarette smoking and age-related macular degeneration in men. *Journal of the American Medical Association, 276,* 1147–1156.

Christie, J. F. (1991). *Psychological research on play: Connections with early literacy development.* Albany: SUNY P.

Chumlea, W. C. (1982). Physical growth in adolescence. In B. B. Wolman (Ed.), *Handbook of developmental psychology.* Englewood Cliffs, NJ: Prentice-Hall.

Cicirelli, V. G. (1976a). Family structure and interaction: Sibling effects on socialization. In M. F. McMillan & S. Henao (Eds.), *Child psychiatry: Treatment and research.* New York: Brunner/Mazel.

Cicirelli, V. G. (1976b). Siblings teaching siblings. In V. L. Allen (Ed.), *Children as teachers: Theory and research on tutoring.* New York: Academic Press.

Cicirelli, V. G. (1977). Relationship of siblings to the elderly person's feelings and concerns. *Journal of Gerontology, 12*(3), 317–322.

Cicirelli, V. G. (1980, December). *Adult children's views on providing services for elderly parents.* Report to the Andrus Foundation.

Cicirelli, V. G. (1981, April). *Interpersonal relationships of siblings in the middle part of the life span.* Paper presented at the biennial meeting of the Society for Research in Child Development, Boston.

Cicirelli, V. G. (1983). Adult children and their elderly parents. In T. H. Brubaker

(Ed.), *Family relationships in later life* (pp. 31–46). Newbury Park, CA: Sage.

Cicirelli, V. G. (1989a). Feelings of attachment to siblings and well-being in later life. *Psychology and Aging, 4*(2), 211–216.

Cicirelli, V. G. (1989b). Helping relationships in later life: A reexamination. In J. A. Mancini (Ed.), *Aging parents and adult children*. Lexington, MA: Heath.

Cicirelli, V. G. (1994). Sibling relationships in cross-cultural perspective. *Journal of Marriage and the Family, 56,* 7–20.

Clark, E. V. (1983). Meanings and concepts. In P. H. Mussen (Ed.), *Handbook of child psychology*. New York: Wiley.

Clark, L. F., & Collins, J. E. (1993). Remembering old flames: How the past affects assessment of the present. *Personality and Social Psychology Bulletin, 19,* 399–408.

Clarke, S. C. (1995, March 22). Advance report of final divorce statistics, 1989 and 1990. *Monthly Vital Statistics Report, 43*(9, supp.). Hyattsville, MD: National Center for Health Statistics.

Clarke-Stewart, A. (1977). *Child care in the family: A review of research and some propositions for policy*. New York: Academic Press.

Clarke-Stewart, A. (1992). Consequences of child care for children's development. In A. Booth (Ed.), *Child care in the 1990s: Trends and consequences*. Hillsdale, NJ: Erlbaum.

Clarke-Stewart, K. A. (1987). Predicting child development from day care forms and features: The Chicago study. In D. A. Phillips (Ed.), Quality in child care: What does the research tell us? *Research Monographs of the National Association for the Education of Young Children*. Washington, DC: National Association for the Education of Young Children.

Clarke-Stewart, K. A. (1989). Infant day care: Maligned or malignant? *American Psychologist, 44*(2), 266–273.

Clarkson-Smith, L., & Hartley, A. A. (1989). Relationship between physical exercise and cognitive abilities in older adults. *Psychology and Aging, 4*(2), 183–189.

Clausen, J. A. (1975). The social meaning of differential physical and sexual maturation. In S. E. Dragastin & G. H. Elder, Jr. (Eds.), *Adolescence in the life cycle*. New York: Halsted.

Clausen, J. A. (1993). *American lives*. New York: Free Press.

Clay, R. A. (1995a, November). Social forces foster workplace violence. *APA Monitor*, p. 37.

Clay, R. A. (1995b, November). Working mothers: Happy or haggard? *APA Monitor*, pp. 1, 37.

Clay, R. A. (1996, February). Beating the "biological clock" with zest. *APA Monitor*, p. 37.

Cleiren, M. P., Diekstra, R. F., Kerkhof, A. D., & van der Wal, J. (1994). Mode of death and kinship in bereavement: Focusing on "who" rather than "how." *Crisis, 14,* 22–36.

Clemens, A. W., & Axelson, L. J. (1985). The not-so-empty nest: Return of the fledgling adult. *Family Relations, 34,* 259–264.

Cobleigh, M. A., Berris, R. F., Bush, T., Davidson, N. E., Robert, N. J., Sparano, J. A., Tormey, D. C., & Wood, W. C. for the Breast Cancer Committee of the Eastern Cooperative Oncology Group. (1994, August 17). Estrogen replacement therapy in breast cancer survivors. *Journal of the American Medical Association, 272,* 540–545.

Cobrinck, P., Hood, R., & Chused, E. (1959). Effects of maternal narcotic addiction on the newborn infant. *Pediatrics, 24,* 288–290.

Cohen, G. D. (1987). Alzheimer's disease. In G. L. Maddox (Ed.), *Encyclopedia of aging* (pp. 27–30). New York: Springer.

Cohen, S. (1996). Psychological stress, immunity, and upper respiratory infections. *Current Directions in Psychological Science, 5,* 86–90.

Cohen, S., Tyrell, D. A. J., & Smith, A. P. (1991). Psychological stress and susceptibility to the common cold. *New England Journal of Medicine, 325,* 606–612.

Cohen, S., Tyrell, D. A. J., & Smith, A. P. (1993). Life events, perceived stress, negative affect and susceptibility to the common cold. *Journal of Personality and Social Psychology, 64,* 131–140.

Cohn, J. F., & Tronick, E. Z. (1983). Three-month-old infants' reaction to simulated maternal depression. *Child Development, 54,* 185–193.

Cohn, L. D. (1991). Sex differences in the course of personality development: A meta-analysis. *Psychological Bulletin, 109,* 252–266.

Coke, M. M. (1992). Correlates of life satisfaction among elderly African-Americans. *Journal of Gerontology: Psychological Sciences, 47*(5), P316–320.

Colby, A., & Damon, W. (1992). *Some do care: Contemporary lives of moral commitment*. New York: Free Press.

Colby, A., Kohlberg, L., Gibbs, J., & Lieberman, M. (1983). A longitudinal study of moral development. *Monographs of the Society for Research in Child Development, 48*(1–2, Serial No. 200).

Colditz, G. A., Hankinson, S. E., Hunter, D. J., Willett, W. C., Manson, J. E., Stampfer, M. J., Hennekens, C., Rosner, B., & Speizer, F. E. (1995). The use of estrogens and progestins and the risk of breast cancer in postmenopausal women. *New England Journal of Medicine, 332,* 1638–1639.

Cole, C., & Rodman, H. (1987). When school-age children care for themselves: Issues for family life educators and parents. *Family Relations, 36,* 92–96.

Cole, M., & Cole, S. R. (1989). *The development of children*. New York: Freeman.

Cole, P. M., Barrett, K. C., & Zahn-Waxler, C. (1992). Emotion displays in two-year-olds during mishaps. *Child Development, 63,* 314–324.

Coleman, J. (1980). Friendship and the peer group in adolescence. In J. Adelson (Ed.), *Handbook of adolescent development*. New York: Wiley.

Coleman, J. S. (1988). Social capital in the creation of human capital. *American Journal of Sociology, 94*(Suppl. 95), S95–120.

Coleman, K. A. (1995). The value of productive activities of older Americans. In S. A. Bass (Ed.), *Older and active: How Americans over 55 are contributing to society*. New Haven: Yale University Press.

Collier, V. P. (1995). Acquiring a second language for school. *Directions in Language and Education, 1*(4), 1–11.

Collins, C. (1994, November 10). Baby walkers: The question of safety. *The New York Times*, p. C2.

Collins, N. L., & Miller, L. C. (1994). Self-disclosure and liking: A meta-analytic review. *Psychological Bulletin, 116,* 457–475.

Collins, R. C., & Deloria, D. (1983). Head Start research: A new chapter. *Children Today, 12*(4), 15–19.

Collins, W. A. (1990). Parent-child relationships in transition to adolescence: Continuity and change in interaction, affect, and cognition. In R. Montemayor, G. R. Adams, & T. P. Gullotta (Eds.), *From childhood to adolescence: A transitional period?* Newbury Park, CA: Sage.

Commonwealth Fund Commission on Elderly People Living Alone. (1986). *Problems facing elderly Americans living alone*. New York: Harris & Associates.

Commonwealth Fund Commission on Elderly People Living Alone. (1992). *Study of elderly people in five countries— U.S., Canada, Germany, Britain, and Japan: Key findings*. New York: Harris & Associates.

Conger, J. J. (1988). Hostages to fortune: Youth, values, and the public interest. *American Psychologist, 43*(4), 291–300.

Conger, R. C., Ge, X., Elder, G. H., Lorenz, F. O., & Simons, R. L. (1994). Economic stress, coercive family processes, and developmental problems of adolescents. *Child Development, 65,* 541–561.

Connecticut Early Childhood Education Council (CECEC). (1983). *Report on full-day kindergarten*. Author.

Connidis, I. A. (1992). Life transitions and the adult sibling tie: A qualitative study. *Journal of Marriage and the Family, 54,* 972–982.

Connidis, I. A., & Davies, L. (1992). Confidants and companions: Choices in later life. *Journal of Gerontology: Social Sciences, 47*(30), S115–122.

Connor, E. M., Sperling, R. S., Gelber, R., et al. (1994). Reduction of maternal-infant transmission of human immunodeficiency virus type 1 with zidovudine treatment. *New England Journal of Medicine, 331*, 1173–1180.

Cooney, T. M., Hutchinson, M. K., & Leather, D. M. (1995). Parenting: Surviving the breakup? Predictors of parent-adult child relations after parental divorce. *Family Relations, 44*, 153–161.

Coons, S., & Guilleminault, C. (1982). Development of sleep-wake patterns and non–rapid eye movement sleep stages during the first six months of life in normal infants. *Pediatrics, 69*(6), 793–798.

Cooper, K. L., & Gutmann, D. L. (1987). Gender identity and ego mastery style in middle-aged, pre- and post-empty nest women. *The Gerontologist, 27*(3), 347–352.

Cooper, R. P., & Aslin, R. N. (1990). Preference for infant-directed speech in the first month after birth. *Child Development, 61*, 1584–1595.

Corbet, A., Long, W., Schumacher, R., Gerdes, J., Cotton, R., & the American Exosurf Neonatal Study Group 1. (1995). Double-blind developmental evaluation at 1-year corrected age of 597 premature infants with birth weights from 500 to 1350 grams enrolled in three placebo-controlled trials of prophylactic synthetic surfactant. *Journal of Pediatrics, 126*, S5–12.

Corbin, C. (1973). *A textbook of motor development.* Dubuque, IA: Brown.

Corbin, C. B., & Pangrazi, R. P. (1992). Are American children and youth fit? *Research Quarterly for Exercise and Sport, 63*(2), 96–106.

Corder, E. H., Saunders, A. M., Strittmatter, W. J., Schmechel, D. E., Gaskell, P. C., Small, G. M., Roses, A. D., Haines, J. L., & Pericak-Vance, M. A. (1993). Gene dose of apolipoprotein E type 4 allele and the risk of Alzheimer's disease in late onset families. *Science, 261*, 921–923.

Coren, S. (1992). *The left-hander syndrome: The causes and consequences of left-handedness.* New York: Free Press.

Coren, S., & Halpern, D. F. (1991). Left-handedness: A marker for decreased survival fitness. *Psychological Bulletin, 109*(1), 90–106.

Corijn, M., Liefbroer, A. C., & Gierveld, J. de J. (1996). It takes two to tango, doesn't it? The influence of couple characteristics on the timing of the birth of the first child. *Journal of Marriage and the Family, 58*, 117–126.

Corliss, J. (1996, October 29). Alzheimer's in the news. *HealthNews*, pp. 1–2.

Cornelius, S. W., & Caspi, A. (1987). Everyday problem solving in adulthood and old age. *Psychology and Aging, 2*, 144–153.

Costa, P. T., Jr., & McCrae, R. R. (1980). Still stable after all these years: Personality as a key to some issues in adulthood and old age. In P. B. Baltes, Jr., & O. G. Brim (Eds.), *Life-span development and behavior* (Vol. 3, pp. 65–102). New York: Academic Press.

Costa, P. T., Jr., & McCrae, R. R. (1988). Personality in adulthood: A six-year longitudinal study of self-reports and spouse ratings on the NEO Personality Inventory. *Journal of Personality and Social Psychology, 54*, 853–863.

Costa, P. T., Jr., & McCrae, R. R. (1994a). Set like plaster? Evidence for the stability of adult personality. In T. F. Heatherton & J. L. Weinberger (Eds.), *Can personality change?* (pp. 21–41). Washington, DC: American Psychological Association.

Costa, P. T., Jr., & McCrae, R. R. (1994b). Stability and change in personality from adolescence through adulthood. In C. F. Halverson, G. A. Kohnstamm, & R. P. Martin (Eds.), *The developing structure of temperament and personality from infancy to adulthood.* Hillsdale, NJ: Erlbaum.

Costa, P. T., Jr., McCrae, R. R., Zonderman, A. B., Barbano, H. E., Lebowitz, B., & Larson, D. M. (1986). Cross-sectional studies of personality in a national sample: 2. Stability in neuroticism, extraversion, and openness. *Psychology and Aging, 1*, 144–149.

Coster, W. J., Gersten, M. S., Beeghly, M., & Cicchetti, D. (1989). Communicative functioning in maltreated toddlers. *Developmental Psychology, 25*(6), 1020–1029.

Council on Ethical and Judicial Affairs. (1990). Black-white disparities in health care. *Journal of the American Medical Association, 263*, 2344–2346.

Council on Scientific Affairs, American Medical Association. (1989). Dyslexia. *Journal of the American Medical Association, 261*, 2236–2239.

Council on Scientific Affairs, American Medical Association. (1995). Female genital mutilation. *Journal of the American Medical Association, 274*(21), 1714–1716.

Courchesne, E., Yeung-Courchesne, R., Press, G. A., Hesselink, J. R., & Jernigan, T. L. (1988). Hypoplasia of cerebellar vermae lobules VI and VII in autism. *New England Journal of Medicine, 318*, 1349–1354.

Cowan, A. L., & Barron, J. (1992, November 22). Executives the economy left behind. *The New York Times*, Section 3, pp. 1, 6.

Cowan, M. W. (1979). The development of the brain. *Scientific American, 241*, 112–133.

Cox, J., Daniel, N., & Boston, B. O. (1985). *Educating able learners: Programs and promising practices.* Austin: University of Texas Press.

Cox, M. J., Owen, M. T., Henderson, V. K., & Margand, N. A. (1992). Prediction of infant-father and infant-mother attachment. *Developmental Psychology, 28*(3), 474–483.

Craft, M. J., Montgomery, L. A., & Peters, J. (1992, October). *Comparative study of responses in preschool children to the birth of an ill sibling.* Nursing seminar series presentation, University of Iowa College of Nursing, Iowa City.

Craik, F. I. M., & Byrd, M. (1982). Aging and cognitive deficits: The role of attentional resources. In F. I. M. Craik & S. Trehub (Eds.), *Aging and cognitive processes* (pp. 191–221). New York: Plenum.

Craik, F. I. M., & Jennings, J. M. (1992). Human memory. In F. I. M. Craik & T. A. Salthouse (Eds.), *Handbook of aging and cognition* (pp. 51–110). Hillsdale, NJ: Erlbaum.

Crain-Thoreson, C., & Dale, P. S. (1992). Do early talkers become early readers? Linguistic precocity, preschool language, and emergent literacy. *Developmental Psychology, 28*(3), 421–429.

Cramer, D. (1986). Gay parents and their children: A review of research and practical implications. *Journal of Counseling and Development, 64*, 504–507.

Crane, D. R., et al. (1995). Gender differences in cognitive and behavioral steps toward divorce. *American Journal of Family Therapy, 23*(2), 99–105.

Cratty, B. J. (1986). *Perceptual and motor development in infants and children* (3d ed.). Englewood Cliffs, NJ: Prentice-Hall.

Crockett, L. J., & Petersen, A. C. (1987). Pubertal status and psychosocial development: Findings from the Early Adolescent Study. In R. M. Lerner & T. T. Foch (Eds.), *Biological-psychosocial interactions in early adolescence: A life-span perspective.* Hillsdale, NJ: Erlbaum.

Cross-National Collaborative Group. (1992). The changing rate of major depression: Cross-national comparisons. *Journal of the American Medical Association, 268*(21), 3098–3105.

Crouter, A. C., MacDermid, S. M., McHale, S. M., & Perry-Jenkins, M. (1990). Parental monitoring and perception of children's school performance and conduct in dual- and single-earner families. *Developmental Psychology, 26*, 649–657.

Crouter, A. C., & McHale, S. M. (1993). Temporal rhythms in family life: Seasonal variation and the relation between parental work and family processes. *Developmental Psychology, 29*, 198–205.

Crow, J. F. (1993). How much do we know about spontaneous human mutation rates? *Environmental and Molecular Mutagenesis, 21,* 122–129.

Crow, J. F. (1994). Spontaneous mutation as a risk factor. *Experimental and Clinical Immunogenetics.*

Crowley, S. L. (1993, October). Grandparents to the rescue. *AARP Bulletin,* pp. 1, 16–17.

Crowley, S. L. (1994a, May). Much ado about menopause: Plenty of information but precious few answers. *AARP Bulletin,* pp. 2, 7.

Crowley, S. L. (1994b, June). Estrogen: Friend or foe? *AARP Bulletin,* pp. 2, 5.

Crown, W. H. (1993). Projecting the costs of aging populations. *Generations, 17*(4), 32–36.

Cruzan v. Director, Missouri Department of Health, 110 S. Ct. 2841 (1990).

Csikszentmihalyi, M., & Larson, R. (1984). *Being adolescent: Conflict and growth in the teenage years.* New York: Basic Books.

Cumming, E., & Henry, W. (1961). *Growing old.* New York: Basic Books.

Cummings, E. M., Iannotti, R. J., & Zahn-Waxler, C. (1989). Aggression between peers in early childhood: Individual continuity and developmental change. *Child Development, 60,* 887–895.

Cunningham, F. G., & Leveno, K. J. (1995). Childbearing among older women—The message is cautiously optimistic. *New England Journal of Medicine, 333,* 1002–1004.

Curtiss, S. (1977). *Genie.* New York: Academic Press.

Cushman, R., Down, J., MacMillan, N., & Waclawik, H. (1991). Helmet promotion in the emergency room following bicycle injury: A randomized trial. *Pediatrics, 88*(1), 43–47.

Cutler, N. E., & Devlin, S. J. (1996). A framework for understanding financial responsibility among generations. *Generations, 20*(1), 24–28.

Cutrona, C., Russell, D., & Rose, J. (1986). Social support and adaptation to stress by the elderly. *Psychology and Aging, 1*(1), 47–54.

Cutz, E., Perrin, D. G., Hackman, R., & Czegledy-Nagy, E. N. (1996). Maternal smoking and pulmonary neuroendocrine cells in sudden infant death syndrome. *Pediatrics, 88,* 668–672.

Cvetanovski, J., & Jex, S. (1994). Locus of control of unemployed people and its relationship to psychological and physical well-being. *Work and Stress, 8*(1), 60–67.

Cytrynbaum, S., Bluum, L., Patrick, R., Stein, J., Wadner, D., & Wilk, C. (1980). Midlife development: A personality and social systems perspective. In L. Poon (Ed.), *Aging in the 1980s.* Washington, DC: American Psychological Association.

Dainoff, M. (1989). Death and other losses. *Humanistic Judaism, 17*(3), 63–67.

Daiute, C., Hartup, W. W., Sholl, W., & Zajac, R. (1993, March). *Peer collaboration and written language development: A study of friends and acquaintances.* Paper presented at the meeting of the Society for Research in Child Development, New Orleans.

Daley, S. (1991, January 9). Little girls lose their self-esteem on the way to adolescence, study finds. *The New York Times,* p. B6.

D'Alton, M. E., & DeCherney, A. H. (1993). Prenatal diagnosis. *New England Journal of Medicine, 32*(2), 114–120.

Dan, A. J., & Bernhard, L. A. (1989). Menopause and other health issues for midlife women. In S. Hunter & M. Sundel (Eds.), *Midlife myths.* Newbury Park, CA: Sage.

Dan, A. J., & Monagle, L. (1994). Sociocultural influences on women's experiences of perimenstrual symptoms. In J. H. Gold & S. K. Severino (Eds.), *Premenstrual dysphorias: Myths and realities* (pp. 201–211). Washington, DC: American Psychiatric Press.

Daniels, D., & Plomin, R. (1985). Origins of individual differences in infant shyness. *Developmental Psychology, 21*(1), 118–121.

Danish, S. J. (1983). Musings about personal competence: The contributions of sport, health, and fitness. *American Journal of Community Psychology, 11*(3), 221–240.

Danish, S. J., & D'Augelli, A. R. (1980). Promoting competence and enhancing development through life development intervention. In L. A. Bond & J. C. Rosen (Eds.), *Competence and coping during adulthood.* Hanover, NH: University Press of New England.

Darlington, R. B. (1991). The long-term effects of model preschool programs. In L. Okagaki & R. J. Sternberg (Eds.), *Directors of development: Influences on the development of children's thinking.* Hillsdale, NJ: Erlbaum.

Datan, N., Rodeheaver, D., & Hughes, F. (1987). Adult development and aging. *Annual Review of Psychology, 38,* 153–180.

Davidson, J., & Smith, R. (1990). Traumatic experiences in psychiatric outpatients. *Journal of Traumatic Stress, 3,* 459–475.

Davidson, J. E., & Sternberg, R. J. (1984). The role of insight in intellectual giftedness. *Gifted Child Quarterly, 28*(2), 58–64.

Davidson, N. E. (1995). Hormone-replacement therapy—Breast versus heart versus bone. *New England Journal of Medicine, 332,* 1638–1639.

Davidson, R. J., & Fox, N. A. (1989). Frontal brain asymmetry predicts infants' response to maternal separation. *Journal of Abnormal Psychology, 948*(2), 58–64.

Davis, K. E. (1985, February). Near and dear: Friendship and love compared. *Psychology Today,* pp. 22–30.

Davis, K. L., et al. (1992). A double-blind placebo-controlled multicenter study of tacrine for Alzheimer's disease. *New England Journal of Medicine, 327,* 1253–1259.

Davis, M., & Emory, E. (1995). Sex differences in neonatal stress reactivity. *Child Development, 66,* 14–27.

Davis-Friedmann, D. (1983). *Long lives: Chinese elderly and the Communist revolution.* Cambridge, MA: Harvard University Press.

Davis-Friedmann, D. (1985). Chinese retirement: Policy and practices. In Z. S. Blau (Ed.), *Current perspectives on aging and the life cycle.* Greenwich, CT: JAI.

Dawson, D. A. (1991). Family structure and children's health and well-being: Data from the 1988 National Health Interview Survey on child health. *Journal of Marriage and the Family, 53,* 573–584.

Dawson, G., Klinger, L. G., Panagiotides, H., Hill, D., & Spieker, S. (1992). Frontal lobe activity and affective behavior of infants of mothers with depressive symptoms. *Child Development, 63,* 725–737.

Dawson, J. M., & Langan, P. A. (1994, July). *Murder in families* (Bureau of Justice Statistics Special Report). Washington, DC: U.S. Government Printing Office.

Dawson-Hughes, B., Dallal, G. E., Krall, E. A., Sadowski, L., Sahyoun, N., & Tannenbaum, S. (1990). A controlled trial of the effect of calcium supplementation on bone density in postmenopausal women. *New England Journal of Medicine, 323,* 878–883.

Day, J., & Curry, A. (1996, August). *Educational attainment in the United States: March 1995* (Current Population Reports, Publication No. P20–489). Washington, DC: U.S. Government Printing Office.

Day, R. D. (1992). The transition to first intercourse among racially and culturally diverse youth. *Journal of Marriage and the Family, 54,* 749–762.

DeAngelis, T. (1994, October). Loving styles may be determined in infancy. *American Psychological Association Monitor,* p. 21.

Deaux, K. (1985). Sex and gender. *Annual Review of Psychology, 36,* 49–81.

DeCasper, A., & Fifer, W. (1980). Newborns prefer their mothers' voices. *Science, 208,* 1174–1176.

DeCasper, A. J., Lecanuet, J.-P., Busnel, M.-C., Granier-Deferre, C., & Maugeais, R. (1994). Fetal reactions to recurrent maternal speech. *Infant Behavior and Development, 17,* 159–164.

DeCasper, A. J., & Spence, M. J. (1986). Prenatal maternal speech influences newborns' perceptions of speech sounds. *Infant Behavior and Development, 9,* 133–150.

DeFrain, J., & Ernst, L. (1978). The psychological effects of sudden infant death syndrome on surviving family members. *Journal of Family Practice,* 6(5), 985–989.

DeFrain, J., Taylor, J., & Ernst, L. (1982). *Coping with sudden infant death,* Lexington, MA: Heath.

DeFries, J. C., Fulker, D. W., & LaBuda, M. C. (1987). Evidence for a genetic etiology in reading disability of twins. *Nature, 329,* 537–539.

DeFries, P. J., Plomin, R., & Fulker, D. W. (1994). *Nature and nurture during middle childhood.* Cambridge, UK: Blackwell.

DeHaan, L. G., & MacDermid, S. M. (1994). Is women's identity achievement associated with the expression of generativity? Examining identity and generativity in multiple roles. *Journal of Adult Development, 1,* 235–247.

Dekovic, M., & Janssens, J. M. A. M. (1992). Parents' child-rearing style and child's sociometric status. *Developmental Psychology, 28,* 925–932.

de Lafuente, D. (1994, September 11). Fertility clinics: Trying to cut the cost of high-tech baby making. *Chicago Sun-Times,* p. 4C.

Delany, E., Delany, S., & Hearth, A. H. (1993). *The Delany sisters' first 100 years.* New York: Kodansha America.

Del Carmen, R. D., Pedersen, F. A., Huffman, L. C., & Bryan, Y. E. (1993). Dyadic distress management predicts subsequent security of attachment. *Infant Behavior and Development, 16,* 131–147.

DeMaris, A., & Swinford, S. (1996). Female victims of spousal violence. *Family Relations, 45,* 98–106.

Deming, W. (1994, February). Work at home: Data from the CPS. *Monthly Labor Review,* pp. 14–20.

Demo, D. H. (1991). A sociological perspective on parent-adolescent disagreements. In R. L. Paikoff (Ed.), Shared views in the family during adolescence. *New Directions for Child Development,* No. 51, pp. 111–118. San Francisco: Jossey-Bass.

Demo, D. H. (1992). Parent-child relations: Assessing recent changes. *Journal of Marriage and the Family, 54,* 104–117.

Denney, N. W. (1972). Free classification in preschool children. *Child Development, 43,* 1161–1170.

Denney, N. W., & Palmer, A. M. (1981). Adult age differences on traditional and practical problem-solving measures. *Journal of Gerontology, 36*(3), 323–328.

Denney, N. W., & Pearce, K. A. (1989). A developmental study of practical problem solving in adults. *Psychology and Aging, 4*(4), 438–442.

Dennis, W. (1960). Causes of retardation among institutional children: Iran. *Journal of Genetic Psychology, 96,* 47–59.

Denny, F. W., & Clyde, W. A. (1983). Acute respiratory tract infections: An overview. In W. A. Clyde & F. W. Denny (Eds.), Workshop on acute respiratory diseases among children of the world. *Pediatric Research, 17,* 1026–1029.

Depression. (1995, March). *Harvard Women's Health Watch,* pp. 2–3.

Desmond, E. W. (1996, April 22). Rarely has a country fallen so far so fast as Japan has in the past five years. What went wrong? *Time,* pp. 60–64.

Dewey, K. G., Heinig, M. J., & Nommsen-Rivers, L. A. (1995). Differences in morbidity between breast-fed and formula-fed infants. *Journal of Pediatrics, 126,* 696–702.

Deykin, E. Y., Alpert, J. J., & McNamara, J. J. (1985). A pilot study of the effect of exposure to child abuse or neglect on adolescent suicidal behavior. *American Journal of Psychiatry, 142*(11), 1299–1303.

Diaz, R. M. (1983). Thought and two languages: The impact of bilingualism on cognitive development. *Review of Research in Education, 10,* 23–54.

Dickinson, D. K., Cote, L., & Smith, M. W. (1993). Learning vocabulary in preschool: Social and discourse contexts affecting vocabulary growth. In C. Daiute (Ed.), The development of literacy through social interaction. *New Directions for Child Development,* No. 61, pp. 67–78. San Francisco: Jossey-Bass.

Dickstein, S., & Parke, R. D. (1988). Social referencing in infancy: A glance at fathers and marriage. *Child Development, 59,* 506–511.

Diehl, M., Coyle, N., & Labouvie-Vief, G. (1996). Age and sex differences in strategies of coping and defense across the life span. *Psychology and Aging, 11*(1), 127–139.

Diehl, M., Willis, S. L., & Schaie, K. W. (1994). *Practical problem solving in older adults: Observational assessment and cognitive correlates.* Unpublished manuscript, Wayne State University, Detroit.

Dien, D. S. F. (1982). A Chinese perspective on Kohlberg's theory of moral development. *Developmental Review, 2,* 331–341.

Dietrich, K. N., Berger, O. G., & Succop, P. A. (1993). Lead exposure and the motor developmental status of urban six-year-old children in the Cincinnati Prospective Study. *Pediatrics, 91,* 301–307.

Dietz, W. H., & Gortmaker, S. L. (1985). Do we fatten our children at the television set? Obesity and television viewing in children and adolescents. *Pediatrics, 75,* 807–812.

DiFranza, J. R., & Lew, R. A. (1995, April). Effect of maternal cigarette smoking on pregnancy complications and sudden infant death syndrome. *Journal of Family Practice, 40,* 385–394.

DiGiulio, J. F. (1992). Early widowhood: An atypical transition. *Journal of Mental Health Counseling, 14,* 97–109.

DiLalla, L. F., Kagan, J., & Reznick, J. S. (1994). Genetic etiology of behavioral inhibition among 2-year-old children. *Infant Behavior and Development, 17,* 405–412.

Dimant, R. J., & Bearison, D. J. (1991). Development of formal reasoning during successive peer interactions. *Developmental Psychology, 27*(2), 277–284.

Dishion, T. J., Patterson, G. R., Stoolmiller, M., & Skinner, M. L. (1991). Family, school, and behavioral antecedents to early adolescent involvement with antisocial peers. *Developmental Psychology, 27*(1), 172–180.

Dittman-Kohli, F., & Baltes, P. B. (1990). Toward a neofunctionalist conception of adult intellectual development: Wisdom as a prototypical case of intellectual growth. In C. N. Alexander & E. J. Langer (Eds.), *Higher stages of human development: Perspectives on adult growth* (pp. 54–78). New York: Oxford University Press.

Dixon, R. A. (1992). Contextual approaches to adult intellectual development. In R. Sternberg & C. A. Berg (Eds.), *Intellectual development.* Cambridge, UK: Cambridge University Press.

Dixon, R. A., & Baltes, P. B. (1986). Toward life-span research on the functions and pragmatics of intelligence. In R. J. Sternberg & R. K. Wagner (Eds.), *Practical intelligence: Nature and origins of competence in the everyday world* (pp. 203–235). New York: Cambridge University Press.

Dixon, R. A., Hultsch, D. F., & Herzog, C. (1988). The metamemory in adulthood (MIA) questionnaire. *Psychopharmacology Bulletin, 24,* 671–688.

Dodge, K. A., Bates, J. E., & Pettit, G. S. (1990). Mechanisms in the cycle of violence. *Science, 250,* 1678–1683.

Dodge, K. A., Coie, J. D., Pettit, G. S., & Price, J. M. (1990). Peer status and aggression in boys' groups: Developmental and contextual analysis. *Child Development, 61,* 1289–1309.

Dodge, K. A., Pettit, G. S., & Bates, J. E. (1994). Socialization mediators of the relation between socioeconomic status and child conduct problems. *Child Development, 65,* 649–665.

Doering, C. H., Kraemer, H. C., Brodie, H. K. H., & Hamburg, D. A. (1975). A cycle of plasma testosterone in the human male. *Journal of Clinical Endocrinology and Metabolism, 40,* 492–500.

Does exercise boost immunity? (1995, April). *Consumer Reports on Health,* pp. 37–39.

Doherty, W. J., & Allen, W. (1994). Family functioning and parental smoking as predictors of adolescent cigarette use: A six-year prospective study. *Journal of Family Psychology, 8*(3), 347–353.

Doka, K. J., & Mertz, M. E. (1988). The meaning and significance of great-grandparenthood. *The Gerontologist, 28*(2), 192–197.

Donnelly, D., & Finkelhor, D. (1992). Does equality in custody arrangement improve the parent-child relationship? *Journal of Marriage and the Family, 54*, 837–845.

Doppelt, J. E., & Wallace, W. L. (1955). Standardization of the Wechsler Adult Intelligence Scale for older persons. *Journal of Abnormal and Social Psychology, 51*, 312–330.

Dore, J. (1975). Holophrases, speech acts, and language universals. *Journal of Child Language, 2*, 21–40.

Doris, J. (1993). Paper presented at the Child Witness Conference. Family Life Development Center, Cornell University, New York.

Dornbusch, S. M., Ritter, P. L., Leiderman, P. H., Roberts, D. F., & Fraleigh, M. J. (1987). The relation of parenting style to adolescent school performance. *Child Development, 58*, 1244–1257.

Dougherty, D. M. (1993). Adolescent health. *American Psychologist, 48*(2), 193–201.

Dove, J. (undated). *Facts about anorexia nervosa.* Bethesda, MD: National Institutes of Health, Office of Research Reporting, National Institute of Child Health and Human Development.

Downs, H. (1993, February 28). My father's new life. *Parade,* p. 12.

Dreher, M. C., Nugent, K., & Hudgins, R. (1994). Prenatal marijuana exposure and neonatal outcomes in Jamaica: An ethnographic study. *Pediatrics, 93*, 254–260.

Dreyer, P. H. (1982). Sexuality during adolescence. In B. B. Wolman (Ed.), *Handbook of developmental psychology.* Englewood Cliffs, NJ: Prentice-Hall.

Dreyfus, H. L. (1993–1994, Winter). What computers still can't do. *Key Reporter,* pp. 4–9.

Dubas, J. S. (1992, March). The long term effects of pubertal timing on achievement, work, and family roles. Poster presented at the biennial meeting of the Society for Research on Adolescence, Washington, DC.

Duncan, B., Ey, J., Holberg, C. J., Wright, A. L., Martinez, F. D., & Taussig, L. M. (1993). Exclusive breast-feeding for at least four months protects against otitis media. *Pediatrics, 91*, 867–872.

Duncan, G. J., Brooks-Gunn, J., & Klebanov, P. K. (1994). Economic deprivation and early childhood development. *Child Development, 65*, 296–318.

Dunham, P. J., Dunham, F., & Curwin, A. (1993). Joint-attentional states and lexical acquisition at 18 months. *Developmental Psychology, 29*, 827–831.

Dunn, J. (1983). Sibling relationships in early childhood. *Child Development, 54*, 787–811.

Dunn, J. (1985). *Sisters and brothers.* Cambridge, MA: Harvard University Press.

Dunn, J. (1991). Young children's understanding of other people: Evidence from observations within the family. In D. Frye & C. Moore (Eds.), *Children's theories of mind: Mental states and social understanding.* Hillsdale, NJ: Erlbaum.

Dunn, J., Brown, J., Slomkowski, C., Tesla, C., & Youngblade, L. (1991). Young children's understanding of other people's feelings and beliefs: Individual differences and antecedents. *Child Development, 62*, 1352–1366.

Dunn, J., & Kendrick, C. (1982). *Siblings: Love, envy and understanding.* Cambridge, MA: Harvard University Press.

Dunne, R. G., Asher, K. N., & Rivara, F. P. (1992). Behavior and parental expectations of child pedestrians. *Pediatrics, 89*(3), 486–490.

DuPont, R. L. (1983). Phobias in children. *Journal of Pediatrics, 102*, 999–1002.

Durlak, J. A. (1973). Relationship between attitudes toward life and death among elderly women. *Developmental Psychology, 8*(1), 146.

Dustman, R. E., Emmerson, R. Y., Steinhaus, L. A., Shearer, D. E., & Dustman, T. J. (1992). The effects of videogame playing on neuropsychological performance of elderly individuals. *Journal of Gerontology: Psychological Sciences, 47*(3), P168–171.

Dwyer, T., Ponsonby, A. L., Blizzard, L., Newman, N. M., & Cochrane, J. A. (1995). The contribution of changes in the prevalence of prone sleeping position to the decline in sudden infant death syndrome in Tasmania. *Journal of the American Medical Association, 273*, 783–789.

Dwyer, T., Ponsonby, A. B., Newman, N. M., & Gibbons, L. E. (1991). Prospective cohort study of prone sleeping position and sudden infant death syndrome. *The Lancet, 337*, 1244–1247.

Dychtwald, K., & Flower, J. (1990). *Age wave: How the most important trend of our time will change your future.* New York: Bantam.

Dykstra, P. A. (1995). Loneliness among the never and formerly married: The importance of supportive friendships and a desire for independence. *Journal of Gerontology: Social Sciences, 50B*, S321–329.

Dyslexia. (1989, September 23). *The Lancet,* pp. 719–720.

Dyson, A. H. (1993). A sociocultural perspective on symbolic development in primary grade classrooms. In C. Daiute (Ed.), The development of literacy through social interaction. *New Directions for Child Development,* No. 61, pp. 25–39. San Francisco: Jossey-Bass.

Easterbrooks, M. A., & Goldberg, W. A. (1984). Toddler development in the family: Impact of father involvement and parenting characteristics. *Child Development, 55*, 740–752.

Eastman, P. (1995, December). The most vulnerable of hearts: Older women and blacks at the greatest risk. *AARP Bulletin,* pp. 1, 13.

Eccles, J. S., Midgley, C., Wigfield, A., Buchanan, C. M., Reuman, D., Flanagan, C., & MacIver, D. (1993). Development during adolescence: The impact of stage-environment on young adolescents' experiences in schools and in families. *American Psychologist, 48*(2), 90–101.

Echeland, Y., Epstein, D. J., St-Jacques, B., Shen, L., Mohler, J., McMahon, J. A., & McMahon, A. P. (1993). Sonic hedgehog, a member of a family of putative signality molecules, is implicated in the regulation of CNS polarity. *Cell, 75*, 1417–1430.

Eckenrode, J., Laird, M., & Doris, J. (1993). School performance and disciplinary problems among abused and neglected children. *Developmental Psychology, 29*(1), 53–62.

Eckerman, C. O., Davis, C. C., & Didow, S. M. (1989). Toddlers' emerging ways of achieving social coordination with a peer. *Child Development, 60*, 440–453.

Eckerman, C. O., & Stein, M. R. (1982). The toddler's emerging interactive skills. In K. H. Rubin & H. S. Ross (Eds.), *Peer relationships and social skills in childhood.* New York: Springer-Verlag.

Edelstein, S. (1990, December–1991, January). Do grandparents have rights? *Modern Maturity,* pp. 40–41.

Edlin, B. R., Irwin, K. L., Farugue, S., McCoy, C. B., Word, C., Serrano, Y., Inciardi, J. A., Bowser, B. P., Schilling, R. F., Holmberg, S. D., & Multicenter Crack Cocaine and HIV Infection Study Team. (1994, November 24). Intersecting epidemics—Crack cocaine use and HIV infection among inner-city young adults. *New England Journal of Medicine, 331*, 1422–1427.

Edson, L. (1968, August 18). To hell with being discovered when you're dead. *The New York Times Magazine,* pp. 26–27, 29–31, 34–36, 41, 44–46.

Edwards, C. P. (1977). The comparative study of the development of moral judgment and reasoning. In R. Monroe, R. Monroe, & B. B. Whiting (Eds.), *Handbook of cross-cultural human development.* New York: Garland.

Effective solutions for impotence. (1994, October). *Johns Hopkins Medical Letter: Health after 50,* pp. 2–3.

Effects of open adoption vary. (1995, May). *The Menninger Letter,* p. 3.

Egbuono, L., & Starfield, B. (1982). Child health and social status. *Pediatrics, 69*(5), 550–557.

Egeland, B., & Farber, E. A. (1984). Infant-mother attachment: Factors related to its development and changes over time. *Child Development, 55,* 753–771.

Egeland, B., Jacobvitz, D., & Sroufe, L. A. (1988). Breaking the cycle of abuse. *Child Development, 59,* 1080–1088.

Egeland, B., & Sroufe, L. A. (1981). Attachment and early maltreatment. *Child Development, 52,* 44–52.

Egertson, H. A. (1987, May 20). Recapturing kindergarten for 5-year-olds. *Education Week,* pp. 28, 19.

Ehrhardt, A. A., & Money, J. (1967). Progestin induced hermaphroditism: I. Q. and psychosocial identity. *Journal of Sexual Research, 3,* 83–100.

Eiberg, H., Berendt, I., & Mohr, J. (1995). Assignment of dominant inherited nocturnal enuresis (ENUR1) to chromosome 13q. *Nature Genetics, 10,* 354–356.

Eichorn, D. H., Clausen, J. A., Haan, N., Honzik, M. P., & Mussen, P. H. (Eds.), (1981). *Present and past in middle life.* New York: Academic Press.

Eiden, R. D., Teti, D. M., & Corns, K. M. (1995). Maternal working models of attachment, marital adjustment, and the parent-child relationship. *Child Development, 66,* 1504–1518.

Eiger, M. S., & Olds, S. W. (1987). *The complete book of breastfeeding* (rev. ed.). New York: Workman.

Eimas, P. (1985). The perception of speech in early infancy. *Scientific American, 252*(1), 46–52.

Eimas, P., Siqueland, E., Jusczyk, P., & Vigorito, J. (1971). Speech perception in infants. *Science, 171,* 303–306.

Einbender, A. J., & Freidrich, W. N. (1989). Psychological functioning and behavior of sexually abused girls. *Journal of Consulting and Clinical Psychology, 57*(1), 155–157.

Eisen, L. N., Field, T. M., Bandstra, E. S., Roberts, J. P., Morrow, C., Larsen, S. K., & Steele, B. M. (1991). Perinatal cocaine effects on neonatal stress behavior and performance on the Brazelton scale. *Pediatrics, 88*(3), 477–480.

Eisen, M., & Zellman, G. L. (1987). Changes in incidence of sexual intercourse of unmarried teenagers following a community-based sex education program. *Journal of Sex Research, 23*(4), 527–544.

Eisenberg, L. (1995, Spring). Is the family obsolete? *Key Reporter,* pp. 1–5.

Eisenberg, N. (1992). *The caring child.* Cambridge, MA: Harvard University Press.

Eisenberg, N., Fabes, R. A., Schaller, M., & Miller, P. A. (1989). Sympathy and personal distress: Development, gender differences, and interrelations of indexes. In N. Eisenberg (Ed.), *Empathy and related emotional responses. New Directions for Child Development,* No. 44. San Francisco: Jossey-Bass.

Eisenson, J., Auer, J. J., & Irwin, J. V. (1963). *The psychology of communication.* New York: Appleton-Century-Crofts.

Elder, G. H., Jr., & Pavalko, E. K. (1993). Work careers in men's later years: Transitions, trajectories, and historical change. *Journal of Gerontology: Social Sciences, 48,* S180–191.

Eley, J. W., Hill, H. A., Chen, V. W., Austin, D. F., Wesley, M. N., Muss, H. B., Greenberg, R. S., Coates, R. J., Correa, O., Redmond, C. K., Hunter, C. P., Herman, A. A., Kurman, R., Blacklow, R., Shapiro, S., & Edwards, B. K. (1994, September 28). Racial differences in survival from breast cancer. *Journal of the American Medical Association, 272,* 199–208.

Elkind, D. (1981). *The hurried child.* Reading, MA: Addison-Wesley.

Elkind, D. (1984). *All grown up and no place to go.* Reading, MA: Addison-Wesley.

Elkind, D. (1986). *The miseducation of children: Superkids at risk.* New York: Knopf.

Elliott, D. S. (1993). Health enhancing and health compromising lifestyles. In S. G. Millstein, A. C. Petersen, & E. O. Nightingale (Eds.), *Promoting the health of adolescents: New directions for the twenty-first century.* New York: Oxford University Press.

Ellis, L., & Ames, M. A. (1987). Neurohormonal functioning and sexual orientation: A theory of homosexuality-heterosexuality. *Psychological Bulletin, 101*(2), 233–258.

Emde, R. N. (1992). Individual meaning and increasing complexity: Contributions of Sigmund Freud and René Spitz to developmental psychology. *Developmental Psychology, 28*(3), 347–359.

Emde, R. N., Plomin, R., Robinson, J., Corley, R., DeFries, J., Fulker, D. W., Reznick, J. S., Campos, J., Kagan, J., & Zahn-Waxler, C. (1992). Temperament, emotion, and cognition at 14 months: The MacArthur longitudinal twin study. *Child Development, 63,* 1437–1455.

Emery, R. E. (1988). *Marriage, divorce, and children's adjustment.* Newbury Park, CA: Sage.

Emery, R. E. (1989). Family violence. *American Psychologist, 44*(2), 321–328.

Emery, R. E. (1995). Divorce mediation: Negotiating agreements and renegotiating relationships. *Family Relations, 44,* 377–383.

Environmental tobacco smoke: Health effects and prevention policies. (1994, October). *Archives of Family Medicine, 3,* 865–871.

Epstein, E., & Gutmann, R. (1984). Mate selection in man: Evidence, theory, and outcome. *Social Biology, 31,* 243–278.

Epstein, L. H., & Wing, R. R. (1987). Behavioral treatment of childhood obesity. *Psychological Bulletin, 101*(3), 331–342.

Epstein, R. A. (1989, Spring). Voluntary euthanasia. *Law School Record* (University of Chicago), pp. 8–13.

Epstein, S. (1990). Cognitive-experiential self-theory. In L. A. Pervin (Ed.), *Handbook of personality theory and research* (pp. 165–192). New York: Guilford.

Erikson, E. H. (1950). *Childhood and society.* New York: Norton.

Erikson, E. H. (1968). *Identity: Youth and crisis.* New York: Norton.

Erikson, E. H. (1973). The wider identity. In K. Erikson (Ed.), *In search of common ground: Conversations with Erik H. Erikson and Huey P. Newton.* New York: Norton.

Erikson, E. H. (1982). *The life cycle completed.* New York: Norton.

Erikson, E. H. (1985). *The life cycle completed* (paperback reprint ed.). New York: Norton.

Erikson, E. H., Erikson, J. M., & Kivnick, H. Q. (1986). *Vital involvement in old age: The experience of old age in our time.* New York: Norton.

Eron, L. D. (1980). Prescription for reduction of aggression. *American Psychologist, 35,* 244–252.

Eron, L. D. (1982). Parent-child interaction, television violence, and aggression in children. *American Psychologist, 37,* 197–211.

Espinosa, M. P., Sigman, M. D., Neumann, C. G., Bwibo, N. O., & McDonald, M. A. (1992). Playground behavior of school-age children in relation to nutrition, schooling, and family characteristics. *Developmental Psychology, 28,* 1188–1195.

Essex, M. J., & Nam, S. (1987). Marital status and loneliness among older women: The differential importance of close family and friends. *Journal of Marriage and the Family, 49,* 93–106.

Ettinger, B., Friedman, G. D., Bush, T., & Quesenberry, C. P. (1996). Reduced mortality associated with long-term postmenopausal estrogen therapy. *Obstetrics & Gynecology, 87,* 6–12.

European Collaborative Study. (1994). Natural history of vertically acquired human immunodeficiency virus-1 infection. *Pediatrics, 94,* 815–819.

Evans, D. A., Funkenstein, H., Albert, M. A., Scherr, P. A., Cook, N. R., Chown, M. J., Hebert, L. E., Hennekens, C. H., & Taylor, J. O. (1989). Prevalence of Alzheimer's disease in a community population of older persons: Higher than previously reported. *Journal of the American Medical Association, 262*(18), 2551–2556.

Evans, G. (1976). The older the sperm ... *Ms., 4*(7), 48–49.

Evans, J. (1994). *Caring for the caregiver: Body, mind and spirit.* New York: American Parkinson Disease Association.

Evans, N., Farkas, A., Gilpin, E., Berry, C., & Pierce, J. P. (1995). Influence of tobacco marketing and exposure to smoking on adolescent susceptibility to smoking. *Journal of the National Cancer Institute, 87,* 1538–1545.

Evans, R. I. (1967). *Dialogue with Erik Erikson.* New York: Harper & Row.

Everson, S. A., Kaplan, G. A., Goldberg, D. E., & Salonen, J. T. (1996). Anticipatory blood pressure response to exercise predicts future high blood pressure in middle-aged men. *Hypertension, 27,* 1059–1064.

Ewigman, B. G., Crane, J. P., Frigoletto, F. D., LeFevre, M. L., Bain, R. P., McNellis, D., & the RADIUS Study Group. (1993). Effect of prenatal ultrasound screening on perinatal outcome. *New England Journal of Medicine, 329,* 821–827.

Fabes, R. A., & Eisenberg, N. (1992). Young children's coping with interpersonal anger. *Child Development, 63,* 116–128.

Fagen, J. W., Morrongiello, B. A., Rovee-Collier, C., & Gekoski, M. J. (1984). Expectancies and memory retrieval in three-month-old infants. *Child Development, 55,* 936–943.

Fagot, B. I., & Hagan, R. (1991). Observations of parent reaction to sex-stereotyped behaviors: Age and sex effects. *Child Development, 62,* 617–628.

Falbo, T., & Polit, D. F. (1986). Quantitative review of the only child literature: Research evidence and theory development. *Psychological Bulletin, 100*(2), 176–189.

Falbo, T., & Poston, D. L. (1993). The academic, personality, and physical outcomes of only children in China. *Child Development, 64,* 18–35.

Fantz, R. L. (1963). Pattern vision in newborn infants. *Science, 140,* 296–297.

Fantz, R. L. (1964). Visual experience in infants: Decreased attention to familiar patterns relative to novel ones. *Science, 146,* 668–670.

Fantz, R. L., Fagen, J., & Miranda, S. B. (1975). Early visual selectivity. In L. Cohen & P. Salapatek (Eds.), *Infant perception: From sensation to cognition: Vol. 1. Basic visual processes* (pp. 249–341). New York: Academic Press.

Fantz, R. L., & Nevis, S. (1967). Pattern preferences and perceptual-cognitive development in early infancy. *Merrill-Palmer Quarterly, 13,* 77–108.

Farlow, M., Graycon, S. I., Hershey, L. A., Lewis, K. W., Sadowsky, C. H., Dolan-Ureno, J., for the Tacrine Study Group. (1992). A controlled trial of tacrine in Alzheimer's disease. *Journal of the American Medical Association, 268,* 2523–2529.

Farnsworth, C. H. (1994, April 5). Quebec bets on subsidized milk, mother's kind. *The New York Times,* p. A4.

Farrell, C., Palmer, A. T., Atchison, S., & Andelman, B. (1994, September 12). The economics of aging: Why the growing number of elderly won't bankrupt America. *Business Week,* pp. 60–68.

Farrell, M. P., & Rosenberg, S. D. (1981). *Men at midlife.* Boston: Auburn.

Farrow, J. A., Rees, J. M., & Worthington-Roberts, B. S. (1987). Health, developmental, and nutritional status of adolescent alcohol and marijuana abusers. *Pediatrics, 79*(2), 218–223.

Farver, J. A. M., Kim, Y. K., & Lee, Y. (1995). Cultural differences in Korean- and Anglo-American preschoolers' social interaction and play behavior. *Child Development, 66,* 1088–1099.

Feagans, L. (1983). A current view of learning disabilities. *Journal of Pediatrics, 102*(4), 487–493.

Federal Bureau of Investigation (FBI). (1991). *Uniform crime reports for the United States: 1990.* Washington, DC: U.S. Government Printing Office.

Federal Glass Ceiling Commission. (1995). *Good for business: Making full use of the nation's human capital: The environmental scam.* Washington, DC: U.S. Department of Labor.

Feifel, H. (1977). *New meanings of death.* New York: McGraw-Hill.

Fein, G. (1981). Pretend play in childhood: An integrative review. *Child Development, 52,* 1095–1118.

Feinman, S., & Lewis, M. (1983). Social referencing at ten months: A second-order effect on infants' responses. *Child Development, 54,* 878–887.

Feldhusen, J. F., & Moon, S. M. (1992). Grouping gifted students: Issues and concerns. *Gifted Child Quarterly, 36*(2), 63–67.

Feldman, H., Goldin-Meadow, S., & Gleitman, L. (1979). Beyond Herodotus: The creation of language by linguistically deprived deaf children. In A. Lock (Ed.), *Action, gesture and symbol: The emergence of language.* New York: Academic Press.

Feldman, R. D. (1982). *Whatever happened to the quiz kids: Perils and profits of growing up gifted.* Chicago: Chicago Review Press.

Feldman, R. D. (1985, August 6). Libraries open the books on local adult illiteracy. *Chicago Sun-Times School Guide,* pp. 10–11.

Feldman, R. D. (1986, April). What are thinking skills? *Instructor,* pp. 62–71.

Feldman, R. S. (1993). *Understanding psychology* (3d ed.). New York: McGraw-Hill.

Fellin, P. A., & Powell, T. J. (1988). Mental health services and older adult minorities: An assessment. *The Gerontologist, 28*(4), 442–446.

Felner, R. D., Brand, S., DuBois, D. L., Adan, A. M., Mulhall, P. F., & Evans, E. G. (1995). Socioeconomic disadvantage, proximal environmental experiences, and socioemotional and academic adjustment in early adolescence: Investigation of a mediated effect. *Child Development, 66,* 774–792.

Felson, D. T., Zhang, Y., Hannan, M., Kiel, D. P., Wilson, P. F. W., & Anderson, J. J. (1993, October 14). The effect of postmenopausal estrogen therapy on bone density in elderly women. *New England Journal of Medicine, 329,* 1141–1146.

Fergusson, D. M., Horwood, L. J., & Shannon, F. T. (1986). Factors related to the age of attainment of nocturnal bladder control: An 8-year longitudinal study. *Pediatrics, 78,* 884–890.

Fernald, A., & Morikawa, H. (1993). Common themes and cultural variations in Japanese and American mothers' speech to infants. *Child Development, 64,* 637–656.

Fernald, A., & O'Neill, D. K. (1993). Peekaboo across cultures: How mothers and infants play with voices, faces, and expectations. In K. MacDonald (Ed.), *Parent-child play* (pp. 259–285). Albany: State University of New York Press.

Feshbach, N. D., & Feshbach, S. (1987). Affective processes and academic achievement. *Child Development, 58,* 1335–1347.

Fiatarone, M. A., Marks, E. C., Ryan, N. D., Meredith, C. N., Lipsitz, L. A., & Evans, W. J. (1990). High-intensity strength training in nonagenarians: Effects on skeletal muscles. *Journal of the American Medical Association, 263,* 3029–3034.

Fiatarone, M. A., O'Neill, E. F., Ryan, N. D., Clemens, K. M., et al. (1994). Exercise training and nutritional supplementation for physical frailty in very elderly people. *New England Journal of Medicine, 330,* 1769–1775.

Fiber bounces back. (1995, March). *Consumer Reports on Health,* pp. 25–28.

Field, D. (1981). Can preschool children really learn to conserve? *Child Development, 52,* 326–334.

Field, D., & Millsap, R. E. (1991). Personality in advanced old age: Continuity or change? *Journal of Gerontology: Psychological Sciences, 46,* P299–308.

Field, D., & Minkler, M. (1988). Continuity and change in social support between young-old and old-old or very-old age. *Journal of Gerontology: Psychological Sciences, 43*(4), P100–106.

Field, D., Minkler, M., Falk, R. F., & Leino, E. V. (1993). The influence of health on family contacts and family functioning in advanced old age: A longitudinal study. *Journal of Gerontology: Psychological Sciences, 48*(1), P18–28.

Field, T. (1991). Quality infant day-care and grade school behavior and performance. *Child Development, 62,* 863–870.

Field, T., Morrow, C., & Adelstein, D. (1993). Depressed mothers' perceptions of infant behavior. *Infant Behavior and Development, 16,* 99–108.

Field, T. M. (1978). Interaction behaviors of primary versus secondary caretaker fathers. *Developmental Psychology, 14,* 183–184.

Field, T. M. (1986). Interventions for premature infants. *Journal of Pediatrics, 109*(1), 183–190.

Field, T. M. (1987). Interaction and attachment in normal and atypical infants. *Journal of Consulting and Clinical Psychology, 55*(6), 853–859.

Field, T. M., & Roopnarine, J. L. (1982). Infant-peer interaction. In T. M. Field, A. Huston, H. C. Quay, L. Troll, & G. Finley (Eds.), *Review of human development*. New York: Wiley.

Field, T. M., Sandberg, D., Garcia, R., Vega-Lahr, N., Goldstein, S., & Guy, L. (1985). Pregnancy problems, postpartum depression, and early infant-mother interactions. *Developmental Psychology, 21*(6), 1152–1156.

Field, T. M., Widmayer, S., Greenberg, R., & Stoller, S. (1982). Effects of parent training on teenage mothers and their infants. *Pediatrics, 69*(6), 703–707.

Field, T. M., Woodson, R., Greenberg, R., & Cohen, D. (1982). Discrimination and imitation of facial expressions by neonates. *Science, 218*, 179–181.

Fillenbaum, G. (1985). Screening the elderly: A brief instrumental activities of daily living measure. *Journal of the American Geriatrics Society, 33*, 698–706.

Fine, M. A., & Kurdek, L. A. (1995). Relation between marital quality and (step) parent-child relationship quality for parents and stepparents in stepfamilies. *Journal of Family Psychology, 9*, 216–223.

Finegan, J. A. K., Quarrington, B. J., Hughes, H. E., Mervyn, J. M., Hood, J. E., Zacher, J. E., & Boyden, N. (1990). Child outcome following midtrimester amniocentesis: Development, behaviour, and physical status at age 4 years. *British Journal of Obstetrics and Gynaecology, 97*, 32.

Fingerhut, L. A., & Kleinman, J. C. (1990). International and interstate comparisons of homicide among young males. *Journal of the American Medical Association, 263*(4), 3292–3295.

Fiore, M. C., Novotny, T. E., Pierce, J. P., et al. (1990). Methods used to quit smoking in the United States: Do cessation programs help? *Journal of the American Medical Association, 263*, 2760–2765.

Fischer, K. (1980). A theory of cognitive development: The control and construction of hierarchies of skills. *Psychological Review, 87*, 477–531.

Fish, M., Stifter, C. A., & Belsky, J. (1993). Early patterns of mother-infant dyadic interaction: Infant, mother, and family demographic antecedents. *Infant Behavior and Development, 16*, 1–18.

Fisher, L., & Lieberman, M. (1994, September). Alzheimer's disease: The impact of the family on spouses, offspring, and in-laws. *Family Process, 33*(3), 305–325.

Fitness Finders. (1984). *Feelin' good*. Spring Arbor, MI: Author.

Fivush, R., Hudson, J., & Nelson, K. (1983). Children's long-term memory for a novel event: An exploratory study. *Merrill-Palmer Quarterly, 30*, 303–316.

Flanagan, C. A., & Eccles, J. S. (1993). Changes in parents' work status and adolescents' adjustment at school. *Child Development, 64*(1), 246–257.

Flavell, J. (1963). *The developmental psychology of Jean Piaget*. New York: Van Nostrand.

Flavell, J. H. (1992). Cognitive development: Past, present, and future. *Developmental Psychology, 28*, 998–1005.

Flavell, J. H. (1993). Young children's understanding of thinking and consciousness. *Current Directions in Psychological Science, 2*, 40–43.

Flavell, J. H., Beach, D., & Chinsky, J. (1966). Spontaneous verbal rehearsal in a memory task as a function of age. *Child Development, 37*, 283–299.

Flavell, J. H., Green, F. L., & Flavell, E. R. (1992). *Young children's knowledge about thinking*. Unpublished manuscript, Stanford University.

Flavell, J. H., Green, F. L., Wahl, K. E., & Flavell, E. R. (1987). The effects of question clarification and memory aids on young children's performance on appearance-reality tasks. *Cognitive Development, 2*, 127–144.

Flavell, J. H., Miller, P. H., & Miller, S. A. (1993). *Cognitive development*. Englewood Cliffs, NJ: Prentice-Hall.

Flavell, J. H., Speer, J. R., Green, F. L., & August, D. L. (1981). The development of comprehension monitoring and knowledge about communication. *Monographs of the Society for Research in Child Development, 46*(5, Serial No. 192).

Flavell, J. H., Zhang, X.-D., Zou, H., Dong, Q., & Qi, S. (1983). A comparison between development of the appearance-reality distinction in the People's Republic of China and the United States. *Cognitive Development, 15*, 459–466.

Flegal, K. M., Troiano, R. P., Pamuk, E. R., Kuczmarski, R. J., & Campbell, S. M. (1995). The influence of smoking cessation on the prevalence of overweight in the United States. *New England Journal of Medicine, 333*, 1165–1170.

Fletcher, A. C., Darling, N. E., Steinberg, L., & Dornbusch, S. M. (1995). The company they keep: Relation of adolescents' adjustment and behavior to their friends' perceptions of authoritative parenting in the social network. *Developmental Psychology, 31*(2), 300–310.

Flint, M., & Samil, R. S. (1990). Cultural and subcultural meanings of the menopause. In M. Flint, F. Kronenberg, & W. Utian (Eds.), *Multidisciplinary perspectives on menopause* (pp. 134–148).

New York: Annals of the New York Academy of Sciences.

Fluoxetine-Bulimia Collaborative Study Group. (1992). Fluoxetine in the treatment of bulimia nervosa: A multicenter placebo-controlled, double-blind trial. *Archives of General Psychiatry, 49*, 139–147.

Folkman, S., & Lazarus, R. S. (1980). An analysis of coping in a middle-aged community sample. *Journal of Health and Social Behavior, 21*, 219–239.

Folkman, S., Lazarus, R. S., Pimley, S., & Novacek, J. (1987). Age differences in stress and coping processes. *Psychology and Aging, 2*, 171–184.

Folsom, A. R., Mink, P. J., Sellers, T. A., Hong, C. P., Zheng, W., & Potter, J. D. (1995). Hormonal replacement therapy and morbidity and mortality in a prospective study of postmenopausal women. *American Journal of Public Health, 85*, 1128–1132.

Folstein, M. F., Bassett, S. S., Anthony, J. C., Romanoski, A. J., & Nestadt, G. R. (1991). Dementia: Case ascertainment in a community survey. *Journal of Gerontology: Medical Sciences, 46*(4), M132–138.

Fonagy, P., Steele, H., & Steele, M. (1991). Maternal representations of attachment during pregnancy predict the organization of infant-mother attachment at one year of age. *Child Development, 62*, 891–905.

Ford, J., Zelnik, M., & Kantner, J. (1979, November). *Differences in contraceptive use and socioeconomic groups of teenagers in the United States*. Paper presented at the meeting of the American Public Health Association, New York.

Forman, B. M., Thotonoz, P., Chen, J., Brun, R. P., Spiegelman, B. M., & Evans, R. M. (1995). 15-deoxy-delta 12, 14-prostaglandin J2 is a ligand for the adipocyte determination factor PPAR gamma. *Cell, 83*, 803–812.

Forteza, J. A., & Prieto, J. M. (1994). Aging and work behavior. In H. C. Triandis, M. D. Dunnette, & L. M. Hough (Eds.), *Handbook of industrial and organizational psychology* (pp. 447–483). Palo Alto, CA: Consulting Psychologists Press.

Fowler, J. (1981). *Stages of faith: The psychology of human development and the quest for meaning*. New York: Harper & Row.

Fowler, J. W. (1989). Strength for the journey: Early childhood development in selfhood and faith. In D. A. Blazer, J. W. Fowler, K. J. Swick, A. S. Honig, P. J. Boone, B. M. Caldwell, R. A. Boone, & L. W. Barber (Eds.), *Faith development in early childhood* (pp. 1–63). New York: Sheed & Ward.

Fowler, M. G., Simpson, G. A., & Schoendorf, K. C. (1993). Families on the move and children's health care. *Pediatrics, 91*, 934–940.

Fox, N. A., Kimmerly, N. L., & Schafer, W. D. (1991). Attachment to mother/attachment to father: A meta-analysis. *Child Development, 62,* 210–225.

Fraga, C. G., Motchnik, P. A., Shigenaga, M. K., Helbock, H. J., Jacob, R. A., & Ames, B. N. (1991). Ascorbic acid protects against endogenous oxidative DNA damage in human sperm. *Proceedings of the National Academy of Sciences of the United States, 88,* 11003–11006.

Frank, S. J., Avery, C. B., & Laman, M. S. (1988). Young adults' perception of their relationships with their parents: Individual differences in connectedness, competence, and emotional autonomy. *Developmental Psychology, 24,* 729–737.

Frankenburg, W. K., Dodds, J., Archer, P., Bresnick, B., Maschka, P., Edelman, N., & Shapiro, H. (1992). *Denver II training manual.* Denver: Denver Developmental Materials.

Frankenburg, W. K., Dodds, J. B., Fandal, A. W., Kazuk, E., & Cohrs, M. (1975). *The Denver Developmental Screening Test: Reference manual.* Denver: University of Colorado Medical Center.

Franks, M. M., & Stephens, M. A. P. (1996). Social support in the context of caregiving: Husbands' provision of support to wives involved in parental care. *Journal of Gerontology: Psychological Sciences, 51B*(1), P43–52.

Fraser, A. M., Brockert, J. F., & Ward, R. H. (1995). Association of young maternal age with adverse reproductive outcomes. *The New England Journal of Medicine, 332* (17), 1113–1117.

Freedman, D. G. (1979, January). Ethnic differences in babies. *Human Nature,* pp. 15–20.

Freedman, D. G., & Freedman, M. (1969). Behavioral differences between Chinese-American and American newborns. *Nature, 224,* 1227.

Freeman, E., Rickels, K., Sondheimer, S. J., & Polansky, M. (1990). Ineffectiveness of progesterone suppository treatment for premenstrual syndrome. *Journal of the American Medical Association, 264,* 349–353.

Freeman, E. W., Rickels, K., Sondheimer, S. J., & Polansky, M. (1995). A double-blind trial of oral progesterone, alprazolam, and placebo in treatment of severe premenstrual syndrome. *Journal of the American Medical Association, 274,* 51–57.

Freeman, S. M., Whartenby, K. A., & Abraham, G. N. (1992). Gene therapy: Applications to diseases associated with aging. *Generations, 16*(4), 45–48.

Fretts, R. C., Schmittdiel, J., McLean, F. H., Usher, R. H., & Goldman, M. B. (1995). Increased maternal age and the risk of fetal death. *New England Journal of Medicine, 333,* 953–957.

Freud, A. (1946). *The ego and the mechanisms of defense.* New York: International Universities Press.

Freud, S. (1953). *A general introduction to psychoanalysis* (J. Riviere, Trans.). New York: Perma-books. (Original work published 1935)

Freud, S. (1964a). New introductory lectures on psycho-analysis. In J. Strachey (Ed. & Trans.), *The standard edition of the complete psychological works of Sigmund Freud* (Vol. 22). London: Hogarth. (Original work published 1933)

Freud, S. (1964b). An outline of psychoanalysis. In J. Strachey (Ed. & Trans.), *The standard edition of the complete psychological works of Sigmund Freud* (Vol. 23). London: Hogarth. (Original work published 1940)

Fricker, H. S., Hindermann, R., & Bruppacher, R. (1989). *The cultural context of infancy: Vol. 1. Biology, culture, and infant development.* Norwood, NJ: Ablex.

Fried, P. A., Watkinson, B., & Willan, A. (1984). Marijuana use during pregnancy and decreased length of gestation. *American Journal of Obstetrics and Gynecology, 150,* 23–27.

Friedan, B. (1993). *The fountain of age.* New York: Simon & Schuster.

Friedman, H. S., Tucker, J. S., Schwartz, J. E., Martin, L. R., Tomlinson-Keasey, C., Wingard, D. L., & Criqui, M. H. (1995). Childhood conscientiousness and longevity: Health behaviors and cause of death. *Journal of Personality and Social Psychology, 68,* 696–703.

Friedman, H. S., Tucker, J. S., Schwartz, J. E., Tomlinson-Keasey, C., Martin, L. R., Wingard, D. L., & Criqui, M. H. (1995). Psychosocial and behavioral predictors of longevity. *American Psychologist, 50,* 69–78.

Friedman, H. S., Tucker, J. S., Tomlinson-Keasey, C., Schwartz, J. E., Martin, L. R., Wingard, D. L., & Criqui, M. H. (1993). Does childhood personality predict longevity? *Journal of Personality and Social Psychology, 65,* 176–185.

Friend, R. A. (1991). Older lesbian and gay people: A theory of successful aging. In J. A. Lee (Ed.), *Gay midlife and maturity* (pp. 99–118). New York: Haworth.

Friend, T. (1994, November 13). Alzheimer's is focus of new developments. *Chicago Sun-Times,* p. 59.

Fries, J. F., & Crapo, L. M. (1981). *Vitality and aging.* San Francisco: Freeman.

Fromkin, V., Krashen, S., Curtiss, S., Rigler, D., & Rigler, M. (1974). The development of language in Genie: Acquisition beyond the "critical period." *Brain and Language, 15*(9), 28–34.

Frone, M. R., Russell, M., & Barnes, G. M. (1996). Work-family conflict, gender, and health-related outcomes: A study of employed parents in two community samples. *Journal of Occupational Health Psychology, 1*(1), 57–69.

Fuchs, C. S., Stampfer, M. J., Colditz, G. A., Giovannucci, E. L., Manson, J. E., Kawachi, I., Hunter, D. J., Hankinson, S. E., Hennekens, C. H., Rosner, B., Speizer, F. E., & Willett, W. C. (1995). Alcohol consumption and mortality among women. *New England Journal of Medicine, 332,* 1245–1250.

Fuchs, D., & Fuchs, L. S. (1986). Test procedure bias: A meta-analysis of examiner familiarity effects. *Review of Educational Research, 56,* 243–262.

Fuchs, L. S., & Fuchs, D. (1986). Effects of systematic formative evaluation of student achievement: A metaanalysis. *Exceptional Children, 53,* 199–205.

Fuhrman, T., & Holmbeck, G. N. (1995). A contextual-moderator analysis of emotional autonomy and adjustment in adolescence. *Child Development, 66,* 793–811.

Fuligni, A. J., & Eccles, J. S. (1993). Perceived parent-child relationships and early adolescents' orientation toward peers. *Developmental Psychology, 29*(4), 622–632.

Fuligni, A. J., & Stevenson, H. W. (1995). Time use and mathematics achievement among American, Chinese, and Japanese high school students. *Child Development, 66,* 830–842.

Fulton, R., & Owen, G. (1987–1988). Death and society in twentieth-century America: Special issue—Research in thanatology. *Omega: Journal of Death and Dying, 18,* 379–395.

Furman, W. (1982). Children's friendships. In T. M. Field, A. Huston, H. C. Quay, L. Troll, & G. E. Finley (Eds.), *Review of human development.* New York: Wiley.

Furman, W., & Bierman, K. L. (1983). Developmental changes in young children's conception of friendship. *Child Development, 54,* 549–556.

Furman, W., & Buhrmester, D. (1985). Children's perceptions of the personal relationships in their social networks. *Developmental Psychology, 21,* 1016–1024.

Furstenberg, F. F., Brooks-Gunn, J., & Morgan, S. P. (1987). Adolescent mothers and their children in later life. *Family Planning Perspectives, 19,* 142–152.

Furstenberg, F. F., & Hughes, M. E. (1995). Social capital in successful development. *Journal of Marriage and the Family, 57,* 580–592.

Furstenberg, F. F., Levine, J. A., & Brooks-Gunn, J. (1990). The children of teenage mothers: Patterns of early child bearing in two generations. *Family Planning Perspectives, 22*(2), 54–61.

Furukawa, S. (1994). *The diverse living arrangements of children: Summer 1991* (U.S. Bureau of the Census, Current Population Reports, Series P70, No. 38). Washington, DC: U.S. Government Printing Office.

Gabiano, C., Tovo, P.-A., de Martino, M., Galli, L., et al. (1992). Mother-to-child transmission of human immunodeficiency virus type 1: Risk of infection and correlates of transmission. *Pediatrics, 90,* 369–374.

Gabriel, T. (1996, January 7). High-tech pregnancies test hope's limit. *The New York Times,* pp. 1, 18–19.

Gaddis, A., & Brooks-Gunn, J. (1985). The male experience of pubertal change. *Journal of Youth and Adolescence, 14,* 61–69.

Gaensbauer, T., & Hiatt, S. (1984). *The psychobiology of affective development.* Hillsdale, NJ: Erlbaum.

Gaertner, S. L., Mann, J., Murrell, A., & Dovidio, J. F. (1989). Reducing intergroup bias: The benefits of recategorization. *Journal of Personality and Social Psychology, 57,* 239–249.

Galambos, N. L., Petersen, A. C., & Lenerz, K. (1988). Maternal employment and sex typing in early adolescence: Contemporaneous and longitudinal relations. In A. D. Gottfried & A. W. Gottfried (Eds.), *Maternal employment and children's development: Longitudinal research.* New York: Plenum.

Galambos, N. L., Sears, H. A., Almeida, D. M., & Kolaric, G. C. (1995). Parents' work overload and problem behavior in young adolescents. *Journal of Research on Adolescence, 5*(2), 201–223.

Gallagher, W. (1993, May). Midlife myths. *The Atlantic Monthly,* pp. 51–68.

Gallagher, W. (1994, September). How we become what we are. *The Atlantic Monthly,* pp. 39–55.

Gallagher-Thompson, D. (1995). Caregivers of chronically ill elders. In G. E. Maddox (Ed.), *The encyclopedia of aging* (pp. 141–144). New York: Springer.

Gallant, S. J., Popiel, D. A., Hoffman, D. M., et al. (1992a). Using daily ratings to confirm premenstrual syndrome/late luteal phase dysphoric disorder, I.: Effects of demand characteristics and expectations. *Psychosomatic Medicine, 54*(2), 149–166.

Gallant, S. J., Popiel, D. A., Hoffman, D. M., et al. (1992b). Using daily ratings to confirm premenstrual syndrome/late luteal phase dysphoric disorder, II: What makes a "real" difference? *Psychosomatic Medicine, 54*(2), 167–181.

Gallo, J. J., Anthony, J. C., & Muthen, B. O. (1994). Age differences in the symptoms of depression: A latent trace analysis. *Journal of Gerontology: Psychological Sciences, 49,* P251–264.

Gallup, G., & Proctor, W. (1982). *Adventures in immortality: A look beyond the threshold of death.* New York: McGraw-Hill.

Gamer, E., Thomas, J., & Kendall, D. (1975). Determinants of friendship across the lifespan. In F. Rebelsky (Ed.), *Life: The continuous process.* New York: Knopf.

Gans, J. E. (1990). *America's adolescents: How healthy are they?* Chicago: American Medical Association.

Garbarino, J., Dubrow, N., Kostelny, K., & Pardo, C. (1992). *Children in danger: Coping with the consequences of community violence.* San Francisco: Jossey-Bass.

Garbarino, J., & Kostelny, K. (1993). Neighborhood and community influences on parenting. In T. Luster & L. Okagaki (Eds.), *Parenting: An ecological perspective* (pp. 203–226). Hillsdale, NJ: Erlbaum.

Garcia-Coll, C., Kagan, J., & Reznick, J. S. (1984). Behavioral inhibition in young children. *Child Development, 55,* 1005–1019.

Gardner, H. (1981, July). Breakaway minds. *Psychology Today,* pp. 64–71.

Gardner, H. (1983). *Frames of mind: The theory of multiple intelligences.* New York: Basic Books.

Gardner, H. (1986, Summer). Freud in three frames. *Daedalus,* 105–134.

Gardner, H. (1988). Creative lives and creative works: A synthetic scientific approach. In R. J. Sternberg (Ed.), *The nature of creativity: Contemporary psychological perspectives* (pp. 298–321). Cambridge, UK: Cambridge University Press.

Garfein, A. J., & Herzog, A. R. (1995). Robust aging among the young-old, old-old, and oldest-old. *Journal of Gerontology: Social Sciences, 50B,* S77–87.

Garland, A. F., & Zigler, E. (1993). Adolescent suicide prevention: Current research and social policy implications. *American Psychologist, 48*(2), 169–182.

Garland, J. B. (1982, March). *Social referencing and self-produced locomotion.* Paper presented at the meeting of the International Conference on International Studies, Austin, TX.

Garmezy, N. (1983). Stressors of childhood. In N. Garmezy & M. Rutter (Eds.), *Stress, coping and development in children.* New York: McGraw-Hill.

Garmezy, N., Masten, A., & Tellegen, A. (1984). The study of stress and competence in children. A building block for developmental psychopathology. *Child Development, 55,* 97–111.

Garner, D. M. (1993). Pathogenesis of anorexia nervosa. *The Lancet, 341,* 1631–1635.

Garwick, A. W., et al. (1994, September). Family perceptions of living with Alzheimer's disease. *Family Process, 33*(3), 327–340.

Geary, D. C. (1993). Mathematical disabilities: Cognitive, neuropsychological, and genetic components. *Psychological Bulletin, 114,* 345–362.

Geber, M. (1962). Longitudinal study and psychomotor development among Baganda children. *Proceedings of the Fourteenth International Congress of Applied Psychology, 3,* 50–60.

Geber, M., & Dean, R. F. A. (1957, June 16). The state of development of newborn African children. *The Lancet,* pp. 1216–1219.

Gecas, V., & Seff, M. A. (1990). Families and adolescents: A review of the 1980s. *Journal of Marriage and the Family, 52,* 941–958.

Geen, R. G. (1994). Television and aggression: Recent developments in research and theory. In D. Zillman, J. Bryant, & A. C. Huston (Eds.), *Media, children, and the family: Social scientific, psychoanalytic, and clinical perspectives.* Hillsdale, NJ: Erlbaum.

Gelfand, D. E. (1982). *Aging: The ethnic factor.* Boston: Little, Brown.

Gelfand, D. M., & Teti, D. M. (1995, November). How does maternal depression affect children? *The Harvard Mental Health Letter,* p. 8.

Geller, J. A. (1992). *Breaking destructive patterns: Multiple strategies for treating partner abuse.* New York: Free Press.

Gelles, R. J., & Maynard, P. E. (1987). A structural family systems approach to intervention in cases of family violence. *Family Relations, 36,* 270–275.

Gelman, R., Bullock, M., & Meck, E. (1980). Preschoolers' understanding of simple object transformations. *Child Development, 51,* 691–699.

Gelman, R., & Gallistel, C. R. (1978). *The child's understanding of number.* Cambridge, MA: Harvard University Press.

Gelman, R., Spelke, A., & Meck, E. (1983). [Work on animism in childhood.]

Gendell, M., & Siegel, J. S. (1996). Trends in retirement age in the U.S., 1955–1993, by sex and race. *Journal of Gerontology: Social Sciences, 51B,* S132–139.

Genevay, B. (1986). Intimacy as we age. *Generations, 10*(4), 12–15.

George, C., Kaplan, N., & Main, M. (1985). *The Berkeley Adult Attachment Interview.* Unpublished protocol, Department of Psychology, University of California, Berkeley.

George, L. K. (1993). Depressive disorders and symptoms in later life. *Generations, 17*(1), 35–38.

Gerhard, G. S., & Cristofalo, V. J. (1992). The limits of biogerontology. *Generations, 16*(4), 55–59.

Gerstel, N., & Gallagher, S. K. (1993). Kinkeeping and distress: Gender, recipients of care, and work-family conflict. *Journal of Marriage and the Family, 55,* 598–607.

Gertner, B. L., Rice, M. L., & Hadley, P. A. (1993). *The influence of communicative competence on peer preferences in a preschool classroom.* Manuscript submitted for publication.

Gesell, A. (1929). Maturation and infant behavior patterns. *Psychological Review, 36,* 307–319.

Getzels, J. W. (1964). Creative thinking, problem-solving, and instruction. In

Yearbook of the National Society for the Study of Education (Part 1, pp. 240–267). Chicago: University of Chicago Press.

Getzels, J. W. (1984, March). *Problem-finding in creativity in higher education.* [The Fifth Rev. Charles F. Donovan, S. J. Lecture]. Boston College, School of Education, Boston.

Getzels, J. W., & Csikszentmihalyi, M. (1968). The value-orientations of art students as determinants of artistic specialization and creative performance. *Studies in Art Education, 10*(1), 5–16.

Getzels, J. W., & Csikszentmihalyi, M. (1975). From problem solving to problem finding. In J. A. Taylor & J. W. Getzels (Eds.), *Perspectives in creativity* (pp. 90–116). Volente, TX: Aldine.

Getzels, J. W., & Csikszentmihalyi, M. (1976). *The creative vision: A longitudinal study of problem finding in art.* New York: Wiley.

Getzels, J. W., & Jackson, P. W. (1962). *Creativity and intelligence: Explorations with gifted students.* New York: Wiley.

Giambra, L. M., & Arenberg, D. (1993). Adult age differences in forgetting sentences. *Psychology and Aging, 8,* 451–462.

Gibbs, N. (1995, October 2). The EQ factor. *Time,* pp. 60–68.

Gielen, U., & Kelly, D. (1983, February). *Buddhist Ladakh: Psychological portrait of a nonviolent culture.* Paper presented at the Annual Meeting of the Society for Cross-Cultural Research: Washington, DC.

Gilbert, L. A. (1994). Current perspectives in dual-career families. *Current Directions in Psychological Science, 3,* 101–105.

Giles-Sims, J., Straus, M., & Sugarman, D. B. (1995). Child, maternal, and family characteristics associated with spanking. *Family Relations, 44,* 170–176.

Gilford, R. (1984). Contrasts in marital satisfaction throughout old age: An exchange theory analysis. *Journal of Gerontology, 39,* 325–333.

Gilford, R. (1986). Marriages in later life. *Generations, 10*(4), 16–20.

Gilford, R., & Bengtson, V. (1979). Measuring marital satisfaction in three generations: Positive and negative dimensions. *Journal of Marriage and the Family, 41,* 387–398.

Gilliand, P. (1989). Evolution of family policy in light of development in western European countries. *International Social Security Review, 42,* 395–426.

Gilligan, C. (1982). *In a different voice: Psychological theory and women's development.* Cambridge, MA: Harvard University Press.

Gilligan, C. (1987a). Adolescent development reconsidered. In E. E. Irwin (Ed.), *Adolescent social behavior and health.* San Francisco: Jossey-Bass.

Gilligan, C. (1987b). Moral orientation and moral development. In E. F. Kittay & D. T. Meyers (Eds.), *Women and moral theory* (pp. 19–33). Totowa, NJ: Rowman & Littlefield.

Gilligan, C., Murphy, J. M., & Tappan, M. B. (1990). Moral development beyond adolescence. In C. N. Alexander & E. J. Langer (Eds.), *Higher stages of human development* (pp. 208–228). New York: Oxford University Press.

Gillman, M. W., Cupples, L. A., Gagnon, D., Posner, B. M., Ellison, R. C., Castelli, W. P., & Wolf, P. A. (1995). Protective effects of fruit and vegetables on development of stroke in men. *Journal of the American Medical Association, 273,* 1113–1117.

Ginsburg, G. S., & Bronstein, P. (1993). Family factors related to children's intrinsic/extrinsic motivational orientation and academic performance. *Child Development, 64,* 1461–1474.

Ginsburg, H., & Opper, S. (1979). *Piaget's theory of intellectual development* (2d ed.). Englewood Cliffs, NJ: Prentice-Hall.

Giordano, P. C., Cernkovich, S. A., & DeMaris, A. (1993). The family and peer relations of black adolescents. *Journal of Marriage and the Family, 55,* 277–287.

Giovannucci, E., Ascherio, A., Rimm, E. B., Stampfer, M. J., Colditz, G. A., & Willett, W. C. (1995). Intake of carotenoids and retinol in relation to risk of prostate cancer. *Journal of the National Cancer Institute, 87,* 1767–1776.

Giovannucci, E., Rimm, E. B., Colditz, G. A., Stampfer, M. J., Ascherio, A., Chute, C. C., & Willett, W. C. (1993). A prospective study of dietary fat and risk of prostate cancer. *Journal of the National Cancer Institute, 85,* 1571–1579.

Gladue, B. A. (1994). The biopsychology of sexual orientation. *Current Directions in Psychological Science, 3,* 150–154.

Glass, R. B. (1986). Infertility. In S. S. C. Yen & R. B. Jaffe (Eds.), *Reproductive endocrinology: Physiology, pathophysiology, and clinical management* (pp. 571–613). Philadelphia: Saunders.

Glass, T. A., Seeman, T. E., Herzog, A. R., Kahn, R., & Berkman, L. F. (1995). Change in productive activity in late adulthood: MacArthur studies of successful aging. *Journal of Gerontology: Social Sciences, 50B,* S65–66.

Gleitman, L. R., Newport, E. L., & Gleitman, H. (1984). The current status of the motherese hypothesis. *Journal of Child Language, 11,* 43–79.

Glenn, N. D. (1991). The recent trend in marital success in the United States. *Journal of Marriage and the Family, 53,* 261–270.

Glenn, N. D., & McLanahan, S. (1981). The effects of offspring on the psychological well-being of older adults. *Journal of Marriage and the Family, 43*(2), 409–421.

Glick, J. (1975). Cognitive development in cross-cultural perspective. In F. Horowitz (Ed.), *Review of child development research* (Vol. 4, pp. 595–654). Chicago: University of Chicago Press.

Glick, P. C., & Lin, S.-L. (1986a). More young adults are living with their parents: Who are they? *Journal of Marriage and the Family, 48,* 107–112.

Glick, P. C., & Lin, S.-L. (1986b). Recent changes in divorce and remarriage. *Journal of Marriage and the Family, 48*(4), 737–747.

Globerman, J. (1996). Motivation to care: Daughters- and sons-in-law caring for relatives with Alzheimer's disease. *Family Relations, 45,* 37–45.

Gold, D., & Andres, D. (1978). Developmental comparison between adolescent children with employed and nonemployed mothers. *Merrill-Palmer Quarterly, 24,* 243–254.

Gold, D. T. (1987). Siblings in old age: Something special. *Canadian Journal on Aging, 6,* 199–215.

Golden, M., Birns, B., & Bridger, W. (1973). *Review and overview: Social class and cognitive development.* Paper presented at the meeting of the Society for Research in Child Development, Philadelphia.

Goldman, L., & Toteson, A. N. A. (1991). Uncertainty about postmenopausal estrogen. *New England Journal of Medicine, 325,* 800–802.

Goldman, L. L., & Rothschild, J. (in press). Healing the wounded with art therapy. In B. Danto (Ed.), *Bereavement and suicide.* Philadelphia: Charles Publishing.

Goldscheider, F., & Goldscheider, C. (1994). Leaving and returning home in 20th century America. *Population Bulletin, 48*(4), 1–35.

Goldsmith, M. F. (1989). "Silent epidemic" of "social disease" makes STD experts raise their voices. *Journal of the American Medical Association, 261*(24), 3509–3510.

Goleman, D. (1990, April 24). Anger over racism is seen as a cause of blacks' high blood pressure. *The New York Times,* p. C3.

Goleman, D. (1992, November 24). Anthropology goes looking in all the old places. *The New York Times,* p. B1.

Goleman, D. (1993, June 11). Studies reveal suggestibility of very young as witnesses. *The New York Times,* pp. A1, A23.

Goleman, D. (1995a, July 1). A genetic clue to bed-wetting is located: Researchers say discovery shows the problem is not emotional. *The New York Times,* p. 8.

Goleman, D. (1995b). *Emotional intelligence: Why it can matter more than IQ.* New York: Bantam.

Golombok, S., Cook, R., Bish, A., & Murray, C. (1995). Families created by the new reproductive technologies:

Quality of parenting and social and emotional development of the children. *Child Development, 66,* 285–298.

Golombok, S., & Tasker, F. (1996). Do parents influence the sexual orientation of their children? Findings from a longitudinal study of lesbian families. *Developmental Psychology, 32,* 3–11.

Gong, Y. L., Koplan, J. P., Feng, W., Chen, C. H., Zheng, P., & Harris, J. R. (1995). Cigarette smoking in China: Prevalence, characteristics, and attitudes in Minhang District. *Journal of the American Medical Association, 274,* 1232–1234.

Gonsiorek, J. C. (1995). Gay male identities: Concepts and issues. In A. R. D'Augelli & C. J. Patterson (Eds.), *Lesbian, gay & bisexual identities over the lifespan: Psychological perspectives.* New York: Oxford University Press.

Gonyea, J. G., Hudson, R. B., & Seltzer, G. B. (1990). Housing preferences of vulnerable elders in suburbia. *Journal of Housing for the Elderly, 7,* 79–95.

Gorbach, S. L., Zimmerman, D. R., & Woods, M. (1984). *The doctors' anti–breast cancer diet.* New York: Simon & Schuster.

Gorman, K. S., & Pollitt, E. (1996). Does schooling buffer the effects of early risk? *Child Development, 67,* 314–326.

Gortmaker, S. L., Must, A., Perrin, J. M., Sobol, A. M., & Dietz, W. H. (1993). Social and economic consequences of overweight in adolescence and young adulthood. *New England Journal of Medicine, 329,* 1008–1012.

Gottesman, I. I. (1993). Origins of schizophrenia: Past and prologue. In R. P. Plomin & G. E. McClearn (Eds.), *Nature, nurture, and psychology.* Washington, DC: American Psychological Association.

Gottman, J. M., & Katz, L. F. (1989). Effects of marital discord on young children's peer interaction and health. *Developmental Psychology, 25*(3), 373–381.

Gottman, J. M., & Krokoff, L. J. (1989). Marital interaction and satisfaction: A longitudinal view. *Journal of Consulting and Clinical Psychology, 57,* 47–52.

Graber, J. A., Brooks-Gunn, J., & Warren, M. P. (1995). The antecedents of menarcheal age: Heredity, family environment, and stressful life events. *Child Development, 66,* 346–359.

Graham, C. J., Dick, R., Rickert, V. I., & Glen, R. (1993). Left-handedness as a risk factor for unintentional injury in children. *Pediatrics, 92*(6), 823–826.

Gralinski, J. H., & Kopp, C. B. (1993). Everyday rules for behavior: Mothers' requests to young children. *Developmental Psychology, 29,* 573–584.

Grant, B. S., Harford, T. C., Dawson, D. A., Chou, P., Dufour, M., & Pickering, R. (1994). Prevalence of *DSM-IV* alcohol abuse and dependency: United States, 1992. *Alcohol, Health, and Research World, 18,* 243–248.

Grantham-McGregor, S., Powell, C., Walker, S., Chang, S., & Fletcher, P. (1994). The long-term follow-up of severely malnourished children who participated in an intervention program. *Child Development, 65,* 428–439.

Grayson, B. (1992–1993). Near-death experiences and antisuicidal attitudes. *Omega, 26,* 81–89.

Grayson, B. (1993). Varieties of near-death experience. *Psychiatry, 56,* 390–399.

Greenberg, J., & Becker, M. (1988). Aging parents as family resources. *The Gerontologist, 28*(6), 786–790.

Greenberger, E., & Steinberg, L. (1986). *When teenagers work.* New York: Basic Books.

Greenfield, P. M. (1984). A theory of the teacher in the learning activities of everyday life. In B. Rogoff & J. Lave (Eds.), *Everyday cognition: Its development in social context.* Cambridge, MA: Harvard University Press.

Greenough, W. T., Black, J. E., & Wallace, C. S. (1987). Experience and brain development. *Child Development, 58,* 539–559.

Greenstein, T. N. (1995). Gender ideology, marital disruption, and the employment of married women. *Journal of Marriage and the Family, 57,* 31–42.

Griep, M. I., Mets, T. F., Vercruysse, A., Cromphout, I., Ponjaert, I., Toft, J., & Massart, D. L. (1995). Food odor thresholds in relation to age, nutritional and health status. *Journal of Gerontology: Biological Sciences, 50*(6), B407–414.

Grodstein, F. (1996). Postmenopausal estrogen and progestin use and the risk of cardiovascular disease. *New England Journal of Medicine, 335,* 453.

Gross, J. (1994, April 5). Blending care and law enforcement, hospitals try to stem child abuse. *The New York Times,* p. A18.

Gross, R. T., & Duke, P. (1980). The effect of early versus late physical maturation on adolescent behavior. In I. Litt (Ed.), Symposium on adolescent medicine [Special issue]. *Pediatric Clinics of North America, 27,* 71–78.

Gruber, A., & Schaie, K. W. (1986, November 21). *Longitudinal-sequential studies of marital assortativity.* Paper presented at the annual meeting of the Gerontological Society of America, Chicago.

Gruber-Baldini, A. L. (1991). *The impact of health and disease on cognitive ability in adulthood and old age in the Seattle Longitudinal Study.* Unpublished doctoral dissertation, Pennsylvania State University.

Grubman, S., Gross, E., Lerner-Weiss, N., Hernandez, M., McSherry, G. D., Hoyt, L. G., Boland, M., & Oleske, J. M. (1995). Older children and adolescents living with perinatally acquired human immunodeficiency virus. *Pediatrics, 95,* 657–663.

Grusec, J. E., & Goodnow, J. J. (1994). Impact of parental discipline methods on the child's internalization of values: A reconceptualization of current points of view. *Developmental Psychology, 30,* 4–19.

Gruson, L. (1992, April 22). Gains in deciphering genes set off effort to guard data against abuses. *The New York Times,* p. C12.

Guemple, L. (1983). Growing old in Inuit society. In J. Sokolovsky (Ed.), *Growing old in different societies* (pp. 24–28). Belmont, CA: Wadsworth.

Guerin, D. W., & Gottfried, A. W. (1994). Temperamental consequences of infant difficultness. *Infant Behavior and Development, 17,* 413–421.

Gui, S.-X. (1989, December). *A new approach to the pension system in Shanghai suburbs.* Paper presented at the International Academic conference on China's Population Aging, Beijing.

Guidubaldi, J., & Perry, J. D. (1985). Divorce and mental health sequelae for children: A two year follow-up of a nationwide sample. *Journal of the American Academy of Child Psychiatry, 24,* 531–537.

Guilford, J. P. (1967). *The nature of human intelligence.* New York: McGraw-Hill.

Guisinger, S., & Blatt, S. J. (1994). Individuality and relatedness: Evolution of a fundamental dialectic. *American Psychologist, 49,* 104–111.

Gunnar, M. R., Larson, M. C., Hertsgaard, L., Harris, M. L., & Brodersen, L. (1992). The stressfulness of separation among nine-month-old infants: Effects of social context variables and infant temperament. *Child Development, 63,* 290–303.

Gutmann, D. (1975). Parenting: A key to the comparative study of the life cycle. In N. Datan & L. H. Ginsberg (Eds.), *Life-span developmental psychology: Normative life crises.* New York: Academic Press.

Gutmann, D. (1977). The cross-cultural perspective: Notes toward a comparative psychology of aging. In J. E. Birren & K. W. Schaie (Eds.), *Handbook of the psychology of aging* (pp. 302–326). New York: Van Nostrand Reinhold.

Gutmann, D. (1985). The parental imperative revisited. In J. Meacham (Ed.), *Family and individual development.* Basel, Switzerland: Karger.

Gutmann, D. (1992). Culture and mental health in later life. In J. E. Birren, R. Sloane, & G. D. Cohen (Eds.), *Handbook of mental health and aging* (pp. 75–96). New York: Academic Press.

Gutmann, D. L. (1974). Alternatives to disengagement: Aging among the highland Druze. In R. LeVine (Ed.), *Culture and personality: Contemporary readings* (pp. 232–245). Chicago: Aldine.

Guyer, B., Strobino, D. M., Ventura, S. J., MacDorman, M., & Martin, J. A. (1996). Annual summary of vital statistics—1995. *Pediatrics, 98,* 1007–1019.

Guyer, B., Strobino, D. M., Ventura, S. J., & Singh, G. K. (1995). Annual summary of vital statistics—1994. *Pediatrics, 96,* 1029–1039.

Haan, N. (1990). Personality at midlife. In S. Hunter & M. Sundel (Eds.). *Midlife myths.* Newbury Park, CA: Sage.

Haas, A. D. (1989, Winter). Adults in college. *Women's American ORT Reporter,* pp. 7, 14.

Hackett, R. D. (1990). Age, tenure, and employee absenteeism. *Human Relations, 43,* 601–619.

Haddow, J. E., Palomaki, G. E., Knight, G. J., Williams, J., Polkkiner, A., Canick, J. A., Saller, D. N., & Bowers, G. B. (1992). Prenatal screening for Down's syndrome with use of maternal serum markers. *New England Journal of Medicine, 327,* 588–593.

Hadeed, A. J., & Siegel, S. R. (1989). Maternal cocaine use during pregnancy: Effect on the newborn infant. *Pediatrics, 84*(2), 205–210.

Hagestad, G. O. (1978). *Patterns of communication and influence between grandparents and grandchildren in a changing society.* Paper presented at the meeting of the World Conference of Sociology, Uppsala, Sweden.

Hagestad, G. O. (1982). *Issues in the study of intergenerational continuity.* Paper presented at the National Council on Family Relations Theory and Methods Workshop, Washington, DC.

Haglund, B. (1993). Cigarette smoking and sudden infant death syndrome: Some salient points in the debate. *Acta Paediatrica, 389*(Suppl.), 37–39.

Haith, M. M. (1986). Sensory and perceptual processes in early infancy. *Journal of Pediatrics, 109*(1), 158–171.

Hakuta, K., Ferdman, B. M., & Diaz, R. M. (1987). Bilingualism and cognitive development: Three perspectives. In S. Rosenberg (Ed.), *Advances in applied psycholinguistics: Vol. 2. Reading, writing, and language learning* (pp. 284–319). New York: Cambridge University Press.

Hakuta, K., & Garcia, E. E. (1989). Bilingualism in education. *American Psychologist, 44*(2), 374–379.

Halaas, J. L., Gajiwala, K. S., Maffei, M., Cohen, S. L., Chait, B. T., Rabinowitz, D., Lallone, R. L., Burley, S. K., & Friedman, J. M. (1995). Weight reducing effects of the plasma protein encoded by the obese gene. *Science, 269,* 543–546.

Hale, J. (1982). *Black children: Their roots, culture, and learning styles.* Provo, UT: Brigham Young University Press.

Hale, S. (1990). A global developmental trend in cognitive processing speed. *Child Development, 61,* 653–663.

Haley, A. (1976). *Roots.* Garden City, NY: Doubleday.

Halfon, N., & Newacheck, P. W. (1993). Childhood asthma and poverty: Differential impacts and utilization of health services. *Pediatrics, 91,* 56–61.

Hall, D. R., & Zhao, J. Z. (1995). Cohabitation in Canada: Testing the selectivity hypothesis. *Journal of Marriage and the Family, 57,* 421–427.

Hall, E. (1983). A conversation with Erik Erikson. *Psychology Today, 17*(6), 22–30.

Hall, G. S. (1916). *Adolescence.* New York: Appleton. (Original work published 1904)

Hall, G. S. (1922). *Senescence: The last half of life.* New York: Appleton.

Hallé, P. A., & de Boysson-Bardies, B. (1994). Emergence of an early receptive lexicon: Infants' recognition of words. *Infant Behavior and Development, 17,* 119–129.

Haltiwanger, J., & Harter, S. (1988). *A behavioral measure of young children's presented self-esteem.* Unpublished manuscript, University of Denver.

Hamer, D. H., Hu, S., Magnuson, V. L., Hu, N., & Pattatucci, A. M. L. (1993). A linkage between DNA markers on the X chromosome and male sexual orientation. *Science, 261,* 321–327.

Hamilton, S. (1990). *Apprenticeship for adulthood.* New York: Free Press.

Hamilton, S., & Crouter, A. (1980). Work and growth: A review of research on the impact of work experience on adolescent development. *Journal of Youth and Adolescence, 9,* 323–338.

Hamon, R. R., & Blieszner, R. (1990). Filial responsibility expectations among adult child–older parent pairs. *Journal of Gerontology: Psychological Sciences, 45*(3), P110–112.

Handy, C. (1991, October–November). Building small fires: Keep life sizzling—diversify! *Modern Maturity,* pp. 35–39.

Handyside, A. H., Lesko, J. G., Tarin, J. J., Winston, R. M. L., & Hughes, M. R. (1992). Birth of a normal girl after in vitro fertilization and preimplantation diagnostic testing for cystic fibrosis. *New England Journal of Medicine, 327*(13), 905–909.

Hanley, R. (1988a, February 4). Surrogate deals for mother held illegal in Jersey. *The New York Times,* pp. A1, B6.

Hanley, R. (1988b, February 4). Legislators are hesitant on regulating surrogacy. *The New York Times,* p. B7.

Hanna, E., & Meltzoff, A. N. (1993). Peer imitation by toddlers in laboratory, home, and day care contexts: Implications for social learning and memory. *Developmental Psychology, 29,* 701–710.

Hanson, L. (1968). *Renoir: The man, the painter, and his world.* New York: Dodd, Mead.

Hardy-Brown, K., & Plomin, R. (1985). Infant communicative development: Evidence from adoptive and biological families for genetic and environmental influences on rate differences. *Developmental Psychology, 21*(2), 378–385.

Hardy-Brown, K., Plomin, R., & DeFries, J. C. (1981). Genetic and environmental influences on rate of communicative development in the first year of life. *Developmental Psychology, 17,* 704–717.

Harkins, E. (1978). Effects of empty nest transition on self-report of psychological and physical well-being. *Journal of Marriage and the Family, 40*(3), 549–556.

Harlow, H. F., & Harlow, M. K. (1962). The effect of rearing conditions on behavior. *Bulletin of the Menninger Clinic, 26,* 213–224.

Harlow, H. F., & Zimmerman, R. R. (1959). Affectional responses in the infant monkey. *Science, 130,* 421–432.

Harper, M. S. (1996, Summer). Mental health of the black elderly. *Dimensions* (Newsletter of American Society on Aging), pp. 1, 7–8.

Harrington, D. M. (1993). Child-rearing antecedents of suboptimal personality development: Exploring aspects of Alice Miller's concept of the poisonous pedagogy. In D. C. Funder, R. D. Parke, C. Tomlinson-Keasey, & K. Widamen (Eds.), *Studying lives through time: Personality and development* (pp. 289–313). Washington, DC: American Psychological Association.

Harris, P. L., Brown, E., Marriott, C., Whittall, S., & Harmer, S. (1991). Monsters, ghosts, and witches: Testing the limits of the fantasy-reality distinction in young children. In G. E. Butterworth, P. L. Harris, A. M. Leslie, & H. M. Wellman (Eds.), *Perspective on the child's theory of mind.* Oxford: Oxford University Press.

Harrison, A. O., Wilson, M. N., Pine, C. J., Chan, S. Q., & Buriel, R. (1990). Family ecologies of ethnic minority children. *Child Development, 61,* 347–362.

Hart, B., & Risley, T. (1996, August). *Individual differences in early intellectual experience of typical American children: Beyond SES, race, and IQ.* Address at the annual convention of the American Psychological Association, Toronto.

Hart, B., & Risley, T. R. (1989). The longitudinal study of interactive systems. *Education and Treatment of Children, 12,* 347–358.

Hart, B., & Risley, T. R. (1992). American parenting of language-learning children: Persisting differences in family-child interactions observed in natural home environments. *Developmental Psychology, 28,* 1096–1105.

Hart, C. H., DeWolf, M., Wozniak, P., & Burts, D. C. (1992). Maternal and paternal disciplinary styles: Relations with preschoolers' playground behavioral orientation and peer status. *Child Development, 63,* 879–892.

Hart, C. H., Ladd, G. W., & Burleson, B. R. (1990). Children's expectations of the outcome of social strategies: Relations with sociometric status and maternal disciplinary style. *Child Development, 61,* 127–137.

Hart, S. N., & Brassard, M. R. (1987). A major threat to children's mental health: Psychological maltreatment. *American Psychologist, 42*(2), 160–165.

Harter, S. (1985). Competence as a dimension of self-worth. In R. Leahy (Ed.), *The development of the self.* New York: Academic Press.

Harter, S. (1990). Causes, correlates, and the functional role of global self-worth: A life-span perspective. In J. Kolligan & R. Sternberg (Eds.), *Competence considered: Perceptions of competence and incompetence across the life-span* (pp. 67–97). New Haven: Yale University Press.

Harter, S. (1993). Developmental changes in self-understanding across the 5 to 7 shift. In A. Sameroff & M. Haith (Eds.), *Reason and responsibility: The passage through childhood.* Chicago: University of Chicago Press.

Harter, S., & Buddin, B. J. (1987). Children's understanding of the simultaneity of two emotions: A five-stage developmental acquisition sequence. *Developmental Psychology, 23,* 388–389.

Hartmann, E. (1981). The strangest sleep disorder. *Psychology Today, 15*(4), 14–18.

Hartup. W. W. (1989). Social relationships and their developmental significance. *American Psychologist, 44,* 120–126.

Hartup, W. W. (1992). Peer relations in early and middle childhood. In V. B. Van Hasselt & M. Hersen (Eds.), *Handbook of social development: A lifespan perspective* (pp. 257–281). New York: Plenum.

Hartup, W. W. (1996). Cooperation, close relationships, and cognitive development. In W. M. Bukowski, A. F. Newcomb, & W. W. Hartup (Eds.), *The company they keep: Friendships and their developmental significance* (pp. 213–237). New York: Cambridge University Press.

Harvey, B. (1990). Toward a national child health policy. *Journal of the American Medical Association, 264,* 252–253.

Haskett, M. E., & Kistner, J. A. (1991). Social interaction and peer perceptions of young physically abused children. *Child Development, 62,* 979–990.

Haskins, R. (1989). Beyond metaphor: The efficacy of early childhood education. *American Psychologist, 44*(2), 274–282.

Haswell, K., Hock, E., & Wenar, C. (1981). Oppositional behavior of preschool children: Theory and prevention. *Family Relations, 30,* 440–446.

Haug, M., Belkgrave, L., & Gratton, B. (1984). Mental health and the elderly: Factors in stability and change over time. *Journal of Health and Social Behavior, 25,* 100–115.

Haugh, S., Hoffman, C., & Cowan, G. (1980). The eye of the very young beholder: Sex typing of infants by young children. *Child Development, 51,* 598–600.

Haurin, R. J. (1992). Patterns of childhood resilience and the relationship to young adult outcomes. *Journal of Marriage and the Family, 54,* 846–860.

Hawkins, H. L., Kramer, A. F., & Capaldi, D. (1992). Aging, exercise, and attention. *Psychology and Aging, 7*(4), 643–653.

Hawkins, J. D., Catalano, R. F., & Miller, J. Y. (1992). Risk and protective factors for alcohol and other drug problems in adolescence and early adulthood: Implications for substance abuse programs. *Psychological Bulletin, 112*(1), 64–105.

Hawley, T. L., & Disney, E. R. (1992). Crack's children: The consequences of maternal cocaine abuse. *Social Policy Report of the Society for Research in Child Development, VI*(4), 1–23.

Hay, D. F., Pedersen, J., & Nash, A. (1982). Dyadic interaction in the first year of life. In K. H. Rubin & H. S. Ross (Eds.), *Peer relationships and social skills in children.* New York: Springer.

Hayes, A., & Batshaw, M. L. (1993). Down syndrome. *Pediatric Clinics of North America, 40,* 523–535.

Hayflick, L. (1974). The strategy of senescence. *The Gerontologist, 14*(1), 37–45.

Hayflick, L. (1981). Intracellular determinants of aging. *Mechanisms of Aging and Development, 28,* 177.

Hayne, H., & Rovee-Collier, C. (1995). The organization of reactivated memory in infancy. *Child Development, 66,* 893–906.

Hayward, M. D., Friedman, S., & Chen, H. (1996). Race inequities in men's retirement. *Journal of Gerontology: Social Sciences, 51B,* S1–10.

Hayward, M. D., & Wang, W. (1993). Retirement in Shanghai. *Research on Aging, 15,* 3–32.

Healy, B. (1991). The Yentl syndrome. *New England Journal of Medicine, 325*(4), 274–276.

Heath, S. B. (1989). Oral and literate tradition among black Americans living in poverty. *American Psychologist, 44,* 367–373.

Helgeson, V. S. (1994). Relation of agency and communion to well-being: Evidence and potential explanations. *Psychological Bulletin, 116,* 412–428.

Heller, R. B., & Dobbs, A. R. (1993). Age differences in word finding in discourse and nondiscourse situations. *Psychology and Aging, 8,* 443–450.

Helmreich, W. (1991). *Against all odds:*

Holocaust survivors and the successful lives they made in America. New York: Simon & Schuster.

Helms, J. E. (1992). Why is there no study of cultural equivalence in standardized cognitive ability testing? *American Psychologist, 47,* 1083–1101.

Helson, R. (1992). Women's difficult times and the rewriting of the life story. *Psychology of Women Quarterly, 16,* 331–347.

Helson, R. (1993). Comparing longitudinal studies of adult development: Toward a paradigm of tension between stability and change. In D. C. Funder, R. D. Parke, C. Tomlinson-Keasey, & K. Widaman (Eds.), *Studying lives through time: Personality and development* (pp. 93–120). Washington, DC: American Psychological Association.

Helson, R., & Moane, G. (1987). Personality change in women from college to midlife. *Journal of Personality and Social Psychology, 53,* 176–186.

Helson, R., & Picano, J. (1990). Is the traditional role bad for women? *Journal of Personality and Social Psychology, 59,* 311–320.

Helson, R., & Wink, P. (1992). Personality change in women from the early 40s to the early 50s. *Psychology and Aging, 7*(1), 46–55.

Hendin, H. (1994, December 16). Scared to death of dying. *The New York Times,* p. A39.

Henker, B., & Whalen, C. K. (1989). Hyperactivity and attention deficits. *American Psychologist, 44,* 216–223.

Henker, F. O. (1981). Male climacteric. In J. G. Howells (Ed.), *Modern perspectives in the psychiatry of middle age.* New York: Brunner/Mazel.

Henly, W. L., & Fitch, B. R. (1966). Newborn narcotic withdrawal associated with regional enteritis in pregnancy. *New York Journal of Medicine, 66,* 2565–2567.

Henrich, J. B. (1992). The postmenopausal estrogen/breast cancer controversy. *Journal of the American Medical Association, 268*(14), 1900–1902.

Herman-Giddens, M. E., Slora, E. J., Wasserman, R. C., Bourdony, C. J., Bhapkar, M. V., Koch, G. G., & Hasemeier, C. M. (1997). Secondary sexual characteristics and menses in young girls seen in office practice: A study from the Pediatric Research in Office Settings network. *Pediatrics, 99,* 505–512.

Herrnstein, R. J., & Murray, C. (1994). *The bell curve: Intelligence and class structure in American life.* New York: Free Press.

Hertzog, C. (1989). Influences of cognitive slowing on age differences in intelligence. *Developmental Psychology, 25*(4), 636–651.

Hertzog, C., & Dixon, R. A. (1994). Metacognitive development in adulthood and old age. In J. Metcalfe & A. P. Shimamura (Eds.), *Metacognition: Knowing about knowing* (pp. 221–251). Cambridge, MA: MIT Press.

Hertzog, C., Dixon, R. A., & Hultsch, D. F. (1990). Relationships between metamemory, memory predictions, and memory task performance in adults. *Psychology and Aging, 5*(2), 215–227.

Hertzog, C., Saylor, L. L., Fleece, A. M., & Dixon, R. A. (1994). Metamemory and aging: Relations between predicted, actual, and perceived memory task performance. *Aging and Cognition, 1,* 203–237.

Herzog, D. B., Keller, M. B., & Lavori, P. W. (1988). Outcome in anorexia nervosa and bulimia. *Journal of Nervous and Mental Disease, 176,* 131–143.

Hess, E. (1996). Discourse, memory and the Adult Attachment Interview: A note with emphasis on the emerging Cannot Classify category. *Infant Mental Health Journal, 17*(1), 4–11.

Hetherington, E. M. (1965). A developmental study of the effects of sex of the dominant parent on sex role preference, identification, and imitation in children. *Journal of Personality and Social Psychology, 2,* 188–194.

Hetherington, E. M. (1980). Children and divorce. In R. Henderson (Ed.), *Parent-child interaction: Theory, research and prospects.* New York: Academic Press.

Hetherington, E. M. (1987). Family relations six years after divorce. In K. Pasley & M. Ihinger-Tallman (Eds.), *Remarriage and parenting today: Research and theory.* New York: Guilford.

Hetherington, E. M. (1989). Coping with family transitions: Winners, losers, and survivors. *Child Development, 60,* 1–14.

Hetherington, E. M., Stanley-Hagen, M., & Anderson, E. (1989). Marital transitions: A child's perspective. *American Psychologist, 44,* 303–312.

Hewlett, B. S. (1987). Intimate fathers: Patterns of paternal holding among Aka pygmies. In M. E. Lamb (Ed.), *The father's role: Cross-cultural perspectives.* Hillsdale, NJ: Erlbaum.

Heyman, R. E., O'Leary, K. D., & Jouriles, E. N. (1995). Alcohol and aggressive personality styles: Potentiators of serious physical aggression against wives? *Journal of Family Psychology, 9*(1), 44–57.

Heyns, B., & Catsambis, S. (1986). Mother's employment and children's achievement: A critique. *Sociology of Education, 59,* 140–151.

Hill, C. D., Thompson, L. W., & Gallagher, D. (1988). The role of anticipatory bereavement in older women's adjustment to widowhood. *The Gerontologist, 28*(6), 792–796.

Hill, J. P. (1987). Research on adolescents and their families: Past and prospect. In E. E. Irwin (Ed.), *Adolescent social be-havior and health.* San Francisco: Jossey-Bass.

Hill, R. D., Storandt, M., & Malley, M. (1993). The impact of exercise training on psychological function in older adults. *Journal of Gerontology, 48*(1), 12–17.

Hilts, P. J. (1991, August 29). Study shows passing AIDS in breast milk is easier than thought. *The New York Times,* p. B13.

Himes, C. L., Hogan, D. P., & Eggebeen, D. J. (1996). Living arrangements of minority elders. *Journal of Gerontology: Social Sciences, 51B,* S42–48.

Hirsch, H. V., & Spinelli, D. N. (1970). Visual experience modifies distribution of horizontally and vertically oriented receptive fields in cats. *Science, 168,* 869–871.

Hirsh-Pasek, K. (1991). Pressure or challenge in preschool? How academic environments affect children. In L. Rescorla, M. C. Hyston, & K. Hirsh-Pasek (Eds.), *Academic instruction in early childhood: Challenge or pressure?* San Francisco: Jossey-Bass.

Hirsh-Pasek, K., Hyson, M. C., & Rescorla, L. (1989, August). *Academic environments in early childhood: Challenge and pressure.* Paper presented at the annual meeting of the American Psychological Association, New Orleans.

Hoff-Ginsberg, E. (1985). Relations between discourse properties of mothers' speech and their children's syntactic growth. *Journal of Child Language, 12,* 367–385.

Hoff-Ginsberg, E. (1986). Function and structure in maternal speech: The relation to the child's development of syntax. *Developmental Psychology, 22*(2), 155–163.

Hoff-Ginsberg, E. (1991). Mother-child conversation in different social classes and communicative settings. *Child Development, 62,* 782–796.

Hoff-Ginsberg, E., & Shatz, M. (1982). Linguistic input and the child's acquisition of language. *Psychological Bulletin, 92*(1), 3–26.

Hoffman, L. W. (1979). Maternal employment. *American Psychologist, 34*(10), 859–865.

Hoffman, L. W. (1986). Work, family, and the child. In M. S. Pallak & R. O. Perloff (Eds.), *Psychology and work: Productivity, change, and employment.* Washington, DC: American Psychological Association.

Hoffman, L. W. (1989). Effects of maternal employment in the two-parent family: A review of recent research. *American Psychologist, 44*(2), 283–292.

Hoffman, M. L. (1970a). Conscience, personality, and socialization techniques. *Human Development, 13,* 90–126.

Hoffman, M. L. (1970b). Moral development. In P. H. Mussen (Ed.), *Carmichael's manual of child psychology* (Vol. 2, 3d ed., pp. 261–360). New York: Wiley.

Hoffman, M. L. (1977). Sex differences in empathy and related behaviors. *Psychological Bulletin, 84,* 712–722.

Hoffman, M. L., & Hoffman, L. W. (Eds.). (1964). *Review of child development research.* New York: Russell Sage Foundation.

Holden, C. (1994). A cautionary genetic tale: The sobering story of D_2. *Science, 264,* 1696–1697.

Holden, C. (1996, July 5). New populations of old add to poor nations' burdens. *Science,* pp. 46–48.

Hollinger, C. L., & Fleming, E. S. (1992). A longitudinal examination of life choices of gifted and talented young women. *Gifted Child Quarterly, 36*(4), 207–212.

Holmes, T. H., & Rahe, R. H. (1976). The social readjustment rating scale. *Journal of Psychosomatic Research, 11,* 213.

Holtzworth-Munroe, A. (1995, August). Marital violence. *Harvard Mental Health Letter,* pp. 4–6.

Holtzworth-Munroe, A., & Stuart, G. L. (1994). Typologies of male batterers: Three subtypes and the differences among them. *Psychological Bulletin, 116*(3), 476–497.

Home, J. (1985). *Caregiving: Helping an aging loved one.* Washington, DC: AARP Books.

Hooker, K., Monahan, D., Shifren, K., & Hutchinson, C. (1992). Mental and physical health of spouse caregivers: The role of personality. *Psychology and Aging, 7*(3), 367–375.

Hooyman, N. R., Rathbone-McCuan, E., & Klingbeil, K. (1982). Serving the vulnerable elderly. *Urban and Social Change Review, 15*(2), 9–13.

Hopper, J. L., & Seeman, E. (1994). The bone density of female twins discordant for tobacco use. *New England Journal of Medicine, 330,* 387–392.

Horbar, J. D., Wright, E. C., Onstad, L., & the Members of the National Institute of Child Health and Human Development Neonatal Research Network. (1993). Decreasing mortality associated with the introduction of surfactant therapy: An observational study of neonates weighing 601 to 1300 grams at birth. *Pediatrics, 92,* 191–196.

Hormone therapy: Is it the right choice for you? (1995, September). *Health after 50: The Johns Hopkins Medical Letter,* pp. 4–6.

Horn, J. (1983). The Texas adoption project: Adopted children and their intellectual resemblance to biological and adoptive parents. *Child Development, 54,* 268–275.

Horn, J. C., & Meer, J. (1987, May). The vintage years. *Psychology Today,* pp. 76–90.

Horn, J. L. (1967). Intelligence—Why it

grows, why it declines. *Transaction, 5*(1), 23–31.

Horn, J. L. (1968). Organization of abilities and the development of intelligence. *Psychological Review, 75,* 242–259.

Horn, J. L. (1970). Organization of data on life-span development of human abilities. In L. R. Goulet & P. B. Baltes (Eds.), *Life-span developmental psychology: Theory and research* (pp. 424–466). New York: Academic Press.

Horn, J. L. (1982a). The aging of human abilities. In B. B. Wolman (Ed.), *Handbook of developmental psychology* (pp. 847–870). Englewood Cliffs, NJ: Prentice-Hall.

Horn, J. L. (1982b). The theory of fluid and crystallized intelligence in relation to concepts of cognitive psychology and aging in adulthood. In F. I. M. Craik & S. Trehub (Eds.), *Aging and cognitive processes* (pp. 237–278). New York: Plenum.

Horn, J. L., & Cattell, R. B. (1966). Age differences in primary mental ability factors. *Journal of Gerontology, 21,* 210–220.

Horn, J. L., & Donaldson, G. (1976). On the myth of intellectual decline in adulthood. *American Psychologist, 31,* 701–719.

Horn, J. L., & Donaldson, G. (1977). Faith is not enough: A response to the Baltes-Schaie claim that intelligence does not wane. *American Psychologist, 32,* 369–373.

Horn, J. L., & Donaldson, G. (1980). Cognitive development: 2. Adulthood development of human abilities. In O. G. Brim & J. Kagan (Eds.), *Constancy and change in human development.* Cambridge, MA: Harvard University Press.

Horn, J. L., & Hofer, S. M. (1992). Major abilities and development in the adult. In R. J. Sternberg & C. A. Berg (Eds.), *Intellectual development.* Cambridge, UK: Cambridge University Press.

Horowitz, F. D. (1992). John B. Watson's legacy: Learning and environment. *Developmental Psychology, 28*(3), 360–367.

Horowitz, F. D., & O'Brien, M. (1986). Gifted and talented children: State of knowledge and directions for research. *American Psychologist, 41*(10), 1147–1152.

Hossain, Z., & Roopnarine, J. L. (1994). African-American fathers' involvement with infants: Relationship to their functioning style, support, education, and income. *Infant Behavior and Development, 17*(2), 175–184.

House, J. D., & Wohlt, V. (1991). Effect of tutoring on voluntary school withdrawal of academically underprepared minority students. *Journal of School Psychology, 29,* 135–142.

House, S. J., Landis, K. R., & Umberson, D. (1988). Social relationships and health. *Science, 241,* 540–544.

Householder, J., Hatcher, R., Burns, W., & Chasnoff, I. (1982). Infants born to narcotics-addicted mothers. *Psychological Bulletin, 92,* 453–468.

Howard, M. (1983). Posponing sexual involvement: A new approach. *SIECUS Report, 11*(4), 5–6, 8.

Howes, C., Hamilton, C. E., & Matheson, C. C. (1994). Children's relationships with peers: Differential associations with aspects of the teacher-child relationship. *Child Development, 65,* 253–263.

Howes, C., & Matheson, C. C. (1992). Sequences in the development of competent play with peers: Social and social pretend play. *Developmental Psychology, 28*(5), 961–974.

Howes, C., Matheson, C. C., & Hamilton, C. E. (1994). Maternal, teacher, and child care history correlates of children's relationships with peers. *Child Development, 65,* 264–273.

Hoyer, W. J., & Rybash, J. M. (1994). Characterizing adult cognitive development. *Journal of Adult Development, 1*(1), 7–12.

Hu, S., Pattatucci, A. M. L., Patterson, C., Li, L., Fulker, D. W., Cherny, S. S., Kruglyak, L., & Hamer, D. H. (1995). Linkage between sexual orientation and chromosome Xq28 in males but not in females. *Nature Genetics, 11,* 248–256.

Hu, Y., & Goldman, N. (1990). Mortality differentials by marital status: An international comparison. *Demography, 27*(2), 233–250.

Hudson, J. I., & Pope, H. G. (1990). Affective spectrum disorder: Does antidepressant response identify a family of disorders with a common pathophysiology? *American Journal of Psychiatry, 147*(5), 552–564.

Huesmann, L. R. (1986). Psychological processes promoting the relation between exposure to media violence and aggressive behavior by the viewer. *Journal of Social Issues, 42,* 125–139.

Hughes, M. (1975). *Egocentrism in preschool children.* Unpublished doctoral dissertation, Edinburgh University, Edinburgh.

Hultsch, D. F. (1971). Organization and memory in adulthood. *Human Development, 14,* 16–29.

Humphrey, L. L. (1986). Structural analysis of parent-child relationships in eating disorders. *Journal of Abnormal Psychology, 95*(4), 395–402.

Humphreys, A. P., & Smith, P. K. (1984). Rough-and-tumble in preschool and playground. In P. K. Smith (Ed.), *Play in animals and humans.* Oxford: Blackwell.

Humphreys, A. P., & Smith, P. K. (1987). Rough and tumble, friendship, and dominance in schoolchildren: Evidence for continuity and change with age. *Child Development, 58,* 201–212.

Hunsaker, S. L., & Callahan, C. M. (1995). Creativity and giftedness: Published instrument uses and abuses. *Gifted Child Quarterly, 39*(2), 110–114.

Hunt, B., & Hunt, M. (1974). *Prime time.* New York: Stein & Day.

Hunt, C. E. (1996). Prone sleeping in healthy infants and victims of sudden infant death syndrome. *Journal of Pediatrics, 128,* 594–596.

Hunt, C. E., & Brouillette, R. T. (1987). Sudden infant death syndrome: 1987 perspective. *Journal of Pediatrics, 110*(5), 669–678.

Huston, A., et al. (1993). *Big world, small screen: The role of television in American society.* Lincoln: University of Nebraska Press.

Huttenlocher, J., Haight, W., Bryk, A., Seltzer, M., & Lyons, T. (1991). Early vocabulary growth: Relation to language input and gender. *Developmental Psychology, 27*(2), 236–248.

Huyck, M. H. (1990). Gender differences in aging. In J. E. Birren & K. W. Schaie (Eds.), *Handbook of the psychology of aging* (3d ed., pp. 124–132). San Diego: Academic Press.

Hwang, C.-P., & Broberg, A. G. (1992). The historical and social context of child care in Sweden. In M. E. Lamb, K. J. Sternberg, C.-P. Hwang, & A. G. Broberg (Eds.). *Child care in context.* Hillsdale, NJ: Erlbaum.

Hwang, S.-J., Beaty, T. H., Panny, S. R., Street, N. A., Joseph, J. M., Gordon, S., McIntosh, I., & Francomano, C. A. (1995). Association study of transforming growth factor alpha (TGF*a*) *Taq*I polymorphism and oral clefts: Indication of gene-environment interaction in a population-based sample of infants with birth defects. *American Journal of Epidemiology, 141,* 629–636.

Hyde, J. S. (1986). *Understanding human sexuality* (3d ed.). New York: McGraw-Hill.

Hyde, J. S., Fennema, E., & Lamon, S. J. (1990). Gender differences in mathematics performance: A meta-analysis. *Psychological Bulletin, 107*(2), 139–155.

Hyde, J., & Linn, M. C. (1988). Gender differences in verbal abilities: A meta-analysis. *Psychological Bulletin, 104*(1), 53–69.

Hyman, B. T., van Hoesen, G. W., Damasio, A. R., & Barnes, C. L. (1984). Alzheimer's disease: Cell-specific pathology isolates hippocampal formation. *Science, 225,* 1168–1170.

Hynd, G. W., & Semrud-Clikeman, M. (1989). Dyslexia and brain morphology. *Psychological Bulletin, 106*(3), 447–482.

Ickovics, J. R., et al. (1994). Limited effects of HIV counseling and testing for women: A prospective study of behavioral and psychological consequences. *Journal of the American Medical Association, 272*(6), 443–448.

Infant Health and Development Program. (1990). Enhancing the outcomes of low-birth-weight, premature infants. *Journal of the American Medical Association, 263*(22), 3035–3042.

Infante-Rivard, C., Fernández, A., Gauthier, R., David, M., & Rivard, G.-E. (1993). Fetal loss associated with caffeine intake before and during pregnancy. *Journal of the American Medical Association, 270,* 2940–2943.

Ingram, D. D., Makuc, D., & Kleinman, J. C. (1986). National and state trends in use of prenatal care, 1970–1983. *American Journal of Public Health, 76*(4), 415–423.

Institute of Medicine, National Academy of Sciences (IOM). (1993, November). *Assessing genetic risks: Implications for health and social policy.* Washington, DC: National Academy of Sciences.

Institute of Medicine, National Academy of Sciences (IOM). (1994). *Overcoming barriers to immunization: A workshop summary.* Washington, DC: National Academy Press.

Isabella, R. A. (1993). Origins of attachment: Maternal interactive behavior across the first year. *Child Development, 64,* 605–621.

Ivy, G. O., MacLeod, C. M., Petit, T. L., & Markus, E. J. (1992). A physiological framework for perceptual and cognitive changes in aging. In F. I. M. Craik & T. A. Salthouse (Eds.), *Handbook of aging and cognition* (pp. 273–314). Hillsdale, NJ: Erlbaum.

Izard, C. E., Haynes, O. M., Chisholm, G., & Baak, K. (1991). Emotional determinants of infant-mother attachment. *Child Development, 62,* 906–917.

Izard, C. E., Huebner, R. R., Resser, D., McGinness, G. C., & Dougherty, L. M. (1980). The young infant's ability to produce discrete emotional expressions. *Developmental Psychology, 16*(2), 132–140.

Izard, C. E., & Malatesta, C. Z. (1987). Perspectives on emotional development I: Differential emotions theory of early emotional development. In J. D. Osofksy (Ed.), *Handbook of infant development* (2d ed.). New York: Wiley.

Izard, C. E., Porges, S. W., Simons, R. F., Haynes, O. M., & Cohen, B. (1991). Infant cardiac activity: Developmental changes and relations with attachment. *Developmental Psychology, 27,* 432–439.

Jackson, J. F. (1993). Human behavioral genetics, Scarr's theory, and her views on interventions: A critical review and commentary on their implications for African American children. *Child Development, 64,* 1318–1332.

Jacobs, R., Hofmann, D. A., & Kriska, S. D. (1990). Performance and seniority. *Human Performance, 3,* 107–121.

Jacobson, J. L., & Wille, D. E. (1986). The influence of attachment pattern on developmental changes in peer interaction from the toddler to the preschool period. *Child Development, 57,* 338–347.

Jacobson, S. W., Jacobson, J. L., Sokol, R. J., Martier, S. S., & Ager, J. W. (1993). Prenatal alcohol exposure and infant information processing ability. *Child Development, 64,* 1706–1721.

Jacques, E. (1967). The mid-life crisis. In R. Owen (Ed.), *Middle age.* London: BBC.

James, W. (1950). *The principles of psychology* (2 vols.). New York: Dover. (Original work published 1890)

Janos, P. M., & Robinson, N. M. (1985). Psychosocial development in intellectually gifted children. In F. D. Horowitz & M. O'Brien (Eds.), *The gifted and talented: Developmental perspectives* (pp. 251–295). Washington, DC: American Psychological Association.

Jaslow, C. K. (1982). *Teenage pregnancy* (ERIC/CAPS Fact Sheet). Ann Arbor, MI: Counseling and Personnel Services Clearing House.

Jason, J. M. (1989). Infectious disease–related deaths of low birth weight infants, United States. 1968 to 1982. *Pediatrics, 84*(2), 296–303.

Jay, M. S., DuRant, R. H., Shoffitt, T., Linder, C. W., & Litt, I. F. (1984). Effect of peer counselors on adolescent compliance in use of oral contraceptives. *Pediatrics, 73*(2), 126–131.

Jefferson, J. W., & Greist, J. H. (1993). *Depression and older people: Recognizing hidden signs and taking steps toward recovery.* Madison, WI: Pratt Pharmaceuticals.

Jendrek, M. P. (1994). Grandparents who parent grandchildren: Circumstances and decisions. *The Gerontologist, 34,* 206–216.

Jenkins, J. M., & Astington, J. W. (1996). Cognitive factors and family structure associated with theory of mind development in young children. *Developmental Psychology, 32*(1), 70–78.

Jensen, A. R. (1969). How much can we boost IQ and scholastic achievement? *Harvard Educational Review, 39,* 1–123.

Jensen, A. R. (1993). Test validity: *g* versus "tacit knowledge." *Current Directions in Psychological Science, 2*(1), 9–11.

Jerger, J., Chmiel, R., Wilson, N., & Luchi, R. (1995). Hearing impairment in older adults: New concepts. *Journal of the American Geriatrics Society, 43,* 928–935.

Jiao, S., Ji, G., & Jing, Q. (1986). Comparative study of behavioral qualities of only children and sibling children. *Child Development, 57,* 357–361.

Jiao, S., Ji, G., & Jing, Q. (1996). Cognitive development of Chinese urban only children and children with siblings. *Child Development, 67,* 387–395.

Johnson, C. L. (1985). *Growing up and growing old in Italian-American families.* New Brunswick, NJ: Rutgers University Press.

Johnson, C. L., & Catalano, D. J. (1981). Childless elderly and their family supports. *The Gerontologist, 21*(6), 610–618.

Johnson, C. L., & Troll, L. (1992). Family functioning in late late life. *Journal of Gerontology: Social Sciences, 47*(2), S66–72.

Johnson, C. L., & Troll, L. E. (1994). Constraints and facilitators to friendships in late late life. *The Gerontologist, 34,* 79–87.

Johnson, M. M. S. (1990). Age differences in decision making: A process methodology for examining strategic information processing. *Journal of Gerontology, Psychological Sciences, 45,* P75–78.

Johnson, M. M. S., Schmitt, F. A., & Everard, K. (1994). *Task driven strategies: The impact of age and information on decision-making performance.* Unpublished manuscript, University of Kentucky, Lexington.

Johnson, R. K., Smiciklas-Wright, H., Crouter, C., & Willits, F. K. (1992). Maternal employment and the quality of young children's diets: Empirical evidence based on the 1987–1988 nationwide food consumption inquiry. *Pediatrics, 90*(2), 245–249.

Johnson, S. J., & Rybash, J. M. (1993). A cognitive neuroscience perspective on age-related slowing: Developmental changes in the functional architecture. In J. Cerella, J. M. Rybash, W. J. Hoyer, & M. L. Commons (Eds.), *Adult information processing: Limits on loss* (pp. 143–175). San Diego: Academic Press.

Johnson, S. L., & Birch, L. L. (1994). Parents' and children's adiposity and eating styles. *Pediatrics, 94,* 653–661.

Johnson, T. E. (1990). Age-1 mutants of *Caenorhabditis elegans* prolong life by modifying the Gompertz rate of aging. *Science, 229,* 908–912.

Johnston, J., & Ettema, J. S. (1982). *Positive images: Breaking stereotypes with children's television.* Newbury Park, CA: Sage.

Johnston, W. B., & Packer, A. H. (1987). *Workforce 2000: Work and workers for the 21st century.* Indianapolis, IN: Hudson Institute.

Jones, C. J., & Meredith, W. (1996). Patterns of personality change across the life span. *Psychology and Aging, 11*(1), 57–65.

Jones, C. L., Tepperman, L., & Wilson, S. J. (1995). *The future of the family.* Englewood Cliffs, NJ: Prentice-Hall.

Jones, D. C., Swift, D. J., & Johnson, M. A. (1988). Nondeliberate memory for a novel event among preschoolers. *Developmental Psychology, 24*(5), 641–645.

Jones, E. (1961). *The life and work of Sigmund Freud.* New York: Basic Books.

Jones, E. F., Forrest, J. D., Goldman, N., Henshaw, S. K., Lincoln, R., Rosoff, J. I., Westoff, C. F., Wulf, W., & Wulf, D. (1985). Teenage pregnancy in developed countries: Determinants and policy implications. *Family Planning Perspectives, 17,* 53–63.

Jones, H., & Conrad, H. (1933). The growth and decline of intelligence: A study of a homogeneous group between the ages of 10 and 60. *Genetic Psychology Monographs, 13,* 223–298.

Jones, H. W., & Toner, J. P. (1993). The infertile couple. *New England Journal of Medicine, 329,* 1710–1715.

Jones, M. C. (1957). The late careers of boys who were early- or late-maturing. *Child Development, 28,* 115–128.

Jones, M. C. (1958). The study of socialization patterns at the high school level. *Journal of Genetic Psychology, 93,* 87–111.

Jouriles, E. N., & Norwood, W. D. (1995). Physical aggression toward boys and girls in families characterized by the battering of women. *Journal of Family Psychology, 9*(1), 69–78.

Jung, C. G. (1953). The stages of life. In H. Read, M. Fordham, & G. Adler (Eds.), *Collected works* (Vol. 2). Princeton, NJ: Princeton University Press. (Original work published 1931)

Jung, C. G. (1961). *Memories, dreams, and reflections.* New York: Random House.

Jung, C. G. (1966). Two essays on analytic psychology. In *Collected works* (Vol. 7). Princeton, NJ: Princeton University Press.

Jung, C. G. (1969). *The structure and dynamics of the psyche.* Princeton, NJ: Princeton University Press.

Jusczyk, P. W., Cutler, A., & Redanz, N. J. (1993). Infants' preference for the predominant stress patterns of English words. *Child Development, 64,* 675–687.

Kaback, M., Lim-Steele, J., Dabholkar, D., Brown, D., Levy, N., Zeiger, K., for the International TSD Data Collection Network. (1993). Tay-Sachs disease—Carrier screening, prenatal diagnosis, and the molecular era. *Journal of the American Medical Association, 270,* 2307–2315.

Kagan, J. (1984). *The nature of the child.* New York: Basic Books.

Kagan, J. (1989). *Unstable ideas: Temperament, cognition, and self.* Cambridge, MA: Harvard University Press.

Kagan, J., Arcus, D., Snidman, N., Wang, Y. F., Hendler, J., & Greene, S. (1994). Reactivity in infants: A cross-national comparison. *Developmental Psychology, 30,* 342–345.

Kagan, J., Reznick, J. S., Clarke, C., Snidman, N., & Garcia-Coll, C. (1984). Behavioral inhibition to the unfamiliar. *Child Development, 55,* 2212–2225.

Kagan, J., Reznick, J. S., & Gibbons, J. (1989). Inhibited and uninhibited types of children. *Child Development, 60,* 838–845.

Kagan, J., & Snidman, N. (1991a). Infant predictors of inhibited and uninhib-

ited behavioral profiles. *Psychological Science, 2,* 40–44.

Kagan, J., & Snidman, N. (1991b). Temperamental factors in human development. *American Psychologist, 46,* 856–862.

Kahana, B., & Kahana, E. (1970). Grandparenthood from the perspective of the developing grandchild. *Developmental Psychology, 3,* 98–105.

Kahana, E. (1982). A congruence model of person-environment interaction. In M. P. Lawton & T. O. Byerts (Eds.), *Aging and the environment: Theoretical approaches* (pp. 97–121). New York: Springer.

Kahn, R. L., & Antonucci, T. C. (1980). Convoys over the life course: Attachment, roles, and social support. In P. B. Baltes & O. G. Brim, Jr (Eds.), *Life-span development and behavior* (pp. 253–286). New York: Academic Press.

Kail, R. (1991). Processing time declines exponentially during childhood and adolescence. *Developmental Psychology, 27,* 259–266.

Kaiser, M. A. (1993). The productive roles of older people in developing countries: What are the implications of economic, social, and cultural participation? *Generations, 17*(4), 65–69.

Kalmuss, D., Davidson, A., & Cushman, L. (1992). Parental expectations, experiences, and adjustment to parenthood: A test of the violated expectations framework. *Journal of Marriage and the Family, 54,* 516–526.

Kalmuss, D. S., & Straus, M. A. (1982). Wife's marital dependency and wife abuse. *Journal of Marriage and the Family, 44,* 277–286.

Kamin, L. J. (1974). *The science and politics of IQ.* Potomac, MD: Erlbaum.

Kamin, L. J. (1981). Commentary. In S. Scarr (Ed.), *Race, social class, and individual differences in I. Q.* Hillsdale, NJ: Erlbaum.

Kandel, D. B., Davies, M., Karus, D., & Yamaguchi, K. (1986). The consequences in young adulthood of adolescent drug involvement. *Archives of General Psychiatry, 43,* 746–754.

Kane, R. I., Wales, J., Bernstein, L., Leibowitz, A., & Kaplan, S. (1984, April 21). A randomized controlled trial of hospice care. *The Lancet,* pp. 890–894.

Kangas, J., & Bradway, K. (1971). Intelligence at middle age: A thirty-eight year follow-up. *Developmental Psychology, 5,* 333–337.

Kaplan, G. (1994). Reflections on present and future research on bio-behavioral risk factors. In S. Blumenthal, K. Matthews, & S. Weiss (Eds.), *New research frontiers in behavioral medicine: Proceedings of the national conference* (p. 124). Washington, DC: NIH Publications.

Kaplan, H., & Dove, H. (1987). Infant development among the Ache of East

Paraguay. *Developmental Psychology, 23*(2), 190–198.

Karlinsky, H., Lennox, A., & Rossor, M. (1994). Alzheimer's disease and genetic testing. *Alzheimer's Disease and Associated Disorders, 8*(2), 63–65.

Karney, B. R., & Bradbury, T. N. (1995). The longitudinal course of marital quality and stability: A review of theory, method, and research. *Psychological Bulletin, 118,* 3–34.

Kastenbaum, R. (1993). Reconstructing death in postmodern society. *Omega, 27,* 75–89.

Katchadourian, H. (1987). *Fifty: Midlife in perspective.* New York: Freeman.

Katz, L. F., & Gottman, J. M. (1993). Patterns of marital conflict predict children's internalizing and externalizing behaviors. *Developmental Psychology, 29,* 940–950.

Katz, S., Branch, L. G., Branson, M. H., Papsidero, J. A., Beck, J. C., & Greer, D. S. (1983). Active life expectancy. *New England Journal of Medicine, 309,* 1218–1224.

Katzev, A. R., Warner, R. L., & Acock, A. C. (1994). Girl or boy? Relationship of child gender to marital instability. *Journal of Marriage and the Family, 56,* 89–100.

Katzman, R. (1993). Education and prevalence of Alzheimer's disease. *Neurology, 43,* 13–20.

Kaufman, A. S., & Kaufman, N. L. (1983). *Kaufman assessment battery for children: Administration and scoring manual.* Circle Pines, MN: American Guidance Service.

Kaufman, J., & Zigler, E. (1987). Do abused children become abusive parents? *American Journal of Orthopsychiatry, 57*(2), 186–192.

Kaufman, T. S. (1993). *The combined family: A guide to creating successful step-relationships.* New York: Plenum.

Kausler, D. H. (1990). Automaticity of encoding and episodic memory processes. In E. A. Lovelace (Ed.), *Aging and cognition: Mental processes, self-awareness, and interventions* (pp. 29–67). Amsterdam: North-Holland, Elsevier.

Kawachi, I., Colditz, G. A., Ascherio, A., Rimm, E. B., Giovannucci, E., Stampfer, M. J., & Willett, W. C. (1994). Prospective study of phobic anxiety and risk of coronary heart disease in men. *Circulation, 89,* 1992–1997.

Kawachi, I., Colditz, G. A., Stampfer, M. J., Willett, W. C., Manson, J. E., Rosner, B., Speizer, F. E., & Hennekens, C. H. (1993). Smoking cessation and decreased risk of stroke in women. *Journal of the American Medical Association, 269,* 232–236.

Kawachi, I., Colditz, G. A., Stampfer, M. J., Willett, W. C., Manson, J. E., Speizer, F. E., & Hennekens, C. H. (1995). Prospective study of shift work and risk of coronary heart disease in women. *Circulation, 92,* 3178–3182.

Kawachi, I., Sparrow, D., Vokonas, P. S., & Weiss, S. T. (1994). Symptoms of anxiety and risk of coronary heart disease: The Normative Aging Study. *Circulation, 90,* 2225–2229.

Kawachi, I., Troisi, R. J., Rotnitzky, A. G., Coakley, E. H., & Colditz, G. A. (1996). Can physical activity minimize weight gain in women after smoking cessation? *American Journal of Public Health, 86,* 999–1004.

Kawai, S. (1996). Japan's national health care system: How do elders fare?—Crises in health care generate changes in national health plan. *Geriatric Nursing, 17*(3), 111–114.

Kaye, W. H., Weltzin, T. E., Hsu, L. K. G., & Bulik, C. M. (1991). An open trial of fluoxetine in patients with anorexia nervosa. *Journal of Clinical Psychiatry, 52,* 464–471.

Kayser-Jones, J. A. (1982). Institutional structures: Catalysts of or barriers to quality care for the institutionalized aged in Scotland and the U.S. *Social Science Medicine, 16,* 935–944.

Keeney, T. J., Canizzo, S. R., & Flavell, J. H. (1967). Spontaneous and induced verbal rehearsal in a recall task. *Child Development, 38,* 953–966.

Keith, P. M. (1983). A comparison of the resources of parents and childless men and women in very old age. *Family Relations, 32,* 403–409.

Kelleher, K. J., Casey, P. H., Bradley, R. H., Pope, S. K., Whiteside, L., Barrett, K. W., Swanson, M. E., & Kirby, R. S. (1993). Risk factors and outcomes for failure to thrive in low birth weight preterm infants. *Pediatrics, 91,* 941–948.

Kellerman, A. L., Rivara, F. P., Somes, G., Reay, D. T., Francisco, J., Banton, J. G., Prodzinski, J., Flinger, C., & Hackman, B. B. (1992). Suicide in the home in relation to gun ownership. *New England Journal of Medicine, 327,* 467–472.

Kellogg, R. (1970). Understanding children's art. In P. Cramer (Ed.), *Readings in developmental psychology today.* Delmar, CA: CRM.

Kelly, J. B. (1982). Divorce: The adult perspective. In B. Wolman (Ed.), *Handbook of developmental psychology.* Englewood Cliffs, NJ: Prentice-Hall.

Kelly, J. B. (1987, August). *Longer-term adjustment in children of divorce: Converging findings and implications for practice.* Paper presented at the annual meeting of the American Psychological Association, New York.

Kelly, J. R. (1987). *Peoria winter: Styles and resources in later life.* Lexington, MA: Lexington.

Kelly, J. R. (1994). Recreation and leisure. In A. Monk (Ed.), *The Columbia retirement handbook* (pp. 489–508). New York: Columbia University Press.

Kelly, J. R., Steinkamp, M., & Kelly, J. (1986). Later life leisure: How they play in Peoria. *The Gerontologist, 26,* 531–537.

Kempe, C. H., Silverman, F. N., Steele, B. N., Droegemueller, W., & Silver, H. K. (1962). The battered child syndrome. *Journal of the American Medical Association, 181,* 17–24.

Kemper, T. L. (1994). Neuroanatomical and neuropathological changes during aging and dementia. In M. L. Albert & J. E. Knoefel (Eds.), *Clinical neurology of aging* (pp. 3–67). New York: Oxford University Press.

Kendall-Tackett, K. A., Williams, L. M., & Finkelhor, D. (1993). Impact of sexual abuse on children: A review and synthesis of recent empirical studies. *Psychological Bulletin, 113*(1), 164–180.

Kendler, K. S., Walters, E. E., Truett, K. R., et al. (1994). Sources of individual differences in depressive symptoms: Analysis of two samples of twins and their families. *American Journal of Psychiatry, 51,* 1605–1614.

Kennedy, R. (1994, December 5). Elizabeth Glaser dies at 47; crusader for pediatric AIDS. *The New York Times,* p. A12.

Kennell, J., Klaus, M., McGrath, S., Robertson, S., & Hinckley, C. (1991). Continuous emotional support during labor in a US hospital. *Journal of the American Medical Association, 265,* 2197–2201.

Kerr, B. A. (1985). *Smart girls, gifted women.* Columbus, OH: Ohio Psychology.

Kessen W., Haith, M., & Salapatek, P. (1970). Infancy. In P. H. Mussen (Ed.), *Carmichael's manual of child psychology* (Vol 1., 3d ed.). New York: Wiley.

Kessler, L. G. (1995). Lung cancer rates in U.S. women. *Journal of the National Cancer Institute, 87,* 79.

Kessler, R. C., McGonagle, K. A., Nelson, C. B., Hughes, M., Swartz, M., & Blazer, D. G. (1994). Sex and depression in the National Comorbidity Survey: 2. Cohort effects. *Journal of Affective Disorders, 30,* 15–26.

Kestenbaum, R., Farber, E. A., & Sroufe, L. A. (1989). Individual differences in empathy among preschoolers: Relation to attachment history. In N. Eisenberg (Ed.), Empathy and related emotional responses. *New Directions for Child Development,* No. 44. San Francisco: Jossey-Bass.

Khan, L. J., & Morrow, P. C. (1991). Objective and subjective underemployment relationships to job satisfaction. *Journal of Business Research, 22*(3), 211–218.

Kiecolt-Glaser, J. K., Fisher, L. D., Ogrocki, P., Stout, J. C., Speicher, C. E., & Glaser, R. (1987). Marital quality, marital disruption, and immune function. *Psychosomatic Medicine, 49,* 13–34.

Kiecolt-Glaser, J. K., Garner, W., Speicher, C. E., Penn, G. M., Holliday, J., & Glaser, R. (1984). Psychosocial modifiers of immunocompetence in medical students. *Psychosomatic Medicine, 46,* 7–14.

Kiecolt-Glaser, J. K., & Glaser, R. (1995). Psychoneuroimmunology and health consequences: Data and shared mechanisms. *Psychosomatic Medicine, 57,* 269–274.

Kiecolt-Glaser, J. K., Glaser, R., Shuttleworth, E. C., Dyer, C. S., Ogrocki, P., & Speicher, C. E. (1987). Chronic stress and immunity in family caregivers of Alzheimer's disease victims. *Psychosomatic Medicine, 49,* 523–535.

Kimmel, D. C. (1988). Ageism, psychology, and public policy. *American Psychologist, 43*(3), 175–178.

Kimmel, D. C., & Sang, B. E. (1995). Lesbians and gay men in midlife. In A. R. D'Augelli & C. J. Patterson (Eds.), *Lesbian, gay, and bisexual identities over the lifespan: Psychological perspectives* (pp. 190–214). New York: Oxford University Press.

King, B. M. (1996). *Human sexuality today.* Englewood Cliffs, NJ: Prentice-Hall.

King, B. M., Camp, C. J., & Downey, A. M. (1991). *Human sexuality today.* Englewood Cliffs, NJ: Prentice-Hall.

King, D. (1993, March). Age-old questions [Letter to the Editor]. *New Woman,* p. 14.

Kinney, H. C., Filiano, J. J., Sleeper, L. A., Mandell, F., Valdes-Dapena, M., & White, W. F. (1995). Decreased muscarinic receptor binding in the arcuate nucleus in Sudden Infant Death Syndrome. *Science, 269,* 1446–1450.

Kinsbourne, M. (1994). Sugar and the hyperactive child. *New England Journal of Medicine, 330,* 355–356.

Kinsella, K., & Gist, Y. J. (1995). *Older workers, retirement, and pensions: A comparative international chartbook* (International Population Center Report IPC/95-2). Washington, DC: U.S. Bureau of the Census.

Kirsch, I. S., Jenkins, L., Jungeblut, A., & Kolstad, A. (1993). *Adult literacy in America: A first look at the results of the National Adult Literacy Survey.* Princeton, NJ: Educational Testing Service.

Kirschenbaum, M. J. (1994, August). Breaking the cycle of domestic violence. *The Menninger Letter,* pp. 1–2.

Kisilevsky, B. S., Muir, D. W., & Low, J. A. (1992). Maturation of human fetal responses to vibroacoustic stimulation. *Child Development, 63,* 1497–1508.

Kistin, N., Benton, D., Rao, S., & Sullivan, M. (1990). Breast-feeding rates among black urban low-income women: Effects of prenatal education. *Pediatrics, 86*(5), 741–746.

Kitson, G. C., & Morgan, L. A. (1990). The multiple consequences of divorce:

A decade review. *Journal of Marriage and Family Therapy, 52,* 913–924.

Kitson, G. C., & Roach, M. J. (1989). Independence and social and psychological adjustment in widowhood and divorce. In D. A. Lund (Ed.), *Older bereaved spouses: Research with practical implications.* New York: Hemisphere.

Kivett, V. R. (1991). Centrality of the grandfather role among older rural black and white men. *Journal of Gerontology: Social Sciences, 46*(5), S250–258.

Kivnick, H. (1982). *The meaning of grandparenthood.* Minneapolis: UMI Research.

Klaus, M. H., & Kennell, J. H. (1976). *Maternal-infant bonding.* St. Louis: Mosby.

Klebanov, P. K., Brooks-Gunn, J., & McCormick, M. C. (1994). Classroom behavior of very low birth weight elementary school children. *Pediatrics, 94,* 700–708.

Kleemeier, R. W. (1962). Intellectual changes in the senium. *Proceedings of the American Statistical Association, 1,* 181–190.

Kleinberg, F. (1984). Sudden infant death syndrome. *Mayo Clinic Proceedings, 59,* 352–357.

Kleinman, J. C., Cooke, M., Machlin, S., & Kessel, S. S. (1983). *Variations in use of obstetric technology* (DHHS Publication No. PHS 84-1232). Washington, DC: U.S. Government Printing Office.

Klerman, G. L., & Weissman, M. M. (1989). Increasing rates of depression. *Journal of the American Medical Association, 261,* 2229–2235.

Klesges, R. C., Klesges, L. M., Eck, L. H., & Shelton, M. L. (1995). A longitudinal analysis of accelerated weight gain in preschool children. *Pediatrics, 95,* 126–130.

Klesges, R. C., Shelton, M. L., & Klesges, L. M. (1993). Effects of television on metabolic rate: Potential implications for childhood obesity. *Pediatrics, 91*(2), 281–295.

Kliegman, R., Madura, D., Kiwi, R., Eisenberg, I., & Yamashita, T. (1994). Relation of maternal cocaine use to the risk of prematurity and low birth weight. *Journal of Pediatrics, 124,* 751–756.

Kliewer, S. A., Lenhard, J. M., Willson, T. M., Patel, I., Morris, D. C., & Lehmann, J. M. (1995). A prostaglandin JZ metabolite binds peroxisome proliferator-activated receptor gamma and promotes adipocyte differentiation. *Cell, 83,* 813–819.

Kline, D. W., Kline, T. J. B., Fozard, J. L., Kosnik, W., Schieber, F., & Sekuler, R. (1992). Vision, aging, and driving: The problems of older drivers. *Journal of Gerontology: Psychological Sciences, 47*(1), P27–34.

Kline, D. W., & Scialfa, C. T. (1996). Visual and auditory aging. In J. E. Birren & K. W. Schaie (Eds.), *Handbook of the*

psychology of aging (pp. 191–208). San Diego: Academic Press.

Kline, M., Johnston, J. R., & Tschann, J. M. (1991). The long shadow of marital conflict: A model of children's post divorce adjustment. *Journal of Marriage and the Family, 53,* 297–309.

Kline, M., Tschann, J. M., Johnston, J., & Wallerstein, J. (1988, March). *Child outcome in joint and sole custody families.* Paper presented at the annual meeting of the American Orthopsychiatry Association, San Francisco.

Klinnert, M. D., Emde, R. N., Butterfield, P., & Campos, J. J. (1986). Social referencing: The infant's use of emotional signals from a friendly adult with mother present. *Developmental Psychology, 22,* 427–432.

Klonoff-Cohen, H. S., Edelstein, S. L., Lefkowitz, E. S., Srinivasan, I. P., Kaegi, D., Chang, J. C., & Wiley, K. J. (1995). The effects of passive smoking and tobacco exposure through breast milk on sudden infant death syndrome. *Journal of the American Medical Association, 273,* 795–798.

Knoop, R. (1994). Relieving stress through value-rich work. *Journal of Social Psychology, 134,* 829–836.

Kochanska, G. (1992). Children's interpersonal influence with mothers and peers. *Developmental Psychology, 28*(3), 491–499.

Kochanska, G. (1993). Toward a synthesis of parental socialization and child temperament in early development of conscience. *Child Development, 64,* 325–437.

Kochanska, G. (1995). Children's temperament, mothers' discipline, and security of attachment: Multiple pathways to emerging internalization. *Child Development, 66,* 597–615.

Kochanska, G., & Aksan, N. (1995). Mother-child positive affect, the quality of child compliance to requests and prohibitions, and maternal control as correlates of early internalization. *Child Development, 66,* 236–254.

Kochanska, G., Aksan, N., & Koenig, A. L. (1995). A longitudinal study of the roots of preschoolers' conscience: Committed compliance and emerging internalization. *Child Development, 66,* 1752–1769.

Kochanska, G., Casey, R. J., & Fukumoto, A. (1995). Toddlers' sensitivity to standard violations. *Child Development, 66,* 643–656.

Koenig, H. G. (1994). *Aging and God.* New York: Haworth.

Koenig, H. G., & Blazer, D. G. (1992). Mood disorders and suicide. In J. E. Birren, R. Sloane, & G. D. Cohen (Eds.), *Handbook of mental health and aging* (pp. 379–407). New York: Academic Press.

Koenig, H. G., George, L. K., & Siegler, I. C. (1988). The use of religion and other emotion-regulating coping strate-

gies among older adults. *The Gerontologist, 28*(3), 303–310.

Koenig, H. G., Kevale, J. N., & Ferrel, C. (1988). Religion and well-being in later life. *The Gerontologist, 28*(1), 18–28.

Koff, E., Rierdan, J., & Sheingold, K. (1982). Memories of menarche: Age, preparation, and prior knowledge as determinants of initial menstrual experience. *Journal of Youth and Adolescence, 11,* 1–9.

Kohlberg, L. (1966). A cognitive-developmental analysis of children's sexrole concepts and attitudes. In E. E. Maccoby (Ed.), *The development of sex differences.* Stanford, CA: Stanford University Press.

Kohlberg, L. (1969). Stage and sequence: The cognitive-developmental approach to socialization. In D. A. Goslin (Ed.), *Handbook of socialization theory and research.* Chicago: Rand McNally.

Kohlberg, L. (1973). Continuities in childhood and adult moral development revisited. In P. Baltes & K. W. Schaie (Eds.), *Life-span developmental psychology: Personality and socialization* (pp. 180–207). New York: Academic Press.

Kohlberg, L. (1981). *Essays on moral development.* San Francisco: Harper & Row.

Kohlberg, L., & Gilligan, C. (1971, Fall). The adolescent as a philosopher: The discovery of the self in a postconventional world. *Daedalus,* pp. 1051–1086.

Kohlberg, L., & Ryncarz, R. A. (1990). Beyond justice reasoning: Moral development and consideration of a seventh stage. In C. N. Alexander & E. J. Langer (Eds.), *Higher stages of human development* (pp. 191–207). New York: Oxford University Press.

Kohlberg, L., Yaeger, J., & Hjertholm, E. (1968). Private speech: Four studies and a review of theories. *Child Development, 39,* 691–736.

Köhler, L., & Markestad, T. (1993). Consensus statement on prevention programs for SIDS. *Acta Paediatrica, 38*(Suppl.), 126–127.

Kohn, M. L. (1980). Job complexity and adult personality. In N. J. Smelser & E. H. Erikson (Eds.), *Themes of work and love in adulthood.* Cambridge, MA: Harvard University Press.

Kolata, G. (1986). Obese children: A growing problem. *Science, 232,* 20–21.

Kolata, G. (1988, March 29). Fetuses treated through umbilical cords. *The New York Times,* p. C3.

Kolata, G. (1995, May 23). Molecular tools may offer clues to reducing risks of birth defects. *The New York Times,* p. C3.

Kolata, G. (1996, October 20). Concerns grow that doctor-assisted suicide would leave the powerless vulnerable. *The New York Times,* p. 14.

Kolb, B. (1989). Brain development, plasticity, and behavior. *American Psychologist, 44*(9), 1203–1212.

Kolbert, E. **(1994, January 11).** Canadians curbing TV violence. *The New York Times,* pp. C15, C19.

Kopp, C. B. **(1982).** Antecedents of self-regulation. *Developmental Psychology, 18*(2), 199–214.

Kopp, C. B., & Kaler, S. R. **(1989).** Risk in infancy: Origins and implications. *American Psychologist, 44*(2), 224–230.

Kopp, C. B., & McCall, R. B. **(1982).** Predicting later mental performance for normal, at-risk, and handicapped infants. In P. B. Baltes & O. G. Brim (Eds.), *Life-span development and behavior* (Vol. 4). New York: Academic Press.

Kornhaber, A. **(1986).** *Between parents and grandparents.* New York: St. Martin's

Kornhaber, A., & Woodward, K. L. **(1981).** *Grandparents/grandchildren: The vital connection.* Garden City, NY: Anchor/Doubleday.

Kosnik, W., Winslow, L., Kline, D., Rasinski, K., & Sekuler, R. **(1988).** Visual changes in daily life throughout adulthood, *Journal of Gerontology: Psychological Sciences, 43*(3), P63–70.

Kottak, C. P. **(1994).** *Cultural anthropology.* New York: McGraw-Hill.

Kraemer, H. C., Korner, A., Anders, T., Jacklin, C. N., & Dimiceli, S. **(1985).** Obstetric drugs and infant behavior: A reevaluation. *Journal of Pediatric Psychology, 10,* 345–353.

Krall, E. A., & Dawson-Hughes, B. **(1994).** Walking is related to bone density and rates of bone loss. *American Journal of Medicine, 96,* 20–26.

Kramer, J., Hill, K., & Cohen, L. **(1975).** Infant's development of object permanence: A refined methodology and new evidence for Piaget's hypothesized ordinality. *Child Development, 46,* 149–155.

Kraus, N., McGee, T. J., Carrell, T. D., Zecker, S. G., Nicol, T. G., & Koch, D. B. **(1996).** Auditory neurophysiologic responses and discrimination deficits in children with learning problems. *Science, 273,* 971–973.

Krause, N. **(1995).** Religiosity and self-esteem among older adults. *Journal of Gerontology: Psychological Sciences, 50B,* P236–246.

Krause, N., & Van Tran, T. **(1989).** Stress and religious involvement among older blacks. *Journal of Gerontology: Social Sciences, 44*(1), S4–13.

Krauss, S., Concordet, J. P., & Ingham, P. W. **(1993).** A functionally conserved homolog of the Drosophila segment polarity gene hh is expressed in tissues with polarizing activity in zebrafish embryos. *Cell, 75,* 1431–1444.

Kreutzer, M., & Charlesworth, W. R. **(1973).** *Infant recognition of emotions.* Paper presented at the meeting of the Society for Research in Child Development, Philadelphia.

Kreutzer, M., Leonard, C., & Flavell, J. **(1975).** An interview study of children's knowledge about memory. *Monographs of the Society for Research in Child Development, 40*(1, Serial No. 159).

Krieger, D. **(1982).** Cushing's syndrome. *Monographs in Endocrinology, 22,* 1–142.

Kristof, N. D. **(1990, December 6).** At 102, he's back in school, with many like him. *The New York Times,* p. A4.

Kristof, N. D. **(1991, June 17).** A mystery from China's census: Where have young girls gone? *The New York Times,* pp. A1, A8.

Kristof, N. D. **(1993, July 21).** Peasants of China discover new way to weed out girls. *The New York Times,* pp. A1, A6.

Kritz-Silverstein, D., & Barrett-Connor, E. **(1996).** Long-term postmenopausal hormone use, obesity, and fat distribution in older women. *Journal of the American Medical Association, 275,* 46–49.

Kroger, J. **(1993).** Ego identity: An overview. In J. Kroger (Ed.), *Discussions on ego identity.* Hillsdale, NJ: Erlbaum.

Kroger, J., & Haslett, S. J. **(1991).** A comparison of ego identity status transition pathways and change rates across five identity domains. *International Journal of Aging and Human Development, 32,* 303–330.

Krueger, J., & Heckhausen, J. **(1993).** Personality development across the adult life span: Subjective conceptions vs. cross-sectional analyses. *Journal of Gerontology: Psychological Sciences, 48,* P100–108.

Krueger, J., Heckhausen, J., & Hundertmark, J. **(1995).** Perceiving middle-aged adults: Effects of stereotype-congruent and incongruent information. *Journal of Gerontology: Psychological Sciences, 50B.* P82–93.

Kruper, J. C., & Uzgiris, I. **(1987).** Fathers' and mothers' speech to young infants. *Journals of Psycholinguistic Research, 16*(6). 597–614.

Ku, L. C., Sonenstein, F. L., & Pleck, J. H. **(1992).** The association of AIDS education and sex education with sexual behavior and condom use among teenage men. *Family Planning Perspectives, 24,* 100–106.

Kübler-Ross, E. **(1969).** *On death and dying.* New York: Macmillan.

Kübler-Ross, E. **(1970).** *On death and dying* [paperback]. New York: Macmillan.

Kübler-Ross, E. (Ed.). **(1975).** *Death: The final stage of growth.* Englewood Cliffs, NJ: Prentice-Hall.

Kuczmarski, R. J., Flegal, K. M., Campbell, S. M., & Johnson, C. L. **(1994).** Increasing prevalence of overweight among U.S. adults: The National Health and Nutrition Examination Surveys, 1960 to 1991. *Journal of the American Medical Association, 272,* 205–211.

Kuczynski, L., & Kochanska, G. **(1995).** Function and content of maternal demands: Developmental significance of early demands for competent action. *Child Development, 66,* 616–628.

Kuhl, P. K., Williams, K. A., Lacerda, F., Stevens, K. N., & Lindblom, B. **(1992).** Linguistic experience alters phonetic perception in infants by 6 months of age. *Science, 255,* 606–608.

Kunkel, S. R., & Applebaum, R. A. **(1992).** Estimating the prevalence of long-term disability for an aging society. *Journal of Gerontology: Social Sciences, 47*(5), S253–260.

Kuntzleman, C. T., & Reiff, G. G. **(1992).** The decline in American children's fitness levels. *Research Quarterly for Exercise and Sport, 63*(2), 107–111.

Kupersmidt, J. B., & Coie, J. D. **(1990).** Preadolescent peer status, aggression, and school adjustment as predictors of externalizing problems in adolescence. *Child Development, 61,* 1350–1362.

Kupfersmid, J., & Wonderly, D. **(1980).** Moral maturity and behavior: Failure to find a link. *Journal of Youth and Adolescence, 9*(3), 249–261.

Kurdek, L. A. **(1995a).** Assessing multiple determinants of relationship commitment in cohabiting gay, cohabiting lesbian, dating heterosexual, and married heterosexual couples. *Family Relations, 44,* 261–266.

Kurdek, L. A. **(1995b).** Lesbian and gay couples. In A. R. D'Augelli & C. J. Patterson (Eds.), *Lesbian, gay and bisexual identities over the lifespan: Psychological perspectives.* New York: Oxford University Press.

Kurdek, L. A., & Schmitt, J. P. **(1987).** Partner homogamy in married, heterosexual cohabiting, gay, and lesbian couples. *Journal of Sex Research, 23,* 212–232.

Kuttner, R. **(1994, August 29).** Where have all the good jobs gone? *Business Week,* p. 16.

Labbok, M. H., & Hendershot, G. E. **(1987).** Does breastfeeding protect against malocclusion? An analysis of the 1981 child health supplement to the National Health Interview Survey. *American Journal of Preventive Medicine, 3, 4.*

Labouvie-Vief, G. **(1985).** Intelligence and cognition. In J. E. Birren & K. W. Schaie (Eds.), *Handbook of the psychology of aging* (pp. 500–530). New York: Van Nostrand Reinhold.

Labouvie-Vief, G. **(1990a).** Modes of knowledge and the organization of development. In M. L. Commons, L. Kohlberg, F. Richards, & J. Sinnott (Eds.), *Beyond formal operations: 2. Models and methods in the study of adult and adolescent thought.* New York: Praeger.

Labouvie-Vief, G. **(1990b).** Wisdom as integrated thought: Historical and development perspectives. In R. J. Sternberg (Ed.), *Wisdom: Its nature, origins,* *and development* (pp. 52–83). Cambridge, UK: Cambridge University Press.

Labouvie-Vief, G., Adams, C., Hakim-Larson, J., Hayden, M., & DeVoe, M. (1987). *Modes of text processing from preadolescence to mature adulthood.* Unpublished manuscript, Wayne State University, Detroit.

Labouvie-Vief, G., & Hakim-Larson, J. (1989). Developmental shifts in adult thought. In S. Hunter & M. Sundel (Eds.), *Midlife myths.* Newbury Park, CA: Sage.

Labouvie-Vief, G., Hakim-Larson, J., & Hobart, C. J. (1987). Age, ego level, and the life-span development of coping and defense processes. *Psychology and Aging, 2,* 286–293.

Lachman, J. L., & Lachman, R. (1980). Age and the actualization of knowledge. In L. W. Poon, J. L. Fozard, L. S. Cermak, D. Arenberg, & L. W. Thompson (Eds.), *New directions in memory and aging* (pp. 313–343). Hillsdale, NJ: Erlbaum.

Lachman, M. E., Lewkowicz, C., Marcus, A., & Peng, Y. (1994). Images of midlife development among young, middle-aged, and older adults. *Journal of Adult Development, 1*(4), 201–211.

Lachs, M. S., & Pillemer, K. (1995). Abuse and neglect of elderly persons. *New England Journal of Medicine, 332,* 437–443.

Lacy, W. B., & Hendricks, J. (1980). Developmental model of adult life: Myth or reality? *Aging and Human Development, 11,* 89–110.

Ladd, G. W. (1990). Having friends, keeping friends, making friends, and being liked by peers in the classroom: Predictors of children's early school adjustment. *Child Development, 61,* 1081–1100.

Ladd, G. W., & Hart, C. H. (1992). Creating informal play opportunities: Are parents' and preschoolers' initiations related to children's competence with peers? *Developmental Psychology, 28,* 1179–1187.

Lagercrantz, H., & Slotkin, T. A. (1986). The "stress" of being born. *Scientific American, 254*(4), 100–107.

Lake, S. R. (1989). *Rematch: Winning legal battles with your ex.* Chicago: Chicago Review Press.

Lamb, M. E. (1977). Father-infant and mother-infant interaction in the first year of life. *Child Development, 48,* 167–181.

Lamb, M. E. (1978). Influence of the child on marital quality and family interaction during the prenatal, perinatal, and infancy periods. In R. Lerner & G. Spanier (Eds.), *Child influences on marital and family interaction: A lifespan perspective.* New York: Academic Press.

Lamb, M. E. (1981). The development of father-infant relationships. In M. E.

Lamb (Ed.), *The role of the father in child development* (2d ed.). New York: Wiley.

Lamb, M. E. (1982a). The bonding phenomenon: Misinterpretations and their implications. *Journal of Pediatrics, 101*(4), 555–557.

Lamb, M. E. (1982b). Early contact and maternal-infant bonding: One decade later. *Pediatrics, 70*(5), 763–768.

Lamb, M. E. (1987a). Predictive implications of individual differences in attachment. *Journal of Consulting and Clinical Psychology, 55*(6), 817–824.

Lamb, M. E. (1987b). *The father's role: Cross-cultural perspectives.* Hillsdale, NJ: Erlbaum.

Lamb, M. E., Frodi, A. M., Frodi, M., & Hwang, C. P. (1982). Characteristics of maternal and paternal behavior in traditional and non-traditional Swedish families. *International Journal of Behavior Development, 5,* 131–151.

Lamb, M. E., & Sternberg, K. J. (1992). Sociocultural perspectives on nonparental childcare. In M. E. Lamb, K. J. Sternberg, C.-P. Hwang, & A. G. Broberg (Eds.). *Child care in context.* Hillsdale, NJ: Erlbaum.

Lamborn, S. D., Mounts, N. S., Steinberg, L., & Dornbusch, S. M. (1991). Patterns of competence and adjustment among adolescents from authoritative, authoritarian, indulgent, and neglectful families. *Child Development, 62,* 1049–1065.

Lampl, M., Veldhuis, J. D., & Johnson, M. (1992). Saltation and stasis: A model of human growth. *Science, 258*(5083), 801–803.

Landers, S. (1992, March). "Second time around families" find aid. *National Association of Social Workers News,* p. 5.

Landesman-Dwyer, S., & Emanuel, I. (1979). Smoking during pregnancy. *Teratology, 19,* 119–126.

Landy, F. J. (1992, February). *Research on the use of fitness tests for police and fire fighting jobs.* Presentation at the Second Annual Scientific Psychology Forum of the American Psychological Association, Washington, DC.

Landy, F. J. (1994, July–August). Mandatory retirement age: Serving the public welfare? *Psychological Science Agenda* (Science Directorate, American Psychological Association), pp. 10–11, 20.

Lange, G., MacKinnon, C. E., & Nida, R. E. (1989). Knowledge, strategy, and motivational contributions to preschool children's object recall. *Developmental Psychology, 25*(5), 772–779.

Langer, E., & Rodin, J. (1976). The effects of choice in enhanced personal responsibility in an institutional setting. *Journal of Personality and Social Psychology, 34*(2), 191–198.

Lanting, C. I., Fidler, V., Huisman, M., Touwen, B. C. L., & Boersma, E. R. (1994). Neurological differences between 9-year-old children fed breast-

milk or formula-milk as babies. *The Lancet, 334,* 1319–1322.

Lapane, K. L., Zierler S., Lasater, T. M., Stein, M., Barbour, M. M., & Hume, A. L. (1995). Is a history of depressive symptoms associated with an increased risk of infertility in women? *Psychosomatic Medicine, 57*(6), 509–513.

LaRossa, R. (1988). Fatherhood and social change. *Family Relations, 34,* 451–457.

LaRossa, R., & LaRossa, M. M. (1981). *Transition to parenthood: How infants change families.* Beverly Hills, CA: Sage.

Larsen D. (1990, December–1991, January). Unplanned parenthood. *Modern Maturity,* pp. 32–36.

Larson, K. (1995, November–1996, February). Poll shows doctors support death with dignity. *Time Lines,* p. 1.

Larson, R., & Lampman-Petraitis, C. (1989). Daily emotional states as reported by children and adolescents. *Child Development, 60,* 1250–1260.

Larson, R., Mannell, R., & Zuzanek, J. (1986). Daily well being of older adults with friends and family. *Psychology and Aging, 1*(2), 117–126.

Larson, R., & Richards, M. H. (1991). Daily companionship in late childhood and early adolescence: Changing developmental contexts. *Child Development, 62,* 284–300.

Latimer, E. J. (1992, February). Euthanasia: A physician's reflections. *Ontario Medical Review,* pp. 21–29.

Laudenslager, M. L., Ryan, S. M., Drugan, R. C., Hyson, R. L., & Maier, S. F. (1983). Coping and immunosuppression: Inescapable but not escapable shock suppresses lymphocyte proliferation. *Science, 221,* 568–570.

Lauer, J., & Lauer, R. (1985). Marriages made to last. *Psychology Today, 19*(6), 22–26.

Laumann, E. O., Gagnon, J. H., Michael, R. T., & Michaels, S. (1994). *The social organization of sexuality: Sexual practices in the United States.* Chicago: University of Chicago Press.

Launer, L. J., Masaki, K., Petrovitch, H., Foley, D., & Havlik, R. J. (1995). The association between midlife blood pressure levels and late-life cognitive function. *Journal of the American Medical Association, 274,* 1846–1851.

Lavee, Y., Sharlin, S., & Katz, R. (1996). The effects of parenting stress on marital quality. *Journal of Family Issues, 17,* 114–135.

Lawson, A., & Ingleby, J. D. (1974). Daily routines of preschool children: Effects of age, birth order, sex and social class, and developmental correlates. *Psychological Medicine, 4,* 339–413.

Lawson, E. J., & Thompson, A. (1995). Black men make sense of marital distress and divorce. *Family Relations, 44,* 211–218.

Lawton, M. P. (1981). Alternate housing.

Journal of Gerontological Social Work, 3(3), 61–79.

Lawton, M. P. (1982). Competence, environmental press, and the adaptation of old people. In M. P. Lawton & T. O. Byerts (Eds.), *Aging and the environment: Theoretical approaches* (pp. 33–59). New York: Springer.

Lawton, M. P., & Nahemow, L. (1973). Ecology and the aging process. In C. Eisdorfer & M. P. Lawton (Eds.), *The psychology of adult development and aging.* Washington, DC: American Psychological Association.

Lazarus, R. S., & Folkman, S. (1984). *Stress, appraisal, and coping.* New York: Springer.

Leadbeater, B. J., & Bishop, S. J. (1994). Predictors of behavior problems in preschool children of inner-city Afro-American and Puerto Rican adolescent mothers. *Child Development,* 65, 638–648.

Leary, W. E. (1994a, March 29). Researchers closing in on a single-dose vaccine for children. *The New York Times,* p. C3.

Leary, W. E. (1994b, April 24). Barriers to immunization peril children, expert says. *The New York Times,* p. A26.

Lederberg, A. R., & Mobley, C. E. (1990). The effect of hearing impairment on the quality of attachment and mother-toddler interaction. *Child Development,* 61, 1596–1604.

Lee, A. M., et al. (1996). Legalizing assisted suicide—Views of physicians in Oregon. *New England Journal of Medicine,* 334, 310–315.

Lee, D. J., & Markides, K. S. (1990). Activity and mortality among aged people over an eight-year period. *Journal of Gerontology: Social Sciences,* 45(1), S39–42.

Lee, G.-H., Proenca, R., Montez, J. M., Carrol, K. M., Darvishzadeh, J. G., Lee, J. I., & Friedman, J. M. (1996). Abnormal splicing of the leptin receptor in *diabetic* mice. *Nature,* 379, 632–635.

Lee, G. R., & Dwyer, J. W. (1996). Aging parent–adult child coresidence. *Journal of Family Issues,* 17, 46–59.

Lee, G. R., Dwyer, J. W., & Coward, R. T. (1993). Gender differences in parent care: Demographic factors and some gender preferences. *Journal of Gerontology: Social Sciences,* 48, S9–16.

Lee, G. R., Netzer, J. K., & Coward, R. T. (1995). Depression among older parents: The role of intergenerational exchange. *Journal of Marriage and the Family,* 57, 823–833.

Lee, G. R., & Shehan, C. L. (1989). Retirement and marital satisfaction. *Journal of Gerontology: Social Sciences,* 44(6), S226–230.

Lee, I.-M., Hsieh, C.-C., & Paffenbarger, R. S. (1995). Exercise intensity and longevity in men. *Journal of the American Medical Association,* 273, 1179–1184.

Lee, I.-M., & Paffenbarger, R. S. (1992). Changes in body weight and longevity. *Journal of the American Medical Association,* 268, 2045–2049.

Lee, J. A. (1987). What can homosexual aging studies contribute to theories of aging? *Journal of Homosexuality,* 13, 43–71.

Lee, P. R., Franks, P., Thomas, G. S., & Paffenbarger, R. S. (1981). *Exercise and health: The evidence and its implications.* Cambridge, MA: Oelgeschlager, Gunn, & Hain.

Lee, T. R., Mancini, J. A., & Maxwell, J. W. (1990). Sibling relationships in adulthood: Current patterns and motivations. *Journal of Marriage and the Family,* 52, 431–440.

Lehmkuhle, S., Garzia, R. P., Turner, L., Hash, T., & Baro, J. A. (1993). A defective visual pathway in children with reading disability. *New England Journal of Medicine,* 328(14), 989–996.

Leichtman, M. D., & Ceci, S. J. (1995). The effects of stereotypes and suggestions on preschoolers' reports. *Developmental Psychology,* 31(4), 568–578.

Leitenberg, H., & Henning, K. (1995). Sexual fantasy. *Psychological Bulletin,* 117, 469–496.

Lelwica, M., & Haviland, J. (1983). Ten-week-old infants' reactions to mothers' emotional expressions. Paper presented at the biennial meeting of the Society for Research in Child Development, Detroit.

Lemish, D., & Rice, M. L. (1986). Television as a talking picture book: A prop for language acquisition. *Journal of Child Language,* 13, 251–274.

Lemon, B., Bengtson, V., & Peterson, J. (1972). An exploration of the activity theory of aging: Activity types and life satisfaction among inmovers to a retirement community. *Journal of Gerontology,* 27(4), 511–523.

Lenneberg, E. H. (1967). *Biological functions of language.* New York: Wiley.

Lenneberg, E. H. (1969). On explaining language. *Science,* 164(3880), 635–643.

Lennox, A., Karlinsky, H., Meschino, J., Buchanan, J. A., Percy, M. E., & Berg, J. M. (1994). Molecular genetic predictive testing for Alzheimer's disease: Deliberations and preliminary recommendations. *Alzheimer Disease and Associated Disorders,* 8, 126–127.

Lenz, E. (1993, August–September). Mirror, mirror . . . : One woman's reflections on her changing image. *Modern Maturity,* pp. 24, 26–28, 80.

Lerner, M. J., Somers, D. G., Reid, D., Chiriboga, D., & Tierney, M. (1991). Adult children as caregivers: Egocentric biases in judgments of sibling contributions. *The Gerontologist,* 31(6), 746–755.

Lerner, J. V., & Galambos, N. L. (1985). Maternal role satisfaction, mother-child interaction, and child temperament: A process model. *Child Development,* 21, 1157–1164.

Lesgold, A. M. (1983). *Expert systems.* Paper represented at the Cognitive Science Meetings, Rochester, NY.

Lester, B. M., Corwin, M. J., Sepkoski, C., Seifer, R., Peuker, M., McLaughlin, S., & Golub, H. L. (1991). Neurobehavioral syndromes in cocaine exposed newborn infants. *Child Development,* 62, 694–705.

Lester, B. M., & Dreher, M. (1989). Effects of marijuana use during pregnancy on newborn cry. *Child Development,* 60, 765–771.

Lester, R., & Van Theil, D. H. (1977). Gonadal function in chronic alcoholic men. *Advances in Experimental Medicine and Biology,* 85A, 339–414.

LeVay, S. (1991). A difference in hypothalamic structure between heterosexual and homosexual men. *Science,* 253, 1034–1037.

Leveno, R. J., Cunningham, F. G., Nelson, S., Roark, M., Williams, M. L., Guzick, D., Dowling, S., Rosenfeld, C. R., & Buckley, A. (1986). A prospective comparison of selective and universal electronic fetal monitoring in 34,995 pregnancies. *New England Journal of Medicine,* 315, 615–619.

Levi, L. (1990). Occupational stress: Spice of life or kiss of death? *American Psychologist,* 45, 1142–1145.

Levin, J. S., & Taylor, R. J. (1993). Gender and age differences in religiosity among black Americans. *The Gerontologist,* 33(1), 16–23.

Levin, J. S., Taylor, R. J., & Chatters, L. M. (1994). Race and gender differences in religiosity among older adults: Findings from four national surveys. *Journal of Gerontology: Social Sciences,* 49, S137–145.

Levine, J. J., & Ilowite, N. T. (1994). Sclerodermalike esophageal disease in children breast-fed by mothers with silicone breast implants. *Journal of the American Medical Association,* 271, 213–216.

Levine, M. D. (1987). *Developmental variation and learning disorders.* Cambridge, MA: Educators Publishing.

Levine, R. (1980). Adulthood among the Gusii of Kenya. In N. J. Smelser & E. H. Erikson (Eds.), *Themes of work and love in adulthood* (pp. 77–104). Cambridge, MA: Harvard University Press.

Levinson, D. (1978). *The seasons of a man's life.* New York: Knopf.

Levinson, D. (1980). Toward a conception of the adult life course. In N. J. Smelser & E. H. Erikson (Eds.), *Themes of work and love in adulthood* (pp. 265–290). Cambridge, MA: Harvard University Press.

Levinson, D. (1986). A conception of adult development. *American Psychologist,* 41, 3–13.

Levinson, D. (1996). *The seasons of a woman's life.* New York: Knopf.

Levitt, M. J., Guacci-Franco, N., & Levitt, J. L. (1993). Convoys of social support in childhood and early adolescence: Structure and function. *Developmental Psychology, 29,* 811–818.

Levy, D. M. (1966). *Maternal overprotection.* New York: Norton.

Levy, G. D., & Carter, D. B. (1989). Gender schema, gender constancy, and gender-role knowledge: The roles of cognitive factors in preschoolers' gender-role stereotype attributions. *Developmental Psychology, 25*(3), 444–449.

Levy-Shiff, R. (1994). Individual and contextual correlates of marital change across the transition to parenthood. *Developmental Psychology, 30,* 591–601.

Levy-Shiff, R., Hoffman, M. A., Mogilner, S., Levinger, S., & Mogilner, M. B. (1990). Fathers' hospital visits to their preterm infants as a predictor of father-infant relationship and infant development. *Pediatrics, 86*(2), 289–293.

Lewin, G. (1994, May 18). Boys are more comfortable with sex than girls are, survey finds. *The New York Times,* p. A20.

Lewin, T. (1988, March 22). Despite criticism, fetal monitors are likely to remain in wide use. *The New York Times,* p. 24.

Lewin, T. (1992, November 7). Doctors consider a specialty focusing on women's health. *The New York Times,* pp. A1, A10.

Lewin, T. (1995, May 30). Family decay global, study says: Troubled households are not just a U.S. phenomenon. *The New York Times,* p. A5.

Lewis, M. (1987). Social development in infancy and early childhood. In J. D. Osofsky (Ed.), *Handbook of infant development* (2d ed.). New York: Wiley.

Lewis, M. (1992). Shame, the exposed self. *Zero to Three, XII*(4), 6–10.

Lewis, M., & Brooks, J. (1974). Self, other, and fear: Infants' reaction to people. In H. Lewis & L. Rosenblum (Eds.), *The origins of fear: The origins of behavior* (Vol. 2). New York: Wiley.

Lewis, M., Worobey, J., Ramsay, D. S., & McCormack, M. K. (1992). Prenatal exposure to heavy metals: Effect on childhood cognitive skills and health status. *Pediatrics, 89*(6), 1010–1015.

Lewis, M. I., & Butler, R. N. (1974). Life-review therapy: Putting memories to work in individual and group psychotherapy. *Geriatrics, 29,* 165–173.

Lewis, R. (1996, October). All the "comforts" of home. *AARP Bulletin,* pp. 2, 13.

Lewit, E. M., Baker, L. S., Corman, H., & Shiono, P. H. (1995). The direct cost of low birth weight. *The Future of Children, 5*(1), 35–56.

Li, C. Q., Windsor, R. A., Perkins, L., Goldenberg, R. L., & Lowe, J. B.
(1993). The impact on infant birth weight and gestational age of cotinine-validated smoking reduction during pregnancy. *Journal of the American Medical Association, 269,* 1519–1524.

Liaw, F., & Brooks-Gunn, J. (1993). Patterns of low-birth-weight children's cognitive development. *Developmental Psychology, 29,* 1024–1035.

Lickona, T. (Ed.). (1976). *Moral development and behavior.* New York: Holt.

Lieberman, M., & Coplan, A. (1970). Distance from death as a variable in the study of aging. *Developmental Psychology, 2*(1), 71–84.

Liebert, R. M. (1972). Television and social learning: Some relationships between viewing violence and behaving aggressively. In J. P. Murray, E. A. Rubinstein, & G. A. Comstock (Eds.), *Television and social behavior* (Vol. 2). Washington, DC: U.S. Government Printing Office.

Liebman, B. (1995, October). Heart disease: How to lower your risk. *Nutrition Action Newsletter,* pp. 1–5.

Lieven, E. M. (1978). Conversations between mothers and young children. In N. Waterson & E. Snow (Eds.), *The development of communication: Social and pragmatic factors in language acquisition.* New York: Wiley.

Light, L. L. (1990). Interactions between memory and language in old age. In J. E. Birren & K. W. Schaie (Eds.), *Handbook of the psychology of aging* (pp. 275–290). San Diego: Academic Press.

Lightfoot-Klein, H. (1989). *Prisoners of ritual.* Binghamton, NY: Haworth.

Lim, L. L. (1996). *More and better jobs for women: An action report.* Geneva: International Labor Office.

Lin, G., & Rogerson, P. A. (1995). Elderly parents and their geographic availability to their adult children. *Research on Aging, 17,* 303–331.

Lindberg, L. D. (1996). Women's decisions about breast feeding and maternal employment. *Journal of Marriage and the Family, 58,* 239–251.

Lindeman, R. D., Tobin, J., & Shock, N. (1985). Longitudinal studies on rate of decline in renal function with age. *Journal of the American Geriatric Society, 33,* 278–285.

Lindenberger, U., & Baltes, P. B. (1994). Sensory functioning and intelligence in old age: A strong connection. *Psychology and Aging, 9,* 339–355.

Linder, K. (1990). *Functional literacy projects and project proposals: Selected examples.* Paris: United Nations Educational, Scientific, and Cultural Organization.

Lindsey, R. (1984, January 15). A new generation finds it hard to leave the nest. *The New York Times,* p. A18.

Linney, J. A., & Seidman, E. (1989). The future of schooling. *American Psychologist, 44*(2), 336–340.

Lipid Research Clinics Program.
(1984a). The lipid research clinic coronary primary prevention trial results: I. Reduction in incidence of coronary heart disease. *Journal of the American Medical Association, 251,* 351–364.

Lipid Research Clinics Program. (1984b). The lipid research clinic coronary primary prevention trial results: II. The relationship of reduction in incidence of coronary heart disease to cholesterol lowering. *Journal of the American Medical Association, 251,* 365–374.

Listening to depression: The new medicines. (1995, January). *Johns Hopkins Medical Letter: Health after 50,* pp. 4–5.

Livson, N., & Peskin, H. (1980). Perspectives on adolescence from longitudinal research. In J. Adelson (Ed.), *Handbook of adolescent psychology.* New York: Wiley.

Lloyd, T., Andon, M. B., Rollings, N., Martel, J. K., Landis, J. R., Demers, L. M., Eggli, D. F., Kieselhorst, K., & Kulin, H. E. (1993). Calcium supplementation and bone mineral density in adolescent girls. *Journal of the American Medical Association, 270,* 841–844.

Lo, Y.-M. D., Patel, P., Wainscoat, J. S., Sampietro, M., Gillmer, M. D. G., & Fleming, K. A. (1989, December 9). Prenatal sex determination by DNA amplification from maternal peripheral blood. *The Lancet,* pp. 1363–1365.

Lock, A., Young, A., Service, V., & Chandler, P. (1990). Some observations on the origin of the pointing gesture. In V. Volterra & C. J. Erting (Eds.), *From gesture to language in hearing and deaf children.* New York: Springer.

Lock, M. (1991). Contested meanings of the menopause. *The Lancet, 337,* 1270–1272.

Lock, M. (1994). Menopause in cultural context. *Experimental Gerontology, 29,* 307–317.

Loda, F. A. (1980). Day care. *Pediatrics in Review, 1*(9), 277–281.

Loeber, R., & Dishion, T. (1983). Early predictors of male delinquency: A review. *Psychological Bulletin, 94,* 68–99.

Lofland, L. H. (1986). When others die. *Generations, 10*(4), 59–61.

Long, L. (1992). International perspectives on the residential mobility of America's children. *Journal of Marriage and the Family, 54,* 861–869.

Longino, C. F. (1987). *The oldest Americans: State profiles for data-based planning.* Coral Gables, FL: University of Miami, Department of Sociology.

Longino, C. F. (1988). Who are the oldest Americans? *The Gerontologist, 28,* 515–523.

Longino, C. F., Jr. (1994). State profiles of the oldest Americans in 1990: Decade cohort changes and the disabled. Winston-Salem, NC: Wake Forest University, Reynolds Gerontology Program.

Longino, C. F., & Earle, J. R. (1996). Who

are the grandparents at century's end? *Generations, 20*(1), 13–16.

Longino, C. F., & Kart, C. S. (1982). Explicating activity theory: A formal replication. *Journal of Gerontology, 37*(6), 713–721.

Lonigan, C. J., Fischel, J. E., Whitehurst, G. J., Arnold, D. S., & Valdez-Menchaca, M. C. (1992). The role of otitis media in the development of expressive language disorder. *Developmental Psychology, 28*(3), 430–440.

Lorenz, K. (1957). Comparative study of behavior. In C. H. Schiller (Ed.), *Instinctive behavior.* New York: International Universities Press.

Louis Harris & Associates. (1986). *American teens speak: Sex, myths, TV and birth control: The Planned Parenthood poll.* New York: Planned Parenthood Federation of America.

Louis Harris & Associates. (1988). *Sexual material on American network television during the 1987–1988 season.* New York: Planned Parenthood Federation of America.

Louis Harris and Associates. (1995). *Women's issues* (Survey conducted for Families and Work Institute and the Whirlpool Foundation). New York: Author.

Lovelace, E. A. (1990). Basic concepts in cognition and aging. In E. A. Lovelace (Ed.), *Aging and cognition: Mental processes, self-awareness, and interventions* (pp. 1–28). Amsterdam: North-Holland, Elsevier.

Lowenthal, M., & Haven, C. (1968). Interaction and adaptation: Intimacy as a critical variable. *American Sociological Review, 33,* 20–30.

Lowry, D. T., & Towles, D. E. (1989). Soap opera portrayals of sex, contraception, and sexually transmitted diseases. *Journal of Communication, 39,* 76–83.

Lozoff, B. (1989). Nutrition and behavior. *American Psychologist, 44,* 231–236.

Lozoff, B., Wolff, A., & Davis, N. S. (1985). Sleep problems seen in pediatric practice. *Pediatrics, 75,* 477–483.

Ludmer-Gliebe, S. (1994, Spring). Can Johnny read? The American illiteracy crisis. *The Reporter* (Women's American ORT), pp. 18–20.

Luecke-Aleksa, D., Anderson, D. R., Collins, P. A., & Schmitt, K. L. (1995). Gender constancy and television viewing. *Developmental Psychology, 31*(5), 773–780.

Luke, B., et al. (1995). The association between occupational factors and preterm birth: A United States nurses' study. *American Journal of Obstetrics and Gynecology, 173,* 849–862.

Lund, D. A. (1993a). Caregiving. In R. Kastenbaum (Ed.), *Encyclopedia of adult development* (pp. 57–63). Phoenix: Oryx.

Lund, D. A. (1993b). Widowhood: The coping response. In R. Kastenbaum (Ed.), *Encyclopedia of adult development* (pp. 537–541). Phoenix: Oryx.

Lund, D. A., Hill, R. D., Caserta, M. S., & Wright, S. D. (1995). Video respite™: An innovative resource for family, professional caregivers, and persons with dementia. *The Gerontologist, 35,* 683–687.

Lund, D. A., Redburn, D. E., Juretich, M. S., & Caserta, M. S. (1989). Resolving problems implementing bereavement self-help groups. In D. A. Lund (Ed.), *Older bereaved spouses* (pp. 203–216). Bristol, PA: Hemisphere/Taylor & Francis.

Luster, T., & McAdoo, H. (1996). Family and child influences on educational attainment: A secondary analysis of the High/Scope Perry Preschool data. *Developmental Psychology, 32*(1), 26–39.

Luster, T., & Small, S. A. (1994). Factors associated with sexual risk-taking among adolescents. *Journal of Marriage and the Family, 56,* 622–632.

Lutjen, P., Trounson, A., Leeton, J., Findlay, J., Wood, C., & Renou, P. (1984). The establishment and maintenance of pregnancy using in vitro fertilization and embryo donation in a patient with primary ovarian failure. *Nature, 307,* 174–175.

Lynn, J., Teno, J. M., Phillips, R. S., Wu, A. W., Desbiens, N., Harrold, J., Claessens, M. T., Wenger, N., Kreling, B., & Connors, A. F., Jr., for the SUPPORT Investigators. (1997). Perceptions by family members of the dying experience of older and seriously ill patients. *Annals of Internal Medicine, 126,* 97–106.

Lyon, T. D., & Flavell, J. H. (1993). Young children's understanding of forgetting over time. *Child Development, 64,* 789–800.

Lyons-Ruth, K., Alpern, L., & Repacholi, B. (1993). Disorganized infant attachment classification and maternal psychosocial problems as predictors of hostile-aggressive behavior in the preschool classroom. *Child Development, 64,* 572–585.

Lyons-Ruth, K., Connell, D. B., & Grunebaum, H. U. (1990). Infants at social risk: Services as mediators of infant development and security of attachment. *Child Development, 61,* 85–98.

Lytton, H., & Romney, D. M. (1991). Parents' differential socialization of boys and girls: A meta-analysis. *Psychological Bulletin, 109*(2), 267–296.

MacAdam, M. (1993). Review of *Caring for an Aging World: International models for long-term care, financing, and delivery. Generations, 17*(4), 77–78.

Maccoby, E. (1980). *Social development.* New York: Harcourt Brace Jovanovich.

Maccoby, E., & Jacklin, C. (1974). *The psychology of sex differences.* Stanford, CA: Stanford University Press.

Maccoby, E. E. (1984). Middle childhood in the context of the family. In W. A. Collins (Ed.), *Development during middle childhood.* Washington, DC: National Academy.

Maccoby, E. E. (1988). Gender as a social category. *Developmental Psychology, 24*(6), 755–765.

Maccoby, E. E. (1990). Gender and relationships: A developmental account. *American Psychologist, 45*(11), 513–520.

Maccoby, E. E. (1992). The role of parents in the socialization of children: An historical overview. *Developmental Psychology, 28,* 1006–1017.

Maccoby, E. E. (1994). Commentary: Gender segregation in childhood. In C. Leaper (Ed.), *Childhood gender segregation: Causes and consequences. New Directions for Child Development,* No. 65, pp. 87–97. San Francisco: Jossey-Bass.

Maccoby, E. E., & Martin, J. A. (1983). Socialization in the context of the family: Parent-child interaction. In P. H. Mussen (Series Ed.) & E. M. Hetherington (Vol. Ed.), *Handbook of child psychology: Vol. 4. Socialization, personality, and social development* (pp. 1–101). New York: Wiley.

MacDonald, W. L., & DeMaris, A. (1995). Remarriage, stepchildren, and marital conflict: Challenges to the incomplete institutionalization hypothesis. *Journal of Marriage and the Family, 57,* 387–398.

MacDonald, W. L., & DeMaris, A. (1996). Parenting stepchildren and biological children. *Journal of Family Issues, 17,* 5–25.

Macfarlane, A. (1975). Olfaction in the development of social preferences in the human neonate. In *Parent-infant interaction* (CIBA Foundation Symposium, 33). Amsterdam: Elsevier.

MacFarquhar, N. (1996, August 8). Mutilation of Egyptian girls: Despite ban, it goes on. *The New York Times,* p. A3.

MacGowan, R. J., MacGowan, C. A., Serdula, M. K., Lane, J. M., Joesoef, R. M., & Cook, F. H. (1991). Breast-feeding among women attending women, infants, and children clinics in Georgia, 1987. *Pediatrics, 87,* 361–366.

Main, M. (1990). Cross-cultural studies of attachment organization: Recent studies, changing methodologies, and the concept of conditional strategies. *Human Development, 33,* 48–61.

Main, M. (1993). *Discourse, prediction, and studies in attachment.* Unpublished manuscript, University of California, Berkeley.

Main, M. (1995). Recent studies in attachment: Overview, with selected implications for clinical work. In S. Goldberg, R. Muir, & J. Kerr (Eds.), *Attachment theory: Social, developmental, and clinical perspectives* (pp. 407–470). Hillsdale, NJ: Analytic Press.

Main, M. (1996). Introduction to the special section on attachment and psychopathology: 2, Overview of the field of attachment. *Journal of Consulting and Clinical Psychology, 64*(2), 237–243.

Main, M., & Goldwyn, R. (1993). *Adult attachment classification system.* Unpublished manuscript, University of California, Berkeley.

Main, M., & Goldwyn, R. (in press). Interview-based adult attachment classifications: Related to infant-mother and infant-father attachment. *Developmental Psychology.*

Main, M., & Hesse, E. (1990). Parents' unresolved traumatic experiences are related to infant disorganized attachment status: Is frightened and/or frightening parental behavior the linking mechanism? In M. T. Greenberg, D. Cicchetti, & E. M. Cummings (Eds.), *Attachment in preschool years: Theory, research, and intervention* (pp. 161–184). Chicago: University of Chicago Press.

Main, M., Kaplan, N., & Cassidy, J. (1985). Security in infancy, childhood and adulthood: A move to the level of representation. In I. Bretherton & E. Waters (Eds.), *Growing points in attachment. Monographs of the Society for Research in Child Development, 50* (1–2), 66–104.

Main, M., & Solomon, J. (1986). Discovery of an insecure, disorganized/disoriented attachment pattern: Procedures, findings, and implications for the classification of behavior. In M. Yogman & T. B. Brazelton (Eds.), *Affective development in infancy.* Norwood, NJ: Ablex.

Makrides, M., Neumann, M., Simmer, K., Pater, J., & Gibson, R. (1995). Are long-chain polyunsaturated fatty acids essential nutrients in infancy? *The Lancet, 345,* 1463–1468.

Malcolm, A. H. (1984, September 23). Many see mercy in ending lives. *The New York Times,* pp. 1, 56.

Malloy, M. H., Rhoads, G. G., Schramm, W., & Land, G. (1989). Increasing cesarean section rates in very low-birth weight infants: Effect on outcome. *Journal of the American Medical Association, 262,* 1475–1478.

Mandler, J. M. (1990). A new perspective on cognitive development in infancy. *American Scientist, 78,* 236–243.

Mangelsdorf, S. C., Shapiro, J. R., & Marzolf, D. (1995). Developmental and temperamental differences in emotion regulation in infancy. *Child Development, 66,* 1817–1828.

Mannell, R. (1993). High investment activity and life satisfaction: Commitment, serious leisure, and flow in the daily lives of older adults. In J. Kelly (Ed.), *Activity and aging.* Newbury Park, CA: Sage.

Manning, W. D., & Landale, N. S. (1996). Racial and ethnic differences in the role of cohabitation in premarital childbearing. *Journal of Marriage and the Family, 58,* 63–77.

Manosevitz, M., Prentice, N. M., & Wilson, F. (1973). Individual and family correlates of imaginary companions in preschool children. *Developmental Psychology, 8*(1), 72–79.

Mansfield, R. S., & Busse, T. V. (1981). *The psychology of creativity and discovery: Scientists and their work.* Chicago: Nelson-Hall.

Manson, J. E., Willett, W. C., Stampfer, M. J., Colditz, G. A., Hunter, D. J., Hankinson, S. E., Hennekens, C. H., & Speizer, F. E. (1995). Body weight and mortality among women. *New England Journal of Medicine, 333*(11), 677–685.

Manton, K. G., & Vaupel, J. W. (1995). Survival after the age of 80 in the United States, Sweden, France, England, and Japan. *New England Journal of Medicine, 333,* 1232–1235.

Maratsos, M. (1973). Nonegocentric communication abilities in preschool children. *Child Development, 44,* 697–700.

March of Dimes Birth Defects Foundation. (1987). *Genetic counseling: A public health information booklet* (rev. ed.). White Plains, NY: Author.

Marcia, J. E. (1966). Development and validation of ego identity status. *Journal of Personality and Social Psychology, 3*(5), 551–558.

Marcia, J. E. (1979, June). *Identity status in late adolescence: Description and some clinical implications.* Address given at a symposium on identity development, Rijksuniversitat Groningen, Netherlands.

Marcia, J. E. (1980). Identity in adolescence. In J. Adelson (Ed.), *Handbook of adolescent psychology.* New York: Wiley.

Marcia, J. E. (1993). The relational roots of identity. In J. Kroger (Ed.), *Discussions on ego identity* (pp. 101–120). Hillsdale, NJ: Erlbaum.

Marcoen, A. (1995). Filial maturity of middle-aged adult children in the context of parent care: Model and measures. *Journal of Adult Development, 2,* 125–136.

Margolin, L., & White, L. (1987). The continuing role of physical attractiveness in marriage. *Journal of Marriage and the Family, 49*(1), 21–27.

Markides, K. S., Coreil, J., & Rogers, L. P. (1989). Aging and health among southwestern Hispanics. In K. S. Markides (Ed.), *Aging and health: Perspectives on gender, race, ethnicity, and class.* Newbury Park, CA: Sage.

Markman, H. J., Renick, M. J., Floyd, F. J., Stanley, S. M., & Clements, M. (1993). Preventing marital distress through communication and conflict management training: A 4- and 5-year follow-up. *Journal of Consulting and Clinical Psychology, 61,* 70–77.

Markoff, J. (1992, October 12). Miscarriages tied to chip factories. *The New York Times,* pp. A1, D2.

Markovitz, J. H., Matthews, K. A., Kannel, W. B., Cobb, J. L., & D'Agostino, R. B. (1993). Psychological predictors of hypertension in the Framingham study. *Journal of the American Medical Association, 270,* 2439–2443.

Marks, N. F. (1996). Caregiving across the lifespan: National prevalence and predictors. *Family Relations, 45,* 27–36.

Marland, S. P., Jr. (1972). *Education of the gifted and talented: Vol. I. Report to the Congress of the United States by the U.S. Commissioner of Education.* Washington, DC: U.S. Government Printing Office.

Marshall, E. (1993). A tough line on genetic screening. *Science, 262,* 984–985.

Marshall, V. W. (1994). Sociology, psychology, and the theoretical legacy of the Kansas City studies. *The Gerontologist, 34,* 768–774.

Martikainen, P., & Valkonen, T. (1996). Mortality after the death of a spouse: Rates and causes of death in a large Finnish cohort. *American Journal of Public Health, 86,* 1087–1093.

Martin, G. B., & Clark, R. D. (1982). Distress crying in neonates: Species and peer specificity. *Developmental Psychology, 18*(1), 3–9.

Martin, L. G. (1988). The aging of Asia. *Journal of Gerontology: Social Sciences, 43*(4), S99–113.

Martocchio, J. J. (1989). Age-related differences in employee absenteeism: A meta-analysis. *Psychology and Aging, 4,* 409–414.

Marwick, C. (1993). Coming to terms with indicators for fetal surgery. *Journal of the American Medical Association, 270,* 2025–2029.

Marx, J. (1996, July 5). Searching for drugs that combat Alzheimer's. *Science,* pp. 50–52.

Marzano, R. J., & Hutchins, C. L. (1987). *Thinking skills: A conceptual framework.* (ERIC Document Reproduction Service No. ED 266436).

Masataka, N. (1996). Perception of motherese in a signed language by 6-month-old deaf infants. *Developmental Psychology, 32,* 874–879.

Maslach, C., & Jackson, S. E. (1985). Burnout in health professions: A social psychological analysis. In G. Sanders & J. Suls (Eds.), *Social psychology of health and illness.* Hillsdale, NJ: Erlbaum.

Maslow, A. (1954). *Motivation and personality.* New York: Harper & Row.

Maslow, A. (1968). *Toward a psychology of being.* Princeton, NJ: Van Nostrand Reinhold.

Masoro, E. J. (1985). Metabolism. In C. E. Finch & E. L. Schneider (Eds.), *Handbook of the biology of aging* (pp. 540–563). New York: Van Nostrand Reinhold.

Masoro, E. J. (1988). Minireview: Food restriction in rodents: An evaluation of its role in the study of aging. *Jour-*

nal of Gerontology: Social Sciences, 43(3), S59–64.

Masoro, E. J. (1992). The role of animal models in meeting the gerontologic challenge of the 21st century. *The Gerontologist, 32*(5), 627–633.

Massey, C. M., & Gelman, R. (1988). Preschoolers' ability to decide whether a photographed unfamiliar object can move itself. *Developmental Psychology, 24*(3), 307–317.

Masters, W. H., & Johnson, V. E. (1966). *Human sexual response*. Boston: Little, Brown.

Masters, W. H., & Johnson, V. E. (1981). Sex and the aging process. *Journal of the American Geriatrics Society, 29*, 385–390.

Matheny, K. B., & Cupp, P. (1983). Control, desirability, and anticipation as moderating variables between life changes and illness. *Journal of Human Stress, 9*(2), 14–23.

Matthews, K. A. (1992). Myths and realities of menopause. *Psychosomatic Medicine, 54*, 1–9.

Matthews, K. A., Shumaker, S. A., Bowen, D. J., Langer, R. D., Hunt, J. R., Kaplan, R. M., Klesges, R. C., & Ritenbaugh, C. (1997). Women's health initiative: Why now? What is it? What's new? *American Psychologist, 52*(2), 101–116.

Matthews, S. H. (1995). Gender and the division of filial responsibility between lone sisters and their brothers. *Journal of Gerontology: Social Sciences, 50B*, S312–320.

Matthews, S. H., Delaney, P. J., & Adamek, M. E. (1989). Male kinship ties: Bonds between adult brothers. *American Behavioral Scientist, 33*, 58–69.

Mauk, J. E. (1993). Autism and pervasive developmental disorders. *Pediatric Clinics of North America, 40*, 567–578.

Maxwell, L. (1987, January). *Eight pointers on teaching children to think* (Research in Brief, IS 87-104 RIB). Washington, DC: U.S. Department of Education, Office of Educational Research and Improvement.

Mayes, L. C., Granger, R. H., Frank, M. A., Schottenfeld, R., & Bornstein, M. H. (1993). Neurobehavioral profiles of neonates exposed to cocaine prenatally. *Pediatrics, 91*, 778–783.

Mayeux, R. (1996). Development of a national prospective study of Alzheimer disease. *Alzheimer Disease and Associated Disorders, 10*(Suppl. 1), 38–44.

McAlister, A. L., Perry, C., & Maccoby, N. (1979). Adolescent smoking: Onset and prevention. *Pediatrics, 63*(4), 650–658.

McAnarney, E. R., & Hendee, W. R. (1989). Adolescent pregnancy and its consequences. *Journal of the American Medical Association, 262*, 74–77.

McCall, R. B., Appelbaum, M. I., & Hogarty, P. S. (1973). Developmental changes in mental performance. *Monographs of the Society for Research in Child Development, 38*(Serial No. 150).

McCall, R. B., & Carriger, M. S. (1993). A meta-analysis of infant habituation and recognition memory performance as predictors of later IQ. *Child Development, 64*, 57–79.

McCann, I. L., & Holmes, D. S. (1984). Influence of aerobic exercise on depression. *Journal of Personality and Social Psychology, 46*(5), 1142–1147.

McCartney, K. (1984). Effect of quality of daycare environment on children's language development. *Developmental Psychology, 20*(2), 244–260.

McClelland, D., Constantian C., Regalado, D., & Stone, C. (1978, January). Making it to maturity. *Psychology Today 12*(1), pp. 42–53, 114.

McClelland, D. C. (1993). Intelligence is not the best predictor of job performance. *Current Directions in Psychological Science, 2*(1), 5–6.

McClenahen, J. S. (1993). A recovery . . . without good jobs. *Industry Week, 242*, 50.

McCord, C., & Freeman, H. P. (1990). Excess mortality in Harlem. *New England Journal of Medicine, 322*, 173–177.

McCord, W. (1993, January/February). Death with dignity. *Humanist*, pp. 26–29.

McCormick, M. E., & Wolf, J. S. (1993). Intervention programs for gifted girls. *Roeper Review, 16*(2), 85–88.

McCrae, R. R., & Costa, P. T., Jr. (1984). *Emerging lives, enduring dispositions*. Boston: Little, Brown.

McCrae, R. R., & Costa, P. T. (1994). The stability of personality: Observations and evaluations. *Current Directions in Psychological Science, 3*(6), 173–175.

McCrae, R. R., Costa, P. T., Jr., & Busch, C. M. (1986). Evaluating comprehensiveness in personality systems: The California Q-set and the five factor model. *Journal of Personality, 54*, 430–446.

McCue, J. D. (1995). The naturalness of dying. *Journal of the American Medical Association, 273*, 1039–1043.

McDaniel, K. D. (1986). Pharmacological treatment of psychiatric and neuro-developmental disorders in children and adolescents (Part 1, Part 2, Part 3). *Clinical Pediatrics, 25*(2, 3, 4), 65–71, 198–224.

McDonald, A. D., Armstrong, B. G., & Sloan, M. (1992). Cigarette, alcohol, and coffee consumption and prematurity. *American Journal of Public Health, 82*, 87.

McDonald, M. A., Sigman, M., Espinosa, M. P., & Neumann, C. G. (1994). Impact of a temporary food shortage on children and their mothers. *Child Development, 65*, 404–415.

McFall, S., & Miller, B. H. (1992). Caregiver burden and nursing home admission of frail elderly patients. *Journal of Gerontology: Social Sciences, 47*, S73–79.

McFarland, R. A., Tune, G. B., & Welford, A. (1964). On the driving of automobiles by older people. *Journal of Gerontology, 19*, 190–197.

McGauhey, P. J., Starfield, B., Alexander, C., & Ensminget, M. E. (1991). Social environment and vulnerability of low birth weight children: A social-epidemiological perspective. *Pediatrics, 88*, 943–953.

McGee, R., Partridge, F., Williams, S., & Silva, P. A. (1991). A twelve-year follow-up of preschool hyperactive children. *Journal of the American Academy of Child and Adolescent Psychiatry, 30*, 224–232.

McGinnis, J. M., & Lee, P. R. (1995). *Healthy People 2000 at mid decade. Journal of the American Medical Association, 273*, 1123–1151.

McGinnis, J. M., Richmond, J. B., Brandt, E. N., Windom, R. E., & Mason, J. O. (1992). Health progress in the United States: Results of the 1990 objectives for the nation. *Journal of the American Medical Association, 268*(18), 2545–2552.

McGue, M. (1993). From proteins to cognitions: The behavioral genetics of alcoholism. In R. P. Plomin & G. E. McClearn (Eds.), *Nature, nurture, and psychology*. Washington, DC: American Psychological Association.

McIntosh, H. (1995). Black teens not smoking in great numbers. *Journal of National Cancer Institute, 87*, 564.

McIntosh, J. L. (1992). Epidemiology of suicide in the elderly. *Suicide and Life-Threatening Behavior, 22*, 15–35.

McKenna, J. J., & Mosko, S. (1993). Evolution and infant sleep: An experimental study of infant-parent co-sleeping and its implications for SIDS. *Acta Paediatrica, 389*(Suppl.), 31–36.

McKenry, P. C., Julian, T. W., & Gavazzi, S. M. (1995). Toward a biopsychosocial model of domestic violence. *Journal of Marriage and the Family, 57*, 307–320.

McKey, R. H., Condelli, L., Ganson, H., Barrett, B. J., McConkey, C., & Plantz, M. C. (1985). *The impact of Head Start on children, families, and communities*. Washington, DC: CSR, Inc.

McKinney, K. (1987, March). *A look at Japanese education today* (Research in Brief, IS 87-107 RIB). Washington, DC: U.S. Department of Education, Office of Educational Research and Improvement.

McKitrick, L. A., Camp, C. J., & Black, F. W. (1992). Prospective memory intervention in Alzheimer's disease. *Journal of Gerontology: Psychological Sciences, 47*(5), P337–343.

McLanahan, S., & Booth, K. (1989). Mother-only families: Problems, prospects, and politics. *Journal of Marriage and the Family, 51*, 557–580.

McLaughlin, I. G., Leonard, K. E., & Senchak, M. (1992). Prevalence and distribution of premarital aggression among couples applying for a marriage license. *Journal of Family Violence, 7*(4), 309–319.

McLoyd, V. (1989). Socialization and development in a changing economy: The effects of paternal job and income loss on children. *American Psychologist, 44,* 293–302.

McLoyd, V. C. (1990). The impact of economic hardship on black families and children: Psychological distress, parenting, and socioemotional development. *Child Development, 61,* 311–346.

McLoyd, V. C., Jayaratne, T. E., Ceballo, R., & Borquez, J. (1994). Unemployment and work interruption among African American single mothers: Effects on parenting and adolescent socioemotional functioning. *Child Development, 65,* 562–589.

McMahon, M. J., Luther, E. R., Bowes, W. A., & Olshan, A. F. (1996). Comparison of a trial of labor with an elective second cesarean section. *New England Journal of Medicine, 335,* 689–695.

Mead, M. (1928). *Coming of age in Samoa.* New York: Morrow.

Mead, M. (1935). *Sex and temperament in three primitive societies.* New York: Morrow.

Meehan, P. J. (1990). Prevention: The endpoint of suicidology. *Mayo Clinic Proceedings, 65,* 115–118.

Meier, D. (1995). *The power of their ideas.* Boston: Beacon.

Melnick, S., Cole, P., Anderson, B. A., & Herbst, A. (1987). Rates and risks of diethylstilbestrol-related clear-cell adenocarcinoma of the vagina and cervix. *New England Journal of Medicine, 316,* 514–516.

Meltzoff, A., & Gopnik, A. (1993). The role of imitation in understanding persons and developing a theory of mind. In S. Baron-Cohen, H. Tager-Flusberg, & D. J. Cohen (Eds.), *Understanding others' minds: Perspectives from autism.* Oxford: Oxford University Press.

Meltzoff, A. N. (1985). Immediate and deferred imitation in fourteen- and twenty-four-month-old infants. *Child Development, 56,* 62–72.

Meltzoff, A. N. (1988a). Infant imitation after a one-week delay: Long-term memory for novel acts and multiple stimuli. *Developmental Psychology, 24*(4), 470–476.

Meltzoff, A. N. (1988b). Infant imitation and memory: Nine-month-olds in immediate and deferred tests. *Child Development, 59,* 217, 225.

Meltzoff, A. N., & Borton, R. W. (1979). Intermodal matching by human neonates. *Nature, 282,* 403–404.

Meltzoff, A. N., & Moore, M. K. (1983). Newborn infants imitate adult facial gestures. *Child Development, 54,* 702–709.

Meltzoff, A. N., & Moore, M. K. (1989). Imitation in newborn infants: Exploring the range of gestures imitated and the underlying mechanisms. *Developmental Psychology, 25*(6), 954–962.

Meltzoff, A. N., & Moore, M. K. (1992). Early imitation within a functional framework: The importance of person identity, movement, and development. *Infant Behavior and Development, 15,* 479–505.

Meltzoff, A. N., & Moore, M. K. (1994). Imitation, memory, and the representation of persons. *Infant Behavior and Development, 17,* 83–99.

Menendez, A. (1995, Fall). Home schooling: The facts. *Voice of Reason* (Newsletter of Americans for Religious Liberty), pp. 6–8.

Menninger Foundation. (1994, March). Grandparenting after divorce still a key role for older persons. *The Menninger Letter,* p. 3.

Meredith, N. V. (1969). Body size of contemporary groups of eight-year-old children studied in different parts of the world. *Monographs of the Society for Research in Child Development, 34*(1).

Merva, M., & Fowles, R. (1992). *Effects of diminished economic opportunities on social stress: Heart attacks, strokes, and crime* [Briefing paper]. Washington, DC: Economic Policy Institute.

Merzenich, M. M., Jenkins, W. M., Johnston, P., Schreiner, C., Miller, S. L., & Tallal, P. (1996). Temporal processing deficits of language-learning impaired children ameliorated by training. *Science, 271,* 77–81.

Meyer, B. J. F., Russo, C., & Talbot, A. (1995). Discourse comprehension and problem solving: Decisions about the treatment of breast cancer by women across the life-span. *Psychology in Aging, 10,* 84–103.

Meyer, D. R., & Bartfeld, J. (1996). Compliance with child support orders in divorce cases. *Journal of Marriage and the Family, 58,* 201–212.

Meyers, A. F., Sampson, A. E., Weitzman, M., Rogers, B. L., & Kayne, H. (1989). School breakfast program and school performance. *American Journal of Diseases of Children, 143,* 1234–1239.

Meyers, H. (1989). The impact of teenaged children on parents. In J. M. Oldham & R. S. Liebert (Eds.), *The middle years.* New Haven: Yale University Press.

Michael, R. T., Gagnon, J. H., Laumann, E. O., & Kolata, G. (1994). *Sex in America: A definitive survey.* Boston: Little, Brown.

Middle age spread. (1995, August). *Harvard Women's Health Watch,* p. 6.

Miedzian, M. (1991). *Boys will be boys: Breaking the link between masculinity and violence.* New York: Doubleday.

Mifflin, L. (1996, February 15). 4 networks plan a ratings system for their shows. *The New York Times,* pp. A1, C24.

Milerad, J., & Sundell, H. (1993). Nicotine exposure and the risk of SIDS. *Acta Paediatrica, 389*(Suppl.), 70–72.

Miles, C., & Miles, W. (1932). The correlation of intelligence scores and chronological age from early to late maturity. *American Journal of Psychology, 44,* 44–78.

Miller, A. (1983). *For your own good: Hidden cruelty in child-rearing and the roots of violence.* New York: Farrar, Straus, & Giroux.

Miller, A. (1984). *For your own good: Hidden cruelty in child-rearing and the roots of violence* (2d ed.). New York: Farrar, Straus, & Giroux.

Miller, B., & Gerard, D. (1979). Family influences on the development of creativity in children: An integrative review. *Family Coordinator, 28*(3), 295–312.

Miller, B. C., & Moore, K. A. (1990). Adolescent sexual behavior, pregnancy, and parenting: Research through the 1980s. *Journal of Marriage and the Family, 52,* 1025–1044.

Miller, D. (1996, January 6). Untying the legal knots of living together. *Cleveland Plain Dealer,* pp. 1E, 4E.

Miller, E., Cradock-Watson, J. E., & Pollock, T. M. (1982, October 9). Consequences of confirmed maternal rubella at successive stages of pregnancy. *The Lancet,* pp. 781–784.

Miller, J. B. (1991). The development of women's sense of self. In J. V. Jordan, A. G. Kaplan, J. B. Miller, I. P. Stiver, & J. L. Surrey (Eds.), *Women's growth in connection: Writings from the Stone Center.* New York: Guilford.

Miller, J. F., Williamson, E., Glue, J., Gordon, Y. B., Grudzinskas, J. G., & Sykes, A. (1980, September 13). Fetal loss after implantation: A prospective study. *The Lancet,* pp. 554–556.

Miller, K., & Kohn, M. (1983). The reciprocal effects of job condition and the intellectuality of leisure-time activities. In M. L. Kohn & C. Schooler (Eds.), *Work and personality: An inquiry into the impact of social stratification* (pp. 217–241). Norwood, NJ: Ablex.

Miller, L. B., & Bizzel, R. P. (1983). Long-term effects of four preschool programs: Sixth, seventh, and eighth grades. *Child Development, 54,* 727–741.

Miller, P. H. (1993). *Theories of personality development* (3d ed.). New York: Freeman.

Miller, R. A. (1996, July 5). The aging immune system: Primer and prospectus. *Science,* pp. 70–74.

Miller, V., Onotera, R. T., & Deinard, A. S. (1984). Denver Developmental Screening Test: Cultural variations in Southeast Asian children. *Journal of Pediatrics, 104*(3), 481–482.

Miller-Jones, D. (1989). Culture and testing. *American Psychologist, 44*(2), 360–366.

Mills, J. L., Graubard, B. I., Harley, E. E.,

Rhoads, G. G., & Berendes, H. W. (1984). Maternal alcohol consumption and birth weight: How much drinking is safe during pregnancy? *Journal of the American Medical Association, 252,* 1875–1879.

Mills, J. L., Holmes, L. B., Aarons, J. H., Simpson, J. L., Brown, Z. A., Jovanovic-Peterson, L. G., Conley, M. R., Graubard, B. I., Knopp, R. H., & Metzger, B. E. (1993). Moderate caffeine use and the risk of spontaneous abortion and intrauterine growth retardation. *Journal of the American Medical Association, 269,* 593–597.

Mills, J. L., McPartlin, J. N., Kirke, P. N., et al. (1995). Homocysteine metabolism in pregnancies complicated by neural tube defects. *The Lancet, 345,* 149–151.

Millstein, S. (in press). Perceptual, attributional, and affective processes in perceptions of vulnerability through the life span. In N. J. Bell & R. W. Bell (Eds.), *Perspectives on adolescent risk taking.* Newbury Park, CA: Sage.

Millstein, S. G., Irwin, C. E., Adler, N. E., Cohn, L. D., Kegeles, S. M., & Dolcini, M. M. (1992). Health-risk behaviors and health concerns among young adolescents. *Pediatrics, 89,* 422–428.

Milne, A. M., Myers, D. E., Rosenthal, A. S., & Ginsburg, A. (1986). Single parents, working mothers, and the educational achievement of school children. *Sociology of Education, 59,* 125–139.

Milunsky, A. (1992). *Heredity and your family's health.* Baltimore: Johns Hopkins Press.

Minkler, H., & Roe, K. (1992). *Forgotten caregivers: Grandmothers raising the children of the crack cocaine epidemic.* Newbury Park, CA: Sage.

Minkler, M., & Roe, K. M. (1996). Grandparents as surrogate parents. *Generations, 20*(1), 34–38.

Miranda, S., Hack, M., Fantz, R., Fanaroff, A., & Klaus, M. (1977). Neonatal pattern vision: Predictor of future mental performance? *Journal of Pediatrics, 91*(4), 642–647.

Miserandino, M. (1996). Children who do well in school: Individual differences in perceived competence and autonomy in above-average children. *Journal of Educational Psychology, 88*(2), 203–214.

Mishel, L., & Bernstein, J. (1994). *The state of working America 1994–1995.* Armonk, NY: Sharp.

Mishell, D. R. (1993). Recurrent abortion. *Journal of Reproductive Medicine, 38,* 250–259.

Mitchell, B. A., Wister, A. V., & Burch, T. K. (1989). The family environment and leaving the parental home. *Journal of Marriage and the Family, 51,* 605–613.

Mitchell, E. A., Ford, R. P. K., Stewart, A. W., Taylor, B. J., Bescroft, D. M. O.,

Thompson, J. M. P., Scragg, R., Hassall, I. B., Barry, D. M. J., Allen, E. M., & Roberts, A. P. (1993). Smoking and the sudden infant death syndrome. *Pediatrics, 91,* 893–896.

Mitchell, V., & Helson, R. (1990). Women's prime of life: Is it the 50s? *Psychology of Women Quarterly, 16,* 331–347.

Miyake, K., Chen, S., & Campos, J. (1985). Infants' temperament, mothers' mode of interaction and attachment in Japan: An interim report. In I. Bretherton & E. Waters (Eds.), Growing points of attachment theory and research. *Monographs of the Society for Research in Child Development, 50*(1-2, Serial No. 109), 276–297.

Moffitt, T. E., Caspi, A., Belsky, J., & Silva, P. A. (1992). Childhood experience and the onset of menarche: A test of a sociobiological model. *Child Development, 63,* 47–58.

Money, J., Ehrhardt, A. A., & Masica, D. N. (1968). Fetal feminization induced by androgen insensitivity in the testicular feminizing syndrome: Effect on marriage and maternalism. *Johns Hopkins Medical Journal, 123,* 105–114.

Monk, A. (1994). Retirement and aging: An introduction to the *Columbia Retirement Handbook.* In A. Monk (Ed.), *The Columbia retirement handbook* (pp. 3–11). New York: Columbia University Press.

Montalbano, W. D. (1995, November 26). Irish vote ends ban on divorce. *Chicago Sun-Times,* p. 3.

Montepare, J. M., & Lachman, M. E. (1989). "You're only as old as you feel": Self-perceptions of age, fears of aging, and life satisfaction from adolescence to old age. *Psychology and Aging, 4*(1), 73–78.

Moon, A., & Williams, D. (1993). Perception of elder abuse and help-seeking patterns among African American, Caucasian American, and Korean American families. *The Gerontologist, 33,* 386–395.

Moon, C., Cooper, R. P., & Fifer, W. P. (1993). Two-day-olds prefer their native language. *Infant Behavior and Development, 16,* 495–500.

Moore, N., Evertson, C., & Brophy J. (1974). Solitary play: Some functional reconsiderations. *Developmental Psychology, 10*(5), 830–834.

Morelli, G. A., Rogoff, B., Oppenheim, D., & Goldsmith D. (1992). Cultural variation in infants' sleeping arrangements: Questions of independence. *Developmental Psychology, 28,* 604–613.

Morison, P., & Masten, A. S. (1991). Peer reputation in middle childhood as a predictor of adaptation in adolescence: A seven-year follow-up. *Child Development, 62,* 991–1007.

Morland, J. (1966). A comparison of race awareness in northern and southern

children. *American Journal of Orthopsychiatry, 36,* 22–31.

Morris, R., & Kralochwill, T. (1983). *Treating children's fears and phobias: A behavioral approach.* Elmsford, NY: Pergamon.

Morrison, D. R., & Cherlin, A. J. (1995). The divorce process and young children's well-being: A prospective analysis. *Journal of Marriage and the Family, 57,* 800–812.

Mortenson, T. G. (1992, April). College participation rates by family income. *Postsecondary Education Opportunity,* pp. 1–4.

Moscovitch, M., & Winocur, G. (1992). The neuropsychology of memory and aging. In F. I. M. Craik & T. A. Salthouse (Eds.), *Handbook of aging and cognition* (pp. 315–372). Hillsdale, NJ: Erlbaum.

Moses, L. J., & Flavell, J. H. (1990). Inferring false belief from actions and reactions. *Child Development, 61,* 929–945.

Mosher, W. D., & Pratt, W. F. (1991). Fecundity and infertility in the United States: Incidence and trends. *Fertility and Sterility, 56,* 192–193.

Moskow-McKenzie, D., & Manheimer, R. J. (1994). *A planning guide to organize educational programs for older adults.* Asheville, NC: University Publications, UNCA.

Moskowitz, B. A. (1978). The acquisition of language. *Scientific American, 239*(5), 92–108.

Moss, M. S., & Moss, S. Z. (1989). The death of a parent. In R. A. Kalish (Ed.), *Midlife loss: Coping strategies.* Newbury Park, CA: Sage.

Motenko, A. K. (1989). Frustrations, gratifications, and well-being of dementia caregivers. *The Gerontologist, 29*(2), 166–172.

Mounts, N. S., & Steinberg, L. (1995). An ecological analysis of peer influence on adolescent grade point average and drug use. *Developmental Psychology, 31*(6), 915–922.

Mufson, S. (1995, August 17). China's elderly population gets cold shoulder. *Chicago Sun-Times,* p. 31.

Mui, A. C. (1992). Caregiver strain among black and white daughter caregivers: A role theory perspective. *The Gerontologist, 32*(2), 203, 212.

Mullen, M. K. (1994). Earliest recollections of childhood: A demographic analysis. *Cognition, 52,* 55–79.

Munck, A., Guyre, P., & Holbrook, N. (1984). Physiological functions of glucocorticoids in stress and their relation to pharmacological actions. *Endocrine Reviews, 5,* 25–44.

Murphy, C. M., & Bootzin, R. R. (1973). Active and passive participation in the contact desensitization of snake fear in children. *Behavior Therapy, 4,* 203–211.

Murphy, D. P. (1929). The outcome of 625 pregnancies in women subjected to pelvic radium roentgen irradiation. *American Journal of Obstetrics and Gynecology, 18,* 179–187.

Murray, A. D., Dolby, R. M., Nation, R. L., & Thomas, D. B. (1981). Effects of epidural anesthesia on newborns and their mothers. *Child Development, 52,* 71–82.

Murray, B. (1996, February). Psychology remains top college major. *APA Monitor,* p. 1.

Murstein, B. I. (1980). Mate selection in the 1970s. *Journal of Marriage and the Family, 42,* 777–792.

Mussen, P. H., & Eisenberg-Berg, N. (1977). *Roots of caring, sharing, and helping: The development of prosocial behavior in children.* San Francisco: Freeman.

Mussen, P. H., & Jones, M. C. (1957). Self-conceptions, motivations, and interpersonal attitudes of late- and early-maturing boys. *Child Development, 28,* 243–256.

Mussen, P. H., & Rutherford, E. (1963). Parent-child relations and parental personality in relation to young children's sex role preferences. *Child Development, 34,* 589–607.

Must, A., Jacques, P. F., Dallal, G. E., Bajema, C. J., & Dietz, W. H. (1992). Long-term morbidity and mortality of overweight adolescents. *New England Journal of Medicine, 327*(19), 1350–1355.

Muuss, R. E. H. (1988). *Theories of Adolescence* (5th ed.). New York: Random House.

Myers, J. E., & Perrin, N. (1993). Grandparents affected by parental divorce: A population at risk? *Journal of Counseling and Development, 72,* 62–66.

Myers, N., & Perlmutter, M. (1978). Memory in the years from 2 to 5. In P. Ornstein (Ed.), *Memory development in children.* Hillsdale, NJ: Erlbaum.

Naeye, R. L., & Peters, E. C. (1984). Mental development of children whose mothers smoked during pregnancy. *Obstetrics and Gynecology, 64,* 601.

Nakonezny, P. A., Shull, R. D., & Rodgers, J. L. (1995). The effect of no-fault divorce rate across the 50 states and its relation to income, education, and religiosity. *Journal of Marriage and the Family, 57,* 477–488.

Nathanielsz, P. W. (1995). The role of basic science in preventing low birth weight. *The Future of Our Children, 5*(1), 57–70.

Nathanson, C. A., & Lorenz, G. (1982). Women and health: The social dimensions of biomedical data. In J. Z. Giele (Ed.), *Women in the middle years.* New York: Wiley.

National Center for Education Statistics (NCES). (1983). High-school dropouts: Descriptive information from high school and beyond. *NCES Bulletin.* Washington, DC: U.S. Department of Education.

National Center for Education Statistics (NCES). (1985). *The relationship of parental involvement to high school grades* (Publication No. NCES-85-205b). Washington, DC: U.S. Government Printing Office.

National Center for Education Statistics (NCES). (1987). *Who drops out of high school? From high school and beyond.* Washington, DC: U.S. Department of Education, Office of Educational Research and Improvement.

National Center for Education Statistics (NCES). (1995a). *Condition of education, 1995.* Washington, DC: U.S. Department of Education.

National Center for Education Statistics (NCES). (1995b). *Digest of education statistics 1995* (NCES 95-029). Washington, DC: U.S. Department of Education.

National Center for Health Statistics. (1990). *Health, United States, 1989 and prevention profile* (DHHS Publication No. 90-1232). Washington, DC: U.S. Public Health Service.

National Center for Health Statistics. (1992). Annual summary of births, marriages, divorces, and deaths: United States, 1991. *Monthly Vital Statistics Report, 40.* Washington, DC: U.S. Public Health Service.

National Center for Health Statistics. (1993). *Health, United States, 1992 and prevention profile.* Washington, DC: U.S. Public Health Service.

National Center for Health Statistics. (1994a). Advance report of final natality statistics, 1992. *Monthly Vital Statistics Report, 43*(5, Suppl.). Hyattsville, MD: U.S. Public Health Service.

National Center for Health Statistics. (1994b). *Health, United States, 1993.* Hyattsville, MD: U.S. Public Health Service.

National Center for Health Statistics. (1995a). *Annual summary of births, marriages, divorces, and deaths—U.S., 1994.* Hyattsville, MD: U.S. Public Health Service.

National Center for Health Statistics. (1995b). Statistics.

National Center for Health Statistics. (1996a, February 29). Advance report of final mortality statistics, 1993. *Monthly Vital Statistics Report, 44*(7, Suppl.). Hyattsville, MD: U.S. Public Health Service.

National Center for Health Statistics. (1996b). *Vital statistics of the United States, 1992: Volume I—Natality.* Hyattsville, MD: U.S. Public Health Service.

National Commission on Excellence in Education. (1983, April). *A nation at risk: The imperative for educational reform* (Stock No. 065-000-00177-2). Washington, DC: U.S. Government Printing Office.

National Commission for the Protection of Human Subjects of Biomedical and Behavioral Research. (1978). Report.

National Commission on Youth. (1980). *The transition to adulthood: A bridge too long.* New York: Westview.

National Committee for Citizens in Education (NCCE). (1986, Winter Holiday). Don't be afraid to start a suicide prevention program in your school. *Network for Public Schools,* pp. 1, 4.

National Hospice Organization. (1996, July 1). *Hospice fact sheet.* Arlington, VA: Author.

National Institute of Mental Health (NIMH). (1982). *Television and behavior: Ten years of scientific progress and implications for the eighties: Vol. 1. Summary report* (DHHS Publication No. ADM 82-1195). Washington, DC: U.S. Government Printing Office.

National Institute on Aging (NIA). (1980). *Senility: Myth or madness.* Washington, DC: U.S. Government Printing Office.

National Institute on Aging (NIA). (1984). *Be sensible about salt.* Washington, DC: U.S. Government Printing Office.

National Institute on Aging (NIA). (1993). *Bound for good health: A collection of Age Pages.* Washington, DC: U.S. Government Printing Office.

National Institute on Aging (NIA). (1994). *Age page: Sexuality in later life.* Washington, DC: U.S. Government Printing Office.

National Institute on Aging (NIA). (1995a). *Aging and your eyes.* Washington, DC: U.S. Government Printing Office.

National Institute on Aging (NIA). (1995b). *Don't take it easy—exercise.* Washington, DC: U.S. Government Printing Office.

National Institute on Aging. (1995c). *Hearing and older people.* Washington, DC: U.S. Government Printing Office.

National Institute on Alcohol Abuse and Alcoholism (NIAAA). (1981, October). *Fact sheet: Selected statistics on alcohol and alcoholism.* Rockville, MD: National Clearinghouse for Alcohol Information.

National Institute on Drug Abuse (NIDA). (1995). *Monitoring the future.* Washington, DC: National Institutes of Health.

National Institutes of Health (NIH). (1992, December 7–9). *Impotence: NIH Consensus Statement, 10*(4), 1–31. Washington, DC: U.S. Government Printing Office.

National Institutes of Health/National Institute on Aging (NIH/NIA). (1993, May). *In search of the secrets of aging* (NIH Publication No. 93-2756). Washington, DC: National Institutes of Health.

National Opinion Research Center. (1996). *General social surveys, 1976, 1996.* Chicago: University of Chicago Press.

National Research Council (NRC). (1993a). *Losing generations: Adolescents in high-risk settings.* Washington, DC: National Academy Press.

National Research Council (NRC). (1993b). *Understanding child abuse and neglect.* Washington, DC: National Academy Press.

National Task Force on the Prevention and Treatment of Obesity. (1993). Very low-calorie diets. *Journal of the American Medical Association, 270,* 967–974.

Needleman, H. L., Riess, J. A., Tobin, M. J., Biesecker, G. E., & Greenhouse, J. B. (1996). Bone lead levels and delinquent behavior. *Journal of the American Medical Association, 275,* 363–369.

Needleman, H. L., & Gatsonis, C. A. (1990). Low-level lead exposure and the IQ of children: A meta-analysis of modern studies. *Journal of the American Medical Association, 263,* 673–678.

Neeley, A. S., & Bäckman, L. (1993). Long-term maintenance gain from memory training in older adults: Two 3½ year follow-up studies. *Journal of Gerontology: Psychological Sciences, 48,* P233–237.

Neeley, A. S., & Bäckman, L. (1995). Effects of multifactorial memory training in old age: Generalizability across tasks and individuals. *Journal of Gerontology: Psychological Sciences, 50B,* P134–140.

Negative stereotypes still plague older workers on the job. (1995, April). *AARP Bulletin,* p. 3.

Neisser, U. (1976). General, academic, and artificial intelligence. In L. Resnick (Ed.), *Human intelligence: Perspectives on its theory and measurement* (pp. 179–189). Norwood, NJ: Ablex.

Neisser, U., Boodoo, G., Bouchard, T. J., Jr., Boykin, A. W., Brody, N., Ceci, S. J., Halpern, D. F., Loehlin, J. C., Perloff, R., Sternberg, R. J., & Urbina, S. (1995). *Intelligence: Knowns and unknowns.* Washington, DC: American Psychological Association.

Nelson, K. (1973). Structure and strategy in learning to talk. *Monographs of the Society for Research in Child Development, 38*(1–2).

Nelson, K. (1981). Individual differences in language development: Implications for development and language. *Developmental Psychology, 17*(2), 170–187.

Nelson, K. (1989). Remembering: A functional developmental perspective. In P. R. Solomon, G. R. Goethels, C. M. Kelly, & B. R. Stephens (Eds.), *Memory: An interdisciplinary approach.* New York: Springer-Verlag.

Nelson, K. (1992). Emergence of autobiographical memory at age 4. *Human Development, 35,* 172–177.

Nelson, K. (1993). The psychological and social origins of autobiographical memory. *Psychological Science, 47,* 7–14.

Nelson, K. B., Dambrosia, J. M., Ting, T. Y., & Grether, J. K. (1996). Uncertain value of electronic fetal monitoring in predicting cerebral palsy. *New England Journal of Medicine, 334,* 613–618.

Nelson, M. E., Fiatarone, M. A., Morganti, C. M., Trice, I., Greenberg, R. A., & Evans, W. J. (1994). Effects of high-intensity strength training on multiple risk factors for osteoporotic fractures: A randomized controlled trial. *Journal of the American Medical Association, 272,* 1909–1914.

Neuffer, E. (1987, November 14). School parents wrestle with Lisa's death. *The New York Times,* p. A29.

Neugarten, B. L. (1967). The awareness of middle age. In R. Owen (Ed.), *Middle age.* London: BBC.

Neugarten, B. L. (1968). Adult personality: Toward a psychology of the life cycle. In B. Neugarten (Ed.), *Middle age and aging.* Chicago: University of Chicago Press.

Neugarten, B. L. (1977). Personality and aging. In J. E. Birren & K. W. Schaie (Eds.), *Handbook of the psychology of aging and the social sciences.* New York: Van Nostrand Reinhold.

Neugarten, B. L., & Hagestad, G. (1976). Age and the life course. In H. Binstock & E. Sharas (Eds.), *Handbook of aging and the social sciences.* New York: Van Nostrand Reinhold.

Neugarten, B. L., Havighurst, R., & Tobin, S. (1968). Personality and patterns of aging. In B. Neugarten (Ed.), *Middle age and aging.* Chicago: University of Chicago Press.

Neugarten, B. L., Moore, J. W., & Lowe, J. C. (1965). Age norms, age constraints, and adult socialization. *American Journal of Sociology, 70,* 710–717.

Neugarten, B. L., & Neugarten, D. A. (1987, May). The changing meanings of age. *Psychology Today,* pp. 29–33.

The new weight guidelines. (1995, November). *Harvard Women's Health Watch,* p. 1.

Newacheck, P. W. (1989). Improving access to health services for adolescents from economically disadvantaged families. *Pediatrics, 84*(6), 1056–1063.

Newacheck, P. W., Stoddard, J. J., & McManus, M. (1993). Ethnocultural variations in the prevalence and impact of childhood chronic conditions. *Pediatrics, 91,* 1031–1047.

Newcomb, A. F., & Bagwell, C. L. (1995). Children's friendship relations: A meta-analytic review. *Psychological Bulletin, 117*(2), 306–347.

Newcomb, A. F., Bukowski, W. M., & Pattee, L. (1993). Children's peer relations: A meta-analytic review of popular, rejected, neglected, controversial, and average sociometric status. *Psychological Bulletin, 113,* 99–128.

Newcombe, N., & Fox, N. A. (1994). Infantile amnesia: Through a glass darkly. *Child Development, 65,* 31–40.

Newman, P. R. (1982). The peer group. In B. Wolman (Ed.), *Handbook of developmental psychology.* Englewood Cliffs, NJ: Prentice-Hall.

Newnham, J. P., Evans, S. F., Michael, C. A., Stanley, F. J., & Landau, L. I. (1993). Effects of frequent ultrasound during pregnancy: A randomised controlled trial. *The Lancet, 342,* 887–891.

Newson, J., Newson, E., & Mahalski, P. A. (1982). Persistent infant comfort habits and their sequelae at 11 and 16 years. *Journal of Child Psychology and Psychiatry, 23,* 421–436.

NICHD Early Child Care Research Network. (1996, April 20). *Infant child care and attachment security: Results of the NICHD study of early child care.* Paper presented at the International Conference on Infant Studies, Providence, RI.

NIH Consensus Development Panel on Physical Activity and Cardiovascular Health. (1996). Physical activity and cardiovascular health. *Journal of the American Medical Association, 276,* 241–246.

Nisan, M., & Kohlberg, L. (1982). Universality and variation in moral judgment: A longitudinal and cross-sectional study in Turkey. *Child Development, 53,* 865–876.

Nishio, H. K. (1994). Japan's welfare vision: Dealing with a rapidly increasing elderly population. In L. K. Olson (Ed.), *The graying of the world: Who will care for the frail elderly?* (pp. 233–260). New York: Haworth.

Nock, S. L. (1995). Commitment and dependency in marriage. *Journal of Marriage and the Family, 57,* 503–514.

Noelker, L. S., & Whitlatch, C. J. (1995). Caregiving. In G. E. Maddox (Ed.), *The encyclopedia of aging* (pp. 144–146). New York: Springer.

Nojima, M. (1994). Japan's approach to continuing education for senior citizens. *Educational Gerontology, 20,* 463–471.

Nolen-Hoeksema, S., & Girgus, J. S. (1994). The emergence of gender differences in depression during adolescence. *Psychological Bulletin, 115*(3), 424–443.

Norton, A. J., & Miller, L. F. (1992). *Marriage, divorce, and remarriage* (Current Population Reports, Series P23-188). Washington, DC: U.S. Government Printing Office.

Norton, A. J., & Moorman, J. E. (1987). Current trends in marriage and divorce among American women. *Journal of Marriage and the Family, 49*(1), 3–14.

Notelovitz, M., & Ware, M. (1983). *Stand tall: The informed woman's guide to preventing osteoporosis.* Gainesville, FL: Triad.

Notzon, F. C. (1990). International differences in the use of obstetric interventions. *Journal of the American Medical Association, 263*(24), 3286–3291.

NOW Legal Defense and Education Fund & Chernow-O'Leary, R. (1987). *The state-by-state-guide to women's legal rights.* New York: McGraw-Hill.

Nozyce, M., Hittelman, J., Muenz, L., Durako, S. J., Fischer, M. L., & Willoughby, A. (1994). Effect of perinatally acquired human immunodeficiency virus infection on neurodevelopment in children during the first two years of life. *Pediatrics, 94,* 883–891.

Nugent, J. K. (1991). Cultural and psychological influences on the father's role in infant development. *Journal of Marriage and the Family, 53,* 475–485.

Nuss, S., Denti, E., & Viry, D. (1989). *Women in the world of work: Statistical analyses and projections to the year 2000.* Geneva: International Labor Office.

Nussbaum, M., Shenker, I. R., Baird, D., & Saravay, S. (1985). Follow-up investigation in patients with anorexia nervosa. *Journal of Pediatrics, 106,* 835–840.

Oakes, J., Gamoran, A., & Page, R. N. (1992). Curriculum differentiation: Opportunities, outcomes, and meanings. In P. W. Jackson (Ed.), *Handbook of research on curriculum* (pp. 570–608). New York: Macmillan.

O'Bryant, S. L. (1988). Sibling support and older widows' well-being. *Journal of Marriage and the Family, 50,* 173–183.

O'Bryant, S. L. (1990–1991). Forewarning of a husband's death: Does it make a difference for older widows? *Omega, 22,* 227–239.

O'Connell, M. (1991). *Late expectations: Childbearing patterns of American women for the 1990s* (Current Population Reports, Series P23-176). Washington, DC: U.S. Government Printing Office.

O'Connor, M. J., Cohen, S., & Parmalee, A. H. (1984). Infant auditory discrimination in preterm and full-term infants as a predictor of 5-year intelligence. *Developmental Psychology, 20,* 159–165.

O'Connor, M. J., Sigman, M., & Kasari, C. (1993). Interactional model for the association among maternal alcohol use, mother-infant interaction, and infant cognitive development. *Infant Behavior and Development, 16,* 177–192.

Offer, D. (1969). *The psychological world of the teenager: A study of normal adolescent boys.* New York: Basic Books.

Offer, D. (1987). In defense of adolescents. *Journal of the American Medical Association, 257,* 3407–3408.

Offer, D., & Church, R. B. (1991). Generation gap. In R. M. Lerner, A. C. Petersen, & J. Brooks-Gunn (Eds.), *Encyclopedia of adolescence* (pp. 397–399). New York: Garland.

Offer, D., & Offer, J. B. (1974). Normal adolescent males: The high school and college years. *Journal of the American College Health Association, 22,* 209–215.

Offer, D., Ostrov, E., & Howard, K. I. (1986). *Normal adolescents' concern with nuclear issues.* Chicago: Michael Reese Hospital and Medical Center.

Offer, D., Ostrov, E., & Howard, K. I. (1989). Adolescence: What is normal? *American Journal of Diseases of Children, 143,* 731–736.

Offer, D., Ostrov, E., Howard, K. I., & Atkinson, R. (1988). *The teenage world: Adolescents' self-image in ten countries.* New York: Plenum.

Offer, D., & Schonert-Reichl, K. A. (1992). Debunking the myths of adolescence: Findings from recent research. *Journal of the American Academy of Child and Adolescent Psychiatry, 31,* 1003–1014.

Office of Juvenile Justice and Delinquency Prevention. (1994). *National crime victimization survey.* Washington, DC: U.S. Bureau of Justice.

O'Grady-LeShane, R. (1993). Changes in the lives of women and their families: Have old age pensions kept pace? *Generations, 17*(4), 27–31.

Okagaki, L., & Sternberg, R. J. (1993). Parental beliefs and children's school performance. *Child Development, 64,* 36–56.

Okun, M. A., Stick, W. A., Haring, M. J., & Witter, R. A. (1984). The social activity/subjective well-being relation: A quantitative synthesis. *Research on Aging, 6,* 45–65.

Okun, S. (1988, January 29). Opera coach died in his "house of worship." *The New York Times,* pp. B1, B3.

O'Leary, K. D., Barling, J., Arias, I., Rosenbaum, A., Malone, J., & Tyree, A. (1989). Prevalence and stability of physical aggression between spouses: A longitudinal analysis. *Journal of Consulting and Clinical Psychology, 57*(2), 263–268.

Oldenhave, A., Jaszman, L. J. B., Haspels, A. A., & Everaerd, W. T. A. M. (1993). Impact of climacteric on well-being. *American Journal of Obstetrics and Gynecology, 168,* 772–780.

Older Women's League. (1994). *Ending violence against midlife and older women.* Washington, DC: Author.

Older workers: The good, the bad, and the truth. (1993, April–May). *Modern Maturity,* p. 10.

Olds, D. L., Henderson, C. R., & Tatelbaum, R. (1994a). Intellectual impairment in children of women who smoke cigarettes during pregnancy. *Pediatrics, 93,* 221–227.

Olds, D. L., Henderson, C. R., & Tatelbaum, R. (1994b). Prevention of intellectual impairment in children of women who smoke cigarettes during pregnancy. *Pediatrics, 93,* 228–233.

Olds, S. W. (1989). *The working parents' survival guide.* Rocklin, CA: Prima.

Oliver, M. B., & Hyde, J. S. (1993). Gender differences in sexuality: A meta-analysis. *Psychological Bulletin, 114,* 29–51.

Oller, D. K., & Eilers, R. (1988). The role of audition in infant babbling. *Child Development, 59,* 441–449.

Olmsted, P. P., & Weikart, D. P. (Eds.). (1994). *Family speak: Early childhood care and education in eleven countries.* Ypsilanti, MI: High/Scope.

Olsen-Fulero, L. (1982). Style and stability in mother conversational behavior: A study of individual differences. *Journal of Child Language, 9,* 543–564.

Olson, P. G. (1994). The changing role of the elderly in the People's Republic of China. In L. K. Olson (Ed.), *The graying of the world: Who will care for the frail elderly?* (pp. 261–288). New York: Haworth.

1 in 4 U.S. kids not vaccinated, survey shows. (1995, August 25). *Chicago Sun-Times,* p. 25.

Opie, I., & Opie, P. (1969). *Children's games in street and playground.* London: Oxford University Press.

Orentlicher, D. (1996). The legalization of physician-assisted suicide. *New England Journal of Medicine, 335,* 663–667.

Oropesa, R. S. (1996). Normative beliefs about marriage and cohabitation: A comparison of non-Latino whites, Mexican Americans, and Puerto Ricans. *Journal of Marriage and the Family, 58,* 49–62.

Orr, D. P., & Ingersoll, G. M. (1995). The contribution of level of cognitive complexity and pubertal timing to behavioral risk in young adolescents. *Pediatrics, 95*(4), 528–533.

Orr, R., & Luszcz, M. (1994). Rethinking women's ways: Gender commonalities and intersections with postformal thought. *Journal of Adult Development, 1,* 225–234.

Orr, W. C., & Sohal, R. S. (1994). Extension of life-span by overexpression of superoxide dimutase and catylase in drosphila melanogaster. *Science, 263,* 1128–1130.

Oshima, S. (1996, July 5). Japan: Feeling the strains of an aging population. *Science,* pp. 44–45.

Oshima-Takane, Y., Goodz, E., & Derevensky, J. L. (1996). Birth order effects on early language development: Do secondborn children learn from overheard speech? *Child Development, 67,* 621–634.

Ostrea, E. M., & Chavez, C. J. (1979). Perinatal problems (excluding neonatal withdrawal) in maternal drug addiction: A study of 830 cases. *Journal of Pediatrics, 94*(2), 292–295.

Oswald, P. F., & Peltzman, P. (1974). The cry of the human infant. *Scientific American, 230*(3), 84–90.

Otten, M. W., Teutsch, S. M., Williamson, D. F., & Marks, J. S. (1990). The effect of known risk factors on the excess mortality of black adults in the United States. *Journal of the American Medical Association, 263*(6), 845–850.

Owens, J. E., Cook, E. W., & Stevenson, I. (1990). Features of "near-death experience" in relation to whether or not patients were near death. *The Lancet, 336,* 1175–1177.

Owens, J. F., Matthews, K. A., Wing, R., & Kuller, L. H. (1992). Can physical activity mitigate the effects of aging in middle-aged women? *Circulation, 85*(3), 1265–1270.

Owens, W. A. (1966). Age and mental abilities: A second adult follow-up. *Journal of Educational Psychology, 57*(6), 311–325.

Owsley, C., Ball, K., Sloane, M. E., Roenker, D. L., & Bruni, J. R. (1991). Visual cognitive correlates of vehicle accidents in older drivers. *Psychology and Aging, 6*(3), 65–70.

Paden, S. L., & Buehler, C. (1995). Coping with the dual-income lifestyle. *Journal of Marriage and the Family, 57,* 101–110.

Padilla, A. M., Lindholm, K. J., Chen, A., Duran, R., et al. (1991). The English-only movement: Myths, reality, and implications for psychology. *American Psychologist, 46*(2), 120–130.

Paganini-Hill, A., & Henderson, V. W. (1994). Estrogen deficiency and risk of Alzheimer's disease in women. *American Journal of Epidemiology, 140,* 256–261.

Pan, W. H.-L. (1994). Children's play in Taiwan. In J. L. Roopnarine, J. E. Johnson, & F. H. Hooper (Eds.), *Children's play in diverse cultures.* Albany: State University of New York Press.

Paneth, N. S. (1995). The problem of low birthweight. *The Future of Children, 5*(1), 19–34.

Papalia, D. (1972). The status of several conservation abilities across the lifespan. *Human Development, 15,* 229–243.

Papola, P., Alvarez, M., & Cohen, H. J. (1994). Developmental and service needs of school-age children with human immunodeficiency virus infection: A descriptive study. *Pediatrics, 94,* 914–918.

Papousek, H. (1959). A method of studying conditioned food reflexes in young children up to age six months. *Pavlovian Journal of Higher Nervous Activity, 9,* 136–140.

Papousek, H. (1960a). Conditioned motor alimentary reflexes in infants: 1. Experimental conditioned sucking reflex. *Ceskoslovenska Pediatrie, 15,* 861–872.

Papousek, H. (1960b). Conditioned motor alimentary reflexes in infants: 2. A new experimental method of investigation. *Ceskoslovenska Pediatrie, 15,* 981–988.

Papousek, H. (1961). Conditioned head rotation reflexes in infants in the first months of life. *Acta Paediatrica, 50,* 565–576.

Pappas, G., Queen, S., Hadden, W., & Fisher, G. (1993). The increasing disparity in mortality between socioeconomic groups in the United States, 1960 and 1986. *New England Journal of Medicine, 329,* 103–109.

Paris, S. G., & Lindauer, B. K. (1976). The role of inference in children's comprehension and memory for sentences. *Cognitive Psychology, 8,* 217–227.

Parish, S., Collins, R., Peto, R., Youngman, L., Barton, J., Jayne, K., Clarke, R., Appleby, P., Lyon, V., Cederholm-Williams, S., Marshall, J., & Sleight, P. for the International Studies of Infarct Survival (ISIS). (1995). Cigarette smoking, tar yields, and non-fatal myocardial infarction: 14,000 cases and 32,000 controls in the United Kingdom. *British Medical Journal, 311,* 471–477.

Park, A. (1995, October 2). One way to test your EQ. *Time,* pp. 64–65.

Park, D. C. (1992). Applied cognitive aging research. In F. I. M. Craik & T. A. Salthouse (Eds.), *Handbook of aging and cognition* (pp. 449–494). Hillsdale, NJ: Erlbaum.

Parke, R. (1977). Some effects of punishment on children's behavior—Revisited. In P. Cantor (Ed.), *Understanding a child's world.* New York: McGraw-Hill.

Parke, R. D., Grossman, K., & Tinsley, B. R. (1981). Father-mother-infant interaction in the newborn period: A German-American comparison. In T. M. Field, A. M. Sostek, P. Viete, & P. H. Leideman (Eds.), *Culture and early interaction.* Hillsdale, NJ: Erlbaum.

Parke, R. D., & Tinsley, B. R. (1981). The father's role in infancy: Determinants of involvement in caregiving and play. In M. E. Lamb (Ed.), *The role of the father in child development* (2d ed.). New York: Wiley.

Parker, J. G., & Asher, S. R. (1987). Peer relations and later personal adjustment: Are low-accepted children at risk? *Psychological Bulletin, 102,* 357–389.

Parmelee, A. H. (1986). Children's illnesses: Their beneficial effects on behavioral development. *Child Development, 57,* 1–10.

Parmelee, A. H., Wenner, W. H., & Schulz, H. R. (1964). Infant sleep patterns: From birth to 16 weeks of age. *Journal of Pediatrics, 65,* 576.

Parmentier, M., Libert, F., Schurmans, S., Schiffmann, S., Lefort, A., Eggerickx, D., Mollereau, C., Gerard, C., Perret, J., et al. (1992). Expression of members of the putative olfactory receptor gene family in mammalian germ cells. *Nature, 355*(6359), 243–269.

Parnes, H. S., & Sommers, D. G. (1994). Shunning retirement: Work experience of men in their seventies and early eighties. *Journal of Gerontology: Social Sciences, 49,* S117–124.

Parrish, K. M., Holt, V. L., Easterling, T. R., Connell, F. A., & LeGerfo, J. P. (1994). Effect of changes in maternal age, parity, and birth weight distribution on primary cesarean delivery rates. *Journal of the American Medical Association, 271,* 443–447.

Parten, M. B. (1932). Social play among preschool children. *Journal of Abnormal and Social Psychology, 27,* 243–269.

Pate, R. R., Pratt, M., Blair, S. N., Haskell, W. L., et al. (1995). Physical activity and public health. *Journal of the American Medical Association, 273,* 402–407.

Patterson, C. J. (1992). Children of lesbian and gay parents. *Child Development, 63,* 1025–1042.

Patterson, C. J. (1995a). Lesbian mothers, gay fathers, and their children. In A. R. D'Augelli & C. J. Patterson (Eds.), *Lesbian, gay, and bisexual identities over the lifespan: Psychological perspectives* (pp. 293–320). New York: Oxford University Press.

Patterson, C. J. (1995b). Sexual orientation and human development: An overview. *Developmental Psychology, 31*(1), 3–11.

Patterson, C. J., Kupersmidt, J. B., & Griesler, P. C. (1990). Children's perceptions of self and of relationships with others as a function of socioeconomic status. *Child Development, 61,* 1335–1349.

Patterson, G. R., DeBaryshe, B. D., & Ramsey, E. (1989). A developmental perspective on antisocial behavior. *American Psychologist, 44*(2), 329–335.

Patterson, G. R., Reid, J. B., & Dishion, T. J. (1992). *Antisocial boys.* Eugene, OR: Castalia.

Patterson, G. R., & Stouthamer-Loeber, M. (1984). The correlation of family management practices and delinquency. *Child Development, 55,* 1299–1307.

Pattison, E. M. (Ed.). (1977). *The experience of dying.* Englewood Cliffs, NJ: Prentice-Hall.

Paveza, G. J., Cohen, D., Eisdorfer, C., Freels, S., Semla, T., Ashford, J. W., Gorelick, P., Hirschman, R., Luchins, D., & Levy, P. (1992). Severe family violence and Alzheimer's disease: Prevalence and risk factors. *The Gerontologist, 32*(4), 493–497.

Pearlin, L. I. (1980). Life strains and psychological distress among adults. In N. J. Smelser & E. H. Erikson (Eds.), *Themes of work and love in adulthood.* Cambridge, MA: Harvard University Press.

Pearson, J. D., Morell, C. H., Gordon-Salant, S., Brant, L. J., Metter, E. J., Klein, L. J., & Fozard, J. L. (1995). Gender differences in a longitudinal study of age-associated hearing loss. *Journal of the Acoustical Society of America, 97,* 1196–1205.

Pease, D., & Gleason, J. B. (1985). Gaining meaning: Semantic development. In J. B. Gleason (Ed.), *The development of language.* Columbus, OH: Merrill.

Peck, R. C. (1955). Psychological developments in the second half of life. In J. E. Anderson (Ed.), *Psychological aspects of aging.* Washington, DC: American Psychological Association.

Pedersen, F. A., Cain, R., & Zaslow, M. (1982). Variation in infant experience associated with alternative family roles. In L. Laosa & I. Sigel (Eds.), *The family as a learning environment.* New York: Plenum.

Pederson, E., Faucher, T. A., & Eaton, W. W. (1978). A new perspective of the effects of first grade teachers on children's subsequent adult status. *Harvard Educational Review, 48,* 1–31.

Pelleymounter, N. A., Cullen, M. J., Baker, M. B., Hecht, R., Winters, D., Boone, T., & Collins, F. (1995). Effects of the obese gene product on body regulation in ob/ob mice. *Science, 269,* 540–543.

Perlmutter, M., Behrend, S. D., Kuo, F., & Muller, A. (1989). Social influences on children's problem solving. *Developmental Psychology, 25,* 744–754.

Perlmutter, M., Kaplan, M., & Nyquist, L. (1990). Development of adaptive competence in adulthood. *Human Development, 33,* 185–197.

Perrucci, C. C., Perrucci, R., & Targ, D. B. (1988). *Plant closings.* New York: Aldine.

Perry, D. (1995, March 3–9). Merciful end? Couple's suicide raises profound questions. *Chicago Jewish News,* p. 10.

Perry, W. G. (1970). *Forms of intellectual and ethical development in the college years.* New York: Holt.

Peskin, H. (1967). Pubertal onset and ego functioning. *Journal of Abnormal Psychology, 72,* 1–15.

Peskin, H. (1973). Influence of the developmental schedule of puberty on learning and ego functioning. *Journal of Youth and Adolescence, 2,* 273–290.

Petersen, A. C. (1991, April). *American adolescence: How it affects girls.* Paper presented at the Gisela Konopka Lecture, University of Minnesota, Minneapolis.

Petersen, A. C. (1993). Presidential address: Creating adolescents: The role of context and process in developmental transitions. *Journal of Research on Adolescents, 3*(1), 1–18.

Petersen, A. C., Compas, B. E., Brooks-Gunn, J., Stemmler, M., Ey, S., & Grant, K. E. (1993). Depression in adolescence. *American Psychologist, 48*(2), 155–168.

Petersen, A. C., Kennedy, R. E., & Sullivan, P. (1991). Coping with adolescence. In. M. E. Colten & S. Gore (Eds.), *Adolescent stress: Causes and consequences* (pp. 93–110). New York: Aldine de Gruyter.

Petersen, A. C., Sarigiani, P. A., & Kennedy, R. E. (1991). Adolescent depression: Why more girls? *Journal of Youth and Adolescence, 20,* 247–271.

Peterson, B. E., & Stewart, A. J. (1996). Antecedents and contexts of generativity motivation at midlife. *Psychology and Aging, 11*(1), 21–33.

Peterson, C. C. (1996). The ticking of the social clock: Adults' beliefs about the timing of transition events. *International Journal of Aging and Human Development, 42*(3), 189–203.

Petitto, L. A., & Marentette, P. F. (1991). Babbling in the manual mode: Evidence for the ontogeny of language. *Science, 251,* 1493–1495.

Pettit, E. J., & Bloom, B. L. (1984). Whose decision was it? The effects of initiator status on adjustment to marital disruption. *Journal of Marriage and the Family, 46*(3), 587–595.

Phillips, D., McCartney, K., & Scarr, S. (1987). Child-care quality and children's social development. *Developmental Psychology, 23*(4), 537–543.

Phillips, D. P. (1992). The birthday: Lifeline or deadline? *Psychosomatic Medicine, 54*(5), 532–542.

Phillips, D. P., & King, E. W. (1988, September 24). Death takes a holiday: Mortality surrounding major social occasions. *The Lancet,* pp. 728–732.

Phillips, D. P., & Smith, D. G. (1990). Postponement of death until symbolically meaningful occasions. *Journal of the American Medical Association, 263,* 1947–1951.

Phinney, J. S. (1993). Multiple group identities: Differentiation, conflict, and integration. In J. Kroger (Ed.), *Discussions on ego identity* (pp. 47–73). Hillsdale, NJ: Erlbaum.

Piaget, J. (1929). *The child's conception of the world.* New York: Harcourt Brace.

Piaget, J. (1932). *The moral judgment of the child.* New York: Harcourt Brace.

Piaget, J. (1951). *Play, dreams, and imitation* (C. Gattegno & F. M. Hodgson, Trans.). New York: Norton.

Piaget, J. (1952). *The origins of intelligence in children.* New York: International Universities Press. (Original work published 1936)

Piaget, J. (1962). Comments on Vygotsky's critical remarks concerning *The Language and Thought of the Child* and *Judgment and Reasoning in the Child.* In L. S. Vygotsky (Ed.), *Thought and language.* Cambridge, MA: MIT Press.

Piaget, J. (1969). *The child's conception of time* (A. J. Pomerans, Trans.). London: Routledge & Kegan Paul.

Piaget, J., & Inhelder, B. (1967). *The child's conception of space.* New York: Norton.

Pickens, J., & Field, T. (1993). Facial expressivity in infants of depressed mothers. *Developmental Psychology, 29,* 986–988.

Pierce, J. P., Lee, L., & Gilpin, E. A. (1994). Smoking initiation by adolescent girls, 1944 through 1988: An association with targeted advertising. *Jour-*

nal of the American Medical Association, 271, 608–611.

Pillemer, K., & Finkelhor, D. (1988). The prevalence of elder abuse: A random sample survey. *The Gerontologist, 28*(1), 51–57.

Pillemer, K., & Moore, D. W. (1989). Abuse of patients in nursing homes: Findings from a survey of staff. *The Gerontologist, 29*(3), 314–320.

Pillemer, K., & Suitor, J. J. (1991). "Will I ever escape my child's problems?" Effects of adult children's problems on elderly parents. *Journal of Marriage and the Family, 53,* 585–594.

Pincus, T., Callahan, L. F., & Burkhauser, R. V. (1987). Most chronic diseases are reported more frequently by individuals with fewer than 12 years of formal education in the age 18–64 United States population. *Journal of Chronic Diseases, 40*(9), 865–874.

Pine, D. S., et al. (1996). Emotional problems during youth and stature in adulthood. *Pediatrics, 87,* 856–863.

Pines, M. (1979, August). Superkids. *Psychology Today,* pp. 53–63.

Pirkle, J. L., Brody, D. J., Gunter, E. W., Kramer, R. A., Raschal, D. C., Flegal, K. M., & Matte, T. D. (1994). The decline in blood lead levels in the United States. *Journal of the American Medical Association, 272,* 284–291.

Plemons, J., Willis, S., & Baltes, P. (1978). Modifiability of fluid intelligence in aging: A short-term longitudinal training approach. *Journal of Gerontology, 33*(2), 224–231.

Plomin, R. (1989). Environment and genes: Determinants of behavior. *American Psychologist, 44*(2), 105–111.

Plomin, R. (1990). The role of inheritance in behavior. *Science, 248,* 183–188.

Plomin, R. (1996). Nature and nurture. In M. R. Merrens & G. G. Brannigan (Eds.), *The developmental psychologist: Research adventures across the life span* (pp. 3–19). New York: McGraw-Hill.

Plomin, R., Owen, M. J., & McGuffin, P. (1994). The genetic bases of behavior. *Science, 264,* 1733–1739.

Plomin, R., Pedersen, N. L., McClearn, G. E., Nesselroade, J. R., & Bergeman, C. S. (1988). EAS temperaments during the last half of the life span: Twins reared apart and twins reared together. *Psychology and Aging, 3,* 43–50.

Plomin, R., & Rende, R. (1991). Human behavioral genetics. In M. R. Rosenzweig and L. W. Porter (Eds.), *Annual review of psychology* (Vol. 42). Palo Alto, CA: Annual Reviews, Inc.

PMS: It's real. (1994, July). *Harvard Women's Health Watch,* pp. 2–3.

Polit, D. F., & Falbo, T. (1987). Only children and personality development: A quantitative review. *Journal of Marriage and the Family, 49,* 309–325.

Pollock, L. A. (1983). *Forgotten children.*

Cambridge, UK: Cambridge University Press.

Poon, L. W. (1985). Differences in human memory with aging: Nature, causes, and clinical implications. In J. E. Birren & K. W. Schaie (Eds.), *Handbook of the psychology of aging* (pp. 427–462). New York: Van Nostrand Reinhold.

Pope, A. W., Bierman, K. L., & Mumma, G. H. (1991). Aggression, hyperactivity, and inattention-immaturity: Behavior dimensions associated with peer rejection in elementary school boys. *Developmental Psychology, 27,* 663–671.

Pope, S. K., Whiteside, L., Brooks-Gunn, J., Kelleher, K. J., Rickert, V. I., Bradley, R. H., & Casey, P. H. (1993). Low-birth-weight infants born to adolescent mothers: Effects of coresidency with grandmother on child development. *Journal of the American Medical Association, 269,* 1396–1400.

Porac, C., & Coren, S. (1981). *Lateral preferences and human behavior.* New York: Springer-Verlag.

Porcino, J. (1983). *Growing older, getting better: A handbook for women in the second half of life.* Reading, MA: Addison-Wesley.

Porcino, J. (1991). *Living longer, living better: Adventures in community housing for the second half of life.* New York: Continuum.

Porcino, J. (1993, April–May). Designs for living. *Modern Maturity,* pp. 24–33.

Posner, J. K., & Vandell, D. L. (undated). *Low-income children's afterschool care: Are there beneficial effects of afterschool programs?* Unpublished manuscript, University of Wisconsin—Madison.

Post, S. G. (1994). Ethical commentary: Genetic testing for Alzheimer's disease. *Alzheimer Disease and Associated Disorders, 8,* 66–67.

Powelson, R. (1995, December 7). AMA seeks ban on tobacco exports. *Cleveland Plain Dealer,* p. 18A.

Power, T. G., & Chapieski, M. L. (1986). Childrearing and impulse control in toddlers: A naturalistic investigation. *Developmental Psychology, 22*(2), 271–275.

Powlishta, K. K., Serbin, L. A., Doyle, A.-B., & White, D. R. (1994). Gender, ethnic, and body type biases: The generality of prejudice in childhood. *Developmental Psychology, 30*(4), 526–536.

Pratt, M. W., Kerig, P., Cowan, P. A., & Cowan, C. P. (1988). Mothers and fathers teaching 3-year-olds: Authoritative parenting and adult scaffolding of young children's learning. *Developmental Psychology, 24*(6), 832–839.

Prechtl, H. F. R., & Beintema, D. J. (1964). The neurological examination of the full-term newborn infant. *Clinics in Developmental Medicine* (No. 12). London: Heinemann.

Prestwood, K. M., Pilbeam, C. C., Burleson, J. A., Woodiel, F. N., Delmas, P. D., Deftos, L. J., & Raisz, L. G. (1994). The short-term effects of conjugated estrogen on bone turnover in older women. *Journal of Clinical Endocrinology and Metabolism, 79,* 366–371.

Prevention Index 1995: A report card on the nation's health. (1995). Emmaus, PA: Rodale.

Prohaska, T. R., Leventhal, E. A., Leventhal, H., & Keller, M. L. (1985). Health practices and illness cognition in young, middle-aged, and elderly adults. *Journal of Gerontology, 40,* 569–578.

Pruchno, R., & Johnson, K. W. (1996). Research on grandparenting: Current studies and future needs. *Generations, 20*(1), 65–70.

Pugh, D. (1983, November 11). Bringing an end to mutilation. *New Statesman,* pp. 8–9.

Purcell, J. H. (1995). Gifted education at a crossroads: The program status study. *Gifted Child Quarterly, 39*(2), 57–65.

Pynoos, R. S., Frederick, C., Nader, K., Arroyo, W., Steinberg, A., Eth, S., Nunez, F., & Fairbanks, L. (1987). Life threat and post-traumatic stress in school-age children. *Archives of General Psychiatry, 44,* 1057–1063.

Quadrel, M. J., Fischoff, B., & Davis, W. (1993). Adolescent (in)vulnerability. *American Psychologist, 48,* 102–116.

Quill, T. E. (1991). Death and dignity: A case of individualized decision making. *New England Journal of Medicine, 324,* 691–694.

Quinby, N. (1985, October). On testing and teaching intelligence: A conversation with Robert Sternberg. *Educational Leadership,* pp. 50–53.

Quinn, J. F. (1993). Is early retirement an economic threat? *Generations, 17*(4), 10–14.

Quinn, J. F. (1996, August). Entitlements and the federal budget: A summary. *Gerontology News* [supplemental brochure].

Quintero, R. A., Abuhamad, A., Hobbins, J. C., & Mahoney, M. J. (1993). Transabdominal thin-gauge embryofetoscopy: A technique for early prenatal diagnosis and its use in the diagnosis of a case of Meckel-Gruber syndrome. *American Journal of Obstetrics and Gynecology, 168,* 1552–1557.

Rabiner, D., & Coie, J. (1989). Effect of expectancy induction on rejected peers' acceptance by unfamiliar peers. *Developmental Psychology, 25,* 450–457.

Racine, A., Joyce, T., & Anderson, R. (1993). The association between prenatal care and birth weight among women exposed to cocaine in New York City. *Journal of the American Medical Association, 270,* 1581–1586.

Raffaelli, M., & Larson, R. W. (1987). *Sibling interactions in late childhood and early adolescence.* Paper presented at the biennial meeting of the Society for Research in Child Development, Baltimore.

Rafferty, Y., & Shinn, M. (1991). Impact of homelessness on children. *American Psychologist, 46*(11), 1170–1179.

Ragozin, A. S., Basham, R. B., Crnic, K. A., Greenberg, M. T., & Robinson, N. M. (1982). Effects of maternal age on parenting role. *Developmental Psychology, 18*(4), 627–634.

Rakowski, W., & Mor, V. (1992). The association of physical activity with mortality among older adults in The Longitudinal Study of Aging. *Journal of Gerontology: Medical Sciences, 47*(4), M122–129.

Rall, L. C., Meydani, S. N., Kehayias, B. D.-H., & Roubenoff, R. (1996). The effect of progressive resistance training in rheumatoid arthritis. *Arthritis and Rheumatism, 39,* 415–426.

Rappaport, L. (1993). The treatment of nocturnal enuresis—Where are we now? *Pediatrics, 92,* 465–466.

Raven, J. C. (1983). *Raven progressive matrices test.* San Antonio, TX: Psychological Corporation.

Ravitch, D. (1983). The education pendulum. *Psychology Today, 17*(10), 62–71.

Raynor, J. O., & Rubin, I. S. (1971). Effects of achievement motivation and future orientation on level of performance. *Journal of Personality and Social Psychology, 17,* 36–41.

Read, C. R. (1991). Gender distribution in programs for the gifted. *Roeper Review, 13,* 188–193.

Redding, R. E., Harmon, R. J., & Morgan, G. A. (1990). Maternal depression and infants' mastery behaviors. *Infant Behavior and Development, 113,* 391–396.

Ree, M. J., & Earles, J. A. (1992). Intelligence is the best predictor of job performance. *Current Directions in Psychological Science, 1*(3), 86–89.

Ree, M. J., & Earles, J. A. (1993). g is to psychology what carbon is to chemistry: A reply to Sternberg and Wagner, McClelland, and Calfee. *Current Directions in Psychological Science, 2*(1), 11–12.

Reese, E., & Fivush, R. (1993). Parental styles of talking about the past. *Developmental Psychology, 29,* 596–606.

Reese, H. W. (1977). Imagery and associative memory. In R. V. Kali & J. W. Hagen (Eds.), *Perspectives on the development of memory and cognition.* Hillsdale, NJ: Erlbaum.

Reid, J. D. (1995). Development in late life: Older lesbian and gay life. In A. R. D'Augelli & C. J. Patterson (Eds.), *Lesbian, gay, and bisexual identities over the lifespan: Psychological perspectives* (pp. 215–240). New York: Oxford University Press.

Reid, J. R., Patterson, G. R., & Loeber, R. (1982). The abused child: Victim, instigator, or innocent bystander? In D. J. Berstein (Ed.), *Response structure and organization.* Lincoln: University of Nebraska Press.

Reid, R. L., & Yen, S. S. C. (1981). Premenstrual syndrome. *American Journal of Obstetrics and Gynecology, 139*(1), 85–104.

Reijo, R., Alagappan, R. K., Patrizio, P., & Page, D. C. (1996). Severe oligozoospermia resulting from deletions of azoospermia factor gene on Y chromosome. *The Lancet, 347*, 1290–1293.

Reiman, E. M., Caselli, R. J., Yun, L. S., Chen, K., Bandy, D., Minoshima, S., Thibodeau, S. N., & Osborne, D. (1996). Preclinical evidence of Alzheimer's disease. *New England Journal of Medicine, 334*(12), 752–758.

Reis, S. (1995). Talent ignored, talent diverted: The cultural contexts underlying giftedness in females. *Gifted Child Quarterly, 39*(3), 162–170.

Reis, S. M. (1989). Reflections on policy affecting the education of gifted and talented students: Past and future perspectives. *American Psychologist, 44*, 399–408.

Reis, S. M. (1991). The need for clarification in research designed to examine gender differences in achievement and accomplishment. *Roeper Review, 13*, 193–198.

Reiss, A. J., Jr., & Roth, J. A. (Eds.). (1994). *Understanding and preventing violence.* Washington, DC: National Academy Press.

Remafedi, G., Resnick, M., Blum, R., & Harris, L. (1992). Demography of sexual orientation in adolescents. *Pediatrics, 89*(4), 714–721.

Rempel, J. (1985). Childless elderly: What are they missing? *Journal of Marriage and the Family, 47*(2), 343–348.

Rennie, J. (1994, June). Grading the gene tests. *Scientific American,* pp. 86–97.

Renzulli, J. S. (1978). What makes giftedness? Reexamining a definition. *Phi Delta Kappan, 60*, 180–184, 261.

Renzulli, J. S., & McGreevy, A. M. (1984). *A study of twins included and not included in gifted programs.* Storrs: University of Connecticut, School of Education.

Report explains increasing number of women in psychology. (1995, December). *APA Monitor,* p. 17.

Rescorla, L. (1991). Early academics: Introduction to the debate. In L. Rescorla, M. C. Hyson, & K. Hirsh-Pasek (1991), Academic instruction in early childhood: Challenge or pressure? *New Directions for Child Development,* No. 53, pp. 5–11. San Francisco: Jossey-Bass.

Research to Prevent Blindness. (1994). Progress report, 1994. New York: Author.

Research shows that women smokers can quit as easily as men. (1992, Spring). *Cancer Center News,* pp. 1, 3–4.

Resnick, L. B. (1989). Developing math-

ematical knowledge. *American Psychologist, 44*, 162–169.

Rest, J. R. (1975). Longitudinal study of the Defining Issues Test of moral judgment: A strategy for analyzing developmental change. *Developmental Psychology, 11*(16), 738–748.

Restak, R. (1984). *The brain.* New York: Bantam.

Reynolds, A. J. (1994). Effects of a preschool plus follow-on intervention for children at risk. *Developmental Psychology, 30*(6), 787–804.

Reynolds, C. R. (1988, Winter). Race differences in intelligence: Why the controversy? *MENSA Research Journal,* pp. 4–7.

Reznick, J. S., Kagan, J., Snidman, N., Gersten, M., Baak, K., & Rosenberg, A. (1986). Inhibited and uninhibited children: A follow-up study. *Child Development, 57*, 660–680.

Rheingold, H. L. (1985). Development as the acquisition of familiarity. *Annual Review of Psychology, 36*, 1–17.

Rhodes, S. R. (1983). Age-related differences in work attitudes and behaviors: A review and conceptual analysis. *Psychological Bulletin, 93*(2), 328–367.

Rhodes, S. R., & Steers, R. M. (1990). *Managing employee absenteeism.* Reading, MA: Addison-Wesley.

Ricciuti, H. M. (1993). Nutrition and mental development. *Current Directions in Psychological Science, 2*(2), 43–46.

Rice, M. L. (1982). Child language: What children know and how. In T. M. Field, A. Huston, H. C. Quay, L. Troll & G. E. Finley (Eds.), *Review of human development research.* New York: Wiley.

Rice, M. L. (1989). Children's language acquisition. *American Psychologist, 44*(2), 149–156.

Rice, M. L., Hadley, P. A., & Alexander, A. L. (1993). Social biases toward children with speech and language impairments: A correlative causal model of language limitations. *Applied Psycholinguistics, 14*, 445–471.

Rice, M. L., Huston, A. C., Truglio, R., & Wright, J. (1990). Words from "Sesame Street": Learning vocabulary while viewing. *Developmental Psychology, 26*, 421–428.

Rice, M. L., Oetting, J. B., Marquis, J., Bode, J., et al. (1994). Frequency of input effects on word comprehension of children with specific language impairment. *Journal of Speech and Hearing Research, 37*(1), 106–121.

Richardson, D. W., & Short, R. V. (1978). Time of onset of sperm production in boys. *Journal of Biosocial Science, 5*, 15–25.

Richardson, J. L., Radziszewska, B., Dent, C. W., & Flay, B. R. (1993). Relationship between after-school care of adolescents and substance use, risk-taking, depressed mood, and academic achievement. *Pediatrics, 92*(1), 32–38.

Richardson, L. (1993, November 25). Adoptions that lack papers, not purpose. *The New York Times,* pp. C1, C6.

Riddle, R. D., Johnson, R. L., Laufer, E., & Tabin, C. (1993). Sonic hedgehog mediates the polarizing activity of the ZPA. *Cell, 75*, 1401–1416.

Riegel, K. F., & Riegel, R. M. (1972). Development, drop, and death. *Developmental Psychology, 6*, 309–316.

Rierdan, J., Koff, E., & Flaherty, J. (1986). Conceptions and misconceptions of menstruation. *Women and Health, 10*(4), 33–45.

Rieser, J., Yonas, A., & Wilkner, K. (1976). Radial localization of odors by human newborns. *Child Development, 47*, 856–859.

Riggs, K. M., Spiro III, A., Tucker K., & Rush, D. (1996). Relations of vitamin B-12, vitamin B-6, folate, and homocysteine to cognitive performance in the Normal Aging Study. *American Journal of Clinical Nutrition, 63*, 306–314.

Riley, M. W. (1994). Aging and society: Past, present, and future. *The Gerontologist, 34*, 436–444.

Rindfuss, R. R., Morgan, S. P., & Swicegood, G. (1988). *First births in America.* Berkeley: University of California Press.

Rindfuss, R. R., & St. John, C. (1983). Social determinants of age at first birth. *Journal of Marriage and the Family, 45*, 553–565.

Ring, K. (1980). *Life at death: A scientific investigation of the near-death experience.* New York: Coward McCann & Geoghegan.

Ritalin improves behavior of ADHD children. (1995, October). *The Menninger Letter,* p. 3.

Ritvo, E. R., Freeman, B. J., Mason-Brothers, A., Mo, A., & Ritvo, A. M. (1985). Concordance for the syndrome of autism in 40 pairs of afflicted twins. *American Journal of Psychiatry, 142*, 74–77.

Rivara, F. P., Bergman, A. B., & Drake, C. (1989). Parental attitudes and practices toward children as pedestrians. *Pediatrics, 84*(6), 1017–1021.

Rivara, F. P., & Grossman, D. C. (1996). Prevention of traumatic deaths to children in the United States: How far have we come and where do we need to go? *Pediatrics, 97*, 791–798.

Rix, S. E. (1994). *Older workers: How do they measure up?* (Pub. No. 9412). Washington, DC: AARP Public Policy Institute.

Roberts, G. C., Block, J. H., & Block J. (1984). Continuity and change in parents' child-rearing practices. *Child Development, 55*, 586–597.

Robertson, L. F. (1984, November). Why we went back to half-days. *Principal,* pp. 22–24.

Robinson, B., & Thurnher, M. (1981). Taking care of aged parents: A family cycle transition. *The Gerontologist, 19*(6), 586–593.

Robinson, I., Ziss, K., Ganza, B., Katz, S., & Robinson, E. (1991). Twenty years of the sexual revolution, 1965–1985: An update. *Journal of Marriage and the Family, 53,* 216–220.

Robinson, J. L., Kagan, J., Reznick, J. S., & Corley, R. (1992). The heritability of inhibited and uninhibited behavior: A twin study. *Developmental Psychology, 28*(6), 1030–1037.

Robinson, L. C., & Blanton, P. W. (1993). Marital strengths in enduring marriages. *Family Relations, 42,* 38–45.

Robison, L. L., Buckley, J. D., Daigle, A. E., Wells, R., Benjamin, D., Arthur, D. C., & Hammond, G. D. (1989). Maternal drug use and risk of childhood nonlymphoblastic leukemia among offspring. *Cancer, 63,* 1904–1911.

Rock, D. A., Ekstrom, R. B., Goertz, M. E., Hilton, T. L., & Pollack, J. (1985). *Factors associated with decline of test scores of high school seniors, 1972 to 1980.* Washington, DC: U.S. Department of Education, Center for Statistics.

Rodehoffer, R. J., Gerstenblith, G., Becker, L. C., Fleg, J. L., Weisfeldt, M. L., & Lakatta, E. G. (1984). Exercise cardiac output is maintained with advancing age in healthy human subjects: Cardiac dilation and increased stroke volume compensate for a diminished heart rate. *Circulation, 69,* 203–213.

Rodin, J., & Ickovics, J. (1990). Women's health: Review and research agenda as we approach the 21st century. *American Psychologist, 45,* 1018–1034.

Rodin, J., Timko, C., & Harris, S. (1985). The construct of control: Biological and psychological correlates. *Annual Review of Gerontology and Geriatrics, 5,* 3–55.

Roe, J. W., et al. (1976). The effect of age on creatinine clearance in men: A cross-sectional and longitudinal study. *Journal of Gerontology, 31,* 155–163.

Rogers, M. F., White, C. R., Sanders, R., Schable, C., Ksell, T. E., Wasserman, R. L., Ballanti, J. A., Peters, S. M., & Wray, B. B. (1990). Lack of transmission of human immunodeficiency virus from infected children to their household contacts. *Pediatrics, 85*(2), 210–214.

Rogers, R. G. (1995). Marriage, sex and mortality. *Journal of Marriage and the Family, 57,* 515–526.

Rogoff, B., & Morelli, G. (1989). Perspectives on children's development from cultural psychology. *American Psychologist, 44,* 343–348.

Roopnarine, J., & Field, T. (1984). Play interaction of friends and acquaintances in nursery school. In T. Field, J. Roopnarine, & M. Segal (Eds.), *Friendships in normal and handicapped children.* Norwood, NJ: Ablex.

Roopnarine, J., & Honig, A. S. (1985, September). The unpopular child. *Young Children,* pp. 59–64.

Roopnarine, J. L., Brown, J., Snell-White, P., & Riegraft, N. B. (1995). Father involvement in children and household work in common-law dual-earner and single-earner Jamaican families. *Journal of Applied Developmental Psychology 16*(1), 35–52.

Roopnarine, J. L., Hooper, F. H., Ahmeduzzaman, M., & Pollack, B. (1993). Gentle play partners: Mother-child and father-child play in New Delhi, India. In K. MacDonald (Ed.), *Parent-child play* (pp. 287–304). Albany: State University of New York Press.

Roopnarine, J. L., Talokder, E., Jain, D., Josh, P., & Srivastav, P. (1992). Personal well-being, kinship ties, and mother-infant and father-infant interactions in single-wage and dual-wage families in New Delhi, India. *Journal of Marriage and the Family, 54,* 293–301.

Roosa, M. W. (1988). The effect of age in the transition to parenthood: Are delayed childbearers a unique group? *Family Relations, 37,* 322–327.

Rose, J. S., Chassin, L., Presson, C. C., & Sherman, S. J. (1996). Prospective predictors of quit attempts and smoking cessation in young adults. *Health Psychology, 15*(4), 261–268.

Rose, R. M., Gordon, T. P., & Bernstein, I. S. (1972). Plasma testosterone levels in the male rhesus: Influences of sexual and social stimuli. *Science, 178*(4061), 643–645.

Rose, S. A., & Feldman, J. F. (1995). Prediction of IQ and specific cognitive abilities at 11 years from infancy measures. *Developmental Psychology, 31*(4), 685–696.

Rose, S. A., Feldman, J. F., Wallace, I. F., & McCarton, C. (1991). Information processing at 1 year: Relation to birth status and developmental outcome during the first 5 years. *Developmental Psychology, 27*(5), 723–737.

Rosen, D. (1996, September 17). Attention deficit disorder. *HealthNews,* p. 4.

Rosenberg, H. M., Ventura, S. J., Maurer, J. D., et al. (1996). *Births and deaths: United States, 1995* (Monthly Vital Statistics Report, Vol. 45, No. 3, Suppl. 2. DHHS Pub. No. 96-1120). Hyattsville, MD: National Center for Health Statistics.

Rosenberg, L., Palmer, J. R., & Shapiro, S. (1990). Decline in the risk of myocardial infarction among women who stop smoking. *New England Journal of Medicine, 322,* 213–217.

Rosenberg, M. S. (1987). New directions for research on the psychological maltreatment of children. *American Psychologist, 42,* 166–171.

Rosenberg, P. S. (1995). Scope of the AIDS epidemic in the United States. *Science, 270,* 1372–1375.

Rosenbluth, S. C., & Steil, J. M. (1995). Predictors of intimacy for women in heterosexual and homosexual couples. *Journal of Social and Personal Relationships, 12*(2), 163–175.

Rosenthal, P. A., & Rosenthal, S. (1984). Suicidal behavior by preschool children. *American Journal of Psychiatry, 141*(4), 520–525.

Rosenthal, R., & Jacobson, L. (1968). *Pygmalion in the classroom.* New York: Holt.

Rosenzweig, M. R. (1984). Experience, memory, and the brain. *American Psychologist, 39,* 365–376.

Rosenzweig, M. R., & Bennett, E. L. (Eds.). (1976). *Neural mechanisms of learning and memory.* Cambridge, MA: MIT Press.

Roses, A. D. (1994, September). *Apolipoprotein E affects Alzheimer's disease expression.* Paper presented at the annual meeting of the Gerontological Society of America, San Diego.

Ross, C. (1995). Reconceptualizing marital status as a continuum of social attachment. *Journal of Marriage and the Family, 57,* 129–140.

Ross, C. E. (1990). Religion and psychological distress. *Journal for the Scientific Study of Religion, 29,* 236–245.

Ross, C. E., Mirowsky, J., & Goldsteen, K. (1990). The impact of the family on health: A decade in review. *Journal of Marriage and the Family, 52,* 1059–1078.

Ross, G., Lipper, E. G., & Auld, P. A. M. (1991). Educational status and school-related abilities of very low birth weight premature children. *Pediatrics, 8,* 1125–1134.

Ross, H. G., Dalton, M. J., & Milgram, J. I. (1980, November). *Older adults' perceptions of closeness in sibling relationships.* Paper presented at the annual meeting of the Gerontological Society of America, San Diego.

Ross Products Division of Abbott Laboratories. (1994). *Ross mothers' survey.* Columbus, OH: Author.

Rossel, C., & Ross, J. M. (1986). *The social science evidence on bilingual education.* Boston: Boston University Press.

Rossi, A. S. (1980). Aging and parenthood in the middle years. In P. B. Baltes & O. G. Brim (Eds.), *Life-span development and behavior.* New York: Academic Press.

Rossi, A. S., & Rossi, P. H. (1990). *Of human bonding: Parent-child relations across the life course.* New York: Aldine de Gruyter.

Rossi, R. (1996, August 30). Small schools under microscope. *Chicago Sun-Times,* p. 24.

Roush, W. (1995). Arguing over why Johnny can't read. *Science, 267,* 1896–1898.

Roush, W. (1996). Live long and prosper? *Science, 273,* 42–46.

Rovee-Collier, C. (1987). Learning and

memory in infancy. In J. D. Osofsky (Ed.), *Handbook of infant development* (2d ed.). New York: Wiley.

Rovee-Collier, C., & Lipsitt, L. (1982). Learning, adaptation, and memory in the newborn. In P. Stratton (Ed.), *Psychobiology of the human newborn*. New York: Wiley.

Rovee-Collier, C., Schechter, A., Shyi, G., & Shields, P. (1992). Perceptual identification of contextual attributes and infant memory retrieval. *Developmental Psychology, 28*(2), 307–318.

Rowe, J. W., et al. (1976). The effect of age on creatinine clearance in men: A cross-sectional and longitudinal study. *Journal of Gerontology, 31,* 155–163.

Roybal, E. R. (1988). Mental health and aging. *American Psychologist, 43*(3), 184–189.

Rubenstein, C. (1993, November 18). Child's play, or nightmare on the field? *The New York Times,* pp. C1, C10.

Rubin, D. H., Krasilnikoff, P. A., Leventhal, J. M., Weile, B., & Berget, A. (1986, August 23). Effect of passive smoking on birth-weight. *The Lancet,* pp. 415–417.

Rubin, K. (1982). Nonsocial play in preschoolers: Necessary evil? *Child Development, 53,* 651–657.

Rubin, K., Maioni, T. L., & Hornung, M. (1976). Free play behaviors in middle-class and lower-class preschoolers: Parten and Piaget revisited. *Child Development, 47,* 414–419.

Rubin, L. B. (1979). *Women of a certain age.* New York: Harper & Row.

Rubin, L. B. (1982). Sex and sexuality: Women at midlife. In M. Kirkpatricks (Ed.), *Women's sexual experiences: Exploration of the dark continent* (pp. 61–82). New York: Plenum.

Rubin, W., Watson, K., & Jambor, T. (1978). Free-play behaviors in preschool and kindergarten children. *Child Development, 49,* 534–536.

Rubinstein, A. (1980). *My many years.* New York: Knopf.

Rubinstein, R. L., Alexander, B. B., Goodman, M., & Luborsky, M. (1991). Key relationships of never married, childless older women: A cultural analysis. *Journal of Gerontology: Social Sciences, 46,* S270–277.

Ruble, D. M., & Brooks-Gunn, J. (1982). The experience of menarche. *Child Development, 53,* 1557–1566.

Rudman, D., Axel, G. F., Hoskote, S. N., Gergans, G. A., Lalitha, P. Y., Goldberg, A. F., Schlenker, R. A., Cohn, L., Rudman, I. W., & Mattson, D. E. (1990). Effects of human growth hormone in men over 60 years old. *New England Journal of Medicine, 323*(1), 1–6.

Rueter, M. A., & Conger, R. D. (1995). Antecedents of parent-adolescent disagreements. *Journal of Marriage and the Family, 57,* 435–448.

Ruff, H. A., Bijur, P. E., Markowitz, M.,

Ma, Y.-C., & Rosen, J. F. (1993). Declining blood lead levels and cognitive changes in moderately lead-poisoned children. *Journal of the American Medical Association, 269,* 1641–1646.

Rule, S. (1981, June 11). The battle to stem school dropouts. *The New York Times,* pp. A1, B10.

Rutter, M. (1979a). Maternal deprivation, 1972–1978: New findings, new concepts, new approaches. *Child Development, 50,* 283–305.

Rutter, M. (1979b). Separation experiences: A new look at an old topic. *Pediatrics, 95*(1), 147–154.

Rutter, M. (1983). Stress, coping, and development: Some issues and some questions. In N. Garmezy & M. Rutter (Eds.), *Stress, coping, and development in children.* New York: McGraw-Hill.

Rutter, M. (1984). Resilient children. *Psychology Today, 18*(3), 57–65.

Rutter, M. (1987). Continuities and discontinuities from infancy. In J. Osofsky (Ed.), *Handbook of infant development.* New York: Wiley.

Ryan, A. S., Craig, L. D., & Finn, S. C. (1992). Nutrient intakes in dietary patterns of older Americans: A national study. *Journal of Gerontology: Medical Sciences, 47*(5), M145–150.

Ryan, A. S., Pratt, W. F., Wysong, J. L., Lewandowski, G., McNally, J. W., & Krieger, F. W. (1991). A comparison of breast-feeding data from the National Surveys of Family Growth and the Ross Laboratories' Mothers Surveys. *American Journal of Public Health, 81,* 1049–1052.

Ryan, M. (1993, September 26). I couldn't bear the silence. *Parade,* p. 14.

Rybash, J. M., Hoyer, W. J., & Roodin, P. A. (1986). *Adult cognition and aging: Developmental changes in processing, knowing, and thinking.* New York: Pergamon.

Ryff, C. D. (1982). Self-perceived personality change in adulthood and aging. *Journal of Personality and Social Psychology, 42*(1), 108–115.

Ryff, C. D., & Baltes, P. B. (1976). Value transition and adult development in women: The instrumentality-terminality sequence hypothesis. *Developmental Psychology, 12*(6), 567–568.

Ryff, C. D., & Heincke, S. G. (1983). Subjective organization of personality in adulthood and aging. *Journal of Personality and Social Psychology, 44*(4), 807–816.

Ryland, E. B., Riordan, R. J., & Brack, G. (1994). Selected characteristics of high-risk students and their enrollment persistence. *Journal of College Student Development, 35,* 54–58.

Rymer, R. (1993). *An abused child: Flight from silence.* New York: HarperCollins.

Sabatelli, R. M., Meth, R. L., & Gavazzi, S. M. (1988). Factors mediating the ad-

justment to involuntary childlessness. *Family Relations, 37,* 338–343.

Sabom, M. B. (1982). *Recollections of death: A medical investigation.* New York: Harper & Row.

Sachs, B. P., McCarthy, B. J., Rubin, G., Burton, A., Terry, J., & Tyler, C. W. (1983). Cesarean section. *Journal of the American Medical Association, 250*(16), 2157–2159.

Sacks, J. J., Smith, J. D., Kaplan, K. M., Lambert, D. A., Sattin, W., & Sikes, K. (1989). The epidemiology of injuries in Atlanta day-care centers. *Journal of the American Medical Association, 262*(12), 1641–1645.

Sadowitz, P. D., & Oski, F. A. (1983). Iron status and infant feeding practices in an urban ambulatory center. *Pediatrics, 72*(1), 33–36.

Sagi, A., & Hoffman, M. (1976). Empathic distress in newborns. *Developmental Psychology, 12*(2), 175–176.

Sahyoun, N. R., Jacques, P. F., & Russell, R. M. (1996). Carotenoids, vitamins C and E, and mortality in an elderly population. *American Journal of Epidemiology, 144,* 501–511.

Sailes, G. A. (1993). An investigation of black student attrition at a large, predominantly white, midwestern university. *Western Journal of Black Studies, 17,* 179–182.

St. George-Hyslop, P. H., Tanzi, R. E., Polinsky, et al. (1987). The genetic defect causing familial Alzheimer's disease maps on chromosome 21. *Science, 235,* 885–890.

Salamone, L. M., Pressman, A. R., Seeley, D. G., & Cauley, J. A. (1996). Estrogen replacement therapy: A survey of older women's attitudes. *Archives of Internal Medicine, 156,* 1293–1297.

Salthouse, T. A. (1984). Effects of age and typing skill. *Journal of Experimental Psychology: General, 113,* 345–371.

Salthouse, T. A. (1985). Anticipatory processing and transcription typing. *Journal of Applied Psychology, 70,* 264–271.

Salthouse, T. A. (1991). *Theoretical perspectives on cognitive aging.* Hillsdale, NJ: Erlbaum.

Salthouse, T. A., & Maurer, T. J. (1996). Aging, job performance, and career development. In J. E. Birren & K. W. Schaie (Eds.), *Handbook of the psychology of aging* (pp. 353–364). San Diego: Academic Press.

Salzinger, S., Feldman, R. S., Hammer, M., & Rosario, M. (1993). Effects of physical abuse on children's social relations. *Child Development, 64,* 169–187.

Samad, A. (1996, August). Understanding a controversial rite of passage: Afterword. *Natural History,* p. 52.

Samadi, A. R., Mayberry, R. M., Zaidi, A. A., Pleasant, J. C., McGhee, N., Jr., & Rice, R. J. (1996). Maternal hypertension and associated pregnancy complications among African-American and other women in the United States. *Obstetrics and Gynecology, 87,* 557–563.

Sandler, D. P., Everson, R. B., Wilcox, A. J., & Browder, J. P. (1985). Cancer risk in adulthood from early life exposure to parents' smoking. *American Journal of Public Health, 75,* 487–492.

Sands, L. P., & Meredith, W. (1992). Blood pressure and intellectual functioning in late midlife. *Journal of Gerontology: Psychological Sciences, 47*(2), P81–84.

Sang, B. (1991). Moving towards balance and integration. In J. W. B. Sang & A. Smith (Eds.), *Lesbians at midlife: The creative transition* (pp. 206–214). San Francisco: Spinsters.

Santer, L. J., & Stocking, C. B. (1991). Safety practices and living conditions of low-income urban families. *Pediatrics, 88*(6), 111–118.

Santrock, J. W., Sitterle, K. A., & Warshak, R. A. (1988). Parent-child relationships in stepfather families. In P. Bronstein & C. P. Cowan (Eds.), *Fatherhood today: Men's changing role in the family.* New York: Wiley.

Sapienza, C. (1990, October). Parental imprinting of genes. *Scientific American,* pp. 52–60.

Sapolsky, R. M. (1992). Stress and neuroendocrine changes during aging. *Generations, 16*(4), 35–38.

Sauer, M. V., Paulson, R. J., & Lobo, R. A. (1990). A preliminary report on oocyte donation extending the reproductive potential to women over forty. *New England Journal of Medicine, 323,* 1157–1160.

Sauer, M. V., Paulson, R. J., & Lobo, R. A. (1993). Pregnancy after age 50: Application of oocyte donation to women after natural menopause. *The Lancet, 341,* 321–323.

Saunders, J. (1981). A process of bereavement resolution: Uncoupled identity. *Western Journal of Nursing Research, 3,* 319–332.

Sax, L. J., Astin, L. W., Korn, W. F., & Mahoney, K. M. (1996). *The American freshman: Norms for fall, 1995.* Los Angeles: UCLA Higher Education Institute.

Saxe, G. B., Guberman, S. R., & Gearhart, M. (1987). Social processes in early number development. *Monographs of the Society for Research in Child Development, 52*(216).

Saywitz, K. J., Goodman, G. S., Nicholas, E., & Moan, S. F. (1991). Children's memories of a physical examination involving genital touch: Implications for reports of child sexual abuse. *Journal of Consulting and Clinical Psychology, 59,* 682–691.

Scandinavian Simvastatin Survival Study Group. (1994). Randomized trial of cholesterol lowering in 4444 patients with coronary heart disease: The

Scandinavian Simvastatin Survival Study (4S). *The Lancet, 344,* 1383–1389.

Scarborough, H. S. (1990). Very early language deficits in dyslexic children. *Child Development, 61,* 1728–1743.

Scarr, S. (1992). Developmental theories for the 1990s: Development and individual differences. *Child Development, 63,* 1–19.

Scarr, S. (1993). Biological and cultural diversity: The legacy of Darwin for development. *Child Development, 64,* 1333–1353.

Scarr, S., Phillips, D., & McCartney, K. (1989). Working mothers and their families. *American Psychologist, 44*(11), 1402–1409.

Scarr, S., & Weinberg, R. (1983). The Minnesota Adoption Study: Genetic differences and malleability. *Child Development, 54,* 260–264.

Schacter, D. L. (1992). Understanding implicit memory: A cognitive neuroscience approach. *American Psychologist, 47,* 559–569.

Schaefer, R. T., & Lamm, R. P. (1995). *Sociology* (5th ed.). New York: McGraw-Hill.

Schaie, K. W. (1977–1978). Toward a stage theory of adult cognitive development. *Journal of Aging and Human Development, 8*(2), 129–138.

Schaie, K. W. (1978). External validity in the assessment of intellectual development in adulthood. *Journal of Gerontology, 33,* 696–701.

Schaie, K. W. (1979). The primary mental abilities in adulthood: An exploration in the development of psychometric intelligence. In P. B. Baltes & O. G. Brim (Eds.), *Life-span development and behavior* (pp. 67–115). New York: Academic Press.

Schaie, K. W. (1983). The Seattle Longitudinal Study: A twenty-one-year investigation of psychometric intelligence. In K. W. Schaie (Ed.), *Longitudinal studies of adult personality development* (pp. 64–155). New York: Guilford.

Schaie, K. W. (1988a). Ageism in psychological research. *American Psychologist, 43,* 179–183.

Schaie, K. W. (1988b). The delicate balance: Technology, intellectual competence, and normal aging. In G. Lesnoff-Caravaglia (Ed.), *Aging in a technological society* (pp. 155–166). New York: Human Sciences Press.

Schaie, K. W. (1989). The hazards of cognitive aging. *The Gerontologist, 29*(4), 484–493.

Schaie, K. W. (1990). Intellectual development in adulthood. In J. E. Birren & K. W. Schaie (Eds.), *Handbook of the psychology of aging* (pp. 291–309). San Diego: Academic Press.

Schaie, K. W. (1994). The course of adult intellectual development. *American Psychologist, 49*(4), 304–313.

Schaie, K. W. (1996). Intellectual development in adulthood. In J. E. Birren & K. W. Schaie (Eds.), *Handbook of the psychology of aging* (4th ed., pp. 266–286). San Diego: Academic Press.

Schaie, K. W., & Baltes, P. B. (1977). Some faith helps to see the forest: A final comment on the Horn-Donaldson myth of the Baltes-Schaie position on adult intelligence. *American Psychologist, 32,* 1118–1120.

Schaie, K. W., & Hertzog, C. (1983). Fourteen-year cohort sequential analyses of adult intellectual development. *Developmental Psychology, 19*(4), 531–543.

Schaie, K. W., & Hertzog, C. (1986). Toward a comprehensive model of adult intellectual development: Contributions of the Seattle Longitudinal Study. In R. J. Sternberg (Ed.), *Advances in human intelligence* (pp. 79–118). Hillsdale, NJ: Erlbaum.

Schaie, K. W., & Strother, C. (1968). A cross-sequential study of age changes in cognitive behavior. *Psychological Bulletin, 70,* 671–680.

Schaie, K. W., & Willis, S. L. (1986). Can decline in adult intellectual functioning be reversed? *Developmental Psychology, 22,* 223–232.

Schaie, K. W., & Willis, S. L. (1991). Adult personality and psychomotor performance: Cross-sectional and longitudinal analysis. *Journal of Gerontology, 46*(6), P275–284.

Schaie, K. W., & Willis, S. L. (1996). Psychometric intelligence and aging. In F. Blanchard-Fields & T. M. Hess (Eds.), *Perspectives on cognitive change in adulthood and aging* (pp. 293–322). New York: McGraw-Hill.

Schanberg, S. M., & Field, T. M. (1987). Sensory deprivation illness and supplemental stimulation in the rat pup and preterm human neonate. *Child Development, 58,* 1431–1447.

Scharlach, A. E. (1987). Relieving feelings of strain among women with elderly mothers. *Psychology and Aging, 2*(1), 9–13.

Scharlach, A. E. (1991). Factors associated with filial grief following the death of an elderly parent. *American Journal of Orthopsychiatry, 61,* 307–313.

Scharlach, A. E., & Fredriksen, K. I. (1993). Reactions to the death of a parent during midlife. *Omega, 27,* 307–319.

Schechtman, V. L., Harper, R. M., Wilson, A. J., & Southall, D. P. (1992). Sleep state organization in normal infants and victims of the sudden infant death syndrome. *Pediatrics, 89,* 865–870.

Schellenberg, G. D., Bird, T., Wijsman, E., et al. (1992). Genetic linkage evidence for a familial Alzheimer's disease locus on chromosome 14. *Science, 258,* 668–671.

Schick, F. L., & Schick, R. (1994). *Statistical handbook on aging Americans, 1994.* Phoenix: Oryx.

Schindler, P. J., Moely, B. E., & Frank, A. L. (1987). Time in day care and social participation in young children. *Developmental Psychology, 23*(2), 255–261.

Schizophrenia update—Part I. (1995, June). *The Harvard Mental Health Letter,* pp. 1–4.

Schlossberg, N. K. (1987, May). Taking the mystery out of change. *Psychology Today,* pp. 74–75.

Schmeck, H. M. (1983, March 22). U.S. panel calls for patients' right to end life. *The New York Times,* pp. A1, C7.

Schmeck, H. M. (1995, June 24). Jonas Salk, whose polio drug altered life in U.S., dies at 80. *The New York Times,* pp. A1, A10.

Schmidt, F. L., Hunter, J. E., & Outerbridge, A. N. (1986). Impact of job experience and ability on job knowledge, work sample performance, and supervisory ratings of job performance. *Journal of Applied Psychology, 71,* 432–439.

Schmitt, B. D., & Kempe, C. H. (1983). Abused and neglected children. In R. E. Behrman & V. C. Vaughn (Eds.), *Nelson textbook of pediatrics* (12th ed.). Philadelphia: Saunders.

Schmitt, M. H. (1970, July). Superiority of breastfeeding: Fact or fancy? *Journal of Nursing,* pp. 1488–1493.

Schnall, P. L., Pieper, C., Schwartz, J. E., Karasek, R. A., Schlussel, Y., Devereaux, R. B., Ganau, A., Alderman, M., Warren, K., & Pickering, T. G. (1990). The relationship between "job strain," workplace diastolic blood pressure, and left ventricular mass index: Results of a case-control study. *Journal of the American Medical Association, 263,* 1929–1935.

Schneider, E. L. (1992). Biological theories of aging. *Generations, 16*(4), 7–10.

Schneider, E. L., & Guralnik, J. M. (1990). The aging of America: Impact on health care costs. *Journal of the American Medical Association, 263*(17), 2335–2340.

Schoen, R. (1992). First unions and the stability of first marriages. *Journal of Marriage and the Family, 54,* 281–284.

Schoendorf, K. C., Hogue, C. J. R., Kleinman, J. C., & Rowley, D. (1992). Mortality among infants of black as compared with white college-educated parents. *New England Journal of Medicine, 326,* 1522–1526.

Schoendorf, K. C., & Kiely, J. L. (1992). Relationship of sudden infant death syndrome to maternal smoking. *Pediatrics, 90*(6), 905–908.

Schonberg, H. C. (1992). *Horowitz: His life and music.* New York: Simon & Schuster.

Schonfeld, D. J., Johnson, S. R., Perrin, E. C., O'Hare, L. L., & Cicchetti, D. V. (1993). Understanding of acquired immunodeficiency syndrome by elementary school children—A developmental survey. *Pediatrics, 92,* 389–395.

Schonfield, D. (1974). Translations in gerontology—From lab to life: Utilizing information. *American Psychologist, 29,* 228–236.

Schor, E. L. (1987). Unintentional injuries: Patterns within families. *American Journal of the Diseases of Children, 141,* 1280.

Schreiber, G. B., et al. (1996). Weight modification efforts reported by preadolescent girls. *Pediatrics, 96*(1), 63–70.

Schuckit, M. A. (1985). Genetics and the risk for alcoholism. *Journal of the American Medical Association, 254*(18), 2614–2617.

Schuckit, M. A. (1987). Biological vulnerability to alcoholism. *Journal of Consulting and Clinical Psychology, 55*(3), 301–309.

Schulman, S. (1986). Facing the invisible handicap. *Psychology Today, 20*(2), 58–64.

Schultz, D. P., & Schultz, S. E. (1986). *Psychology and industry today* (4th ed.). New York: Macmillan.

Schulz, R. (1978). *A psychology of death, dying, and bereavement.* Reading, MA: Addison-Wesley.

Schulz, R., Bookwala, J., Knapp, J. E., Scheier, M., & Williamson, G. M. (1996). Pessimism, age, and cancer mortality. *Psychology and Aging, 11,* 304–309.

Schulz, R., & Heckhausen, J. (1996). A life span model of successful aging. *American Psychologist, 51,* 702–714.

Schvaneveldt, J. D., Lindauer, S. L. K., & Young, M. H. (1990). Children's understanding of AIDS: A developmental viewpoint. *Family Relations, 39,* 330–335.

Schweinhart, L. J., Barnes, H. V., & Weikart, D. P. (1993). *Significant benefits: The High/Scope Perry Preschool Study through age 27* (Monographs of the High/Scope Educational Research Foundation, No. 10). Ypsilanti, MI: High/Scope.

Schweinhart, L. J., Weikart, D. P., & Larner, M. B. (1986). A report on the High/Scope preschool curriculum comparison study. *Early Childhood Research Quarterly, 1,* 15–45.

Scott, C. (1993). *Decade of the executive woman.* New York: Korn/Ferry International.

Scott, J. P., & Roberto, K. A. (1981, October). *Sibling relationships in late life.* Paper presented at the annual meeting of the National Council on Family Relations, Milwaukee.

Sears, R. R., Maccoby, E. E., & Levin, H. (1957). *Patterns of child rearing.* New York: Harper & Row.

Seccombe, K. (1991). Assessing the costs and benefits of children: Gender comparisons among childfree husbands and wives. *Journal of Marriage and the Family, 53,* 191–202.

Seddon, J. M., Willett, W. C., Speizer, F. E., & Hankinson, S. E. (1996). A prospective study of cigarette smoking and age-related macular degeneration in women. *Journal of the American Medical Association, 276,* 1141–1146.

Sedlak, A. J., & Broadhurst, D. D. (1996). Executive summary of the third national incidence study of child abuse and neglect (NIS-3). Washington, DC: U.S. Department of Health and Human Services.

Seidman, S. N., & Rieder, R. O. (1994). A review of sexual behavior in the United States. *American Journal of Psychiatry, 151,* 330–341.

Seifer, R., Schiller, M., Sameroff, A. J., Resnick, S., & Riordan, K. (1996). Attachment, maternal sensitivity, and infant temperament during the first year of life. *Developmental Psychology, 32*(1), 12–25.

Seiner, S. H., & Gelfand, D. M. (1995). Effects of mother's simulated withdrawal and depressed affect on mother-toddler interactions. *Child Development, 60,* 1519–1528.

Seligman, M. E. P. (1991). *Learned optimism.* New York: Knopf.

Seligman, M. E. P. (1996, August). *Predicting and preventing depression.* Paper presented at the 104th annual convention of the American Psychological Association, Toronto.

Selkoe, D. J. (1991). The molecular pathology of Alzheimer's disease. *Neuron, 6*(4), 487–498.

Selkoe, D. J. (1992). Aging brain, aging mind. *Scientific American, 267,* 135–142.

Sen, A. (1993). The economics of life and death. *Scientific American, 268,* 40–47.

Serbin, L. A., Moller, L. C., Gulko, J., Powlishta, K. K., & Colburne, K. A. (1994). The emergence of gender segregation in toddler playgroups. In C. Leaper (Ed.), Childhood gender segregation: Causes and consequences. *New Directions for Child Development,* No. 65, pp. 7–17. San Francisco: Jossey-Bass.

Sexton, M., & Hebel, R. (1984). A clinical trial of change in maternal smoking and its effect on birth weight. *Journal of the American Medical Association, 251*(7), 911–915.

Sexual side effects of Prozac and other SSRIs. (1994, May). *The Menninger Letter,* p. 7.

Shafer, M. B., & Moscicki, A. (1991). Sexually transmitted disease. In W. R. Hendee (Ed.), *Health of adolescents: Understanding and facilitating biological behavior and social development* (pp. 211–249). San Francisco: Jossey-Bass.

Shannon, D. C., & Kelly, D. H. (1982a). SIDS and near-SIDS (Part 1). *New England Journal of Medicine, 306*(16), 959–965.

Shannon, D. C., & Kelly, D. H. (1982b). SIDS and near-SIDS (Part 2). *New England Journal of Medicine, 306*(17), 1022–1028.

Shannon, L. W. (1982). *Assessing the rela-*

tionship of adult criminal careers to juvenile careers. Iowa City: University of Iowa, Iowa Urban Community Research Center.

Shapiro, P. (1994, November). My house is your house: Advanced planning can ease the way when parents move in with adult kids. *AARP Bulletin,* p. 2.

Shatz, M., & Gelman, R. (1973). The development of communication skills: Modifications in the speech of young children as a function of listener. *Monographs of the Society for Research in Child Development, 38*(5, Serial No. 152).

Shaw, M. P. (1989). The eureka process: A structure for the creative experience in science and engineering. *Creativity Research Journal, 2,* 286–298.

Shaw, M. P. (1992a). Affective components of scientific creativity. In M. P. Shaw & M. A. Runco (Eds.), *Creativity and affect.* Norwood, NJ: Ablex.

Shaw, M. P. (1992b). Reason, emotionality, and creative thinking. *Humanistic Judaism, 20*(4), 42–44.

Shay, K. A., & Roth, D. L. (1992). Association between aerobic fitness and visuospatial performance in healthy older adults. *Psychology and Aging, 7*(1), 15–24.

Shaywitz, B. A., Sullivan, C. M., Anderson, G. M., Gillespie, S. M., Sullivan, B., & Shaywitz, S. E. (1994). Aspartame, behavior, and cognitive function in children with attention deficit disorder. *Pediatrics, 93,* 70–75.

Shaywitz, S. E., Shaywitz, B. A., Fletcher, J. M., & Escobar, M. D. (1990). Prevalence of reading disability in boys and girls. *Journal of the American Medical Association, 246*(8), 998–1002.

Shea, S., Basch, C. E., Stein, A. D., Contento, I. R., Irigoyen, M., & Zybert, P. (1993). Is there a relationship between dietary fat and stature or growth in children three to five years of age? *Pediatrics, 92*(4), 579–586.

Shepherd, J., Cobbe, S. M., Ford, I., et al. (1995). Prevention of coronary heart disease with pravastatin in men with hypercholesterolemia. *New England Journal of Medicine, 333,* 1301–1307.

Sherman, E. (1991). *Reminiscence and the self in old age.* New York: Springer.

Sherman, E. (1993). Mental health and successful adaptation in late life. *Generations, 17*(1), 43–46.

Sherman, E., & Peak, T. (1991). Patterns of reminiscence and the assessment of late life adjustment. *Gerontological Social Work, 16,* 59–74.

Sherman, L. W., & Berk, R. A. (1984, April). The Minneapolis domestic violence experiment. *Police Foundation Reports,* pp. 1–8.

Sherman, L. W., & Cohn, E. G. (1989). The impact of research on legal policy: The Minneapolis domestic violence experiment. *Law and Society Review, 23*(1), 118–144.

Shiavi, R. (1990). Sexuality and aging in men. *Annual Review of Sex Research, 1,* 227–249.

Shiavi, R., Mandeli, J., & Schreiner-Engel, P. (1994). Sexual satisfaction in healthy aging men. *Journal of Sex and Marital Therapy, 20,* 3–13.

Shields, P. J., & Rovee-Collier, C. (1992). Long-term memory for context-specific category information at six months. *Child Development, 63,* 245–259.

Shiono, P. H., & Behrman, R. E. (1995). Low birth weight: Analysis and recommendations. *The Future of Children, 5*(1), 4–18.

Ship, J. A., & Weiffenbach, J. M. (1993). Age, gender, medical treatment, and medication effects on smell identification. *Journal of Gerontology: Medical Sciences, 48*(1), M26–32.

Shipp, E. R. (1988, February 4). Decision could hinder surrogacy across nation. *The New York Times,* p. B6.

Should you take estrogen to prevent osteoporosis? (1994, August). *Johns Hopkins Medical Letter: Health after 50,* pp. 4–5.

Shu, X.-O., Ross, J. A., Pendergrass, T. W., Reaman, G. H., Lampkin, B., & Robison, L. L. (1996). Prenatal alcohol consumption, cigarette smoking, and risk of infant leukemia: A Children's Cancer Group Study. *Journal of the National Cancer Institute, 88,* 24–31.

Shulik, R. N. (1988). Faith development in older adults. *Educational Gerontology, 14,* 291–301.

Siegel, O. (1982). Personality development in adolescence. In B. B. Wolman (Ed.), *Handbook of developmental psychology.* Englewood Cliffs, NJ: Prentice-Hall.

Siegler, I., McCarty, S. M., & Loge, P. E. (1982). Wechsler memory scale scores, selective attribution, and distance from death. *Journal of Gerontology, 37,* 176–181.

Siegler, R. S., & Richards, D. (1982). The development of intelligence. In R. Sternberg (Ed.), *Handbook of human intelligence.* London: Cambridge University Press.

Siegrist, J. (1996). Adverse health effects of high-effort/low-reward conditions. *Journal of Occupational Health Psychology, 1*(1), 27–41.

Sigelman, C., Alfeld-Liro, C., Derenowski, E., Durazo, O., Woods, T., Maddock, A., & Mukai, T. (1996). Mexican-American and Anglo-American children's responsiveness to a theory-centered AIDS education program. *Child Development, 67,* 253–266.

Sigman, M., Neumann, C., Jansen, A. A. J., & Bwibo, N. (1989). Cognitive abilities of Kenyan children in relation to nutrition, family characteristics, and education. *Child Development, 60,* 1463–1474.

Sigman, M. D., Kasari, C., Kwon, J.-H., & Yirmiya, N. (1992). Responses to the negative emotions of others by autistic, mentally retarded, and normal children. *Child Development, 63,* 796–807.

Silverman, W. K., LaGreca, A. M., & Wasserstein, S. (1995). What do children worry about? Worries and their relation to anxiety. *Child Development, 66,* 671–686.

Silverstein, B., Perdue, L., Peterson, B., et al. (1986). The role of the mass media in promoting a thin standard of bodily attractiveness for women. *Sex Roles, 14*(9/10), 519–532.

Silverstein, B., Peterson, B., & Perdue, L. (1986). Some correlates of the thin standard of bodily attractiveness for women. *International Journal of Eating Disorders, 5*(5).

Silverstein, M., Parrott, T. M., & Bengtson, V. L. (1995). Factors that predispose middle-aged sons and daughters to provide social support to older parents. *Journal of Marriage and the Family, 57,* 465–475.

Simmons, R. G., Blyth, D. A., & McKinney, K. L. (1983). The social and psychological effect of puberty on white females. In J. Brooks-Gunn & A. C. Petersen (Eds.), *Girls at puberty: Biological and psychological perspectives.* New York: Plenum.

Simmons, R. G., Blyth, D. A., Van Cleave, E. F., & Bush, D. M. (1979). Entry into early adolescence: The impact of school structure, puberty, and early dating on self-esteem. *American Sociological Review, 44*(6), 948–967.

Simmons, R. G., Burgeson, R., Carlton-Ford, S., & Blyth, D. A. (1987). The impact of cumulative change in early adolescence. *Child Development, 58,* 1220–1234.

Simner, M. L. (1971). Newborn's response to the cry of another infant. *Developmental Psychology, 5,* 135–150.

Simon-Rusinowitz, L., Krach, C. A., Marks, L. N., Piktialis, D., & Wilson, L. B. (1996). Grandparents in the workplace: The effects of economic and labor trends. *Generations, 20*(1), 41–44.

Simons, C. (1987, March). They get by with a lot of help from their *kyoiku* mamas. *Smithsonian,* pp. 44–52.

Simons, M. (1993, February 10). Dutch parliament approves law permitting euthanasia. *The New York Times,* p. A10.

Simonton, D. K. (1983). Dramatic greatness and content: A quantitative analysis of 82 Athenian and Shakespearean plays. *Empirical Studies of the Arts, 1,* 109–123.

Simonton, D. K. (1986). Popularity, content, and context in 37 Shakespearean plays. *Poetics, 15,* 493–510.

Simonton, D. K. (1989). The swan-song phenomenon: Last-works effects for 172 classical composers. *Psychology and Aging, 4,* 42–47.

Simonton, D. K. (1990). Creativity and wisdom in aging. In J. E. Birren & K. W. Schaie (Eds.), *Handbook of the psychology of aging* (pp. 320–329). New York: Academic Press.

Simpson, G. A., & Fowler, M. G. (1994). Geographic mobility and children's emotional/behavioral adjustment and school functioning. *Pediatrics, 93,* 303–309.

Simpson, J. L., & Elias, S. (1993). Isolating fetal cells from maternal blood: Advances in prenatal diagnosis through molecular technology. *Journal of the American Medical Association, 270,* 2357–2361.

Simpson, K. H. (1996). Alternatives to physician-assisted suicide. *Humanistic Judaism, 24(4),* 21–23.

Simpson, R., Kelly, S. F., Atkinson, H. P., Turner, M., Greiser, K., & Zhao, D. (1991). Abstract. *Circulation, 84(4),* 11–334.

Singer, D. G., & Singer, J. L. (1990). *The house of make-believe: Play and the developing imagination.* Cambridge, MA: Harvard University Press.

Singer, J. L., & Singer, D. G. (1981). *Television, imagination, and aggression: A study of preschoolers.* Hillsdale, NJ: Erlbaum.

Singer, L. T., Yamashita, T. S., Hawkins, S., Cairns, D., Baley, J., & Kliegman, R. (1994). Increased incidence of intraventricular hemorrhage and developmental delay in cocaine-exposed, very low birth weight infants. *Journal of Pediatrics, 124,* 765–771.

Singer, M. I., Anglin, T. M., Song, L. Y., & Lunghofer, L. (1995). Adolescents' exposure to violence and associated symptoms of psychological trauma. *Journal of the American Medical Association, 273,* 477–482.

Singer, P. A. (1988, June 1). Should doctors kill patients? *Canadian Medical Association Journal, 138,* 1000–1001.

Singer, P. A., & Siegler, M. (1990). Euthanasia—A critique. *New England Journal of Medicine, 322,* 1881–1883.

Singh, G. K., Mathews, T. J., Clarke, S. C., Yannicos, T., & Smith, B. L. (1995, October 23). Annual summary of births, marriages, divorces, and deaths: United States, 1994. *Monthly Vital Statistics Report, 43(13).* Hyattsville, MD: National Center for Health Statistics.

Singh, S., Forrest, J. D., & Torres, A. (1989). *Prenatal care in the United States: A state and country inventory.* New York: Alan Guttmacher Institute.

Sinnott, J. (1996). The developmental approach: Postformal thought as adaptive intelligence. In F. Blanchard-Fields & T. M. Hess (Eds.), *Perspectives on cognitive change in adulthood and aging* (pp. 358–386). New York: McGraw-Hill.

Sinnott, J. D. (1984). Postformal reasoning: The relativistic stage. In M. L. Commons, F. A. Richards, & C. Armon (Eds.), *Beyond formal operations: Late adolescence and adult cognitive development* (pp. 357–380). New York: Praeger.

Sinnott, J. D. (1989a). A model for solution of ill-structured problems: Implications for everyday and abstract problem-solving. In J. D. Sinnott (Ed.), *Everyday problem solving: Theory and applications* (pp. 72–99). New York: Praeger.

Sinnott, J. D. (1989b). Life-span relativistic postformal thought: Methodology and data from everyday problem-solving studies. In M. L. Commons, J. D. Sinnott, F. A. Richards, & C. Armon (Eds.), *Adult development: Vol. 1. Comparison and application of developmental models* (pp. 239–278). New York: Praeger.

Sinnott, J. D. (1991). Limits to problem solving: Emotion, intention, goal clarity, health and other factors in postformal thought. In J. D. Sinnott & J. C. Cavanaugh (Eds.), *Bridging paradigms: Positive development in adulthood and cognitive aging* (pp. 169–202). New York: Praeger.

Sisodia, S. S., Koo, E. H., Beyreuther, K., Unterbeck, A., & Price, D. L. (1990). Evidence that B-amyloid protein in Alzheimer's disease is not derived by normal processing. *Science, 248,* 492–495.

Skaff, M. M., & Pearlin, L. I. (1992). Caregiving: Role engulfment and the loss of self. *The Gerontologist, 32(5),* 656–664.

Skinner, B. F. (1938). *The behavior of organisms: An experimental approach.* New York: Appleton-Century.

Skinner, B. F. (1957). *Verbal behavior.* New York: Appleton-Century-Crofts.

Sklar, L. S., & Anisman, H. (1981). Stress and cancer. *Psychological Bulletin, 89(3),* 369–406.

Skoe, E. E., & Diessner, R. E. (1994). Ethic of care, justice, identity, and gender: An extension and replication. *Merrill-Palmer Quarterly, 40,* 272–289.

Skoe, E. E., & Gooden, A. (1993). Ethics of care and real-life moral dilemma content in male and female early adolescents. *Journal of Early Adolescence, 13(2),* 154–167.

Skolnick, A. A. (1993). 'Female athlete triad' risk for women. *Journal of the American Medical Association, 270,* 921–923.

Skoog, I., Nilsson, L., Palmertz, B., Andreasson, L., & Svanborg, A. (1993). A population-based study of dementia in 85-year-olds. *New England Journal of Medicine, 328,* 153–158.

Slap, G. B., Vorters, D. F., Chaudhuri, S., & Centor, R. M. (1989). Risk factors for attempted suicide during adolescence. *Pediatrics, 84,* 762–772.

Sleek, S. (1995, December). Rallying the troops inside our bodies. *APA Monitor,* pp. 1, 24–25.

Slemenda, C. W. (1994). Cigarettes and the skeleton. *New England Journal of Medicine, 330,* 430–431.

Slobin, D. (1973). Cognitive prerequisites for the acquisition of language. In C. Ferguson & D. Slobin (Eds.), *Studies of child language development.* New York: Holt, Rinehart, & Winston.

Slobin, D. (1983). Universal and particular in the acquisition of grammar. In E. Wanner & L. Gleitman (Eds.), *Language acquisition: The state of the art.* Cambridge, UK: Cambridge University Press.

Slobin, D. I. (1971). Universals of grammatical development in children. In W. Levett & G. B. Flores d'Arcais (Eds.), *Advances in psycholinguistic research.* Amsterdam: New Holland.

Slomkowski, C. L., Nelson, K., Dunn, J., & Plomin, R. (1992). Temperament and language: Relations from toddlerhood to middle childhood. *Developmental Psychology, 28,* 1090–1095.

Smelser, N. J. (1980). Issues in the study of work and love in adulthood. In N. J. Smelser & E. H. Erikson (Eds.), *Themes of work and love in adulthood.* Cambridge, MA: Harvard University Press.

Smetana, J. G., Yau, J., Restrepo, A., & Braeges, J. L. (1991). Adolescent-parent conflict in married and divorced families. *Developmental Psychology, 27,* 1000–1010.

Smilansky, S. (1968). *The effects of sociodramatic play on disadvantaged preschool children.* New York: Wiley.

Smith, A. D., & Earles, J. L. (1996). Memory changes in normal aging. In F. Blanchard-Fields & T. M. Hess (Eds.), *Perspectives on cognitive change in adulthood and aging* (pp. 165–191). New York: McGraw-Hill.

Smith, D. W., & Brodzinsky, D. M. (1994). Stress and coping in adopted children: A developmental study. *Journal of Clinical Child Psychology, 23(1),* 91–99.

Smith, J., & Baltes, P. B. (1990). Wisdom-related knowledge: Age/cohort differences in response to life planning problems. *Developmental Psychology, 26(3),* 494–505.

Smith, J. B., & Fenske, N. A. (1996). Cutaneous manifestations and consequences of smoking. *Journal of the American Academy of Dermatology, 34,* 717.

Smith, M. M., & Lifshitz, F. (1994). Excess fruit juice consumption as a contributing factor in nonorganic failure to thrive. *Pediatrics, 93,* 438–443.

Smith, T. E. (1981). Adolescent agreement with perceived maternal and paternal educational goals. *Journal of Marriage and the Family, 43,* 85–93.

Smith, T. W. (1994). *The demography of sexual behavior.* Menlo Park, CA: Henry J. Kaiser Family Foundation.

Snarey, J. R. (1985). Cross-cultural universality of social-moral development: A critical review of Kohlbergian research. *Psychological Bulletin, 97,* 202–232.

Snarey, J. R., Reimer, J., & Kohlberg, L. (1985). Development of social-moral reasoning among kibbutz adolescents: A longitudinal cross-cultural study. *Developmental Psychology, 21,* 3–17.

Snow, C. E. (1972). Mother's speech to children learning language. *Child Development, 43,* 549–565.

Snow, C. E. (1977). Mother's speech research: From input to interaction. In C. E. Snow & C. A. Ferguson (Eds.), *Talking to children: Language input and acquisition.* London: Cambridge University Press.

Snow, C. E. (1990). The development of definitional skill. *Journal of Child Language, 17,* 697–710.

Snow, C. E. (1993). Families as social contexts for literacy development. In C. Daiute (Ed.), The development of literacy through social interaction. *New Directions for Child Development,* No. 61, pp. 11–24. San Francisco: Jossey-Bass.

Snow, C. E., Arlman-Rupp, A., Hassing, Y., Jobse, J., Jootsen, J., & Verster, J. (1976). Mother's speech in three social classes. *Journal of Psycholinguistic Research, 5,* 1–20.

Snow, M. E., Jacklin, C. N., & Maccoby, E. E. (1983). Sex-of-child differences in father-child interaction at one year of age. *Child Development, 54,* 227–232.

Snyder, C. J., & Barrett, G. V. (1988). The Age Discrimination in Employment Act: A review of court decisions. *Experimental Aging Research, 14,* 3–47.

Snyder, M. (1987). *Public appearance/private realities: The psychology of self-monitoring.* New York: Freeman.

Society for Assisted Reproductive Technology, The American Fertility Society. (1993). Assisted reproductive technology in the United States and Canada: 1991 results from the Society for Assisted Reproductive Technology generated from The American Fertility Society Registry. *Fertility and Sterility, 59,* 956–962.

Sohal, R. S., & Weindruch, R. (1996). Oxidative stress, caloric restriction, and aging. *Science, 273,* 59–63.

Soldo, B. J., Wolf, D. A., & Agree, E. M. (1990). Family, households, and care arrangements of frail older women: A structural analysis. *Journal of Gerontology: Social Sciences, 45,* S238–249.

Solomon, M. (1993). Report of survey of doctors and nurses about treatment of terminally ill patients. *American Journal of Public Health, 83*(1), 23–25.

Solomons, H. (1978). The malleability of infant motor development. *Clinical Pediatrics, 17*(11), 836–839.

Sonenstein, F. L., Pleck, J. H., & Ku, L. C. (1991). Levels of sexual activity among adolescent males in the United States. *Family Planning Perspectives, 23*(4), 162–167.

Song, M., & Ginsburg, H. P. (1987). The development of informal and formal mathematical thinking in Korean and U.S. children. *Child Development, 58,* 1286–1296.

Sontag, L. W., & Richards, T. W. (1938). Studies in fetal behavior: Fetal heart rate as a behavioral indicator. *Child Development Monographs, 3*(Whole No. 4).

Sontag, L. W., & Wallace, R. I. (1934). Preliminary report on the Fels fund: A study of fetal activity. *American Journal of Diseases of Children, 48,* 1050–1057.

Sontag, L. W., & Wallace, R. I. (1936). Changes in the heart rate of the human fetal heart in response to vibratory stimuli. *American Journal of Diseases of Children, 51,* 583–589.

Sophian, C. (1988). Early developments in children's understanding of number: Inferences about numerosity and one-to-one correspondence. *Child Development, 59,* 1397–1414.

Sorce, J. F., Emde, R. N., Campos, J., & Klinnert, M. D. (1985). Maternal emotional signalling: Its effect on the visual cliff behavior of 1-year-olds. *Developmental Psychology, 21,* 195–200.

Sorensen, T., Nielsen, G., Andersen, P., & Teasdale, T. (1988). Genetic and environmental influence of premature death in adult adoptees. *New England Journal of Medicine, 318,* 727–732.

Speece, M. W., & Brent, S. B. (1984). Children's understanding of death: A review of three components of a death concept. *Child Development, 55,* 1671–1686.

Spence, A. P. (1989). *Biology of human aging.* Englewood Cliffs, NJ: Prentice-Hall.

Spencer, M. B., & Markstrom-Adams, C. (1990). Identity processes among racial and ethnic minority children. *Child Development, 61,* 290–310.

Spiker, D., Ferguson, J., & Brooks-Gunn, J. (1993). Enhancing the maternal interactive behavior and child social competence in low birth weight, premature infants. *Child Development, 64,* 754–768.

Spindler, A. M. (1996, June 9). It's a face-lifted, tummy-tucked jungle out there: Fearing the axe, men choose the scalpel. *The New York Times,* pp. 1, 8–9.

Spirduso, W. W., & MacRae, P. G. (1990). Motor performance and aging. In J. E. Birren & K. W. Schaie (Eds.), *Psychology of aging* (3d ed., pp. 183–200). New York: Academic Press.

Spitz, M. R., & Johnson, C. C. (1985). Neuroblastoma and paternal occupation: A case-control analysis. *American Journal of Epidemiology, 121*(6), 924–929.

Spitz, R. A. (1945). Hospitalism: An inquiry into the genesis of psychiatric conditioning in early childhood. In D. Fenschel et al. (Eds.), *Psychoanalytic studies of the child* (Vol. 1, pp. 53–74). New York: International Universities Press.

Spitz, R. A. (1946). Hospitalism: A follow-up report. In D. Fenschel et al. (Eds.), *Psychoanalytic studies of the child* (Vol. 1, pp. 113–117). New York: International Universities Press.

Spitze, G., & Miner, S. (1992). Gender differences in adult child contact among elderly black parents. *The Gerontologist, 32,* 213–218.

Spitzer, M. E. (1988). Taste acuity in institutionalized and noninstitutionalized elderly men. *Journal of Gerontology, 43*(3), 71–74.

Spock, B., & Rothenberg, M. B. (1985). *Baby and child care.* New York: Pocket Books.

Spohr, H.-L., Willms, J., & Steinhausen, H.-C. (1993). Prenatal alcohol exposure and long-term developmental consequences. *The Lancet, 341,* 907–910.

Spurlock, J. (1990). Single women. In J. Spurlock & C. B. Robinowitz (Eds.), *Women's progress: Promises and problems* (pp. 23–33). Washington, DC: American Psychiatric Association.

Squire, L. R. (1992). Memory and the hippocampus: A synthesis of findings with rats, monkeys, and humans. *Psychological Review, 99,* 195–231.

Squire, L. R. (1994). Declarative and nondeclarative memory: Multiple brain systems supporting learning and memory. In D. L. Schacter & E. Tulving (Eds.), *Memory systems 1994* (pp. 203–232). Cambridge, MA: MIT Press.

Sroufe, L. A. (1977). Wariness of strangers and the study of infant development. *Child Development, 48,* 731–746.

Sroufe, L. A. (1979). Socioemotional development. In J. Osofsky (Ed.), *Handbook of infant development.* New York: Wiley.

Sroufe, L. A. (1983). Individual patterns of adaptation from infancy to preschool. In M. Perlmutter (Ed.), *Proceedings of the Minnesota symposium on child psychology.* Hillsdale, NJ: Erlbaum.

Sroufe, L. A., Bennett, C., Englund, M., Urban, J., & Shulman, S. (1993). The significance of gender boundaries in preadolescence: Contemporary correlates and antecedents of boundary violation and maintenance. *Child Development, 64,* 455–466.

Sroufe, L. A., Carlson, E., & Shulman, S. (1993). Individuals in relationships: Development from infancy through adolescence. In D. C. Funder, R. D. Parke, C. Tomlinson-Keasey, & K. Widaman (Eds.), *Studying lives through time: Personality and development* (pp. 315–342). Washington, DC: American Psychological Association.

Sroufe, L. A., Fox, N. E., & Pancake, V. R. (1983). Attachment and dependency in a developmental perspective. *Child Development, 54,* 1615–1627.

Sroufe, L. A., & Waters, E. (1976). The ontogenesis of smiling and laughter: A perspective on the organization of development in infancy. *Psychological Review, 83,* 173–189.

Sroufe, L. A., & Wunsch, J. (1972). The development of laughter in the first year of life. *Child Develop., 43,* 1326–1344.

Stack, S. (1994). The effect of geographic mobility on premarital sex. *Journal of Marriage and the Family, 56,* 204–208.

Stadtman, E. R. (1992). Protein oxidation and aging. *Science, 257,* 1220–1224.

Stamler, J., Dyer, A. R., Shekelle, R. B., Neaton, J., & Stamler, R. (1993). Relationship of baseline major risk factors to coronary and all-cause mortality, and to longevity: Findings from long-term follow-up of Chicago cohorts. *Cardiology, 82*(2–3), 191–222.

Stamler, R., Stamler, J., & Garside, D. (undated). *The 20-year story of the Chicago Heart Association Detection Project in Industry.* Chicago: Am. Heart Association of Metro. Chicago.

Stampfer, M. J., Colditz, G. A., Willett, W. C., Manson, J. E., Rosner, B., Speizer, F. E., & Hennekens, C. H. (1991). Postmenopausal estrogen therapy and cardiovascular disease. *New England Journal of Medicine, 325,* 756–762.

Stanley, A. (1990, May 7). Prodigy, 12, fights skeptics, hoping to be a doctor at 17. *The New York Times,* pp. A1, B2.

Stanton, C. K., & Gray, R. H. (1995). Effects of caffeine consumption on delayed conception. *American Journal of Epidemiology, 142,* 1322–1329.

Starfield, B. (1991). Childhood morbidity: Comparisons, clusters, and trends. *Pediatrics, 88*(3), 519–526.

Starfield, B., Katz, H., Gabriel, A., Livingston, G., Benson, P., Hankin, J., Horn, S., & Steinwachs, D. (1984). Morbidity in childhood—a longitudinal view. *New England Journal of Medicine, 310,* 824–829.

Starr, B. D. (1995). Sexuality. In G. L. Maddox (Ed.), *The encyclopedia of aging* (pp. 854–857). New York: Springer.

Stattin, H., & Magnusson, D. (1990). *Pubertal maturation in female development.* Hillsdale, NJ: Erlbaum.

Staub, S. (1973). *The effect of three types of relationships on young children's memory for pictorial stimulus pairs.* Unpublished doctoral dissertation, Harvard University Graduate School of Education.

Steele, C. M., & Aronson, J. (1995). Stereotype threat and intellectual test performance of African-Americans. *Journal of Personality and Social Psychology, 69,* 797–811.

Steinbach, U. (1992). Social networks, institutionalization, and mortality among elderly people in the United States.

Journal of Gerontology: Social Sciences, 47(4), S183–190.

Steinberg, K. K., Smith, S. J., Thacker, S. B., & Stroup, D. F. (1994). Breast cancer risk and duration of estrogen use: The role of the study design in meta-analysis. *Epidemiology, 5,* 415–421.

Steinberg, L. (1981). Transformations in family relations at puberty. *Developmental Psychology, 17,* 833–840.

Steinberg, L. (1987). Impact of puberty on family relations: Effect of pubertal status and pubertal timing. *Developmental Psychology, 23*(3), 451–460.

Steinberg, L. (1988). Reciprocal relation between parent-child distance and pubertal maturation. *Developmental Psychology, 24*(1), 122–128.

Steinberg, L., & Darling, N. (1994). The broader context of social influence in adolescence. In R. Silberstein & E. Todt (Eds.), *Adolescence in context.* New York: Springer.

Steinberg, L., Dornbusch, S. M., & Brown, B. B. (1992). Ethnic differences in adolescent achievement: An ecological perspective. *American Psychologist, 47,* 723–729.

Steinberg, L., Fegley, S., & Dornbusch, S. M. (1993). Negative impact of part-time work on adolescent adjustment: Evidence from a longitudinal study. *Developmental Psychology, 29,* 171–180.

Steinberg, L., Lamborn, S. D., Dornbusch, S. M., & Darling, N. (1992). Impact of parenting practices on adolescent achievement: Parenting, school involvement, and encouragement to succeed. *Child Development, 47,* 723–729.

Steinberg, L., & Silverberg, S. B. (1987). Influences on marital satisfaction during middle stages of the family life cycle. *Journal of Marriage and the Family, 49,* 751–760.

Steiner, J. E. (1979). Human facial expressions in response to taste and smell stimulation. *Advances in Child Development and Behavior, 13,* 257.

Stephens, M. A. P., & Franks, M. (1995). Spillover between daughters' roles as caregiver and wife: Interference or enhancement? *Journal of Gerontology: Psychological Sciences, 50B,* P9–17.

Steptoe, A., & Butler, N. (1996). Sports participation and emotional wellbeing in adolescents. *The Lancet, 347,* 1789–1792.

Stern, M., & Hildebrandt, K. A. (1986). Prematurity stereotyping: Effects on mother-infant interaction. *Child Development, 57,* 308–315.

Sternberg, R. J. (1984, September). How can we teach intelligence? *Educational Leadership,* pp. 38–50.

Sternberg, R. J. (1985a). *Beyond IQ: A triarchic theory of human intelligence.* New York: Cambridge University Press.

Sternberg, R. J. (1985b, August). *A triangular theory of love.* Paper presented at the annual meeting of the American Psychological Association, Los Angeles.

Sternberg, R. J. (1985c, November). Teaching critical thinking, Part I: Are we making critical mistakes? *Phi Delta Kappan,* pp. 194–198.

Sternberg, R. J. (1986). *Intelligence applied: Understanding and increasing your intellectual skills.* San Diego: Harcourt Brace.

Sternberg, R. J. (1987, September 23). The use and misuse of intelligence testing: Misunderstanding meaning, users over-rely on scores. *Education Week,* pp. 28, 22.

Sternberg, R. J. (1995). Love as a story. *Journal of Social and Personal Relationships, 12*(4), 541–546.

Sternberg, R. J., & Barnes, M. L. (1985). Real and ideal other in romantic relationships: Is four a crowd? *Journal of Personality and Social Psychology, 49,* 1586–1608.

Sternberg, R. J., & Grajek, S. (1984). The nature of love. *Journal of Personality and Social Psychology, 47,* 312–329.

Sternberg, R. J., & Lubart, T. I. (1995). *Defying the crowd: Cultivating creativity in a culture of conformity.* NY: Free Press.

Sternberg, R. J., & Wagner, R. K. (1993). The *g*-ocentric view of intelligence and job performance is wrong. *Current Directions in Psychological Science, 2*(1), 1–4.

Sternberg, R. J., Wagner, R. K., Williams, W. M., & Horvath, J. A. (1995). Testing common sense. *American Psychologist, 50,* 912–927.

Sterns, H. L., Barrett, G. V., & Alexander, R. A. (1985). Accidents and the aging individual. In J. E. Birren & K. W. Schaie (Eds.), *Handbook of the psychology of aging* (pp. 703–724). New York: Van Nostrand Reinhold.

Stevens, J. C., Cain, W. S., Demarque, A., & Ruthruff, A. M. (1991). On the discrimination of missing ingredients: Aging and salt flavor. *Appetite, 16,* 129–140.

Stevens, J. H., & Bakeman, R. (1985). A factor analytic study of the HOME scale for infants. *Developmental Psychology, 21*(6), 1106–1203.

Stevenson, D. L., & Baker, D. P. (1987). The family-school relation and the child's school performance. *Child Development, 58,* 1348–1357.

Stevenson, H. W., Chen, C., & Lee, S.-Y. (1993). Mathematics achievement of Chinese, Japanese, and American children: Ten years later. *Science, 258*(5081), 53–58.

Stevenson, H. W., Lee, S., Chen, C., & Lummis, M. (1990). Mathematics achievement of children in China and the United States. *Child Development, 61,* 1053–1066.

Stevenson, H. W., Lee, S., Chen, C., Stigler, J. W., et al. (1990). Contexts of achievement: A study of American, Chinese, and Japanese children. *Monographs of the Society for Research in Child Development, 55*(1–2, Serial No. 221).

Stevenson, H. W., Stigler, J. W., Lee, S., Lucker, G. W., Kitamura, S., & Hsu, C. (1985). Cognitive performance and academic achievement of Japanese, Chinese, and American children. *Child Development, 56,* 718–734.

Stevenson, M. R., & Black, K. N. (1988). Paternal absence and sex-role development: A meta-analysis. *Child Development, 59,* 793–814.

Stewart, I. C. (1994, January 29). Two-part message [Letter to the editor]. *The New York Times,* p. A18.

Stewart, M. A., & Olds, S. W. (1973). *Raising a hyperactive child.* New York: Harper & Row.

Stewart, R. B. (1983). Sibling attachment relationships: Child-infant interactions in the strange situation. *Developmental Psychology, 19*(2), 192–199.

Stewart, W., Kawas, C., Corrada, M., & Metler, E. J. (in press). Risk of Alzheimer's disease and duration of NSAIDs. *Neurology.*

Sticht, T. G., & McDonald, B. A. (1990). *Teach the mother and reach the child: Literacy across generations—Literacy lessons.* Geneva: International Bureau of Education.

Stifter, C. A., Coulehan, C. M., & Fish, M. (1993). Linking employment to attachment: The mediating effects of maternal separation anxiety and interactive behavior. *Child Development, 64,* 1451–1460.

Stigler, J. W., Lee, S., & Stevenson, H. W. (1987). Mathematics classrooms in Japan, Taiwan, and the United States. *Child Development, 58,* 1272–1285.

Stipek, D., Feiler, R., Daniels, D., & Milburn, S. (1995). Effect of different instructional approaches on young children's achievement and motivation. *Child Development, 66,* 209–233.

Stipek, D. J., Gralinski, H., & Kopp, C. B. (1990). Self-concept development in the toddler years. *Developmental Psychology, 26*(6), 972–977.

Stocker, C., Dunn, J., & Plomin, R. (1989). Sibling relationships: Links with child temperament, maternal behavior, and family structure. *Child Development, 60,* 715–727.

Stones, M. J., & Kozma, A. (1996). Activity, exercise, and behavior. In J. E. Birren & K. W. Schaie (Eds.), *Handbook of the psychology of aging* (4th ed., pp. 338–352). San Diego: Academic Press.

Strahan, G. W. (1997). *An overview of nursing homes and their current residents: Data from the 1995 National Nursing Home Survey* (Advance Data from Vital and Health Statistics, No. 280). Hyattsville, MD: National Center for Health Statistics.

Straus, M. A., & Donnelly, D. A. (1993). Corporal punishment of adolescents by American parents. *Youth and Society, 24,* 419–442.

Strauss, M., Lessen-Firestone, J., Starr, R., & Ostrea, E. (1975). Behavior of narcotics-addicted newborns. *Child Development, 46,* 887–893.

Strawbridge, W. J., & Wallhagen, M. I. (1991). Impact of family conflict on adult child caregivers. *The Gerontologist, 31*(6), 770–777.

Strawn, J. (1992). The states and the poor: Child poverty rises as the safety net shrinks. *Social Policy Report of the Society for Research in Child Development, VI*(3).

Streissguth, A. P., Aase, J. M., Clarren, S. K., Randels, S. P., LaDue, R. A., & Smith, D. F. (1991). Fetal alcohol syndrome in adolescents and adults. *Journal of the American Medical Association, 265,* 1961–1967.

Streissguth, A. P., Martin, D. C., Barr, H. M., Sandman, B. M., Kirchner, G. L., & Darby, B. L. (1984). Intrauterine alcohol and nicotine exposure: Attention and reaction time in 4-year-old children. *Developmental Psychology, 20*(4), 533–541.

Stroebe, M., Gergen, M. M., Gergen, K. J., & Stroebe, W. (1992). Broken hearts or broken bonds: Love and death in historical perspective. *American Psychologist, 47*(10), 1205–1212.

Strom, R., Collinsworth, P., Strom, S., & Griswold, D. (1992–1993). Strengths and needs of black grandparents. *International Journal of Aging and Human Development, 36,* 255–268.

Strong, M. (1988). *Mainstay.* Boston: Little, Brown.

Strube, M. J., & Barbour, L. S. (1984). Factors related to the decision to leave an abusive relationship. *Journal of Marriage and the Family, 46,* 837–844.

Stubbs, M. L., Rierdan, J., & Koff, E. (1989). Developmental differences in menstrual attitudes. *Journal of Early Adolescence, 9*(4), 480–498.

Stunkard, A., Harris, J. R., Pedersen, N. L., & McClearn, G. E. (1990). The body-mass index of twins who have been reared apart. *New England Journal of Medicine, 322*(21), 1483–1487.

Stunkard, A. J., Foch, T. T., & Hrubec, Z. (1986). A twin study of human obesity. *Journal of the American Medical Association, 256*(1), 51–54.

Sue, S., & Okazaki, S. (1990). Asian-American educational achievements: A phenomenon in search of an explanation. *American Psychologist, 45*(8), 913–920.

Suicide: Part 1. (1986, February). *Harvard Medical School Health Letter,* pp. 1–4.

Suicide—Part I. (1996, November). *The Harvard Mental Health Letter,* pp. 1–5.

Suicide—Part II. (1996, December). *The Harvard Mental Health Letter,* pp. 1–5.

Suitor, J. J., & Pillemer, K. (1987). The presence of adult children: A source of stress for elderly married couples? *Journal of Marriage and the Family, 49,* 717–725.

Suitor, J. J., & Pillemer, K. (1988). Explaining intergenerational conflict when adult children and elderly parents live together. *Journal of Marriage and the Family, 50,* 1037–1047.

Suitor, J. J., & Pillemer, K. (1993). Support and interpersonal stress in the social networks of married daughters caring for parents with dementia. *Journal of Gerontology: Social Sciences, 41*(1), S1–8.

Sullivan, H. S. (1953). *The interpersonal theory of psychiatry.* New York: Norton.

Sullivan-Bolyai, J., Hull, H. F., Wilson, C., & Corey, L. (1983). Neonatal herpes simplex virus infection in King County, Washington. *Journal of the American Medical Association, 250,* 3059–3062.

Suomi, S., & Harlow, H. (1972). Social rehabilitation of isolate-reared monkeys. *Developmental Psychology, 6*(3), 487–496.

Super, D. E. (1957). *The psychology of careers.* New York: Harper & Row.

Super, D. E. (1985). Coming of age in Middletown: Careers in the making. *American Psychologist, 40,* 405–414.

The SUPPORT Principal Investigators. (1995). A controlled trial to improve care for seriously ill hospitalized patients: The Study to Understand Prognoses and Preferences for Outcomes and Risks of Treatments (SUPPORT). *Journal of the American Medical Association, 274,* 1591–1598.

Swain, I. U., Zelazo, P. R., & Clifton, R. K. (1993). Newborn infants' memory for speech sounds retained over 24 hours. *Developmental Psychology, 29*(2), 312–323.

Swann, W. B. (1983). Self-verification: Bringing social reality into harmony with the self. In J. Suls & A. B. Greenwald (Eds.), *Psychological perspectives of the self* (pp. 33–66). Hillsdale, NJ: Erlbaum.

Swann, W. B. (1987). Identity negotiations: Where two roads meet. *Journal of Personality and Social Psychology, 53,* 1038–1051.

Swedo, S., Rettew, D. C., Kuppenheimer, M., Lum, D., Dolan, S., & Goldberger, E. (1991). Can adolescent suicide attemptors be distinguished from at-risk adolescents? *Pediatrics, 88*(3), 620–629.

Sweetland, J. D., & DeSimone, P. A. (1987). Age of entry, sex, and academic achievement in elementary school children. *Psychology in the Schools, 24,* 406–412.

Szinovacz, M. (1996). Couples' employment/retirement patterns and perceptions of marital quality. *Research on Aging, 18,* 243–268.

Tabor, A., Philip, J., Masden, M., Bang, J., Obel, E. B., & Norgaard-Pedersen, B. (1986, June 7). Randomized controlled trial of genetic amniocentesis in 4606 low-risk women. *The Lancet,* pp. 1287–1293.

Takanishi, R. (1993). The opportunities of adolescence—Research, interventions, and policy. *American Psychologist, 48*, 85–87.

Tallal, P., Miller, S. L., Bedi, G., Byma, G., Wang, X., Nagarajan, S. S., Schreiner, C., Jenkins, W. M., & Merzenich, M. M. (1996). Language comprehension in language-learning impaired children improved with acoustically modified speech. *Science, 271*, 81–84.

Tamir, L. M. (1989). Modern myths about men at midlife: An assessment. In S. Hunter & M. Sundel (Eds.), *Midlife myths.* Newbury Park, CA: Sage.

Tamis-LeMonda, C. S., & Bornstein, M. H. (1993). Antecedents of exploratory competence at one year. *Infant Behavior and Development, 16*(4), 423–440.

Tanfer, K., & Horn, M. C. (1985). Contraceptive use, pregnancy and fertility patterns among single American women in their 20's. *Family Planning Perspectives, 17*(1), 10–19.

Tang, M., Jacobs, C., Stern, Y., Marder, K., Schofield, P., Gurland, B., Andrews, H., & Mayeux, R. (1996). Effect of oestrogen during menopause on risk and age at onset of Alzheimer's disease. *The Lancet, 348*, 429–433.

Tanner, J. M. (1978). *Fetus into man: Physical growth from conception to maturity.* Cambridge, MA: Harvard University Press.

Tanner, J. M. (1989). *Fetus into man: Physical growth from conception to maturity* (2d ed.). Cambridge, MA: Harvard University Press.

Targ, D. B. (1979). Toward a reassessment of women's experience at middle-age. *Family Coordinator, 28*(3), 377–382.

Tartaglia, L. A., Dembski, M., Weng, X., Deng, N., Culpepper, J., Devos, R., Richards, G. J., Campfield, L. A., Clark, F. T., Deeds, J., Muir, C., Sanker, S., Moriarty, A., Moore, K. J., Smutko, J. S., Mays, G. G., Woolf, E. A., Monroe, C. A., & Tepper, R. I. (1995). Identification and expression cloning of a leptin receptor, Ob-R. *Cell, 83*, 1263–1271.

Tashman, B. (1995, August). Misreading dyslexia: Researchers debate the causes and prevalence of the disorder. *Scientific American,* pp. 14, 16.

Taylor, A. R., Asher, S. R., & Williams, G. A. (1987). The social adaptation of mainstreamed mildly retarded children. *Child Development, 58*, 1321–1334.

Taylor, H. (1995, January 30). *Doctor-assisted suicide: Support for Doctor Kevorkian remains strong, and 2-to-1 majority approves Oregon-style assisted suicide bill.* New York: Harris & Associates.

Taylor, J. A., Krieger, J. W., Reay, D. T., Davis, R. L., Harruff, R., & Cheney, L. K. (1996). Prone sleep position and the sudden infant death syndrome in King's County, Washington: A case-control study. *Journal of Pediatrics, 128,* 626–630.

Taylor, J. A., & Sanderson, M. (1995). A reexamination of the risk factors for sudden infant death syndrome. *Journal of Pediatrics, 126,* 887–891.

Taylor, M., Cartwright, B. S., & Carlson, S. M. (1993). A developmental investigation of children's imaginary companions. *Developmental Psychology, 28*(2), 276–285.

Taylor, R. D., & Roberts, D. (1995). Kinship support in maternal and adolescent well-being in economically disadvantaged African-American families. *Child Development, 66,* 1585–1597.

Taylor, S. E. (1989). *Positive illusions: Creative self-deception and the healthy mind.* New York: Basic Books.

Taylor, W. R., & Newacheck, P. W. (1992). Impact of childhood asthma on health. *Pediatrics, 90*(5), 657–662.

Techner, D. (1994, February 6). *Death and dying.* Seminar presentation for candidates in Leadership Program, International Institute for Secular Humanistic Judaism, Farmington Hills, MI.

Teicher, M., et al. (1996). Objective measurements of hyperactivity and attention problems in ADHD. *Journal of the American Academy of Child and Adolescent Psychiatry, 35*(3), 334–342.

Teller, D. Y., & Bornstein, M. H. (1987). Infant color vision and color perception. In P. Salapatek & L. B. Cohen (Eds.), *Handbook of infant perception: Vol. 1. From sensation to perception* (pp. 185–236). Orlando, FL: Academic Press.

Terman, D. L., Larner, M. B., Stevenson, C. S., & Behrman, R. E. (1996). Special education for students with disabilities. *The Future of Children, 6*(1), 4–24.

Terman, L. M., & Oden, M. H. (1959). *Genetic studies of genius: Vol. 5. The gifted group at mid-life.* Stanford, CA: Stanford University Press.

Termine, N. T., & Izard, C. E. (1988). Infants' responses to their mothers' expressions of joy and sadness. *Developmental Psychology, 24*(2), 223–229.

Tessler, M. (1986). *Mother-child talk in a museum: The socialization of a memory.* Unpublished manuscript, City University of New York, Graduate Center.

Tessler, M. (1991). *Making memories together: The influence of mother-child joint encoding on the development of autobiographical memory style.* Unpublished doctoral dissertation, City University of New York, Graduate Center.

Testing for Alzheimer's disease. (1995, January). *Harvard Women's Health Watch,* p. 1.

Teti, D. M., & Ablard, K. E. (1989). Security of attachment and infant-sibling relationships: A laboratory study. *Child Development, 60,* 1519–1528.

Teti, D. M., Gelfand, D. M., Messinger, D. S., & Isabella, R. (1995). Maternal depression and the quality of early attachment: An examination of infants, preschoolers, and their mothers. *Developmental Psychology, 31*(3), 364–376.

te Velde, E. R., & van Leusden, H. A. I. M. (1994). Hormonal treatment for the climacteric: Alleviation of symptoms and prevention of postmenopausal disease. *The Lancet, 343,* 654–656.

Thacker, S. B., Addiss, D. G., Goodman, R. A., Holloway, B. R., & Spencer, H. C. (1992). Infectious diseases and injuries in child day care. Opportunities for healthier children. *Journal of the American Medical Association, 268,* 1720–1726.

Tharp, R. G. (1989). Psychocultural variables and constants: Effects on teaching and learning in schools. *American Psychologist, 44,* 349–359.

Thelen, E. (1995). Motor development: A new synthesis. *American Psychologist, 50*(2), 79–95.

Thelen, E., & Fisher, D. M. (1982). Newborn stepping: An explanation for a "disappearing" reflex. *Developmental Psychology, 18,* 760–775.

Thelen, E., & Fisher, D. M. (1983). The organization of spontaneous leg movements in newborn infants. *Journal of Motor Behavior, 15,* 353–377.

Thomas, A., & Chess, S. (1977). *Temperament and development.* New York: Brunner/Mazel.

Thomas, A., & Chess, S. (1984). Genesis and evolution of behavioral disorders: From infancy to early adult life. *American Journal of Orthopsychiatry, 141*(1), 1–9.

Thomas, A., Chess, S., & Birch, H. G. (1968). *Temperament and behavior disorders in children.* New York: New York University Press.

Thomas, D. (1985). The dynamics of teacher opposition to integration. *Remedial Education, 20*(2), 53–58.

Thomas, J. L. (1986). Gender differences in satisfaction with grandparenting. *Psychology and Aging, 1*(3), 215–219.

Thomas, R. (1979). *Comparing theories of child development.* Belmont, CA: Wadsworth.

Thomas, W. P., & Collier, V. P. (1995). *Language minority student achievement and program effectiveness.* Manuscript in preparation.

Thompson, B., Wasserman, J. D., Gyurke, J. S., Matula, K., Mitchell, J. H., & Carr, B. (1994, January). *The validity of mental and motor scores from the new Bayley Scales of Infant Development—II: A second-order factor analysis.* Paper presented at the annual meeting of the Southwest Educational Research Association, San Antonio, TX.

Thompson, L. (1992). Fetal transplants show promise. *Science, 257,* 868–870.

Thompson, L., & Walker, A. J. (1989).

Gender in families: Women and men in marriage, work, and parenthood. *Journal of Marriage and the Family, 51,* 845–871.

Thompson, L. A., Fagan, J. F., & Fulker, D. W. (1991). Longitudinal prediction of specific cognitive abilities from infant novelty preference. *Child Development, 62,* 530–538.

Thompson, R. A., Lamb, M. E., & Estes, D. (1982). Stability of infant-mother attachment and its relationship to changing life circumstances in an unselected middle-class sample. *Child Development, 53,* 144–148.

Thomson, E., & Collela, U. (1992). Cohabitation and marital stability: Quality or commitment? *Journal of Marriage and the Family, 54,* 259–267.

Thornton, A. (1989). Changing attitudes toward family issues in the United States. *Journal of Marriage and the Family, 51,* 873–893.

Thun, M. J., Day-Lally, C. A., Calle, E. E., Flanders, W. D., & Heath, C. W., Jr. (1995). Excess mortality among cigarette smokers: Changes in a 20-year interval. *American Journal of Public Health, 85,* 1223–1230.

Thurstone, L. L. (1938). Primary mental abilities. *Psychometric Monographs,* No. 1.

Timiras, P. S. (1972). *Developmental psychology and aging.* New York: Macmillan.

Tisdale, S. (1988). The mother. *Hippocrates, 2*(3), 64–72.

Tobin, J. J., Wu, D. Y. H., & Davidson, D. H. (1989). *Preschools in three cultures: Japan, China, and the United States.* New Haven: Yale University Press.

Tobin-Richards, M. H., Boxer, A. M., McKavrell, S. A., & Petersen, A. C. (1984). Puberty and its psychological and social significance. In R. M. Lerner & N. L. Galambos (Eds.), *Experiencing adolescence: A sourcebook for parents, teachers, and teens.* New York: Garland.

Tobin-Richards, M. H., Boxer, A. M., & Petersen, A. C. (1983). The psychological significance of pubertal change: Sex differences in perceptions of self during early adolescence. In J. Brooks-Gunn & A. C. Petersen (Eds.), *Girls at puberty: Biological, social, and psychological perspectives.* New York: Plenum.

Tomasello, M., Mannle, S., & Kruger, A. C. (1986). Linguistic environment of 1- and 2-year-old twins. *Developmental Psychology, 22*(2), 169–176.

Toner, B. B., Garfinkel, P. E., & Garner, D. M. (1986). Long-term follow-up of anorexia nervosa. *Psychosomatic Medicine, 48*(7), 520–529.

Torrance, E. P. (1966). *The Torrance Tests of Creative Thinking: Technical-norms manual* (research ed.). Princeton, NJ: Personnel Press.

Torrance, E. P. (1974). *The Torrance Tests of Creative Thinking: Technical-norms*

manual. Bensonville, IL: Scholastic Testing Service.

Torrance, E. P. (1988). The nature of creativity as manifest in its testing. In R. J. Sternberg (Ed.), *The nature of creativity: Contemporary psychological perspectives* (pp. 43–75). Cambridge, UK: Cambridge University Press.

Torrance, E. P., & Ball, O. E. (1984). *Torrance Tests of Creative Thinking: Streamlined (revised) manual, Figural A and B.* Bensonville, IL: Scholastic Testing Service.

Tower, R. B., & Kasl, S. V. (1996). Gender, marital closeness, and depressive symptoms in elderly couples. *Journal of Gerontology: Psychological Sciences, 51B,* P115–129.

Tramontana, M. G., Hooper, S. R., & Selzer, S. C. (1988). Research on the preschool prediction of later academic achievement: A review. *Developmental Review, 8,* 89–146.

Travis, J. (1996, January 6). Obesity researchers feast on two scoops. *Science News,* p. 6.

Treas, J. (1995, May). Older Americans in the 1990s and beyond. *Population Bulletin, 50*(2). Washington, DC: Population Reference Bureau.

Treffers, P. E., Eskes, M., Kleiverda, G., & van Alten, D. (1990). Home births and minimal medical interventions. *Journal of the American Medical Association, 246*(17), 2203, 2207–2208.

Troll, L. E. (1975). *Early and middle adulthood.* Monterey, CA: Brooks/Cole.

Troll, L. E. (1980). Grandparenting. In L. W. Poon (Ed.), *Aging in the 1980s.* Washington, DC: American Psychological Association.

Troll, L. E. (1983). Grandparents: The family watchdogs. In T. H. Brubaker (Ed.), *Family relationships in later life.* Beverly Hills, CA: Sage.

Troll, L. E. (1985). *Early and middle adulthood* (2d ed.). Monterey, CA: Brooks/Cole.

Troll, L. E. (1986). Parents and children in later life. *Generations, 10*(4), 23–25.

Troll, L. E. (1989). Myths of midlife intergenerational relationships. In S. Hunter & M. Sundel (Eds.), *Midlife myths.* Newbury Park, CA: Sage.

Troll, L. E., Miller, S., & Atchley, R. (1979). *Families in later life.* Belmont, CA: Wadsworth.

Tronick, E. (1972). Stimulus control and the growth of the infant's visual field. *Perception and Psychophysics, 11,* 373–375.

Tronick, E. Z. (1980). On the primacy of social skills. In D. B. Sawin, L. O. Walker, & J. H. Penticuff (Eds.), *The exceptional infant: Psychosocial risk in infant environment transactions.* New York: Brunner/Mazel.

Tronick, E. Z. (1989). Emotions and emotional communication in infants. *American Psychologist, 44*(2), 112–119.

Tronick, E. Z., & Gianino, A. F. (1986). The transmission of maternal depression to the infant. In E. Z. Tronick & T. Field (Eds.), *Maternal depression and infancy disturbance.* San Francisco: Jossey-Bass.

Tronick, E. Z., Morelli, G. A., & Ivey, P. (1992). The Efe forager infant and toddler's pattern of social relationships: Multiple and simultaneous. *Developmental Psychology, 28,* 568–577.

Trotter, R. J. (1983). Baby face. *Psychology Today, 17*(8), 14–20.

Trotter, R. J. (1986, August). Profile: Robert J. Sternberg: Three heads are better than one. *Psychology Today,* pp. 56–62.

Trotter, R. J. (1987). You've come a long way, baby. *Psychology Today, 21*(5), 34–45.

Tschann, J., Johnston, J. R., & Wallerstein, J. S. (1989). Resources, stressors, and attachment as predictors of adult adjustment after divorce: A longitudinal study. *Journal of Marriage and Family Therapy, 51,* 1033–1046.

Tubman, J. G., Windle, M., & Windle, R. C. (1996). The onset and cross-temporal patterning of sexual intercourse in middle adolescence: Prospective relations with behavior and emotional problems. *Child Development, 67,* 327–343.

Tucker, M. B., Taylor, R. J., & Mitchell-Kernan, C. (1993). Marriage and romantic involvement among aged African Americans. *Journal of Gerontology: Social Sciences, 48,* S123–132.

Tuma, J. M. (1989). Mental health services for children: The state of the art. *American Psychologist, 44,* 188–199.

Turkington, C. (1983, May). Child suicide: An unspoken tragedy. *APA Monitor,* p. 15.

Turner, H., & Finkelhor, D. (1996). Corporal punishment as a stressor among youth. *Journal of Marriage and the Family, 58,* 155–156.

Turner, P. H., et al. (1985, March). *Parenting in gay and lesbian families.* Paper presented at the first meeting of the Future of Parenting Symposium, Chicago.

Turner, P. J., & Gervai, J. (1995). A multidimensional study of gender typing in preschool children and their parents: Personality, attitudes, preferences, behavior, and cultural differences. *Developmental Psychology, 31*(5), 759–772.

Tyler, P. E. (1994, January 11). Chinese start a vitamin program to eliminate a birth defect. *The New York Times,* p. C3.

Uhlenberg, P. (1988). Aging and the social significance of cohorts. In J. E. Birren & V. L. Bengtson (Eds.), *Emergent theories of aging* (pp. 405–425). New York: Springer.

Uhlenberg, P., Cooney, T., & Boyd, R. (1990). Divorce for women after midlife. *Journal of Gerontology, 45*(1), 53–61.

Uhlenberg, P., & Myers, M. A. P. (1981). Divorce and the elderly. *The Gerontologist, 21*(3), 276–282.

Umberson, D. (1992). Relationships between adult children and their parents: Psychological consequences for both generations. *Journal of Marriage and the Family, 54,* 664–674.

Umberson, D., & Chen, M. D. (1994). Effects of a parent's death on adult children: Relationship to salience and reaction to loss. *American Sociological Review, 59,* 152–168.

Umberson, D., Wortman, C. B., & Kessler, R. C. (1992). Widowhood and depression: Explaining long-term gender differences in vulnerability. *Journal of Health and Social Behavior, 33,* 10–24.

UNICEF (1992). *State of the world's children.* New York: Oxford University Press.

UNICEF (1996). *State of the world's children.* New York: Oxford University Press.

United Nations. (1991). *The world's women 1970–1990: Trends and statistics.* New York: Author.

United Nations Educational, Scientific, and Cultural Organization (UNESCO). (1989). *International literacy year (ILY), 1990.* Paris: Author.

United Nations International Labor Organization (UNILO). (1993). *Job stress: The 20th-century disease.* New York: United Nations.

United States Environmental Protection Agency. (1994). *Setting the record straight: Secondhand smoke is a preventable health risk* (EPA Publication No. 402-F-94-005). Washington, DC: U.S. Government Printing Office.

Upjohn Company. (1984). *Writer's guide to sex and health.* Kalamazoo, MI: Author.

Urbano-Marquez, A., Estruch, R., Fernandez-Sola, J., Nicolas, J. M., Pare, J. C., & Rubin, E. (1995). The greater risk of alcoholic cardiomyopathy and myopathy in women compared with men. *Journal of the American Medical Association, 274,* 149–154.

U.S. Advisory Board on Child Abuse and Neglect. (1995, October). *A nation's shame: Fatal child abuse and neglect in the United States.* Washington, DC: U.S. Government Printing Office.

U.S. Bureau of the Census. (1990). *Who's minding the kids? Child care arrangements: 1986–1987* (Current Population Reports, Series P-70, No. 20). Washington, DC: U.S. Government Printing Office.

U.S. Bureau of the Census. (1991a). *Household and family characteristics, March 1991* (Publication No. AP-20-458). Washington, DC: U.S. Government Printing Office.

U.S. Bureau of the Census. (1991b). *1990 census of population and housing.* Washington, DC: Data User Service Division.

U.S. Bureau of the Census. (1992a). *Marital status and living arrangements: March 1991* (Current Population Reports, Series P-20-461). Washington, DC: U.S. Government Printing Office.

U.S. Bureau of the Census. (1992b). *Sixty-five plus in America.* Washington, DC: U.S. Government Printing Office.

U.S. Bureau of the Census. (1992c, October). *When families break up* (Statistical Brief). Washington, DC: U.S. Government Printing Office.

U.S. Bureau of the Census. (1993a). *Sixty-five plus in America.* Washington, DC: U.S. Government Printing Office.

U.S. Bureau of the Census. (1993b). *Statistical Abstract of the United States, 1993.* Washington, DC: U.S. Government Printing Office.

U.S. Bureau of the Census. (1993c). Statistics on characteristics of single-parent households.

U.S. Bureau of the Census. (1994, May). *Who's minding the kids? Child care arrangements: Fall 1991* (Current Population Reports, Series P-70-36, Table B). Washington, DC: U.S. Government Printing Office.

U.S. Bureau of the Census. (1995a). *Sixty-five plus in the United States.* Washington, DC: U.S. Government Printing Office.

U.S. Bureau of the Census. (1995b). *Statistical Abstract of the United States, 1995.* Washington, DC: U.S. Government Printing Office.

U.S. Bureau of the Census. (1995c). Statistics.

U.S. Bureau of the Census. (1996a, February). *How we're changing: Demographic state of the nation: 1996* (Current Population Reports, Special Studies, Series P-23-191). Washington, DC: U.S. Government Printing Office.

U.S. Bureau of the Census. (1996b). *Marital status and living arrangements: March 1994* (Current Population Reports, Series P-20-484). Washington, DC: U.S. Government Printing Office.

U.S. Bureau of the Census. (1996c). *Sixty-five plus in the United States* (Current Population Reports, P-23-190). Washington, DC: U.S. Government Printing Office.

U.S. Bureau of the Census. (1996d). *Statistical Abstract of the United States: 1996.* Washington, DC: U.S. Government Printing Office.

U.S. Bureau of the Census. (1996e). Statistics.

U.S. Bureau of the Census. (1996f). See Casper, 1996.

U.S. Bureau of Justice Statistics. (1994, November). *Selected findings: Violence between intimates.* Washington, DC: U.S. Government Printing Office.

U.S. Consumer Product Safety Commission. (1991). Statistics on shopping cart safety.

U.S. Department of Agriculture. (1992). *Expenditures on the child by families, 1992.* Hyattsville, MD: USDA Family Economics Research Group.

U.S. Department of Education. (1986a). *Participation in adult education, May 1984* (Office of Educational Research and Improvement Bulletin CS 86-308B). Washington, DC: Center for Education Statistics.

U.S. Department of Education. (1986b). *What works: Research about reading and learning.* Washington, DC: Office of Educational Research and Improvement. (Available from What Works, Pueblo, CO 81009)

U.S. Department of Education. (1992). *Dropout rates in the U.S., 1991* (Publication No. NCES 92-129). Washington, DC: U.S. Government Printing Office.

U.S. Department of Health and Human Services (USDHHS). (1982). *Prevention 82.* (DHHS Publication No. PHS 82-50157). Washington, DC: U.S. Government Printing Office.

U.S. Department of Health and Human Services (USDHHS). (1985). *Health, United States, 1985* (DHHS Publication No. PHS 86-1232). Washington, DC: U.S. Government Printing Office.

U.S. Department of Health and Human Services (USDHHS). (1987). *Smoking and health: A national status report* (DHHS/PHS/Child Development Publication No. 87-8396). Washington, DC: U.S. Government Printing Office.

U.S. Department of Health and Human Services (USDHHS). (1988, June 21). *HHS News.*

U.S. Department of Health and Human Services (USDHHS). (1990). *Health, United States, 1989* (DHHS Publication No. PHS 90-1232). Washington, DC: U.S. Government Printing Office.

U.S. Department of Health and Human Services (USDHHS). (1992). *Health, United States, 1991, and Prevention Profile* (DHHS Publication No. PHS 92-1232). Washington, DC: U.S. Government Printing Office.

U.S. Department of Health and Human Services (USDHHS). (1993). *Cataract patient's guide* (Publication No. PHS A93-0544). Washington, DC: U.S. Government Printing Office.

U.S. Department of Health and Human Services (USDHHS). (1995). *Health, United States, 1994* (DHHS Publication No. PHS 95-1232). Washington, DC: U.S. Government Printing Office.

U.S. Department of Health and Human Services (USDHHS). (1996). *Health, United States, 1995* (DHHS Publication No. PHS 96-1232). Washington, DC: U.S. Government Printing Office.

U.S. Department of Health and Human Services (USDHHS), Public Health Service Expert Panel on the Content

of Prenatal Care. (1989). *Caring for our future: The content of prenatal care.* Washington, DC: U.S. Government Printing Office.

U.S. Department of Justice. (1988). Press release on juvenile offenders.

U.S. Department of Justice. (1995). *Crime in the United States—1994: Uniform crime reports.* Washington, DC: U.S. Government Printing Office.

U.S. Department of Labor. (1992). Statistics on employed civilians detailed by occupation, sex, race, and Hispanic origin. *Handbook of labor statistics.* Washington, DC: U.S. Government Printing Office.

U.S. Department of Labor, Bureau of Labor Statistics. (1996a, January). *Employment & earnings.* Washington, DC: U.S. Government Printing Office.

U.S. Department of Labor, Bureau of Labor Statistics. (1996b). *Employment situation: August, 1996* (USDL 96-365, Table A-2). Washington, DC: U.S. Government Printing Office.

U.S. Department of Labor, Bureau of Labor Statistics. (1996c). Unpublished tabulations from the Current Population Survey—1995, Annual Averages, Table A-17.

U.S. Department of Labor, Women's Bureau. (1994). *Working women count.* Washington, DC: U.S. Government Printing Office.

U.S. Department of Labor, Women's Bureau. (1995). *Facts on working women.* Washington, DC: U.S. Government Printing Office.

U.S. Office of Technology Assessment. (1992). *The menopause, hormone therapy, and women's health.* Washington, DC: U.S. Government Printing Office.

U.S. Public Health Service. (1995). *Healthy People 2000: Mid-course review and 1995 revisions.* Hyattsville, MD: U.S. Department of Health and Human Services.

Vachon, M., Lyall, W., Rogers, J., Freedmen-Letofky, K., & Freeman, S. (1980). A controlled study of self-help intervention for widows. *American Journal of Psychiatry, 137*(11), 1380–1384.

Vaillant, G. E. (1977). *Adaptation to life.* Boston: Little, Brown.

Vaillant, G. E. (1989). The evolution of defense mechanisms during the middle years. In J. M. Oldman & R. S. Liebert (Eds.), *The middle years.* New Haven: Yale University Press.

Vaillant, G. E. (1993). *The wisdom of the ego.* Cambridge, MA: Harvard University Press.

Vaillant, G. E., & Vaillant, C. O. (1990). Natural history of male psychological health: 12. A 45-year study of predictors of successful aging. *American Journal of Psychiatry, 147,* 31–37.

Valaes, T., Petmezaki, S., Henschke, C., Drummond, G. S., & Kappas, A. (1994). Control of jaundice in preterm newborns by an inhibitor of bilirubin production: Studies with tin-mesoporphyrin. *Pediatrics, 93,* 1–11.

Valdez-Menchaca, M. C., & Whitehurst, G. J. (1992). Accelerating language development through picture book reading: A systematic extension to Mexican daycare. *Developmental Psychology, 28,* 1106–1114.

Valkenburg, P. M., & van der Voort, T. H. A. (1994). Influence of TV on daydreaming and creative imagination: A review of research. *Psychological Bulletin, 116*(2), 316–339.

Van de Perre, P., Simonon, A., Msellati, P., Hitimana, D.-G., Vaira, D., Bazubagira, A., Van Goethem, C., Stevens, A.-M., Karita, E., Sondag-Thull, D., Dabis, F., & Lepage, P. (1991). Postnatal transmission of human immunodeficiency virus type 1 from mother to infant. *New England Journal of Medicine, 325,* 593–598.

van der Maas, P. J., Pijnenborg, L., & van Delden, J. J. M. (1995). Changes in Dutch opinions on active euthanasia, 1966 through 1991. *Journal of the American Medical Association, 273,* 1411–1414.

van Noord-Zaadstra, B., et al. (1991). Delayed childbearing: Effect of age on fecundity and outcome of pregnancy. *British Medical Journal, 302,* 1361–1365.

Vandell, D. L., & Corasaniti, M. A. (1988). The relation between third graders' after-school care and social, academic, and emotional functioning. *Child Development, 59,* 868–875.

Vandell, D. L., & Ramanan, J. (1991). Children of the National Longitudinal Survey of Youth: Choices in after-school care and child development. *Developmental Psychology, 27,* 637–643.

Vandell, D. L., & Ramanan, J. (1992). Effects of early and recent maternal employment on children from low-income families. *Child Development, 63,* 938–949.

Van IJzendoorn, M. H. (1995). Adult attachment representations, parental responsiveness, and infant attachment: A meta-analysis on the predictive validity of the Adult Attachment Interview. *Psychological Bulletin, 117*(3), 387–403.

VanTassel-Baska, J. (1992). Educational decision making on acceleration and grouping. *Gifted Child Quarterly, 36*(2), 68–72.

Vasudev, J. (1983). *A study of moral reasoning at different stages in India.* Unpublished manuscript, University of Pittsburgh, PA.

Vaughn, B. E., Goldberg, S., Atkinson, L., Marcovitch, S., MacGregor, D., & Seifer, R. (1994). Quality of toddler-mother attachment in children with Down syndrome: Limits to interpretation of Strange Situation behavior. *Child Development, 65,* 95–108.

Vaughn, B. E., Stevenson-Hinde, J., Waters, E., Kotsaftis, A., et al. (1992). Attachment security and temperament in infancy and early childhood: Some conceptual clarifications. *Developmental Psychology, 28,* 463–473.

Ventura, S. J., Taffel, S. M., Mosher, W. D., Wilson, J. B., & Henshaw, S. (1995, May 25). *Trends in pregnancies and pregnancy rates: Estimates for the United States, 1980–92* (Monthly Vital Statistics Report, Vol. 43, No. 11S). Washington, DC: Centers for Disease Control and Prevention/National Center for Health Statistics.

Verbrugge, L. M., Gruber-Baldini, A. L., & Fozard, J. L. (1996). Age differences and age changes in activities: Baltimore Longitudinal Study of Aging. *Journal of Gerontology: Social Sciences, 51B,* S30–41.

Verhaeghen, P., Marcoen, A., & Goossens, L. (1992). Improving memory performance in the aged through mnemonic training: A meta-analytic study. *Psychology and Aging, 7*(2), 242–251.

Verloove-Vanhorick, S. P., Veen, S., Ens-Dokkum, M. H., Schreuder, A. M., Brand, R., & Ruys, R. H. (1994). Sex differences in disability and handicap at five years of age in children born at very short gestation. *Pediatrics, 93,* 576–579.

Verschuren, W. M. M., Jacobs, D. R., Bloemberg, B. P. M., Kromhout, D., Menotti, A., Aravanis, C., Blackburn, H., Buzina, R., Dontas, A. S., Fidanza, F., Karvonen, M. J., Nedeljkovic, S., Nissinen, A., & Toshima, H. (1995). Serum total cholesterol and long-term coronary heart disease mortality in different cultures. *Journal of the American Medical Association, 274,* 131–136.

Vinick, B. (1978). Remarriage and old age. *Family Coordinator, 27,* 359–363.

Visher, E. B., & Visher, J. S. (1983). Stepparenting: Blending families. In H. I. McCubbin & C. R. Figley (Eds.), *Stress and the family: 1. Coping with normative transitions.* New York: Brunner/Mazel.

Visher, E. B., & Visher, J. S. (1989). Parenting coalitions after remarriage: Dynamics and therapeutic guidelines. *Family Relations, 38,* 65–70.

Visher, E. B., & Visher, J. S. (1991). *How to win as a step-family* (2d ed.). New York: Brunner/Mazel.

Voelker, R. (1993). The genetic revolution: Despite perfection of elegant techniques, ethical answers still elusive. *Journal of the American Medical Association, 270,* 2273–2277.

Voelker, R. (1995). Ames agrees with mom's advice: Eat your fruits and vegetables. *Journal of the American Medical Association, 273,* 1077–1078.

Volling, B. L., & Feagans, L. V. (1995). Infant day care and children's social competence. *Infant Behavior and Development, 18,* 177–188.

Vosniadou, S. (1987). Children and metaphors. *Child Development, 58,* 870–885.

Voydanoff, P. (1987). *Work and family life.* Newbury Park, CA: Sage.

Voydanoff, P. (1990). Economic distress and family relations: A review of the eighties. *Journal of Marriage and the Family, 52,* 1099–1115.

Voyer, D., Voyer, S., & Bryden, M. P. (1995). Magnitude of sex differences in spatial abilities: A meta-analysis and consideration of critical variables. *Psychological Bulletin, 117*(2), 250–270.

Vuori, L., Christiansen, N., Clement, J., Mora, J., Wagner, M., & Herrera, M. (1979). Nutritional supplementation and the outcome of pregnancy: 2. Visual habitation at 15 days. *Journal of Clinical Nutrition, 32,* 463–469.

Vygotsky, L. S. (1956). *Selected psychological investigations.* Moscow: Izdstel'sto Akademii Pedagogicheskikh Nauk USSR.

Vygotsky, L. S. (1962). *Thought and language.* Cambridge, MA: MIT Press.

Vygotsky, L. S. (1978). *Mind in society: The development of higher psychological processes.* Cambridge, MA: Harvard University Press.

Wagner, R. K., & Sternberg, R. J. (1985). Practical intelligence in real-world pursuits: The role of tacit knowledge. *Journal of Personality and Social Psychology, 49,* 436–458.

Wagner, R. K., & Sternberg, R. J. (1986). Tacit knowledge and intelligence in the everyday world. In R. J. Sternberg & R. K. Wagner (Eds.), *Practical intelligence: Nature and origins of competence in the everyday world.* Cambridge, UK: Cambridge University Press.

Walasky, M., Whitbourne, S. K., & Nehrke, M. F. (1983–1984). Construction and validation of an ego-integrity status interview. *International Journal of Aging and Human Development, 81,* 61–72.

Walfish, S., Antonovsky, A., & Maoz, B. (1984). Relationship between biological changes and symptoms and health and behavior during the climacteric. *Maturitas, 6,* 9–17.

Walford, R. L. (1983). *Maximum life span.* New York: Norton.

Walford, R. L. (1986). *The 120-year-diet.* New York: Simon & Schuster.

Walk, R. D., & Gibson, E. J. (1961). A comparative and analytical study of visual depth perception. *Psychology Monographs, 75*(15).

Walker, A. J., & Allen, K. R. (1991). Relationships between caregiving daughters and their elderly mothers. *The Gerontologist, 31*(3), 389–396.

Walker, D., Greenwood, C., Hart, B., & Carta, J. (1994). Prediction of school outcomes based on early language production and socioeconomic factors. *Child Development, 65,* 606–621.

Walker, L. J. (1984). Sex differences in the development of moral reasoning: A critical review. *Child Development, 55,* 677–691.

Walker, L. J., & Taylor, J. H. (1991). Family interactions and the development of moral reasoning. *Child Development, 62,* 264–283.

Wallace, D. C. (1992). Mitochondrial genetics: A paradigm for aging and degenerative diseases? *Science, 256,* 628–632.

Wallach, M. A., & Kogan, M. (1965). *Modes of thinking in young children: A study of the creativity-intelligence distinction.* New York: Holt.

Wallerstein, J. S. (1983). Children of divorce: The psychological tasks of the child. *American Journal of Orthopsychiatry, 53,* 230–243.

Wallerstein, J. S. (1987). Children of divorce: Report of a ten-year follow-up of early latency-age children. *American Journal of Orthopsychiatry, 57,* 199–211.

Wallerstein, J. S., & Blakeslee, S. (1995). *The good marriage: How and why love lasts.* Boston & New York: Houghton Mifflin.

Wallerstein, J. S., & Kelly, J. B. (1980). *Surviving the break-up: How children actually cope with divorce.* New York: Basic Books.

Walls, C., & Zarit, S. (1991). Informal support from black churches and well-being of elderly blacks. *The Gerontologist, 31,* 490–495.

Walsh, D. A., & Hershey, D. A. (1993). Mental models and the maintenance of complex problem solving skills into old age. In J. Cerella & W. Hoyer (Eds.), *Adult information processing: Limits on loss* (pp. 553–584). New York: Academic Press.

Walter, H. J., Vaughan, R. D., & Cohall, A. T. (1991). Psychosocial influences on acquired immunodeficiency syndrome risk-behaviors among high school students. *Pediatrics, 88,* 846–852.

Wannamethee, S. G., Shaper, A. G., Whincup, P. H., & Walker, M. (1995). Smoking cessation and the risk of stroke in middle-aged men. *Journal of the American Medical Association, 274,* 155–160.

Ward, R., Logan, J., & Spitze, G. (1992). The influence of parent and child needs on coresidence in middle and later life. *Journal of Marriage and the Family, 54,* 209–221.

Ward, R., & Spitze, G. (1996). Will the children ever leave? Parent-child coresidence history and plans. *Journal of Family Issues, 17,* 514–539.

Warr, P. (1994). Age and employment. In H. C. Triandis, M. D. Dunnette, & L. M. Hough (Eds.), *Handbook of industrial and organizational psychology* (Vol. 4, pp. 485–550). Palo Alto, CA: Consulting Psychologists Press.

Warren, J. A., & Johnson, P. J. (1995). The impact of workplace support on work-family role strain. *Family Relations, 44,* 163–169.

Wasik, B. H., Ramey, C. T., Bryant, D. M., & Sparling, J. J. (1990). A longitudinal study of two early intervention strategies: Project CARE. *Child Development, 61,* 1682–1696.

A waste of talent. (1993). *American Demographics, 15*(8), 6.

Waters, E., & Deane, K. E. (1985). Defining and assessing individual differences in attachment relationships: Q-methodology and the organization of behavior in infancy and early childhood. *Monographs of the Society for Research in Child Development, 50,* 41–65.

Waters, E., Wippman, J., & Sroufe, L. A. (1979). Attachment, positive affect, and competence in the peer group: Two studies in construct validation. *Child Development, 50*(3), 821–829.

Waters, K. A., Gonzalez, A., Jean, C., Morielli, A., & Brouillette, R. T. (1996). Face-straight-down and face-near-straight-down positions in healthy prone-sleeping infants. *Journal of Pediatrics, 128,* 616–625.

Watson, J. B., & Rayner, R. (1920). Conditioned emotional reactions. *Journal of Experimental Psychology, 3,* 1–14.

Wayler, A. H., Kapur, K. K., Feldman, R. S., & Chauncey, H. H. (1982). Effects of age and dentition status on measures of food acceptability. *Journal of Gerontology, 37*(3), 294–299.

Weathers, W. T., Crane, M. M., Sauvain, K. J., & Blackhurst, D. W. (1993). Cocaine use in women from defined populations: Prevalence at delivery and effects on growth in infants. *Pediatrics, 91,* 350–354.

Webb, W. B. (1987). Disorders of aging sleep. *Interdisciplinary Topics in Gerontology, 22,* 1–12.

Weg, R. B. (1987). Intimacy and the later years. In G. Lesnoff-Caravaglia (Ed.), *Handbook of applied gerontology.* New York: Human Sciences Press.

Weg, R. B. (1989). Sensuality/sexuality of the middle years. In S. Hunter & M. Sundel (Eds.), *Midlife myths.* Newbury Park, CA: Sage.

Wegman, M. E. (1992). Annual summary of vital statistics—1991. *Pediatrics, 90*(6), 835–845.

Wegman, M. E. (1993). Annual summary of vital statistics—1992. *Pediatrics, 92,* 743–754.

Wegman, M. E. (1994). Annual summary of vital statistics—1993. *Pediatrics, 94,* 792–803.

Weinberg, R. A. (1989). Intelligence and IQ: Landmark issues and great debates. *American Psychologist, 44*(2), 98–104.

Weindruch, R., & Walford, R. L. (1988). *The retardation of aging and disease by dietary restriction.* Springfield, IL: Thomas.

Weinstein, R. S., Marshall, H. H., Sharp,

L., & Botkin, M. (1987). Pygmalion and the student: Age and classroom differences in children's awareness of teacher expectation. *Child Development, 58,* 1079–1093.

Weishaus, S., & Field, D. (1988). A half century of marriage: Continuity or change? *Journal of Marriage and the Family, 50,* 763–774.

Weisman, S. R. (1988, July 20). No more guarantees of a son's birth. *The New York Times,* pp. A1, A9.

Weisner, T. S. (1993). Ethnographic and ecocultural perspectives on sibling relationships. In Z. Stoneman & P. W. Berman (Eds.), *The effects of mental retardation, visibility, and illness on sibling relationships* (pp. 51–83). Baltimore: Brooks.

Weiss, B., Dodge, K. A., Bates, J. E., & Pettit, G. S. (1992). Some consequences of early harsh discipline: Child aggression and a maladaptive social information processing style. *Child Development, 63,* 1321–1335.

Weiss, G. (1990). Hyperactivity in childhood. *New England Journal of Medicine, 323*(20), 1413–1415.

Weissman, M. M., Klerman, G. L., Markowitz, J. S., & Ouelette, R. (1989). Suicidal ideation and suicide attempts in panic disorders and attacks. *New England Journal of Medicine, 321,* 1209–1214.

Weisz, J. R., Sigman, M., Weiss, B., & Mosk, J. (1993). Parent reports of behavioral and emotional problems among children in Kenya, Thailand, and the United States. *Child Development, 64,* 98–109.

Weisz, J. R., Weiss, B., Han, S. S., Granger, D. A., & Morton, T. (1995). Effects of psychotherapy with children and adolescents revisited: A meta-analysis of treatment outcome studies. *Psychological Bulletin, 117*(3), 450–468.

Weitzman, M., Gortmaker, S., & Sobol, A. (1992). Maternal smoking and behavior problems of children. *Pediatrics, 90*(3), 342–349.

Wellington, N., & Rieder, M. J. (1993). Attitudes and practices regarding analgesia for newborn circumcision. *Pediatrics, 92,* 541–543.

Wellman, H., & Lempers, J. (1977). The naturalistic communicative abilities of two-year-olds. *Child Development, 48,* 1052–1057.

Werker, J. F., Pegg, J. E., & McLeod, P. J. (1994). A cross-language investigation of infant preference for infant-directed communication. *Infant Behavior and Development, 17,* 323–333.

Werner, E., Bierman, L, French, F. E., Simonian, K., Conner, A., Smith, R., & Campbell, M. (1968). Reproductive and environmental casualties: A report on the 10-year follow-up of the children of the Kauai pregnancy study. *Pediatrics, 42,* 112–127.

Werner, E. E. (1985). Stress and protective factors in children's lives. In A. R. Nichol (Ed.), *Longitudinal studies in child psychology and psychiatry.* New York: Wiley.

Werner, E. E. (1987, July 15). *Vulnerability and resiliency: A longitudinal study of Asian Americans from birth to age 30.* Invited address at the Ninth Biennial Meeting of the International Society for the Study of Behavioral Development, Tokyo.

Werner, E. E. (1989). Children of the garden island. *Scientific American, 260*(4), 106–111.

Werner, E. E. (1993). Risk and resilience in individuals with learning disabilities: Lessons learned from the Kauai longitudinal study. *Learning Disabilities Research and Practice, 8,* 28–34.

Werner, E. E. (1995). Resilience in development. *Current Directions in Psychological Science, 4*(3), 81–85.

Wertz, D. C., Fanos, J. H., & Reilly, P. R. (1994). Genetic testing for children and adolescents: Who decides? *Journal of the American Medical Association, 272,* 875–881.

West Berlin Human Genetics Institute. (1987). Study on effects of nuclear radiation at Chernobyl on fetal development. Berlin: Author.

Wharton, D. (1993, June–July). Through the glass ceiling: Minorities, women, and corporate America's human resource needs. *The National Voter,* pp. 10–11.

Whiffen, V. E., & Gotlib, I. H. (1989). Infants of postpartum depressed mothers: Temperament and cognitive status. *Journal of Abnormal Psychology, 98*(3), 274–279.

Whitbourne, S. K. (1985). *The aging body.* New York: Springer-Verlag.

Whitbourne, S. K. (1987). Personality development in adulthood and old age: Relationships among identity style, health, and well-being. In K. W. Schaie (Ed.), *Annual review of gerontology and geriatrics* (pp. 189–216). New York: Springer.

Whitbourne, S. K. (1996). *The aging individual: Physical and psychological perspectives.* New York: Springer.

White, B. L. (1971, October). *Fundamental early environmental influences on the development of competence.* Paper presented at the Third Western Symposium on Learning: Cognitive Learning, Western Washington State College, Bellingham, WA.

White, B. L., Kaban, B., & Attanucci, J. (1979). *The origins of human competence.* Lexington, MA: Heath.

White, J. M. (1992). Marital status and well-being in Canada: An analysis of age group variations. *Journal of Family Issues, 13,* 390–409.

White, K. R. (1982). The relation between socioeconomic status and academic achievement. *Psychological Bulletin, 91*(3), 461–481.

White, L., & Edwards, J. N. (1990). Emptying the nest and parental well-being: An analysis of national panel data. *American Sociological Review, 55,* 235–242.

White, L. K. (1990). Determinants of divorce: A review of research in the eighties. *Journal of Marriage and the Family, 52,* 904–912.

White, N., & Cunningham, W. R. (1988). Is terminal drop pervasive or specific? *Journal of Gerontology, 43*(6), 141–144.

Whitehurst, G. I., Fischel, J. E., Caulfield, M., DeBaryshe, B. D., & Valdez-Menchaca, M. C. (1989). Assessment and treatment of early expressive language delay. In P. R. Zelazo & R. G. Barr (Eds.), *Challenges to developmental paradigms: Implications for theory, assessment and treatment.* Hillsdale, NJ: Erlbaum.

Whitehurst, G. J., Falco, F. L., Lonigan, C. J., Fischel, J. E., DeBaryshe, B. D., Valdez-Menchaca, M. D., & Caufield, M. (1988). Accelerating language development through picture book reading. *Developmental Psychology, 24*(4), 552–559.

Whitehurst, M., Groo, D., & Brown, L. E. (1996). Prepubescent heart response to indoor play. *Pediatric Exercise Science, 8*(3), 245–250.

Whitehurst, M., Groo, D., Brown, L. E., & Findley, B. W. (1995). Prepubescent heart rate response to indoor play. *Medicine and Science in Sport and Exercise, 27*(5), S115.

Whitson, J. S., Selkoe, D. J., & Cotman, C. W. (1989). Amyloid B protein enhances survival of hippocampal neurons in vitro. *Science, 243,* 1488–1490.

WHO Brief Intervention Study Group. (1996). A cross-national trial of brief interventions with heavy drinkers. *American Journal of Public Health, 86,* 948–955.

Wickelgren, I. (1996, July 5). For the cortex, neuron loss may be less than thought. *Science,* pp. 48–50.

Wideman, M. V., & Singer, J. F. (1984). The role of psychological mechanisms in preparation for childbirth. *American Psychologist, 34,* 1357–1371.

Widom, C. S. (1989). The cycle of violence. *Science, 244,* 160–166.

Wiggins, S., Whyte, P., Higgins, M., Adams, S., et al. (1992). The psychological consequences of predictive testing for Huntington's disease. *New England Journal of Medicine, 327,* 1401–1405.

Wilcox, A. J., Weinberg, C. R., & Baird, D. D. (1995). Timing of sexual intercourse in relation to ovulation: Effects on the probability of conception, survival of the pregnancy, and sex of the baby. *New England Journal of Medicine, 333,* 1563–1565.

Wilcox, A. J., Weinberg, C. R., O'Connor, J. F., Baird, D. D., Schlatterer, J. P., Canfield, R. E., Armstrong, E. G., & Nisula, B. C. (1988). Incidence of early loss of pregnancy. *New England Journal of Medicine, 319*(4), 189–194.

Wiley, D., & Bortz, W. M. II. (1996). Sexuality and aging—Usual and successful. *Journal of Gerontology: Medical Sciences, 51A*(3), M142–146.

Willett, W. C. (1994). Diet and health: What should we eat? *Science, 264,* 532–537.

Willett, W. C., Hunter, D. J., Stampfer, M. J., Colditz, G., Manson, J. E., Spiegelman, D., Rosner, B., Hennekens, C. H., & Spiezer, F. E. (1992). Dietary fat and fiber in relation to risk of breast cancer. *Journal of the American Medical Association, 268,* 2037–2044.

Willett, W. C., Stampfer, M. J., Colditz, G. A., Rosner, B. A., & Speizer, F. E. (1990). Relation of meat, fat, and fiber intake to the risk of colon cancer in a prospective study among women. *New England Journal of Medicine, 323,* 1664–1672.

Williams, B. C. (1990). Immunization coverage among preschool children: The United States and selected European countries. *Pediatrics, 86*(Suppl.), 1052–1056.

Williams, B. C., & Miller, C. A. (1991). *Preventive health care for young children: Findings from a 10-country study and directions for United States policy.* Arlington, VA: National Center for Clinical Infant Programs.

Williams, B. C., & Miller, C. A. (1992). Preventive health care for young children: Findings from a 10-country study and directions for the United States policy. *Pediatrics, 89*(5), Supplement.

Williams, E. R., & Caliendo, M. A. (1984). *Nutrition: Principles, issues, and applications.* New York: McGraw-Hill.

Williams, G. (1991, October–November). Flaming out on the job: How to recognize when it's all too much. *Modern Maturity,* pp. 26–29.

Williams, J., Best, D., & Boswell, D. (1975). The measurement of children's racial attitudes in the early school years. *Child Development, 46,* 494–500.

Williams, J. E., & Best, D. L. (1982). *Measuring sex stereotypes: A thirty-nation study.* Beverly Hills, CA: Sage.

Williams, S. B. (1987). A comparative study of black dropouts and black high school graduates in an urban public school system. *Education and Urban Society, 19,* 311–319.

Williams, T. F. (1992). Aging versus disease: Which changes seen with age are the result of "biological aging"? *Generations, 16*(4), 21–25.

Williams, W. M., & Sternberg, R. J. (in press). *Success acts for managers.* Orlando, FL: Harcourt Brace.

Williamson, D. F., Kahn, H. S., Remington, P. L., & Anda, R. F. (1990). The 10-year incidence of overweight and major weight gain in U.S. adults. *Archives of Internal Medicine, 150,* 665–672.

Willinger, M. (1995). Sleep position and sudden infant death. *Journal of the American Medical Association, 273*(10), 818–819.

Willinger, M., Hoffman, H. T., & Hartford, R. B. (1994). Infant sleep position and risk for sudden infant death syndrome: Report of meeting held January 13 and 14, 1994. *Pediatrics, 93,* 814–819.

Willis, S. L. (1985). Towards an educational psychology of the older learner: Intellectual and cognitive bases. In J. E. Birren & K. W. Schaie (Eds.), *Handbook of the psychology of aging* (2d ed., pp. 818–847). New York: Van Nostrand Reinhold.

Willis, S. L. (1990). Current issues in cognitive training research. In E. A. Lovelace (Ed.), *Aging and cognition: Mental processes, self-awareness, and intervention* (pp. 263–280). Amsterdam: North-Holland, Elsevier.

Willis, S. L., Blieszner, R., & Baltes, P. B. (1981). Intellectual training research in aging: Modification of performance on the fluid ability of figural relations. *Journal of Educational Psychology, 73,* 41–50.

Willis, S. L., Jay, G. M., Diehl, M., & Marsiske, M. (1992). Longitudinal change and prediction of everyday task competence in the elderly. *Research on Aging, 14,* 68–91.

Willis, S. L., & Nesselroade, C. S. (1990). Long-term effects of fluid ability training in old-old age. *Developmental Psychology, 26,* 905–910.

Willis, S. L., & Schaie, K. W. (1986a). Practical intelligence in later adulthood. In R. J. Sternberg & R. K. Wagner (Eds.), *Practical intelligence: Nature and origins of competence in the everyday world* (pp. 236–268). New York: Cambridge University Press.

Willis, S. L., & Schaie, K. W. (1986b). Training the elderly on the ability factors of spatial orientation and inductive reasoning. *Psychology and Aging, 2,* 239–247.

Wilson, G. L. (1991). Comment: Suicidal behavior—Clinical considerations and risk factors. *Journal of Consulting and Clinical Psychology, 59,* 869–873.

Wilson, G., McCreary, R., Kean, J., & Baxter, J. (1979). The development of preschool children of heroin-addicted mothers: A controlled study. *Pediatrics, 63*(1), 135–141.

Wingfield, A., & Stine, E. A. L. (1989). Modeling memory processes: Research and theory on memory and aging. In G. C. Gilmore, P. J. Whitehouse, & M. L. Wykle (Eds.), *Memory, aging, and dementia: Theory, assessment, and treatment* (pp. 4–40). New York: Springer.

Winick, M. (1981, January). Food and the fetus. *Natural History,* pp. 16–81.

Wink, P., & Helson, R. (1993). Personality change in women and their partners. *Journal of Personality and Social Psychology, 65,* 597–606.

Winsborough, H. H., Bumpass, L. L., & Aquilino, W. S. (1991). *The death of parents and the transition to old age.* Paper presented at the annual meeting of the Population Association of America, Washington, DC.

Wiseman, E. J., & Souder, E. (1996). The older driver: A handy tool to assess competence behind the wheel. *Geriatrics, 51*(7), 36–43.

Wittrock, M. C. (1980). Learning and the brain. In M. C. Wittrock (Ed.), *The brain and psychology.* New York: Academic Press.

Wolf, M. (1968). *The house of Lim.* Englewood Cliffs, NJ: Prentice-Hall.

Wolfe, D. A. (1985). Child-abusive parents: An empirical review and analysis. *Psychological Bulletin, 97*(3), 462–482.

Wolfe, R., Morrow, J., & Fredrickson, B. L. (1996). Mood disorders in older adults. In L. L. Carstensen, B. A. Edelstein, & L. Dornbrand (Eds.), *The practical handbook of clinical gerontology* (pp. 274–303). Thousand Oaks, CA: Sage.

Wolff, P. H. (1963). Observations on the early development of smiling. In B. M. Foss (Ed.), *Determinants of infant behavior* (Vol. 2). London: Methuen.

Wolff, P. H. (1966). The causes, controls, and organizations of behavior in the newborn. *Psychological Issues, 5*(1, Whole No. 17), 1–105.

Wolff, P. H. (1969). The natural history of crying and other vocalizations in early infancy. In B. M. Foss (Ed.), *Determinants of infant behavior* (Vol. 4). London: Methuen.

Wolff, R. (1993). *Good sports: The concerned parent's guide to Little League and other competitive youth sports.* New York: Dell.

Wolraich, M. L., Lindgren, S. D., Stumbo, P. J., Stegink, L. D., Appelbaum, M. I., & Kiritsky, M. C. (1994). Effects of diets high in sucrose or aspartame on the behavior and cognitive performance of children. *New England Journal of Medicine, 330,* 301–307.

Wolraich, M. L., Wilson, D. B., & White, J. W. (1995). The effect of sugar on behavior or cognition in children: A meta-analysis. *Journal of the American Medical Association, 274*(20), 1617–1621.

Women in legal profession make progress, but problems persist. (1996, January 8). Associated Press.

Wong, N. D., Hei, T. K., Qaqundah,

P. Y., Davidson, D. M., Bassin, S. L., & Gold, K. V. (1992). Television viewing and pediatric hypercholesterolemia. *Pediatrics, 90*(1), 75–79.

Wong, P. T. P., & Watt, L. M. (1991). What types of reminiscences are associated with successful aging? *Psychology and Aging, 6*(2), 272–279.

Wood, D. (1980). Teaching the young child: Some relationships between social interaction, language, and thought. In D. Olson (Ed.), *The social foundations of language and thought.* New York: Norton.

Wood, D., Bruner, J., & Ross, G. (1976). The role of tutoring in problem solving. *Journal of Child Psychiatry and Psychology, 17,* 89–100.

Wood, D. L., Hayward, R. A., Corey, C. R., Freeman, H. E., & Shapiro, M. F. (1990). Access to medical care for children and adolescents in the United States. *Pediatrics, 86*(5), 666–673.

Wood, P. R., Hidalgo, H. R., Prihoda, T. J., & Kromer, M. E. (1993). Hispanic children with asthma. *Pediatrics, 91,* 62–69.

Woodhead, M. (1988). When psychology informs public policy: The case of early childhood intervention. *American Psychologist, 43,* 443–454.

Woodruff, D. S. (1985). Arousal, sleep and aging. In J. E. Birren & K. W. Schaie (Eds.), *Handbook of the psychology of aging* (pp. 261–295). New York: Van Nostrand Reinhold.

Woodward, A. L., Markman, E. M., & Fitzsimmons, C. M. (1994). Rapid word learning in 13- and 18-month olds. *Developmental Psychology, 30*(4), 553–566.

Working Women Education Fund. (1981). *Health hazards for office workers.* Cleveland: Author.

World Features Syndicate. (1996, January 6). Marriage customs around the world. *Cleveland Plain Dealer.*

World Health Organization. (1991). *World health statistics annual, 1990.* Geneva: Author.

Worldwatch Institute. (1994). *Vital signs.* New York: Norton.

Worobey, J. L., & Angel, R. J. (1990). Functional capacity and living arrangements of unmarried persons. *Journal of Gerontology: Social Sciences, 45,* S95–101.

Wortman, C. B., & Silver, R. C. (1989). The myths of coping with loss. *Journal of Consulting and Clinical Psychology, 57*(3), 349–357.

Wright, A. L. (1983). A cross-cultural comparison of menopausal symptoms. *Medical Anthropology, 7,* 20–35.

Wright, A. L., Holberg, C. J., Martinez, F. D., Morgan, W. J., & Taussig, L. M. (1989, October 14). Breast-feeding and lower respiratory tract illness in the first year of life. *British Medical Journal, 299,* 946–949.

Wright, J. C., Huston, A. C., Truglio, R., Fitch, M., Smith, E., & Piemyat, S. (1995). Occupational portrayals on television: Children's role schemata, career aspirations, and perceptions of reality. *Child Development, 66,* 1706–1718.

Wright, J. T., Waterson, E. J., Barrison, I. G., Toplis, P. J., Lewis, I. G., Gordon, M. G., MacRae, K. D., Morris, N. F., & Murray Lyon, I. M. (1983, March 26). Alcohol consumption, pregnancy, and low birth weight. *The Lancet,* pp. 663–665.

Wright, L. (1995, August 7). Double mystery. *The New Yorker,* pp. 45–62.

Wright, L. (1996, January 15). Silent sperm. *The New Yorker,* pp. 42–55.

The Writing Group of PEPI Trial. (1995). Effects of estrogen or estrogen/progestin regimens on heart disease risk factors in postmenopausal women. *Journal of the American Medical Association, 273,* 199–208.

Wu, Z. (1995). The stability of cohabitation relationships: The role of children. *Journal of Marriage and the Family, 57,* 231–236.

Wudunn, S. (1996, March 23). Japan's single mothers face discrimination. *Cleveland Plain Dealer,* p. 5E.

Wykle, M. L., & Musil, C. M. (1993). Mental health of older persons: Social and cultural factors. *Generations, 17*(1), 7–12.

Wynn, K. (1992). Evidence against empiricist accounts of the origins of numerical knowledge. *Mind and Language, 7,* 315–332.

Yamazaki, J. N., & Schull, W. J. (1990). Perinatal loss and neurological abnormalities among children of the atomic bomb. *Journal of the American Medical Association, 264,* 605–609.

Yang, B., Ollendick, T. H., Dong, Q., Xia, Y., & Lin, L. (1995). Only children and children with siblings in the People's Republic of China: Levels of fear, anxiety, and depression. *Child Development, 66,* 1301–1311.

Yarrow, M. R. (1978, October). *Altruism in children.* Paper presented at program, Advances in Child Development Research, New York Academy of Sciences, New York.

Yazigi, R. A., Odem, R. R., Polakoski, K. L. (1991). Demonstration of specific binding of cocaine to human spermatozoa. *Journal of the American Medical Association, 266,* 1956–1959.

Yllo, K. (1984). The status of women, marital equality, and violence against women: A contextual analysis. *Journal of Family Issues, 5,* 307–320.

Yllo, K. A. (1993). Through a feminist lens: Gender, power, and violence. In R. J. Gelles & D. R. Loseke (Eds.), *Current controversies on family violence* (pp. 47–62). Newbury Park, CA: Sage.

Yogman, M. J. (1984). Competence and performance of fathers and infants. In A. MacFarlane (Ed.), *Progress in child health.* London: Churchill Livingston.

Yogman, M. J., Dixon, S., Tronick, E., Als, H., & Brazelton, T. B. (1977, March). *The goals and structure of face-to-face interaction between infants and their fathers.* Paper presented at the meeting of the Society for Research in Child Development, New Orleans.

Yoshikawa, H. (1994). Prevention as cumulative protection: Effects of early family support and education on chronic delinquency and its risks. *Psychological Bulletin, 115*(1), 28–54.

Youngblade, L. M., & Belsky, J. (1992). Parent-child antecedents of 5-year-olds' close friendships: A longitudinal analysis. *Developmental Psychology, 28*(4), 700–713.

Youngstrom, N. (1992, January). Inner-city youth tell of life in "a war zone." *APA Monitor,* pp. 36–37.

Zabin, L. S., & Clark, S. D. (1983). Institutional factors affecting teenagers' choice and reasons for delay in attending a family planning clinic. *Family Planning Perspectives, 15,* 25–29.

Zabin, L. S., Emerson, M. R., Ringers, P. A., & Sedivy, V. (1996). Adolescents with negative pregnancy test results. *Journal of the American Medical Association, 275*(2), 113–117.

Zahn-Waxler, C., & Kochanska, G. (1990). The origins of guilt. In R. Thompson (Ed.), *The 36th National Symposium on Motivation: Socioemotional development* (pp. 183–258). Lincoln: University of Nebraska Press.

Zahn-Waxler, C., Radke-Yarrow, M., Wagner, E., & Chapman, M. (1992). Development of concern for others. *Developmental Psychology, 28,* 126–136.

Zahn-Waxler, C., Robinson, J. L., & Emde, R. N. (1992). The development of empathy in twins. *Developmental Psychology, 28,* 1038–1047.

Zakariya, S. B. (1982, September). Another look at the children of divorce: Summary report of the study of school needs of one-parent children. *Principal,* pp. 34–37.

Zametkin, A. J. (1995). Attention-deficit disorder: Born to be hyperactive. *Journal of the American Medical Association, 273*(23), 1871–1874.

Zarate, A. O. (1994). *International mortality chartbook: Levels and trends, 1955–1991.* Hyattsville, MD: U.S. Public Health Service.

Zarbatany, L., Hartmann, D. P., & Rankin, D. B. (1990). The psychological functions of preadolescent peer activities. *Child Development, 61,* 1067–1080.

Zelazo, N. A., Zelazo, P. R., Cohen, K. M., & Zelazo, P. D. (1993). Specificity of practice effects on elementary neuromotor patterns. *Developmental Psychology, 29,* 686–691.

Zelazo, P. R., Zelazo, N. A., & Kolb, S. (1972). "Walking" in the newborn. *Science, 176,* 314–315.

Zell, E. R., Dietz, V., Stevenson, J., Cochi, S., & Bruce, R. H. (1994). Low vaccination levels of U.S. preschool and school-age children. *Journal of the American Medical Association, 271,* 833–839.

Zelnik, M., Kantner, J. F., & Ford, K. (1981). *Sex and pregnancy in adolescence.* Beverly Hills, CA: Sage.

Zelnik, M., & Shah, F. K. (1983). First intercourse among young Americans. *Family Planning Perspectives, 15,* 64–72.

Zentella, A. C. (1981). Language variety among Puerto Ricans. In C. A. Ferguson & S. B. Heath (Eds.), *Language in the USA* (pp. 218–238). New York: Cambridge University Press.

Zeskind, P. S., & Iacino, R. (1984). Effects of maternal visitation to preterm infants in the neonatal intensive care unit. *Child Development, 55,* 1887–1893.

Zhang, Y., Proenca, R., Maffei, M., Barone, M., Leopold, L., & Friedman, J. M., (1994). Positional cloning of the mouse obese gene in its human homologue. *Nature, 372,* 425–431.

Zigler, E., & Styfco, S. J. (1993). Using research and theory to justify and inform Head Start expansion. *Social Policy Report of the Society for Research in Child Development, VII*(2).

Zigler, E., & Styfco, S. J. (1994). Head Start: Criticisms in a constructive context. *American Psychologist, 49*(2), 127–132.

Zigler, E., Taussig, C., & Black, K. (1992). Early childhood intervention: A promising preventative for juvenile delinquency. *American Psychologist, 47,* 997–1006.

Zigler, E. F. (1987). Formal schooling for four-year-olds? *North American Psychologist, 42*(3), 254–260.

Zimiles, H., & Lee, V. E. (1991). Adolescent family structure and educational progress. *Developmental Psychology, 27*(2), 314–320.

Zimmerman, D. (1993). Genital mutilation of women now is a challenge in the U.S. *Probe: David Zimmerman's Newsletter on Science, Media, Public Policy, and Health, 2*(4), 1, 4–5.

Zimmerman, M. A., Salem, D. A., & Maton, K. I. (1995). Family structure and psychosocial correlates among urban African-American adolescent males. *Child Development, 66,* 1598–1613.

Zimrin, H. (1986). A profile of survival. *Child Abuse and Neglect, 10,* 339–349.

Zoglin, R. (1994, February 28). Murder, they wheezed. *Time,* pp. 60–62.

Zube, M. (1982). Changing behavior and outlook of aging men and women: Implications for marriage in the middle and later years. *Family Relations, 31*(1), 147–156.

Zuckerman, B., Frank, D., Hingson, R., Amaro, H., Levenson, S. M., Kayne, H., Parker, S., Vinci, R., Aboagye, K., Fried, L., Cabral, H., Timperi, R., & Bauchner, H. (1989). Effects of maternal marijuana and cocaine use on fetal growth. *New England Journal of Medicine, 320*(12), 762–768.

Zuckerman, B. S., & Beardslee, W. R. (1987). Maternal depression: A concern for pediatricians. *Pediatrics, 79*(1), 110–117.

Zuckerman, D. M., & Zuckerman, B. S. (1985). Television's impact on children. *Pediatrics, 75,* 233–240.

Zuckerman, M. (1994). Impulsive unsocialized sensation seeking: The biological foundation of a basic dimension of personality. In J. E. Bates & T. D. Wachs (Eds.), *Temperament: Individual differences at the interface of biology and behavior* (pp. 219–255). Washington, DC: American Psychological Association.

ACKNOWLEDGMENTS

TEXTUAL CREDITS

Chapter 2

Table 2-1: Adapted from Fahey, V., "The Gene Screen: Looking in on baby," in Tisdale, "The Mother," *Hippocrates*, Vol. 2, No. 3, 1988, pp. 68–69. Reprinted with permission from *Hippocrates*, © 1988.

Table 2-2: From Milunsky, A., *Heredity and Your Family's Health*, by A. Milunsky, p. 122. © 1992 The Johns Hopkins University Press.

Chapter 3

Table 3-1: From Timiras, P. S., 1972, *Developmental Physiology and Aging*. Macmillan Publishing Co. Reprinted by permission of the author.

Table 3-3: From Apgar, V., "A proposal for a new method of evaluation of the newborn infant," *Current Research in Anesthesia & Analgesia*, 32, 1953, pp. 260–267. Reprinted by permission of Williams & Williams.

Table 3-4: American Academy of Pediatrics. Reproduced by permission of *Pediatrics*, Vol. 98, pp. 158–159. Copyright 1996.

Table 3-6: From Wegman, M. E., "Annual summary of vital statistics—1992." Reproduced by permission of *Pediatrics*, Vol. 92, pp. 743–754. Copyright 1993; and "Annual summary of vital statistics—1993." Reproduced by permission of *Pediatrics*, Vol. 94, pp. 792–803. Copyright 1994.

Table 3-8: Adapted from Frankenburg, W. K., J. Dodds, P. Archer, B. Bresnick, P. Maschka, N. Edelman, and H. Shapiro, *Denver II Training Manual*, Denver Developmental Materials, Inc., 1992.

Chapter 4

Box Table 4-1: From Fernald, A., and D. K. O'Neill, "Peekaboo across cultures: How mothers and infants play with voices, faces, and expectations," in *Parent-Child Play*, edited by K. MacDonald, State University of New York Press, 1993, pp. 259–285.

Table 4-2: From Kessen, W., M. Haith, and P. Salapatek, "Infancy," in *Carmichael's Manual of Child Psychology*, Vol. 1, Third Edition, edited by P. H. Mussen. Copyright © 1970. Reprinted by permission of John Wiley & Sons, Inc.

Chapter 5

Quote, p. 149: From Hartford, J., "Life Prayer." Copyright © 1968 by Ensign Music Corporation.

Table 5-1: Adapted from Sroufe, L. A., "Socioemotional development," in *Handbook of Infant Development*, edited by J. Osofsky. Copyright © 1979. Reprinted by permission of John Wiley & Sons, Inc.

Table 5-2: Adapted from Izard, C. E., and C. Z. Malatesta, "Perspectives on emotional development I: Differential emotions theory of early emotional development," in *Handbook of Infant Development*, Second edition. Copyright © 1987. Reprinted by permission of John Wiley & Sons, Inc.; and Lewis, "Shame: the exposed self," *Zero to Three*, XII(4), 1992, pp. 6–10. Reprinted with permission from ZERO TO THREE: NC/TF.

Table 5-3: From Thomas, A., and S. Chess, "Genesis and evolution of behavioral disorders: From infancy to early adult life," *American Journal of Psychiatry*, 141(1), pp. 1–9. Copyright 1984 American Psychiatric Association. Adapted by permission.

Table 5-4: From Ainsworth, M. D. S., M. C. Blehar, E. Waters, and S. Wall, *Patterns of Attachment: A Psychological Study of the Strange Situation*. Lawrence Erlbaum, Associates, Inc., 1978, p. 37.

Chapter 6

Table 6-1: Adapted with permission from Charles B. Corbin, *A Textbook of Motor Development.* Copyright © 1973 Wm. C. Brown Publishers, Dubuque, Iowa.

Box 6-3: From Tobin, J. J., D. Y. H. Wu, and D. H. Davidson, *Preschools in Three Cultures: Japan, China, and the United States.* Copyright © 1989. Reprinted by permission of Yale University Press.

Chapter 7

Table 7-1: Adapted from Parten, M. B., "Social play among preschool children," *Journal of Abnormal and Social Psychology*, 27. 1932, pp. 243–269. Copyright © 1932 by the American Psychological Association. Adapted with permission.

Table 7-2: From Papalia, D., and S. Olds, *A Child's World: Infancy to Adolescence*, Sixth Edition, p. 387. Copyright © 1992. Reproduced with permission of The McGraw-Hill Companies.

Table 7-3: From Kendall-Tackett, K. A., L. M. Williams, and D. Finkelhor, "Impact of sexual abuse on children: A review and synthesis of recent empirical studies," *Psychological Bulletin*, 113, 1993, pp. 164–180. Copyright © 1993 by the American Psychological Association. Reprinted with permission.

Tables 7-4, 7-5, & 7-6: From Harrington, D. M. "Child-rearing antecedents of suboptimal personality development: Exploring aspects of Alice Miller's concept of the poisonous pedagogy," in *Studying Lives Through Time: Personality and Development*, edited by D. C. Funder, et al., pp. 289–313. Copyright © 1983 by Allyn and Bacon. Reprinted by permission.

Table 7-7: From Morris, R. J., and T. R. Kratochwill, "Childhood Fears," in *Treating Children's Fears and Phobias: A Behavioral Approach* by R. J. Morris and T. R. Kratochwill, p. 2. Copyright © 1983 by Allyn and Bacon. Reprinted by permission.

Chapter 8

Table 8-1: From Bryant J. Cratty, *Perceptual and Motor Development in Infants and Children*, Second Edition, © 1979, p. 222. Adapted by permission of Prentice Hall, Englewood Cliffs, New Jersey.

Table 8-2: From Newacheck, P. W., J. J. Stoddard, and M. McManus, "Ethnocultural variations in the prevalance and impact of childhood chronic conditions." Reproduced by permission of *Pediatrics,* Vol. 91, pp. 1031–1047. Copyright 1993.

Table 8-3: From Hoffman, M. L., "Moral development," in *Carmichael's Manual of Child Psychology, Vol. 2,* edited by P. H. Mussen, pp. 261–360. Copyright © 1970. Reprinted by permission of John Wiley & Sons, Inc.

Table 8-4: From Chomsky, C. S., *The Acquisition of Syntax in Children from Five to Ten.* Copyright © 1969. Reprinted by permission of MIT Press.

Chapter 9

Table 9-1: From Zarbatany, L., D. P. Hartmann, and D. B. Rankin, "The psychological functions of preadolescent peer activities," *Child Development, 61,* 1990, pp. 1067–1080. © The Society for Research in Child Development.

Table 9-2: Adapted from Garbarino, J., N. Dobrow, K. Kostelny, and C. Pardo, *Children in Danger: Coping with the Consequences of Community Violence,* pp. 51–52. Copyright 1992 Jossey-Bass Inc., Publishers.

Chapter 10

Tables 10-1 & 10-3: From Papalia, D., and S. Olds, *A Child's World: Infancy to Adolescence,* Sixth Edition, pp. 556, 560. Copyright © 1992. Reproduced with the permission of The McGraw-Hill Companies.

Table 10-6: From Kohlberg, L., "Stage and sequence: The cognitive-developmental approach to socialization," in *Handbook of Socialization Theory and Research* by David A. Goslin, Rand McNally, 1969. Reprinted by permission of David A. Goslin; and from Lickona, Thomas, *Moral Development and Behavior.* Holt, Rinehart and Winston, 1976. Reprinted by permission of Thomas Lickona.

Table 10-8: Furstenberg, F. F., and M. E. Hughes, "Social capital in successful development," *Journal of Marriage and the Family, 57,* 1995, pp. 580–592. Copyrighted 1995 by the National Council on Family Relations, 3989 Central Ave. NE, Suite 550, Minneapolis, MN 55421. Reprinted by permission.

Box 10-2: From American Foundation for the Prevention of Venereal Disease, Inc., *Sexually Transmitted Disease (Venereal Disease): Prevention for Everyone,* 16th Edition, 1988. Reprinted by permission; and from Upjohn Company, *Writer's Guide to Sex and Health.* Reprinted by permission of Upjohn Company.

Chapter 11

Quote, p. 367: From *A Sky full of Poems* by Eve Merriam. Copyright © 1964, © 1970, 1973, 1986 by Eve Merriam. © renewed Eve Merriam. Reprinted by permission of Marian Reiner.

Table 11-1: From Marcia, J. E., "Development and validation of ego identity status," *Journal of Personality and Social Psychology, 3*(5), 1966, pp. 551–558. Copyright 1966 by the American Psychological Association. Adapted by permission.

Table 11-2: From Marcia, J. E., "Identity in adolescence," in *Handbook of Adolescent Psychology,* edited by J. Adelson. Copyright © 1980. Reprinted by permission of John Wiley & Sons, Inc.

Table 11-3: From Kroger, J., "Ego identity: An overview," in *Discussions of Ego Identity,* edited by J. Kroger. Lawrence Erlbaum Associates, Inc., 1993.

Table 11-4: From Miller, B. C., and K. A. Moore, "Adolescent sexual behavior, pregnancy, and parenting: Research through the 1980s," *Journal of Marriage and the Family, 52,* 1990, pp. 1025–1044. Copyrighted 1990 by the National Council on Family Relations, 3989 Central Ave. NE, Suite 550, Minneapolis, MN 55421. Reprinted by permission; and Sonnenstein, F. L., J. H. Pleck, and L. C. Ku. Reproduced with permission of the Alan Gutmaker Institute from "Levels of sexual activity among adolescent males in the United States," *Family Planning Perspectives, 23*(4), July/August 1991, pp. 162–167.

Chapter 12

Table 12-1: From McGinnis, J. M., and P. R. Lee, "Healthy people 2000 at mid decade," *Journal of the American Medical Association 273,* 1995, pp. 1123–1151. Copyright 1995, American Medical Association.

Table 12-2: From Brody, J. E., "Trying to reconcile exercise findings," *The New York Times,* April 12, 1995, p. 22L. Copyright © 1995 by The New York Times Co. Reprinted by permission.

Table 12-3: Adapted from Sternberg, R. J., R. K., Wagner, W. W. Williams, and J. A. Horvath, "Testing common sense," *American Psychologist, 50,* 1995, pp. 912, 927. Copyright © 1995 by the American Psychological Association. Adapted by permission.

Table 12-4: Reprinted by permission of the publishers from *In A Different Voice* by Carol Gilligan, Cambridge, Mass.: Harvard University Press, copyright © 1982 by Carol Gilligan.

Chapter 13

Table 13-2: From Sternberg, R. J., "A Triangular Theory of Love," *Psychological Review, 93,* pp. 119–135. Copyright © 1986 by the American Psychological Association. Reprinted with permission.

Table 13-3: From Michael, R. T., J. H. Gagnon, E. O. Laumann, and G. Kolata, *Sex in America: A Definitive Survey.* Little, Brown and Co., 1994.

Table 13-4: From Schoen, R., "First unions and the stability of first marriages," *Journal of Marriage and the Family, 54,* 1992, pp. 281–284. Copyrighted 1990 and 1992 by the National Council on Family Relations, 3989 Central Ave. NE, Suite 550, Minneapolis, MN 55421. Reprinted by permission; and from White, L. K., "Determinants of divorce: A review of research in the eighties," *Journal of Marriage and the Family, 52,* 1990, pp. 904–912. Copyrighted 1990 by the National Council on Family Relations, 3989 Central Ave. NE, Suite 550, Minneapolis, MN 55421. Reprinted by permission.

Chapter 14

Table 14-1 & Box 14-3: From Papalia, D., C. Camp, and R. Feldman, *Adult Development and Aging,* pp. 105, 274–275. Copyright © 1995(?). Reproduced with permission of The McGraw-Hill Companies.

Table 14-2: Reprinted with permission from the *Journal of Psychosomatic Research,* Vol. 11, T. H. Holmes and R. H. Rahe, "Social Readjustment Rating Scale," 1967, Elsevier Science Inc.

Table 14-3: From Working Women Education Fund, 1981, p. 9. Reprinted by permission of National Association for Working Women.

Chapter 15

Quote, p. 505: From "Dream Deferred," *The Panther and the Lash* by Langston Hughes. Copyright 1951 Langston Hughes. Reprinted by permission of Alfred A. Knopf, Inc.

Table 15-2: From Helson, R., and P. Wink, "Personality change in women from the early 40s to the early 50s," *Psychology and Aging 7*(1), 1992, pp. 46–55. Copyright © 1992 by the American Psychological Association. Reprinted by permission.

Table 15-3: From Hamon, R. R., and R. Blieszner, "Filial responsibility expectations among adult child-older parent pairs," *Journal of Gerontology,* Vol. 45, P110–P112, 1990. Copyright © The Gerontological Society of America.

Box 15-3: Home, J., "A Caregiver's Bill of Rights," *Caregiving: Helping an Aging Loved One*, 1985, p. 299. Reprinted with the permission of the American Association of Retired Persons.

Chapter 16

Table 16-2: From *Vital Signs 1994: The Trends that are Shaping Our Future* by Lester R. Brown, Hal Kane, and David Malin Roodman, eds. Copyright © 1994 by Worldwatch Institute. Reprinted by permission of W. W. Norton & Company, Inc.

Table 16-3: Adapted from *Is It Alzheimer's? Warning Signs You Should Know*, 1993. This information was adapted with permission from the Alzheimer's Association. For more information on Alzheimer's disease, Alzheimer's Association, or to contact the Association chapter nearest you, call (800) 272-3900.

Table 16-4: From Schaie, K. W., "The hazards of cognitive aging," *The Gerontologist*, 29(4), 1989, pp. 484–493. Copyright by The Gerontological Society of America. Used with permission.

Chapter 17

Quote, p. 575: From Duskin, R., "Haiku," *Sound and Light*, 1987.

Table 17-1: From Koenig, H. G., L. K. George, and I. C. Siegler, "The use of religion and other emotion-regulating coping strategies among older adults," *Gerontologist*, Vol. 28, pp. 303–310, 1988. Copyright © The Gerontological Society of America.

Chapter 18

Table 18-2: Reprinted with permission from *Omega*, Vol. 27, 1993. A. E. Scharlach and K. I. Fredericksen, "Reactions to the death of a parent during midlife," p. 311, Copyright 1993, with kind permission from Elsevier Science Ltd., The Boulevard, Langford Lane, Kidlington OX5 1GB, UK.

ILLUSTRATIONS

Chapter 2

Figure 2-9: From Brody, J., "Preventing birth defects even before pregnancy," *The New York Times*, June 28, 1995, p. C10. Copyright © 1995 by The New York Times Co. Reprinted by permission.

Chapter 3

Figure 3-1: From Lagercrantz, H., and T. A. Slotkin, "The 'stress' of being born," *Scientific American*, 254(4), 1986, pp. 100–107. Copyright © 1986 by Scientific American, Inc. All rights reserved.

Figure 3-2: Figure 3.1 "Fetal Brain Development," from *The Brain* by Richard Restak, M.D., copyright © 1984 by Educational Broadcasting Corporation and Richard M. Restak, M.D. Used by permission of Bantam Books, a division of Bantam Doubleday Dell Publishing Group, Inc.

Chapter 4

Figure 4-2: From Baillargeon, R., and J. DeVos, "Object permanence in young infants: Further evidence," *Child Development*, Vol. 62, 1991, pp. 1227–1246. © Society for Research in Child Development.

Figure 4-3: From Wynn, K., "Evidence against empiricist accounts of the origins of numerical knowledge," *Mind and Language, 7*, 1992, pp. 315–332.

Figures 4-4 & 4-5: From Baillargeon, R., "How do infants learn about the physical world?" *Current Directions in Psychological Science*, Vol. 3, No. 5, 1994, pp. 133–139. Reprinted with the permission of Cambridge University Press.

Box Figure 4-2: From Petitto, L. A., and P. F. Marentette, "Babbling in the manual mode: Evidence for the ontogeny of language," *Science, 251*, 1991, pp. 1493–1495. Copyright 1991 American Association for the Advancement of Science.

Chapter 6

Figure 6-2: From Bassuk, E. L., "Homeless families," *Scientific American, 265*(6), 1991, pp. 66–74. Copyright © 1991 by Scientific American, Inc. All rights reserved.

Figure 6-3: From Gelman, R., M. Bullock, and E. Meck, "Preschoolers' understanding of simple object transformations," *Child Development, 51*, 1980, pp. 691–699. © The Society for Research in Child Development.

Chapter 7

Cartoon, p. 237: Drawing by Bernard Schoenbaum. © 1996 The New Yorker Magazine, Inc.

Chapter 9

Figure 9-2: From Burns, A., "Mother-headed families: An international perspective and the case of Australia," *Social Policy Report of the Society for Research in Child Development, VI*(1), Spring, 1992. Reprinted by permission of the Society for Research in Child Development.

Figure 9-3: From Long, L., "International perspectives on the residential mobil-

ity of America's children," Journal of Marriage and the Family, 54, 1994, pp. 861–869. Copyrighted 1994 by the National Council on Family Relations, 3989 Central Ave. NE, Suite 550, Minneapolis, MN 55421. Reprinted by permission.

Chapter 10

Figure 10-1: From Elliot, D. S., *Promoting the Health of Adolescents: New Directions for the Twenty-First Century*, edited by Susan G. Millstein, Anne C. Petersen, et al. Copyright © 1994 by Oxford University Press, Inc. Used by permission of Oxford University Press, Inc.

Chapter 12

Figure 12-2: From Stamler, R., J. Stamler, and D. Garside, *The 20-Year Story of the Chicago Heart Association Detection Project in Industry*, American Heart Association of Metropolitan Chicago. Reprinted by permission of Rose Stamler.

Figure 12-3: From Sen, A., "The economics of life and death," *Scientific American*, Vol. 268, 1993, p. 45. Copyright © 1993 by Scientific American, Inc. All rights reserved.

Figure 12-4: From O'Grady-LeShane, R., "Changes in the lives of women and their families: Have old age pensions kept pace?" *Generations, 17*(4), 1993, pp. 27–31. Reprinted with permission from *Generations*, 833 Market St., Suite 511, San Francisco, CA 94103. Copyright 1993, American Society on Aging.

Chapter 13

Figure 13-1: Costa, P. T., Jr., and R. R. McCrae, "Still stable after all these years: Personality as a key to some issues in adulthood and old age," *Life-span Development and Behavior*, Vol. 3, edited by P. B. Baltes, Jr., and O. G. Brim, 1980, pp. 65–102. Reprinted by permission of Academic Press.

Figure 13-3: "Maslow's Hierarchy of Needs" from *Motivation and Personality*, 3rd Edition by Abraham H. Maslow, Revised by Robert Frager, James Fadiman, Cynthia McReynolds, and Ruth Cox. Copyright © 1954, 1987 by Harper & Row, Publishers, Inc. Copyright © 1970 by Abraham H. Maslow. Reprinted by permission of Addison-Wesley Educational Publishers, Inc.

Figure 13-4: From *The Social Organization of Sexuality* by R. T. Michael, E. O. Laumann, J. Gagnon, and S. Michaels. Copyright © 1994. Reprinted by permission of The University of Chicago Press; and from Michael, R. T., J. H. Gagnon, E. O. Laumann, and G. Kolata, *Sex in America: A Definitive Survey*. Little, Brown and Co., 1994.

Figure 13-5: From Burns, A., "Mother-headed families: An international perspective and the case of Australia," *Social Policy Report of the Society for Research in Child Development, VI*(1), Spring, 1992. Reprinted by permission of the Society for Research in Child Development.

Chapter 14

Figure 14-1: From Stamler, R., J. Stamler, and D. Garside, *The 20-Year Story of the Chicago Heart Association Detection Project in Industry,* American Heart Association of Metropolitan Chicago. Reprinted by permission of Rose Stamler.

Figure 14-2: From *Understanding Psychology,* Third Edition, by R. S. Feldman. Copyright © 1993. Reprinted by permission of McGraw-Hill, Inc.

Figure 14-3: From *Raven's Standard Matrices* by J. C. Raven. Reprinted by permission of J. C. Raven Ltd.

Figure 14-4: From Horn, J. L., and G. Donaldson, "Cognitive development: Adulthood development of human abilities." Reprinted by permission of the publishers from *Constancy and Change in Human Development,* edited by Orville G. Brim and Jerome Kagan, Cambridge, Mass.: Harvard University Press, Copyright © 1980 by the President and Fellows of Harvard College.

Figure 14-5: From Riley, M. W., "Aging and society: Past, present, and future," The *Gerontologist,* Vol. 33, pp. 436–444, 1994. Copyright © 1994 The Gerontological Society of America.

Figure 14-6: From Papalia, D., C. Camp, and R. Feldman, *Adult Development and Aging,* p. 105. Copyright © 1995(?). Reproduced with permission of The McGraw-Hill Companies.

Chapter 15

Figure 15-1: Cutler, N. E., and S. J. Devlin, "A framework for understanding financial responsibility among generations," *Generations, 20*(1), 1996, p. 24–28. Reprinted with permission from *Generations,* 833 Market St., Suite 511, San Francisco, CA 94103. Copyright 1996, American Society on Aging.

Figure 15-2: From *The New American Grandparent* by A. Cherlin and F. F. Furstenberg, Jr., Basic Books, 1986, p. 74. Reprinted by permission of the authors.

Cartoon, p. 522: Drawing by Koren. © 1995 The New Yorker Magazine, Inc.

Chapter 16

Figure 16-1: Adapted from *A Profile of Older Americans,* 1995. Reprinted by permission of the American Association of Retired Persons.

Figures 16-2, 16-4, & 16-5: From *Fifty: Midlife in Perspective* by Katchadourian. © 1987 by Herant Katchadourian. Used with permission of W. H. Freeman and Company.

Figure 16-7: From Schaie, K. W., "The course of adult intellectual development," *American Psychologist, 49*(4), 1994, pp. 303–313. Copyright © 1994 by the American Psychological Association. Reprinted with permission.

Chapter 17

Figure 17-1: From Lawton, M. P., and L. Nahemow, "Ecology and the aging process," in *The Psychology of Adult Development and Aging,* edited by C. Eisdorfer and M. P. Lawton, 1973, p. 661. Copyright © 1973 by the American Psychological Association. Reprinted with permission.

Figure 17-3: From Kaiser, M. A., "The production roles of older people in developing countries: What are the implications of economic, social and cultural participation," *Generations,* Vol. 17, No. 4, 1993. Reprinted with permission from *Generations,* 833 Market St., Suite 511, San Francisco, CA 94103. Copyright 1993, American Society on Aging; and from Commonwealth Fund, "Commonwealth Fund Commission on elderly people living alone," *Study of Elderly People in Five Countries—U.S., Canada, Germany, Britain, and Japan: Key Findings,* 1992. Reprinted by permission of Louis Harris & Associates.

Figure 17-6: Adapted from *A Profile of Older Americans,* 1995. Reprinted by permission of the American Association of Retired Persons.

Chapter 18

Figure 18-1: From Siegler, E., S. M. McCarty, and P. E. Logue, "Wechsler Memory Scale scores, selective attribution, and distance from death," *Journal of Gerontology,* Vol. 37, pp. 176–181, 1982. Copyright © The Gerontological Society of America.

Figure 18-2: From McIntosh, J. L., "Epidemiology of suicide in the elderly," *Suicide and Life-threatening Behavior,* Vol. 22, 1992. Reprinted by permission of The Guilford Press.

PHOTOS

Chapter 2

Box Figure 2-1: Courtesy of Integrated Genetics.

NAME INDEX

SUBJECT INDEX